Complete A+ Guide to IT Hardware and Software

A CompTIA® A+ Core 1 (220-1101) & CompTIA A+ Core 2 (220-1102) Textbook

NINTH EDITION

CHERYL A. SCHMIDT
CHRISTOPHER A. LEE
FLORIDA STATE COLLEGE AT JACKSONVILLE

PEARSON IT
CERTIFICATION

Complete A+ Guide to IT Hardware and Software, Ninth Edition

ISBN-13: 978-0-13-767044-4
ISBN-10: 0-13-767044-3

Library of Congress Control Number: 2022906025

1 2022

Trademarks

All terms mentioned in this book that are known to be trademarks or service marks have been appropriately capitalized. Pearson IT Certification cannot attest to the accuracy of this information. Use of a term in this book should not be regarded as affecting the validity of any trademark or service mark.

Warning and Disclaimer

Every effort has been made to make this book as complete and as accurate as possible, but no warranty or fitness is implied. The information provided is on an "as is" basis. The authors and the publisher shall have neither liability nor responsibility to any person or entity with respect to any loss or damages arising from the information contained in this book.

Special Sales

For information about buying this title in bulk quantities, or for special sales opportunities (which may include electronic versions; custom cover designs; and content particular to your business, training goals, marketing focus, or branding interests), please contact our corporate sales department at corpsales@pearsoned.com or (800) 382-3419.

For government sales inquiries, please contact governmentsales@pearsoned.com.

For questions about sales outside the U.S., please contact intlcs@pearson.com.

Editor-in-Chief
Mark Taub

Director, ITP Product Management
Brett Bartow

Executive Editor
James Manly

Development Editor
Ellie C. Bru

Managing Editor
Sandra Schroeder

Project Editor
Mandie Frank

Copy Editor
Kitty Wilson

Indexer
Ken Johnson

Proofreader
Debbie Williams

Technical Editor and Contributors
Chris Crayton
Jeff Burns
Melodie Schmidt
Karl Schmidt
Elizabeth Drake
Christine Farrington
David Brown

Publishing Coordinator
Cindy Teeters

Cover Designer
Chuti Prasertsith

Compositor
Tricia Bronkella

Art Production
Justin Ache
Marc Durrence
Katherine Martin
Amanda McIntosh
KC Frick
Donna McAfee Tucker
Vived Graphics

Photographers
Raina Durrence
Jennifer Cansler
George Nichols

Pearson's Commitment to Diversity, Equity, and Inclusion

Pearson is dedicated to creating bias-free content that reflects the diversity of all learners. We embrace the many dimensions of diversity, including but not limited to race, ethnicity, gender, socioeconomic status, ability, age, sexual orientation, and religious or political beliefs.

Education is a powerful force for equity and change in our world. It has the potential to deliver opportunities that improve lives and enable economic mobility. As we work with authors to create content for every product and service, we acknowledge our responsibility to demonstrate inclusivity and incorporate diverse scholarship so that everyone can achieve their potential through learning. As the world's leading learning company, we have a duty to help drive change and live up to our purpose to help more people create a better life for themselves and to create a better world.

Our ambition is to purposefully contribute to a world where

- Everyone has an equitable and lifelong opportunity to succeed through learning
- Our educational products and services are inclusive and represent the rich diversity of learners
- Our educational content accurately reflects the histories and experiences of the learners we serve
- Our educational content prompts deeper discussions with learners and motivates them to expand their own learning (and worldview)

While we work hard to present unbiased content, we want to hear from you about any concerns or needs with this Pearson product so that we can investigate and address them.

Please contact us with concerns about any potential bias at https://www.pearson.com/report-bias.html.

Credits

Figure	Credits
Chapter Opener	agsandrew/Shutterstock
Figure 1-8	scanrail/123RF
Figure 1-14	MNI/Shutterstock
Figure 1-13	Sergey Tikhomirov/123RF
Figure 1-15	norikko/Shutterstock
Figure 1-16	AlexLMX/Shutterstock
Figure 1-17	Oleksiy Mark/Shutterstock
Figure 1-18	BonD80/Shutterstock
Figure 1-21	Petr Malyshev/Shutterstock
Figure 1-35 (3)	Unkas Photo/Shutterstock
Figure 1-5A, Figure Lab 1-1-Figure Lab 1-8, Figure 4-9-Figure 4-11, Figure 4-15, Figure 6-6, Figure 6-7, Figure 6-17, Figure 6-18, Figure 7-34, Figure 7-40, Figure 7-43, Figure 7-45, Figure 7-46, Figure 8-5, Figure 8-16, Figure 8-17, Figure 9-21-Figure 9-24, Figure 9-33-Figure 9-37, Figure 9-39, Figure 9-40, Figure 9-43, Figure 9-48, Figure 9-49, Figure 9-50, Figure 10-50, Figure 10-51, Figure 10-58, Figure 10-79, Figure 12-1, Figure 12-16, Figure 12-21, Lab Figure 12-1, Figure 13-34, Figure 13-40, Figure 13-55, Figure 13-58, Figure 13-59, Figure 13-63, Figure 13-67, Figure 13-69, Figure 13-72, Figure 13-77-Figure 13-79, Figure 13-82, Figure 13-86 -Figure 13-100, Chapter 14, Logo of Windows, Figure 14-2A, Figure 14-2B, Figure 14-3-Figure 14-24, Figure 14-27-Figure 14-34, Figure 15-1, Figure 15-3, Figure 15-4, Figure 15-6-Figure 15-13, Figure 16-1, Figure 16-6-Figure 16-11, Figure 16-12A, Figure 16-12B, Figure 16-14, Figure 16-15A, Figure 16-15B, Figure 16-16-Figure 16-50, Figure 16-52-Figure 16-59, Figure 16-61-Figure 16-68, Figure 18-17-Figure 18-29, Figure 18-35, Figure 18-36, Figure 18-38, Figure 18-42, Figure 18-43, Figure 18-48, Figure 18-49, Lab Figure 18-1	Microsoft Corporation
Figure 1-5B, Figure 10-13, Figure 10-31, Figure 10-35, Figure 10-37, Figure 10-80, Figure 10-87, Figure 17-2-Figure 17-15	Apple Inc
Figure 1-5C, Chapter 14, Logo of Linux	Linus Torvalds
Figure 1-5D, Figure 9-45, Figure 10-12, Figure 10-34, Figure 10-36, Figure 10-81, Chapter 14, Logo of Android	Google LLC
Figure 1-7	MaverickLEE/Shutterstock
Figure 1-10	NAN728/Shutterstock
Figure 1-12	Sashkin/Shutterstock
Figure 1-24A	Robert Milek/Shutterstock
Figure 1-24B	magraphics/123RF
Figure 1-24C	CactusG/Shutterstock
Figure 1-25	Agenturfotografin/Shutterstock
Figure 1-34	alexlmx/123RF
Figure 1-35	Equipoise/Shutterstock
Figure 2-2A	kanvag/Shutterstock
Figure 2-2C	kanvag/Shutterstock
Figure 2-4	Adam Wasilewski/Shutterstock
Figure 2-7B	Peter Gudella/Shutterstock
Figure 2-9	Ruslan Kudrin/Shutterstock
Figure 2-16	Shawn Hempel/Shutterstock
Figure 2-29	Mau Horng/Shutterstock
Figure 2-34A	Ferhat/Shutterstock
Figure 2-34B	Alexey Rotanov/Shutterstock
Figure 2-39	Mr. Pairoj Sroyngern/123RF
Figure 2-40A	Aleh Datskevich/123RF
Figure 2-40B	Mikhail hoboton Popov/Shutterstock

Figure	Credits
Figure 2-45	Unkas Photo/Shutterstock
Figure 2-49I	Peter Gudella/Shutterstock
Figure 2-3	normaals/123RF
Figure 2-1	Montree Saowang/Shutterstock
Figure 2-6	ericlefrancais/Shutterstock
Figure 2-8A	ravl/Shutterstock
Figure 2-8B	Feng Yu/Shutterstock
Figure 2-13	Mehmet Cetin/Shutterstock
Figure 2-14B	volodymyrshtun89/123RF
Figure 2-15	Tuomas Lehtinen /Shutterstock
Figure 2-24A	arnut09job/123RF
Figure 2-27	kanvag/Shutterstock
Figure 2-36	samsonovs/123RF
Figure 2-37	gefufna/123RF
Figure 2-46 (2)	Gareth Boden/Pearson Education Ltd
Figure 2-48	PVLGT/Shutterstock
Figure 2-49A	MRS. NUCH SRIBUANOY/Shutterstock
Figure 2-49C	ericlefrancais/Shutterstock
Figure 2-49D	Nata-Lia/Shutterstock
Figure 2-49E	ericlefrancais/Shutterstock
Figure 2-49F	Tuomas Lehtinen /Shutterstock
Figure 2-49G	1125089601/Shutterstock
Figure 2-49H	Mikhail hoboton Popov/Shutterstock
Figure 2-49J	Coleman Yuen/Pearson Education Asia Ltd
Figure 3-17	ruslanlytvyn/123RF
Figure 3-18	anmbph/123RF
Figure 3-28	naskami/123RF
Figure 3-37	Unkas Photo/Shutterstock
Figure 3-14	Denis Dryashkin/Shutterstock
Figure 3-20	anykeen/123RF
Figure 3-21	mark800/123RF
Figure 3-22	Denis Dryashkin/Shutterstock
Figure 3-23	Georgii Shipin/Shutterstock
Figure 3-26	Unkas Photo/Shutterstock
Figure 3-1	Aleksei Lazukov/Shutterstock
Figure 3-2	KsanderDN/Shutterstock
Figure 3-29	Zadorozhnyi Viktor/Shutterstock
Figure 3-34	BonD80/Shutterstock
Figure 3-38	wavebreakmedia/Shutterstock
Figure 4-1	daniidfoto/123RF
Figure 4-19	Stokkete/Shutterstock
Figure 4-6	BonD80/Shutterstock
Figure 4-3, Figure 4-4, Figure 4-5, Figure 4-20, Figure 4-21	UEFI Forum
Figure 4-8	lapis2380/123RF

Figure	Credits
Figure 5-1	dmitr1ch/123RF
Figure 5-6	ironstuff/123RF
Figure 5-22	dmitryi/123RF
Figure 5-32	Dmytro Skrypnykov/123RF
Figure 5-4	StockPhotosArt/Shutterstock
Figure 5-7	Lolostock/Shutterstock
Figure 5-8A	cristi180884/Shutterstock
Figure 5-8B	BonD80/Shutterstock
Figure 5-13	thodonal/123RF
Figure 5-14	wavebreakmedia/Shutterstock
Figure 5-19	chokmoso/Shutterstock
Figure 5-20	Richard z/Shutterstock
Figure 5-21	thodonal/123RF
Figure 5-27A	Olga Popova/Shutterstock
Figure 5-27B	cristi180884/Shutterstock
Figure 5-34	Brazhnykov Andriy/Shutterstock
Figure 5-36	House@Brasil Art Studio/Shutterstock
Figure 5-37A	cristi180884/Shutterstock
Figure 5-18	anakeseenadee/123RF
Figure 5-29	stasysk/123RF
Figure 5-35	patpataor/123RF
Figure 6-19	diegomaravilla/123RF
Figure 6-21	shaffandi/123RF
Figure 6-14	Joseph Scott Photography/Shutterstock
Figure 6-20	Svitlana Kataieva/Shutterstock
Figure 6-1	nemalo/123RF
Figure 6-3	S.Dashkevych/Shutterstock
Figure 6-4	vetkit/Shutterstock
Figure 6-22	ESB Professional/Shutterstock
Figure 7-3	scyther5/123RF
Figure 7-16	daniidfoto/123RF
Figure 7-20A	Maxim Blinkov/123RF
Figure 7-26	paylessimages/123RF
Figure 7-48	justoomm/123RF
Figure 7-1	photka/123RF
Figure 7-8	SvedOliver/Shutterstock
Figure 7-14	kitaec/123RF
Figure 7-18A	servantes/Shutterstock
Figure 7-18B	vvetc1/Shutterstock
Figure 7-19A	ravl/Shutterstock
Figure 7-19B	scorpion26/123RF
Figure 7-19C	Crepesoles/Shutterstock
Figure 7-20B	Lipowski Milan/Shutterstock
Figure 7-24	CyberVam/Shutterstock
Figure 7-29	igorspb/123RF
Figure 7-41	concept w/Shutterstock

Figure	Credits
Figure 7-2	Visual Generation/Shutterstock
Figure 7-6	mbongo/123RF
Figure 7-11	Artush/Shutterstock
Figure 7-17	svedoliver/123RF
Figure 7-21	mbnq/123RF
Figure 7-27	yemelyanov/123RF
Figure 7-30	believeinme33/123RF
Figure 7-31	maxkyth/123RF
Figure 7-50	Studio 8/Pearson Education Ltd
Figure 8-3	kitaec/123RF
Figure 8-11	Denis Dryashkin/Shutterstock
Figure 8-12	Oleksandr Lysenko/Shutterstock
Figure 8-15	yanalesnyk/123RF
Figure 8-20	pathdoc/Shutterstock
Figure 8-24	anaken2012/Shutterstock
Figure 8-27	bacho12345/123RF
Figure 8-29	Oleksiy Mark/Shutterstock
Figure 8-30	Olha Vlasiuk/Shutterstock
Figure 8-32	Valeriy Lebedev/Shutterstock
Figure 8-33	Gustavo Frazao/Shutterstock
Figure 8-2	golibtolibov/123RF
Figure 8-7	Jan Mika/Shutterstock
Figure 8-9	Istvan Csak/Shutterstock
Figure 8-18	DenisProduction.com/Shutterstock
Figure 8-25	magraphics/123RF
Figure 8-31	Logitech
Figure 9-19	Zern Liew/Shutterstock
Figure 9-25	kitaec/123RF
Figure 9-27	esbobeldijk/Shutterstock
Figure 9-38	singkham/123RF
Figure 9-46	kitaec/123RF
Figure 9-2	burnel1/123RF
Figure 9-5	Sinisa Botas/Shutterstock
Figure 9-9	manaemedia/Shutterstock
Figure 9-10	Michal Vitek/Shutterstock
Figure 9-11	manaemedia/123RF
Figure 9-12	vetkit/Shutterstock
Figure 9-14	Suljo/123RF
Figure 9-44	Daniel Krason/Shutterstock
Figure 9-47	Michael Pettigrew/Shutterstock
Figure 9-1	ProstoSvet/Shutterstock
Figure 9-15	asharkyu/123RF
Figure 9-16	korolyok/123RF
Figure 9-26	Gareth Boden/Pearson Education Ltd
Figure 9-29	artranq/123RF
Figure 9-32	krivich/123RF

Figure	Credits
Figure 9-41	ldprod/123RF
Figure 9-51	Rocketclips, Inc/Shutterstock
Figure 10-26	fkdkondmi/Shutterstock
Figure 10-59	The Loupe Project/Shutterstock
Figure 10-62B	Piotr Adamowicz/123RF
Figure 10-82	hit003/123RF
Figure 10-89	kovalska/123RF
Figure 10-90	weerapat/123RF
Figure 10-1	multicanarias/123RF
Figure 10-2	dolgachov/123RF
Figure 10-4	forest71/Shutterstock
Figure 10-5	Alexey Rotanov/Shutterstock
Figure 10-7	3DMAVR/Shutterstock
Figure 10-8	Renars 2013/Shutterstock
Figure 10-9	Oleg Troino/Shutterstock
Figure 10-10	Olga Popova/Shutterstock
Figure 10-19	prykhodov/123RF
Figure 10-22	Anton Starikov/Shutterstock
Figure 10-24	highwaystarz/123RF
Figure 10-30	leaf/123RF
Figure 10-32	ProStockStudio/Shutterstock
Figure 10-33	Christos Georghiou/Shutterstock
Figure 10-38	mazirama/123RF
Figure 10-42	Kilroy79/Shutterstock
Figure 10-48A	fserega/123RF
Figure 10-48B	ratmaner/123RF
Figure 10-49A	NET_Photog/Shutterstock
Figure 10-49B	JIPEN/Shutterstock
Figure 10-53	Romash Denis/Shutterstock
Figure 10-55	mickyso/Shutterstock
Figure 10-57	Joggie Botma/Shutterstock
Figure 10-64	JIPEN/Shutterstock
Figure 10-72	Rashevskyi Viacheslav/Shutterstock
Figure 10-75	Antlii/Shutterstock
Figure 10-78	tab62/Shutterstock
Figure 10-84	Yomka/Shutterstock
Figure 10-85	kulyk/Shutterstock
Figure 10-88	Olinchuk/Shutterstock
Figure 10-92	pixssa/Shutterstock
Figure 10-93	Denis Cristo/Shutterstock
Figure 10-94	grafvision/Shutterstock
Figure 10-3	RHJPhtotos/Shutterstock
Figure 10-6	RomboStudio/Shutterstock
Figure 10-11	dolgachov/123RF
Figure 10-15A	Blackboard/Shutterstock
Figure 10-15B	Eric Buell Photography/Shutterstock

Figure	Credits
Figure 10-17	Brian A Jackson/Shutterstock
Figure 10-23A	Monstar Studio/Shutterstock
Figure 10-23B	Remus Rigo/Shutterstock
Figure 10-25	Bluetooth SIG, Inc
Figure 10-27	Oleksiy Mark/Shutterstock
Figure 10-29	Albert Lozano/Shutterstock
Figure 10-39	Matt Hafner
Figure 10-41	Andrey_Popov/Shutterstock
Figure 10-62A	Piotr Adamowicz/123RF
Figure 10-65	kuprevich/123RF
Figure 10-71	Designua/Shutterstock
Figure 10-83	arka38/Shutterstock
Figure 10-86	selinofoto/Shutterstock
Figure 10-91	Pasko Maksim/Shutterstock
Figure 10-96	Yomka/Shutterstock
Figure 11-1	artellia/123RF
Figure 11-2	Corepics VOF/Shutterstock
Figure 11-3	Dejan Stanic Micko/Shutterstock
Figure 11-4	Stocked House Studio/Shutterstock
Figure 11-5	300dpi/123RF
Figure 11-6	MilousSK/Shutterstock
Figure 11-7	Kittichai/Shutterstock
Figure 11-8	improvize/Shutterstock
Figure 11-9	RAJ CREATIONZS/Shutterstock
Figure 11-10	mikeledray/Shutterstock
Figure 11-11	DeSerg/Shutterstock
Figure 11-12	Natalia Siverina/Shutterstock
Figure 11-13	Andrey_Popov/Shutterstock
Figure 11-14	Phovoir/Shutterstock
Figure 11-15	sheelamohanachandran2010/ Shutterstock
Figure 11-17	Galyna Andrushko/Shutterstock
Figure 11-20	Cartoon Resource/Shutterstock
Figure 11-22	Sashkin/Shutterstock
Figure 11-26	pathdoc/Shutterstock
Figure 12-14	Dmitriy Shpilko/123RF
Figure 12-22	Marishatti/Shutterstock
Figure 12-7	rocketclips/123RF
Figure 12-3	Evan Lorne/Shutterstock
Figure 12-4	Roman Pyshchyk/Shutterstock
Figure 12-5	S1001/Shutterstock
Figure 12-6	Suti Stock Photo/Shutterstock
Figure 12-11	federicofoto/123RF
Figure 12-17	JustAnotherPhotographer/Shutterstock
Figure 12-19	Zern Liew/Shutterstock
Figure 12-26	stockasso/123RF

Figure	Credits
Lab Figure 12-2	© 2022 VMware, Inc
Lab Figure 12-3	© 2022 Oracle
Figure 13-12	Georgios Alexandris/Shutterstock
Figure 13-25	SeventyFour/Shutterstock
Figure 13-38	Christos Georghiou/Shutterstock
Figure 13-54	Andrey Moisseyev/123RF
Figure 13-103A	Maximumm/Shutterstock
Figure 13-103C	Andrew Park/Shutterstock
Figure 13-103D	svetlanaangelus/123RF
Figure 13-103E	dotshock/Shutterstock
Figure 13-5	amoklv/123RF
Figure 13-16A	svart/123RF
Figure 13-16B	svart/123RF
Figure 13-17	Fotofermer/Shutterstock
Figure 13-18	ludinko/Shutterstock
Figure 13-19A	Everything I Do/Shutterstock
Figure 13-24	eugenesergeev/123RF
Figure 13-26	svetlanaangelus/123RF
Figure 13-27	hxdyl/123RF
Figure 13-29	Plus69/Shutterstock
Figure 13-39	diabl/123RF
Figure 13-80	nemalo/123RF
Figure 13-81	ultramcu/123RF
Figure 13-83	Riverlim/123RF
Figure 13-84	aleksanderdn/123RF
Figure 13-103B	Oleksiy Mark/Shutterstock
Figure 13-1	karelnoppe/123RF
Figure 13-3	siiixth/Shutterstock
Figure 13-4	TechnoVectors/Shutterstock
Figure 13-6	Lia Gloss/Shutterstock
Figure 13-7	Arjuna Kodisinghe/Shutterstock
Figure 13-8	kubais/Shutterstock
Figure 13-11	Piyawat Nandeenopparit/Shutterstock
Figure 13-15	zhekoss/Shutterstock
Figure 13-19B	Anthony O'Donnell/Shutterstock
Figure 13-20	Plus69/Shutterstock
Figure 13-30	gregg williams/Shutterstock
Figure 13-41	Oleksiy Mark/Shutterstock
Figure 13-44, Figure 13-52A, Figure 13-52B, Figure 13-60, Figure 13-61, Figure 18-50, Figure 18-52	TP-Link Corporation Limited
Figure 13-66	alphaspirit.it/Shutterstock
Figure 13-73	PGMart/Shutterstock

Figure	Credits
Figure 13-85	elenabsl/Shutterstock
Figure 13-102	Peter Kotoff/Shutterstock
Figure 13-105	Nikonaft/Shutterstock
Lab Figure 13-1	Aliaksandr Bukatsich/Shutterstock
Lab Figure 13-2	darkwisper/123RF
Lab Figure 13-3	Georgios Alexandris/Shutterstock
Lab Figure 13-4	a_v_d/Shutterstock
Lab Figure 13-5	samsonovs/Shutterstock
Chapter 14, Logo of Open office	Apache
Chapter 14, Logo of Adobe	Adobe
Figure 15-14	calado/Shutterstock
Figure 15-15	Yury Zap/Shutterstock
Figure 16-2	Iurii Motov/123RF
Figure 16-51	ojogabonitoo/123RF
Figure 16-60	siiixth/123RF
Figure 16-3	binaryproject/123RF
Figure 16-4	scanrail/123RF
Figure 16-5	jijomathaidesigners/Shutterstock
Figure 16-31	anyaberkut/123RF
Figure 16-69	AntiMartina/Shutterstock
Figure 17-1	belchonock/123RF
Figure 17-16-Figure 17-24	Canonical Ltd
Figure 18-33	lukassek/123RF
Figure 18-2	gifted/Shutterstock
Figure 18-3	patrimonio designs ltd/Shutterstock
Figure 18-4	Agnieszka Jonik/123RF
Figure 18-6	Jim Pruitt/123RF
Figure 18-7	Demetrio Zimino/Shutterstock
Figure 18-8	mariok/123RF
Figure 18-9	liudmilachernetska/123RF
Figure 18-10	Buchachon Petthanya/123RF
Figure 18-11	alexmit/123RF
Figure 18-12	ocusfocus/123RF
Figure 18-13	Cartoon Resource/Shutterstock
Figure 18-14	B Studio/Shutterstock
Figure 18-1	Jules Selmes/Pearson Education Ltd
Figure 18-15	untitled/Shutterstock
Figure 18-16	JustAnotherPhotographer/Shutterstock
Figure 18-30	escova/Shutterstock

Figure	Credits
Figure 18-32	Bedrin/Shutterstock
Figure 18-37	kmls/Shutterstock
Figure 18-39	baur/Shutterstock
Figure 18-40	Oez/Shutterstock
Figure 18-41	Grasko/Shutterstock
Figure 18-46	marigranula/123RF
Figure 18-53	iqoncept/123RF
Figure 19-1	Rawpixel.com/Shutterstock
Figure 19-12	Bert Folsom/123RF
Figure 19-2	ESB Professional/Shutterstock
Figure 19-3	photosync/Shutterstock
Figure 19-4	Niwan Nuntasukkasame/123RF
Figure 19-5	petovarga/123RF
Figure 19-7	wk1003mike/Shutterstock
Figure 19-11	Boris Alexeev/123RF
Figure 19-14a	Mile Atanasov/Shutterstock
Figure 19-14b	vetkit/Shutterstock
Figure 19-29	lemonadeserenade/123RF
Figure 19-30	Pavel Karpovskii/123RF
Figure 19-32	iqoncept/123RF
Figure 19-34	Cartoonresource/Shutterstock
Figure 19-35	Rawpixel.com/Shutterstock
Figure 19-36	Valeriy Kachaev/123RF
Figure 19-37	andrew grossman/123RF
Figure 19-38	simmmax/123RF
Figure 19-39	Jan Mika/Shutterstock
Figure 19-40	Jane Kelly/Shutterstock
Figure 19-6	petovarga/123RF
Figure 19-8	enterphoto/Shutterstock
Figure 19-9	Gareth Boden/Pearson Education Ltd
Figure 19-10	rumruay/Shutterstock
Figure 19-13	Winai Tepsuttinun/Shutterstock
Figure 19-19	Yury Asotov/Shutterstock
Figure 19-20	Travelpixs/Shutterstock
Figure 19-23	Oez/Shutterstock
Figure 19-25	Benjamin Haas/Shutterstock
Figure 19-26	Kheng Guan Toh/Shutterstock
Figure 19-27	desdemona72/Shutterstock
Figure 19-28	Cartoon Resource/Shutterstock
Figure 19-31	Noppadol Anaporn/123RF

Contents at a Glance

Introduction ... xxvii
Features of this Book ... xxviii
Chapter 1: Introduction to the World of IT ... 1
Chapter 2: Connectivity ... 31
Chapter 3: On the Motherboard ... 67
Chapter 4: Introduction to Configuration ... 109
Chapter 5: Disassembly and Power ... 143
Chapter 6: Memory ... 187
Chapter 7: Storage Devices ... 223
Chapter 8: Video and Multimedia Devices ... 279
Chapter 9: Printers and Multifunction Devices ... 317
Chapter 10: Mobile Devices ... 375
Chapter 11: Computer Design and Troubleshooting Review ... 473
Chapter 12: Internet Connectivity, Virtualization, and Cloud Technologies ... 515
Chapter 13: Networking ... 551
Chapter 14: Introduction to Operating Systems ... 651
Chapter 15: Introduction to Scripting ... 697
Chapter 16: Advanced Windows ... 763
Chapter 17: macOS and Linux Operating Systems ... 857
Chapter 18: Computer and Network Security ... 899
Chapter 19: Operational Procedures ... 977
Appendix A: Subnetting Basics ... 1021
Appendix B: Certification Exam Objectives (Online)
Glossary ... 1025
Index ... 1075

Contents

Introduction xxvii

Features of this Book xxviii

Chapter 1: Introduction to the World of IT 1

Who Needs This Book? 2
Technician Qualities 2
Breaking into IT with the CompTIA A+ Certification 5
Basic Skills for This Course 5
Types of Computers 8
Basic Computer Hardware 8
Mice and Keyboards 14
Common Peripherals 17
1s and 0s 18
Safety Notes 21
Chapter Summary 22
Key Terms 23
Review Questions 24
Exercises 26
Exercise 1.1 Identifying Tower Computer Parts 26
Exercise 1.2 Identifying Computer Parts 28
Activities 28
Internet Discovery 28
Soft Skills 29
Critical Thinking Skills 29

Chapter 2: Connectivity 31

Introduction to Connectivity 32
External Connectivity 32
Mouse and Keyboard Ports 32
Video Ports 33
Audio Ports 44
eSATA Ports 45
Modem and Serial Ports 45
Network Ports 47
Network Cabling 48
Integrated Motherboard Ports 54
Getting to Know Ports 54
Wireless Connectivity for Input Devices 56
Chapter Summary 57
Key Terms 59
Review Questions 60
Exercises 61
Exercise 2.1 Identifying Computer Ports 61
Exercise 2.2 Identifying More Computer Ports 62
Exercise 2.3 Identifying Display Ports 62
Exercise 2.4 Identifying USB Ports 63
Exercise 2.5 Identifying Cables 63

Activities ... 64
Internet Discovery ... 64
Soft Skills ... 65
Critical Thinking Skills ... 65

Chapter 3: On the Motherboard ... 67
Introduction to the Motherboard ... 68
Processor Overview ... 68
Processor Basics ... 69
Speeding Up Processor Operations Overview ... 71
Clocking ... 72
Cache ... 73
Threading Technology ... 73
Connecting to the Processor ... 74
Multicore Processors ... 74
Graphics Processing Unit (GPU) ... 76
Introduction to Virtualization ... 76
Intel Processors ... 77
AMD Processors ... 78
CPU Sockets ... 79
Processor Cooling ... 80
Installing a Processor ... 82
Upgrading Processors ... 84
Overclocking Processors ... 84
Installing CPU Thermal Solutions ... 85
Troubleshooting Processor Issues ... 86
Expansion Slots ... 87
PCI (Peripheral Component Interconnect) ... 88
AGP (Accelerated Graphics Port) ... 88
PCIe (Peripheral Component Interconnect Express) ... 89
Motherboard Security Options ... 93
Types of Motherboards ... 94
Upgrading and Replacing Motherboards ... 95
Motherboard Troubleshooting ... 96
Chapter Summary ... 99
Key Terms ... 101
Review Questions ... 102
Exercises ... 104
Exercise 3.1 Identifying ATX Motherboard Parts ... 104
Exercise 3.2 Motherboard Analysis ... 105
Activities ... 106
Internet Discovery ... 106
Soft Skills ... 107
Critical Thinking Skills ... 107

Chapter 4: Introduction to Configuration ... 109
Configuration Overview ... 110
BIOS Overview ... 110
The Setup Program ... 111
Flash BIOS ... 112

BIOS/UEFI Configuration Settings....113
CMOS Memory....117
Motherboard Battery....118
Firmware Updates: Flashing/Clearing the BIOS/UEFI....118
Other Configuration Parameters....120
Hardware Configuration Overview....123
Installing a USB Device....124
Installing an eSATA Card....128
Installing a Network Interface Card....129
Troubleshooting Configurations....130
Chapter Summary....133
Key Terms....133
Review Questions....134
Exercises....136
Exercise 4.1 System Expansion....136
Exercise 4.2 BIOS/UEFI Options....138
Activities....140
Internet Discovery....140
Soft Skills....141
Critical Thinking Skills....141

Chapter 5: Disassembly and Power....143
Disassembly Overview....144
Electrostatic Discharge (ESD)....144
Electromagnetic Interference (EMI)....146
Tools....147
Disassembly....148
Reassembly....156
Preventive Maintenance....156
Basic Electronics Overview....159
Power Supply Overview....163
Replacing or Upgrading a Power Supply....170
Power Protection....172
Symptoms of Power Supply Problems....173
Chapter Summary....177
Key Terms....179
Review Questions....180
Exercises....182
Exercise 5.1 Identifying Power Supply Connectors....182
Exercise 5.2 Recognizing Computer Replacement Parts....183
Exercise 5.3 Describing Computer Parts....183
Activities....184
Internet Discovery....184
Soft Skills....185
Critical Thinking Skills....185

Chapter 6: Memory....187
Memory Overview....188
Memory Physical Packaging....188
Planning a Memory Installation....189

Installing Memory Overview 200
Virtual RAM 202
Monitoring Memory Usage in Windows 203
Older Applications in Windows 204
Troubleshooting Memory Problems 205
Removable Storage 207
Chapter Summary 211
Key Terms 212
Review Questions 213
Exercises 215
Exercise 6.1 Configuring Memory on Paper 215
Exercise 6.2 Configuring Memory on Paper 216
Exercise 6.3 Configuring Memory on Paper 218
Exercise 6.4 Configuring Memory on Paper 220
Activities 221
Internet Discovery 221
Soft Skills 222
Critical Thinking Skills 222

Chapter 7: Storage Devices 223
Storage Devices Overview 224
Hard Drive Overview 225
Solid-State Drive (SSD) Overview 227
Mechanical Drive Interfaces Overview 229
M.2 and NVMe 230
PATA, SATA, and SAS Connectivity 231
Storage Device Configuration Overview 235
System BIOS/UEFI Configuration for Storage Devices 241
Hard Drive Preparation Overview 242
Windows Disk Management 250
Fault Tolerance 253
Windows Storage Spaces 255
Disk Caching/Virtual Memory 256
Troubleshooting Storage Devices Overview 258
Data Loss and Corruption 260
Troubleshooting New Storage Device Installation 260
Troubleshooting Previously Installed Storage Devices 262
RAID Issues 265
SSD Issues 266
Chapter Summary 268
Key Terms 271
Review Questions 272
Exercises 274
Exercise 7.1 Planning Storage Device Installation and Configuration 274
Exercise 7.2 Configuring a SATA Hard Drive on Paper 275
Activities 277
Internet Discovery 277
Soft Skills 278
Critical Thinking Skills 278

Chapter 8: Video and Multimedia Devices 279
Multimedia Devices Overview 280
Video Overview 280
Video Cards 280
Projectors 287
Introduction to Audio 289
Installing Sound Cards 292
Sound Cards Using Windows 293
Speakers 295
Troubleshooting Sound Problems 296
Optical Drive Overview 297
Optical Drive Installation 300
Troubleshooting Optical Drive Issues 300
Scanners 302
Other Multimedia Devices 305
Chapter Summary 309
Key Terms 310
Review Questions 311
Exercises 313
Exercise 8.1 Video and Multimedia Device Research 313
Exercise 8.2 Which One Will You Buy? 314
Activities 315
Internet Discovery 315
Soft Skills 316
Critical Thinking Skills 316

Chapter 9: Printers and Multifunction Devices 317
Printer/Multifunction Device Overview 318
Categories of Printers 318
Impact Printers 319
Inkjet Printers 321
Laser Printers 323
Thermal Printers 327
3-D Printers 329
Paper 332
Virtual Printing 334
Refilling Cartridges, Re-inking Ribbons, and Recycling Cartridges 335
Upgrading Printers 336
Printer Maintenance 336
Printer Installation Overview 342
Installing Multifunction Devices 343
USB Printer Installation 343
Printers in the Windows Environment 344
Printer Sharing 349
Cloud Printing/Scanning 354
General Printer Troubleshooting 355
USB-Attached Printer Troubleshooting 359
Windows Printer Troubleshooting 359
Impact Printer Troubleshooting 362

Inkjet Printer Troubleshooting 363
Laser Printer Troubleshooting 363
Chapter Summary 366
Key Terms 368
Review Questions 369
Exercises 371
Exercise 9.1 Research a Local Printer 371
Exercise 9.2 Printer Driver Research 371
Activities 372
Internet Discovery 372
Soft Skills 372
Critical Thinking Skills 373

Chapter 10: Mobile Devices 375
Mobile Device Overview 376
Using Mobile Devices 382
Cell Phones 385
Mobile Apps 387
Mobile Device Wired Connectivity 390
Mobile Device Wireless Connectivity 393
Mobile Device Email Configuration 399
Mobile Device Synchronization and Backup 401
Other Mobile Software Tools 408
Laptops Overview 410
Laptop Hardware 410
Laptop Power 415
Laptop Repairs Overview 418
Laptop Display 433
Mobile Device Security 440
Mobile Device Travel and Storage 447
Mobile Device Troubleshooting Overview 447
Chapter Summary 462
Key Terms 465
Review Questions 466
Exercises 468
Exercise 10.1 Identifying Laptop Parts 468
Exercise 10.2 Identifying Common Laptop Keys 469
Exercise 10.3 Identifying Cell Phone Parts 469
Activities 470
Internet Discovery 470
Soft Skills 471
Critical Thinking Skills 471

Chapter 11: Computer Design and Troubleshooting Review 473
Design Overview 474
Computer System Design 474
Motherboard and Associated Component Design 481
Power Supply and Case Design 481
Storage Subsystem Design 483

Audio Subsystem Design 483
Display Subsystem Design....484
Troubleshooting Overview....485
Step 1. Identify the Problem....486
Step 2. Establish a Theory of Probable Cause (Question the Obvious)....487
Step 3. Test the Theory to Determine the Cause 495
Step 4. Establish a Plan of Action to Resolve the Problem and Implement the Solution....497
Step 5. Verify Full System Functionality and, If Applicable, Implement Preventive Measures....497
Step 6. Document the Findings, Actions, and Outcomes....497
Sample Troubleshooting Flowcharts....498
Chapter Summary 502
Key Terms....504
Review Questions....505
Exercises 506
Exercise 11.1 Recommending Computer System Design....506
Exercise 11.2 Understanding Design Components....508
Exercise 11.3 Understanding Subsystem Design Components....509
Exercise 11.4 Determining the Troubleshooting Theory Step....511
Activities....511
Internet Discovery....511
Soft Skills 513
Critical Thinking Skills....513

Chapter 12: Internet Connectivity, Virtualization, and Cloud Technologies 515
Internet Connectivity Overview 516
Dial-up Connectivity 516
Cable Modems....518
xDSL Modems....519
VoIP 520
Fiber Networks 522
Satellite Modems....524
Mobile Connectivity Overview 525
Web Browsers 528
Basic Web Browser Issues....531
Introduction to Virtualization....533
Desktop Virtualization Basics....534
Cloud Computing....537
Chapter Summary 543
Key Terms....545
Review Questions....546
Exercises 547
Exercise 12.1 Exploring Internet Connectivity Options 547
Exercise 12.2 Exploring the *Internet Options* Window 548
Activities....549
Internet Discovery....549
Soft Skills 549
Critical Thinking Skills....550

Chapter 13: Networking 551
Networking Overview 552
Network Media Overview 559
Ethernet over Power 568
Protecting Your Network and Cable Investment 569
The OSI Model 573
The TCP/IP Model 575
Network Addressing 577
More IPv4 Addressing 578
Wireless Networks Overview 581
Wireless Network Standards 582
Wireless Network Components 583
Wireless Network Design 585
Antenna Basics 590
Wireless and Wired Client Device Configuration Overview 594
Configuring an End Device: IP Addressing 594
Adding a Computer to a Windows Domain 601
Wireless NIC–Specific Settings 601
Advanced NIC Properties 603
NIC Configuration When Using Virtualization 603
Thin or Thick Client Installation Overview 605
Wireless AP/Router Configuration 607
WWAN Cellular Configuration 608
IoT and Smart Devices 609
Network Troubleshooting 611
Troubleshooting Cable and DSL Modems 619
Networking Multifunction Devices 619
Network Servers 621
Embedded, SCADA, and Legacy Systems 622
Software-Defined Networking 623
Network Terminology 624
The TCP/IP Model in Action 625
More Windows Network Settings 627
Introduction to Shared Folders 632
Chapter Summary 635
Key Terms 637
Review Questions 639
Exercises 642
Exercise 13.1 Understanding Wireless AP Paper Configuration 642
Exercise 13.2 Understanding T568B Color Sequence 642
Exercise 13.3 Recognizing Network Devices 643
Exercise 13.4 Identifying Basic Wireless Network Parts 644
Exercise 13.5 Creating a Wireless Network 644
Exercise 13.6 Practicing with Network Numbers and Broadcast Addresses 645
Exercise 13.7 Practicing with CIDR Notation 646
Exercise 13.8 Determining the Default Gateway 646

Activities 648
Internet Discovery 648
Soft Skills 649
Critical Thinking Skills 649

Chapter 14: Introduction to Operating Systems 651
Operating Systems Overview 652
User Interaction with Operating Systems 653
Overview of Popular Operating Systems 654
32-Bit vs. 64-Bit Operating Systems 655
Windows 10 and Windows 11 Versions 656
Workstation Operating Systems 657
Operating Systems for Mobile Devices 657
End-of-Life (EOL) Concerns 658
Update Limitations 658
Compatibility Concerns 659
Corporate Operating System Needs 660
Basic Windows Usage Overview 661
Windows 10 and Windows 11 Desktop Components 663
Shortcuts and Tiles 669
Recycle Bin 670
Interactions Within a Window 670
Managing Windows Files and Folders 672
Searches and Indexing 678
Attributes, Compression, and Encryption 679
Introduction to Windows Control Panel Utilities 682
Determining the Windows Version 685
Windows Registry 686
Editing the Windows Registry 687
Backing Up Data 688
WinRE 688
Recovering the Windows OS 688
Chapter Summary 690
Key Terms 691
Review Questions 692
Exercises 693
Exercise 14.1 693
Exercise 14.2 694
Exercise 14.3 694
Activities 695
Internet Discovery 695
Soft Skills 695
Critical Thinking Skills 696

Chapter 15: Introduction to Scripting 697
Scripting Overview 698
Command Prompt Overview 699
Command Prompt Basics 699
Moving Around from a Command Prompt 701

The md and rd Commands 705
Two Useful Commands: del and type 706
Copying Files 706
The attrib Command 708
Why Learn Commands? 708
PowerShell 708
Other Commands You Should Look Over 709
Command Format 710
Introduction to Scripting 734
Script File Types 735
Use Cases for Scripting 736
Mitigating Consequences of Scripting 737
Environment Variables 738
Script Syntax 740
Introduction to Script Programming 741
Variables 741
Data Types 743
Examples of Using Variables 744
Comments Within Scripts 745
Basic Script Constructs 746
Decisions: The Selection Structure 746
Compound Conditions and Logical Operators 750
Loops: The Repetition Structure 751
A Brief Look at VBScript and PowerShell 753
Chapter Summary 756
Key Terms 757
Review Questions 758
Exercises 759
Exercise 15.1 Identifying command-line commands 759
Exercise 15.2 Scripting Concepts 760
Activities 760
Internet Discovery 760
Soft Skills 761
Critical Thinking Skills 761

Chapter 16: Advanced Windows 763
Advanced Windows Overview 764
Preinstallation of Windows 764
Installation/Upgrade of Windows 774
Corporate Windows Deployment 775
Verifying the Installation 776
Troubleshooting a Windows Installation 777
Reloading Windows 779
Windows Updates 780
Backing Up the Windows Registry and Data 781
Configuring Windows Overview 783
Configuring Windows 784
Adding Devices 784
Installing/Removing Software 792

Computer Management Console 796
System Tools 797
User Account Management 801
Managing Storage 807
Managing Services and Applications 811
Data Sources (ODBC) 812
Print Management Console 813
Overview of the Windows Boot Process 814
System Restore 815
Windows Recovery Environment (WinRE) 816
Startup Settings Menu 819
System Configuration Utility 820
Task Manager 824
Speeding Up the Windows Boot Process 826
Troubleshooting the Windows Boot Process 827
Black Screen/Video Issues 829
Troubleshooting a Service That Does Not Start 831
Slow Boot 832
Troubleshooting Windows Network Settings 833
Windows Reboots/System Instability 835
Shutdown Problems 835
Summary of Troubleshooting Steps 836
Power Options 836
Monitoring System Performance 838
Supporting Windows Computers Remotely 843
Preventive Maintenance for Your Operating System 846
Chapter Summary 848
Key Terms 850
Review Questions 851
Exercises 852
Exercise 16.1 Windows Tools 852
Exercise 16.2 Task Manager Tabs 853
Exercise 16.3 System Configuration Tabs 854
Activities 854
Internet Discovery 854
Soft Skills 855

Chapter 17: macOS and Linux Operating Systems 857
Introduction to macOS 858
Navigating the User Interface 859
Basic System Usage, Updates, and Backups 862
Management and Troubleshooting Tools 866
Utilities 869
Introduction to Linux 878
Navigating the GNOME User Interface 879
Basic System Usage, Updates, and Backups 880
Command-Line Interface 883
macOS and Linux Best Practices 892

Chapter Summary 893
Key Terms 894
Review Questions 895
Exercises 896
Exercise 17.1 896
Exercise 17.2 896
Activities 897
Internet Discovery 897
Soft Skills 897
Critical Thinking Skills 898

Chapter 18: Computer and Network Security 899
Security Overview 900
Security Policy 900
Physical Security 901
Logical Security 908
Considering the End User 912
Licensing 912
Security Threats and Vulnerabilities 915
Protecting Access to Local and Network Resources 920
Permissions 928
Folder Options 934
Protecting the Operating System and Data 935
Internet Security 942
Remote Access to Network Devices 955
Internet Appliances 956
Wireless Network Security Overview 957
Security Incident Response 964
A Final Word About Security 966
Chapter Summary 968
Key Terms 969
Review Questions 971
Exercises 973
Exercise 18.1 Examining the Security Incident Response 973
Exercise 18.2 Wireless Security 974
Exercise 18.3 Data Security 974
Activities 975
Internet Discovery 975
Soft Skills 976
Critical Thinking Skills 976

Chapter 19: Operational Procedures 977
Operational Procedures Overview 978
Proper Power Handling and Adverse Power Conditions 986
IT Documentation 994
Change Management 999
Chapter Summary 1012
Key Terms 1014
Review Questions 1015

Exercises 1017
Exercise 19.1 Determining a Power Solution 1017
Exercise 19.2 Determining the Type of Documentation Needed 1018
Activities 1018
Internet Discovery 1018
Soft Skills 1019
Critical Thinking Skills 1020

Appendix A: Subnetting Basics 1021
Exercise 1024
Exercise A.1 Subnet Practice Exercise 1024

Appendix B: Certification Exam Objectives (Online)

Glossary 1025

Index 1075

About the Authors

Cheryl Schmidt is a professor of Network Engineering Technology at Florida State College at Jacksonville. Prior to joining the faculty ranks, she oversaw LAN and PC support for the college and other organizations. She started her career as an electronics technician in the U.S. Navy. She teaches computer repair and various networking topics, including CCNA, network management, and network design. She has published other works with Pearson, including *IP Telephony Using CallManager Express* and *Routing and Switching in the Enterprise Lab Guide*.

Cheryl has won awards for teaching and technology, including Outstanding Faculty of the Year, Innovative Teacher of the Year, Cisco Networking Academy Instructor Excellence Award, and Cisco Networking Academy Stand Out Instructor. She has presented at U.S. and international conferences. Cheryl keeps busy maintaining her technical certifications and teaching but also loves to travel, hike, do all types of puzzles, and read.

Christopher Lee teaches Information Technology and Electronics at Florida State College at Jacksonville. A native of Greenville, South Carolina, Chris earned a bachelor's degree and a master's degree in Electrical Engineering from Georgia Institute of Technology. He taught his first computer programming classes at age 14! Since then, he has worked for a variety of companies including IBM, Nortel Networks, Evans Solutions, Convergys Corporation, NGA Human Resources, and himself. His experience spans several industries: Telecommunications, Youth Outside the Educational Mainstream, Information Technology, Higher Education, Human Resources Outsourcing, and Community Development.

Chris has devoted countless volunteer hours in technology outreach. He enjoys helping children and adults (especially those in underserved communities) learn the skills or access the resources they need to be competitive in today's technological society. He has built strong partnerships with and implemented successful programs in organizations such as National Society of Black Engineers Jr (NSBE Jr), For Inspiration and Recognition in Science and Technology (FIRST) LEGO League, Northeast Florida STEM2 Hub, Tristan's Acceleration Academy, and Renaissance JAX.

Dedications

A Note to Instructors from Cheryl:

I was a teacher long before I had the title professor. Sharing what I know has always been as natural as walking to me, but sitting still to write what I know is not as natural, so composing this text has been one of my greatest challenges. Thank you so much for choosing this text. I thank you for sharing your knowledge and experience with your students. Your dedication to education is what makes the student experience so valuable.

A Note to Students:

Writing a textbook is really different from teaching class. I have said for years that my students are like my children, except that I don't have to pay to send them through college. I am happy to claim any of you who have this text. I wish that I could be in each classroom with you as you start your IT career. How exciting!

IT support is an ever-changing field. You have to be excited about the never-ending changes to be good in this field. You can never stop learning, or you will not be very good anymore. I offer this important piece of advice:

> Consistent, high-quality service boils down to two equally important things: caring and competence.
> —Chip R. Bell and Ron Zemke

Acknowledgments

From Cheryl Schmidt:

I am so thankful for the support of my family during the production of this book. My husband, Karl, daughters, Raina and Karalina, and son-in-law, Marc, were such a source of inspiration and encouragement. My grandsons, Gavin, Riley, Logan, and Liam, and my granddaughters, Brie and Liv, are a constant source of wonderment for me. Thanks to my mother who recently passed away, Barbara Cansler, who taught me to love words, and my brother, Jeff Cansler, for just listening. Thanks to my walking buddy, Kellie, for the miles of letting me work through knotty sections. Thanks to my colleagues, adjuncts, and students at my college who offered numerous valuable suggestions for improvement and testing the new material. Thanks to my colleagues Pamela Brauda and David Singletary for inspiring me as a teacher. Finally, I want to thank my co-author and a great teacher, Chris Lee, as well as my personal technical team, Justin Ache, Raina Durrence, Marc Durrence, and Jeff Burns.

Many thanks are also due the folks at Pearson. The professionalism and support given during this edition was stellar. Thank you so much, Pearson team, especially James Manly, Eleanor Bru, Kitty Wilson, Mandie Frank, and Chris Crayton. I thank the whole team so much for your conscientious efforts.

Finally, thank you to the students who have taken the time to share their recommendations for improvement. You are the reason I write this book each time. Please send me any ideas and comments you may have. I love hearing from you and of your successes. I may be reached at cheryl.schmidt@fscj.edu.

From Chris Lee:

I am thankful for the lifetime of support and guidance that have allowed me to achieve my dreams and contribute to this book. My parents, Brenda McClinton and Herman Brown, have always encouraged me to follow my own path. They have also been my favorite remote "clients," as they have embraced computer technology whereas many of their peers find it intimidating. My grandparents, Roosevelt and Bettye Nelson, are my biggest cheerleaders; they're always excited to hear about my latest projects during our weekly phone calls. I appreciate the patience and motivation from my son, Jawara, as he discovers his own niche within the world of computer science and in life itself.

Some very special teachers also deserve recognition. Mr. William Marshall at the Phyllis Wheatley Community Center allowed me to make or build whatever I wanted in the Arts and Crafts room. He saw the budding engineer in me and allowed me to discover my passion. Mrs. Linda Dillard at Duncan Chapel Elementary School instilled the discipline that I needed to stay focused amid so many distractions. Mrs. Jeanne Perkinson at Wade Hampton High School took my B.A.S.I.C. programming to the next level and introduced me to structured programming. Dr. George Lee Cain helped me weather my first term at Georgia Tech. OMED Student Services and Dr. Gary S. May at Georgia Tech gave me numerous resources to navigate college life and exposed me to several opportunities to develop my skills and serve my community.

We Want to Hear from You!

As the reader of this book, *you* are our most important critic and commentator. We value your opinion and want to know what we're doing right, what we could do better, what areas you'd like to see us publish in, and any other words of wisdom you're willing to pass our way.

We welcome your comments. You can email or write to let us know what you did or didn't like about this book—as well as what we can do to make our books better.

Please note that we cannot help you with technical problems related to the topic of this book.

When you write, please be sure to include this book's title and author as well as your name and email address. We will carefully review your comments and share them with the author and editors who worked on the book.

Email: community@informit.com

Introduction

Complete A+ Guide to IT Hardware and Software, ninth edition, is a textbook and optional lab manual intended for one or more courses geared toward CompTIA A+ Certification and computer repair. It covers all the material needed for the CompTIA A+ Core 1 (220-1101) and CompTIA A+ Core 2 (220-1102) exams. The book is written so that it is easy to read and understand, with concepts presented in building-block fashion. The book focuses on hardware, software, mobile devices, virtualization, basic networking, and security.

Some of the best features of the book include the coverage of difficult subjects in a step-by-step manner, carefully developed graphics that illustrate concepts, photographs that demonstrate various technologies, reinforcement questions, critical thinking skills, soft skills, and hands-on exercises at the end of each chapter. Also, this book is written by teachers who understand the value of a textbook as we both are very active in the classroom and community.

What's New in the Ninth Edition?

This edition has been revised to include more relevant coverage of hardware, including SSD migration and a few new network concepts, such as updated wireless standards, updated browser security settings, and DNS material. Some references to Windows 7 were left where it is quite different from Windows 8, 10, or 11. More scripting is included as well. The following are a few of the many new features of this edition:

- This book conforms with the latest CompTIA A+ exam requirements, including those of the CompTIA A+ Core 1 (220-1101) and CompTIA A+ Core 2 (220-1102) exams.
- Chapter 2 now includes information on Cat 8 and direct burial cable, as well as updated graphics showing motherboard ports.
- Chapter 3 now includes information regarding ARM processors.
- The video information in Chapter 4 has been moved to Chapter 8. Chapter 4 introduces TPM, which is covered in more depth in Chapter 18.
- The book has always been filled with graphics and photos, but even more have been added to target those naturally drawn to the IT field. This edition is full color.
- There are questions at the end of each chapter, and even more questions are available in the test bank available from the Pearson Instructor Resource Center.

Organization of the Text

The text is organized to allow thorough coverage of all topics and also to be a flexible teaching tool. It is not necessary to cover all the chapters, nor do the chapters have to be covered in order.

- **Chapter 1** provides an introduction to IT and careers that need the information in this book. It identifies computer parts. Chapter 1 does not have a specific soft skills section, as do the other chapters. Instead, it focuses on common technician qualities that are explored in greater detail in the soft skills sections of later chapters. Finally, Chapter 1 provides a great introduction to using Notepad, the Windows Snipping Tool, and internet search techniques.
- **Chapter 2** is about connecting things to a computer and port identification. Details are provided on video, USB, and sound ports. The soft skills section is on using appropriate titles.
- **Chapter 3** details components, features, and concepts related to motherboards, including processors, caches, expansion slots, and chipsets. Active listening skills are the focus of the soft skills section.
- **Chapter 4** deals with system configuration basics. BIOS options, UEFI BIOS, and system resources are key topics. The soft skills section covers the importance of doing one thing at a time when replacing components.

- **Chapter 5** steps through how to disassemble and reassemble a computer. Tools, ESD, EMI, and preventive maintenance are discussed. Subsequent chapters also include preventive maintenance topics. Basic electronics and computer power concepts are also included in this chapter. The soft skills section involves written communication.
- **Chapter 6** covers memory installation, preparation, and troubleshooting. The importance of teamwork is emphasized as the soft skill.
- **Chapter 7** deals with storage devices, including SATA SCSI, SAS, and SSDs. RAID is also covered. Phone communication skills are covered in the soft skills section of this chapter.
- **Chapter 8** covers video and multimedia devices, including optical drives, sound cards, cameras, scanners, and speakers. The chapter ends with a section on having a positive, proactive attitude.
- **Chapter 9** provides details on printers and multifunction devices. A discussion of work ethics finishes the chapter.
- **Chapter 10** is on mobile devices, including details on mobile device operating systems, configuration, backup, security, and troubleshooting. The soft skills section takes a brief foray into professional appearance.
- **Chapter 11** covers computer design. Not only are the specialized computers and components needed within the types of systems covered, but computer subsystem design is also included. Because design and troubleshooting use higher levels of critical thinking skills, the chapter also includes a review of troubleshooting, including logic, error codes, and troubleshooting flowcharts. The soft skills section provides recommendations for dealing with irate customers.
- **Chapter 12** handles internet connectivity, virtualization, and cloud technologies. It covers internet browser configuration, along with the soft skill mentoring
- **Chapter 13** introduces networking. Basic concepts, terminology, and exercises make this chapter a favorite. Appendix A provides an introduction to subnetting that can be used in conjunction with this chapter. The focus of the soft skills section is being proactive instead of reactive.
- **Chapter 14** provides an introduction to operating systems in general and discusses basic differences between the Windows versions and how to function in the various Windows environments. The soft skills section includes tips on how to stay current in this fast-paced field.
- **Chapter 15** provides an introduction to scripting and includes how to function from the command prompt and the basics of scripting in Python, JavaScript, shell scripting, VBScript, batch files, and PowerShell. The soft skills section discusses looking at a problem from the user's perspective and being more empathetic.
- **Chapter 16** covers Windows 8, 10, and 11. Details include how to install, configure, and troubleshoot the environment. Avoiding burnout is the soft skill discussed in this chapter.
- **Chapter 17** discusses the basics of macOS and Linux. It provides a basic introduction to these two environments to help a technician become familiar with the environment and a few tools. The soft skills section talks about being humble.
- **Chapter 18** describes computer, mobile device, and network security. The soft skills section is on building customer trust.
- **Chapter 19** guides the student through operational procedures such as workplace safety, recycling, disposal, a review of power protection, change management, and soft skills.
- **Appendix A** is an introduction to subnetting and variable length subnet mask (VLSM).

Features of This Book

The following key features of the book are designed to enable a better learning experience:

- **Objectives:** Each chapter begins with both chapter objectives and the CompTIA A+ exam objectives.
- **Graphics and photographs:** Many more full-color images and all-new graphics have been added to better illustrate the concepts.
- **Tech Tips:** The chapters are filled with Tech Tips that highlight technical issues and certification exam topics.
- **Key terms in context:** As you read the chapter, terms that appear in blue are considered key terms and are defined in the glossary.

- **Key Terms list:** At the end of the chapter, all key terms are listed, along with page numbers to which to refer for context.
- **Soft Skills:** Technology is not the only thing you must learn and practice; each chapter offers advice, activities, and examples of how to be a good tech, an ethical tech, a good work mate, a good communicator, and so on.
- **Chapter Summary:** The summary recaps the key concepts of the chapter, and you can use it for review to ensure that you've mastered the chapter's learning objectives.
- **A+ Certification Exam Tips:** Read through these tips on the CompTIA A+ exams so you aren't caught off guard when you sit for the exam.
- **Review Questions:** Hundreds of review questions, including true/false, multiple choice, matching, fill-in-the-blank, and open-ended questions, assess your knowledge of the topics taught in each chapter.
- **Applying your knowledge:** This book provides hundreds of exercises and activities to help you put into practice what you are learning:
  - **Exercises:** Sometimes called "paper labs," the exercises need no lab devices to complete in the classroom or for homework.
  - **Activities:** The activities provide extensive practice with internet discovery, soft skills, and critical thinking skills to round out your technical knowledge so that you can be prepared for IT work. These can be used to "Flip the Classroom" so that instruction is interactive and in the hands of the students.
- **Lab Exercises:** The separate companion *Complete A+ Guide to IT Hardware and Software Lab Manual* (on the companion web page) contains more than 140 labs in total. These hands-on labs enable you to link theory to practical experience.

Companion Website

Register this book to get access to the **lab manual** plus additional bonus content to help you succeed with this course and the certification exam. Check this site regularly for any updates or errata that might become available for this book. Be sure to check the box indicating that you would like to hear from us to receive news of updates and exclusive discounts on related products.

To access this companion website, follow the steps below:

1. Go to *www.pearsonITcertification.com/register* and log in or create a new account.
2. Enter the ISBN 9780137670444.
3. Answer the challenge question as proof of purchase.
4. Click the *Access Bonus Content* link in the Registered Products section of your account page to be taken to the page where your downloadable content is available.

Please note that many of our companion content files can be very large, especially image and video files.

If you are unable to locate the files for this title by following the steps above, please visit www.pearsonITcertification.com/contact and select the *Site Problems/Comments* option. Our customer service representatives will assist you.

CompTIA A+ Exam Objectives

To earn CompTIA A+ certification, you must pass both the CompTIA A+ Core 1 (220-1101) and CompTIA A+ Core 2 (220-1102) certification exams.

Tables I.1 and I.2 summarize the domain content for each exam.

TABLE I.1 CompTIA A+ Core 1 (220-1101) exam

Domain	Percentage of examination
1.0 Mobile Devices	15%
2.0 Networking	20%
3.0 Hardware	25%
4.0 Virtualization and Cloud Computing	11%
5.0 Hardware and Network Troubleshooting	29%
Total	100%

TABLE I.2 CompTIA A+ Core 2 (220-1102) exam

Domain	Percentage of examination
1.0 Operating Systems	31%
2.0 Security	25%
3.0 Software Troubleshooting	22%
4.0 Operational Procedures	22%
Total	100%

Table I.3 shows a summary of the exam domains addressed in each chapter. Each chapter lists the certification objectives it covers in the chapter opener. See Appendix B on the companion website for a detailed table that identifies where you can find all the CompTIA A+ exam objectives covered in this book.

TABLE I.3 Summary of exam domains by chapter

Table of contents	220-1101 domains	220-1102 domains
Chapter 1: Introduction to the World of IT	3	4
Chapter 2: Connectivity	1, 2, 3	4
Chapter 3: On the Motherboard	3, 5	4
Chapter 4: Introduction to Configuration	3, 5	
Chapter 5: Disassembly and Power	3, 5	4
Chapter 6: Memory	3, 5	1
Chapter 7: Storage Devices	3, 5	1, 2, 3, 4
Chapter 8: Video and Multimedia Devices	3	1, 4
Chapter 9: Printers and Multifunction Devices	2, 3, 5	1, 3, 4
Chapter 10: Mobile Devices	1, 2, 3, 5	1, 2, 3
Chapter 11: Computer Design and Troubleshooting Review	3, 5	4
Chapter 12: Internet Connectivity, Virtualization, and Cloud Technologies	2, 3, 4	1, 2, 3
Chapter 13: Networking	2, 3, 4, 5	1, 2, 3, 4
Chapter 14: Introduction to Operating Systems		1, 2, 3

Table of contents	220-1101 domains	220-1102 domains
Chapter 15: Introduction to Scripting		1, 3, 4
Chapter 16: Advanced Windows		1, 2, 3, 4
Chapter 17: macOS and Linux Operating Systems		1, 3
Chapter 18: Computer and Network Security	2, 3	1, 2, 3, 4
Chapter 19: Operational Procedures		4

1 Introduction to the World of IT

In this chapter you will learn:

- > Qualities a technician should have
- > Basic skills needed to function in the Windows environment and in the technical world
- > Important computer parts
- > Basic computer terms

CompTIA Exam Objectives:

- ✓ 1101-3.1 Explain basic cable types and their connectors, features, and purposes.
- ✓ 1101-3.6 Given a scenario, deploy and configure multifunction devices/printers and settings.
- ✓ 1102-4.4 Given a scenario, use common safety procedures.
- ✓ 1102-4.7 Given a scenario, use proper communication techniques and professionalism.

Who Needs This Book?

More types of people than you might first think need this book. People who obviously need this information are those who will fix computers or work on a help desk or support desk. However, there are other types of users who might not be so obvious. Many folks who break into the information technology (IT) world do so through jobs that require the A+ certification. Consider medical electronics technicians who repair common equipment used in hospitals. These technicians need this material because many medical devices connect to a PC or have PC-based software that controls the device. Further, the medical devices commonly attach to wired and wireless networks.

Look at Figure 1.1 to see the types of jobs and people who need the information in this book. It might also give you ideas about something you might like to do for a career.

FIGURE 1.1 IT roles

Technician Qualities

Each chapter includes a small bit of space on qualities a technician should possess or strive toward. Spending a little brain power on improving what many call your "soft skills" will pay off in promotions. Three of the most important qualities of a technician are active listening skills, a good attitude, and logic. Active listening means that you truly listen to what a person is saying. **Active listening skills** involve good eye contact, nodding your head every now and then to show that you are following the conversation, taking notes on important details, and avoiding distractions such as incoming calls or text messages. **Clarify customer statements** by asking pertinent questions and avoid interrupting. Listen to the entire problem. Ask **open-ended questions**—questions that allow the user to expand on the answer rather than answer with a single word, such as *yes* or *no*. Figure 1.2 illustrates this point.

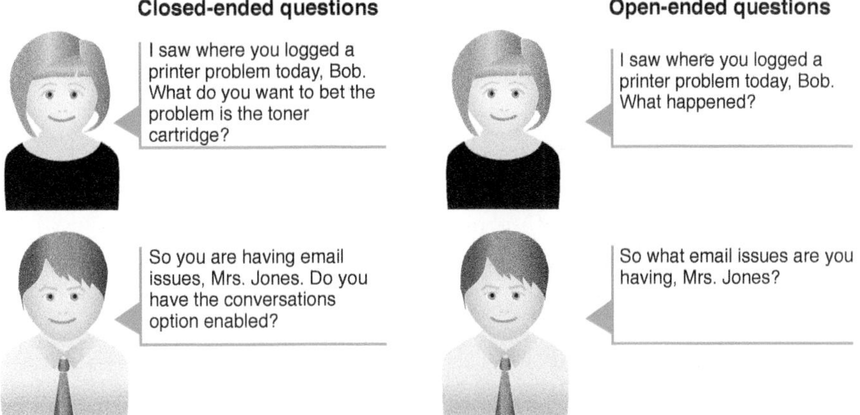

Allow the users to state the problem without leading them toward a solution. Restate the problem to ensure understanding and ask questions for clarity and to narrow your understanding.

FIGURE 1.2 Asking technical questions

A positive attitude is probably the best quality a technician can possess. A technician with a positive attitude does not diminish the customer's problem; every problem is equally important to the computer user. A positive attitude is critical for being successful in the computer service industry. Figure 1.3 shows how negative attitudes affect your success.

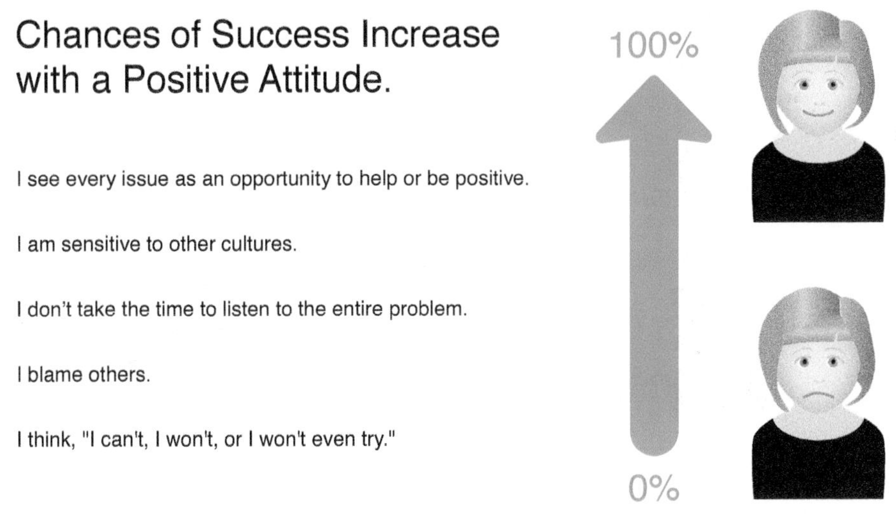

FIGURE 1.3 Have a positive attitude

Avoid developing tunnel vision (that is, thinking that there is only one answer to a problem). Step back and look at the problem so that all possible issues can be evaluated. Be logical in your assessment and the methods used to troubleshoot and repair. This book will help you with all of this by explaining computer terminology in easy-to-understand terms and providing analogies that can be used when dealing with customers.

Before delving into computer topics, you should remember that a class can't fully prepare you for every aspect of a job. You must learn things on your own and constantly strive to update your skills so you do not become obsolete. The IT field changes rapidly. Figure 1.4 illustrates this concept. Finally, you will find that you must be a jack of all trades, as shown in Figure 1.5.

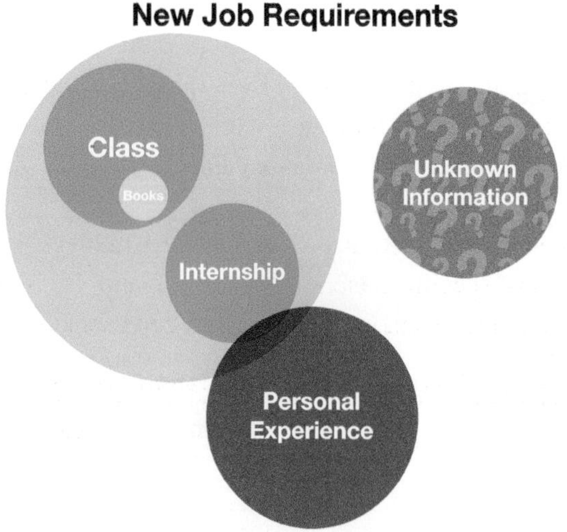

FIGURE 1.4 Preparing for IT job requirements

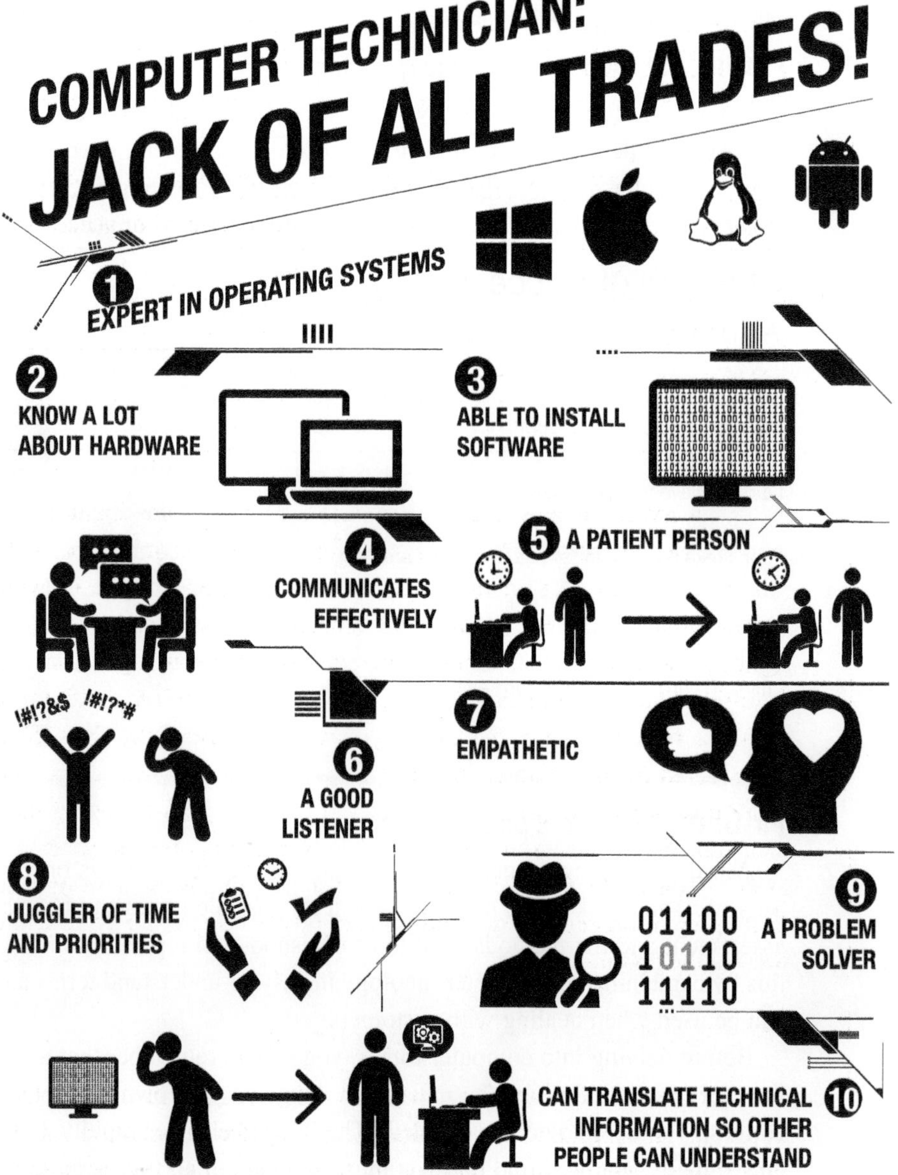

FIGURE 1.5 Computer technician skills

Breaking into IT with the CompTIA A+ Certification

Many IT-related jobs require the A+ certification. Even if not required, the certification shows that you have a good understanding of how computers work. This certification does not guarantee you a job, but it does open doors in that a company may interview you if you lack IT experience but have the A+ certification.

A+ certification requires that you take two exams: Core 1 (220-1101) and Core 2 (220-1102). Each of these exams covers specific material. Tables 1.1 and 1.2 show the major categories (domains) for each exam and the extent to which they are represented.

TABLE 1.1 CompTIA Core 1 (220-1101) A+ certification domains

Domain	Percentage of examination	Chapter(s)
1.0 Mobile Devices	15%	10
2.0 Networking	20%	12–13
3.0 Hardware	25%	1–9, 11
4.0 Virtualization and Cloud Computing	11%	3, 12
5.0 Hardware and Network Troubleshooting	29%	1–13

TABLE 1.2 CompTIA Core 2 (220-1102) A+ certification domains

Domain	Percentage of examination	Chapter(s)
1.0 Operating Systems	31%	14–17
2.0 Security	25%	18
3.0 Software Troubleshooting	22%	14–18
4.0 Operational Procedures	22%	19

"What are the exams like?" you might ask. The exams include multiple-choice and performance-based questions. A performance-based question might be a drag-and-drop scenario or might ask you to do something specific on a particular device or within a particular operating system environment. Each exam is 90 minutes long and contains a maximum of 90 questions. The testing system allows you to bookmark questions that you might want to return to at the end if you have time. More information can be found on the CompTIA website (www.comptia.org).

At the beginning of each chapter, you will see a list of the CompTIA A+ exam objectives that are covered in that chapter. At the end of each chapter, we've provided some A+ certification exam tips—tips to definitely pay attention to if you plan on taking the A+ exams. I recommend that you review the exam objectives, study material specific to them, and take some practice exams. Pearson IT Certification, the publisher of this book, develops many different certification exam prep resources that suit various study styles. Go to http://pearsonitcertification.com/aplus to browse the options.

Basic Skills for This Course

In order to repair a computer, you need a few basic skills that include being familiar with the keyboard and inputting information, searching for information on the internet, and capturing information. Just because you may not be a good typist does not mean that you will not be good in an IT-related field.

Searching for Information on the Internet

IT people need to use all available resources, including online resources. As noted, you need to be capable of searching for information online. Figure 1.6 illustrates various online resources that IT people search all the time.

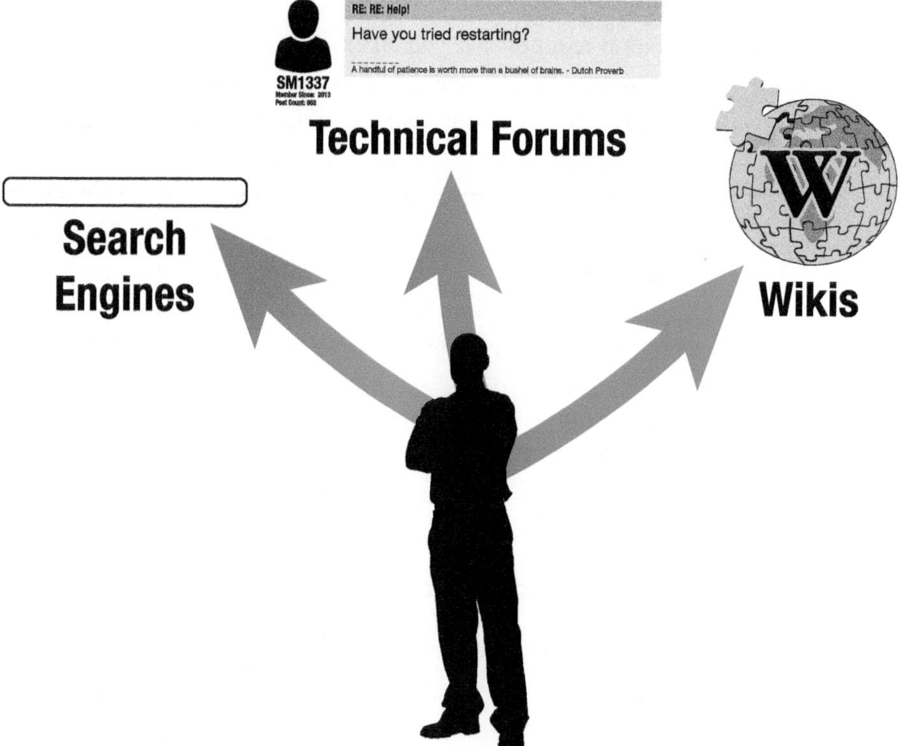

FIGURE 1.6 Search skills

Each chapter in the book has an activity at the end of it that enables you to practice searching the internet for information relevant to the chapter. Tips for searching include the following:

- Search engines use different algorithms, so if one does not work, try another one. Examples of search engines are Google, Bing, Yahoo, and Ask. To access a search engine, open a web browser and type one of the search engine names followed by `.com`. Figure 1.7 shows where you enter the search engine name in the address bar.

FIGURE 1.7 Web browser address bar

- Use descriptive key words.
- Do not include common words like *the*, *in*, *at*, or *for* because search engines tend to skip these words anyway. If you do want to use one of them, put a plus sign (+) in front of the word.

- Avoid using a complex version, plural, or past tense of a word to avoid eliminating pages that are relevant. For example, to search for how to install a Bluetooth headset, avoid using the word *installation*, *installed*, or *installing* in the search window. Simply include the word *install*.
- If several words are used together (an exact phrase), such as Windows 10, put quotation marks around the phrase—**`"Windows 10"`**.
- Use as many distinguishing words as possible.
- If two words have the same meaning and are commonly used, use the word *or* in the search. For example, to search for generic information on a dot matrix printer, which is sometimes called an impact printer, you might search as follows: `"dot matrix" or "impact printer"`. Note that the vertical bar (|), which is the key above the Enter key, can be used instead of the word *or*, as follows: `"dot matrix"` | `"impact printer"`.
- If a particular term can have two meanings (such as the word *memory* relating to something inside a computer or else relating to a brain function), you can use the minus sign in order to keep some information from being displayed. `memory -brain`, for example, would be a search for memory without any brain function results included.
- If a particular term (such as *memory*) is generic, you can add a word and use the word *AND* in order to clarify the search, such as `computer AND memory`.
- When searching for technical information, include the hardware or software manufacturer. A search for `Microsoft Windows 10` provides different results than a search for `Windows 10`.
- If nothing relevant is on the first page of links, change the key words used in your search.

Consider the situation of a keyboard that intermittently works on a Microsoft Surface computer. The keyboard does not come standard as part of a Surface purchase. You do not own a Surface yourself and are unfamiliar with the tablet but must support it. An example of what might be typed into a search engine is `Microsoft Surface intermittent keyboard`.

Screen Capturing

Sometimes, part of technical documentation is being able to capture what is on the screen. Windows versions come with the Snipping Tool and Snip & Sketch; you can access these tools by holding down the Windows key, pressing and holding the Shift key, and pressing the S key. This makes documenting problems easy, and you can copy what you capture into other applications. It doesn't matter what IT job you may have when you enter the workforce; documentation is a part of all IT jobs.

Creating a Text File

Another part of documentation might involve creating or using a text file, known as a .txt file. You might need to send it as an attachment, or you might need to create a text file as part of the job. Sometimes a text file is the easiest type of file to create, especially on a mobile device. Text files can be created using a word processor and the *Save As* process, or they can be created using an app. Text files are popular because they can be opened by many apps. Text files commonly include only text, without multiple fonts or graphics. Windows has Notepad, and Apple has TextEdit, which can be used to create or open text files.

Types of Computers

The simplest place to start to learn about technical support is with the devices themselves. The **PC**, or personal computer, comes in desktop, tower, and all-in-one models, as well as mobile models such as laptops, smartphones, and tablets. Figure 1.8 shows some of the devices technical staff are expected to support.

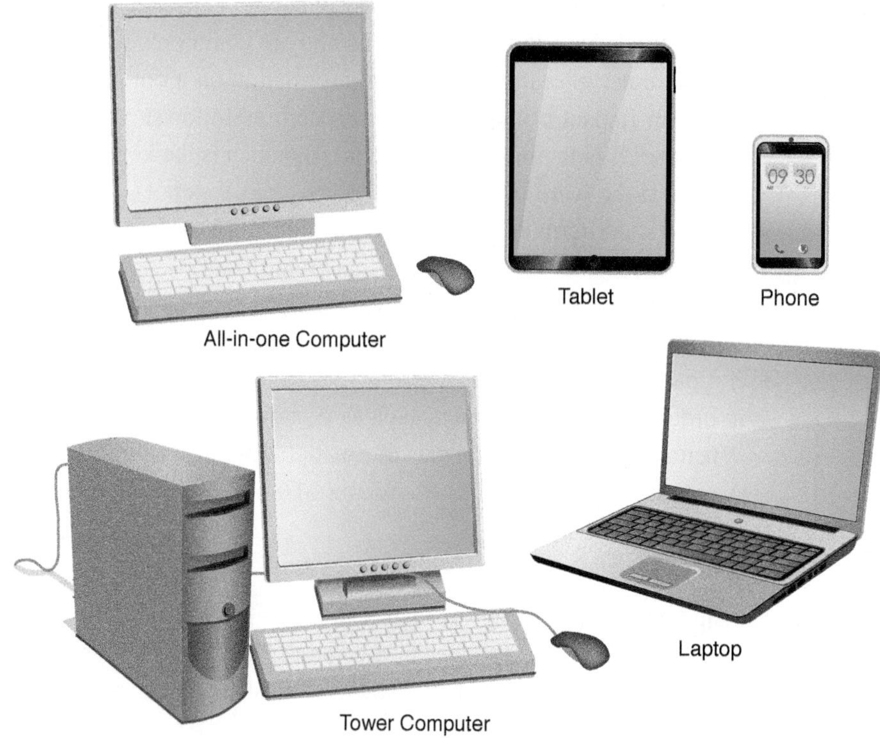

FIGURE 1.8 Types of computers

Basic Computer Hardware

Computer systems include hardware, software, and firmware. **Hardware** is something you can touch and feel, like the physical computer and the parts inside the computer. The monitor, keyboard, and mouse are hardware components. **Software** interacts with the hardware. Windows, Linux, macOS, Microsoft 365, Google Chrome, Adobe Acrobat Reader, Intuit TurboTax, and WordPerfect are examples of software.

Without software that directs the hardware to do something, a computer is useless. Every computer needs an important piece of software called an **operating system**, which coordinates the interaction between hardware and software applications. The operating system also handles the interaction between a user and the computer. Examples of operating systems include Windows 10 and 11, macOS, and various Linux systems, such as Red Hat and Ubuntu.

A **device driver** enables the operating system to recognize, control, and use a hardware component. Device drivers are hardware and operating system specific. For example, a printer requires a specific device driver when connected to a computer that used to have Windows 7 installed. The same printer might require a different device driver when using Windows 10 or 11. That Windows print driver would not work on an Apple computer. Each piece of installed hardware requires a device driver for the operating system being used. Figure 1.9 shows how hardware and software must work together.

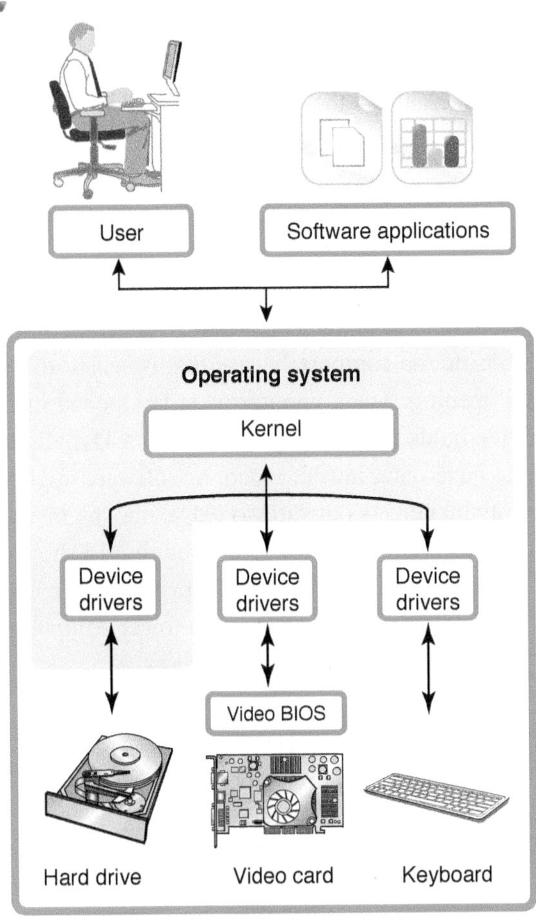

FIGURE 1.9 Hardware and software

Notice in Figure 1.9 the operating system kernel. The kernel is the central part of an operating system. The kernel is the connection between hardware and the applications being used.

A PC typically consists of a case (chassis), a keyboard that allows users to provide input into the computer, a **monitor** that outputs or displays information (shown in Figure 1.10), and a mouse that allows data input or is used to select menus and options. Figure 1.10 shows a computer monitor, which may also be called a flat panel, display, or screen.

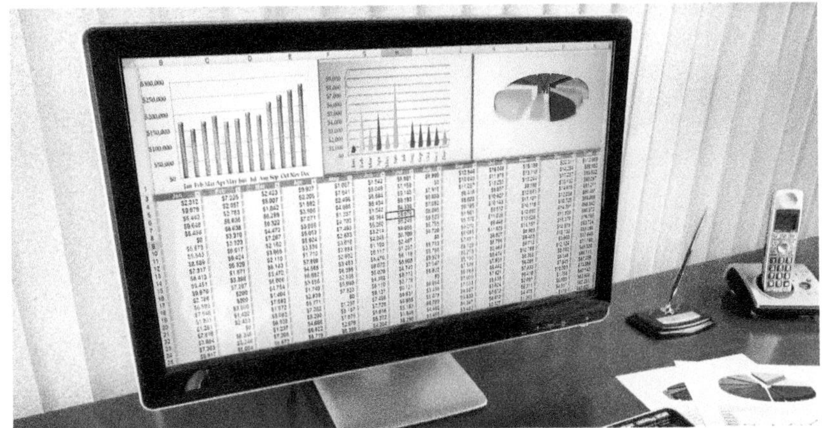

FIGURE 1.10 Computer monitor

When the computer cover or side is opened or removed, the parts inside can be identified. The easiest part to identify is the **power supply**, which is the metal box normally located in a back corner of a case. A power cord connects the power supply to a wall outlet or surge strip. One purpose of the power supply is to convert the outlet AC voltage to DC voltage used internally in the PC. The power supply distributes this DC voltage using cables that connect to the various internal computer parts. A fan located inside the power supply keeps the computer cool to prevent damage to the components.

A PC usually has a device to store software applications and files. Two examples of storage devices are the hard drive and optical drive. The **hard drive**, sometimes called the hard disk, is a rectangular box normally inside the computer's case that is sealed to keep out dust and dirt. The hard drive has no external opening. The computer must be opened in order to access an internal hard drive. An **optical drive** holds discs (compact discs, or CDs), digital versatile discs (DVDs), or Blu-ray discs (BDs) that have data, music, video, or software applications on them. The front of the optical drive has a tray that ejects outward so a disc may be inserted. Figure 1.11 shows the major components of a tower computer. Figures 1.12 through 1.14 show components as they would look before being installed. Figure 1.12 shows a hard drive. Figure 1.13 shows an optical drive. Figure 1.14 shows a power supply. Figure 1.15 shows a tower computer case.

FIGURE 1.11 Tower computer

FIGURE 1.12 Hard drive

FIGURE 1.13 DVD or optical drive

FIGURE 1.14 Power supply

FIGURE 1.15 Tower case

The **motherboard** is the main circuit board inside a PC and contains the most electronics. It is normally located on the bottom of a desktop or laptop computer and mounted on the side of a tower computer. Other names for the motherboard include mainboard, planar, or system board. External devices connect directly to the back of the motherboard or ports on the front of the computer. Figure 1.16 shows a motherboard when it is not installed inside a computer as well as memory and an adapter, which are covered next.

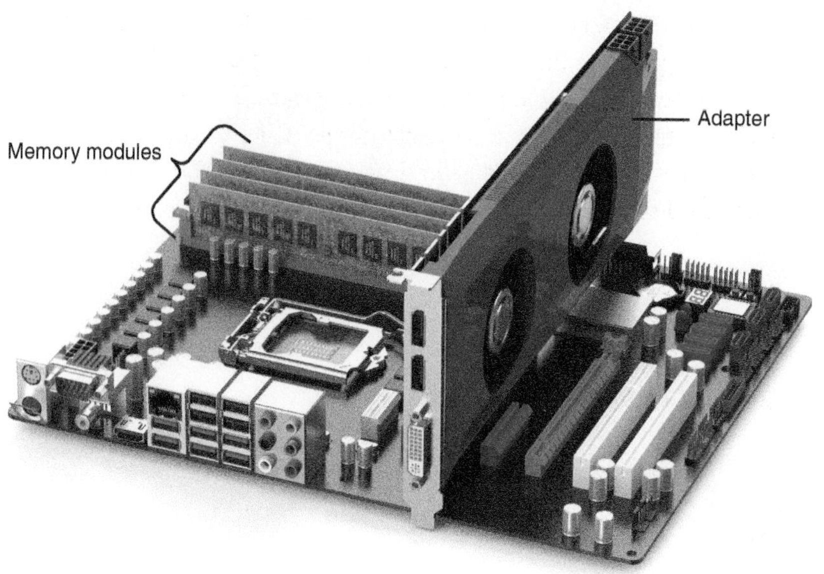

FIGURE 1.16 Computer motherboard

The motherboard holds memory modules. **Memory** modules hold applications, part of the operating system, and user documents. Random-access memory (**RAM**) is the most common type of memory on the motherboard and is volatile; that is, the data inside the module is lost when power is removed. When a user types a document in a word processing program, both the word processing application and the document are in RAM. If the user turns the computer off without saving the document to removable media or the hard drive, the document is lost because the information does not stay in RAM. (Note that some applications have the ability to periodically save a document, but this is not a guarantee that it has the latest information.) Figure 1.17 shows memory modules when they are not installed into the motherboard memory slots. Memory is covered in great detail in Chapter 6, "Memory."

FIGURE 1.17 Memory modules

A device may have a cable that connects the device to the motherboard. Other devices require an adapter. An **adapter** is an electronic card that plugs into an **expansion slot** on the motherboard. Other names for an adapter are controller, card, controller card, circuit card, circuit board, and adapter board. Adapters allow someone to add functionality or an enhancement that is not provided through the ports on the motherboard, such as better sound or video graphics or additional ports of some type in order to connect external devices. Figure 1.18 shows an adapter. Notice how the contacts at the bottom are a particular shape. Chapter 3, "On the Motherboard," goes into more detail about the types of expansion slots and adapters. You can also look back to Figure 1.16 to see a video card/adapter installed into a motherboard expansion slot.

FIGURE 1.18 Adapter

TECH TIP

How to identify an adapter's function

Tracing the cable attached to an adapter or looking at the device connected to an adapter can help identify the adapter's function.

The following are the generic steps for installing adapters:

Step 1. Always follow the manufacturer's installation directions. Use an antistatic wrist strap when handling adapters. Electrostatic discharge (ESD) can damage electronic parts. (See Chapter 5, "Disassembly and Power," for more details on ESD.)

Step 2. Be sure the computer is powered off and unplugged.

Step 3. Remove any brackets from the case or plastic covers from the rear of the computer that may prevent adapter installation. Install the adapter in a free expansion slot and reattach any securing hardware.

Step 4. Attach any internal device cables that connect to the adapter, as well as any cables that go to an external port on the adapter.

Step 5. Attach any internal or external devices to the opposite ends of the cable, if necessary.

Step 6. Power on any external devices connected to the adapter, if applicable.

Step 7. Reattach the computer power cord and power on the computer.

Step 8. Load any application software or device drivers needed for the devices attached to the adapter.

Step 9. Test the device connected to the adapter.

See Figure 1.19 for an illustration of a motherboard, expansion slots, memory, and an adapter in an expansion slot.

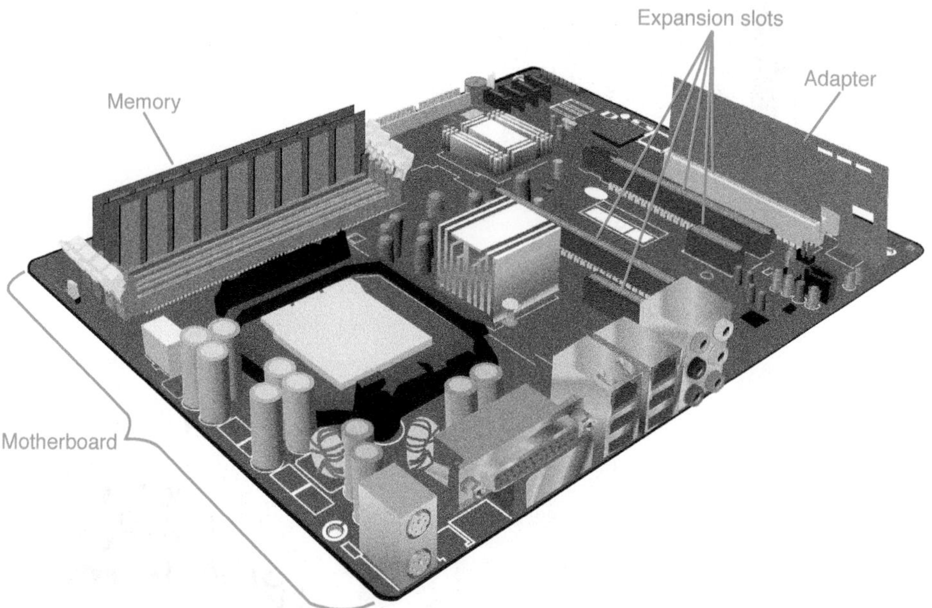

FIGURE 1.19 Motherboard with expansion slots and an adapter

Mice and Keyboards

Input devices, such as the mouse and keyboard, attach to the motherboard. The most common type of **mouse** is an optical mouse, which has optical sensors that detect the direction in which the mouse moves. It uses reflections from light-emitting diodes (LEDs) from almost any surface to detect the mouse location. Mice commonly can be adjusted for sensitivity—how far you have to move the mouse to move the cursor on the screen a desired amount. Figure 1.20 shows a photo of the bottom of an optical mouse.

A **keyboard** is an input device that connects to a port on the motherboard or attaches wirelessly. Features users look for in a keyboard include a separate numeric keypad for those who have to input a great deal of numbers, adjustable tilt legs, and spill resistance. Figure 1.21 shows the type of keyboard and mouse that are commonly used with a tower, desktop, or all-in-one computer.

FIGURE 1.20 Optical mouse

FIGURE 1.21 Keyboard and mouse

Mouse and Keyboard Preventive Maintenance

Mouse cleaning kits are available in computer stores, but normal household supplies also work. Use the following procedures to clean an optical mouse:

Step 1. Wipe the bottom with a damp, lint-free cloth.

Step 2. Use compressed air to clean the optical sensors.

Keyboards also need periodic cleaning. Figure 1.22 shows keyboard cleaning techniques.

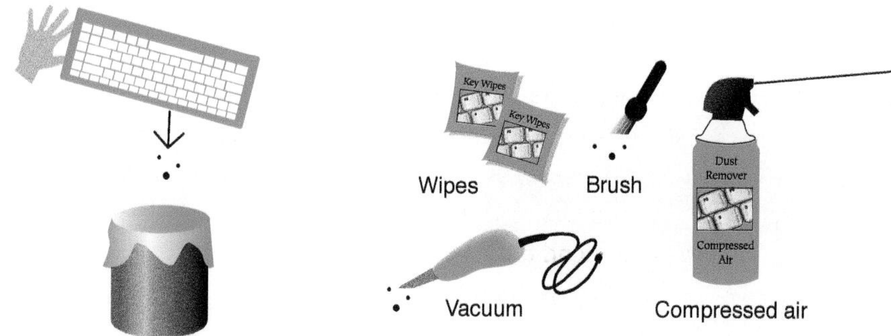

1. Turn keyboard upside down and gently shake out debris

2. Clean the keyboard (several options shown)

FIGURE 1.22 Keyboard cleaning techniques

Keyboard/Mouse Troubleshooting

One of the easiest ways to determine whether a keyboard is working is to press the Caps Lock or Num Lock key and watch to see if the keyboard light illuminates. Sometimes an application setting may be causing what appears to be a keyboard problem. Use another application to see if the keyboard is the problem. Keyboards can have LED lights that indicate particular functions. Table 1.3 lists the most common lights. Note that different vendors label the lights in various ways.

TABLE 1.3 Common keyboard lights

Associated toggle key	Keyboard light	Description
Num Lock	Number lock (NUM LOCK)	Toggles the 10-key pad between digits 0 through 9 and various functions, such as HOME, PG UP, PG DOWN, END, and various arrow keys.
Caps Lock	Capital letters lock (CAPS LOCK)	Toggles between all uppercase and lowercase letters.
Scroll Lock	Scroll lock	A rarely used key used to prevent scrolling and use of the arrow keys to progress through information displayed.

TECH TIP

One key doesn't work

If a particular key is not working properly, remove the key cap. A small, flat-tipped screwdriver can assist with this. After removing the key cap, use compressed air around the sticky or malfunctioning key.

If coffee or another liquid spills into a PC keyboard, all is not lost, but unplug it quickly and away from the computer, turn it over. Use paper towels to get up what water you can. Afterward, the keyboard can be disassembled and/or scrubbed with lint-free swabs or cloths. However, PC keyboards and mice are normally considered throw-away technology. It is cheaper to get a new one than to spend a lot of time trying to repair a keyboard or mouse.

Common Peripherals

Many devices connect to a computer to provide input, such as a mouse or keyboard, or output, such as a display. Some devices can be both input and output devices, such as smart TVs, Musical Instrument Digital Interface– (MIDI–) enabled devices (which are electronic musical devices), touch screens, or printers. In the case of a printer, data is sent from a computer to the printer, and the printer can send data (information), such as an out-of-ink message, back to the computer. Figure 1.23 shows some common input and output devices.

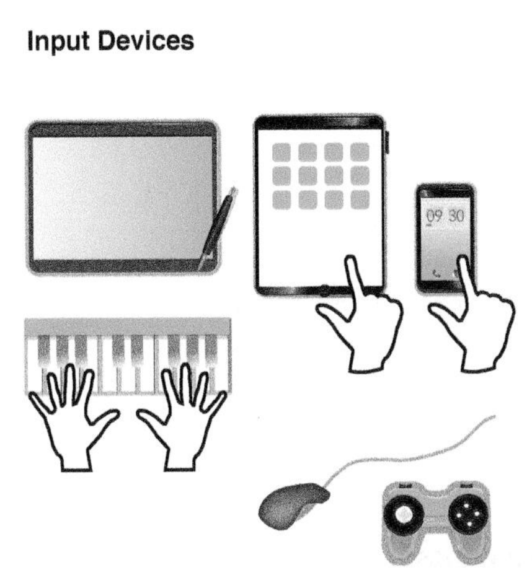

Mouse, Keyboard, Digital Pen, Digital Tablet, Finger, Signature, Pad, Touch Screen, Track Pad, Touchpad, Trackball, Track Stick, Stylus, Barcode Reader, Digitizer, Game Pad/Console, Joystick, Scanner, Camera

Printer, Speakers, Display Devices

FIGURE 1.23 Input and output devices

Table 1.4 lists various peripherals that you will see used and attached to computers today. We will be examining some of these devices in more depth and learn how to configure them, but this is a good chapter to get the basics.

TABLE 1.4 Common peripherals

Peripheral	Description
Printer	An output device that transfers information such as text and graphics from a computer onto paper or other media (see Figure 1.24).
Flatbed scanner	An input device that digitizes words or graphics and can be used as a copier. A scanner may have an automatic document feeder (**ADF**) that allows one or more documents to be fed into the scanner (see Figure 1.24).
All-in-one printer	A device that has a printer, scanner, copier, and sometimes fax capabilities. Sometimes known as a multifunction printer (see Figure 1.24).
Camera/ webcam	An input device used to provide live video feed such as when you participate in a video conference or capture video images or motion (see Figure 1.25). More information can be found in Chapter 8, "Video and Multimedia Devices."
Microphone	An input device used to capture sound (see Figure 1.25). More information can be found in Chapter 8.
Headset	An input/output device that commonly has a microphone and headphones, as shown in Figure 1.25.

FIGURE 1.24 Printer, scanner, and all-in-one printer

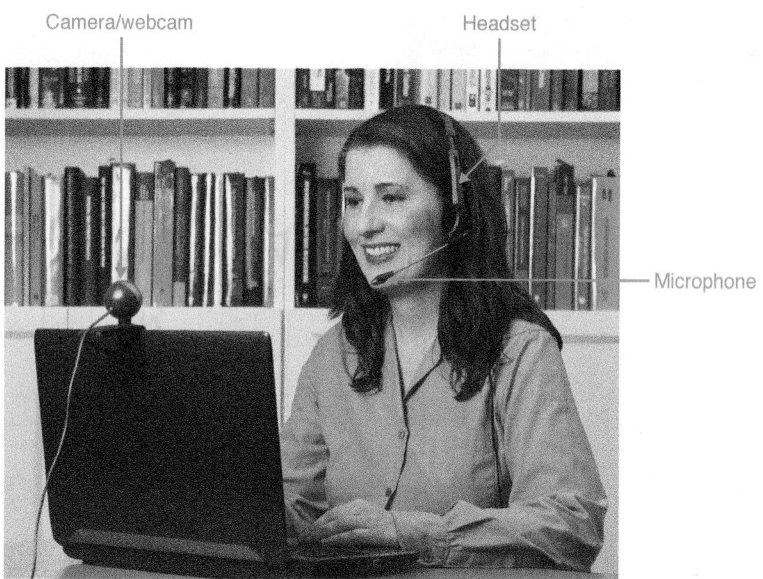

FIGURE 1.25 Camera/webcam, headset, and microphone

1s and 0s

Computers are digital devices. That means they understand 1s and 0s. One 1 or one 0 is known as a **bit**. In actuality, a 1 is simply a voltage level. So, when we type characters into a word processing application, the keyboard translates those characters into voltage levels. Figure 1.26 shows this concept. Notice that each letter is represented by a combination of eight 1s and 0s. Each 1 is a voltage level sent to the motherboard (and components on it). Each 0 is simply the absence of a voltage level.

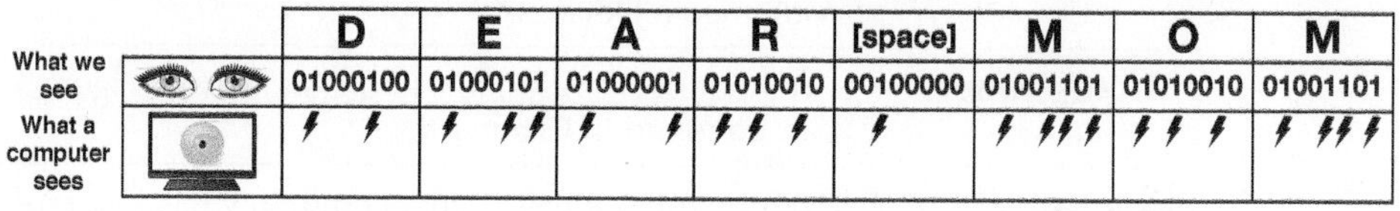

		D	E	A	R	[space]	M	O	M
What we see		01000100	01000101	01000001	01010010	00100000	01001101	01010010	01001101
What a computer sees									

FIGURE 1.26 Binary bits

Technicians need to be able to describe capacities such as hard drive capacities and available drive space. Eight bits grouped together are a **byte**. Figure 1.27 shows a hot dog divided into eight sections (which make a big old "byte").

Approximately 1,000 bytes is a **kilobyte** (kB), as shown in Figure 1.28. 1 kB is 1,024 bytes to be exact, but industry folks simply round off the number to the nearest thousand for ease of calculation. Approximately 1 million bytes is a **megabyte** (MB), but a true megabyte is 1,048,576 bytes. 540 megabytes is abbreviated 540 MB, or 540 M. Notice in Figure 1.29 that a megabyte stores a lot more 1s and 0s than a kilobyte.

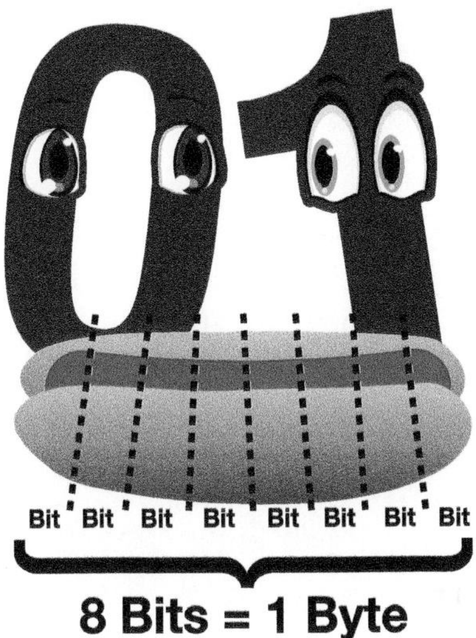

FIGURE 1.27 A byte

FIGURE 1.28 A kilobyte

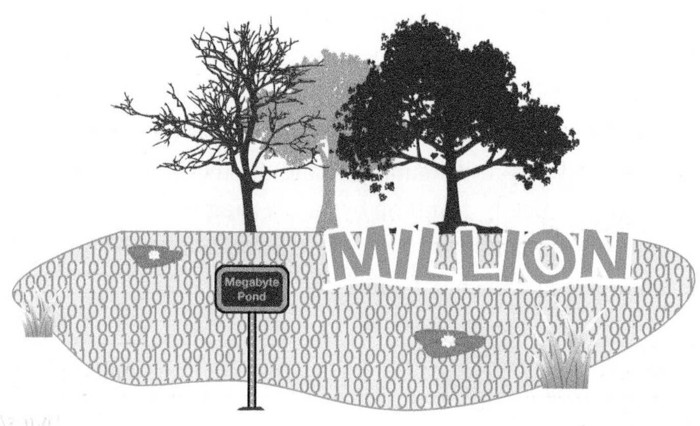

FIGURE 1.29 A megabyte

Approximately 1 billion bytes (1,073,741,824 bytes) is a **gigabyte** (GB), which is shown as 1 GB or 1 G. Approximately 1 trillion bytes (1,099,511,627,776 bytes) is a **terabyte**, which is shown as 1 TB or 1 T. Figures 1.30 and 1.31 show how storage capacities get larger.

FIGURE 1.30 A gigabyte

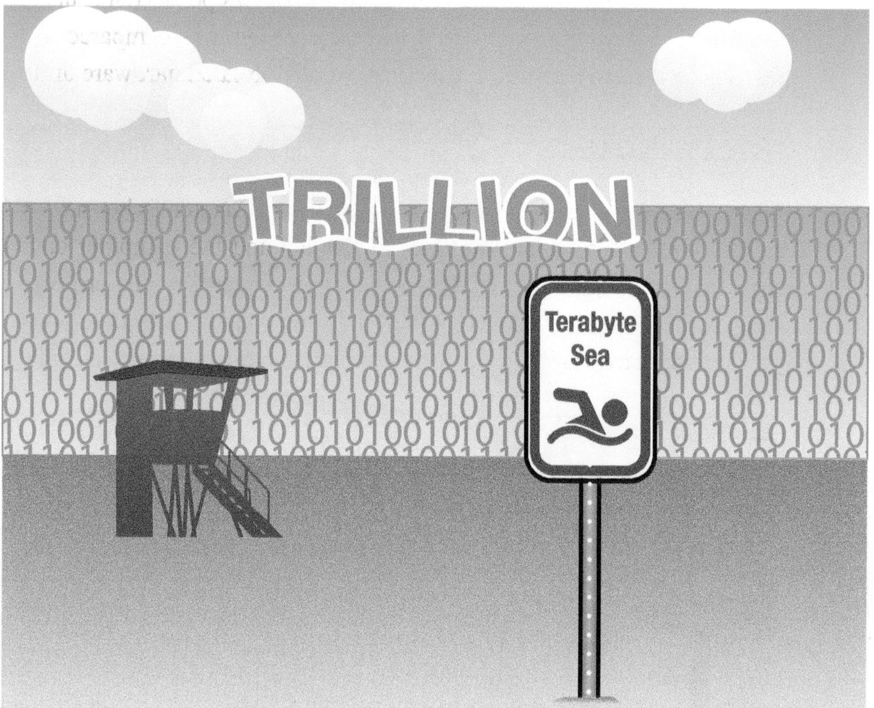

FIGURE 1.31 A terabyte

When information needs to be expressed exactly, binary prefixes are used. For example, when describing the value 2^{10} (1,024), instead of saying this is 1 kilobyte, which people tend to think of as approximately 1,000 bytes, the term kibibyte (KiB) is used. When describing the value 2^{20}, or 1,048,576, the term mebibyte (MiB) is used. Table 1.5 shows the terms used with computer storage capacity and binary prefixes when exact measurements are needed.

TABLE 1.5 Storage terms and binary prefixes

Term	Abbreviation	Description
Kilobyte/kibibyte	kB/KiB	~1 thousand bytes/2^{10} bytes
Megabyte/mebibyte	MB/MiB	~1 million bytes/2^{20} bytes
Gigabyte/gibibyte	GB/GiB	~1 billion bytes/2^{30} bytes
Terabyte/tebibyte	TB/TiB	~1 trillion bytes/2^{40} bytes
Petabyte/pebibyte	PB/PiB	~1,000 trillion bytes/2^{50} bytes
Exabyte/exbibyte	EB/EiB	~1 quintillion bytes/2^{60} bytes
Zettabyte/zebibyte	ZB/ZiB	~1,000 exabytes/2^{70} bytes
Yottabyte/yobibyte	YB/YiB	~1 million exabytes/2^{80} bytes

Frequencies are also important measurements in computers because people want to know how fast their computers, processors, memory, and other parts are operating. Frequencies are shown in similar measurements, but instead of bits (b) or bytes (B), speeds are shown in hertz (Hz). A hertz is a measurement of cycles per second. Something that operates at approximately 1 million cycles per second is said to operate at 1 megahertz (1 MHz). For 1 billion cycles per second, the measurement is known as 1 gigahertz, or 1 GHz. Transfer speeds are commonly shown in bits per second, such as gigabits per second, or Gb/s, or bytes per second, such as in megabytes per second, or MB/s. Notice the capital letter B to indicate bytes as compared to the lowercase b to indicate bits. These measurements are used in a lot of IT-related hardware and software.

Safety Notes

Safety is covered in each chapter, especially in Chapter 5, but no book on computer repair can begin without stating that both the technician and the computer can be harmed by poor safety habits. Before beginning any PC service, remove jewelry. To protect yourself and the computer, make sure to power off the computer and remove the power cord when disassembling, installing, or removing hardware or when doing preventive maintenance (cleaning).

TECH TIP

Some things should be left alone

Never take apart an older cathode ray tube (CRT) monitor or any power supply unless you have been specifically trained on these components.

Technicians can also be harmed when doing menial tasks such as lifting a computer or heavy laser printer. Lifting is a common requirement listed in IT job advertisements and explained during interviews. Technical jobs frequently specify a maximum lifting requirement of 40 to 50 pounds. Use proper safety precautions, such as those shown in Figure 1.32.

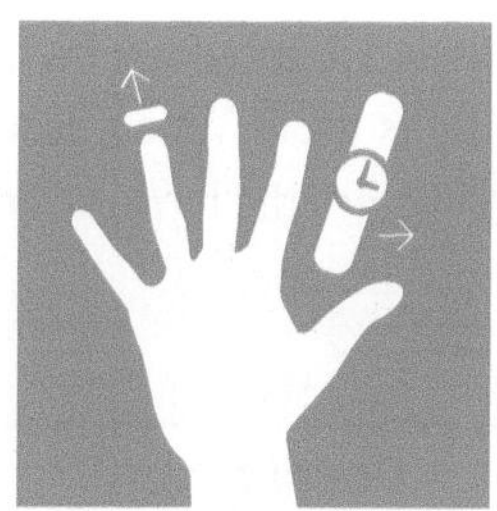

Remove jewelry before working inside of a computer

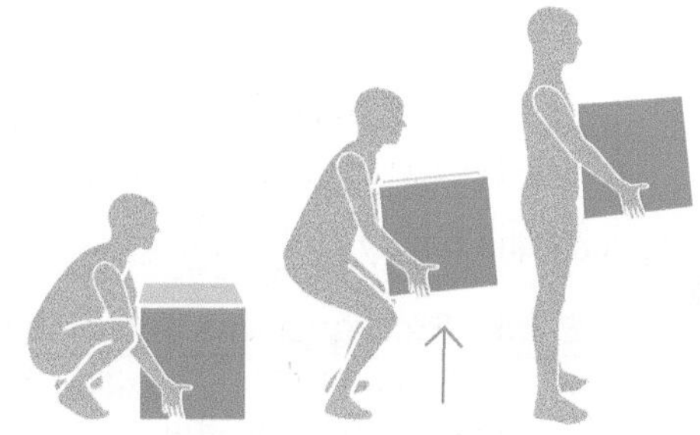

- Bend at the knees
- Use your legs to lift
- Use lifting aids when possible
- Ask for assistance when possible

FIGURE 1.32 Safety tips

Chapter Summary

> Many IT roles require detailed knowledge of PC hardware and software.

> Computer technicians should actively listen, have a positive attitude, and use logic when solving problems.

> The CompTIA A+ certification requires two exams: Core 1 (220-1101) and Core 2 (220-1102). Many people break into the IT field with this certification.

> IT staff must be proficient at searching for information on the internet, capturing files, and documenting technical information.

> Computers consist of hardware (the physical parts) and software (the operating system and applications).

> A technician needs to be able to identify important computer parts installed in a computer and as standalone parts: case, keyboard, mouse, motherboard, monitor, power supply, hard drive, optical drive, adapter, and memory.

> A technician needs to know the purposes of common peripherals used in the industry: printer, flatbed scanner with ADF, camera/webcam, microphone, and headset.

> Mice and keyboards are important input devices. To clean a keyboard, turn it over to remove debris. Then use a vacuum, compressed air, or wipes to clean it.

> Safety is important when working on a computer. Power it down and remove the power cord before working inside it.

> Use proper lifting techniques when servicing equipment.

A+ CERTIFICATION EXAM TIPS

- ✓ Get a good night's rest the night before the exam.
- ✓ Ensure that you are knowledgeable about and proficient with all of the terms and technologies listed in the official CompTIA A+ exam objectives. Some students study for a particular exam by going through the objectives one by one and reviewing the material as they go through.
- ✓ Ensure that you can identify the basic parts of a computer and explain the purpose of each one. Ensure that you know the following parts: hard drive, optical drive, power supply, motherboard, and RAM.
- ✓ Know common hardware so you will be familiar with future chapters that go into the details of installing, configuring, and troubleshooting these devices: printer, flatbed scanner, ADF, monitor, optical drive, mouse, keyboard, trackpad, drawing pad, camera/webcam, microphone, speakers, and headset.
- ✓ Know the following safety procedures: disconnect power, remove jewelry, lifting techniques, and weight limitations.
- ✓ Review the "Soft Skills" section at the end of the chapter. Make sure you know what open-ended questions are.

Key Terms

active listening skills 2
adapter 13
ADF 17
bit 18
byte 19
camera 17
clarify customer statements 2
device driver 8
expansion slot 13
flatbed scanner 17
gigabyte 20
hard drive 10
hardware 8
headset 17
keyboard 14
kilobyte 19
megabyte 19
memory 12
microphone 17
monitor 9
motherboard 11
mouse 14
open-ended question 2
operating system 8
optical drive 10
PC 8
power supply 10
printer 17
RAM 12
software 8
terabyte 20
webcam 17

Review Questions

1. Match each part to the appropriate description.

____ motherboard	a. Converts AC to DC
____ RAM	b. Holds the most data
____ DVD drive	c. Has the most electronics
____ hard drive	d. Fits in an expansion slot
____ adapter	e. Contents disappear when power is off
____ power supply	f. Holds a disc

2. A technician has been asked to provide support to an administrative assistant who is participating in a video conferencing session. Which peripheral would be used in video conferencing more so than in normal daily operational tasks?

   [mouse | webcam | all-in-one-printer | hard drive]

3. Which of the following are important suggested internet search tips? (Choose two.)

   a. Try another search engine if the first one does not provide satisfactory results.

   b. Use as many common words as possible, like the, in, at, or for.

   c. Put quotation marks around two or more words that might be found consecutively in output.

   d. Use as few words as possible.

   e. Avoid using the name of the equipment manufacturer.

4. What is the acronym used to describe memory that is commonly found on a motherboard?

   ____

5. When lifting a heavy computer, you should squat, bend at the knees, and use your legs to lift. [T | F]

6. How many tests must a person take in order to be A+ certified?

   [0 | 1 | 2 | 3 | 4]

7. Is the following question open ended or closed ended? You say your computer has been running slowly since Monday. Which applications have you installed this week? [open ended | closed ended]

8. List one example of having a positive attitude.

   ____

9. Which of the following devices are common output devices? (Select all that apply.)

   [digital piano | speakers | display | stylus | track stick | barcode reader | printer]

10. People who work with computers might be expected to lift up to how many pounds?

    [10 to 20 | 20 to 30 | 30 to 40 | 40 to 50]

11. Which Microsoft Windows application could be used to create a text file?

    [Textpad | Notepad | WriteIt | NoteIt]

12. Which Windows tool can be used to capture the screen?

    [Notepad | Bluetooth | Microsoft Edge | Snip & Sketch]

13. Rewrite the following conversation into an open-ended question.

    Technician: Good morning. I have a service log that states you are getting an error message whenever you access a PDF file. Have you done your Acrobat updates lately?

    ____

    ____

    ____

14. List one procedure you would do to help an erratic optical mouse.

    ____

    ____

15. Match the capacity to the description.

____ bit	a. 8 bits
____ kilobyte	b. a 1 or a 0
____ megabyte	c. approximately 1,000 bytes
____ byte	d. approximately 1 million bytes
____ gigabyte	e. approximately 1 trillion bytes
____ terabyte	f. approximately 1 billion bytes

16. Match the device to the description. Note that each description will best fit only one answer.

____ flatbed scanner	a. has an ADF
____ adapter	b. used to feed multiple sheets of paper one page at a time
____ ADF	c. used to capture video
____ power supply	d. inserts into an expansion slot
____ webcam	e. converts AC to DC

17. Which of the following is a feature of an optical mouse?

    a. LED

    b. contacts

    c. volatility

    d. electrical conversion

18. Which device is normally found inside a computer?

    [ADF | printer | headset | hard drive]

19. Which device normally can be seen if looking inside a desktop computer with the cover off and when normally looking at the front of a desktop computer?

    [hard drive | motherboard | optical drive | RAM]

20. Where can you find the motherboard in a tower computer?

    a. inside the power supply

    b. on the side of the case

    c. below the hard drive

    d. beside the RAM

Exercises

Exercise 1.1 Identifying Tower Computer Parts

Objective: To identify various computer parts correctly

Procedure: Identify each computer part in Figure 1.33. Match the part to the number in Figure 1.34.

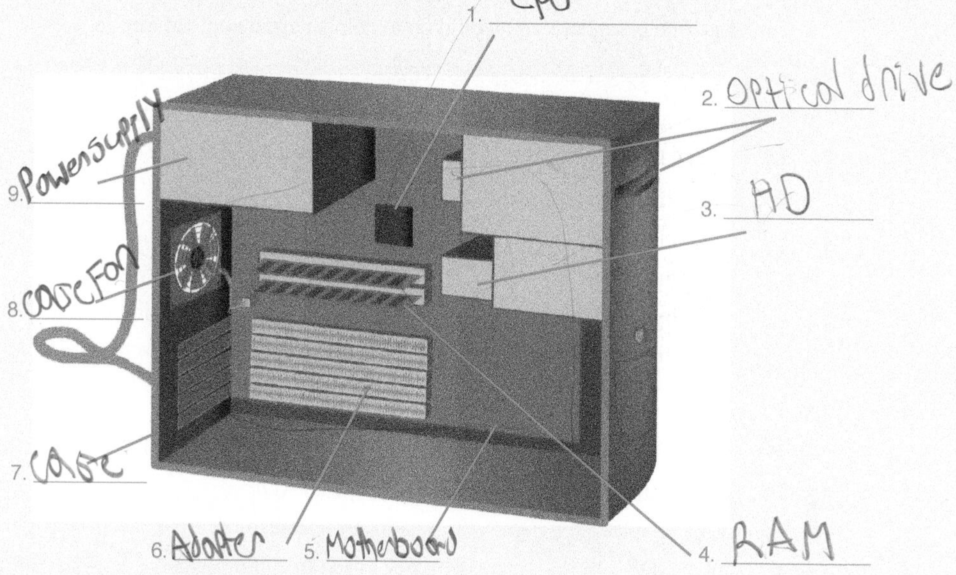

FIGURE 1.33 Tower computer parts identification

1. CPU
2. Optical drive
3. Hard drive
4. RAM
5. Motherboard
6. Adapter
7. Case
8. Case Fan
9. Power supply

FIGURE 1.34 Second tower computer parts identification

1.	_______	**a.**	Motherboard
2.	_______	**b.**	RAM
3.	_______	**c.**	Power supply
4.	_______	**d.**	Case fan
5.	_______	**e.**	Adapter
6.	_______	**f.**	Optical drive
7.	_______	**g.**	Case

Introduction to Connectivity

Now that we've discussed the basic parts of a PC, we are ready to dive into the technical details. Some of the ports may be challenging at first, but it is important that people going into the IT field know how to connect devices to ports and the purpose of each port.

External Connectivity

A **port** is a connector on a motherboard or on a separate adapter that allows a device to connect to a computer. Ports can be found all around a computer or mobile device. Figure 2.1 shows a motherboard with some of the ports we will be covering. See how many you can already identify and then return to this figure after finishing the chapter. IT professionals should be able to recognize and identify the common ports used today.

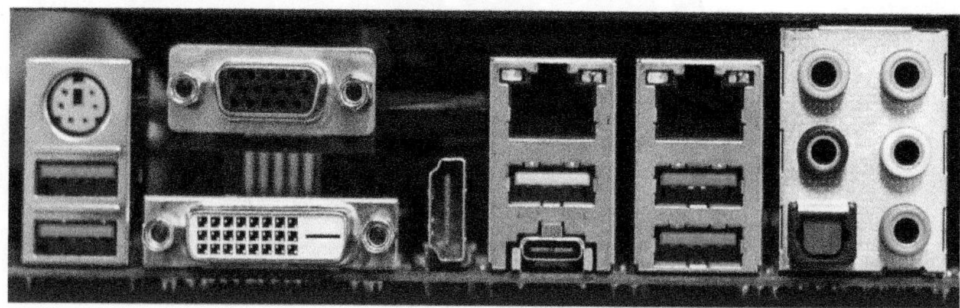

FIGURE 2.1 Motherboard ports

Mouse and Keyboard Ports

Mouse ports and **keyboard ports** were traditionally 6-pin **mini-DIN** ports that are sometimes called **PS/2 ports**. Most ports are keyed so the cable can only be inserted one way. Today, USB ports are more commonly used for mouse and keyboard connectivity, but some gaming motherboards still have the mini-DIN port(s). Manufacturers color code the mouse port as green and the keyboard port as purple; they may put a small diagram of a keyboard or a mouse by each connector. Figure 2.2 shows mouse and keyboard connectivity options.

6-pin mini-DIN PS/2 ports

or

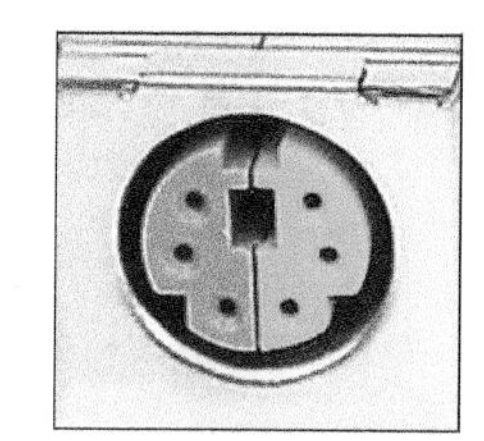

6-pin mini-DIN combo port

or

USB ports

FIGURE 2.2 Mouse and keyboard ports

Video Ports

A video port is used to connect a monitor. Video output can be the older method of an **analog signal** (varying levels, such as seen with an audio signal) or the newer output that uses a **digital signal** (1s and 0s). Because a computer uses digital signals, sending 1s and 0s is more efficient than converting an analog signal to a digital signal. This is relevant because there are still video ports around that are designed for analog signals. Figure 2.3 shows the difference between analog and digital signals.

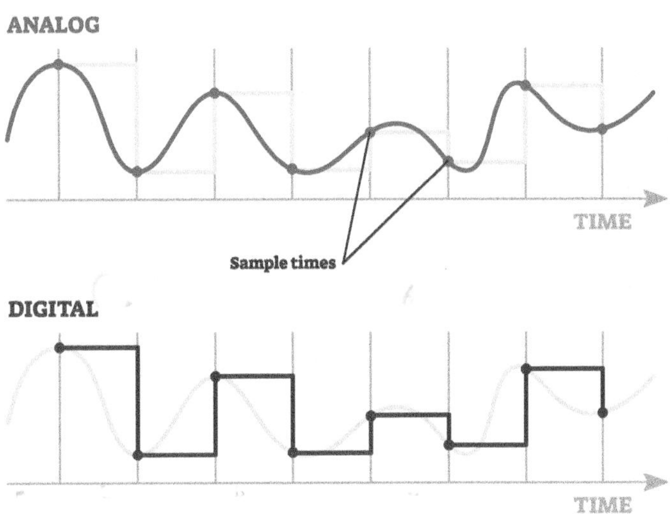

FIGURE 2.3 Analog and digital signals

The most common video ports used today are VGA, DVI, DisplayPort, and HDMI. These are all covered in this section. In addition, multipurpose ports such as USB-C, Thunderbolt, and Lightning are also used for video. The multipurpose ports are covered separately since they can transmit more than just audio and video.

Video Graphics Array (VGA)

The video graphics array port, or **VGA port**, was designed for analog output to an old cathode ray tube (CRT) monitor. VGA ports are easy to identify because they have three rows of holes—15 holes in total. Ports that have holes are known as female ports. The VGA port is sometimes seen in documentation as an HD15, DE15, or D-sub port. The "D" in these names comes from the VGA connector being a D-shell connector. Look at the VGA port in Figure 2.4 and imagine that port turned sideways so it looks like the letter D. The VGA cable has a DB15 male end that attaches to the DE15 female port.

Digital Visual Interface (DVI)

A newer port is the Digital Visual Interface port, or **DVI port**, that has three rows of square holes. Some monitors can also connect to the older VGA port. Some video adapters also enable you to connect a video device (such as a television) that has an **S-Video port**. Figure 2.4 shows a video adapter with the DVI port as the left connector, the S-Video port in the center, and a VGA port on the right.

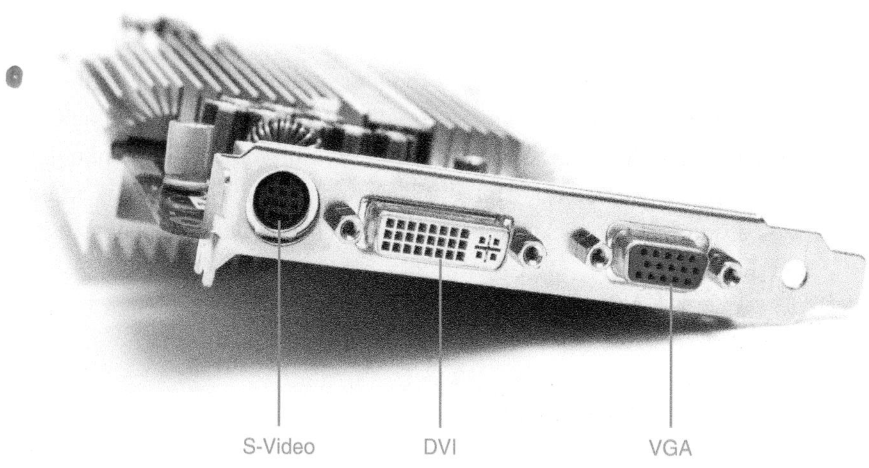

FIGURE 2.4 DVI, S-Video, and VGA ports

There are several types of DVI connectors. The one used depends on the type of monitor attached. Two terms used with DVI connectors are single link and dual link. A single link connection allows lower video resolutions than a dual link connection because a dual link port has more pins. The two major types of connectors are DVI-D and DVI-I. **DVI-D** is used for digital video connectivity only. **DVI-I** can be used for both digital and analog monitors, and it is the most common. A less common type is DVI-A, which is used for analog connectivity (and is not shown in Figure 2.5). Figure 2.6 shows both a DVI cable and a VGA cable.

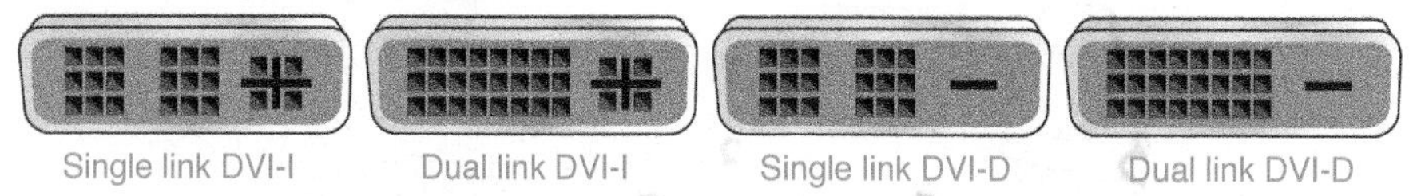

FIGURE 2.5 DVI connectors

FIGURE 2.6 DVI and VGA cables

TECH TIP

Match a monitor to the port type

Be careful when installing a monitor. For example, ensure that the video port matches the DVI connection type for the monitor. Converters can be purchased to adapt a monitor to a different type of port.

DisplayPort

The **DisplayPort** developed by VESA (Video Electronics Standards Association) can send and receive video, audio, or both types of signals simultaneously to monitors, televisions, and home theaters. Figure 2.7 shows the DisplayPort and a cable that would connect to this port.

FIGURE 2.7 DisplayPort

HDMI

Another upgrade over DVI is High-Definition Multimedia Interface (**HDMI**), a digital interface that can carry audio and video over the same cable. HDMI ports are found on cable TV boxes, televisions, video adapters, laptops, desktops, and tablets. Smaller miniHDMI or microHDMI connectors are used with devices such as cameras, tablets, and smartphones. Figure 2.8 shows an HDMI port and cable. Table 2.1 describes the different HDMI ports.

FIGURE 2.8 HDMI port and cable

TABLE 2.1 HDMI ports

HDMI connector type	Description
A	19-pin port found on a TV or PC that can have a Category 1 (standard) or Category 2 (high-speed) cable attached
B	29-pin port used with very high-resolution displays
C	19-pin miniHDMI port found on mobile devices
D	19-pin microHDMI port found on mobile devices

Figure 2.9 shows a video card that would be used in a gaming computer. On top is a dual link DVI-D port. On the bottom, from left to right, are a DisplayPort, an HDMI port, and a dual link DVI-I port. Table 2.2 summarizes important PC video ports. Note that Thunderbolt, Lightning, and

USB cables can also carry video signals; these ports and cables are covered in the "Multipurpose Ports" section, later in this chapter.

FIGURE 2.9 Video ports, including a DisplayPort, an HDMI port, and two DVI ports

TABLE 2.2 Video port summary

Port type	Analog, digital, or both	Max transfer speed	Carries audio?	Maximum cable lengths
VGA	Analog	N/A	No	Depends on resolution
DVI-D	Digital	Dual link 7.92 Gb/s	No	Up to 15 feet (4.57 m) for display resolutions up to 1920×1200
DVI-I	Both	Single or dual link	No	Not in the standards, but a general rule of thumb is up to 15 feet (4.57 m) for display resolutions up to 1920×1200
DisplayPort	Digital	80 Gb/s	Yes	9.8 feet (3 m) for passive and 108 feet (32.9 m) for active
HDMI	Digital	48 Gb/s	Yes	Not in the standards, but a general rule of thumb is up to 16 feet (4.88 m) for standard cable and up to 49 feet (14.9 m) for high-speed, good-quality cable and connectors

Video Adapters and Converters

Converters can be purchased for video ports to convert from one of the major types to another type. For example, Figure 2.10 shows a **DVI-to-HDMI adapter** (with both ends visible).

FIGURE 2.10 DVI-to-HDMI adapter

Multipurpose Ports

Some ports/cables can be used for multiple devices, including USB 2.0, USB 3.x, USB 4, USB-C, Thunderbolt, and Lightning. The USB port is probably the one people are most familiar with, but the Thunderbolt and Lightning ports are also considered multipurpose ports. Let's explore these ports.

USB Ports

USB stands for Universal Serial Bus and is one of the most popular ports. A USB port allows up to 127 connected devices to transmit at speeds up to 10 Gb/s (10 billion bits per second), 20 Gb/s, or even 40 Gb/s. Devices that connect to a USB port include printers, scanners, mice, keyboards, joysticks, optical drives, game pads, cameras, modems, speakers, telephones, video phones, data gloves, and digitizers. Additional ports can sometimes be found on the front of a PC case or on the side of a mobile device. Figure 2.11 shows some USB ports.

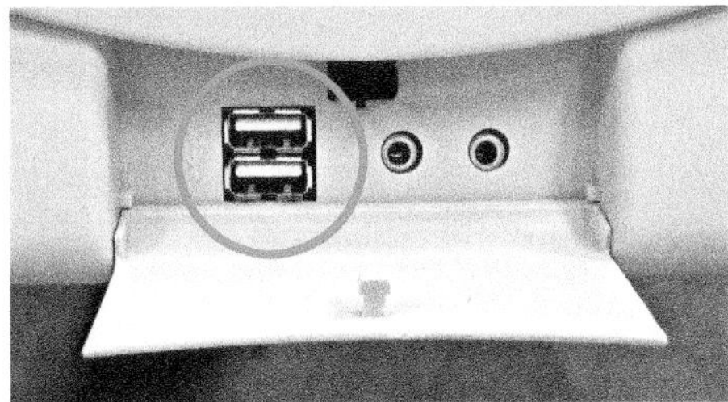

FIGURE 2.11 USB ports

USB Versions

USB ports come in several versions: USB 1.0/1.1, **USB 2.0** (Hi-Speed), **USB 3.0** (3.2 Gen 1 SuperSpeed and 3.2 Gen 2 SuperSpeed+), and 4.x. Figure 2.12 shows the different USB versions and speed symbols.

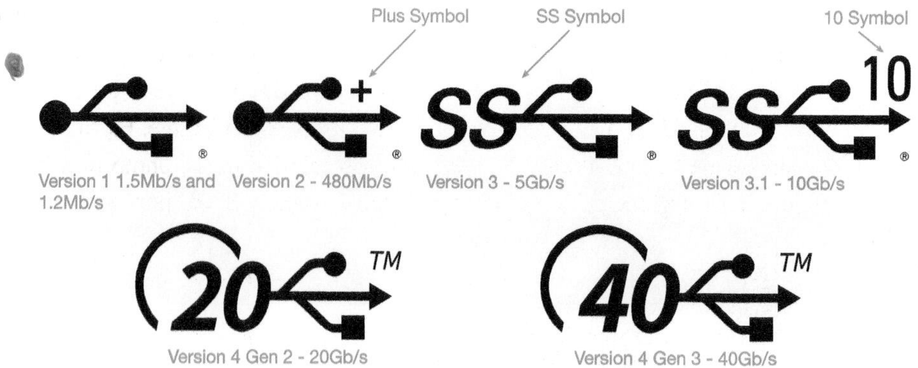

FIGURE 2.12 USB versions, speeds, and symbols

> **TECH TIP**
>
> **Documentation can be key to USB speed**
>
> A port does not have to be labeled, and sometimes looking at the technical specifications for a computer or motherboard is the only way to determine the port speed.

USB Power Delivery (USB-PD)

USB ports have been able to provide 5V at 500mA for 2.5 watts of power to devices since version 2.0. The newest USB standard, Power Delivery (**PD** or **USB-PD**), can provide up to 20V at 5A for 100 watts of power. The standard actually has five levels of power delivery: 10W, 18W, 36W, 60W, and 100W. All USB4 connections allow charging a USB device.

USB Cables

Each USB standard has a maximum cable length (shown in Table 2.3, later in the chapter). USB cables can be longer than these specifications, but longer cables may not work well. You can use an active USB extension cable (repeater cable) or a powered USB hub, covered later in the chapter, to go further distances.

If a USB port provides power to a device, then the maximum cable length shortens. For example, if a USB 2.0 PD device is being used, the maximum cable length is less than 13 feet (4 m). If a USB 3.1 PD device is used with a USB Type-C cable, then the cable length should be less than 3.3 feet (1 m). A PD device requires a Type-C cable, but not all ports or cables support PD.

USB Connectors

Older USB ports are commonly known as **USB Type-A** and **USB Type-B**. A USB printer cable, for example, has a Type-A male connector on one end and a Type-B male connector on the other end. The port on the computer is a Type-A port. Figure 2.13 shows Type-A and Type-B connectors.

FIGURE 2.13 USB Type-B and Type-A connectors

The **USB Type-C** (sometimes called **USB-C**) connector is the latest type and will eventually replace the Type-A and Type-B connectors. With older devices, it is possible to use an adapter in order to attach to a Type-C connector. Many USB 3.0 ports are Type-C connectors, but they do not have to be as USB 3.1 and higher ports require a Type-C cable. Figure 2.14 shows a USB Type-C connector and cable alongside a Type-A port. Notice in the photo of a USB Type-C connector in Figure 2.14 that the cable could be inserted into the USB-C port with either side facing up.

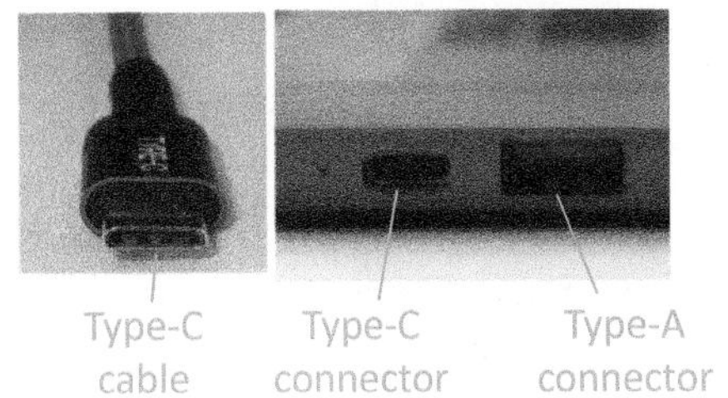

FIGURE 2.14 USB Type-C cable and connector and Type-A port

MiniUSB and MicroUSB

Two smaller USB ports used on portable devices such as hubs, external hard drives, digital cameras, and smartphones are the **miniUSB** and **microUSB** ports. There are several types of these smaller USB ports: mini-A, mini-AB, micro-B, and micro-AB. The mini-AB and micro-AB ports accept either a mini-A/micro-A or a mini-B/micro-B cable end. Figure 2-15 shows the standard Type-A USB cable that would be inserted into a PC port compared to the miniUSB and microUSB cables used with mobile devices. Figure 2.16 shows a USB 3.0 micro-B port and connector.

FIGURE 2.15 MicroUSB, miniUSB, and USB Type-A cables

FIGURE 2.16 USB 3.0 micro-B port and connector

USB Hubs

A USB port can have more than one device attached to the port through the use of a USB hub. Many hubs can operate in two power modes—self-powered and bus powered. A powered hub (sometimes called a self-powered hub) has an external power supply attached. A bus-powered hub has no external power supply. Once USB devices attached to a hub are tested, the hub's power supply can be removed, and the devices can be retested. If all attached devices work properly, the power supply can be left disconnected. Figure 2.17 shows USB hub connectivity, and Figure 2.18 shows USB cabling rules.

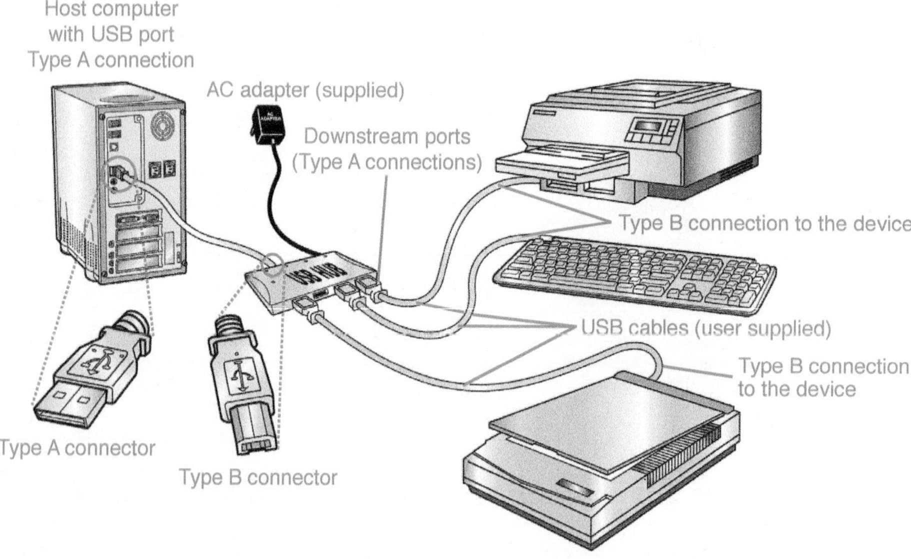

FIGURE 2.17 USB hub connectivity

USB cabling rules
• 5 hubs maximum (total max range of 88.5 feet or 27 meters)
• 127 devices maximum connected to up to 5 hubs
• Maximum distance between 2 USB hubs
high-speed devices – 16.4 feet or 5 meters
low-speed devices – 9.8 feet or 3 meters

FIGURE 2.18 USB cabling rules

USB ports have always been able to provide power to unpowered devices, such as flash drives. A **charging USB port** is a port designed to be able to provide power and charge attached devices. Note that not all USB devices can be powered on while charging. With a **sleep-and-charge USB port**, the port provides power to charge the device even when the computer is powered off. See the computing device's specifications to see if a USB port supports this feature. Table 2.3 summarizes USB types, alternate names, speeds, port colors, and cable requirements.

TECH TIP

Safely removing USB devices

To remove a USB device, do not simply unplug it from the port. Instead, click on the *Safely Remove Hardware* icon (Windows 7) or *Safely Remove Hardware and Eject Media* (Windows 8/10/11) from the notification area and then select the USB device to remove. On a Mac, right-click the desktop icon for the device and select *Eject x* (where *x* is the device name) or drag the desktop icon to the trash can. In Ubuntu Linux, locate the device in Files or File Explorer. Click the small eject icon. The operating system prompts when it is safe to unplug the device.

TABLE 2.3 USB port summary

Port type and alternate name	Maximum transmission speed	Port color	Cable type/length and alternate name
USB 1.x	1.5 Mb/s and 12 Mb/s	Usually white	9.8 feet (3m) Type-A 1.0 low speed 1.1 full speed
USB 2.0	480 Mb/s	Black	9.8 feet (3m) Type-A Hi-Speed
USB 3.0	5 Gb/s	Blue	9.8 feet (3m) Type-A or Type-C SuperSpeed
USB 3.1 Gen 1	5 Gb/s	Blue	9.8 feet (3m) Type-A or Type-C SuperSpeed
USB 3.1 Gen 2	10 Gb/s	Teal	9.8 feet (3m) Type-C SuperSpeed+
USB 3.2 Gen 1 (3.2 Gen 1x1 1 lane) (3.2 Gen 1x2 2 lanes)	5 Gb/s and 10 Gb/s	Red	9.8 feet (3m) Type-C SuperSpeed USB 5Gbps SuperSpeed USB 10Gbps
USB 3.2 Gen 2 (3.2 Gen 2x1 1 lane) (3.2 Gen 2x2 2 lanes)	10 Gb/s and 20 Gb/s	Red	9.8 feet (3m) Type-C SuperSpeed USB 10Gbps SuperSpeed USB 20Gbps
USB4 Gen 2 (2 lanes)	20 Gb/s	N/A	9.8 feet (3m) Type-C
USB4 Gen 3 (2 lanes)	40 Gb/s	N/A	9.8 feet (3m) Type-C
USB sleep-and-charge	N/A	Yellow, orange, or red	N/A

USB Converters

Converters are available to convert a USB port to a different type of connector (or vice versa), such as the **USB-to-Ethernet converter** used to connect a device, such as a tablet that has a USB port, to a wired Ethernet network (see Figure 2.19).

FIGURE 2.19 USB-to-Ethernet converter

Installing Extra USB Ports

Sometimes people want more USB ports and do not want to add another hub. Many motherboards support adding two or more USB ports by using a cable that attaches to an internal USB connector on the motherboard, also known as a USB header. The term **header** simply means a set of motherboard pins for a specific purpose, like USB 2.0, USB 3.0, USB Type-C, SATA, eSATA, RGB LEDs (lights), and TPM (Trusted Platform Module). The ports mount in an expansion slot space, but they do not have a card that plugs into an expansion slot. Even if a motherboard has such pins, the ports and cable assembly might have to be purchased separately. Figure 2.20 shows sample USB ports that attach to a motherboard.

FIGURE 2.20 Installing extra USB ports

Thunderbolt

A **Thunderbolt port** is a type of port that is used primarily for video, uses some of the DisplayPort video port technology, and can carry power, audio, video, and data to external storage devices. The Thunderbolt interface was developed by Intel with support from Apple. The Thunderbolt port used on Apple computers is the same connector as the miniDisplayPort; however, Thunderbolt 3 uses the USB Type-C connector, discussed earlier in this chapter, in the "USB Connectors" section. Thunderbolt 3 is the first Thunderbolt version to support USB.

A Thunderbolt cable can have data speeds up to 80 Gb/s. Thunderbolt allows daisy-chaining up to six devices. Figure 2.21 shows a Thunderbolt port and cable. Look back at Figure 2.14 to see the Type-C connector and cable that Thunderbolt 3 and 4 use.

FIGURE 2.21 Thunderbolt cable and port

TECH TIP

Can a Thunderbolt 3 or 4 device work in a USB-C port?

Even if a Thunderbolt 3 or 4 device can attach to a USB-C port, it may not work. If the device does work, it will work at USB-C speed. However, USB-C devices can function and connect to a Thunderbolt 3 or 4 port.

Lightning

The last multipurpose port to cover is the **Lightning port** and associated cable. The Lightning port, developed by Apple, is an 8-pin port that accepts the cable with either side facing up (that is, it is reversible). The Lightning port can carry data and power from mobile devices to other devices, such as cameras, external monitors, and external storage devices. An adapter/converter can be used to allow the cable to be used with the older Apple 30-pin connector, USB, HDMI, VGA, or SD cards. The Lightning port supports USB data and USB charging, but the Lightning port or cable is not interchangeable with USB-C. Note that some MacBook computers have USB-C, not Lightning, connectors. Figure 2.22 shows a Lightning cable. Table 2.4 shows a comparison of the three multipurpose ports.

FIGURE 2.22 Lightning cable

TABLE 2.4 Multipurpose port comparison

Port type	Maximum transmission speed	Type of connector	Platforms	What it carries
USB4 Gen 3	40 Gb/s	USB Type-C 24-pin reversible connector	Found on Apple and PCs	Data and power
Thunderbolt 4	80 Gb/s	USB Type-C 24-pin reversible connector	Intel and Apple developed	Data and power
Lightning	Speeds up to USB 3.0, but normally 480 Mb/s	8-pin reversible connector	Apple-proprietary	Data and power

Audio Ports

A **sound card** (sometimes called an audio card) converts digital computer signals to sound and sound to digital computer signals (see Figure 2.3). Sound ports are commonly integrated into the motherboard, but some people want better sound, and so they add a card. The most common sound ports include a port for a microphone and one or more ports for speakers. The ports can accept analog or digital signals.

The traditional analog sound ports are 3.5 mm (see Figure 2.23). The newer Sony/Phillips Digital interface (**S/PDIF**) in/out ports, on the left in Figure 2.23, are used to connect to various devices, such as digital audio tape players/recorders, DVD players/recorders, and external disc players/recorders. There are two main types of S/PDIF connectors: an **RCA** jack (last port on the left) used to connect a coaxial cable and a fiber-optic port for a **TOSLINK** cable connection (two optical ports beside the RCA/Digital Out jack in Figure 2.23). Sound cards are popular because people want better sound quality than what is available with the ports integrated into a motherboard.

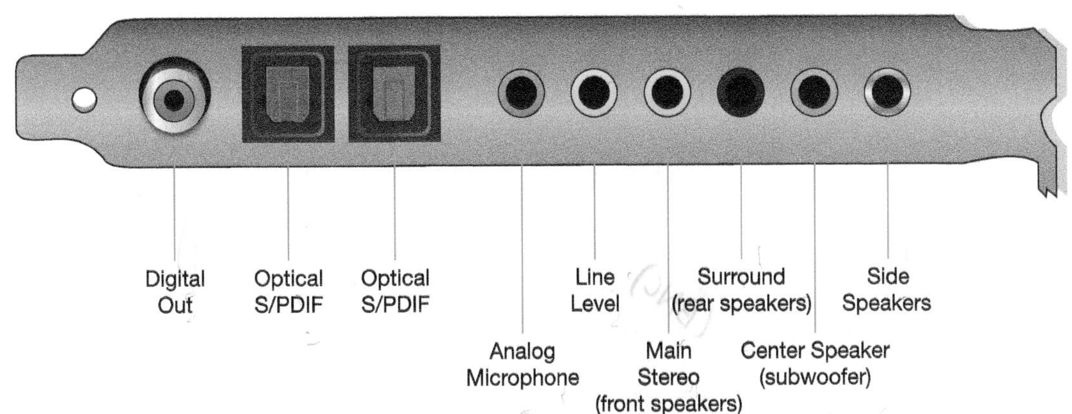

FIGURE 2.23 Sound card ports

eSATA Ports

SATA connections are commonly used for internal and external storage devices. A 7-pin non-powered external serial AT attachment, or **eSATA**, port is used for connecting external storage. Desktop computers commonly have an SATA header so that an eSATA port can be easily added. eSATA can transfer data at 6 Gb/s. Devices can connect at a maximum of approximately 6.6 feet (2 m). If the internal SATA drive has crashed, an external drive connected to an eSATA or USB port can be used to boot and troubleshoot the system.

A variation of the eSATA port is the **eSATAp port**, which is also known as eSATA/USB, or power over eSATA. This variation can accept eSATA or USB cables and provides power when necessary. Figure 2.24 shows a standard **eSATA cable**, an eSATA port, and an eSATAp (eSATA/USB combination) port.

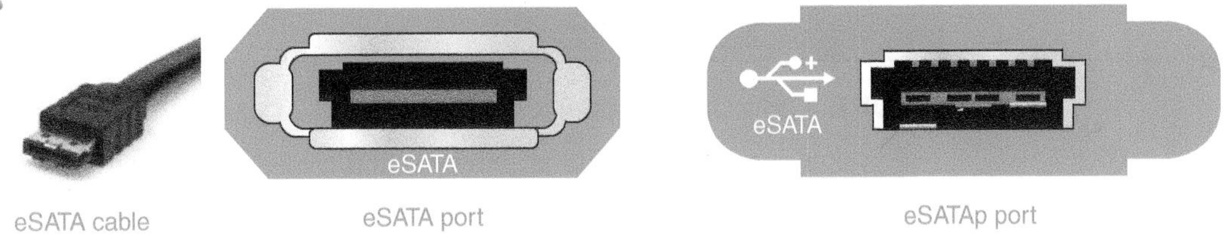

FIGURE 2.24 eSATA cable and eSATA/eSATAp ports

Modem and Serial Ports

A modulator/demodulator, or **modem**, connects a digital computer to a different type of network, such as a phone line or an internet connection. An internal modem used to connect a computer to a phone network is an adapter that has one or two **RJ11** phone jack ports. The RJ11 port labeled *Line* is for the connection to the wall jack; the one labeled *Phone* is for a phone connection, if needed. Figure 2.25 shows an internal modem with two RJ11 ports.

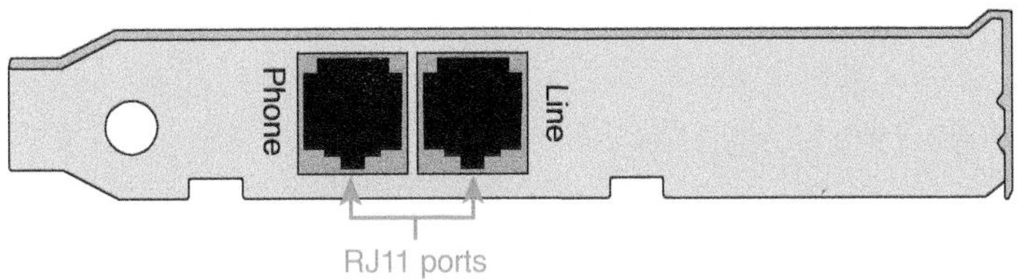

FIGURE 2.25 An internal modem with two RJ11 ports

The same type of RJ11 port with four conductors is used with a cable modem used to connect a home network to the internet, and the RJ11 port is used to connect a phone. Figure 2.26 shows this port labeled as Phone Lines 1&2.

FIGURE 2.26 Cable modem with RJ11 port

Serial ports are found on older modems and motherboards, network equipment, alarm systems, automation systems, communication systems, and single-board systems like the Raspberry Pi and ASUS Tinker Board. Serial ports are 9-pin male (that is, they have pins instead of holes) and are sometimes called **DB9** or RS-232 ports. Figure 2.27 shows the DB9 serial ports on an older computer. Figure 2.28 shows an example of a **serial cable**. The DB9 female connector would attach to the DB9 male connector on a device or motherboard. Figure 2.29 shows a USB-to-serial converter cable you might need to connect an external modem to a modern motherboard.

FIGURE 2.27 DB9 serial ports

FIGURE 2.28 Serial cable ends

FIGURE 2.29 USB-to-serial port converter

Network Ports

A **network port** is used to connect a device such as a computer or printer to a network. The most common type of network port is an **Ethernet port**, also known as an **RJ45** port. A network cable inserts into an Ethernet port to connect a computing device to a wired network. A network port is sometimes called a **NIC** (network interface card or controller). Notice the 8 conductors (wires) in the RJ45 Ethernet port shown in Figure 2.30.

FIGURE 2.30 An RJ45 Ethernet port

An RJ45 port looks very similar to an RJ11 phone jack (see Figures 2.25 and 2.26). However, the RJ45 connector has 8 conductors (wires) instead of 4. Look closely at the connectors in Figure 2.31 to see the difference. The RJ11 connector is on the left.

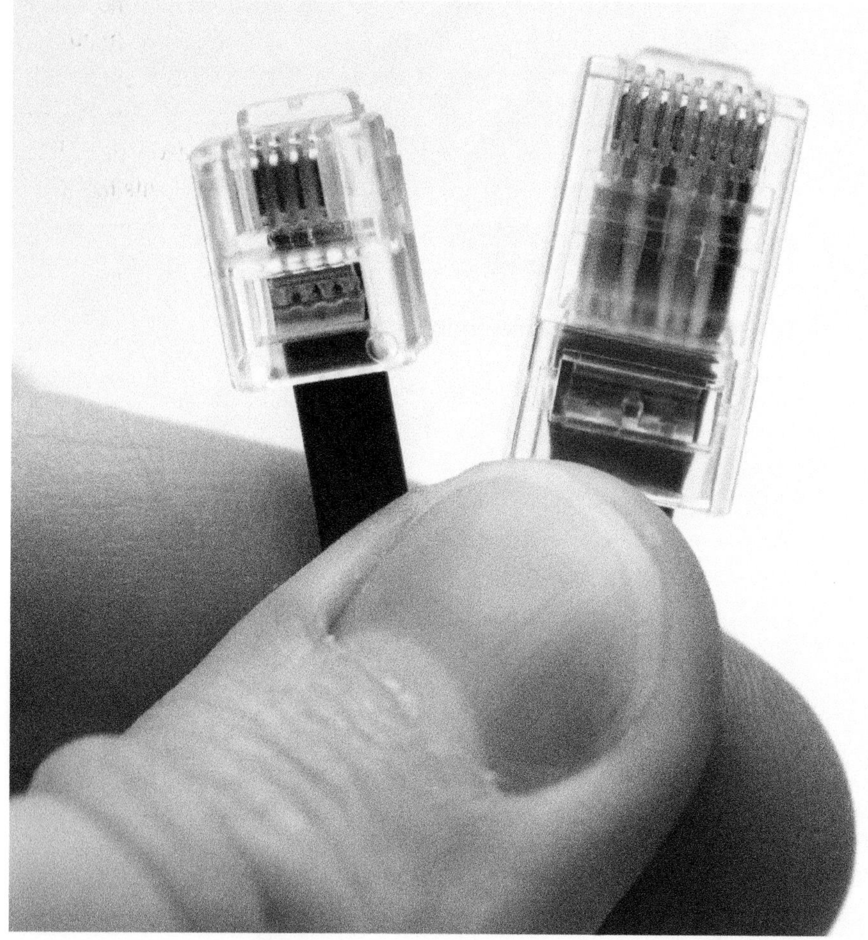

FIGURE 2.31 RJ11 and RJ45 connectors

TECH TIP

Ethernet port symbols

An Ethernet port commonly has LEDs on top or near the port to indicate data activity. This port may also have one of the following symbols:

Network Cabling

People who work in IT have all types of devices—including PCs, printers, servers, projectors, and displays—that connect to the network. This is a good time to make sure you know what type of cable might be used. We will start with **copper cabling**, which sends electrical pulses to create the digital 1s and 0s, and then look at fiber-optic cabling that uses light instead.

Coaxial

A type of connector you might see associated with video, but more likely with cable TV or when attaching a wireless network antenna to a connector, is a Bayonet Neill–Concelman (BNC) connector. A **BNC connector** is used with a **coaxial** cable that is found in video networks such as a school where multiple TVs connect to the same distribution center or in a home that obtains TV channels through a cable provider. A BNC connector has a center conductor that pushes onto the receptacle and is surrounded by insulation. Outside the insulation is a shield of copper braid, a metallic foil, or both, to protect the center conductor from outside noises called electromagnetic interference (EMI), as shown in Figure 2.32. Figure 2.33 shows the front of a BNC connector already attached to the coax cable.

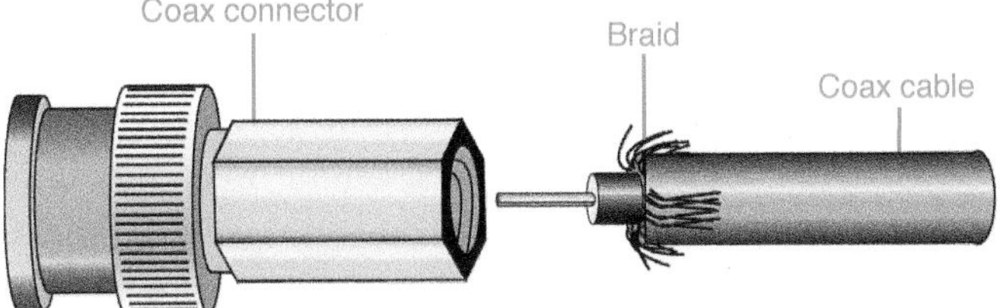

FIGURE 2.32 Coaxial cable with a BNC connector

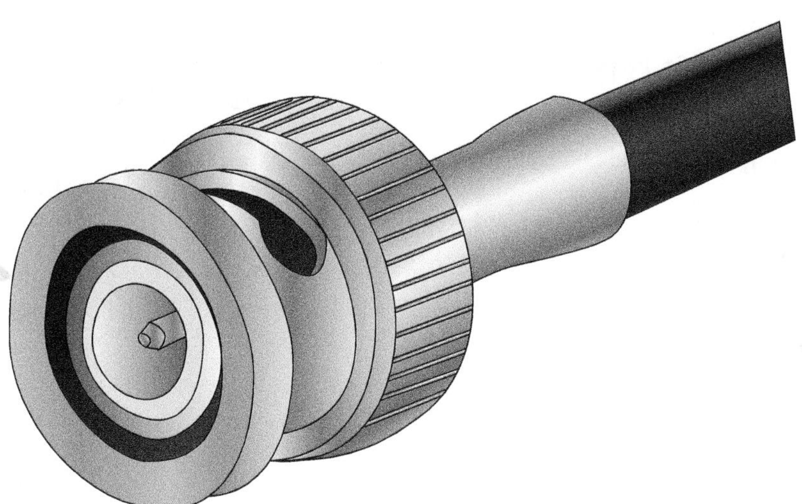

FIGURE 2.33 BNC connector

Figure 2.34 shows two popular coax connectors: BNC and F. Notice that the BNC connector has a notched side to turn and twist onto the receiving connector. The **F type** connector simply screws onto the receiving connector. Table 2.5 lists types of coax cables.

FIGURE 2.34 Coaxial BNC and F connectors

TABLE 2.5 Coax cable types

Coax cable type	Description
RG-6*	This is the type of cable least likely to be used in a network. It is a 75-ohm cable suitable for distributing signals for cable TV, satellite dishes, or rooftop antennas. It has better shielding than RG-59, so it is larger in diameter. Typical distances are 1000 feet (305 m) to 1500 feet (457 m). It can carry frequencies up to 2200 MHz.
RG-59	This type of 75-ohm cable is not used in LANs but is used in video installations. Typical distances are 750 feet (225 m) to 1000 feet (305 m). It can carry frequencies up to 1000 MHz.

*RG stands for radio grade.

If a coaxial cable of different impedance attaches to another coaxial cable, signal loss results. Coaxial cable is rated according to whether it will be used in an interior or exterior space. Use the appropriate cable type for the installation. Be careful when bending the cable. When there is a problem and the right type of cable and connector are used, the most common issue is that the coax connector is not attached properly.

Ethernet Cable

Ethernet is the most common type of wired network seen in homes and in companies. An Ethernet cable attaches to an RJ45 Ethernet port. The most common type of network cable is **unshielded twisted pair (UTP)**. UTP comes in several types: **Cat 5**, **Cat 5e**, **Cat 6**, and **Cat 6a**. Cat 7 and Cat 8 are also available. The *Cat* in these cable names is short for *category*.

UTP cable has 8 wires that are twisted to prevent data that is traveling along one wire from interfering with an adjacent wire; this type of interference is called *crosstalk*. Figure 2.35 shows a Cat 6 cable and a Cat 5e cable. Notice that the Cat 6 cable is thinner. Table 2.6 shows a comparison of the cable types. Cat 6a has more cable twists to reduce crosstalk. Cat 6a cabling might also have a thicker conductor and jacket.

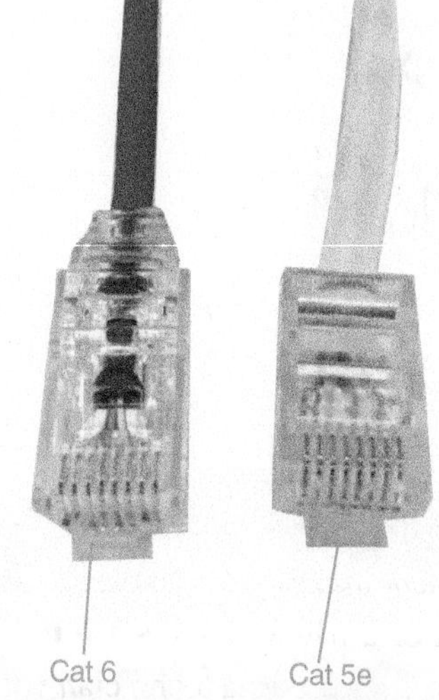

FIGURE 2.35 Cat 6 and Cat 5e cables

TABLE 2.6 Ethernet cable comparison

Ethernet cable type	Maximum transmission speed	Bandwidth	Distance limitation
Cat 5	100 Mb/s	100 MHz	328 feet (100 m)
Cat 5e	1000 Mb/s, or 1 Gb/s	100 MHz	328 feet (100 m)
Cat 6	1000 Mb/s, or 1 Gb/s*	250 MHz	328 feet (100 m)
Cat 6a	10,000 Mb/s, or 10 Gb/s	500 MHz	328 feet (100 m)
Cat 7	10,000 Mb/s, or 10 Gb/s	600 MHz	328 feet (100 m)
Cat 8	25,000/40,000 Mb/s or 25/40 Gb/s	2000 MHz	328 feet (100 m)

*Cat 6 can support speeds of 10 Gb/s at lengths up to 165 feet (55 m).

The alternative to UTP is **shield twisted pair (STP)** cable, which is used in manufacturing, with security alarm systems, for audio connections, between buildings, and in harsh environments where the cabling needs a little more shielding to keep the data intact. The shielding is provided by a foil wrapped around all the cables as well as around each grouping of two cables, which makes STP cabling thicker than UTP. Cat 7 and Cat 8 cabling use this type.

STP is also used with direct burial and underground cable in an outdoor environment. **Direct burial cable** is designed to be used underground without any extra protection provided (like tubing, piping, or extra covering) because this type of cabling has extra insulation, cover, and waterproofing added. UTP direct burial cable is also available and designed to protect against moisture.

Both UTP and STP use the RJ45 connector, which has a tang on one side. To remove a cable from an Ethernet port, press on the tang to release the cable from the port. When inserting the cable, ensure that the cable is oriented properly and then push the cable firmly into the port until you hear a click of the tang fitting snuggly into the port. Figure 2.36 shows the top and bottom of an Ethernet cable connector.

FIGURE 2.36 Ethernet RJ45 connector with tang

Ethernet cabling in a corporate environment makes use of a patch panel to get cabling from one part of a building to the next. On the back of a patch panel is a **punchdown block** that is also found in traditional phone networks. Figure 2.37 shows a technician using a **punchdown tool** to firmly attach a wire into a punchdown block.

FIGURE 2.37 Connecting a wire on a punchdown block using a punchdown tool

A special type of UTP or STP cable is **plenum cable**. A plenum is a building's air circulation space for heating and air conditioning systems. Plenum cable is treated with Teflon or alternative fire-retardant materials to reduce the fire risk. Plenum cable produces less smoke and is less toxic when it burns than regular networking cable.

An alternative to plenum cable is polyvinyl chloride (**PVC**) cable, which has a plastic cable insulation or jacket. PVC is cheaper than plenum cable, and it can have flame-retardant chemicals added to make it compliant with building codes. PVC is usually easier to install than plenum cable.

To avoid extra troubleshooting time, most businesses install their network cable according to the ANSI/TIA/EIA-568-A or 568-B (commonly shown as **T568A** and **T568B** or **568A/B**) standard. These standards specify how far the cable can extend, how to label it, what type of connectors to use, and so forth. Figure 2.38 shows that the colored wires within a connector must be in a particular order. Chapter 13, "Networking," shows how to make cables according to the T568A and T568B standards.

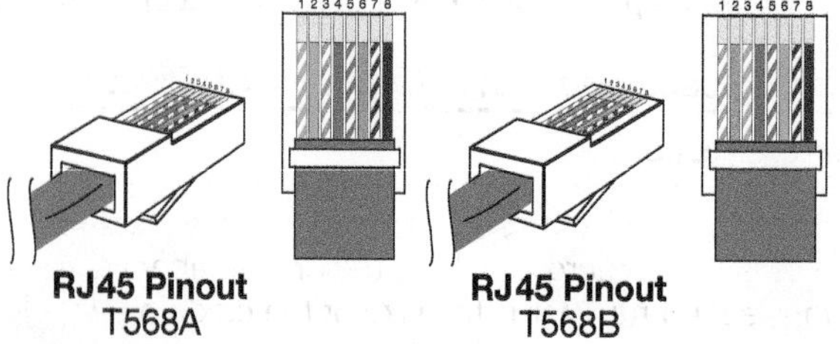

FIGURE 2.38 ANSI/TIA/EIA T568A and T568AB wiring standards

Fiber Media

Fiber cable, also known as **optical cable** or fiber-optic cable, is made of glass or a type of plastic fiber and is used to carry light pulses. Fiber cable can be used to connect a workstation to another device, but in industry, the most common uses of fiber-optic cable are to connect networks forming the network backbone, networks between buildings, service provider high-speed networks, and homes to a service provider. Figure 2.39 shows fiber switch connections. Notice that the fibers are grouped in pairs.

FIGURE 2.39 Fiber connections

There are many different types of fiber connectors, and some of them are proprietary. Four of the most common connectors used with fiber-optic cable are Mechanical Transfer Registered Jack, or MT-RJ (common in home installations), **straight tip (ST) connector**, **subscriber connector (SC)**, and **Lucent connector (LC)**. Figure 2.40 shows three of these connectors.

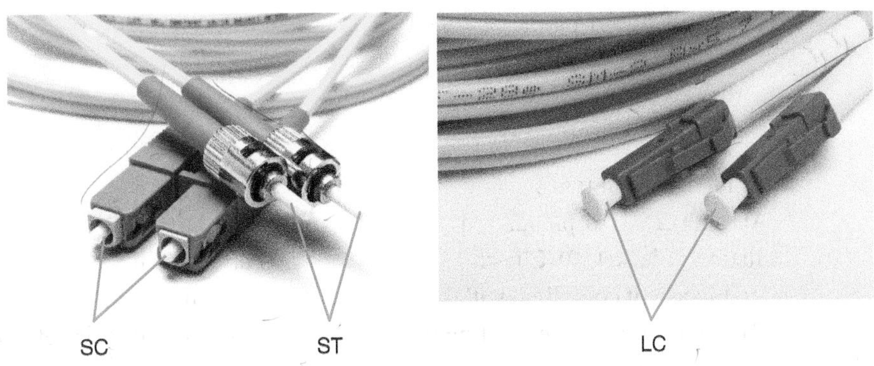

FIGURE 2.40 Fiber-optic connector types

The two major classifications of fiber are single-mode and multi-mode. **Single-mode fiber** cable has only one light beam sent down the cable. **Multi-mode fiber** allows multiple light signals to be sent along the same cable. Table 2.7 describes the characteristics of the two types. (Note that fiber's maximum speeds keep increasing as technology keeps changing.)

TABLE 2.7 Fiber cable speed and transmission characteristics

Type	Characteristic
Single-mode	Classified by the size of the fiber core and the cladding. Common sizes include 8/125 to 10/125 microns, where the first number represents the size of the core, and the second number is the size of the cladding. Single-mode cable allows for distances more than 50 miles (80 km) at speeds more than 100 Gb/s.
Multi-mode	Sizes include 50/125 and 62.5/125 microns. Can support distances more than 1 mile (2 km) and speeds up to 10 Gb/s. ST connectors are used more with multi-mode fiber than with single-mode.

TECH TIP

Choosing the correct fiber type

Multi-mode fiber is cheaper and more commonly used than single-mode fiber and is good for shorter-distance applications; however, single-mode fiber can transmit a signal farther than multi-mode and supports the highest bandwidth.

Integrated Motherboard Ports

An integrated motherboard provides expandability because ports are built in and do not require separate adapters. If a motherboard includes USB, network, sound, keyboard, mouse, and video ports, there is more space available for other adapters. The number of available expansion slots in a system depends on the motherboard manufacturer. Figure 2.41 shows integrated motherboard ports including ports to attach two Wi-Fi 6 wireless antennas.

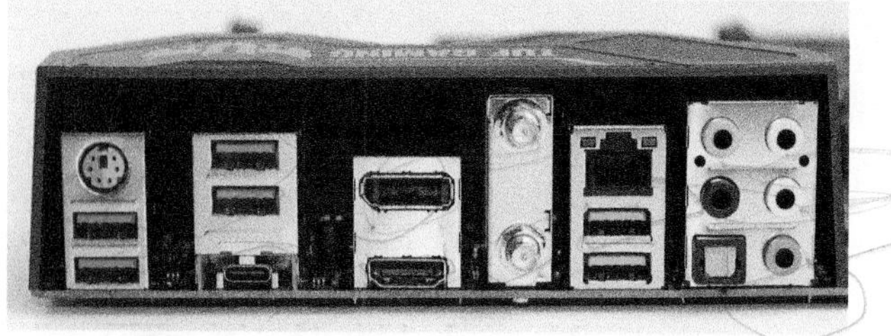

FIGURE 2.41 Integrated motherboard ports

Ports built into a motherboard are faster than those on an expansion board. All adapters in expansion slots run more slowly than the motherboard components. Computers with integrated motherboards are easier to set up because you do not have to install an adapter or configure the ports. Normally, systems with integrated motherboards are easier to troubleshoot because the components are on one board. The drawback is that when one port goes bad, you have to add an adapter that has the same type of port as the one that went bad. Furthermore, ports found on an adapter might be of higher quality or might have more capabilities than an integrated port. See Figure 2.42.

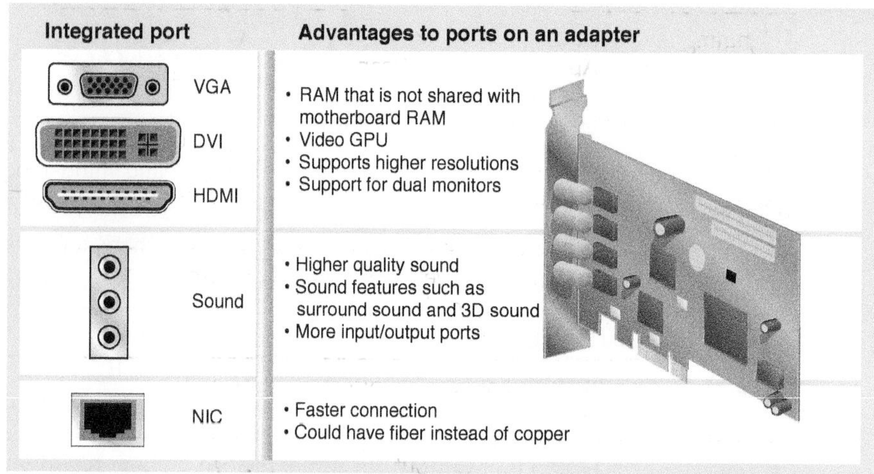

FIGURE 2.42 Advantages of adapters

Getting to Know Ports

Being able to identify ports quickly and accurately is a critical skill in computer repair. Table 2.8 lists the most common computer ports.

TABLE 2.8 Common ports

Port	Usage	Port color code	Common connector
PS/2 mouse	Mouse	Green	6-pin mini-DIN
PS/2 keyboard	Keyboard	Purple	6-pin mini-DIN
VGA	Video for an analog monitor	Blue	3-row 15-pin female D-shell or mini-VGA port
DVI	Video for a DVI digital or analog monitor	White	3-row 18- or 24-pin female DVI, mini-DVI, or micro-DVI
DVI-D	Video for a DVI digital monitor	White	3-row 18- or 24-pin female DVI, mini-DVI, or micro-DVI
DVI-A	Video for a DVI analog monitor	White	3-row 18- or 24-pin female DVI, mini-DVI, or micro-DVI
HDMI	Digital audio and video monitor	N/A	19- or 29-pin HDMI, mini-HDMI, or micro-HDMI
DisplayPort	Digital audio and video monitor	N/A	20-pin DisplayPort or mini-DisplayPort
USB	Multipurpose port for data, video, audio, and power	Black, blue, teal, or red	USB Type-A, Type-B, Type-C, miniUSB, microUSB
Thunderbolt	Multipurpose port that can carry data, video, audio, and power	N/A	20-pin DisplayPort, mini-DisplayPort, or USB Type-C connector
Lightning	Multipurpose port for Apple devices that can carry data and power	N/A	8-pin connector
Audio	Analog audio input	Light pink	1/8 inch (3.5 mm) jack
Audio	Analog line level audio input	Light blue	1/8 inch (3.5 mm) jack
Audio	Analog line level audio output from main stereo signal	Lime green	1/8 inch (3.5 mm) jack
Audio	Analog line level audio for right-to-left speaker	Brown	1/8 inch (3.5 mm) jack
S/PDIF	Audio input/output	Orange	RCA jack (coax) or TOSLINK (fiber)
RJ45	UTP Ethernet network	N/A	8-conductor
RJ11	Internal/external modem or phone	N/A	4-conductor
DB9	RS232 serial port found on older computers and some networking equipment	N/A	9-pin port
eSATA	External storage devices	N/A	7-pin nonpowered port
eSATAp	External devices	N/A	Combination eSATA/USB port

Wireless Connectivity for Input Devices

Many input devices, such as keyboards, mice, game pads, touchpads, and headphones, have wireless connectivity. Technologies used to connect without a cord include infrared, radio, Bluetooth, and near field communication (NFC). Many computing devices, especially smartphones and other mobile devices, have cordless connectivity integrated into the device; otherwise, a transceiver is connected to a USB port to allow connectivity to the computing device. Figure 2.43 shows a wireless presenter used with a computing device and a projector.

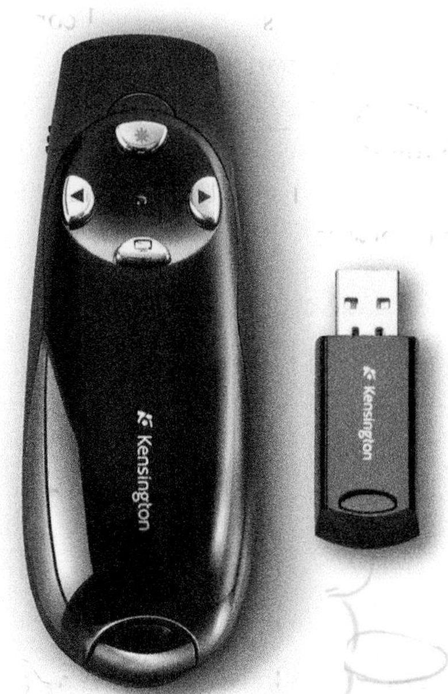

FIGURE 2.43 Wireless presenter

Table 2.9 summarizes the various wireless technologies used with input and output devices.

TABLE 2.9 Wireless input/output technologies

Technology	Description
Infrared (**IR**)	Used for very short distances. Cheaper than other technologies.
Radio	Works in the 27 or 900 MHz, or 2.4, 5, or 60 GHz radio frequency ranges. Longer distances are supported than with infrared.
Bluetooth	Includes 128-bit security and works in the 2.4 GHz range. There are four classes of devices, with ranges up to 1.6 feet (0.5 m), 3 feet (1 m), 33 feet (10 m), and 328 feet (100 m). Note that Bluetooth 5 supports a connection between two devices up to 800 feet (242 meters) away. Up to eight devices can be connected with only one device controlling the other devices.
Near field communication (**NFC**)	Used to print from a phone or a camera or to transfer data between two smartphones that are positioned very close to one another (less than 6 inches [15.24 cm]). Also used in payment systems. Works in the 13.56 MHz range at transfer speeds up to 424 kb/s.

SOFT SKILLS: USING APPROPRIATE TITLES

The internet and mobile devices have brought new methods of communication. In today's social media world, communication tends to be more casual, with people using colloquialisms, slang, and other language habits that aren't necessarily professional. In addition, some people regularly use acronyms, such as HAGD, LOL, BTW, NRN, TYVM, and YMMD, to communicate in emails, notes, text messages, and memos.

Many places of business are returning to the basics when it comes to customer service, and these businesses expect you as an IT professional to use professional communication methods. People expect the IT department to use more professional communication skills, and improved soft skills are therefore emphasized during the hiring process. For example, IT personnel are expected to use appropriate titles, such as Dr., Mr., Professor, and Ms. when talking to non-IT personnel, including external vendors. In the work environment, you should use a person's title, sir, or ma'am until the person you are addressing tells you otherwise. Figure 2.44 shows a couple of examples.

FIGURE 2.44 At work, use appropriate salutations

Chapter Summary

- A technician must be able to identify a variety of ports, including mouse and keyboard PS/2, VGA, DVI, HDMI, DisplayPort, Thunderbolt, Lightning, USB, RJ45, RJ11, 3.5 mm sound jack, TOSLINK, RCA, DB9, eSATA, and eSATAp ports.
- USB is the most popular connection type for adding devices to desktops, laptops, and tablets.
- USB provides power: 10W, 18W, 36W, 60W, and 100W. All USB4 ports support charging a USB device.
- Add additional USB ports by connecting a hub that can be self-powered or bus powered. Up to five hubs can be daisy-chained to one port.
- Connect an internal USB cable from a motherboard connector to a metal plate that mounts in an empty expansion slot for more USB ports.
- Adapters are available to convert between different types of display ports, such as DVI and VGA or DVI and HDMI.
- Converters are available for USB ports, such as USB-to-Ethernet if the Ethernet port goes bad on a computer.
- Audio ports can be analog or digital. S/PDIF ports are digital. There are two types of S/PDIF ports: TOSLINK and fiber.

Review Questions

1. Match the port to the description.

_____	DVI	a. Ethernet
_____	VGA	b. TOSLINK
_____	Thunderbolt	c. up to 127 devices
_____	USB	d. daisy-chain up to 6 devices
_____	NIC	e. older monitor
_____	S/PDIF	f. digital signals to monitor

2. Which connectors are used with fiber-optic cabling? (Choose all that apply.)
   [BNC | DVI | ST | Lightning | LC | Thunderbolt | UTP]
3. What is a visual indication that a port is USB version 3.0?
   ____
4. Which port uses an RJ45 connector?
   [modem | Ethernet | Lightning | S/PDIF]
5. What feature does an eSATAp port have that makes it different from an eSATA port?
   ____
6. When considering VGA, HDMI, DVI, and DisplayPort, which video port can output both digital audio and video signals and is the most technologically advanced?
   [DisplayPort | DVI | HDMI | VGA]
7. What is the most common DVI port?
   [DVI-A | DVI-D | DVI-C | DVI-I]
8. Which has the faster transfer time, a USB 3.0 or 1000 Mb/s Ethernet port?
   [USB 3.0 | 1000 Mb/s Ethernet]
9. What is the maximum cable length for an Ethernet UTP cable?
   [100 meters | 150 meters | 200 meters | 1000 meters]
10. Which color of sound port would be used to attach a speaker?
    [black | green | pink | white]
11. List two titles that might be used in the workplace that are not sir or ma'am.
    ____
12. You see a port on a computer that you have never seen before. There are no markings. How will you determine the purpose of the port?
    ____
13. What type of port uses an RJ11 connector?
    [Ethernet | internal modem | display | keyboard]
14. Which port is more likely found on an Apple computer than any other type of PC?
    [Ethernet | RJ45 | Lightning | USB-C]
15. On which type of cable would you find an F type connector?
    [VGA | Thunderbolt | Lightning | coaxial]
16. On which type of card would a DB9 connector be found?
    [serial | NIC | video | audio]

17. Which cable can carry video and audio signals and can be used to connect external storage devices?

[Type-A | DVI-I | Thunderbolt | mini-DIN]

18. In which of the following situations would Bluetooth most likely be used?

a. To connect to a corporate wireless network

b. To attach a keyboard to a PC

c. To connect a PC to a phone line

d. To connect a flash drive to a camera

19. List one advantage of having an adapter rather than an integrated motherboard port.

____

20. What are two commonly used connectors on coaxial cable used in video distribution systems? (Choose two.)

[RG-6 | RG-11 | RG-59 | RJ11 | RJ45]

Exercises

Exercise 2.1 Identifying Computer Ports

Objective: To identify various computer ports correctly

Procedure: Identify each computer port in Figure 2.45.

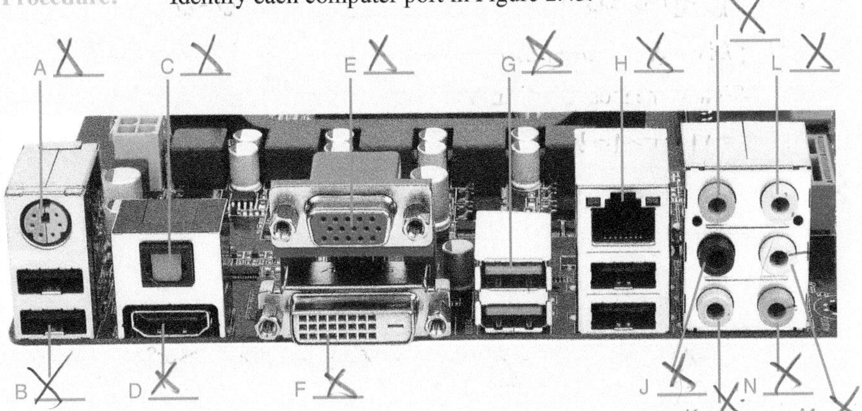

FIGURE 2.45 Identify motherboard ports

A. ______________________________
B. ______________________________
C. ______________________________
D. ______________________________
E. ______________________________
F. ______________________________
G. ______________________________
H. ______________________________
I. ______________________________
J. ______________________________
K. ______________________________
L. ______________________________
M. ______________________________
N. ______________________________

Exercise 2.2 Identifying More Computer Ports

Objective: To identify various computer ports using graphics

Procedure: Identify each computer port in Figure 2.46.

FIGURE 2.46 Identify computer ports

1. Thunderbolt
2. DB-9
3. Optical S/PDIF
4. RJ45 (Ethernet)
5. RJ11 (Telephone)
6. USB 3.0
7. eSATAp
8. USB-C
9. PS/2 Keyboard
10. Side speakers Sound

Exercise 2.3 Identifying Display Ports

Objective: To identify various display ports correctly

Procedure: Identify each display port in Figure 2.47.

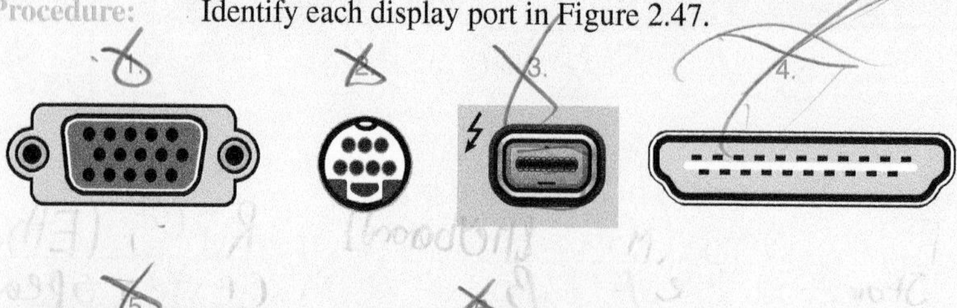

FIGURE 2.47 Identify video ports

1. VGA
2. S-Video
3. Thunderbolt
4. ~~SATA~~ ← HDMI
5. Display Port
6. DVI-I (Dual)

Exercise 2.4 Identifying USB Ports

Objective: To identify various USB ports correctly

Procedure: Identify each display port in Figure 2.48.

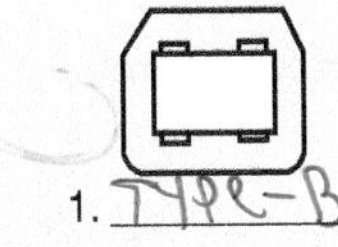

1. Type-B

2. TypeA

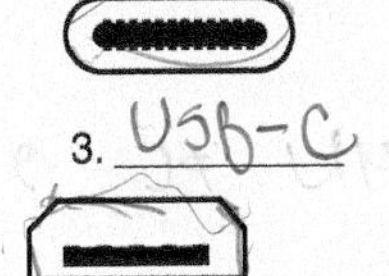

3. USB-C

4. Mini-USB

5. Micro-USB

FIGURE 2.48 Identify USB ports

1. Type-B
2. Type-A
3. USB-C
4. Mini-USB
5. Micro-USB

Exercise 2.5 Identifying Cables

Objective: To identify various cables

Procedure: Identify each cable in Figure 2.49.

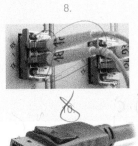

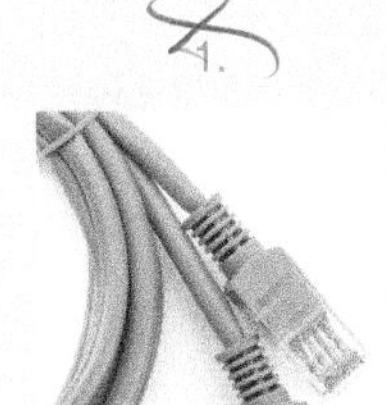

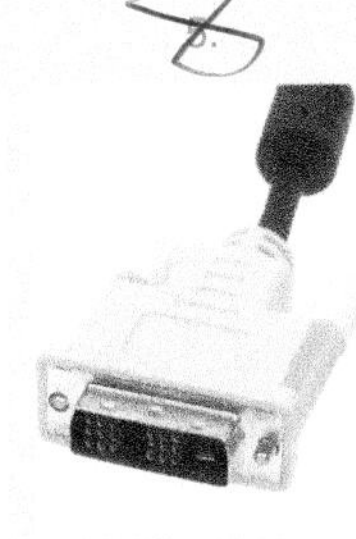

8.

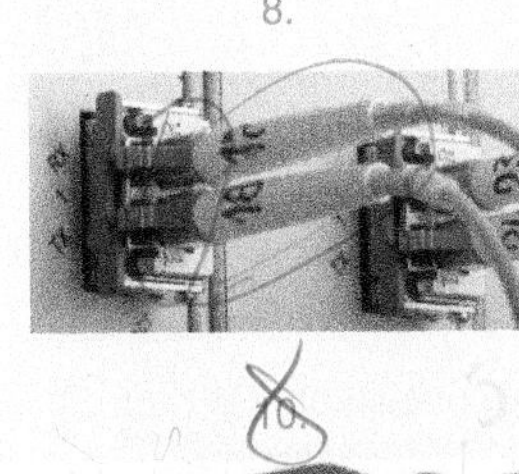

FIGURE 2.49 Identify cables

1. RJ-45
2. USB-C
3. VGA
4. HDMI
5. Singlelink DVI-D
6. Standard type-a
7. F-Connector
8. LC
9. DB-9 (Serial)
10. DisplayPort

Activities

Internet Discovery

Objective: To obtain specific information from the internet regarding a computer or its associated parts

Parts: Computer with internet access

Procedure: Complete the following procedure and answer the accompanying questions.

Questions: For Questions 1–4: Obtain technical information about a particular computer (maybe your own computer or a model number given by the instructor). Answer the following questions based on the information. You may need to obtain more documents, or you may need to select a different computer model to answer questions. Please use only one computer model.

1. Which ports are available on the front of the computer?

   ___

2. Which ports are available on the back of the computer?

   ___

3. How many drive bays are available to install devices such as hard drives, optical drives, tape drives, and so on?

   ___

4. Were the photos in the documentation clear enough to differentiate between the different ports? If not, explain what is wrong.

   ___

5. List 10 acronyms and what they stand for that would be appropriate in a text message to a family member but inappropriate to use when communicating (even texting) with an employee from a non-IT department who is not a close friend but a professional acquaintance. Also, provide the URL(s) where this information is found.

   ___

6. Using the internet, list one fact about NFC that was not in the chapter and the URL where you found this information.

   ___

Soft Skills

Objective: To enhance and fine-tune a future technician's ability to listen, communicate in both written and oral forms, and support people who use computers in a professional manner

Procedure:

1. In teams of two, one student writes a professional note that contains internet acronyms that are commonly used for texting. The other student tries to then guess what the acronyms mean. Together, rewrite the note so it is more professional.
2. Draft an email to a pretend computer customer that you just met yesterday for the first time. You did not have the part needed to repair the computer, but now the part has come in. Be sure you use professionalism in your email.

Critical Thinking Skills

Objective: To analyze and evaluate information as well as apply learned information to new or different situations

Procedure:

1. Find an advertisement for a computer in a local computer flyer, in a newspaper, in a magazine, in a book, or on the internet. List which ports you know in one column and the ports you do not know in the other column. Select one port you do not know and research that component. Write the new information and share it with at least one other person.
2. Work in groups of three. As a group, do you think future computers will only have wireless connections or continue to have both wired and wireless connectivity? Why do you think this? What might be some hindrances to future computers having only have wireless connections?
3. Provide five tips that might help someone identify the different computer ports. If possible, each person in the class should state a tip without duplicating someone else's tip.

Introduction to the Motherboard

The motherboard contains the most electronics and is important to any type of device including a computer. Figure 3.1 shows some of the key motherboard components we will be covering.

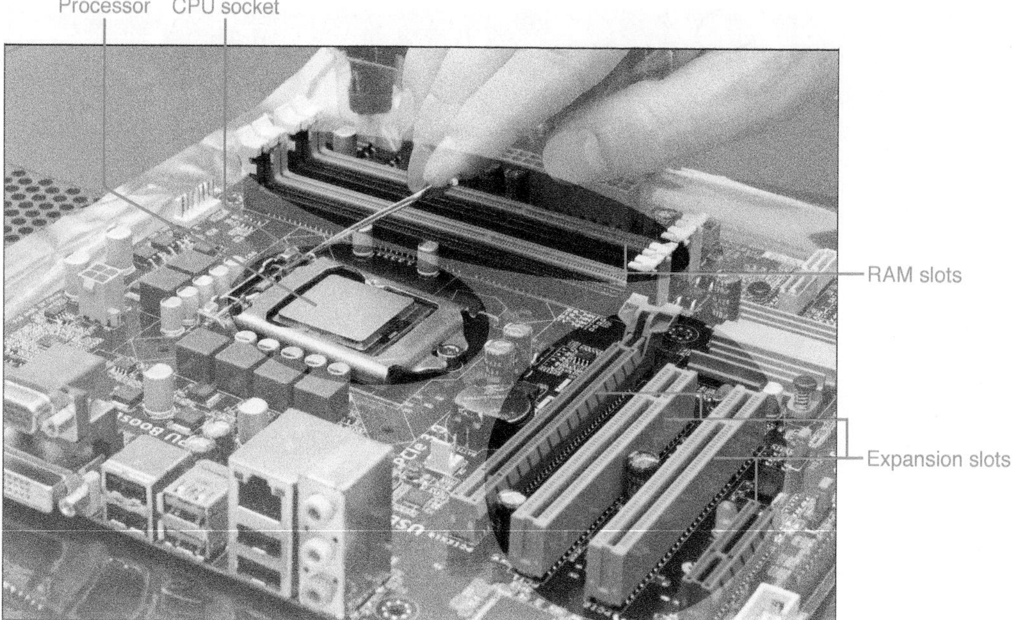

FIGURE 3.1 Key motherboard components

Processor Overview

At the heart of every computer is the **processor**, which determines, to a great extent, the power of the computer. The processor is also called the central processing unit (**CPU**), or microprocessor. The processor executes instructions, performs calculations, and coordinates input/output operations. Each motherboard has chips that work with the CPU and that are designed to exact specifications. The major processor manufacturers today are Intel, Motorola, VIA, Samsung, NVIDIA, Apple Inc., Qualcomm, and AMD (Advanced Micro Devices, Inc.). **Intel** and **AMD** are the predominant manufacturers for desktop and laptop processors. A term you might hear related to Intel and AMD CPUs is x86-64. The **x86** relates to the Intel 8086 processor, and the 64, or **x64**, reflects the update to a 64-bit version. Intel has its own patented CPU architecture called Intel 64, and AMD has the patented architecture AMD64.

ARM processors are used on mobile devices like smartphones, tablets, and laptops, but can also be used with desktop computers and servers. ARM used to be an acronym for Acorn RISC (reduced instruction set computing) Machine and then Advanced RISC Machines, but today it is just an architecture used in processors and microcontrollers. ARM processors can be 32- or 64-bit. ARM processors take less power, produce less heat, and cost less than AMD or Intel processors. The company Arm Ltd. also licenses its own designs to other companies that create their own products.

A motherboard accepts the processors of one or more specific manufacturers; for example, a motherboard that accepts an Intel processor will not support an AMD processor. Figure 3.2 shows a processor.

FIGURE 3.2 Intel processor

Processor Basics

Processors come in a variety of speeds, measured in gigahertz (GHz). Hertz is a measurement of cycles per second. One hertz, written 1 Hz, equals 1 cycle per second. One gigahertz, or 1 GHz, is 1 billion cycles per second. Today's processors can run at speeds near 5 GHz.

Buses

Processors operate on 1s and 0s. The 1s and 0s must travel from one place to another inside the processor, as well as outside to other chips. To move the 1s and 0s around, electronic lines called a bus are used. The electronic lines inside the CPU are known as the **internal data bus**, or system bus. In the Intel 8086 (from which the term x86 architecture originated), the internal data bus comprises 16 separate lines, with each line carrying a single 1 or a single 0. In today's processors, 64 or 128 internal data bus lines operate concurrently.

For a CPU to communicate with devices in the outside world, such as a printer, the 1s and 0s travel on the **external data bus**. The external data bus connects the processor to adapters, the keyboard, the mouse, storage, and other devices. You can see the external data lines by looking between the expansion slots on the motherboard. Today's processors have 64- and 128-bit external data paths. Figure 3.3 shows the internal and external data buses.

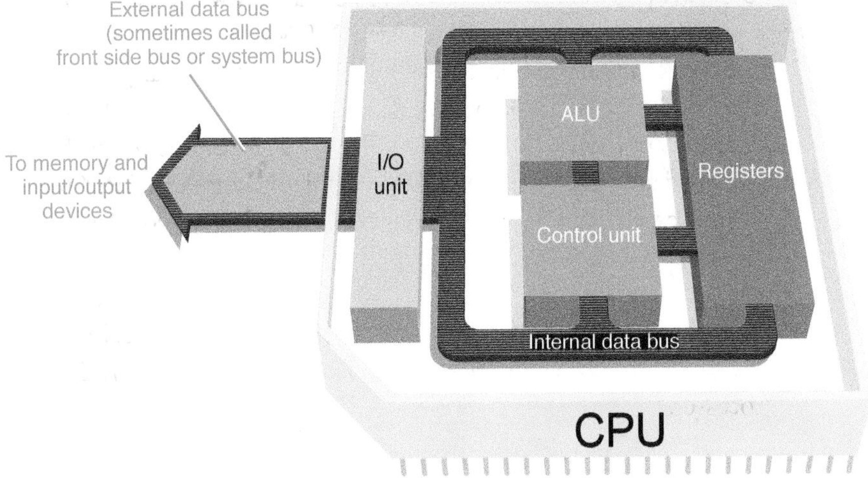

FIGURE 3.3 Internal and external data buses

ALUs

A processor has a special component called the arithmetic logic unit (ALU), which does all the calculations and comparison logic that the computer needs. Figure 3.3 shows the basic idea of how the ALU connects to the registers, control unit, and internal bus. The control unit coordinates activities inside the processor. The I/O unit manages data entering and leaving the processor. The registers in the CPU make up a high-speed storage area for 1s and 0s before the bits are processed.

Processing Data

To understand how a computer processes data, consider a letter typed on a computer that starts out *DEAR MOM*. To the computer, each letter of the alphabet is a different combination of eight 1s and 0s. For example, the letter *D* is 01000100, and the letter *E* is 01000101. Figure 3.4 demonstrates that the size of the bus greatly increases performance on a computer much the way increasing the number of lanes of a highway decreases congestion.

DEAR MOM,

The larger the bus (more lanes), the better the performance.

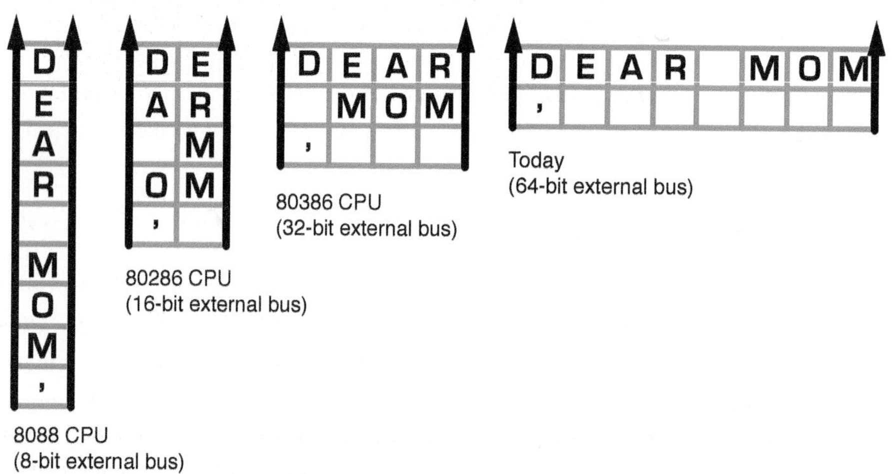

FIGURE 3.4 Bus performance

Pipelines

Processors have multiple pipelines (separate internal buses) that operate simultaneously. To understand pipelining, take the example of a fast-food restaurant. In the restaurant, assume that there are five steps involved in making a burger and giving it to the customer. To make this burger process go faster, you could (maybe) do one of the things shown in Figure 3.5.

To relate this to processors, you could increase the CPU clock speed, you could change the structure of the CPU pipeline in terms of how many steps are in each pipeline, and/or the CPU could have multiple pipelines. For example, if a processor has two pipelines, the Dear Mom letter can be in one pipeline, while a photo upload using a different application can be in the other pipeline.

2. Break the tasks into smaller tasks

1. Make your employees work faster

3. Have more lines of people doing exactly the same process tasks

FIGURE 3.5 Ways to get faster processes

Speeding Up Processor Operations Overview

You can determine the speed of a processor by looking at the model number on the chip, but processors frequently have devices attached to them for cooling, which makes it difficult to see the writing on the chip. A processor commonly does not use its maximum speed all the time in order to save power or stay cool. Also, a processor is not always functioning at its maximum potential for a lot of reasons, including coding used within an application, the user switching from application to application, inadequate bus width, or the amount of RAM installed. A processor can also operate beyond its rated specifications to handle periods of increased workload.

TECH TIP

Locating processor speed

An easy way to tell processor speed with Windows is to go to File Explorer and right-click *This PC* and select *Properties*.

We have already taken a look at how increasing the CPU pipeline can, to some extent, improve processor operations, but other technologies also exist. We start by defining some of the terms that relate to this area and associating those terms with concepts and the various technologies used. Table 3.1 list some terms related to speed.

TABLE 3.1 Motherboard speed terms

Term	Explanation
Clock or **clock speed**	The speed of the processor's internal clock, measured in gigahertz.
Front side bus (**FSB**)	The speed (commonly called motherboard speed) between the CPU and some of the motherboard components. Sometimes listed in megatransfers per second, or MT/s. With MT/s, not only is the speed of the FSB considered, but also how many processor transfers occur each clock cycle. A 266 MHz FSB that can do four transfers per second could be listed as 1064 MT/s.
Back side bus	The speed between the CPU and the L2 cache located outside the main CPU but on the same chip.
PCI bus speed	The speed used to deliver data on the PCI bus. Common speeds for the PCI bus are 33 and 66 MHz, allowing bandwidths up to 533 MB/s.
PCIe bus speed	The speed used to deliver data on the PCIe bus (the main bus used on the motherboard). Common data transfer rates follow. Note that to find the total throughput, multiply the transfer rate by the number of lanes. For example, with PCIe 4.x transfer rate of 16.0 GT/s (gigatransfers per second), the throughput on a 1x card is 1.6 GB/s and on a 16x card is 128 GB/s: > PCIe 1.1: 2.5 GT/s > PCIe 2.x: 5 GT/s > PCIe 3.x: 8 GT/s > PCIe 4.x: 16 GT/s > PCIe 5.x: 32 GT/s > PCIe 6.x: 64 GT/s
AGP bus speed	The speed used to deliver data on the AGP bus, an older standard used for video cards.
CPU speed	The speed at which the CPU operates; it can be changed on some motherboards.
CPU throttling	Reducing the clock frequency to slow the CPU in order to reduce power consumption and heat. This is especially useful in mobile devices.

Clocking

A motherboard generates a clock signal that is used to control the transfer of 1s and 0s to and from the processor. One clock cycle is from one point on the sine wave to the next point that is located on the same point on the sine wave later in time. In older computers, data was sent to the CPU only once during a clock cycle. Today, data is sent four times during a single clock cycle, as shown in Figure 3.6.

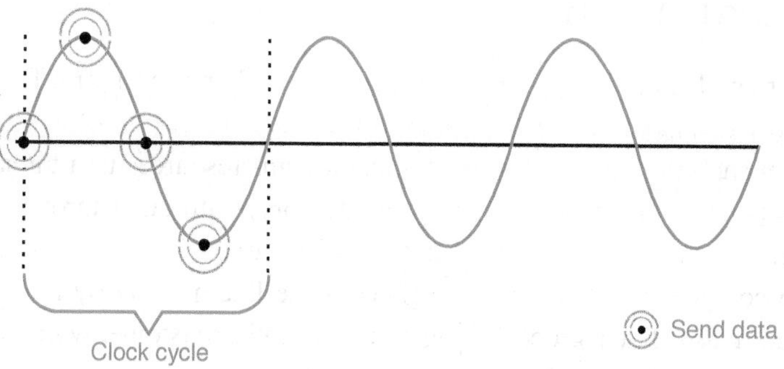

FIGURE 3.6 Clock cycle that clocks data four times per cycle

Cache

An important concept related to processor speed is keeping data flowing into the processor. The data or instruction the CPU needs to process is usually found in one of four places: cache memory, motherboard memory (main memory), a solid-state drive (SSD, which is also memory), or the hard drive.

Cache memory is a very fast type of memory designed to increase the speed and efficiency of processor operations. Cache provides the fastest access. If the information is not in cache memory, the processor looks for the data in motherboard RAM. If the information is not there, it is retrieved from the hard drive and placed into the motherboard memory or the cache. Hard drive access is the slowest of the three. Table 3.2 lists the types of cache. Figure 3.7 shows the hierarchy of where the CPU looks for data.

TABLE 3.2 Types of cache

Type	Explanation
L1 cache	Cache memory integrated into the processor and the fastest type
L2 cache	Cache in the processor packaging but not part of the CPU; also called on-die cache
L3 cache	Usually found in more powerful processors and can be located in the CPU housing (on-die) or on the motherboard

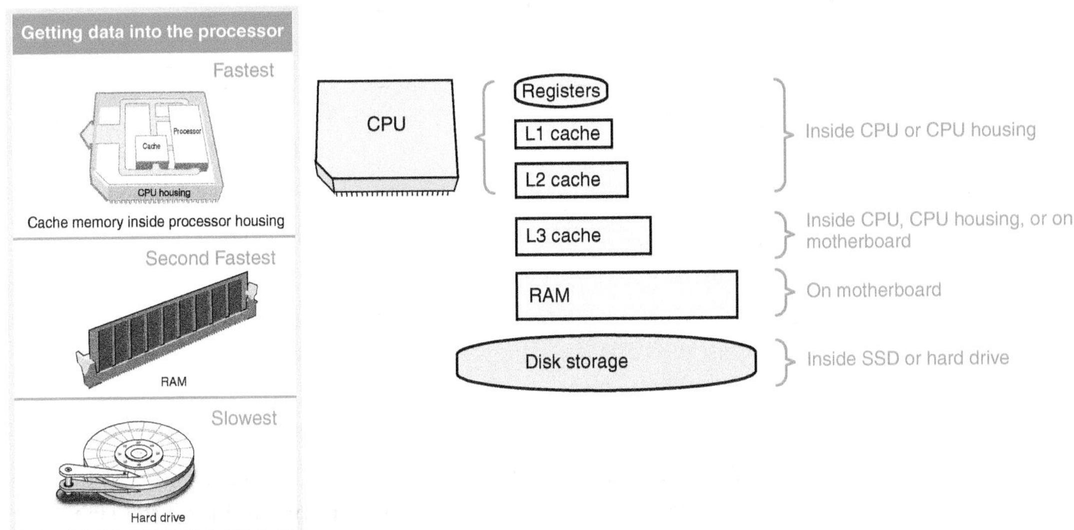

FIGURE 3.7 CPU data sources and data access hierarchy

Threading Technology

Two common threading techniques are used to speed up processor efficiency: multithreading and HT (Hyperthreading Technology). A **thread** is a small piece of an application process. An operating system such as Windows schedules and assigns resources to a thread. Each thread can share resources (such as the processor or cache memory) with other threads. A thread in the pipeline might have a delay due to waiting on data to be retrieved or awaiting access to a port or another hardware component. **Multithreading** keeps the line moving by letting another thread execute some code. This is like a grocery cashier taking another customer while someone goes for a forgotten loaf of bread. Figure 3.8 shows this concept.

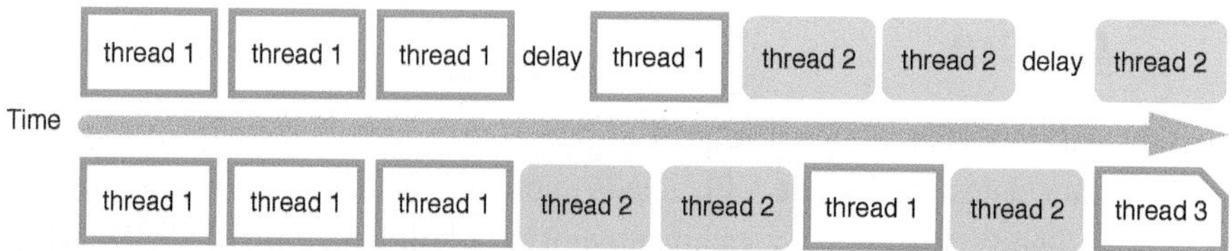

FIGURE 3.8 Multithreading

Intel's HT (**Hyperthreading**, Hyper-Threading, or HT Technology) allows a single processor to handle two separate sets of instructions simultaneously. To the operating system, HT makes the system appear as if it has multiple processors. Intel claims that the system can have up to a 30% increase in performance, but studies have shown that the increase is application dependent.

Connecting to the Processor

Accessing L2 cache and motherboard components was a bottleneck in older systems. The solution to this problem is to use two buses: a back side bus and a front side bus. The back side bus connects the CPU to the L2 cache. The front side bus (see Figure 3.9) connects the CPU to the motherboard components. The front side bus is considered the speed of the motherboard.

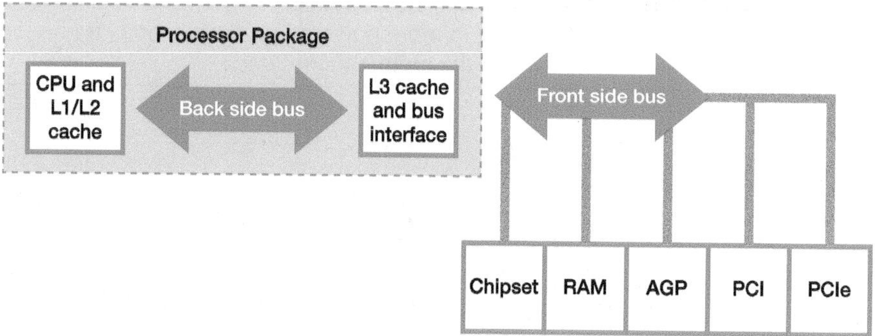

FIGURE 3.9 Front side bus and back side bus

Many people think that the higher the CPU speed, the faster the computer. This is seldom true. Several factors contribute to the speed of a computer. One factor is bus speed. Bus speed describes how fast the CPU can communicate with motherboard components, such as memory, the chipset, or the PCI/PCIe bus.

Intel and AMD have technologies to replace the front side bus in some parts. AMD's solution is Direct Connect. Direct Connect allows each of the processor cores to connect directly to memory, to the other motherboard components such as the expansion slots, and to other processor cores by using a high-speed bus called **HyperTransport** (see Figure 3.11, later in the chapter). AMD is upgrading HyperTransport to Infinity Fabric. Intel has Ultra Path Interconnect (UPI), Serial Peripheral Interface (SPI), and Direct Media Interface (DMI), which are point-to-point connections between the processor and one or more motherboard components.

Multicore Processors

A **single-core processor** is just one processor. Both Intel and AMD provide **multicore** processors, which means more than one CPU in the same housing (see Figure 3.10). Each core can execute programs or threads. One Intel Core i9 CPU has 18 cores, and AMD's Ryzen Threadripper has 64 cores and 128 threads. Figure 3.10 shows how multiple Intel processors connect. Figure 3.11 shows how each AMD CPU accesses RAM and where the HyperTransport bus is used for connectivity.

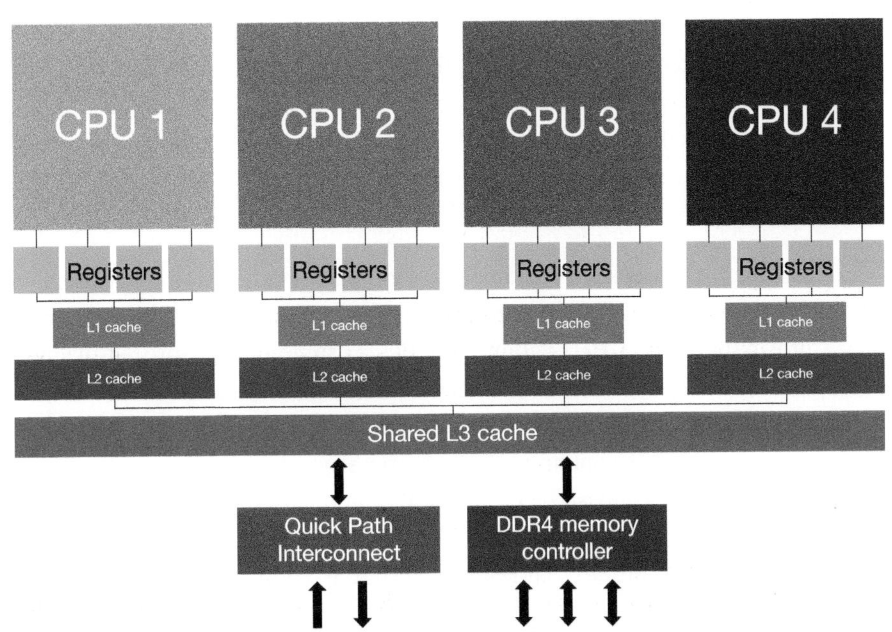

FIGURE 3.10 Intel multicore architecture

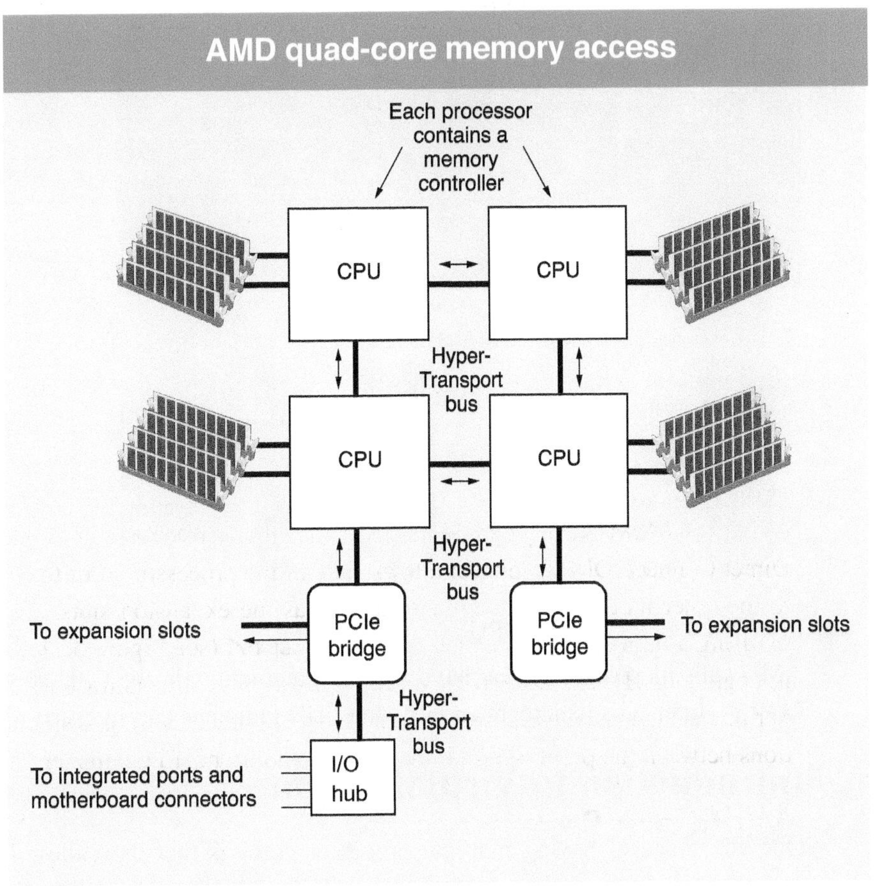

FIGURE 3.11 AMD quad-core memory access

TECH TIP

How many cores and threads do you have?

Right-click on Windows taskbar > *Task Manager* > *Performance* tab > *CPU* > look for *Cores, Logical processors, and Threads.*

A logical processor can execute its own set of instructions. All applications can take advantage of the multicore technology and the background processes that are associated with the operating system and applications. This improves operations when multitasking or when running powerful applications that require many instructions to be executed, such as drawing applications and games.

Graphics Processing Unit (GPU)

Another bottleneck for computer performance is video. Computer users who want better video performance buy a separate video adapter that contains a GPU. Both Intel and AMD have a graphics processing unit (**GPU**) within the CPU on some of their processor models. With an **integrated GPU** (iGPU), sometimes called an integrated graphics processor (IGP), an external video card with a GPU is not required, and graphical data is processed quickly with reduced power consumption.

Today's CPUs contain multicore processors, and GPUs contain hundreds of smaller core processors. GPUs can also be used for other purposes that are not directly related to graphics but that increase system performance. These GPUs are sometimes referred to as general-purpose GPUs (GPGPUs). Figure 3.12 shows how an IGP is within the same housing as the CPU cores.

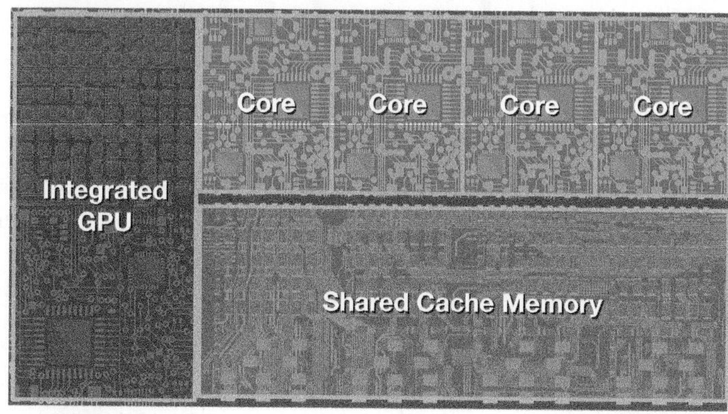

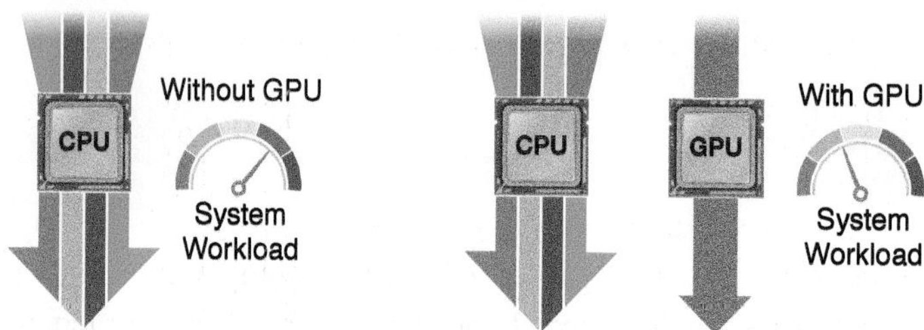

FIGURE 3.12 CPU vs. GPU

AMD calls its processors that have a GPU integrated with the CPU accelerated processing units (**APUs**). Intel calls its integrated GPU Intel HD Graphics and Intel Iris Graphics.

Introduction to Virtualization

One advantage of having multiple processor cores is that they allow both home and business computers to take advantage of virtual technology. **Virtualization** allows you to have one or more virtual machines (**VMs**) on the same computer. Virtualization software, such as VMware Workstation, Oracle VM VirtualBox, or Microsoft Hyper-V, enables one computer to act as if it were two or more computers. The computer can have two or more operating systems installed through the use of the virtualization software. Each operating system has no knowledge of the other operating system(s) on the computer (see Figure 3.13).

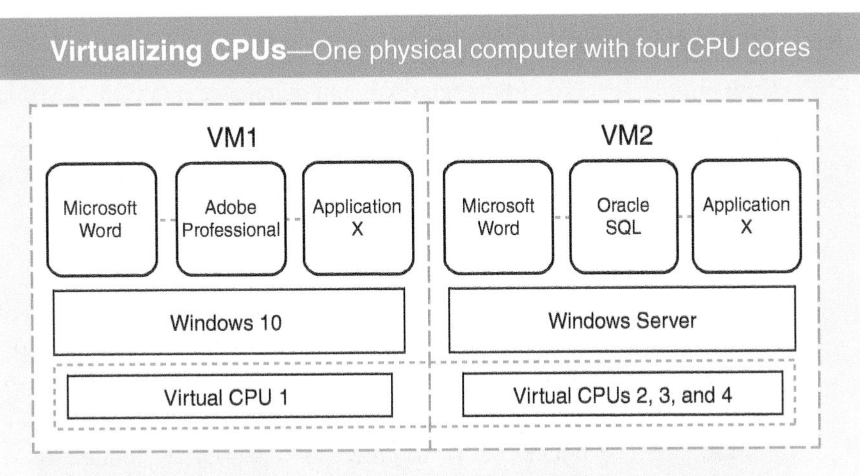

FIGURE 3.13 The concept of virtualization

Windows 8, 10, and 11 have Hyper-V, which allows an application to run in a virtual environment as if an older operating system had been installed. Businesses often use virtualization so they can use legacy software on newer machines but keep it separate from the main operating system or another virtualized machine on the same computer. Reduced costs and physical space are benefits of virtualization. Home computer users can install multiple operating systems in separate VMs (virtual machines) within the same physical box, with each VM being seen as a separate computer. To better prepare yourself for the CompTIA A+ certification exams, you could install Windows 10 or 11 and Linux.

Selecting a motherboard and processor is important when in a virtual environment. Refer to the virtualization software documentation to determine whether the CPU used is supported. Be sure to enable **virtualization support** in the firmware (covered in Chapter 4, "Introduction to Configuration"). Another issue regarding processors and virtualization is licensing. For virtualization software that must be purchased (that is, is not freeware), the software manufacturer may charge on a per-processor or per-socket license basis or on a per-core basis.

Intel Processors

Traditionally, Intel has rated its processors by GHz, and people have compared processors based on speed alone. Now, Intel arranges its products by family numbers. In a family of processors, you can compare attributes such as speed and the amount of cache memory and other technologies. Table 3.3 shows Intel's processor families. Figure 3.14 shows a close-up of a processor installed into a motherboard. Figure 3.15 shows how to decipher Intel processor models.

TABLE 3.3 Intel processor families

Processor family*	Comments
Xeon	CPU for server and professional PCs that need ECC memory, large amounts of memory, larger cache, more cores, and multiple sockets.
Core X	18-core processor (at press time) for high performance, extreme gaming, intensive content creation, and megatasking.
Core i9	Powerful multicore processor for gaming and intensive content creation as well as megatasking.
Core i7	Multicore with cache memory shared between cores and on-board memory controller. Good for virtualization, graphic/multimedia design and creation, and gaming.

Processor family*	Comments
Core i5	Midrange dual- and quad-core processor. Used for video, photos, email, and internet access.
Core i3	Low-end desktop and mobile processor used for common tasks such as word processing and internet access.

*Intel is constantly upgrading processors. For more information, visit www.intel.com.

FIGURE 3.14 Installed processor

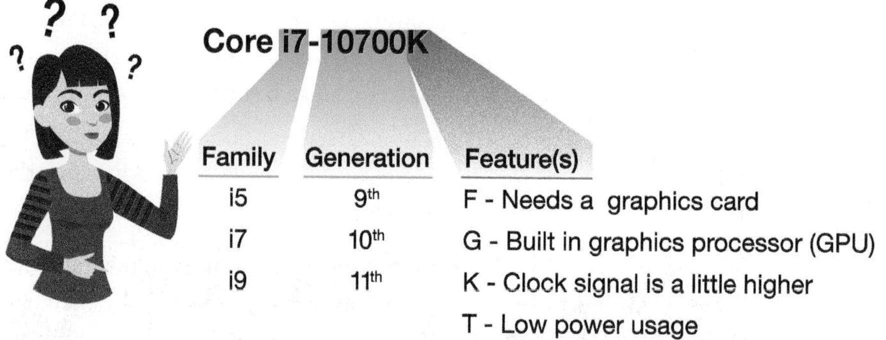

FIGURE 3.15 Deciphering Intel processor model numbers

AMD Processors

AMD is Intel's largest rival in computer processors. Anyone buying a processor should research all models and vendors. Table 3.4 lists the AMD processor families, and Figure 3.16 shows how to make sense of the AMD CPU model numbers.

TABLE 3.4 AMD processor families

Processor family	Comments
Ryzen Threadripper	8 to 64 cores, 128 processing threads, and 20 to 292 MB cache for extremely high-end desktop processor
Ryzen 9	8 to 16 cores, 32 processing threads, and up to 72 MB cache for gaming or creating multimedia
Ryzen 7	8 cores, 16 processing threads, 20 MB cache for gaming, high-end content creation, and megatasking
Ryzen 5	4 to 6 cores, up to 12 processing threads, and up to 20 MB cache for workplace or home computing use
Ryzen 3	4 cores and up to 18 MB cache for standard computing use

Ryzen 7 3700X

Family	Generation	Performance Level	Feature(s)
3	1st	1-3	X - High performance
5	2nd	4-5	WX - High core count workstation
7	3rd	6-7	G - Desktop + IGP
9	4th	8	E - Low-power desktop
THREADRIPPER	5th	9	GE - Low-power desktop + IGP
			XT - Extreme

FIGURE 3.16 Deciphering AMD processor model numbers

CPU Sockets

A processor inserts into a **CPU socket**. There are different types of sockets, but each socket has a specific number of pins and only accepts specific CPUs. A motherboard that can take more than one CPU will show in the documentation/specifications as a **multisocket** motherboard. Typically, it is motherboards on a server, a more powerful computer used in networks, that has a multisocket motherboard. Figure 3.17 shows a desktop motherboard CPU socket.

FIGURE 3.17 CPU socket

Processor sockets are also called zero insertion force sockets, or **ZIF sockets**, and they come in different sizes. A ZIF socket has a small lever to the side that, when lifted, brings the processor slightly up and out of the socket holes. When installing a processor, you align the CPU over the socket and press the lever down to bring the processor into the socket with equal force. In Figure 3.17, notice the lever beside the socket that is used to lift the metal cover.

TECH TIP

Buying the right CPU

If you buy a motherboard and processor separately, it is important to ensure that the motherboard CPU socket is the correct type for the processor.

Intel sockets: LGA 1151, 1155, 1156, 1200, 2066, 3647

AMD sockets: AM5, AM4, TR4, TRX4

Processor Cooling

Keeping a CPU cool is critical. Both Intel and AMD have technologies that reduce processor energy consumption (and heat) by turning off unused parts of the processor or slowing down the processor when it starts to overheat. But these measures alone are not enough. Today's systems use one or more of the methods listed in Table 3.5. Figure 3.18 shows a heat sink and a fan.

TABLE 3.5 Processor cooling methods

Method	Description
Heat sink	A heat sink is a block of metal (usually aluminum or copper), metal bars, or metal fins that attach to the top of the processor or other motherboard components. Heat from the processor is transferred to the heat sink and then blown away by the air flow throughout the computer case.
Fan	Fans can be attached to the processor, beside the processor, and in the case.
Thermal paste or **thermal pad**	Thermal paste, compound, or grease can be applied to the top of a processor before a heat sink is attached. Some heat sinks and fans have thermal paste pre-applied. A thermal pad provides uniform heat dispersion and lies between the processor and the heat sink.
Liquid cooling	Liquid is circulated through the system, including through a heat sink that is mounted on the CPU. Heat from the processor is transferred to the cooler liquid. The now-hot liquid is transported to the back of the system, converted to heat, and released outside the case. CPU temperature remains constant, no matter the usage. Some systems require the liquid to be periodically refilled.
Phase-change cooling (vapor cooling)	This expensive option uses a technique similar to a refrigerator: A gas is converted to a liquid that is converted back to gas.

The largest chip on the motherboard with a fan or a heat sink attached is easily recognized as the processor. Figure 3.19 shows an Intel Core i7 that has a fan and a heat sink installed. Notice the heat pipes that are used as part of the heat sink.

FIGURE 3.18 Heat sink and fan

FIGURE 3.19 CPU with heat sink and fan attached

TECH TIP

Cooling the CPU

Do not apply power to a computer until the CPU and the heat sink, fan, and/or cooling unit are installed. Running the CPU without installing appropriate cooling mechanisms will overheat the CPU and destroy or weaken it.

Additional motherboard components can also have heat sinks attached. They are normally the chipset and/or the I/O (input/output) controller chips. Figure 3.20 shows a motherboard with these cooling elements.

FIGURE 3.20 Motherboard heat sinks

> **TECH TIP**
>
> **When thermal paste acts like glue**
>
> Over time, thermal paste can act like glue, making a processor hard to separate from a heat sink. You can use a thermal paste cleaner, acetone, or denatured alcohol to separate the two parts. Do not pry them apart!

Installing a Processor

Processors are sold with installation instructions. In addition, motherboard manuals (or other documentation) include the steps to upgrade or install the CPU. The following are the parts and the general steps for installing a processor:

Parts: Proper processor for the motherboard (refer to motherboard documentation)
Antistatic materials

Step 1. Ensure that power to the computer is off and the computer is unplugged.

Step 2. Place an antistatic wrist strap around your wrist and attach the other end to a ground or an unpainted metal part of the computer. Alternatively, use an antistatic glove.

Step 3. Push the retention lever down and outward to release the CPU retention plate. Move the handle backward until the retention plate is fully open. Do not touch the CPU socket. If a plastic cover is installed in the CPU socket, remove it.

Step 4. Remove the processor from packaging, taking care to hold it by the edges and never touch the bottom metal portion of the processor. Remember that a CPU fits only one way into the socket. Look at the processor and the socket before inserting the chip to ensure proper alignment. A socket and CPU normally have a triangle marking or dot to indicate pin 1, as shown in Figure 3.21. The processor also has notches on each side that align with the socket. Insert the CPU into the socket by aligning it with the socket and lowering it until it is flush with the socket, as shown in Figure 3.22. (Do not force it!)

FIGURE 3.21 Pin 1 and notch on a processor

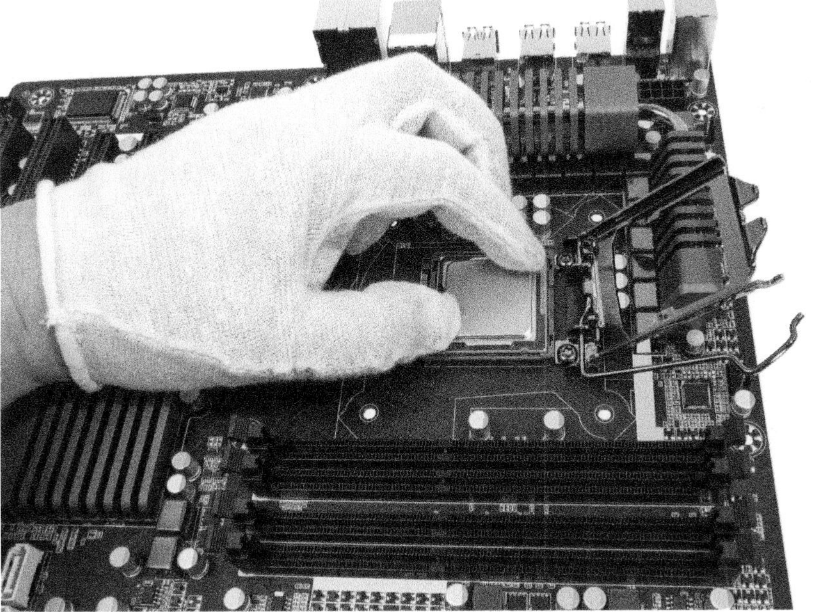

FIGURE 3.22 Installing a CPU

TECH TIP

Handling the CPU

Always hold a CPU by the edges to avoid bending or touching the pins underneath. Do not touch a CPU until you are ready to install it in the socket.

Upgrading Processors

Two common questions asked of technicians are "Can a computer be upgraded to a higher or faster processor?" and "Should a computer be upgraded to a higher or faster processor?" Whether or not a computer can be upgraded to a higher or faster processor depends on the capability of the motherboard. When a customer asks if a processor should be upgraded, the technician should ask, "What operating system and applications are you using?" The newer the operating system, the more advanced the processor should be. Some games and applications that must perform calculations, as well as graphic-oriented applications, require a faster, more advanced processor. The motherboard's documentation is very important when considering a CPU upgrade. Read this documentation to determine whether the motherboard can accept a faster processor.

TECH TIP

Upgrading a CPU

Do not upgrade a processor unless the documentation or manufacturer states that the motherboard supports a newer or faster processor.

Throttle management is the process of controlling the speed of a CPU by slowing it down when it is not being used heavily or when it is hot. Usually this feature is controlled by a system BIOS/UEFI setting and the Windows *Power Options* Control Panel. Some users may want performance to be at a maximum and so may not use CPU throttling. Laptop users, on the other hand, may want to conserve power whenever possible to extend the time the computer can be used on battery power. Use the *Battery* Windows Settings link to control how apps affect battery performance.

Upgrading components other than the processor can also increase speed in a computer. Installing more memory and/or higher capacity and faster storage commonly improve a computer's performance more than installing a new processor. All devices and electronic components must work together to transfer the 1s and 0s efficiently.

Overclocking Processors

Overclocking involves changing the front side bus speed and/or multiplier to boost CPU and system speed. Overclocking has some issues:

- The processor, motherboard, memory, and other components can be damaged by overclocking.
- Applications may crash, the operating system may not boot, and/or the system may hang (lock up) when overclocking.
- You may void the warranty on some CPUs if you overclock.
- When you increase the speed of the CPU, the processor's heat increases. Extra cooling, using fans and larger heat sinks, is essential.
- Input/output devices may not react well to overclocking.
- The memory chips may need to be upgraded to be able to keep up with the faster processing.
- You need to know how to reset the system BIOS/UEFI in case the computer will not boot properly after you make changes. This process is covered in Chapter 4.

TECH TIP

Being ready to cool

The primary problem with overclocking is insufficient cooling. Make sure you purchase a larger heat sink and/or extra fans before starting the overclocking process.

Many motherboard manufacturers do not allow changes to the CPU, multiplier, and clock settings. The changes to the motherboard are most often made through BIOS/UEFI Setup. However, CPU manufacturers may provide tuning tools in the form of applications installed on the computer for overclocking configuration. Keep in mind that overclocking is a trial-and-error situation. There are websites geared toward documenting specific motherboards and overclocked CPUs.

Installing CPU Thermal Solutions

A CPU may come with a thermal solution such as a heat sink and/or fan. The thermal solution commonly comes with a pre-applied thermal paste or an attached thermal pad. Heat sinks and fans attach to the processor using different methods, such as screws, thermal compound, and clips. Clips can involve retaining screws, pressure release, or a retaining slot. The type of heat sink and/or fan installed must fit the processor and case. Additional hardware may have to be installed on the motherboard to be able to attach a CPU thermal solution. Figure 3.23 shows a CPU cooler being installed.

FIGURE 3.23 CPU heat sink/fan installation

TECH TIP

Take a photo of the CPU

Before attaching a heat sink and/or fan to a CPU, take a picture of the markings on top. You might need to use these markings if you ever need technical support and need the exact specifications. Techs often take pictures to document motherboard replacements and wiring.

If a thermal solution is being installed, then the thermal pad or old thermal paste should be removed and new thermal paste applied. Do not scratch the surface of a heat sink. Use a plastic scribe or tool to remove a thermal pad or old paste. A thermal paste cleaner, acetone, or denatured alcohol with a lint-free cloth can be used to remove residual paste.

When installing thermal paste, apply the prescribed amount in the center of the processor. Spread the compound evenly in a fine layer over the center portion of the CPU that comes in contact with the heat sink. When the heat sink is attached to the processor, the thermal compound will spread (hopefully not over the edges). Always follow the heat sink installation directions.

A CPU fan is likely to have a 3- or 4-pin cable that attaches to the motherboard. The motherboard might have a 3- or 4-pin connector. A 3-pin fan can be attached to a 4-pin motherboard connector, and a 4-pin fan cable can be connected to a 3-pin motherboard connector, as shown in Figure 3.24. Note that when a 3-pin cable attaches to 4-pin connector, the fan is always on and cannot be controlled, as a 4-pin cable to a 4-pin connector can.

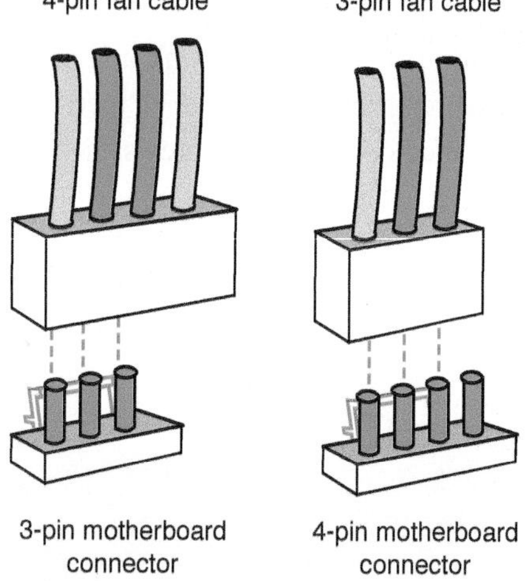

FIGURE 3.24 CPU fan connectivity

Troubleshooting Processor Issues

Processor issues can appear in different ways, as illustrated in Figure 3.25.

The following tips can help you solve CPU issues:

> The number-one issue related to processor problems is heat. Ensure that all fans work. Listen for a **grinding noise** indicating that something is caught in the fan, lack of oil, or a failing fan. Adding fans costs very little compared to replacing a processor and/or a motherboard. Ensure that the computer has adequate circulation/cooling. Vacuum dust from the motherboard/CPU. Cool the room more.

> Many BIOS/UEFI screens show the CPU temperature. (This is covered in more detail in Chapter 4.)

> Research any visual codes shown on the motherboard LEDs or listen for audio beeps as the computer boots. Refer to the computer or motherboard manufacturer's website.

Processor issues are difficult to troubleshoot, and it is often very challenging to determine whether a problem is a CPU or motherboard issue. If you have power to the system (that is, the power supply has power coming out of it), the hard drive works (try it in a different computer), and the monitor works (try it on a different computer), then the motherboard and/or CPU are prime suspects.

Use your senses when troubleshooting processor problems.

- Nothing on the screen (and the power supply and monitor work)
- System powers on, but turns off quickly
- BSOD (blue screen of death)
- An error code that the documentation shows as a CPU problem

- Hear the fan(s) going frantically, but the system won't boot or boots and then shuts off
- System powers on briefly, but then shuts off
- A series of beeps that the manual shows as a CPU problem

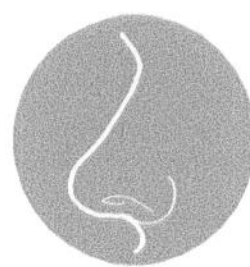

- Smell something burning (fan might be out, causing the CPU to shut down)

FIGURE 3.25 Detecting processor problems

Expansion Slots

If a computer is to be useful, the CPU must communicate with the outside world, including other motherboard components and adapters plugged into the motherboard. An expansion slot is used to add an adapter to the motherboard. Figure 3.26 shows expansion slots on a motherboard.

FIGURE 3.26 Motherboard expansion slots

A technician must be able to distinguish among adapters and expansion slots and must be able to identify the adapters/devices that use expansion slots. A technician must also realize the abilities and limitations of each type of expansion slot when installing upgrades, replacing parts, and making recommendations. Let's start with the oldest type and move forward.

PCI (Peripheral Component Interconnect)

A previously popular expansion slot is Peripheral Component Interconnect (**PCI**). There was also an upgrade to the PCI bus called PCI-X that was commonly found in servers and is not covered except in comparison here. Figure 3.27 shows the most common type of PCI expansion slot.

FIGURE 3.27 PCI expansion slot

AGP (Accelerated Graphics Port)

AGP (Accelerated Graphics Port) is a bus interface for graphics adapters developed from the PCI bus. Intel provided the majority of the development for AGP. With AGP, the video subsystem is isolated from the rest of the computer. Figure 3.28 shows an illustration of an AGP slot compared with PCI expansion slots. Both of these expansion slot types have been replaced by PCIe (covered next), but you still see both as a technician.

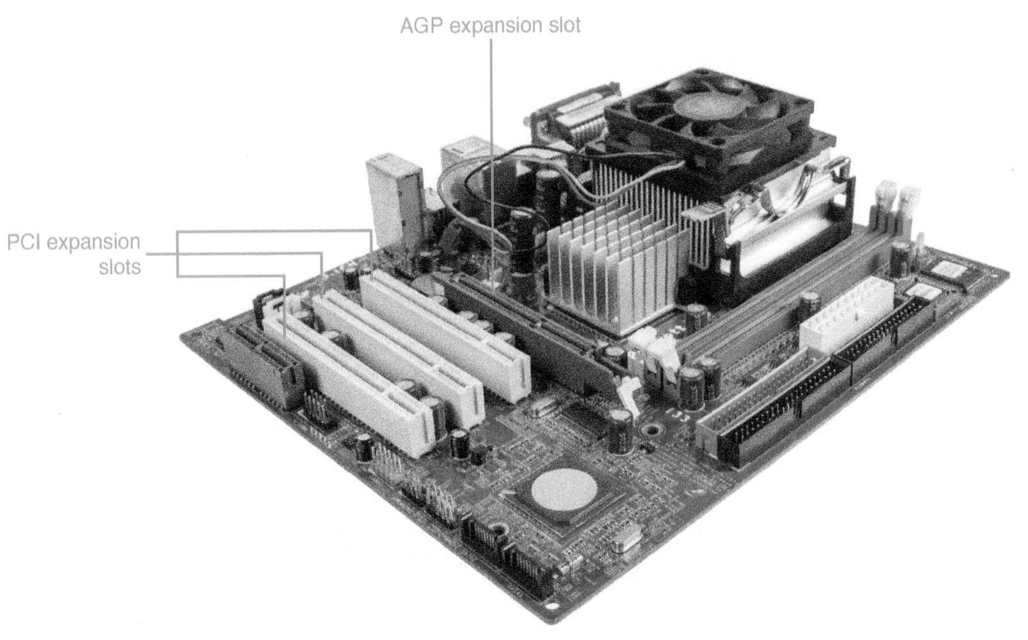

FIGURE 3.28 AGP and PCI expansion slots

PCIe (Peripheral Component Interconnect Express)

PCI and AGP have been replaced with **PCIe** (PCI Express), which is also sometimes written PCI-E. PCIe outperforms all other types of PCI expansion slots. Figure 3.29 shows PCIe expansion slots, and Table 3.6 lists the different PCIe versions.

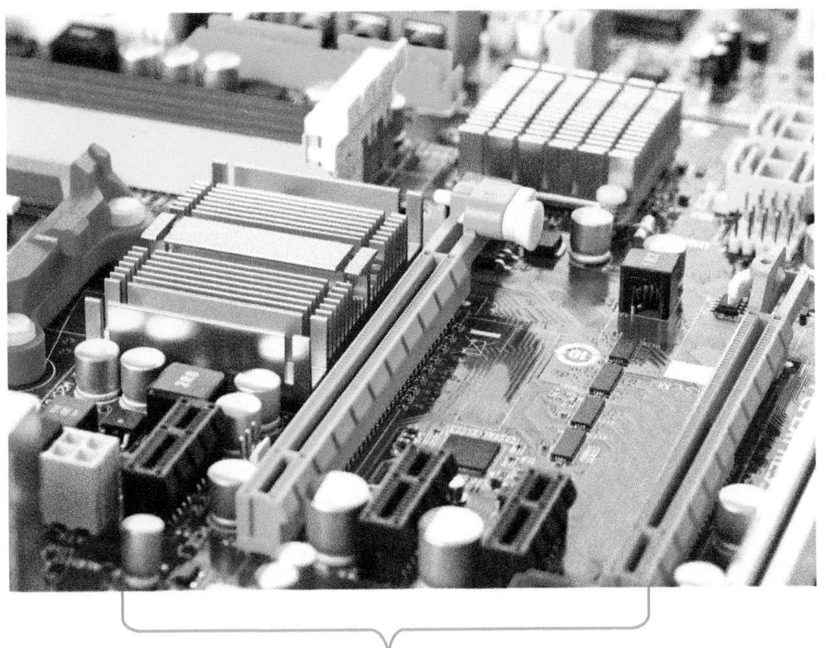

FIGURE 3.29 PCIe expansion slots

TABLE 3.6 PCIe versions

PCIe version	Speed (per lane per direction)
1.0	2.5 GT/s (gigatransfers per second) or 250 MB/s
2.0	5 GT/s or 500 MB/s
3.0	8 GT/s or 1 GB/s
4.0	16 GT/s or 2 GB/s
5.0	32 GT/s or 4 GB/s
6.0	64 GT/s or 8 GB/s

The older PCI standard is half-duplex bidirectional, which means that data is sent to and from the PCI card using only one direction at a time. PCIe sends data full-duplex bidirectionally; in other words, it can send and receive at the same time. Figure 3.30 shows this concept.

TECH TIP

PCI cards in PCIe slots

Older PCI and AGP adapters will not work in any type of PCIe slots.

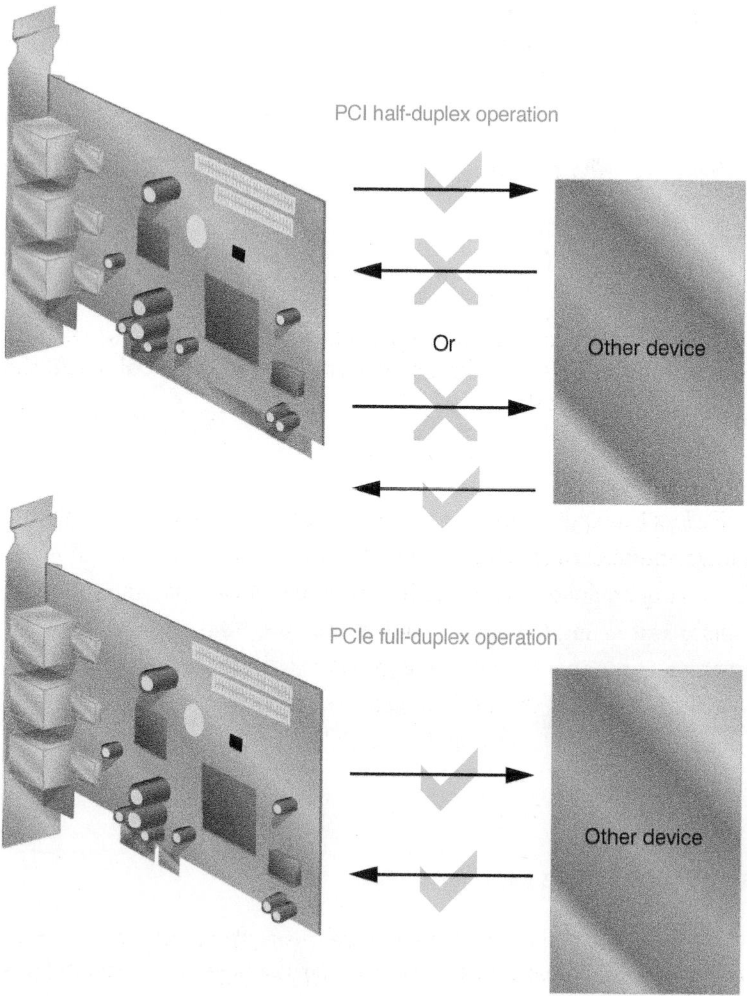

FIGURE 3.30 A comparison of PCI and PCIe transfers

Another difference between PCI and PCIe is that PCIe slots come in different versions, depending on the maximum number of lanes that can be assigned to the card inserted into the slot. For example, an x1 slot can have only one transfer lane used by the x1 card inserted into the slot; x2, x4, x8, and x16 slots are also available. The standard supports an x32 slot, but these slots are rare because of the length. An x16 slot accepts up to 16 lanes, but fewer lanes can be assigned. Figure 3.31 shows the concept of PCIe lanes. Notice that one lane has two unidirectional communication channels. Also note that only seven lanes are used. PCIe has the capability to use a reduced number of lanes if one lane experiences a failure or a performance issue.

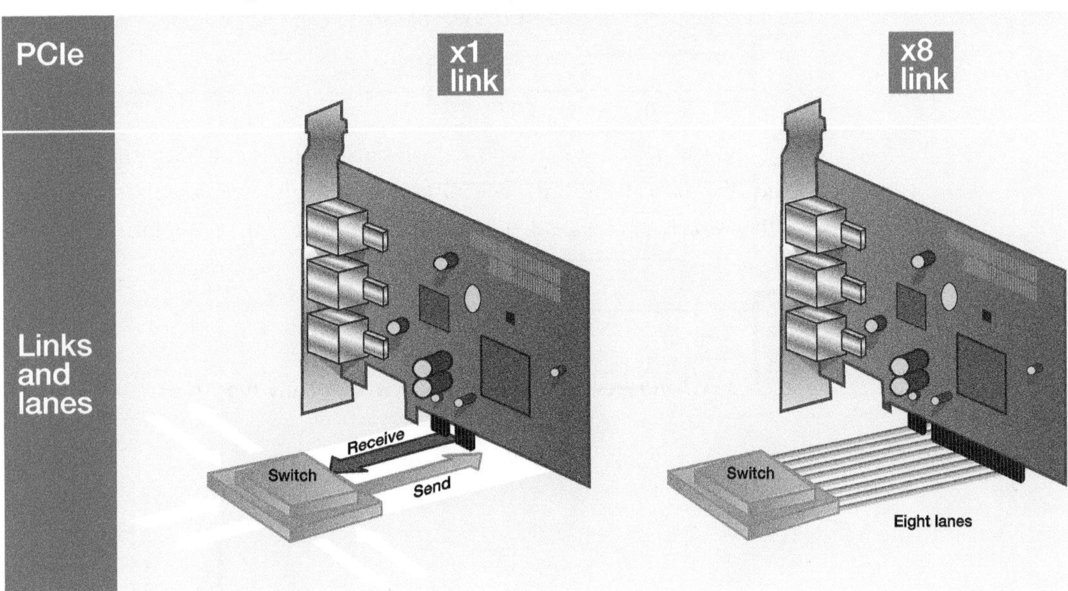

FIGURE 3.31 PCIe lanes

TECH TIP

Beware of the PCIe fine print

Some motherboard manufacturers offer a larger slot size (such as x8), but the slot runs at a slower speed (x4, for example). This keeps the cost down. The manual would show such a slot as x8 (x4 mode) in the PCIe slot description.

A PCIe x1 adapter can fit in an x1 or higher slot. A larger card, such as a PCIe x16, cannot fit in a lower-numbered (x8, x4, x2, or x1) slot. Figure 3.32 shows this concept.

Removing an adapter is normally just a matter of removing a retaining screw or lifting a retention plate and lifting the adapter out of the slot. Some expansion slots have retention levers. You move the retention lever to the side in order to lift the adapter from the expansion slot. Figure 3.33 shows an example of the PCIe adapter removal process. Figure 3.34 shows a motherboard with two PCIe x1, two PCIe x16, and three PCI expansion slots. Notice that the PCIe x16 slots have a retention lever.

TECH TIP

Removing PCIe adapters

PCIe x16 adapters commonly have release levers. You must press the lever while pulling the adapter out of the expansion slot, or you may damage the board (and possibly the motherboard).

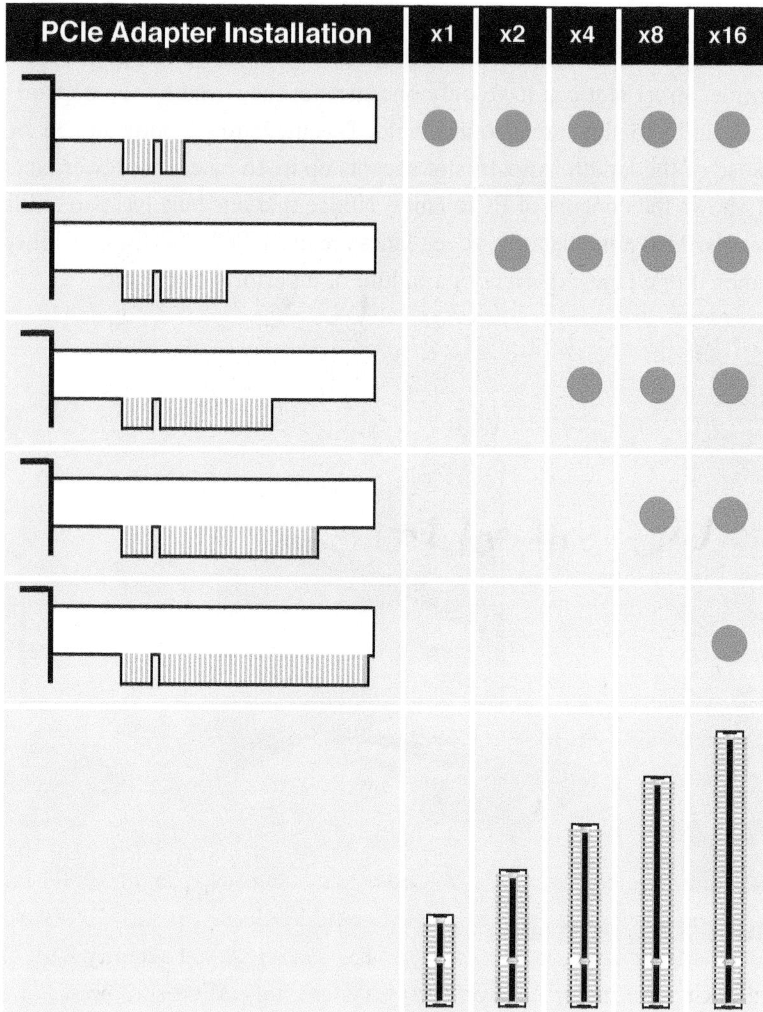

FIGURE 3.32 Correct slots for PCIe cards

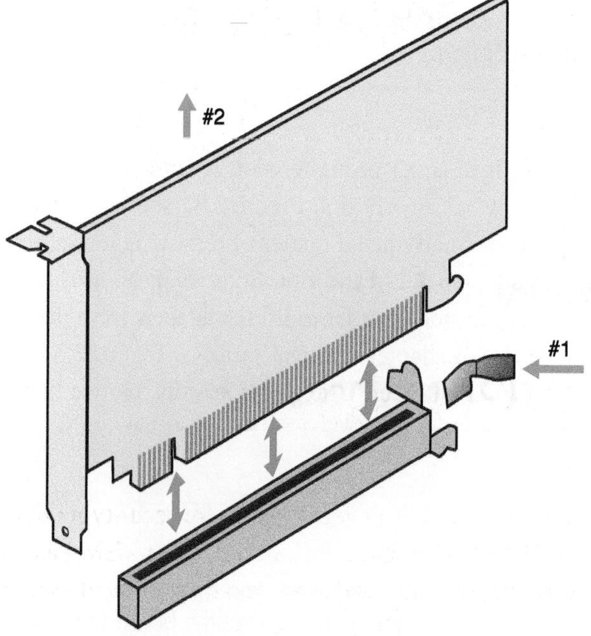

FIGURE 3.33 PCIe adapter removal

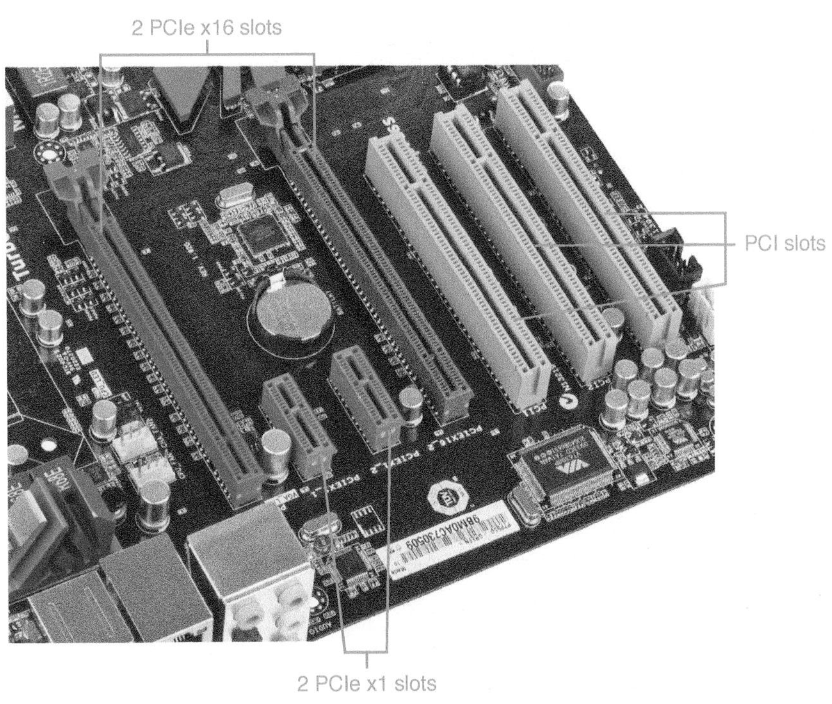

FIGURE 3.34 Motherboard with PCIe and PCI slots

Motherboard Security Options

Motherboards can contain security options that can help provide more security for applications and data. A motherboard might contain a Trusted Platform Module (TPM) or a connector to install one. A **TPM** can be used when securing data, storing digital security certificates, storing passwords, or checking the integrity of operating system files. Microsoft Windows 11 requires a TPM to be installed before the operating system will function. The TPM is enabled and configured through the BIOS/UEFI, which is covered in Chapter 4. Figure 3.35 shows a TPM.

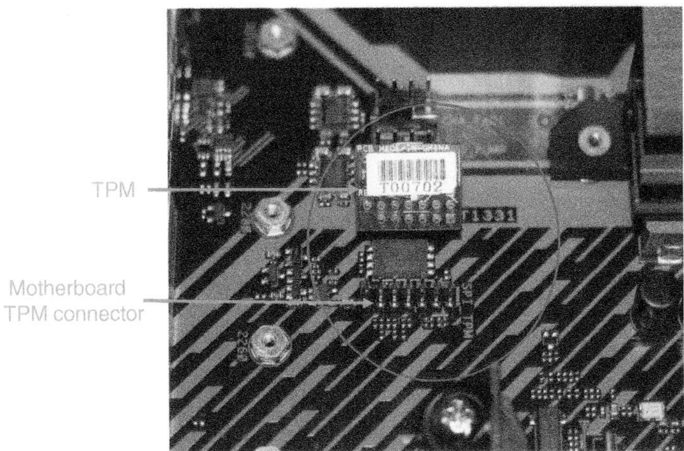

FIGURE 3.35 TPM

Another similar security option is an **HSM** (hardware security module) that can be installed as an adapter to do some of the same functions as a TPM. An HSM has a cryptoprocessor or other chips that are used to create, manage, and store security keys and used in encryption of data and storage devices.

Types of Motherboards

Motherboards come in different sizes, known as **form factors**. The most common desktop computer motherboard form factor is Advanced Technology Extended (**ATX**). Other ATX form factors include **micro-ATX** (sometimes written µ ATX or mATX), mini-ATX, FlexATX, EATX, WATX, nano-ATX, pico-ATX, and mobileATX.

A motherboard form factor that is larger and has better air flow (but that is not as popular as ATX and micro-ATX) is Balanced Technology eXtended (BTX). A smaller form factor is Information Technology eXtended (**ITX**), which comes in mini-ITX, nano-ITX, and pico-ITX sizes. Figure 3.36 shows some of the motherboard form factors, and Table 3.7 provides consolidated information on the main form factors. Figure 3.37 shows a motherboard with many of the motherboard components labeled.

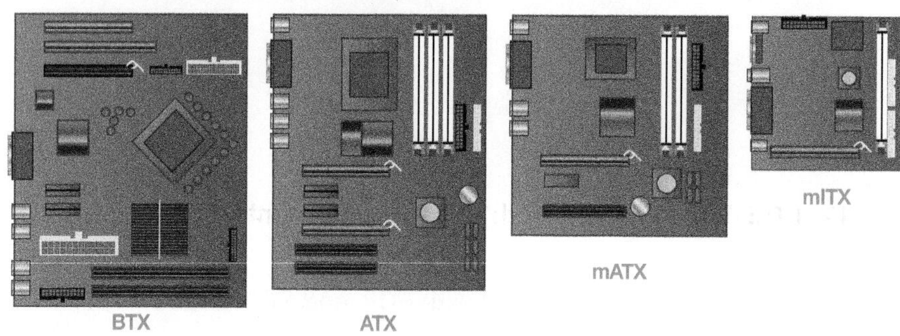

FIGURE 3.36 Motherboard form factors

TABLE 3.7 Motherboard form factor comparison

Form factor	Description	Size
BTX	Used in desktop computers	12.8×10.5 inches (32.5×26.7 cm)
ATX	Used in desktop computers	12×9.6 inches (30.5×24.4 cm)
mATX	MicroATX—a smaller desktop motherboard	9.6×9.6 inches (24.4×24.4 cm)
ITX or mITX	Used in very small computers and set-top boxes	6.7×6.7 inches (17×17 cm)

TECH TIP

Matching the motherboard form factor and case

The case used for a computer must match the motherboard form factor. Some cases can accommodate different form factors, but you should always check. When you are building a computer or replacing a motherboard, it is important to obtain the correct form factor.

Manufacturers sometimes design a case so that it requires a proprietary motherboard. With such a design, a replacement motherboard must be purchased from the original manufacturer and is usually more expensive than a generic option.

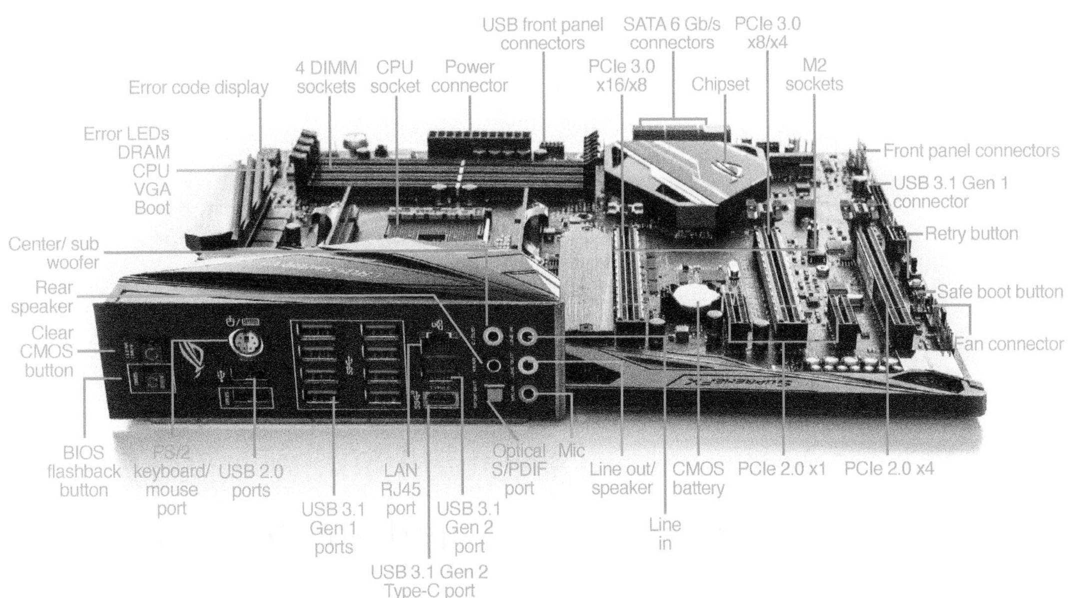

FIGURE 3.37 Gaming motherboard components

Upgrading and Replacing Motherboards

The following list guides you through making the decision (or helping a customer make the decision) about whether to upgrade a motherboard:

- Why is the computer being upgraded? Sometimes upgrading the motherboard does not help unless the other computer components are upgraded. If software access is slow, the solution might not be a new motherboard but a faster and larger hard drive, new/high-capacity SSD, or more RAM.
- Which type of expansion slot (PCI, AGP, or PCIe) and how many adapters of each type are needed from the old motherboard? Does the new motherboard have the required expansion slots?
- Is the motherboard compatible? Check which CPU manufacturer and models are supported. Will the new motherboard fit in the current computer case, or is a new one required?
- If upgrading the CPU, will the motherboard support the new CPU?
- Will the old memory chips work in the new motherboard or with the new CPU?

TECH TIP

Motherboards in other types of devices

Note that **server motherboards**, laptop motherboards, and other **mobile device motherboards** tend to be proprietary, and you have to buy a replacement from the manufacturer.

Before replacing a motherboard, it is important to do all the following:

- Remove the CPU and CPU fan.
- Remove adapters from expansion slots.
- Remove memory chips from expansion slots.
- Disconnect power connectors.
- Disconnect ribbon cables.
- Disconnect external devices such as mouse, keyboard, and monitor.

Replacement motherboards do not normally come with RAM, so the old modules are removed from the bad/older motherboard. A motherboard usually does not come with a CPU. When upgrading any component or an entire computer, remember that the older part can be donated to a charity or an educational institution.

TECH TIP

Use good antistatic measures when installing a motherboard

When replacing a motherboard, place the motherboard on a nonconductive surface such as an antistatic mat or the antistatic bag that came with the motherboard.

Motherboard Troubleshooting

Common symptoms of motherboard issues are similar to symptoms of CPU problems: The system has a **blank screen** or **black screen** on bootup (which could mean the video cable is not attached well or the system is not powered/turned on); an error code appears; one or more beeps occur; the system experiences **unexpected shutdown**, **intermittent shutdown**, or **system lockup**; the system might do **continuous reboots**; a Windows BSOD (**blue screen of death**) appears; or one or more of the ports, expansion slots, or memory modules fails. Note that unexpected/intermittent shutdowns, system lockups, and continuous reboots can also be symptoms of a CPU or power supply problem.

Motherboard problems and power problems are probably the most difficult issues to troubleshoot. Because various components are located on the motherboard, many things can cause errors. **POST** (power-on self-test) is one of the most beneficial aids for troubleshooting a motherboard and may include a series of **POST beeps**. The meaning of any code that appears on the screen should be researched. If multiple POST error codes appear, you should troubleshoot them in the order in which they are presented. Chapter 11, "Computer Design and Troubleshooting Review," describes common beeps and errors, but note that manufacturers could have their own **proprietary crash screens** and errors.

The following list helps with motherboard troubleshooting:

> Is the motherboard receiving power? Check the power supply to see if the fan is turning. If the CPU or motherboard has a fan, see if it is turning. Check voltages going from the power supply to the motherboard. See Chapter 5, "Disassembly and Power," for directions.
> Check the BIOS/UEFI settings (covered in Chapter 4) for accuracy.
> Check for **overheating**, which might point to a problem with the CPU or motherboard. Is the motherboard hot to the touch or emitting a **burning smell**? Power down the computer and allow the computer to cool. Power on the computer with the cover off. See if the CPU fan is turning.
> Check the motherboard for **capacitor swelling**—small components that might appear to be bulging. If you look again at Figure 3.34, you can see the metal cylinders (which are capacitors) in the bottom-right corner and beside the expansion slots. If you see that such a capacitor is bulging, replace the motherboard as soon as possible.
> Reseat the CPU, adapters, and memory chips.
> Remove unnecessary adapters and devices and boot the computer.
> Plug the computer into a different power outlet and circuit, if possible.
> Check to determine whether the motherboard is shorting out on the frame.
> Check the CMOS battery. (See Chapter 5 for how to take voltage readings.)

> With a motherboard that has diagnostic LEDs, check the output for any error code. Refer to the motherboard documentation or online documentation for the problem and possible solution.

TECH TIP

These concepts relate to Apple computers, too

Even though this book focuses on PCs, concepts related to CPUs, motherboards, expansion slots, cache, and chipsets also apply to Apple computers. Apple computers and PCs have similar CPU and memory requirements.

SOFT SKILLS: ACTIVE LISTENING

Active listening is participating in a conversation where you focus on what the customer is saying—in other words, listening more than talking. For a technician, active listening has the following benefits:

- Enables you to gather data and symptoms quickly
- Enables you to build rapport with the customer
- Improves your understanding of the problem
- Enables you to solve the problem more quickly because you understand the problem better
- Provides mutual understanding between you and the customer
- Provides a means of having a positive, engaged conversation rather than having a negative, confrontational encounter
- Focuses on the customer rather than the technician
- Provides an environment in which the customer might be more forthcoming with information related to the problem

Frequently, when a technician arrives onsite or contacts a customer who has a technical problem, the technician is rushed; thinking of other things, including the problems that need to be solved; assuming that he or she knows exactly what the problem is, even though the user has not finished explaining the problem; or more interested in the technical problem than in the customer and the issues. Active listening changes the focus from the technician's problems to the customer's problems.

A common but ineffective service call involves a technician doing most of the talking and questioning, using technical jargon and acronyms and a flat or condescending tone. A customer who feels vulnerable experiences a heightened anxiety level. Active listening changes this scenario by helping you build a professional relationship with your customers. Figure 3.38 shows a technician actively listening. The list that follows outlines some measures that help you implement active listening.

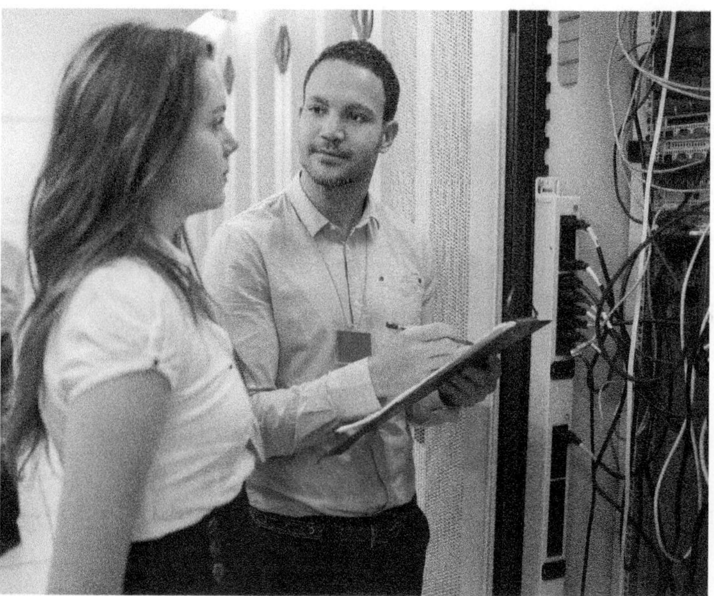

FIGURE 3.38 Active listening

Have a positive, engaged professional attitude when talking and listening to customers:

> Leave your prejudices behind; be polite and aware of other cultures and customs; be open-minded and nonjudgmental.
> Have a warm and caring attitude.
> Do not fold your arms in front of your chest because doing so distances you from the problem and the customer.
> Do not blame others or talk badly about other technicians.
> Do not act as if the problem is not your responsibility.

Focus on what the customer is saying:

> Turn off or ignore your electronic devices.
> Maintain eye contact; don't let your mind wander.
> Allow the customer to finish explaining the problem; do not interrupt; avoid arguing with the customer or being defensive.
> Stop all irrelevant behaviors and activities.
> Mentally review what the customer is saying.
> Refrain from talking to coworkers unnecessarily while interacting with customers.
> Avoid personal interruptions or distractions.

Participate in the conversation in a limited but active manner:

> Maintain a professional demeanor (suspend negative emotions); do not minimize or diminish the customer's problem.
> Acknowledge that you are listening by occasionally nodding and making comments such as "I see."
> Use positive body language such as leaning slightly forward or taking notes.
> Observe the customer's behavior to determine when it is appropriate to ask questions.

Briefly talk with the customer:

> Speak using a positive tone; use a tone that is empathetic and genuine, not condescending.
> Restate or summarize points made by the customer.
> Ask nonthreatening, probing questions related to the customer's statements or questions.
> Do not jump between topics.
> Do not use technical jargon.
> Clarify the meaning of the customer's situation.
> Identify clues to help solve the problem and reduce your troubleshooting time by listening carefully to what the customer says.
> Follow up with the person at a later date to ensure that the problem is solved and to verify satisfaction.
> Offer different repair or replacement options, if possible.

Chapter Summary

> Important motherboard parts include the following: CPU, RAM slots, RAM, expansion slots (PCI, PCIe, and AGP), and cooling devices.
> ARM processors are popular in mobile devices (but can be used for desktops and servers), take less power, produce less heat, and cost less than Intel or AMD processors. Desktop processors can be multicore and can contain very fast cache memory: L1, L2, and L3.

> Intel processors use Hyperthreading to make efficient use of processor time as the CPU executes separate sets of instructions simultaneously.
> Processors must be kept cool with fans and/or heat sinks. A thermal paste or pad is applied between a heat sink and a processor. Never turn on a computer without some type of cooling installed.
> The clock speed refers to the processor's internal clock. This is not the same as the FSB or bus speed.
> CPU throttling slows down the processor to prevent overheating.
> PCI is a 32- and 64-bit parallel bus. PCI and AGP have been replaced with the serial PCIe bus.
> PCIe slots have a specific number of bidirectional lanes that are the maximum a card can use. A PCIe adapter can fit in a slot of the same number of lanes or a slot that has the ability to process a larger number of lanes.
> An integrated GPU is on-die with the CPU and processes graphics-related functions.
> When replacing a motherboard, ensure that the form factor, CPU socket, and number/types of expansion slots are appropriate.
> A TPM or HSM increases security by storing digital security certificates and passwords and securing data.
> Use POST in troubleshooting motherboard or CPU issues. Symptoms of CPU or motherboard issues include swollen capacitors, unexpected/intermittent shutdowns, system lockups, blank screen on bootup, continuous reboots, and overheating.
> Active listening is an important skill for a technician. Avoid getting distracted by people or technology and do take notes, make good eye contact, and ask directed questions when appropriate.

A+ CERTIFICATION EXAM TIPS

✓ Know the following motherboard connector types: PCI, PCIe, eSATA, socket types (including the term multisocket), and headers. Know that server and mobile motherboards are frequently proprietary items.

✓ Know the following CPU architecture features: x64/x86, ARM, single-core, multicore, multithreading, and virtualization support.

✓ Review diagrams for PCI and PCIe expansion slots. Use the internet to view motherboards to see if you can determine the type of expansion slot. Do the same for other motherboard components, including the processor. Be ready to label graphics on the exam.

✓ Know that Intel and AMD are two prominent CPU manufacturers that require an appropriate motherboard and socket in order to install the processor.

✓ Review the types of CPU cooling methods: fan, heat sink, liquid, and thermal paste/pads.

✓ Be able to install a CPU and cooling system. Know how and where to connect a CPU fan.

✓ Know the differences between and be able to identify ATX, ITX, and BTX motherboard form factors.

✓ Know the differences between a TPM and an HSM.

✓ Know symptoms of processor and motherboard issues: swollen capacitor, unexpected/intermittent shutdowns, system lockups, blank or black screen on bootup, continuous reboots, overheating, and a burning smell. Use POST codes to help with troubleshooting.

Key Terms

active listening 98
AGP 88
AMD 68
APU 76
ARM processor 68
ATX 94
black screen 96
blank screen 96
blue screen of death 96
burning smell 96
cache memory 73
capacitor swelling 96
clock 72
clock speed 72
continuous reboot 96
CPU 68
CPU socket 79
CPU speed 72
CPU throttling 72
external data bus 69
fan 80
form factor 94
FSB 72
GPU 76
grinding noise 86
heat sink 80
HSM 93
Hyperthreading 74
HyperTransport 74
integrated GPU 76
Intel 68
intermittent shutdown 96
internal data bus 69
ITX 94
L1 cache 73
L2 cache 73
L3 cache 73
liquid cooling 80
micro-ATX 94
mobile device motherboard 95
multicore 74
multisocket 79
multithreading 73
overclocking 84
overheating 96
PCI 88
PCIe 89
POST 96
POST beeps 96
processor 68
proprietary crash screen 96
server motherboard 95
single-core processor 74
system lockup 96
thermal pad 80
thermal paste 80
thread 73
throttle management 84
TPM 93
unexpected shutdown 96
virtualization 76
virtualization support 77
VM 76
x64 68
x86 68
ZIF socket 80

Review Questions

1. Which component can be located both on a video card and on a motherboard?

   [TPM | PCIe expansion slot | PCI expansion slot | GPU]

2. Which expansion slot is best for a video card in a new desktop computer?

   [PCIe | PCI | USB | AGP]

3. A motherboard has a PCIe x16 expansion slot. Which PCIe adapter(s) will fit in this slot? (Choose all that apply.)

   [x1 | x2 | x4 | x8 | x16 | x32]

4. Match the motherboard part with the appropriate description.

____ L1 cache	**a.** Mounted on top of the CPU
____ CPU	**b.** Memory found in the CPU
____ FSB	**c.** Executes software instructions
____ heat sink	**d.** Bus between the CPU and motherboard components
____ HT	**e.** Slows the CPU to cool it
____ throttling	**f.** Allows one processor to handle multiple instructions simultaneously

5. What is the front side bus?

   a. The internal data bus that connects the processor core to the L1 cache

   b. The internal data bus that connects the processor core to the L2 cache

   c. The external data bus that connects the processor to the motherboard components

   d. The external data bus that connects the processor to the L2 cache

6. A customer wants to upgrade the L2 cache. Which of the following does this definitely require?

   a. A motherboard purchase

   b. A CPU purchase

   c. A video card purchase

   d. A RAM module purchase

7. Match the expansion slot to its definition.

____ AGP	**a.** 32- or 64-bit parallel bus
____ PCI	**b.** Just for video cards
____ PCIe	**c.** Has a varying number of lanes

8. What is the difference between Hyperthreading and HyperTransport?

   ____

   ____

   ____

9. What should a technician do if a swollen capacitor is found on a motherboard?

   a. Replace the capacitor.

   b. Replace the motherboard.

   c. Check the voltages coming from the power supply.

   d. Replace the power supply.

10. Which of the following statements is true regarding PCIe?
    a. A PCIe slot will not accept a PCI card.
    b. PCIe is a parallel bus technology.
    c. PCIe is a 32- or 64-bit bus technology.
    d. PCIe is being replaced by PCI-X.
11. [T | F] A PCIe x8 adapter always transmits using eight lanes.
12. What is the significance of a motherboard specification that states the following: 1 PCIe x16 (x8 mode) slot?
    a. The slot accepts x8 or x16 cards.
    b. The slot can transmit traffic using 8 or 16 lanes.
    c. The slot can transmit in bursts of 8 or 16 bytes at a time.
    d. The slot accepts x16 cards but uses only 8 lanes.
13. What are two security options that would help with password management and encryption? (Choose two.)

    [CPU | TPM | PCIe standard | GPU | HSM]
14. A technician for a college is going to repair a problem in another building. A professor stops the technician to talk about her slow computer. The technician gives a little eye roll but then stops and listens to the professor. The professor comments, "I can't get my email or even type my tests. The computer takes at least 20 minutes just to boot." The technician looks around, a little exasperated, and says, "Uh huh." "I logged this problem over a week ago," continues the professor, "and no one has dropped by." "Uh huh," replies the technician again. "Do you know when you folks might get to that issue or have an idea about what might be the problem?" the professor asks. The technician looks at the professor and says, "It is probably a virus that has been going around. Jim was supposed to get to those. We will get to you as soon as we can." The technician's phone rings, and he walks away to get to the phone.

    List three active listening techniques and good customer support procedures that could improve this situation.

    ____

    ____

    ____

    ____

    ____
15. Explain how a technician might be culturally insensitive.

    ____

    ____

    ____
16. Which component can be adjusted to overclock?

    [heat sink | CPU | expansion slot | chipset]
17. [T | F] When installing a CPU, orient pin 1 to pin 1 on the socket and align the other pins. Lower the ZIF socket lever and lock. Power on the computer to ensure that the CPU works. Power down the computer and install the heat sink and/or fan.
18. What is applied between a processor and a heat sink to increase heat dissipation?

    [a capacitor | thermal paste | a fan | cache memory]

19. When looking over the specifications for the motherboard, you see LGA 2066. Which component is being referenced?

    [RAM | HSM | processor | expansion slot]

20. Which method is not used to cool a processor?

    [CPU fan | case fan | heat sink | thermal tank]

Exercises

Exercise 3.1 Identifying ATX Motherboard Parts

Objective: To identify various motherboard parts

Parts: None

Procedure: Identify each of the ATX motherboard parts in Figure 3.39.

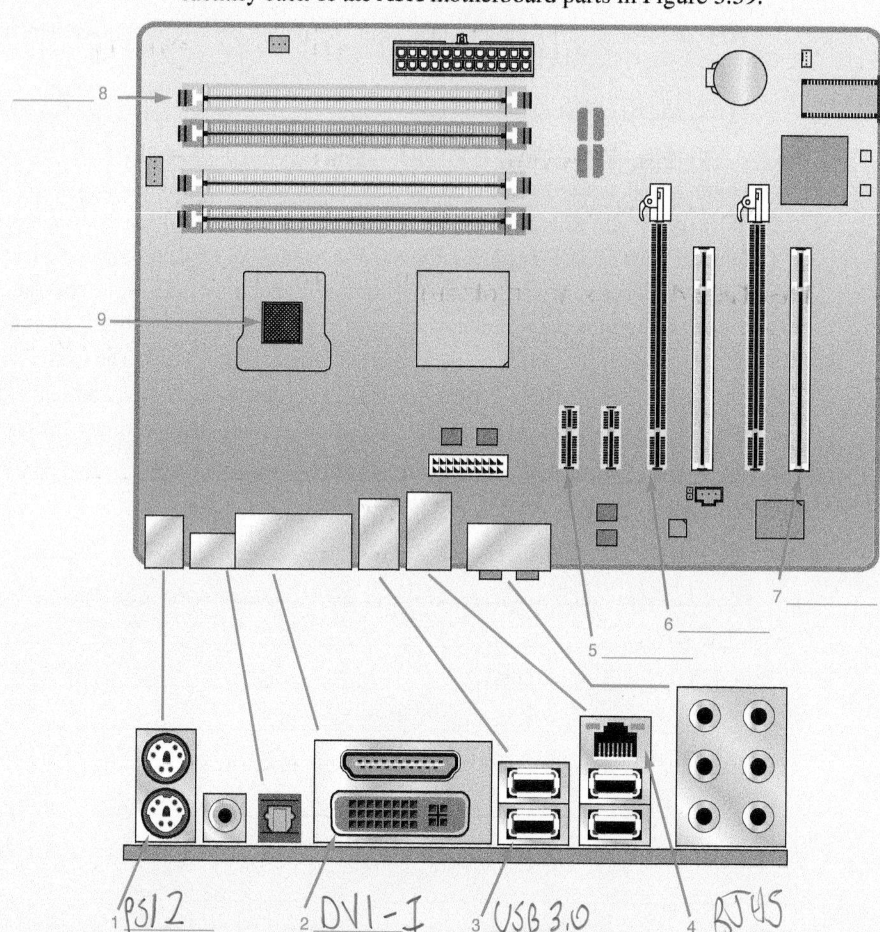

FIGURE 3.39 Motherboard ports, slots, and parts

1. __________
2. __________
3. __________
4. __________
5. __________
6. __________
7. __________
8. __________
9. __________

(last 5)

Exercise 3.2 Motherboard Analysis

Objective: To identify various motherboard parts

Parts: None

Procedure: Using the information you learned in this chapter and related to the specifications found in Figure 3.40, answer the questions that follow.

XYZ Motherboard Specifications

Form factor	ATX
Power connector	24-pin
CPU	
CPU socket type	LGA1155
CPUs supported	Celeron, Pentium, Core i3, i5, i7
Chipset	Intel Z77
Graphics	
Integrated GPU	Multi-VGA output support: HDMI/DVI/ RGB/DisplayPort ports
Memory	
Memory	4x240-pin
Memory standard	DDR3 2600(O.C.), 2400(O.C.), 2200(O.C.), 2133(O.C.), 1866(O.C.), 1800(O.C.), 1600, 1333
Maximum memory	32GB
Memory channel	Dual channel
Expansion slots	
PCIe 3.0/2.0 x16	2 (single x16 or dual x8)
PCIe 2.0 x16	1 (x4 mode)
PCIe 2.0 x1	2
PCI	2
Onboard LAN	
Max LAN speed	10/100/1000Mb/s
Wireless LAN	WiFi 802.11 b/g/n
Rear ports	
PS/2	1 x PS/2 keyboard/mouse port
Video	D-sub + DVI
HDMI	1 x HDMI
DisplayPort	1 x DisplayPort
USB 1.1/2.0	2 x USB 2.0
USB 3.0	4 x USB 3.0
S/PDIF out	1 x optical
Audio	6 ports

FIGURE 3.40 Desktop motherboard advertisement

1. If you were buying this motherboard, what type of case would you need to purchase?

____

2. What does LGA1155 tell you about this motherboard?

____

3. Does this motherboard come with a CPU installed?

   [Yes | No | Cannot tell from the information presented]

4. What motherboard component controls the maximum number of USB 3.0 ports this motherboard could have?

   [CPU | RAM | chipset | FSB]

5. What processor(s) does this motherboard accept?

____

6. What do you think the letters O.C. after some of the memory chips mean in relationship to this motherboard?

____

____

7. What is the most significant difference between a version 2.0 PCIe slot and a version 3.0 PCIe expansion slot?

____

____

CHAPTER 3

8. What does the PCIe 3.0/2.0 x16 line that states "2 (single x16 or dual x8)" mean?
   - **a.** The adapter that goes into this slot can use a single lane that goes at x16 speeds or two lanes that go at x8 speeds.
   - **b.** One single x16 adapter and/or one single x8 adapter can go into the expansion slots.
   - **c.** One x16 adapter can go into one of the version 3.0 slots and achieve 3.0 speeds, or two x16 adapters can be installed, but they can transfer only eight lanes at a time at 3.0 speeds.
   - **d.** A single x16 adapter can be installed in one of the version 3.0 slots, or two x8 adapters can be installed in the two version 3.0 slots.
9. What device cable can be inserted into the PS/2 port? (Choose the best answer.)
   [speaker | mouse or keyboard | display | external storage]
10. Which type of video port is described as a D-sub in this documentation?
    [DisplayPort | DVI | HDMI | VGA]
11. What is an advantage of having an integrated GPU in the CPU?
    It lessens the load for the CPU.
12. What is the most likely reason this motherboard manufacturer chose to include two PCI expansion slots?
    To support legacy adapters allowing the manufacturer to sell to older motherboard users.
13. How many different video port types does this motherboard have? List them.
    (1) D-sub + DVI, (2) HDMI, (3) DisplayPort
14. What is the purpose of the S/PDIF out port?
    [video | audio | wireless networking | input device connectivity]
15. Is this motherboard a multisocket motherboard? How can you tell?
    [Yes | No]
    It didn't specify in the motherboard specifications as it should.

Activities

Internet Discovery

Objective: To obtain specific information on the internet regarding a computer or its associated parts

Parts: A computer with internet access

Procedure: Locate documentation on the internet for a ASUS Prime Z590-A motherboard to answer Questions 1–12. Continue your internet search to answer Questions 13 and 14.

Questions:

1. Does the motherboard support an Intel or AMD processor? ______
2. Which chipset is used? ______
3. How many expansion slots are on the motherboard? ______
4. Which form factor does this motherboard use? ______
5. Which processors can be used on this motherboard?
   ______
6. Does the motherboard support having an integrated GPU in the CPU? How can you tell whether it does or not? ______
   ______

7. Which type of CPU socket does the motherboard have? ______________________

8. How many and of what type of PCIe slots does it have?

____

____

9. Is there any other type of slot on this motherboard? If so, what is it?

____

10. Does this motherboard have an integrated USB 3.2 port? ______________________

11. What are the maximum number and type of USB ports available on the rear of the motherboard?

____

____

____

____

12. Write the URL where you found the motherboard information.

____

____

13. Find a vendor for an AMD motherboard that uses the AM4 socket and supports the Ryzen 2000, 3000, and 5000 desktop processors. Document the motherboard model and vendor.

____

14. Find an internet site that describes the dimensions of the extended ATX motherboard form factor. List the dimensions and the website.

____

Soft Skills

Objective: To enhance and fine-tune a future technician's ability to listen, communicate in both written and oral forms, and support people who use computers in a professional manner

Activities:

1. On a piece of paper or an index card, list three ways you can practice active listening at school. Share this information with your group. Consolidate ideas and present five of the best ideas to the class.
2. In a team environment, come up with two examples of situations you have experienced in which a support person (a PC support person, salesclerk, checkout clerk, person being asked directions, and so on) could have provided better service if he or she had been actively listening. Share your findings with the class.
3. In teams of two, have one person tell a story and the other person practice active listening skills. The person telling the story should critique the listener. The pair should then change roles.

Critical Thinking Skills

Objective: To analyze and evaluate information and to apply learned information to new or different situations

Activities:

1. Find an advertisement for a computer in a local computer flyer, newspaper, magazine, book, or on the internet. Determine all the information about the motherboard and ports that you can from the ad. Write down any information you do not understand. Research this information and share your findings with a classmate.

2. Your parents want to give you a new computer as a present. The one they are considering has a GPU integrated into the CPU. List at least one argument you might use for getting a different computer model.

____

____

____

3. Why do you think a motherboard has different buses that operate at different speeds?

____

____

4 Introduction to Configuration

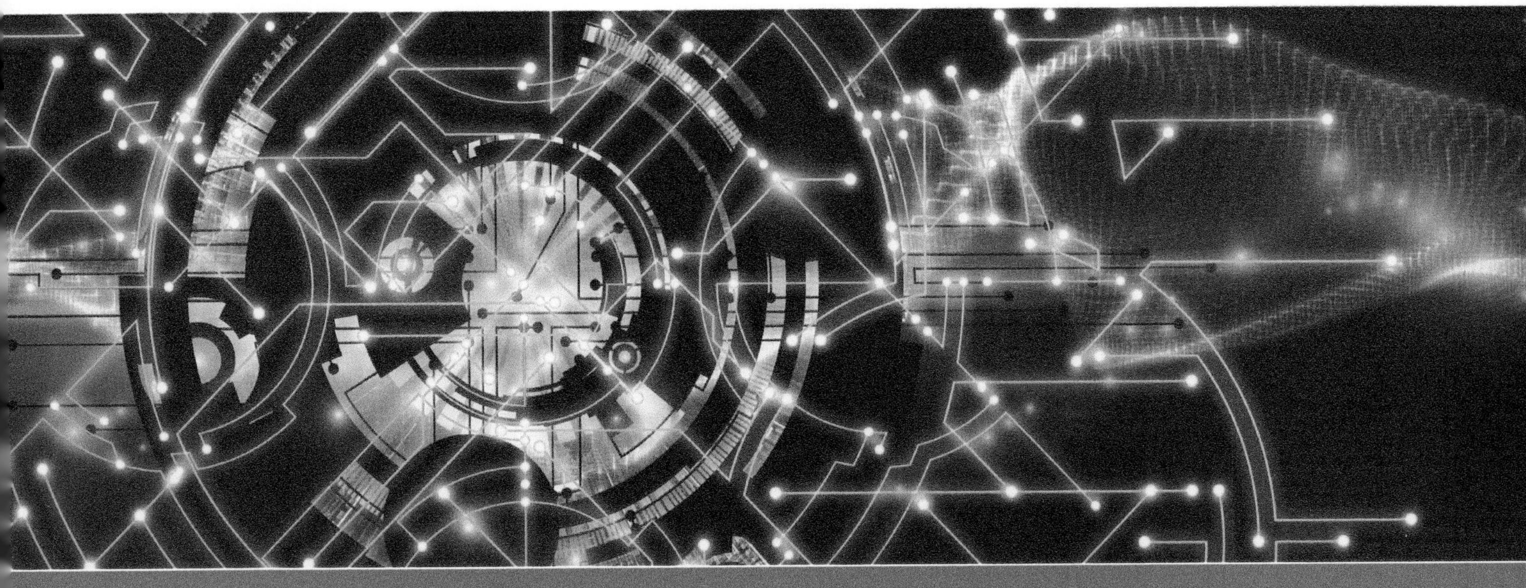

In this chapter you will learn:

- > The importance of BIOS and UEFI
- > How to replace a motherboard battery
- > What system resources are and how to view/change them
- > Basics steps needed to install, configure, and verify common peripheral devices and USB, eSATA, and network cards
- > How to troubleshoot configuration and device issues

CompTIA Exam Objectives:

✓ 1101-3.1 Explain basic cable types and their connectors, features, and purposes.

✓ 1101-3.4 Given a scenario, install and configure motherboards, central processing units (CPUs), and add-on cards.

✓ 1101-5.2 Given a scenario, troubleshoot problems related to motherboards, RAM, CPU, and power.

Configuration Overview

Installing and configuring the motherboard, processor, RAM, or other devices can involve using the system BIOS/UEFI **Setup** program or the operating system. It also enables you to set performance options.

BIOS Overview

The basic input/output system (BIOS) is an important motherboard component that is commonly soldered to the motherboard, as shown in Figure 4.1. The BIOS is also known as the Unified Extensible Firmware Interface (UEFI) and sometimes simply as EFI, BIOS/UEFI, or UEFI/BIOS. The **BIOS** has the following functions:

- Holds and executes power-on self-test (**POST**)—a program that identifies, tests, and initializes hardware components.
- Holds a basic routine called a bootstrap program that locates an operating system and launches it, allowing the operating system to then control the system.
- Holds Setup, which is a program that allows viewing and management of settings related to the display, date/time, processor, memory, and drives. Other names used for Setup include BIOS Setup, System Setup, and CMOS Setup.
- Optionally, turns control over to an adapter's onboard BIOS so that the card can initialize during the computer boot process.

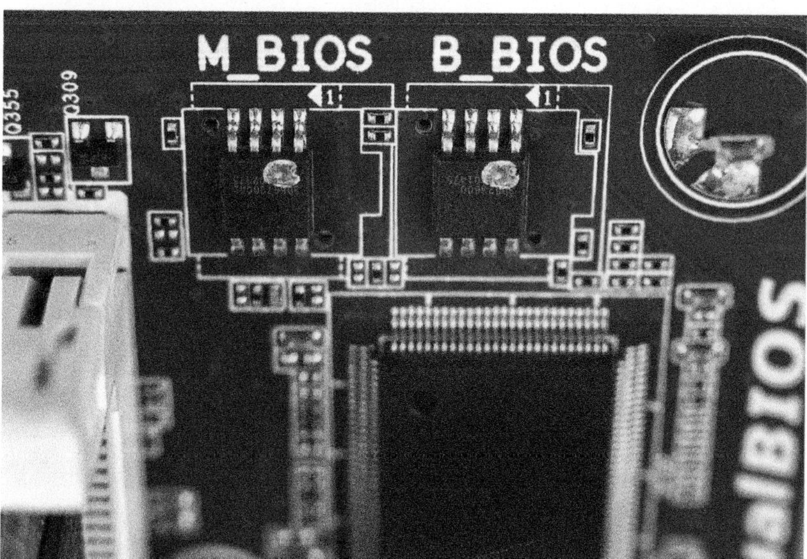

FIGURE 4.1 Motherboard BIOS

POST performs basic tests of individual hardware components, such as the motherboard, RAM modules, keyboard, optical drive, and hard drive. POST runs when a cold boot is performed (powering on the computer). An indication that POST is running is that the indicator lights on the keyboard momentarily flash on and then off.

TECH TIP

Speed up boot time

BIOS can be configured to limit the number of devices checked by POST, thus reducing boot time.

In contrast, restarting the computer is known as a warm boot. In Windows, right-click the *Start* button > *Shut down or sign out* > *Restart*. Warm booting causes any changes that have been made to take effect without putting as much strain on the computer as a cold boot does. A warm boot does not execute POST.

The Setup program is held in BIOS, and through the Setup program, you can see and possibly configure or disable such things as RAM, the type and number of drives installed, where the computer looks for its boot files, the current date and time, and so on.

There are two main ways to configure a system or an adapter: through the Setup program held in system BIOS and through the operating system. Let's examine using the Setup program first.

TECH TIP

What if you can't get into Setup?

If nothing appears on the monitor and the display has power and you have a good connection to the video port, check the motherboard for any LEDs (CPU, RAM, display/VGA, boot, and so on) and research what it means if the LED stays on. Check CPU, CPU fan, and RAM installation.

The Setup Program

Computers have Setup software built into the system BIOS chip on the motherboard that you can access with specific keystrokes (such as Esc, Insert, Del, F1, F2, F10, or the key combination Ctrl+Alt+some other key), determined by the BIOS manufacturer. During the boot process, most computers display a message stating which keystroke(s) will launch the Setup program. The message shown is usually in one of the four corners of the screen (see Figure 4.2).

TECH TIP

Accessing BIOS Setup from within Windows 10/11

To access BIOS Setup in Windows, access *Settings > Update and Security* (10) *or System* (11) *> Recovery > Restart Now.*

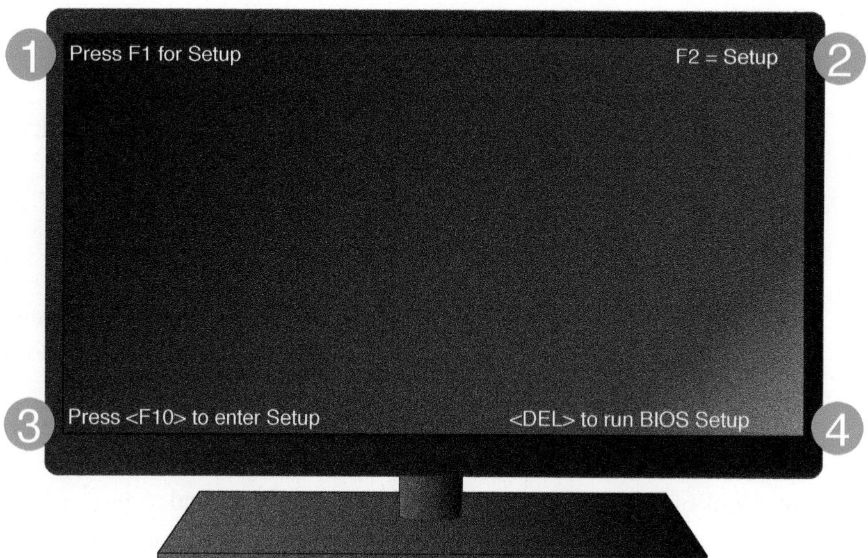

FIGURE 4.2 Setup keystrokes

Flash BIOS

Flash BIOS allows you to upgrade (or downgrade) the BIOS without installing a new chip or chips. Common computer BIOS/UEFI manufacturers include AMI (American Megatrends, Inc.), Phoenix Technologies, Byosoft (Nanjing Byosoft Co., Ltd.), and Insyde Software.

An upgrade of the BIOS normally involves removing all BIOS software and settings stored in CMOS. Some manufacturers provide utilities that enable you to save the current CMOS settings before upgrading the BIOS. Two things should be done before upgrading the flash BIOS if possible: Back up current CMOS settings and back up the current BIOS.

UEFI

Unified Extensible Firmware Interface (**UEFI**) is the interface between the operating system and firmware, which can be the traditional BIOS, or UEFI can replace the BIOS. The traditional BIOS always checks for certain things, such as a keyboard, before allowing the system to boot. Traditional BIOS made configuring kiosks and other touch screen technologies difficult. UEFI fixed these issues.

With UEFI, you can boot into a special environment. Many manufacturers have moved to the UEFI type of BIOS for the following reasons:

- It is a graphical environment that provides mouse support.
- It enables you to use a virus-scanning utility that is not operating system dependent.
- It offers software that is not just configuration screens.
- It offers optional internet access for troubleshooting or download capabilities.
- It offers better system support for cooling, voltage levels, performance, and security.
- It provides support for increased hard drive capacities and ability to divide the hard drive into sections that are not subject to the limitations of the traditional BIOS.
- It commonly has data related to temperature, voltage, CPU speed, bus speed, and fan speed.
- It can have a boot manager instead of relying on a boot sector. See Chapter 7, "Storage Devices," for more information on the GUID partition table (GPT) and boot sector. Figure 4.3 shows an example of a UEFI environment.

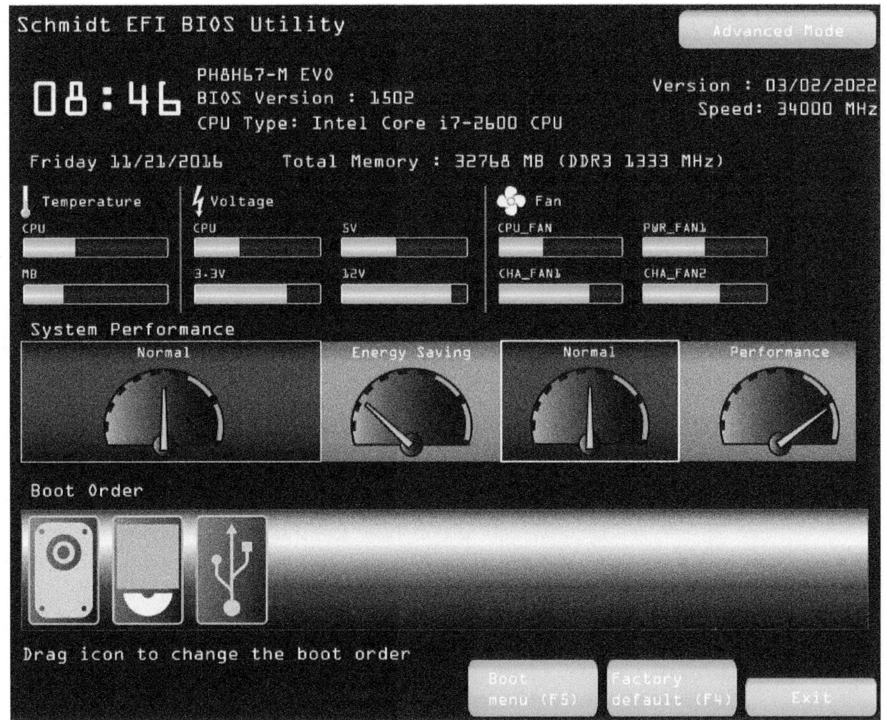

FIGURE 4.3 Sample UEFI main menu

From the BIOS/UEFI main menu, there might be icons you can use to access utilities or more advanced configurations, as shown in Figure 4.4.

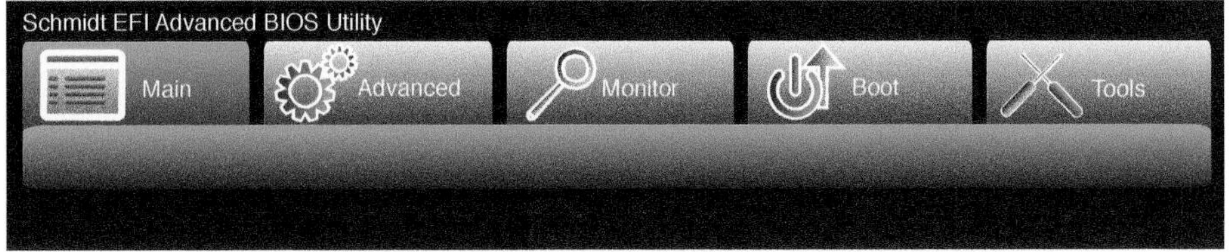

FIGURE 4.4 Sample UEFI advanced menu

BIOS/UEFI Configuration Settings

BIOS/UEFI options vary according to manufacturer, but many options are similar. Table 4.1 shows some common settings and briefly explains each one. Note that the key term items are on the CompTIA A+ certification exam. A technician should be familiar with these common BIOS/UEFI setup options, especially the starred **security settings**.

TECH TIP

Using Setup to disable ports and connectors

Motherboards include connectors for hard drives, optical drives, and so on. If one of these connectors fails, you can disable it through Setup and obtain a replacement adapter just as you would if an integrated port failed. Setup can also be used to disable integrated motherboard ports.

TABLE 4.1 Common BIOS/UEFI Setup options

Setup option	Description
System Information	Displays general information, such as the processor, processor speed, amount of RAM, type and number of hard drives and optical drives installed, BIOS/UEFI manufacturer, and BIOS/UEFI date.
General Optimization	Allows faster booting through the disabling of features such as memory checking, booting to the network, and booting from removable drives.
Boot Options, Boot Sequence, Boot Drive Order, or Boot Menu	Prioritizes devices in the order in which the computer looks for an operating system. Changed when a **system attempts to boot to an incorrect device**.
CPU Configuration or Advanced CPU Settings	Contains settings such as CPU TM function, which affects CPU throttle management (slowing the CPU when overheated); clock speed, which may not be changeable; PECI (Platform Environment Control Interface), which affects how the thermal sensors report the core temperature of your CPU; Max CPUID, which is used for compatibility with older operating systems; CPU Ratio control, which sets the CPU multipliers; and Vanderpool Technology, which is used with Intel virtualization.
Fan Control	Enables the configuration of case and/or CPU fans, including the ability to place the fans in silent mode or control fan speed.
Video Options	Enables configuration such as DVMT (dynamic video memory technology) to control video memory, aperture size (the amount of system RAM dedicated for the video adapter use), and which video controller is primary or secondary.
Onboard Device Configuration	Allows modification of devices built into the motherboard, such as audio, Bluetooth wireless, network, USB, or video ports.
* **Passwords**, **Boot Password**, Power on Password, Password Options, Supervisor Password, **Administrator Password** or User Password	Allows protection of the BIOS/UEFI menu options, specifically configuration of a password to enter the Setup program, to allow the computer to boot, or to distinguish between someone who can make minor changes such as alterations to boot options or date and time (user password), or someone who can view and change all Setup options (supervisor or administrator password). Other vendors might have the following levels: full access (all screens except supervisor password), limited access, view-only access, or no access.
* Virus Protection	Runs a small virus-scanning application located in BIOS/UEFI. Some operating systems and software updates require this option to be disabled for the upgrade to proceed.
Numlock On/Off	Allows default setting (enabled or disabled) of the Num Lock key option after booting.
USB Permissions	Allows modification of USB speed options and the number of ports to enable.
Hyper-Threading	Allows enabling/disabling of Hyper-Threading technology.
Integrated Peripherals (enabling/disabling devices and ports)	Allows enabling/disabling and configuration of motherboard-controlled devices such as PATA/SATA ports and integrated ports including USB, audio, and network. Sets the amount of RAM dedicated for video use. If the computer has an ample amount of RAM, increasing this setting can increase performance, especially in applications (such as games) that use high-definition graphics.

Setup option	Description
Advanced BIOS Options	Allows configuration of options such as CPU and memory frequencies, CPU, front side bus, north bridge, south bridge, chipset, and memory voltage levels.
Interface Configurations	Either indicates a category or lists an individual interface (for example, IDE Configuration, SATA Configuration, PCI Configuration, PCIe Configuration).
IDE Configuration	Allows manual configuration of IDE devices, such as PATA, hard drives, and optical drives.
SATA Configuration	Allows viewing of Serial ATA values assigned by BIOS/UEFI and changing of some of the related options, as well as RAID configuration.
PCI/PnP Configuration	Allows viewing and changing of PCI slot configuration, including IRQ and DMA assignments.
PCIe Configuration	Allows manual configuration of the PCIe version.
Devices	Allows configuration of USB, SATA, video, onboard devices, and PCI, where the M.2 slot might need to be enabled so the SSD will be recognized.
Virtualization Support	Also known as Virtualization Technology or Secure Virtual Machine Mode. Enables/disables virtualization so the virtualization software can access additional hardware capabilities.
ACPI (Advanced Configuration and Power Interface)	Determines what happens if power is lost, power options if a call comes into a modem, and power options when directed by a PCI or PCIe device or by mouse/keyboard action.
Hardware Monitor	Allows viewing of CPU and motherboard temperature monitoring as well as the status of CPU, chassis, voltages, clock speeds, fan speeds, bus speeds, chassis intrusion detection/notification, and power supply fans.
* **Disable Execute Bit**, Execute Disable, or No Execute	Prevents executable code (viruses) from being executed from a specific marked memory area.
* **Drive Encryption**	Specifies that a secret key is used to encrypt the data on the hard drive. The computer will not boot without the correct password. The drive cannot be moved to another computer unless the correct password is entered.
* **LoJack**	Allows security settings to perform tasks such as locating the device, locking the device remotely, displaying an "if lost" message, or deleting data if stolen.
* **Intrusion Detection/ Notification**	Also known as Chassis Intrusion. Allows notification if the cover has been removed.
* **Secure Boot**	Checks every driver before launching the drivers and the operating system. Prevents an unauthorized operating system or software from loading during the boot process.

Setup option	Description
iGPU	Allows configuration of how much memory is allocated for the integrated GPU.
Built-in Diagnostics	Provides access to hardware components, the hard drive, memory, the battery, and other diagnostic tests.
* Trusted Platform Module (**TPM**)	Might also be seen as a PTT option. Allows enabling the TPM motherboard chip that generates and stores cryptographic keys and passwords. You can also clear the saved data using the TPM Clear option. Note that you might also see a **fTPM** (firmware TPM) option if the TPM function uses the CPU and not a separate chip to provide this function.

* Security options

TECH TIP

System boots from the wrong device

If a computer tries to boot from the wrong device, change the *Boot Sequence* setting in BIOS/UEFI. It is also possible that an optical disc is in the drive or a non-bootable USB drive is attached, and that is the first boot option currently selected.

Figure 4.5 shows a sample BIOS/UEFI screen where you can set the administrator or user password. Note that this is not a Windows or corporate network password.

FIGURE 4.5 Password security menu

You must save your changes whenever you make configuration changes. Some manufacturers allow saving screen captures to a USB flash drive. Exiting without saving changes is a common mistake. Table 4.2 lists sample BIOS/UEFI exit options.

TABLE 4.2 Sample configuration change options

Option	Description
Save & Exit Setup	Saves all changes and leaves the Setup program.
Exit Without Saving	Closes without saving any changes that have been made. Used when changes have been made in error or more research is needed.
Load Fail-Safe Defaults	Sets the default settings programmed by the manufacturer. Used when unpredictable results occur after changing an option.
Load Optimized Defaults	Has more aggressive settings than the Load Fail-Safe Defaults option. This option is programmed by the manufacturer.

TPM Considerations

TPM comes in two main versions: 1.2 and 2.0. The 2.0 version is a worldwide standard, but each computer manufacturer's UEFI options could be listed differently. When you enable TPM through the UEFI, you select and enable the TPM module that can be a physical module or done through the firmware. You can also clear the TPM.

TECH TIP

Clearing TPM invalidates security keys and causes data loss

If you clear the TPM, TPM is turned off and all existing security keys are invalidated, and this can cause access to encrypted data to be lost. Ensure all data is backed up before clearing the TPM. You can keep all security keys and data if you just disable (turn off) the TPM instead of clearing it.

On a Windows computer, each component is checked for boot drivers, rootkits, and malware, and the TPM stores this information. The UEFI Secure Boot option, BitLocker Drive Encryption, and Windows Defender make use of the TPM. Once the TPM is enabled, you can start the TPM initialization wizard by typing `tpm.msc` in the Windows Search textbox. You will be prompted to create a TPM owner password. This password can be saved to removable media and/or printed. Note that this is very important information and cannot be recovered.

CMOS Memory

Settings changed in system BIOS/UEFI are recorded and stored in a complementary metal-oxide semiconductor (**CMOS**) found in the motherboard chipset. CMOS is memory that requires a small amount of power provided by a coin-sized lithium battery (**CMOS battery**) when the system is powered off. The memory holds the settings configured through BIOS/UEFI. When the battery dies, all configuration information in CMOS is lost and must be re-entered or relearned after the battery is replaced.

TECH TIP

Incorrect Setup information causes POST errors

If you incorrectly input configuration information, POST error codes or error messages that would normally indicate a hardware problem appear.

Motherboard Battery

The most common CMOS battery used today is a CR2032 lithium battery, which is about the size of a nickel. Figure 4.6 shows a photo of a lithium battery installed on a motherboard.

FIGURE 4.6 Motherboard battery

> **TECH TIP**
>
> **Date, time, or settings reset**
>
> A first indication that a battery is failing is **inaccurate system date/time** on the computer.

No battery lasts forever. High temperatures shorten a battery's life span (which is typically three to eight years).

> **TECH TIP**
>
> **Using a battery recycling program**
>
> Many states have environmental regulations regarding battery disposal. Many companies also have battery recycling programs. The earth911.com website provides information regarding recycling and disposing of batteries and computer components by zip code or city/state.

Firmware Updates: Flashing/Clearing the BIOS/UEFI

Firmware updates are needed to obtain new features and address security flaws that might arise. The terms used for this process are "flashing the BIOS" and "updating or upgrading the firmware." A computer may need a BIOS/UEFI upgrade for a variety of reasons, including the following:

> To provide support for new or upgraded hardware such as a processor or a faster USB port
> To provide support for a higher-capacity hard drive

> For increased virus protection
> For optional password protection
> To solve problems with the current version
> To provide a security patch

Viruses can infect the BIOS/UEFI, so you should keep the BIOS write-protected until you need to update it. The following procedure is one example of how to flash the BIOS/UEFI:

Step 1. After the system BIOS/UEFI upgrade is downloaded from the internet, execute the update by double-clicking on the filename.

Step 2. Follow the directions on the screen or from the manufacturer.

Step 3. Reboot the computer.

At times, you might need to reset the BIOS, and there are four common ways this might be done: CMOS jumper, CMOS reset button, remove CMOS battery, BIOS/UEFI setting to reset to factory defaults. A **jumper** is a small piece of plastic that fits over pins. A jumper can be used to enable or disable a particular feature. Figure 4.7 shows an enlarged jumper and a CMOS password jumper. Figure 4.8 shows a CMOS reset button.

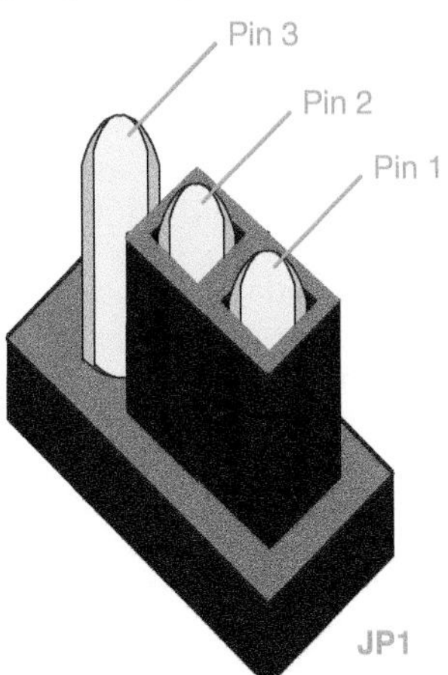

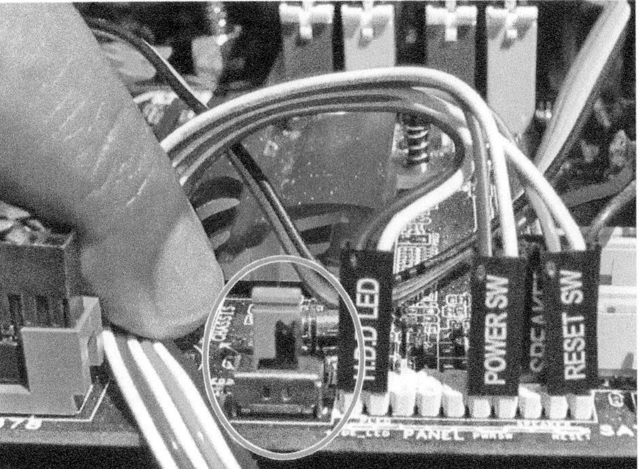

FIGURE 4.7 JP1 jumper block with pins 1 and 2 jumpered together and CMOS password jumper

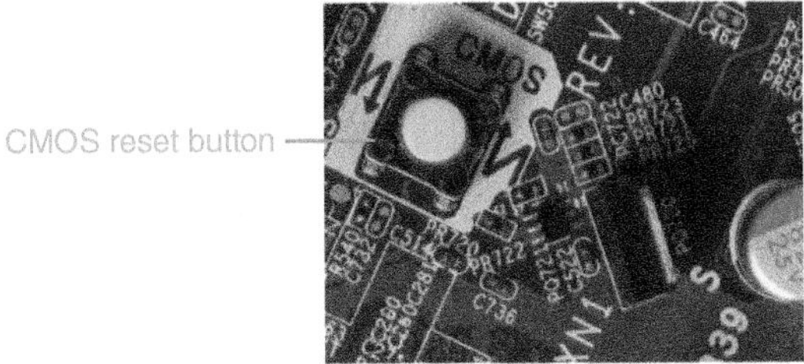

FIGURE 4.8 A CMOS reset button

> **TECH TIP**
>
> **Don't clear CMOS after a BIOS/UEFI update**
>
> Do not clear the CMOS immediately after upgrading the BIOS/UEFI. Power down the system and then power it back on before clearing CMOS data.

If flashing a laptop BIOS/UEFI, ensure that the laptop battery is fully charged or—better yet—connect the laptop to AC power. If the BIOS is downloaded (and not saved locally), connect the laptop to a wired network to do the download to ensure connectivity during the download process.

Keep in mind that not all vendors provide a method of recovering a BIOS/UEFI if a flash update does not go well. A computer without an operational BIOS/UEFI cannot boot, and a new motherboard must be purchased. You should therefore have a good reason for flashing the BIOS/UEFI and research the backup method the motherboard uses before flashing the BIOS/UEFI.

Other Configuration Parameters

Other possible parameters contained and set via the Setup program or operating system are interrupt requests (IRQs), input/output (I/O) addresses, direct memory access (DMA) channels, and memory addresses. These parameters are assigned to adapters and ports. No matter how the parameters are assigned, collectively they are known as **system resources**. Let's take a look at IRQs, I/O addresses, and memory addresses. Table 4.3 briefly describes these resources.

TABLE 4.3 System resources

Type	Description
IRQ	A number assigned to an adapter, a port, or a device so that orderly communication can occur between it and the processor. For example, when a key is pressed at the same time the mouse is moved, the keyboard has the highest priority because of its IRQ number.
I/O address	A unique address that allows an adapter, a port, or a device to exchange data with a processor. These addresses enable the processor to distinguish among the devices with which it communicates.
Memory address	A unique address assigned to a memory chip installed anywhere in the system. The CPU uses these addresses when it accesses information inside the memory chip.

IRQs

Imagine being in a room of 20 students when 4 students want the teacher's attention. The teacher needs an orderly process to acknowledge each request, prioritize the requests (which student is first), and then answer each question. A similar situation arises when multiple devices want the attention of the CPU. For example, which device gets to go first if a key on the keyboard is pressed and the USB mouse is moved simultaneously? The answer lies in the interrupt request assigned to the keyboard and the mouse. Every device requests permission to do something by interrupting the processor (which is similar to a student raising a hand). The CPU has a priority system to handle such situations.

TECH TIP

How IRQs are assigned to multiple-device ports

Ports such as USB that support multiple devices require only one interrupt per port. For example, a single USB port can support up to 127 devices but needs only one IRQ for however many devices connect to a USB hub.

Adapter and device interrupts are viewed and set by using Device Manager in Windows or using various Control Panels. Technicians need to know how to use **Device Manager**, which shows the status of installed hardware. Here are the various ways to access Device Manager:

> Type **`devmgmt.msc`** from a command prompt or search textbox.
> Type **`device manager`** from the search textbox on the taskbar.
> Select *Settings* > type **`device manager`** in the *Find a setting* search textbox.
> Select *Devices and Printers* Control Panel > *Device Manager* link.
> Select *System and Security* Control Panel > *Administrative Tools* > *Computer Management* > *Device Manager.*
> Right-click the *Start* button > *Device Manager.*

Within Device Manager select *View* > *Resources by Type* and expand the *Interrupt request (IRQ)* section. Some interrupts have multiple entries. Multiple entries do not always indicate a resource conflict; they are allowed because devices may share IRQs.

In order to access specifics in Device Manager, use the *View* > *Devices by Type* option. Then expand any specific section, such as Network Adapters, right-click on a particular device or adapter, and select *Properties*. Figure 4.9 shows an integrated network card's properties, which cannot be changed through Device Manager, as indicated by the Change Setting button being grayed out. (However, properties might be able to be modified through the system BIOS/UEFI Setup program.)

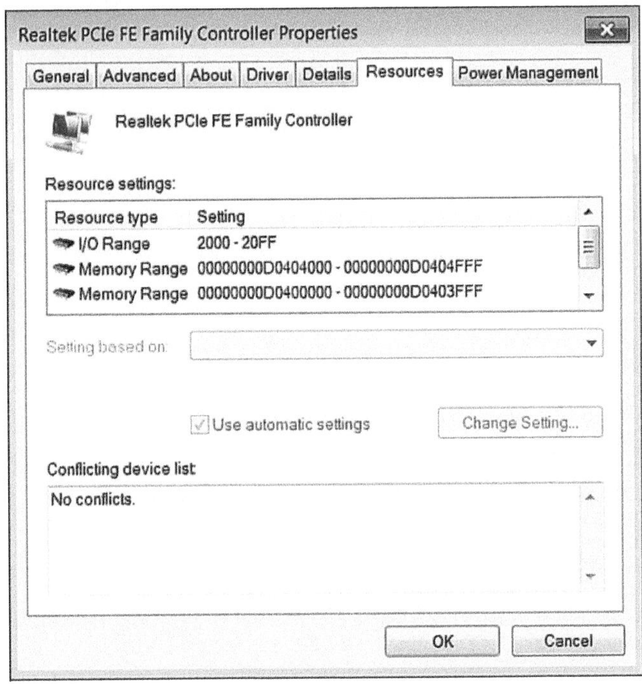

FIGURE 4.9 Resources tab in Device Manager

TECH TIP

What to do when a conflict occurs

If you suspect a resource conflict with a card, reboot the computer. The BIOS/UEFI and operating system will try to work things out. This may take multiple reboots. In addition, if an adapter is installed, moving it to another slot can resolve the situation.

I/O (Input/Output) Addresses

An I/O address, also known as an input/output address or port address, enables a device and a processor to exchange data. An I/O address is like a mailbox number; it must be unique. I/O addresses are simply addresses the processor can use to distinguish among the devices with which it communicates.

> **TECH TIP**
>
> **When is an I/O address needed?**
>
> Remember that every device must have a separate I/O address. Otherwise, the CPU cannot distinguish between installed devices.

I/O addresses are shown in hexadecimal format (base 16), from 0000 to FFFF. Some outputs are shown with eight positions, such as 00000000 to FFFFFFFF. Hexadecimal numbers are 0, 1, 2, 3, 4, 5, 6, 7, 8, and 9, as well as the letters A, B, C, D, E, and F. An example of an I/O address is 390h. Normally, devices need more than one hexadecimal address location.

Memory Addresses

A memory address is a unique address assigned to a memory chip installed anywhere in the system. The CPU uses a memory address when it accesses information inside the chip. Memory addresses are shown as a range of hexadecimal addresses in Device Manager (see Figure 4.10).

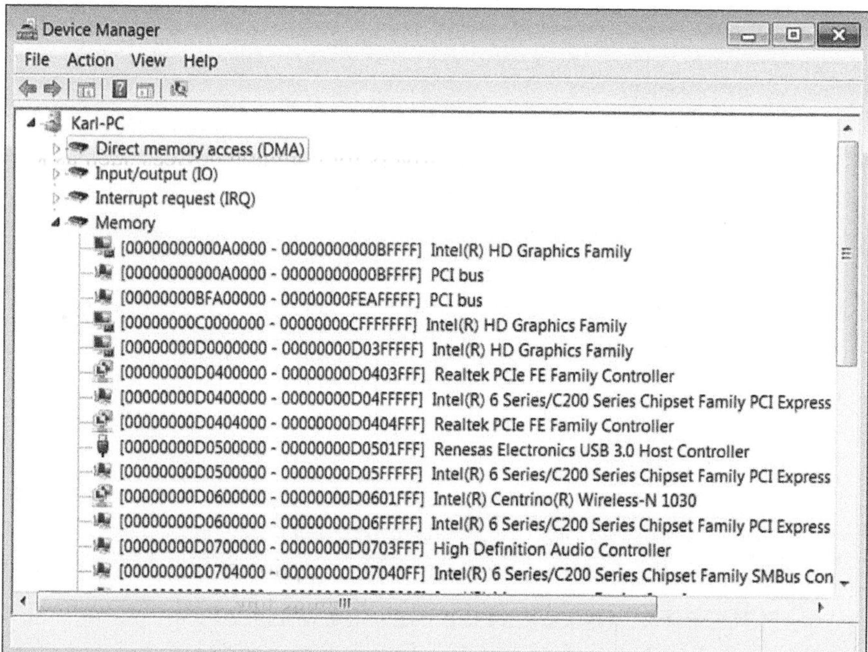

FIGURE 4.10 Memory addresses in Device Manager

Hardware Configuration Overview

Configuration of adapters and other hardware is easy if you follow the documentation and know how to obtain device drivers. Documentation for installation is frequently available on the internet, as are many device drivers. Device drivers are also provided as part of the Windows update process.

The system BIOS/UEFI plays an important role as part of the startup routine. Not only does it check hardware for errors as part of POST, it also detects installed adapters and devices. The BIOS/UEFI, along with the operating system, determines what resources to assign to a device or an adapter. This information is stored in a part of CMOS known as the Extended System Configuration Data (**ESCD**) area. After information is configured in the ESCD area, the information stays there and does not have to be recomputed unless another device is added.

After resources are allocated, the BIOS looks in the saved settings of CMOS to determine which device it should look to first for an operating system. This part of the BIOS/UEFI routine is known as the bootstrap loader. If the BIOS/UEFI cannot locate an operating system in the first location specified in the saved settings, it tries the second device and continues on, looking to each device specified in the saved settings for an operating system. When an operating system is found, the operating system loads.

Installing Drivers

When installing hardware or an adapter in the Windows environment, a driver is required. Remember that a driver is software that allows the operating system to control hardware. The operating system detects the adapter or hardware installation and adds the device's configuration information to the registry. The **registry** is a central database in Windows that holds hardware information and other data. All software applications access the registry for configuration information instead of going to the adapter.

Windows comes with many drivers for common devices such as keyboards, mice, printers, and displays. Here are some processes used to install a driver:

- You might be prompted to install or search for the driver as part of the installation process. You may have to designate where the driver is located, such as on media that comes with the hardware. You might also be required to download it and designate where the downloaded file is located.
- Use Device Manager to install a driver. Open *Device Manager* > expand the relevant particular hardware category > right-click the device > *Update Driver Software*, as shown in Figure 4.11.
- Use File Explorer to locate an executable file that comes with the hardware. Double-click on the Setup file provided to install software and/or a driver.
- Use the *Add a Device* Control Panel Option or *Add Bluetooth or other device* (Windows 10)/*Add a device* (Windows 11) Settings link.
- Use the Add Hardware Wizard by typing **`hdwwiz`** in the Windows search textbox.

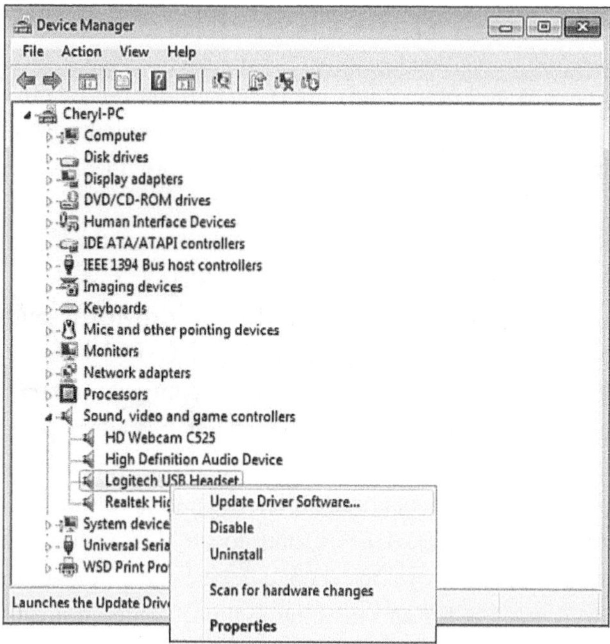

FIGURE 4.11 Update Driver Software option in Device Manager

Installing a USB Device

To install a USB device, perform the following steps:

Step 1. Power on the computer.

Step 2. Optionally, install the USB device's software. Note that some manufacturers require that software and/or device drivers be installed before the USB device is attached.

Step 3. Optionally, power on the device. Not all USB devices have external power adapters or a power button because they receive power from the USB bus.

Step 4. Locate a USB port on the rear or front of the computer or on a USB hub. Plug the USB device into a free port. The operating system normally detects the USB device and loads the device driver. You may have to browse to the driver.

Step 5. Verify installation in Device Manager.

TECH TIP

Ignoring manufacturer's advice gets you in trouble

If a manufacturer recommends installing the device driver before attaching the USB device, follow the instructions! Failure to do so may require uninstallation of the driver and then reinstallation using recommended procedures, in order for the device to work properly.

Installing/Configuring USB Cards

Additional USB ports can be added by using a USB hub or connecting a **USB expansion card**, which is a metal plate that has additional USB ports that connect to motherboard pins. The plate inserts where an expansion card goes, but it does not have connectors that fit into an expansion slot. The metal plate simply slides into the spot where a card would normally go. Figure 4.12

shows one of these plates; this one has two USB ports and an eSATA port. You can also review Figure 2.20 to see how to attach the cables to the motherboard.

FIGURE 4.12 USB and eSATA bracket/ports that connect to motherboard pins

Keep in mind that if a motherboard does not have any pins, you can add more USB ports by purchasing a PCI or PCIe USB adapter with multiple ports. The adapter might not have the capability of providing power unless the adapter supports having a power cable from the power supply attached to the card.

It is possible to install a USB card to add additional USB ports to a computer. USB ports are powered; therefore, a USB card normally has a place to connect power. If the power supply does not have the appropriate power connector, a power adapter may have to be purchased. Generic instructions follow:

Step 1. Power down the computer and remove the power cord.

Step 2. Remove the computer cover. Locate an empty expansion slot. You may have to remove a screw or raise a retaining bar to be able to use the expansion slot (see Figure 4.13).

Step 3. Using proper antistatic procedures (see Chapter 5, "Disassembly and Power"), ground yourself or use antistatic gloves.

Step 4. Add a cable to the motherboard if using a USB bracket. Optionally, attach a power connector to the adapter.

Step 5. Ensure that the proper expansion slot is being used and insert the card firmly into the slot (see Figure 4.14). Ensure that the card is fully inserted by pressing firmly down on the adapter and visually inspecting it afterward. The card should be at a 90-degree angle from the PC. It should not tilt at either end. Ensure that the card fits firmly in the expansion slot.

Step 6. Lower the expansion bar or attach a screw, if needed.

Step 7. Reinstall the computer cover, reattach the power cord, and power on the computer. Install drivers as necessary.

Step 8. Test by attaching a USB device to each port.

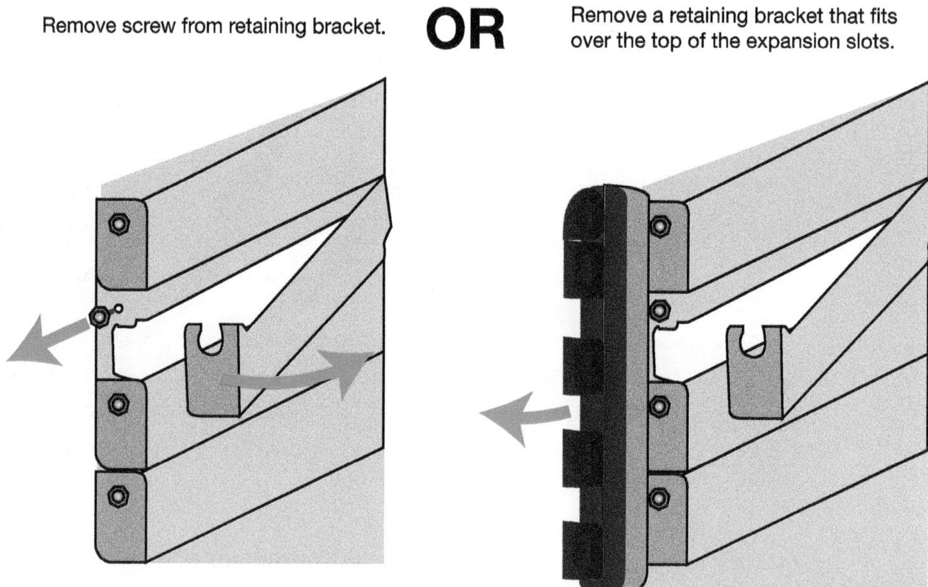

Remove screw from retaining bracket.
OR
Remove a retaining bracket that fits over the top of the expansion slots.

FIGURE 4.13 Adapter screw or retainer bar

FIGURE 4.14 Inserting an adapter directly into an expansion slot

Troubleshooting USB

To troubleshoot USB device problems, check the obvious first: the cabling and power. Verify whether any USB device that plugs into a USB hub works. If no devices work, swap the hub or attach to a different USB port. If some hub ports work and some do not, attach an external power source to the hub, change its configuration if necessary, and retest the devices. Restart the computer and retest the USB device.

USB ports can provide power at different levels such as 2A at 5V (10W), 5A at 12V (60W), and 5A at 20V (100W). Not all USB-C cables can provide 100W power either. Ensure you are using a 5A-rated USB-C to USB-C cable.

You can verify how much power a USB device is using by using external software like USBDeview. You can view the power state using Device Manager using these steps.

Step 1. Expand the *Universal Serial Bus Hub Controllers* section.

Step 2. Right-click on each *Generic USB Hub* option and select *Properties.*

Step 3. Access the *Details* tab and use the *Property* dropdown arrow to select *Power data.*

Step 4. In the *Current power state* section, notice the D0 through D3 state. A D0 state is fully on state and D3 is the lowest power state (sleep mode even if it has devices attached).

A USB device could be drawing more power than is allowed. If this is the case, the computer can disable the port. The only way to re-enable the port is to restart the computer. If a device is using less than 50 mA of power, the USB port never becomes active. Try plugging the USB device into a different USB port or verifying that the device works on another computer.

In Windows 10 and 11, in the USB hub *Properties* > *Power Management* tab, it is possible to allow (the default setting) or disallow the computer to shut the USB port/hub off to save power (see Figure 4.15).

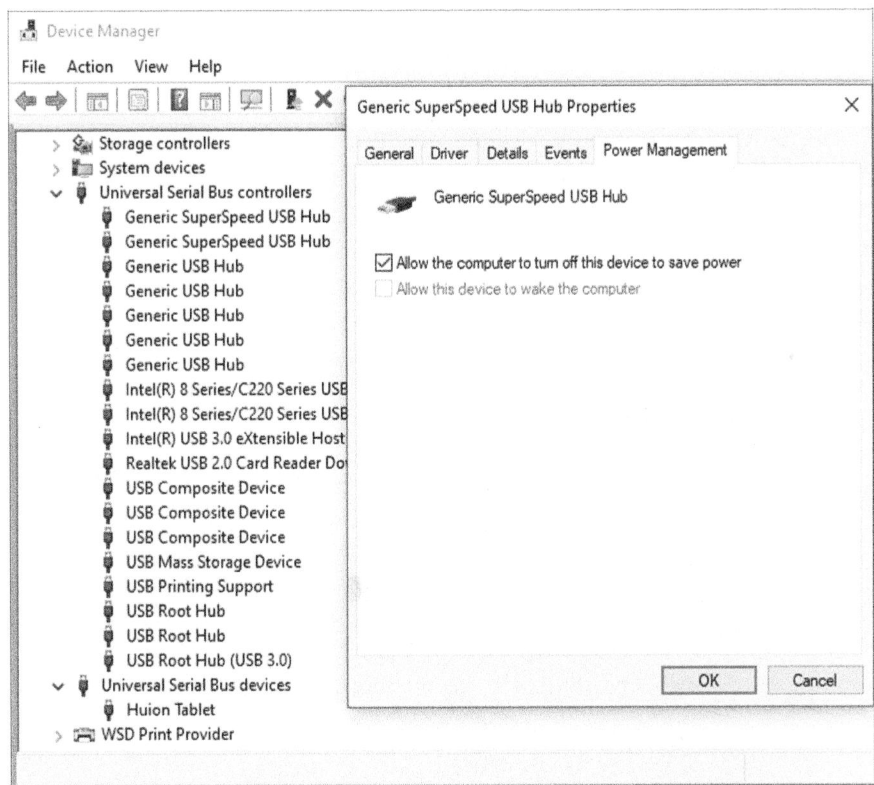

FIGURE 4.15 USB port Windows power management

A USB device requires a driver that may be loaded automatically. An incorrect or outdated driver could be loaded and causing problems. The following list can also help when troubleshooting USB devices:

- Use Device Manager to ensure that a hub is functioning properly.
- Ensure that the BIOS/UEFI firmware is up-to-date.
- Use Device Manager to ensure that no USB device has an IRQ assigned and shared with another non-USB device.
- USB devices sometimes do not work in Safe mode and require hardware support configured through the BIOS/UEFI.

- Sometimes a USB device stops working on a hub that has an external power source. In such a case, remove the hub's external power source and retest.
- If a self-powered USB hub gets its power disconnected, the hub becomes a bus-powered hub and outputs only lower power on each port. Reattach the power cord or remove the hub and then reattach it.
- If a newly attached USB device reports that it is attached but does not work properly, upgrade the driver.
- Do not connect USB devices to a computer that is in standby mode or sleep mode. Doing so may prevent the computer from coming out of standby mode.
- For intermittent USB device problems, disable power management to see if doing so solves the problem.
- Test a device connected to a USB hub by connecting it directly to a USB port that has nothing else attached. The problem may be caused by other USB devices or a USB hub.
- Remove the USB device's driver and reinstall it. Sometimes you must reboot the computer to give the new drivers priority over the general-purpose drivers.
- If a USB device is running slowly, try attaching it to a different port that has fewer devices connected to the same port.
- Verify that the USB port is enabled in BIOS/UEFI if integrated into the motherboard or attached to the motherboard through an adapter cable.
- Refer to the USB device manufacturer's website for specific troubleshooting details.

Installing an eSATA Card

A Serial ATA (SATA) port allows connection of a SATA storage device such as a hard drive or an optical drive. External SATA (eSATA) ports allow connectivity of storage devices outside the computer or laptop. If a computer has no eSATA ports or does not have enough of them, two options exist. The first option is that you can install an **eSATA bracket**, as shown in Figure 4.16. Notice that SATA cables are simply attached to the backs of the ports. Each SATA cable attaches to a port on the motherboard. For the bracket shown, the motherboard needs to have two available SATA ports in order to have two external ports.

FIGURE 4.16 eSATA bracket with cables

The second option is to have a PCIe **eSATA card**, as shown in Figure 4.17. Notice that this card doesn't have any cables that come with it, as an eSATA bracket does, and it has ports at the top of the card as well as external ones. You could attach a SATA cable from the top of this card to an internal device or attach an eSATA cable from one of the external ports to an external eSATA device.

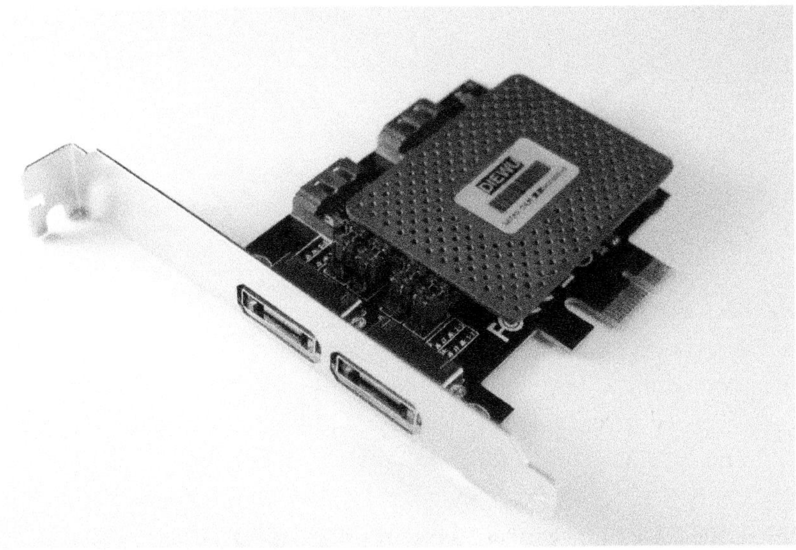

FIGURE 4.17 eSATA PCIe card

To install an eSATA card or bracket, perform the following steps:

Step 1. Power off the computer and unplug it.

Step 2. Remove the computer cover and locate an unused expansion slot. You may have to remove a screw or raise a retaining bar to be able to use the expansion slot.

Step 3. Remove the slot cover.

Step 4. Using proper antistatic procedures (see Chapter 5), ground yourself or use antistatic gloves.

Step 5. Ensure that the proper expansion slot is being used. Insert the card firmly into the expansion slot. If only a bracket is being used, insert the bracket between the motherboard and the back of the case where there is an empty expansion slot.

Step 6. Lower the expansion bar or attach a screw to keep the card or bracket firmly in place.

Step 7. If a bracket is being used, attach each SATA cable to an available SATA motherboard port. Make note of which SATA port is being used as each one may need to be enabled within BIOS/UEFI.

Step 8. Reinstall the computer cover, reattach the power cord, and power on the computer. Go into BIOS/UEFI and enable the appropriate SATA ports as necessary. Install any software that came with the card.

Step 9. Test by attaching an eSATA device to each port.

Installing a Network Interface Card

Almost all devices connect to a wired or wireless network by using a network interface card (NIC). Many devices have wired and wireless NICs built into the device, but if such a NIC fails, a new NIC must be installed, such as the Ethernet NIC shown in Figure 4.18.

FIGURE 4.18 Ethernet network interface card

You must take several steps as part of the installation process before connecting to the network:

Step 1. Determine that an appropriate expansion slot is available.

Step 2. Remove the computer cover and locate an unused expansion slot. Remove the slot cover.

Step 3. Ground yourself and ensure that the proper expansion slot is being used. Insert the card firmly into the expansion slot. Secure the card.

Step 4. Reinstall the computer cover, reattach power, and power on the computer. Download and install the latest driver.

Step 5. Give the computer a unique name and optionally join a workgroup or domain.

Step 6. Configure TCP/IP addressing information, as described in Chapter 13, "Networking."

Troubleshooting Configurations

The following are possible indications that a device is not working:

> A new device is installed, and the new device or a previously installed device does not work.
> The computer locks up or restarts when performing a specific function, such as when playing or recording audio.
> The computer hangs during startup or shutdown.
> A device does not work properly or fails to work at all.

TECH TIP

Verifying hardware with Device Manager

A small down arrow by a device's icon in Device Manager means the device is disabled, and an exclamation point (!) on a yellow field usually indicates a resource conflict or driver problem. An "i" indicates that the Use Automatic Settings feature is not being used for the device, and resources were manually configured.

In Device Manager, if an exclamation point (!) appears, the hardware device is not working properly, and you should check for cabling issues, resource conflicts, and configuration issues. If a yellow question mark appears, Windows does not recognize the device, and you can try one of the following:

> Perform a Windows update to ensure that you have the latest drivers, security updates, and fixes.

> Manually update the driver by right-clicking the device in *Device Manager* and selecting *Properties* > *Driver* tab > *Update Driver*. You can download this driver from the device manufacturer's website or let Windows try to find the driver.

TECH TIP

Using the General tab for troubleshooting

On the *General* tab of the Properties dialog for any adapter or port, check the *Device Status* section for any error codes, including those for resource conflicts.

With any Device Manager issue, you can right-click the device and select *Properties*. Look at the *General* tab to see if there are error codes.

Configuration problems can also be associated with specific BIOS/UEFI settings. Table 4.4 lists some problems and how you might be able to solve them.

TABLE 4.4 Troubleshooting BIOS/UEFI-related issues

Issue	Things to try
Message appears stating that the date and time are not set, the clock is not set, or all saved BIOS/UEFI settings are lost, or unexpected issues occur in more than one application.	Check the date and time through the operating system. Replace the motherboard CMOS battery.
Cannot configure a system for virtualization.	Enable virtualization in BIOS/UEFI.
Attached device does not work.	If the device connects to a motherboard port, ensure that the port is not disabled in BIOS/UEFI. Ensure that the device connects to the correct port, including a possible port on an adapter instead of the motherboard. If the device connects to a port on an adapter that is the same type of port as one found on the motherboard, the integrated port may need to be disabled in BIOS/UEFI.
System locks up sporadically.	If overclocking, put the system back to its original settings.
System is slow to boot or boots from the wrong device.	Check the BIOS/UEFI boot order setting.

SOFT SKILLS: A GOOD TECHNICIAN PRACTICE: CHANGE ONLY ONE THING AT A TIME AND DOCUMENT

The least effective type of computer technician is a "gun slinger." The term *gun slinger* brings to mind images of Wild West ruffians who had shooting matches with other gangsters in the town's main street. Gun slingers drew their guns frequently and with little provocation. They did not put much thought into their method or consider other possible resolutions. You must strive *not* to be this type of technician.

A gun slinger technician changes multiple things simultaneously. For example, if there is no display on the output, the technician might swap out the monitor, disable the onboard video port, add a new video adapter, power on the computer, and, when output appears, call the problem "solved." If a computer problem is repaired using such a technique, the technician never knows exactly what solved the problem. A gun slinger technician might get frustrated easily because it is easy to forget what has been tried when multiple things have been tried simultaneously—and it is almost impossible to know which one worked (see Figure 4.19).

FIGURE 4.19 A gun slinger technician in action

A good technician, on the other hand, makes a list of symptoms (even if it is simply a mental list) followed by a list of things to try. Then the technician tries the possible solutions, starting with the simplest one (the one that costs the least amount of time to the computer user). The technician documents each step. After each approach that does not fix the problem, the technician puts the system back to the original configuration before attempting the next possible solution. This method keeps the technician focused on what has been tested, and if another technician takes over, the steps do not have to be repeated. Best of all, when one of the possible solutions fixes the problem, the exact solution is known.

Gun slinger technicians do not learn as fast as other technicians because they do not determine the real causes of problems. Each time they are presented with a problem similar to one they have seen in the past, gun slinger technicians use the same haphazard troubleshooting method. These technicians are actually dangerous to an organization because they are not good at documenting what they have done and determining exactly what fixes a particular problem. A good computer technician should methodically troubleshoot a problem by making only one change at a time and reverting the change if the change does not solve the problem. Furthermore, the technician needs to document the issue and its resolution for future problems.

Chapter Summary

- The BIOS/UEFI is used to enable/disable, configure, and troubleshoot motherboard components, expansion slots, and ports, and it sets power-on and BIOS/UEFI passwords.
- An updated type of BIOS is BIOS/UEFI, which allows the use of a mouse and a graphical environment. Security options, support for larger hard drives, antivirus software, remote management, and utilities may also be included.
- When a computer is off, a motherboard battery holds saved settings in CMOS. If a computer does not keep the date and time, replace the battery.
- The TPM can be enabled or cleared through UEFI. Note that if you clear the TPM, all digital security certificates, passwords, and encrypted data are lost. Consider disabling TPM instead.
- Each port and card uses system resources such as interrupts, I/O addresses, and memory addresses.
- System resources can be viewed and changed using Device Manager. You can also use Device Manager to see that a device is working properly.
- A USB card, eSATA card or bracket, or NIC can be added to a computer to provide additional ports.

A+ CERTIFICATION EXAM TIPS

- ✓ A lot of questions from both exams can come from this chapter, especially in the troubleshooting areas. Review the troubleshooting bullets. Research issues on the internet and read people's postings. Their stories and frustrations (and successes) will stick in your mind and help you with the exam.
- ✓ Using at least one computer, go through the BIOS/UEFI menus. Review what types of things can be configured through BIOS/UEFI. Important settings include the following: boot options, USB settings including permissions and the ability to disable the ports, fan options, security settings (passwords including a boot password), and TPM settings.
- ✓ Be able to install and configure a network interface card (NIC) and other adapters.
- ✓ Know what to do if a system tries to boot to an incorrect device or if the system date/time is incorrect.

Key Terms

Administrator Password 114
BIOS 110
Boot Options 114
boot password 114
CMOS 117
CMOS battery 117
Device Manager 121
Disable Execute Bit 115
Drive Encryption 115
eSATA bracket 128
eSATA card 128
ESCD 123
Fan Control 114
firmware update 118
flash BIOS 112
fTPM 116
I/O address 120
inaccurate system date/time 118
Intrusion Detection/Notification 115
IRQ 120
jumper 119
LoJack 115
memory address 120
Passwords 114
POST 110
registry 123
Secure Boot 115
security settings 113
Setup 110
system attempts to boot to an incorrect device 114
system resources 120
TPM 116
UEFI 112
USB expansion card 124
USB Permissions 114
Virtualization Support 115

Review Questions

1. When would a technician flash a BIOS/UEFI?
   a. When the date and time start to be incorrect
   b. When a port or motherboard component does not perform at its maximum potential
   c. When the driver for a motherboard port is out of date
   d. When the motherboard has an upgrade, such as a new processor, extra RAM, or an additional adapter installed in an expansion slot
2. What is the effect of setting an administrator password in BIOS/UEFI?
   a. It prevents the computer from having multiple devices that can boot the system.
   b. It prevents the BIOS/UEFI from being infected with a virus.
   c. It prevents a user from accessing the computer operating system.
   d. It prevents a user from changing system Setup settings.
3. Which program is used to determine the driver version being used for a card installed in a computer?

   [BIOS | CMOS | Task Manager | Device Manager | system Setup]
4. Which program is commonly used to verify that a new piece of hardware is recognized by the operating system, functions, and the system resources assigned?

   [BIOS/UEFI | CMOS | manufacturer-provided application | Device Manager]
5. Where would a CR2032 lithium battery most likely be used in a tower PC?
   a. As a Bluetooth battery
   b. Inside the processor
   c. As a component on the motherboard
   d. In the CMOS
6. Which BIOS/UEFI option might need to be modified in order to boot a Windows computer from a flash drive that contains Ubuntu, a Linux-based operating system?

   [LoJack | Secure Boot | Virus Protection | USB Configuration | Hyper-Threading]
7. What is a TPM?
   a. A method of sharing resources between adapters
   b. A physical module that stores passwords and digital certificates
   c. The technique used by a USB hub when multiple devices are attached to it
   d. A type of lithium battery used to keep current Setup configuration data
8. A technician is looking at a used computer that was recently purchased by someone, and the computer is requesting a password before the operating system loads. What can the technician do to remove the password?
   a. Press Esc key to enter BIOS
   b. Press the F8 key as the computer boots
   c. Remove the CMOS battery for a minute and then reinstall it
   d. Hold the power button down for 10 seconds as the computer is booting
9. Which tab of a device's Properties dialog window has a Device Status section that might contain helpful troubleshooting information or the status of the device?

   [General | Advanced | Driver | Details | Management]

10. A technician receives a complaint about a computer being slow to respond to typed keystrokes. The technician installs more memory and a new keyboard. The customer is happy. What, if anything, could have been done better?

____

____

____

11. What is the maximum wattage that can be provided by a USB port?

[100 | 5 | 2.5 | 4.5]

To answer Questions 12–15, consider the following BIOS/UEFI configuration menu options.

Main menu	Onboard devices	Boot device priority
BIOS Information	PCIe	1st Boot Device
BIOS Version	LAN1 Controller	2nd Boot Device
Build Date	USB 2.0 Controller	3rd Boot Device
EC F/W Version	USB 3.0 Controller	4th Boot Device
CPU Information	Audio	
Memory Information	OnChip SATA Controller	
System Information	SATA	
System Language	HDMI/DVI	
System Date		
System Time		

12. Which menu would you use to determine whether the system should be flashed?
    a. Main menu
    b. Onboard devices
    c. Boot device priority
13. A computer is mounted inside a cabinet, and you want to know if the USB 3.0 port has been disabled. Which menu would you use?
    a. Main menu
    b. Onboard devices
    c. Boot device priority
14. Which menu would you use to determine whether the particular SATA port you used to connect to an eSATA bracket is enabled?
    a. Main menu
    b. Onboard devices
    c. Boot device priority
15. A technician wants to boot from an eSATA external hard drive. Which submenu item should she use?

    [OnChip SATA controller | SATA | PCIe Training | 1st Boot Device]
16. A technician keeps having to configure the date and time. What component is suspect?

    [CPU | BIOS/UEFI | battery | chipset | CMOS]

CHAPTER 4

17. What are three ways to get more USB ports? (Choose three.)
    a. Connect a USB hub to an existing USB port.
    b. Connect a network hub to an existing USB port.
    c. Install a PCIe adapter that has USB ports.
    d. Install an AGP adapter that has USB ports.
    e. Install a USB bracket that has USB ports and attaches to motherboard pins.
    f. Use a USB port multiplexer.
18. When would a technician use UEFI?
    a. When managing configuration through Device Manager
    b. When the date and/or time continues to be wrong
    c. When an adapter has just been installed
    d. When replacing a motherboard
19. A computer is being used in a medical office. For security reasons, the technician has been asked to reasonably ensure that no one attaches any external media. What would the technician probably do?
    a. Password protect the BIOS/UEFI and disable unused ports.
    b. Swap out the motherboard for one that doesn't have extra ports.
    c. Assign user rights through user passwords on the computer.
    d. Encrypt the hard drive.
    e. Flash the chipset.
20. A technician for a small company set a BIOS/UEFI password on every computer. The technician leaves the company, and the replacement technician needs to access the BIOS/UEFI. What should the new technician do?

    ____

    ____

    ____

Exercises

Exercise 4.1 System Expansion

Objective: To be able to explore different ways to expand a system

Parts: None

Procedure: Use the documentation in Table 4.5 to answer the questions.

TABLE 4.5 Motherboard specifications

Component	Description
CPU	Support for Intel Celeron, Core i3, and Core i5
Chipset	Intel B150 Express
Memory	2 DDR4 DIMM sockets supporting up to 32 GB Dual-channel support Support for DDR4 2133 MHz
Onboard graphics	Integrated Graphics Processor 2 HDMI ports Maximum shared memory of 512 MB

Component	Description
Audio	Realtek ALC887 codec 2/4/5.1/7.1-channel Support for S/PDIF out
LAN	2 Intel GbE LAN chips that support 10/100/1000 Mb/s
Expansion slots	1 PCIe 3.0 x16 slot 1 M.2 Socket 1 connector for wireless module
USB	Chipset: 4 USB 2.0/1.1 ports (2 on back and 2 through the internal USB header) 6 USB 3.0/2.0 ports (4 on back and 2 ports through the internal USB header)
Internal connectors	1 24-pin ATX main power connector 1 4-pin ATX 12 V power connector 6 SATA 6 Gb/s connectors 1 M.2 Socket 3 connector 1 CPU fan header 1 system fan headers 1 front panel header 1 front panel audio header 1 USB 3.0/2.0 header 1 USB 2.0/1.1 header 4 serial port headers 1 S/PDIF Out header 1 speaker header 1 clear CMOS jumper
Back panel connectors	2 USB 2.0/1.1 ports 1 PS/2 keyboard/mouse port 2 Wi-Fi antenna connectors 2 HDMI ports 4 USB 3.0/2.0 ports 2 RJ45 ports 6 audio jacks

1. The computer that uses this motherboard has one SATA hard drive attached. The person who owns this computer wants to use an eSATA drive.

   Based on the documentation given, can the user attach an eSATA drive to the computer as it is configured now?

   [Yes | No]

2. The technician wants to use an eSATA bracket that has two eSATA ports/cables in addition to one internal SATA device.

   Does the motherboard support this? Explain how you know.

   ____

   ____

CHAPTER 4

3. The user who owns the computer does not like to use USB hubs.

   What is the maximum number of devices the user can connect to the back of the computer without using USB hubs? What advice might you give the user regarding these ports?

   ____

   ____

   ____

   ____

   ____

4. The user wants additional USB ports on the back of the computer. The technician would like to use a USB bracket to provide two additional ports.

   Based on the documentation, can a USB bracket be used with this motherboard? How can you tell? Be specific.

   ____

   ____

Exercise 4.2 BIOS/UEFI Options

Objective: Use information found on the BIOS/UEFI screen to determine which option to use

Parts: None

Procedure: Use Figures 4.20 and 4.21 to answer the questions.

Use Figure 4.20 to answer Questions 1–5.

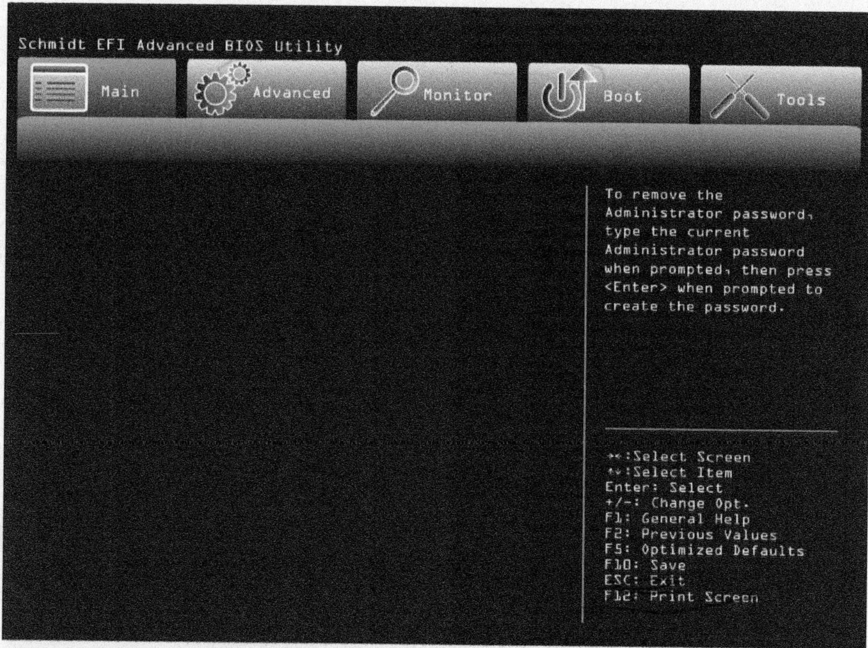

FIGURE 4.20 Sample BIOS/UEFI window 1

1. The user has modified BIOS/UEFI options to the point where half the ports don't work and the computer is running slowly.

   Which menu option or keystroke should the technician use in order to solve this problem?

   ____

2. The technician has modified some settings but now wants to research some alternatives and doesn't want to keep the settings he just changed.

   Which menu option or keystroke should the technician use in this situation?

   ____

3. The computers in the research lab have to have extra security. A technician configuring a new computer for that lab is using the BIOS/UEFI to disable all USB ports on the front and rear panels.

   Which menu option is used to complete this task?

   [Main | Advanced | Monitor | Boot | Tools]

4. The technician wants to see the last time anyone opened the case.

   Which menu option is used to complete this task?

   [Main | Advanced | Monitor | Boot | Tools]

5. The user has complained that the system takes too long to boot. One thing a prior technician did was to always have the system try to boot from an external drive used to reimage the computer. If the external drive wasn't found, then it used the internal hard drive to load the operating system.

   Which menu option should the new technician use to change the system to use the internal hard drive to load the operating system as the computer's first choice?

   [Main | Advanced | Monitor | Boot | Tools]

Use Figure 4.21 to answer Questions 6–10.

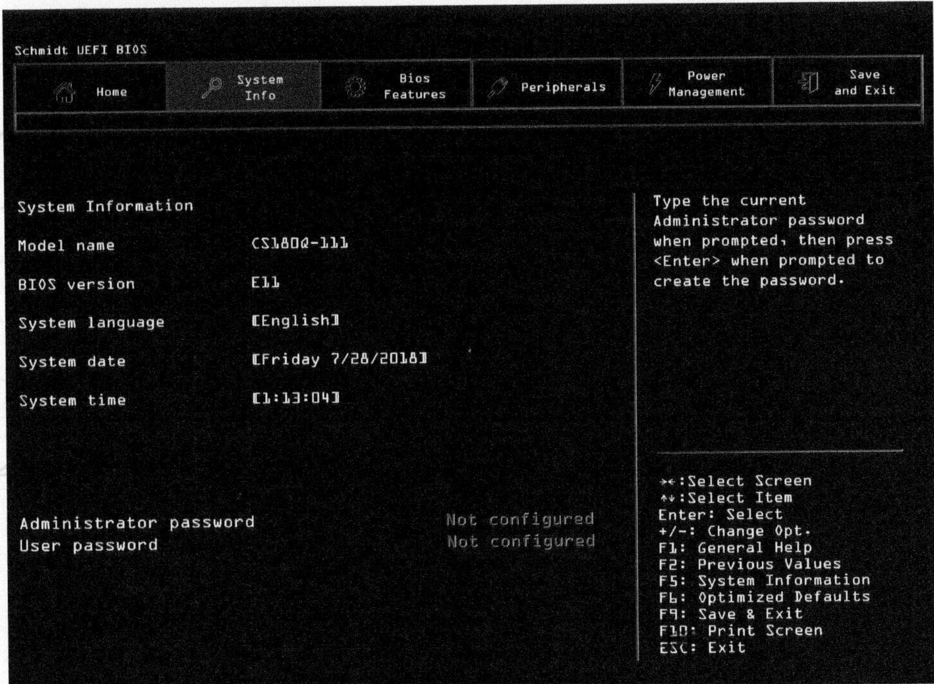

FIGURE 4.21 Sample BIOS/UEFI window 2

6. The technician wants to stop the user from changing BIOS/UEFI settings.

   Which menu option or keystroke should the technician use in order to set a BIOS/UEFI administrator password?

   [Home | System Info | Peripherals | Power Management]

7. A week ago, a user complained about the computer time being wrong. The technician changed the time and date. Now the user has complained again that the date and time are incorrect. If the technician changes the time again and checks the computer the next day and finds it off again, what should the technician do?

   a. Flash the BIOS/UEFI.
   b. Replace the motherboard.
   c. Replace the motherboard battery.
   d. Reset the time a third time.

8. A gamer has been adjusting timing features on this motherboard to make the system go faster. Which keystroke could the user use in order to take a screenshot of the current settings?

   ____

9. The technician has been modifying BIOS/UEFI settings.

   What keystroke should the technician use when exiting the Setup screen?

   ____

10. The technician wants to enable two SATA ports so a two-port eSATA bracket can be cabled to the motherboard.

    Which menu option should the technician use to ensure that the two SATA ports are enabled?

    [Home | System Info | Peripherals | Power Management]

Activities

Internet Discovery

Objective: To obtain specific information on the internet regarding a computer or its associated parts

Parts: Computer with internet access

Procedure: Use the internet to answer the following questions. Assume that the customer owns an Asus M241 all-in-one computer when answering Questions 1 and 2.

Questions:

1. A customer owns an Asus M241 all-in-one computer. Determine the procedure for accessing the computer's Setup program. Write the key(s) to press and the URL where you find this information.

   ____

   ____

2. What is the latest BIOS/UEFI version for the Asus M241?

   ____

3. A Windows 10 Asus computer owner wants to know if this model can be upgraded to Windows 11? Provide the URL where you found this information.

   ____

   ____

4. A customer owns a Tyan S7025 motherboard. How many and which type of PCIe slots does this motherboard have? Write the answer and the URL where you find the answer.

   ____

   ____

5. On the same Tyan S7025 motherboard as in Question 4, which motherboard jumper is used to clear CMOS? Write the answer and the URL where you find the information.

____

6. On the same Tyan S7025 motherboard as in Question 4, which BIOS/UEFI menu option is used to configure the order in which the system looks for devices to boot the computer? Write the answer and the URL where you find the answer.

____

____

Soft Skills

Objective: To enhance and fine-tune a future technician's ability to listen, communicate in both written and oral forms, and support people who use computers in a professional manner

Activities:

1. In teams, come up with a troubleshooting scenario that involves a computer technician who uses gun slinging techniques and the same scenario involving a technician who is methodical. Explain what each technician type does and how each one solves the problem. Also, detail how these two technicians treat the customer differently. Determine ways that a gun slinging technician might be harmful to a computer repair business. Either demonstrate or report on your findings.
2. After exploring the BIOS/UEFI options, turn to a fellow student, pretend he or she is a customer over the phone, and walk the student through accessing Setup. Explain the purposes of at least five of the options. Reverse roles and cover five other options. Be sure to act like a typical computer user when playing the customer role.
3. Brainstorm a troubleshooting scenario in which you fix a problem that involves accessing the Setup program and/or an adapter. Document the problem using a word processing application. Create an invoice using either a word processing or spreadsheet application. Share your documents with others in the class.

Critical Thinking Skills

Objective: To analyze and evaluate information as well as apply learned information to new or different situations

Activities:

1. Describe a situation where you think adding an eSATA card makes sense.

____

____

____

2. Compare and contrast a post office with IRQs, I/O addresses, and memory addresses shown in Device Manager. For example, how might something that happens in a post office relate to an IRQ in a PC (or I/O address or memory address)?

3. Your parents have a new computer, and they see a message to press F2 to enter Setup. They do this, and they want you to explain what they are looking at.

5 Disassembly and Power

In this chapter you will learn:

- How to prevent static electricity, RFI, and EMI from harming or interfering with a computer
- The tools needed to work on computers
- How to take apart a computer and put it back together
- How to perform basic voltage and continuity checks
- How to install, upgrade, or replace a power supply
- Tips for good written communication

CompTIA Exam Objectives:

- ✓ 1101-3.1 Explain basic cable types and their connectors, features, and purposes.
- ✓ 1101-3.4 Given a scenario, install and configure motherboards, central processing units (CPUs), and add-on cards.
- ✓ 1101-3.5 Given a scenario, install or replace the appropriate power supply.
- ✓ 1101-5.2 Given a scenario, troubleshoot common problems related to motherboards, RAM, CPU, and power.
- ✓ 1102-4.4 Given a scenario, use common safety procedures.
- ✓ 1102-4.5 Summarize environmental impacts and local environmental controls.
- ✓ 1102-4.7 Given a scenario, use proper communication techniques and professionalism.

Disassembly Overview

It is seldom necessary to completely disassemble a computer. However, when a technician is first learning about PCs, disassembly can be both informative and fun. A technician might disassemble a computer when it has a problem of undetermined cause or a grounding problem. An **equipment grounding** problem occurs when the motherboard or adapter is not properly installed and a trace (a metal line on the motherboard or adapter) touches the computer frame, causing the adapter and possibly other components to stop working.

Electrostatic Discharge (ESD)

You must take precautions when disassembling a computer. The electronic circuits located on the motherboard and adapters are subject to ESD. Electrostatic discharge (**ESD**) is a difference of potential between two items that causes static electricity. Static electricity can damage electronic equipment. The average person cannot feel static discharge until it reaches 3,000 volts. An electronic component can be damaged with as little as 30 volts. Some electronic components might not be damaged the first time static electricity occurs. However, the effects of static electricity can be cumulative, weakening or eventually destroying a component. An ESD event is not recoverable: Nothing can be done about the damage it induced. Electronic chips and memory modules are most susceptible to ESD strikes

TECH TIP

Atmospheric conditions affect static electricity

When humidity is low, the potential for ESD is greater than at any other time; however, too much humidity is bad for electronics. Keep humidity between 45% and 55% to reduce the threat of ESD.

A technician can prevent ESD by using a variety of methods. The most common tactic is to use an **antistatic wrist strap**, also called an **ESD strap**. An antistatic wrist strap allows a technician and a computer to be at the same voltage potential. As long as the technician and the computer or electronic part are at the same potential, static electricity does not occur. See Figure 5.1.

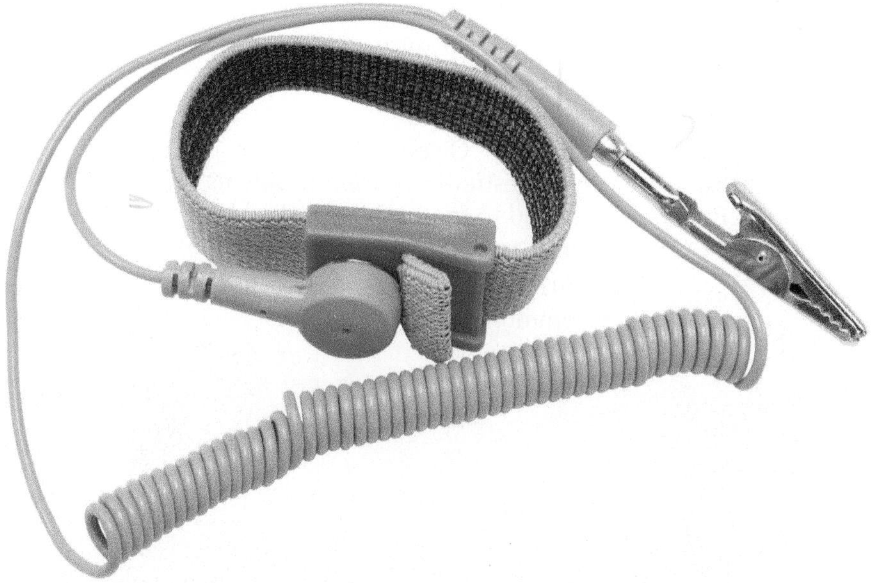

FIGURE 5.1 Antistatic wrist strap

One end encircles the technician's wrist, and the other end attaches to the computer. The clip attaches to a grounding post or a metal part such as the power supply or case, as shown in Figure 5.2. You might see the electronic symbol for ground, ⏚, near a ground post.

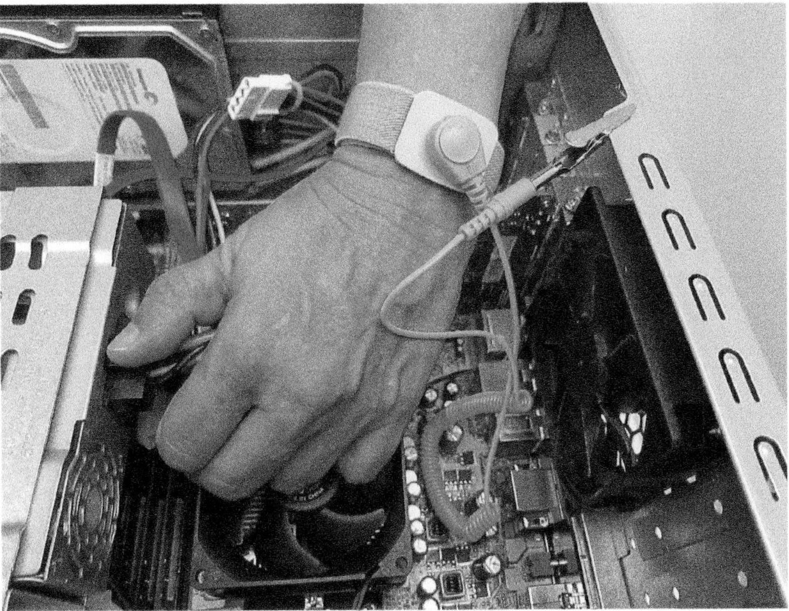

FIGURE 5.2 Where to attach an antistatic wrist strap

> **TECH TIP**
>
> **When *not* to wear an antistatic wrist strap**
>
> Technicians should not wear an ESD wrist strap when working inside a cathode ray tube (CRT) monitor or power supply because of the high voltages there. Of course, a technician should not be inside these devices unless properly trained in electronics.

Antistatic gloves (see Figure 5.3) can be used instead of an antistatic wrist strap. Laptops and other mobile devices frequently do not have good places to attach a wrist strap, and in such a case, antistatic gloves work better.

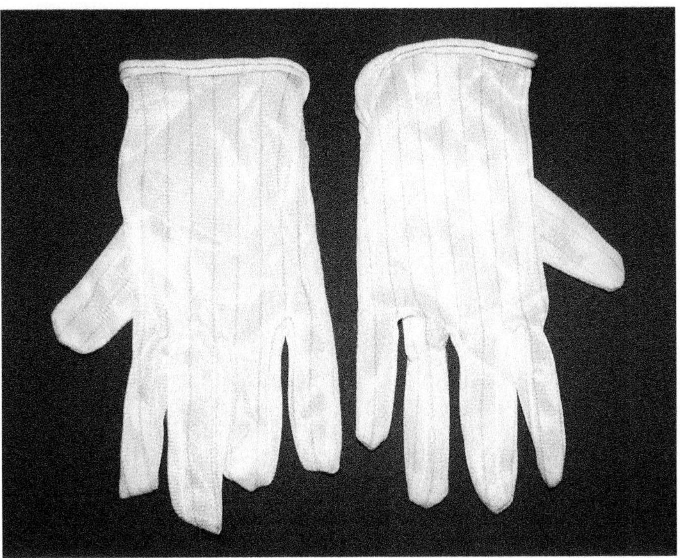

FIGURE 5.3 Antistatic gloves

Antistatic bags are good for storing spare adapters and motherboards when the parts are not in use. However, antistatic bags lose their effectiveness after a few years. Figure 5.4 shows an antistatic bag with an adapter inside it. **ESD mats** are available to place underneath a computer being repaired, and such a mat might have a snap for connecting an antistatic wrist strap.

FIGURE 5.4 Antistatic bag

If an antistatic wrist strap is not available, you can still reduce the chance of ESD damage. After removing the computer case, stay attached to an unpainted metal computer part such as the power supply. Remove the computer parts one by one, always keeping your elbow (or some other bare part of your arm) touching the power supply. This **self-grounding** method is an effective way of keeping a technician and a computer at the same voltage potential, thus reducing the chance of ESD damage. However, it is not as safe as using an antistatic wrist strap. Also, remove the power cable from the back of the computer because a power supply provides a small amount of power to the motherboard even when the computer is powered off. Always unplug the computer and use an antistatic wrist strap when removing or replacing parts inside a computer!

TECH TIP

Good news about ESD

Electronics manufacturers are designing components that are less susceptible to ESD. However, you should still ground yourself using any means possible. Each zap weakens a component!

Electromagnetic Interference (EMI)

Electromagnetic interference (**EMI**) is noise caused by electrical devices, such as a computer, a pencil sharpener, a motor, a vacuum cleaner, an air conditioner, and fluorescent lighting. The electrical devices around the computer case, including speakers, cause more EMI problems than the computer.

A specific type of electromagnetic interference that negatively affects computers is radio frequency interference (**RFI**). RFI is simply noises that occur in the radio frequency range. If a computer has an intermittent problem, check the surrounding devices for the source of that problem. EMI problems are very hard to track to the source. Any electronic device, including computers and printers, can be a source of EMI or RFI. EMI can also come through power lines. Move the computer to a different wall outlet or to a totally different circuit to determine whether the power outlet is the problem source. EMI can also affect files on a hard drive.

TECH TIP

Replacing empty slot covers

To help with EMI and RFI problems, replace slot covers for expansion slots that are no longer being used. Slot covers are shown in Figure 4.13 (refer to Chapter 4, "Introduction to Configuration"). Slot covers also keep out dust and improve the airflow within the case.

Tools

No chapter on disassembly and reassembly would be complete without mentioning tools. Tools are used in removing/replacing field replaceable units (FRUs), which are parts of the computer or other electronic devices such as the power supply or motherboard.

Many technicians do not go on a repair call with a full tool case. The vast majority of all repairs are completed with the following basic tools that are shown in Figure 5.5:

> Small and medium flat-tipped screwdrivers
> #0, #1, and #2 Phillips screwdrivers
> 1/4- and 3/16-inch hex nut drivers
> Small diagonal cutters
> Needle-nose pliers

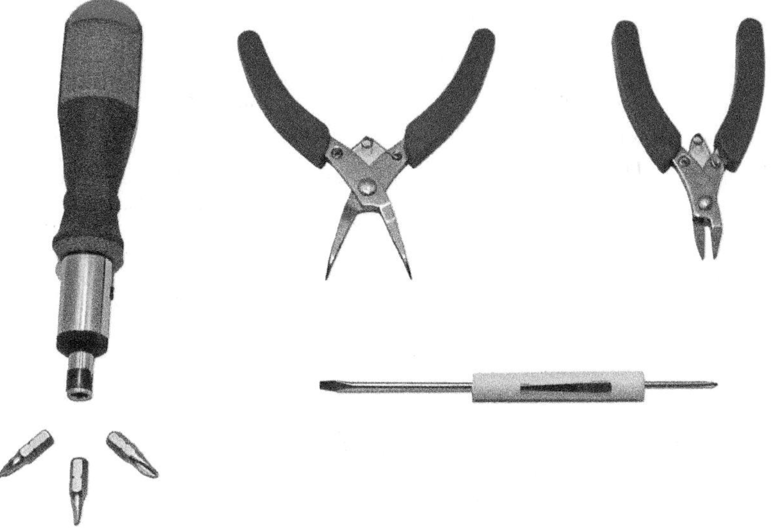

FIGURE 5.5 Basic PC technician tools

Screwdrivers take care of most disassemblies and reassemblies. Sometimes manufacturers place tie wraps on new parts, new cables, or the cables inside the computer case. Diagonal cutters are great for removing these tie wraps without cutting cables or damaging parts. Needle-nose pliers are good for straightening bent pins on cables or connectors, and they are useful for doing a million other things. Small tweaker screwdrivers and needle-nose pliers are indispensable.

TECH TIP

Getting those wayward screws

Magnetic screwdrivers are handy for picking up dropped screws. However, they can affect memory, so avoid using them, if possible. If a screw rolls under the motherboard and cannot be reached, tilt the computer so that the screw rolls out.

Disassembly

Before a technician disassembles a computer, the following disassembly steps should be considered:

> Do not remove the motherboard battery; if you do, the configuration information in CMOS will be lost.
> Use proper grounding procedures to prevent ESD damage.
> Keep paper, a pen, a cell phone, or a digital camera nearby for note taking, diagramming, and photo taking. Even if you have taken apart computers for years, you might find something unique or different inside worth noting.
> Have ample flat and clean workspace.
> When removing adapters, do not stack the adapters on top of one another.
> If possible, place removed adapters inside a special ESD protective bag.
> Handle each adapter, motherboard, or processor on the side edges. Avoid touching the gold contacts on the bottom of adapters. Sweat, oil, and dirt cause problems.
> Remember that hard drives require careful handling. A very small jolt can cause damage to stored data.
> You can remove a power supply but do not disassemble a power supply without proper training and tools.
> Document screw and cable locations. Label them if possible.

The following section describes the steps in disassembling a computer.

Step 1. Remove Power and External Cables

The first step in disassembling a computer is to remove the power cord. A small amount of power is sent to the motherboard even when the computer is powered off so that the computer can be "woken up" in a corporate environment and updates can be applied. Next is removing external cables. Make notes about which cable attaches to each specific port. Figure 5.6 shows the back of the computer where this is done.

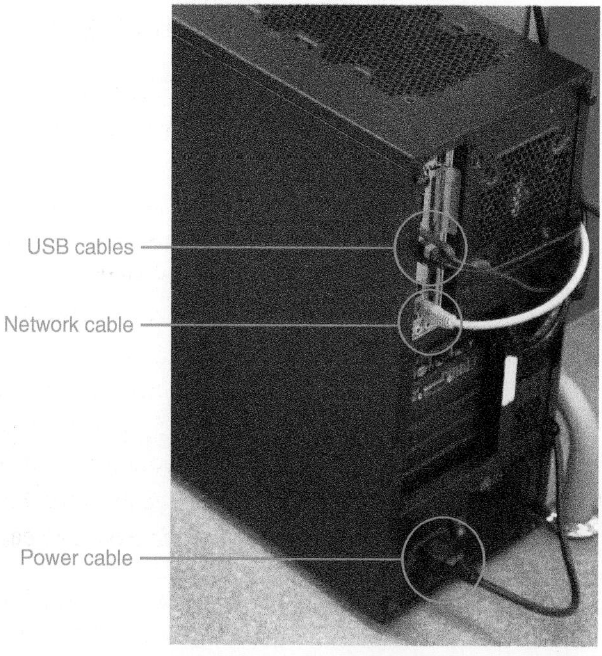

FIGURE 5.6 Removing power and external cables

Step 2. Open the Case

Opening or removing the case is sometimes the hardest part of disassembly. Some manufacturers have tabs or covers over the retaining screws, and others have retention levers or tabs that have to be pressed before the cover slides open or away. For some computers, you must press downward on a tab on top of the computer while simultaneously pressing upward on a tab on the bottom of the computer. Once the tabs are pressed, the cover can be pried open.

Some cases have screws that loosen but do not have to be removed all the way to remove or open the case. For all computer screws, make diagrams and place the screws in an egg carton with each section of the carton labeled with where you got the screws. Remember that to remove or loosen a screw, turn the screwdriver to the left. When possible, refer to the manufacturer's directions when opening a case. Most of the time, you can access inside the computer by simply removing the screws that hold down the side panel, as shown in Figure 5.7.

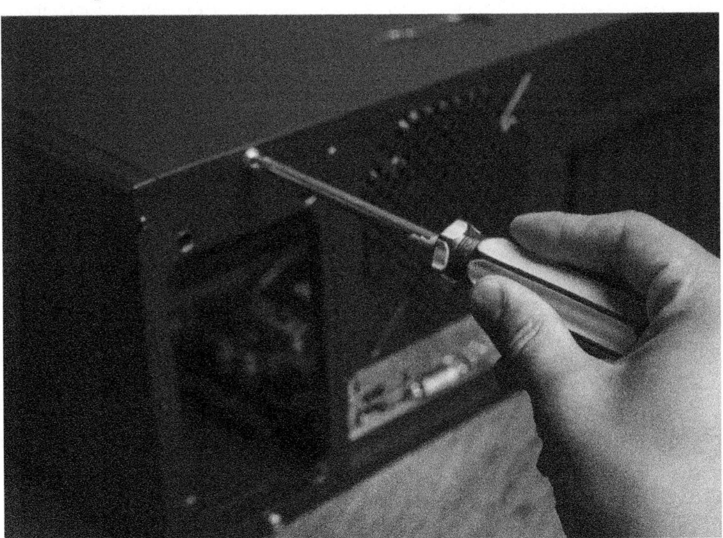

FIGURE 5.7 Removing case screws

Step 3. Remove Internal Cables and Connectors

Internal cables commonly connect from a device to the motherboard, the power supply to a device, the motherboard to the front panel buttons or ports, and/or from a card that occupies an expansion space to a device. Cables can be tricky. Inserting a cable backward into a device or an adapter can damage the device, motherboard, or adapter. Most cables are keyed so the cable inserts only one way into the connector. However, some cables or connectors are *not* keyed.

Some cables have a pull tab or plastic piece used to remove the cable from the connector and/or device. Use this if possible or firmly grip the connector, not the cable. If a connector has a locking tab, release the tab *before* disconnecting the cable to prevent damage to the cable and/or connector.

Be careful with drive cables. Some of the narrow drive cables, such as Serial Advanced Technology Attachment (SATA) cables, are not very sturdy and do not connect as firmly as some of the other computer cables. Also, with this particular cable type, it does not matter which cable end attaches to the device. A 90°-angled version of this cable (see Figure 5.8) might attach to devices in a case that has a limited-space design and might have a release latch.

FIGURE 5.8 SATA cables including 90°-angled cable with a latch on the right

TECH TIP

Snug connections

When connecting cables to a motherboard or internal components, ensure that each cable is connected tightly, evenly, and securely.

Motherboard connectors are usually notched so that the cable inserts only one way; however, not all cables are notched. Some motherboards have pin 1 (or the opposite pin) labeled. Always refer to the motherboard documentation for proper orientation of a cable into a motherboard connector.

Each cable has a certain number of pins, and all cables have a **pin 1**. Pin 1 on a cable connects to pin 1 on a connector. The cable connector usually has an arrow etched into its molding showing the pin 1 connection. Figure 5.9 shows pin 1 on an Internal Drive Electronics (**IDE**) **cable**.

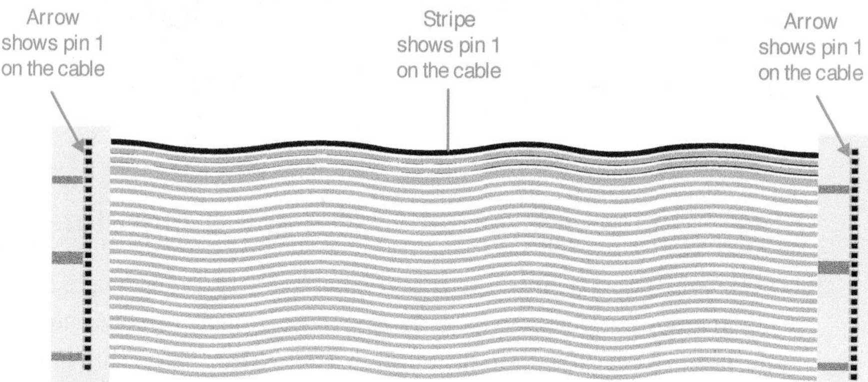
Arrow shows pin 1 on the cable
Stripe shows pin 1 on the cable
Arrow shows pin 1 on the cable

FIGURE 5.9 Pin 1 on a 40-pin IDE PATA ribbon cable

Figure 5.10 shows the motherboard **SATA connectors** used for the cables in Figure 5.8 that connect to hard drives and/or optical drives. Figure 5.11 shows two other motherboard connectors: The top connector is an IDE connector for older Parallel ATA (PATA) drives, and the bottom one is for motherboard power. Notice that the top connector has a notch (opening) to prevent the cable from being installed incorrectly. Also notice that the bottom connector has certain connector openings that are different from the square ones to prevent inserting the cable in the wrong direction.

FIGURE 5.10 Motherboard SATA drive connectors

FIGURE 5.11 Two motherboard connectors (older IDE on top and motherboard power on bottom)

Specific cables connect from the motherboard **front panel connectors** to lights, ports, or buttons on the front panel. These include the power button, a reset button, USB ports, a microphone port, a headphone port, speakers, fans, the drive activity light, and the power light, to name a few. Be very careful when removing and reinstalling these cables. Usually, each one of them has a connector that must attach to the appropriate motherboard pins. Be sure to check all ports and buttons after you have reconnected these cables. Refer to the motherboard documentation if your diagramming, photos, or notes are incomplete. Figure 5.12 shows the motherboard pins and the cables.

FIGURE 5.12 Motherboard front panel cables

> **TECH TIP**
>
> **Carefully connecting front panel cables**
>
> Ensure that you connect the front panel cables to the appropriate pins and in the correct direction. Some manufacturers label the cables. As shown in Figure 5.12, once you have one oriented correctly (such as the words appearing toward the outside of the motherboard), the others are commonly oriented in the same direction. Also notice in this figure that all the white cables orient in the same direction.

The motherboard also contains pins that are used to connect cables such as those that go to the CPU or case fans. Look back at Figure 3.24 (refer to Chapter 3, "On the Motherboard") to see how fans connect to pins on the motherboard.

Step 4. Remove Adapters

Adapters commonly have retaining screws or a bar that keeps the adapters firmly in the case. (Refer to Figure 4.13 in Chapter 4 for an illustration of these two methods.) Use the edges of the adapter to pull it upward out of the expansion slot. Do not touch the contacts on the bottom of the adapter. Never pile adapters on top of one another. If an adapter will not be reinstalled, insert an expansion slot blank cover in the empty expansion slot so proper airflow will be maintained within the case. Figure 5.13 shows an adapter being removed.

FIGURE 5.13 Adapter removal

Step 5. Remove Storage Devices

Mechanical hard drives must be handled with care when disassembling a computer. Inside traditional hard drives are hard platters with tiny read/write heads located just millimeters above the platters. If dropped, the read/write heads might touch the platter, causing damage to the platter and/or the read/write heads. Today's drives have self-parking heads that pull the heads away to a safe area when the computer is powered off or in a power-saving mode. Even with self-parking heads, improper handling can cause damage to the hard drive.

A solid-state drive (SSD) does not contain fragile heads. However, these drives are susceptible to ESD. Use proper antistatic handling procedures when removing/installing them. Store a solid-state drive in an antistatic bag when not in use.

A drive slides into a drive bay. Some cases require the drive to have rails that attach to the side of the drive. Other cases require that the drive be screwed into the hard drive bay. Figure 5.14 shows a hard drive being removed. You can see that this particular case requires screws to secure drives inserted into the drive bays.

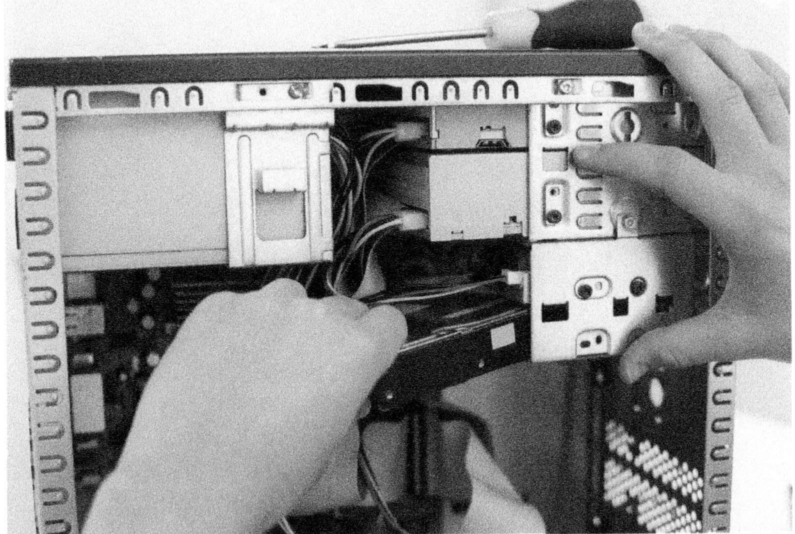

FIGURE 5.14 Removing a hard drive

Figure 5.15 shows a hard drive that has a guide rail attached and a different set of guide rails below the drive. When replacing a drive, the drive rails would have to be removed from the old drive and attached to the replacement drive. When installing a new drive, drive rails might have to be purchased.

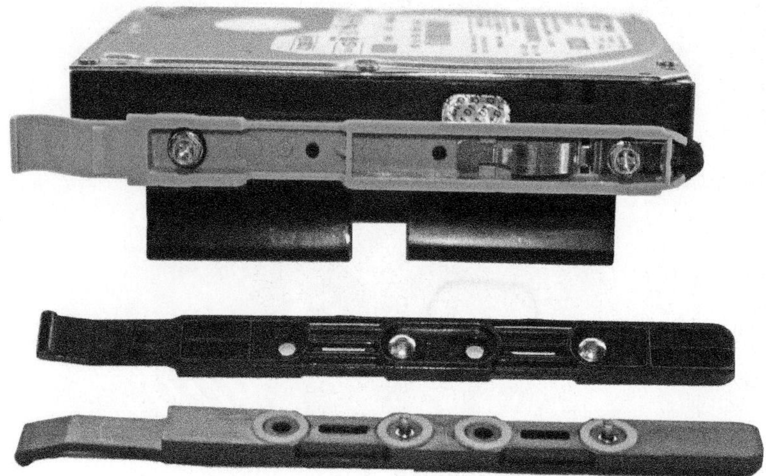

FIGURE 5.15 Hard drive rails

Step 6. Remove the Motherboard

Chapter 3 covers motherboard replacement extensively, so here we discuss issues related to building a computer from scratch or disassembling a computer. Some cases include a standard I/O panel shield that might need to be removed to install the I/O shield that comes with some motherboards. The **I/O shield** is a part that allows for optimum airflow and grounding for the motherboard ports. The I/O shield helps ensure that the motherboard is installed correctly and properly aligned with the case. Figure 5.16 shows a motherboard I/O shield.

FIGURE 5.16 Motherboard I/O shield

Some computer cases have plastic or metal (commonly brass) **standoffs** that allow the motherboard to be screwed into the case without the motherboard solder joints touching and grounding to the computer case, causing the motherboard not to work. Some standoffs are plastic, and they slide into slots on the computer case. Do not remove these types of standoffs; just leave them attached and slide the motherboard out of the slots. One type of metal standoff screws into the case; this standoff has a threaded side that the motherboard sits on and a screw that attaches the motherboard to the standoff, as shown in Figure 5.17.

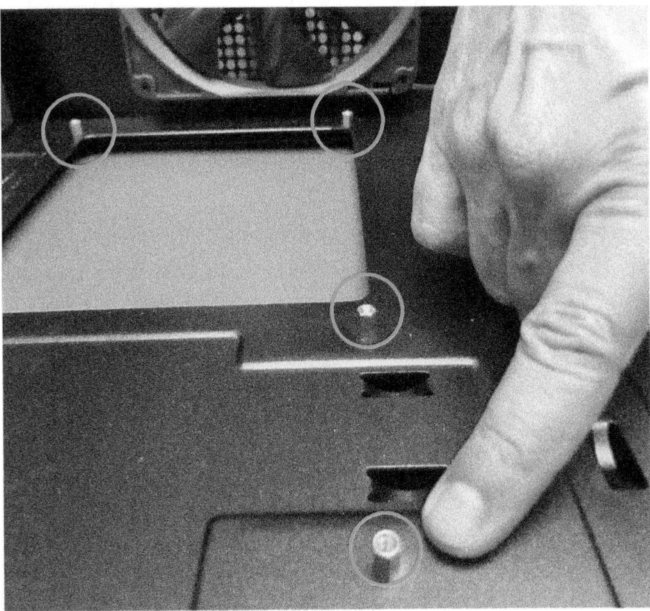

FIGURE 5.17 Motherboard standoff

Some motherboards have not only screws that attach them to the metal standoffs but also one or more retaining clips. A retaining clip might need to be pressed down, lifted up, or bent upward in order to slide the motherboard out of the case. The case might contain one or more notches, and the motherboard might have to be slid in a particular direction (usually in the direction going away from the back I/O ports) before being lifted from the case.

All-in-One Computers

The same disassembly concepts apply to all-in-one computers as to desktop computers regarding cabling, storage device removal, RAM removal, motherboard removal, and power. The difference is the space in which the devices are installed: An all-in-one computer has everything installed on the back of the display, as shown in Figure 5.18.

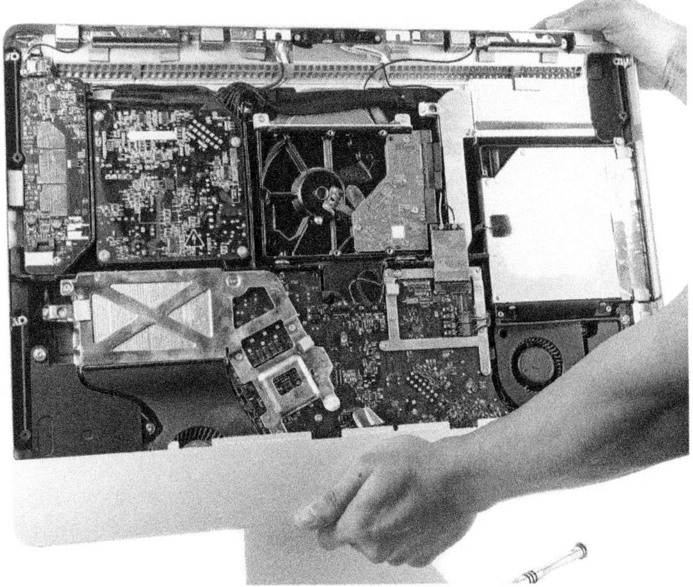

FIGURE 5.18 All-in-one computer parts

Reassembly

Reassembling a computer is easy if the technician is careful and properly documents the disassembly. Simple tasks such as inserting the optical drive in the correct drive bay become confusing after many parts have been removed. Writing reminders or taking photos takes less time than having to troubleshoot a computer because of poor reassembly. A technician should reinsert all components into their proper places, being careful to replace all screws and parts and to install missing slot covers, if possible.

When reinstalling a motherboard, reverse the procedure used during disassembly. Ensure that the motherboard is securely seated into the case and that all retaining clips and/or screws are replaced. Visual inspection can also help. Ensure that the ports extend fully from the case through the I/O shield. As a final step, ensure that the drives and cover are aligned properly when the case is reinstalled.

Cables and connectors are the most common sources of reassembly problems once the motherboard is installed. Ensure that cables are fully attached to devices and the same motherboard connector. Ensure that power cables are securely attached.

Preventive Maintenance

In the course of daily usage, computers get dirty (see Figure 5.19), especially inside. Dust accumulates, thus creating insulation and increasing the amount of heat generated. Additional heat can cause electronic components to overheat and fail. It can also cause the processor to consistently run at a lower speed. Dust is an enemy of computers.

FIGURE 5.19 Dust inside a compartment

Preventive maintenance includes procedures performed to prolong the life of a computer. A computer in a normal working environment should be cleaned at least once a year. Typical preventive measures include vacuuming the computer and cleaning the optical drive laser, keyboard keys, printer, and display screen. Be sure to power down a computer and remove the power cord, remove the battery and AC adapter for a laptop or other mobile device, and allow a laser printer to cool before accessing internal parts. Preventive measures for many individual devices are described in their respective chapters. For example, the steps detailing how to clean optical discs are included in Chapter 8, "Video and Multimedia Devices." This section gives an overview of a preventive maintenance program and some general tips about cleaning solvents.

TECH TIP

Carefully cleaning LCD monitors and laptop displays

Use one of the following to clean LCD monitors and laptop displays: (1) wipes specifically designed for LCDs or (2) a soft lint-free cloth dampened with either water or a mixture of isopropyl alcohol and water. Never put liquid directly on the display and ensure that the display is dry before closing the laptop.

When performing preventive maintenance, power on the computer to be certain it operates. Perform an audio and visual inspection of the computer as it boots. Ensure that the room temperature is appropriate for the device. Electronic equipment such as PCs and mobile devices is designed to operate at room temperature (around 73°F [23°C]). Anything above 80°F (27°C) should warrant additional cooling methods for the device.

It is a terrible feeling to perform preventive maintenance on a computer but then power it on and find that it does not work. You will wonder if the cleaning you performed caused the problem or if the computer had a problem before the preventive maintenance.

Manufacturers sometimes have a preventive **maintenance kit** for service calls. The kit normally includes the components listed and described in Table 5.1.

TABLE 5.1 Preventive maintenance items

Item	Description
Portable vacuum	Used to suck dirt from inside a computer. Be sure to use nonmetallic attachments. With a vacuum cleaner that has the ability to blow air, vacuum first and then set the vacuum cleaner to blow to get dust out of hard-to-reach places. Hold fan blades in place while vacuuming.
Toner vacuum	Used to clean computers and laser printers. Special vacuum bags are used to prevent the toner from melting and potentially damaging the vacuum cleaner.
Special vacuum bags	Used for laser printers so that the toner does not melt on the vacuum motor.
Compressed air	Used to remove dust in hard-to-reach places (preferably after vacuuming).
Urethane swabs	Used to clean between keys on a keyboard. If a key is sticking, disconnect the keyboard before spraying or using contact cleaner on it.
Monitor wipes	Used on the front of the display. Wipes with an antistatic solution work best.
Lint-free cloths	Used to clean laptop touchpads and other components. Dampen the cloth to remove residual finger oil.
General-purpose cloths	Used to clean the outside of the case and to clean the desktop areas under and around a computer.
General-purpose cleanser	Used with soft lint-free cloths or lint-free swabs. Never spray or pour liquid on any computer part.
Denatured alcohol	Used on rubber rollers, such as those inside printers.
Antistatic brush	Used to brush dirt from hard-to-reach places.

Electronics: Terminology

Voltage, current, power, and resistance are terms commonly used in the computer industry. **Voltage**, which is a measure of the pressure pushing electrons through a circuit, is measured in **volts** and shown as a value followed by a capital V. A power supply's output is measured in volts. Power supplies typically put out +3.3 volts, +5 volts, +12 volts, and –12 volts. You will commonly see these output voltages shown in power supply documentation as +3.3V, +5V, or +12V. Another designation is +5VSB. This is for the computer's standby power, which is always provided, even when the computer is powered off. This supplied voltage is why you have to unplug a computer when working inside it.

TECH TIP

Polarity is important only when measuring DC voltage

When a technician measures the voltage coming out of a power supply, the black meter lead (which is negative) connects to the black wire from the power supply (which is ground). The red meter lead connects to either the +5 or +12 volt wires from the power supply.

The term *volts* is also used to describe voltage from a wall outlet. Wall outlet voltage is normally 120VAC (120 volts AC). A multimeter is a tool used to take voltage readings such as from power supply connectors and wall outlets. Figure 5.22 shows a multimeter being used to take a DC voltage reading on the power connectors coming from a power supply. When the meter leads are inserted correctly, the voltage level shown is of the correct polarity. A mutlimeter can also be used to measure current (amps) and resistance (ohms), which are discussed next.

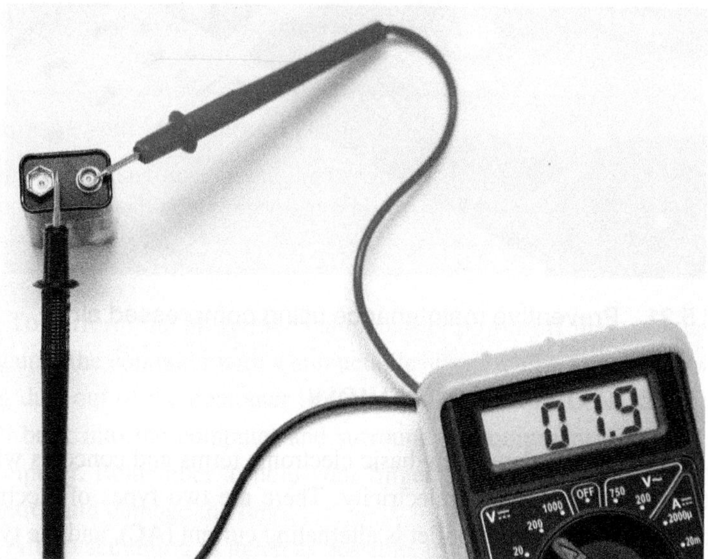

FIGURE 5.22 DC voltage reading

The reading on the meter could be the opposite of what it should be if the meter's leads are reversed. Polarity is not important when measuring AC. Figure 5.23 shows rules to observe when working with meters.

Power supplies, flat panel displays, and mobile device displays also contain high voltage levels. 120 volts AC is present inside the power supply of a desktop computer. Power supplies and monitors have capacitors inside them. A capacitor is a component that holds a charge even after the computer is turned off.

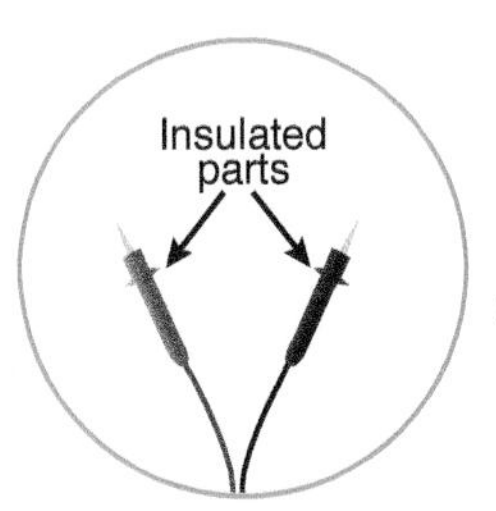

Meter probes

1. Select AC or DC on the meter (some meters automatically select AC or DC).

   VAC or ACV or ~ or Ṽ

   VDC or DCV or — or ⎓ or V̄

2. Select the appropriate voltage range (0-10V, 0-100V, etc). The meter can be damaged if you measure a high voltage in a low range (but not the reverse). Use the highest range for unknown voltages.

3. Touch only the insulated parts of the meter probes.

FIGURE 5.23 Meter rules

Current is measured in **amps** (amperes), which is the number of electrons going through a circuit every second. In a water pipe analogy, voltage is the amount of pressure applied to force the water through the pipe, and current is the amount of water flowing. Every device needs a certain amount of current to operate. A power supply is rated for the amount of total current (in amps) it can supply at each voltage level. For example, a power supply could be rated at 20 amps for the 5 volt level and 8 amps for the 12 volt level.

Power is measured in **watts**, which is a measurement of how much work is being done. It is determined by multiplying volts by amps. Power supplies are described as providing a maximum number of watts or having a specific wattage rating. It is the sum of all outputs (for example, [5 volts × 20 amps] + [12V × 8 amps] = 100 watts + 96 watts = 196 watts).

TECH TIP

Current is what kills people when an electrical shock is received

Voltage determines how much current flows through the body. A high-current and low-voltage situation is the most dangerous.

Resistance is measured in **ohms**, which is the amount of opposition to current in an electronic circuit. The resistance range on a meter can be used to check continuity or check whether a fuse is good. A **continuity** check is used to determine whether a wire has a break in it. A conductor (wire) in a cable or a good fuse will have very low resistance to electricity (close to 0 ohms). A broken wire or a bad fuse will have a very high resistance (millions of ohms, sometimes shown as infinite ohms, or OL). For example, a cable is normally made up of several wires that go from one connector to another. If you measure the continuity from one end of a wire to the other, it should show no resistance. If the wire has a break in it, the meter shows infinite resistance. Figure 5.24 shows examples of a good wire reading and a broken wire reading.

TECH TIP

Always unplug a computer before working inside it

The power supply provides power to the motherboard, even if the computer is powered off. Leaving the power cord attached can cause damage when replacing components such as the processor or RAM.

Digital meters have different ways of displaying infinity. Always refer to the meter manual. When checking continuity, the meter is placed on the ohms setting, as shown in Figure 5.24. The ohms setting is usually illustrated by an omega symbol (Ω).

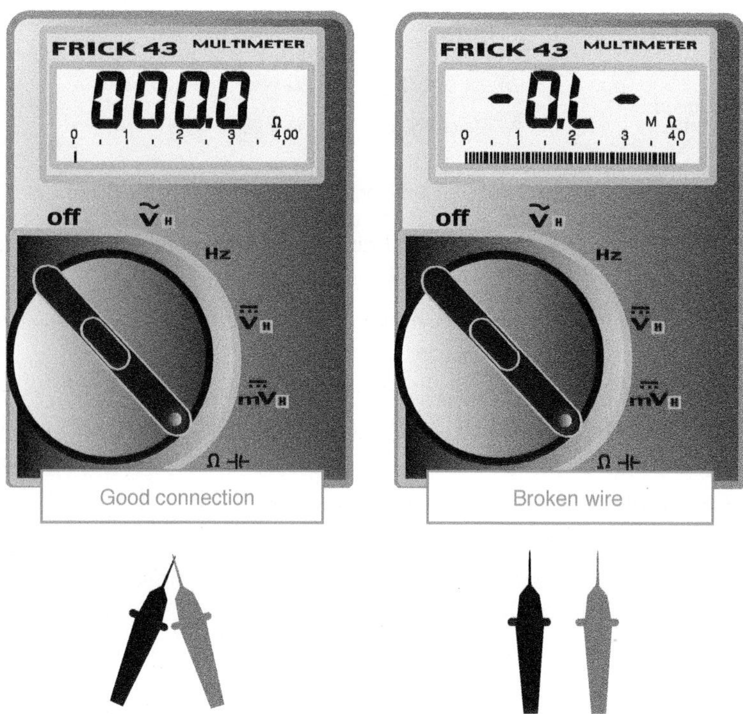

FIGURE 5.24 Sample resistance meter readings

> **TECH TIP**
>
> **Dealing with small connections and a meter**
>
> With connectors that have small pin connections, use a thin meter probe or insert a thin wire, such as a paper clip, into the hole and touch the meter to the wire to take your reading.

Polarity is not important when performing a continuity check. Either meter lead (red or black) can be placed at either end of the wire. However, you do need a pin-out diagram (wiring list) for the cable before you can check continuity because pin 1 at one end could connect to a different pin number at the other end.

A technician needs to be familiar with basic electronics terms and checks. Table 5.2 consolidates this information.

TABLE 5.2 Basic electronics terms

Term	Value	Usage
Voltage	Volts	Voltage is relevant when checking AC voltage from a wall outlet (typically 120VAC) and when checking the DC output voltage from a power supply (typically ±12, +3.3, and ± 5VDC).
Current	Amps (amperes)	Each device needs a certain amount of current to operate. A power supply is rated for total current in amps for each voltage level (such as 24 amps for 5-volt power and 50 amps for 12-volt power).
Resistance	Ohms	Resistance is the amount of opposition to electric current. Resistance measurements are used to check continuity on cables and fuses. A cable that shows little or no resistance has no breaks in it. A good fuse shows no resistance. If a cable has a break in it or if a fuse is bad, the resistance is infinite.
Wattage (power)	Watts	Watts is a measure of power and is derived by multiplying amps by volts. Power supply output is measured in watts.

Power Supply Overview

A power supply is an essential component within a computer; no internal computer component/device works without it. A power supply converts AC to DC, distributes lower-voltage DC power (**3.3V**, **5V**, and **12V** output voltage) to components throughout the computer, and provides cooling through the use of a fan located inside the power supply. The AC voltage a power supply accepts is normally either 100 to 120 volts or 200 to 240 volts. Note that the A+ certification exam objectives list this as **110V vs. 220V input voltage**. Some dual-voltage power supplies can accept either. This type of power supply might have a selector switch on the back or may be able to automatically detect the input voltage level.

Power supplies can also be auto-switching. An auto-switching power supply monitors the incoming voltage from the wall outlet and automatically switches itself accordingly. Auto-switching power supplies accept voltages from 100 to 240VAC at 50 to 60 Hz. These power supplies are popular in mobile devices and are great for international travel.

TECH TIP

Powering on a power supply without anything attached could damage the power supply

Do not power on a power supply without connecting to the motherboard and possibly a device such as an optical drive or a hard drive. An ATX power supply usually requires a motherboard connection at a minimum.

Power Supply Form Factors

Just as motherboards come in different shapes and sizes, so do power supplies. Today's power supply form factors are ATX, ATX12V, and micro-ATX. The ATX power supply form factor was the first type to allow a small amount of voltage to be provided to the motherboard so that both hardware and software could be used to "wake up" the device and/or reduce the voltage to conserve power. This was known as a soft switch.

The micro-ATX power supply form factor is a smaller version than a full-sized ATX power supply to fit in smaller cases. Other form factors include LFX12V (low profile), SFX12V (small form factor), EPS12V (used with server motherboards), CFX12V (compact form factor), SFX12V (small form factor), TFX12V (thin form factor), WTX12V (workstation form factor for high-end workstations and select servers), and FlexATX (for smaller systems).

Intel, AMD, and video card manufacturers certify specific power supplies that work with their processors and video cards. A computer manufacturer can also have a proprietary power supply form factor that is not compatible with different computer models or other vendors' machines. Laptop power supplies are commonly proprietary.

Power Supply Connectors

Table 5.3 lists the possible ATX power supply connectors, and Figure 5.25 shows them.

TABLE 5.3 ATX power supply connectors

Connector	Notes	Voltage(s)
24-pin main power	Main ATX power connector to the motherboard	+3.3, +5, +12, -12
15-pin SATA power	Internal SATA power connector	+3.3, +5, +12
8-pin 12V	12V for CPU used with an ATX12V v1 power supply	+12

Connector	Notes	Voltage(s)
8-pin PCIe	PCIe video; connects to a PCIe video adapter (Note that some connectors are 6+2-pin, meaning they accept either the 6- or 8-pin cable.)	+12
6-pin PCIe	PCIe video; connects to PCIe video adapter	+12
6-pin	Sometimes labeled AUX; connects to the motherboard if it has a connector	+3.3, +5
4-pin **Molex**	Connects to peripheral devices such as hard drives and CD/DVD drives	+5, +12
4-pin Berg	Connects to peripheral devices such as a floppy drive	+5, +12
4-pin 12V	Sometimes labeled AUX or 12V; connects to the motherboard for the CPU	+12
3-pin	Used to monitor fan speed	N/A

TECH TIP

The motherboard, case, and power supply must be size compatible

The motherboard and case form factor and the power supply form factor must fit in the case and must work together. For optimum performance, research what connectors and form factors are supported by both components.

FIGURE 5.25 ATX power supply connectors

Figure 5.26 illustrates the ATX **24-pin motherboard connector** standards. Older power supplies had a 20-pin motherboard connector that you could plug straight into the 24-pin motherboard socket (leaving pins 11, 12, 23, and 24 empty), or you could buy a **20-pin to 24-pin motherboard adapter**. Notice in Figure 5.26 that the power cable is only one connector, and the cable inserts into the connector one way only. Also notice that a power good signal (labeled PWR_OK in Figure 5.26) goes to the motherboard. When the computer is turned on, part of POST is to allow the power supply to run a test on each of the voltage levels. The voltage levels must be correct before any other devices are tested and allowed to initialize. If the power is okay, a power good signal is sent to the motherboard. If the power good signal is not sent from the power supply, a timer chip on the motherboard resets the CPU. Once a power good signal is sent, the CPU begins executing software from the BIOS/UEFI. Figure 5.26 also shows the +5VSB connection to provide standby power for features such as Wake on LAN or Wake on Ring (covered later in this chapter).

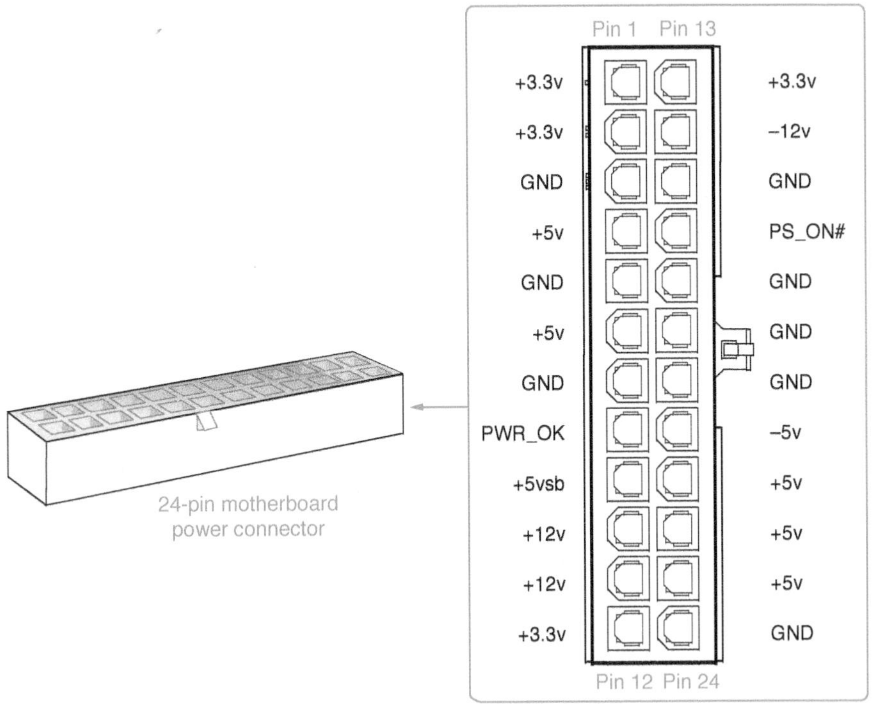

FIGURE 5.26 ATX 24-pin motherboard connectivity

The quantity and type of connectors available on a power supply depend on the power supply manufacturer. If a video card needs a PCIe connector and two Molex power connectors are free, a dual Molex-to-PCIe converter can be purchased. If a SATA device needs a power connection and only a Molex cable is free, a Molex-to-SATA converter is available. Figure 5.27 shows a dual Molex-to-PCIe converter on the left and a Molex-to-SATA converter on the right.

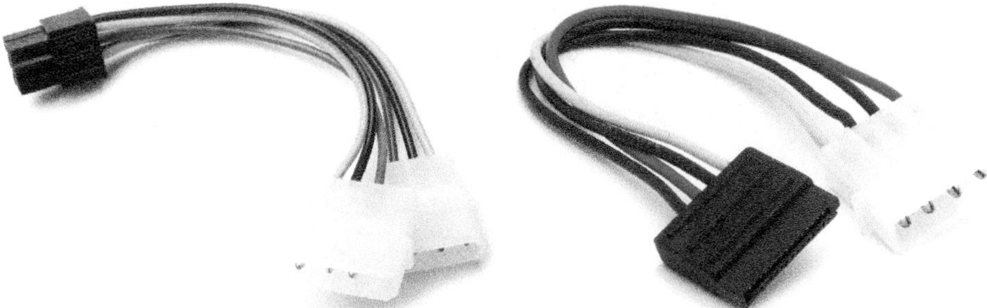

FIGURE 5.27 Dual Molex-to-PCIe and Molex-to-SATA converters

Power supply connectors can connect to any device; there is not a specific connector for the hard drive, the optical drive, and so on. If there are not enough connectors from the power supply for the number of devices installed in a computer, a Y power connector can be purchased at a computer or electronics store.

Purposes of a Power Supply

The power from a wall outlet is high-voltage AC. The type of power computers need is low-voltage DC. All computer parts (the electronic chips on the motherboard and adapters, the electronics on the drives, and the motors in the hard drive and optical drive) need DC power to operate. Power supplies in general come in two types: linear and switching. Computers use switching power supplies. The main functions of a power supply include the following:

- Convert AC to DC
- Provide DC voltage to the motherboard, adapters, and peripheral devices
- Provide cooling and facilitate airflow through the case

TECH TIP

Checking the input voltage selector

Some power supplies and laptops have input voltage selectors; others have the ability to accept input from 100 to 240 volts for use in various countries (dual-voltage). Ensure that a power supply accepts or is set to the proper input voltage.

Another purpose of a power supply is to distribute proper DC voltage(s) to each component. Several cables with connectors come out of the power supply. With ATX motherboards, there is only a 24-pin connector used to connect power to the motherboard. The power connector inserts only one way into the motherboard connector. Figure 5.28 shows an ATX connector being inserted into a motherboard.

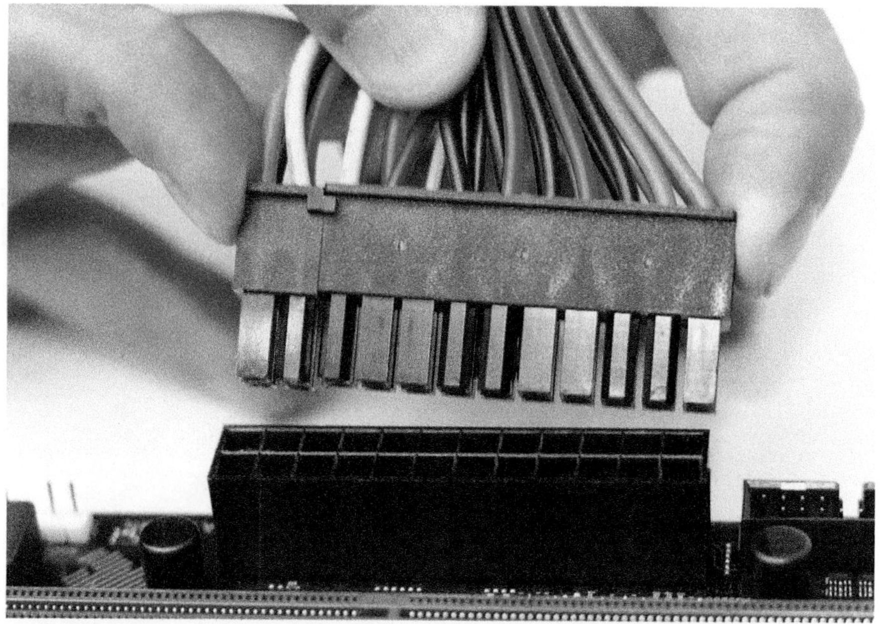

FIGURE 5.28 Installing an ATX power connector on a motherboard

Another purpose of a power supply is to provide cooling for the computer. The power supply's fan circulates air throughout the computer. Most computer cases have air vents on one side, on both sides, or in the rear. The ATX-style power supply blows air inside the case instead of out the back; with this reverse-flow cooling method, the air blows over the processor and memory to keep them cool. This type of power supply keeps the inside of the computer cleaner than older styles.

TECH TIP

Don't block air vents

Whether a computer is a desktop model, a tower model, or a desktop model mounted in a stand on the floor, ensure that nothing blocks the air vents in the computer case.

Because heat sinks generate a lot of heat, it is important to have the proper amount of airflow and in the right direction. Additional fans can be installed to provide additional cooling for a PC. Figure 5.29 shows extra cooling fans installed as well as LED lights that are popular in cases today.

FIGURE 5.29 Computer case auxiliary fan with LED lighting

TECH TIP

Airflow and ventilation

Airflow should be through the computer and over the motherboard to provide cooling for the motherboard components.

Cases have different numbers of and locations of mounting spots for the case fan(s). Figure 5.30 shows two possible installation sites for an additional fan.

TECH TIP

Being careful when installing an auxiliary fan

Place a fan so the outflow of air moves in the same direction as the flow of air generated by the power supply. If an auxiliary fan is installed inside a case in the wrong location, the auxiliary airflow could work against the power supply airflow, reducing the cooling effect.

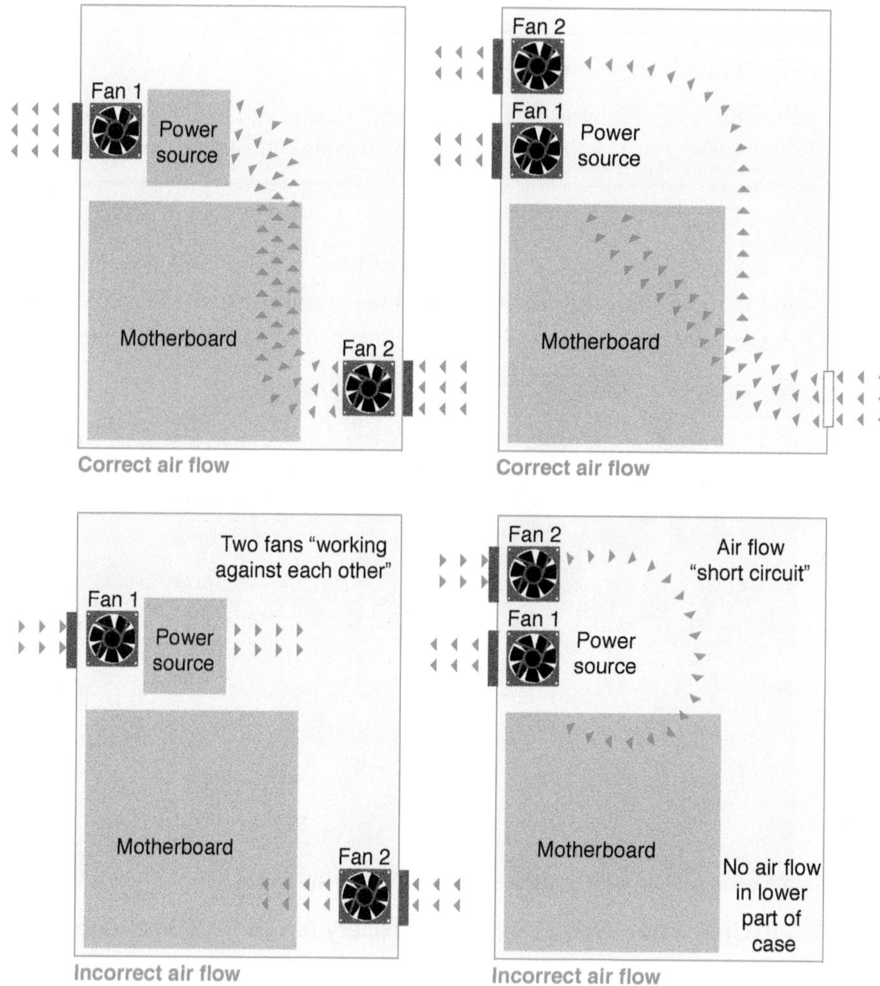

FIGURE 5.30 Placement of auxiliary fans

Advanced Configuration and Power Interface (ACPI)

Advanced Configuration and Power Interface (**ACPI**) gives the BIOS/UEFI and operating system control over various devices' power and modes of operation. ACPI has various operating states, as shown in Table 5.4.

TABLE 5.4 ACPI operating states

Global system state	Sleep state	Description
G0 Working	S0	The computer is fully functional. Software, such as the autosave function used with Microsoft products, can be optimized for performance or to reduce battery usage.
G1 Sleeping		Requires less power than the G0 state and has multiple sleep states: S1, S2, S3, and S4.
	S1	CPU is still powered, and unused devices are powered down. RAM is still being refreshed. Hard drives are not running.
	S2	CPU is not powered. RAM is still being refreshed. System is restored instantly upon user intervention.

Global system state	Sleep state	Description
	S3	Power supply output is reduced. RAM is still being refreshed. Some information in RAM is restored to the CPU and the cache.
	S4	Lowest-power sleep mode, which takes the longest to come up. Information in RAM is saved to nonvolatile memory such as a hard drive or flash media. Some manufacturers call this the hibernate state.
G2 Soft off	S5	Power consumption is almost zero. Requires the operating system to reboot. No information is saved anywhere.
G3 Mechanical off		Also called off. This is the only state in which the computer can be disassembled. You must power on the computer to use it again.

ACPI allows apps to work with the operating system to manage power, such as when an application is set to automatically save a document but might not do so until the hard drive is being used for something else in order to conserve power in a laptop. In the Windows environment, the sleep mode (also known as suspend mode) uses one of the G1 sleeping ACPI states to allow the device to be awakened to continue working. The hibernate mode uses the G1 S4 mode and takes the longest to bring a device back to a working state.

TECH TIP

Which power option to select: standby or hibernate?

Most people who want to quickly re-access a device would select the standby option. However, the hibernate mode saves more energy.

Two common BIOS/UEFI and adapter features that take advantage of ACPI are Wake on LAN and Wake on Ring. The **Wake on LAN** feature allows a network administrator to control the power to a workstation remotely and directs the computer to come out of sleep mode. Software applications can also use the Wake on LAN feature to perform updates, upgrades, and maintenance tasks. The feature can also be used to bring up computers immediately before the business day starts. Wake on LAN can be used with web or network cameras to start recording when motion is detected or to bring up a network printer so that it can be used when needed.

Wake on Ring allows a computer to come out of sleep mode when the telephone line has an incoming call. It lets the computer receive phone calls, faxes, and emails when the user is not present.

TECH TIP

Why leave computers on at the office?

In Windows, when a computer is shut down, it is put in soft off, or S5, state. Wake on LAN is not officially supported from this state, and for this reason, corporate environments request that users leave their computers turned on but logged off on specific days or every day.

Replacing or Upgrading a Power Supply

Power supplies are rated in watts. Today's computers have power supplies with a **wattage rating** ranging from 250 to 500 watts, although powerful computers, such as network servers or higher-end gaming systems, can have power supplies rated 600 watts or higher. Internal and external devices powered by a particular type of port, such as USB, are affected by the number of amps available from the +5 and +12V DC power supply output and the total amount of wattage available.

Each device inside a computer uses a certain amount of power, and the power supply must provide enough power to run all the devices. The power each device or adapter requires is usually defined in the documentation for the device or adapter or on the manufacturer's website. The computer uses the wattage needed, not the total capacity of a power supply.

TECH TIP

Watching the wattage

Many manufacturers overstate the wattage. The wattage advertised is *not* the wattage available at higher temperatures, such as when mounted inside a computer. Research a model before purchasing.

Some power supplies are listed as being dual or triple (or tri) rail. A **dual-rail power supply** has two +12V output lines that are monitored for an over-current condition. A triple-rail power supply simply has three +12V output lines monitored. Keep in mind that most manufacturers do not have two or more independent 12V sources; they all derive from the same 12V source but have independent output lines. Figure 5.31 shows how the +12V rails might be used.

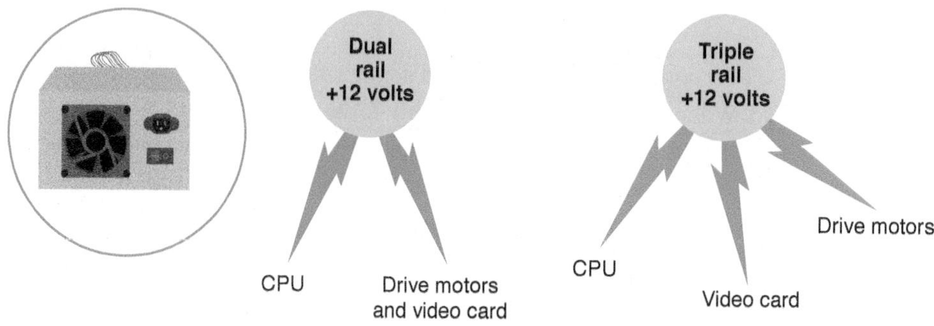

FIGURE 5.31 12V rails

Some people are interested in exactly how much power their system is consuming. Every device in a computer consumes power, and each device may use one or more different voltage levels (for example, +5V, –5V, +12V, –12V, and +3.3V). A power supply has a maximum amperage for each voltage level (for example, 30 amps at +5 volts and 41 amps at +12V). To determine the maximum power being used, in watts, multiply the amps by the volts. If you add all the maximum power levels, the amount will be greater than the power supply's rating. This means that you cannot use the maximum power at every single voltage level; however, because –5V and –12V are not used very often, normally this is not a problem.

Number of Devices/Types of Devices to Be Powered

To determine the power being consumed, you must research every device to determine how much current it uses at a specific voltage level. Power calculators are available on the internet to help with this task. It is important to have a power supply powerful enough for the number of devices and types of devices installed in the computer. Table 5.5 lists sample computer component power requirements.

TABLE 5.5 Sample computer component power requirements

Component	Power consumption
Motherboard (without processor)	5W to 150W
Processor	10W to 140W
PATA IDE hard drive	3W to 30W
SATA hard drive	2W to 15W
Optical drive	10W to 30W
Nonvideo adapter	4W to 25W
AGP video adapter	20W to 50W
PCIe video card with one power connector	50W to 150W
PCIe video card with two power connectors	100W to 300W
Extra fan	3W
RAM module	15W

Choosing a Power Supply

When choosing a power supply, the first things to consider are size and form factor because the power supply has to fit in the case. Different physical sizes of power supplies are available, and some computers (especially servers or network equipment) have a **redundant power supply** that can be used if one power supply fails. The second thing to consider is wattage: You should buy a power supply that has the same or more wattage than the original power supply. Finally, do not forget to ensure that the on/off switch on the new power supply is in a location that fits in the computer case.

TECH TIP

All power supplies are not created equal

A technician needs to replace a power supply with one that provides an equal or greater amount of power. Search the internet for power supply reviews. A general rule of thumb is that if two power supplies are equal in wattage, the heavier one is better because it uses a bigger transformer, bigger heat sinks, and higher-quality components.

The 80 PLUS is a power supply efficiency rating system that has been incorporated into ENERGY STAR specifications. Efficiency involves converting more AC to DC. The rating system consists of six levels of efficiency with 80 PLUS Titanium being the highest. Each level must provide a particular level of efficiency at a specific amount of load (number of components being used simultaneously that require power).

Just because a power supply is not certified as 80 PLUS does not mean that it is not an energy-efficient power supply, but the level does give you an idea of the difference between power supplies. When choosing a power supply, the most important things to consider are as follows:

> Size and form factor
> Wattage
> Number and type of connectors
> Energy efficiency
> Number of 12V rails monitored for an over-current condition

Some people like extra features such as colored lights inside the power supply, power supply fan, and/or ports. A **modular power supply** comes with detachable cables (see Figure 5.32) so that cables that are not used are simply not attached to the power supply to aid in cable management.

FIGURE 5.32 Modular power supply with detachable cable ports

TECH TIP

Power values for energy-efficient monitors

Always keep the screen saver timeout value shorter than the power saver timeout value, especially with green (energy-efficient) monitors!

Power Protection

Power supplies have built-in protection against adverse power conditions. However, the best protection for a computer is to unplug it during a power outage or thunderstorm. Surge protectors and uninterruptible power supplies (UPSs) are commonly used to protect against adverse power conditions. A line conditioner can also be used. Each device has a specific purpose and guards against certain conditions. A technician must be familiar with each device in order to make recommendations for customers. Figure 5.33 shows a surge protector, and Chapter 19, "Operational Procedures," covers these devices in more detail.

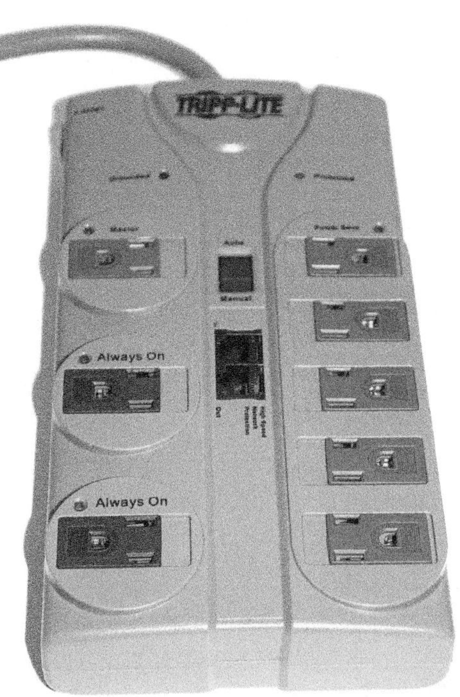

FIGURE 5.33 Tripp Lite surge protector

Symptoms of Power Supply Problems

The power supply is sometimes a source of unusual problems. The effects of the problems can range from those not noticed by the user to those that shut down the system. The following is a list of symptoms of power supply problems:

- The power light is off and/or the device won't turn on (**no power or black screen**)
- The power supply fan does not turn when the computer is powered on.
- The computer sounds a continuous beep. (This could also be a bad motherboard or a stuck key on the keyboard.)
- When the computer powers on, it does not beep at all. (This could also be a bad motherboard.)
- When the computer powers on, it sounds repeating short beeps. (This could also be a bad motherboard.)
- During POST, a 02*X* or parity POST error code appears (where *X* is any number); one of the POST checks is a power good signal from the power supply, and a 021, 022, … error message indicates that the power supply did not pass the POST.
- The **computer reboots,** powers down without warning, has **intermittent shutdowns**, or reboots continuously.
- The power supply fan is noisy (emits a loud or **grinding noise**).
- The power supply is too hot to touch.
- The computer emits a **burning smell**, emits **smoke**, or is **overheating.**
- The power supply fan spins, but no power goes to other devices.
- The monitor has a power light, but nothing appears on the monitor, and no PC power light illuminates.

Checking Power Supply Voltages

Refer to Figure 5.26 and notice how +3.3V, +5V, –5V, +12V, and –12V are output and supplied to the motherboard (with +5V and +12V being the most common voltages supplied to devices).

The motherboard and adapters use +3.3V and +5V, but –5V is seldom used. Mechanical drives commonly use +5V and +12V. The +12V voltage is used to operate the device motors found in drives, the CPU, internal cooling fans, and the graphics card. Chips use +5V and +3.3V, and +3.3V is also used for memory, AGP/PCI/PCIe adapters, and some laptop fans. The negative voltages are seldom used.

A technician must occasionally check voltages in a system. There are four basic checks for power supply situations: (1) wall outlet AC voltage, (2) DC voltages going to the motherboard, (3) DC voltages going to a device, and (4) ground or lack of voltage with an outlet tester. A **power supply tester** can be used to check DC power levels on the different power supply connectors. Figure 5.34 shows a PC power supply tester. The type of connectors varies from vendor to vendor, so make sure you get a tester that can handle Molex, SATA, and main system power at a minimum.

FIGURE 5.34 PC power supply tester

Solving Power Supply Problems

When you suspect that a power supply is causing a problem, swap the power supply, make the customer happy, and be on your way! Power problems are not usually difficult to detect or troubleshoot.

TECH TIP

Do not disassemble a power supply

Power supplies are not normally disassembled. Manufacturers often rivet them shut. Even when a power supply can be disassembled, you should not take it apart unless you have a background in electronics.

Do not overlook the most obvious power supply symptoms. Start by checking the computer power light. If it is off, check the power supply's fan by placing your palm at the back of the computer. If the fan is turning, it means the wall outlet is providing power to the computer, and you can assume that the wall outlet is functioning. Check the motherboard for LEDs and refer to the manual for their meaning. Test the power outlet with another device. Ensure that the power cord is inserted fully into the wall outlet and the computer. If you suspect that the wall outlet is faulty, use an **AC circuit tester** to verify that the wall outlet is wired properly.

The following troubleshooting questions can help you determine the location of a power problem:

> Did the power supply work before? If not, check the input voltage selector switch on the power supply and verify that it is on the proper setting.
> Is the power supply's fan turning? If yes, check voltages going to the motherboard. If they are good, maybe just the power supply fan is bad. If the power supply's fan is not turning, check the wall outlet for proper AC voltages.
> Is a surge strip used? If so, check to see whether the surge strip is powered on and then try a different outlet in the surge strip or replace the surge strip.
> Is the computer's power cord okay? Verify that the power cord plugs snugly into the outlet and into the back of the computer. Swap the power cord to verify that it is functioning.
> Is the front panel power button stuck?
> Are the voltages going to the motherboard at the proper levels? If they are low, something might be overloading the power supply. Disconnect the power cable to one device and re-check the voltages. Replace the power cable to the device. Remove the power cable from another device and recheck the motherboard voltages. Continue doing this until the power cord for each device has been disconnected and the motherboard voltages have been checked. A single device can short out the power supply and cause the system to malfunction. Replace any device that draws down the power supply's output voltage and draws too much current. If none of the devices is the cause of the problem, replace the power supply. If replacing the power supply does not solve the problem, replace the motherboard.

If a computer does not boot properly but does boot when you press Ctrl+Alt+Del, the power good signal is likely the problem. Some motherboards are more sensitive to the power good signal than others. Try replacing the power supply.

TECH TIP

Checking the power good signal

Check the power supply documentation to see whether the power supply outputs a power good (OK) signal rather than the normal +5V. Turn on the computer. Check the power good signal on the main motherboard power connector (attached to the power supply). A power supply with a power good signal below +3V needs to be replaced.

Sometimes, when a computer comes out of sleep mode, not all devices respond, and the computer's power or reset button has to be pressed to reboot the computer. The following situations can cause this to happen:

> Set the screen saver to *None* to see if it is causing the problem.
> One or more adapters/devices are not ACPI compliant.
> An adapter/device has an outdated driver.
> The system BIOS/UEFI or an installed adapter BIOS needs to be updated.

To see whether the screen saver causes a problem, use the Windows *Personalization* Settings > *Screen saver settings* link and set the screen saver option to *None*. Identifying a problem adapter, device, or driver requires internet research. Check each adapter, device, and driver individually. Use the *Power Options* Control Panel to change the power scheme. For each device, check for a *Power Management* tab on the *Properties* dialog box and make changes if needed.

SOFT SKILLS: WRITTEN COMMUNICATIONS SKILLS

When technicians are in school, they seldom think that the skills they should be learning involve writing. However, in the workplace, technicians use **written communication** skills when they document problems and use email (see Figure 5.35). Advisory committees across the country say that in addition to having technical knowledge, it is important that technicians be able to communicate effectively both in writing and orally, and they should be comfortable working in a team environment. In addition, technicians should possess critical thinking skills—that is, be able to solve a problem without having been taught about the specific problem.

FIGURE 5.35 Technicians must frequently provide written communication

Regardless of the size of a company, documentation is normally required. The documentation might be only the number of hours spent on a job and a basic description of what was done, but most companies require a bit more. Documentation should be written so others can read and understand it. Keep in mind that if another technician must handle another problem from the same customer, good documentation saves time and money. The following is a list of complaints from managers who hire technicians:

- Avoids doing documentation in a timely manner
- Does not provide adequate or accurate information on what was performed or tried
- Has poor spelling, grammar, capitalization, and punctuation skills
- Writes in short, choppy sentences, using technical jargon
- Does not provide updates on the status of a problem

You can use this list to know where to improve your skills and avoid making the same mistakes.

Email is a common means of communication for technicians. However, most technicians do not take the time to communicate effectively using email. The following is a list of guidelines for effective email communication:

- Do not use email when a meeting or a phone call is more appropriate.
- Include a short description of the email topic in the subject line.
- Do not write or respond to an email when you are angry.
- Send email only to the appropriate people; do not copy others unnecessarily.

- Stick to the point; do not digress.
- Use a spelling and grammar checker; if one is not included in the email client, write the email in a word processing application, check it, and then paste the document into the body of the email.
- Use proper grammar, punctuation, and capitalization; do not write in all uppercase or all lowercase letters.
- Smile when you are typing. Your good attitude will come across in your writing.
- Focus on the task at hand. Read your note out loud if it is a critical one.
- Write each email as if you were putting the message on a billboard (see Figure 5.36); you never know how the content might be used or who might see it.

The number-one complaint about technical support staff is not their lack of technical skills but their lack of communication skills. Spend as much of your education practicing your communication skills as you do your technical skills.

FIGURE 5.36 Consider what you write in written communications; it could be publicized

Chapter Summary

- Wearing a wrist strap or staying in contact with unpainted metal keeps you and a computing device at the same electrical potential so you won't induce current into any part and weaken/damage it.
- EMI and RFI cause issues. Move a computer or an offending device and replace all slot covers/openings.
- When removing parts, have the right tools, lighting, and antistatic items, as well as ample workspace. Take notes. Don't use magnetized tools. Avoid jarring hard drives.
- Be careful when installing an I/O shield and be aware of standoffs when dealing with the motherboard.
- Preventive maintenance procedures prolong the life of a computer. Vacuum before spraying compressed air.
- An MSDS/SDS describes disposal and storage procedures and contains information about toxicity and health concerns. Cities/states have specific disposal rules for chemicals, batteries, electronics, and so on. Always know the disposal rules in the area where you work.
- AC power goes into a power supply or mobile device power brick. DC power is provided to all internal parts of a computing device. AC and DC voltage checks can be done, and only with DC power does polarity matter. Use the highest meter setting possible with unknown voltage levels. Power is measured in watts.
- Continuity checks are done on cabling, and a good wire shows close to 0 ohms.

> A power supply converts AC to DC, distributes DC throughout a unit, and provides cooling. The power supply must be the correct form factor and able to supply the correct amount of wattage for a particular voltage level, such as +5V or +12V. Multiple "rails" are commonly available for +12V because the CPU commonly needs its own connection. The numbers and types of connectors vary, but converters can be purchased.
> Use ACPI to control power options through the BIOS/UEFI and the operating system. Wake on LAN and Wake on Ring are power features that allow a device to be powered up from a lowered power condition for a specific purpose.
> AC circuit testers, multimeters, and power supply testers are tools used with power problems.
> In all communications and written documentation, be professional and effective. Use proper capitalization, grammar, punctuation, and spelling.

A+ CERTIFICATION EXAM TIPS

✓ Review the chapter summary. Don't forget that other chapters have preventive maintenance tips, too, including the chapters on storage devices, multimedia devices, printers, and other peripherals.

✓ Always remember to power down a computer, remove the power cord/power brick/battery, and allow a laser printer to cool before performing maintenance.

✓ Be familiar with proper component handling and storage, including the use of self-grounding techniques, antistatic bags, ESD straps, and ESD mats.

✓ Know the purpose of an MSDS.

✓ Know that both with safety issues and when dealing with chemicals and components that could have potential environmental impact, IT personnel must comply with local government regulations.

✓ Know the purpose of an antistatic ESD strap, ESD mats, antistatic bags, and self-grounding techniques. Don't use an antistatic ESD strap when working inside an old CRT monitor or power supply.

✓ Wear safety goggles and an air filtration mask for protection from airborne particles.

✓ Be aware of temperature risks, effects of humidity on electronic equipment, and when ventilation is needed.

✓ Be able to identify and explain basic SCSI, SATA, eSATA, and IDE hard drive cables (including power, as discussed in Chapter 7, "Storage Devices").

✓ Know that older power supplies have a 20-pin motherboard cable that can be used on a 24-pin motherboard connector, or a 20- to 24-pin motherboard adapter can be purchased.

✓ Identify common connector types, such as a Molex connector.

✓ Know that the power supply outputs 3.3V, 5V, and 12V and that electronics commonly use 5V and motors use 12V. If a computer is to be used internationally, ensure that it supports an auto-switching power supply that accepts either 110V or 220VAC as input voltage.

✓ Understand computer component power requirements and that the power supply must be powerful enough to power the number of devices and types of devices installed in the computer.

✓ Be familiar with common power problem symptoms, including the fan spinning but no power being provided to other devices, lack of power, noisy or inoperative fan, and the computer rebooting or powering down without warning.

✓ Be familiar with motherboard connections to the top and front panels (USB, audio, power button, power light, drive activity lights, and reset button).

✓ The following communication and professionalism skills are part of the 220-1102 exam: Use proper language and avoid jargon, acronyms, and slang when applicable; and provide proper documentation on the services provided.

Key Terms

3.3V 163
5V 163
4-pin 12V 164
6-pin PCIe 164
8-pin PCIe 164
12V 163
20-pin to 24-pin motherboard adapter 164
24-pin motherboard connector 164
110V vs. 220V input voltage 163
AC 159
AC circuit tester 174
ACPI 168
air filtration mask 158
amp 161
antistatic bag 146
antistatic wrist strap 144
black screen 173
burning smell 173
compressed air 157
computer reboot 173
continuity 161
DC 159
dual-rail power supply 170
EMI 146
equipment grounding 144
ESD 144
ESD mat 146
ESD strap 144
front panel connector 151
grinding noise 173
I/O shield 154
IDE cable 150
intermittent shutdown 173
maintenance kit 157
modular power supply 172
Molex 164
MSDS 158
no power 173
ohm 161
overheating 173
pin 1 150
power 161
power supply tester 174
preventive maintenance 156
redundant power supply 171
resistance 161
RFI 146
safety goggles 158
SATA connector 150
SDS 158
self-grounding 146
smoke 173
standoff 154
toner vacuum 157
volt 160
voltage 160
Wake on LAN 169
Wake on Ring 169
watt 161
wattage rating 170
written communication 176

Review Questions

1. What would happen if you removed the battery from a motherboard by accident?

____

2. List three tasks commonly performed during preventive maintenance.

____

____

____

3. Computers used in a grocery store warehouse for inventory control have a higher part failure rate than do the other company computers. Which of the following is most likely to help in this situation?
   a. an antistatic wrist strap
   b. a preventive maintenance plan
   c. antistatic pads
   d. high-wattage power supplies
4. Which of the following can prolong the life of a computer and conserve energy? (Choose all that apply.)
   a. a preventive maintenance plan
   b. antistatic mats and pads
   c. upgraded power supply
   d. a power plan
   e. Li-ion replacement batteries
   f. extra case fans
5. Which power component has a 24-pin connector?
   a. main motherboard connector
   b. power supply fan
   c. case fan
   d. AUX power for the CPU
6. An optical drive randomly becomes unavailable, and after replacing the drive, the technician now suspects that the drive may not be getting 5 volts consistently. What could help in this situation?
   a. a UPS
   b. a surge protector
   c. antistatic wipes
   d. a preventive maintenance plan
   e. a power supply tester
7. When disassembling a computer, which tool will help you remove the memory module?
   a. magnetic screwdriver
   b. needle-nose pliers
   c. #1 or #2 Phillips screwdriver
   d. antistatic wrist strap
8. A user had a motherboard problem last week, and a technician fixed it. Now the same computer has a different problem. The user reports that the USB ports on the front do not work anymore. What is the first thing you should check?
   a. power supply
   b. power connection to the front panel
   c. motherboard connections to the front panel
   d. voltage output from the power supply to the USB connectors

9. Which of the following items would be specialized for use with a laser printer?

   [surge strip | vacuum | power supply tester | antistatic wrist strap]

10. Which two of the following would most likely cause a loud noise on a desktop computer? (Choose two.)

    [motherboard | USB drive | power supply | case fan | memory | PCIe adapter]

11. A computer will not power on. Which of the following would be used to check the wall outlet?

    [power supply tester | UPS | multimeter | POST]

12. A computer will not power on. After checking the wall outlet and swapping the power cord, what would the technician use next?

    a. resistance

    b. power supply tester

    c. antistatic wrist strap

    d. magnetic screwdriver

    e. nonmagnetic screwdriver

13. Which of the following is affected by the power supply wattage rating?

    a. number of adapters and internal storage devices

    b. number of power supply connectors

    c. speed of the processor

    d. type of processor

    e. type of power supply connectors

14. Which of the following would help with computer heat?

    a. increasing the power supply wattage

    b. upgrading to a larger power supply form factor

    c. unplugging unused power connectors

    d. installing case fans

15. [T | F] Power supply disassembly is a common requirement of a PC technician.

16. Consider the following email.

From: Cheryl a. Schmidt To: Network Engineering Technology Faculty Subj: [None] We have little time to get the PMS done on the PCs and N/W gear. What software do you want?

    Reword this email to illustrate good written communication skills.

17. List three recommendations for good technical written communication.

____

____

____

____

____

18. A computer is doing weird things, such as shutting down unexpectedly and hanging. You suspect a power problem. You check the power good (power OK) signal on the power supply's main motherboard connector. The voltage reading shows that you have power (+2.5 volts). What are you going to do next?
    - **a.** Check the voltage coming out of a Molex or SATA connector.
    - **b.** Check the wall outlet voltage.
    - **c.** Replace the power supply.
    - **d.** Check the power supply cable for resistance.
19. What is the purpose of the I/O shield?
    - **a.** It prevents dust and dirt from coming in through the front computer ports.
    - **b.** It provides grounding for motherboard ports.
    - **c.** It prevents dust and dirt from coming into the power supply.
    - **d.** It protects a technician from shocks.
20. Which two items would help a technician maintain personal safety while working on PCs and printers in an extremely dusty warehouse? (Choose two.)

    [vacuum | toner vacuum | safety goggles | antistatic wrist strap | air filtration mask]

Exercises

Exercise 5.1 Identifying Power Supply Connectors

Objective: To be able to identify the purposes of common power supply connectors

Procedure: Identify the power supply connectors in Figure 5.37.

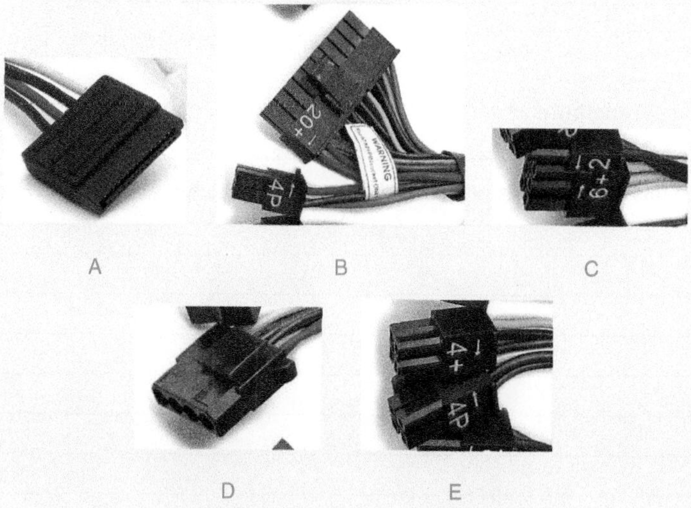

A B C

D E

FIGURE 5.37 Identifying power connectors

____ 1. Molex for older optical drive

____ 2. SATA for hard drive

____ 3. PCIe video

____ 4. Main motherboard

____ 5. CPU

Exercise 5.2 Recognizing Computer Replacement Parts

Objective: To be able to recognize parts from a computer

Procedure: Use the following information to answer the questions.

The following parts were ordered by someone building his or her own computer:

a. Intel Core i7 4.4 GHz

b. ASUS Rampage V Extreme X99 (does not include USB 3.1 headers)

c. Triage 8 GB

d. Micro-ATX with two 3.5" internal and two 5.25" external drive bays

e. EVA 450W

1. What part is designated by the letter a?

[memory | hard drive | optical drive | CPU]

2. What part is designated by the letter b?

[motherboard | processor | memory | hard drive]

3. What part is designated by the letter c?

[motherboard | optical drive | RAM | SATA hard drive | SSD]

4. What part is designated by the letter d?

[RAM | case | all storage devices | power supply]

5. What part is designated by the letter e?

[case | SSD | optical drive | power supply]

Exercise 5.3 Describing Computer Parts

Objective: To be able to recognize computer parts based on a description

Procedure: Match the description to the computer part affected during disassembly.

____ 1. 24-pin connector	a. Power supply to motherboard cable
____ 2. 40-pin ribbon cable	b. Front panel to motherboard cable
____ 3. Antistatic bag	c. Hard drive to motherboard cable
____ 4. ESD strap	d. Motherboard to IDE PATA device
____ 5. Grounding	e. Attaches to wrist and computer
____ 6. Hard drive	f. Holds an adapter when not in use
____ 7. HDD LED	g. Helps with EMI
____ 8. SATA 3	h. Keeping in contact with the computer
____ 9. Slot cover	i. Attaches motherboard to case
____ 10. Standoffs	j. Might need guide rails

Activities

Internet Discovery

Objective: To obtain specific information on the internet regarding a computer or its associated parts

Parts: Computer with internet access

Procedure: Complete the following procedure and answer the following questions.

1. Locate an internet site that provides tips for doing computer preventive maintenance.

   Write two of the best tips and the URL where you found the information.

   ____

   ____

   ____

2. Locate an internet site where you can buy a computer toolkit that includes an antistatic wrist strap.

   List the URL where you found the toolkit and at least three sizes of screwdrivers or bits provided.

   ____

   ____

   ____

3. Locate a power supply tester that includes a SATA connector.

   List the manufacturer and model.

   ____

   ____

4. Find a website on good netiquette.

   Give three recommendations and the name of the website (not the URL).

   ____

   ____

   ____

   ____

   ____

5. You have just started working at a place that uses the HP Elite 800 G2 23-inch nontouch all-in-one computer.

   You have been sent to do power checks on the power supply of one of these units. How do you get the cover off? Explain in detail, using complete sentences.

   ____

   ____

   ____

   ____

   What recommendation does HP give for cleaning stubborn stains that might be found on the cases of computers in the maintenance shop?

   ____

According to the documentation, what is different about removing an AMD processor than removing an Intel processor?

____

____

____

Soft Skills

Objective: To enhance and fine-tune a future technician's ability to listen, communicate in both written and oral forms, and support people who use computers in a professional manner

Activities:

1. Prepare a business proposal for a replacement power supply for a specific computer. State the computer and present your proposal to the class.
2. Write an informal report on the skills learned while taking apart a computer and reassembling it. Share your best practices with a small group.
3. Work in teams to decide the best way to inform a customer about the differences between an ATX power supply and an SFX power supply. Present your description to the class as if you were talking to the customer. You might consider showing motherboards and cases to help illustrate your point. Each team member must contribute. Each classmate votes for the best team explanation.

Critical Thinking Skills

Objective: To analyze and evaluate information as well as apply learned information to new or different situations

Activities:

1. Use the internet to find a description of a particular computer that lists each device that is installed and the type of motherboard, integrated ports, and so on. Then locate a power supply calculator. Find a replacement power supply, based on the calculations performed. Write the details of what you looked for in the replacement power supply, the power supply, vendor, number and type of connectors, and cost.

   ____

   ____

2. For one of the computers in the classroom, locate the documentation on how to disassemble it. Look through the documentation and find at least three good tips that you might not have thought of immediately if you were disassembling the computer. Then find at least three safety tips. Place all of this information in an outline. An alternative is to be creative and present the tips graphically on one page or presentation slide.

6 Memory

In this chapter you will learn:

> Different memory technologies
> How to plan for a memory installation or upgrade
> How to install and remove memory modules
> How to optimize memory for Windows platforms
> Best practices for troubleshooting memory problems
> The benefits of teamwork

CompTIA Exam Objectives:

✓ 1101-3.2 Given a scenario, install the appropriate RAM.

✓ 1101-3.3 Given a scenario, select and install storage devices.

✓ 1101-5.2 Given a scenario, troubleshoot problems related to motherboards, RAM, CPU, and power.

✓ 1102-1.3 Given a scenario, use features and tools of the Microsoft Windows 10 operating system (OS).

✓ 1102-1.4 Given a scenario, use the appropriate Microsoft Windows 10 Control Panel utility.

✓ 1102-4.7 Given a scenario, use proper communication techniques and professionalism.

Memory Overview

Computer systems need software to operate, and software resides in computer memory. A technician must understand memory terminology, determine the optimum amount of memory for a system, install the memory, and troubleshoot and solve any memory problems.

The main type of memory found on the motherboard is random-access memory (**RAM**), specifically dynamic RAM (**DRAM**). The other type of RAM is static RAM (**SRAM**). DRAM is less expensive but slower than SRAM. With DRAM, the 1s and 0s inside the chip must be refreshed. Over time, the charge, which represents information inside a DRAM chip, leaks out. The information, which is stored in 1s and 0s, is periodically rewritten to the memory chip through the refresh process. The refreshing is accomplished inside the DRAM while other processing occurs. Refreshing is one reason DRAM chips are slower than SRAM.

Most memory on a motherboard is DRAM, but a small amount of SRAM can be found inside the processor, just outside the processor inside the processor housing, and sometimes on the motherboard. SRAM is also known as **cache memory**. Cache memory holds the most frequently used data so the CPU does not return to the slower DRAM chips to obtain the data. Figure 6.1 shows a motherboard with DRAM and a processor that contains SRAM.

FIGURE 6.1 DRAM and SRAM

As noted in Chapter 3, "On the Motherboard," to determine memory requirements, you must consider the operating system, applications, and installed hardware. Memory is one of the most critical things on the motherboard that can easily be upgraded. Let's start with the physical memory module.

TECH TIP

Don't forget hard drive space and video memory

RAM is only one piece of the puzzle. All of a computer's parts—including RAM, hard drive space, and video memory—must work together to provide good (optimal) system performance.

Memory Physical Packaging

The memory used on motherboards today comes in packaging known as a dual in-line memory module (**DIMM**), which has 168, 184, 240, or 288 pins. Memory can also be called a memory stick, or a technician might call one memory module a stick of memory or simply RAM. Laptops and printers use a smaller DIMM called a small outline DIMM (**SODIMM**). Figure 6.2 shows the progression of memory packaging. Figure 6.3 shows a SODIMM.

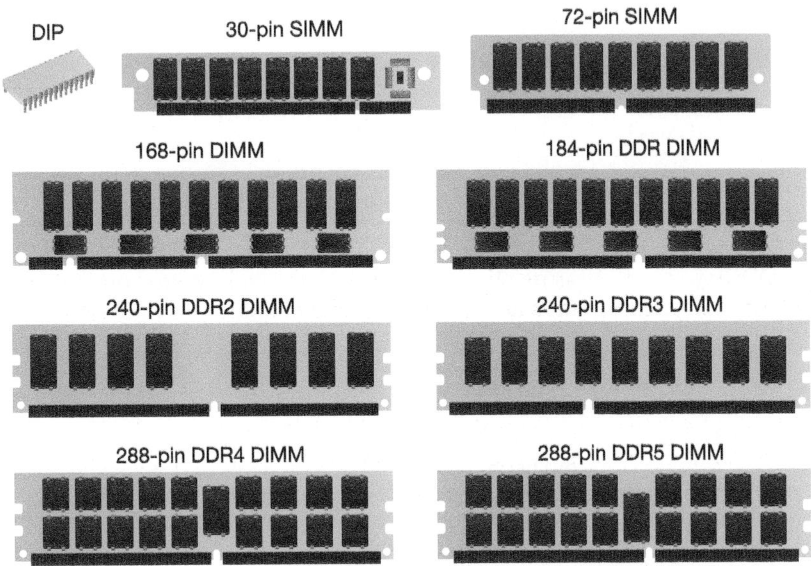

FIGURE 6.2 Memory chips/modules

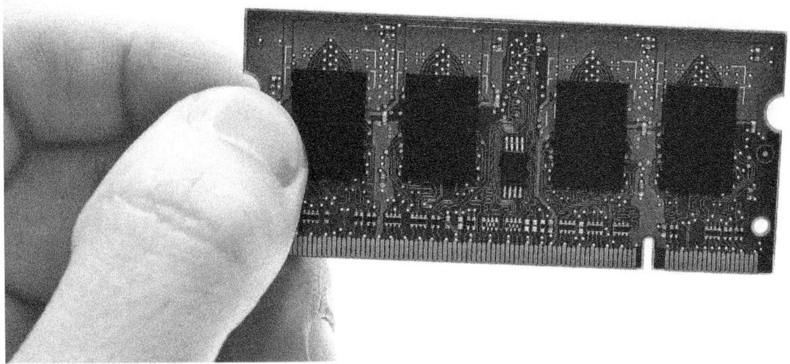

FIGURE 6.3 SODIMM

Planning a Memory Installation

Now that you know a little about memory types, let us look at how to go about planning a memory installation. Some key points follow:

- Refer to the system or motherboard documentation to see what type of memory is supported.
- Determine what features are supported.
- Determine how much memory is needed.
- Determine what memory module(s) you need and how many of them.
- Research prices and purchase the memory module(s) you need.

Planning the Memory Installation: Memory Module Types

Technology has provided faster DRAM speeds without increasing the cost too greatly. Table 6.1 lists some of the memory technologies available today.

TABLE 6.1 Memory module types

Technology	Explanation
Synchronous DRAM (SDRAM)	Performs very fast burst memory access. New memory addresses are placed on the bus but before the prior memory address retrieval and execution is complete. SDRAM synchronizes its operation with the CPU clock signal to speed up memory access. Used with DIMMs.
Double data rate (DDR)	Sometimes called DDR SDRAM or DDR RAM. DDR memory can send twice as much data because data is transmitted on both sides of the clock signal (that is, on the rising and falling edges instead of just on the rising edge).
DDR2	Sometimes called DDR2 RAM. DDR2 uses 240-pin DIMMs and is not compatible with DDR.
DDR3	Uses 240-pin DIMMs and is not compatible with DDR2 or DDR. Supports multicore processor-based systems and more efficient power utilization (1.5V).
DDR4	Operates at a lower voltage (1.2V) and faster speeds than DDR3 modules. DDR4 uses 288-pin DIMMs and is not compatible with DDR, DDR2, or DDR3.
DDR5	Operates at a lower voltage (1.1V) and faster speeds than DDR4 modules. Uses 288 pins like DDR4 but cannot be inserted into a DDR4 slot.

TECH TIP

Using a lower-voltage chip

DDR3 and DDR4 memory can be purchased as a module that uses a lower voltage than a standard module. The motherboard must support this feature. These modules have an L at the end (DDR4L, for example).

Even though some DDR modules have a different numbers of pins, they are the same physical size. A DDR5 module does not fit in a DDR2, DDR3, or DDR4 slot because the notches are different. Most people cannot tell the difference among DDR memory modules. You have to make sure you have the right kind of module for the motherboard. Figure 6.4 shows DDR4 DIMMs. Notice in Figure 6.4 the metal casing, called a **heat spreader**, on the outside of the memory module. Aluminum or copper is commonly used on heat spreaders in order to dissipate heat away from the memory

FIGURE 6.4 DDR4 DIMMs

TECH TIP

Using the right type of memory chips

The chipset and motherboard design are very specific about what type, speed, and features the memory chips can have. Refer to the motherboard documentation.

Table 6.2 lists some examples of DIMM models.

TABLE 6.2 DIMMs

Memory type	Alternative name	Clock speed	Data rate
PC3-16000	DDR3-2000	1000 MHz	2 GT/s
PC3-17000	DDR3-2133	1066 MHz	2.13 GT/s
PC4-1866	DDR4-1866	933 MHz	1.86 GT/s
PC4-2400	DDR4-2400	1200 MHz	2.4 GT/s
PC4-2666	DDR4-2666	1333 MHz	2.66 GT/s
PC4-3000	DDR4-3000	1500 MHz	3 GT/s
PC4-25600	DDR4-3200	1600 MHz	3.2 GT/s

Because a DIMM can be shown with either the PC*X*- or DDR*X*- designation, which type you buy can be confusing. A brief explanation might help. DDR3-2000 is a type of DDR3 memory that can run on a 1000 MHz front side bus (the number after DDR3 divided in half). Another way of showing the same chip would be to use the designation PC3-16000, which is the theoretical bandwidth of the memory chip in MB/s. The good news about DDR4 and DDR5 is that the module names now match the standard names.

Planning the Memory Installation: Memory Features

In addition to determining what type of memory chips are going to be used, you must determine what features the memory chips might have. The computer system or motherboard documentation delineates what features are supported. Table 6.3 helps characterize memory features.

TABLE 6.3 Memory features

Feature	Explanation
Non-parity	Chips that do not use any error checking. If an advertisement doesn't say parity or ECC, the memory module is non-parity and the most common type.
Error correction code (**ECC**)	Uses a mathematical algorithm to verify data accuracy. ECC can detect up to 4-bit memory errors and correct 1-bit memory errors in higher-end computers and network servers.
Unbuffered memory	Memory in which data is sent immediately through the memory chip. It is the opposite of registered memory and is faster than registered or fully buffered memory.
Buffered memory (registered memory)	A memory module that has extra chips (registers) near the bottom of the module that delay all data transfers to ensure accuracy in servers and high-end computers. These modules are sometimes advertised as fully buffered DIMMs (FBDIMMs).

Feature	Explanation
Serial presence detect (**SPD**)	A module that has an extra EEPROM that holds information about the DIMM (capacity, voltage, refresh rates, and so on). The BIOS/UEFI reads and uses this data for best performance. Some modules have thermal sensors (sometimes listed as TS in advertisements) that monitor and report memory heat conditions.
Dual-voltage memory	A module that might be listed with an L and that can operate at a lower voltage level (thus with less heat).
Extreme memory profile (XMP)	A module that allows the BIOS/UEFI to configure voltage and timing settings in order to overclock the memory.

A memory module might use more than one of the categories listed in Tables 6.2 and 6.3. For example, a DIMM could be a DDR4 module, could be registered, and could support ECC for error detection and correction. Most registered memory also uses the ECC technology. Memory modules can support either ECC or non-ECC, and they can be registered or unbuffered memory. It is important that you research this *before* you purchase memory.

TECH TIP

If error correction isn't mentioned in the advertisement...

If error correction is not mentioned, the chip is a non-parity chip. Most memory modules today are non-parity because the memory controller circuitry provides error correction.

Planning for Memory: How Much Memory to Install

When you want to improve the performance of a computer, adding memory is one of the easiest upgrades. The amount of memory needed depends on the operating system, applications, number of applications open at the same time, type of computer, and maximum amount allowed by the motherboard.

Memory modules come in specific capacities, such as the ones shown in Figure 6.5. Notice how the capacities double. If someone installed four 512 MB modules, for example, the total amount installed would be 2 GB (as two 512 MB modules equals 1 GB). If a motherboard had four memory expansion slots and the maximum the motherboard supported was 8 GB, then the largest-capacity memory module you could put in any slot would be a 2 GB module.

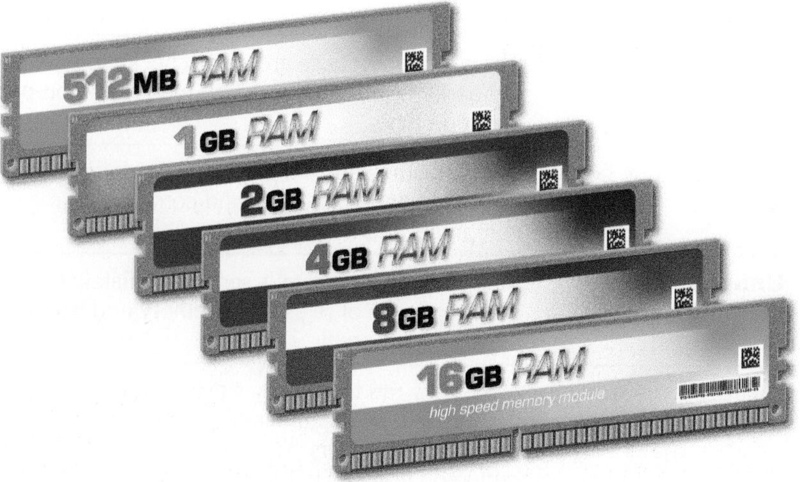

FIGURE 6.5 Memory module capacities

The operating system you use determines to a great extent the starting point for the amount of memory to have. Generally, the older or less powerful your operating system, the smaller amount of RAM you need. Table 6.4 provides a starting point for calculating memory requirements. Remember that as you want to run more applications simultaneously and the higher the application function (such as gaming or photo/video/sound manipulation), the more memory you will need. Also note that the memory recommendations shown in Table 6.4 are not the minimum requirements listed by the operating system creators. Notice that Apple computers (macOS) have similar memory recommendations to PCs.

TABLE 6.4 Minimum operating system starting memory recommendations

Operating system	Minimum amount of RAM to start calculations
Windows 10	2 GB
Windows 11	4 GB
macOS Sierra/High Sierra/Mojave	2 GB
macOS Sierra/Catalina/Big Sur	4 GB
Linux	Depending on the version, from 64 MB

When upgrading memory, you need to know a couple of key pieces of information:

> How much memory are you starting with?
> How many motherboard RAM slots are currently being used, and are there any slots free?
> What is the maximum amount of memory that your motherboard supports?

TECH TIP

Windows might have memory limitations

Even if the motherboard allows more memory, your operating system has limitations. Upgrade the operating system if this is the case. Table 6.5 shows the Windows memory limits.

TABLE 6.5 Windows memory limits

Operating system	Memory limit
Windows 10 Home	128 GB
Windows 10 Pro/Enterprise	2 TB

To see the amount of installed memory, access the *System Information* window from a command prompt by typing **`msinfo32`** and pressing Enter. Scroll down to see the memory information. Figure 6.6 shows the System Information window for a computer system that currently has 24 GB of RAM installed (24.0 GB Total Physical Memory).

TECH TIP

Every motherboard has a maximum

Each motherboard supports a maximum amount of memory. You must check the computer or motherboard documentation to see how much this is. There is not a workaround for this limitation. If you want more memory than the motherboard allows, you must upgrade to a different motherboard.

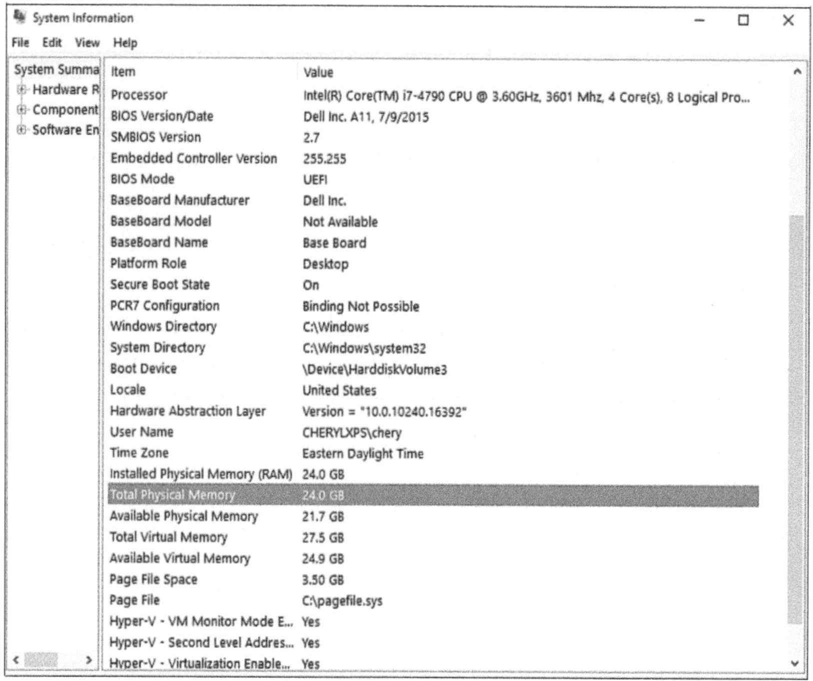

FIGURE 6.6 System Information window

Figure 6.7 shows a sample advertisement for a micro-ATX motherboard. The *Specifications* tab commonly shows the type of memory supported (and may also show the exact speeds supported), the maximum amount of memory, and the number of memory slots.

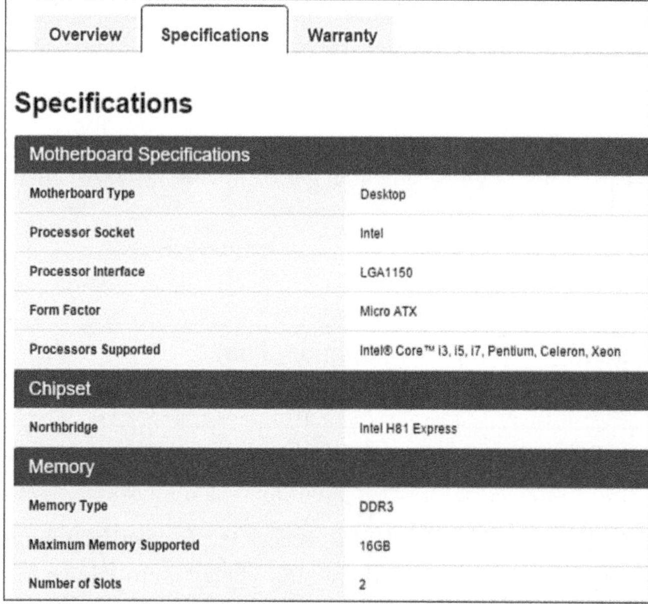

FIGURE 6.7 Sample motherboard memory specifications

To determine how many slots you are currently using and whether you have any free, you need to either (1) access the BIOS/UEFI to see this information; (2) use the *Task Manager > Performance* tab in Windows; or (3) remove the computer cover and look at the motherboard to see which memory slots have installed modules and whether there are any free slots. Some memory sales websites have a software program that determines the type of memory you are using and makes recommendations.

Planning for Memory: How Many of Each Memory Type?

A motherboard has a certain number of memory slots, determined by its manufacturer. The type of memory module that inserts into a slot and the features that the module has are determined by the motherboard manufacturer.

Most motherboards support dual-channel memory. **Dual-channel** means that the motherboard memory controller chip handles processing of memory requests more efficiently by handling two memory paths simultaneously. For example, say that a motherboard has four memory slots. Traditionally, the memory controller chip, commonly called the MCH (memory controller hub), had one channel through which all data from the four slots traveled. With dual-channeling, the four slots are divided into two channels, and each channel has two slots. Figure 6.8 shows this concept.

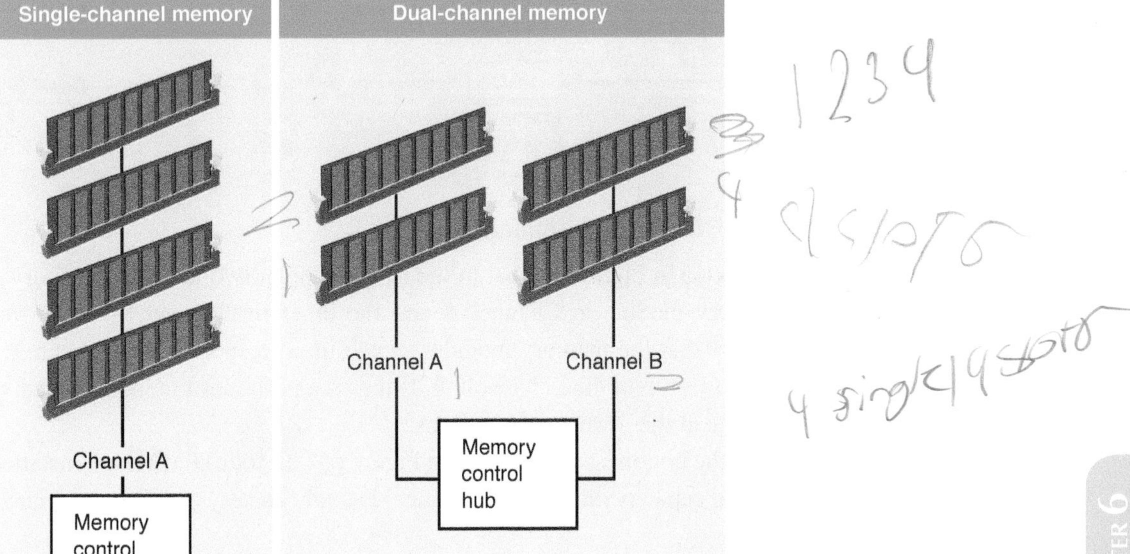

FIGURE 6.8 Dual-channel memory

Dual-channeling increases a system's performance. However, it speeds things up on some motherboards only if the memory modules match exactly—same memory type, same memory features, same speed, and same capacity. Note that on some motherboards, the memory modules on Channel A and Channel B do not have to have the same capacities, but the total capacity of the memory module in Channel A should match the total capacity of the memory modules installed in Channel B. Some motherboards require this. Figure 6.9 illustrates this concept.

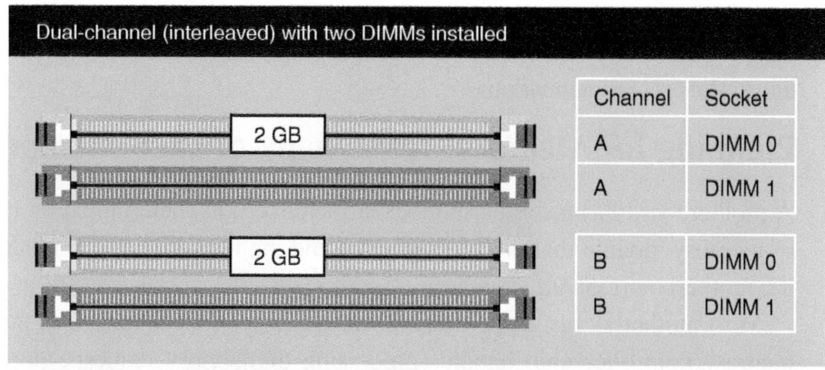

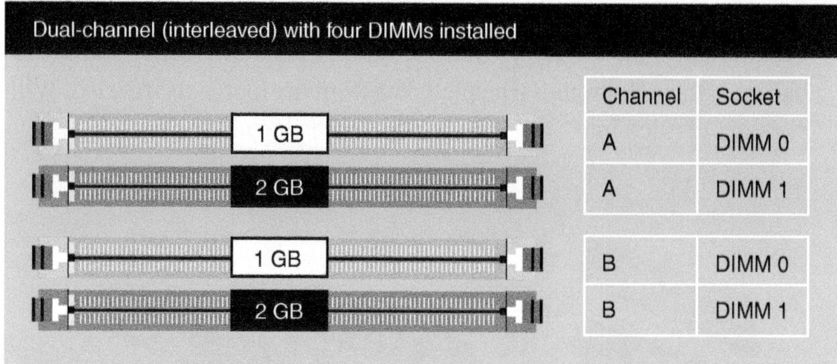

FIGURE 6.9 Dual-channeling

Notice in Figure 6.9 that in the first example, two identical memory modules are inserted: one memory module in Channel A and the other in Channel B. Some motherboard manufacturers require that the memory modules match in all respects—manufacturer, timing, and capacity—in order to support dual-channeling. If they support ones that don't match perfectly, the channel will operate at the lower specifications.

In the bottom section shown in Figure 6.9, all four DIMMs are installed. Notice that the Channel A total capacity matches the Channel B total capacity (3 GB in both channels, for a total of 6 GB).

TECH TIP

Dual-channel should use exact memory module pairs

Channel A and Channel B (sometimes labeled Channel 0 and Channel 1) should have matching memory modules. Buy a kit (a package of pre-tested memory modules that are guaranteed to work together) to ensure that the two modules are the same.

To plan for the correct amount of memory, you must refer to the motherboard documentation. An example helps with this concept. Figure 6.10 shows a motherboard layout with four memory slots that has different labeling than shown in Figure 6.9. Remember that motherboard manufacturers can label their motherboards any way they want. This is one of the reasons documentation is so important.

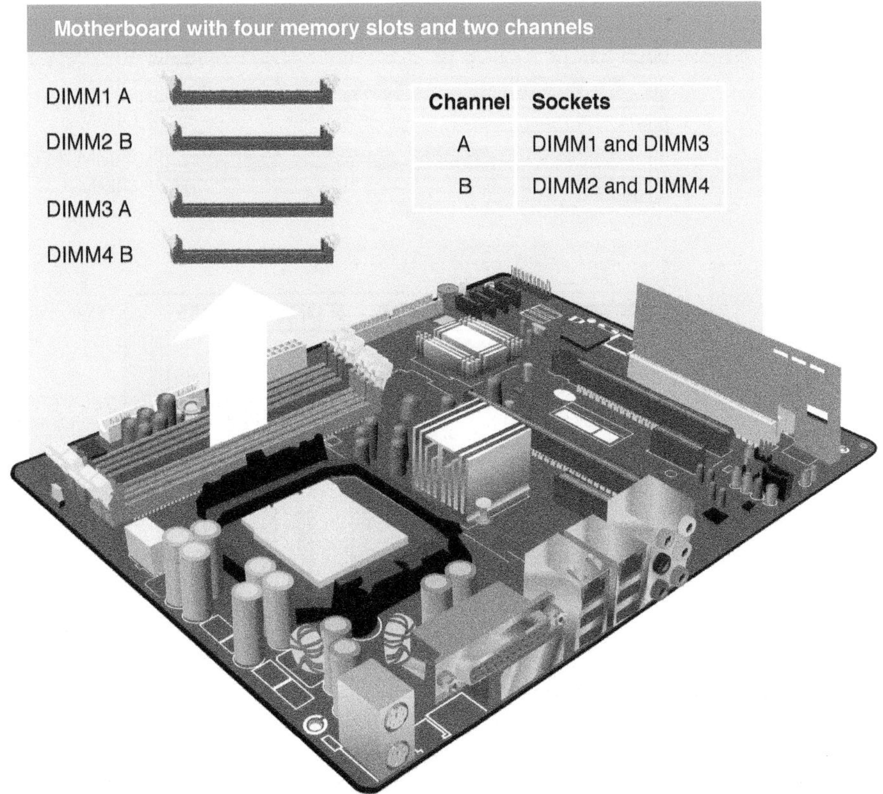

FIGURE 6.10 Motherboard with four memory slots and two channels

The motherboard in Figure 6.10 allows 512 MB, 1 GB, and 2 GB unbuffered non-ECC DDR3 DIMMs, for a maximum of 8 GB. Pretend the customer wants 2 GB of RAM. What could you do? How many memory modules would you buy, and what capacities? Table 6.6 shows the possible solutions. The best solution is the second one because it has the largest-capacity chips and takes advantage of dual-channeling, with slots left over for more upgrading.

TABLE 6.6 Possible solutions

Solution	Number and size of memory module(s) needed
1	Four 512 MB DIMMs installed in DIMM1, DIMM2, DIMM3, and DIMM4 slots (dual-channeling)
2*	Two 1 GB DIMMs installed in DIMM1 and DIMM2 slots (dual-channeling)
3	Two 1 GB DIMMs installed in DIMM1 and DIMM3 slots (not dual-channeling)
4	One 2 GB DIMM installed in DIMM1 (not dual-channeling)

*Best solution

Many newer motherboards and server motherboards support **triple-channel** memory, where three memory modules work together, or **quad-channel** memory, where four memory modules are accessed simultaneously. This feature is most commonly found on server motherboards. Figure 6.11 shows a motherboard that has six memory expansion slots and that supports triple-channeling.

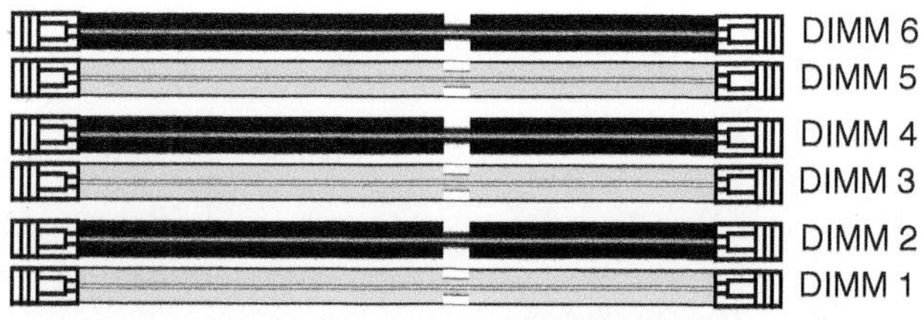

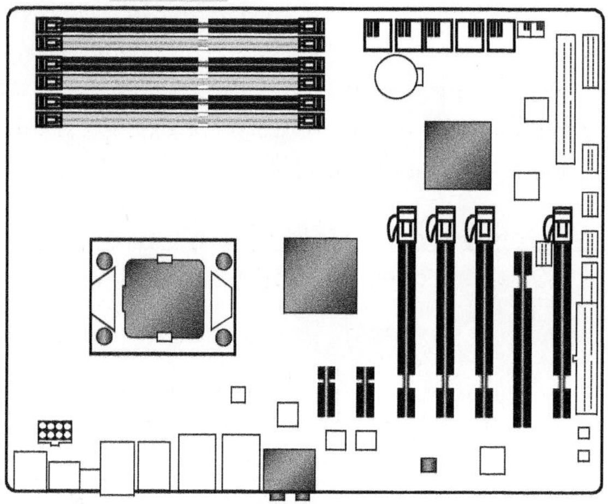

Dual-channel Configuration

	DIMM 1	DIMM 2	DIMM 3	DIMM 4	DIMM 5	DIMM 6
Two modules	X		X			
Four modules	X	X	X	X		

Triple-channel Configuration

	DIMM 1	DIMM 2	DIMM 3	DIMM 4	DIMM 5	DIMM 6
Three modules	X		X		X	
Six modules	X	X	X	X	X	X

FIGURE 6.11 Motherboard with six memory slots and three channels

Planning for Memory: Researching and Buying Memory

The researching and buying step in the process of planning for a memory installation/upgrade is the step most likely to make your head spin. Different websites list memory differently. Some give you too much information and some too little. A few, such as Kingston Technology (www.kingston.com) and Crucial (www.crucial.com), specialize in memory and make it as painless as possible. They even provide tools that will scan your computer and recommend compatible memory or storage upgrades! Nevertheless, as a technician, you should be familiar with all aspects of memory and memory advertisements.

TECH TIP

Buying the fastest type of memory a motherboard allows

Buying memory that is faster than the motherboard allows is like taking a race car on a one-lane unpaved road: The car has the ability to go faster, but it is not feasible with the type of road being used. Sometimes you must buy faster memory because the older memory is no longer sold. This is all right, as long as it is the correct type, such as DDR3, DDR4, or DDR5.

A confusing aspect of buying memory is memory speed. Memory speed can be represented as MHz or the PC rating. The higher the number, the faster the speed of the module. To further understand memory, it is best to look at some examples. Table 6.7 shows examples of how different amounts of memory might be advertised.

TABLE 6.7 Sample DIMM advertisements

Memory module	How it might be advertised
2 GB	DDR3 PC3-10600 > CL9 > UNBUFFERED > NON-ECC > DDR3-1333 > 1.35V > 256 Megx64
2 GB kit (1 GBx2)	DDR3 PC3-10600 > CL9 > REGISTERED > ECC > DDR3-1333 > 1.5V > 128 Megx72
4 GB	PC4-17000 2133MHz uDIMM single-rank
16 GB (2x8GB)	DDR4 3200MHz Desktop Memory Kit CL16

Notice in Table 6.7 how the ads either list the memory module as a DDR4 or PC4 for DDR4 type. If an ad doesn't mention ECC, then you can assume the memory is non-parity and that it does no error checking. Today's electronics are very accurate, and for most non-financial applications, non-parity memory is fine. If you see uDIMM, it is for unregistered or unbuffered memory.

The second and fourth rows in Table 6.7 list kits for motherboards that have dual-channeling capabilities. The 2 GB kit includes two 1 GB memory modules, for a total of a 2 GB memory gain. Sometimes you might see the words *dual-rank* in an advertisement. This is like having two modules combined into one module. These modules frequently have memory on both sides of the module. Dual-rank will only work if the motherboard supports it. The third row mentions a memory module that is single-rank, which just means it is a normal memory module.

Another listing in the memory advertisement shown in Table 6.7 is the **CL rating**. CL (column address strobe [CAS] latency) is the amount of time that passes before the processor moves on to the next memory address. RAM is made up of cells that hold data. A cell is the intersection of a row and a column. (It is much like a cell in a spreadsheet application.) The CAS signal picks which memory column to select, and a signal called RAS (row address strobe) picks which row to select. The intersection of the two is where the data is stored.

TECH TIP

CL ratings and speed

The lower the CL rating, the faster the memory. Think of access time like a track meet: The person with the lowest time wins the race and is considered to be the fastest. Chips with a lower CL rating are faster than those with higher numbers.

Installing Memory Overview

Memory is an important part of computer performance. Installation involves planning, installing, and possibly removing some older modules. Lack of planning can lead to less-than-optimal performance.

The following is the best process for determining which memory chips to install in each bank:

Step 1. Determine which chip capacities can be used for the system. Look in the documentation included with the motherboard or computer for this information.

Step 2. Determine how much memory is needed. Ask the users which operating system is installed and which applications they are using (or look yourself). Refer to documentation for each application to determine the amount of RAM recommended. Plan for growth.

Step 3. Determine the capacity of the chips that go in each bank by drawing a diagram of the system, planning the memory population on paper, and referring to the system or motherboard documentation.

Some memory modules might need to be removed in order to put higher-capacity ones into the bank. Look at what is already installed in the system, refer to the documentation, and remove any existing modules, as necessary, to upgrade the memory.

> **TECH TIP**
>
> **Memory safety reminder**
>
> Before installing a memory module, power off the computer, disconnect the power cord from the back of the computer, and use proper antistatic procedures. Memory modules are especially susceptible to ESD. If ESD damages a memory module, a problem might not appear immediately and could be intermittent and hard to diagnose.

Removing/Installing Memory

When removing a DIMM, push down on the retaining tabs that clasp over the DIMM. Be careful not to overextend the tabs when pushing on them. The DIMM lifts slightly out of the socket. Always ensure that you are grounded to prevent ESD by using an antistatic wrist strap or maintaining contact between a bare part of your arm and metal within the computer (self-grounding). Figure 6.12 shows the steps involved in removing a DIMM.

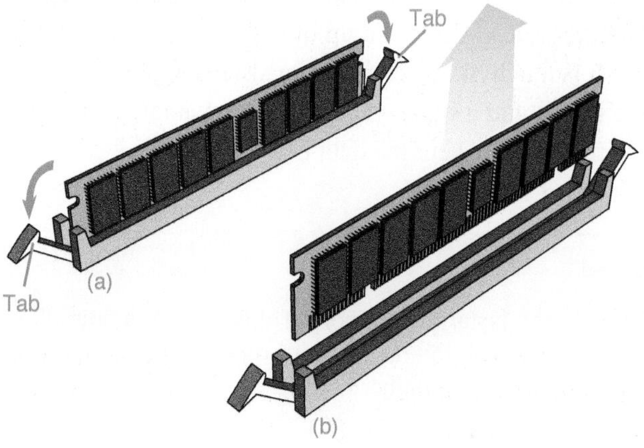

FIGURE 6.12 DIMM removal

A DIMM has one or more notches on the bottom, so that the module inserts into the memory socket only one way. Verify that the notches on the bottom of the module align with the notches in the motherboard memory slot. The DIMM will not insert into the memory socket unless it is oriented properly.

Make sure the side tabs are pulled out before you insert the DIMM and close the tabs over the DIMM once it is firmly inserted into the socket. If the DIMM does not go into the slot easily, do not force it and check for correct alignment. Once the DIMM is aligned correctly into the slot, push the DIMM firmly into the slot, and the tabs should naturally close over the DIMM or on the sides of the DIMM. Figure 6.13 illustrates how to insert a DIMM. Figure 6.14 shows a close-up of how the tab needs to fit securely in the memory module notch.

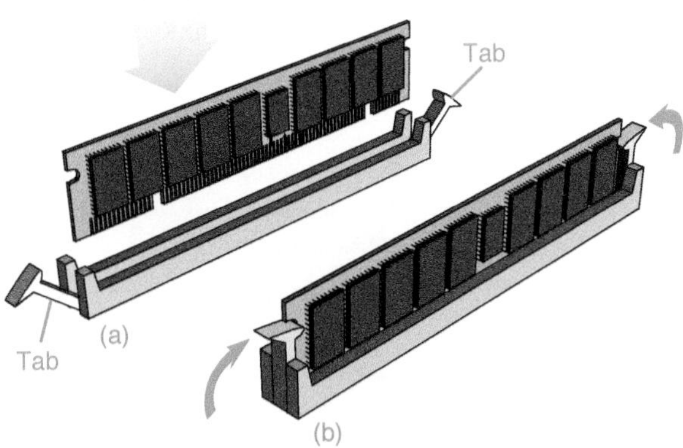

FIGURE 6.13 DIMM installation

FIGURE 6.14 Secure DIMM tab

TECH TIP

POST error codes are normal after a memory installation/upgrade

Some computers show a POST error message or automatically go into the Setup program. This is normal. The important thing to notice during POST is that the memory shown in the BIOS/UEFI should equal the amount of memory installed.

Adding more RAM can make a noticeable difference in computer performance (up to a point, of course). When a computer user is sitting in front of a computer waiting for a document to appear or waiting to go to a different location within a document, it might be time to install more RAM. If you have several opened applications on the taskbar, click one of them. If you have to wait several seconds before it appears, it might be a good idea to upgrade your RAM.

Virtual RAM

Virtual RAM (virtual memory) involves using hard drive space as if it were RAM. Virtual memory allows the operating system to run larger applications and manage multiple applications that are loaded simultaneously. The amount of hard drive space used is dynamic—that is, it increases or decreases as needed. If the system begins to page frequently and is constantly swapping data from RAM to the hard drive, the size automatically shrinks. See Figure 6.15 and notice how each application has its own memory space.

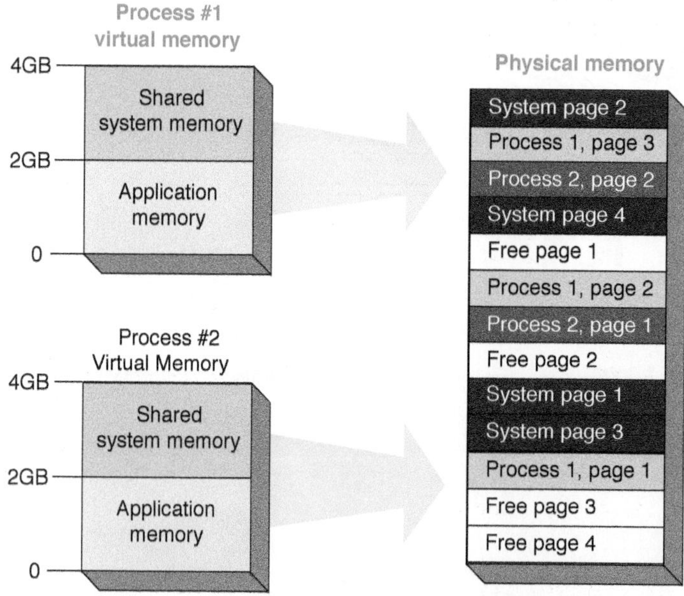

FIGURE 6.15 Windows virtual memory usage

A **paging file** is a block of hard drive space that applications use like RAM. Other names for the paging file include pagefile, pagefile.sys, page file, and swap file. Look back at Figure 6.6, which shows the System Information screen, and you can see the data related to the paging file next to Total Virtual Memory, Available Virtual Memory, and Page File Space. For optimum performance in any Windows operating system, set aside as much free hard drive space as possible to allow ample room for virtual memory and caching. Keep the hard drive cleaned of temporary files and outdated files/applications.

TECH TIP

Hard drive paging file tips

If multiple hard drives are available, a technician might want to move the paging file to a different drive. Always put the paging file on the fastest hard drive unless that hard drive lacks space.

The amount of virtual memory is dynamically created by the operating system and does not normally need to be set manually. In Windows, search for the word **`performance`** > select the *Adjust the Appearance and Performance of Windows* link > *Advanced* tab > *Change* button. Change the parameters and click *OK* twice. Figure 6.16 shows how virtual memory relates to RAM and hard drive space.

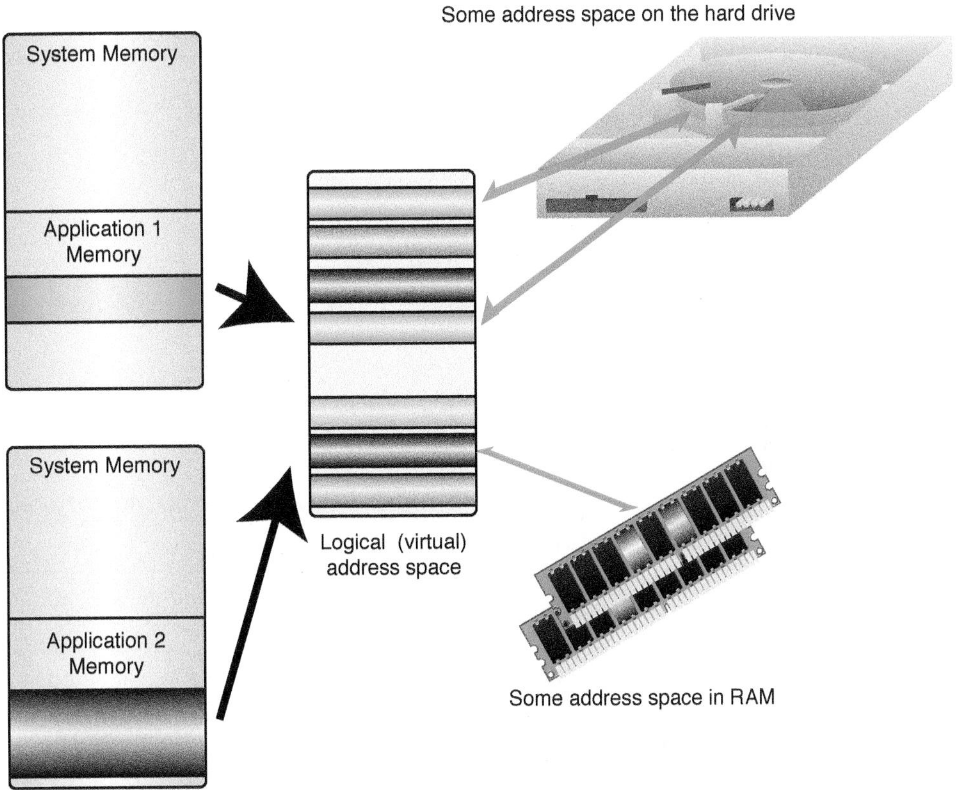

FIGURE 6.16 Virtual memory

Monitoring Memory Usage in Windows

Windows has a **Performance utility** in Task Manager for monitoring memory usage. To access Task Manager, press Ctrl+Alt+Del. Select the *Performance* tab, which has graphs that visually demonstrate the CPU and memory usage.

Figure 6.17 shows Task Manager, and Table 6.8 details some of the fields related to memory. Note that in order to see the memory-related data, you must click the Memory option in the left pane. In the Memory Composition section, there are several sections separated by vertical bars. You can place the pointer inside a space, and the name of the section appears. The sections, from left to right, are as follows:

> *In Use:* The amount of memory currently being used
> *Modified:* Memory that holds data that must be written to the drive before the memory location can be used by something else
> *Standby:* The amount of memory that is cached and currently is not being used
> *Free:* The available memory to be used

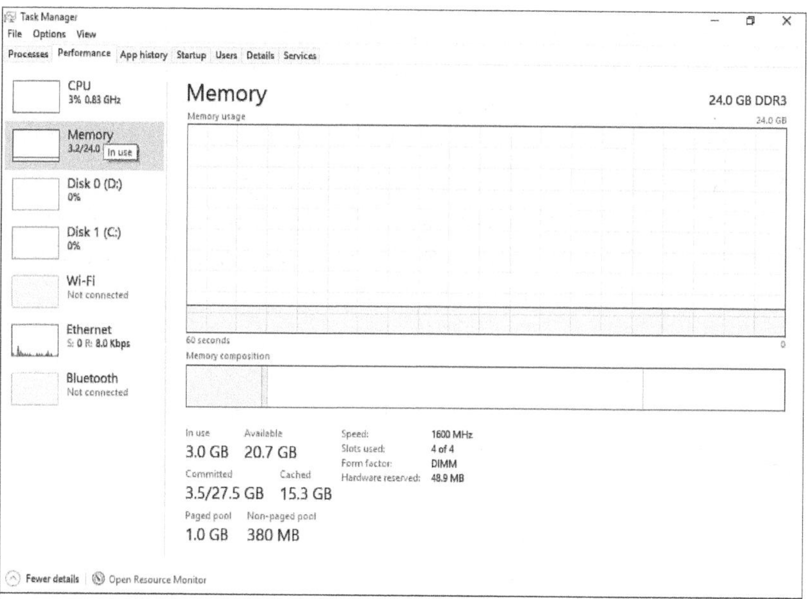

FIGURE 6.17 Windows Task Manager Performance tab—Memory

TABLE 6.8 Windows Task Manager Performance tab memory-related fields

Field	Description
In Use	The amount of memory currently being used by applications, the operating system, drivers, and processes.
Available	The amount of physical memory for application/operating system use.
Committed	This is shown as two numbers. The first number is how much memory the operating system has identified from open applications and processes that need memory (and that might get removed or paged out of RAM if other, more important, processes need the space). The second number is the amount of physical and virtual memory available.
Cached	The memory space that includes data that needs to be written to disk before being available, as well as cached data that is currently not being used.
Paged Pool	Memory set aside for operating system functions or device drivers that could be written to disk, if necessary.
Non-Paged Pool	Memory set aside for operating system functions or device drivers that must remain in physical memory (that is, cannot be paged out).
Speed	Speed of the RAM chips.
Slots Used	Number of memory slots used for memory modules and total number of slots.
Form Factor	Type of memory module, such as DIMM or SODIMM (used in laptops). Chapter 11, "Computer Design and Troubleshooting Review," covers mobile devices and SODIMMs.
Hardware Reserved	Memory reserved for device drivers or firmware that cannot be used by Windows for any other function.

Older Applications in Windows

Older applications are sometimes challenging in the newer versions of Windows. Some dated applications do not operate in the newer Windows versions because these programs frequently make direct calls to hardware, which Windows 7 and higher do not allow. These programs might also require that you change the color depth and resolution settings through the Display Control Panel or Settings link.

For Windows 7 and higher, Microsoft states that some older software might not run properly and offers **Compatibility mode**. Right-click the application icon from the *Start* menu or right-click the program executable file and select *Properties*. Use the *Compatibility* tab to select the Windows version for which the application was written. If you do not know the version, you can select the *Run Compatibility Troubleshooter* button and then select the *Try Recommended Settings* link. Figure 6.18 shows the Compatibility tab.

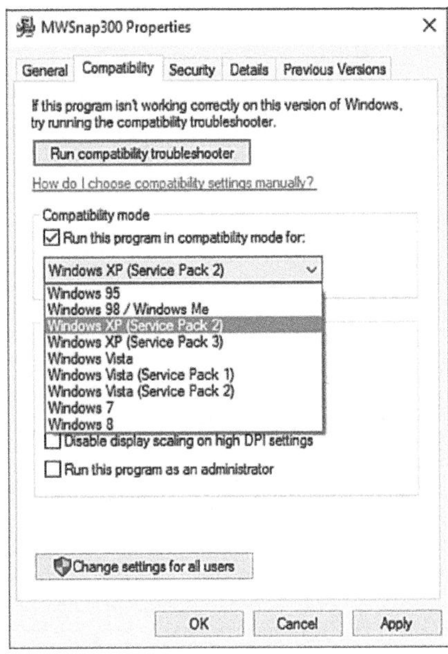

FIGURE 6.18 Windows Compatibility tab

You can also configure virtual machines by using virtualization software such as Microsoft's Virtual PC or Hyper-V, Oracle VM VirtualBox, or VMware Workstation to run older operating systems as well as run older applications. A **virtual machine** (VM) allows you to reduce hardware costs by running multiple operating systems simultaneously on a single computer (without one interfering with the other). Virtualization is covered in more detail in Chapter 12, "Internet Connectivity, Virtualization, and Cloud Technologies."

Troubleshooting Memory Problems

You can get "out of memory" errors, **POST beeps**, motherboard diagnostic lights or codes, system lockups (**intermittent shutdowns**), **sluggish performance**, spinning **pinwheel** (indicating an application is hung), and **application crashes** due to memory problems. With any of these problems, no matter which operating system is being used, check the amount of available memory and free hard drive space. Sometimes you must close all applications, reboot the computer, and open only the application that was running when the out-of-memory error occurred because some applications do not release the memory space they hold. Use Task Manager or the Apps setting to halt the application.

The following tips and troubleshooting steps help with memory management:

- Add more RAM. To see the amount of physical memory (RAM) currently installed, access *File Explorer*, right-click *This PC*, and select *Properties*.
- If you just installed new memory and an error appears, this is normal. Enter *Setup* because the system BIOS/UEFI knows something has changed.
- If you just installed new memory and the computer will not boot, check your installation by carefully pushing harder on the memory module (after shutting down and removing power,

of course) to ensure that the module is fully seated into the slot. Check for loosened cables near the memory module(s). Ensure that you are installing the right memory type.

> Use the **Windows Memory Diagnostic Tool**, by using one of the following methods:
  > In Windows, search using the words **`memory diagnostic`**. Select the *Windows Memory Diagnostic* (Windows 10/11) link.
  > Boot into the *Advanced Boot Options* menu (by pressing F8 upon startup). Press Esc. Press Tab to move to the *Tools* section > *Windows Memory Diagnostic Tool.*
  > Use the original Windows operating system disc to boot the computer. Enter the language requirements and then click the *Repair Your Computer* link. From the *System Recovery Options* window, select *Windows Memory Diagnostic Tool.*
  > Use the command **`mdsched`**.

> Delete files/applications that are no longer needed and close applications that are not being used. Empty the Recycle Bin.

> Adjust the size of the virtual memory.

> Do not put the paging file on multiple partitions that reside on the same hard drive. Use multiple hard drives, if necessary.

> Put the paging file on a hard drive partition that does not contain the operating system.

> Put the paging file on the fastest hard drive.

> Remove the desktop wallpaper scheme or use a plain one.

> Adjust your Temporary Internet Files setting. For Microsoft Edge in Windows, search for Internet Explorer (not Microsoft Edge) and select the *Tools* > *Internet Options* > *Settings* button. Adjust how much drive space is set aside for caching web pages.

> Defragment the hard drive. See Chapter 7, "Storage Devices," for the steps.

TECH TIP

Upgrading memory is an easy solution

Upgrading memory is one of the easiest ways to solve performance issues. Keep in mind that sometimes you simply must buy more RAM, but you should try the previously mentioned tips before resorting to that.

If you receive a message that SPD device data is missing or inconclusive, your motherboard is looking for SPD data that it cannot receive from the memory module. If this is a new module, ensure that it supports SPD. If it is an older module, you need to replace one of your memory modules.

POST usually detects a problem with a memory chip, and most systems show an error code or message. The motherboard might also contain diagnostic lights or a code. In either case, turn off the computer, remove the cover, press down on any memory modules, and reboot. Another option is to clean the memory module slots with compressed air and reinstall the module. The key to good memory chip troubleshooting is to divide and conquer. Narrow the problem to a suspected memory module and then swap banks, if possible.

TECH TIP

When adding more memory doesn't help

Today's operating systems rely almost as much on hard drive space as they do on RAM because of multitasking. Lack of hard drive space is almost as bad as not having enough RAM. If the system still runs slowly after adding RAM, look at used hard drive space and delete files to free up space, upgrade drive storage, or add another drive.

Removable Storage

Removable storage is very important to users today, for PCs, laptops, mobile devices, cameras, and smartphones. Removable memory comes in many forms and capacities. Common removable storage includes flash drives and memory cards.

Flash memory is a type of nonvolatile, solid-state memory that holds data even when the computer power is off. Network devices, smartphones, and tablets use flash memory to store the operating system and instructions. Some tablets can use external flash media for storage. Solid-state drives (SSDs) also use flash memory (see Chapter 7). Digital cameras use flash memory to store pictures. Unlike DRAM, flash memory does not have to be refreshed, and unlike SRAM, it does not need constant power. Figure 6.19 shows various flash memory devices.

USB **flash drives** (sometimes called thumb drives, memory bars, or memory sticks) allow storage up to 1 TB, and higher capacities are expected in the near future. In Figure 6.19, the blue and two white items are USB flash drives, and the rest are storage for devices such as digital cameras and recorders. After attaching a flash drive to a USB port, a drive letter is assigned by the operating system, and File Explorer can be used to manipulate files on the drive.

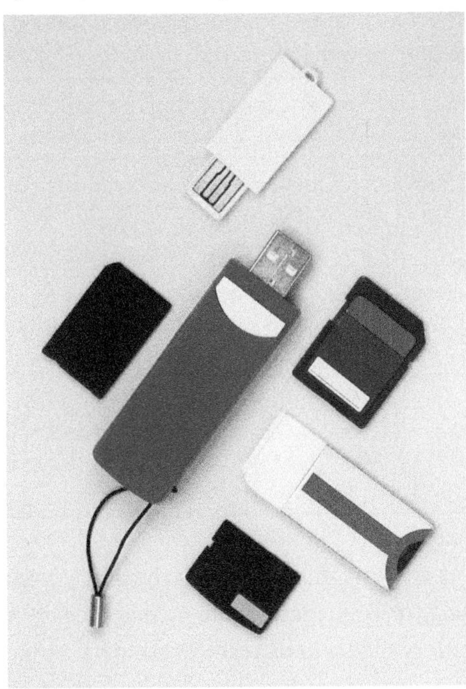

FIGURE 6.19 Flash memory

TECH TIP

The number-one cause of flash drive failure is improper removal

When you are finished using a flash drive, double-click the *Remove Hardware* icon located in the notification area. Click *Safely Remove Hardware and Eject Media*. Select the appropriate flash drive. When you see a message appear that says you can safely remove the drive, remove the flash drive from the USB port.

Figure 6.20 shows the interior of a flash drive. Chapter 11 goes into more detail about the types of flash memory used with such devices.

FIGURE 6.20 Inside a USB flash drive

Memory cards contain flash memory and are used in cell phones, digital recorders, cameras, and just about any type of mobile device you can find. Table 6.9 lists memory cards you might see or need to install.

TABLE 6.9 Memory cards

Storage type	Comments
CompactFlash (CF)	Introduced by SanDisk; uses flash memory; does not require a battery to store photos after power is removed; includes CF-I and CF-II
SmartMedia	Developed by Toshiba; smaller and lighter than CF; adapter cards with PC Card/ExpressBus ATA are available for data transfers
Memory Stick	Created by Sony; small in size; can read/write with a Memory Stick reader; includes Memory Stick (MS), Memory Stick Duo (MSD), Memory Stick Micro (M2)
Secure Digital	Size of a postage stamp; does not require power to retain data; uses flash memory technology; supports cryptographic security; different types include SD, miniSD, microSD, and SDHC
MMC (multimedia card)	A type of flash memory used in many portable devices, including cameras; works in many devices that support SD cards and is less expensive; types include MMC, eMMC, RS-MMC, MMCmicro, dual voltage (DV-MMC), MMCplus, MMCmobile, and MiCard

Related to removable storage is copying data that is on the card. A **memory card reader** or multi-card reader attaches externally or is integrated into a computer or laptop. A reader has multiple slots that allow different memory media to be read. These devices have many names, such as 15-in-1 reader, 8-in-1 reader, or 5-in-1 reader (depending on how many different slots or types of memory modules the device accepts). A memory card reader instantly recognizes inserted memory cards, whose contents can be copied to the computer and manipulated. The media card slots are assigned drive letters that are accessible through File Explorer. Figure 6.21 shows one of these readers.

TECH TIP

No drive letter

If the media does not appear in Windows/File Explorer, the reader may have been temporarily uninstalled. Use the Safely Remove Hardware and Eject Media tool in the notification area, unplug the cable from the port, and re-insert the cable to ensure that the operating system recognizes the reader. If the card reader or ports are still not available or if they are integrated into the computer, restart the computer.

FIGURE 6.21 Memory card reader

Memory is one of the most critical components of a computer, and it is important for a technician to be well versed in the different memory technologies. Because memory is one of the most common upgrades, becoming proficient and knowledgeable about populating memory is important.

SOFT SKILLS: TEAMWORK

Technicians tend not to like working in teams as much as they like working on their own. Much of a technician's job is done alone. However, a technician normally has one or more peers, a supervisor, and a network of partners involved with the job, such as suppliers, subcontractors, and part-time help. It is easy to have tunnel vision in a technical support job and lose sight of the mission of the business. Many technical jobs have the main purpose of generating revenue—solving people's computer and network problems for the purpose of making money. Other technicians have more of a back-office support role—planning, installing, configuring, maintaining, and troubleshooting technologies the business uses to make money.

Technicians must focus on solving customers' problems and ensuring that customers feel that their problems have been solved professionally and efficiently. However, you cannot lose sight of the business-first mentality; remember that you play a support role whether you generate revenue or not. You are a figure on someone's balance sheet, and you need to keep your skills and attitudes finely tuned to be valuable to the company. No matter how good you are at your job, you are always better to a company if you are part of a team than if you're on your own. Make sure to **be on time, maintain a positive attitude, and project confidence**. Being a person who is late, takes off early, chats too much with customers, blames others, and so on, is not being a good team member. If you are going to be late for work or leave early, inform your supervisor and coworkers so they can take care of any issues that arise while you're gone. If you are going to be late for a customer appointment, contact the customer and let him or her know you are running late.

Technicians need to be good team players and see themselves as a reflection of their company when on the job (see Figure 6.22). Employers see **teamwork** as an important part of a technician's skill set—just as important as technical skills. Think of ways that you can practice teamwork even as a student and refine those skills when you join the workforce.

FIGURE 6.22 Teamwork

Chapter Summary

- Memory on a motherboard is SDRAM, a type of RAM that is cheaper and slower than SRAM, the type of memory inside the CPU and processor housing.
- Each type of DDR module will only fit in that type of module's motherboard slot. For example, a DDR5 module requires a DDR5 slot.
- Unbuffered non-parity memory is the memory normally installed in computers.
- ECC is used for error checking and is commonly found in high-end computers and servers.
- The CL rating or the timing sequence's first number shows how quickly the processor can access data in sequential memory locations. The lower the first number, the faster the access.
- SPD is a technology used so the memory module can communicate specifications to the BIOS/UEFI.
- Dual-rank memory is one module that acts like two modules. Single-rank memory is the norm, and an advertisement will not normally use this term.
- Before installing memory, plan your strategy: Read the manual to determine the type of memory; determine the total amount of memory; determine whether any memory is to be removed; determine the memory to purchase; and be mindful of getting the most out of your memory by implementing dual-, triple-, or even quad-channeling.
- When implementing dual-, triple-, or quadruple-channeling, buy matching memory modules.
- Particular versions of Windows have memory limitations.
- RAM is very susceptible to ESD events. Use proper handling procedures, including using an antistatic wrist strap.
- Before removing or installing memory, disconnect the power cord and remove the battery on a mobile device.
- Having as much RAM in a system as possible is an important performance factor, and so is having free hard drive space because hard drive space is used as memory. This is called virtual memory, and the information stored temporarily on a hard drive is stored in an area known as a paging file, page file, or swap file. The paging file should be on the fastest drive that has the most free storage.
- Use Task Manager to monitor memory performance.
- Use POST, motherboard LED/display output codes, BIOS/UEFI diagnostics, and the Windows Memory Diagnostic Tool to diagnose memory problems.
- Flash media is used to provide memory or additional storage space for computing devices and includes USB flash drives.
- A technician is part of a business and should contribute to the team. A technician should professionally represent a company.

A+ CERTIFICATION EXAM TIPS

- ✓ Be able to install the correct RAM. Know the pin numbers of DDR3, DDR4, and DDR5 for both DIMMs and SODIMMs and that a DDR3 socket, for example, will not accept a DDR4 or DDR5 module.
- ✓ Know that adding memory is one of the easiest ways to improve computer performance.
- ✓ Know how to calculate what memory is needed for an upgrade or a new install.
- ✓ Be able to identify memory slots on a motherboard.
- ✓ Know how to populate memory when single-, dual-, triple-, or quad-channeling is being implemented.
- ✓ When populating memory, consult the motherboard documentation before you go any further.
- ✓ Be able to describe the difference between non-parity and error correction code (ECC) memory.
- ✓ Know that memory chips are especially susceptible to ESD and how to prevent ESD damage when installing or removing memory. Review Chapter 5, "Disassembly and Power," for tips on handling ESD.
- ✓ Remember that if any application is slow to respond, the computer may need more RAM. POST error codes, application crashes, and intermittent shutdowns can indicate a memory problem.
- ✓ Review the troubleshooting symptoms and tips at the end of the chapter.
- ✓ Know when and how to use Compatibility mode and the Windows Memory Diagnostic Tool.
- ✓ Keep in mind that the following professionalism skills are part of the 220-1102 exam: (1) Maintain a positive attitude, (2) project confidence, (3) be on time, and (4) if you will be late, contact the customer.

Key Terms

application crash 205
be on time 210
buffered memory 191
cache memory 188
CL rating 199
Compatibility mode 205
DDR3 190
DDR4 190
DDR5 190
DIMM 188
DRAM 188
dual-channel 195
ECC 191
flash drive 207
flash memory 207
heat spreader 190
intermittent shutdown 205
maintain a positive attitude 210
memory card 208
memory card reader 208
non-parity 191
paging file 202
Performance utility 203
pinwheel 205
POST beep 205
project confidence 210
quad-channel 197
RAM 188
sluggish performance 205
SODIMM 188
SPD 192
SRAM 188
teamwork 210
triple-channel 197
unbuffered memory 191
virtual machine 205
virtual RAM 202
Windows Memory Diagnostic Tool 206

Review Questions

The following specifications for motherboard RAM are used for Questions 1–5:

> Four DDR4 SDRAM DIMM sockets arranged in two channels and supporting up to 128 GB (32 GB single DIMM capacity) of system memory

> Support for DDR4 3200/2933/2667/2400/2133 MHz memory modules DIMMs

> Support for ECC unbuffered DIMM 1Rx8/2Rx8 memory modules

> Support for non-ECC unbuffered DIMM 1Rx8/2Rx8/1Rx16 memory modules

> Support for extreme memory profile (XMP) memory modules

> Support for up to 16 GB of system memory

1. Of the given features, which one(s) would be applicable to this computer? (Choose all that apply.)

   [unbuffered | registered | 204-pin SO-DIMM | 288-pin DDR5 DIMM | 288-pin DDR4 DIMM | ECC | non-ECC | single rank | dual rank]

2. Pretend that this computer has 4 GB of memory installed. Write all combinations of memory population in the slots.

   ____

3. [T | F] The technician that is recommending memory for this motherboard could recommend memory that does not perform error checking.

4. What does the statement "four DDR4 SDRAM DIMM sockets arranged in two channels" mean?

   ____

   ____

5. Would there be an issue if this motherboard contained 6 GB of RAM and the computer had 32-bit Windows 10 installed? If so, explain the issue.

   ____

   ____

Consider the following memory advertisements for desktop memory used in Questions 6–11:

a. 2 GB 240-pin SDRAM DDR3L 1600 (PC3L 12800) Desktop Memory

b. 4 GB DDR3-1600 (PC3-12800) CL11 240-pin DIMM

c. 4 GB ECC registered DDR3 SDRAM CAS latency 9

d. 4 GB 240-pin DDR3 SDRAM 1333 (PC3 10600) CAS 9

e. 8 GB (1x8 GB) 1333MHz PC3-10600 CL9 ECC registered dual-rank low power

f. 8 GB (2x4 GB) DDR4 SDRAM 2133 (PC4 17000)

g. 16 GB PC4L-2666

h. 16 GB kit (2x8 GB) DDR4 2666 MHz PC4-21300 CL19 unbuffered non-ECC 1.2V UDIMM

i. 16 GB 1Rx16 DDR4 UDIMM 3200MHz

6. In these advertisements, which DDR4 option(s) would hold the most data in a single memory module and be best suited for a desktop computer?

   ____

   ____

   ____

7. In option g, what does the L in PC4L mean?

   ____

   ____

   ____

8. A customer wants to dual-channel 8 GB of DDR4 RAM on a desktop computer. Which memory module(s) would be best to buy, given the following documentation from the motherboard manual? (Memory module slots are in order from closest to the CPU: 1, 3, 2, and 4.)
   > Do not install ECC memory modules.
   > The memory configurations are as follows:
   > A pair of matched modules in DIMM connectors 1 and 2
   > A pair of matched modules in DIMM connectors 1 and 2 and another pair in connectors 3 and 4
   > If you install mixed pairs, the memory modules function at the speed of the slowest memory module installed.

   ____

   ____

9. Considering the answer given to Question 8, which motherboard DIMM connectors would be used?

   ____

10. What type of memory feature will be needed if data accuracy is paramount for a new computer?
    [buffered | ECC | registered | XMP]
11. When comparing options b and d and imagining that both modules cost the same, which one would be the better purchase? Explain your reasoning.

    ____

    ____

12. What method is most effective for preventing an ESD event when installing RAM?
    a. placing the computer on an antistatic mat
    b. wearing an antistatic wrist strap
    c. staying in contact with an unpainted metal part of the computer
    d. wearing rubber-soled shoes and using the buddy system by having another technician standing by
13. Which of the following would be the first sign that a computer needs more RAM?
    a. The computer is slow to respond.
    b. The computer makes a ticking noise.
    c. A POST error message appears.
    d. A recommendation to use the *Windows Memory Diagnostic Tool* appears.
14. How can you tell the maximum amount of memory a motherboard can support?
    a. Look at the memory options in BIOS/UEFI.
    b. Use the Windows Task Manager > *Performance* tab.
    c. Use the Windows Memory tool.
    d. Look at the motherboard documentation.
15. List one easy way to tell how much RAM is installed in a computer.

    ____

    ____

16. [T | F] A DDR4 DIMM can fit in a DDR3 memory expansion slot.
17. You have just added two new memory modules to a computer, but now the system will not boot and is beeping multiple times. What will you check first?

    ____

    ____

    ____

18. Give an example of how a technician might project confidence while working on a help desk.

____

____

____

19. A system already has two 2666 MHz memory modules installed, and a technician adds two more modules that operate at 3200 MHz. What will be the result of this action?

 a. The computer won't boot.

 b. The computer might freeze at times.

 c. The memory will operate at the 2666 MHz speed.

 d. All memory will operate at the 3200 MHz speed.

20. A technician has received a complaint that a computer is not performing as well as it used to. Which Windows 10 tool would the technician get the user to open to quickly tell how much RAM is currently being used by the open applications?

 [Performance Monitor | Device Manager | System Information Tool | Task Manager]

Exercises

Exercise 6.1 Configuring Memory on Paper

Objective: To be able to determine the correct amount and type of memory to install on a motherboard

Parts: Internet access or access to magazines or ads that show memory prices

Procedure: Refer to Table 6.10 to answer the questions. This motherboard supports 1600/1333/1066 MHz DDR3 memory modules. The capacities supported are 1, 2, 4, and 8 GB, for a total of 16 GB maximum. Memory channel speed is determined by the slowest DIMM populated in the system.

TABLE 6.10 Motherboard single-/dual-channel combinations

		Sockets	
Mode	**Scenario**	**DIMM1**	**DIMM2**
Single	1	Populated	
	2		Populated
Dual-channel	1	Populated	Populated

1. What memory modules are needed if the customer wants 5 GB of RAM? What capacities and how many modules of each capacity are required?

____

2. How many memory slots does this motherboard have? [1 | 2 | 3 | 4]

3. Using the internet, a computer parts magazine, or a list of memory modules, determine the exact part numbers and quantities of memory modules that you would buy to populate this motherboard with 5 GB of RAM. List them as well as the location where you obtained the information.

____

____

4. This motherboard already has 4 GB of RAM installed in the DIMM1 slot. The customer would like to upgrade to 8 GB total memory, use the existing module if possible, and use dual-channeling. This question requires two answers. What capacity and number of memory modules are needed to get up to the 8 GB total? List any concerns to consider.

____

____

____

5. What memory slot will be used to install the memory module, based on the documentation provided?

____

____

6. What does the documentation mean when referencing DDR3 1600/1333/1066 MHz RAM?

____

____

7. How do you know which one of the 1600, 1333, or 1066 modules to use?

____

____

____

____

____

8. Using the internet, a computer parts magazine, or a provided list of memory modules, determine the exact part numbers and quantities of memory modules that you would buy to get this computer from 4 GB to 8 GB. List the module information along with the location where you obtained the information.

____

____

Exercise 6.2 Configuring Memory on Paper

Objective: To be able to determine the correct amount and type of memory to install on a motherboard

Parts: Internet access or access to magazines or ads that show memory prices

Procedure: Refer to Figure 6.23 and Table 6.11 to answer the questions. This motherboard supports the following memory configurations:

- Up to 64 GB memory
- Support for DDR4 26666/2400/2133 MHz memory modules
- Support for ECC unbuffered DIMM 1Rx8/2Rx8 memory modules (operate in non-ECC mode)
- Support for non-ECC unbuffered DIMM 1Rx8/2Rx8/1Rx16 memory modules

The desktop board supports either single- or dual-channel memory configurations. The board has four DDR4 SDRAM DIMM connectors with gold-plated contacts.

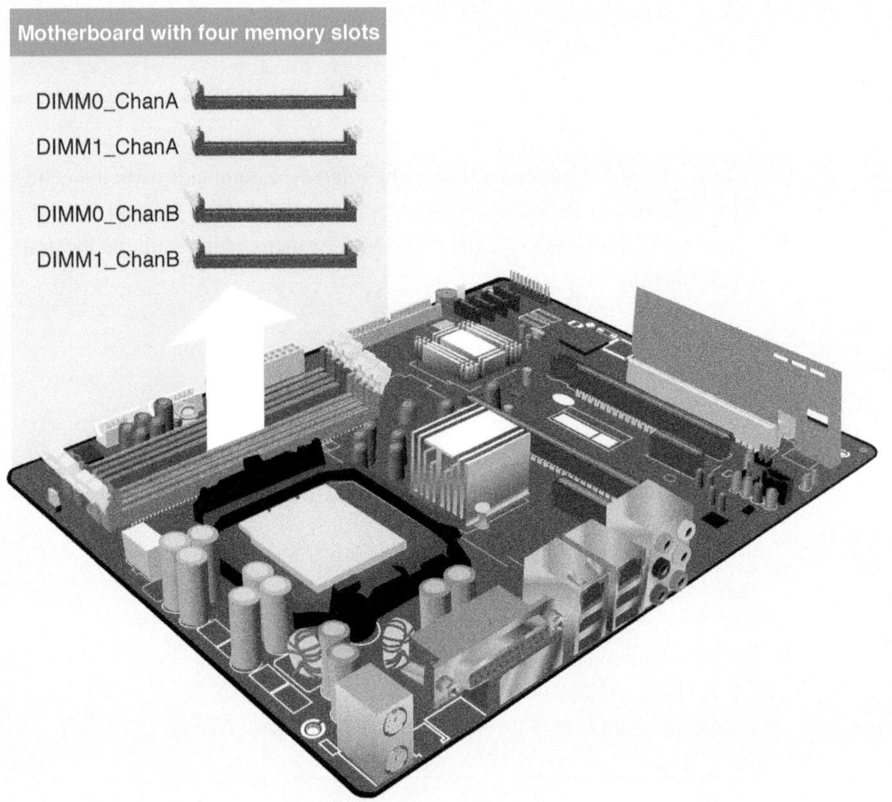

FIGURE 6.23 Motherboard with four memory slots and two channels

TABLE 6.11 Motherboard single-/dual-channel guidelines

Installed memory	Guidelines
2 DIMMs dual-channel	Install a matched pair of DIMMs equal in speed and size in DIMM0 of both Channel A and Channel B.
4 DIMMs dual-channel	Follow the directions for two DIMMs and add another matched pair of DIMMs in DIMM1 of both Channels A and B.
3 DIMMs dual-channel	Install a matched pair of DIMMs equal in speed and size in DIMM0 and DIMM1 of Channel A. Install a DIMM equal in speed and total size of the DIMMs installed in Channel A in either DIMM0 or DIMM1 of Channel B.
Single-channel	All other memory configurations result in single-channel memory operation.

CHAPTER 6

1. Within the documentation what does 1Rx8/2Rx8/1Rx16 mean?

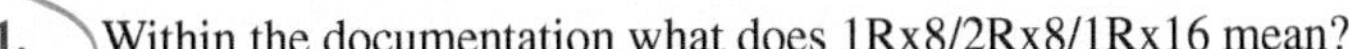

____

____

2. What memory features, if any, can be used? (Choose all that apply.)

   [non-ECC | non-parity | ECC | registered | fully buffered | unbuffered | SPD]

3. What memory modules are needed if the customer wants 32 GB of dual-channel RAM? (What capacities and how many of each capacity are required?)

____

4. What memory slots will be used to install the 32 GB of dual-channeled memory, based on the information provided?

5. This requires two answers. Using the internet, a computer parts magazine, or a list of memory modules, determine the exact part numbers and quantities of memory modules you would buy to populate this motherboard with 32 GB of RAM. List them, along with the location where you obtained the information.

6. What does *unbuffered* mean?

7. This question requires two answers. Can DDR3 memory modules be used with this motherboard? How can you tell?

8. If this motherboard already has 8 GB of RAM installed in the DIMM0_ChanA slot and the customer would like to upgrade to 16 GB of dual-channel RAM, what memory modules are needed? (What capacities and how many of each capacity are required?)

9. What concerns would you have regarding dual-channeling before researching prices?

10. What memory slots will be used to install the 16 GB of total memory, based on the information provided and the upgrade scenario presented in Question 8?

11. Using the internet, a computer parts magazine, or a list of memory modules, determine the exact part numbers and quantities of memory modules that you would buy to get to the total of 16 GB (from 8 GB) and do dual-channeling. List them, along with the location where you obtained the information.

Exercise 6.3 Configuring Memory on Paper

Objective: To be able to determine the correct amount and type of memory to install on a motherboard

Parts: Internet access or access to magazines or ads that show memory prices

Procedure: Refer to Figure 6.24 to answer the questions. The motherboard supports the following memory configurations:

> 1 GB, 2 GB, 4 GB unbuffered and non-ECC DDR3 DIMMs can be used in the DIMM slots (1, 2, 3, and 4) for a total of 32 GB max using DDR3 1066/1333 MHz modules.

> Recommended memory configurations are modules in DIMMs 1 and 3 or modules in DIMMs 1, 2, 3, and 4.

> Single- and dual-channel modes are supported.

> You may install different sizes in Channel A and B. The dual-channel configuration will be the total size of the lowest-sized channel. Any excess memory will operate in single-channel mode.

>>1.65V DIMMs are recommended.

>Use the same CAS latency and obtain from the same vendor, if possible.

>The default memory operation frequency is dependent on SPD.

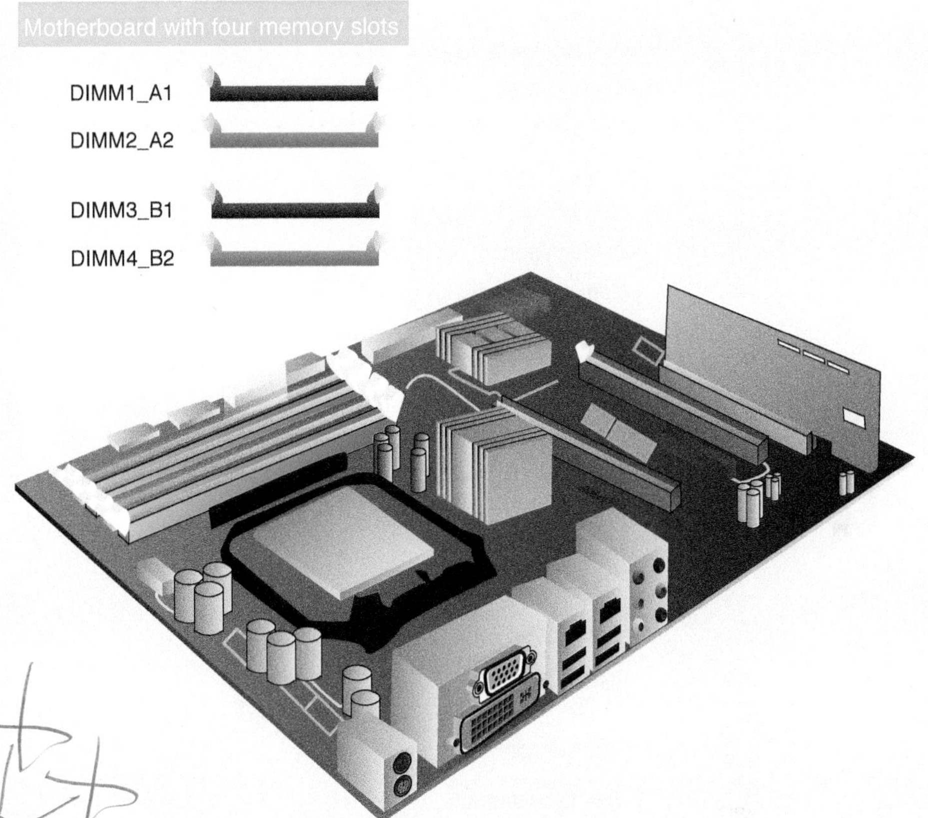

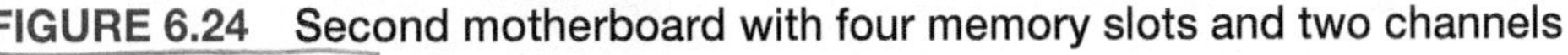
FIGURE 6.24 Second motherboard with four memory slots and two channels

1. What memory features, if any, are used? (Choose all that apply.)

   [parity | non-parity | ECC | registered | unbuffered | SPD]

2. The customer wants 4 GB of RAM. What memory modules are needed? (What capacities and how many of each capacity are required?)

   ____

3. What memory slots will be used to install the memory suggested in Question 2?

   ____

   ____

4. Using the internet, a computer parts magazine, or a list of memory modules provided by the instructor, determine the exact part numbers and quantities of memory modules that you would buy. List them, along with the location where you obtained this information.

   ____

5. In what type of systems would ECC modules most likely be required and used?

   [student desktop | smartphones | tablets | servers | laptops]

6. What is the purpose of ECC modules?

   ____

7. What is the purpose of SPD?

   ____

Exercise 6.4 Configuring Memory on Paper

Objective: To be able to determine the correct amount and type of memory to install on a motherboard

Parts: Internet access or access to magazines or ads that show memory prices

Procedure: Refer to Figure 6.25 to answer the questions. The motherboard supports the following memory configurations:

> Max memory supported: 16 GB

> Memory types: DDR4-4600/4400/4266/4200

> Memory channels: 3

> Number of DIMMs: 4

> ECC supported: Yes

> Connectors use gold-plated contacts

> Unbuffered, non-registered single- or double-sided SPD DIMMs with a voltage rating of 1.65V or less

> Optimal performance can be achieved by installing three matching DIMMs in the ChanA, ChanB, and ChanC memory slots.

> Dual-channel operation can be achieved by installing matching DIMMs in ChanB and ChanC or all four memory slots.

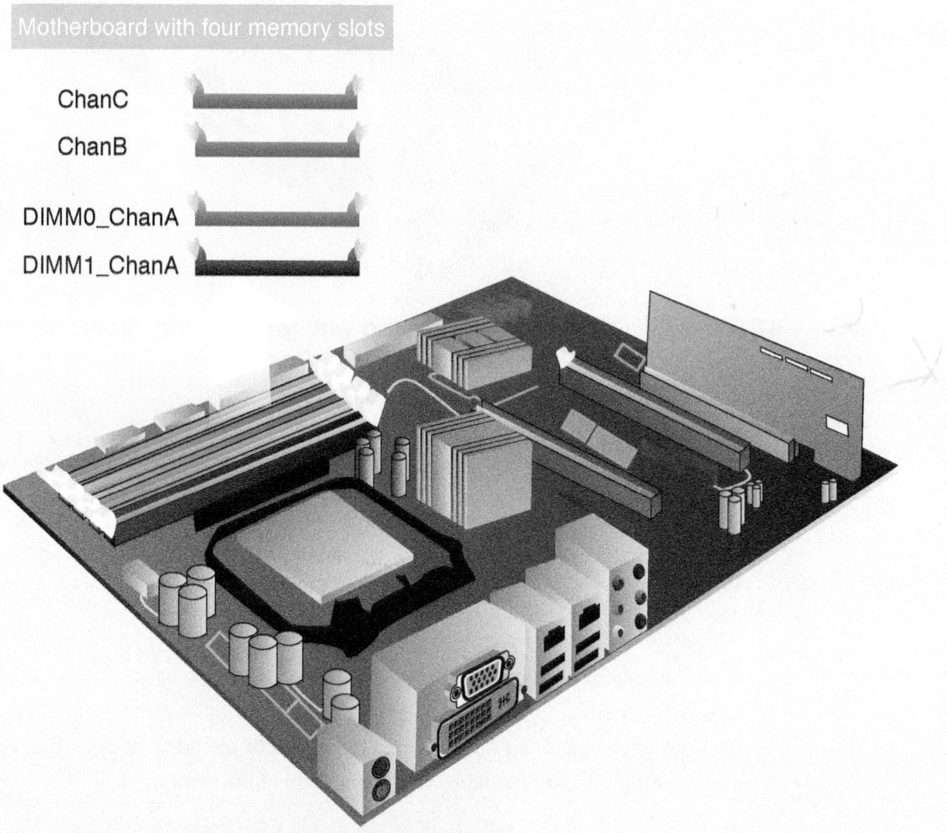

FIGURE 6.25 Triple-channel motherboard

1. What memory features, if any, are used? (Choose all that apply.)
   [parity | non-parity | ECC | registered | unbuffered | SPD]
2. The customer wants 8 GB of RAM performing triple-channeling. Can this be done? Why or why not? [Yes | No]

____

____

3. What memory modules are needed to put 8 GB of memory on the motherboard? (What capacities and how many of each capacity are required?) Justify your choice.

____

____

____

____

4. What memory slots will be used to install the memory suggested in Question 3?

____

____

5. Using the internet, a computer parts magazine, or a list of memory modules provided by the instructor, determine the exact part numbers and quantities of memory modules that you would buy. List them, along with the location where you obtained this information.

____

6. The user has 32-bit Windows 10 installed on this computer. Will there be any issues with the 8 GB of RAM? If so, what might those issues be?

____

____

7. List one method a technician could use to ensure that the 8 GB is recognized by the system.

____

____

Activities

Internet Discovery

Objective: To become familiar with researching memory chips using the internet

Parts: A computer with internet access

Procedure: Use the internet to complete the following procedure:

> Power on the computer and start an internet browser.

> Using any search engine, locate two vendors that sell memory chips.

> Create a table like the one below and fill in your findings for each of the memory sites.

	Site 1	Site 2
URL		
Type of DIMM		
Largest-capacity DIMM		
Pros of website		
Cons of website		

Soft Skills

Objective: To enhance and fine-tune a future technician's ability to listen, communicate in both written and oral forms, and support people who use computers in a professional manner

Activities:

1. On your own, use the internet to find a utility that tests soft skills or your personality. Compare your scores with those of others in the class. Make a list of how you might improve in specific weak areas. Present your findings to a group and share your group findings with another group.
2. Note that this activity requires two computers. In groups of two, have one person describe in great detail to the other person how to upgrade the computer's memory by removing memory from one computer and adding it to the other. The person doing the physical installation can do nothing except what the partner describes how to do. Reverse roles for removing the memory and reinstalling back in the original computer. At the end of the exercise, the two participants describe to the teacher what they experienced.
3. In small groups, find a video that describes how to do something on a computer. Critique the video in terms of how the speaker might do a better job communicating to people who are not technicians. Share the video with the class, along with your recommendations for doing it better. As an option, script a short presentation for how to do something. Tape/record it if possible and have the class critique each group's presentation.

Critical Thinking Skills

Objective: To analyze and evaluate information as well as apply learned information to new or different situations

Activities:

1. Using the documentation of any computer, compare and contrast two dual-channeling scenarios/solutions for a pretend customer. List three recommendations you would have for the customer. Write a list of your findings and share them with the class.

   ____

   ____

   ____

2. List the repercussions of discovering that a motherboard supports both single-rank and dual-rank memory modules. How does a single-rank memory module compare with a dual-rank memory module?

   ____

   ____

   ____

   ____

   ____

3. Download a motherboard manual from the internet or use one provided in the classroom. Find the memory section and make a list of any terms or directions that are given that you do not understand. In groups of four or five, share your lists and come up with as many solutions as possible. Share your group list with the class. Write any unsolved questions on the board and bring the answers to those questions back in a week.

7 Storage Devices

In this chapter you will learn:

> Basic storage terms
> About IDE (PATA), SATA, eSATA, SSD, and SSHD technologies
> How to install and configure storage devices, including RAID
> How to fix storage device problems
> How to keep a drive healthy
> How to create and troubleshoot a RAID array
> How to create and use Windows Storage Spaces
> Effective phone communication

CompTIA Exam Objectives:

✓ 1101-3.1 Explain basic cable types and their connectors, features, and purposes.

✓ 1101-3.3 Given a scenario, select and install storage devices.

✓ 1101-5.3 Given a scenario, troubleshoot and diagnose problems with storage drives and RAID arrays.

✓ 1102-1.2 Given a scenario, use the appropriate Microsoft command-line tool.

✓ 1102-1.3 Given a scenario, use features and tools of the Microsoft Windows 10 operating system (OS).

✓ 1102-1.8 Explain common OS types and their purposes.

✓ 1102-1.9 Given a scenario, perform OS installations and upgrades in a diverse OS environment.

✓ 1102-2.8 Given a scenario, use common data destruction and disposal methods.

✓ 1102-3.1 Given a scenario, troubleshoot common Windows OS problems.

✓ 1102-4.7 Given a scenario, use proper communication techniques and professionalism.

Storage Devices Overview

Storage devices hold the data we are so fond of generating and keeping—photos, PDFs, movies, documents, spreadsheets, and whatever else we can think to save. Data can be stored on optical media, flash media, or magnetic media such as hard drives, as shown in Figure 7.1.

FIGURE 7.1 Storage devices

Many folks, especially those who travel frequently, use data storage servers at their company. Data can also be stored "in the cloud." This means that there are storage devices available on remote servers to store data. Some storage is provided by an internet provider or as a service for a mobile device. Companies such as Amazon, Microsoft, Google, SugarSync, and Dropbox provide cloud storage. Some companies charge for cloud storage, and others offer limited amounts of cloud storage for free and have an option to pay for more. This is known as *cloud storage* or *offsite storage*. More information on how to do this is provided in Chapter 12, "Internet Connectivity, Virtualization, and Cloud Technologies." Figure 7.2 illustrates this concept, but keep in mind that "in the cloud" is just a ton of hard drives, servers, and other devices in some remote location.

FIGURE 7.2 Cloud storage

Hard Drive Overview

A hard drive can be mounted inside a computer case or attached externally to a USB, IEEE 1394 (FireWire), eSATA, or eSATAp port. Hard drive capacities extend into the terabytes. Hard drives are frequently upgraded in computers, so it is important for you to understand all the technical issues, including recognizing the parts of the hard drive subsystem, how the operating system and the BIOS/UEFI work together with a hard drive, and how to configure and troubleshoot a hard drive.

Hard drives come in different physical sizes (form factors). For desktop and small server models, 5.25-inch (not very popular) and **3.5-inch drives** are available. The **2.5-inch drive** form factor is designed for laptops. A 1.8-inch form factor is available for use and can be found for solid-state drives (SSDs), tablets, and portable devices. Figure 7.3 shows two hard drive sizes.

FIGURE 7.3 Desktop hard drive form factors

A hard drive can also be placed inside an external enclosure and attached using a USB, eSATA, eSATAp combo, or FireWire port. Figure 7.4 shows a Sabrent hard drive enclosure that includes a cooling fan with a filter that protects the fan from dust particles.

FIGURE 7.4 Sabrent external hard drive enclosure

Magnetic Hard Drive Geometry

Traditional mechanical hard drives are magnetic devices. These hard drives have multiple hard metal surfaces called *platters*. Each platter typically holds data on both sides and has two read/write heads: one for the top and one for the bottom. The read/write heads float on a cushion of air without touching the platter surface. Data is written by using electromagnetism. A charge is applied to the read/write head, creating a magnetic field. The metal hard drive platter has magnetic particles that are affected by the read/write head's magnetic field, allowing 1s and 0s to be "placed" or "induced" onto the drive. Figure 7.5 shows the major components inside a mechanical hard drive.

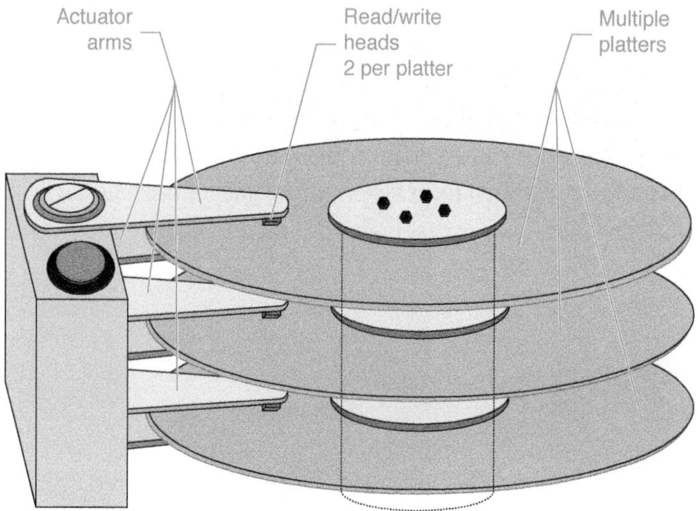

FIGURE 7.5 Hard drive geometry

A magnetic hard drive typically has two motors: one to turn the platters and one to move the read/write heads. A hard drive spins at different rotational rates called *revolutions per minute* (*RPMs*). Common speeds are **5,400 RPM**, **7,200 RPM**, **10,000 RPM**, and **15,000 RPM**. The higher the drive RPM number, the faster the transfer rate and generally the higher the cost.

If a read/write head touches the platter, a **head crash** occurs. This is sometimes called HDI (head-to-disk interference), and it can damage the platters or the read/write head, causing data corruption. Another important concept is mean time between failures (**MTBF**)—the average number of hours before a drive is likely to fail. Mechanical hard drives do fail, and that is why it is so important to back up the data stored on them. Figure 7.6 shows the inside of a hard drive. You can see the top read/write head and the platters. Keep in mind that you should not remove the cover from a hard drive because by doing so, you could allow particles into the sealed drive area.

FIGURE 7.6 Hard drive with cover removed

The magnetic hard drive surface is metallic and has concentric circles, each of which is called a *track*. Tracks are numbered starting with the outermost track, which is called track 0. One corresponding track on all surfaces of a hard drive is a *cylinder*. Figure 7.7 shows the difference between tracks and cylinders. Each track is further separated into sectors. Normally, each sector stores 512 bytes.

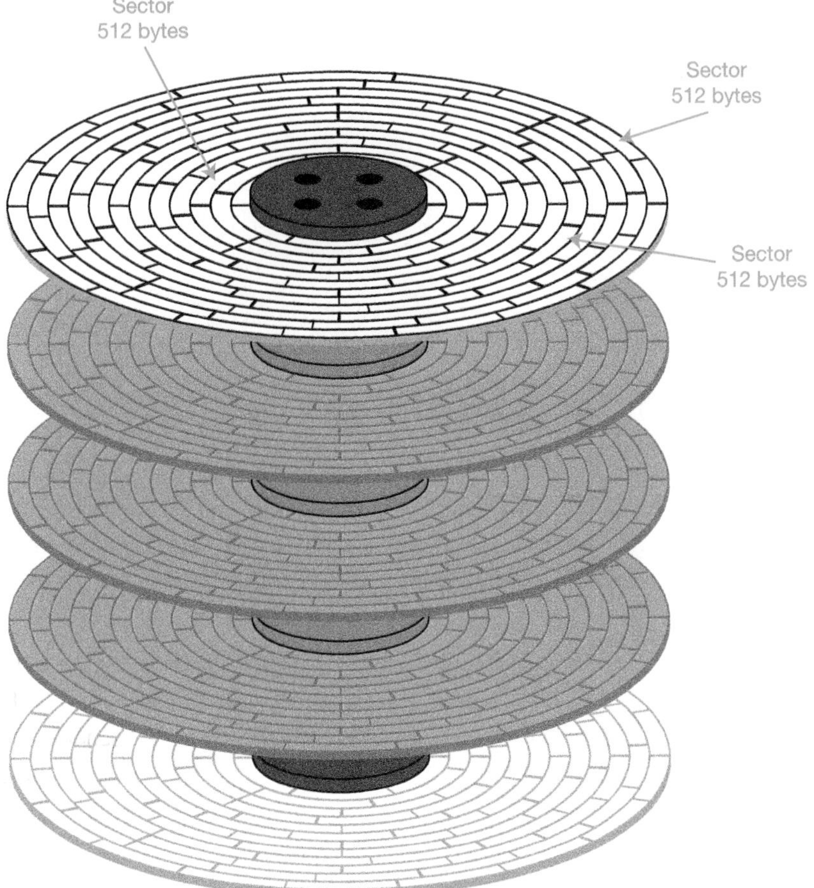

FIGURE 7.7 Cylinders, tracks, and sectors

Solid-State Drive (SSD) Overview

SSDs are storage devices that use nonvolatile flash memory technologies instead of traditional mechanical hard drive technologies. SSDs eliminate the number-one cause of hard drive failure: moving parts. SSDs produce little heat and are reliable, quiet, secure, long-lasting, and fast. SSDs are installed in laptops and desktop models as internal and external units. SSDs are common in tablets and some mobile devices. They are also used in environments such as temperature extremes or where a drive might be jolted. SSDs can be used in conjunction with mechanical hard drive storage.

TECH TIP

Don't use an SSD for archival storage

SSDs slowly lose their charge if left for a long time without power.

The main drawback to SSDs is cost. SSDs are expensive compared to mechanical hard drives. As with flash drives, each memory block of an SSD has a finite number of reads and writes. An SSD that writes data across the entire memory capacity will last longer. Some companies include software with the drive that helps with installation, configuration, performance, and monitoring and that tracks or estimates end of life. Figure 7.8 shows the inside of an SSD.

FIGURE 7.8 Solid-state drive without a cover

Today, hybrid SSDs are available. A hybrid SSD, or solid-state hybrid drive (**SSHD**), provides a combination of mechanical and flash technologies. The SSHD has some flash memory integrated with a traditional mechanical drive (see Figure 7.9).

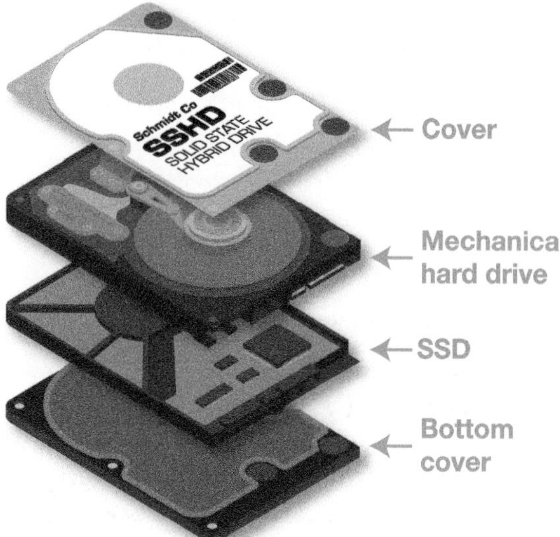

FIGURE 7.9 SSHD

The flash memory in an SSHD typically contains the most frequently used data that would be sent to the host interface. Advanced algorithms are used to predict this data. Only if requested data is not in flash memory will data be pulled from the slower mechanical drive. SSHDs provide the best of both worlds: Costs are lower per byte because you have a little bit of really fast memory storage, thanks to the SSD, and there is a lot of storage space, thanks to the traditional mechanical drive. You also do not require a faster RPM traditional drive with an SSHD.

Mechanical Drive Interfaces Overview

A hard drive system must use a set of rules in order to operate. These rules make up a standard called an *interface* that governs communication with the hard drive. There are two major hard drive interfaces: Integrated Drive Electronics (**IDE**)—also known as the AT Attachment (ATA) or Enhanced IDE (**EIDE**) standard—and Small Computer System Interface (SCSI). IDE is the most common in home and office computers. SCSI is more commonly found in storage networks or used with servers.

Note that other interfaces can also be used to attach external storage devices. Almost everyone has seen a flash drive or an external hard drive attached to a USB port. This chapter focuses more on the internal storage interfaces.

Both IDE and SCSI started out as parallel architectures, in which multiple bits are sent over multiple paths. Such an architecture requires precise timing as transfer rates increase. With both IDE and SCSI, multiple devices can attach to the same bus. Whereas parallel IDE, or parallel ATA (PATA), supports only two devices, parallel SCSI supports more. When multiple devices share the same bus, they have to wait their turn to access the bus, and there are configuration issues with which to contend.

In contrast, a serial architecture is a point-to-point bus in which each device has a single connection back to the controller. Bits are sent one at a time over a single link. More devices can attach to this type of architecture because it scales easily and is easy to configure. Figure 7.10 shows the concept of parallel and serial transfers.

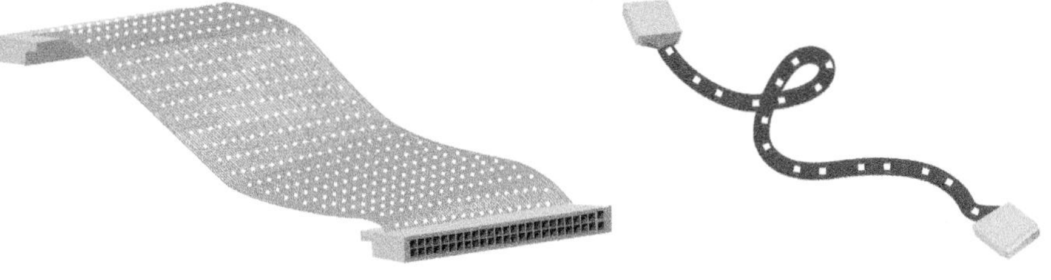

FIGURE 7.10 Parallel vs. serial data transfers

Today serial architectures are used. Both the IDE and SCSI standards have serial architectures available. The ATA serial standard is known as Serial ATA (**SATA**), and the SCSI serial standard is known as Serial Attached SCSI (**SAS**). SATA drives are used with laptops and PCs.

Both SATA and SAS drives are used with network-attached storage (NAS) devices, servers, and storage area networks (SANs). A **NAS drive** runs at higher RPMs, stores data for one or more servers and/or computers, and is designed to run 24/7 with optimized performance. Figure 7.11 shows SAS drives used in a data center.

FIGURE 7.11 SAS drives

M.2 and NVMe

SATA in laptops is being replaced by an interface known as M.2. An **M.2** slot allows SSDs and Wi-Fi/Bluetooth modules of varying sizes to be connected. An M.2 slot can interface with SATA 3.0 and higher, PCIe 3.0 and higher, and USB 3.0 and higher. Note that currently a single M.2 slot can use a maximum of four PCIe lanes and may use fewer. Refer to the motherboard documentation for the exact specifications.

Common card sizes include 2242, 2260, 2280, and 22110. In these sizes, 22 refers to the width, in millimeters, and the next two or three numbers refer to the length. The device or motherboard documentation indicates which sizes are accepted.

M.2 devices are also keyed, which means there are separations between the gold connectors. The three most common keys used are B, M, and B+M. A module using the B key uses up to two PCIe lanes, and the M key uses up to four PCIe lanes. Figure 7.12 shows four sizes of M.2 cards with one of the cards with an M key and the other cards with the B+M key.

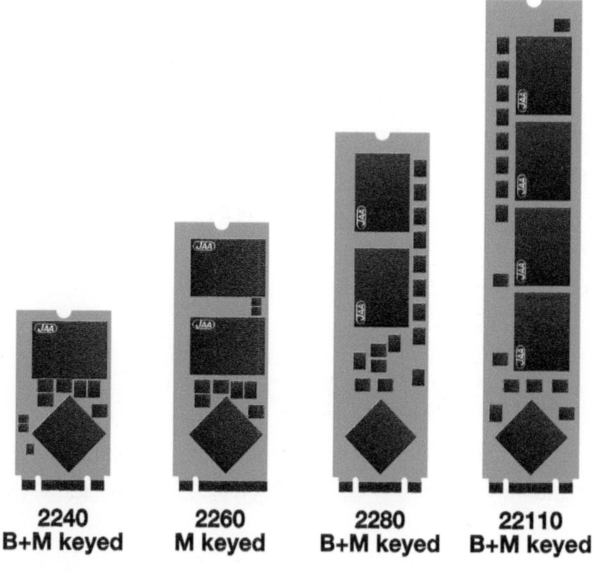

FIGURE 7.12 M.2 SSD sizes and keys

TECH TIP

SSDs that are B+M keyed fit in B or M slots

Any SSD that is B+M keyed can fit in a socket that is B keyed or in a socket that is M keyed.

SSDs can also use Non-Volatile Memory Express (**NVMe**), which provides faster performance when accessing the flash memory in SSDs. SSDs perform better when attached to the PCIe four-lane NVMe standard. To use NVMe, an SSD is usually mounted on a PCIe card or attached through an M.2 connector (see Figure 7.13). Make sure the motherboard supports an NVME SSD before buying and installing one.

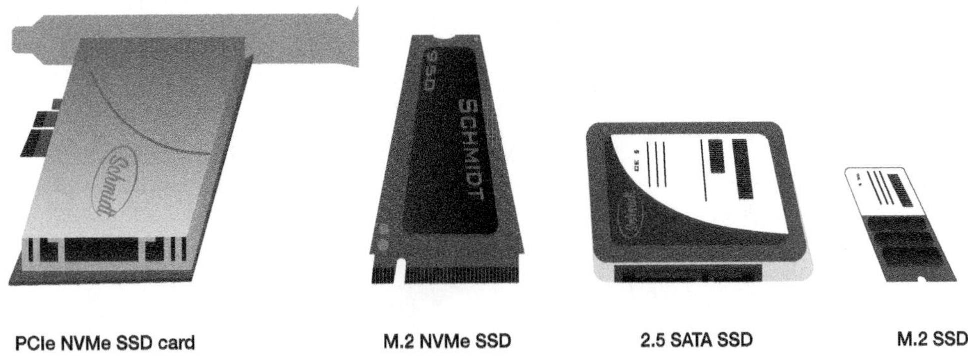

FIGURE 7.13 NVMe and non-NVMe SSDs

PATA, SATA, and SAS Connectivity

PATA uses a 40-pin IDE cable that connects the hard drive to an adapter or the motherboard and transfers 16 bits of data at a time. The SATA connector has seven conductors (four lines used for data in pairs of two). Figure 7.14 shows both a PATA **IDE cable** and a **SATA cable**.

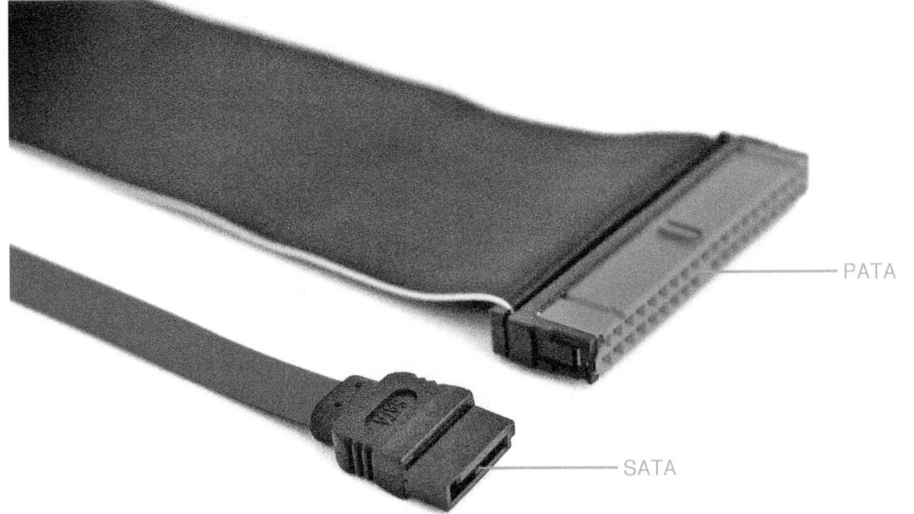

FIGURE 7.14 SATA and PATA data cables

Each PATA motherboard connector allows two devices to be attached through the IDE cable. A SATA connector attaches to only one device. Figure 7.15 shows the difference between PATA and SATA motherboard connectors.

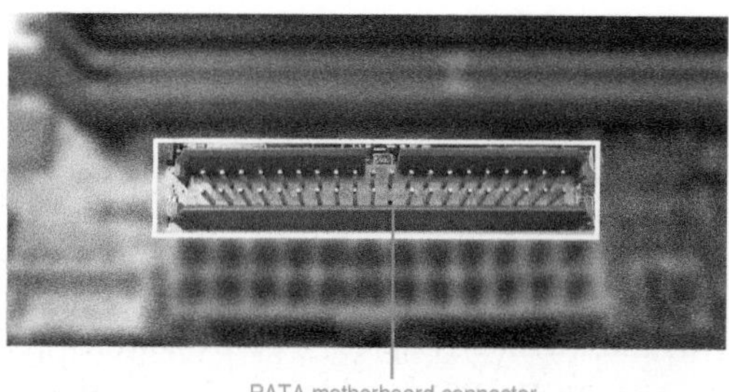

FIGURE 7.15 PATA and SATA motherboard connectors

The original SATA specification transfers data at 1.5 Gb/s and is called SATA 1 or SATA I. The 3 Gb/s version is known as SATA 2 or SATA II, and the latest release, SATA 3 or SATA III, runs at a maximum of 6 Gb/s. These devices are commonly seen marked as SATA 1.5 Gb/s, 3 Gb/s, and 6 Gb/s.

SATA is a point-to-point interface, which means that each device connects to the host through a dedicated link, and each device has the bandwidth of the entire interface. SATA supports both internal and external devices. Figure 7.16 shows three internal SATA drives with the data cable attached. The data connector and cable are to the left of the power connector (which doesn't have a power cable attached in Figure 7.16).

FIGURE 7.16 SATA hard drive and data cable

Desktop motherboards, laptops, and mobile devices can make use of an mSATA connector for installation of an SSD. Whereas the M.2 form factor can make use of SATA or PCIe, the **mSATA** standard only allows use of the SATA standard. Figure 7.17 shows an installed mSATA SSD.

An internal SATA device commonly uses a 15-pin SATA power connector rather than the Molex connector used by older hard drives. However, some drives do ship with Molex connectors. A Molex-to-SATA converter can be purchased Figure 7.18 shows an older Molex power connector and an internal SATA power connector.

FIGURE 7.17 mSATA SSD and connector

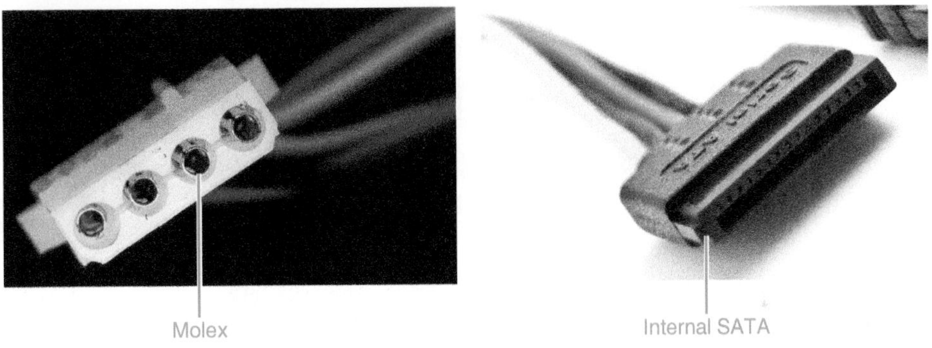

FIGURE 7.18 Hard drive power connectors

Internal SATA data cables are limited to a maximum of 3.3 feet (1 meter). An internal SATA data cable is more likely to be inadvertently unplugged or partially unplugged than is a PATA cable. Special cables with locking mechanisms are in an L shape for hard-to-reach places, and low-profile form factor cases can also be purchased. Figure 7.19 shows these 7-pin internal SATA device cables.

FIGURE 7.19 Internal SATA data cables

External SATA (**eSATA**) provides external device connectivity. It allows shielded cable lengths up to 6.56 feet (2 meters), with faster connections than USB 2.0 or 3.0. However, the standard eSATA connection does not provide power to external devices, but an eSATAp combo (USB and eSATA) port can provide power. Note that eSATA is currently not faster than USB 3.1 gen 2.

Figure 7.20 shows an eSATA port and eSATA cable. An eSATA cable can be rated for 1.5 Gb/s, 3 Gb/s, or 6 Gb/s. eSATA cables are limited to 3.3 feet (1 meter) for 1.5 Gb/s devices and 6.56 feet (2 meters) for 3 Gb/s or 6 Gb/s transfers.

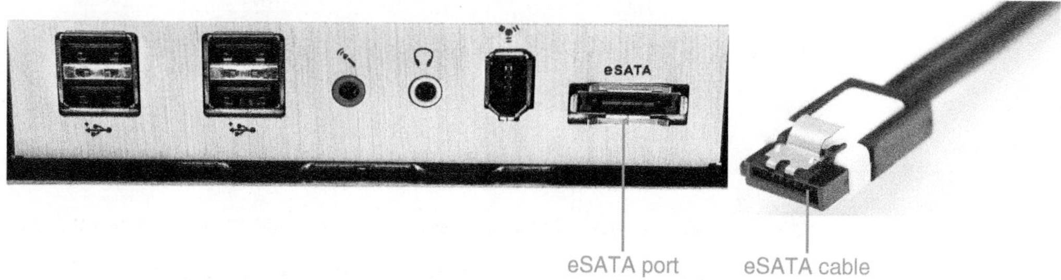

FIGURE 7.20 eSATA port and cable

There are several connectors for SCSI drives, but the one most commonly seen by PC technicians is the SCSI connector for a Serial-Attached SCSI (SAS) drive. The SAS connector looks similar to the connectors on a SATA drive, as shown in Figure 7.21.

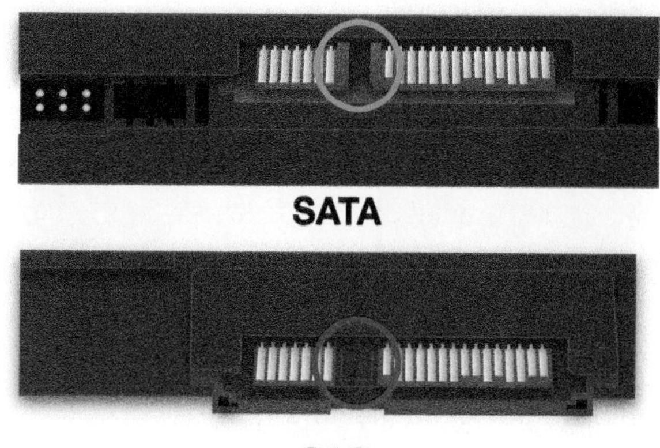

FIGURE 7.21 Serial-Attached SCSI (SAS) connector

A Serial-Attached **SCSI cable**, or SAS cable, is used to connect hard drives or tape drives to a SAS controller. The cable shown in Figure 7.22 is used to connect a SAS hard drive to a SATA controller that supports SAS drives. One cable provides both power and data connections.

FIGURE 7.22 SAS (Serial-Attached SCSI) cable

Storage Device Configuration Overview

Drive configuration sometimes includes setting jumpers on the drive. However, individual drive manufacturers may develop their own configuration steps. Refer to the documentation included with the drive, adapter, or motherboard for configuration and installation information. The overall steps for installing a storage device are as follows:

Step 1. Keep the drive in the protective antistatic bag until you are ready for the installation. Then use proper antistatic handling procedures when installing the drive and handle the drive by the edges; avoid touching the drive electronics and connectors.

Step 2. Turn off the computer and remove the computer power cord before installing the drive.

Step 3. Physically mount and secure the device in the computer and attach the proper cable.

Step 4. Reconnect the power cord and power on the computer. Configure the BIOS/UEFI, if necessary.

Step 5. If a hard drive is being installed, prepare the drive for data, as described later in this chapter.

PATA Physical Installation

A PATA cable allows two storage devices to connect to a single motherboard connector. PATA devices are configured using jumpers. The most common option used is cable select. When one device is used, set the jumper to cable select and attach to the black connector that is at the end. Attach the blue connector to the motherboard. If two devices are to be used, set the jumper on each device to cable select. Figure 7.23 illustrates how multiple PATA devices connect to the motherboard.

> **Note** Use of the terms *master* and *slave* is ONLY in association with the official terminology used in industry specifications and standards and in no way diminishes Pearson's commitment to promoting diversity, equity, and inclusion and challenging, countering, and/or combating bias and stereotyping in the global population of the learners we serve.

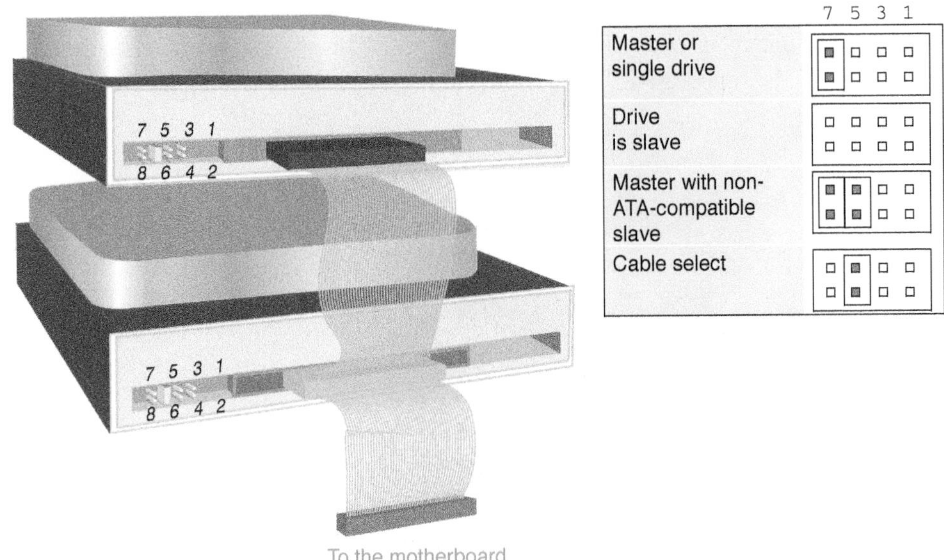

FIGURE 7.23 Two PATA devices configured with cable select

SATA Physical Installation

SATA drives are easy to install. A 7-pin data connector attaches from the motherboard or SATA adapter to the internal SATA drive. A 15-pin cable connects power to the drive. The internal SATA power connector is unique but could possibly be an older Molex connector. A cable converter can be obtained if a Molex connector is the only one available from the power supply. Figure 7.24 shows how cables connect to an internal SATA drive. Figure 7.25 shows how two SATA drives attach to a motherboard that has two SATA connectors.

FIGURE 7.24 SATA data (left) and power (right) cabling

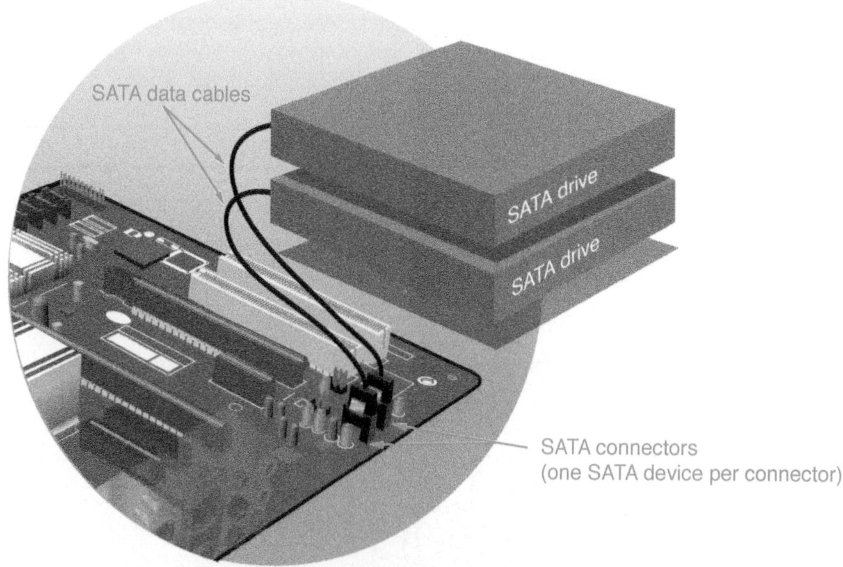

FIGURE 7.25 SATA connectivity

Figure 7.26 shows a SATA adapter that has two internal ports on the far end and one eSATA port. To install a SATA host adapter, power off the computer and remove the computer power cord. Remove the computer cover and locate an open expansion slot. Some adapters have jumpers for configurable options. For most adapters the default settings will work but refer to the adapter's documentation for details.

FIGURE 7.26 eSATA card

TECH TIP

Enabling a SATA port in BIOS/UEFI

Some manufacturers require that you enable the motherboard port through the system BIOS/UEFI before any device connected to the port is recognized.

To install an internal SATA hard drive, power off the computer and remove the computer's power cord. Physically mount the drive into a drive bay. Note that you may have to install rails on the side of the drive to slide it into the case or attach screws to the case and hard drive to mount the drive, as shown in Figure 7.27.

FIGURE 7.27 Installed SATA hard drive

To add an mSATA module, power off the computer, remove the cover, and locate the mSATA motherboard connector. Insert the card into the connector and attach screws at the opposite end, as shown in Figure 7.28. Power on the computer and make sure the BIOS/UEFI recognizes it.

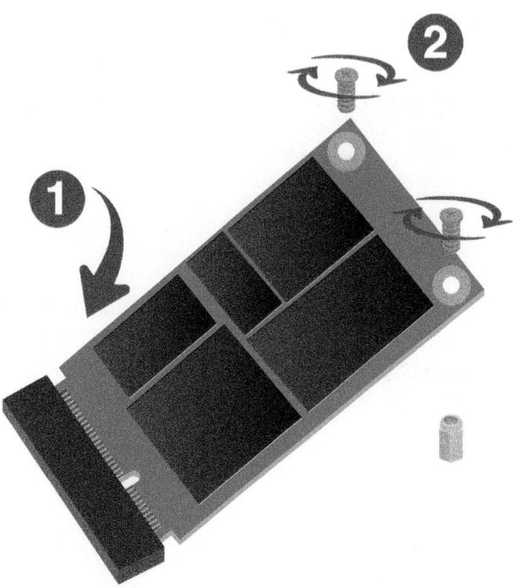

FIGURE 7.28 mSATA Installation

An external (eSATA) drive normally has no jumpers, terminators, or switches to configure. However, when connecting a faster drive to a slower port—such as when installing a 3.0 Gb/s drive in a 1.5 Gb/s port—a jumper may need to be configured so the drive is compatible with the port. Refer to the drive manufacturer's documentation when installing a drive. Attach the power cord to the drive, if applicable, and insert the other end of the power cord into a wall outlet. Attach one end of the eSATA cable to the drive. Plug the other end of the cable into an eSATA port on the computer. Figure 7.29 shows an external hard drive that supports IEEE 1394 (FireWire), eSATA, and USB, as you can see from the ports on the back of the unit.

FIGURE 7.29 External hard drive

Before switching on eSATA drive power, ensure that the drive is positioned where it will stay during operation and that all data and power cords are attached securely. Switch on the drive power. The drive **mounts**. When a drive mounts, a communications channel is opened between the drive and the operating system. Whenever the drive is to be disconnected, it is to be unmounted. Use the Windows *Disk Management* tool to ensure that the drive is recognized. The Disk Management tool is covered later in this chapter.

TECH TIP

Unmounting an eSATA drive

To unmount an eSATA drive, click the *Safely Remove Hardware* icon in the notification area and select the appropriate drive letter. Remove the drive when prompted by the operating system. If you cannot find this icon in Windows, use *File Explorer* to locate the drive, right-click it, and select *Eject*.

SSD Physical Installation

For a desktop computer, an SSD can be installed using several methods that can be combined:

- Internally mounted and connected to a SATA (or even PATA) motherboard port and installed the same as any other SATA device
- Inserted into an mSATA connector, as described earlier
- As an NVMe module on a PCIe card or inserted into an M.2 slot
- As a SATA SSD module inserted into an M.2 slot
- As an external device connected to an eSATA, eSATAp, or USB port

Figure 7.30 shows an internal SSD that connects to a SATA port and that is mounted in a drive slot. Figure 7.31 shows an NVMe module being inserted into an M.2 slot. Be sure the computer is powered off and press the module firmly into the slot. Usually, a screw is needed to attach the far end of the module.

FIGURE 7.30 Internal SATA SSD

FIGURE 7.31 Internal NVMe SSD in an M.2 slot

SSDs do not normally require special drivers. Refer to the SSD mounting directions provided by the manufacturer. The following steps are generic ones:

Step 1. Power off the computer, remove the power cord, and locate an empty drive bay, mSATA connector, M.2 connector, or PCIe expansion slot, depending on the type of SSD you are installing. If SATA, ensure that there is an available power connector.

Step 2. Use proper antistatic procedures. If installing into a drive bay, attach mounting brackets to the SSD, which may have to be purchased separately, may be provided with the drive, or may be provided with the computer.

Step 3. Slide the SSD into the drive bay, connector, or expansion slot and secure, if necessary.

Step 4. If a SATA drive is being installed, connect the data cable from the motherboard or adapter to the drive and attach a power connector.

Step 5. Reinstall the computer cover, reattach the power cord, and power on the computer.

Step 6. Ensure that BIOS/UEFI recognizes the drive.

TECH TIP

Beware of static electricity

SSDs are flash memory and are susceptible to static electricity. Use proper ESD handling procedures when installing an SSD.

If installing an external SSD, use the following steps:

Step 1. Attach the appropriate USB or eSATA cable from the drive to the computer.

Step 2. Power on the SSD. The system should recognize the new drive.

TECH TIP

Wanting to upgrade an SSD with another SSD?

When upgrading an SSD that already has the operating system installed on it, you need some space on the original SSD to clone (copy) the drive and some cloning software that may come with the new drive. During the process, you may need to ensure that the software knows that an SSD drive is being used. If the clone process doesn't go well, you might need to boot from a Linux flash drive and use `GParted` to remove the sections of the drive before trying the process again. Consider cloning the drive and then resizing the partition.

System BIOS/UEFI Configuration for Storage Devices

A hard drive is configured through the system BIOS/UEFI Setup program. Setup is accessed via keystrokes during the boot process. In today's computers, the BIOS/UEFI automatically detects the hard drive type. The drive type information is saved in CMOS.

TECH TIP

Configure BIOS/UEFI according to the drive manufacturer's instructions

Drive manufacturers normally include documentation describing how to configure the drive in BIOS/UEFI Setup. Also, they provide software for any system that does not recognize the drive.

Hard drives are normally configured using the auto-detect feature, which determines the drive type for the system. Table 7.1 shows the most commonly used storage device settings. SATA drives can be set in different modes of operation:

> *Legacy mode:* This mode is used in a system that does not have SATA drivers natively.
> *Advanced Host Controller Interface (**AHCI**) mode:* When enabled, AHCI mode allows SATA drives to be inserted/removed when power is on and enables you to use commands to allow the host circuits to communicate with attached devices in order to implement advanced SATA features.
> *RAID mode:* RAID is discussed later in this chapter.

Note that the BIOS/UEFI is also where you select the drive that will boot the system.

TABLE 7.1 Common storage device BIOS/UEFI settings

Device type	BIOS/UEFI setting
IDE PATA/SATA/SCSI/SAS	AUTO
SATA	SATA mode: IDE mode (no AHCI or RAID)
SATA	SATA mode: SATA or AHCI (AHCI enabled)
SATA	SATA mode: RAID (AHCI and RAID enabled)
mSATA	AUTO
NVMe SSD	May have to set the PCIe bandwidth to x2 or x4
M.2 SSD	May have to enable; may have to go into a specific PCIe slot and configure the mode to M.2

It is important to ensure the BIOS/UEFI recognizes a device before you prepare the device to accept data or attempt to have the device store data. No matter the type of storage device, go into BIOS/UEFI and ensure that the device is recognized and configured as needed. You may have to use the advanced settings to access the storage device options.

Hard Drive Preparation Overview

After a hard drive is installed and configured properly and the hard drive type is recognized and seen within the Setup program, the drive must be prepared to accept data. The two steps of hard drive preparation are as follows:

Step 1. Partition the drive.

Step 2. Perform a high-level format on the hard drive.

> **TECH TIP**
>
> **Low-level formatting**
>
> Low-level formatting may be done at the hard drive factory. Some manufacturers provide software that enables you to do low-level formatting on the drive, but you should do this only at the direction of the manufacturer.

Partitioning a hard drive involves allowing a drive letter to be assigned to one or more sections of the hard drive. **High-level formatting** involves preparing the drive for use for a particular file system and allows the drive to accept data from the operating system. A drive cannot be used until it has been partitioned and had high-level formatting done; thus, technicians must be very familiar with these steps.

Partitioning

As just mentioned, the first step in preparing a hard drive for use is partitioning. Partitioning a hard drive means dividing the drive into separate sections so the computer system sees the hard drive as more than one drive. Each drive section gets a drive letter. Figure 7.32 shows a hard drive platter with some colored sections. Each section between the colored lines can be a volume and can receive a different drive letter.

Partitioning can be done during the Windows installation process or by using the Windows **Disk Management** program. Similarly, the `diskpart` utility can be used from the command prompt. Disk Management is normally used to partition additional hard drives and to manage all of them. The first hard drive in a system is normally partitioned as part of the Windows installation process. Additional partitions can be created using Disk Management after the operating system is installed.

Partitioning provides advantages such as the following:

- Dividing a hard drive into separate subunits that are then assigned drive letters, such as `C:` or `D:`, by the operating system
- Organizing the hard drive to separate multiple operating systems, applications, and data
- Providing data security by placing data in a different partition to allow ease of backup as well as protection
- Using the hard drive to its fullest capacity

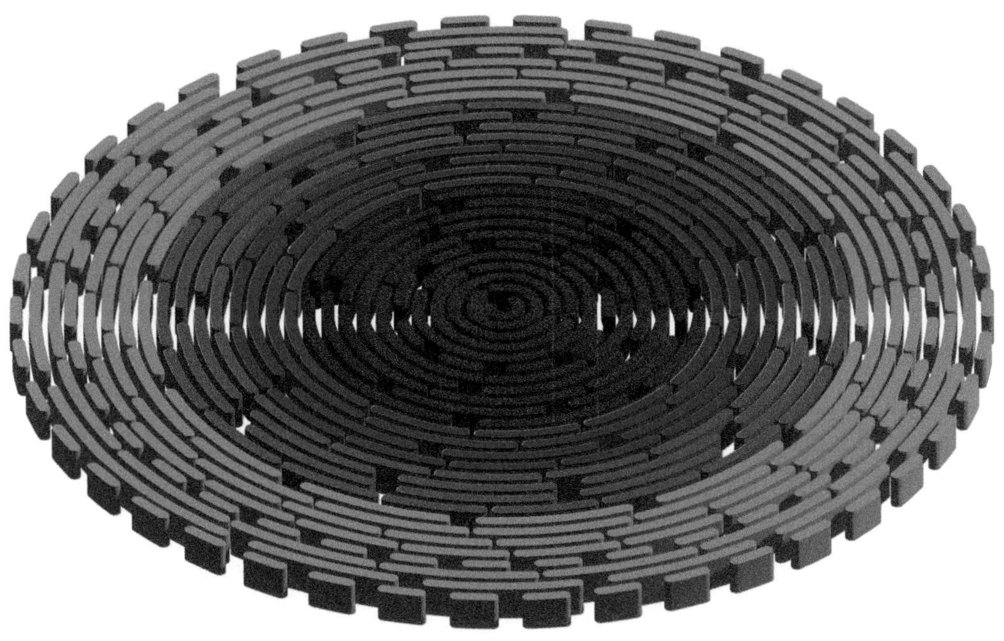

FIGURE 7.32 Visualization of partitioning

TECH TIP

How to determine what file system is being used

Right-click any drive in *Windows Explorer* (Windows 7) or *File Explorer* (Windows 8/10/11) and select *Properties*. The *General* tab shows the type of file system being used.

The original purpose of partitioning was to make it possible to load multiple operating systems. This is still a good reason today because placing each operating system in its own partition eliminates the crashes and headaches caused by multiple operating systems and multiple applications coexisting in the same partition. The type of partition and how big the partition can be depends on the file system being used. A **file system** defines how data is stored on a drive. The most common Windows file systems are FAT16, FAT32, exFAT, and NTFS. What file system can be used depends on what operating system is installed, whether the device is an internal device or external, and whether files are to be shared. Table 7.2 lists file systems and explains a little about each one.

TABLE 7.2 File systems

File system	Description
FAT	Also called FAT16. Used with all versions of Windows. 2 GB partition limitation with old operating systems. 4 GB partition limitation with XP and higher versions of Windows.
FAT32	Supported with all versions of Windows. Commonly used with removable flash drives. Supports drives up to 2 TB. Can recognize volumes greater than 32 GB but cannot create them that big.
exFAT	Commonly called FAT64. A file system made for removable media (such as flash drives and SD cards) that extends drive size support up to 64 ZB in theory, but 512 TB is the recommended max. Made for copying large files such as disk images and media files. Supported by all versions of Windows.

File system	Description
NTFS	Used with Windows 7, 8, and 10. Supports drives up to 16 EB (16 exabytes, which equals 16 billion gigabytes), but in practice is only 16 TB. Supports file compression and file security (encryption). NTFS allows faster file access and uses hard drive space more efficiently compared to FAT (FAT16) and FAT32. Supports individual file compression and has the best file security.
Apple File System (**APFS**)	Owned by Apple, designed with encryption in mind, and works across all Apple platforms. It uses GPT partitions, covered later in this chapter, and allows disk cloning.
ext3	Also known as third extended file system. Used in Linux-based operating systems and is a journaling file system (which means it tracks changes in case the operating system crashes, allowing it to be restarted without reloading).
ext4	An update to ext3 that allows for larger volumes and file sizes within Linux-based operating systems.

An even better reason for partitioning than loading multiple operating systems or separating the operating system from data is to partition the hard drive for more efficient use of space. An operating system sets aside at least one cluster for every file. A **cluster** is the smallest amount of space reserved for one file, and it is made up of a specific number of sectors. Figure 7.33 illustrates the concept of a cluster. Keep in mind that the number of hard drive sectors per track varies. The outer tracks hold more information (that is, have more sectors) than the inner tracks.

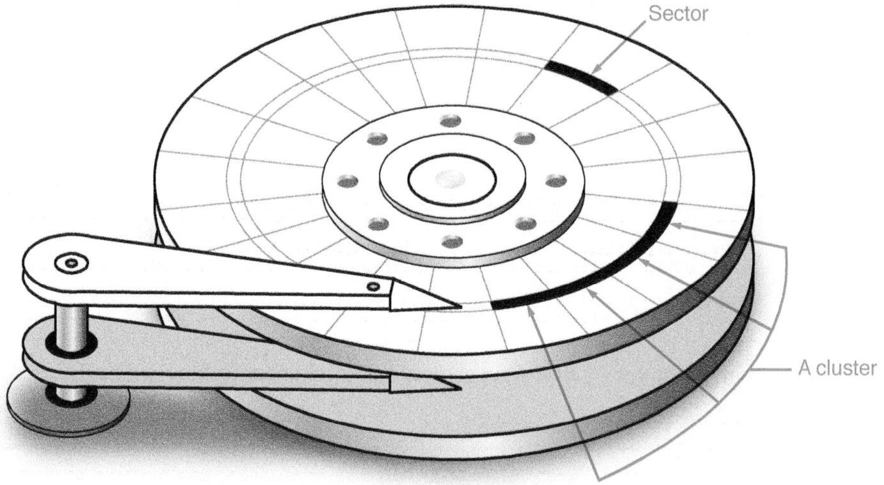
Sector
A cluster
One cluster is the minimum amount of space for a file.

FIGURE 7.33 Cluster

TECH TIP

How to convert partitions

Use the `convert` program in Windows to convert a FAT16, FAT32, or exFAT partition to NTFS without loss of data. Access a command prompt window and type the command `convert x: /fs:ntfs`, where *x* is the drive letter of the partition being converted to NTFS.

Press Enter and then press Y and press Enter. You can add a `/V` switch to the end of the command for a more verbose operation mode.

Any type of partition conversion requires free hard drive space. The amount depends on the size of the partition. Table 7.3 shows that partitioning large drives into one FAT partition wastes drive space. An efficiently partitioned hard drive allows more files to be saved because less space on the hard drive is wasted.

TABLE 7.3 Sample FAT16 partitions and cluster sizes

Partition size	Number of sectors	Cluster size
0–32 MB	1	512 bytes
1 GB–2 GB	64	32 kB
2 GB–4 GB	128	64 kB

A best practice is to put applications in a separate partition from data files. The following are some good reasons for partitioning a hard drive and separating data files from application files:

- Multiple partitions on the same hard drive divide the drive into smaller subunits, which makes it easier and faster to back up the data (which should be backed up more often than applications).
- The data is protected from operating system failures, unstable software applications, and any unusual software problems that occur between the application and the operating system.
- The data is in one location, which makes backing up, organizing, and locating the files easier and faster.

FAT32 partitions have been around a long time and are still used. Flash drives are commonly formatted for FAT32 due to the NTFS "lazy write," which prolongs a write and might not release an external drive for some time. The FAT32 file system makes more efficient use of the hard drive than FAT16. NTFS is an efficient file system. Table 7.4 lists the default cluster sizes for all versions of Windows 7 and higher.

TABLE 7.4 NTFS partition and cluster sizes

Partition size	Number of sectors	Cluster size
0–16 TB	8	4 kB
16 TB–32 TB	16	8 kB
>32 TB–64 TB	32	16 kB
>64 TB–128 TB	64	32 kB
>128 TB–256 TB	128	64 kB

Figure 7.34 shows a screen capture of the Windows 10 Disk Management window that has multiple drives (Disk 0, Disk 1, Disk 2) and multiple partitions on Disk 1 and Disk 2.

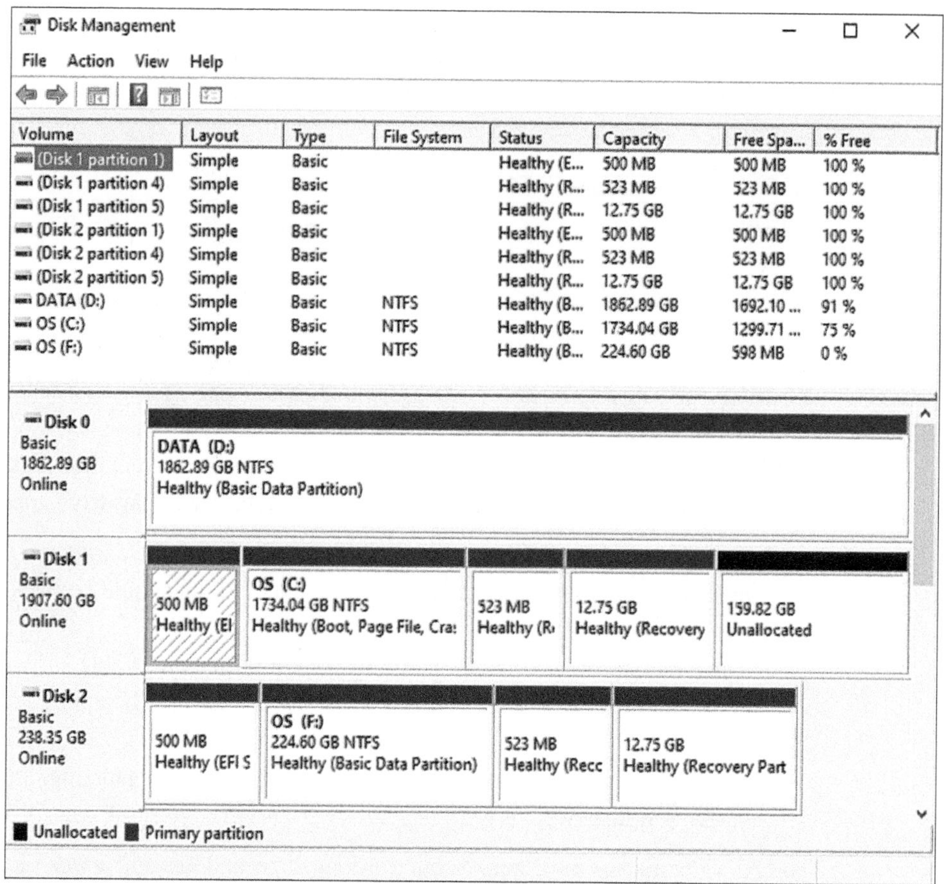

FIGURE 7.34 Windows Disk Management tool

> **TECH TIP**
>
> **Benefits of NTFS**
>
> NTFS supports disk quotas, which means that individual users can be limited in the maximum amount of usable hard drive space. NTFS can also automatically repair disk problems. For example, when a hard drive sector is going bad, NTFS moves the entire cluster to another cluster.

Partitions are defined as primary and extended. If there is only one hard drive installed in a system and the entire hard drive is one partition, it is the **primary partition**. The primary partition on the first detected hard drive is assigned the drive letter `C:`.

> **TECH TIP**
>
> **eSATAs are already partitioned**
>
> Most eSATA drives are already partitioned and formatted, but these drives can be repartitioned and reformatted as necessary via the *Disk Management* tool.

If a drive is divided, only part of the drive is the primary partition. In older operating systems, the rest of the cylinders can be designated as the **extended partitions**. An extended partition allows a drive to be further divided into **logical drives**. A logical drive is sometimes called a **volume**. A volume is assigned a drive letter and can include a logical drive and removable media such as a CD, DVD, BD, or flash drive. There can be only one extended partition per drive. In operating systems, a single hard drive could be divided into a maximum of four primary partitions. Remember that a partition is a contiguous section of storage space that functions as if it is a separate drive. Figure 7.35 illustrates how one hard drive can be divided into partitions.

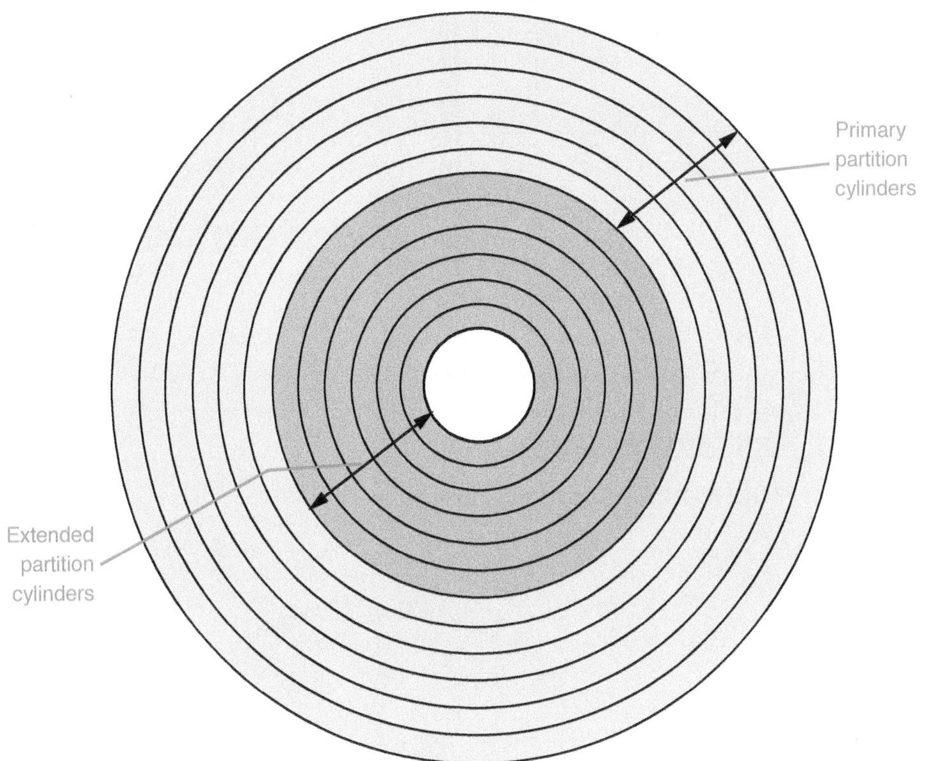

FIGURE 7.35 Hard drive partitioning

The first hard drive in a computer system must have a primary partition, but an extended partition is not required. If the drive has an extended partition, it can be further subdivided or split into logical drives that appear as separate hard drives to the computer system. Logical drives created in the extended partition are assigned drive letters such as `D:` or `E:`. The only limit for logical drives is the number of drive letters. Figure 7.36 illustrates a hard drive divided into a primary partition and an extended partition that is further subdivided into two logical drives.

If two hard drives are installed in a computer, the first hard drive *must* have a primary partition. The second hard drive is not required to have a primary partition and may simply have a single extended partition. If the second hard drive does have a primary partition, it can have an extended partition, too. Today, more than four primary partitions can exist, and the sections are simply called *volumes*.

When a hard drive is first installed and partitioned, the outermost track on the platter (cylinder 0, head 0, and physical sector 1) is reserved for the partition table. The partition table holds information about the types of partitions created and in what cylinders those partitions reside. The partition table is part of the master boot record (**MBR**), which contains a program that reads the partition table, looks for the primary partition marked as active, and goes to that partition to boot the system. Figure 7.37 shows the locations of important parts of the hard drive that allow booting, reading partitions, and accessing files.

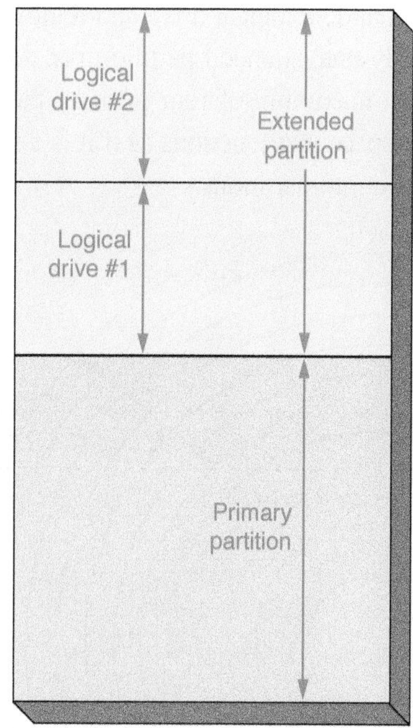

FIGURE 7.36 Two logical drives

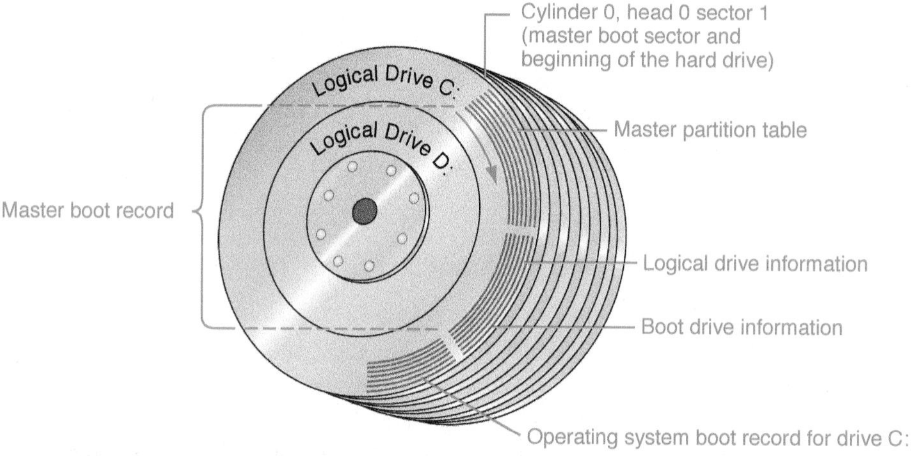

FIGURE 7.37 Hard drive structure

NTFS has two additional terms that you need to be aware of as a technician:

> **System partition**: The partition on the hard drive that holds the hardware-specific files needed to load the operating system
> **Boot partition**: The partition on the hard drive that contains the operating system

In Windows, the boot partition and the system partition can be on the same partition.

TECH TIP

What happens when different types of partitions are deleted?

When a partition is deleted, all information in the partition is lost. When logical drives in an extended partition are deleted, all data is lost. The other logical drives within the extended partition retain their information.

The Host Protected Area (**HPA**) is a hidden area of a hard drive that is used to hold a copy of the operating system; sometimes installed applications use the HPA when the operating system becomes so corrupt that a reinstallation is necessary. Many manufacturers provide a BIOS/UEFI setting or a keystroke that can be used when the system boots in order to access this area.

The GUID, or globally unique identifier, partition table (**GPT**) is available with 64-bit Windows operating systems. GPT partitioning is accomplished using the Disk Management tool or using the `diskpart` command-line utility. Table 7.5 compares MBR with GPT disks.

TABLE 7.5 MBR and GPT disk features

Feature	MBR	GPT
Partition size	Up to 2 TB	Up to 9.4 ZB
Types of partitions	Up to 4 primary; supports extended partitions	Up to 128 primary
Firmware	BIOS or UEFI	UEFI
Operating system	Windows	Windows 7/8/10/11 64-bit or higher
Partition table	Only one partition table	Has a backup partition table

TECH TIP

You lose data when converting to GPT

MBR-based partitions can be converted to GPT and vice versa, but data is not preserved. This is seen only with systems that have a UEFI BIOS. Back up data if you convert!

Special products can be used to partition a hard drive and also repartition without any data loss. Examples include Acronis's Disk Director, EaseUS's Partition Master, and Avanquest's Partition Commander.

How Drive Letters Are Assigned

An operating system assigns drive letters to hard drives during the partitioning step. The order in which partitions are assigned drive letters depends on three factors: the number of hard drives, the type of volume on the hard drives (primary or extended), and the operating system.

Note that if a new drive is installed, drive letters for devices, volumes, partitions, or logical drives are added afterward. Drive letters can be changed through the Disk Management tool or by using the `diskpart` command-line utility. Be careful, though, because some applications have pointers to specific files on specific drive letters.

High-Level Formatting

As mentioned earlier, the second step in preparing a hard drive for use is high-level formatting. High-level formatting must be performed on all primary partitions, logical drives located within extended partitions, and GPT partitions before data can be written to the hard drive. The high-level format sets up the file system so it can accept data.

NTFS allows support for multiple data streams as well as support for every character in the world. NTFS also automatically remaps bad clusters to other sections of the hard drive without any additional time or utility. During the installation process, Windows allows for a **quick format** (where you see the word "(quick)" after the option) or a full format (sometimes called a standard format). A **full**

format scans for and marks bad sectors. This prevents the operating system from being installed on a sector that may cause operating system issues. A quick format simply prepares the drive for data and takes a lot less time than a full format. Use a full format if you suspect that a drive has issues.

Figure 7.38 shows the NTFS partition structure once it has been set up and the high-level formatting is completed.

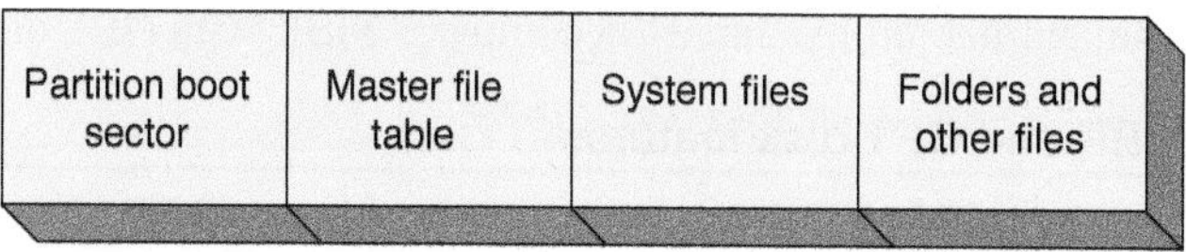

FIGURE 7.38 NTFS volume structure

High-level formatting creates two file allocation tables (FATs): one primary and one secondary. The formatting process also creates the root directory that renumbers the sectors. The **FAT** keeps track of the hard disk's file locations. It is similar to a table of contents in a book as it lists where the files are located in the partition. Table 7.6 shows the differences between the file systems.

TABLE 7.6 Comparing Windows file systems

Specification	FAT16	FAT32	NTFS	exFAT
Maximum file size	4 GB	4 GB	~16 TB	~16 EB
Maximum volume (partition) size	4 GB (2 GB, if shared with a really old computer)	32 GB (max format)	2 TB (or greater)	64 ZB (512 TB recommended)
Maximum files per volume	~64,000	~4 million	~4 billion	Not defined (but 1,000 per directory)

High-level formatting can be performed using the `format` command or by using the Windows Disk Management tool. The area of the disk that contains information about the system files, the DOS boot record (**DBR**), is located on the hard drive's cylinder 0, head 1, sector 1. The more common term for this today is **boot sector**, or volume boot record.

Additional drive partitions and drives installed after the first hard drive partition is created use the Windows Disk Management tool to apply high-level formatting to the drive. The first hard drive partition normally has high-level formatting done as part of the operating system installation process.

Windows Disk Management

In the Windows environment, storage devices are managed with the Disk Management tool. With Windows, there are two types of storage: basic storage and dynamic storage. The big difference between these two is that you can make partitions and resize changes with a dynamic disk but not with a basic disk. Table 7.7 explains these and other associated terms. Figure 7.39 shows some of these concepts.

TECH TIP

Hibernation affects disk space

Whenever you put your computer in sleep/hibernate mode, information in RAM is stored temporarily on the hard drive. This requires free hard drive space.

TABLE 7.7 Logical disk management terms

Term	Description
Basic storage	One of the two types of storage. This is what has traditionally been known as a partition. It is the default that is used by all operating systems.
Basic disk	Any drive that has been partitioned and set up for writing files. A basic disk has primary partitions, extended partitions, and logical drives contained within the extended partitions.
Dynamic storage	The second type of storage; contrast with basic storage. Allows you to create primary partitions, logical drives, and dynamic volumes on storage devices. It is more powerful than basic storage in that it allows creation of simple, spanned, or striped volumes using dynamic disks.
Dynamic disk	A disk made up of volumes. A volume can be the entire hard disk, parts of the hard disk combined into one unit, and other specific types of volumes, such as single, spanned, or striped volumes. Cannot be on a removable drive.
Simple volume	Disk space allocated from one hard drive. The space does not have to be contiguous.
Spanned volume	Disk space created from multiple hard drives. Also known as "just a bunch of disks" (**JBOD**). Windows writes data to a spanned volume in such a way that the first hard drive is used until the space is filled. Then, the second hard drive's space is used for writing. This continues until all hard drives in the spanned volume are utilized.
Striped volume	Disk space in which data is written across 2 to 32 hard drives. It is different from a spanned volume in that the drives are used alternately. Another name for this is striping, or RAID 0 (covered in the next section).
System volume	Disk space that holds the files needed to boot the operating system.
Boot volume	Disk space that holds the remaining operating system files. Can be the same volume as the system volume.
RAW volume	A volume that has never had high-level formatting performed and that does not contain a file system.

A basic disk, simple volume, or spanned volume can be resized, shrunk, or expanded without affecting data. When working within Disk Management, right-click on a drive to see all the available options, such as viewing the properties of the drive, marking a partition as active, changing the drive letter and paths, formatting, extending a volume, shrinking a volume, adding a mirror, or deleting a volume.

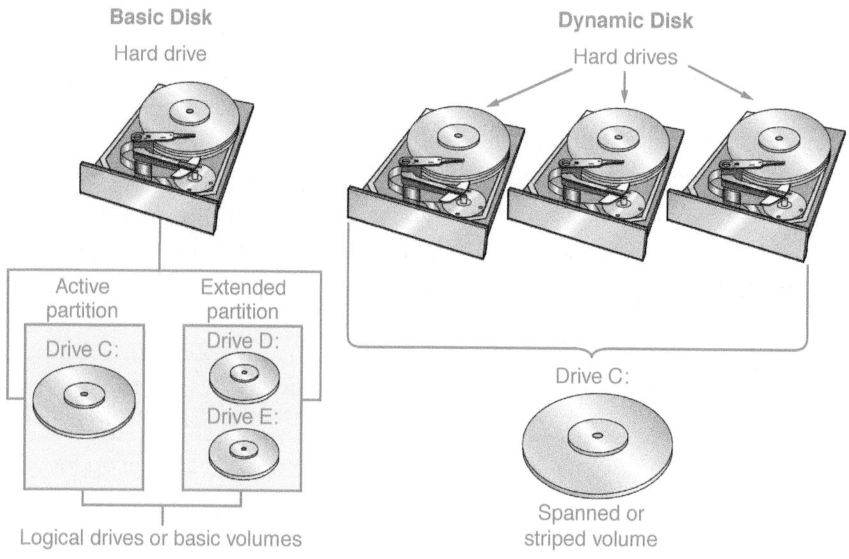

FIGURE 7.39 Disk Management concepts

> **TECH TIP**
>
> **Managing disks and partitions**
>
> Use the *Disk Management* tool (from the *Computer Management* console, or by right-clicking the Start button in Windows 10 and selecting *Disk Management*, or by using the `diskmgmt.msc` command) to determine what type of partition you have, to work with dynamic disks, or to convert a basic disk to a dynamic one. This conversion process cannot be reversed.

To extend (make larger), split (break into two sections), or shrink (reduce the size of) a partition, use the following steps:

Step 1. Access the Windows *Disk Management* tool.

Step 2. Right-click on the drive volume.

Step 3. Select either *Shrink Volume* or *Extend Volume*.

Figure 7.40 shows a hard drive partition and settings used to shrink it so that another partition can be created.

Shrink E: ×

Total size before shrink in MB:	953867
Size of available shrink space in MB:	950745
Enter the amount of space to shrink in MB:	22000
Total size after shrink in MB:	931867

You cannot shrink a volume beyond the point where any unmovable files are located. See the "defrag" event in the Application log for detailed information about the operation when it has completed.

See "Shrink a basic volume" in Disk Management help for more information

Shrink | Cancel

FIGURE 7.40 Resizing a partition

Fault Tolerance

With a **drive array**, two or more hard drives are configured for speed, redundancy, or both (see Figure 7.41). Redundant array of independent (or inexpensive) disks (**RAID**) allows reading from and writing to multiple hard drives for larger storage areas, better performance, and fault tolerance. Fault tolerance is the ability to continue functioning after a hardware or software failure. A RAID array can be implemented with hardware or software. Hardware RAID is configured through the BIOS/UEFI.

FIGURE 7.41 RAID

Generic steps for configuring hardware RAID are as follows:

Step 1. Ensure that the motherboard ports that you want to use are enabled.

Step 2. Ensure that you have RAID drivers for the hard drives used in the RAID.

Step 3. Physically install and cable the hard drives.

Step 4. Enter BIOS/UEFI and enable RAID.

Step 5. Configure RAID in BIOS/UEFI or through a special key sequence to enter the RAID BIOS configuration.

Step 6. Install Windows on a RAID by using the *Custom (Advanced) Installation* option.

Software RAID is configured through Windows or through software provided by the RAID adapter manufacturer. If you want to be able to control RAID through Windows and resize the volumes or make adjustments, use software RAID.

RAID can also be implemented with flash cache modules (FCMs) and a traditional mechanical hard drive. Software on the host device and/or device drivers provides optimization and oversight.

RAID comes in many different levels, but the ones implemented in the Windows environment are 0, 1, and 5. The ones on the A+ certification exam are RAID levels 0, 1, 5, and 10. Some motherboards support "nested" RAID, in which RAID levels are combined. This method also increases the complexity of the hard drive setup. Table 7.8 explains the RAID levels.

TABLE 7.8 RAID

RAID level	Description
0	Also called **disk striping** or disk striping without parity. Data is alternately written on two or more hard drives, which increases system performance. These drives are seen by the system as one logical drive. **RAID 0** does not protect data when a hard drive fails. It is not considered fault tolerant. It has the fastest read and write performance.
1	Also called **disk mirroring** or disk duplexing, **RAID 1** protects against hard drive failure by using two or more hard drives and one disk controller. The same data is written to two drives so that if one drive fails, the system continues to function. Disk duplexing is similar except that two disk controllers are used. With disk duplexing, performance is slightly degraded when writing data because it has to be written to two drives.
0+1	A striped set and a mirrored set combined. At least four hard drives are required, and they need to have an even number of disks. A second striped set mirrors a primary striped set of disks. Also called RAID 01, this mode can read from the drive quickly, but there is a slight degradation when writing.
1+0	A mirrored set and a striped set combined with at least four hard drives. The difference between 1+0 and 0+1 is that 1+0 has a striped set from a set of mirrored drives. This mode, also called **RAID 10**, can read from the drive quickly but has a slight degradation when writing.
5	Also called disk striping with parity. **RAID 5** writes data to three or more hard drives. Included with the data is parity information. If a drive fails, the data can be rebuilt based on the information from the other two drives. This level can read and write data quickly.

Figure 7.42 shows the different types of RAID. With RAID 0, blocks of data (B1, B2, B3, and so on) are placed on alternating drives. With RAID 1, the same block of data is written to two drives. RAID 5 has one drive that contains parity information (P) for particular blocks of data such as B1 and B2.

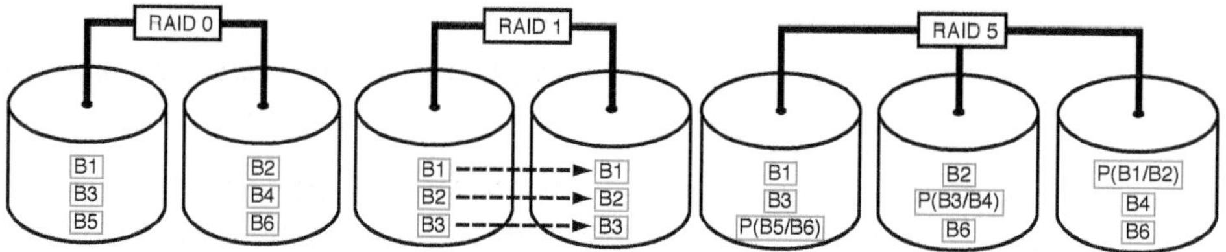

FIGURE 7.42 RAID concepts

Windows 7 Professional and higher versions support simple, spanned, striped, and mirrored volumes. Keep in mind that a spanned volume does not provide redundancy or fault tolerance, as most of the RAID levels do.

RAID drives are often hot swappable; that is, they can be removed or installed while power is applied to the computer. USB, SATA, and SAS all support hot swapping, but RAID is not required to be supported. Refer to the drive and computer manual before hot swapping any hard drive. RAID rebuilds are time and input/output (I/O) intensive. Be prepared for the system to be out of commission for a while; the amount of time the system will be unavailable depends on the size of the drive and the RAID type.

Hardware RAID for home or business computers used to require a separate RAID adapter and software to perform the RAID. Now many motherboards support RAID, and so do the Windows 7 and higher operating systems. Many times, you must configure the motherboard BIOS/UEFI for

RAID as part of your initial configuration. Table 7.9 shows some common RAID BIOS configuration parameters.

TABLE 7.9 RAID BIOS/UEFI configuration settings

BIOS/UEFI setting	Description
SATA mode: AHCI Mode	A mode that may mean that hot swapping is supported. A set of commands can be used to increase storage performance.
SATA mode: RAID Mode or Discrete SATA Mode	Allows you to select a particular RAID level and the drives associated with the RAID.
SATA drives: Detected RAID Volume	Usually an information screen that shows the type of RAID configured, if any.
SATA drives: eSATA Controller Mode	Allows configuration of RAID through the eSATA port.
SATA drives: eSATA Port x Hot Plug Capability	Allows hot swapping to be enabled or disabled for eSATA ports.

Windows Storage Spaces

Microsoft Windows 8 and Windows 10 support **Windows Storage Spaces**, which combine drives into a flexible data storage option. An administrator first creates a storage pool, which is two or more physical disks that can be different types, such as a SATA drive and a USB drive. A storage space is a virtual disk created from available space in a storage pool. There are three types of storage spaces:

> *Simple:* Data is striped across physical disks. No resiliency is provided. This type of storage space provides the highest performance, but there is a loss of data if one disk fails.

> *Parity:* Data is striped across the physical disks and includes parity information. This type of storage space slows performance.

> *Mirror:* Data is striped across multiple disks, and the same data is copied for the highest level of resiliency.

Unlike with RAID, if you add a drive to a storage space, the data is not rewritten to include the new drive. Instead, new data uses all of the drives. To create a storage space, follow these steps:

Step 1. Access the *Storage Spaces* Windows Control Panel link. Select *Create a new pool and storage space*.

Step 2. Select the drives to be used and then select *Create Pool* (see Figure 7.43).

Step 3. Name the storage space and select the drive letter, file system, resiliency type, and pool size and then select *Create Storage Space*.

When the storage space is created, the storage drive letter appears in File Explorer.

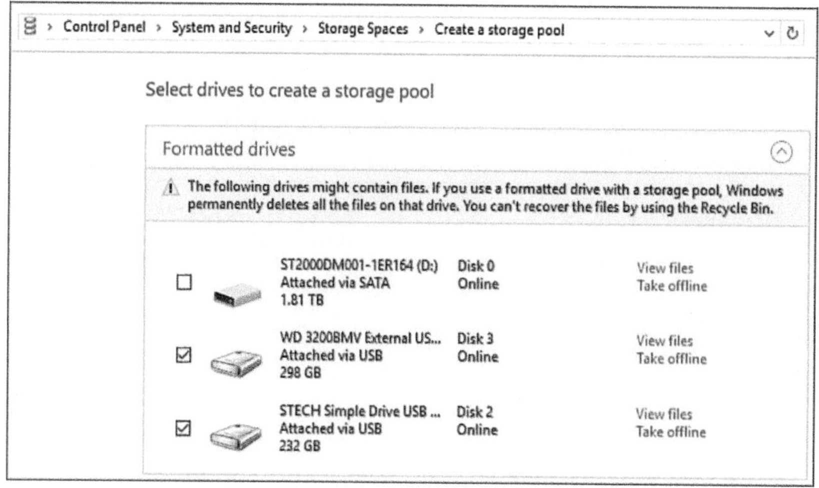

FIGURE 7.43 Windows Storage Spaces: Creating a storage pool

Disk Caching/Virtual Memory

When you buy a hard drive, an optical drive, or an SSD, one feature you should look at when choosing between drives is the amount of cache on the drive. The **disk cache** (sometimes called a data buffer) is SRAM on the drive that takes data in and holds it there until the drive has time to write the data. The cache can also be used when data is requested from the drive. The drive reads more data than requested and holds that data until needed without returning to the hard drive. Figure 7.44 shows this concept.

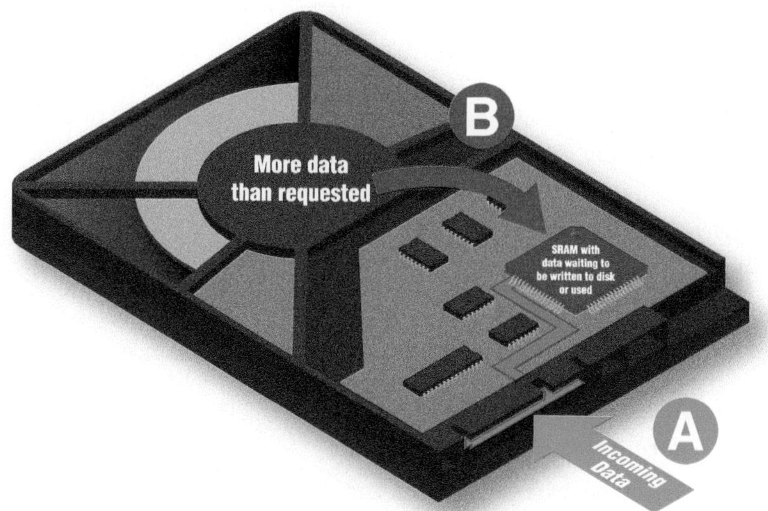

FIGURE 7.44 Disk cache

A different way of using a hard drive is with virtual memory or using hard drive space as if it were RAM. The amount of RAM installed in a system is not enough to handle the operating system and the multiple applications that are opened and being used. Only the program and data of the application that is currently being used is in RAM. The rest of the open applications and data are stored in a paging file (also called a swap file, `pagefile.sys`, or page file) on the hard drive. When you switch over to a different app that is held in the swap file, data is moved from RAM into the swap file, and the data you need to look at is moved into RAM for faster access and data manipulation.

The disk cache is dynamic, which means it increases and decreases the cache size as needed. If the system begins to page (that is, constantly swap data between RAM and the hard drive), the cache size automatically shrinks. In Windows, the virtual memory swap file is called `pagefile.sys`. Here is how to adjust it in Windows 10/11: Access *Settings*. In the *Find a setting* search textbox, type **`performance`**. Select the *Adjust the appearance and performance of Windows* link > *Advanced* tab > *Change* button (as shown in Figure 7.45). Change the parameters and click the *OK* button twice.

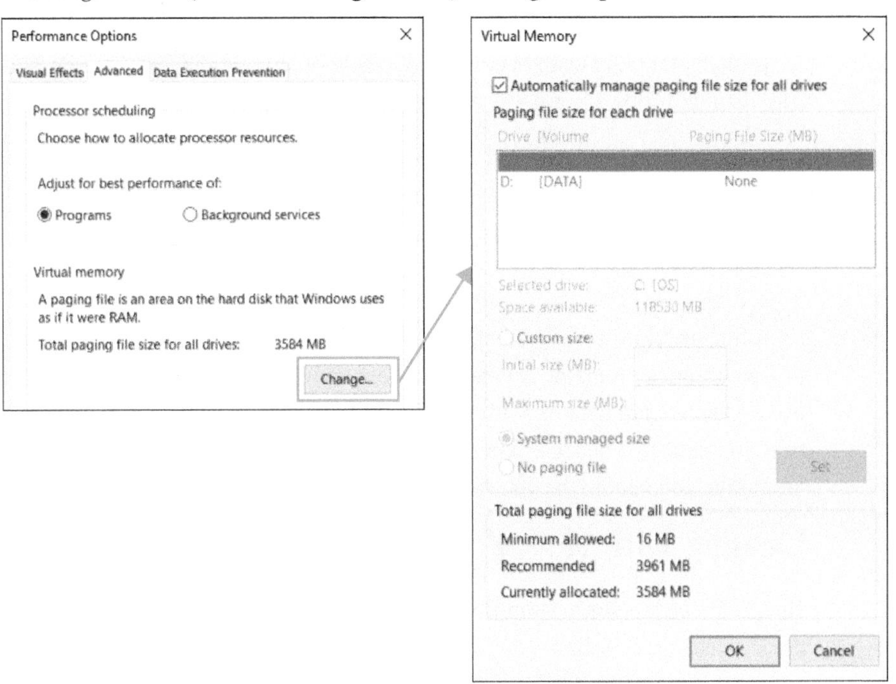

FIGURE 7.45 Windows 10 virtual memory manager

TECH TIP

Where to keep a swap file

If multiple hard drives are available, a technician might want to move the swap file to a different drive. Put the swap file on the fastest hard drive unless that hard drive lacks space. The swap file can reside on multiple hard drives. It is best to keep the swap file on a hard drive that does not contain the operating system.

Memory space is divided into 4 KB blocks of memory called *pages*. The operating system allocates as much available RAM as possible to an application. Then the operating system swaps, or pages, the application to and from the temporary swap file as needed. The operating system determines the optimum setting for this swap file; however, the swap file size can be changed.

The page file can also get corrupted. If it does, in Windows, hold down Shift while selecting *Restart* from the power icon > *Troubleshoot* > *Advanced Options* > *Startup Repair*.

TECH TIP

Adding more physical RAM helps with caching

One of the most effective ways to speed up a computer is to reduce the amount of data that has to be swapped from the hard drive to RAM. This is done by increasing the amount of motherboard RAM.

Troubleshooting Storage Devices Overview

Storage devices are critical to computer users because they hold users' data. Sadly, users do not back up their data or system frequently. Blackblaze (www.blackblaze.com) did a study of more than 25,000 mechanical drives and found that over a four-year period, 78% of the drives lasted longer than four years, but 22% of them failed during the first four years. Mechanical drives have moving parts, and moving parts fail. Expect it!

Tools that a technician needs to troubleshoot storage devices include both hardware and software. The list that follows is a good starting point:

> Screwdriver to loosen or remove screws.
> External hard drive enclosure to be able to check a drive from another system or be able to determine whether the problem is the drive or the motherboard port (refer to Figure 7.4 to see one).
> Access to operating system commands and Windows tools to check a drive for physical and file structure errors and attempt to fix them.

Two things to remember when troubleshooting a storage device are to be patient and be kind to the user. A technician dealing with storage devices is often faced with angry users. Stay calm and do the best you can. Just because a system will not boot from the hard drive does not mean it is bad. There are things you can do, as you will soon see.

Dealing with Slow Performance

Keeping a computer system in a clean and cool operating environment extends the life of the hard drive. Hard drive failures are due to problems with moving parts (heads and motors), power fluctuations, and/or failures. Performing preventive maintenance on the entire computer is good for all components inside the computer, including the hard drive subsystem.

Windows has three great tools to use in hard drive preventive maintenance: error checking (*Check Now* or the *Check* button), Disk Cleanup, and Disk Defragmenter. In Windows, you can use a disk tool to locate **lost clusters**, which are clusters that have become disassociated from data files but still occupy disk space. Error checking/Check Now is also good for dealing with intermittent read/write errors. Locate the drive in File Explorer, right-click the drive, and then select *Properties* > *Tool* tab > *Check*.

The Windows program **Disk Cleanup** removes temporary files, removes offline internet files, empties the Recycle Bin, compresses unused files, and removes unused programs—and it prompts you before doing any of this. To access Disk Cleanup, follow these steps:

Step 1. Access *File Explorer*.

Step 2. Right-click on the drive letter (commonly `C:`) and select *Properties*.

Step 3. On the *General* tab, select the *Disk Cleanup* button.

Step 4. In the Disk Cleanup window, select the checkboxes for the options desired and click *OK* (as shown in Figure 7.46).

TECH TIP

Running Disk Cleanup from a command prompt

To run Disk Cleanup from a command prompt, type **`cleanmgr.exe`** and then press Enter.

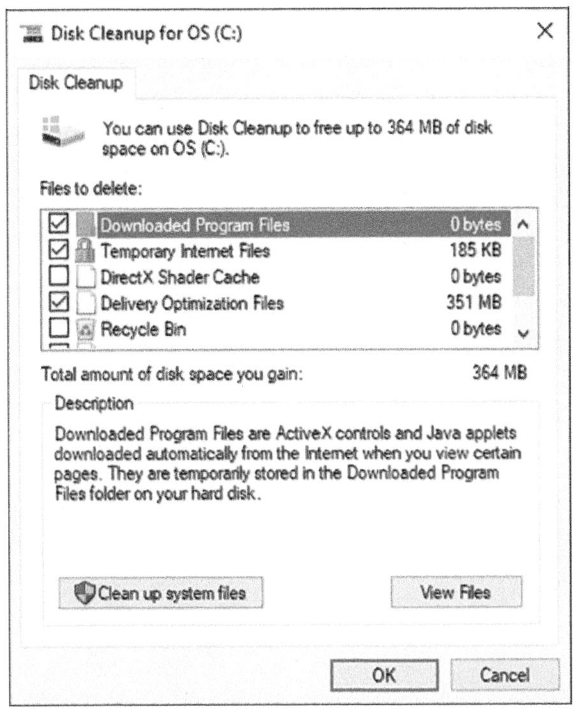

FIGURE 7.46 Disk Cleanup window

Drive performance affects system and application performance. Some vendors list the number of input/output operations per second (**IOPS**) as a measure of storage performance, but this is not a consistent measurement. If a drive is slow to respond or has **extended read/write times**, you can use *Task Manager* > *Performance* tab > click on the drive and look at the average response time, read speed, and write speed data. There is also a link there that you can use, or you can open *Windows Resource Monitor* (`resmon.exe`) > *Disk* tab to see the specifics on the data.

Over time, as files are added to a hard drive, the files become fragmented, which means the clusters that make up a file are not adjacent to one another. Fragmentation slows down a hard drive in two ways: The FAT has to keep track of scattered clusters, and the hard drive read/write head assembly must move to different locations on the drive's surface to access a single file. Figure 7.47 illustrates fragmentation of three files (F1, F2, and F3) and the results after defragmentation has been executed on the hard drive. **Defragmentation** is the process of placing files in contiguous sectors. Notice the results of the defragmentation process in Figure 7.47:

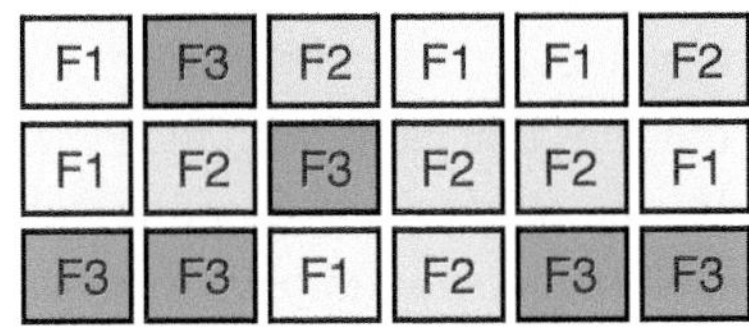

Three fragmented files

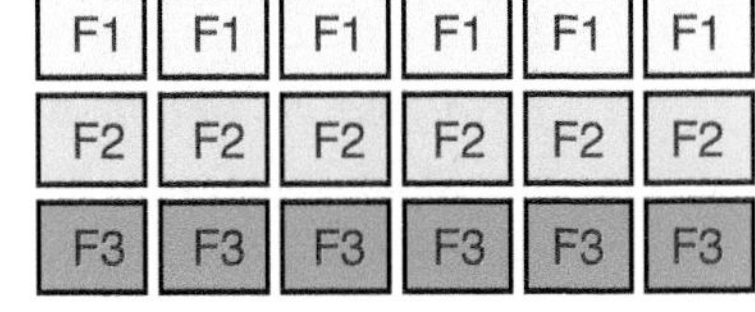

Three contiguous files

FIGURE 7.47 Fragmented hard drive/defragmented hard drive

TECH TIP

Tool order matters

Use the error checking (Check Now or Check) and Disk Cleanup tools before running the Disk Defragmenter tool.

Defragmenting a hard drive makes for faster hard disk access. This process also extends the life of the hard drive by reducing the drive's mechanical movements. Windows 7 automatically schedules a hard drive to be defragmented every Wednesday at 1 a.m. Windows 8 and higher perform hard drive optimization as needed. You can manually execute optimization by using the Disk Defragmenter tool using one of the following methods:

> In Windows, open *File Explorer*, locate a hard drive letter and right-click on it > select *Properties* > *Tools* tab > *Optimize*.
> From a command prompt or search textbox, use the `defrag` command.
> From a command prompt or search textbox, use the `dfrgui.exe` command

TECH TIP

SSD defragmentation kills

Do not defragment an SSD as you would a magnetic hard drive. Defragmentation causes more reads and writes, which reduces the life span of the SSD.

Data Loss and Corruption

A hard drive typically has a warranty of three years, but people use their computers longer than that. Hard drives fail, and data is lost or becomes corrupted. The best prevention is to back up your drive. You can buy a drive that will back up your entire drive with one click. You can also use free cloud storage such as Google Drive or Microsoft OneDrive for data storage from a variety of storage devices.

In the corporate world, companies can buy **file recovery software** or hire other companies to provide it as a service. Technicians who do not have this software should at least have the name of a company they recommend or use.

Hard drives have built in technology to mark bad sectors and move the data to a different location on the drive. That data may be corrupted even though it is moved. Here are some recommendations for repairing corrupt data.

> Restore corrupt data from a backup.
> If the corrupt data is one or more system files, use the **System File Checker** tool or the `sfc /scannow` command.
> If the `sfc` command does not work, you can reinstall the operating system by using the *Refresh your PC* option, which keeps the apps that came with the PC and the apps installed from the Microsoft Store. You can also use the *Reset this PC* option, which allows you to choose whether to keep your personal files. Note that you do have to reinstall your applications.
> Use the `chkdsk` command. Use the `/f` option to fix any errors found on the disk. Use the `/R` option to locate bad sectors and recover any readable information.

Troubleshooting New Storage Device Installation

Most problems with new drive installation stem from improper configuration of jumpers on PATA drives or problems with cabling. BIOS/UEFI and the operating system can display a multitude of symptoms, including POST error codes, beeps, and messages, such as the following:

> Hard drive not found
> No boot device available

> Hard drive not present
> Inaccessible boot device
> Invalid boot disk

The following tips assist with checking possible problems when **drive not recognized** errors occur in the system or a **motherboard LED** indicates a drive or boot failure:

> Check the physical settings (such as the power cable, jumper settings, secure data cable, data cable pin 1 orientation, and device placement on the data cable).
> Check the drive type setting in BIOS/UEFI Setup and ensure that the ports (especially SATA ports) are enabled.
> If everything works well, but the **drive activity LED** doesn't blink when storing/retrieving data, check your front panel cable connection to the motherboard.
> If after you have configured the drive, installed it, and powered it on, the BIOS/UEFI shows the drive type as "None" or "Not installed," or if it displays all 0s in the drive parameters even though you set it to automatically detect the drive, then the BIOS/UEFI is not able to detect it. Check the BIOS/UEFI SATA mode and BIOS/UEFI version. Check all jumper settings, check the cable connection(s), and check the power connection. In Setup, reduce any advanced features to their lowest values or disable them. Increase the amount of time the computer takes to initialize the hard drive by going into Setup and modifying features such as hard drive boot delay or setting the boot speed to the lowest value. This gives the hard drive more time to spin up and reach the appropriate RPM before data is read from it. Make sure the motherboard port is enabled.
> If the BIOS/UEFI recognizes the device but you have a **missing drive in the OS**, the drive may not have been initialized or partitioned. Use the Windows Disk Management tool to fix.
> Determine whether the drive has been partitioned and one partition has been marked as the active partition. Also determine whether high-level formatting has been applied to the drive.
> If the hard drive does not format to full capacity, your BIOS/UEFI may not support the larger drive and/or the BIOS/UEFI must be upgraded, you may have selected a file system that does not support larger partitions, or you may need an updated driver.
> If during power-on the hard drive does not spin up or if the hard drive spins down after a few seconds, check the power connector, the data cable, the drive recognized in BIOS/UEFI, jumper settings, energy management jumpers or settings in Setup, and any software that came with the drive that enables power management. Disable power management in BIOS/UEFI and/or the operating system. Try installing the drive in another system.
> If the system locks or you get a blue screen of death (**BSOD**), write down the message or code, if any, and try a warm boot (Ctrl+Alt+Del). If the drive is recognized after the warm boot, the Setup program may be running too fast for the drive to initialize. Refer to the hard drive documentation to see if the hard drive has a setting to help with this problem.
> Verify that the mounting screw to hold the drive in the case is not too tight. Loosen the screw and power up the computer. Figure 7.48 shows the mounting screws for a hard drive installed in a tower case.

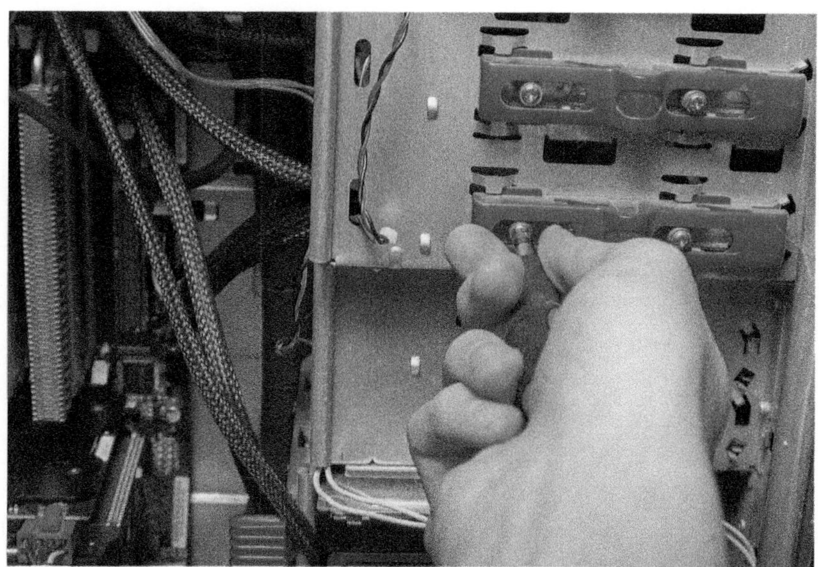

FIGURE 7.48 Hard drive mounting screws

Troubleshooting Previously Installed Storage Devices

Previously installed boot devices can have all of the same symptoms as a newly installed storage device plus the following additional ones:

> **Clicking sounds**
> Read/write errors
> Slow to respond
> Blue screen of death (BSOD) or pinwheel (macOS and Windows)

Because many drives are mechanical devices, they make noises. Sometimes these noises occur because the hard drive is being used too much as virtual memory due to a lack of physical RAM. Some noises are normal, and others indicate problems, as shown in Figure 7.49.

Normal noises	Abnormal noises
Whining noise on spin up	High-pitched whining sound
Periodic clicking or whirling sounds when the drive is being accessed	Repeated clicking or tapping sounds when computer is idle
Clicking sound made by heads parking during power saving modes or when powering off	High-frequency vibration in mounting hardware
	Hard drive clicks and/or a POST error

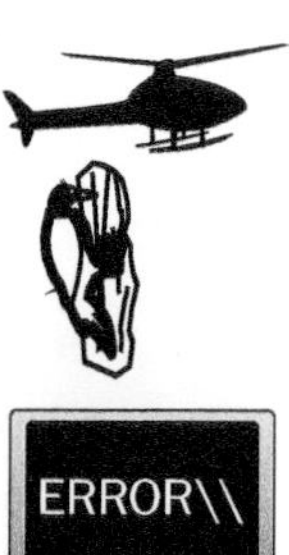

ERROR\\

FIGURE 7.49 Hard drive noises

When a hard drive starts making that loud clicking, tapping, or **grinding noise**, back up the drive immediately and go ahead and purchase a replacement drive. The drive is failing!

The following are generic guidelines for hard drives that have worked but that are now having problems or for when a computer **fails to boot**:

> Run a virus-checking program after booting from virus-free boot media. Many viruses are specifically designed to attack hard drives. If you have to wipe a hard drive to ensure that

the virus is erased before reinstalling the operating system, applications, and data, ensure that you do a full format and not a quick one as part of the operating system installation process.

> Has there been a recent cleaning of the computer, or has someone recently removed the top from the computer? If so, check all cables and verify that they connect correctly. Check the power connection to the hard drive.

TECH TIP

Does your hard drive stick?

Place a hand on top of the drive as you turn on the computer. Does the drive spin at all? If not, the problem is probably a "sticky" drive or a bad drive. A hard drive must spin at a certain RPM before the heads move over the surface of the hard drive. To check to see whether the drive is sticking, remove the drive and try spinning the spindle motor by hand. If it is not moving, remove the drive, hold the drive in your hand, and give a quick jerk with your wrist. Another trick that may work is to remove the hard drive from the case, place the drive in a plastic bag, and put it in the freezer for a couple of hours. Then remove the drive and allow it to warm up to room temperature and reinstall the drive into the system and try it.

> If the hard drive light flashes quickly on bootup, the controller is trying to read the partition table in the master boot record. If this information is not found, various symptoms are possible, such as the error messages "Invalid boot disk," "Inaccessible boot device," "Invalid partition table," "Error loading operating system," "Missing operating system," or "No operating system found." Use the `diskpart` command from the Windows Recovery Environment (WinRE) to see whether the hard drive partition table is okay. Here are a few commands to try within this utility: `list disk`, `list volume`, `list partition`, `detail disk`, `detail volume`, and `detail partition`. Try running `bootrec /fixmbr` or use a hard drive utility to repair the partition table.

> A common problem is that the operating system cannot be found, which is indicated with the **bootable device not found** or **no OS found** message (or other messages, such as "Disk Boot Failure," "Non-System Disk," and "Disk Error" that may indicate a boot record problem). The solution is to boot from a bootable disc or USB flash drive to see if drive `C:` is available. When doing so, change the BIOS/UEFI boot order settings to boot to your removable media. The operating system may have to be reloaded. Also, verify that the primary partition is marked as active and that there is not nonbootable media such as a disc or USB flash drive inserted into or attached to the system. Check the first boot option setting in BIOS/UEFI and make sure it is set to the appropriate drive.

> If you receive a message such as "Hard drive not found," "No boot device available," "Fixed disk error," or "Disk boot failure," the BIOS/UEFI cannot find the hard drive. Check cabling. Place the drive in an external enclosure and attach it to a working computer.

> If a self-monitoring, analysis, and reporting technology (**S.M.A.R.T.**) error appears, back up data and research the error to take immediate action. S.M.A.R.T. is used to monitor both mechanical hard drives and SSDs. A S.M.A.R.T. error may appear immediately before a failure. Table 7.10 lists a few of the S.M.A.R.T. errors. Keep in mind that drive manufacturers may have their own errors as well.

TABLE 7.10 S.M.A.R.T. errors

Error	Description
Reallocated sectors count	The number of sectors that were marked as bad, causing the data within those sectors to be moved
Spin retry	The number of times the drive was not up to speed in order to read and write from the drive
SATA downshift error count or runtime bad block count	The number of data blocks that contained uncorrectable errors
Reported uncorrectable errors	The number of uncorrectable errors detected
Reallocation event	How many times data had to be remapped
Soft read error rate or TA counter detected	The number of off-track errors

> When Windows has startup problems, the Windows Recovery Environment (WinRE) and *Advanced Options* menu (press F8 on startup) are used. With Windows devices, if the system boots too quickly to access this menu, hold down Shift while restarting the system. Then select *Troubleshoot* > *Advanced Options* > *Startup Repair* or *Command Prompt*. Startup problems are often due to viruses. Other utilities that help with MBR, boot sector, and system files are System File Checker (SFC) and the *Advanced Boot Options* menu. Use `bootrec /fixmbr` or `bootrec /fixboot` from WinRE.

TECH TIP

Using System File Checker

You can run the System File Checker program from the command prompt by typing **`sfc /scannow`**. The System File Checker should also be run after removing some viruses.

> When Windows has startup problems due to incompatible hardware or software or a corrupted installation process, the Advanced Boot Options menu can help.

> If an insufficient disk space error appears or if the user is experiencing **sluggish performance** (that is, if the computer takes a long time to respond), delete unnecessary files, including `.tmp` files, from the hard drive, empty the Recycle Bin, and save files to an optical disc, a flash drive, or an external hard drive and remove the moved files from the hard drive. Use the Disk Cleanup and Defragmenter tool. Another option is to add another hard drive and move some (or all) data files to it.

> For eSATA drives, check the power cabling and data cabling. Ensure that the data cable is the correct type for the port and device being used. Partition and format the drive before data is written to it. Ensure that the port is enabled through BIOS. The BIOS/UEFI may require an update, or a device driver may be required (especially if the drive is listed under Other Devices in Device Manager). Note that some operating systems report SATA drives as SCSI drives.

> If the computer reports that the hard drive may have a defective area or if you start getting **read/write failure** notices, right-click on the hard drive volume > *Properties* > *Tools* tab > *Check Now* (Windows 7)/*Check* (8/10/11). The drive may need to be replaced soon.

> If drives fail frequently in a particular computer, check for heat problems, power fluctuations, vibrations, improper mounting screws or hardware that might cause vibrations, and

environmental issues such as dust, heat, magnetic fields, smoke, and nearby motors. Consider using an SSD if the computer is in a harsh environment.

> If a USB drive is the boot device and the system will not boot, unplug the drive, reattach it, and restart the system.

> If a **spinning pinwheel**, ball, hourglass, or other application-specific icon appears; if a message that an application is not responding (sometimes asking you if you want to wait or kill the application) appears; or if a drive takes a long time to respond within an application, use the Disk Management tool to view the status of the drive. (Note that the Mac's colored spinning pinwheel is covered in Chapter 17, "macOS and Linux Operating Systems.") Table 7.11 shows some of the normal and problem **drive status** messages seen in the Windows Disk Management tool. These status messages can help with drive management, troubleshooting, and recovery.

TABLE 7.11 Disk Management status states

Status state	Description
Active	The bootable partition, usually on the first hard drive, is ready for use.
Dynamic	An alternative to the basic disk, the dynamic disk has volumes instead of partitions. Types of volumes include simple volumes, volumes that span more than one drive, and RAID volumes.
Failed	The basic disk or dynamic volume cannot be started; the disk or volume could be damaged; the file system could be corrupted; or there may be a problem with the underlying physical disk (turned on, cabled correctly) or with an associated RAID drive. Right-click the disk and select *Reactivate Disk*. Right-click the dynamic volume and select *Reactivate Volume*.
Foreign	A dynamic disk from another computer has just been installed. Right-click the disk and select *Import Foreign Disks*.
Healthy	The drive is ready to be used.
Not Initialized	A basic disk is not ready to be used. Right-click the disk and select *Initialize Disk*. The **Initialize Disk** option enables a disk so that data can be stored.
Invalid	The operating system cannot access the dynamic disk. Convert the disk to a basic disk (by right-clicking the disk number and selecting *Convert to Basic Disk*).
Offline	Ensure that the physical disk is turned on and cabled correctly. Right-click it and select *Reactivate Disk* or *Activate*.
Online (errors)	Use the hard drive error checking tool. In Windows Explorer/File Explorer, right-click the hard drive partition and then select *Properties*, the *Tools* tab, and *Check Now* (Windows 7)/*Check* (8/10) button.
Unallocated	Space on a hard drive has not been partitioned or put into a volume.
Unknown	A new drive has not been initialized properly. Right-click the drive and select *Initialize Disk*. The volume boot sector may be corrupted or infected by a virus.
Unreadable	The drive has not had time to spin up. Restart the computer and rescan the disk (using the *Action* menu item).

RAID Issues

When two or more drives are configured in a RAID, they are seen as one volume and managed as one volume. Because of the different types of RAID and the number of hard drives involved in the RAID, a lot of problems could occur. Symptoms of RAID problems are similar to those that occur with a hard drive failure (read/write failure, RAID partition lost, slow system performance, loud clicking noise, failure to boot, drive not recognized, operating system not found, or a BSOD).

The following issues can help you with RAID configurations:

> If you have done RAID through the BIOS/UEFI, you cannot manage RAID through Windows (it is grayed out and shows as no fault tolerance). If you want to manage RAID through Windows, you have to break the RAID in BIOS/UEFI (remove the RAID) and then re-create the RAID in Windows. Back up your data before doing this.

> Sometimes as part of the RAID configuration, you need driver media for the Windows installation or RAID failure troubleshooting process. Follow the motherboard or RAID adapter's manufacturing directions on how to create this media (usually via a USB drive or optical disc, even though the directions on the screen may say floppy disk).

> If Windows doesn't allow you or give you the option to create a RAID array, check the BIOS/UEFI settings and ensure that AHCI has been enabled for the drives.

> If disk mirroring is not an option in Windows Disk Management, check your Windows version. You must have Windows Professional or a higher edition to create a RAID array.

> If Windows no longer boots, a BSOD appears, and the Windows boot drive is part of a RAID array, reinstall Windows if you want to keep the RAID array. You may have to get drivers before doing this. If you do not care about RAID and just want Windows to boot again, remove the hardware RAID. You can also use the BSOD code shown to research the error.

> If a RAID partition suddenly goes missing, check for a virus.

> If you receive a message such as **RAID not found**, check the hardware or software configuration (depending on which type of RAID was configured). A power surge can corrupt a hardware RAID configuration done through BIOS/UEFI Setup. A system upgrade, application upgrade, or new application can affect software RAID.

> If you have a **RAID failure**, use the Windows Disk Management tool to check the status of the drives. Then check the RAID configuration if the drives are okay.

SSD Issues

The BIOS should recognize an internally installed SSD. If it does not, go into the system BIOS/UEFI Setup and ensure that the connector to which the SSD attaches is enabled. Be especially careful with SATA ports and port numbering. Configure the system to automatically detect the new drive, save the settings, and reboot the system. Here are some things to try, but remember that other hard drive tips still apply, such as those related to the computer not booting or the operating system not being found:

> Restart the PC.

> Try another SATA port or cable.

> Uninstall/reinstall the driver.

> Use cloning software from the SSD manufacturer or purchased from another vendor.

> Turn off the Wake on LAN BIOS option.

SOFT SKILLS: PHONE SKILLS

Technicians must frequently use the phone in the normal course of business to speak with customers, vendors, and technical support staff. A technician's job may involve communication via the telephone full time.

Phone communication skills are different from the skills needed for in-person communication because on the phone, you have only your words and voice intonation to convey concepts, professionalism, and technical assistance.

When dealing with someone in person, you can use some of the following techniques that are not as effective in a phone conversation:

- Gesture to emphasize points.
- Draw a graphic to illustrate a concept.
- Perform steps needed for troubleshooting faster because you can do them rather than step someone through them.
- Show empathy more easily with your body language, actions, and voice.

When dealing with someone on the phone, the following pointers can help. Some of the tips apply to everyday technical support as well:

- Identify yourself clearly and pleasantly.
- Smile even though they cannot see you (see Figure 7.50). It will make a difference in your tone.

FIGURE 7.50 Telephone communication skills

- Avoid using a condescending tone.
- Be patient and speak slowly when giving directions.
- Use active listening skills (covered in Chapter 2, "Connectivity"); avoid doing other tasks when on a call with someone.
- Avoid using acronyms and technical jargon.
- Avoid being accusatory or threatening.
- If the customer is irate, try to calm the customer down and help him or her; however, if the customer continues to be belligerent, turn the call over to your supervisor.
- Escalate the problem if it is beyond your skill level; do not waste the customer's time.
- Do not leave people on hold for extended periods without checking back with them and updating them.
- Speak clearly and loudly enough to be heard easily.
- Avoid having a headset microphone pulled away so it is hard to hear you; if you are asked to repeat something, speak louder or adjust the microphone or handset.
- Avoid eating, drinking, or chewing gum when on the phone.

Good interpersonal skills are even more important when on the phone than with face-to-face interactions. Before getting on the phone, take a deep breath and check your attitude. Every customer deserves your best game, no matter what type of day you have had or what type of customer you have previously spoken to.

Chapter Summary

- Hard drive form factors include 5.25-, 3.5-, 2.5-, and 1.8-inch drives. Hard drives come in different speeds: 5,400, 7,200, 10,000, and 15,000 RPM. Faster RPM rates mean more expensive drives but also faster data transfers.
- Common drives today are PATA, SATA, and SSD for desktop and mobile computers.
- A PATA drive is internal only and connects to a 40-pin ribbon cable that can have two devices per motherboard connector/cable.
- SATA drives can be internal or external and connect using a 7-pin 3.3-foot (1 meter) maximum internal connector, an external eSATA connector (3.3-foot [1-meter] maximum for 1.5 Gb/s devices and 6.56-foot [2-meter] maximum for 3 or 6 Gb/s devices), or an eSATAp combo eSATA/USB port. SATA 1 (I) drives operate at a maximum of 1.5 Gb/s, SATA 2 (II) drives at 3 Gb/s, and SATA 3 (III) drives at 6 Gb/s. SATA internal drives use a unique SATA power connector. A Molex-to-SATA converter can be purchased, but 3.3V is not supplied to the drive; most drives do not use the 3.3V line. External drives use an external power source unless plugged into an eSATAp combo port, which can provide power.
- A SATA drive requires no jumper, and only one device can connect to a SATA motherboard/adapter port.
- SSDs have become more common in desktops, laptops, and tablets. They are often used in harsh environments, dirty environments, heavy movement environments, and harsh temperature environments. They are extremely fast but expensive. They connect using SATA, mSATA, eSATA, M.2, PCIe, or USB connections.
- SSDs erase data in blocks instead of by marking available clusters in the FAT with traditional drives. SSDs should not be defragmented. SSDs use various technologies to ensure functionality, such as using all the memory evenly (wear leveling) and using reserved spare memory blocks.
- An SSHD is a combination of a mechanical hard drive and flash memory that holds the most frequently used data.

- Hard drives must be partitioned and have high-level formatting applied before they can be used to store data.
- Partitioning separates a drive into smaller sections (volumes) that can receive drive letters. The smaller the volume, the smaller the cluster size. A cluster is the smallest space in which a single file can reside. A cluster consists of four or more sectors, and each sector contains 512 bytes.
- Partitioning can be done through the Windows installation process or by using the Disk Management tool.
- A simple volume is the most common type of partition volume created.
- To create a spanned volume (otherwise known as JBOD), space from two or more hard drives is seen as one drive letter. One drive is filled before any other hard drives are used.
- A striped volume writes data to two or more drives but does not provide redundancy.
- The system volume (usually `C:`) holds files needed to boot the operating system.
- The boot volume (usually `C:`) holds the majority of the operating system files.
- Computer manufacturers may use an HPA or a protected partition for system recovery.
- Multiple drives can be configured in a hardware or software RAID implementation. Hardware RAID is done using the BIOS/UEFI or a RAID adapter. Software RAID is done using the Windows Disk Management tool.
- RAID 0, or disk striping, does not provide fault tolerance, but it does provide fast, efficient use of two or more drives.
- RAID 1 is disk mirroring, and this method does provide fault tolerance by ensuring an exact copy of a drive in case one drive fails.
- RAID 5 is disk striping with parity, where parity data is kept on one of the three or more drives. This parity data can be used to rebuild one drive if one of the three or more drives fails.
- RAID 10 is a mirrored set and a striped set combined with four hard drives at a minimum. This mode can read from the drive quickly but with slight degradation when writing.
- Windows Storage Spaces can use a variety of drive types to create a single storage space that can have RAID-like qualities.
- File systems in use are FAT16 (FAT), FAT32, exFAT, NTFS, APFS, ext3, and ext4. FAT32 and exFAT are used for external drives, such as flash thumb drives. NTFS, which is used for internal drives, provides features such as better cluster management, security, compression, and encryption. ext3 and ext4 are used in Linux-based systems.
- Two ways of changing from one file system to another are by using the `convert` command and by formatting the drive. The `convert` command preserves existing data. High-level formatting does not preserve any saved data.
- If a drive fails to be recognized as a new installation, check cabling and BIOS/UEFI settings, especially for a disabled SATA port.
- Normal mechanical drive noises include a clicking when going into sleep mode or being powered down due to self-parking heads.
- Abnormal drive noises include a couple of clicks with a POST beep and/or error, repeated clicking noises, grinding noise, high-frequency vibration due to improper or poor mounting hardware, and a high-pitched whining sound.
- If a drive fails after operating for a while, check for a virus. See if the BIOS has a virus checker. Try a warm boot to see whether the drive has not spun up to speed yet. Check cabling, especially on SATA. Review any recent changes. Use the Windows Advanced Boot Options menu, Windows Recovery Environment (WinRE), System File Checker (SFC), and the `bootrec /fixmbr` and `bootrec /fixboot` commands. Boot from an alternate source and check Disk Management for status messages related to the hard drive.

> Hard drive space used as RAM is known as virtual memory. Ensure that enough free storage space is available.

> When speaking on the phone to anyone, be clear in your statements, don't use technical jargon, keep your tone professional, and do not do other tasks, including eating or drinking.

A+ CERTIFICATION EXAM TIPS

- ✓ Be able to select, install, and configure SATA and SSD (mSATA, PCIe, M.2, and NVMe), drives.
- ✓ Make sure you know about and can recognize SATA, eSATA, IDE (PATA), and SCSI (SAS) cabling.
- ✓ Be able to recommend a hard drive based on speed (5,400, 7,200, 10,000, and 15,000 RPM) or form factor (2.5-inch vs. 3.5-inch).
- ✓ Be able to recommend an SSD based on interface used (NVMe, SATA, or PCIe) as well as form factor (M.2 or mSATA).
- ✓ Know the purposes of the error checking (Check Now/Check), Disk Cleanup, and Disk Defragmenter tools.
- ✓ Use a computer to review the disk tools and how to get to them.
- ✓ Review all the troubleshooting tips right before taking the exam.
- ✓ Be familiar with the following Disk Management concepts: understanding drive status and what to do if the status is not healthy, mounting, extending partitions, splitting partitions, assigning drive letters, adding drives, and adding arrays.
- ✓ Know what a normal hard drive sounds like and what sounds a hard drive in trouble makes. Ensure that you back up the data before a drive fails.
- ✓ Know the difference between RAID levels 0, 1, 5, and 10.
- ✓ Know the various file systems, including exFAT, FAT32, NTFS, APFS, ext3, and ext4.
- ✓ Know the difference between a quick format and a full format.
- ✓ Know the differences between basic and dynamic disks and understand primary, extended, and logical partitions and volumes.
- ✓ Be able to troubleshoot common symptoms, such read/write failures, sluggish performance, grinding noises, clicking sounds, failure to boot, drive not found or recognized, missing drives in the OS, RAID not found, and RAID not working.
- ✓ Know the difference between normal LED behavior for drive activity and unusual behavior. Know that some motherboards have LEDs that can help when troubleshooting drives.
- ✓ Be familiar with BSOD and spinning pinwheel proprietary crash screens.
- ✓ Know how and when to use Microsoft command-line tools such as `format`, `diskmgmt.msc`, `resmon.exe`, `cleanmgr.exe`, `dfrgui.exe`, `diskpart`, `SFC`, and `chkdsk`.
- ✓ Install a couple of practice drives for the exam. Misconfigure the BIOS/UEFI and leave a cable unplugged or the drive power removed so you see the POST errors and symptoms.
- ✓ Know how and when to configure RAID and the differences between the various RAID levels.
- ✓ Be able to initialize a drive, convert a file system, convert a drive to a dynamic disk, create a simple volume, and select a particular file system.
- ✓ Know how to speak on the phone professionally.

Key Terms

2.5-inch drive 225
3.5-inch drive 225
5,400 RPM 226
7,200 RPM 226
10,000 RPM 226
15,000 RPM 226
AHCI 241
APFS 244
basic disk 251
basic storage 251
boot partition 248
boot sector 250
boot volume 251
bootable device not found 263
`bootrec` 263
BSOD 261
`chkdsk` 260
clicking sound 262
cluster 244
`convert` 244
DBR 250
`defrag` 260
defragmentation 259
`dfrgui.exe` 260
disk cache 256
Disk Cleanup 258
Disk Management 242
disk mirroring 254
disk striping 254
`diskpart` 242
drive activity LED 261
drive array 253
drive not recognized 261
drive status 265
dynamic disk 251
dynamic storage 251
eSATA 233
exFAT 243
ext3 244
ext4 244
extended partition 246
extended read/write time 259
fail to boot 262
FAT (file system type) 243
FAT (file allocation table) 250
FAT32 243
file recovery software 260
file system 243
`format` 250
full format 249
GPT 249
grinding noise 262
head crash 226
high-level formatting 242
HPA 249
IDE 229
IDE cable 231
Initialize Disk 265
IOPS 259
JBOD 251
logical drive 246
lost cluster 258
M.2 230
MBR 247
missing drive in the OS 261
motherboard LED 261
mount 239
mSATA 232
MTBF 226
NAS drive 229
no OS found 263
NTFS 244
NVMe 231
partitioning 242
phone communication skills 267
primary partition 246
quick format 249
RAID 253
RAID 0 254
RAID 1 254
RAID 5 254
RAID 10 254
RAID failure 266
RAID not found 266
RAW volume 251
read/write failure 264
SAS 229
SATA 229
SATA cable 231
SCSI cable 234
`sfc` 260
simple volume 251
sluggish performance 264
S.M.A.R.T. 263
spanned volume 251
spinning pinwheel 265
SSD 227
SSHD 228
striped volume 251
System File Checker 260
system partition 248
system volume 251
volume 246
Windows Storage Spaces 255

Review Questions

Consider the following internal hard drive specifications when answering Questions 1–7:

> SATA 6 Gb/s transfer rate
> 1 TB capacity
> Minimizes noise to levels near the threshold of human hearing
> 3.5-inch 7,200 RPM
> 32 MB buffer size

1. Which SATA version is being used?

   [1 | 2 | 3 | cannot be determined from the information given]

2. Which Windows file system should be placed on this drive if encryption will be used?

   [exFAT | FAT | FAT32 | NTFS]

3. Which drive preparation steps are required to be done if this drive is added as a new drive? (Select all that apply.)

   [defragmentation | low-level format | high-level format | error checking | RAID | virus checking | partitioning | striping | duplexing]

4. This drive is meant to be quiet. List two noises that the drive could make that would indicate issues to you.

   ____

   ____

   ____

5. Is this drive internal or external? Explain your reasoning.

   [Internal | External | cannot be determined]

   ____

   ____

6. What is this drive's form factor?

   [6 Gb/s | 1 TB | 3.5-inch | 7,200 RPM | 32 MB]

7. How many other devices could be on the same cable that connects this device to the motherboard?

   [0 | 1 | 2 | 3 | cannot be determined]

8. If only two drives are available, which RAID levels can be used? (Choose all that apply.)

   [0 | 1 | 5 | 10]

9. A technician has been called to help with a problem. A S.M.A.R.T. error appears, and the user reports that the system has been running slowly for several months. Which two tools or actions should the technician use immediately?

   [chkdsk | partition the drive | apply high-level formatting to the drive | `convert` | `diskpart` | back up the data | attach external drives and configure Storage Spaces]

10. What is the difference between spanning and striping?

    a. Spanning is done in hardware, and striping is done in software.

    b. Spanning is done within RAID, and striping is done in Windows or through BIOS/UEFI.

    c. Spanning takes two drives, and striping takes three drives.

    d. Spanning fills one drive before moving to the next drive, whereas striping alternates between the drives.

    e. Spanning is RAID 0, and striping is RAID 1.

11. A tile and carpet warehouse uses several computers for the inventory process. The computers in the warehouse area have a higher hard drive failure rate than those in the office area. Which solution will help this company?

    a. Replace the hard drives with SSDs.

    b. Place antistatic mats under the computers and on the floor where people stand or sit to use the computer.

    c. Install more powerful power supplies.

    d. Install additional CPU fans.

    e. Replace the drives with higher-RPM drives.

A user wants to add an SSD to a computer. Consider the following SSD specifications for the drive being purchased and the user's motherboard documentation when answering Questions 12–16.

Specifications:

> 1 TB capacity

> PCIe 3.0 x4 interface

> M.2 2280

Motherboard documentation

> 1 x M.2_1 socket 3 with M key, type 2242/2260/2280/22110 storage devices support (SATA and PCIe 3.0 x4 mode)

> 1 x M.2_2 socket 3 with M key type 2242/2260/2280/22110 storage devices support SATA and PCIe 4.0 x4 mode)

12. Is this drive internal or external? How can you tell?

    [internal | external]

13. Will the SSD be able to be installed in the computer based on the specifications given?

    [Yes | No | Cannot be determined from the information provided]

14. When considering the motherboard documentation, what do the numbers 2242/2260/2280/22110 mean?

    ____

15. What is a drawback of SSDs?

    [installation time | MTBF | maintenance requirements | cost | speed | reliability]

16. Would the SSD work in the M.2_2 socket?

    [Yes | No | Cannot be determined from the information given]

17. Which tool do most Windows users use to check for lost clusters?

    [error checking (Check/Check Now) | `diskpart` | Disk Defragmenter | Disk Cleanup]

18. How would a technician use the drive LED to troubleshoot a hard drive?

    ____

    ____

    ____

19. [T | F] If you have enough RAM installed, the hard drive will not be used as cache memory.

20. You are speaking on the phone to a customer who is upset. The customer curses and starts yelling. What should you do?

- **a.** Hang up on the caller.
- **b.** Ask the caller if you can put her on hold while she calms down.
- **c.** Speak to the customer using a calm, professional tone.
- **d.** Stay calm but raise your voice level a little to show the importance and professionalism of your technical response.

Exercises

Exercise 7.1 Planning Storage Device Installation and Configuration

Objective: To be able to use motherboard documentation to plan for various storage device scenarios.

Procedure: Refer to the following figure and answer the accompanying questions.

Questions: See Figure 7.51 to answer Questions 1–10.

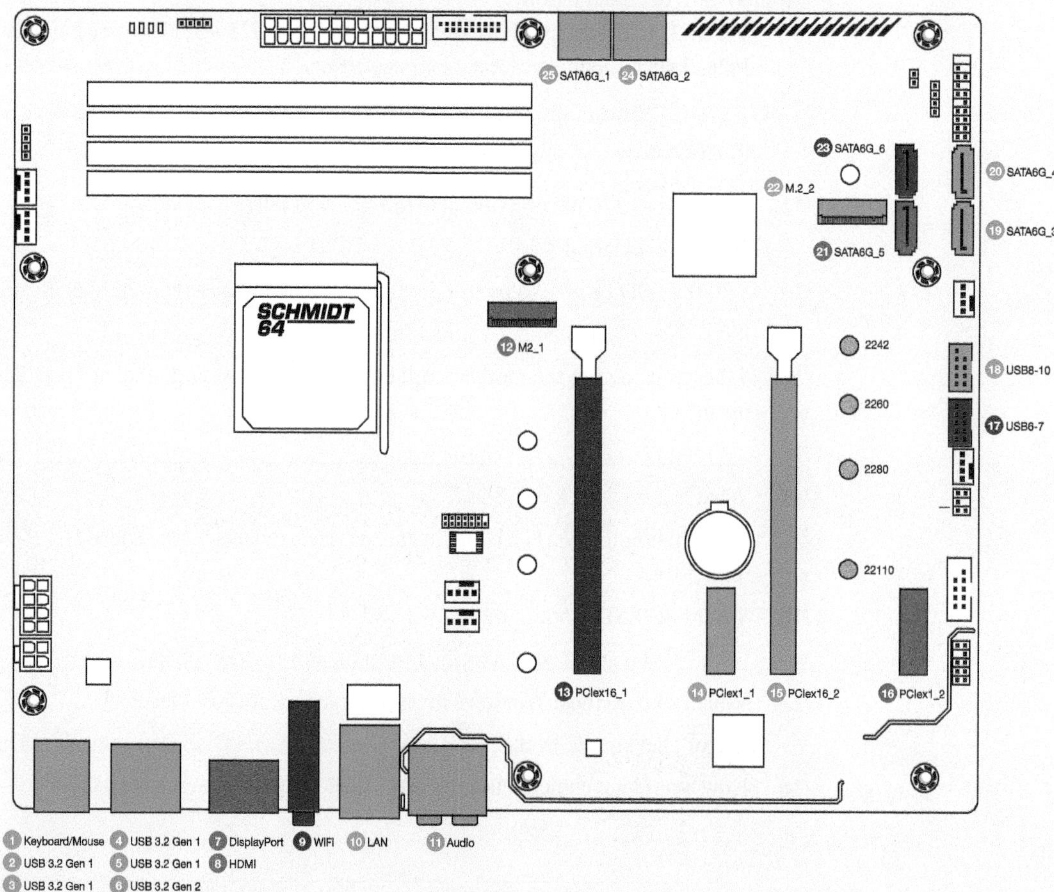

FIGURE 7.51 Exercise 7.1 documentation

1. A user has the motherboard shown and wants to install two internal hard drives. Using Figure 7.51, determine which ports should be used to connect the hard drives. (List two ports.)

____

____

2. Now the user wants to add a third drive, an internal SSD. List all ports that the user could use that have not been used already.

____

____

____

3. If the user is considering an external SSD and wants to use eSATA, how would the user cable up to this motherboard that does not have an eSATA port?

____

____

4. What is the significance of the 2242, 2260, 2280, and 22110 numbers on the motherboard?

____

5. Could either of the M.2 slots be used for an internal mechanical hard drive?

[Yes | No]

6. Could either of the M.2 slots be used for an internal SSD?

[Yes | No]

7. If the motherboard documentation states that an NVMe SSD is supported, which ports/slots could be used?

____

8. What is the maximum number of mechanical hard drives that could be installed using this motherboard? How did you determine the maximum number?

____

9. Which external ports could be used for an external mechanical hard drive? List all that apply.

____

10. Which external ports could be used for an external SSD? List all that apply.

____

Exercise 7.2 Configuring a SATA Hard Drive on Paper

Objective: To be able to configure SATA hard drive jumpers

Parts: Computer with internet access

Procedure: Refer to the following figures and answer the accompanying questions

Questions: See Figure 7.52 to answer Questions 1–3.

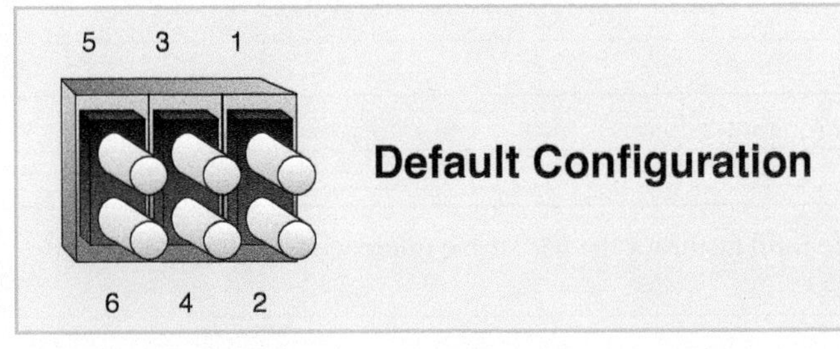

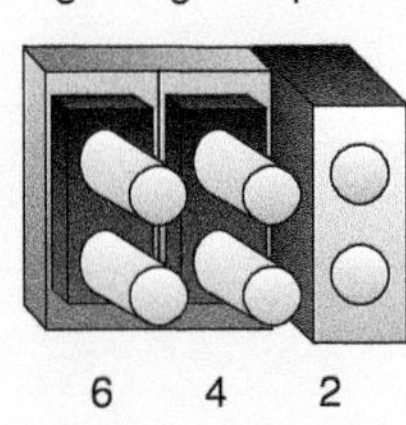

PHY Mode
Limit transfer to 1.5 Gbps

FIGURE 7.52 Exercise 7.2 documentation, part 1

1. Considering the information provided, when would you change the jumpers on this drive?

2. If the drive has pins 1 and 2 jumpered, what version of SATA is the drive using?
[SATA 1 | SATA 2 | SATA 3]

3. If this hard drive were to be installed in a desktop model, what would the form factor of this drive most likely be?

4. Refer to Figure 7.53. The information provided is for a laptop computer used in a business environment. What do you think would be the effects of installing a jumper on pins 1 and 2 on this drive?

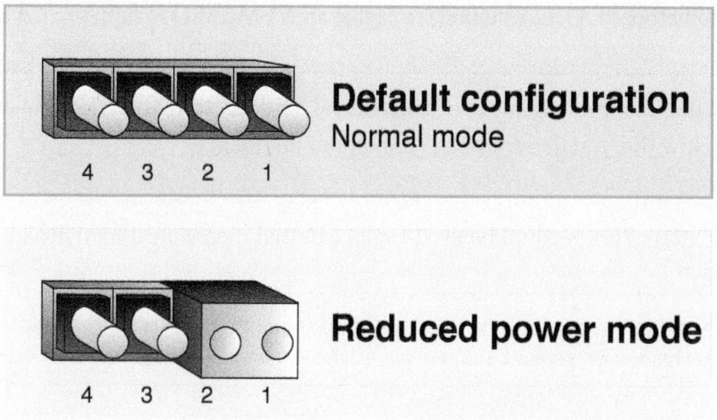

FIGURE 7.53 Exercise 7.2 documentation, part 2

5. Use the internet to determine SATA jumper settings for a particular vendor's replacement hard drive. Write the jumper settings and explanation for the jumpers. Write the URL where you found this information.

6. What is the form factor for the hard drive referenced in Question 5?

Activities

Internet Discovery

Objective: To use the internet to obtain specific information regarding a computer or its associated parts

Parts: Computer with internet access

Questions: Use the internet to answer the following questions. Write the answers and the URL of the site where you found the information for each answer. In answering Questions 1–3, assume that you have just purchased a Seagate Barracuda 3 TB 7,200 RPM 6 Gb/s hard drive.

1. What types of cables are needed for this drive? Do they come with the drive? Write the answers and the URL where you found this information.

   ____

   ____

2. How much cache does this drive have?

   ____

3. If the computer does not have an available SATA connector, what one recommendation could you make?

   ____

   ____

   ____

4. A customer has a Western Digital WD Blue SN550 NVMe M.2 500 GB 3D NAND internal SSD. What is the minimum PCIe version needed to install this card? List the website where you found this answer.
   [1 | 2 | 3 | 4]

   ____

5. Based on the same drive as in Question 4 and information you learned in this chapter, what slot size must the motherboard support in order to install this drive?

   [550 | 5502 | 2400 | 2280 | 22110]

6. Find an eSATA and an internal SATA hard drive that are equal or close to equal in capacity. What is the price difference between the two? Write the answer and the URL where you found this information.

   ____

   ____

Watch the *How to use all capacities of a new hard drive over 2TB*? DFI knowledgebase video, at https://us.dfi.com/knowledge/video/17, to answer Questions 7–10. (If this link does not work when you try to use it, find a video that shows how to install a GPT partition or search for this video at youtube.com.)

7. Which Windows tool was used to convert the partition to a GPT partition?
   [Task Manager | Disk Management | Device Manager | command prompt]

8. Even though the Disk 1 drive was originally unpartitioned, before the presenter did anything to the drive, the drive showed as having how many unallocated sections?

   [1 | 2 | 3]

9. If a drive has already been partitioned and has data on it, what must you do before converting the drive to a GPT disk?

   ____

   ____

10. List one comment that you found interesting and informative.

    ____

Soft Skills

Objective: To enhance and fine-tune a technician's ability to listen, communicate in both written and oral forms, and support people who use computers in a professional manner

Activities:

1. In groups of two, pretend one of you has a hard drive problem. The other student should pretend to help the first student on the phone. Share your phone conversation with two other groups. Select the best group and scenario.
2. With two other classmates, come up with 10 additional tips for good phone support that were not listed in the chapter. Share your ideas with the class.
3. As a team, plan the installation of three storage devices. The boot device will be a SATA SSD with a mechanical internal SSD used for data storage as well as an external USB mechanical drive. In your plan, detail what drives you are using for the plan, what things you will check for, how you will obtain the documentation, and what obstacles could appear as part of the installation process. The user also would like some type of redundancy. What choices might you present to the user? Share your plan with other teams.

Critical Thinking Skills

Objective: To analyze and evaluate information as well as apply learned information to new or different situations

Activities:

1. List three things that could cause a computer to lock up periodically that relate to the hard drive. What could you do to fix, check, or verify these three things?
2. A customer wants to either upgrade or replace his hard drive. Go through the steps you would take from start to finish to accomplish this task.
3. Your team supports a department with 20 workstations. Some people store very important information on their local hard drives. Use the internet to research redundancy options as well as options presented in the chapter. Develop a list of possible redundancy plans for the department.

8 Video and Multimedia Devices

In this chapter you will learn:

- > Basics steps needed to install, configure, and troubleshoot video cards, sound cards, and projectors
- > How to install, configure, and troubleshoot optical drives and scanners
- > How to use Windows to verify optical drives, sound cards, and scanners
- > How to provide support with a positive, proactive attitude

CompTIA Exam Objectives:

- ✓ 1101-3.3 Given a scenario, select and install storage devices.
- ✓ 1101-3.4 Given a scenario, install and configure motherboards, central processing units (CPUs), and add-on cards.
- ✓ 1101-5.3 Given a scenario, troubleshoot and diagnose problems with storage drives and RAID arrays.
- ✓ 1101-5.4 Given a scenario, troubleshoot video, projector, and display issues.
- ✓ 1102-1.4 Given a scenario, use the appropriate Microsoft Windows 10 Control Panel utility.
- ✓ 1102-1.5 Given a scenario, use the appropriate Windows settings.
- ✓ 1102-4.7 Given a scenario, use proper communication techniques and professionalism.

Multimedia Devices Overview

Video is an integral part of a computer system, and many jobs require different video specifications. Video is also part of multimedia production. The term *multimedia* has different meanings. This chapter focuses on the most popular areas—optical drive technologies, projectors, sound cards, scanners, cameras, and speakers. These devices collectively enable you to create and output sound, music, video, and movies. The chapter is not intended to be a buyer's guide or an electronics "how it works" chapter; instead, it is a guide for technicians with an emphasis on installation and troubleshooting.

Video Overview

Technicians must look at video as a subsystem that consists of the display, the electronic circuits that send the display instructions, and the cable that connects them. Note that the video subsystem can also be built into the motherboard. Figure 8.1 illustrates a computer video subsystem.

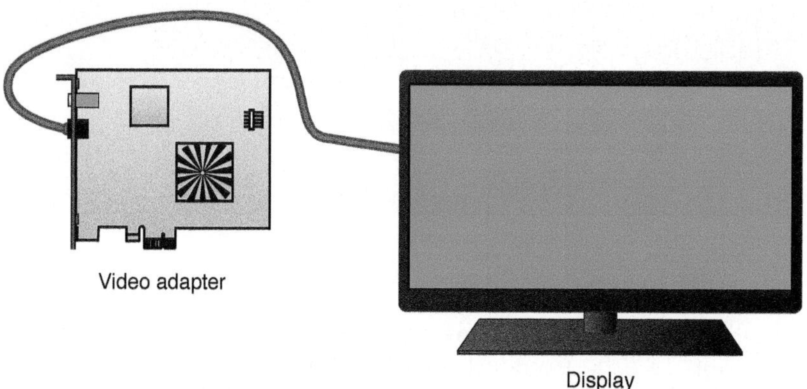

FIGURE 8.1 Video subsystem

Video Cards

The **video card** (also known as a video adapter) controls most of the display output. Video cards are commonly installed into PCIe expansion slots.

A PCIe video card may require either a 6- or 8-pin connector from the power supply. A 6-pin cable can provide an additional 75W of power, while an 8-pin cable can provide an additional 150W. A PCIe video card could require multiple power cables. Figure 8.2 shows a video card and its power cable.

A CPU that has the ability to send video signals to motherboard ports is known as an integrated graphics processor (IGP). In contrast, a video adapter has its own processor, called the graphics processing unit (**GPU**). Other names include video processor, video coprocessor, or video accelerator. Video is processed on the adapter rather than within the motherboard CPU. Figure 8.3 shows a video adapter with a video processor. GPUs commonly have fans and/or heat sinks attached.

FIGURE 8.2 Video card power connector

FIGURE 8.3 Video card with GPU

TECH TIP

You might need a video card with an AMD processor

Be careful when buying or replacing AMD processors as some of the processor descriptions say "requires discrete graphics card." What this means is that the system will not work without a video card installed. The processor does not have graphics capability and cannot send video signals to integrated motherboard video ports. Look for a G in the AMD model number if you want a processor that has an IGP.

A special type of PCIe or external device you may see is a **video capture card** that allows video to be taken from a video source such as a camera, game console (like Xbox or PlayStation), TV channel, or video recorder and saved, put into a presentation or archived file, or streamed onto the internet or a home network. Teachers might use such a device to record or stream a lesson. Not all video capture cards support audio. You can buy video capture cards and devices that have specific input connectors like component video, S-video, or HDMI and an output connector that is commonly USB and/or HDMI. Figure 8.4 shows an external video capture device.

FIGURE 8.4 Video capture device

Video Memory

One of the most important functions of a video processor is to transfer data to and from a video adapter's memory. Memory on a video adapter can be just like motherboard memory or specialized video graphics double data rate (GDDR) modules.

Video RAM is RAM that is used for video exclusively. When video RAM is insufficient for the task being performed, motherboard RAM is used. When motherboard RAM is being used in addition to video card RAM, the amount of motherboard RAM being used is known as **shared system memory**, or shared video memory. You see this when you examine the video display properties. Some systems allow customization through system BIOS/UEFI or a special control panel provided by the video adapter manufacturer. Figure 8.5 shows the properties of a video card that has 2 GB of RAM installed (listed under Dedicated GPU Memory). The Shared GPU Memory amount is how much motherboard RAM is allowed to be used by the video card (and the operating system and the applications). This is frequently limited to half the total amount of installed motherboard RAM.

TECH TIP

Checking how much video memory you have

Use *Task Manager > Performance* tab to see the amount of video memory and any shared system memory. you can also use the `dxdiag` command.

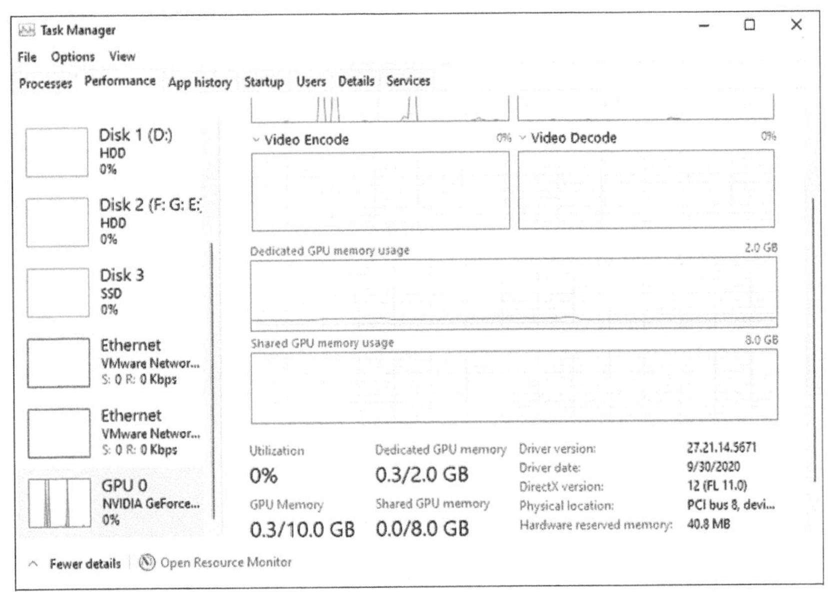

FIGURE 8.5 Shared system memory for video

Installing a Video Adapter

Before installing a video adapter, do your homework:

> Make sure you have the correct interface type and an available motherboard slot. PCIe is the most common, but AGP can still be found.
> Use an antistatic strap or grounding techniques. You may need a screwdriver.
> Download the latest drivers for the video adapter from the manufacturer.
> Ensure that the power supply can supply enough power when the adapter is added. Some adapters require a PCIe 6- or 8-pin or AGP Molex power connector.

TECH TIP

Installing a new video adapter

When you install a new video adapter, if it does not work, disable the onboard video port by accessing system BIOS/UEFI settings.

Before installing an adapter, power off the computer and unplug it. Use an antistatic wrist strap or antistatic gloves. Remove any previously installed video adapters (if performing an upgrade). Locate the expansion slot (PCIe or AGP).

Line up the video adapter's metal connectors with the slot. Push the adapter into the expansion slot. Figure 8.6 shows a video adapter being installed. Notice that a cable from the motherboard S/PDIF out connector attaches to this video card for audio output. Make sure sections of the adapter's gold connectors are not showing and that the card is not skewed. Re-install the retaining screw, if necessary. Connect the monitor to the external video connector. Power on the monitor and computer.

A video card has a set of drivers or software to enable the adapter to work to its full potential. Individual software drivers from the manufacturer provide system compatibility and performance boosts. The internet is used to obtain current video drivers from adapter manufacturers. Be sure to use the proper video driver for the operating system. Always follow the adapter manufacturer's instructions for installing drivers.

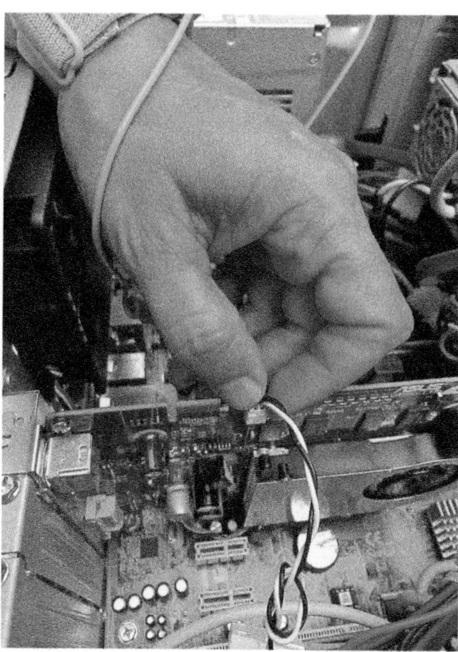

FIGURE 8.6 Video card installation with audio cable

Troubleshooting Video

As with other troubleshooting, when troubleshooting a video problem, check simple solutions first. Do not assume anything! Verify that the monitor's power light is on. If it is not, check the power cable connectors, surge strip, and wall outlet. Verify that the brightness and contrast settings have not been changed. Check or disable power-saving features while you're troubleshooting. Check the monitor cable connected to the video port. Use the built-in diagnostics that some monitors have. Ask the user if any new or upgraded software or hardware has recently been installed, including an operating system automatic update.

TECH TIP

Keep in mind the video system

If a piece of video hardware is defective, then it is the display, adapter, motherboard port, or cable. If replacement is necessary, always attempt the easiest solution first.

Many video problems involve a software driver or improperly configured settings. The best way to be sure is to download the exact driver for the monitor and the display adapter/port from the internet or obtain it from the manufacturer. Some troubleshooting tips related to video follow. Remember that these are only suggestions. Research and, if necessary, contact the manufacturer of the monitor, motherboard, or video adapter for specific instructions on troubleshooting the equipment.

Common video problems include the following:

> **Physical cabling issues** that include the cable not pushed fully into the connector or bent/broken video pins can cause a flickering or **flashing screen**, horizontal or vertical lines, **incorrect colors** and/or **fuzzy images**. Use needle-nose pliers to straighten bent pins. If video cables are okay, try resetting the display to factory default settings and/or refresh rate.

- If you suspect a video driver problem, access *Device Manager* and expand the *Display Adapters* section. Locate the video card and look for any visual indications of problems. Right-click the video adapter > *Properties* > *General* tab to check the device status section to see if the status indicates that the device is working properly. Check for a video driver update.
- For video problems in Windows, search and access the *Change advanced startup options* > *Advanced Startup* (to restart) > *Troubleshoot* > *Advanced options* > *Startup settings* in order to use the low-resolution video option to see if the problem is resolved and to determine whether it is a software driver problem.
- For oversized images and icons, check the resolution setting.
- **A dead pixel** is a pixel that does not light up on an LCD screen and can be (usually is) present on LCDs—even new ones. LCD panels with dead pixels can still be used and are common. If there are too many dead pixels, replace the display. Note that LCDs can also have bright spots when pixels are permanently stuck in the on position.
- If the display doesn't seem to look correct, set the display to the native resolution (that is, the resolution for which the display was made).

TECH TIP

What to do if a display goes black, red, dim, or pink

Check cabling. The backlight bulb might be faulty. Try swapping monitors.

- If a cursor appears momentarily before the computer boots and then nothing is displayed or a distorted display appears, check for a video driver problem.
- Sometimes a **dim image** seems to be evident or no image is displayed, but you can hear the hard drive. In such a case, ensure that the display has power, reset the display to the factory defaults, and try adjusting the brightness and contrast. If these steps do not help, the inverter (the component that converts DC to AC for the backlight) most likely needs to be replaced.

TECH TIP

What to do if a display is dark

Check to see whether the computer is in sleep mode or won't come out of sleep mode. Check the video cable. Hold down the power button and try restarting. Check the power management settings.

- If video is a problem while working in Windows, use the Safe Mode, Last Known Good Configuration, or Enable Low-Resolution Video option and then load the correct driver. You can also use the Driver Rollback option if a new driver has just been installed.
- If audio cannot be heard through the display, check cabling, ensure that the correct sound output device is selected, and check the volume controls and muting.
- If a blue screen of death (BSOD) appears, log any error message or code that appears (see Figure 8.7) and try rebooting the computer. Do not take a hammer to it. Researching the error is a much more productive way of repairing the computer. You can also boot to safe mode or low-resolution video mode and reload a video driver from there.

To connect a projector to a PC and a monitor, you need a video distribution (sharing) device, two video ports from a PC, or a video port splitting cable/device. A laptop frequently has a video port available for connecting an external monitor or a projector. Table 8.1 lists key features to look for in a professional projector.

TABLE 8.1 Projector features

Projector feature	Comments
Brightness or luminance	How much light a monitor or projector can produce. Two factors affect brightness: how much light the projector outputs and the reflective properties of the screen being used. Some projectors have optimization, so you can't base comparisons just on lumens ratings.
Lumens	A measure of light output or brightness—how much visible light is coming out of equipment, such as lamps, lighting equipment, or projectors. This measure is important when comparing products for a room that has lots of exposure to sunlight, for example.
Resolution	The number of pixels used to create an image. The more pixels, the higher the resolution. Shown using two numbers, where the first number indicates the number of horizontal pixels used and the second number indicates the number of vertical pixels.
Wired Ethernet capability	The ability for a projector to be connected through an RJ45 port to an Ethernet network.
Wireless	The ability for a projector to be connected through an 802.11 wireless network.
Remote control or desk controller	The ability to control a projector through either a remote control or a control panel mounted near a computer in the room.

Projector Maintenance

Do not immediately unplug the power to a projector after a presentation; instead, allow the projector to cool down first. You can turn off the projector, but the fan still runs on some models to quickly cool the projector. Keep the filter clean to extend the life of the projector bulb. Keep a spare bulb in stock.

Projector Troubleshooting

Troubleshooting projectors can be tricky sometimes because they might be connected through a control console, they might be mounted in the ceiling (where verifying cabling may not be easy), and they have multiple input ports. Review the "Troubleshooting Video" section, earlier in this chapter, which contains many tips that may be the issue when sending video through a projector. Other troubleshooting tips:

> Verify the input source. An **incorrect data source** is a common issue. Use the remote or projector buttons (see Figure 8.9) to cycle through the inputs. You should also check for tightened cables, if possible.

> If a projector is showing nothing, check that it is powered. If it has recently been turned on and then off, you may have to wait a few minutes to be able to turn it back on again. Check for a **burned-out bulb**. If the projector has power and the correct data source is chosen, then a burned-out bulb is a likely culprit.

FIGURE 8.9 Selecting the input source on a projector

- If the projector has **audio issues** such as not playing sound, check the sound on the computer being used to project and ensure that the volume is not muted or set low. Use the *Sound* setting in Windows. Verify the input source and check the projector mute setting by using the projector remote. Adjust the projector's volume settings. Verify the audio settings in the projector software, if applicable. Never forget that if this is the first time sound has played through the projector, cabling could be an issue.
- If you see a dim image, you might have to adjust the projector brightness/contrast, clean a dirty lens, or replace a failing lamp.
- For presentation software, the *Display* Control Panel/Setting may need to have the *Duplicate the Display* option enabled. Ensure that the projector light shows (that is, that the bulb is good). If flickering occurs, check cabling.
- If you have **intermittent projector shutdowns** or the projector shuts off unexpectedly, check that power is securely attached or that there are batteries, if they are used for power. If the projector has gone into standby mode due to inactivity, press the projector power button to wake the projector. If the projector has been used for an extended period of time, then the projector must have time to cool before re-energizing. Check status indicators, if possible, for an indication of a particular overheating fault. If this occurs and the projector has not been on long, clean and/or replace the air filter.

Introduction to Audio

No multimedia chapter would be complete without mentioning sound. Sound is important to the end user, but sound is also important to a technician in many instances, such as when a computer does not boot. A motherboard might have a small speaker that allows POST sounds to be heard even if the more advanced sound system is not working. Figure 8.10 shows a motherboard speaker.

On a motherboard, external ports for speakers and headphones are typically 1/8-inch (3.5 mm) connectors that accept TRS (tip ring sleeve) connectors. Figure 8.11 shows common motherboard sound ports.

Theory of Sound Card Operation

Sound cards can include a variety of options, such as an input from a microphone, an output to a speaker, and the ability to generate music (for example, bringing sound into the computer through a microphone connected to a sound card). Computers work with digital signals (1s and 0s), so a sound card must convert an analog signal to a digital format to send the sound into a computer. Sound cards can also take the digital data from a computer and output the sound to speakers. To convert an analog waveform to 1s and 0s, samples of the data are taken. The more samples taken, the truer the reproduction of the original signal. Figure 8.14 shows 16-bit sampling.

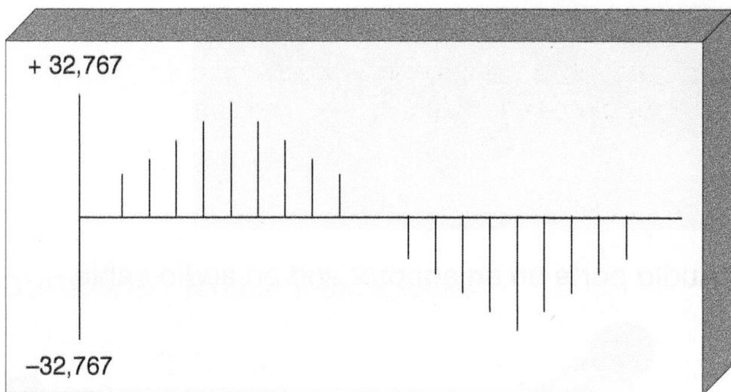

FIGURE 8.14 16-bit sampling

The sound card frequency response is dependent on the sample rate (also known as sample frequency). For a good reproduction of sound, the sound wave is sampled at twice the range desired. The frequency response for a music CD is 44,100 samples per second—a good-quality sound reproduction for human ears. DVDs require a 48 kHz or 96 kHz sampling rate for audio output. Figure 8.15 shows digitized sound samples.

FIGURE 8.15 Digitized sound

Installing Sound Cards

The steps involved in installing a sound card are similar to the steps involved in installing any other adapter. Refer to the manufacturer's instructions when installing devices and adapters. The basic steps are as follows:

Step 1. Power off the computer, remove the computer cover and power cord, and locate an empty expansion slot (making sure it is the appropriate type of slot).

Step 2. Attach the appropriate cables, such as the audio cable, from the optical drive to the adapter.

Step 3. Attach external devices, such as speakers. Attach power to the external devices as necessary.

Step 4. Power on the computer. Windows should detect that new hardware has been installed.

Step 5. Load the appropriate device drivers for the sound card.

After a sound card is installed, there are normally other programs and utilities from the sound card manufacturer that you can install.

TECH TIP

Disabling motherboard sound when installing an adapter

If you install a sound card into a computer that has sound built into the motherboard, you should disable the onboard sound before installing the new adapter.

Sound Cards Using Windows

With Windows the *Hardware and Sound* Control Panel or *Sound* setting is used to change sound and adjust multimedia settings. Most people control volume through a notification area volume control icon located in the lower-right portion of the screen.

TECH TIP

Check for muting

If sound is not coming from a computer, look for an x over the sound icon located in the notification area and ensure that the volume is not muted.

You can tell whether a device has integrated sound or a sound adapter installed by inspecting the *Sound, Video and Game Controllers* category in Device Manager. Figure 8.16 shows a screen capture of Device Manager from a computer that has integrated sound on the motherboard. Note that integrated sound may be located in the *System Devices* category or the *Other Devices* category.

Microphones are commonly used for conference calls. A microphone can be attached to a headset, or it can be a separate device, integrated into the computer display, or integrated into the device (as with mobile devices). To see microphone settings on a Windows device, use the *Settings* > *Sound* option. Figure 8.17 shows the Windows choices shown when you click on the down arrow in the *Sound* from the Input section and both a headset and a webcam have microphone capabilities.

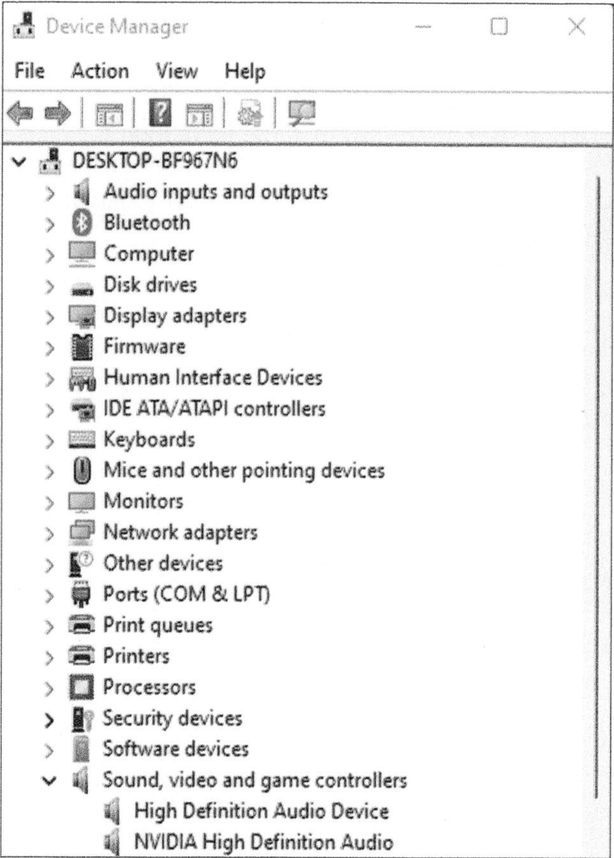

FIGURE 8.16 Integrated sound in Device Manager

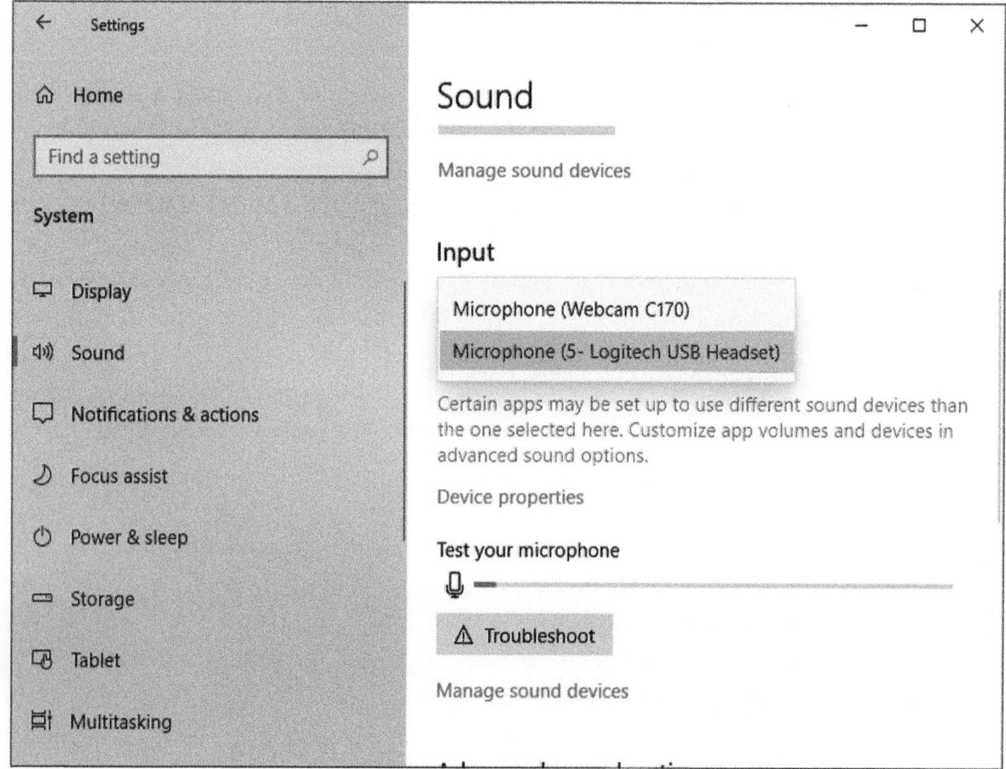

FIGURE 8.17 Choosing a microphone within Windows

Speakers

Most people connect speakers to a sound card or an integrated sound port. Others use a headset, as shown in Figure 8.18. The quality of sound is personal; sounds that are acceptable to one person are not always acceptable to others. Table 8.3 shows some features to look for in speakers.

FIGURE 8.18 Sound quality is personal

TABLE 8.3 Speaker features

Feature	Description
Amplification	Increases the strength of the sound. Amplification output is measured in watts, and most sound cards provide up to 4 watts of amplification (which is not enough for full-bodied sound). Many speakers have built-in amplifiers to boost the audio signal for a much fuller sound.
Power rating	Indicates how loud the volume can go without distorting the sound. This is expressed in watts per channel. Look for the root-mean-square (RMS) power rating; 10 to 15 watts per channel is an adequate rating for most computer users.
Frequency response range	Indicates the range of frequency (sounds) that a speaker can reproduce. Humans can hear from 20 Hz to 20 kHz, and the range varies for each person. Therefore, whether a computer speaker is appropriate depends on the person listening to the speaker. Speaker quality is subjective. Room acoustics and speaker placement also affect sound quality.
Shielding	Cancels out magnetic interference and keeps magnetic interference away from other devices. A speaker may have a magnet inside it that can cause distortion to a device such as a monitor. These magnets can also cause damage to disks and other storage media.

Computer systems can come with internal or external speakers. The external speakers could be battery or AC powered, which might not be desired. Some speakers have an external volume control. Be mindful of this as it is another thing to check for when sound does not occur. Figure 8.19 shows computer speakers that are USB powered that connect to the sound port (green cable into green port).

FIGURE 8.19 USB speakers

TECH TIP

How to choose speakers

Listen to them without headphones, using an audio disc.

Troubleshooting Sound Problems 

The best place to start troubleshooting sound problems is to check the easy potential problems first. Here are some basic areas to get started:

- Are the speakers plugged into the correct port on the sound card?
- Is the volume control muted? If it is, take it off mute.
- Is the volume control on the speakers turned up?
- From within Windows, check whether the device appears to be playing without sound being heard. In this case, the problem is definitely in the sound system.
- Do the speakers have power?

The following is a list of common sound problems and solutions:

- If a speaker is emitting unwanted sounds, make sure there are no empty adapter slots in the computer. Move the speakers farther away from the computer. If the speakers produce a humming noise and are AC powered, move the speaker power cord to a different wall outlet.
- If the sound card is not working, check Device Manager to see whether the sound card is listed twice. If there are two entries for the same sound card, remove both of them by clicking each entry and clicking the *Remove* button. Restart Windows.
- In Windows, if you do not see a sound icon on the screen, right-click a blank area of the taskbar > *Taskbar Settings* > *Select which icons appear on the taskbar* link > locate the *Volume* icon > select the *On* side.
- If the computer emits no sound, use the Windows audio troubleshooter. Search the Windows Control Panel by typing the word **`sound troubleshooting`**.

> If the audio volume is low no matter what sound is played (see Figure 8.20), the speakers may not be amplified speakers, or they may not be connected to the correct sound card port.

FIGURE 8.20 Low or no sound

Optical Drive Overview

Compact disc (CD), digital versatile disc or digital video disc (DVD), and Blu-ray disc (BD) drives are collectively called **optical drives**, or optical disk drives (ODDs). Optical discs are used when creating or playing music CDs or movie DVDs and also for backing up data. CDs are the older technology, but they are still in use today in combination with DVD and BD technologies. Blu-ray discs tend to be used for movie distribution and for video games. Drives can be obtained that can handle CD, DVD, and BD media. Figure 8.21 shows a BenQ CD drive and its various front panel controls.

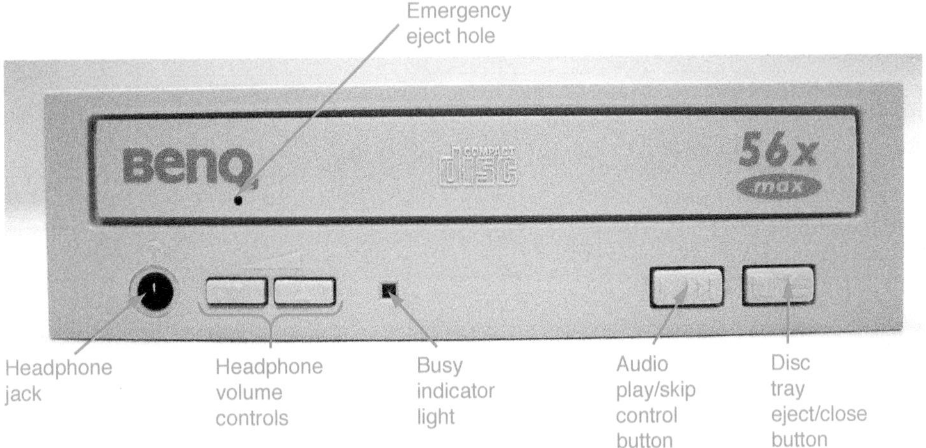

FIGURE 8.21 BenQ CD drive front panel controls

Reading information from a disc involves shining a light through the protective coating to an aluminum alloy layer, where data is stored. CD and DVD drives use red laser technology, whereas Blu-ray drives use blue-violet laser technology for higher disc capacities. Figure 8.22 shows the inside view of a CD drive. The other technologies operate in a similar fashion.

TECH TIP

Some optical drives cannot read Blu-ray discs

Some optical drives cannot read Blu-ray discs because CD/DVD drives use a red laser, and Blu-ray drives use a blue-violet laser. Drives that have both lasers are available.

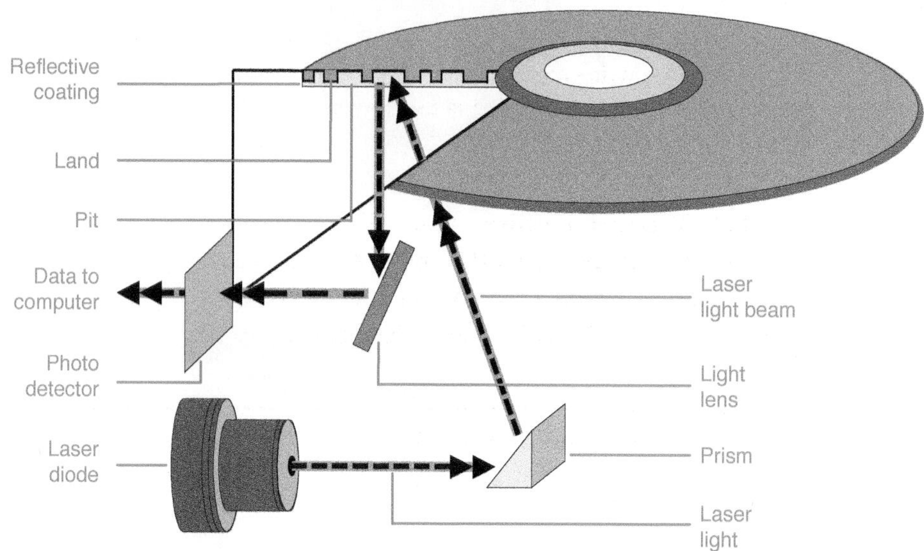

FIGURE 8.22 Inside a CD drive

Optical Drive Features

Optical drives that have an "R" designation can read only from a disk. Drives that have an "RW" or "RE" designation can perform both reads and writes. Drives with a "DL" designation use dual-layer technology, so that two physical layers are available on the same side of the disc. Table 8.4 lists common media types.

TABLE 8.4 Optical writable media

Media type	Capacity
CD	650 or 700 MB
CD-RW	650 or 700 MB
DVD-5/RW	4.7 GB single-sided single layer
DVD-9/RW (DVD-9DL)	8.5 GB single-sided dual-layer
DVD-10/RW	9.4 GB double-sided single-layer
DVD-18/RW (DVD-18DL)	17.1 GB double-sided dual-layer
BD/BD-RE	25 GB single-layer
BD DL/BD-RE DL	50 GB dual-layer
BD XL	100 or 128 GB multi-layer
Mini BD	7.8 GB single-layer
Mini BD DL	15.6 GB dual-layer

Optical drives come in a variety of types, classified by an x factor: 1x (single-speed), 2x (double-speed), 32x, 48x, 52x, and higher. Optical drives do not operate at just a single speed, though; the speed varies depending on the type of media being read and whether writing is being done.

TECH TIP

How to read the numbers

ODDs are frequently shown with three consecutive factor numbers, such as 52x32x52. The first number is the write speed, the second number is the read/write speed, and the third number is the maximum read speed that is used when reading a disc.

Both DVD and BD drives have **region codes**. The world is divided into six regions for DVD drives and three regions for BD drives. A drive must be set for the correct region code, or an optical disc made for that area will not work. Some drives allow the region code to be changed a specific number of times. Table 8.5 shows the region codes for DVD and Blu-ray drives.

TABLE 8.5 DVD and Blu-ray region codes

DVD region code	Geographic area	Blu-ray region code	Geographic area
1	United States and Canada	A	North/Central/South America, Southeast Asia, Taiwan, Hong Kong, Macau, and Korea
2	Europe, Near East, Japan, and South Africa	B	Europe, Africa, Southwest Asia, Australia, and New Zealand
3	Southeast Asia	C	Central/South remaining Asian countries, China, and Russia
4	Australia, Middle America, and South America		
5	Africa, Asia, and Eastern Europe		
6	China		

Many drive features or capabilities can be determined by looking at the symbols on the front of the drive, as shown in Figure 8.23.

FIGURE 8.23 Optical drive symbols

TECH TIP

Using an ISO file

An ISO file/image is commonly used when installing an operating system. If you need to download and install software or an OS, then you can download the ISO image, right-click on the filename in File Explorer, and select *Burn disc image*. ISO images can also be used to boot an OS.

Optical Drive Interfaces and Connections

An optical drive can be internally mounted and attached to a SATA interface, or the drive can be externally attached to a USB, eSATA, or eSATAp (combo SATA/USB) port. The SATA interface is the most common for internal devices, and USB is most common for external devices.

Optical Drive Installation

One thing to be concerned about with an optical drive is whether the drive is to be installed horizontally or vertically. Not all drives can be installed vertically.

The steps for installing an internal optical drive are almost identical to the steps for installing a hard drive:

Step 1. Download the latest drivers before installation.

Step 2. Install any necessary mounting brackets.

Step 3. Ensure that a proper port/interface is available. Ensure that a power connector is available. Refer to the drive documentation.

Step 4. Turn off the power. Remove power cords.

Step 5. Install the drive.

Step 6. Attach the power and data cables.

Step 7. Enter BIOS/UEFI to check the drive status. Ensure that the port is enabled. Ensure that the drive is recognized.

Step 8. If necessary, install drivers and/or software as part of the installation process.

TECH TIP

Always test the installation

Test the installation by using the device to play something or write to a disc that you bring along. Ensure that the customer tries the disc and is comfortable with the changes caused by the installation.

Troubleshooting Optical Drive Issues

Windows has troubleshooting tools. Search for the word `troubleshoot` in the Search textbox.

TECH TIP

Checking the easy stuff first

Verify that the correct type of disc is in the drive, is inserted correctly (label side up), and is not dirty or damaged. Test the disc in another drive. Verify that the ODD has a drive letter. Check Device Manager for errors.

The following is a list of problems, along with possible solutions and recommendations:

- If a drive tray cannot be opened, make sure there is power. Use File Explorer to locate the drive, right-click the drive, and select *Eject*. Some drives have an emergency eject button or a hole you can insert a paper clip into to eject the disc. Refer to Figure 8.21 to see an example of the eject hole.
- If a drive is not recognized by the operating system, check cables, the power cord, and the port enabled in BIOS/UEFI.
- If you hear **grinding noises** or **clicking sounds**, check disc for alignment in the holder.
- If a drive cannot read a disc, ensure that the drive supports the disc being used and that the disc label faces up. Ensure that the disc is clean and free of scratches. Try the disc in another machine or try a different disc to see if the problem is with the drive or the disc.
- If a DVD soundtrack works, but video is missing or distorted, check the cabling. Verify the video drivers. Try changing the display resolution and the number of colors.
- If a message appears about an illegal DVD or BD region error or region code error, change the region, if possible. You can't use the disc without using a drive that matches.

TECH TIP

Seeing video but hearing no audio

If you can see video but can't hear audio or vice versa, check cabling and verify that the computer has the hardware and software requirements for DVD playback. Update the driver.

- Some optical drive problems are resolved by using DirectX. **DirectX** allows people who write software to not have to write code to access specific hardware directly. Access the DirectX Diagnostic Tool in Windows by entering **`dxdiag`** in the Search dialog box.

Preventive Maintenance for ODDs and Discs

CDs and DVDs have a protective coating that helps protect the disc. Fingerprints, dust, and dirt can still negatively affect CD and DVD performance. BDs are less likely to need preventive maintenance than other optical formats.

TECH TIP

Handling discs with care

Always handle a disc by the edges and keep the disc in a sleeve or case to aid in good performance. Never touch a disc's surface. Store discs in a cool location.

When reading information, the optical drive laser beam ignores the protective coating and shines through to the data layer. If dust or dirt completely blocks the laser beam, the laser beam could be reflected or distorted, causing distortion or data corruption. Special cleaning discs, cloths, and kits are available for cleaning optical discs. A soft lint-free cloth and water or glass cleaner works, too. Figure 8.24 shows proper handling during the cleaning process.

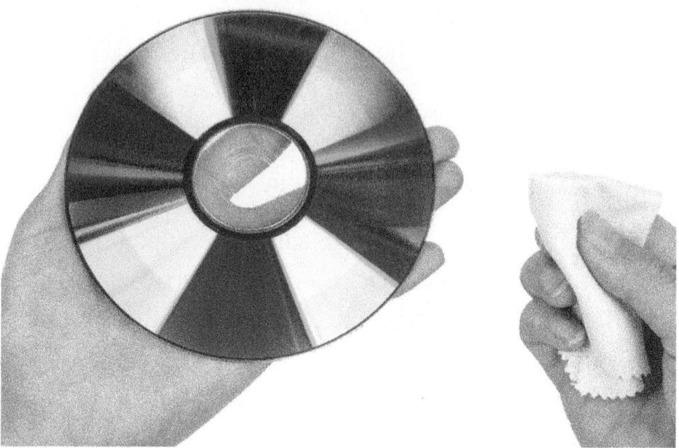

FIGURE 8.24 Disc cleaning

> **TECH TIP**
>
> **Cleaning discs**
>
> When using a cleaning cloth, wipe the disc from the inside (near the center hole) to the outside of the disc (not in a circular motion) on the side of the disc that holds data.

The laser lens is responsible for reading information from discs. If the laser lens gets dust, dirt, or moisture on it, the drive may report data or read errors. Use a laser lens cleaning kit or use an air blower like ones used on a camera lens.

Scanners

A scanner is an input device that allows documents including text and pictures to be brought into a computer and displayed, printed, emailed, written to an optical disc, and so on. A scanner is commonly built into a multifunction device (MFD) such as a printer, scanner, copier, and/or fax machine. These are also called all-in-one (AIO) devices. The most common types of scanners are listed in Table 8.6. Figure 8.25 shows a flatbed scanner, and Figure 8.26 shows how it works. Figure 8.27 shows a handheld scanner used to read barcodes.

TABLE 8.6 Types of scanners

Scanner type	Comments
Flatbed scanner (sometimes called desktop scanner)	Can scan books, paper, photographs, and so on; can take up desk space
ADF scanner (automatic document feeder) or sheetfeeder	Enables a document to be fed through an automatic document feeder similar to a copier; good for scanning multiple-page documents
Handheld scanner	Slowly moves across the document; user must have patience and a steady hand; portable unit
Barcode scanner	A handheld device that reads a code displayed as a series of vertical lines or a quick response (QR) code that is a square that has embedded information such as a website within the displayed pattern.

FIGURE 8.25 Flatbed scanner

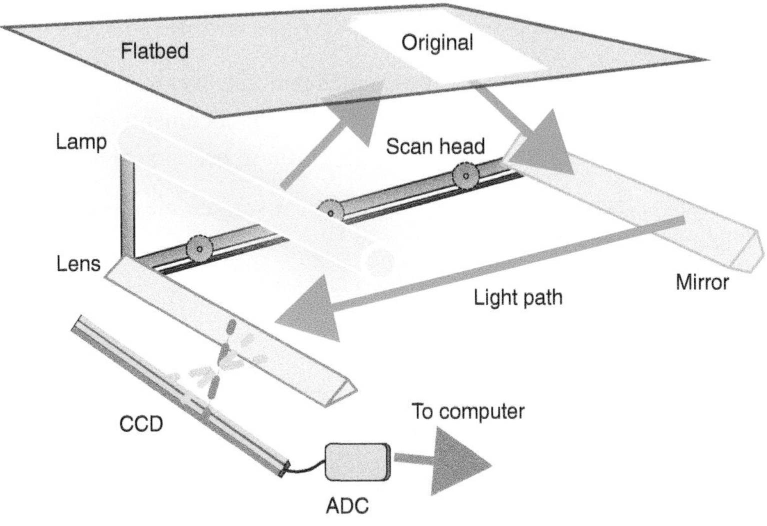

FIGURE 8.26 How a flatbed scanner works

FIGURE 8.27 Barcode reader

A scanner normally attaches to a computer using one of the following options:

- USB
- RJ45 Ethernet
- Wireless

USB is the most common connectivity option. To install a USB scanner, always follow the manufacturer's directions. The following steps are generic:

Step 1. Install software and drivers.

Step 2. Unpackage and unlock or remove special packaging.

Step 3. Connect the data or network cable as well as the power cable.

Step 4. Power on the scanner. Some scanners have a calibration process that needs to be performed. There may be a special switch or push button that locks/unlocks the scan head.

Step 5. Configure options and default settings.

Step 6. Scan a document to test the scanner.

Step 7. Ensure that the customer is trained and has all scanner documentation.

A scanner's plate glass needs to be cleaned periodically (see Figure 8.28). To test whether cleaning has been successful, scan a full page without a document loaded onto the scanner. See if the results yield any smudges or streaks. Consider these best practices:

- The best cleaning method is to put optical surface cleaning fluid on an antistatic cleaning cloth and then wipe the glass.
- Never spray cleaner directly on the glass.
- Do not use rough paper towels.
- A commercial glass cleaner or water can be used.
- Always remove all cleaner residue from the glass.
- Do not press down on the glass.
- Do not use an abrasive or corrosive solvent.
- Keep the glass dust free.

TECH TIP

Protecting scanner glass

Be careful with sharp objects such as staples around a scanner. A scratched or damaged glass surface results in marks on all scanned images.

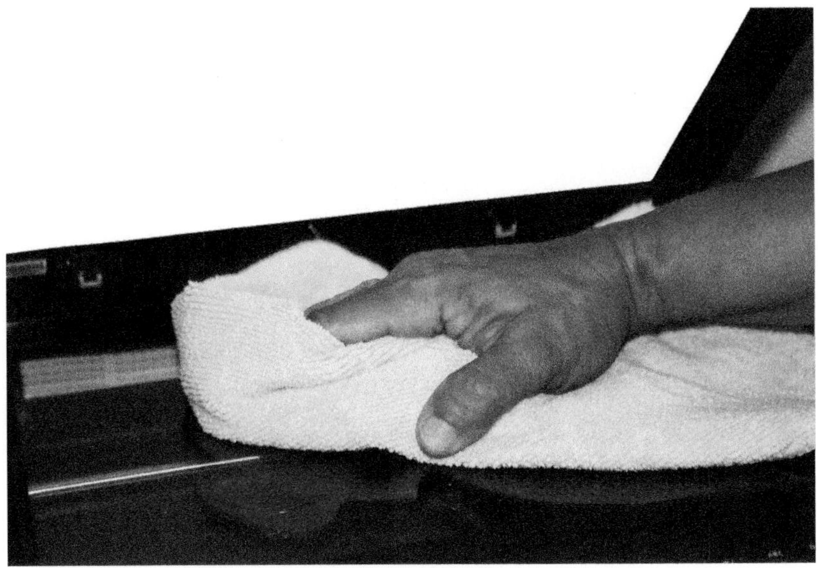

FIGURE 8.28 Scanner glass cleaning

Other Multimedia Devices

There are many multimedia devices today, and almost everything can connect to a computer. Video recording capabilities can be built into a computer or a mobile device, can be attached to a computer, or can be standalone devices such as digital cameras or camcorders used for the purpose of taking photographs or recording movies. Other multimedia devices include webcams and digitizers.

Digital Cameras

Some folks still have a digital camera or use one for work instead of using their personal cell phone and storage. Digital cameras can commonly be attached to a computer using a USB port, or the storage media can be removed and inserted into a slot, a special adapter for that slot, or a multi-card reader.

TECH TIP

Caring for a digital camera

Remove disposable (alkaline) batteries from a digital camera when it's not being used for an extended period so they do not leak battery fluid into the camera.

Many multimedia devices, including cameras, store photographs or movies on removable storage/flash media (miniSD, microSD, xD, CompactFlash, and so on) or hard drives, usually in the JPEG file format, but some cameras can save in RAW or TIFF formats. Figure 8.29 shows a digital camera with removable flash memory cards.

FIGURE 8.29 Digital camera with flash memory

Webcams

Another popular type of digital camera is a **webcam**, which is short for web camera—a digital camera that attaches to a PC for use in transmitting live video or recording video. Web cameras can also attach to VoIP phones and activate when a phone session occurs for instant web conferencing. A webcam may have a small visor that can be flipped over the lens to prevent video when desired. Figure 8.30 shows a wired webcam, but keep in mind that webcams can connect wirelessly or can be integrated into displays or mobile devices.

FIGURE 8.30 Webcam

To access an integrated camera in a flat panel display, you normally use the *Devices and Printers* Control Panel or the *Privacy* Windows Settings link > *Camera*, or software that comes with the camera, such as the Logitech Webcam Software shown in Figure 8.31. If you ever get a "Bandwidth exceeded" message when a camera is being used, try reducing the camera's resolution in whatever software is being used.

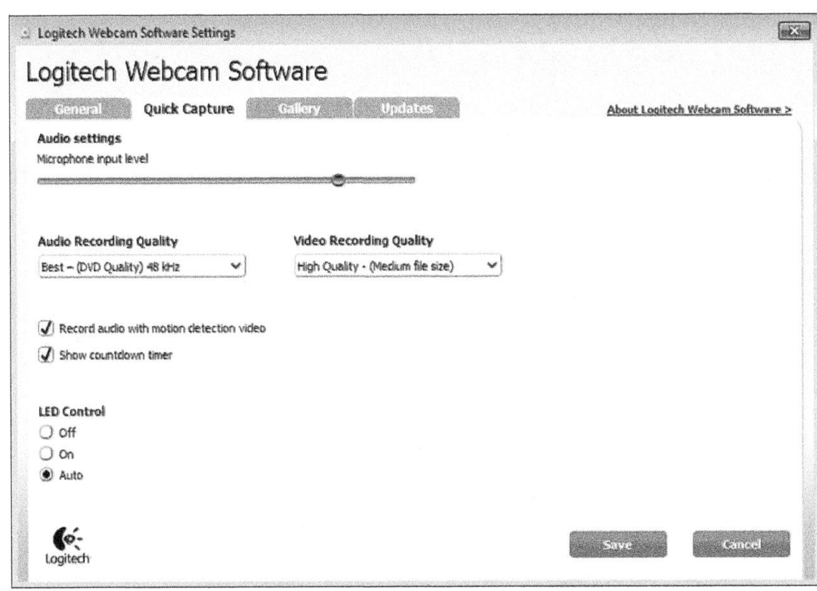

FIGURE 8.31 Logitech Webcam control software

Regardless of whether multimedia devices are integrated into a computer or connect to a computer, all devices attach and install similarly. When installing a new device for a customer, don't forget to allow the customer to test the device while you are still there. Also, remember to leave all documentation related to the installation with the customer. The customer paid for the device and is entitled to the documentation.

Digitizers

A **digitizer** (see Figure 8.32) provides input into documents such as architectural drawings, technical plans, and photos. It can also be used to draw electronic pictures. Online teachers use a digitizer to annotate a presentation or document.

FIGURE 8.32 Digitizer

A digitizer comes with a pen that may or may not need a battery. Some pens have replaceable ends. Digitizers either connect through a wired USB connection or can be wireless. A digitizer tablet comes with software that commonly allows the pen and digitizer tablet buttons to be customized in terms of what a button does and the speed at which a button reacts. Some digitizers come with diagnostics as part of the software.

SOFT SKILLS: ATTITUDE

A technician's **attitude** (see Figure 8.33) is one of his or her greatest assets. Some consider having a good attitude as simply being positive at work, but that is not the entire picture.

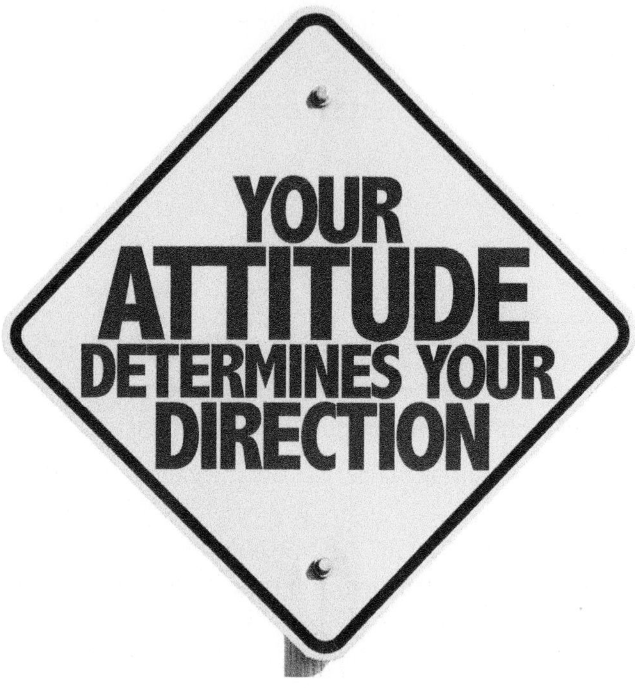

FIGURE 8.33 Your attitude is important

A technician with a good attitude has the following traits:

- *Is proactive, not reactive:* A good technician actively looks for a solution rather than waiting for someone to instruct him or her.
- *Projects confidence:* A technician who lacks confidence is easily spotted by end users. A confident technician isn't arrogant but instead is secure in the knowledge that a problem can be solved.
- *Seeks solutions instead of providing excuses:* A positive person does not continually apologize or talk in a subservient tone. For example, a positive technician explains issues such as late deliveries in a professional, positive manner.
- *Accepts responsibility for actions taken:* If you forget something or take a misstep, you should apologize and explain to the customer what happened. Truth goes a long way with customers. A positive technician does not constantly shift blame to other departments or technicians. Even if the other department or technician is responsible, a person with a positive attitude handles the customer and then talks to the other department or technician about the problem.
- *Deals with priority changes professionally:* In the IT field, computer and network problems may require tasks to be reprioritized weekly, daily, and even hourly. These are normal occurrences, and a person with a positive attitude understands this.
- *Cooperates and works well with others:* A positive attitude is contagious, and others like being around it.
- *Maintains professionalism even when working with a coworker who is unethical, unprofessional, or uncooperative:* A technician with a good attitude does not let someone else's poor attitude be a negative influence.

> *Embraces problems as challenges to learn and develop skills:* Sometimes, after joining the IT field, a technician becomes complacent and does not seek new skills. The IT field requires that you constantly improve and refine your skills. See a tough problem as a challenge, not as a burden. With such an attitude, problems will not frustrate you but will serve as catalysts for advancement and make you a better technician.

You should exhibit all these traits consistently to establish a positive mental attitude and make it part of your daily habits.

Chapter Summary

> A video card uses an AGP or PCIe slot and may require additional power.
> Video memory can be separate from motherboard RAM, can be shared system memory, or can be a combination of both.
> When a computer shows a blank screen, check the power source, the display cable, the power cable, and the surge protector. Try rebooting and using the *Safe* mode or *Enable low resolution video* boot option.
> If an artifact appears, check for heat problems.
> If an LCD or plasma display has burn-in, try turning off the display for a few hours. Create an all-white image in a graphics program and use it as the screen saver. Turn the display brightness to low and leave the monitor on for a few hours.
> If geometric distortion occurs or the screen is not centered correctly, check video cables or reset the display to the factory default settings.
> If the display image is dim or blank, try adjusting the brightness controls and contrast. Reset to the factory defaults. Replace the inverter.
> If the display flickers, check the video cable or refresh rate. Check for external radio or other interference sources.
> Projectors come with a variety of ports, including VGA, DVI, HDMI, composite, and component/RGB.
> Check power, input source, and computer output source if nothing outputs to a projector. The bulb may be burned out.
> A motherboard normally has a small speaker used for POST codes when sound does not work properly.
> If a sound card is installed, disable the motherboard sound ports.
> The higher the sampling rate, the better the audio quality.
> For sound issues, check muting, volume controls, cables, and device conflicts.
> Install ODDs using the same rules of configuration as for SATA and PATA hard drives.
> Use the appropriate media for the type of drive installed.
> Optical drives and discs have region codes that must match.
> For stuck optical discs, use the *Eject* option from Windows/File Explorer or the emergency eject hole.
> Keep the laser lens clean.
> Wipe dirty discs in an inward-to-outward (not circular) motion.
> Scanners commonly connect using USB, an RJ45 network port, or through a wireless network.
> Do not spray cleaner directly on scanner glass but do keep the glass clean.
> Digital cameras commonly have storage media that can be removed and attached directly to a PC or mobile computer, using a memory card reader.

> Webcams can be integrated into a display or mobile device or an external unit that is used for conference calls or for recording video.

> When installing and configuring common peripheral devices, always follow manufacturers' directions. Software is commonly provided to configure device options.

> A technician should have a positive attitude and project confidence, be proactive, and maintain professionalism when working with others.

A+ CERTIFICATION EXAM TIPS

✓ Be able to install and configure a sound card, a video card, and a capture card.

✓ Be able to select and install an optical drive and a flatbed scanner.

✓ Recognize symptoms and what to do when the following video problems occur: cabling issues, fuzzy image, burn-in, dead pixels, flashing screen, incorrect color, audio issues (if the display has this capability), and a dim image.

✓ Note that projector troubleshooting has similar issues that require additional troubleshooting—like dim image, cabling issues, audio issues, and fuzzy image—but can also have problems like incorrect data source, burned-out bulb, and intermittent shutdown.

✓ Recognize that an optical drive can make grinding or clicking noises if the disc is inserted incorrectly.

✓ Maintaining a positive attitude and projecting confidence are professionalism and communication skills that are part of the 220-1102 exam.

Key Terms

ADF scanner 302
attitude 308
audio issue 289
burn-in 286
burned-out bulb 288
clicking sound 301
component/RGB video 287
dead pixel 285
digitizer 307
dim image 285
DirectX 301
`dxdiag` 282
flashing screen 284
flatbed scanner 302
frequency response range 295
fuzzy image 284
GPU 280
grinding noise 301
incorrect color 284
incorrect data source 288
intermittent projector shutdown 289
lumens 288
optical drive 297
physical cabling issue 284
power rating 295
region code 299
shared system memory 282
sound card 290
video capture card 282
video card 280
webcam 306

Review Questions

Consider the following optical drive specifications as you answer Questions 1–7:

> SATA interface half-height internal BD-ROM
> Maximum 4x BD-ROM/BD-RE SL and 4x BD-ROM/BD-R/BD-RE DL CAV reading
> Maximum 8x DVD-ROM/+R/+RW/+RDL/-R/-RW/-RW DL CAV reading
> Maximum 32x CD-ROM/R/RW CAV reading
> Random access times: BD, 250 ms; DVD, 160 ms; CD, 150 ms
> Buffer size 2 MB
> System requirements for HD Blu-ray playback: 3.0 GHz, 1 GB+ of RAM, Windows 7 or higher, HDCP capable display, or TV for digital output.

1. Which SATA version is being used?

   [1 | 2 | 3 | Cannot be determined from the information given]

2. Can Blu-ray discs be created on this unit? How can you tell?

   ____

3. Pretend you are adding this device to a computer. What is the maximum number of devices (if any) that can be on the same cable that connects this drive to the motherboard?

   [None | 1 | 2 | Cannot be determined from the information given]

4. What would the computer have to have in order to install this device?

   ____

5. If the non-used SATA motherboard ports are disabled by default, how would a technician enable them before installing this device? ______________________________

6. Can a DVD±RW disc be read in this drive? How can you tell?

   ____

7. What does BD-RE DL mean?

   ____

   ____

8. A technician for a computer store is examining a computer that a client has just built and brought into the store. The AMD-based system will not output video even though the system has an HDMI port and a new HDMI cable attaches to a new display that works on another system and is powered. What is a likely problem?

   a. The cable is bad.

   b. The monitor is bad.

   c. The system RAM needs to be inserted properly.

   d. The system needs a video adapter.

9. Select the non-sound port.

   [RJ45 | S/PDIF | TOSLINK | RCA | 1/8-inch TRS]

10. Which optical media has the highest capacity? [DVD | CD | BD]

11. Which drive would have two lasers?

    a. a drive that can handle an 8.5 GB single-sided dual-layer disc

    b. a drive that can handle a double-sided single-layer disc

    c. a drive that can handle a 25 GB dual-layer disc

    d. a drive that can handle a DVD or a Blu-ray disc

12. A PCIe sound card is being installed. Which two steps are most likely going to be done by the technician? (Choose two.)
    - **a.** Upgrade the power supply.
    - **b.** Install a driver.
    - **c.** Flash the BIOS/UEFI.
    - **d.** Disable the integrated ports in BIOS/UEFI.
    - **e.** Configure jumpers on the adapter.
    - **f.** Delete the integrated port drivers.
13. Which utility is best used to troubleshoot sound issues?

    [Disk Management | DirectX | BIOS/UEFI diagnostics | Device Manager]
14. A projector is not outputting sound. What are three likely issues? (Choose three.)
    - **a.** burned-out bulb
    - **b.** mute button
    - **c.** faulty projector filter
    - **d.** projector volume setting
    - **e.** projector fan
    - **f.** projector battery low
    - **g.** computer volume setting
15. A user has attempted a scanner installation to the computer's front USB ports because all the back ports were taken. However, the scanner will not function. What should the technician try next?
    - **a.** Replace the scanner.
    - **b.** Replace the USB port.
    - **c.** Reattach the USB cable that leads from the front panel to the motherboard.
    - **d.** Add a version 2.0 or higher USB hub to the back USB port.
16. [T | F] A technician can clean a scanner using paper towels.
17. [T | F] Part of the installation process for a tablet is to calibrate the camera.
18. A user has heard about dead pixels and has brought in a recently purchased display, suspecting that the display has this issue. What should the technician do?
    - **a.** Replace the display.
    - **b.** Connect the display to a computer and use the burn-in process to check the display for this problem.
    - **c.** Test the display and explain that dead pixels are common and as long as there are not too many of them, they will not interfere with the output.
    - **d.** Tell the user to update the video driver and the BIOS/UEFI version.
19. An administrative assistant who commonly uses a specific meeting room complains that the projector is shutting down after five minutes each time it is used. What is a likely issue?

    [bulb | power supply | input source | filter]

20. Which scenario is one that most shows a positive attitude?
    a. A technician returns a borrowed disc to a team member after having the disc more than six months.
    b. A technician leaves documentation for a newly installed optical drive with the customer, even though the customer treated the technician poorly during the installation.
    c. A technician eagerly helps reorganize a wiring closet for the company.
    d. A technician smiles when an angry customer is taking out her computer problems on the technician.

Exercises

Exercise 8.1 Video and Multimedia Device Research

Objective: To be able to use the internet to locate device drivers and technical specifications

Parts: A computer that has internet access

Procedure: Using the internet, find the cost, latest device driver, and most important technical specification for the devices listed in Table 8.7.

TABLE 8.7 Multimedia device information

Device type	Cost	Device driver version	Most important technical specification
Flatbed scanner	______	______	______
Barcode reader	______	______	______
Video card	______	______	______
Projector	______	______	______
Digitizer	______	______	______
Digital camera	______	______	______
Webcam	______	______	______
Sound card	______	______	______
Speakers	______	______	______

Exercise 8.2 Which One Will You Buy?

Objective: To be able to use the internet to locate multimedia devices for a specific purpose

Parts: A computer that has internet access

Procedure: Using the internet, find a device to meet the user specifications

1. A 10-person conference room has an oval table. A computer is in the corner. The company would like to add to the room a projector and a projection screen. Do the following:
   > List three criteria you looked for in the projector.
   > List at least one projector you recommend.

   ____

   ____

2. A 25-person computer training room needs a scanner. The people who use the room scan forms completed by trainees. Each person completes a three-page form. Because of the nature of the information, the form cannot be put onto a web page.
   > List three criteria you looked for in the scanner.
   > List at least one scanner you recommend to the company.

   ____

   ____

   ____

3. A person owns a home business creating movies for events such as weddings, receptions, showers, and so on and providing a digital copy of each edited video. Previously, the owner provided the digital copy on an external drive, but now the owner wants to offer optical media as well. Even though folders are backed up to a remote site, what type of optical drive and media supported by the drive would you recommend for this home business owner?
   > List the type of optical drive you recommend and give at least two reasons for why you chose this type.
   > Would you recommend an internal or external drive? Describe why you chose this type.
   > List at least one drive you would recommend for this desktop computer. Include the part number and website where you found the drive.

   ____

   ____

   ____

Activities

Internet Discovery

Objective: To obtain specific information on the internet regarding a computer or its associated parts

Parts: Computer with access to the internet

Questions: Use the internet to answer the following questions.

1. Find a website that sells external optical drives. List the cost of one drive and the website URL.

____

2. Find three recommended replacement PCIe 3.0 x16 video cards with a minimum of 4 GB of video RAM for a gamer who can spend a maximum of $300. List the three models and the website URL where you found each one.

____

____

____

3. Find the driver version for a Sound BlasterX AE-5 PCIe adapter that is going in a 64-bit Windows 10 computer. Document the driver download filename and URL where you find this information.

____

____

____

____

4. A business is using the NEC NP-UM352W projector. Whenever they use the projector, the picture suddenly becomes dark. List the recommended steps and the URL where you found this information.

____

____

____

5. The president of a company purchased a Canon EOS Rebel T4i digital camera. Which type of memory media does this camera accept? Write the answer and URL where you find the answer.

____

____

6. A customer has a Plextor PX-891SAF CD-RW, DVD+/-RW drive. How much buffer memory does the drive contain, and which interface(s) does it support? Write the answers and website URL where you find the information.

____

____

Soft Skills

Objective: To enhance and fine-tune a technician's ability to listen, communicate in both written and oral forms, and support people who use computers in a professional manner

Activities:

1. List some tips for determining whether a computer has an optical drive installed, as if you were stepping through it over the phone with a customer who is not a technician. Using your instructions, practice with a classmate.

____

____

____

____

____

____

____

2. With the class divided into groups of five, each group makes a list of three categories that relate to multimedia devices. The five groups share their lists and determine which group works on which category. In 30 minutes, each team comes up with five answers with corresponding questions for their category. The answers are rated from 100 to 500, with 100 being the easiest. The teams play *Jeopardy!*, with the rule that each team cannot choose its own category.

Critical Thinking Skills

Objective: To analyze and evaluate information and apply information to new or different situations

Activities:

1. For this activity, you need an advertisement for a sound card, including the technical specifications. Make a list of all terms used in this ad that you do not know. Using books, the internet, or other resources, research these terms and define them.
2. Form teams of two and obtain several multimedia devices. The devices are numbered. Each team selects a number and installs, configures, and tests the associated device. Each team documents its installation and shares its experience (including lessons learned) with the rest of the class.

9 Printers and Multifunction Devices

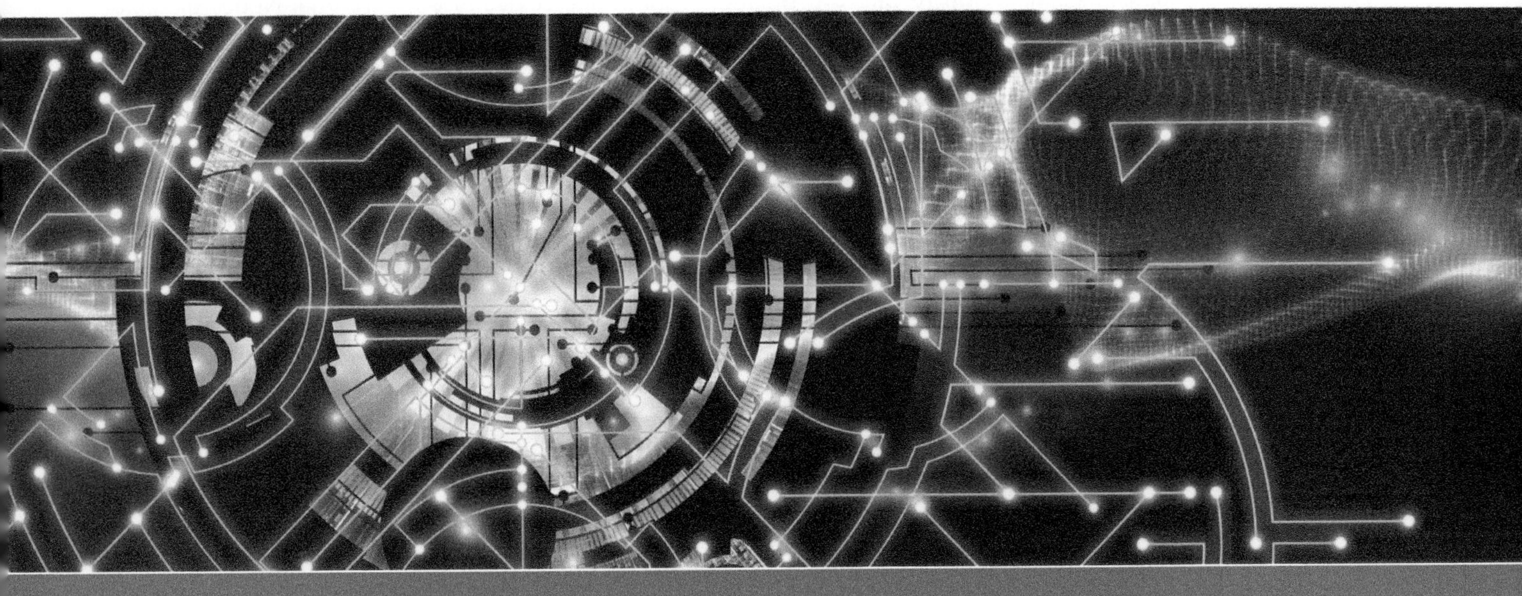

In this chapter you will learn:

- How each type of printer operates
- The steps required to install a printer or multifunction device
- Preventive printer maintenance
- How to control printers/multifunction devices from Windows and make printer adjustments
- How to solve common printer/multifunction device problems
- Techniques for ethical and professional behavior

CompTIA Exam Objectives:

✓ 1101-2.4 Summarize services provided by networked hosts.

✓ 1101-3.6 Given a scenario, deploy and configure multifunction devices/printers and settings.

✓ 1101-3.7 Given a scenario, install and replace printer consumables.

✓ 1101-5.6 Given a scenario, troubleshoot and resolve printer issues.

✓ 1102-3.1 Given a scenario, troubleshoot common Windows OS problems.

✓ 1102-4.7 Given a scenario, use proper communication techniques and professionalism.

Printer/Multifunction Device Overview

Printers are commonly used output devices and can be a source of frustration for users. Printers frequently have other functions, such as scanning, copying, and faxing. A printer that can do other things is called a **multifunction device**, or all-in-one device (see Figure 9.1). Notice the automatic document feeder (**ADF**) on top, which is used to feed papers to be copied, scanned, or faxed.

FIGURE 9.1 Multifunction device

TECH TIP

Dealing with sensitive printed material

If any printouts are on a printer, ask the user to remove them and put them away. Demonstrate professionalism any time you are exposed to corporate or personal information that might be found on printers or desks or within documents.

Categories of Printers

Printers can be categorized according to how they put an image on paper. There are five main categories of printers: impact, inkjet, laser, thermal, and 3-D. There are other types, but these five account for the majority of printers used in businesses and homes. Computer users normally choose a printer based on the type of printing they need to do. Table 9.1 describes the five major printer categories.

TABLE 9.1 Printer categories

Type of printer	Description
Impact printer	Also known as a dot matrix printer, good for printing multiple copies of text, but has limited graphics capabilities. Uses ribbons. It is the only printer that can do multiple-part forms using paper/forms and supports the 132-column paper needed in some industries.
Inkjet printer	Much quieter and produces higher-quality graphics than an impact printer. Uses an ink cartridge that costs $10 to $60 and can print a varying number of pages, depending on the manufacturer, the size of the cartridge, what is printed, and print quality settings. Inkjet printers are best for color printing.

Type of printer	Description
Laser printer	Produces the highest-quality output at the fastest rate. Uses a toner cartridge that can cost $20 to $350. Common in the corporate network environment. Used for graphic design and computer-generated art where high-quality printing is a must. Some can produce color but at a much higher cost.
Thermal printer	Uses special thermal paper that is sensitive to heat. An image is created where the heat is applied. Commonly used as ticket printers or receipt printers in retail outlets and gas stations.
3-D printer	Used to create 3-D objects using various types of materials, including plastics, resin, filament, thermoplastics, clay, alloys, rubber, stainless steel, and metal alloys.

Impact Printers

Impact printers (see Figure 9.2) are also called dot matrix printers because of the way they create an image on paper. Such a printer has an **impact print head** that holds tiny wires called print wires. Figure 9.3 shows an Oki Data Americas, Inc., print head. The print wires are shown on the front of the print head. The print wires can get out of alignment and produce malformed characters.

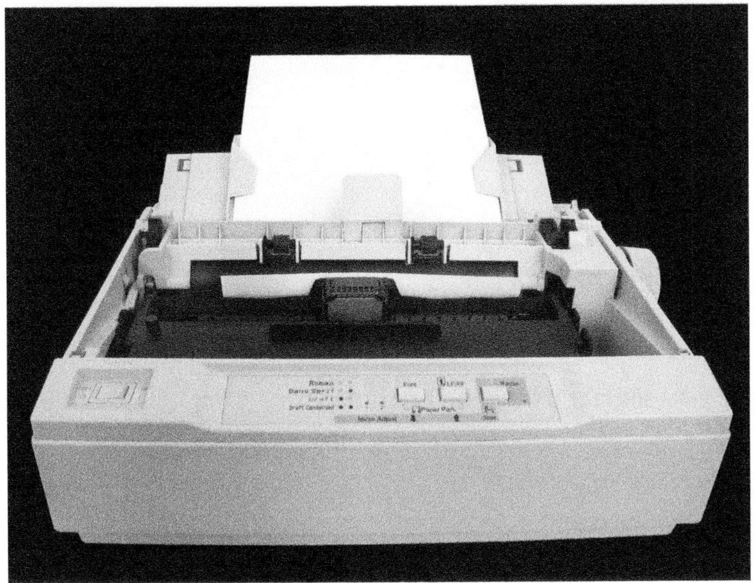

FIGURE 9.2 Impact printer

The wires individually strike a **print ribbon** hard enough to create a dot on the paper. The dots collectively form letters or images. The speed at which the print head can place characters on a page is its characters per second (cps) rating. The number of print wires in the print head determines the quality of printing: The more print wires, the better the print quality. The most common numbers of print wires are 9, 18, and 24.

The impact of the printer physically striking the ribbon, which in turn touches the paper, causes impact printers to be noisy. Figure 9.4 shows an impact printer print head. To show the individual print wires, the casing that covers the print wires has been removed from the illustration.

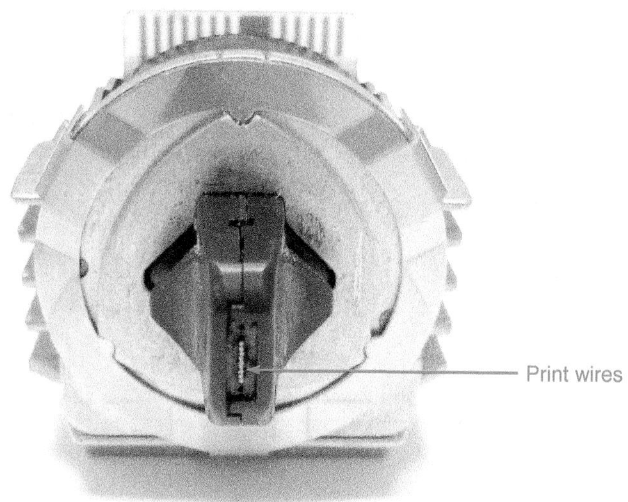

FIGURE 9.3 Impact printer head

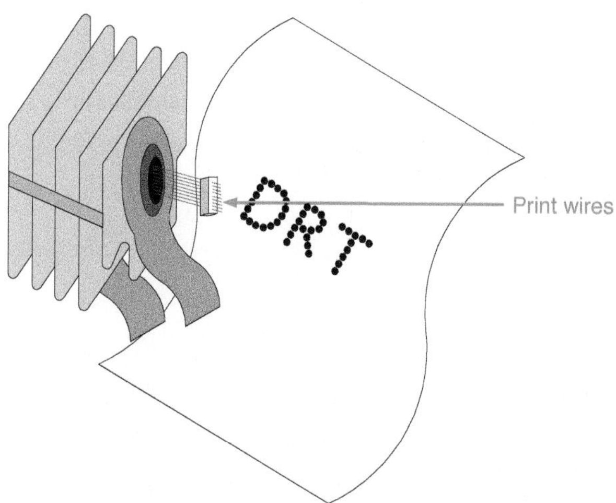

FIGURE 9.4 Impact print head operation

TECH TIP

Printing in one direction is not a problem

Most impact printers print bidirectionally. When the print head gets too hot, the printer prints only in the left-to-right direction. This is normal.

Because the print wire impacts the ribbon, one of the most common points of failure with impact printers is the print head. It can be expensive to replace print heads frequently in a high-usage situation; however, refurbished print heads are available at a reduced price.

Impact printers are the workhorses of printers. One advantage of an impact printer is that it can print multiple-part forms and wide forms. Special **impact paper** can be purchased so duplicates are made each time a print job is sent. Laser and inkjet printers cannot produce multiple-part forms; they can only make multiple copies of the same document.

TECH TIP

Don't stack

Don't stack things on top of a printer, especially an impact printer. Keep a printer in a cool environment to avoid overheating.

Inkjet Printers

Inkjet printers are much quieter than impact printers and are used to print black-and-white, grayscale, and color output. An inkjet printer also has an **inkjet print head** that has many tiny nozzles that squirt ink onto the paper. Each nozzle is smaller than a strand of human hair. There are up to 6,000 nozzles for better quality than the impact printer. Figure 9.5 shows an **ink cartridge**. Notice the three rows of nozzles on the cartridge on the left.

FIGURE 9.5 Inkjet print cartridge

Inkjet printers, also called bubble jet printers, use thermal (heat) technology to place the ink on the paper. Each print nozzle attaches to a small ink chamber that attaches to a larger ink reservoir. Once the ink boils, a vapor bubble forms. As the bubble gets hotter, it expands and goes out through the print cartridge's nozzle onto the paper.

An alternative for producing the ink dots is to use piezo-electric technology, which uses pressure, rather than heat, to eject the ink onto the paper. Some companies use this technology to obtain high resolutions. DPI is the number of dots per inch a printer outputs. The higher the DPI, the better the quality of inkjet or laser printer output. Figure 9.6 shows the basic principle of how an inkjet printer works. Table 9.2 lists the major parts found inside an inkjet printer.

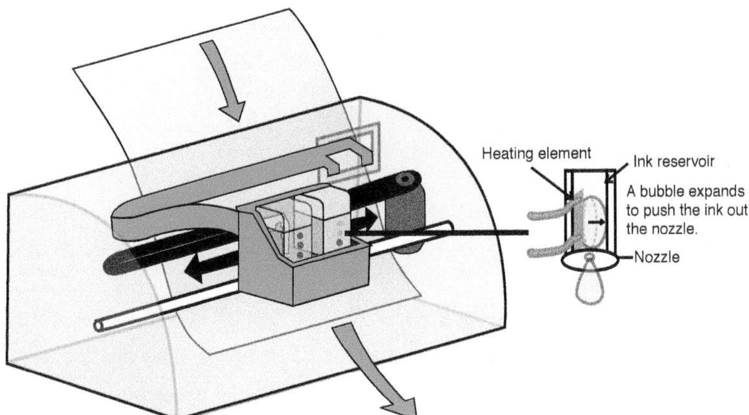

FIGURE 9.6 How an inkjet printer works

TABLE 9.2 Inkjet parts

Part	Description
Print head	Contains nozzles used to dispense ink
Print head assembly	Holds the print head and possibly the ink cartridge(s)
Ink cartridge	Also known as a print cartridge or simply as a cartridge; may be one color or may have sections for separate colors and may include the print head
Stepper motor	Used to move the print head/ink cartridge from one side of the printer and back as well as move the print head assembly (see Figure 9.7)
Carriage belt	A belt that connects to the stepper motor and print head assembly to move the print head and ink cartridge from one side of the printer to the other side (see Figure 9.7)
Power supply	Converts wall outlet AC to DC for inside the printer
Carriage	The part that moves from one side of the printer and back; includes the belt, stabilizer bar, and print head assembly, as well as the print head that may be included with the ink cartridge(s) (see Figure 9.7)
Paper tray and/or paper **feeder**	Holds paper (see Figure 9.7)
Roller	Moves paper through the printer (see Figure 9.7)
Duplexing assembly	Supports two-sided printing (see Figure 9.20, later in the chapter)

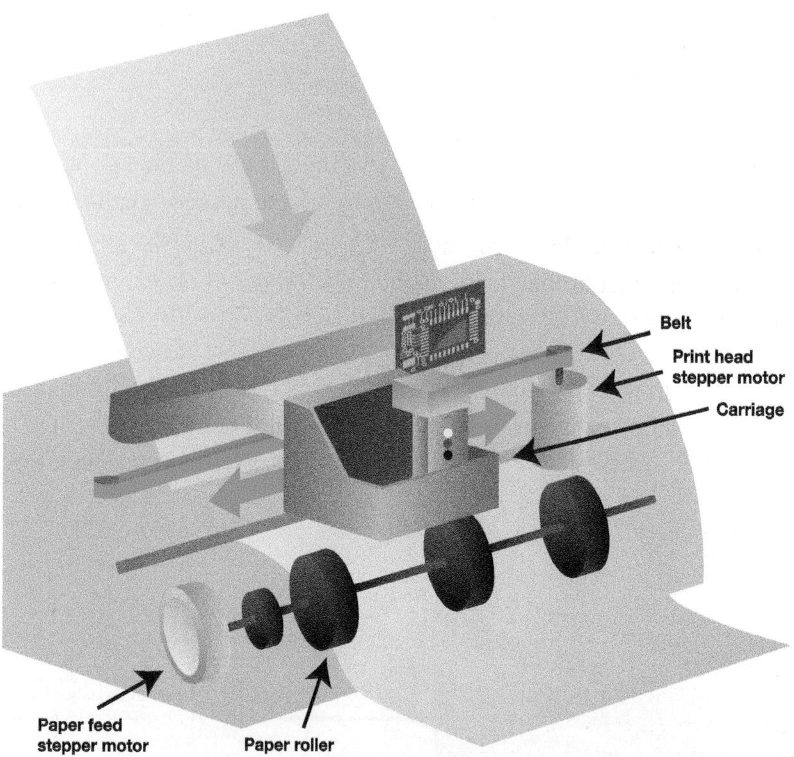

FIGURE 9.7 Major inkjet printer parts

Most inkjet printers have different modes of printing. The draft mode uses the least amount of ink, and the NLQ mode uses the most ink. The quality produced by an inkjet printer is equal to or sometimes higher than that of a laser printer, and inkjet printers print in color, whereas most laser printers print only in monochrome (black and white).

TECH TIP

Be aware of optimized DPI

Many inkjet printers now show their DPI as *optimized* DPI. Optimized DPI describes not how many drops of liquid are in an inch but how many are in a specific grid.

Color inkjet printers usually have a black cartridge for text printing and a separate color cartridge or separate cartridges for colored ink. Buying an inkjet printer that uses a single cartridge for all colors means a lower-priced initial printer purchase but is more expensive in the long run. Models do exist that have separate cartridges for black ink and for colored ink.

There are some alternatives to inkjet technology. Table 9.3 outlines four of them.

TABLE 9.3 Other printer technologies

Type of printer	Description
Solid ink printer	Sometimes called a phase change or hot melt printer; uses colored wax sticks to create vivid color output. This type of printer can print more colors, is faster, has fewer mechanical parts, and is cheaper than color laser printers but is more expensive than normal inkjet printers.
Dye sublimation printer	Also known as a dye diffusion thermal transfer printer; uses four film ribbons that contain color dyes. The quality is high, but the printers are expensive.
Thermal wax transfer printer	Uses wax-based inks like a solid ink printer but prints at lower resolutions.
Large-format inkjet printer	A wide printer to print large-scale media such as CAD drawings, posters, and artwork.

A drawback to using an inkjet printer is that sometimes the ink smears. Ink manufacturers vary greatly in how they respond to this problem. If the paper gets wet, some inkjet output becomes messy. The ink also smears if you touch the printed page before the ink dries. The ink can also soak into and bleed down the paper. Using good-quality paper and ink in the ink cartridge helps with this particular problem. See the section "Paper," later in this chapter, for more information on choosing the correct paper for different printers.

Laser Printers

A laser printer uses a process similar to a copy machine's electrophotographic process. Before exploring how a laser printer works, identifying the major parts inside the printer helps to understand how it works. Figure 9.8 shows a side view of a laser printer.

TECH TIP

Knowing the dangers inside laser printers

Be very careful when working inside a laser printer. There are high voltages and high temperatures in various parts. Turn off the printer and let it cool down before servicing it. Remove power from the printer before working on it, when possible.

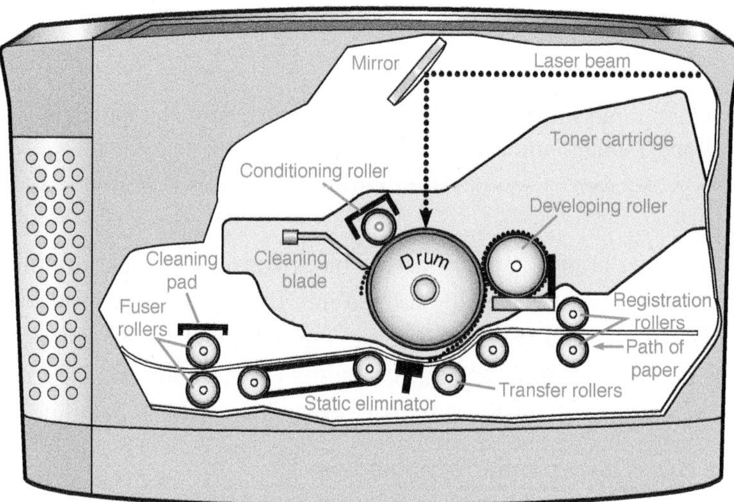

FIGURE 9.8 Inside a laser printer

The computer sends 1s and 0s to the printer. The data is converted into dots, and sent through an array of LEDs or through a laser beam. The light beam strikes the photosensitive imaging drum located inside the toner cartridge (see Figure 9.9). Laser toner particles are attracted to the drum. The paper feeds through, and the toner transfers to the paper. The toner is then fused or melted onto the paper. Table 9.4 summarizes the seven-step laser printer **imaging process.**

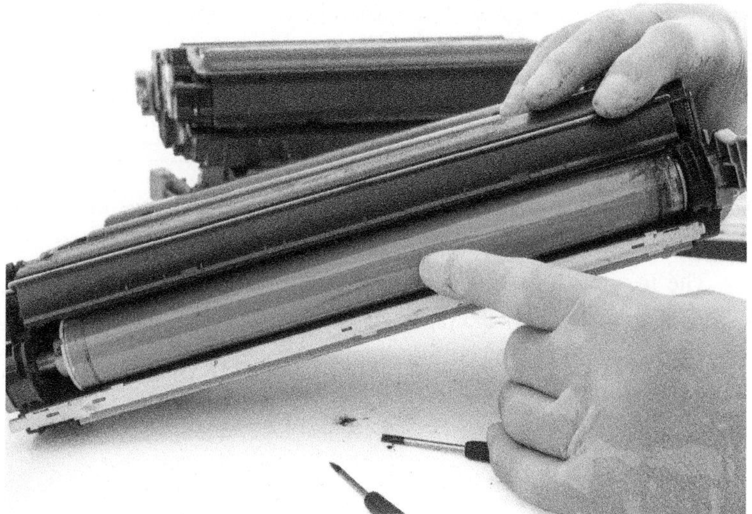

FIGURE 9.9 Laser imaging drum

TABLE 9.4 Laser printer imaging process

Step	Description
Processing	Gets the data ready to print. The laser printer converts the data from the printer language into a bitmap image. The laser printed page is made up of very closely spaced dots.
Charging	Also known as conditioning, as it conditions or gets the drum ready for use. Before any information goes onto the drum, the entire drum must have the same voltage level. The primary (main) corona or conditioning roller has up to –6,000VDC applied to it and anywhere from –600V to –1,000V applied to the drum surface as a uniform electrical charge.

Step	Description
Exposing	Also known as the writing phase, puts 1s and 0s on the drum surface. Light reflects to the drum surface in the form of 1s and 0s. Every place the beam touches, the drum's surface voltage is reduced. The image on the drum is nothing more than dots of electrical charges and is invisible at this point.
Developing	Gets toner on the drum (develops the image). A developing cylinder or roller is inside the toner cartridge (right next to the drum) and contains a magnet that runs the length of the cylinder. When the cylinder rotates, toner is attracted to the cylinder because the toner has iron particles in it. The toner receives a negative electrostatic charge. The magnetized toner particles are attracted to the places on the drum where the light beam strikes. The image is now black on the drum surface.
Transferring	Transfers an image to paper. A **transfer belt** (or an equivalent part, such as a **transfer roller**, corona, or pad) is located at the bottom of the printer and places a positive charge on the back of the paper. The positive charge attracts the negatively charged toner particles from the drum. The particles leave the drum and go onto the paper. At this point, the image is on the paper, but the particles are held only by their magnetic charge.
Fusing	The **fuser assembly** melts the toner onto the paper. Heat and pressure make the image on the paper permanent. The paper, with the toner particles clinging to it, immediately passes through fusing rollers or a belt that applies pressure to the toner. The top roller applies intense heat (350°F) to the toner and paper that literally squeezes and melts the toner into the paper fibers. Figure 9.10 shows an example of a fuser assembly and the motor used with it.
Cleaning	Wipes off any toner left on the drum. Some books list this as the first step, but the order does not matter because the process is a continuous cycle. During the cleaning stage, a wiper blade or brush clears the photosensitive drum of any excess toner. Then an erase lamp neutralizes any charges left on the drum so the next printed page begins with a clean drum.

FIGURE 9.10 Laser printer parts

A mnemonic (where the first letter of a saying helps you remember another word) for the laser printer imaging process is as follows: Printers Can Expediently Do Tasks For Companies.

TECH TIP

Laser printers *do* make weird noises

A laser printer frequently makes an unusual noise that is a result of the fusing rollers turning when the printer is not in use. If the rollers didn't turn like this, they would have an indentation on one side. Users not familiar with laser printers sometimes complain about this noise, but it is a normal function of a laser printer.

Table 9.5 lists the major parts of a laser printer and briefly describes the purpose of each part.

TABLE 9.5 Laser printer parts

Part	Purpose
AC power supply	Acts as the main power supply for the printer
Cleaning blade	Wipes away excess toner from the drum before printing the next page
Cleaning pad	Applies oil to the fusing roller to prevent sticking; also removes excess toner during the fusing stage
Conditioning roller	Used instead of a primary corona wire to apply a uniform negative charge to the drum's surface
Control panel assembly	Acts as the user interface on the printer
Density control blade	Controls the amount of toner allowed on the drum (usually user adjustable)
Developing cylinder	Rotates to magnetize the toner particles before they go on the drum (also called the developing roller)
Drum (photosensitive)	Also known as **imaging drum**; accepts light beams (data) from LEDs or a laser; can be permanently damaged if exposed to light; humidity can adversely affect it
Duplexing assembly	Supports two-sided printing
ECP (electronic control package)	The main board for a printer that usually holds most of the electronic circuitry, the CPU, and RAM
Erase lamp	Neutralizes any residual charges on the drum before printing the next page
Fuser (fusing) assembly	Holds the fusing roller, conditioning pad, pressure roller, and heating unit
Fusing roller	Applies pressure and heat to fuse the toner into the paper
High-voltage power supply	Provides a charge to the primary corona or conditioning roller, which puts a charge on the drum
Main motor	Provides the power to drive several smaller motors that drive the gears, rollers, and drum
Pickup rollers (feed rollers)	Rollers used along the paper path to feed paper through the laser printer
Primary corona (main corona)	Applies a uniform negative charge to the drum's surface
Registration assembly	Holds the majority of the rollers and gears to move paper through the unit

Part	Purpose
Separation pad	A bar or pad in a laser printer that can have a rubber or cork surface that rubs against the paper as it is picked up
Scanner unit	Includes a laser or an LED array that is used to write the 1s and 0s onto the drum surface
Toner	Powder made of plastic resin particles and organic compounds bonded to iron oxide
Toner cartridge (EP cartridge)	Holds the conditioning roller, cleaning blade, drum, developing cylinder, and toner; always remove the toner cartridge before shipping a laser printer
Transfer corona wire (transfer belt or roller)	Applies a positive charge on the back of the paper to pull the toner from the drum onto the paper

Figure 9.11 shows the inside of a toner cartridge.

FIGURE 9.11 Inside a laser printer cartridge

TECH TIP

A word about spilled toner

Toner melts when warmed; small toner spills outside a printer can be wiped using a cold, damp cloth. Toner spills inside a printer require a special type of vacuum with special bags. Toner on clothing can normally be removed by washing in cold water. Do not put the clothing in a dryer if the toner has not yet been removed, or the toner will melt into the clothing and become impossible to remove.

Thermal Printers

Thermal printers are used in a lot of retail establishments and at kiosks, gas pumps, trade shows, and basically anywhere someone needs a little printer to print a document, such as a receipt. IT staff commonly service thermal printers. Thermal printers are also known as point of sale (POS) or cash register printers.

A thermal printer uses **special thermal paper** that is sensitive to heat. A print head has closely spaced **heating elements** that appear as closely spaced dots on the heat-sensitive paper. A **feed assembly** is used to move the thermal paper through the printer. Figure 9.12 shows examples of thermal printers. Figure 9.13 shows how a thermal printer works.

FIGURE 9.12 Thermal printers

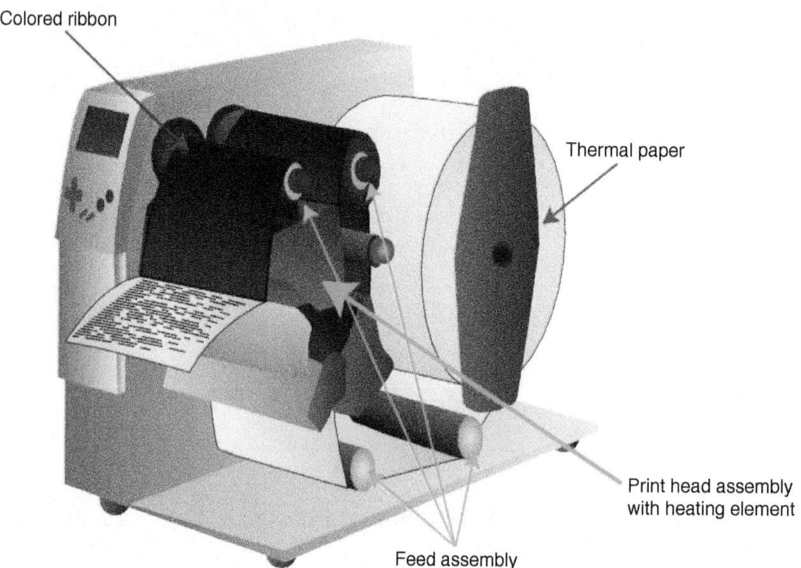

FIGURE 9.13 Inside a thermal printer

A technician must be sure to warn the user about the **high sensitivity of thermal paper** and to store the paper in a cool location. Most thermal printing situations—such as parking receipts and bar codes—require high-sensitivity thermal paper that does not last long. Other situations—such as certain sales receipts, warehouse labeling, and supermarket weigh scale labels—require low-sensitivity thermal paper that is not as affected as much by high temperatures or exposure to the sun.

The thermal print head is one of the most important parts of a thermal printer. The print head can be damaged in several ways:

- Residue or material buildup can cause uneven printing or missing dots.
- Opening the print mechanism while printing can damage the print head.
- Poor-quality thermal paper can damage the print head.
- A dirty environment can damage the print head.
- Other objects (stuck labels, staples, paper clips, and debris) can damage the print head.

- ESD—even very little voltage—can damage the print head. Use self-grounding or an anti-static wrist strap when handling the print head.
- Excessive moisture, such as in high-humidity environments, can damage the print head.

3-D Printers

3-D printers are used to "print" 3-D solid objects out of various types of materials. A 3-D image is scanned into the computer, drawn, or downloaded from the internet. Software slices the image into thousands of layers. The printer "prints" each layer until the object is formed. Think of the possibilities—from being able to print a toy, a cat dish, or that hard-to-get-plastic piece that always breaks on the pool vacuum. Figure 9.14 shows a 3-D printer.

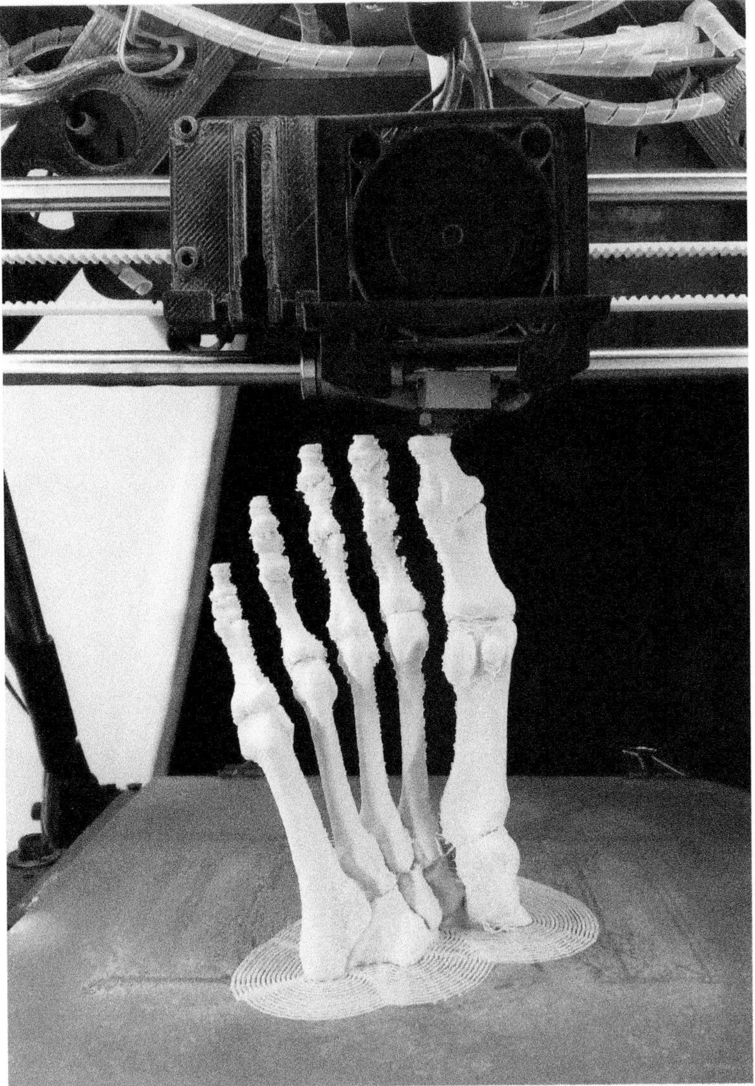

FIGURE 9.14 3-D printing

The place where the 3-D object is built is known as the **print bed** and is commonly made of glass, aluminum, or plastic. The print bed affects whether or not the 3-D object releases easily from the printer. Some find that using an adhesive helps to prevent a bond between the object and the print bed.

3-D Filament and Resin Printing

3-D printers commonly use plastic known as **plastic filament**, or printer **filament**, that comes in different types and colors. The type you need depends on the 3-D printer model and the type of object being created. Two common types of plastic filament are acrylonitrile butadiene styrene (ABS) and polylactic acid (PLA). Figure 9.15 shows what plastic filament looks like on the reel.

FIGURE 9.15 3-D printing filament

An alternative to using plastic filament is to use liquid **resin** and a stereolithography/digital light processing (SLA/DLP) printer. These printers use a tank of resin and light to create more detailed objects as shown in Figure 9.16.

FIGURE 9.16 3-D printing using resin

Always follow the manufacturer's instructions and safety precautions for replacing/installing the plastic filament in a 3-D printer. The following are generic instructions:

Step 1. Use side cutters to trim the end of the filament to create a sharp taper.

Step 2. Mount the reel onto the printer, ensuring that the filament spool unwinds in the correct direction.

Step 3. Use a printer menu to select the load filament option. Some models use options such as *Material* > *Change*. On printers that allow multiple reels, you might need to choose which reel is being loaded, such as right or left, as shown in the Figure 9.17 menus.

Step 4. After the printer preheats the extruder (the part that ejects material to create the 3-D object), insert the end of the filament into the hole on the 3-D printer, as shown in Figure 9.18. Note that you might have to insert the filament through a sleeve before doing this. You should see the filament come out of the printer if it is feeding properly.

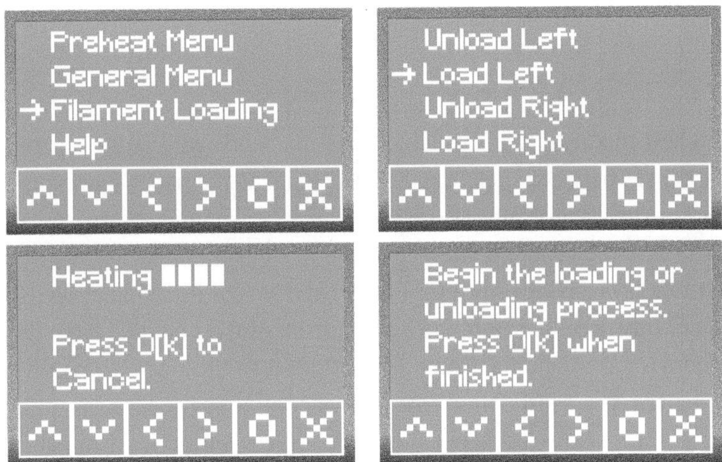

FIGURE 9.17 Sample 3-D printer menu options

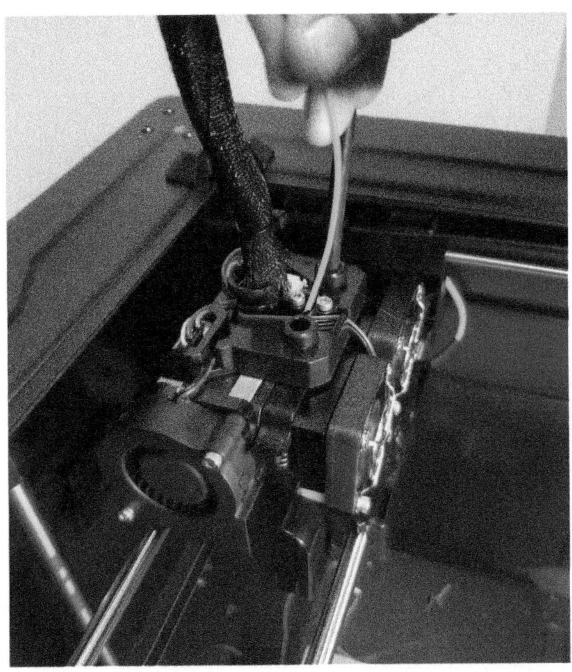

FIGURE 9.18 Inserting plastic filament into a 3-D printer

Paper

The type of paper used in a printer can affect its performance and cause problems. Because inkjet printers spray ink onto the paper, the quality of paper determines how well the ink adheres. For a laser printer, how well the paper heats and absorbs the toner affects the printed output.

Erasable-bond paper does not work well in laser printers because the paper does not allow the toner to fuse properly. Recycled paper may cause printer jams, but some manufacturers have a jam-free percentage shown. Another factor in the printed output is the brightness rating, a measurement of how much light the paper reflects. The higher the number, the more white the paper appears and the more crisp the printed output appears.

TECH TIP

Paper and pounds

Paper is rated in pounds (abbreviated lb) and shown as 20 lb or 20# (a good weight for standard use). A higher number indicates heavier, thicker paper.

The highest-quality paper available does not work well if the surrounding area is too humid. Humidity causes paper to stick together and reduces the paper's strength, which causes feed problems. For best printing results, store paper in a non-humid storage area and fan the paper before you insert it into the printer's bin.

A multifunction device or printer might have two or three paper feeds: from the rear paper tray, from a paper tray accessed from the bottom front of the unit, and from the top, which is commonly used for copying or scanning. Some impact printers allow you to remove the normal paper feeder and attach a **tractor feed** option that allows continuous-feed paper to be fed through the printer. Figure 9.19 shows how the paper with holes feeds through an impact printer. Both impact and inkjet printers have special feeders or a slide bar to feed envelopes or unusual-sized paper through. Laser printers sometimes ship with additional trays and must be configured for this option.

FIGURE 9.19 Tractor-fed paper

Another paper option is a duplexing assembly that enables two-sided printing. You may have seen and heard a duplexing assembly in action on a copier. A duplexing assembly is more commonly purchased for a laser printer than any other printer types, but specific inkjet printers can also have this optional part. The duplexer is integrated into the printer or attached to the bottom or rear of the printer and selected through the *Print* menu of any application. Figure 9.20 shows a duplexing assembly.

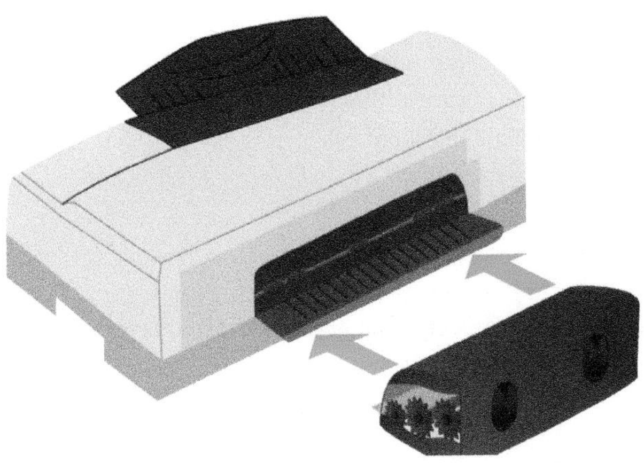

FIGURE 9.20 Duplexing assembly

TECH TIP

How to control printer trays and manual feed options

In Windows, the *General* tab on the *Printer properties* window is commonly used to view the current paper settings. Click the *Preferences* button to configure where you want the printer to look for paper to be used (see Figure 9.21).

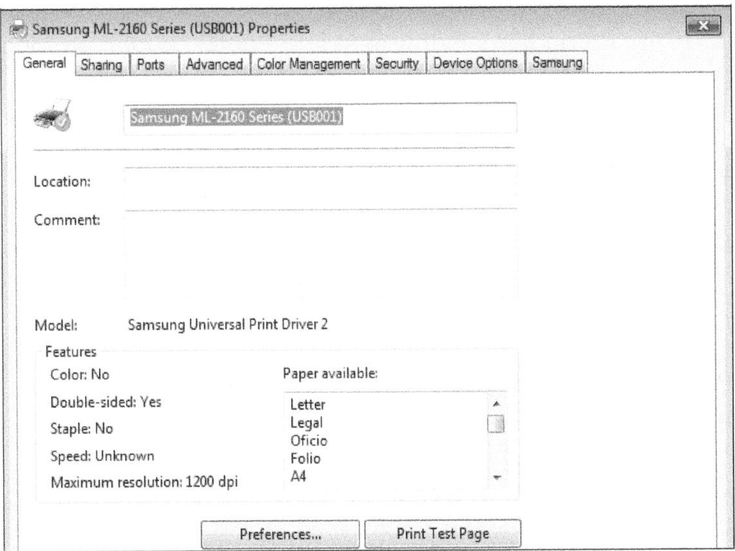

FIGURE 9.21 Paper options for a printer

Most printers allow you to set a default order in which the printer looks for paper. You can typically configure this through either manufacturer-provided software or the *Printer properties* window. Many printers have both *Properties* and *Printer properties* options (see Figure 9.22). Figure 9.23 shows the difference between the windows these options bring up. You will most likely want the *Printer properties* option shown on the right.

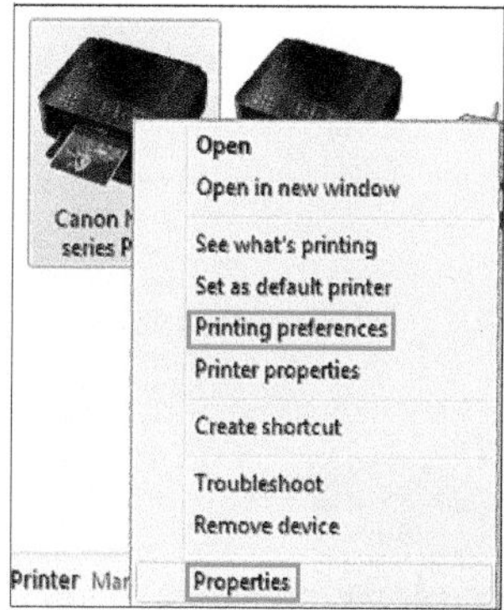

FIGURE 9.22 Right-click menu options for a printer

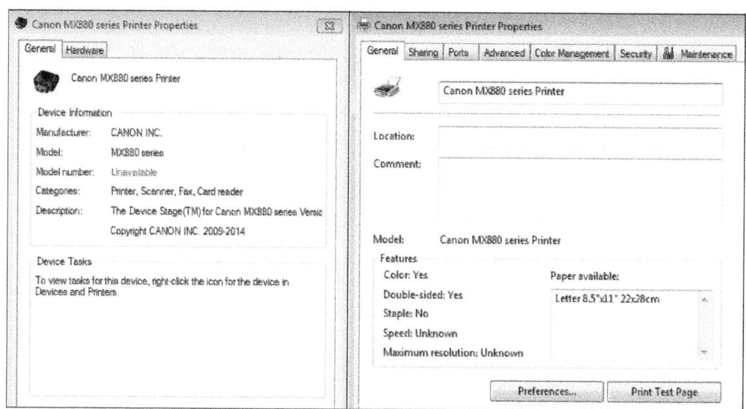

FIGURE 9.23 Properties window (left) and Printer properties window (right)

Virtual Printing

Printing of any type takes information formatted in a specific application (web browser, word processor, spreadsheet, photo viewer, and so on) and puts it into a format the printer understands. **Virtual printing** means printing to somewhere other than the directly connected printer and commonly to a specific file type so the file can be viewed, saved, or even emailed instead of printed or eventually sent to a printer. Four common virtual printing techniques are outlined in Table 9.6.

TABLE 9.6 Virtual printing options

Virtual printing type	Description
Print to file	Saves a print job as a .prn file to be printed later. Not all printers support this. *File* > *Print* > select *Print to File* checkbox > *OK*.
Print to PDF	Saves a print job as a Portable Document Format (.pdf) file (see Figure 9.24) that can be sent or printed to any printer later. If it is not shown, search for the *Advanced Printer Setup* Control Panel link > *The Printer That I Want Isn't Listed* link > *Add a Local Printer or Network Printer with Manual Settings* radio button > *Next* > from the *Use an Existing Port* drop-down menu, select *File: (Print to File)* > *Next*. From any application, select *File* > *Print* > select *Microsoft Print to PDF* > *OK*.
Print to XPS	Saves a file as a Microsoft XPS file that allows a document to be printed on any printer but not modified. From any application, *File* > *Print* > select *Microsoft XPS Document Writer*.
Print to image	Saves a file to an image file. When documents cannot print to PDF due to a poor download or damaged content, print to image is a great option. Some software allows you to save as a JPEG, TIFF, or PNG.

FIGURE 9.24 Microsoft Print to PDF option

Refilling Cartridges, Re-inking Ribbons, and Recycling Cartridges

If you refill ink cartridges, you should add new ink before an old cartridge runs completely dry. Also, be sure the refill ink emulates the manufacturer's ink. Some ink refill companies use inferior ink that, over time, has a corrosive effect on the cartridge housing. A leaky cartridge or one that bursts, causing ink to get into the printer, is trouble.

Some manufacturers offer a continuous ink system (CIS) that does not require changing out ink cartridges so often. Other companies sell a product that modifies a printer to use a CIS. Figure 9.25 shows a CIS.

FIGURE 9.25 Refilling a CIS

When it comes to laser cartridge remanufacturing, the most important components are the drum and the wiper blade that cleans the drum. Many laser cartridge remanufacturers use the same parts repeatedly. A quality refill company will disassemble the cartridge and inspect each part. When the drum and wiper blade are worn, they are replaced with new parts. Some states have disposal requirements for inkjet and laser printer cartridges.

TECH TIP

Beware of toner cartridges

Toner powder is harmful if inhaled. Wear a mask when refilling. Also, wear disposable gloves when replacing or refilling a toner cartridge to prevent toner from entering your skin pores.

Re-inking an impact printer ribbon is not a good idea. It can cause a mess, and the ink is sometimes an inferior quality that causes deterioration of the print head over time.

Upgrading Printers

Printers can be upgraded in many ways, and the options available are vendor and printer dependent. The most common upgrades include memory and tray/paper feed options. Printer memory is important so that the documents can be sent and stored away from the computer that requested the print job. This frees up the computer's memory and hard drive space to do other tasks.

Paper storage trays and feeders are another common upgrade. Special paper feed options can be purchased that are mounted onto a printer for rolls or different sizes of paper. With the increased popularity of digital photography, these printer options are quite popular.

Printer Maintenance

Maintenance is important for all types of electronics, but printers have maintenance and preventive maintenance requirements that are a bit different than those of other devices. For some printers, preventive maintenance kits are available for purchase. Quality printer replacement parts and preventive maintenance kits are important to a technician. Let's examine the maintenance procedures associated with each printer type.

Impact Printer Maintenance

A technician may be required to do the following maintenance on an impact printer:

- Replace the ribbon (see Figure 9.26)
- Replace the print head
- Replace paper
- Clear and clean the paper path

FIGURE 9.26 Impact printer ribbon

You know it is time to **replace the ribbon** when the print output is consistently light. Generic ribbon replacement instructions are to pull straight up on the ribbon assembly to lift it out of the printer. Insert the new ribbon into the grooves in the frame and push downward until it clicks into place.

The time to **replace the print head** is when the output shows one or more white horizontal lines. When replacing the printer print head, always follow the manufacturer's instructions. Generic steps to install an impact printer print head are as follows:

Step 1. Power off the printer and allow the print head to cool.

Step 2. Press the release lever or button that allows the print head to be removed.

Step 3. Insert the replacement print head.

Step 4. Power on the printer and send a sample print job to ensure that the print head is firing all pins.

To **replace paper**, simply insert the paper inside the paper tray. If continuous paper or forms are installed, you may be required to clear and clean the paper path. Ensure that the paper aligns properly and evenly to the pins in the continuous (tractor-fed) paper.

Impact printers usually require cleaning more often than any other type of printer because they are frequently used for continuously fed paper or multiform paper and are often installed in industrial environments. Paper chafe, dust, and dirt cause an insulating layer of heat to form on the printer components, which causes them to fail. It is important to vacuum impact printers more often than other printers as a preventive maintenance task.

Inkjet Printer Maintenance

On inkjet printers, a technician may need to do the following maintenance:

> Replace the cartridge (see Figure 9.27)
> Calibrate colors and print head alignment
> Clear paper jams
> Clean the print head

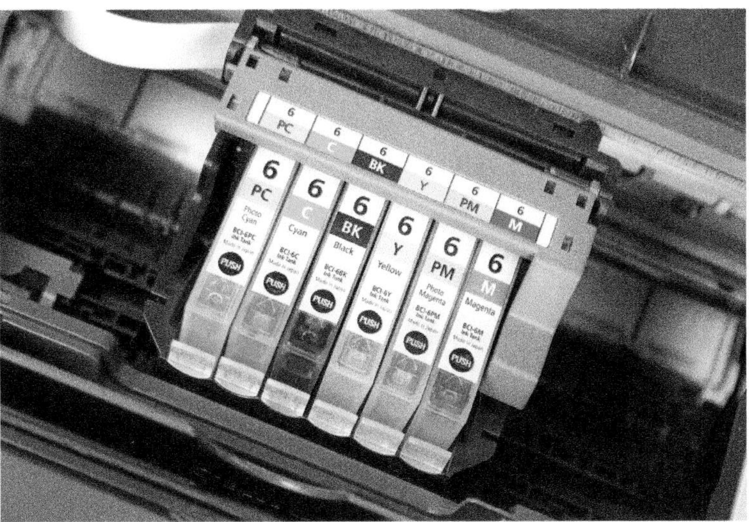

FIGURE 9.27 Inkjet ink cartridge assembly

You know it is time to **replace an ink cartridge** when the print output is consistently light, a particular color does not print, or a message appears. The generic steps to install an ink cartridge are as follows, but always refer to the manufacturer's directions:

Step 1. Ensure that the printer is powered on.

Step 2. Open the printer cover or door to gain access to the print cartridge assembly. Most printers automatically move the assembly to a place where access is easiest. Give the printer time to complete this process.

Step 3. Release the old print cartridge. There might be a release lever to access the cartridge. Some cartridges require pressing down to eject or simply pulling out, pulling out and then up, or lifting up.

Step 4. Remove the protective tape from the new cartridge. Be careful not to touch any ink nozzles and/or the copper contacts on the cartridge.

Step 5. Insert the new cartridge, reversing the removal procedure.

Step 6. Replace the printer cover or access door.

Step 7. Print a test page.

On most inkjet printers you have to **calibrate** in order to do a print head alignment process and adjust colors to ensure quality output. Many inkjet printers come with their own optional software that can be installed to perform this process. Each inkjet printer has a different calibration process, but the generic steps are as follows:

Step 1. Locate the printer in the Printers & scanners Windows Settings option.

Step 2. Right-click the printer and select *Properties* or *Printer properties.*

Step 3. Locate the calibration function, which is commonly found on a *Tools*, *Maintenance*, or *Advanced* tab.

Step 4. Perform the calibration, which normally involves printing a page and then selecting specific values through another menu. See Figure 9.28 for an example of the calibration or print head alignment page that is printed as part of the calibration process.

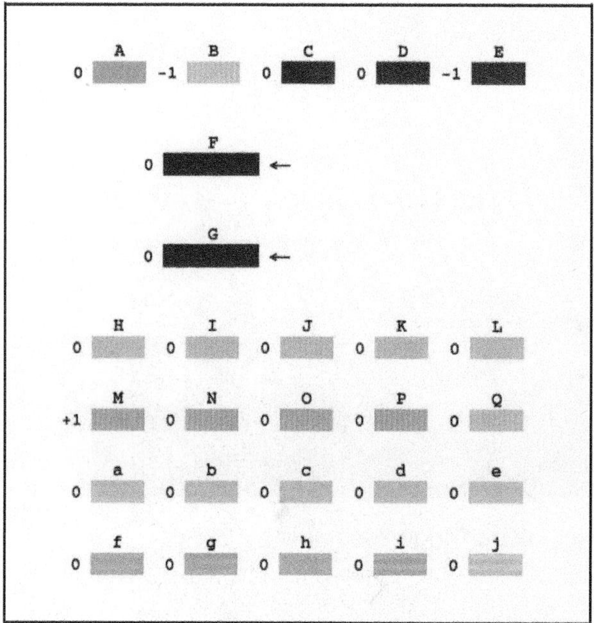

FIGURE 9.28 Sample inkjet print head/calibration output page

Inkjet printers require little preventive maintenance. Keep the interior and exterior clean of dust and particles. Use a soft brush or nonmetallic vacuum nozzle to remove dust. Do not use any type of lubricants on the print cartridge bar. Use the printer's software or maintenance procedure for aligning the print cartridge each time it is replaced.

Some printers have a "clean" maintenance procedure that can be done through the software that ships with the printer. Some of these processes do not **clean the print head** well enough, and the print head may clog with use. In such a case, remove the print head and clean it with a lint-free cloth or with a dampened cotton swab. Allow the cartridge to dry thoroughly before reinstalling it.

Laser Printer Maintenance

Technicians commonly do maintenance on a laser printer such as the following:

- Replace a toner cartridge
- Apply a maintenance kit
- Perform calibration
- Clear paper jams
- Clean the printer

To **replace the toner cartridge** on a laser printer, always refer to the manufacturer's instructions. These are the generic steps:

Step 1. Power off the printer.

Step 2. Access the toner cartridge. This may involve lifting the top cover or opening an access door.

Step 3. Remove the old cartridge by lifting up or sliding forward and then lifting up (see Figure 9.29). If this model has a release tab, press it.

Step 4. If the original covering and bag are available, attach the covering and insert the cartridge inside the bag. Recycle if possible.

Step 5. Remove the new cartridge from the box. Avoid doing this in sunlight. Avoid touching the cartridge drum. Many cartridges have a plastic strip that must be pulled out and thrown away. Remove the protective drum covering.

Step 6. Install the new cartridge and ensure that it snaps securely in place.

Step 7. Close the top cover or access door.

Step 8. Print a test page to ensure that the printer works well.

FIGURE 9.29 Replacing a laser printer cartridge

A **laser printer maintenance kit** is available for some models. The contents of the kit are vendor specific and might include any of the following: separation pad, pickup roller, transfer roller, charge roller, and fuser assembly. Always follow the manufacturer's directions for installing a maintenance kit. The separation pad and pickup rollers commonly require removal of an e-clip that holds rollers tightly on a bar. An e-clip looks like the letter C or letter E, as shown in Figure 9.30.

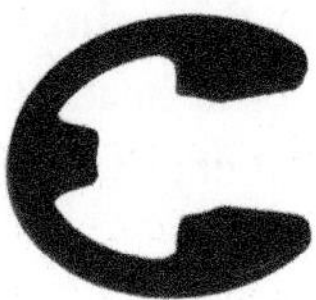

FIGURE 9.30 E-clip

There is a specific tool for removing e-clips, but needle-nose pliers and a small flat-tip screwdriver can work, too. Hold the closed side of the e-clip tightly with the pliers and use the tip of the screwdriver to gently pry the e-clip off the bar.

A common process done at the end of applying the maintenance kit is to reset the **maintenance counter**. This counter is used to count the number of pages until the next time the message to apply the maintenance kit appears. Usually this counter is reset through the laser printer menu, but some printers require you to press a special button sequence.

TECH TIP

Allow laser printer to cool

Before working on a laser printer, allow the printer to cool down. Look for warnings where hot components are located.

A laser printer may have software options for cleaning and calibration. The cleaning mode cleans the paper path so that no random specks appear on the output. When you **calibrate** a laser printer, you adjust for print density or how dark the print appears. Calibration can help with environmental issues (see the bulleted point on ozone that follows) or print cartridge quality issues. Cleaning mode and calibration are commonly accessed through the printer menu or from manufacturer-specific software on a PC. Some laser printers have automatic calibration and also allow it to be done manually.

Laser printers do require some periodic maintenance. The list that follows can help:

- Be careful about using compressed air to **clean a laser printer** that has loose toner in it. The compressed air could push the toner into hard-to-reach places or into parts that heat up, causing the parts to fail. Be sure to vacuum up laser printer toner before using compressed air inside a laser printer.
- If a transfer corona is used, clean it when replacing the toner cartridge. Some printers include a small cleaning brush for this purpose. Some toner cartridges include a cotton swab. The transfer corona wire is normally in the bottom of the printer, protected by monofilament wires. Be extremely careful not to break the wires or the transfer corona.

TECH TIP

Laser printer preventive maintenance is important

If any toner appears inside a laser printer, do *not* use a normal vacuum cleaner to get it out. Toner particles can seep through the vacuum cleaner bag and into the vacuum's motor, where the particles melt. Also, the toner can become electrically charged and ignite a fire. Special high-efficiency particulate air (HEPA) vacuum bags are available for some computer and/or laser printer vacuum cleaners.

> Laser printers that use a corona wire can produce ozone gas that causes headaches, sore eyes, dry throat, nausea, irritability, and depression. Some printers have an ozone filter that removes the ozone gas as well as any toner and paper dust particles. The ozone filter needs to be replaced after a specific number of usage hours. Check the printer documentation for the filter replacement schedule. Most home and small office laser printers do not have ozone filters so recommend adequate ventilation.
> The fuser cleaning pad sits above the top fusing roller and is normally replaced at the same time as the toner cartridge. However, the cleaning pad sometimes becomes dirty before it is time to replace the cartridge. If the cleaning pad needs to be cleaned, remove it and hold it over a trash can. Use the shaft of a small flat-tipped screwdriver to rub along the felt pad. Replace the cleaning pad and wipe the screwdriver with a cloth.
> The fusing roller sometimes has particles cling to it. When the assembly cools, *gently* scrape the particles from the roller. A small amount of isopropyl alcohol on a soft, lint-free cloth or an alcohol pad can help with stubborn spots.

Thermal Printer Maintenance

Maintenance done on a thermal printer commonly involves doing the following tasks:

> Replace special thermal paper
> Clean the print head/heating element
> Remove debris
> Check the feed assembly

If a company uses thermal printers, you might be required to **replace paper**. Look back at Figure 9.13 to see how the paper is threaded through the rollers. Commonly, there are arrows that show you the path or a picture. Ensure the proper size and type of thermal paper is being used.

You also need to **clean the heating element**. The heating element is part of the print head, and you can use a thermal printer cleaning pen that contains isopropyl alcohol. Isopropyl alcohol or premoistened thermal cleaning swabs can be used to clean the thermal print head and rollers. **Remove debris** inside the printer and use compressed air if needed. It is recommended that with some thermal printers, you use a cleaning card, cleaning file, cleaning pen, or cleaning swabs. Remember to allow the thermal printer to cool before performing preventive maintenance.

Printer Maintenance Conclusion

Printers are critical to some users. Keeping a printer well maintained and recommending a maintenance routine is part of the routine for many technicians. If any type of printer must be sent out for repair, for warranty work, or for some other reason, make sure to remove the toner cartridge, platen knobs, and power cords before packing the printer in a box (or remind the user to do so). Check with the receiving company to see if you should send the toner cartridge separately.

TECH TIP

What if you just performed maintenance on a printer, and now the printing looks bad?

After performing preventive maintenance on a printer, the pages may appear smudged or slightly dirty. Run a few print jobs through the printer to allow the dust to settle (so to speak). Never perform any maintenance on any computer part or peripheral without testing the results.

Printer Installation Overview

Always refer to the printer documentation for exact installation and configuration specifics (see Figure 9.31).

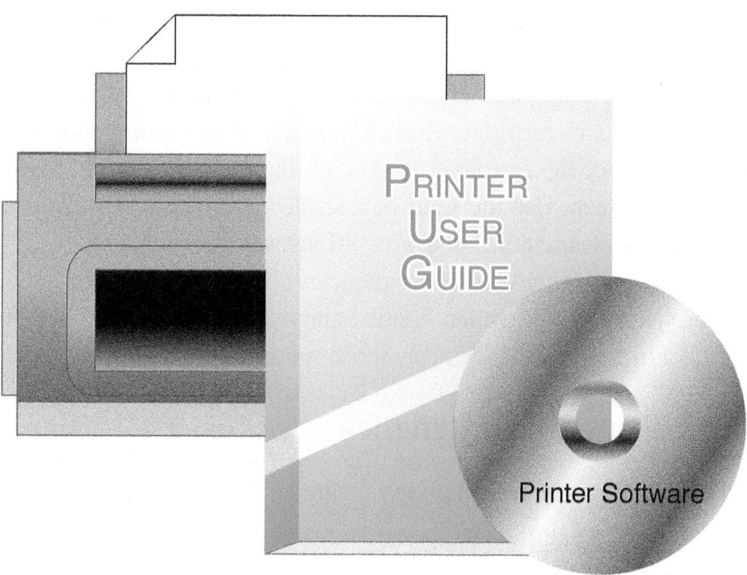

FIGURE 9.31 Printer installation, using software and a manual

As with any other device, do your homework first by deciding on the **setup location**. Ensure that the location is free from debris and nothing blocks device vents. Then determine if the printer is going to be wired or wireless. If wired, determine if the printer will connect through a USB port or through the wired network. Ensure that you have the proper cable on hand. If wireless, determine if it will connect to Bluetooth or the Wi-Fi network. Table 9.7 describes some tips for the various connectivity types.

TABLE 9.7 Printer device connectivity types

Connectivity type	Notes
USB	If software was installed before attaching the cable, Windows should detect it and automatically start the installation process.
Wired network	To set up a printer on a wired network, use the *Devices > Add a printer or scanner* link. A prompt asks whether the printer is local or networked. A local printer is directly attached to the computer, and a networked printer is attached to another workstation, a print server, or directly to the network.
Wireless network	Setting up a printer on a wireless network is similar to setting up a printer on a wired network except that you have to know a few details about the wireless network, such as the wireless network name (SSID) and security password.
Bluetooth	Bluetooth may have to be enabled first through a switch on the computer or through the Bluetooth & other devices Settings link. Bluetooth must be enabled on the printer to make it discoverable. Note that some Bluetooth devices are always in discovery mode.

Properly unbox the device, making sure the shipping container is not damaged and documenting if it is. You should also ensure that there are no damaged parts; if there are, you need to document them and return the printer. Usually there is a quick start guide that has pictures to tell you what to do, such as remove all tape that holds down the covers, install any print cartridge(s), adjust paper guides to the proper size, insert paper, and, if not already attached, attach the power cord to the printer and plug the other end into the wall outlet.

Remember that with Windows, if a printer is not discovered, you can use the *Settings* > *Devices* > *Printers & scanners* > *Add a printer or scanner* link. If the printer does not appear, you can select the link *The printer that I want isn't listed* > *Add a local printer or network printer with manual settings* link > *Next* > *Use an existing port* > select the appropriate port > select the manufacturer and printer model from the list or click the *Have Disk* button to browse to the downloaded file.

Be sure to test all functionality and train the user. Have the user print from an application. Be sure the printer is the default, if applicable. This is covered later in the chapter. Be sure to test the ADF capability, if installed.

Installing Multifunction Devices

Multifunction devices (sometimes called all-in-one printers) connect with a cable or wirelessly the same as a printer does, but they support printing, scanning, copying, and sometimes faxing. You have to remove protective materials from the scanner glass before using.

Installing a multifunction device is different from installing a printer in that you have more configuration to do. In addition to doing a printer and scanner calibration, you may have to connect the device using a phone cable between the RJ11 port on the device and a phone jack on the wall and configure/test the fax function. You should also test the copy function.

USB Printer Installation

The following steps explain how to install a printer that attaches to a USB port:

Step 1. Take the printer out of its box and remove the shipping materials. Remember to remove all the shipping safeguards. Set the printer in an appropriate area.

Step 2. Connect the power cord from the printer to the wall outlet, surge protector, or UPS outlet.

Step 3. Load paper and the ribbon, ink, and cartridge into the printer, according to the manufacturer's instructions.

Step 4. Turn on the printer and verify that the power light is on.

Step 5. Install the print driver by following the manufacturer's instructions for the particular operating system being used.

Step 6. Attach the USB cable to the printer and to the computer, as shown in Figure 9.32. Note that this cable might not be provided with the printer.

Step 7. Configure options and default settings.

Step 8. Verify that the operating system recognizes the printer. Perform a test print to verify communication between the computer and printer. Perform the calibration/print head alignment procedure.

Step 9. Train the user on printer operation and leave all printer documentation with the customer.

FIGURE 9.32 USB connection to the back of a printer

TECH TIP

Educating the user on printer functionality and print cartridges

As part of the installation process, ask the user to print something and show him or her any unique features. Inform the user that the cartridge that comes with the printer does not last long and to order a new one as soon as possible.

Printers in the Windows Environment

The operating system plays a big part in controlling a printer. When working in a Windows environment, there are three essential areas for a technician to know (besides knowing how to print): (1) configuration utilities, (2) managing the print driver, and (3) printer settings. Sometimes these areas overlap.

To print in Windows, use one of the following methods:

- Open the file in the appropriate application. Click the *File* menu item and click the *Print* option.
- Drag the file to print to the printer's icon in the *Printers* folder.
- Create a shortcut icon on the desktop for a specific printer and drag the file to that icon.
- Right-click the filename and select the *Print* option.
- Open the file in the appropriate application and press Ctrl+P to bring up the *Print* window.
- Open the file in the appropriate application and click the printer icon located under the menu bar.

TECH TIP

Using the printer icon in the notification area

When a print job occurs, Windows normally shows an icon of a printer in the notification area (the right side of the taskbar). When the print job is still accessible, you can double-click the printer icon, click the document, and pause or cancel the print job by using the *Documents* menu option.

You can use the *Settings > Devices > Printers & scanners* link to add a printer, remove a printer, temporarily halt a print job (that is, pause the printer), and define or change printer settings, such as resolution, paper type, and paper orientation. Note that you can also use the *Devices and Printers* Control Panel (*Add a printer* link) as well. A Windows utility starts automatically when Windows detects a newly connected printer. After the wizard starts, you must select whether the printer is a local printer (used by only one computer) or a network printer. If the local printer option is selected, you have to install a print driver. (Device sharing and networking printers are covered later in this chapter.) For best performance, always use the latest driver from the printer manufacturer for the operating system installed.

A **default printer** is a printer that applications use without any configuration changes. Even if you reply *No* to this prompt, you can change a printer to the default printer at a later date. Using the *Settings > Devices > Printers & scanners* link allows you to select a specific printer icon > *Manage* and gives you access to the *Printer properties* link. In this window, several tabs are available, depending on the printer model. Common tabs include *General*, *Sharing*, *Ports*, and *Advanced*. Figure 9.33 shows an example of this window. Notice that the *General* tab has a *Print Test Page* button that can be used to test connectivity between the computer and the printer, and the test can be used to ensure that the print driver is working.

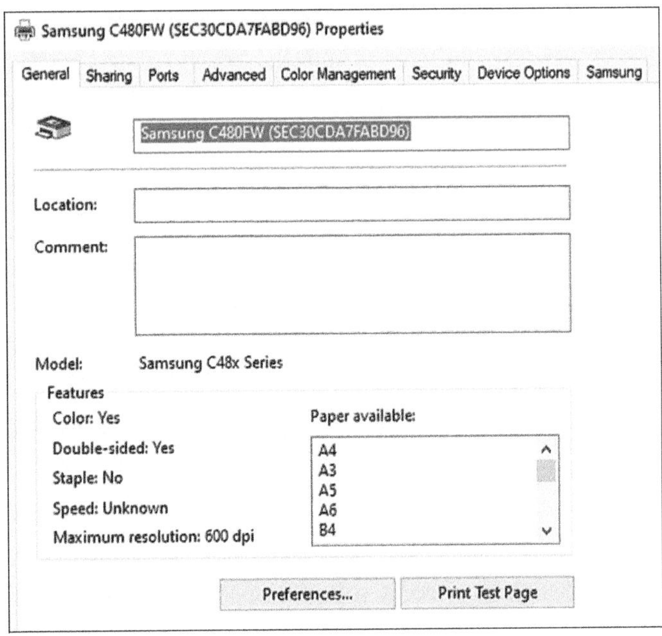

FIGURE 9.33 Printer properties window

TECH TIP

Setting a printer as the default printer

Click on the printer > *Manage* > *Set as default printer*. The default printer has a check mark next to the printer icon.

A specific printer's *Printer properties* window contains useful tools and settings. Table 9.8 lists the common tabs and their general purposes.

TABLE 9.8 Printer properties window tabs

Tab	Description
General	Displays the printer name and has a button for printing a test page
Sharing	Shares the printer over a network
Ports	Sets the LPT port number or displays the current port
Advanced	Allows setting of resolution, graphics intensity (darkness), graphics mode, spooling (transmission delay), and defaults
Maintenance	Printer type dependent; contains links to various maintenance functions, including cleaning, calibration, print head alignment, nozzle check, roller cleaning, and quiet mode
Fonts	Displays and installs printer fonts
Device Options	Adjusts print density and quality, displays the amount of RAM installed in the printer, and adjusts printer memory tracking

TECH TIP

Print Test Page button on the Printer properties window _General_ tab

The *General* tab is normally where you find a button that allows communication between the PC and the printer to be tested with a test page.

TECH TIP

I want my print job now!

If multiple print jobs are in the printer queue, you can reorder them by right-clicking on a document and selecting *Properties*. On the *General* tab, change the priority. A lower number, such as 1, indicates a lower priority than a higher number, such as 3.

How an application outputs to a printer is determined by the operating system used. A **print driver** or printer driver is a piece of software specifically written for a particular printer for a specific operating system. If you upgrade the operating system or move the printer to a different computer, a different printer driver is required. The print driver enables the printer's specific features and allows an application to communicate with the printer via the operating system. Windows applications use one print driver per printer.

TECH TIP

Using the latest print driver

For best results and performance, use the manufacturer-provided driver that is designed for the operating system being used.

The print driver and software from the printer manufacturer provide customizable configuration settings for a particular operating system. These settings can be accessed by right-clicking on the printer within the *Printers & scanners Settings* link, select the printer > *Manage* and selecting *Printing Preferences*. Commonly used configuration settings include the following:

- **Orientation** *(see Figure 9.34):* The vertical or horizontal presentation of the document. Portrait orientation is taller than it is wide, and landscape is wider than it is tall.
- **Duplex** *(see Figure 9.34)*: Also known as double-sided printing. Note that the printer featured in Figure 9.34 does not have a duplexer assembly, so printing on two sides would require turning the paper over and sending it back through the printer.
- **Collate** *(see Figure 9.35):* The collation setting affects the order in which the pages are printed when multiple copies of a multipage document are being made. For example, if you want to make three copies of a 10-page document, with collation enabled, you get the first copy of the 10-page document, then the second copy, and finally the third copy. Without collation enabled, you would get three copies of the first page, three copies of the second page, and so on.
- **Quality** *(see Figure 9.36):* This setting controls the resolution (DPI for example) and amount of ink/toner used.
- **Tray settings***:* These settings may be under the Paper/Quality or Paper tab and include different paper sizes, percentage output, tray switching, and tray priorities.
- **Paper source***:* This setting controls where the printer pulls from. The printer may have an Auto Select function where it uses paper from the appropriate source based on the paper size chosen within the document. Otherwise, you can select a specific tray that is to be used by default.

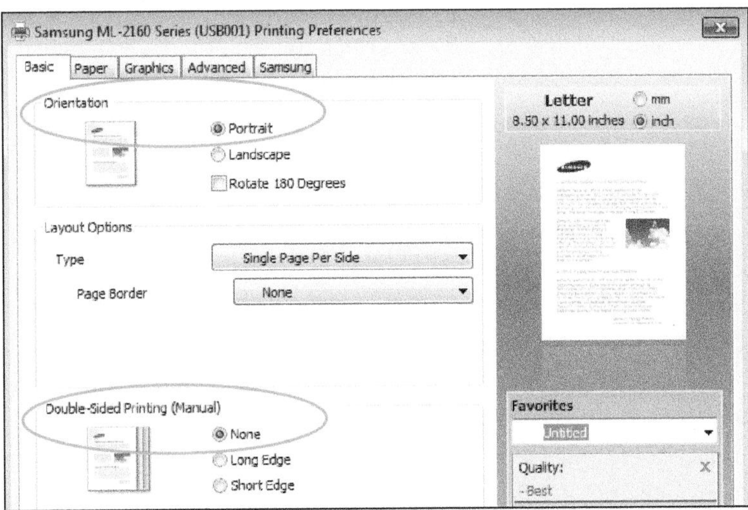

FIGURE 9.34 Printer orientation and duplex settings

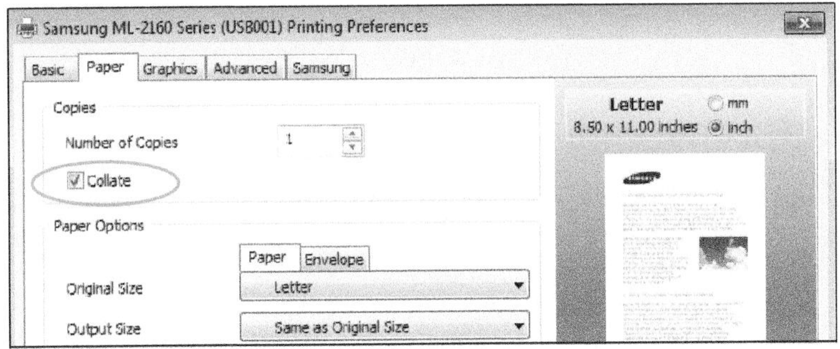

FIGURE 9.35 Printer collate option

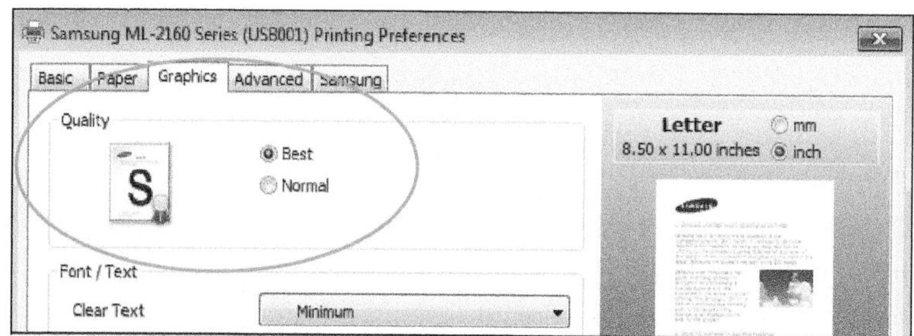

FIGURE 9.36 Printer print quality option

Each printer has its own Page Description Language (**PDL**) that is a translator between the computer and the printer. The PDL handles the overall page look and has commands that treat the entire document as a single graphic. The two most popular page description languages are Adobe Systems Inc.'s **PostScript** and Hewlett-Packard's Printer Control Language (**PCL**). Both are used by other printer manufacturers. PCL uses the printer hardware to do the translation, which speeds up the printing process no matter which operating system you are using. The drawback to using a PCL printer is that when you print the document on a different PCL printer, the quality may not be the same. In contrast, PostScript provides higher-quality output even if printed on two PostScript printers. Note that when *Auto* is selected for the printer language, the printer switches to the most appropriate printer language, depending on the type of information within the document.

TECH TIP

Which driver should I use, PostScript or PCL?

Some manufacturers may provide both a PCL driver and a PostScript driver. If the user does mostly word processing or spreadsheets, then use the PCL driver. If they print graphics and need higher-quality output, then the PostScript driver will serve them better.

Printers accept as much data as possible from a computer, process that data, output it, communicate to the computer the need for more data, accept more data, and repeat the process. With Windows, a print spooler is used. A **print spooler**, or print manager, is a software program that intercepts an application's request to print. Instead of going directly to the printer, the data goes on the hard drive. A print spooler allows multiple print jobs to be queued on the hard drive so that other work can be performed while the printer prints. If you select *Printer properties* for a particular printer, you can control the print spooler from the *Advanced* tab, as shown in Figure 9.37.

A print spooler runs as a service in Windows, relies on another service, called the Remote Procedure Call (RPC) service, and, optionally, the HTTP service. To verify whether the services are running, type `services.msc` at a command prompt or from the search textbox to ensure these services are running. Note that if a printer is shared for use by other computers, spooling must be enabled.

TECH TIP

When not to use spooling

If you have less than 300 MB of hard drive space, turn off spooling because the system needs the free drive space to operate. Remove files from the hard drive and clean up if possible or add more storage so spooling can be re-enabled.

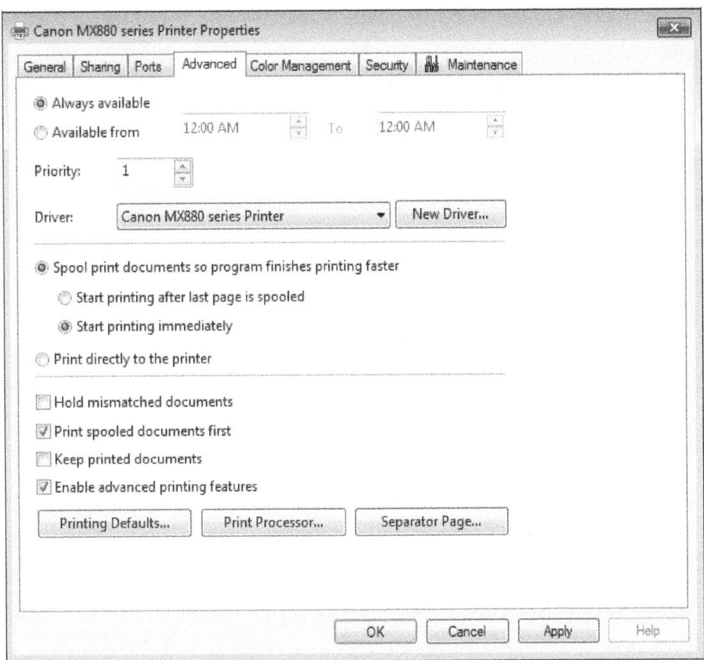

FIGURE 9.37 Spooling settings

Printer Sharing

Many home users and almost all businesses use printing device sharing (that is, printers that can be used by more than one computer). Printers can be shared using the following methods:

- Connect a printer to a USB port on a computer that is connected to the wired or wireless network and share the printer.
- Connect a printer with a wired or wireless NIC directly on the network. Some printers can be upgraded to have a wired or wireless network port added to them. Figure 9.38 shows a module that can be inserted into a printer so that the Ethernet port connects the printer to a wired network.
- Set up a computer or device that is designated as a print server. Connect the printer to the print server. Connect the print server to the network.
- Use public/shared devices.

FIGURE 9.38 Printer module with a wired network port

A networked printer can reduce costs. Laser printers can be expensive—especially ones that produce high-speed, high-volume, high-quality color output. Buying one printer and allowing users to access it from their individual desktops, laptops, and mobile devices can be cost-effective. It also reduces the amount of office or home space needed. Network printing is a viable alternative to using a computer's USB port. Wired printers can connect to a computer and then be shared or can connect to a wired network so that everyone on the network can use the printer.

Sharing Through Windows

To share a workstation-connected printer across the network, follow these steps:

Step 1. Enable *File and Print Sharing* by selecting the *Network and Sharing Center* Control Panel > *Change advanced sharing settings* > expand the current network profile > *Turn on File and printer sharing* > *Save changes* (see Figure 9.39).

Step 2. To share a directly connected printer so others can access it, right-click the printer to be shared > *Properties* (or possibly *Printer properties*) > *Sharing* tab > enable (select) the *Share this printer* option so it is checked > in the *Share name* textbox, type a name for the printer > *OK* (see Figure 9.40).

Notice in Figure 9.40 that you can install additional drivers for other Windows operating systems so that when other computers access this shared printer, they do not have to download and install the driver for this printer.

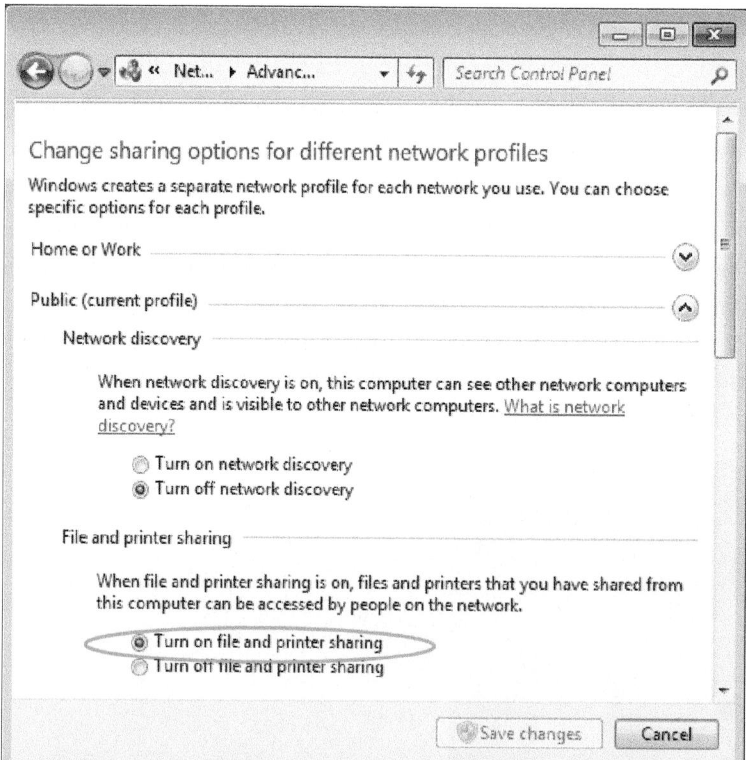

FIGURE 9.39 Enable printer sharing

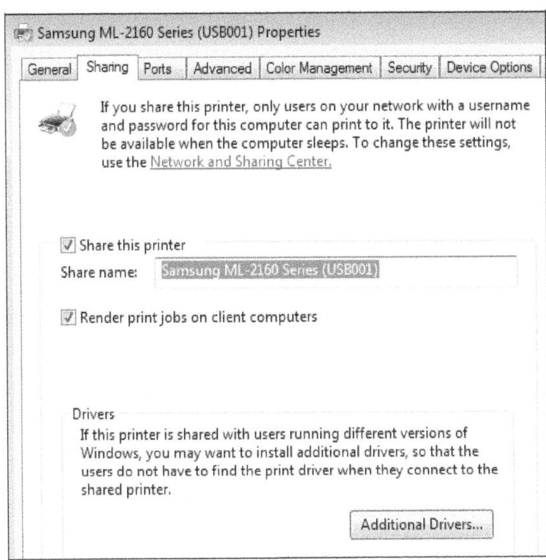

FIGURE 9.40 Printer Sharing tab

Wireless Printers

A PC can use different methods to connect wirelessly to a printer:

> The printer can have an 802.11 wireless NIC installed, or the NIC can attach to a USB port.
> The printer can have integrated Bluetooth capabilities or a Bluetooth adapter attached via a USB port.
> The wireless printer can communicate directly with another wireless device.
> The print server to which the printer connects can have wireless capabilities, and wireless PCs and devices can connect to the printer through the print server (as discussed in the next section).

Printers with wireless capabilities are common. Refer to Chapters 13, "Networking," and 14, "Introduction to Operating Systems," for more information on wireless networking theory and issues related to installing wireless devices.

An 802.11 wireless network has an 802.11 access point or combination access point and router that coordinates communication between all devices on the wireless network, including the wireless printer, as shown in Figure 9.41.

FIGURE 9.41 Wireless printing

TECH TIP

Doing your wireless homework

When installing an 802.11 wireless network printer, obtain the SSID and security information before starting the installation.

There are different types of 802.11 networks (a, b, g, n, ac, and ax). Each type has its own frequency and rules of operation. The wireless NICs in all the devices on a wireless network must be of compatible types. See Chapter 13 for more information on wireless types and obtaining a network IP address.

The steps for installing a wireless printer are similar to the steps for installing a wired network printer once the printer is attached to the wireless network. Before installing a wireless printer, you need to ensure that a functional wireless network is in the area. You need to know the SSID and any security settings configured on the wireless network. Normally, you can configure wireless printers using one of the following methods:

- Install software that comes with the printer *before* connecting the printer. Then use the software to enter the wireless network SSID and optional security parameters.
- Use the controls on the front panel of the printer to configure the wireless settings.
- Use a USB connection to the printer until the wireless network configuration options are entered.

Some Bluetooth printers are configured by first connecting them via USB and then configuring the Bluetooth option. To install a Bluetooth printer, always follow the manufacturer's directions, but the following generic steps are provided:

Step 1. Install the print driver for the operating system version being used.

Step 2. Ensure that Bluetooth is enabled on the computer or mobile device.

Step 3. Ensure that Bluetooth is enabled on the printer (usually through a front panel control). Note that you may have to set the visibility option to *Visible to All.*

Step 4. If in Windows, use the *Settings > Devices > Bluetooth & other devices* link to access the *Add Bluetooth or other devices* link. On a device, something may have to be tapped or pushed in order to start pairing with the Bluetooth printer.

Step 5. Ensure that the two devices pair properly and that the print function works.

Print Server

A **print server** connects to a network and allows any computer that is also connected to a network to print to it if the networks are the same or connected to one another. Some print servers can handle both wired and wireless connections. In such a case, the print server attaches to a network switch, and a network wireless router or wireless access point attaches to the same switch. Any PCs (wired or wireless) can print to the printer that attaches to the print server. Figure 9.42 illustrates this concept.

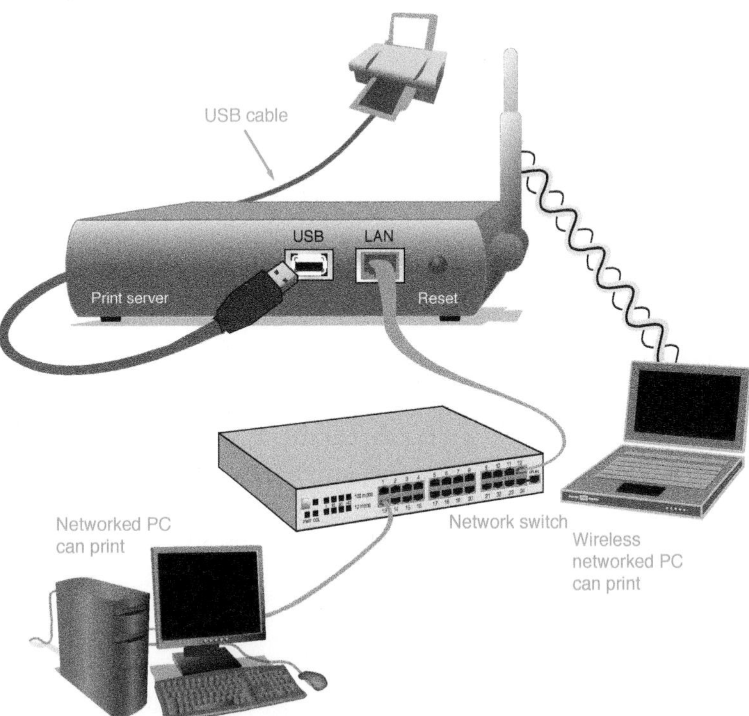

FIGURE 9.42 Wireless and wired print server connectivity

Accessing a Network, Wireless, or Bluetooth Printer

To access a networked printer, use the Windows *Settings > Devices > Printers and scanners >Add a printer or scanner > The printer that I want isn't listed* link. The available options include (see Figure 9.43):

- The *My printer is a little older. Help me find it.* option
- Browse for a network printer
- Type the path to the printer
- Enter the IP address or printer hostname
- Add a Bluetooth, wireless, or network discoverable printer
- Manually add a printer

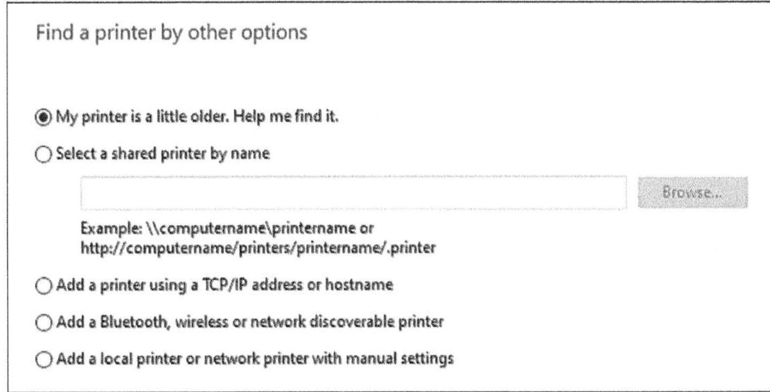

FIGURE 9.43 Finding a shared printer

An older PC can be used as a software print server. Software such as Apple's AirPrint or Bonjour can also be used to create a print server. Bonjour allows Apple and Windows devices to share printers without any configuration. See Chapter 13 for more information on configuring network devices.

Cloud Printing/Scanning

What if a company wants to be able to print something in a remote location or if a user is on a wired computer and wants to print to a wireless printer? Other companies might want users to be able to scan a document and store it so others can retrieve or view that document. **Cloud services** support network scanning and retrieval as well as printing to remote devices, whether the user connects to the network where the printer is located or not. Some all-in-one devices support scanning or printing directly to an online cloud storage provider or emailing a copy directly to someone, as do some copiers.

Cloud printing/scanning can be done through a service provided by the device manufacturer or through a provider such as Google. People already access email, files, music, and other devices by using the cloud, so it makes sense that an app can allow a print job or scanned document to do the same. Figure 9.44 shows how a document or a photo can be printed from a cell phone if cloud printing is enabled.

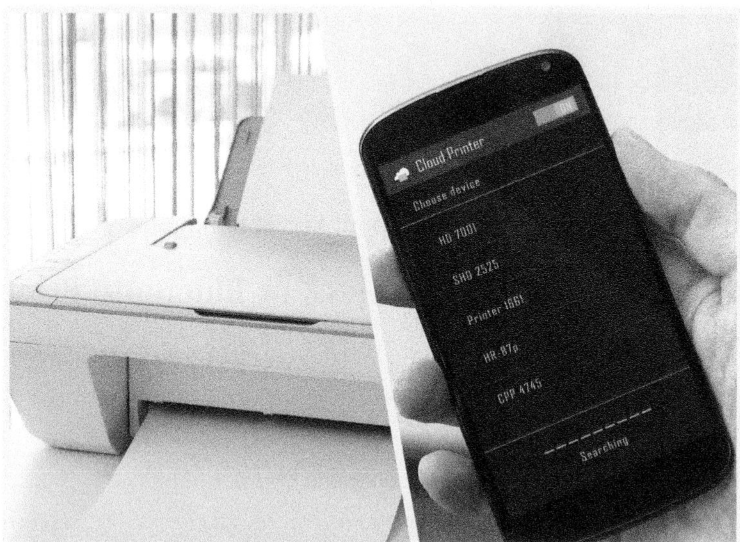

FIGURE 9.44 Cloud printing

Google Cloud Print allows printing from any device to a Google Cloud Print–connected printer. This means you can print a picture or a document from your phone or mobile device. To determine whether a printer is Google Cloud ready, open a Chrome web browser window. In the address bar, type **`chrome://devices`**. You then see a list of any Google Cloud devices. To add a printer, click *Add Printers*. Select whatever printers you would like to add to Google Cloud Print and click the *Add Printer(s)* button (see Figure 9.45). In the resulting screen, click *Manage My Printers* to see the options within Google Cloud Print.

Once you have printers registered to the cloud, you can download an app on your phone or mobile device. Many printer manufacturers have their own cloud-based print solutions and apps.

You can also scan and have the scan be sent to someone's email address or to a network folder that can be accessed by others. Every all-in-one printer is different, but look for the option to scan and send or email, and you will be allowed to enter an email address. Once the scan begins, it is sent through the network to a person's email inbox. See Chapter 13 for how to configure an all-in-one device or networked scanner for this feature.

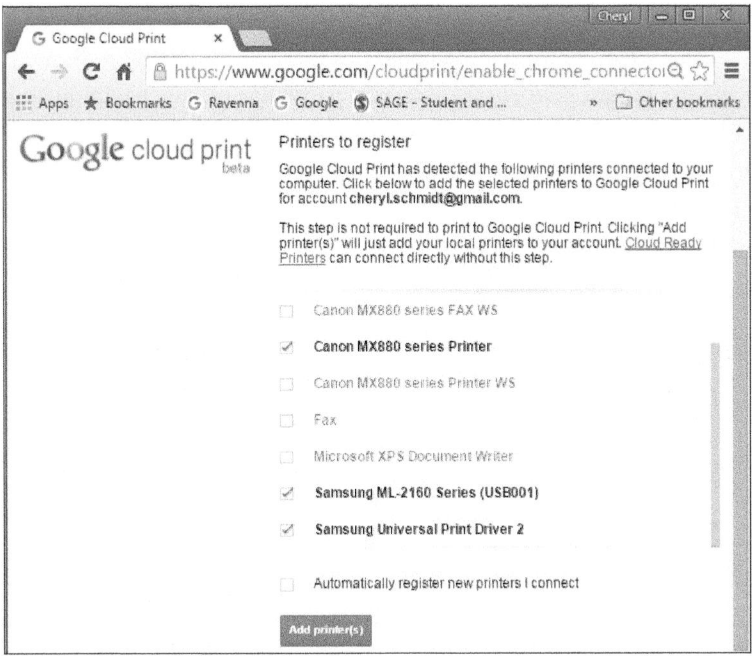

FIGURE 9.45 Viewing Google Cloud printers to register

Printing/Scanning Data Privacy

Printers can be a security weakness in a corporate environment. People might leave printouts on the printer, unauthorized users might use the copier or printer, and hackers use access to networked printers as a way to gain access to other network devices. One way to protect a printer that connects to the network is to require **user authentication** and require the user to input a user ID/password, input a PIN, or use badging as an access control method where the user scans their ID in order to print.

Another option might be to use **secure print**, which might be a security option on a networked printer, copier, or all-in-one unit from within the *Printer properties* window > *Printing options*, *Output method*, or other drop-down menu. Commonly you are required to enter a passcode and that same passcode is used in order to get the printout(s) from the printer.

Technicians need to be aware of the drawbacks to printing to a shared, public, or cloud-based printer:

- Printers shared through a PC require that the PC be powered on at all times.
- Sharing a printer through a PC means that print jobs are spooled to the PC hard drive (hard drive caching). If someone sends an inappropriate print job or prints something that is sensitive corporate information, a technician must realize that the spooled data can be recovered even after the print job completes.
- Privacy can be an issue. For wireless printers that are shared, it may be necessary to give the wireless network password to anyone who wants to print. Printers involved in cloud-based printing require a user to authenticate and register with the app being used.

General Printer Troubleshooting

The printing hardware subsystem consists of the printer and connectivity method such as cable, and communications port or wireless. If something is wrong with the hardware, the problem is normally in one of these areas. Always check the connections and power. The printer is a mechanical device with motors, plastic gears, rollers, and moving parts. If an error code or message appears on the front panel, refer to the manual or online documentation. Some printers beep or have indicator lights. Figure 9.46 shows that one particular printer has indications for low ink in specific cartridges (the lights for B, C, M, and Y).

A printer normally has a self-test routine. Refer to a printer's documentation to determine how to run the test. If a printer's self-test operates properly, the printer is operational. In this case, any remaining print problem has to do with the port, cable, or software.

FIGURE 9.46 Printer indicator lights

Running the self-test from the computer shows that printer connectivity works (the computer can issue a command to the printer, and the printer gets it). The self-test is commonly run from the printer's *Properties* or *Printer properties* option from the *Printers & scanners* Windows *Settings* link. Access the *General* tab > *Print Test Page* button. Refer to Figure 9.33.

TECH TIP

The paper is not feeding

If a printer is having trouble with the **paper not feeding**, you should look to see how far the paper went along the paper path before it jammed or could not go any farther. Check paper quality and efficiency of the rubber rollers that move the paper along the paper path. Over time, rollers can become slick from use and stop working properly.

If a printer makes a **grinding noise** or has **paper jams**, check that there is paper in the paper tray. Then look for paper bits or misfed paper along the paper path once you have powered off the printer. Check for paper clips or staples that might have been accidently fed into the printer and are along the paper path. Also check for labels that are causing a jam. Sometimes to **clear a jam** pull gently backward on the paper from the paper tray (although it is always best to try to take the paper through the natural direction of the paper path), fanning through the paper in the paper tray to loosen one piece of paper from other pieces, or pulling the paper the rest of the way through. Do not tug; do not tear the paper, if possible, as doing so will make fixing the jam more difficult for you. Needle-nose pliers and tweezers are great tools for stuck paper. The grinding noise might also be gears located inside a toner cartridge. Replace the cartridge to verify.

If using an ADF and the paper doesn't feed or if you have a **multipage misfeed**, check the paper path through the ADF for a foreign object, something stuck to the rollers, slick rollers, the paper guides being the correct width, and forgotten paper on the scanner glass. For a multipage misfeed coming from a paper tray, fan the paper thoroughly. Check for damp paper.

If a printer will not print, check the following:

> If the printer attaches to a computer, see if any message appears on the computer.
> See if any message appears on the printer's front panel.
> Determine whether the correct printer was chosen.
> Ensure that the printer was configured for the correct port or for wireless and that the wireless network is available.
> Ensure that the printer has ink or toner and paper.

TECH TIP

The paper could be the culprit

If a printer has trouble feeding paper, ensure that you're using the correct type of paper. Many paper jams are due to inferior paper quality, paper damage due to humidity, or operator-related problems such as the **incorrect paper size** selected in the software program.

If you are unable to install a printer using the manufacturer's instructions, try the following steps:

Step 1. Check the cabling and power.

Step 2. Reread the manufacturer's directions and ensure that they have been followed.

Step 3. Delete the print driver and try the installation again, following the manufacturer's instructions.

Step 4. Download a different print driver and try the installation again.

Step 5. Research the error on the printer manufacturer's website. In some cases, it may be necessary to back up the registry, modify the registry, and restart the print spooler to repair the issue.

If there is no image on the printer display, check that the printer is powered on. Also check the wall outlet by plugging a known working device into the same socket; if applicable, check the power surge strip. The printer power brick may be faulty.

TECH TIP

Mixed-up output

If you see **garbled print** on the output, check the cable and then the print driver.

If a printer gives a "paper out" message (see Figure 9.47), but the paper is installed in the printer, check the paper sensor. Take out the paper and reinsert it. Ensure that there is no blockage. Dust and debris can cause both blockage and sensor sticking.

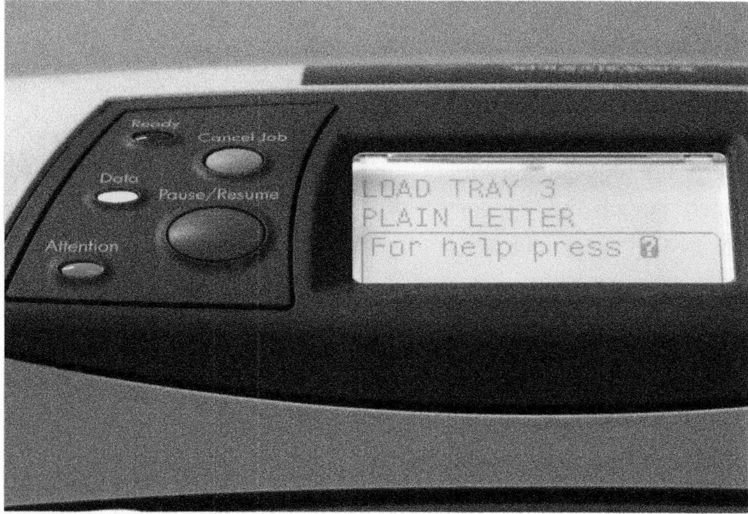

FIGURE 9.47 Printer front panel message

TECH TIP

Faded or totally missing print

When the print output is **faded print** or blank, check the ribbon (if using impact or thermal printers), ink levels (in inkjet printers), or toner (in laser printers). Check the quality setting. In a thermal printer, reduce the print head energy or print head pressure setting; ensure that the ribbon and media are compatible. Check the print driver as you may have to roll back the driver in Device Manager if a Windows update has just occurred.

If the printer outputs creased paper, check the following:

- Ensure that the paper guides in the paper tray are set to the correct size and do not push too tightly against the paper.
- Fan the paper before printing.
- Ensure that the paper being used meets the printer manufacturer's specifications.
- Check for staple jams and jams due to using paper that has been **hole punched** or the paper bits/dust from hole-punched paper.
- Check the paper path for obstructions, such as a label or paper clip.

Another problem could be that the printer is not configured for the correct port. Check that the printer is configured for the proper port. Refer to the printer's documentation for specifics on how to configure the printer for a specific port. To verify which port is currently configured, access the printer manufacturer's software or use Windows *Printer properties* from Settings or Control Panel > *Ports* tab. You can also connect a working printer to the port, install the proper print driver, and verify that the port works.

TECH TIP

What to do with slick printer rollers

Special rubber cleaners/rejuvenators are available for rubber printer rollers. Some printers have a special cleaning page for cleaning rollers. Refer to the printer's manual for exact procedures. If a cleaner is unavailable, scrub the rollers with a wire brush or sandpaper to roughen them up a bit or use the end of a paper clip to roughen up the rubber part of the roller. Vacuum all debris before using the printer.

Another problem is that a printer may not have enough memory and may display a low memory message or just blink as if it is accepting data. Then the printer quits blinking, and nothing appears or the printer prints only half the page. This could also be caused by insufficient free hard drive space when spooling is enabled.

TECH TIP

What if a printer needs more memory?

Alternatives to adding memory are to send fewer pages of the print job at a time, reduce the printer resolution, reduce the size of the graphics, or standardize the fonts (by not using as many font types, styles, or font sizes). Also ensure free drive space on the computer used to send the print job.

USB-Attached Printer Troubleshooting

If a printer that uses a USB port is exhibiting problems, consult the following list of troubleshooting options:

- If the computer stops responding and the USB device is suspect, power off the device and then turn it back on again. Go into *Device Manager* and ensure that there is only one listing for the USB printer.
- The BIOS/UEFI settings may have to be enabled for USB devices. Different BIOS/UEFI manufacturers list the USB settings differently, such as *Enabling Onboard USB* or within the PCI section.
- Use *Device Manager* to check whether USB is listed. Look at the *Universal Serial Bus Controllers* section. If USB is not listed, check the BIOS/UEFI settings or update the BIOS. If the USB device is listed, ensure that there are no resource conflicts.
- If there is a USB hub connected to the USB port, disconnect the hub and connect the USB printer directly to the USB port to see if the hub is the problem.
- Disconnect the USB printer while the computer is powered on. Power down the computer. Then power on the computer. Insert the USB printer cable into the USB port. The system should automatically detect and install the printer.
- Verify that the USB device works by plugging it into another USB port or another computer's USB port.
- Check that the proper USB cable is being used.

On the software side, troubleshooting involves narrowing down the problem to the print driver. Because Windows uses one print driver for a specific printer within all applications, check the printing from within several software apps. Use a simple text program such as Notepad to see if simple text will print. Printers need memory to print multiple pages of complex graphics. If a printer prints a couple pages and then stops, or if it prints half a page, ejects the paper, and then prints the other half of the page and ejects the paper, free up hard drive space. If printing does not occur in all the software packages tested, the problem is most likely the software driver. See the next section for specific Windows printer troubleshooting tips.

Windows Printer Troubleshooting

The most common printing test is a test page from an application or from a specific printer's *Properties* or *Printer properties* window, using the *General* tab. Remember that Windows uses a single print driver for all applications. Windows has a troubleshooting tool you can use by searching for and selecting *Troubleshoot* > *Additional troubleshooters* link > *Printer* > *Run the troubleshooter* button > follow the directions on the screen.

If the Windows troubleshooting tool does not help, run a self-test on your printer by following the manufacturer's directions. If the self-test works, the printer is likely fine, and the problem lies in the cable, port, software driver, or printer settings.

TECH TIP

Print from Notepad

If a printer self-test works, try printing from Notepad. If the file prints, your problem may be a print problem that affects only one application, or the printer may not have enough memory for complex output, such as high-end graphics.

Free hard drive space is important for print spooling. Insufficient free space can cause problems with print jobs. Even if there appears to be enough hard drive space to spool a print job, the printer may still need more RAM installed to print a large or complex document.

A print spooler and/or associated services, such as RPC and HTTP, can cause problems and can be stopped or paused. Locate the Print Spooler, RPC, or HTTP service used by the printer (by typing **`services.msc`**). Right-click on the service and select *Properties*. In the window that appears, you can start, stop, pause, or resume a service. Figure 9.48 shows the Print Spooler Properties window. Because the service is started automatically, the only button currently available is *Stop*. If the printer works, then you know the printer, port, and printer cable are all operational, and the problem is in the operating system.

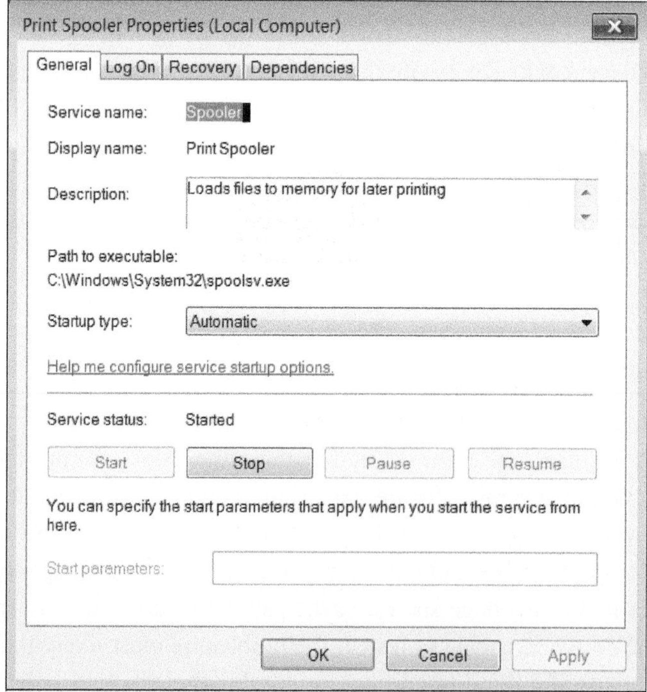

FIGURE 9.48 Managing the Print Spooler service

If you reload a printer driver, the old version of the printer driver must be removed first. Some manufacturers have specific instructions for removing their drivers. Always follow their directions. Most of them say to do something similar to the following: Right-click the specific printer icon and click the *Delete* option. Click the *Yes* button when prompted if all the associated printer files are to be deleted. To reinstall the printer, use the *Add Printer Wizard*.

The print queue sometimes causes problems. A single document may be in the queue but not print for some reason, causing other print jobs added later to fail to print. Always check the print queue to see if there are **multiple print jobs pending** in the queue. Multiple failed print jobs indicate a problem with the printer such as a paper jam or lack of paper, being out of ink/toner, and so on. Check the printer's front panel to see if it indicates any errors.

After a problem is rectified, the print queue might need to be cleared. Depending on what rights the user has, sometimes a technician must clear the print queue. The following methods can be used:

- Open the *Printers & scanners* Windows Settings option. Right-click the specific printer icon > *Open*. Right-click the first document (the one that is causing the problem) > *Cancel*. To cancel all print jobs, select *Cancel All Documents* from the *Printer* menu option.
- If the print job has already gone to the printer and is no longer stored on the hard drive, you may not be able to use the first method. In this case, use the *Printer* menu or *Cancel* function on the printer to cancel the print job.
- Clear and restart the print spooler service.
- Turn the printer off and back on again.

Note that if you get an access denied message, it means you must be logged on as an administrator to control the print queue. If a user gets the access denied message, then the user account must be added to the printer. Access *Printer properties* > *Security* tab > add the user account.

You can use Windows Event Viewer to both set up and check the print **audit log** (sometimes called a print log). Access *Event Viewer* > expand *Applications and Services* > expand *Microsoft* > expand *Windows* > expand *Print Service* > right-click on *Operational* > *Enable Log*. Return to this same area to view information related to printing problems.

Another Windows problem relates to setting the correct paper size. If someone has changed the Windows *Region* setting, it affects the default paper size. Change the setting back using the *Printer properties* link. The tab chosen is vendor dependent, but Figure 9.49 shows an example of the various paper size options.

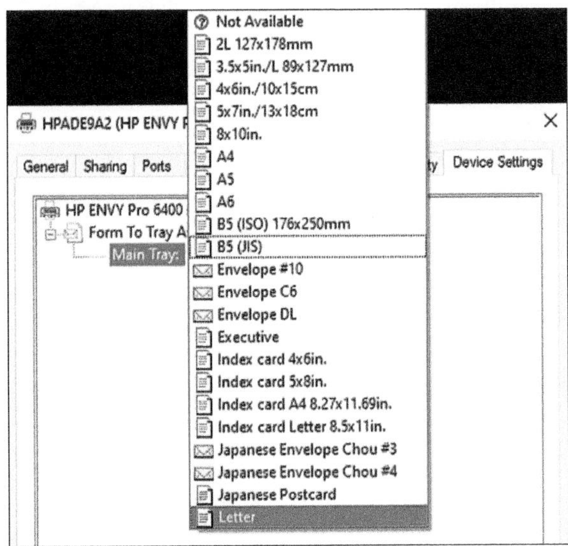

FIGURE 9.49 Printer paper size options

Another option available through *Printer properties* that can cause a problem is having the **incorrect orientation**. The two choices are landscape and portrait. Portrait prints the page with the long side of the paper on the left, whereas landscape prints the page with the long side of the paper across the top. Figure 9.50 shows how the *Preferences* button is commonly used to access the paper orientation.

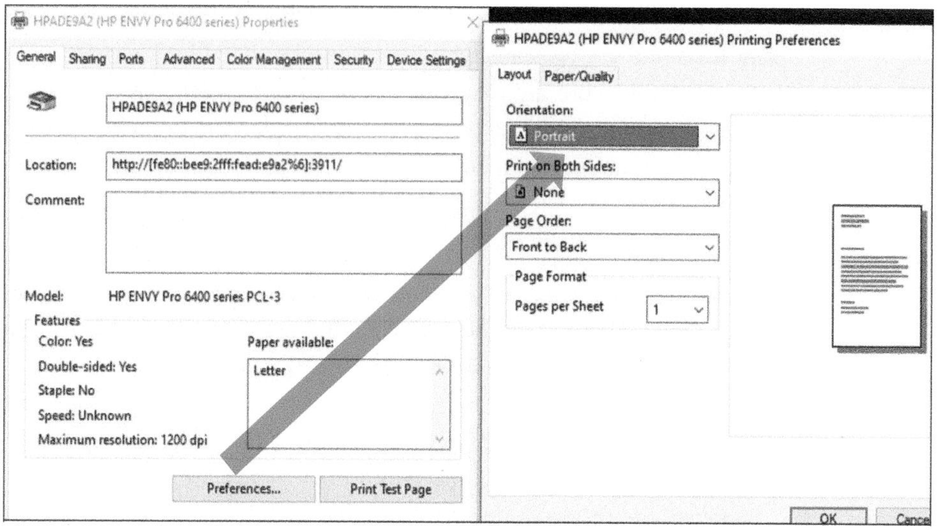

FIGURE 9.50 Printer Preferences > Orientation

If you are having trouble sharing a printer, ensure that Windows Firewall is not blocking printer sharing. Take these steps if Windows Firewall is being used (for another vendor's firewall, follow directions from the vendor):

Step 1. Open the *Windows Firewall* Control Panel or *Windows Defender Firewall* Settings link.

Step 2. In Windows, select the *Allow an app or feature through Windows Defender Firewall* link.

Step 3. Locate and check (enable) the *File and printer sharing* option. Click *OK*.

TECH TIP

Network printers

If a printer can be seen on the network but cannot be printed to, verify that the printer is on and shows no error conditions on the front panel or LEDs. Print a test page using the front panel menu, if possible. Verify that the network printer has a static IP address and is not configured for DHCP. These concepts are covered in Chapter 13.

Impact Printer Troubleshooting

When technicians state that a print head is not firing, this means that one or more of the print wires are not coming out of the print head to impact the ribbon. A print head that is not firing is evidenced by one or more white lines appearing where the printed dots should be. The most likely problem is the print head. However, the problem could be the printer's main board or a loose print head cable. Because the print head is a mechanical part, it is the most suspect.

If the print is light and then dark, the printer ribbon may not be advancing properly. There is a motor that handles ribbon movement, and it may need to be replaced. A faulty ribbon can also cause the carriage to seize up. Remove the ribbon and power up the printer. If the carriage moves when the ribbon is removed, but it will not move when the ribbon is installed, replace the ribbon. Some printers have belts that move the print head across the page. A worn, loose, or slipping belt can cause erratic printing.

TECH TIP

How to fix light printing

Light printing can be caused by several issues. Adjust the print head gap to place the print head closer to the ribbon or replace the ribbon. Also, the platen could be misaligned with the bottom paper-feed rollers.

If the printer prints continuously on the same line, be sure the setting for tractor-fed paper or friction-fed paper is correct. Or, the motor that controls paper movement may need to be replaced. If the printer moves the paper up a small bit after printing, the model may have the Auto Tear Off feature enabled. The Auto Tear Off feature is used with the perforated forms that are needed in many businesses. See the printer's documentation to disable this feature.

Inkjet Printer Troubleshooting

Most inkjet printer troubleshooting involves the print head. Inkjet printers frequently have a built-in print head cleaning routine. Access the routine through the printer's buttons or through software. Most manufacturers recommend cleaning an inkjet cartridge only when there is a problem, such as lines or dots missing from the printed output. Otherwise, cleaning an inkjet cartridge with this method wastes ink and shortens the life span of the print cartridge. If speckling or random spots appear, check ink cartridges for a leak and replace.

Usually, inkjet manufacturers include an alignment program to align the dots more precisely. Use the alignment program when **vertical lines** or characters do not align properly. If the colors do not appear correctly (for example, the printed output has an **incorrect chroma** display), check ink levels and run the printer manufacturer–provided color calibration routine. Some printers have a chroma optimizer that increases the black density and has better color tone gradations. Refer to the printer's documentation for troubleshooting programs, such as the print head cleaning, calibration, and alignment routines.

TECH TIP

Troubleshooting color

If a page does not print in color, check the printer properties to see if the grayscale option is selected.

Laser Printer Troubleshooting

Laser printers have more mechanical and electronic circuitry than the other printer types, which means more things can go wrong. The following list contains some common symptoms and possible solutions:

> If black **streaks** appear on the paper, the problem may be the drum, toner cartridge, fusing assembly, or paper. The drum can be part of the toner cartridge or might be a separate unit. The toner cartridge is the easiest thing to replace to see if the streaks stop. Allow the printer to cool and check the fuser cleaning pad for toner particles and then use a small screwdriver to scrape off excess particles. Finally, the paper might have a static charge, especially on low-humidity days, so fan the paper before re-inserting it.

- If speckling appears or if output appears darker in some spots than others, remove the toner cartridge. Gently rock the toner cartridge back and forth to redistribute the toner. If this does not fix the problem, turn down the toner density by using the *Printers & scanners* Settings link or software provided by the printer manufacturer. Try replacing the toner cartridge and paper type as it may be too smooth.
- If printing appears light, adjust the darkness setting on the printer or through the printer's operating system settings. The toner could be low. Damp paper could also cause this symptom. If the print appears consistently dark, adjust the darkness setting.
- If a horizontal line appears periodically throughout the printout, the problem is one of the rollers. The rollers in a laser printer are not all the same size; the distance between the lines is the circumference of the roller.
- When white vertical lines appear, the corona wires may have paper bits or something else stuck on them. Or something might be caught in the developer unit (located in the cartridge). Replace the cartridge to see if this is the problem.
- If the back side of the printed page is smudged, the fuser could be faulty or need an adjustment, the wrong type of paper could be being used, or the toner might be leaking. Some printers allow temperature adjustments. Increase the temperature if the image smears; decrease the temperature if the paper curls or if burn marks appear.

Many laser printer problems involve the toner cartridge, which is a good thing because the cartridge is a part that people normally have on hand. Various symptoms can occur because of the toner cartridge, including **double images** (ghost or **echo images**), smearing, horizontal streaking, vertical streaking, faded printing, one vertical black line, one horizontal black line, a white streak on one side, and a wavy image. One of the easiest things to do is to remove the toner cartridge, hold the cartridge in front of you with both hands, and rock the cartridge away from you and then back toward you. Re-insert the cartridge into the printer and test it.

Sometimes, the primary corona wire or the conditioning roller inside the toner cartridge needs to be cleaned. Clean the corona wires with the provided brush or with a cotton swab. Dampen the cotton swab with alcohol, if necessary. Clean the conditioning roller with a lint-free cloth and dampen the cloth with alcohol, if necessary.

When **toner is not fused** to the paper, you need to determine whether the problem is in the fuser assembly or elsewhere in the printer. Send any output to the printer. When the printer is through with the writing stage and before the toner fuses to the paper, open the laser printer cover and remove the paper. If the paper is error free, the problem is most likely in the transfer corona/roller or fusing assembly.

Experience is the best teacher when it comes to printers. If you work on a couple impact models, a couple inkjet printers, and a couple laser printer models, you will see the majority of problems. A printer has a limited number of electronic parts. Normally, the problems are in the moving parts or are software related.

SOFT SKILLS: WORK ETHICS

Ethics is a set of morals by which you live or work. Employers want employees to possess high ethical standards. This means they want people who are honest, trustworthy, and dependable. IT technicians are exposed to many personal things—passwords, private data, and visited internet sites, just to name a few. Employers do not want to worry about technicians taking things that belong to others, looking at data that does not relate to the computer problem at hand (such as the information that might be on the desk shown in Figure 9.51 or printed material in the printer tray), or taking/giving away things from the office.

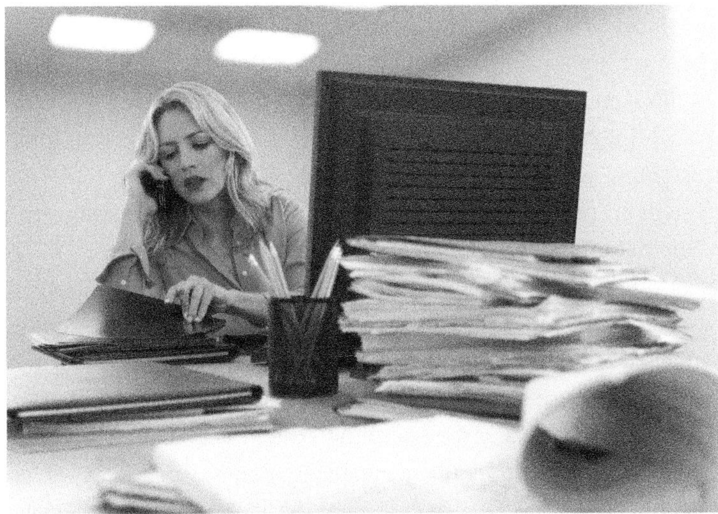

FIGURE 9.51 Work ethics: Do not look at or take information when working in an office

The best guideline in terms of ethics is to always be professional. For example, if you are in a situation where someone asks you to share another person's password, ask yourself whether divulging the information is professional. When opening a customer's documents and reading them, ask yourself whether you are being professional. If the answer is no, stop reading. If you are in a customer's office and accidentally see the person's password taped to a keyboard, let the person know that you have seen it, suggest that passwords should not be kept in a conspicuous place, and recommend that the password be changed right away. One of the biggest assets an IT professional can have is his or her reputation. Being ethical at work goes a long way in establishing a good reputation.

Finally, every IT person can probably remember at least one instance in which he or she was asked to do something unethical—charge for more time than was actually spent on a job, provide access to a room or an area where access is normally restricted, or grant privileges that others at the same level do not have. When put in such a situation, there are a few options: (1) Politely refuse, (2) adamantly refuse, or (3) report the person to a supervisor. Recommending what to do is difficult, but for most offenses, politely refusing is the best course of action and is the most professional. If a request is against corporate policy or could hurt others in the company, you need to report it to a company manager or security. Your own boss may be the best person to inform.

Chapter Summary

- Five types of printers commonly seen in businesses are impact, inkjet, laser, thermal, and 3-D printers.
- A multifunction device commonly has the ability to copy, print, scan, and possibly fax.
- Laser and inkjet printers do high-quality printing. A laser printer's supplies cost more than other printers' supplies, but laser printers last longer, and the cost per page is lower than for other types of printers.
- Printers can be shared using the operating system and a computer connected to a network.
- With wired networking, the printer has a direct connection to the network. Wireless networking includes 802.11 and Bluetooth technologies. A print server might be used to control and manage multiple printers. Printers can be registered through an app and managed/directed from that app to provide remote printing.
- Impact printers use print wires to impact a ribbon and are commonly used when multipart forms/output is needed.
- The steps in printing from a laser printer include processing the data, charging, exposing, developing, transferring, fusing, and cleaning.
- Impact printers can use normal-sized paper and fan-folded paper with pin holes that are fed by a tractor. Laser printers can have extra drawers for paper. A duplexing assembly option can be attached to allow a printer to print on both sides of the paper without human intervention. Impact printers use special heat-sensitive paper.
- Print drivers must match the operating system version.
- A printer uses a print spooler or hard drive space that keeps data flowing to the printer in large print jobs. The print spooler can be stopped and started using the Services window (`services.msc`).
- If a printer doesn't work, check the printer display, check the computer for any messages, and ensure that the correct printer was chosen.
- A laser printer maintenance kit includes parts from a manufacturer that need to be changed after the printer has been used for a given number of hours. The contents of such a kit are vendor specific. The maintenance counter must be reset after a maintenance kit has been applied.
- Virtual printing can be accomplished through the print to file, print to PDF, print to XPS, and print to image options.
- Common printer problems include light print, ghost images, toner not fusing to the paper, paper path issues, problems with wired or wireless connectivity to the printer, print driver problems, security settings, and error codes that appear on the printer display.
- Print security can be enhanced by ensuring that a person is authorized to print. Authentication can be provided through a user ID/password, an employee badge, by entering an authorization PIN, or using secure print.
- A computer technician needs to behave ethically around customers and peers.

A+ CERTIFICATION EXAM TIPS

- ✓ Know how impact, inkjet, laser, thermal, and 3-D printers work and the basic parts within each one. Know how to properly unbox a printer or multifunction device and understand considerations for device location.
- ✓ Know the parts of a laser printer: imaging drum, fuser assembly, transfer belt, transfer roller, pickup rollers, separation pads, and duplexing assembly. Some printers allow adjustments to the fuser assembly. The temperature should be hotter if the image smears and turned down if the paper curls or has burn marks.
- ✓ Know the laser imaging process: processing, charging, exposing, developing, transferring, fusing, and cleaning.
- ✓ Know the parts of an inkjet printer: ink cartridge, print head, roller, feeder, duplexing assembly, and carriage belt.
- ✓ Know the parts of a thermal printer: feed assembly, heating element, and special thermal paper that is sensitive to heat and must be stored in a cool place.
- ✓ Know the parts of an impact printer: print head, ribbon, tractor feeder, and impact paper.
- ✓ Know that a document can be scanned and sent to an email or remote scanning can occur using cloud services.
- ✓ Know how to operate and install a device that has an automatic document feeder (ADF).
- ✓ Know appropriate laser printer maintenance techniques, including replacing toner, applying a maintenance kit, calibrating, and cleaning.
- ✓ Know appropriate thermal printer maintenance techniques, including replacing paper, cleaning the heating element, and removing debris.
- ✓ Know appropriate impact printer maintenance techniques, including replacing the ribbon, replacing the print head, and replacing paper.
- ✓ Know appropriate inkjet printer maintenance techniques, including cleaning the heads, replacing cartridges, calibrating the print head for color, and clearing jams.
- ✓ Be able to describe the steps needed to install/replace the plastic filament in a 3-D printer, install resin, and recommend products for the print bed.
- ✓ Be able to configure and troubleshoot printer options, including duplex, tray settings, paper size, orientation, and quality settings.
- ✓ Know how to review and control the print driver and print spooler.
- ✓ Know how to network a printer by using a print server and printer sharing.
- ✓ Be aware of data privacy issues, including user authentication that may be required using a user ID/password, PIN, badge, and secure print; hard drive caching; and access to corporate/private information that may be onscreen or printed.
- ✓ Review all the troubleshooting sections (especially the key terms) before taking the exam. Know how to troubleshoot and resolve paper jams, staple jams, and hole punch issues. Know how to resolve vertical lines in output, garbled prints, toner not fusing to the paper, multipage misfeeds, multiple print jobs pending in the queue, speckling, double images, and grinding noises.

Key Terms

3-D printer 319
ADF 318
audit log 361
calibrate (inkjet) 338
calibrate (laser printer) 340
carriage belt 322
charging 324
clean a laser printer 340
clean the heating element 341
clean the print head 339
cleaning 325
clear a jam 356
cloud services 354
collate 347
default printer 345
developing 325
double image 364
duplex 347
duplexing assembly 326
echo image 364
exposing 325
faded print 358
feed assembly 328
feeder 322
filament 330
fuser assembly 325
fusing 325
garbled print 357
grinding noise (printer) 350
heating element 328
high sensitivity of thermal paper 328
hole punch 358
imaging drum 326
imaging process 324
impact paper 320
impact print head 319
impact printer 318
incorrect chroma 363
incorrect orientation 361
incorrect paper size 357
ink cartridge 321
inkjet print head 321
inkjet printer 318
laser printer 319
laser printer maintenance kit 340
maintenance counter 340
multifunction device 318
multipage misfeed 356
multiple print jobs pending 361
orientation 347
paper jam 356
paper not feeding 356
paper source 347
PCL 348
PDL 348
pickup rollers 326
plastic filament 330
PostScript 348
print bed 329
print driver 346
print ribbon 319
print server 352
print spooler 348
processing 324
quality 347
remove debris 341
replace an ink cartridge 338
replace paper (impact) 337
replace paper (thermal) 341
replace the print head (impact) 337
replace the ribbon 337
replace the toner cartridge 339
resin 330
roller 322
secure print 355
separation pad 327
setup location 342
special thermal paper 328
streak 363
thermal printer 319
toner is not fused 364
tractor feed 332
transfer belt 325
transfer roller 325
transferring 325
tray settings 347
unbox the device 342
user authentication 355
vertical lines 363
virtual printing 334

Review Questions

1. What method does a technician normally use to print a test page to prove that connectivity exists between a computer and a printer and to prove that the driver is working properly?
   a. Use a self-test button on the printer.
   b. Use Notepad and print.
   c. Use at least two applications and print.
   d. Use the *Print Test Page* button from the *General* tab of the Printer Properties window.
2. Which type of printer would a glass blower who sells art at trade shows most likely use to print receipts? [impact | inkjet | thermal | laser]
3. Which program is used to restart the print spooler in Windows?
   [Device Manager | Services | System Information | DirectX]
4. A Samsung laser printer is showing an error message on the screen that says that the paper is out, but the user shows you that there is plenty of paper in the bin. What should you do?
   a. Turn the printer off and back on again.
   b. Check the paper sensor for debris or dust.
   c. Use the reset sensor to reset the printer paper counter.
   d. Use the Print Test Page button in Windows to verify connectivity.
5. Which type of printer contains a fuser assembly?
   [impact | inkjet | laser | thermal]
6. Which type of printer has a print bed?
   [impact | inkjet | laser | thermal | 3-D]
7. For what do you use a printer-duplexing assembly?
   a. two-sided printing
   b. multiple paper trays
   c. wired and wireless network connectivity
   d. rasterization
8. Which component causes ghost images on laser printer output?
   [drum | fusing assembly | LED array/laser | pickup rollers | paper sensor]
9. An inkjet printer print head appears to be stuck, and the printer is making a grinding noise. Which part(s) should the technician check first?
   a. print cartridge
   b. paper feeder
   c. carriage and carriage belt
   d. printer mainboard
10. One of the technicians in your shop frequently swaps parts that do not fix the problem. The parts taken out of customer machines are taken to build private customer computers. This is an example of poor _____.
    [communication skills | work ethics | relations | troubleshooting skills]
11. Which type of printer maintenance commonly requires resetting a maintenance counter?
    [impact | thermal | laser | inkjet]

12. Which printer option allows multiple copies of a document to be printed in page 1, 2, 3 order instead of all the page 1s to be printed, then all the page 2s, and then all the page 3s?

    [fusing | collating | duplexing | conditioning]

13. A networked printer is visible through the network, but no one can print to it. What is the first thing the technician should check?

    a. print spooler setting

    b. printer IP address

    c. errors or indicators on the printer

    d. cabling

14. A laser printer outputs streaks on the paper. What is the issue?

    [drum | roller | ink cartridge | laser]

15. An inkjet printer's output appears to have missing elements. What is the first thing a technician should try if the ink cartridge appears to be full?

    ____

16. A printer menu displays the message "Filament Loading." Which type of printer is being used?

    [3-D | impact | inkjet | laser]

17. What is the purpose of the roller in an inkjet printer?

    a. It limits the amount of paper fed through the printer to one page.

    b. It controls the amount of ink allowed onto the paper.

    c. It moves the paper through the paper path.

    d. It moves the carriage from one side to the other.

18. What happens if a heating element on a thermal printer fails?

    a. missing printed output

    b. paper failing to feed through

    c. incorrect color output

    d. garbled output

19. How is laser printer calibration commonly performed?

    a. with a multimeter

    b. with a special tool that is part of the maintenance kit

    c. through the printer menu

    d. with calipers

20. The printed output prints about three-quarters down the page and then starts printing the rest on the next page. A technician has been contacted to help. On which option does the technician need to instruct the user?

    [duplexing | paper size | collating | orientation | finishing]

Exercises

Exercise 9.1 Research a Local Printer

Objective: To use the internet or a magazine to research information about a printer

Parts: A computer with internet access

Notes: A printer is not required to be attached to the computer for this exercise to be executed.

Procedure: Complete the following procedure and answer the accompanying questions.

A business user is interested in purchasing two printers. Details for the printers are as follows:

Printer A: A printer to be shared by all employees through the wired Ethernet network. Output should be high-quality black-and-white, grayscale, or color. The printer will not be used for huge print jobs but to print a proposal for a client or a few handouts for a small number of participants in a presentation. Speed is not an issue.

Printer B: A printer model that will be standard for those who need a printer attached to their workstations. The printer should be able to support wired connectivity to the Ethernet LAN or IEEE 802.11 wireless connectivity. The printer might be shared with computers that do not have a local printer attached. The printer should support quality black-and-white, grayscale, or color. The printer will not be used for a large number of copies. Speed is not an issue. A scanner needs to be part of the printer, too. The cost of supplies is a concern.

1. Using the internet, provide the business user with three suggestions for Printer A. List the model number and at least five facts related to the criteria. Find three price quotes for each suggested model and the name of the company for each one.

   ____

   ____

2. Using the internet, provide the business user with three suggestions for Printer B. List the model number and at least five facts related to the criteria. Find three price quotes for each suggested model and the name of the company for each one.

   ____

   ____

   ____

Exercise 9.2 Printer Driver Research

Objective: To use the internet to research information about three printer drivers

Parts: A computer with internet access

Notes: A printer is not required to be attached to the computer for this exercise to be executed.

Procedure: Complete the following procedure and answer the accompanying questions.

Locate the latest driver for each of the following printers and operating systems. Write the driver version in the third column.

Printer model	Operating system	Latest print driver version
HP OfficeJet Pro 8720 all-in-one	Windows 10 (64-bit)	
Lexmark C3224dw color laser	Windows 7 (64-bit) PostScript	
Okidata ML1120 dot matrix	Windows 10 (64-bit)	

Activities

Internet Discovery

Objective: To obtain specific information on the internet regarding a computer or its associated parts

Parts: Computer with access to the internet

Questions: Use the internet to answer the following questions.

1. A customer has a broken USB inkjet printer that would cost more to repair than to replace. The customer is considering an Epson Expression XP-440 all-in-one printer as a replacement. The customer would also like to have wireless connectivity, individual color cartridges, and the ability to print from a camera memory card. Will this printer meet the customer's needs? Explain your answer and write the URL where the information was found.

____

____

2. What is the latest print driver version for a Canon PIXMA MG3120 printer if the customer has 64-bit Windows 10 installed? Note that you just want to reload the printer driver. Write the version number and the URL where you found the information.

____

____

3. A customer has a Lexmark E460 laser printer connected to a computer that runs 32-bit Windows 7. Does Lexmark provide a Windows 7–capable printer driver for this printer? Write the answer and the URL where you found the solution.

____

____

4. How do you reset the HP LaserJet P2035 to factory default settings? Write the answer and list the URL where you found the answer.

____

____

5. You had to replace the drum on a Brother HL-L8250CDN color laser printer. What process is used to reset the drum unit counter?

____

____

____

____

Soft Skills

Objective: To enhance and fine-tune a technician's ability to listen, communicate in both written and oral forms, and support people who use computers in a professional manner

Activities:

1. The class is divided into seven groups. Each group is assigned a laser printing process. The group has 20 minutes to research the process. At the end of 20 minutes, each team explains its process to the rest of the class.

2. Pretend you have a job as a computer technician. You just solved a printer problem. Using good written communication skills, document the problem as well as the solution in a professional format. Exchange your problem/solution with a classmate and critique each other's writing. Based on suggestions and your own background, refine your documentation. Share your documentation with the rest of the class.

____

____

____

____

____

____

____

____

____

Critical Thinking Skills

Objective: To analyze and evaluate information as well as apply learned information to new or different situations

Activities:

1. Two networked PCs and a printer are needed for this activity. Connect a printer to a PC. Install the printer, configure the default settings to something different from the current settings, share the printer, and then print from another PC that connects to the same network.
2. Interview a technician regarding a printing problem. List the steps the technician took and make notes about how he or she might have done the steps differently, based on what you have learned. Share the experience with the class.

10 Mobile Devices

In this chapter you will learn:

> About the operating systems mobile devices use
> How to configure mobile devices
> How to back up and secure mobile devices
> How to troubleshoot mobile devices
> The importance of appearance in the IT field

CompTIA Exam Objectives:

✓ 1101-1.1 Given a scenario, install and configure laptop hardware and components.

✓ 1101-1.2 Compare and contrast the display components of mobile devices.

✓ 1101-1.3 Given a scenario, set up and configure accessories and ports of mobile devices.

✓ 1101-1.4 Given a scenario, configure basic mobile-device network connectivity and application support.

✓ 1101-2.1 Compare and contrast Transmission Control Protocol (TCP) and User Datagram Protocol (UDP) ports, protocols, and their purposes.

✓ 1101-2.2 Compare and contrast networking hardware.

✓ 1101-2.3 Compare and contrast protocols for wireless networking.

✓ 1101-2.5 Given a scenario, install and configure basic wired/wireless small office/home office (SOHO) networks.

✓ 1101-2.7 Compare and contrast internet connection types, network types, and their features.

✓ 1101-2.8 Given a scenario, use networking tools.

✓ 1101-3.1 Explain basic cable types and their connectors, features, and purposes.

✓ 1101-3.2 Given a scenario, install the appropriate RAM.

✓ 1101-3.3 Given a scenario, select and install storage devices.

✓ 1101-3.4 Given a scenario, install and configure motherboards, central processing units (CPUs), and add-on cards.

✓ 1101-5.5 Given a scenario, troubleshoot common issues with mobile devices.

✓ 1101-5.7 Given a scenario, troubleshoot problems with wired and wireless networks.

✓ 1102-1.4 Given a scenario, use the appropriate Microsoft Windows 10 Control Panel utility.

✓ 1102-1.5 Given a scenario, use the appropriate Windows settings.

✓ 1102-1.8 Explain common OS types and their purposes.

✓ 1102-2.1 Summarize various security measures and their purposes.

✓ 1102-2.5 Given a scenario, manage and configure basic security settings in the Microsoft Windows OS.

✓ 1102-2.7 Explain common methods for securing mobile and embedded devices.

✓ 1102-2.9 Given a scenario, configure appropriate security settings on small office/home office (SOHO) wireless and wired networks.

✓ 1102-3.4 Given a scenario, troubleshoot mobile OS and application issues.

✓ 1102-3.5 Given a scenario, troubleshoot common mobile OS and application security issues.

✓ 1102-4.7 Given a scenario, use proper communication techniques and professionalism.

Mobile Device Overview

Mobile devices are an integrated part of today's society. Wearable devices such as smartwatches, fitness monitors, glasses, and headsets allow us to take our technology wherever we go. New laptop features, tablets, Android phones and tablets, Apple iPhones and iPads, and other electronics are continuously being introduced. Many mobile devices are all-in-one units. Mobile devices are designed to be quick, light, durable, and portable (see Figure 10.1), and in some cases, a mobile device is a user's main computer. Table 10.1 lists characteristics of various mobile devices.

FIGURE 10.1 Mobile devices

TABLE 10.1 Mobile devices

Device	Description
Tablet	A tablet is a mobile device that has a touch screen, camera(s), microphone, and possibly one or more ports (see Figure 10.2). Tablets connect to the internet; they can be used to take, send, receive, and store pictures and video. Apple's tablet is known as an iPad, and there are variations such as the iPad mini, iPad Air, and iPad Pro.
Drawing pad	A drawing pad is a device used to draw, annotate an existing document, or drawing, type, or write. Also known as a drawing tablet or graphics tablet. Drawing pads are used by teachers, graphic artists, space planners, and engineers.
GPS	The Global Positioning System (GPS) is a series of satellites that provide location, movement, and time information to a single device or to a component integrated into a mobile device.
Smartphone	A smartphone has the capability to make calls and run apps, play music, track movement using GPS, connect to wireless networks, connect wirelessly to other devices, connect to the internet through the phone network or wireless network, and take high-resolution pictures and videos. Two popular smartphone operating systems are Android and Apple iOS.

Device	Description
Phablet	A phablet, which is a cross between a smartphone and a tablet, tends to have a larger screen than a smartphone (see Figure 10.3). Phablets are designed for taking notes and viewing documents more easily. A phablet may include a stylus.
E-reader	Also known as an e-book reader, an e-reader has an LCD screen designed for reading and storing digital books, magazines, and other online materials.
Smart camera	A smart camera has one or more extra capabilities beyond what a digital camera has and is used for such things as facial recognition, measuring, inspection for quality assurance, surveillance, and robot guidance. A smart camera may include a mobile operating system, have internet access, and have support for wired and wireless networking. Figure 10.4 shows a smart camera attached to a drone.

FIGURE 10.2 Tablet

FIGURE 10.3 Phablet

FIGURE 10.4 Smart camera

Mobile Operating System Basics and Features

A mobile device, like any other computer, needs an operating system (OS). The mobile operating system can be proprietary to a particular vendor, but four common mobile operating systems are all based on Linux: Android, iOS, Windows, and Chrome.

Android is an open source OS that is based on the Linux kernel and used mainly on phones and tablets but that is also available on laptops and PCs. Open source operating systems allow vendors to use the core source code and customize the operating system. Google, Inc. purchased Android in 2005, and it continues to be one of the most popular mobile operating systems in the world.

Apple's **iOS** is used only on Apple devices, and **iPadOS** is used on Apple tablets. Microsoft Windows operating systems are used on many laptops and tablets. Microsoft used to have its own mobile operating systems, including a phone operating system, but those have all been discontinued. Windows 10 IoT Core operating system is used on ARM devices.

Many are familiar with Chrome as a browser option, but **Chrome OS** is also an operating system that was developed by Google as an open source project (called the Chromium OS project). Developers can use or modify the code developed from this group, but Chrome OS is supported by Google and Google partners. Laptops that use Chrome OS, known as Chromebooks, are very popular in schools and commonly use cloud-based apps. The Chrome OS is also used on ARM mobile devices.

Mobile Storage

A mobile device needs a place to store data, and mobile storage uses the same technology as some PC storage, but of course, the storage media is smaller. Mobile devices do have RAM. For example, laptops commonly have as much laptop RAM as desktops. Sometimes this RAM is not upgradable in mobile devices such as tablets and smartphones. However, mobile devices commonly use flash memory. **Flash memory** is a type of nonvolatile, solid-state memory that holds data even when the computer power is off. Smartphones, tablets, and other mobile devices use flash memory to store the operating system, apps, and data/video. Flash memory cards for mobile devices include various types of Secure Digital (**SD**) cards: SD, miniSD, microSD, SDHC, miniSDHC, microSDHC, SDXC, microSDXC, Extreme Digital (xD), and probably more since this book has been published. On some phones, reaching the micro memory chip requires removing the back cover of the phone and the battery.

Another flash technology used with mobile devices is CompactFlash (CF). CF cards can be inserted directly into many devices, such as cameras, smartphones, network devices, and tablet PCs. A CF card uses flash memory, which does not require a battery to keep the data saved to it. A CF card can also be installed into a computer with a CF card reader. The CF technology is also used in solid-state drives. Figure 10.5 shows three flash memory cards.

FIGURE 10.5 Flash storage

TECH TIP

Don't format CF cards with Windows

If Windows is used to format a CF card, it will place a different file system on the card. Windows can be used to read files from a CF card or place files on a CF card, but best practice is to use the formatting option on the device instead of using Windows to format a CF card.

Flash memory cards, or storage cards, are used in mobile devices and laptops, as well as in desktop computers. In Apple and Android products, use the *Settings* > *Storage* option to view the internal memory capacity and any additional memory storage.

A device may have an SD card slot built in, as in the case of the laptop shown in Figure 10.6. Sometimes in order to insert a microSD card into a laptop or tablet, an adapter may have to be purchased so that the microSD card can be used. Figure 10.7 shows how the microSD card inserts into an adapter. That adapter must match the slot size of the mobile device.

Some people like to use a **smart card reader** (also known as a multi-card reader, media card reader, or flash/flash **memory card reader**) to quickly and easily transfer pictures, data, movies, and so on to a PC. Some card readers accept 75 different types of media storage. A card reader attaches to a USB port or is integrated into a laptop. Look at Figure 10.8 to see some of the media slots. Once a smart card is inserted, the OS assigns a drive letter to the reader.

FIGURE 10.6 Laptop SD card slot

FIGURE 10.7 Flash media adapter

FIGURE 10.8 Smart card reader

Mobile Accessories

Mobile devices have some accessories that are unlike PC accessories. Table 10.2 describes various mobile accessories a technician may need to know about and discuss with customers.

TABLE 10.2 Mobile accessories

Accessory	Description
Headset	A headset can use a wired or wireless connection to provide sound and typically fits over one (see Figure 10.9) or both ears. See the "Bluetooth" section, later in this chapter, for wireless headset configuration.
Webcam	A webcam is an integrated or wired device used to record or provide live video and optionally sound. A few webcams connect via Bluetooth. A webcam usually comes with software from the manufacturer and is typically detected by operating systems and software that might make use of the device. A privacy slide may be used to block a webcam lens.
Speaker	Speakers are built in to mobile devices and displays; some devices have audio ports for external speakers. Speakers can be wired or wireless. See the "Bluetooth" section, later in this chapter, for wireless speaker configuration. Use *Settings* to control or mute a speaker.
Touch pen	Also known as a stylus or an active pen, a touch pen might be vendor specific and is used to provide input into a mobile screen. Cases or screen covers can interfere with touch pens. Some pen tips are replaceable. Use *Settings* to ensure that a touch pen device is enabled.
Mobile docking station	A mobile docking station provides a stable environment for mobile computers while traveling, such as for a laptop in a police car or for military operations. Docking stations are also available to charge one or more mobile devices. Some docking stations also synchronize devices with each other or with applications while charging. Figure 10.10 shows a mobile docking station.
Track pad	A track pad is integrated into a laptop or a USB or wireless device (see Figure 10.11) used to input and interact with the operating system and software.

FIGURE 10.9 Wireless headset

FIGURE 10.10 Mobile docking station

FIGURE 10.11 Track pad integrated into a laptop

Using Mobile Devices

A mobile operating system is different from other operating systems in that, instead of primarily using a mouse or keyboard to interact with the operating system, a finger, a stylus, spoken word, or multiple fingers are used. A home page might be displayed or a system bar might extend across the bottom of a mobile device's screen. There might also be a mobile notification area, which contains icons for information such as the battery life, wireless signal strength, time, and external media connectivity. Note that on a smartphone (refer to Figure 10.12), the notification area and settings are commonly available with a swipe from the top of the display. Figure 10.13 shows an Apple iPhone home screen. An older Apple iPad or iPhone has a physical home button (not an icon to tap) beside or below the screen.

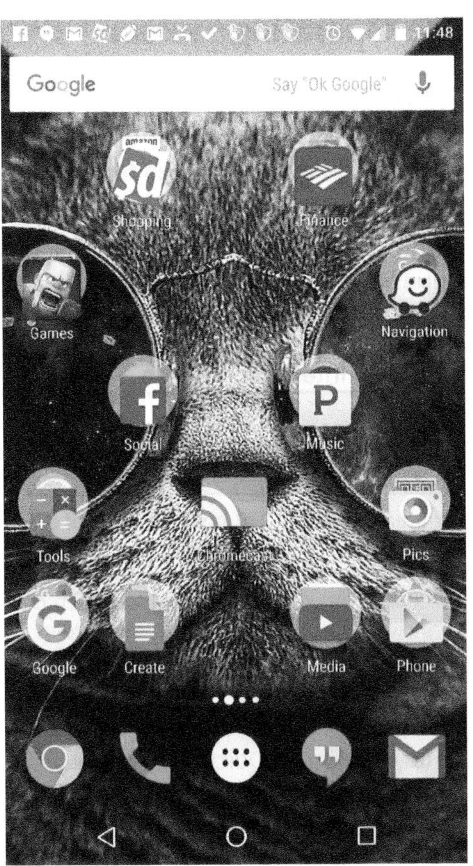

FIGURE 10.12 Android smartphone home screen

FIGURE 10.13 iPhone home screen

Some people disable the GPS capability until they want to use it to prevent geotracking. Geotracking involves tracking the location and movement of a mobile device (see Figure 10.18). Social media and other applications, known as **cellular location services** or **locator applications**, rely on such data to "publish" your current location or the locations of friends you have selected. Vendors have plans that include the ability to track family members. Companies use geotracking to locate lost and stolen mobile devices. Note that some devices also use a geotagging feature; for example, a camera app may use geotagging to include with a photo information such as where the photo was taken. It is possible to disable the geotagging feature, and may users do so for privacy reasons.

FIGURE 10.18 Geotracking

Configure Android devices for GPS by using the *Settings > Biometrics and security > Location* option. For Apple iOS devices, use *Settings > Privacy > Location Services* option.

Because a mobile device screen is used to interact with the operating system, screen calibration may need to be performed. Android users use the *Settings* app. Windows users use *Settings > Calibrate the Screen for Pen and Touch Input > Calibrate.* You can also download an app to perform screen calibration tasks, such as color, sensitivity, one-hand configuration, or motion/gestures configuration. Table 10.6 explains some mobile operating system features.

TABLE 10.6 Mobile operating system features

Feature	Description
Internet calling	Use an app such as Skype, Google Hangouts, or WhatsApp to call another person.
Wi-Fi calling	Make a call using a Wi-Fi connection rather than the cell phone network; beneficial when the phone network has a weak signal or to avoid using cell phone network minutes or roaming. Some vendors offer this as a built-in service.
Virtual assistant	Use voice commands to obtain information such as directions or current sports scores and to dictate emails or texts; examples include Apple's Siri, Microsoft's Cortana, Google Assistant, and Amazon Alexa.
Emergency notification	Obtain wireless emergency alerts (WEA); a U.S. method for propagating emergency alerts such as announcements from the National Weather Service, presidential messages, and emergency operations center messages to mobile devices.
Mobile payment service	Pay for services or goods by using a mobile device instead of with cash or a credit card. Such services are especially popular in developing countries where banking is not as prevalent as it is in developed nations. Transactions can be conducted using technologies such as near field communication (NFC), Wireless Application Protocol (WAP), direct mobile billing, and Short Message Service (SMS). Popular mobile payment apps include Apply Pay and Google Pay. See Figure 10.19.

FIGURE 10.19 Mobile wallet

Obtaining, Installing, and Removing Apps

Mobile device apps are obtained from a source such as Google Play, Apple's App Store (or iTunes), the Microsoft Store, Amazon's Appstore for Android, and a host of other content sources. There are other ways to get an app: by manually installing it (called *side loading*), using a USB cable (which commonly requires a file management app), using your storage media and a media reader, using an app such as Bump to transfer an application, or using a quick response (QR) code between two devices. For an example of a QR code, look at the bottom of the cell phone screen in Figure 10.19. Note that whatever method you use to install an app, you must ensure that the app is from a trusted source or a trusted app developer. Table 10.7 lists tasks that are commonly conducted by using apps.

TABLE 10.7 Mobile device tasks*

Task	Android	iOS or iPadOS	Windows
Delete an app	Press and hold the app's icon and drag it to the trash can.	Press and hold the app's icon until it jiggles and press the *X* that appears beside the icon. Press the menu key to stop the jiggling.	Press and hold the app's icon > tap *Uninstall* > *Yes*.
Close an app/ force it to stop	*Settings* > *Applications* > *Manage Applications* > tap the specific application name > tap *Force Stop*.	Press the Home button quickly two times or swipe up on iPhone X > swipe left to locate the app if using the Home button > swipe upward on the app preview.	Swipe down from the top of the screen and drag the app to beyond the bottom of the screen.
Install an app	Access Google *Play* Store > locate and select the app to download > tap *Install*.	Access *App Store* > locate and select the app to install > tap *Install*.	Access *Microsoft Store/ Marketplace* > locate and select the app to install > tap *Install*.
Move an app icon	Press and hold the app icon until it jiggles and drag the icon to another location.	Press and hold the app icon until it jiggles and drag the icon to another location.	Press and hold the tile until the app bar appears. Then drag the tile to the new location.
Create a folder to hold apps	Press an empty part of the home screen and select *Folder*.	Press and hold the app icon until it jiggles. Drag the icon onto another app icon. A folder is created that contains both icons.	From the *Start* screen, tap and drag one tile on top of another.

*Because Android is open source, the exact steps may vary. Also, Apple devices are constantly being updated/upgraded.

Two important terms related to apps are APK and SDK. Android application package (**APK**) is the file format used to distribute and install Android apps. So if you download an app, it is an APK file. A software development kit (SDK) is a set of tools (application programming interfaces [APIs], documentation, programming tools, analytic tools, sample code, and so on) used to develop an app for a specific mobile OS or platform. You can use **developer mode** on an Android device through the *Settings* option. This is a security risk and may cause issues on the device or cause the device operating system to be unstable. Be sure your apps are from a secure and trusted source or trusted app developer.

Mobile Device Wired Connectivity

Mobile devices have many of the same ports as computers but in smaller versions. **Proprietary vendor-specific ports** are primarily for power connections or provide communication options. Let's explore these ports in a little more detail, starting with the ports you are most familiar with: USB and Lightning ports.

Mobile USB and Lightning Ports

Mobile devices frequently have either a USB, **microUSB**, **miniUSB**, or **USB-C** port. Figure 10.20 shows the standard Type-A USB port found on a PC and the miniUSB, microUSB, and USB-C ports found on mobile devices. The USB-C port is now a standard interface for smartphones.

FIGURE 10.20 USB Type-A, mini, micro, and USB-C ports

Apple has an 8-pin **Lightning port** for its devices, but Apple is moving to the USB Type-C port. Both the Lightning port and USB-C cables can be inserted either face up or face down because they are non-directional. Figure 10.21 shows a Lightning connector and port. Figure 10.22 shows Apple's two connectors on the left, along with the microUSB, miniUSB, and traditional USB connectors.

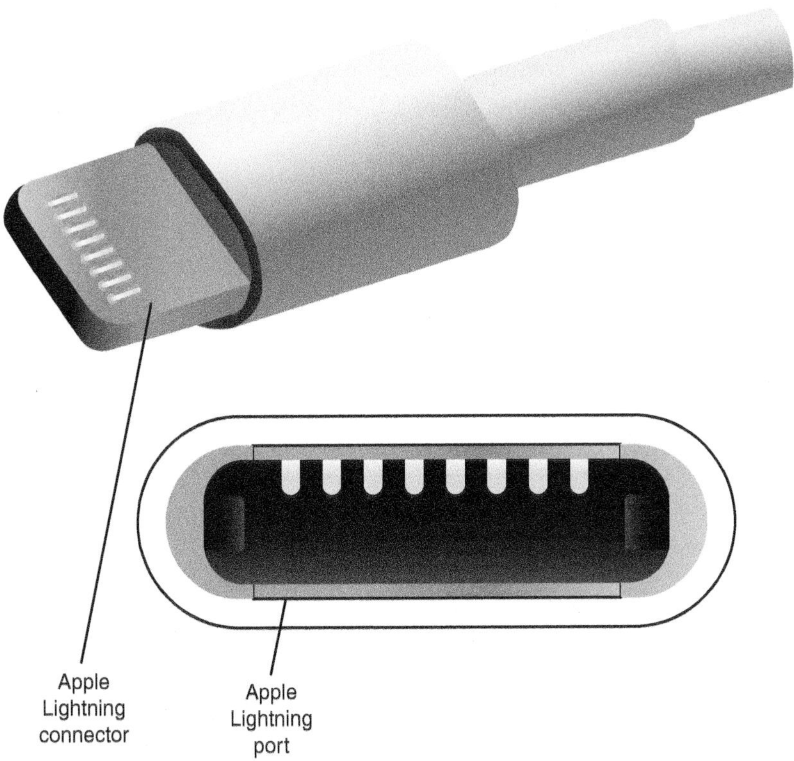

FIGURE 10.21 Apple Lightning port and connector

FIGURE 10.22 Mobile connectors

With a device that doesn't have a wired RJ45 network connection but that does have a USB port, a USB-to-RJ45 converter can be used. Wired network connections are faster than wireless connections and are commonly found on laptops, but other mobile devices lack RJ45 jacks. Refer to Figure 2.19 for a photograph of a USB-to-RJ45 (Ethernet) dongle.

Mobile Serial Ports

Single-board computers and microcontrollers like Arduino, Dwengo, and Raspberry Pi are small devices that have integrated ports and expansion capabilities and may include 9-pin male or female RS232 serial ports (see Figure 10.23). Other handheld mobile or network devices might also have serial ports. Use a serial-to-USB converter (refer to Figure 2.29) to transfer data from such a device to a computer. There are also devices that allow multiple serial connections to attach to a wired Ethernet network.

FIGURE 10.23 RS232 ports

Mobile Device Wireless Connectivity

The whole purpose of having a mobile device is to be able to move around with it. However, mobility is only part of the picture. The other part involves connecting to some type of network, such as a cellular, satellite (for GPS), wireless (Wi-Fi), or Bluetooth network.

Note that because Android devices are created using an open source operating system, configuration options can be different from one device to another. Apple and Windows have different versions of their mobile operating systems. By default, when most mobile devices are configured for wireless networks, the devices connect. If you walk out of range of a wireless network and another one is configured, your device is likely to switch over to the second wireless network. If no wireless networks are within range, the mobile device switches over to the cellular network if you are connected to it.

Bluetooth

Bluetooth is a radio-based wireless technology used to connect two or more devices that are within close range of one another. This type of connectivity is called a wireless personal area network (PAN). Bluetooth operates in the unlicensed 2.4 GHz range. Bluetooth includes 128-bit security and supports a data rate up to 24 Mb/s. Up to eight devices can be connected. Bluetooth has three classes of devices:

- *Class 1:* Range up to 328 feet (100 meters)
- *Class 2:* Range up to 33 feet (10 meters)
- *Class 3:* Range up to 3 feet (1 meter)

Note that the Bluetooth 5 standard supports a longer range of up to 800 feet (242 meters). The Bluetooth standards do not define the maximum range. Rather, the range depends on the type of Bluetooth radio installed. Most mobile devices use a Class 2 radio but seldom can have connectivity more than 33 feet away.

Many mobile devices support Bluetooth. Refer to Figure 10.9 to see a Bluetooth headset used with a cell phone. Figure 10.24 shows controls in a car to enable Bluetooth connectivity. The Bluetooth symbol is shown in Figure 10.25.

FIGURE 10.24 Enabling Bluetooth connectivity

FIGURE 10.25 Bluetooth symbol

The basic concept behind configuring Bluetooth is that each device must have Bluetooth enabled and must "pair," or connect, with another Bluetooth-enabled device. Once enabled, Bluetooth broadcasts a wireless signal that other Bluetooth-enabled devices can detect. The basic steps for configuration are as follows:

Step 1. Enable Bluetooth.

Step 2. Ensure that pairing is enabled.

Step 3. Pair with another Bluetooth-enabled device.

Step 4. Enter the security PIN code.

Step 5. Test connectivity.

To enable Bluetooth on an Android phone, you can swipe from the top and tap the *Bluetooth* icon. On an iPhone, swipe up from the bottom edge of the screen to display the *Control Center*. Then tap the *Bluetooth* button to enable/disable it.

Laptops frequently use a function (Fn) key along with a key that has the Bluetooth symbol (F1–F12) to activate Bluetooth. In Windows, search for **`bluetooth`** > *Change Bluetooth Settings* option > *Options* tab > ensure that the *Allow Bluetooth Devices to Find This Computer* checkbox is enabled.

Table 10.8 shows basic Bluetooth configurations for the various operating systems after a device is powered on and ready for pairing.

TABLE 10.8 Bluetooth installation steps

Windows	Apple iOS	Android
Ensure that Bluetooth is enabled. Use the *Add a Bluetooth device* link > select the device > *Next*. If the device is a Bluetooth printer, use the *Add a printer or scanner* link. You may have to enter a passkey or PIN.	Access *Settings* > *General* > *Bluetooth* > *ON*. In the *Devices* field, you should see the name of the device. Select the device > *Pair*. You may have to enter a passkey or PIN.	Access *Settings* > *Wireless and Network* > *Bluetooth Settings*. Ensure that Bluetooth is enabled > *Scan Devices*. Select the device once it appears > *Accept*. You may have to enter a passkey or PIN.

Laptops commonly have Bluetooth installed. To determine whether Bluetooth is installed in Windows, open the *Devices* Settings option. If Bluetooth is installed, a Bluetooth on/off setting appears. Bluetooth can be used to share photos or files between Android devices. To share a photo, open the photo and tap the *Share* icon > *Bluetooth* and select the Bluetooth device to share with. To share a file, open *File Manager* and select the file > tap the *Share* icon > *Bluetooth* and select the device to share with.

If a device does not have Bluetooth capability or if the Bluetooth circuitry fails and the device has a USB port, a USB-to-Bluetooth adapter can be obtained and used. Plug the dongle into a USB port on your laptop. In Windows, use the *Settings* > *Devices* > *Bluetooth* option. Your Bluetooth device displays > select *Next* > follow any additional instructions such as entering a PIN. Be sure to follow the manufacturer's directions.

IEEE 802.11 Wireless

The 802.11 wireless standard is used when connecting a mobile device to a wireless network that operates in the **2.4 GHz** and/or **5 GHz** range. A wireless access point is used to coordinate and connect multiple wireless devices in the immediate area. Data rates depend on the distance from the access point and what type of walls and materials are between the mobile device and the access point. 802.11 wireless networks are commonly referred to as Wi-Fi. Table 10.9 shows the 802.11 standards related to wireless and the frequency range/speed used with each type.

TABLE 10.9 IEEE 802.11 wireless standards

Standard	Frequency range and speed
802.11a	5 GHz up to 54 Mb/s
802.11b	2.4 GHz up to 11 Mb/s
802.11g	2.4 GHz up to 54 Mb/s
802.11n	2.4 GHz and 5 GHz up to 600 Mb/s
802.11ac (Wi-Fi 5)	5 GHz up to 1+ Gb/s
802.11ax (Wi-Fi 6)	2.4, 5, and 6 GHz up to 14 Gb/s

The reason it is important to know the frequency is so you can determine whether a mobile device can attach to the wireless network. If an 802.11n access point is used, it has the capability to be programmed in both the 2.4 and 5 GHz ranges, but someone could just configure it to operate in one of these ranges, such as 2.4 GHz. That would mean a mobile device would have to support the 802.11b, 802.11g, or 802.11n standard. The access point could also be configured to support only 802.11n devices (but this is not common except perhaps within a company). The more devices that connect and transmit/receive data on a wireless network, the worse the network's performance. Some access points allow a limited number of wired connections in addition to all the wireless devices connected to it, as shown in Figure 10.26.

FIGURE 10.26 IEEE 802.11 wireless network

To configure a wireless mobile device for IEEE 802.11 wireless networking, ensure that the *Wi-Fi* option is enabled. The basic configuration steps for accessing 802.11 wireless networks are as follows:

Step 1. Enable Wi-Fi through the device's *Settings* option.

Step 2. Select the Wi-Fi wireless network to join.

Step 3. Enter the security password, if required.

For a wireless network that does not broadcast the SSID (see Chapter 13, "Networking," for more information on that), the network can be manually configured on a mobile device. To manually add a wireless network on an Android device, use *Settings > Add Network* and manually enter the SSID, security type, and password. Similarly, on an iOS device, use *Settings > Wi-Fi* and follow the same process.

If the 802.11 Wi-Fi circuitry fails or is unavailable on a mobile device, and the device has a USB port, a USB Wi-Fi network card (see Figure 10.27) can be obtained and installed.

FIGURE 10.27 USB wireless NIC

Airplane Mode

Airplane Mode allows you to disable all wireless communication: Wi-Fi, mobile broadband, Bluetooth, GPS or GNSS (Global Navigation Satellite System), and NFC. In this mode, you can still view a movie or play a game, as long as doing so does not require internet, cellular, or wireless connectivity. To turn on Airplane Mode, use the *Settings > Airplane Mode* option. Airplane Mode saves on power, secures your mobile device because no wireless communication can occur, and is used on airplanes (hence the name) and in other communication-sensitive situations.

Table 10.10 lists the basic network connectivity configuration options for Android and Apple iOS devices.

TABLE 10.10 Mobile device network configuration options

Connectivity method	Android	iOS
802.11 wireless	*Settings > Wireless and Networks > Wi-Fi*	*Settings > Wi-Fi*
Bluetooth	*Settings > Wireless and Networks > Bluetooth*	*Settings > Bluetooth*

Connectivity method	Android	iOS
Cellular	*Settings > Wireless and Networks > More Networks > Mobile Networks*	*Settings > General > Cellular Data*
GPS	*Settings > Location Services > Location*	*Settings > Location*
Airplane Mode	*Settings > Wireless and Networks > Flight Mode > Airplane Mode*	*Settings > Privacy > Location Services*

Hotspot/Tethering

A Wi-Fi **hotspot** is a wireless network that provides internet access. Hotspots can be found in cities, parks, stores, restaurants, hotels, libraries, government buildings, airports, and schools; they can also be made through cell phones or cell provider devices. Security can be a concern with hotspots if no encryption or authentication is required.

To configure an Android device as a hotspot, access *Settings > Hotspot > Configure*. For an iPhone, access *Settings > General > About* and name the personal hotspot; then return to *Settings* and turn on *Personal Hotspot* and configure password settings.

Another way of gaining access to the internet is through tethering. Say you are at a gas station and need to look up something on the internet on your PC. There is no free Wi-Fi in the area, but your phone has internet connectivity. In such a case, you can get access the internet on the PC by tethering it to your phone. **Tethering** allows sharing of an internet connection with other mobile devices in the nearby area. Tethering might also be considered to be a hotspot. Common methods of using tethering are through Bluetooth, Wi-Fi, or a wired USB connection. Some phone vendors charge for the tethering option.

Configure tethering on an Android device by using the *Settings > Wireless & Networks* option. Then select whether you are using USB, Wi-Fi, or Bluetooth to tether. On an iPhone, access *Settings* > enable *Personal Hotspot* > the directions for connecting through Wi-Fi, Bluetooth, and USB appear. Figure 10.28 shows wired tethering through USB and the concept of wireless tethering. Note that companies might implement bandwidth throttling to limit the amount of data sent over the corporate wireless network.

FIGURE 10.28 Wireless tethering

Radio Frequency Identification (RFID)

With radio frequency identification (**RFID**), wireless radio waves are used to locate something. RFID is used to track and locate shipped goods or items in a warehouse, clothing in a store, pets, and people. RFID tags are also used in devices that mount in cars and are used for toll collection as the cars pass through toll booths.

RFID tags can be active or passive. An active tag has a battery and periodically sends out a signal. A passive tag does not have a battery and gets its power from the RFID reader. Figure 10.29 shows an RFID tag like one you might have seen in your textbook when you bought it.

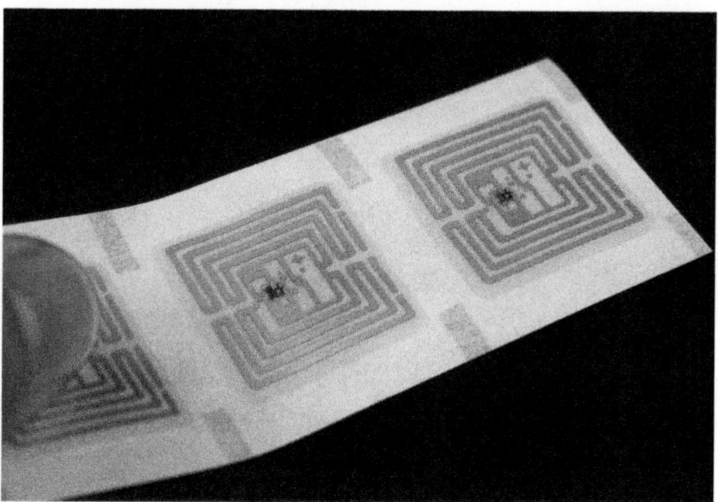

FIGURE 10.29 RFID tag

Near Field Communication (NFC)

Near field communication (**NFC**) is a radio-based wireless technology similar to RFID that allows two devices that are close together in proximity to exchange information either by being near and doing a tap, bumping the two devices, or swiping the device against an NFC reader/scanner. There are three modes of NFC operation:

> *NFC card emulation:* Enables a mobile device to act like a smart card and perform business transactions such as wireless payment-related or ticket purchases, display, inspection, or invalidation transactions
> *NFC reader/writer:* Allows an NFC device to read information from a tag
> *NFC peer-to-peer:* Allows two NFC-enabled devices to exchange information

The devices must be within close proximity of one another (1.5 inches or less) which in itself is a security feature; in addition, a user has to initiate the payment process within the mobile device and sometimes has to use **two-factor authentication** with a passcode and/or **biometric** features such as a fingerprint or face scan. Be sure to put security features in place with any device used for NFC; for example, use a password on the device, don't store username or login information within the mobile device, and have antivirus/anti-malware software installed.

NFC is also used to allow keyless entry into cars, buildings, and rooms; connect speakers; and provide wireless charging. If your phone has NFC capability and your printer supports NFC, then you can stand next to the printer, tap the *Print* option, and send something to the printer. Figure 10.30 shows someone making a payment for purchases by using an NFC-enabled smartphone. Note that NFC transactions are secure and commonly include a haptic (vibration) and/or audio feedback indicating that a transaction has occurred.

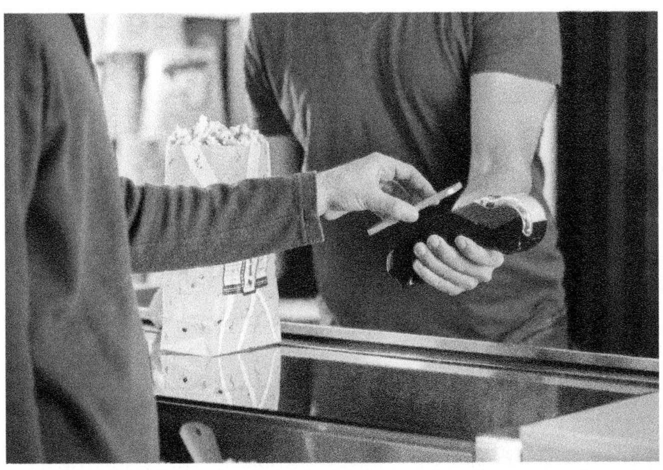

FIGURE 10.30 NFC transaction

To configure an Android device for NFC, go to *Settings > NFC* and ensure that it is turned on. To be able to pay using your phone, you need to have an app such as Google Wallet or Samsung Pay installed. To configure an iOS device for NFC and Apple Pay, go to *Settings > Wallet & Apple Pay* > add a credit or debit card and follow the directions for the type of card chosen.

Infrared

Infrared (**IR**) is a radio-based wireless technology that operates in the 300 GHz to 430 THz range, but many devices use either 2.4 GHz or 27 MHz. IR is used for very short distances and is cheaper than other wireless technologies. IR requires line of sight; anything from a human to a chair can get in the way and cause lack of connectivity. For that reason, IR is commonly used for short distances to connect wireless devices such as motion detectors, intrusion detectors, TV remotes, hand scanners, a mouse, or a keyboard.

Cellular Data

Cellular data usage is usually tracked, and unless you have an unlimited data plan, charged for. Cellular data is any type of data sent over a cellular network. Two methods for sending data over a cellular network are Short Message Service (SMS) and Multimedia Message Service (MMS). SMS is used for text messages. MMS is used for visual data such as photos or video.

Many phone providers charge for these services, so some users disable them. On an iOS device, use *Settings > General > Cellular Data*. On an Android device, access *Wireless and Networks Settings > Mobile Networks > Data*. A **data cap** is a limit on the amount of data that can be used by an internet subscriber. Some vendors throttle or slow down internet access once the data cap has been reached, and some impose additional fees. Using nearby wireless networks for data transmission instead of the cellular network helps with reducing cellular data usage.

Mobile apps can be set to use cellular data, and a high number of ads will increase data usage. To block ads on an Android, use *Settings > Site settings > Pop-ups and redirects > Ads blocked*. For an iPhone or iPad, use *Settings > Privacy > Apple Advertising*. You can also use an ad blocker.

Mobile Device Email Configuration

Many people want to check their email on a mobile device. Email can be accessed and delivered using a variety of protocols, including the following:

- *Post Office Protocol version 3 (***POP3***):* Used to retrieve email using TCP port 110; saves email to the local device.

> *Internet Message Access Protocol* (**IMAP**)*:* Used to retrieve email using TCP port 143; good when two or more people check the same account or a user wants email access from multiple devices.

> *Secure Sockets Layer (SSL)/Transport Layer Security (TLS):* Used to encrypt data between an email client and the email server.

> *Simple Mail Transfer Protocol (SMTP):* An older protocol used to send emails using TCP port 25.

> *Multipurpose Internet Mail Extensions (MIME) and Secure MIME (S/MIME):* Used along with SMTP so that pictures and attachments are supported; S/MIME allows encryption and signing of MIME data.

> *Exchange Online:* Microsoft's application that uses the messaging application programming interface (MAPI) to connect to Microsoft Exchange servers for email, calendar, and contact information. Microsoft supports storing copies of messages or calendar events in personal storage table (`.pst`) files, such as when items from the Microsoft Exchange server are archived and stored locally.

The email server used determines which email client may be used on a mobile device. Several key pieces of information are commonly needed to configure the client (see Table 10.11). Some organizations configure the email server to support autoconfiguration (sometimes called autodiscovery) so that all you have to enter is a username and password, and all of the other configuration parameters are automatically provided to the device. Not all email client apps support autoconfiguration. You might have to get the email configuration parameters from the IT support staff, an FAQ page, or a website.

TABLE 10.11 Email configuration parameters

Parameter	Description
Email address	The address used to send you an email, such as cheryl.schmidt@gmail.com.
Email protocol	The protocol(s) used to send and receive email.
Server name or host name	The name of the incoming or outgoing mail server (which you can get from network staff).
Username	The name assigned to you by the company that hosts the email server. This may be your email address.
Password	The password used in conjunction with a username to access an email account.
Domain	The network domain name.
SSL/TLS	Secure Sockets Layer (SSL)/Transport Layer Security (TLS), when enabled, is used to encrypt data between the mobile device and the email server.

Most mobile devices include email configuration as part of the mobile OS. Common email providers include Yahoo, Outlook, AOL Mail, Microsoft Exchange (included with Microsoft 365) Google/Inbox, and iCloud, as well as other commercial email providers, such as Zoho Mail, GMX Mail, Guerrilla Mail, Chimpmail, and Proton Mail.

When you first configure an Android device, you are prompted to either enter your Google account information or create a Google account. The email app that comes with the phone simply opens Gmail. You can add an account by selecting *Settings > Email* option. Use the *Personal (IMAP/POP)* option for selecting which protocol is used to access email. Use the *Exchange* option for configuring Microsoft Exchange.

Similarly, on Apple iOS devices, use *Settings* > *Passwords & Accounts* (or *Mail, Contacts, Calendars* on older versions, as in Figure 10.31) > select *Add Account* > select the particular type of account desired (Exchange, Google, Yahoo, and so on).

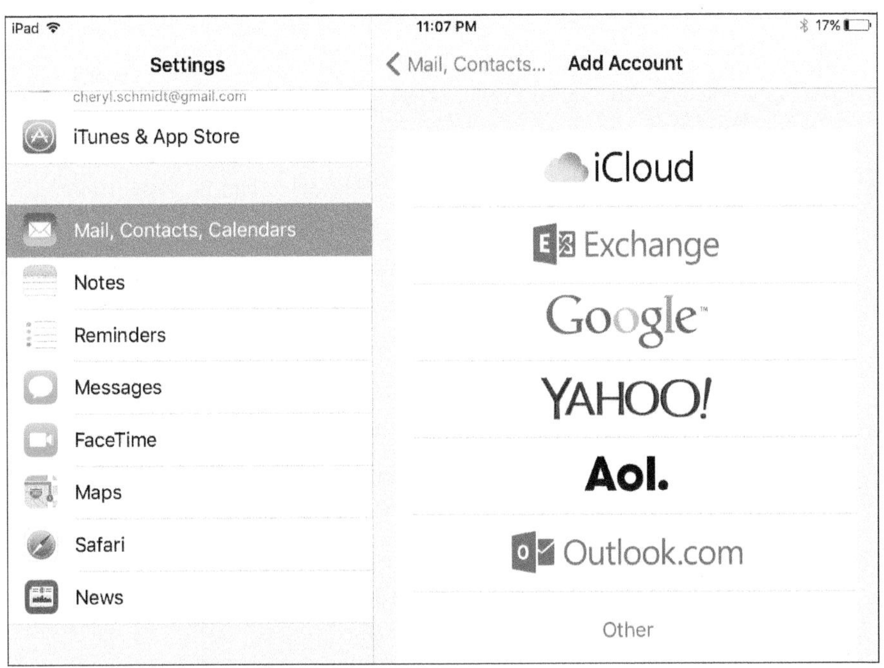

FIGURE 10.31 Email configuration on an iOS device

Mobile Device Synchronization and Backup

Synchronization means making the same data available on multiple devices and/or at multiple locations. This is sometimes known as a **remote backup**, cloud backup, or cloud storage. The types of data synchronized include personal contacts, applications, email, pictures, music, videos, calendar appointments, browser bookmarks, documents, folders, location data, social media data, e-books, and passwords.

Synchronization makes life easier because you do not have to log in to a work computer or bring up a web browser in order to see what is scheduled tomorrow. You can also synchronize your fitness results and maintain them on both your cell phone and mobile fitness device or smart watch.

TECH TIP

Think before you sync

Be careful about synchronizing cached passwords (that is, passwords you have directed the browser, operating system, or app to save) across the cloud as such transmissions can have security ramifications. There are also issues syncing music files due to file formats and multiple platforms (Apple, PC, car, mobile device, for example). Be sure to research your synchronization method.

Synchronization Methods

Synchronization can be done through a particular operating system, browser, email provider, applications, and/or third-party vendors. For example, Microsoft uses **ActiveSync** to synchronize data such as files and website bookmarks between a mobile device and Windows desktop computer.

Exchange ActiveSync is used to synchronize a person's contacts, calendar, and email. Use *Settings > Mail > Accounts* on an iPhone or iPad to configure Exchange ActiveSync. Use *Settings > Accounts > Sync* on an Android device to configure it.

People commonly use one or more of the following synchronization methods for mobile devices:

> *Synchronize to the cloud:* It is possible to store data in a remote location where it can be viewed, retrieved, saved, shared, and/or forwarded based on the cloud vendor used and user preferences (see Figure 10.32).

> *Synchronize to the desktop:* A mobile device can be synchronized with one or more desktop computers using an app, software, the operating system, or a combination of these.

> *Synchronize to the automobile:* It is possible to connect and synchronize a Bluetooth headset, smartphone, or other mobile device to a car. A Ford vehicle, for example, can sync to a cell phone, and the address book is transferred to the car and kept in an internal database. Many vehicles support text-to-speech and can read text messages.

Note that whichever type is used, it is important that the software requirements needed to install the app and actually synchronize the data are met on each of the devices that have data to be synchronized.

FIGURE 10.32 Synchronization to the cloud

TECH TIP

Use vCards for syncing contacts

A vCard (also known as a virtual contact file [VCF]) is used for electronic contact information; it is basically an e-business card. A vCard file can have the extension `.vcf` or `.vcard`. If a vCard is imbedded in an email, you can normally right-click on it and add to your contacts.

Synchronization Connection Types

In order for devices to synchronize data, they have to establish connectivity with each other. Synchronization commonly occurs using one of three types of connections:

- *Wired USB connection:* Two devices may attach to one another using a USB port on each device. An example is an iOS device connected via USB to a computer and using iTunes to synchronize music.
- *Wireless connection:* Devices can attach to one another using any wireless method, including 802.11 Wi-Fi connections and cellular networks.
- *Wired network connection:* Devices can attach to a wired network and access the internet and a cloud-based solution through a web browser.

Figure 10.33 shows synchronization between a mobile phone and a desktop computer.

FIGURE 10.33 Synchronization between a mobile phone and a PC

Synchronization on Android Devices

Google software is commonly used to synchronize data between an Android device and other devices. Google Drive can be used to store and share documents for free. The Google Chrome browser allows synchronization of bookmarks. Google Photos allows storage and sharing of photos. When you use Google software to synchronize, an Android user authenticates once in order to access multiple services. This is known as mutual authentication for multiple services or single sign-on (SSO), and it is available through the other mobile operating systems as well. When you use a third-party product to synchronize data, you may be required to install an app on one or more mobile devices and PCs.

An Android device is configured with a Google ID and password using the *Settings* > *Accounts* option, and then the three vertical dots in the top-right corner can be tapped to select what to synchronize. Figure 10.34 shows the synchronization settings for email (which is turned on).

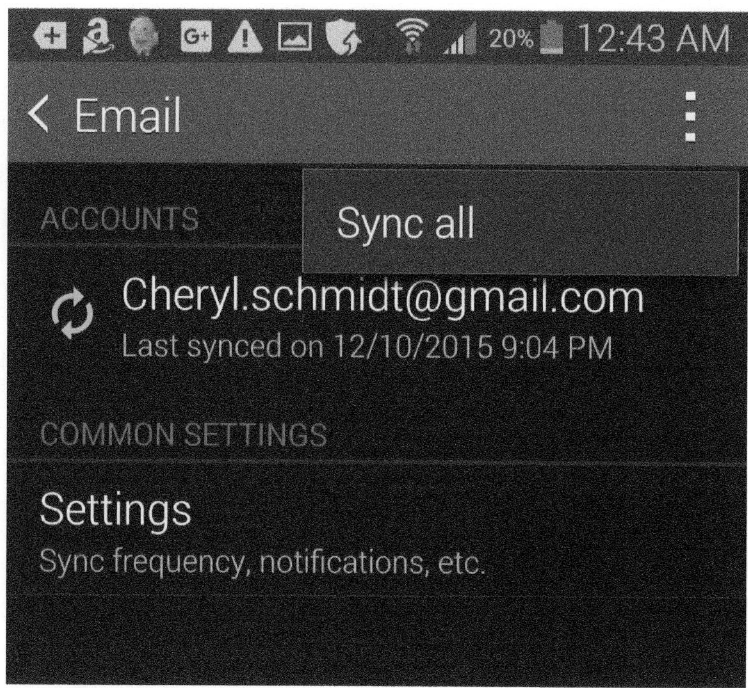

FIGURE 10.34 Android email synchronization

Synchronization on iOS Devices

iOS devices can use Google Gmail and other apps to synchronize Google contacts and calendar. An individual app may also support synchronization with Google. You can view and add apps by using *Settings* > *Personal* (which is not used on some Android devices) > *Accounts and Sync* or whatever method is used by the particular application.

However, iOS users tend to use Apple solutions, such as iCloud and iTunes, for synchronization. iCloud is used to store, share, and manage data from any device, including contacts, calendar, ringtones, photos/videos, and data. Apple provides iCloud Photo Library for photos and video and iCloud Drive for document storage. Apple provides free storage with the option to pay for more. A Windows device requires download and installation of iCloud for Windows in order to access data stored there. Figure 10.35 shows the configuration for iCloud on an iOS device.

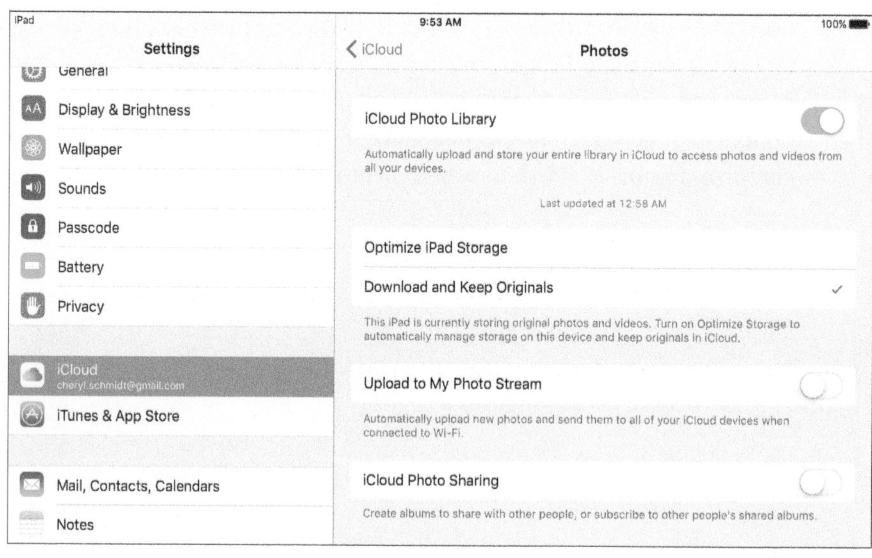

FIGURE 10.35 iCloud configuration screen

iTunes can be used to synchronize Apple devices and to play and manage music, video, books, and lectures. iTunes used to require a USB connection between a mobile device and a PC or Mac but now supports Wi-Fi connectivity. Through iTunes, you can back up personal data (settings, messages, voicemails, and so on) and the Apple device operating system.

iTunes has a 64-bit version for Windows. There is no such application for Android devices. However, you can connect an Apple mobile device to an Android device and use the Android *File Transfer* app to transfer files such as music files (found on the Apple device in the folder *Music > iTunes > iTunes Media*).

To use iTunes, open it from an Apple device that runs macOS or connect the Apple device to a computer or PC. Select the device by choosing the correct device icon in the upper-left corner of the iTunes window. In the left panel of the *Settings* area are various sections (such as Music, Movies, TV Shows, Info, Podcasts, iTunes U, Books, AudioBooks, Tones, and Photos), based on the types of items in the iTunes library. Each section can be accessed to sync that particular type of content. iTunes cannot sync browser email accounts, bookmarks, and other such information.

Backup and Restore Overview

Synchronization of apps is one way of backing up information, but it doesn't provide an operating system backup. A mobile device should have the system backed up in case of an operating system update failure, a virus infection, or inability to remove malware. Apps are available that allow you to remotely back up a mobile device. Backup and restore techniques are just as important in the mobile environment as they are in the desktop arena.

Android-Based Backup and Restore

Android devices have different backup options based on the type of data you want to back up and/or restore. Table 10.12 lists the major ones.

TABLE 10.12 Android backup options

Type of data to back up	Method
Photos/videos	Use Auto Backup. Open *Google Photos* app > top left, access the menu icon (three horizontal bars) > *Settings* > *Back Up & Sync* > enable or disable. Important note: Turning off the backup settings affects all apps that use Back Up & Sync, such as Google Drive.
Files, folders, images, videos	Use Google Drive. Open a web browser and go to https://drive.google.com. Use the menu to create new folders or upload files or drag and drop files/folders into the window.
Data	Use Android Backup Service: *Settings* > *Backup and Reset* > enable *Back up my data*. Figure 10.36 shows this screen.

The Android Backup Service backs up the following data and settings: Google Calendar, Wi-Fi networks and passwords, home screen wallpaper, Gmail settings, apps installed through Google Play and backed up using the Play Store app, display settings, language settings, input settings, date and time, and some third-party app settings and data.

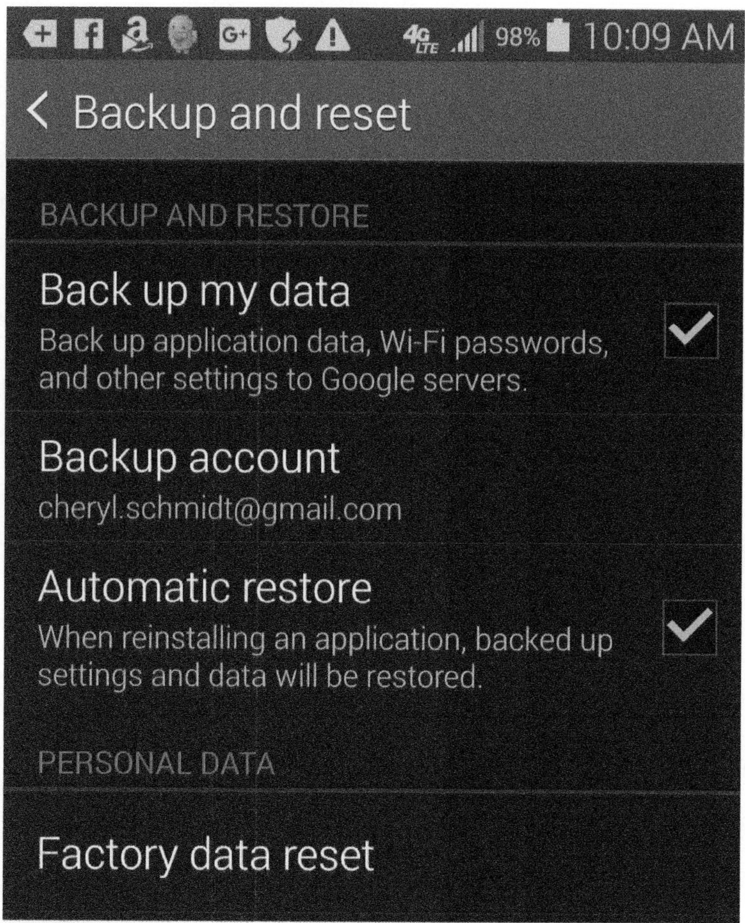

FIGURE 10.36 Android Backup and Reset screen

Notice in Figure 10.36 that you can also use this screen to perform a factory reset. A **factory reset** is used when a device cannot be repaired using any other method. As the name of the option implies, it resets the mobile device to the original settings. Android phones keep the OS separate from the apps and data. The OS is read-only. A factory reset resets only the apps and data. That is why you need to back them up. Generic steps to back up an Android-based mobile device are as follows:

Step 1. Boot the device into *Recovery Mode*, which is typically accessed by holding down two or more specific buttons (such as the power, volume, and/or home buttons) while the device boots. See the mobile device manufacturer's website for specific instructions.

Step 2. From the boot menu, select *Backup & Restore > Backup*.

Step 3. When the backup is complete, restart the device and boot normally.

The generic steps for the restore process are as follows:

Step 1. Boot the device into *Recovery Mode*.

Step 2. From the boot menu, select *Backup & Restore > Restore*.

Step 3. When the restore is complete, reboot the device to ensure that it boots normally.

Note that there are other apps that can be used to back up the operating system and the installed apps.

iOS-Based Backup and Restore Overview

With iOS you can back up your operating system using iCloud or iTunes. If you use iCloud, the backup is stored in the cloud (up to 5 GB free at press time), it is encrypted, and it can be accomplished wirelessly. With iTunes, the backup is stored on a Mac or PC, the storage limit is based on storage available on that Mac or PC, and encryption is optional.

iCloud Backup and Restore Overview

iCloud backups do not include data that is already in the cloud, data from other cloud services, Apple Pay information, Touch ID, or content that you got from other vendors (even if available in iTunes or Books). In order to make a backup using iCloud, ensure that the device connects to a Wi-Fi network > *Settings* > *iCloud Backup/Storage & Backup* > enable (turn on) *iCloud Backup* > *Back Up Now*.

You can verify that the backup is stored by using the following steps: *Settings* > *iCloud* > *Storage* > *Manage Storage* > select the device. The details shown include the date, time, and backup file size. Backups are automatically made on a daily basis if the device meets the following criteria:

- The device connects to a power source.
- The device connects to a Wi-Fi network.
- The device has a locked screen
- iCloud storage space is available.

To reset and restore an iOS device using iCloud, follow these generic steps:

Step 1. Boot the device and look for a hello screen. Note that if the device is still functional, you cannot restore from an iCloud backup if the device is configured. Use the *Settings > Erase All Content and Settings option* to wipe the device.

Step 2. Follow the directions on how to set up the device, including the requirement of joining a Wi-Fi network.

Step 3. Select *Restore from an iCloud Backup* and sign in to iCloud.

Step 4. Select a backup. Do not disconnect from the Wi-Fi network. Note that this may take a period of time.

iTunes Backup and Restore Overview

Use the following steps to make a backup of an iOS device using iTunes:

Step 1. Open the iTunes application on a Mac or PC.

Step 2. Connect the iOS device to the Mac or PC, using a USB cable. The device icon should display in the top-left corner, as shown in Figure 10.37.

Step 3. Make a backup of content downloaded from the iTunes Store or Apple App Store by using *File > Devices > Transfer Purchases*. Note that when the file transfer is complete, you might need to press Ctrl+B.

Step 4. Select whether the backup is to be kept in the cloud (by selecting the *iCloud* radio button) or on the PC or Mac (by selecting the *This Computer* radio button). See Figure 10.37.

Step 5. On a Mac, select *Back Up Now* (as shown in Figure 10.37). On a Windows PC, use *File > Devices > Back Up*.

Step 6. When the process is finished, use the iTunes *Summary* option to see the date and time of the backup. In Windows, use *Preferences > Devices*. If the file is encrypted, you see a lock icon beside the device name.

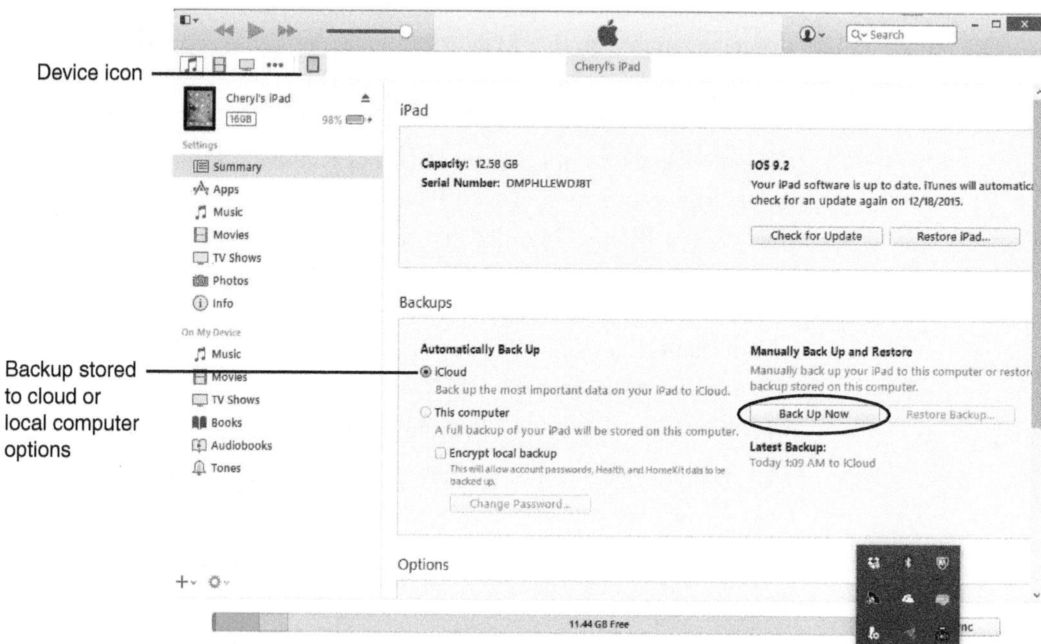

FIGURE 10.37 iTunes backup options

A reinstallation of the operating system is known as a **clean install**. To restore a device using iTunes, connect the device to the Mac or PC that contains the backup using a cable. Open iTunes. Select *File > Devices > Restore from Backup*. Select the latest backup and click *Restore*. Note that the file transfer can take some time.

OneDrive

Microsoft has a product called **OneDrive** that can be used for synchronization and/or backup and restore operations. People who use Microsoft Outlook through an Exchange server from any mobile operating system can save files and photos to OneDrive and then access them through a web browser or mobile device app. Microsoft reserves the right to monitor any content saved in OneDrive and can remove any files that do not adhere to its strict policy.

Other Mobile Software Tools

Mobile devices sometimes require other tools for troubleshooting and management. You might also have to download apps to perform specific tasks or to help with troubleshooting. You might consider installing some of the apps described in the following sections as a standard in a business environment.

Mobile Device Management

Mobile device management (**MDM**) is the ability to view and manage multiple mobile devices (see Figure 10.38). In the corporate environment, mobile devices are challenging for IT staff. Some companies purchase software in order to push updates, track, and remotely wipe data and configurations. Mobile application management (**MAM**) is used to control corporate applications on mobile devices. MAM allows new apps to be pushed out after testing, allows updates to be controlled, and enables additional device management and/or security features such as two-factor authentication where the user has to enter two pieces of information such as a password as well as a code that was texted or emailed to them.

FIGURE 10.38 Mobile device management

The free Apple Configurator app is an example of an MDM product. It allows business support staff to configure settings on iOS-based devices before issuing them to users. Using configuration profiles, IT personnel can install specific iOS versions and ensure that security policies are applied. Apple Configurator can also be used to wipe a device and provide basic management of deployed devices. Similar products can be purchased to allow more corporate management capabilities.

Mobile Antivirus/Anti-malware

Mobile devices can have **malware** (software that causes a device to misbehave or spy on the user) installed just as desktop computers can. See Chapter 18, "Computer and Network Security," for more details on security issues such as malware. Some products, such as Malwarebytes for anti-malware or AVG Antivirus security for multiple security threats, are available for mobile devices. Free versions typically have antivirus and/or anti-malware. Paid versions add features such as app backup, app locks, SIM locking, antitheft, anti-phishing, tracking, and secure web browsing.

App Scanner

One way of preventing malware and preventing apps from revealing your personal information is to install an app scanner. An app scanner is an online tool in which you can type the name of an app to see whether any of your data is at risk and generate a risk score to get an idea of how risky the app is. Other app scanners may be part of security apps, such as Sophos Mobile Security. There are also app scanners that manage particular apps and ensure compliance, cloud-based management for specific mobile devices, and enterprise-based mobile device management.

Wi-Fi Analyzer

A **Wi-Fi analyzer** app (sometimes known as a wireless locator, Wi-Fi scanner, or wireless scanner) is used to identify what wireless networks are in the area and what frequencies (channels) are being used and to find less crowded channels for any wireless installations, hotspot, or tethering that may be needed in a particular area. Some Wi-Fi analyzers give you additional feedback, such as a quality rating based on the channel you might select. One optional feature is a signal meter to see the wireless range of a particular wireless network. Wi-Fi analyzers are particularly useful to technicians in allowing them to identify potential sources of other wireless interference. See Chapter 13 for more detail on wireless networks and wireless configuration. Figure 10.39 shows a Wi-Fi analyzer designed for Windows 10 devices that is available in the Microsoft Store.

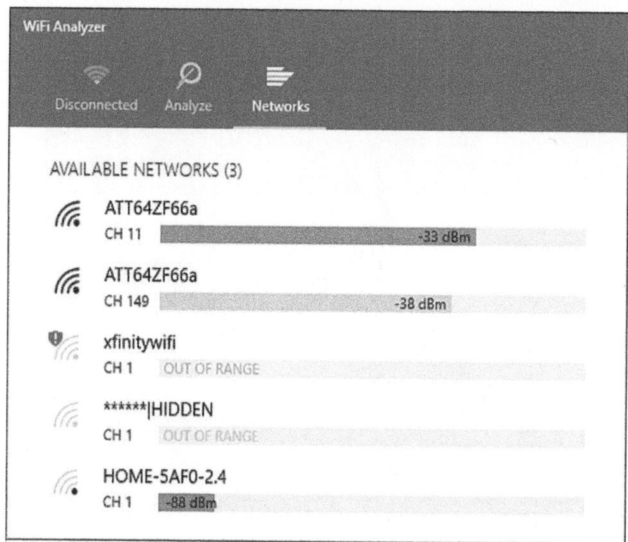

FIGURE 10.39 WiFi Analyzer app screen

Cell Tower Analyzer

A cell tower analyzer app (also known as a cell signal analyzer) provides details about the cell phone network and possibly wireless networks. The information can include signal strength, data state, data activity, mobile network code (MNC), mobile country code (MCC), IP address, roaming state, phone type, and so on. You can use other apps to see all the cell towers in the area in order to get an idea of cell phone coverage in the areas most used.

Laptops Overview

Mobile devices are fun to explore, but let's move on to laptops now. Laptops were the first mobile devices that technicians had to support. They are an integral part of the IT scene. Anyone in an IT position is expected to know some technical laptop basics. Technical support staff are expected to know more. Keep in mind that every laptop is different. Consult a particular computer manufacturer's website for instructions on replacing anything on a laptop.

Laptop Hardware

A laptop has similar parts and ports to a desktop computer, but some of these components are, naturally, smaller. Figure 10.40 shows common laptop parts. Notice in the figure how many of the components are built into the laptop motherboard.

Whenever taking anything out of a laptop, one of the major issues is that tiny screws could be hidden under plastic or rubber caps; most screws are accessible from the bottom of the laptop (see Figure 10.41). Use a magnetic screwdriver to remove the screws or place the screws on a magnetized tray. Some manufacturers label the types of screws or locations for ease of explaining disassembly. Keep like screws together (in containers or an egg carton) and take notes and photos. All the parts are manufacturer dependent, but the following explanation and graphics/photos should help.

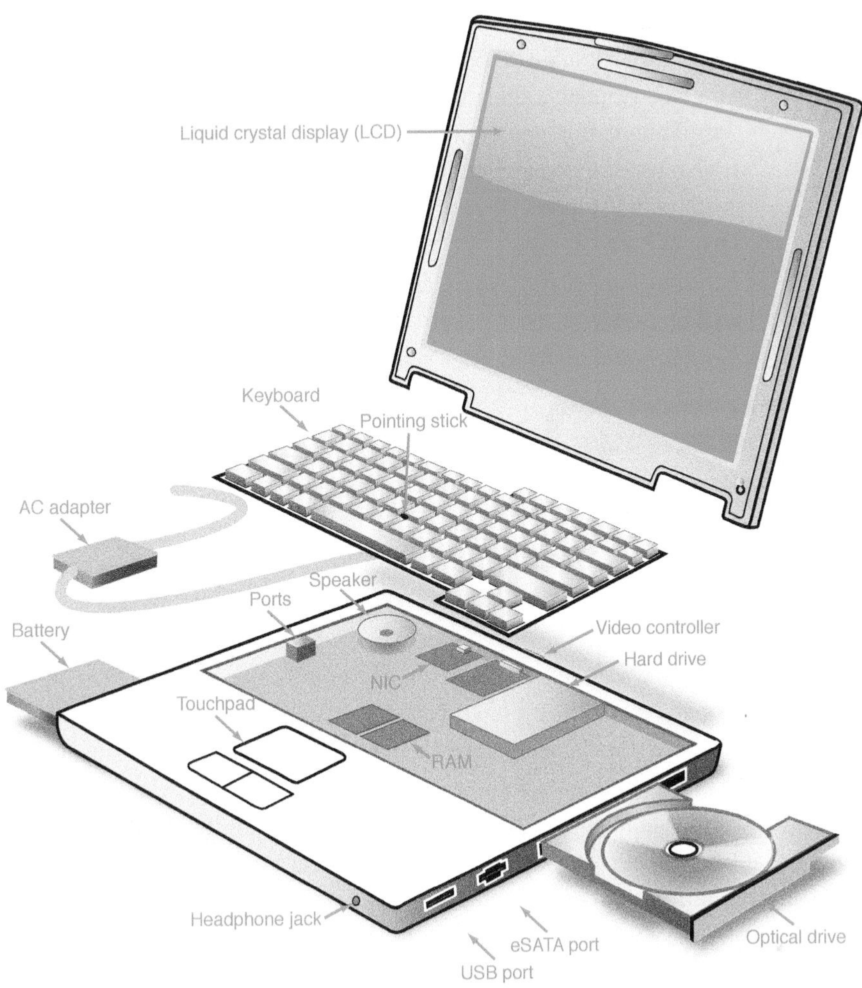

FIGURE 10.40 Laptop parts

FIGURE 10.41 Laptop screws and covers

External Laptop Devices

Laptops might also have external devices attached. The USB port is the port used most commonly for external connectivity. For laptops that do not have a free USB port, you can use an eSATA port for an external device or add a USB hub. Types of external connectivity include the following:

> *External monitor:* An external monitor attaches to a video or USB port. Common video ports on laptops include USB, VGA, HDMI, Thunderbolt, and DisplayPort. HDMI can carry audio and video signals. Thunderbolt can carry not only video but data and power as well. That is why Thunderbolt can be used for other connections besides video connections. Thunderbolt is also used to connect to docking stations (covered next). Some devices have miniature versions of these ports. Figure 10.42 shows the difference between a DisplayPort and a mini DisplayPort.

> *External hard drive:* An external hard drive commonly connects to a USB, Thunderbolt, or eSATA port.

> *External optical drive:* An external optical drive commonly connects to a USB port.

FIGURE 10.42 DisplayPort and mini DisplayPort

Some people like having more expandability when in the office than when traveling with a laptop. For these folks, two devices can help: a docking station and a port replicator. A **laptop docking station** allows a laptop computer to be more like a desktop system. A **docking station** can have ports for charging devices and connections for a full-size monitor, keyboard, mouse, and printer. In addition, a docking station can have expansion slots or cards and storage bays.

Docking stations tend to be vendor proprietary, which means that if you have a particular brand of laptop, you must use the same brand of docking station. Typically, to install a laptop into a docking station, you close the laptop and slide the laptop into the docking station. Figure 10.43 shows the concept of a laptop docking station and the ports that can be found on the back.

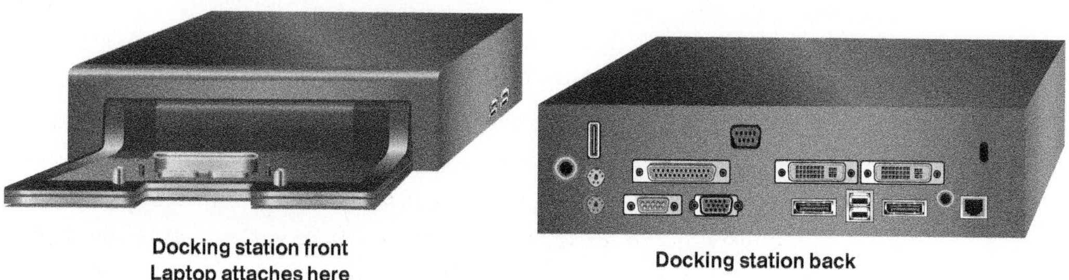

FIGURE 10.43 Laptop docking station

A **port replicator** (see Figure 10.44) is similar to a docking station but does not normally include expansion slots or drive storage bays. A port replicator attaches to a laptop and allows more devices to be connected, such as an external monitor, keyboard, mouse, and printer. Port replicators can be proprietary or may support multiple laptop vendors.

FIGURE 10.44 Port replicator

Other Laptop Expansion Options

Laptops can also be expanded by adding expansion cards. The **miniPCIe** is a 52-pin card that fits in the bottom of a laptop or on the motherboard/system board (but not in a tablet). Two uses are to install a wireless card or a cellular card. A **wireless card** is used to connect a laptop to an IEEE 802.11 or Bluetooth wireless network. A **cellular card** is used to connect a laptop to the cell phone network. Note that some adapters have both wireless and cellular abilities built into the same card. Also, these adapters could be attached via a USB port instead of a miniPCIe adapter.

To install a miniPCIe adapter, you may have to disassemble the laptop or remove a screw from the bottom, as shown in Figure 10.45, or you may have to lift a lid to access the slot. An expansion slot is shown in Figure 10.46.

FIGURE 10.45 Laptop underside

FIGURE 10.46 Laptop adapter

M.2 and NVMe

A type of expansion slot found in both laptops and desktop computers is M.2. The **M.2** expansion slot is quite flexible in that the specification allows different module sizes, including widths of 12, 16, 22, and 30 mm and lengths of 16, 26, 30, 38, 42, 60, 80, and 110 mm. Usually a longer slot allows the short cards to be installed. You will see a card size that is made up of both numbers—for example, 2280. M.2 cards are also keyed, with B, M, and B+M being the most common keys. A card with the B key uses two PCIe lanes, and an M key uses up to four PCIe lanes. Look back at Figure 7.12 in Chapter 7, "Storage Devices," to see this again.

M.2 expansion cards in laptops and desktop computers are used for Wi-Fi, Bluetooth, and cellular network cards as well as solid-state drives (SSDs). The support of various card lengths and advanced technology makes M.2 an attractive expansion capability option for SSDs and cards in all computer systems and mobile devices. Figure 10.47 shows an M.2 Wi-Fi expansion card and an SSD.

SSD storage comes in the form of 2.5-inch cases, mounted on a PCIe card for desktops, on an M.2 card, and on a Non-Volatile Memory Express (**NVMe**) card. For a laptop, an SSD on an NVMe is the fastest option. M.2 and the 2.5-inch case connect to a µSATA (microSATA) connection. The NVMe card uses the PCIe bus and provides a faster connection but is more expensive. Look back at Figure 7.13 to see an NVMe card (and SSD).

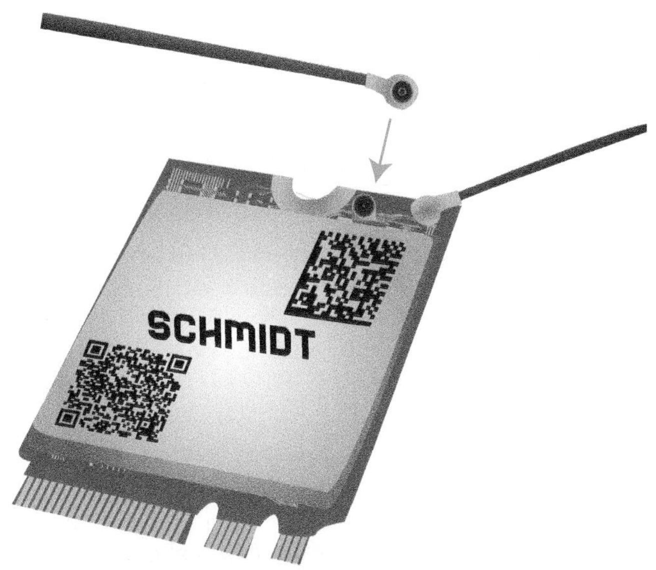

FIGURE 10.47 M.2 wireless card and SSD

Laptop Power

A laptop normally uses a battery as its power source, but a laptop can also be powered through an AC wall outlet connection that recharges the laptop battery. A power adapter (sometimes called a wall adapter) converts the AC power from the wall outlet to DC and connects to the rear of the laptop (near where the battery is located). The port sometimes has a DC voltage symbol below or beside it. This symbol is a solid line with a dashed line below it (⎓). Figure 10.48 shows an example of a power adapter that would be connected between the laptop and the AC outlet and the power connection on a laptop.

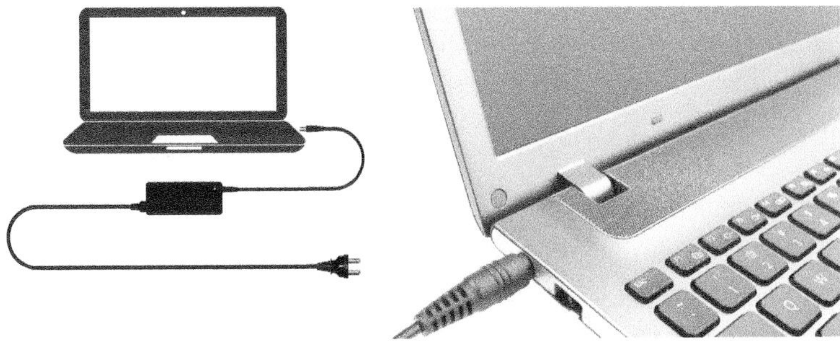

FIGURE 10.48 Laptop power adapter and power connector

When purchasing a new power supply for a laptop or a battery for a mobile device, ensure that it has the same specifications as the one from the manufacturer. Less expensive models might not provide the same quality as approved models. Ensure that the replacement has a power jack that does not wiggle when it is inserted into the device. Ensure that a laptop power brick has the appropriate DC voltage required by the laptop. Current (amperage) should be equal to or greater than in the original power brick.

TECH TIP

Do not power on after a temperature change

Computers are designed to work within a range of temperatures, and sudden change is not good for them. If a mobile device is in a car all night and the temperature drops, allow the device to return to room temperature before powering it on. Avoid direct sunlight. It is usually 40°F hotter inside the computer case than outside it.

Laptop Battery Removal

Laptop batteries fail and have to be replaced. Ensure that you disconnect the AC adapter and power off a laptop before removing the battery. You may have to turn the laptop over to access the battery compartment. Laptop batteries are normally modules that have one or two release latches that are used to remove the module (see Figure 10.49).

FIGURE 10.49 Release latch for laptop battery removal

Laptops and other mobile devices use lithium-ion (Li-ion) batteries, which are very light and can hold a charge longer than any other type. These batteries lose their charge over time, even if they are not being used. Some vendors recommend not leaving a laptop with a Li-ion battery plugged into an AC outlet all the time.

TECH TIP

Keep Li-ion batteries cool

Li-ion batteries last longer if they are kept cool (not frozen). When you store a Li-ion battery, the battery should be only 40% charged and placed in a refrigerator to prolong its life.

Li-ion polymer batteries are similar to other Li-ion batteries except that they are packed in pouched cells. This design allows for smaller batteries and more efficient use of space, which is important in the portable computer and mobile device industries. For environmentalists, the zinc-air battery is the one to watch. AER Energy Resources, Inc., has several patents on a battery that uses oxygen to generate electricity. Another upcoming technology is fuel cells. Fuel cells used for a laptop can provide power for 5 to 10 hours.

Getting the Most from Your Laptop Battery

Mobile devices rely on their batteries to provide mobility. The following tips can help you get more time out of your batteries:

> Most people do not need a spare Li-ion battery. If you are not using a Li-ion battery constantly, it is best not to buy a spare. The longer the spare sits unused, the shorter the life span it will have.
> Buy the battery recommended by the laptop manufacturer.
> For a mobile device or smartphone, use an AC outlet rather than a USB port for faster charging.
> If using a USB port for charging a mobile device or smartphone, unplug all unused USB devices. Note that not all USB ports can provide a charge if the host device is in sleep mode.
> Avoid using an optical player when running on battery power.
> Turn off the wireless adapter if a wireless network is not being used.
> In the power options, configure the mobile device for hibernation rather than standby.
> Save work only when necessary and turn off the autosave feature.
> Reduce the screen brightness.
> Avoid using external USB devices such as flash drives or external hard drives.
> Install more RAM to reduce swapping of information from the hard drive to RAM to CPU or to just be more efficient.
> In mobile devices, keep battery contacts clean with a dab of rubbing alcohol on a lint-free swab once a month.
> Avoid running multiple programs.
> If possible, disable automatic updates.
> Avoid temperature extremes.
> Turn off location services.
> The laptop manufacturer might also support a wireless charging mat that allows a laptop battery to be charged without an AC adapter.

Select the *Power & sleep* Settings Windows link for a laptop: *On battery power, turn off after*, *When plugged in, turn off after*, *On battery power, PC goes to sleep after*, *When plugged in, PC goes to sleep after*, or *When my PC is asleep and on battery power, disconnect from the network*. Users and technicians should adjust these settings to best fit how the laptop or mobile device is used. The *Additional power settings* link opens up the Power Options Control Panel and allows customization of a power plan, as shown in Figure 10.50.

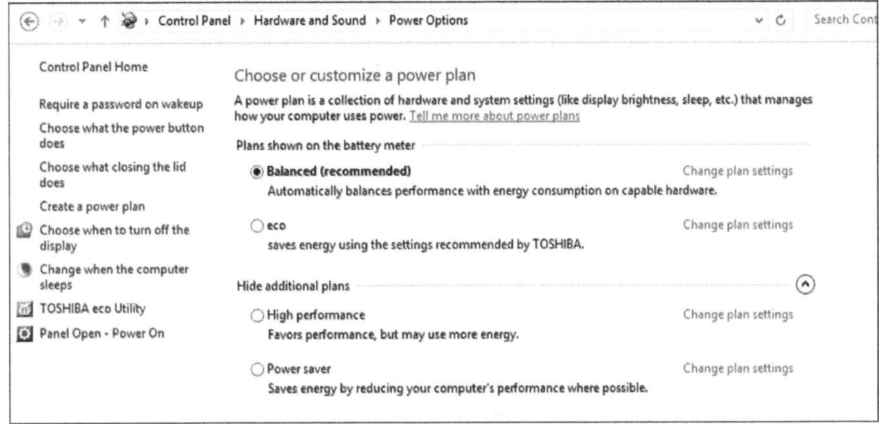

FIGURE 10.50 Laptop power settings

Another way to control the power settings on a Windows laptop is through the battery meter in the bottom-right corner of the screen on the taskbar. By clicking on the meter, you can change the power option or adjust the screen brightness. Figure 10.51 shows the screen that appears when the battery meter icon is clicked.

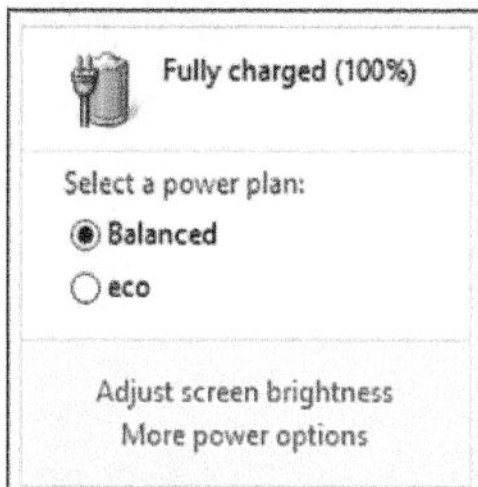

FIGURE 10.51 Laptop battery meter

Laptop Repairs Overview

It is a bit more difficult to get replacement or upgrade parts in a laptop than in a desktop PC because the parts are smaller and a bit different due to manufacturers keeping the laptops light, portable, and maintaining speeds equal to those of desktop computers. Most laptop parts (but not storage devices and memory) are manufacturer dependent. Laptop repairs require more attention to detail than do desktop repairs because there are so many screws, the screws are much smaller, and there is little space in which to work. Be patient. The following is a good list of items to remember when disassembling and reconnecting everything in a laptop:

- Use proper antistatic procedures. There are not always good places to attach an antistatic wrist strap. Consider using antistatic gloves (refer to Figure 5.3). Maintain skin contact when touching parts if no other antistatic tools are used; this is known as self-grounding.
- Organize your parts. Use an egg carton and label individual sections for screws of like length and type, as well as where the screws came from. Otherwise, place like screws on tape sticky side up to and make notes to go with them.
- Take photos.
- Take notes.
- Use appropriate tools. Scribes, described shortly, are very handy when removing plastic pieces. Very thin needle-nose pliers are great with laptop connectors. It is important to have #1 and #0 Phillips screwdrivers.
- Refer to the manufacturer's directions when removing and installing parts. Having a tablet or phone you can use to pull up this documentation while you work is fine. Use your resources. No person can know all models of all machines they work on.

Some laptop and mobile device compartments require levering the compartment cover away from the case or removing plastic parts such as the cover or frame that fits over a mobile computer keyboard. A plastic **scribe** is the best tool to use for this levering. Figure 10.52 shows a plastic scribe being used to lift the plastic part that is between the keyboard and the laptop case.

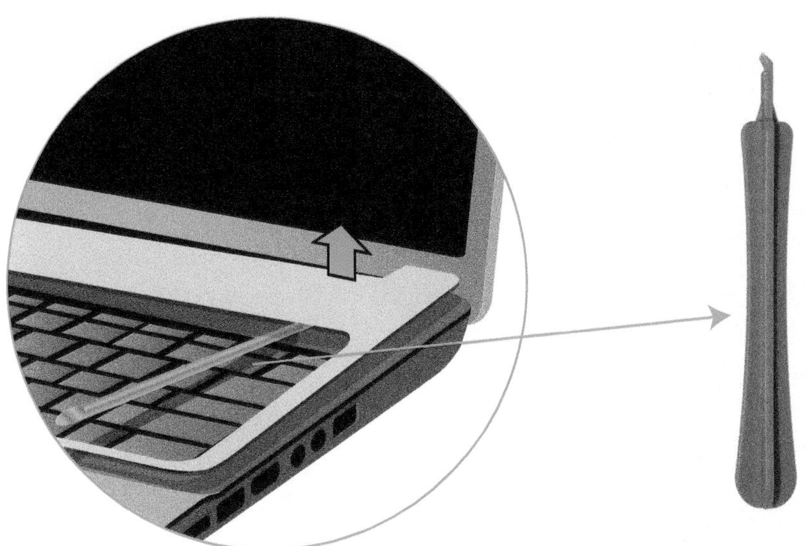

FIGURE 10.52 Plastic scribe

Laptop Motherboard/Processor Replacement

A laptop or **mobile motherboard** (system board) is similar to a desktop motherboard. It holds the majority of the electronics, contains a processor, has memory, is usually vendor specific, and supports having ports attached. The processor on a mobile device is typically not as powerful as the processor on a desktop model, it might have less memory that may not be upgradable, and it has fewer ports. However, some powerful laptops have more power, upgradability, and ports than some low-end desktop models.

In order to get to the motherboard, at a minimum, screws from the underside of the laptop have to be removed. Sometimes a hard drive, a drive that inserts on the side, the keyboard, and memory must be removed before you can remove the motherboard. Figure 10.53 shows a laptop system board.

Before replacing a motherboard, it is important to do all the following:

- Disconnect the AC power connector.
- Remove the battery.
- Disconnect external devices, such as the mouse, keyboard, and monitor.
- Remove adapters.
- Remove memory from expansion slots.
- Disconnect cables, taking care to use any release tabs and not to pull on the cables but on the connector. Needle-nose pliers or tweezers may be needed.
- Remove the optical drive, SSD, and/or hard drive.
- Remove the processor and cooling assembly. Note that this may be done after removing the motherboard. Store the processor in an antistatic bag. It will have to be reinstalled, and some new thermal paste may need to be applied when the new motherboard is installed.
- Remember that replacement motherboards do not come with RAM, a processor, or adapters.
- Make a note or take a photo of the CPU orientation before removing it from the bad/older motherboard.

FIGURE 10.53 Laptop motherboard

Laptop processors are not normally upgraded, but they do sometimes have to be replaced. Refer to the laptop documentation for motherboard removal procedures. Power off a laptop and remove the laptop battery before working inside the machine. Use proper grounding procedures. A laptop processor may have a heat sink and/or fan assembly attached (refer to Figure 10.53). Furthermore, some processor sockets may need to be loosened or a screw may need to be loosened/removed before you lift the processor from the socket, as shown in Figure 10.54. Figure 10.55 shows a processor being removed.

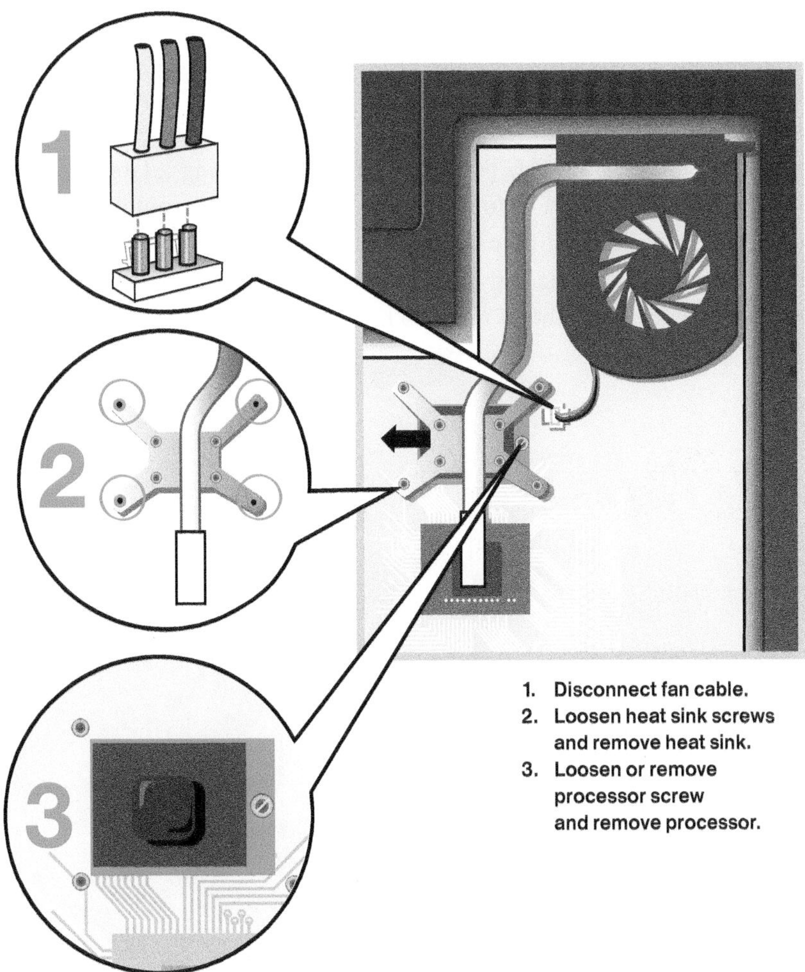

1
2
3
1. Disconnect fan cable.
2. Loosen heat sink screws and remove heat sink.
3. Loosen or remove processor screw and remove processor.

FIGURE 10.54 Laptop processor removal steps

FIGURE 10.55 Laptop processor removed

Laptop Keyboards/Touchpad

Laptops usually have integrated keyboards and a variety of mouse replacement devices, such as a touch stick, touchpad, and/or one or two buttons used for clicking and right-clicking. You should remove the battery and AC power cord before removing a laptop keyboard or any other internal laptop part. To remove a laptop keyboard, you commonly remove screws from the top or bottom of the laptop and slide or lift the keyboard out of the case. Refer to the manufacturer's documentation before removing or replacing a laptop keyboard. Figure 10.56 shows the laptop keyboard removal process. Figure 10.57 shows a laptop keyboard that has been removed.

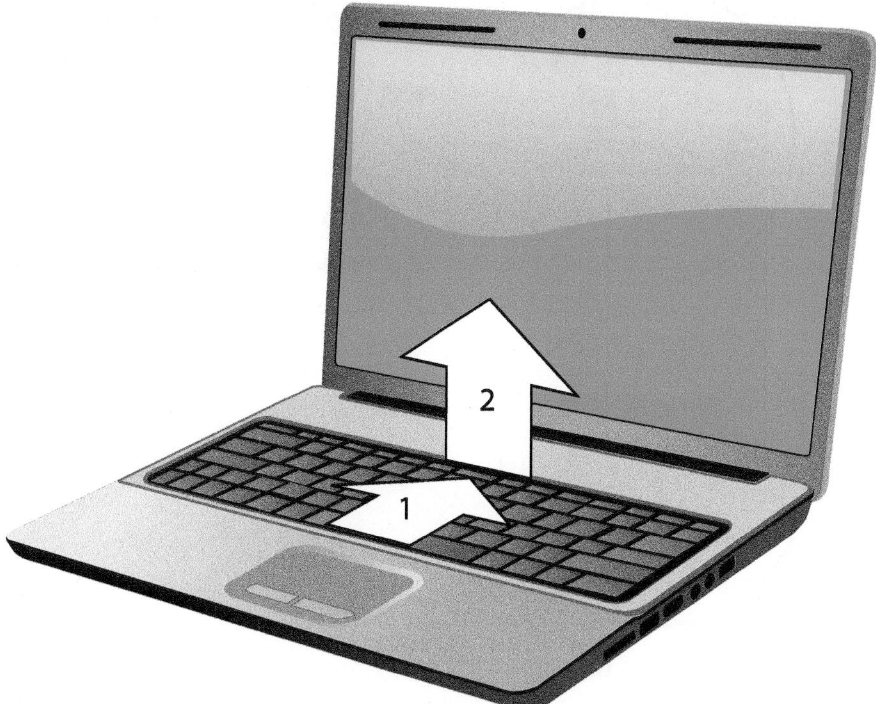

FIGURE 10.56 Laptop keyboard removal process

TECH TIP

These concepts relate to Apple computers, too

Even though this book focuses on PCs, concepts related to CPUs, motherboards, expansion slots, caches, and chipsets also apply to Apple computers. Apple computers and PCs have similar CPU and memory requirements.

Replacing the touchpad or a mouse-like device on a laptop requires a little more work and disassembly than are required for replacing a keyboard. Sometimes an internal drive, memory, the keyboard, the wireless network card, and/or the system board must be removed before you can access the part(s) that hold the touchpad in place. Sometimes the keyboard must be turned upside down to get to the touch stick. Look at Figure 10.57, and you can see the blue touch stick attached to the keyboard.

FIGURE 10.57 Removed laptop keyboard

Touchpads are also sensitive and may need to be adjusted through the operating system during regular use or after replacement. For a Mac, use the Apple icon in the upper-left corner to select *System Preferences > Trackpad*. The touchpad settings in Windows are accessed through either the *Mouse* Control Panel or the *Touchpad* setting, as shown in Figure 10.58. Some vendors have their own touchpad Control Panel.

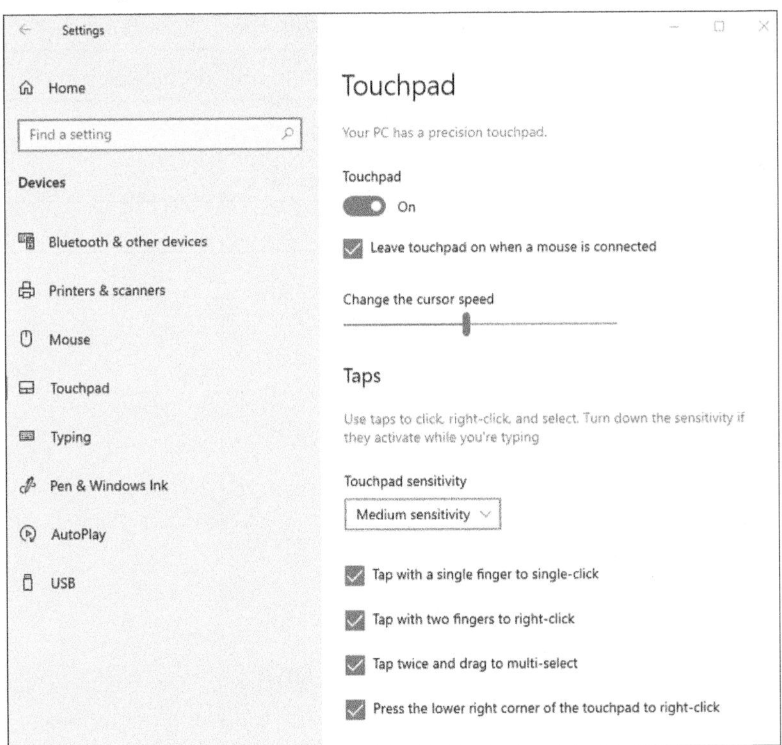

FIGURE 10.58 Touchpad configuration from Windows Settings

TECH TIP

What to do if a laptop keyboard or touchpad goes bad

You can replace mobile keyboards/pointing devices or use external wired or wireless ones.

Laptops have **special function keys**. These keys are in the uppermost part of the keyboard. They are labeled F1, F2, and so on through F10 or F12. They allow you to quickly control screen brightness and hibernation, turn Wi-Fi on/off, mute sound, and perform other functions. For example, on some laptops when you press the Fn key (on the lower-left side of keyboard) while simultaneously pressing the F8 key, your screen brightness increases. Refer to your particular device's user manual or look at the symbols on the keyboard for a clue about what they can do when combined with the Fn key. Table 10.13 lists one vendor's function keys. Figure 10.59 shows a close-up of some of the laptop function keys. See if you can guess what features they perform.

TABLE 10.13 Sample laptop function keys

Fn +____	Description
F1	Mute the speaker
F2	Decrease sound
F3	Increase sound
F4	Turn the system off
F5	Refresh the browser window
F6	Enable/disable the touchpad
F7	Decrease display brightness
F8	Increase display brightness
F9	Switch display output to an external device
F10	Switch power modes
F11	Enable/disable Bluetooth
F12	Enable/disable Wi-Fi

FIGURE 10.59 Laptop special function keys

Other function keys may be available for the following operations:

> Enable/disable cellular
> Enable/disable the touchpad
> Change the screen orientation
> Enable/disable GPS
> Enable/disable Bluetooth
> Enable/disable Airplane Mode
> Enable/disable keyboard backlighting
> Media options such as fast forward and rewind for videos or audio playback

> Video controls such as dual displays, external display, laptop display and external display, and blanking the display (See Figure 10.60 for a couple examples of video controls that require the use of a function key.)

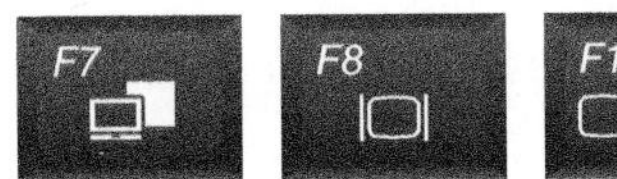

FIGURE 10.60 Laptop video output special function keys

Laptop Memory

Laptop RAM (random-access memory) modules are different from the ones used in desktop or tower computers. Laptops use a special form factor called a small-outline DIMM (**SODIMM**). Other types exist (microDIMMs and small-outline RIMMs [SORIMMs]), but SODIMMs are the most popular, and they come in 144-, 200-, 204-, 260-, or 262-pin versions for up to 64-bit transfers. Figure 10.61 shows the difference between DDR2, DDR3, DDR4, and DDR5 SODIMMs. Each type of SODIMM is notched differently and cannot fit in another type of slot (so, for example, a DDR4 module requires a DDR4 SODIMM memory slot).

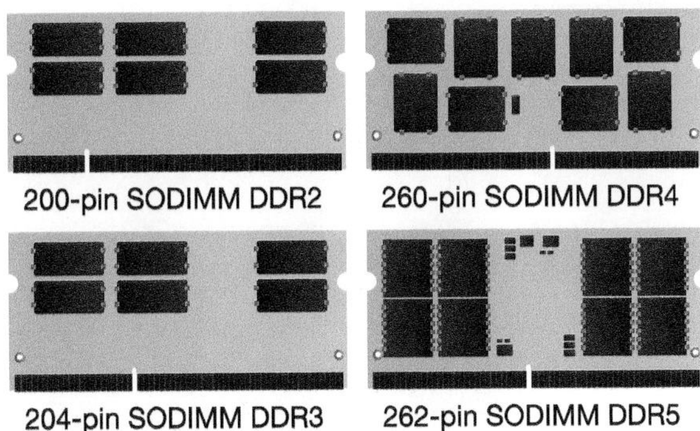

FIGURE 10.61 SODIMM form factors

Some laptops cannot be upgraded. A laptop that has only one memory slot requires replacement of the current module with a higher capacity one. Some smartphones, tablets, and laptops can be upgraded with flash memory cards.

Planning a Laptop Memory Upgrade

When upgrading memory on a laptop, in addition to determining what type of memory chips are going to be used, you must determine what features the memory chip might have. The computer system or motherboard documentation delineates what features are supported. Refer to Table 6.3 in Chapter 6, "Memory," for a refresher on memory technologies and features. Laptop memory advertisements are similar to desktop memory advertisements, as shown in Table 10.14.

TABLE 10.14 Sample SODIMM advertisements

Memory	Advertisement
2 GB	204-pin SODIMM DDR3 1333 Unbuffered 1.35V CAS Latency 9
4 GB	204-pin SODIMM DDR3 1333 Unbuffered 1.5V CAS Latency 10
16 GB kit (2×8 GB)	260-pin SODIMM DDR4 2,400 MHz (PC4-19200) CL16 (16-16-16-39) Non-ECC Unbuffered 1.2V
3 2 GB (2x16 GB)	260-pin SODIMM (PC4-19200) DDR4 2400 CL16-16-16-39 1.20V

Notice in Table 10.14 that the 2 GB memory module runs at 1.35V, and the others run at 1.5V or 1.2V (or some other voltage that is not listed). Some motherboards support **dual-voltage memory**, which means the motherboard supports the memory module that runs at the lower 1.35V, 1.2V, or 1.1V level. The lower voltage memory modules use less power and generate less heat than do the other types. Note that all memory modules must be at the same lower voltage to operate at that particular voltage level.

Laptop Memory Removal/Installation

Refer to the manufacturer's documentation when replacing or upgrading RAM. Before installing or removing laptop memory, turn off the laptop, disconnect the AC power cord (if installed), and remove the battery.

Determine the parts that must be removed in order to access the memory slots. Be sure the laptop memory notch fits into the memory slot key. Laptop memory is normally installed at a 45-degree angle into the slot. Press down on the module until it locks into the side clips. Figure 10.62 shows how to access the memory module in a laptop and the installation process. Notice that the laptop battery has been removed.

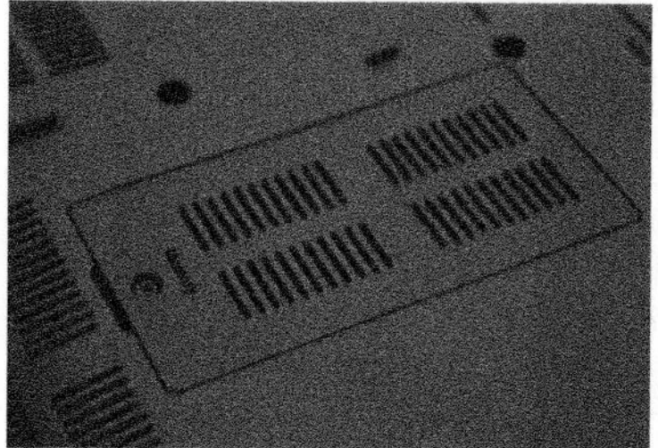

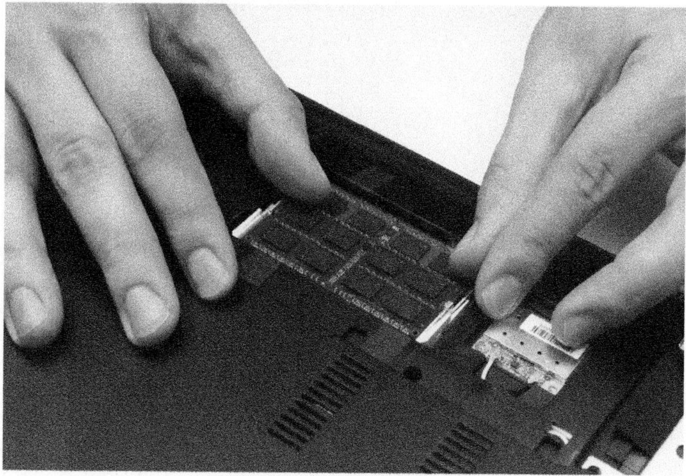

FIGURE 10.62 Accessing and installing a laptop memory module

Laptop Storage

Laptop hard drives come in two major form factors: 1.8-inch and 2.5-inch. The 2.5-inch form factor is designed for laptops. The 1.8-inch form factor is found in laptops, ultrabooks, and ultra-portable devices such as MP3 players, and it is also used for SSDs. Figure 10.63 shows a 2.5-inch hard drive installed in a laptop.

TECH TIP

What to do if you want more storage space for a laptop

A laptop typically does not allow a second hard drive. However, you can add an additional hard drive to the USB, eSATA, or combo eSATAp port.

FIGURE 10.63 Installed 2.5-inch laptop hard drive

Hard drives in laptops tend to be one of three types, as described in Table 10.15.

TABLE 10.15 Laptop hard drive types

Type	Description
Mechanical drive	This is a traditional drive that requires a motor to spin and has read/write heads that float over the hard drive platters. Most modern laptops have moved away from mechanical drives in favor of SSDs.
SSD	An SSD uses flash memory technology to store data. It has no moving parts and produces less heat than a mechanical drive. It is very fast but more expensive than a mechanical drive.
Hybrid drive	This type of drive is sometimes known as a solid-state hybrid drive (SSHD). Part of the drive is an SSD to store the operating system, and the other part is a traditional mechanical drive to hold user data.

Internal Laptop Drives

Laptops traditionally had a PATA or SATA hard drive installed, but today they commonly have an SSD instead of or in addition to these drive types. Other mobile devices, such as tablets, use SSDs as well. A miniPCIe adapter, μSATA (microSATA), **mSATA** (miniSATA) (refer to Figure 7.17) connector, or M.2 (refer to Figure 7.13) connector can be used to connect a drive to the system. Additional storage can be provided by devices that connect to USB, eSATA, or eSATAp ports.

External Drives

An external drive may need to be attached to external power. Some USB devices use external power, some are powered and connect to one USB port, and still others require two USB ports. Some manufacturers may require you to install software before attaching an external drive. Once a drive is attached, use *Device Manager* to ensure that the drive is recognized by the operating system.

Replacing a Hard Drive

Two installation methods are used with hard drives installed in portable computers: proprietary or removable. With a proprietary installation, the hard drive is installed in a location where it cannot be changed, configured, or moved very easily. Proprietary cables and connectors are used. With removable hard drives, the laptop has a hard drive bay that allows installation/removal through a single connector that provides power as well as data signaling. Otherwise, the drive could have separate data and power connectors.

To remove a laptop hard drive, follow the manufacturer's instructions. Also ensure that you are replacing the drive with the correct size and interface before starting the process. The following are generic steps for removing/replacing a laptop hard drive:

Step 1. Power down the laptop and remove the battery.

Step 2. Turn the computer upside down and locate the panel used to access the hard drive. Take appropriate antistatic precautions. Note that some laptop models have hard drives that release to the side of the computer.

Step 3. Remove any screws to gain access to the drive. A sliding lock release may also allow access to the drive area. Do not lose these screws as screws may not come with the replacement drive.

Step 4. Slide the drive out of the connector and remove it from the unit. Do not force it. Some units have release levers, are mounted on a frame, and/or are mounted on rubber feet. You may need to gently rock a drive back and forth while pulling gently to ease the drive out of the laptop. Remember that this drive has probably never been removed since it was initially installed.

Reverse the process to install a new drive that has the same form factor. Figure 10.64 shows a SATA hard drive being mounted inside a frame before being installed in a laptop.

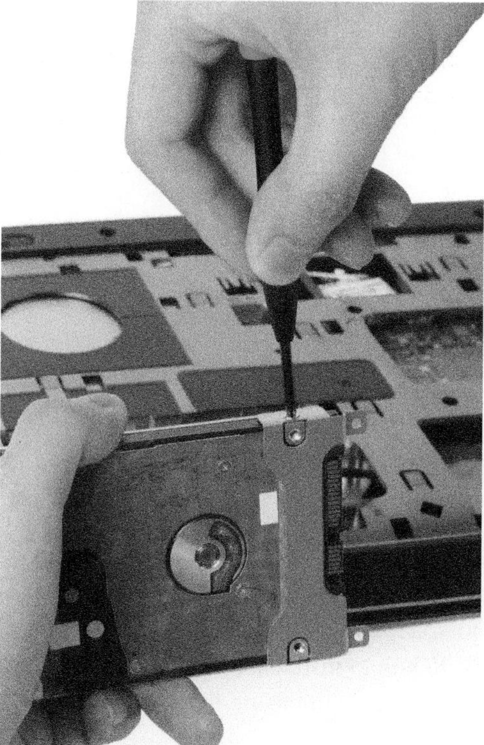

FIGURE 10.64 Installing a laptop hard drive

Migrating/Upgrading a Hard Drive to an SSD

When replacing a laptop hard drive with an SSD because there is only one drive bay, an external drive enclosure that holds the SSD is needed for the installation process. The enclosure might later be used for the current hard drive to make it an external drive. Also, it is best to use third-party software that clones your computer and allows you to move selected applications over to the SSD without reinstallation of the software.

Figure 10.65 shows an M.2 SSD being installed in a laptop. Remember to remove battery and AC power while installing and running from AC power attached during this process. The following are generic steps used to migrate a hard drive with an SSD:

Step 1. Delete any unneeded files and folders. Uninstall any unneeded, unwanted, or unused applications.

Step 2. Defragment the existing hard drive or run Disk Cleanup.

Step 3. Create a system image.

Step 4. Put the SSD in an external enclosure, if necessary, and connect it to the laptop or install the M.2 SSD into the M.2 slot.

Step 5. Use the *Disk Management* tool to verify that Windows recognizes the drive. If the drive is listed as "Not initialized," right-click on the drive and select *Initialize Disk*. Also ensure that the used space on the current hard drive is less than the space available on the SSD. Depending on the software you use, you may have to shrink your current hard drive partition that has the operating system installed to less than that of the SSD. If you do, reboot the computer after all operations to ensure that the hard drive is still working properly.

Step 6. Use third-party software to clone the current hard drive to the SSD.

Step 7. If you used an external enclosure, power off the laptop. Remove the old hard drive and install the SSD.

Step 8. Power on the laptop and ensure that the SSD boots and all applications work. For more information, refer to Chapter 7.

FIGURE 10.65 Installing a laptop SSD

TECH TIP

A noisy hard drive can be a warning

Mechanical hard drives tend to give indicators that failure is imminent. They make noises, the laptop fails to boot, data blocks are marked as bad, data access might be slow, or error messages appear. SSDs, on the other hand, might fail with no advance warning.

Laptop Wireless/Bluetooth Card Replacement

The laptop wireless card is commonly located under the keyboard or accessible from the underside of the laptop. Figure 10.66 shows an 802.11ac Wi-Fi and Bluetooth card. Note that Wi-Fi and Bluetooth cards can also use an M.2 connector.

FIGURE 10.66 802.11ac Wi-Fi and Bluetooth laptop card

Refer to the manufacturer's website for the exact laptop wireless/Bluetooth card replacement procedures. The generic removal steps are as follows:

Step 1. Disconnect the AC power and remove the battery. Take appropriate antistatic precautions.

Step 2. Locate the wireless card. See an example in Figure 10.67.

Step 3. Disconnect the wireless antenna cable(s) from the card (like shown in Figure 10.67). Notice that the wires attach to posts on the wireless NIC. A small flat-tipped screwdriver, small needle-nose pliers, or tweezers might be used for this task. Be very careful with this step. Cables are not typically included with a replacement wireless card. Take a picture or make a note about which cable attaches to which connector if multiple cables are used.

Step 4. Ease the wireless card out of the laptop. Note that a lever or tab may be used, depending on the vendor. Make a note or take a photo of how the wireless card inserts into the slot.

Simply reverse these steps to install the replacement card.

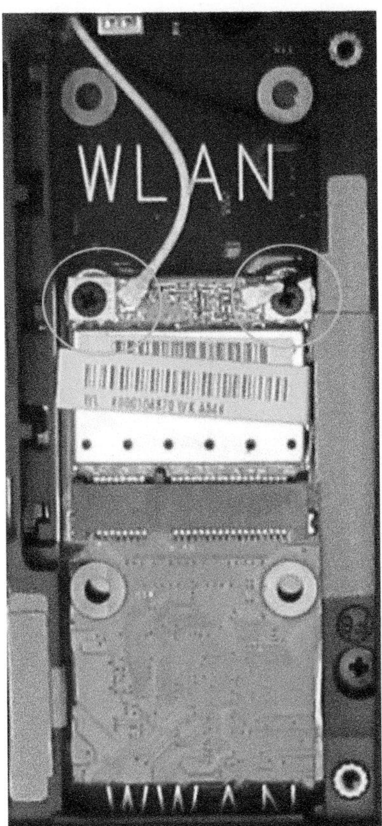

FIGURE 10.67 Laptop wireless NIC

TECH TIP

Where is the wireless antenna on a laptop?

For laptops that have integrated wireless NICs, the wireless antenna is usually built into the laptop display for best connectivity. This is because the display is the tallest point of the laptop and is therefore closest to the wireless receiving antenna. The quality of integrated antennas varies.

Laptop DC Jack Replacement

Because of the numerous times the AC-to-DC power brick is attached to a laptop, it makes sense that laptop power jacks need to be replaced sometimes. The **DC jack** is where you attach power to the laptop. You know the jack is problematic when a new power brick doesn't work, when you can see a broken pin or loose pin in the DC jack, or when you use a multimeter to test the DC voltage level coming out of the power brick, and it is fine but the laptop will not power using the DC cord.

Figure 10.68 shows how a DC connector might connect. Disconnect the power brick and remove the battery before starting any repair. Note that the cable attached to the DC jack may have retaining clips or might be threaded through a very narrow space. Do not damage adjacent parts.

Document any parts that you have to remove in order to remove the defective DC jack. Refer to the manufacturer's replacement steps.

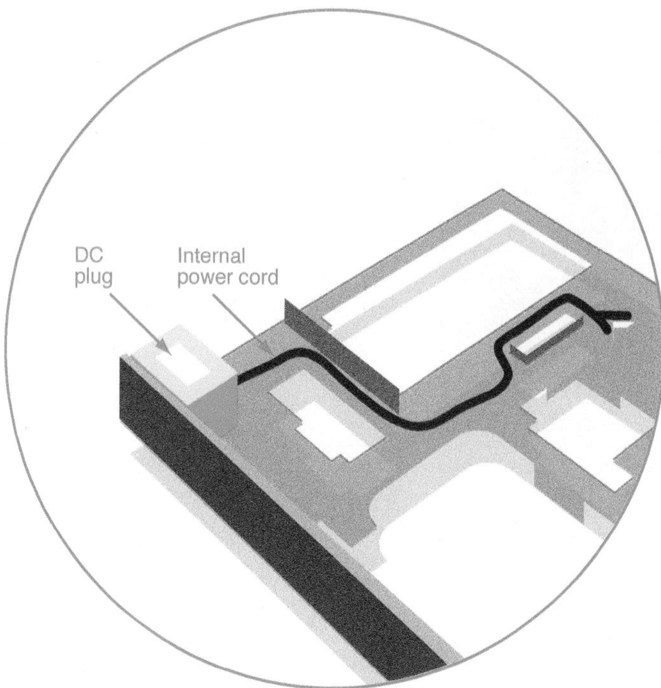

FIGURE 10.68 Laptop DC jack (plug) and power cable

Mobile Device Sound

Laptop speakers are not always of the highest quality. Compared to desktop computers, mobile devices are limited in their sound options. A mobile device normally has an integrated microphone, a line out connector for headphones, and sound integrated into the system board. Laptop devices normally allow the user to control sound with buttons above the keypad or by selecting a combination of Fn and another key.

For Android mobile devices, use the *Setting > Sound* option to mute and modify the ringtone. Optionally, you can also select sounds to be played, such as when the screen unlocks or when switching between screens.

For Apple iOS devices, use the *General > Settings > Sounds* option. The speaker volume and sounds indicating email, phone calls, reminders, keyboard clicks, and so on are set on this screen. Both Android and Apple iOS-based mobile devices have volume controls on the sides.

Consider using wireless or USB speakers if a laptop speaker fails. Keep in mind that if a sound device is powered by the USB port, this shortens battery life. Laptop speakers are commonly located in the sides or back corners of a laptop. Figure 10.69 shows two different types of mobile device speakers.

When replacing laptop speakers, be careful when tracing and removing the speaker wires. Refer to the manufacturer's directions. Speaker wires must sometimes be wiggled gently in order to detach them. They commonly screw into the motherboard. Inspect the speaker wire path before removing the wire. Other parts may have to be removed in order to remove faulty speakers.

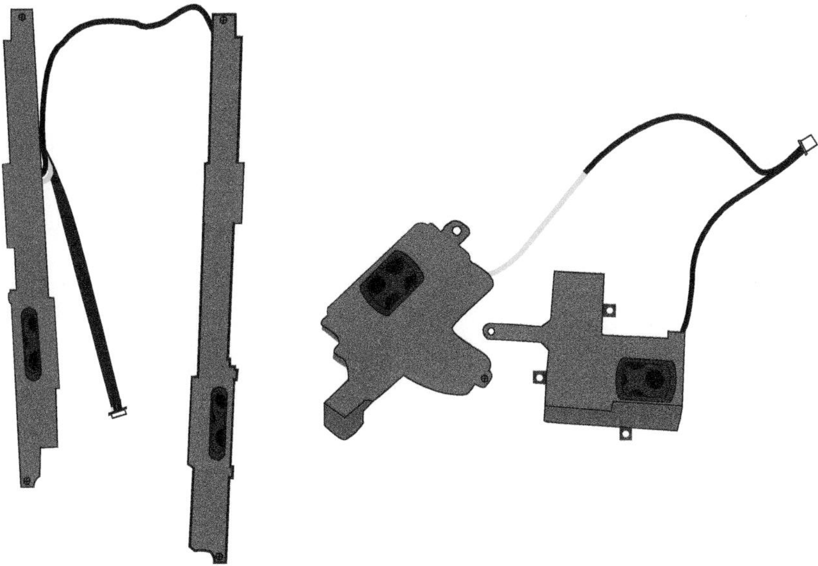

FIGURE 10.69 Internal laptop speakers

Laptop Video Card Replacement

A laptop is likely to have a GPU built into the motherboard or soldered onto the motherboard. Video cards are not a common replacement item because replaceable video cards make the laptop heavier and thicker. You can achieve extra graphics output to additional external displays by using a USB-to-HDMI (see Figure 10.70) or USB-to-DVI external adapter.

FIGURE 10.70 USB-to-HDMI adapter

Laptop Display

The laptop display is one of the most complex parts of a laptop. Three of the most popular display technologies are described in Table 10.16.

TABLE 10.16 Video output technology

Technology	Description
Liquid crystal display (**LCD**)	Technology used in laptops, flat panel monitors, TVs, tablets, smartphones, and projectors. A **backlight** (which can be a cold cathode fluorescent lamp [**CCFL**] or LED technology) extends behind the combined glass assembly, and the light is always on. This is why an LCD monitor appears to sometimes glow even when it's off and why crystals are needed to block some of the light to create the intensities of light.
Light-emitting diode (**LED**)	A low-power, low-heat, long-lasting electronic device used in many technologies, including calculators; home, business, and auto lighting; fiber optics; and displays. LED displays use liquid crystals as well as an LED backlight instead of a CCFL. LED displays have better color accuracy than LCDs, are thinner than the LCDs that use CCFLs, and are commonly used for large displays.
Organic LED (**OLED**)	OLED technology does not require a backlight, as LCD does, but has a film of organic compounds placed in rows and columns that can emit light. OLED technology is lightweight and has a fast response time, low power usage, and a wide viewing angle; it is used in TVs, mobile phones, and handheld gaming consoles.

LCDs use liquid crystals embedded into the display materials (see Figure 10.71) to create the images once the CCFL or backlight illuminates them. Liquid crystals are sensitive to temperature changes, so mobile device displays may appear distorted in cold or hot temperatures.

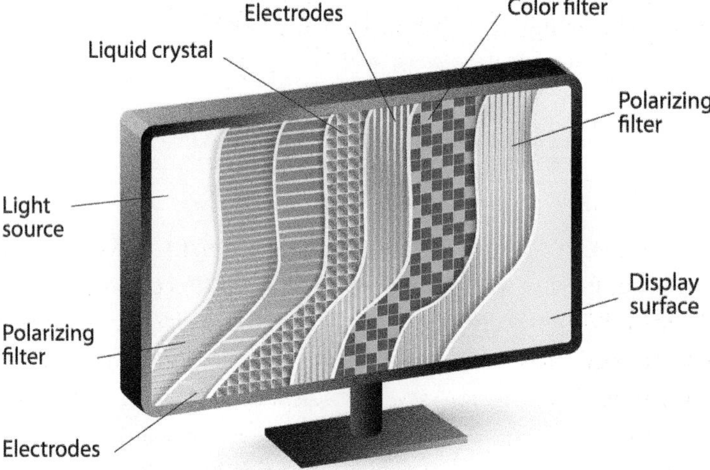

FIGURE 10.71 Inside an LCD

There are three main types of LCDs:

> *Twisted Nematic (***TN***):* Cheapest to make, most common, and fastest to display the image, but it is best viewed from straight on (not at an angle).

> *Vertical Alignment (***VA***):* Slowest response time but better color and wider viewing angles than TN.

> *In-Plane Switching (***IPS***):* Best type for viewing from an angle, quality, and color, but slow response time. Good for those in graphics design or any profession that needs consistent color reproduction.

TECH TIP

Liquid crystals are poisonous

Be careful with cracked LCDs. If liquid crystals (which are not actually liquid) get on you, wash with soap and water and seek medical attention.

A laptop may have a rotating/removable screen. If the display is removable, it normally can be used as a tablet. A laptop with a rotating display is useful in offices where information is to be shared or shown to a person sitting in front of a desk. The display can be rotated in the opposite direction or just turned a bit, as shown in Figure 10.72.

FIGURE 10.72 Laptop with rotating screen

To rotate the screen, follow the manufacturer's instructions. Many models have a display release latch located near the area where the display connects to the part of the laptop case where the keyboard is located. With such a model, press the release latch and turn the display.

If a laptop doesn't have a display that physically rotates but you want to change the orientation of the information on the screen, you can adjust the rotation through Windows. In Windows, use the *Display* Settings link, and if multiple monitors are present, select the one to be changed, locate the *Orientation* drop-down box and select the orientation you would like, and click *Apply*. Note that if you have a special graphics card, you may use an application like the Intel Graphics Media Accelerator to configure the graphics properties.

Besides the laptop screen, the display assembly contains other parts, and some of them have nothing to do with the screen. Table 10.17 outlines some common components found in a laptop display.

TABLE 10.17 Mobile display components

Component	Description
Wi-Fi antenna	An antenna that attaches to the WLAN card (which is commonly under the computer and/or attached to the system board) in order to receive/transmit wireless signals.
Webcam	A camera used for video conferencing (and as a camera/video recorder in other mobile devices). Some laptops have the ability to use the integrated camera for facial recognition as a security measure. However, because the biometric software cannot distinguish between a living face and a digitized image, it is possible to fool the software by using a photograph.
Microphone	A device used to digitize voice into 1s and 0s so that sound may be heard on a conference call or in a recording. Microphones are tested through the *Sound* Windows Setting *Input* section.
Inverter	A component that converts DC to AC for the CCFL backlight.
Touch screen/ digitizer	In a touch screen display, a thin layer of plastic that translates pressure, swipes, or other touch actions into digital signals. Replacement is sometimes difficult but is usually cheaper than replacing the display.

A laptop has a video cable that connects the LCD to the motherboard. Either a CCFL or LED backlight bulb is used on many models so images on the screen can be seen. The CCFL type connects to an inverter (see Figure 10.73). The inverter converts low DC voltage to high AC voltage for the backlight bulb. Screens larger than 15.4 inches may need two CCFL backlight bulbs. An LCD with an LED backlight does not need an inverter. An OLED display doesn't need an inverter or a backlight.

The lid close detector (displayed in Figure 10.73) can be a physical switch or a magnetic switch located close to the back edge of the keyboard portion of a laptop. A laptop can be configured through power management configuration to go into hibernation, sleep, or standby mode when the laptop is closed.

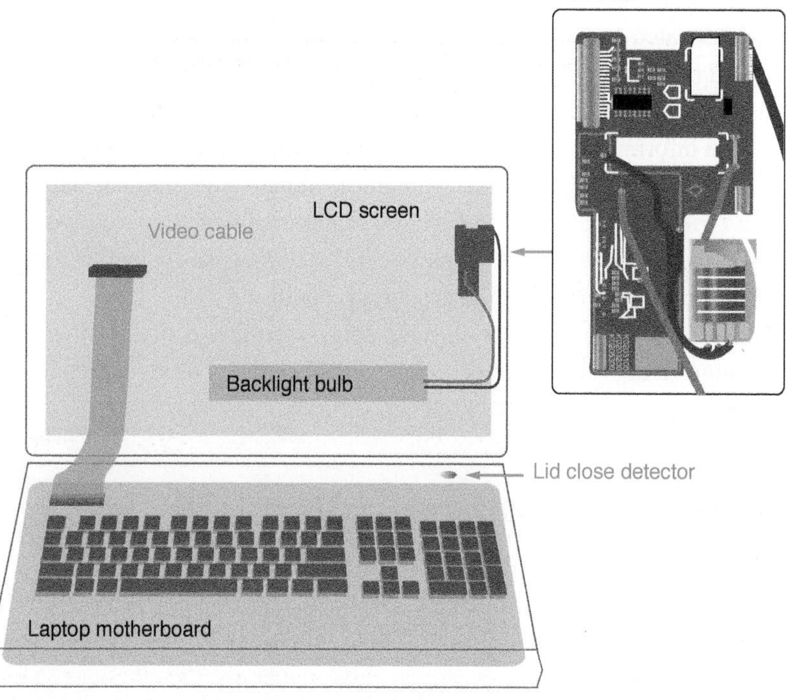

FIGURE 10.73 Laptop video connectivity

TECH TIP

Is it worth fixing a laptop display?

Laptop displays might be too expensive to repair, but if the inverter or backlight is the faulty part, the repair cost is negligible.

A laptop display may need to be replaced as part of a repair or due to a **broken screen**. When removing a laptop display, refer to the directions from the computer manufacturer. The following steps are generic:

Step 1. Use proper antistatic precautions and remove the screws that hold the screen bezel in place.

Step 2. If you have a display that is inside the plastic cover (and does not go right to the edge of the laptop), you must gently pry the plastic bezel that protects the screen edge from the case. Note that there may be little covers over screws. Remove the covers and then the screws, if necessary. There is a light adhesive, and you might want to use a hair dryer on low heat to warm up the adhesive so it is easier to pry off. The screen might also be held in place by hinge covers. Turn the laptop upside down and use a tool to separate the hinge cover at the seam.

Step 3. Remove the screen's retaining screws.

Step 4. Gently lift the screen from the case. Be very careful with the connectors. Flip the screen so the back of the screen is visible.

Step 5. Notice the ribbon cable that runs up the back of the display. Gently disconnect the cable at the top of the display and the cable that connects to the motherboard. With some cables you must squeeze to release; others have pull tabs or need to be gently pulled from the socket. Figure 10.74 shows the back side of an LCD that uses a CCFL backlight.

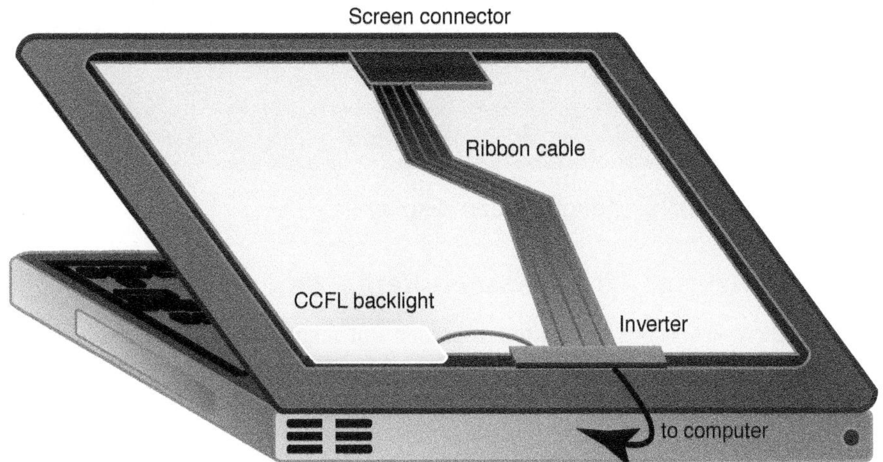

FIGURE 10.74 LCD cabling with a CCFL backlight

TECH TIP

What is the best resolution for a laptop display?

Set a laptop to the native resolution (the resolution for which the LCD was made).

Touch Screens

Touch screen displays are used with PCs, tablets, and smartphones. They respond to contact on the screen rather than keyboard or mouse input. Touch screens are commonly used in situations where information is to be controlled and in public areas, such as for kiosks at airports, malls, and entrance areas at schools or businesses. Special drivers and software are used to control the monitor.

Several technologies are used to manufacture a touch screen display. The two most common ones are resistive and capacitive. A resistive touch screen has a flexible membrane stretched over the face of the display. The membrane contains a special metal oxide coating and has spacers that are used to locate the touched spot on the screen. Resistive touch screens are good in manufacturing and in the medical industry, where personnel wear gloves. A stylus can also be used with both types of displays.

Capacitive touch screens are more durable than resistive screens. They respond to a touch or multiple touches on the display and easily detect contact. Most touch screens are the capacitive type. Some mobile devices allow you to calibrate the screen or lock the screen orientation by using the Windows *Settings* > *Display* option. Figure 10.75 shows a touch screen.

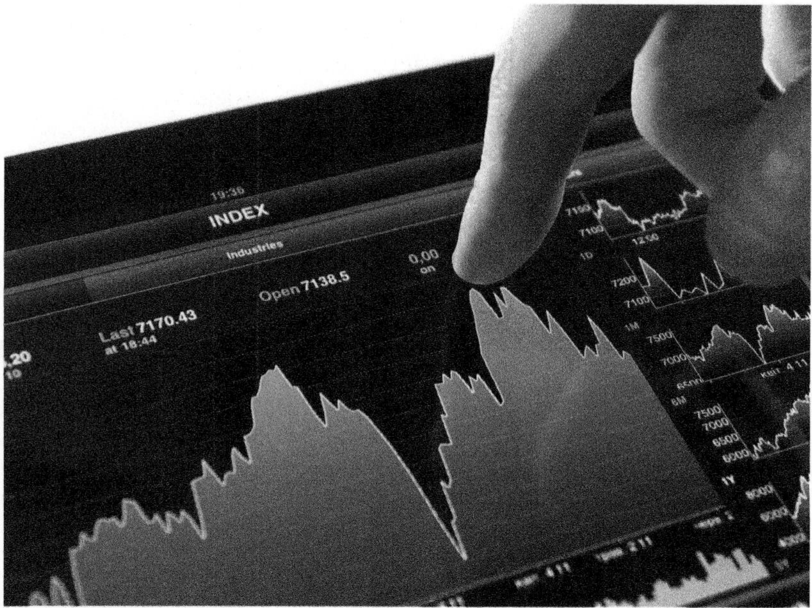

FIGURE 10.75 Touch screen display

Digitizer or Touch Screen Replacement

If there are issues with a touch screen not responding to input or if applications randomly open, **digitizer** issues might be the culprit. Try restarting the device or powering off and back on before trying anything else. If the device was dropped or jarred, the cable that connects the digitizer to the mainboard might be loose or disconnected. Dirt, dust, particles, scratches, cracks (that might allow particles down between the digitizer and the LCD), and so on might cause issues. If you have to replace the digitizer, follow the manufacturer's directions. You might need some double-sided foam tape to keep the digitizer from touching the LCD screen.

A touch screen may be part of an LCD, and if it is, you just replace the LCD as described earlier. Alternatively, a touch screen may be a separate assembly, in which case you remove the retaining screws and lean the screen backward so that the screen doesn't fall forward when all screws are removed. The screen may have to be pried from the outside casing, using a metal or plastic prying tool that has a small flat edge. Gently lean the screen forward and notice the cable/connector that connects to the screen. There may be a retaining bar and/or tape or a tab on the connector.

Figure 10.76 shows a touch screen that has just been removed. One cable is the video cable that goes to the motherboard. The other cables connect to the Wi-Fi/Bluetooth and cellular cards.

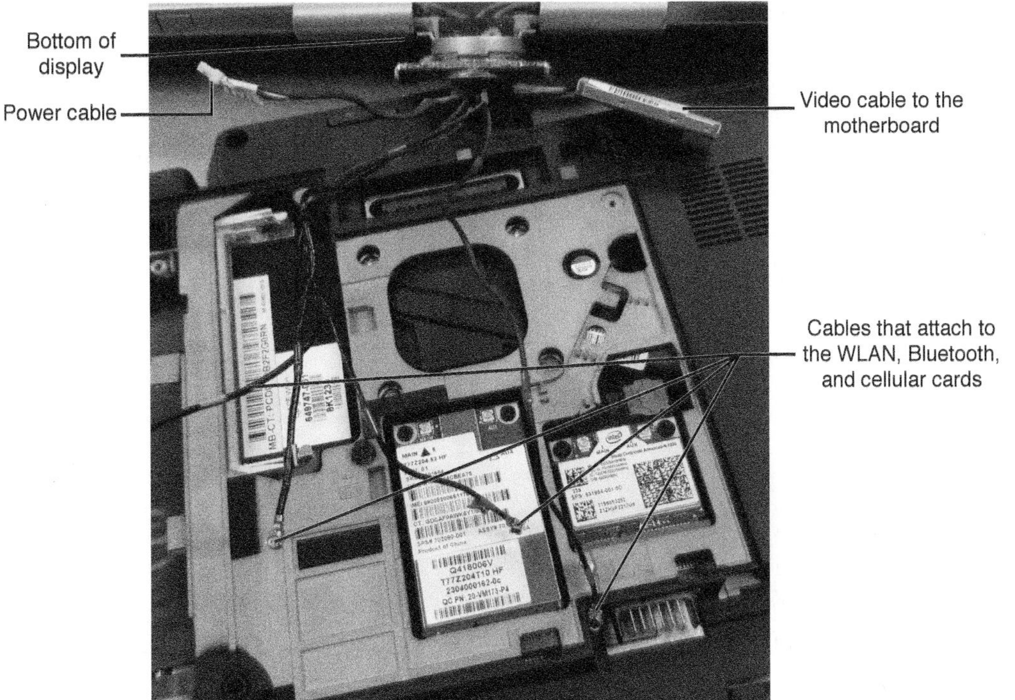

FIGURE 10.76 Removing a touch screen from a motherboard

After a touch screen is replaced, use Device Manager to verify that it is recognized by the operating system. Expand the *Human Interface Devices* (HID) section to ensure that the device and driver are shown. Most manufacturers provide their updates through Windows updates, but you might want to check the manufacturer's website to see if there is a newer driver. If a new touch screen does not function, make sure the replacement screen is really a touch screen and ensure that the digitizer cables are attached.

The technologies that enable touch screens allow users to interact with mobile devices and displays of all types. A touch screen has multiple configurations that can be controlled, including how swiping operates. After replacing a touch screen, you might need to calibrate it. In Windows, search for the word `calibrate` and select *Calibrate Display Color*. To calibrate a Mac display, access the Apple menu > *System Preferences* > *Displays* > *Color* > click *Calibrate*. You can also refer to the "Touch Screen Does Not Respond or Is Inaccurate" section, later in the chapter.

Microphone and Camera/Webcam Replacement

Microphones in tablets normally do not have controls, as those in laptops and PCs do. Instead, a tablet microphone is controlled through an application that supports a microphone. External microphones can be added using wireless Bluetooth connectivity, USB, or a microphone jack. Smartphones, of course, have integrated microphones.

If a webcam and microphone are built into the display, they are commonly on the same circuit board. Before replacing a webcam or microphone, make sure that the part is actually faulty. Start by checking to see if Device Manager recognizes it. If you just upgraded the operating system, such as to Windows 10 or 11, you might need an updated driver rather than a new webcam. Try another application with it, use a different browser with the application, use a website that provides a free tool to test the webcam, or try a video chat session with a friend. You might also consider adding an external device by using USB or Bluetooth instead of repairing the built-in device.

If a webcam or an integrated microphone really is faulty, consult the documentation provided by the manufacturer. The generic directions for dealing with a microphone or webcam that is built into the display are as follows:

Step 1. Remove the screen bezel, as described earlier in this chapter, to expose the webcam (see Figure 10.77).

Step 2. If the webcam is held by a screw or a horizontal connector that has light adhesive holding it to the back of the display case, use a flat-tipped screwdriver or plastic scribe to pry the webcam from the case.

Replace the device by reversing this process.

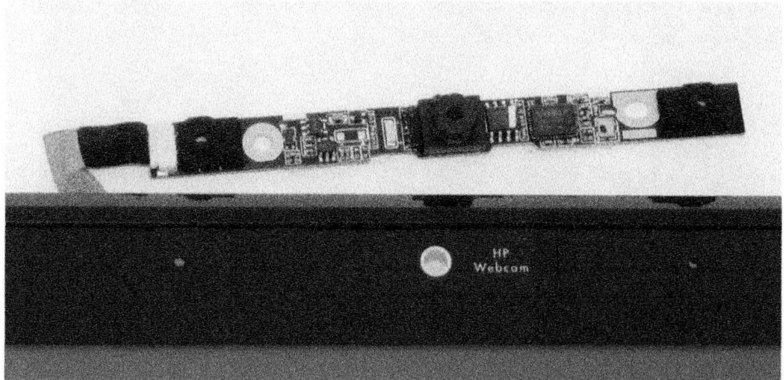

FIGURE 10.77 Webcam removed from the back of an HP laptop

Display Inverter Replacement

If an inverter needs to be replaced, follow the installation directions provided by the manufacturer. Generic instructions for replacement are as follows:

Step 1. Remove the screen bezel, as described earlier in this chapter, to expose the inverter at the bottom of the display.

Step 2. If the inverter has a connector on either side of it, remove those cables from the inverter.

Step 3. Remove the retaining screw, if necessary.

Step 4. Remove the bad inverter.

Reverse this process to install the replacement part.

Mobile Device Security

Laptops have special physical security needs, and locking and tracking devices are available for them. Use a nondescript bag to carry a laptop to reduce the chance of theft. Have an engraved permanent asset tag attached. A physical laptop lock or laptop locking station can be purchased and installed on a desk. A user can place a laptop into the locking station without worrying about someone coming by and taking it.

Another option is to use the universal security slot (USS), which allows a cable lock or laptop alarm to be attached. Special software packages enable a laptop to automatically contact a tracking center in case of theft. Figure 10.78 shows a cable lock attached to the USS on a laptop computer.

FIGURE 10.78 Laptop cable lock

Many people think that devices that do not have a storage device do not need antivirus or anti-malware software. This is a misconception. It is important to install antivirus/anti-malware software on mobile devices.

Bootleg apps are pirated software that could cause security issues and/or OS issues. A **malicious app** is malware that can install a virus, ransomware, or spyware onto the mobile device and cause many types of issues. Just because an app is in the Play Store or App Store, does not mean it is a legitimate app. With **application spoofing**, a mobile app pretends to be another app, has ads that are not from a trusted source, obtains and steals information about/from the device, and/or provides location information without the user having a choice. Do your research before downloading an app. Check reviews, the version history, and the app name and app developer carefully.

Here are some more security suggestions:

- Mobile devices can run each app in a sandbox—a space separated from other apps. Using a sandbox provides a natural security mechanism for applications.
- Mobile device **OS updates** and upgrades are just as important as updates on a full-sized computer. Connect a device to AC power if possible during an OS update.
- A device exhibiting **sluggish response time** could be a security risk. Check if there are any OS updates available. Consider whether any apps have been added or updated recently. Malware may be present. Restart the device or power it off and back on.
- Many mobile devices have GPS tracking capability that can be used to locate a lost or stolen device. This may be a paid service.
- A paid service or an app on a phone can provide the capability to perform a remote lock or a remote wipe. The remote lock disables the phone so it cannot be accessed. The remote wipe deletes all data from the device. A **remote wipe** uses software to send a command to a mobile device to do one or any of the following: delete data, do a factory reset, remove everything from the device so it cannot be used, or overwrite data storage to prevent forensic data recovery.
- Beware of **fake security warnings** that could come through the OS, app, or browser. Don't call the number, tap or click on the link, or respond to the text. A result of interacting with one of these could also result in a high number of ads.
- Doing a factory reset can help when some of the app issues and resolutions discussed in this section do not work.

> Verify that the phone firmware is the latest version as an update may fix a security issue.
> A mobile device may have a lost mode option that enables you to display messages on the screen for anyone who might find the device.

Most mobile devices have the ability to do some of the following types of locks or **screen locks**: have a **swipe lock**, **PIN code**, passcode lock, **security pattern**, **facial recognition lock** or unlock, **fingerprint lock**, or password enabled that activates when the device is inactive. **Authenticator apps** can also be downloaded.

Biometrics are security settings associated with unique physical characteristics such as fingerprint scanning or facial recognition. To configure biometrics in Windows, 10, you can use *Windows Hello*, which is available through *Settings > Accounts > Sign-in options* (see Figure 10.79). Note that you might not be able to control or configure these sign-in options on a corporate-owned laptop.

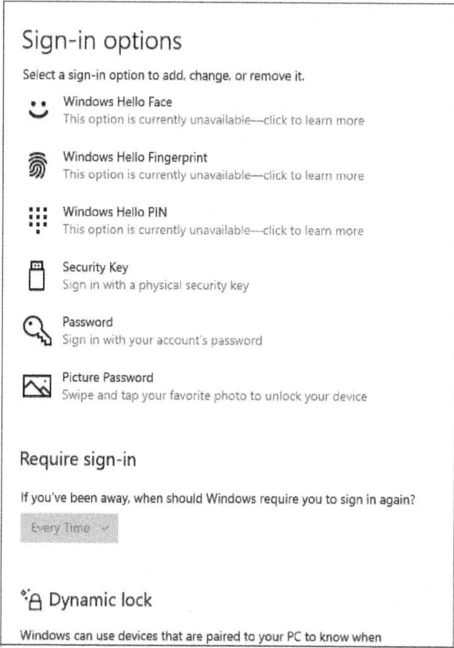

FIGURE 10.79 Windows Hello options

Let's take a look at the different Windows Hello options:

> *Windows Hello Face:* Uses facial recognition and requires an infrared camera that can do 3D depths. If the user changes appearance such as hair style often, you might consider recommending one of the other options.
> *Windows Hello Fingerprint:* Configures a fingerprint lock and requires an internal fingerprint reader or an external one.
> *Windows Hello PIN:* Configures a security PIN.
> *Security Key:* Requires a physical device such as a USB device or an NFC device like a phone or security access card and is used in addition to a fingerprint lock or PIN.
> *Password:* Uses common alphanumeric characters to unlock/login to the mobile device.
> *Picture Password:* Uses a photo and requires three gestures to be performed on the photo (for example, a click, swipe, circled object, or drawn line).

To configure basic mobile security, perform the following:

> *Android: Settings > Location & Security > Set Up Screen Lock.*
> *iOS: Settings > General > Passcode Lock On* option. Use *Settings > Passcode* for more passcode options. You can also configure the *Auto-Lock* time. On an iPad, you can use the *iPad Cover Lock/Unlock On* option.

Failed Login Attempts or Unauthorized Account Access

Some mobile devices have configuration settings for when the security method fails, such as an incorrectly entered password or **system lockout**. Some devices allow a default number of attempts. For extra security, some devices can be configured to take an action after a set number of failed attempts, such as disabling the device or even erasing the data. Most mobile device users who have this capability enabled have the data backed up to the cloud or onto a machine.

On an Android device, perform a factory reset from the Android system recovery menu. In iOS, you can use the *Passcode Lock* setting (refer to Figure 10.80) to set how long the system waits for the passcode (*Require Passcode* setting). After 6 failed attempts, the iOS mobile device will be disabled for 1 minute; after 7 failed attempts, it will be disabled for 5 minutes; after 9 failed attempts, it will be disabled for an hour. If you enable the *Erase Data* option, the device will be wiped after 11 failed attempts.

So what happens if someone gets into your account? Change your password immediately. Change the credit card used on the account. Notify the vendor (Apple, Microsoft, Google, and so on). If possible, enable two-step verification to prevent future issues. Some email products allow you to view account activity. Many vendors have an option to send you an email when an unusual device is used to access your account.

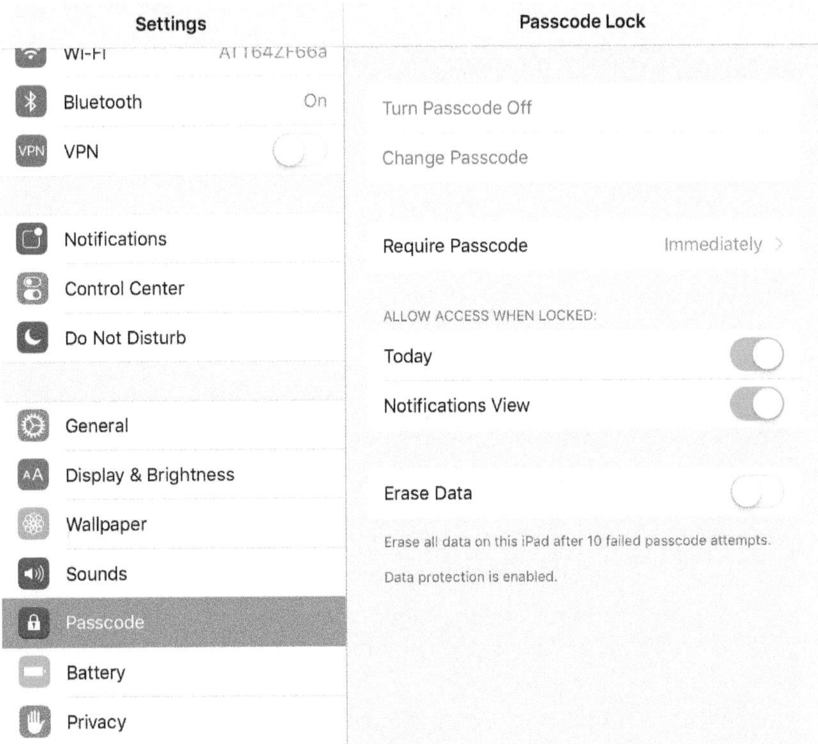

FIGURE 10.80 iOS passcode settings

Unauthorized Location Tracking

Although not all mobile devices have GPS, they can obtain information from other networks and browsers to provide location services. Apps that use location services also use battery life. To turn location services on and off, use the following:

> *On Android: Settings > Location.*
> *On iOS: Settings > Privacy > Location Services.* (Note that you can use the *System Services* option to select which services are allowed to track your location.) You can also use *Settings*

> *Privacy* > *Advertising* > enable *Limit Ad Tracking* and *Reset Advertising Identifier* in order to be prompted for which apps can track your location. Another option is to change your Safari or other browser settings. To disable tracking in Safari, *Settings* > *Safari* > enable *Do Not Track.*

Android and iOS have apps for dealing with mobile devices that have been lost or stolen:

> *Android: Settings* > *Security* > *Device Administration*
> *iOS: Settings* > *Find My iPhone*

In addition, other free and paid apps are available for dealing with mobile devices that have been lost or stolen.

Leaked Personal Files/Data

The way to protect personal files and/or data on a mobile device is to protect the device itself by securing the device, encrypting the files, or encrypting the entire device. Don't enable Bluetooth or GPS except when you need it. If you think data has already been compromised, change all passwords on all accounts and devices. Watch accounts and notify credit companies, if applicable. You can also do a factory reset on the device.

Unauthorized Camera/Microphone Activation

As discussed earlier in this chapter, some apps intentionally gather information about you by using your location and possibly the integrated camera and microphone. One app has the capability of figuring out where you are, who is in the room, and the sounds being heard and then correlating the data with others in the same vicinity to create a social network environment. Other apps are used for spying on people. Research each app that you or the customer installs.

Every Android app is supposed to state what access permissions are required by the app. With Android, you can ensure that *Android Device Manager* is enabled (*Settings* > *Security* > *Device Administration*). It is enabled by default. See Figure 10.81.

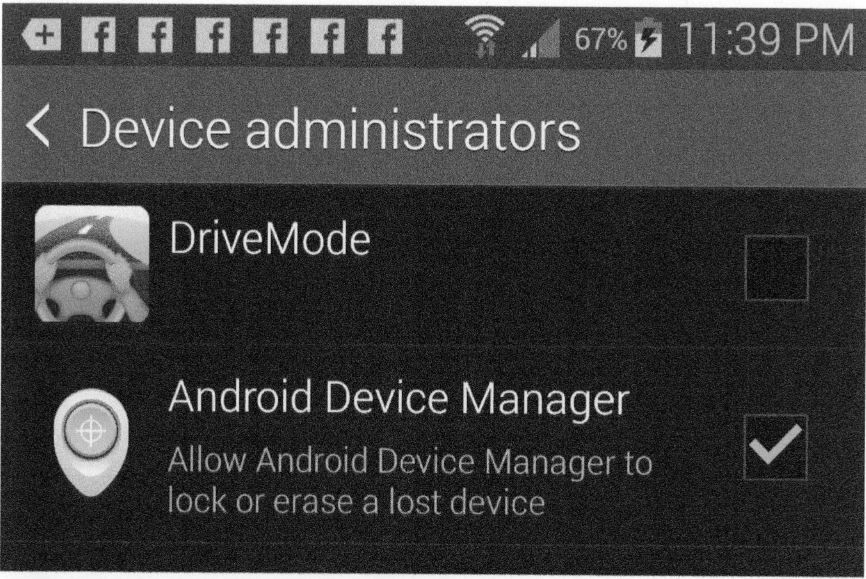

FIGURE 10.81 Android Device Manager

With iOS devices, use *Settings > Privacy > Camera/Microphone* to show what apps have requested access to either the camera or the microphone.

Not all reported activity occurs through an app. So how can you tell if someone has accessed your phone and potentially your camera and microphone as well? Here are some signs:

> Look for strange Short Message Service (SMS) text messages.
> Look for increased phone bills.
> Take notice of any weird activity on your phone, such as apps locking or opening mysteriously or slow performance.
> Take note of battery life to see if the battery is losing its charge faster than normal.

Data-Usage Limit Notification

Many mobile devices that connect to the cellular network have a specific amount of text, photo, and video allowed in the user's specific rate plan. A **high number of ads** can use up data on the rate plan. Refer to the "Cellular Data" section, earlier in this chapter, for recommendations on blocking ads. Be sure to check mobile device privacy, browser, and application settings for notifications, pop-ups, and advertising settings (*Settings > Privacy*). Also check settings or system preferences for location-based ads and services.

To view how much data has been used in a specific period or to turn off cellular data, use these steps:

> *Android: Settings > Data Usage* (optionally, you can set the mobile data limit)
> *iOS: Settings > Cellular > Cellular Data*

Unauthorized Root Access

A user who has unauthorized root access has access to the mobile device's file system (see Figure 10.82). Through the file system, malicious programs can be installed, files can be downloaded and copied, and private information can be gleaned. **Jailbreak** (iOS) and **root access** (Android) are two terms that mean that the operating system has been compromised in such a way that the user has an increased level of privilege on the phone. On Android, this is known as having root access. For iOS devices, users bypass some of the restrictions placed on the device. People do this for several reasons, including to be able to remove apps that are preinstalled and typically unremovable, to gain free access to features such as tethering that typically might require an additional charge, to enable the device to operate faster, to ensure that the device is not tied to or monitored by the operating system vendor or the phone vendor, and/or to modify the operating environment.

Android is an open source operating system, and vendors are allowed to make modifications and customize it. For both iOS and Android devices, security and operating system releases are not received by phones that have been rooted or jailbroken. Rooting or jailbreaking a device may void the manufacturer's warranty; makes a device more susceptible to viruses, malware, and security issues; and increases the possibility of access to the root directory (the starting place for all files). If an iOS device has been jailbroken, the original iOS can be restored by using iTunes.

FIGURE 10.82 Gaining root access to a mobile phone

VPN

A virtual private network (**VPN**) is used to connect one device to another device through a public network such as the internet. Figure 10.83 shows an example of the concept. A salesperson might have a tablet in order to demonstrate a product as well as input customer information. To upload the customer information, the salesperson might need to establish a VPN, and a technician might be required to configure this on a phone or another mobile device. Specific network information is required from the network support staff in order to create this type of connection.

The general steps to start the VPN configuration are as follows:

> *iOS: Settings* > *General* > *VPN*
> *Android: Settings* > *More* (from the *Wireless & Networks* section) > *VPN* > + (plus sign)

In order to use the VPN, the user has to connect using his or her own username and password:

> *iOS: Settings* > set *VPN* to on
> *Android: Settings* > *General* > *VPN*

FIGURE 10.83 Concept of a VPN

Mobile Device Travel and Storage

When traveling with a laptop, check that drive doors and devices are securely latched. Ensure that the mobile device is powered off or in hibernation mode (not in sleep/suspend or standby power mode).

Carry the device in a padded case. When placing the device on an airport security conveyor belt, ensure that the device is not placed upside down, which can cause damage to the display. Never place objects on top of a mobile device or pick up a laptop by the edges of the display when the laptop is opened. When shipping a mobile device, place it in a properly padded box.

The United States has regulations about lithium batteries on airplanes. If the battery contacts come in contact with metal or other batteries, the battery could short-circuit and cause a fire. For this reason, any lithium batteries are to be kept in original packaging. If original packaging is not available, place electrical tape over the battery terminals or place each battery in an individual bag. Spare lithium batteries are not allowed in checked baggage but can be taken in carry-on bags.

Mobile Device Troubleshooting Overview

Troubleshooting mobile devices is similar to troubleshooting desktop devices. Whether Android, iOS, or Windows is being used as an operating system, you use *Settings* or various system preferences in order to make changes to or adjust configuration settings on a device.

If a port does not work properly, check/clean the port of any dirt, corrosion, or obstruction. If the port has corrosion, disconnect power, remove the battery, and use an electronic contact cleaner solution. If it is the charging port, try a different cable. If you have a **physically damaged port**, see if the device is still under warranty. If the device is a laptop or tablet, you may have to replace the motherboard/mainboard. If a smartphone, you could buy a replacement circuit board (see Figure 10.84). Don't rule out using a repair shop.

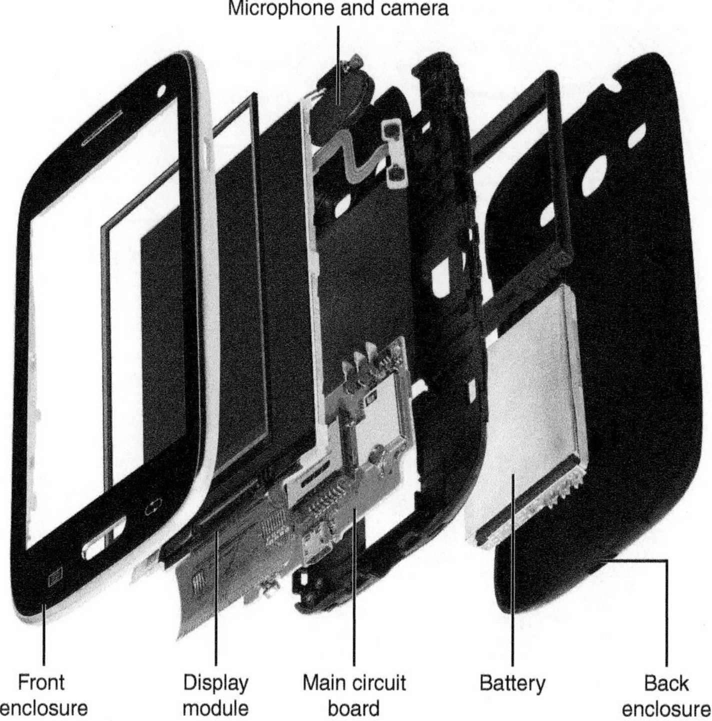

FIGURE 10.84 Disassembled smartphone

If you drop a device in water and have **liquid damage**, remember that the term *water resistant* does not mean *waterproof.* There are companies that specialize in drying out mobile devices. Putting the device in rice and/or letting it dry for 24 hours are not good solutions as you cannot get all the water from the electronics.

The software and hardware of mobile devices are similar to those of desktop devices. For example, things that go wrong in a mobile device touch screen are similar to those that occur on a laptop touch screen. Overheating, a power issue, a misbehaving app, and/or the OS can all cause a device to **randomly reboot**, and you just have to eliminate each of these issues one by one to see which one it is. Let's dive deeper into some of the issues.

Hard and Soft Resets

Sometimes a simple soft reset is all it takes to fix a problem. A **soft reset** is simply a restart of a mobile device. Some phones have a restart option. You commonly see a soft reset after an OS update. In some instances, a phone might not restart, and you might need to remove the battery in order to power off the device. Reasons to do a soft reset include the following abnormal behaviors:

- Unresponsive touch screen
- Slow system response
- Inability to receive, make, send, and/or receive text messages or calls
- Audio issues
- Error codes (in which case you should record the codes before restarting; see Figure 10.85)

FIGURE 10.85 Cell phone error

In contrast to a soft reset, a **hard reset** is a factory reset. (Hard resets for Android devices are covered earlier in this chapter.) You may need to do a hard reset if no other solution helps with the problem, if you have forgotten your password, if the screen is unresponsive and a soft reset does not help, or if you installed a software app that you cannot uninstall or that causes erratic behavior that cannot be solved in any other way.

In Android, boot the device into *Recovery Mode* (typically accessed by holding down two or more specific buttons, such as the power, volume, and/or home buttons) while the device boots > *Wipe Data/Factory Reset* (press *Power* button to select) > *Yes – Erase All User Data.* In iOS, you perform a hard reset with *Settings > General > Reset > Erase All Content and Settings > Erase iPhone/iPad.*

In Windows, depending on the manufacturer, holding down the power button (or the power button and the increase volume button) for several seconds may prompt a hard reset. Sometimes, you might have to disconnect the AC power cord and remove the battery.

Some devices can be fixed by removing the power brick (wall adapter) and the battery and leaving the battery out for about 30 seconds. On some Apple devices, you must hold the power button down for 5 seconds afterward. This is known as a System Management Controller (SMC) reset. Apple devices also keep configuration settings such as volume, date, and time in parameter RAM (PRAM). A small separate battery keeps these settings current. To reset these settings on an Apple laptop, hold down the following keys at the same time while the system is booting: ⌘+Option+P+R.

The following sections discuss troubleshooting of mobile devices by area of concern. Remember that the internet has a wealth of technical information available. Research is an important troubleshooting step that can help you see how others have solved similar problems.

OS Fails to Update

Operating system updates (see Figure 10.86) install important security patches and new features. If a mobile device **OS fails to update**, try a hard reset. If that doesn't work, check the following:

> Make sure the device is powered/fully charged and connected to a Wi-Fi network.
> Free up some space by removing apps, photos, and files that are no longer used. Store photos and files in the cloud or back them up and then remove them.
> If the device is an older one, check to see if the model is still supported by the manufacturer.
> Turn off Bluetooth and try the update again.
> Try the download again at a different time.
> On an Android device, clear the data and cache of the Play Store app using *Settings > Applications > Google Play Store > Clear data > Clear cache.*
> On an iOS device go to *Settings > General > Storage* and find the update in the list. Select *Update > Delete Update*. Then go back into the *General* setting and select *Software Update* and try again.
> Perform a factory reset using the mobile device manufacturer's directions.

FIGURE 10.86 Cell phone OS update

Mobile Device App Concerns

An app problem can show various symptoms, including causing the device to be slow to respond or other apps not to load. Many apps that are free (and even some that you pay for) do not play well with one another, have **unexpected app behavior**, or have issues with specific operating system versions. In order to troubleshoot apps, sometimes you need to stop an app (that is, perform a forced stop) or stop other apps because the mobile device is slow to respond due to high resource utilization (that is, apps taking all of the memory and processor power). Also, an app may be a malicious app and could pose a security risk.

Here are the generic steps for stopping an application if an **app fails to close**, but remember that Android is open source, so vendors can implement things differently, and iOS and Windows have different versions, and the exact steps may be different than those shown:

> *Android: Settings* > *Apps/Application Manager* > locate and select a particular application > *Force Stop*

> *iOS:* Press the *Home* button two times quickly or swipe up from the bottom > swipe to find the app to close > swipe up on the app's preview to close it

You might also be required to uninstall and reinstall an app if the app fails to respond or is not working. There are free app managers that allow you to do this easily, but mobile operating systems allow you to delete apps, too. (However, some apps that come with a mobile device can be installed but may be disabled.) Deleting an app deletes the data and settings. These are the generic steps for deleting an app:

> *Android: Settings* > *Apps/Application Manager* > locate and select a particular app > *Uninstall/Disable*

> *iOS:* Press and hold on top of the app icon until all the icons shake (see Figure 10.87) > tap the *x* in the corner of the icon > *Delete*

FIGURE 10.87 iOS app deletion

Depending on the type of mobile device, you might be able to use the operating system to check for app log errors. In Windows, use *Event Viewer*. On a Mac, access the *Utilities* folder from within the *Applications* folder. Ensure that the sidebar is shown (and click the leftmost button in the toolbar if the sidebar is not shown). Select *All Messages* from the tab bar. There are also log files located in the *Library* > *Logs* > *DiagnosticReports* folder. You might also try restarting or power the device off and back on again.

App Not Installing or Updating

When an app does not install, ensure that your hardware/operating system is compatible with the app and has storage space available. Some apps do not run well from an SD card and might need to be installed onto the phone's internal storage. Ensure that an antivirus program isn't blocking app installation/upgrade. If an app hangs during the installation or upgrade process, ensure that you have a connection to a Wi-Fi or cellular network, restart the device, and start the process again.

Try downloading the app from a different Wi-Fi network. Follow these generic steps when apps are not installing:

> *Android: Settings > Apps/Application Manager > All >* locate and tap on *Market > Clear Data > Clear Cache.*
> *iOS:* Try resetting the network settings: *Settings > General > Reset* and try again. You could reset all settings or take the device to an Apple Store.

App Not Loading

When you are faced with an app not loading, see if the mobile device believes it to be running already. Windows has *Task Manager*, and Android has *Settings > Apps/Application Manager.* With iOS, some apps refresh their content automatically. You can see these settings with *Settings > General > Background App Refresh.* You can also try closing the app and opening it again. Try restarting the mobile device. Try powering down the device and restarting it. Check for operating system updates as well as app updates. If all else fails, delete the app and reinstall it.

Unable to Decrypt Email

On a mobile device, a user may not be able to open an email because the device is unable to decrypt email. With iOS devices, you can use S/MIME to send and possibly receive encrypted email messages. Use the *Passwords & Accounts* (or *Mail, Contacts, Calendars* on older versions) option > select the appropriate email account > *Account* > depending on the email account type, you can set the S/MIME setting there or go into *Advanced.* Some vendors allow encryption of all messages by default.

Within Android, support for S/MIME is built in to email clients and can be accessed through the email app > *Settings* option. Also, web browser add-ons can be used. Some email apps might require that a security certificate (file) be obtained and copied to the *root directory* (see Chapter 17, "macOS and Linux Operating Systems," for more information on this) or the *Download* folder. Then access your email account > *Settings > Security Options > Email Certificate >* + (plus sign) > select the certificate.

TECH TIP

Email not current on your smartphone?

Check connectivity. If you have internet/cellular access, restart the phone.

AirDrop Not Working

AirDrop is used to transfer documents or photos between two Apple devices. If it is not working, ensure that the two devices are within Bluetooth range or connect to a Wi-Fi network and ensure that the wireless method being used (Bluetooth or Wi-Fi) is enabled. Ensure that Personal Hotspot is turned off. Check both devices for the AirDrop receiving setting. If it is set to Contacts Only, then the sending device must be in the contacts either with the person's Apple ID's email address or a mobile number.

Mobile Device Keyboard/Trackpad Issues

Sometimes when symptoms appear, the solution is not simply to replace the part. The key to such issues is to research what others have done when the particular problem has occurred. For example, software updates sometimes fix hardware issues.

Keyboard Issues

Not all devices have keyboards. Mobile devices can have wireless keyboards, optional keyboards, and wired keyboards. Three common keyboard issues are Num Lock indicator light, sticking keys, and ghost cursor/pointer drift.

The Num Lock key is used to allow keys on the numeric pad to be used as something besides numbers (arrow keys, a Home key, Page Up and Page Down keys, Delete key, Insert key, and End key). See Figure 10.88. Pressing the Num Lock key so the Num Lock indicator light illuminates on the keyboard causes numbers to be used. Again pressing the Num Lock key so the indicator turns off causes the keys to be used for arrow keys and the like. Configure the system BIOS/UEFI for the default action (enabled or not enabled) per the customer's preference.

FIGURE 10.88 Num Lock and numeric keypad

Mobile devices that have keyboards can get dirtier than desktop systems. For sticking keys, follow the same process you would use for a desktop keyboard. Shake out the dirt and spray with compressed air, as shown in Figure 1.22 in Chapter 1, "Introduction to the World of IT." Keys might have to be removed in order to get to the dirt or debris, to clean, or to spray compressed air. Figure 10. 89 shows a close-up of a laptop key that has been removed. Peek under the key to see how it attaches before prying off the key.

FIGURE 10.89 Removed laptop key

Trackpad Issues

The trackpad is commonly problematic for someone who is not used to a laptop. Performing a **touch calibration** or adjusting the sensitivity settings can solve most problems. However, an annoying problem is the illustrious ghost cursor or **cursor drift**, in which the pointer moves across the screen even if no one is touching it. Cursor drift can often be fixed by adjusting the touchpad sensitivity settings or updating the touchpad driver. Malware or a virus can also cause this symptom. In Windows, you can search for `troubleshoot touchpad` for guidance. Some users disable the touchpad and use a wired mouse.

Mobile Device Display Issues

Displays are critical to mobile devices. They get viewed, touched, and swiped more than any other part. Screens can be stuck and may fail to rotate; a display may go out, dim, stop responding, flicker, or in some other way cause user dissatisfaction. Let's tackle some of the common issues.

Screen Does Not Autorotate

Not all apps support screen rotation and work only in landscape mode. But on a screen that **does not autorotate**, it is time to check the settings. On an Android device, go into *Settings* and ensure that the autorotate setting is on and not locked in portrait or landscape mode. On an iOS device, open *Control Center* and check that portrait orientation is turned off. On Windows use the *System* Settings link > *Display* > check the *Lock* rotation and ensure it is in the *Off* position. An app could be causing problems, so close all apps and then open the app you want to rotate after you have ensured that the app supports autorotation. Also see if the OS needs to be updated or whether the G-sensor or accelerometer is faulty.

Dim Display, No Display, or Flickering Display

A **dim display** is commonly caused by a lack of interaction, the display setting, or a low battery. Move the pointer or tap the screen, adjust display settings, and attach AC power to see if the problem is a battery-related issue. On a laptop, the problem could also be caused by an improperly adjusted backlight or sticky lid actuator switch (the switch that detects when the laptop is closed or opened).

If a device has **no display**, attach an external display if possible and use the appropriate Fn key combination to send the output to the external display. If you cannot display to an external monitor or if showing a presentation, you might have to use the Windows *Display* Settings link to adjust the output to duplicate what is showing on the screen. Check video cabling. Also use the appropriate Fn key combination, even if an external display is not available in case the settings have been changed by mistake.

Check the laptop close switch that is located in the main part of the laptop, near the back, where the display attaches to the laptop. The lid close detector can be a physical switch or a magnetic switch located near the back edge of the keyboard portion of a laptop. A laptop and some mobile devices can be configured to go into hibernation, sleep, or standby mode when the laptop is closed. Check the power management settings. Also check the video cable from the laptop system board to the display.

TECH TIP

What to do if a laptop display goes black, red, dim, or pink

If a laptop display goes black, red, dim, or pink, most likely this is because the backlight bulb is faulty. Otherwise, the problem is the DC-to-AC inverter. Connect an external monitor to the laptop external video port. If the external monitor works, most likely the backlight bulb is the culprit.

For a mobile device, try turning it off and back on. On a laptop or tablet, see if the device appears to boot normally. If the device has recently been exposed to liquid, power off the device, remove the battery, and allow the device to dry thoroughly before trying to power it back on again. A bad LCD backlight or inverter can cause a dim or blank display, too.

A flickering display can sometimes be fixed by simply adjusting the resolution (to the native resolution) or refresh rate or tightening the display cable. If you have recently changed the display, check the driver. Move the display to see if the flicker is related to display movement. An inverter and backlight can also cause this problem or show horizontal/vertical lines. Refer to Figure 10.74 to see how the display attaches.

TECH TIP

What to do if the top of a web browser or File Explorer is missing

If the top part of a web browser window where you can enter a URL is missing, try pressing F11, which takes the window out of full-screen mode. If that doesn't work or if the top part of File Explorer is missing, try using Ctrl+Shift+Windows+B to restart the video.

Touch Screen Does Not Respond or Is Inaccurate

The touch screen is a critical part of a mobile device. Users get frustrated by **touch screen non-responsive** issues. The following list suggests things to try if a touch screen is non-responsive or doesn't respond the way you expect it to:

- Close some apps to free up memory.
- Determine whether the problem is app specific, if possible.
- Restart the device. Force a shutdown even if doing so requires disconnecting the AC power cord and/or removing the battery.
- If the display has had any liquid on it, turn off the device and remove the battery. Allow the device to dry thoroughly before powering it on.
- If a screen protector is in place, remove it.
- Shut down the device and remove any memory cards, the SIM card, and the battery for about 60 seconds. Reinstall these items and power up.
- Use a calibration utility, if available, to calibrate for touch input. On an Android device, try *Settings > Display*. In Windows, search for and use *Calibrate the screen for pen and touch input > Calibrate*. For iOS devices, try resetting the phone.
- Perform a factory restart.

If the touch screen is broken, you should be able to still see what is on the device. When the LCD is damaged and cracks appear or when the screen has dark spots, the touch screen might still work in places. Screens can be ordered and replaced. Some repair shops specialize in mobile device displays.

Slow Performance

Slow performance means a system is not responding as fast as it normally does. The problem can be a lot of things, but some folks first notice the responsiveness of a touch screen or delays when waiting for data to download. If you suspect that the touch screen is the problem, troubleshoot that. But if you have ruled out the touch screen, consider the following tips:

- Check the battery power level.
- Close apps that aren't being used.

- Close services (Wi-Fi, GPS, location services, Bluetooth, and so on) that are not being used. Put the device in Airplane Mode.
- Attach to a Wi-Fi network.
- Move closer to the wireless access point if attached to Wi-Fi.
- On newer Android devices, use the option to reduce the amount of data needed by the Chrome browser: *Settings > (Advanced) Data Saver.*

Mobile Device Power Issues

A mobile device quickly becomes useless if it has power issues. Power is required for a device to be mobile. Power issues can include extremely short battery life, no power, swollen battery, and the **battery not charging**.

Battery Issues

A battery is critical for the operation of a mobile device. A battery that has **poor battery health** (that is, it won't hold a charge for long or drains quickly) commonly needs to be replaced. However, the problem could be that many apps, wireless, location services, GPS, and Bluetooth settings are turned on. Check the display settings. Set the brightness/contrast to a lower setting instead of Auto. Inspect the battery to see if it is swollen. A **swollen battery** is a battery that bulges and might even leak (see Figure 10.90). Most batteries that won't hold a charge need to be replaced; a battery that is swollen should be replaced immediately. Also verify that the phone shows the battery actually being charged. Don't just assume that it is charged, based on the amount of time it has been plugged in. The physical connection to the charger could be a tenuous one. The charger could be faulty, too.

FIGURE 10.90 Swollen battery in a cell phone

Battery Not Charging

Improper charging could be due to the battery, the charger, or the connection on the phone. Inspect the connection on the phone first. Do you see any debris or dirt, or do you see pins that look like they do not align with the other pins? If so, power off the device, remove the battery, and clean it with compressed air; gently try to align pins that are misaligned. Do the same inspection on the charge connector. Take a voltage reading on the charger, if possible. See if it is outputting power. See if the same cable and/or charger can charge other devices that require the same voltage and connector type. Try to charge with a different connector, such as a car adapter.

No Power or Frozen System

An electronic device that has no power or is a frozen system is useless. Try the following when troubleshooting a mobile device that will not power up:

> Check for the power light.
> Ensure that the device has not gone into sleep mode. Try waking up the device or powering it down and then powering it up again.
> Check for a misbehaving app. Close all apps and only have one open at a time to see which one might be causing the symptoms.
> Attach the device to an AC adapter and power it up.
> Disconnect the AC power brick, remove the battery, and hold down the power button for a few seconds. Replace the battery and reconnect to AC. Try to power on the laptop again.
> Inspect the power button and think about whether it has felt strange lately.
> When you attach the power brick to the mobile device, does the connector attach easily, or does it wiggle? If the device is a laptop, consider replacing the DC power jack.
> Check the display brightness.
> If the device is a laptop, check the lid close sensor.
> If the device is a laptop or a tablet with a keyboard, try closing the display and opening it back up fully.
> Check for malware or viruses.

Overheating: Warm/Hot to the Touch

Heat is one of the worst enemies of electronic devices. Symptoms of **overheating** include the device being warm or hot (see Figure 10.91) to the touch, losing battery strength faster than normal, and shutting down unexpectedly. Leaving mobile devices in hot vehicles and in the sun is bad. If a device is overheating, power down the device and let it cool. Do not just move it to a cooler spot.

FIGURE 10.91 Overheated laptop

See if you can determine a specific spot on the device that is getting hotter than other places. Determine whether that spot is where the battery or power is located or whether it is another spot on the mobile device. If it is near the battery, troubleshoot power problems after the device has cooled completely.

Check the battery health icon on the device. Inspect the battery. Replace the battery if you think it is the cause. Close unneeded apps and services. Remove the device from its case, if applicable. Ensure that you are not covering the device's air vents, such as by placing it on a lap or pillow. Place a laptop on something that elevates it from the desk, such as drink coasters. In addition, pads, trays, and mats can be purchased with fans that are AC powered or USB powered. Research the device vendor to determine if others are having similar issues.

Mobile Device Sound Issues

Mobile devices, like desktop computers, can have sound issues. If the problem is no sound from speakers, verify that the speakers are plugged into the correct port. Determine whether the volume is muted or low. Is the correct output selected? Do the speakers require external power, and is that power being provided?

For headphone issues, ensure that the cable attaches to the correct line out port. Determine whether you want the speakers disabled. Normally, if you plug into the headphones line out port, the speakers cut off. For Android or iOS devices, check the volume control and whether the device is muted. On tablets or smartphones, check whether other applications are using the microphone.

Another common complaint is that, when headphones are attached, sound still comes through the speakers. Ensure that the headphones connect to the device securely. Power off the device, remove the battery, and clean the headphone jack. Also try these steps:

- *Android:* Press and hold the power/lock button to change the sound setting to mute everything except the media sound. Close unused apps.
- *iOS:* Try muting sound and then re-enabling it.

Mobile Device Network Issues

Chapter 13 goes into more details on networking, but this chapter presents some basic trouble-shooting techniques you can perform on mobile devices without providing more involved details about how these technologies work. The issues are broken down into four areas: Wi-Fi, GPS, Bluetooth, and NFC.

Wi-Fi Issues

Use the following list when troubleshooting Wi-Fi issues such as **intermittent wireless** or **no wireless connectivity** on a mobile device:

- Ensure that the mobile device is not in Airplane Mode.
- Ensure that Wi-Fi is enabled.
- Ensure that the correct Wi-Fi network is chosen. If prompted, provide the appropriate security/login credentials.
- Turn off Wi-Fi and then re-enable it.
- If a laptop always has low signal strength, ensure that the wires are attached to the wireless NIC. If the display has been replaced recently, ensure that all connectors have been reattached properly and have not been damaged.
- For any device that has low signal strength, one issue might be **high network traffic**. Move around and try to see if you get more signal bars by moving. The more bars you see, the better the signal strength and speed of transmission. See Figure 10.92.
- With some laptops, you must turn the laptop to a different angle to attach to an access point or find a stronger signal strength (which means faster transfers). Antenna placement is important in a wireless network. Antennas on mobile devices tend to be in the edges or built into the displays.

- If the internet connection shows **limited connectivity** or you have **no internet connectivity**, try rebooting the device or the router that connects to the internet if in a home or small business network. With a wireless connection, check security settings and ensure that wireless (Wi-Fi) connectivity is enabled. If on a wired network, the cable could be an issue.
- If a mobile device connects to a Wi-Fi network unintentionally, turn off Wi-Fi. Some mobile devices have the ability to automatically switch between Wi-Fi and mobile networks in order to keep a solid internet connection. To disable this in iOS, use *Settings* > *Wi-Fi* > disable *Auto-Join*. On Android devices that have Wi-Fi enabled, use *Settings* > *Wi-Fi* > select and hold on the wireless network that is not wanted > *Forget Network*.
- Whenever a question mark appears at the top of a mobile device, it means there are Wi-Fi networks in the area, and you need to select the one that you want to attach to. A lock next to a wireless network name means you need a password to access the wireless network.
- Slow or intermittent transmissions can be related to distance to the access point, external interference, other Wi-Fi networks and devices, and the number of devices attached to the same wireless access point.

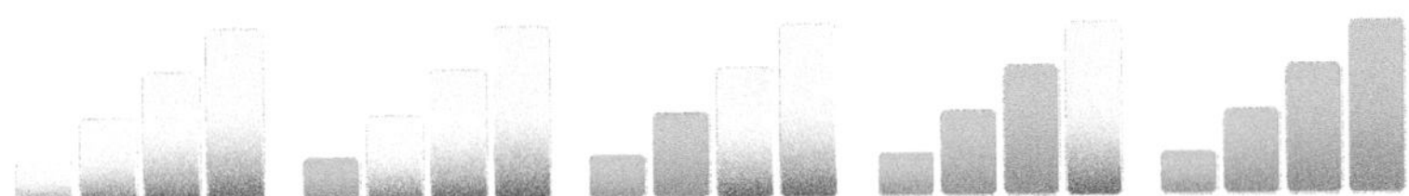

FIGURE 10.92 Wireless signal strength

GPS Issues

GPS is not provided in all mobile devices. The geographic environment affects GPS reception and can cause intermittent connectivity. If GPS is installed, but the problem is GPS not functioning properly, try turning off *Location Services* and then turning it back on. If that fails, restart the device. Some Android devices have assisted GPS, which uses GPS satellites, cell towers, and Wi-Fi networks to provide location services. The device might be in an area where connectivity is limited or missing. Ensure that *Use Wireless Networks* and *Use GPS Satellites* are enabled on an older phone. Some phones have a *High Accuracy* setting instead. Another problem is that the user might have denied a particular app the right to have access to location services, and an app like Google Maps might not be very useful without location services. Access the app settings to verify that location services are enabled. You can try uninstalling and reinstalling the app. Turn off any apps that are using GPS but are not needed.

Bluetooth Issues

If you have **no Bluetooth connectivity**, the suggestions are the same as for all other network connectivity issues: Turn the device off and back on again, move the device closer to the other Bluetooth device(s), and put the device in Airplane Mode and then turn off Airplane Mode to toggle off all radios and then re-enable them. Other troubleshooting hints are as follows:

- Check for interference from other devices, including wireless devices on the same frequency. Also look for Windows, Apple iOS, or Android configuration issues.
- If a Bluetooth device is not working in Windows, try the following: Select the Bluetooth icon ( ) in the notification area on the taskbar and select *Show Bluetooth Devices*. If the device is not listed there, select *Add a Device* and try to add it.
- Ensure that the Bluetooth device is charged, powered on, and in the appropriate mode to pair with another Bluetooth device, such as a computing device or car with Bluetooth capability.

- Ensure that other wireless devices, such as wireless networks, automatic lighting and remote controls, cell phones and other portable phones, and microwave ovens, are not interfering with the device.
- Remove unused USB devices.
- If passkeys (PINs) are used, ensure that the keys match on both devices.
- If a Bluetooth transceiver is used, move the transceiver to another USB port.
- Remove all other Bluetooth devices to aid in troubleshooting the problematic device.
- In Windows, ensure that Bluetooth services are enabled. See Chapter 16, "Advanced Windows," for more information on Windows services.
- In Windows, ensure that Device Manager shows no issues with the Bluetooth transceiver driver (under the *Bluetooth Radios* section) or the Bluetooth device (sometimes shown under the *Other Devices* category). The Bluetooth driver for the host computer may need to be updated for a newer device.
- You can use similar tricks with Apple iOS and Android devices: Ensure that the device is powered, ensure that Bluetooth is enabled, and ensure that no other wireless networks/devices are nearby (by moving to another location to see if they appear).
- A common method used with Bluetooth devices is to restart the pairing mode on the Bluetooth device or rescan for a device from the iOS/Android computing device.
- If a mobile device unintentionally pairs with another Bluetooth device, turn off Bluetooth—and keep it off except when you are using it. Move the mobile device closer to the Bluetooth device.

NFC Issues

The most common cause of NFC not working is that it is turned off/disabled. If you recently did a restart of the mobile device, it may have disabled NFC. Check the battery level. Some devices do not allow NFC to be used if the battery does not have a specific (high) battery charge level. Sometimes a specific style of case may interfere with NFC operations. Check to ensure the device is not in Airplane Mode. Try restarting the device or powering off and back on.

SOFT SKILLS: A WORD ABOUT APPEARANCE

Whether you like it or not, you are sometimes judged on your personal appearance. Why does appearance matter so much? Research shows that we form opinions about each other within mere seconds of meeting. And some people decide whether you are trustworthy in less than a second! Look at Figure 10.93 and imagine that each of these people is a technician coming in to fix your computer. What would be your impression of each person, based only on his or her attire?

FIGURE 10.93 Professional attire options

To make good impressions on your boss and your customers, strive to project a competent and professional appearance and demeanor. A good rule of thumb is to dress to the level of the client. For example, you would probably dress more professionally for a job in a law office or doctor's office than you would for a job at Joe the plumber's business. If you knew you were going to be working on laser printers, you probably wouldn't want to wear your best clothes, or you might wear a lab coat to protect your clothes.

Be aware of generational bias. In the United States today, four generations have different values. The Traditionalists, or silent generation, born 1925–1945, value suits, coats, and ties for men and dresses for women. Most of these people are now age 75+, so there are few of them left in workplaces. The Baby Boomers, 1946–1964, are a little more relaxed about dress codes but still believe in good appearance (think business casual). Now aged in their 60s to 70s, they are likely to be bosses and senior managers. Next come the GenXers, generally born 1965–1980, who value flexibility and freedom and are even more relaxed—even casual. Finally, GenYers, or Millennials—born between 1981 and 1996—value change, diversity, and individual freedom. These are the workers most likely to express themselves with tattoos, piercings, extreme grooming, and so on. To Millennials, dress codes are much less important than they are to members of the other generations.

The following are some common-sense guidelines:

- Above all, avoid tattered jeans, sneakers, and t-shirts, as you could run the risk of looking too scruffy to be taken seriously.
- If your job involves dirty work, such as pulling fiber-optic cables through the overhead space or working on laser printers, jeans and button-down shirts are acceptable. Or consider wearing a lab coat. It doesn't hurt to let the client know upon checking in that you are dressed for a dirty job.

- Watch your haircuts and (for men) beards. Don't forget to groom your hands and nails, which will be noticed (either consciously or unconsciously) by your boss and customers.
- Women are more likely to be better liked and trusted if they use moderate makeup and little to no perfume.

Table 10.18 lists recommendations for attire according to the environment.

TABLE 10.18 Attire in specific environments

Environment	Recommended attire
Business dress or formal	Men: Coat and tie. Women: Dress, skirt, pant suit.
Business casual	Men: Dress shirt (tie optional). Women: Dress, skirt/blouse, pants/shirt.
Casual	Men: Collared shirt, polo shirt, nice pants, slacks. Women: Pants, polo shirt.

TECH TIP

The colors you wear send subliminal messages

Colors can profoundly affect how other people view you. Here are some of the main ones to bear in mind:

- *Black or dark gray:* Represents authority and confidence
- *Blue:* Suggests trust and traditional values
- *Green:* Portrays empathy and tranquility
- *Red:* Conveys that you are passionate and likely to be an extrovert
- *Brown:* Says that you are loyal and reliable

It is usually the subconscious mind that notices how others look. So even if you don't consider appearances to be very important, keep in mind that, without your realizing it, appearances have helped you form an opinion of just about everyone you have ever met. Don't underestimate the importance of dressing appropriately on the job but don't let your wardrobe impede your ability to do the job.

Chapter Summary

- Mobile devices are used for different purposes and therefore come in a variety of types, including laptops, tablets, drawing pads, smartphones, wearable technology, e-readers, and cameras.
- Mobile devices have the following common hardware parts: display, flash memory, battery, DC jack, speaker, microphone, speaker, wireless antenna, system board, processor, and expansion options. Other parts that may be more for laptops or tablets include ExpressCards; SODIMMs; storage that could be mechanical, SSD, and/or hybrid; ports and adapters; keyboards; miniPCI/PCIe cards; touchpads; and touch screens.

- Mobile devices have various methods of expansion and connectivity, including the following: NFC, proprietary, serial, hotspot, USB, miniUSB, microUSB, Lightning, infrared, tethering, Bluetooth, GPS, cellular, satellite, Wi-Fi, miniPCI/PCIe, docking stations, and port replicators.
- Mobile devices commonly have accessories that need to be installed and/or attached, including headsets, touchpads, webcam, speakers, game pads, battery packs/chargers, and memory.
- Mobile device operating systems include the open source Android, p Apple iOS and iPadOS, Chrome OS, and various Microsoft Windows-based mobile operating systems.
- Laptops use Fn to control specific functions, such as Wi-Fi, Bluetooth, speakers, display output, and keyboard backlighting.
- Mobile devices need to have their operating system and data backed up. Two common methods to do this are to back them up to another device or use storage in the cloud.
- Mobile devices need security. All mobile devices need operating system security, personal file and identity security, anti-malware, and antivirus. Remote data wiping can be configured to protect the data on devices that are compromised or stolen.
- A plastic scribe helps with prying off plastic parts and covers. Laptop speakers and DC power plugs frequently have cables that run along the back or sides of the device. Keep screws separated and take notes and photos for any parts that are removed.
- Conserve mobile device power by adding more RAM, turning off wireless/Bluetooth, turning off unnecessary apps, configuring power options, reducing screen brightness, and avoiding temperature extremes.
- Li-ion batteries are used with mobile devices. If a device must be attached to AC power or a USB port in order to work, replace the battery with the correct DC power jack, appropriate DC voltage level, and current (amperage) equal to or higher than the original power brick.
- Before removing or installing memory, disconnect the power cord and remove the battery on a mobile device.
- Laptops can sometimes be upgraded with SODIMMs. Tablets and smartphones can sometimes be upgraded and gain additional storage through flash memory cards.
- AC power goes into the power supply or mobile device power brick. DC power is provided to all internal parts of a computing device.
- Secure a mobile device with a PIN, facial recognition, a password, or a passcode/pattern.
- When replacing a laptop motherboard, additional components may have to be removed.
- Troubleshooting mobile devices commonly includes a soft reset or a restart or a hard reset, which is another name for a factory reset. Android and iOS devices use *Settings* to manage most configurations. Windows uses either various Control Panels or *Settings*.
- Troubleshooting commonly involves disabling apps, connectivity, and features.
- Troubleshooting sometimes involves removing AC power and the battery from a mobile device.
- Mobile device repairs commonly require different tools, including scribes, antistatic gloves, and smaller tools.

19. A mobile device continuously attaches to a nearby Bluetooth-enabled computer that is not the computer the user wants to attach to. What should be done?

    a. Disconnect the Bluetooth adapter from the nearby computer.

    b. Move the Bluetooth device closer to the desired computer.

    c. Power off the nearby computer.

    d. Put the mobile device in Airplane Mode.

20. A technician suspects a mobile device has a security issue due to a rogue APK source because the user admits to just having updated the OS. Which type of mobile device is the technician working on? [Windows laptop | iPad | Apple laptop | Android device]

Exercises

Exercise 10.1 Identifying Laptop Parts

Objective: To identify various laptop parts correctly

Procedure: Identify each part in Figure 10.94 by matching the component name to the identified part in the photo.

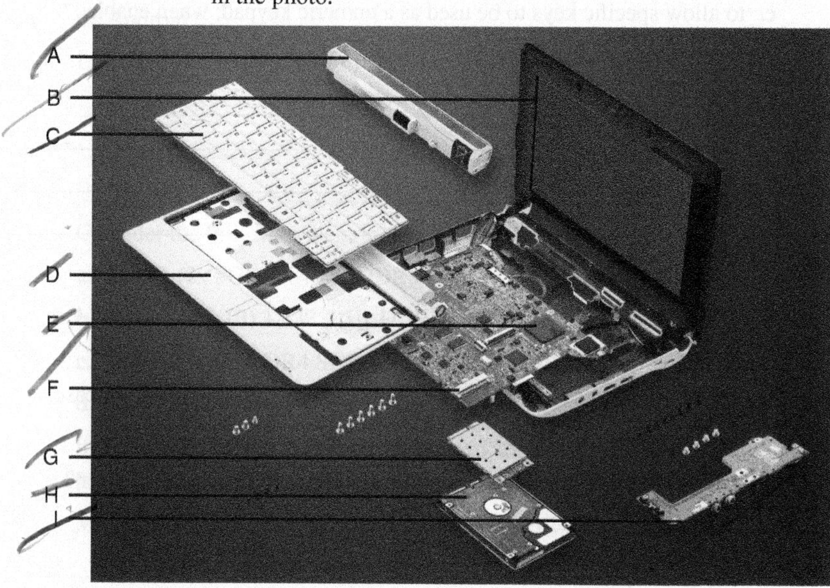

FIGURE 10.94 Laptop part identification photo

Components

LCD	Keyboard
Ports assembly	System board
Mounting bracket for touchpad	Processor
Hard drive	Palm rest assembly
Battery	

A. ____________ F. ____________

B. ____________ G. ____________

C. ____________ H. ____________

D. ____________ I. ____________

E. ____________

Exercise 10.2 Identifying Common Laptop Keys

Objective: To identify various keys used on a laptop

Procedure: Match each laptop function key in Figure 10.95 to the description in Table 10.19.

FIGURE 10.95 Laptop function key identification photo

TABLE 10.19 Keyboard function key usage

a.	Increase volume	**g.**	Mute
b.	Decrease display brightness	**h.**	Increase display brightness
c.	Enable keyboard backlight	**i.**	Display mode
d.	Pair with Bluetooth Device	**j.**	Enable touchpad
e.	Disable webcam	**k.**	Decrease volume
f.	Put in sleep mode	**l.**	Disable touchpad

F1 _______	F4 _______	F7 _______	F10 _______
F2 _______	F5 _______	F8 _______	F11 _______
F3 _______	F6 _______	F9 _______	F12 _______

Exercise 10.3 Identifying Cell Phone Parts

Objective: To identify various cell phone parts correctly

Procedure: Identify each part in Figure 10.96 by matching the component name to the identified part in the photo. Note that not all identified parts are used. Write your answers in Table 10.20.

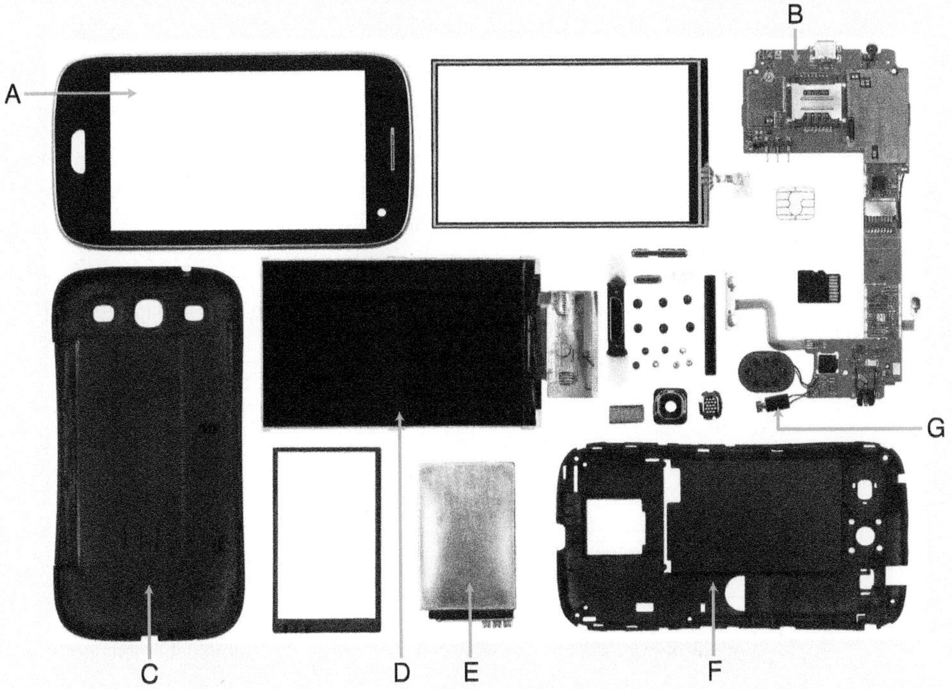

FIGURE 10.96 Cell phone parts identification

TABLE 10.20 Cell phone parts

Part	Corresponding letter
Front enclosure	
Display	
Microphone and camera	
Back enclosure	
Main printed circuit board	
Battery	

Activities

Internet Discovery

Objective: To obtain specific information from the internet regarding a computer or its associated parts

Parts: Computer with internet access

Procedure: Complete the following procedure and answer the accompanying questions.

Questions:

Watch the laptop hard drive replacement video at the following URL to answer Questions 1–5: https://www.youtube.com/watch?v=wSa3Owia-2k. (If this link does not work, find a video that shows a laptop hard drive replacement.)

1. List one piece of software mentioned in the video that might be obtained or purchased in order to clone the operating system.

____

2. Use the internet to find an alternative cloning software that could be used. Detail why you think this software would be appropriate and why you chose it.

____

3. What were the two locations for the hard drives in the two laptops, and how were they removed?

____

____

____

____

____

4. What power safety procedures were recommended?

____

5. What power procedure was recommended in the chapter that was not done in this video?

____

A customer owns a Toshiba Satellite R845-ST6N02 laptop. Use the Toshiba troubleshooting assistant program to help with a battery problem. Use information from this program to answer Questions 6–9.

6. What output values should be on the AC adapter?

____

7. Assume that the values on the AC power brick match those required on the computer. How long should the power button be held down after the external power and battery have been removed from the computer?

____

8. Which two colors can be used for the power indicator light (if it is working, of course)?

____

9. Assume that you have power, and you shut down the computer and remove the AC adapter. What might you do before assuming that the battery is dead?

____

10. A student has an ASUS ROG gaming laptop, and the function keys are not working. Use the internet to find what some people have done. List one or two solutions.

____

____

Soft Skills

Objective: To enhance and fine-tune a future technician's ability to listen, communicate in both written and oral forms, and support people who use computers and mobile devices in a professional manner

Activities:

1. In groups of three, each person finds a video that shows a particular model of laptop being taken apart. Share your findings with the others. Each team selects the best video to share with the class or submits the web link to the teacher.
2. Record yourself describing a mobile device problem and what you did to fix it, in three minutes or less. If you have never had a mobile device problem, use the internet to find someone else's problem and then describe it in your own words. No reading aloud. Tell the story.
3. In groups of six, three people must each find a cartoon or story that describes a funny mobile device situation. The other three people should find a cartoon or story that illustrates the need to dress professionally in the IT field. Each person must share findings with the group. Have a category for mobile and a category for appearance. Each person rates each cartoon or story. Summarize your findings in electronic format or verbally.
4. Each group is assigned one of the following laptop parts: (1) processor and heat solution; (2) mechanical, SSD, or hybrid storage device; (3) display; (4) system board; (5) inverter; (6) backlight. Work in teams to outline in words and illustrations how to replace the part and issues related to the replacement. Present your group's work to the class.
5. Find a graphic or photograph that shows how you think a computer or mobile device technician might appear when professionally dressed. Then find another one that shows inappropriate attire.

Critical Thinking Skills

Objective: To analyze and evaluate information as well as apply learned information to new or different situations

Procedure:

1. Locate two laptop manuals from two different manufacturers. They cannot just be two models from the same manufacturer. Compare and contrast how the CPU is replaced in each one.

____

____

____

2. Select a laptop that has a mechanical hard drive and pretend it is yours and has been yours for at least a year. Now pretend that you are upgrading to an SSD or a hybrid drive. Select what hardware and software you might need and price it all out. Develop a step-by-step plan of action of how you are going to do this.
3. On a separate piece of paper, describe why Wi-Fi networks are so important to cell phone users. Are there any drawbacks to using them?
4. Find a technical job at monster.com, dice.com, or indeed.com. Then look online for at least three graphics or photos showing clothes you think someone would wear to the interview for this job. Find another three graphics or photos that depict what someone would wear on a daily basis for the job.

11 Computer Design and Troubleshooting Review

In this chapter you will learn:

- > To select computer components based on the customer's needs
- > The components best suited for a particular computing environment
- > How to design for specific computer subsystems, such as the video or storage subsystem
- > How to perform basic troubleshooting procedures
- > How BIOS/UEFI controls the boot sequence and how that helps when troubleshooting
- > The purpose of POST error codes
- > How to deal with difficult customers or situations

CompTIA Exam Objectives:

- ✓ 1101-2.8 Given a scenario, use networking tools.
- ✓ 1101-4.2 Summarize aspects of client-side virtualization.
- ✓ 1101-5.1 Given a scenario, apply the best practice methodology to resolve problems.
- ✓ 1101-5.2 Given a scenario, troubleshoot problems related to motherboards, RAM, CPU, and power.
- ✓ 1102-4.7 Given a scenario, use proper communication techniques and professionalism.

Design Overview

Why would employers want technicians to be able to design computers? If you needed a car repaired, wouldn't it be nice to have a person who could design cars to advise you? A designer would know the best engines, the most fuel-efficient body design, what parts might not work well with other parts, and so on. A designer would know a lot about all parts of the car. The same is true about those who can design computers: They know a lot about computer parts and how those parts interact with one another.

When you first learn about computers, you learn the language, or lingo. You learn terms such as *RAM* and *CPU*. Later, when you hear such words, you form images in your mind. You do more than just recognize the words; you actually know what different parts look like. You can explain to someone else what a part does. You continue to grow in a particular area. Designing something is right up there with troubleshooting something well: It requires knowing what you are talking about.

Benjamin Bloom chaired a committee that created a classification of learning objectives that was named Bloom's Taxonomy. Look at Figure 11.1 to see how people normally progress through the learning process from the bottom to the top. Notice that creating is at the top. Of course, employers want people who can design: They are the folks who know all the things it takes to be able to design.

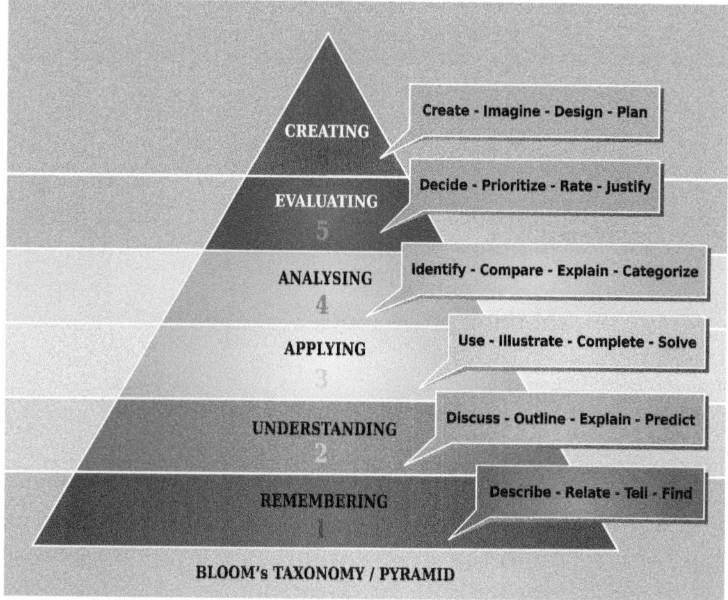

FIGURE 11.1 Bloom's Taxonomy

This chapter helps you learn how to select components within subsystems, such as video or audio, and the components needed for complete computer builds, based on the type of customer and the customer's needs. Even if you are designing just a subset of a computer, such as the video subsystem or an optical drive subsystem, you must know how that subset interacts with other components that might need to be upgraded as well. Be sure to check out the exercises at the end of the chapter, which help put all this together. Practice is one of the best teachers.

Computer System Design

Computer users need different types of computer systems. What the user does with a computer dictates the components and peripherals needed. Looking at computer systems by purpose is a good place to start with design.

Graphic/CAD/CAM Design Workstations

Engineers and design engineers use computer-aided design (CAD) and computer-aided manufacturing (CAM) systems in manufacturing plants to create things. Graphic design personnel also use a similar type of system (see Figure 11.2). A **graphic/CAD/CAM design workstation** needs the following key components:

- Powerful multicore processor(s)
- Maximum system RAM
- A solid-state drive (SSD)
- High-end video card(s) with maximum video RAM and a graphics processing unit (GPU)
- A large display or dual displays
- Large-capacity hard drive(s)
- Optional peripherals such as digital tablets, scanners, plotters, and 3-D printers
- Good-quality mouse or input device

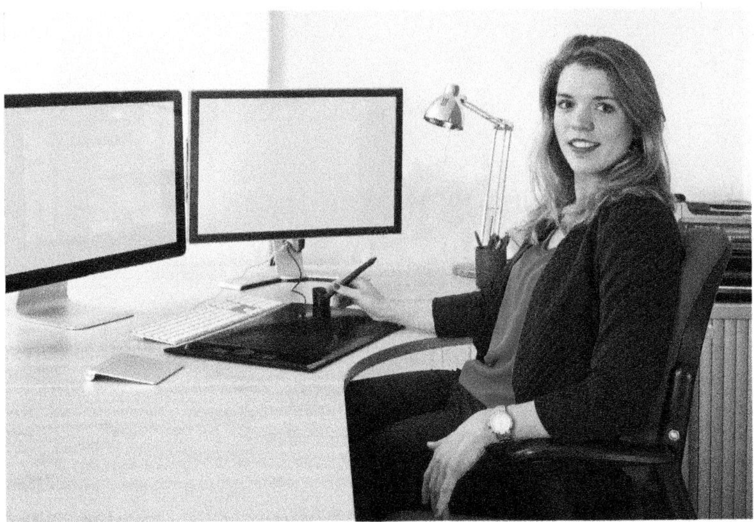

FIGURE 11.2 CAD/CAM design workstation

Gaming PCs

A gaming computer is a unique type of PC. Gamers frequently build their own systems, but some computer manufacturers make gaming PCs. A **gaming PC** (see Figure 11.3) tends to have the following key components:

- Powerful multicore processor(s)
- High-end video cards (with maximum video RAM and specialized GPU)
- High-definition sound card and speakers
- High-end system cooling
- An SSD
- A large amount of RAM
- A large display or dual displays
- Quality mouse
- Optional gaming console
- Headphones with microphone
- Optional 3-D glasses (if supported by the video card and monitor)

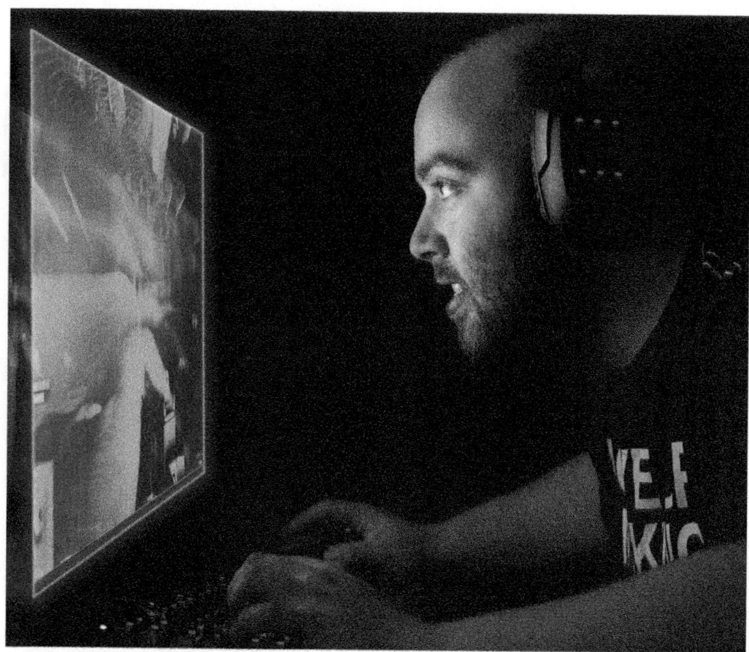

FIGURE 11.3 Gaming PC

Audio/Video Editing Workstations

An **audio/video editing workstation** (see Figure 11.4) is used to manipulate sounds (shorten, add, overlay, and so on) or video. This type of system requires a lot of hard drive space and RAM. These are the most common configuration elements for such a computer:

- Specialized video card with maximum video RAM and GPU
- Sound card and speakers
- Fast and large-capacity hard drive
- Dual monitors
- Powerful multicore processor(s)
- A large amount of system RAM
- Quality mouse
- Possible digital tablet or scanner

FIGURE 11.4 Audio/video editing workstation

Network-Attached Storage (NAS) Devices

A network-attached storage (**NAS**) device can be a single box that contains multiple hard drives used for storing photos, movies, and files from multiple computers in a home or small office environment (see Figure 11.5). It is commonly used for media streaming of videos and music and file sharing in the home environment. A diskless NAS is a storage container that comes without disks so you can add your own mechanical drives or SSDs.

FIGURE 11.5 Home or small business NAS

A NAS can also be rows of hard drives in a larger company environment (see Figure 11.6). These drives provide storage for multiple servers and users and are commonly configured in a RAID array for data recovery in case one drive fails.

FIGURE 11.6 Corporate NAS

Virtualization Workstations

A **virtualization workstation** has at least one operating system, in its own **virtual machine** that is separate from the host operating system (see Figure 11.7). Remember that because each virtual machine has its own operating system, each one needs to have its own applications and security installed. Note that a controlled virtualized workstation in a business is known as a virtual desktop and that is covered in the next chapter.

A virtualization workstation has the following components:

> Maximum CPU cores
> Maximum RAM
> Multiple, fast, large-capacity hard drives
> Possible SSDs
> Possible network-attached storage for increased storage space that can be shared with other devices

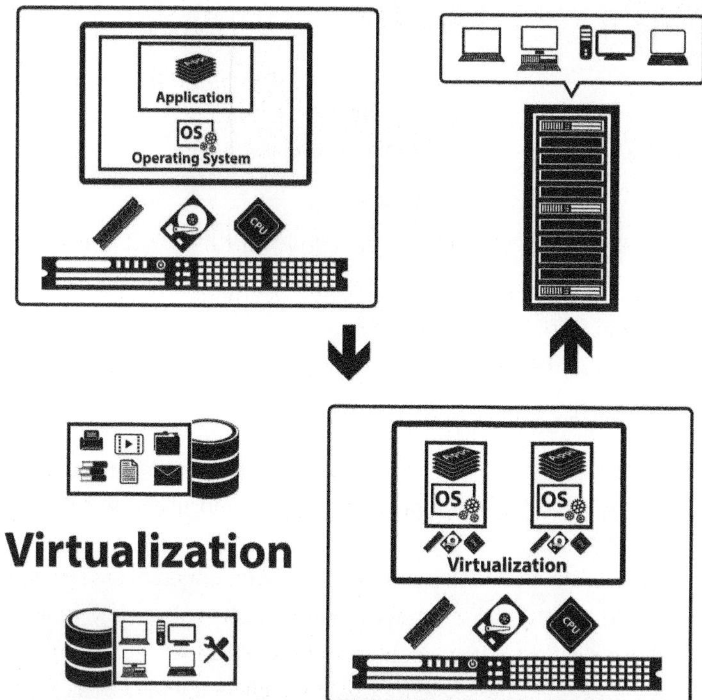

FIGURE 11.7 Virtualization workstation concepts

Thin Client Workstations

A **thin client** workstation is a desktop or laptop that has a display, mouse, keyboard, and network connectivity and runs applications from a server. There is very little software added to the computer. Thin client computers provide better security to critical data and applications and are commonly used in airports, hotels, and corporate areas where the information accessed or software used is centralized.

Thin client computers are less expensive than normal workstations; however, the network infrastructure (for example, servers, software, storage area network [SAN]) to support thin clients costs money. Storage tends to be cloud based or on remote storage media. Both the hardware and software environments can be virtualized (commonly referred to as desktop virtualization) in order to provide a controlled environment. Corporations, medical offices, and call centers commonly use thin clients (see Figure 11.8).

FIGURE 11.8 Thin client workstations

Characteristics to look for in a thin client computer include the following:

> Meets minimum requirements for selected operating system
> Network connectivity (1 Gb/s preferred)
> Only used for basic applications, such as word processing, spreadsheet manipulation, and web-based apps
> Optional display privacy screen

Standard Thick Client Workstations

In contrast to a thin client workstation, a **thick client** computer is the most common type of desktop or laptop in the work environment. Applications are installed, and documents are commonly stored on the local hard drive. An all-in-one computer could be a thick client computer. Computers in small businesses tend to be thick client workstations. A thick client computer has the following characteristics:

> Meets minimum hardware requirements for the selected operating system
> Desktop applications (each one should meet recommended hardware and software requirements)
> Optional display privacy screen
> Optional dual displays

Home Servers

A **home server** computer is used to store data; function as a web server, print server, or file server; control media streaming; be accessible from outside the home; control devices; and manage backups of other computers. Notice in Figure 11.9 that the home server in the top-right corner can be used to back up files from other home devices, such as a laptop. Servers and networks are discussed in Chapter 13, "Networking." Typical components found in a home server include the following:

> Multiple hard drives in a RAID array configuration
> 1 Gb/s (1000 Mb/s) NIC
> Medium to large case
> Multiple processors or multiple cores in the processor
> 8 GB or more RAM
> Server applications, including media streaming, file sharing, and print sharing applications

> Optional NAS
> Optional KVM switch

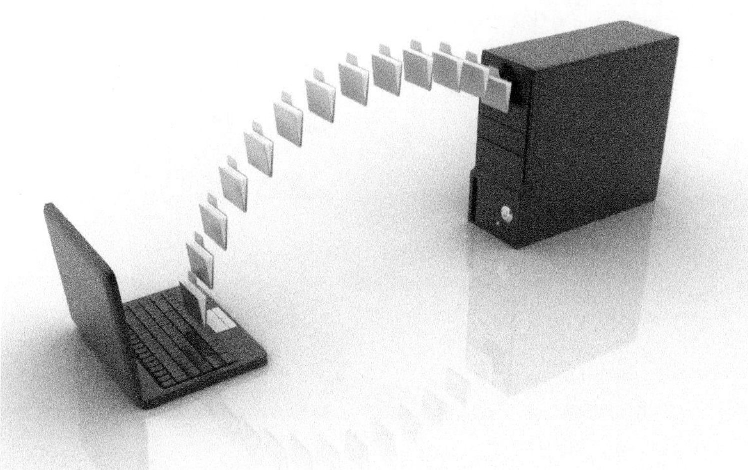

FIGURE 11.9 Home server

Go Green

Keep in mind that there are many ways to go green and conserve energy in computer design. The company requesting a design may require green specifications. Cases, motherboards, processors, power supplies, printers, displays, and other computing devices can be designed with energy conservation in mind. The Electronic Product Environmental Assessment Tool (EPEAT) can help with that.

The **EPEAT rating system** was designed to work with the EPA in identifying products that have a green (and clean) design. **ENERGY STAR** is another program that requires strict energy efficiency. Products that earn the ENERGY STAR rating today have low total energy requirements, low-power modes, and efficient power supplies.

Another aspect of being green is recycling old components. Check with the local disposal regulations and requirements and find places that can recycle your old electronics (see Figure 11.10).

You can also be conscientious of energy requirements when designing a subsystem. Upgrade requests might be for a computer subsystem. In such a case, the best practice is to look at the subsystem as a unit. The following sections examine the various computer subsystems.

FIGURE 11.10 Computer parts recycling

Motherboard and Associated Component Design

The motherboard, chipset, and CPU are all directly related to one another and should be designed in conjunction with one another. If you buy an Intel motherboard, then you have to get an Intel processor; alternatively, you can use an AMD motherboard and processor. Newer technologies may influence your choices.

TECH TIP

Don't forget the cooling

If you select a high-end CPU, you must have appropriate cooling for it.

Memory ties into processor technology because the type of motherboard/chipset dictates the type of memory supported, the maximum amount of memory the motherboard manufacturer might consider putting on the motherboard, and the maximum memory speed that can be used. Whenever a technician is upgrading or replacing a motherboard, compatibility with existing components is a requirement.

The most important design consideration for memory is to take advantage of dual, triple, and quad channeling, when possible. Ensure that the memory modules are purchased together and installed according to the recommendations set forth in the motherboard/computer manual. Encourage the end user to buy as much RAM as he or she can initially afford. This area is one of the most influential considerations on the user computing experience. Beef up this subsystem component as much as possible.

When dealing with the motherboard, consider the form factor, chipset, whether the CPU is included, CPU size, motherboard socket size, nanotechnology used with the processor and/or chipset (14 nm, 22 nm, 32 nm, 45 nm, and so on), CPU cooling, RAM, and the number and type of memory slots/CPU sockets.

Power Supply and Case Design

When selecting a power supply, the main concerns are size (form factor), wattage for specific voltage levels, number of connectors, and power efficiency. One issue you must consider is how many connectors connect to the same cable. When you have several high-powered devices, you want to be able to connect them with separate power cables, if possible, instead of using two connectors along the same cable. Also, be careful with cables that do not have at least four wires. These are peripheral cables to power 12-volt fans and are normally labeled as fan connectors. Some power supplies have detachable cables that connect between a power supply connector and a device connector. You attach the number and type of cables you need. Buy additional cables of a specific type, as needed. Figure 11.11 shows detachable cables.

When replacing, upgrading, or purchasing a power supply, considerations include the number of power cables needed for video cards, number and type of power cables, form factor, wattage for the 12-volt line, total wattage (determined using an online power-use calculator), quietness, mean time between failures (MTBFs), overvoltage, overcurrent, undervoltage and short-circuit protection, as well as warranty period.

The power supply, case, and motherboard have to be the same form factor. Some cases accept multiple motherboard form factors. Most cases have at least two locations for fans: one fan at the front of the case and one at the rear. Fans tend to come in 40, 60, 80, 90, 92, 120, or 140 mm sizes. Look for the following key features in a new case: size, type (desktop or tower), number and type of front panel ports, number and placement of fans, cable management, expansion slots, drive bays, and ease of cover removal.

FIGURE 11.11 Detachable cables for some power supplies

Table 11.1 lists recommendations for cases and power supplies for different types of users.

TABLE 11.1 Power supply and case design

Use	Design considerations
Graphic/CAD/CAM, gaming PC, home server PC, audio/video editing computer, or virtualization computer	500W or higher power supply ATX mid- or full-sized tower Two or more case cooling fans
Thin client	300W or higher power supply Mini-ATX or micro-ATX tower
Standard thick client or normal user	300W or higher power supply ATX, mini-ATX, micro-ATX, or mid-sized ATX tower

Figure 11.12 shows a computer case that has removable drive trays for internal hard drives.

FIGURE 11.12 Case with removable internal hard drive trays

Storage Subsystem Design

The storage subsystem consists of magnetic or flash technologies for internal or external hard drives, flash storage (including SSDs), or optical drives. When adding, replacing, or building a storage subsystem, you must take into account the customer needs, how long the customer plans on storing the data, and how long the customer thinks the storage subsystem will be in use before being upgraded or replaced. Table 11.2 helps with the storage device options.

TABLE 11.2 Storage subsystem design considerations

Feature	Design considerations
Internal connectivity	SATA or M.2
Internal power	Molex or SATA power connector
Internal physical size	1.8, 2.5, 3.5, or 5.25 inches, with an available expansion slot in the case
External connectivity	USB, IEEE 1394 (FireWire), eSATA, or eSATAp port NIC, if required, for cloud (internet) storage Media reader for flash media, if needed
External power	Either external power cord or power provided by the USB, IEEE 1394, or eSATAp port
Storage technology	Magnetic (hard drive or optical drive); SATA 1.5, 3, or 6 Gb/s (SATA1, SATA2, or SATA3), M.2, flash memory (SSD, flash drives, and flash media), or hybrid (magnetic and SSD)
Special storage considerations	Multiple drives, if RAID is used NAS to share storage with other computers
Storage device speed	5,400, 5,900, 7,200, 10,000, or 15,000 RPM for magnetic drives Transfer rate for SSDs Input/output operations per second (**IOPS**) for both magnetic drives and SSDs, which is a measurement that takes into account sequential reads/writes as well as random reads/writes
Optical drive features	Read-only or read/write; red-violet and/or blue laser(s)
Drive buffers	Buffers in storage drives that can increase data transfer rates

Audio Subsystem Design

The audio design subsystem consists of the audio ports and speakers. When upgrading or building an audio subsystem, let the customer listen to the speakers, if possible. Table 11.3 lists audio design considerations.

TABLE 11.3 Audio subsystem design considerations

Feature	Design considerations
Number of speakers	Two for a casual user or gamer; three to seven for a music, video, or gaming enthusiast 5.1 surround-sound system: center channel speaker, two front channel speakers for left/right audio, two rear channel speakers for left/right audio, and a subwoofer for low-frequency (bass) sound effects 7.1 surround-sound system: the same speakers as 5.1, with two additional center channel speakers for left/right audio

Feature	Design considerations
Microphone	Integrated into the display, headset, or external, with a headset being best for conference calls
2.0 or 2.1	2.0 audio subsystem: two channels (left and right), with an amplifier within one of the two speakers 2.1 audio subsystem: two speakers and a subwoofer for lower-frequency sounds
Port connectivity	3.5 mm mini-plug, S/PDIF TOSLINK, S/PDIF fiber, or wireless
Sound card	PCI, PCIe, or integrated into the motherboard Number and type of sound ports matching the speaker connectivity
Logistics	Elimination of trip hazards Shelving, wall plates, wall inserts, wall hangers Speaker location planning

Display Subsystem Design

Displays are important to the computing experience. With respect to replacing, upgrading, and installing displays, design specifications are important. Many consider multiple displays in the work environment the norm. Some jobs require many displays, as shown in Figure 11.13.

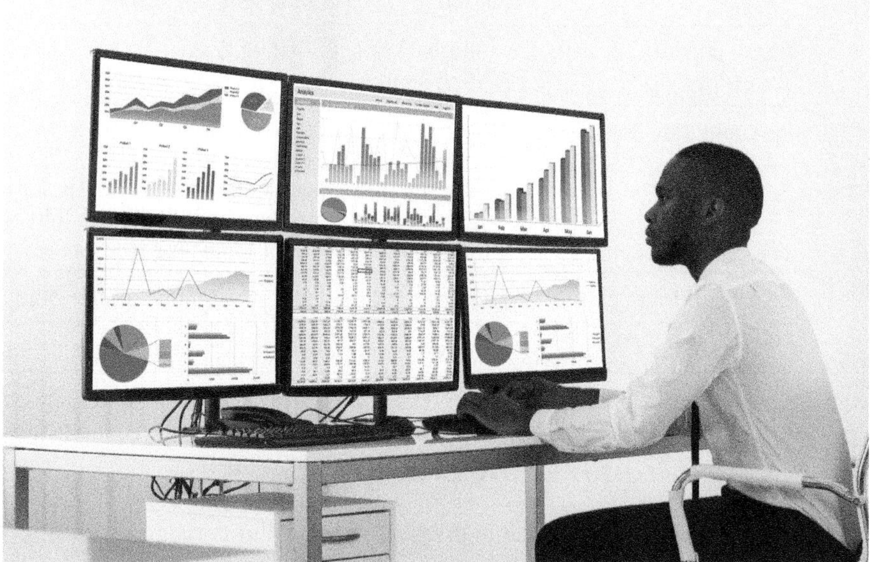

FIGURE 11.13 Multiple displays

Table 11.4 lists some design considerations for displays.

TABLE 11.4 Display subsystem design considerations

Feature	Design considerations
Size/aspect ratio	Common determining factors include physical location, available space, and cost Common aspect ratios: 4:3, 16:9, 16:10, and 1.9:1
Number of displays	Two displays or a single widescreen display
Type of display	Plasma, LCD with CCFL backlight, LCD with LED backlight (LED), or OLED Touchscreen

Feature	Design considerations
Display conferencing features	Integrated microphone or webcam
Contrast ratio	A higher number is better and keep in mind that not all vendors give true numbers
Video adapter	Number and type of ports Number of cards and support for sharing of resources (for example, SLI, CrossFire) Memory GPU Power and cooling requirements Power connectivity requirements

Troubleshooting Overview

When a computer does not work properly, technicians must exhibit one essential trait: the will to succeed. The main objective is to return a computer or peripheral to service as quickly and economically as possible. When a computer is down, a business loses revenue and productivity. Therefore, a technician must have a good attitude and a large amount of perseverance and drive to resolve the problem at hand quickly, efficiently, and in a professional, helpful manner.

TECH TIP

Back up data

Before any changes are made to a system, ensure that its data is backed up, if possible.

Technicians must use all available resources, including documentation for a particular peripheral, motherboard, or computer; the internet; their five senses; other technicians; corporate documentation; textbooks; experience with similar problems; training materials; previous service history on a particular customer/computer; information from users or those around them (see Figure 11.14); or an online database provided by a company or partner. Technicians can be stubborn, but they must keep in mind that time is money, and solving a problem quickly and with the least amount of downtime to the customer is a critical component of a computer support job.

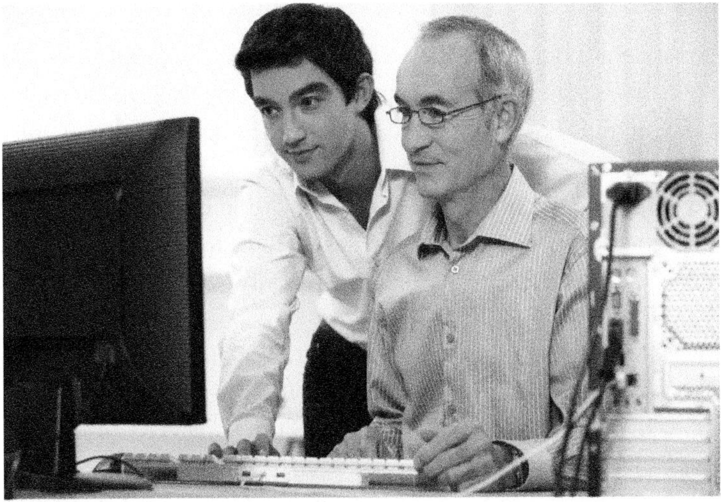

FIGURE 11.14 Technician gathering information from a computer user

TECH TIP

Before making changes...

Always consider corporate policies, procedures, and impacts before implementing changes.

Evaluating and solving a technology problem is a high-level objective in Bloom's Taxonomy, as shown earlier in the chapter (refer to Figure 11.1). Teaching someone to troubleshoot is challenging. Not every problem can be described in a step-by-step fashion. Troubleshooting is easier if a technician uses reasoning and takes logical steps. Logical troubleshooting can be broken down into six simple steps:

Step 1. Identify the problem.

Step 2. Establish a theory of probable cause. (Question the obvious.)

Step 3. Test the theory to determine the cause.

Step 4. Establish a plan of action in order to resolve the problem and implement the proposed solution.

Step 5. Verify full system functionality and, if applicable, implement preventive measures.

Step 6. Document findings, actions, and outcomes.

When following these steps, do not forget to consider company policies, procedures, and how any changes may impact company functions.

Step 1. Identify the Problem

Computer problems come in all shapes and sizes. As part of step 1, you gather information from the user and see if the user has changed anything. Many problems relate to the people who operate computers—the users. Users may fail to choose the correct printer, press the wrong key for a specific function, or issue an incorrect command.

Have the user demonstrate or re-create the problem. Because the user is often the problem, you can save a great deal of time by taking this step. Do not assume anything! A user may complain that "my hard drive does not work" when, in fact, there is no power to the computer. Often users repeat computer terms they have heard or read, but they do not use them correctly or in the right context. By asking a user to re-create a problem, a technician has a chance to see the problem as the client sees it. This should be done even during a phone consultation. Whether diagnosing a problem on the phone or in person, be sure to follow these guidelines:

- Do not assume anything; ask the user to re-create the problem step-by-step.
- Question the user. Ask the user if anything has been changed. Do not be threatening; you want the user to be forthright and honest. Ask open-ended questions to get an idea of what is wrong. Use closed-ended questions (those that require a yes or no answer) to narrow the problem. Refer to Figure 1.2 in Chapter 1, "Introduction to the World of IT," to see examples of these techniques.
- Inquire about any environmental or infrastructure changes in the work environment. Has anything been added to the computer or network recently? Has any maintenance work been done in the area?
- Verify obvious conditions, such as power to the monitor or speakers muted through the settings.
- Do not assume that there is not a problem if the user cannot re-create it. Some problems occur intermittently.
- Use all your senses. Listen for noises such as from the power supply, case/CPU fans, speaker feedback, hard drive, or optical drive. Power off if you detect a burning smell.
- **Back up data**, if possible, before making changes (see Figure 11.15).

FIGURE 11.15 Back up user data before making changes

Step 2. Establish a Theory of Probable Cause (Question the Obvious)

In order to establish a theory of probable cause, you have to have heard or seen the problem as explained by the user. A lot of times, you establish a theory based on analyzing the problem and determining whether the problem is hardware or software related (or both) by using your senses. Sight, hearing, and smell can reveal a great deal. Smell for burning components. Watch the computer boot, look for lights, listen for beeps, and take notes.

Review system and application logs. Operating system logs document what occurs during normal and abnormal conditions. Applications also log issues. For hardware issues such as those related to motherboards, RAM, CPU, or power, make sure you examine log entries and error messages displayed. Use the Windows *System Configuration* window > *Boot* tab and enable the *Boot log* checkbox > *Apply* > *OK* > *Restart.* Within the Options window select *Enable Boot Logging* > *Reboot* > and examine the logging file `ntbtlog.txt` (by opening the *Run* option and searching for **`C:\Windows\nbtlog.txt`**).

Finally, use internal resources such as coworkers or your boss. Use external resources including the internet to research symptoms. Do not forget to question the obvious.

The Boot Process

One thing that might help you establish a theory of probable cause is to examine the boot process. Frequently, a hardware problem is detected during the power-on self-test (POST) executed by the BIOS/UEFI when the computer is first powered on. Remember that the traditional BIOS is looking for the boot loader (a small bit of code on a drive). The computer is configured with a specific device boot order. Knowing the steps taken during the boot process can help you troubleshoot an older machine that has a traditional BIOS:

Step 1. The power supply sends a power good signal.

Step 2. The CPU looks in BIOS for software.

Step 3. The CPU executes POST from BIOS. Note that any errors are usually audio or motherboard LEDs or codes at this point.

Step 4. System resources (I/O address, memory addresses, and interrupts) are retrieved from nonvolatile RAM (NVRAM), (which is RAM that can be changed but where data is not lost when power is removed) and assigned to ports, devices, and adapters.

Step 5. Video is initialized, and a cursor appears.

Step 6. POST continues to check hardware and error messages, and/or codes can now appear on the display.

Step 7. Based on the boot order configuration in System Setup, the system checks for an operating system from the specified devices.

Step 8. The computer loads an operating system found from the first device that contains an operating system or displays an error.

On a newer computer that has a UEFI BIOS, things can be a bit different. A UEFI BIOS can optionally have a BIOS compatibility mode in which the computer behaves as previously described. However, if the system is natively booting using UEFI, the UEFI standards require a common format for executable code. This allows much more flexibility in the boot process, as UEFI has to be able to interpret (not just recognize) globally unique identifiers (GUID) partition table (GPT) partitions and the traditional master boot record (MBR). UEFI supports larger drives and partitions.

UEFI has a boot manager. This boot manager can load UEFI drivers and applications and is customizable. These are not operating system drivers. This means that if the operating system has issues, you can still use your mouse and other devices that have UEFI drivers within the UEFI environment and with UEFI applications that could help with troubleshooting. Refer to Chapter 4, "Introduction to Configuration," for a refresher on the UEFI BIOS. Figure 11.16 shows the boot sequence for a UEFI-based device.

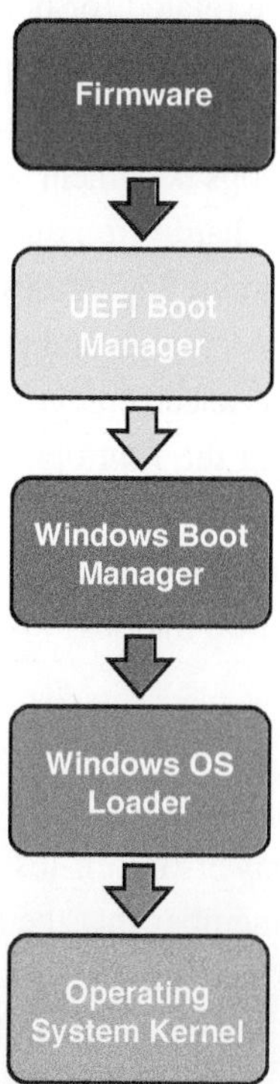

FIGURE 11.16 UEFI boot order

POST Codes and Error Messages

During the firmware phase—whether UEFI or BIOS is used—POST checks out the hardware in a sequential order, and if it finds an error, the BIOS/UEFI issues a beep, displays a numeric error code, or displays an **error message**. Make note of any error codes, beeps, or messages. The number or duration of beeps, the meaning of numeric error codes, and the type of error messages that appear are different for different computers.

TECH TIP

Audio POST code: Checking video and RAM first

Have you ever been working on a computer and gotten a POST code that you didn't want to take the time to look up? Audio codes are frequently related to video and memory. Check connections and reset the card or module.

The secret is knowing the BIOS/UEFI chip manufacturer. The computer or motherboard documentation sometimes contains a list of codes or beeps used for troubleshooting. A single beep is a common tone heard on a successful completion of POST because hardware errors were not detected. Listening is an important part of troubleshooting.

Table 11.5 lists the audio beeps heard on Dell computers. Look at the first line. The 1-1-2 means the computer beeps once, pauses, beeps again, pauses, and then beeps two times. Table 11.6 lists audio beeps for computers that have an AMI BIOS/UEFI chip installed. Table 11.7 lists the audio beeps heard on a computer with a Phoenix BIOS/UEFI chip installed.

TABLE 11.5 Dell computer POST audio beeps

Beeps	Description of problem
1-1-2	Processor register failure
1-1-3	NVRAM
1-1-4	BIOS checksum failure
1-3-1 through 2-4-4	Memory modules not identified or used
3-2-4	Keyboard controller test failure
3-3-1	NVRAM power loss
3-3-2	NVRAM configuration
3-3-4	Video memory test failure
3-4-1	Screen initialization failure
4-3-4	Time-of-day clock stopped

TECH TIP

Troubleshoot the first POST code heard or seen

If multiple POST errors occur, start by troubleshooting the first one you hear or see.

TABLE 11.6 AMI BIOS/UEFI audio beeps

Beeps	Description of problem
1, 2, or 3	Memory error
4, 5, 6, or 7	Motherboard component
8	Video issue
1 long 3 short	Memory test failure
1 long 8 short	Display test failure
2 short	POST failure

TABLE 11.7 Phoenix audio beep codes

Beeps	Description
1-2-2-3	BIOS ROM (flash the BIOS/motherboard)
1-3-1-1	Memory refresh (RAM contacts/RAM)
1-3-1-3	8742 keyboard controller (keyboard/motherboard)
1-3-4-1	Memory address line error (RAM contacts/RAM/power supply/motherboard)
1-3-4-3	Memory error (RAM contacts/RAM/motherboard)
1-4-1-3	CPU bus clock frequency
2-2-3-1	Unexpected interrupt (adapter/motherboard)
2-4-2-3	Keyboard error
3-1-1-1	Onboard I/O port issue

Don't get frustrated about error messages that appear on the screen. Error messages are good things in that they assist you in troubleshooting. Table 11.8 lists the POST error messages sometimes seen on other computers.

TABLE 11.8 BIOS/UEFI POST error messages

Message	Description
BIOS ROM checksum error—System halted	The BIOS/UEFI has a problem and needs to be replaced.
CMOS battery failed/error	Replace the motherboard battery.
CMOS checksum error—Defaults loaded	CMOS has detected a problem. Check the motherboard battery.
CMOS timer error	The system date/time has not been set. Check/replace the motherboard battery if this is not the first time this computer has been powered on.
Hard disk install failure	The BIOS/UEFI could not find or initialize the hard drive. Check the hard drive connectivity and power.
Intruder detection error	The computer chassis has been opened.
Keyboard error or no keyboard present	The keyboard could not be found. Check the cabling.

Message	Description
Keyboard is locked out—Unlock the key	Ensure that nothing rests on the keys during the POST.
Memory test fail	A RAM error occurred. Swap the memory modules.
Memory size decrease error	The amount of system RAM has decreased. Check to see whether RAM has been stolen, needs to be reseated, or needs to be replaced.
Memory optimal error	The amount of memory in channel A is not equal to channel B. For optimal memory performance, the channels should have equal memory. See Chapter 6, "Memory," for more details.
Override enabled—Defaults loaded	The current settings in CMOS could not be loaded, and the BIOS/UEFI defaults are used. Check the battery and CMOS settings.

A BIOS/UEFI can be sold to various computer manufacturers that are then allowed to create their own error codes and messages. Look in the motherboard/computer manual or on the manufacturer's website for a list of exact error messages.

TECH TIP

Check motherboard manual or website for the latest error codes

Manufacturers constantly produce BIOS/UEFI upgrades, and you can use the internet to verify POST errors that occur and the recommended actions to take.

In addition to generating audio tones or numeric error codes or written messages, additional troubleshooting information might be provided, such as the following:

> You might see a **proprietary crash screen** or a screen showing something that is unique to a specific manufacturer.

> In Windows, you might see a blue screen of death (**BSOD**) with a numeric code and/or a message. You might also see the system display a message saying a particular application is not responding or nothing is happening at all. Use *Task Manager* to stop the application or give the application more time to complete the task. Close other open applications. See Chapter 16, "Advanced Windows," for more Windows troubleshooting.

> On macOS or Linux operating systems, you might see a colored **pinwheel** that appears to turn forever. Use *Activity Monitor* to check for processor and RAM performance and free disk space and/or to stop the problematic application. See Chapter 17, "macOS and Linux Operating Systems," for more troubleshooting tips on Mac and Linux systems.

When a numeric code appears or when certain lights illuminate, you have to use the internet or motherboard/computer manual to determine the issue. Some motherboards have a numeric display or colored indicators that display as part of the POST. The meaning of the visual clues can be found in the motherboard or computer manual.

Other Diagnostics

Some technicians carry a POST card as part of their toolkit. A **POST card** is a PCI/PCIe adapter or USB-attached card that performs hardware diagnostics and displays the results as a series of codes on an LED display or LED light(s). These are not as popular today as they once were because many UEFI-based motherboards include powerful diagnostics (see Table 11.9) that can be executed or downloaded from the computer manufacturer's website. However, a POST card is useful if a system does not boot and no other symptoms appear.

TABLE 11.9 UEFI diagnostic types

Diagnostic	Description
Express, start, or system test	Similar to POST, checks the main hardware components needed to load the operating system.
Component test	Allows selection of individual parts to test.
Hard drive test	Checks the drive for bad areas and has the capability to mark an area and not use it in the future.
Memory test	Performs multiple reads/writes to memory locations.
Battery test	Checks the battery's power level.

Some motherboard LEDs are used in conjunction with switches that can be pressed to test components. Figure 11.17 shows a motherboard LED, and Figure 11.18 shows some common uses of motherboard LEDs.

FIGURE 11.17 Motherboard LED

Examples of Motherboard Switches and LEDs

Switch	LED	Explanation
MemOK!	MemOK	Depress the MemOK switch to determine if the RAM modules are compatible. The MemOK LED illuminates if so.
EPU	EPU	Enable the EPU switch or enable through BIOS to allow the motherboard to moderate power consumption. When enabled, the EPU LED is lit.
	RAM	The RAM LED illuminates for a memory error.
	Power	The power LED commonly illuminates when power is applied, or if the computer is in either the sleep or soft off power mode.

FIGURE 11.18 Motherboard switches and LED usage

Hardware Errors

Hardware errors sometimes occur. For example, a display might suddenly go black, an optical drive's access light might not go on when it attempts to access the optical disc, or a printer might repeatedly flash an error code. If you suspect a physical port problem, you can use a loopback plug to test the port. A **loopback plug** sends a signal out one or more electrical pins and allows the signal to come back in on one or more different pins. One of the most common uses for a loopback plug is to test a communication circuit port or an RJ45 loopback plug to test network port functionality.

Hardware errors are usually obvious because of POST error codes or errors that occur when accessing a particular device. Also, some peripherals, such as hard drives and printers, include diagnostics as part of the software that is loaded when the device is installed. These diagnostics are frequently accessed through the device's *Properties* window.

Intermittent Device Failure

Sometimes, none of the hardware troubleshooting actions described so far work. In such a case, a grounding problem might be the issue. Symptoms of a grounding problem include intermittent or unexplained shutdowns.

To troubleshoot an **intermittent device failure**, build the computer outside the computer case on an antistatic mat, if possible. Start with only the power supply, motherboard, and speaker connected. Even though it will normally produce a POST audio error, verify that the power supply fan turns. Most power supplies issue a click before the audio POST beeps. Next, verify the voltages from the power supply. If the fan turns and the voltages are correct, power down the machine and add a video adapter and monitor to the system. If the machine does not work, put the video adapter in a different expansion slot and try again. If placing the video adapter in a different expansion slot does not work, swap out the video adapter.

If the video adapter works, continue adding devices one by one and checking the voltages. Just as any one device can prevent a system from operating properly, so can any adapter. If one particular adapter causes a system to malfunction, try a different expansion slot before trying a different adapter. If the expansion slot proves to be a problem, check the slot for foreign objects. If none are found, but the problem still occurs, place a note on the expansion slot so that no one will use it.

An intermittent device failure is one of the hardest things to troubleshoot. Devices commonly associated with intermittent device failure are the motherboard, RAM, processor, and power supply; however, a failing hard drive can also present as an intermittent device failure if the drive is starting to have problems.

When considering the motherboard, RAM, processor, and power supply, RAM is the easiest to troubleshoot of these four components if there are multiple memory modules installed. Before trying anything else, remove power to the system and push firmly on the memory modules. They can creep up a bit even with the side locking levers in place. Power on and see if the problem reappears. If it doesn't, swap the modules to see whether symptoms change or remove one of the modules. If the system stays stable, re-insert the module and see whether the intermittent failure returns.

For intermittent power issues, first check the power output with a power supply tester. Also check the power supply wattage and ensure that it is adequate for the number of installed devices. Inspect power connectors to ensure that they have not gotten caught or crimped in the cover.

Determining whether a problem is a motherboard or a processor is tough. The easiest thing to do is check the processor on a different (compatible) motherboard. You might see whether you can use a particular UEFI diagnostic to do an extended test on the motherboard and processor.

Software Errors

Software errors occur when a computer user accesses a particular application or file or when the system boots. Applications sometimes present error messages like POST does, but they are application specific. Sometimes an application restarts itself or needs to be manually stopped through Task Manager. Then you can open the application again.

Some software errors relate to hardware, such as a USB-to-serial adapter. If the application being used with such an adapter locks, unplugging the USB cable and re-inserting may cause the hardware and software to start working again.

Sometimes a software problem can be resolved with a **warm boot**. Warm booting causes any changes that have been made to take effect without putting as much strain on the computer as a cold boot does. A warm boot can be performed in various ways, but one way is through the *Start* button > *Power* option > *Restart*.

Files that affect the booting process, such as files in the Startup folder, are dependent on the operating system. If in doubt as to whether a problem is hardware or software related, use Windows *Device Manager* to test the hardware to eliminate that possibility. Every software program has problems (bugs). Software manufacturers typically offer software **patches** or **service releases** to fix known problems. Patches or service releases are usually available on the internet from the software manufacturer. It is important to keep applications and the operating system patched. A **service pack** usually contains multiple patches and installs them at the same time rather than in multiple downloads.

Take your time with this step, gathering all the details you can to come up with what the problem could be. Figure 11.19 shows some problem-solving strategies you can use during this part of the troubleshooting process.

FIGURE 11.19 Problem-solving strategies

Step 3. Test the Theory to Determine the Cause

Once you have a theory or suspect a general area and your theory is confirmed, you need to determine the next steps needed to resolve the problem. If you go through a series of steps and the problem is still unresolved, you might have to step back and re-evaluate the problem. From there, you can establish a new theory or, if needed, escalate the problem to a more senior technician.

Divide the problem into logical areas and continue subdividing the problem until you have isolated it. For example, if an error appears each time the computer user tries to write data to a flash drive, the logical places to look are the user's flash drive, the port that it connects to, potentially a cable that connects the port to the motherboard, the motherboard circuits that control that port, the BIOS/UEFI settings where the port could be disabled, and the software program currently being used. Any of these may be the cause of the problem.

Ernie Friend, a technician of many years, advises students to divide a problem in half, and then divide it in half again, and then continue to divide it until the problem is manageable. This way of thinking carries a technician a long way. Also, keep in mind that you will eventually beat the problem at hand! You are smarter than any problem!

TECH TIP

Reinstall the original part if it does not fix the problem

Reinstall the original part if the symptoms do not change after changing out that part. Then continue troubleshooting.

Here's how you could use Ernie's philosophy with a flash drive problem: Divide the problem in half by determining whether the problem is hardware or software related. To determine whether the software application is causing the problem, try saving a file to the flash drive from another application. If the second application works, then the problem is in the first application. If both applications have problems, the problem is most likely in the hardware or the BIOS/UEFI. The next easiest thing to eliminate as a suspect is the flash drive. Try a different flash drive. If a different flash drive works, then the first flash drive was the problem. If neither drive accepts data, the problem is the port, cable, motherboard, or BIOS/UEFI settings. Try a different port. If that works, then something is wrong with the port or the cable that goes from a front panel port to the motherboard, the port is disabled (check Device Manager), or the port is disabled in the BIOS/UEFI settings.

If a hardware problem is evident after a POST error or peripheral access/usage error occurs, consider the problem a subunit of the entire computer. For example, if a POST error occurs for the optical drive, the subunit is the optical drive subsystem, which consists of the drive, the cable, and the controlling circuits that may be on an adapter or the motherboard.

If a problem is software related, narrow it to a specific area. For example, determine whether the problem is related to printing, saving, or retrieving a file. This may give you a clue about what section of the application is having a problem or may even lead you back to considering other hardware components as the cause of the problem.

TECH TIP

Change or check the easy stuff first

When isolating a problem to a specific area, be practical; change or check the easy stuff first (see Figure 11.20). Time is money—to the company or person whose computer is down and to the company that employs the technician.

"It could be that it's not plugged in, but that would be too easy."

FIGURE 11.20 Check the easy stuff first

When multiple things could cause a problem, make a list of possibilities and eliminate the potential problems one by one. If a display is faulty, swap the display with another one before opening the computer and replacing the video adapter.

Also, check with the computer user to see whether anything about the computer has changed recently. For example, ask if anyone installed or removed something from the computer or if new software was loaded before or has been loaded since the problem started. If the problem is hardware related, you can use the Device Manager and Windows troubleshooting wizards to narrow it down to a subunit.

If you do not hear any unusual audio beeps or see any POST error codes and you suspect a software error, reboot the computer. Before Windows starts, press the F8 key to bring up the *Advanced Boot Options* menu. Select a menu option, such as *Repair Your Computer*, *Safe Mode*, or *Last Known Good Configuration*. On newer computers, it is not always easy to press the F8 key fast enough during startup to get to the Advanced Startup options. Here's how to do this for Windows: Access *Settings* > *Update & Security* > *Recovery* > locate the *Advanced Startup* section > click the *Restart Now* button.

Determining what the problem is usually takes longer than fixing it. Software problems frequently involve reloading software applications and software drivers or getting software updates and patches from the appropriate vendor. The internet is an excellent resource for these files and vendor recommendations. Hardware problem resolution simply involves swapping the damaged part.

If swapping a part or reloading the software does not solve the problem, go back to logical troubleshooting. Step 2 reminds you to divide the problem into hardware- and software-related issues. Go back to that step, if necessary.

Step 4. Establish a Plan of Action to Resolve the Problem and Implement the Solution

Every repair should involve a plan of action. Having a plan helps you through the problem-resolution process. The plan of action should take you through resolving the problem and implementing the solution. Refer to the vendor's support site and instructions for guidance in how to proceed.

Some repairs take multiple steps. You might have to apply a BIOS/UEFI update before installing a new adapter. You might have to update the operating system or remove a virus before reinstalling or upgrading an application. Having a plan instead of just doing things in a random order saves time—and time is money!

Step 5. Verify Full System Functionality and, If Applicable, Implement Preventive Measures

Do not assume that a single hardware component or software repair fixes a computer. The computer can have multiple problems, or one repair may not offer a complete solution. Verify full system functionality and have the user test the computer in normal conditions to ensure that the problem is indeed solved. You may need to implement preventive measures, such as cleaning the computer or device or installing a legal copy of antivirus/anti-malware software and making sure that software is updated. Preventive measures also include using disk maintenance utilities to clean up the hard drive, cleaning the optical drive laser lens, scheduling disk maintenance, and creating a recovery image.

Step 6. Document the Findings, Actions, and Outcomes

Many technicians feel that their work is done once a problem is solved, but it is not. It is important to document the steps taken to resolve a problem in a clear, concise manner. A lot of times, this documentation is put in a customer's record, or an invoice is generated as a result of the repair. Having easy-to-read and easy-to-understand documentation is important for nontechnical users who see this documentation as well as any follow-up repairs that you or another technician must do. The old adage that a job is not done until the paperwork is done is still true, even though the paperwork is now usually electronic documentation, as shown in Figure 11.21. Documentation remains an important last step.

The best computer technicians can repair problems, build trust with users, and explain problems in a way customers can understand. A repair is not finished until the user is informed. Technical training on new equipment or a procedure/process may be necessary. Realize that computer users are intelligent, even if they are not proficient in technical terminology.

A good recommendation is to follow up with a customer a week after a repair to make sure the customer is satisfied and verify that the problem is solved. If the customer is unhappy, jump at the chance to redo the repair. The best advertising is good referrals from satisfied customers. Keep in mind that the general rule of thumb is that if a customer is satisfied, he or she will tell 1 or 2 other people about the service, but if a customer is dissatisfied, he or she will tell 10 other people about the problem.

Each computer repair is a different scenario because of the plethora of vendors, products, and standards in the marketplace. But this is part of what makes a technician's job so interesting and challenging. Break down each problem into manageable tasks, isolate the specific issue, and use all available resources—including other technicians, documentation, and the internet—to solve a problem. Keep a "can do" attitude with intermittent problems, which are the most difficult-to-solve types of problems. Don't forget to tell the user what was done.

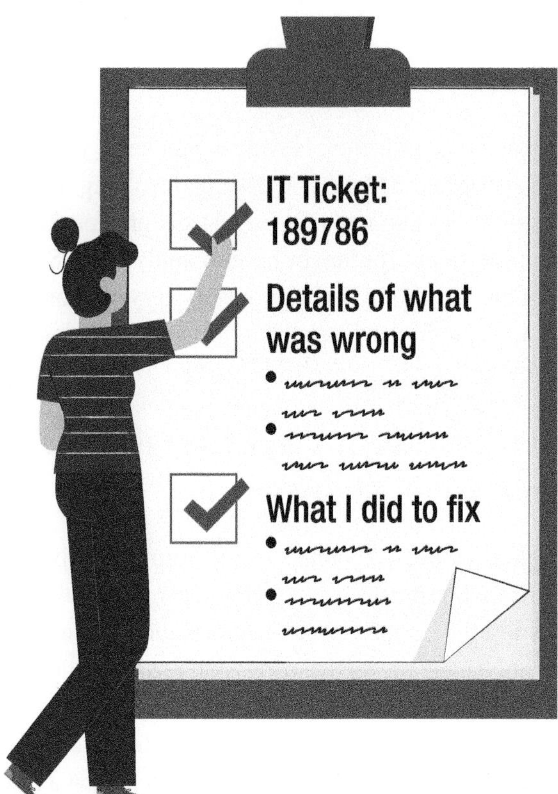

FIGURE 11.21 Document the findings, actions, and outcomes

Sample Troubleshooting Flowcharts

Technical documentation commonly includes troubleshooting flowcharts. Learning how to read and use them is helpful. Figure 11.22 shows a flowchart that does not have any words in it. The symbols in the sample flowchart are as follows:

- The powder blue and dark orange rectangles with rounded edges are terminal blocks that show where to start or where to end. Not all flowcharts have these blocks.
- The lime green parallelogram shows input or output, which could be generating a report or receiving some type of diagnostic data.
- The yellow rectangle is the most common shape you will see in a flowchart. It shows an action to take, a task to do, or an operation to perform.
- The purple diamond is a decision box. Which direction you take out of the decision box depends on what happens. Notice in Figure 11.22 that there are three results that could occur from the decision box. If they were Yes, No, and Not applicable, and whatever you did resulted in the question posed in the purple box having an answer of yes, the left output from the purple decision box could lead to another action box, labeled Yes. If the answer were not applicable and the bottom of the purple decision box were labeled N/A, then you would terminate and be done (drop to the orange terminal block). If the answer out of the purple decision box were no and the right side of the decision box were labeled No, you would do the action listed in the blue action box on the right

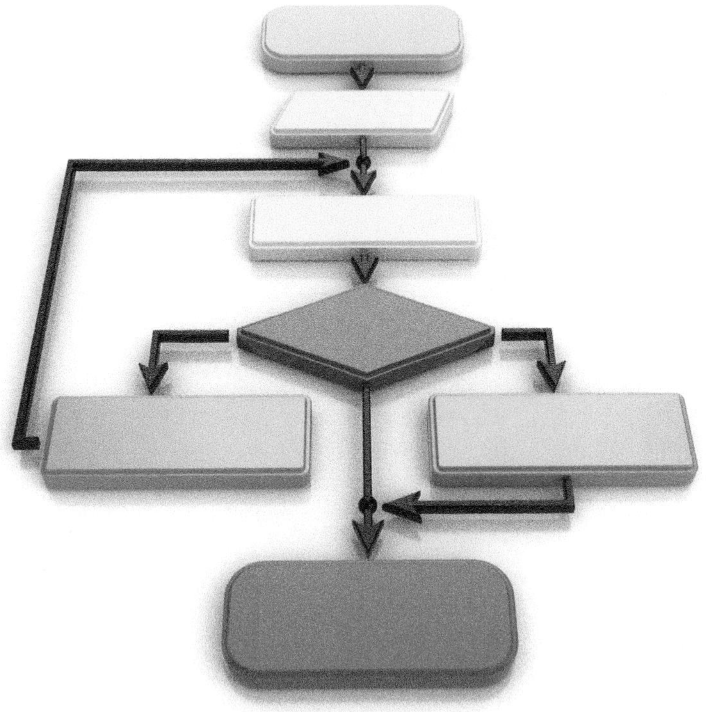

FIGURE 11.22 Sample flowchart

Figure 11.23 shows a simple troubleshooting flowchart, and Figure 11.24 shows a USB troubleshooting flowchart.

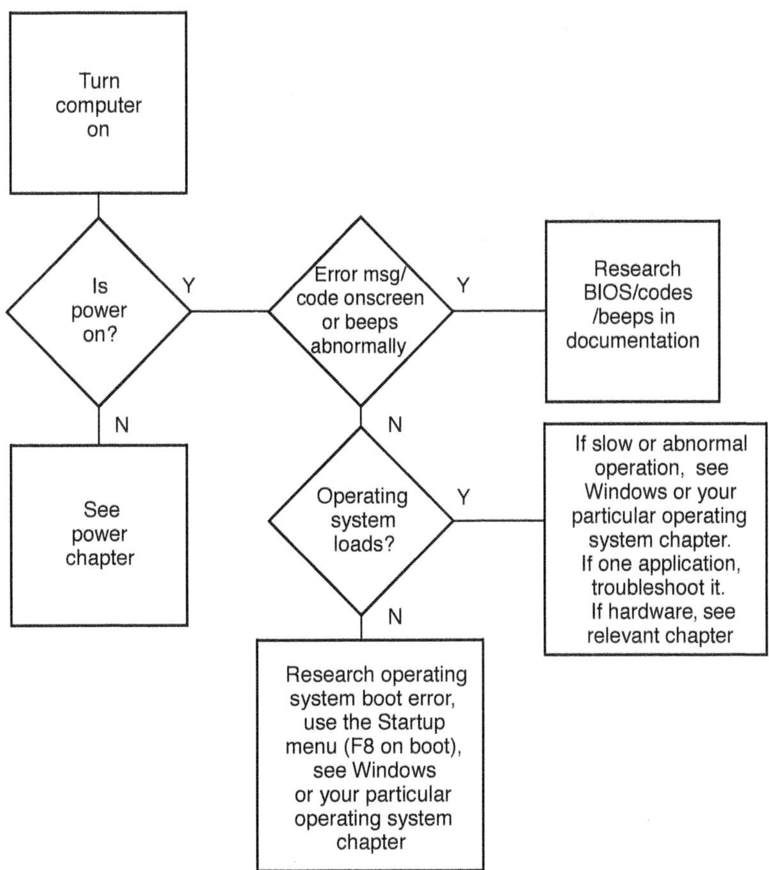

FIGURE 11.23 Basic troubleshooting flowchart

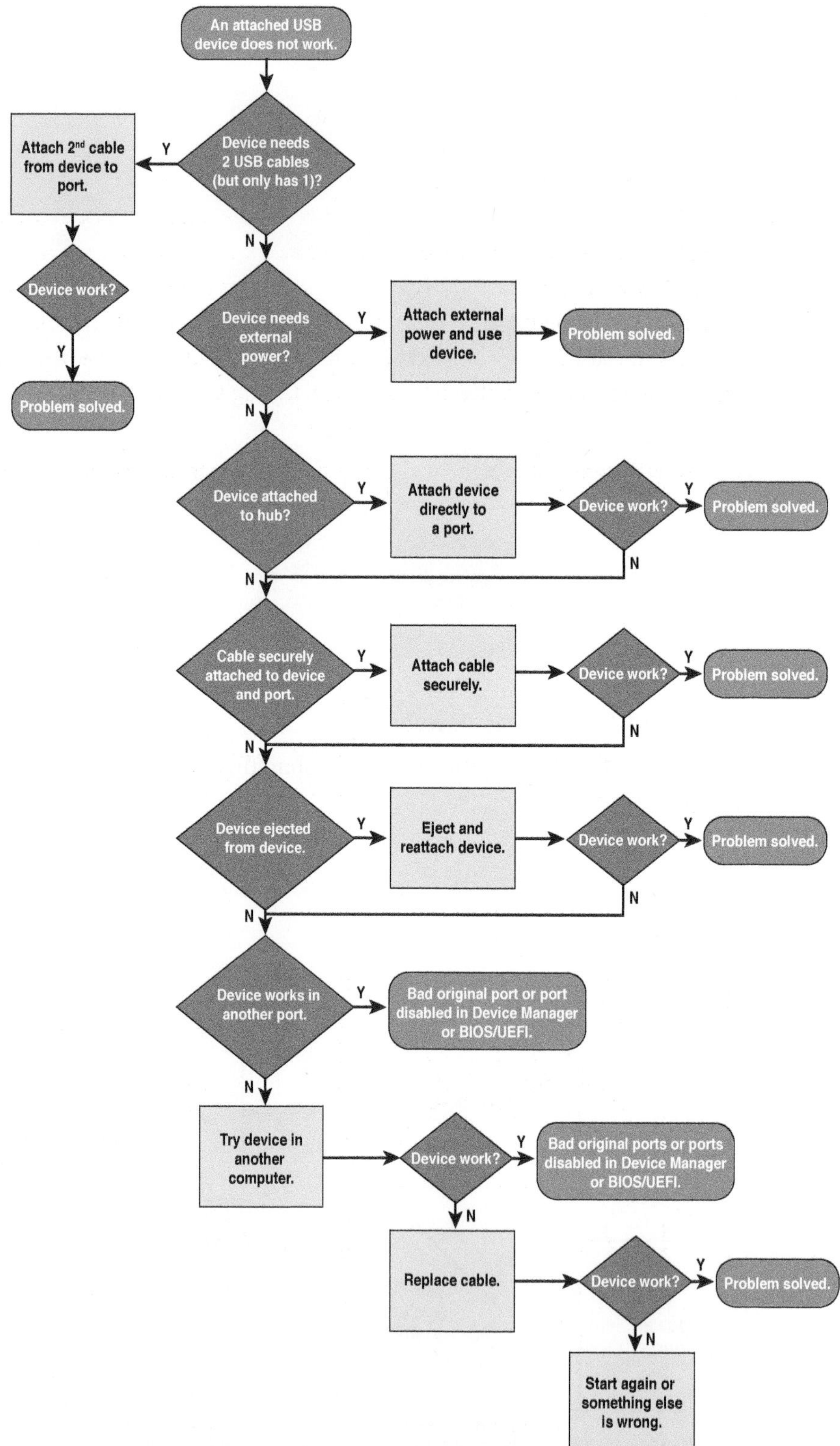

FIGURE 11.24 USB troubleshooting flowchart

Keep in mind that each chapter of this book has one or more troubleshooting sections to help with problems. In addition, the chapters toward the end of this book address problems related to operating systems. Review the troubleshooting sections of the CompTIA A+ 220-1101 certification exam objectives and review each chapter's troubleshooting sections before taking the exam.

SOFT SKILLS: DEALING WITH DIFFICULT CUSTOMERS

One of the most difficult tasks a technician faces is dealing with people who are angry, upset, or frustrated. This is a common issue for those who come to help or try to troubleshoot a problem over the phone. Dealing with irate customers is a skill that you can fine-tune. Listening to peer technicians tell how they have successfully (or unsuccessfully) dealt with difficult customers can also help. Realize that not only do customers want their computer problems fixed, they sometimes just need to vent and be heard. Because a technician is the person with the knowledge for at least the start of the resolution and the technician is in front of or on the phone with the person who is not able to do something on the computer, the technician may be a scapegoat and must try to listen to the irritated customer. Some key tips for dealing with customers are shown in Figure 11.25.

FIGURE 11.25 Dealing with irate customers

The last suggestion in Figure 11.25 about being assertive is one that many people do not understand. Aggression involves dominating a conversation or situation by threatening, bullying, being sarcastic, or showing belittling behavior and/or actions. Some technicians consistently demonstrate aggressive behavior. This reflects poorly on the technician and the company that the technician represents. Passive behavior involves letting others dominate you and expressing yourself apologetically. Technicians who are passive frequently apologize while the customer is trying to explain the problem. Assertive behavior involves being respectful of another person but not allowing him or her to take advantage or dominate the situation. This is the middle ground you want to strive for when dealing with customers. It would be appropriate to raise a hand to indicate that you want an irate customer to stop what he or she is doing (see Figure 11.26). This would be an assertive way to show that the current behavior is inappropriate.

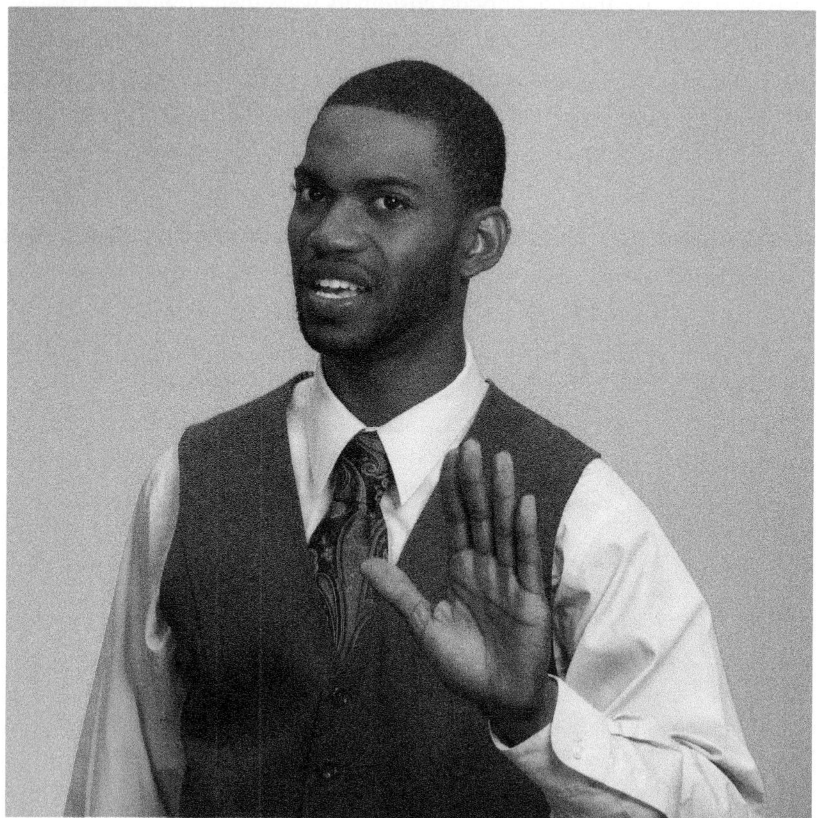

FIGURE 11.26 Being assertive with an irate customer

When dealing with an irate customer, you want to stay calm and maintain your professionalism. Once the customer has calmed down a bit, you can glean more information about the problem with less anger mixed into the conversation. Dealing with angry customers is an important part of a technician's job, as it is for anyone else who works in a service industry. Consider customers' points of view and don't forget that they are the ones who must use the devices that you repair.

Chapter Summary

- A graphic/CAD/CAM design workstation needs multiple powerful multicore processors, maximum RAM, a high-end video card with maximum RAM and GPU, a large display/multiple displays, a large-capacity hard drive(s), an SSD, and a good input device(s).
- A gaming PC needs an SSD, a large amount of RAM, a high-definition sound card and speakers, additional system (high-end) cooling, a large display and/or multiple displays, high-end video/specialized GPU, and good input/output devices.

- An audio- or video-editing workstation needs powerful multicore processors, maximum RAM, a good video card with maximum RAM and GPU, a specialized sound card, a fast and large-capacity hard drive, dual monitors, and good input device(s).
- A virtualization workstation needs maximum multicore processors, maximum RAM, multiple fast hard drives, an SSD, and at least a 1 Gb/s NIC.
- A thick client computer supports desktop applications and meets recommended requirements for the selected OS.
- A thin client computer supports basic applications and meets minimum requirements for the selected OS. A thin client must also have network connectivity.
- A network-attached storage (NAS) device can be used for media streaming and file sharing. It should include a gigabit NIC, a RAID array, and a large hard drive.
- A home server PC has a medium to large case, multiple powerful multicore processors, lots of RAM, RAID, a 1 Gb/s NIC, and server applications such as media streaming, file sharing, and print sharing applications.
- When designing a motherboard, the CPU size and motherboard CPU socket must match.
- The power supply, motherboard, and case form factors must match.
- A power supply must have the correct wattage for a specific power level and an appropriate number/type of power cables.
- Display design should include considerations about physical space; type of display; features that might be integrated into the display (such as a microphone or camera), video port, and memory; GPU; and additional power requirements.
- The six steps of troubleshooting are as follows: (1) Identify the problem, (2) establish a theory, (3) test the theory, (4) establish a plan of action, (5) verify full system functionality and, if applicable, implement preventive measures, and (6) document the findings, actions, and outcomes and provide feedback.
- BIOS/UEFI controls the boot process. Knowing the traditional BIOS steps can help with the troubleshooting process.
- Like a traditional BIOS, UEFI checks the hardware, but the UEFI boot manager can load drivers that allow devices such as the mouse and NIC to be used with UEFI applications.
- POST codes or motherboard LEDs can give you clues in troubleshooting an issue.
- The BIOS/UEFI can contain advanced diagnostics.
- Reinstall parts if replacing them does not solve a problem.
- Document a problem as part of the troubleshooting process. Give users the appropriate documentation. Be professional in your oral and written communication. Tell the user what was done.

A+ CERTIFICATION EXAM TIPS

✓ Know that to test a port or a connection such as the internet connection a loopback plug is used.

✓ For troubleshooting motherboards, RAM, CPU, and power, know what to do when these symptoms appear: POST beeps, proprietary crash screens, BSOD, pinwheel, black screen, no power, sluggish performance, overheating, burning smell, intermittent shutdown, application crashes, grinding noise, capacitor swelling, and inaccurate system date/time.

✓ Focus on display/projector, storage device, and RAID symptoms: incorrect data source, physical cabling issued, burned-out bulb, fuzzy image, display burn-in, dead pixels, flashing screen, incorrect color, audio issues, dim image, intermittent projector shutdown, LEDs, grinding noises, clicking sounds, bootable device not found, data loss/corruption, RAID failure, S.M.A.R.T. failure, extended read/write times, IOPS, and missing drives in OS.

✓ If you know any technicians, ask them to tell you about the problems they have solved this week. Another idea is to get them to tell you a problem and you see if you can guess the top things that could cause that problem.

✓ Review the section "Soft Skills: Dealing with Irate Customers" for communication skills best practices. The communication questions can sometimes have answers that are very similar. Use the review questions at the end of the chapter to help practice with those types of questions.

✓ The 220-1102 exam focuses on very specific criteria for proper communication and professionalism, including difficult customers and situations. Avoid arguing with a customer and/or being defensive. Do not minimize a customer's problem. Avoid being judgmental. Clarify customer statements by asking open-ended questions (which allow the customer to freely explain the situation) to narrow the scope of the problem and by restating the issue or question to verify your understanding. Do not disclose work-related experiences via social media.

✓ Know the six steps in resolving problems and ensure that you consider company policies, procedures, and impacts before implementing any changes. Even though these steps are logical, when the steps are placed into written questions, they can become tricky. On the 220-1101 exam, the six troubleshooting steps could be applied to specific troubleshooting scenarios. Try to think of the computer problems and relate them to the best practice methodology six troubleshooting steps:

Step 1. Identify the problem. Gather information from the user, identify user changes, and do a backup before making changes. Check whether any environmental or infrastructure changes have been made, such as network modifications or installers in the area.

Step 2. Establish a theory of probable cause. (Question the obvious.) If necessary, conduct internal/external research based on the symptoms.

Step 3. Test the theory to determine the cause. If the theory is confirmed, determine the next steps to take. If you cannot confirm a theory, find a new theory or escalate the problem.

Step 4. Establish a plan of action to resolve the problem and implement the proposed solution. Refer to the manufacturer's instructions for guidance.

Step 5. Verify full system functionality and, if applicable, implement preventive measures.

Step 6. Document the findings, actions, and outcomes.

Key Terms

audio/video editing workstation 475
back up data 486
BSOD 491
ENERGY STAR 480
EPEAT rating system 480
error message 489
gaming PC 475
graphic/CAD/CAM design workstation 475
home server 479
intermittent device failure 493
IOPS 483
loopback plug 493
NAS 477
patch 494
pinwheel 491
POST card 491
proprietary crash screen 491
service pack 494
service release 494
thick client 479
thin client 478
virtual machine 477
virtualization workstation 477
warm boot 494

Review Questions

1. _____ executes POST. [BIOS/UEFI | CMOS | NAS | RAM]
2. Which technology is most likely to require dual monitors as part of the configuration?

   [virtual computer | home server | audio/video editing workstation | NAS]
3. A person comes into a computer store wanting a custom-built computer. The customer will be using the computer to stream video; to video chat with remote family; and for standard computer usage such as word processing, spreadsheet, and internet browsing. In addition, a child will use the computer to play games. Which computer component will the technician focus on to satisfy this customer?

   [500 GB hard drive | RAID array | multicore processor | 10G NIC]
4. Before making any changes to a computer that has a problem, what is the first thing you should do?
   - **a.** Inform your supervisor of the steps you are taking.
   - **b.** Back up any data that is stored locally on the computer that is not backed up elsewhere.
   - **c.** Inform the user of any possibilities that might be causing the problem.
   - **d.** Use a loopback plug to run diagnostics.
5. Which of the following would most likely be a design consideration for a gaming PC rather than a computer used for virtualization?
   - **a.** high amount of RAM
   - **b.** NAS
   - **c.** multiple fast, large-capacity hard drives
   - **d.** additional system cooling
6. If a computer beeps once during POST, what does this commonly mean to a technician?
   - **a.** There is not a problem.
   - **b.** A CPU register test is occurring.
   - **c.** A DRAM refresh is occurring.
   - **d.** A video initialization error has occurred.
7. An adapter or a USB device that performs diagnostics and displays a code or illuminates LEDs is known as a _____.

   [DIGI card | probe | torx | POST card]

8–10. Group the following computer components into three design subsystems. In other words, group the components that need to be considered together when designing a subsystem of a computer. Each group must include at least two components. All components are used.

power supply	CPU	chipset
video card	case	CPU cooling
motherboard	display	RAM

Group 1 components: ______________________________

Group 2 components: ______________________________

Group 3 components: ______________________________

11. A motherboard advertisement lists UEFI as one of the motherboard features. What is UEFI?
    a. a port
    b. a BIOS replacement
    c. an internal interface
    d. a type of storage device
12. Which design environments would have the largest display needs? (Choose three.)
    [CAD | gaming | audio/video editing | virtualization | thick client | home server]
13. Which type of computer design would be implemented if a workstation ran both Linux and Windows as operating systems?
    [CAD | home theater | virtualization | thin client | thick client]
14. When designing a tower computer, with what computer component would you consider physical space more than any other part?
    [hard drive | motherboard | display | CPU | power supply | air filter]
15. Which components could have an ATX form factor? (Choose two.)
    [hard drive | motherboard | display | CPU | power supply | air filter]
16. Place the six steps of troubleshooting in the order in which they occur.
    ____ Step 1 **a.** Test the theory to determine cause.
    ____ Step 2 **b.** Establish a theory of probable cause.
    ____ Step 3 **c.** Document and provide feedback.
    ____ Step 4 **d.** Identify the problem.
    ____ Step 5 **e.** Verify system functionality and, if applicable, implement preventive measures.
    ____ Step 6 **f.** Establish a plan of action to resolve the problem and implement the solution.
17. [T | F] During the troubleshooting phase in which you test the theory, you might be required to escalate the problem to a more experienced technician.
18. A _____ is used to test a communications circuit or RJ45 port.
    [multimeter | probe | torx | loopback plug]
19. Which computer design environment would have the most need for a laptop enclosure?
    [industrial | gaming | virtualization | mobile | home server]
20. [T | F] When dealing with an irate customer, it is best to listen to the customer vent.

Exercises

Exercise 11.1 Recommending Computer System Design

Objective: To be able to recommend a complete system based on the customer's needs or placement of the system

Parts: Computer with internet access

Procedure: Use the internet to research specific computers, based on the given scenario.

1. A homebound elderly person has just had her hard drive fail. The drive was installed in a really old computer, and the person has decided to replace the computer rather than fix the broken one. The elderly person uses the computer to shop for family members, check email, play basic computer card games with others online, and view pictures on CDs or DVDs sent by family members. Internet access is through a DSL modem that connects to the USB port and still works. Find a suitable computer on the internet. The customer would like to keep the cost around $700, including installation, if possible. Write the computer model, basic description, cost, and cost of installation.

2. A graphic artist would like a second computer as a mobile solution and would like your assistance finding a suitable laptop. The graphic artist does mostly video graphics creation but would like to be able to work while traveling. Find three possible solutions. Provide the computer model, basic description, and costs of the three laptops.

3. A sports complex wants to have a kiosk with a touchscreen and that holds a computer that runs specialized software. The software allows people to search for events and get detailed walking directions to the events and/or a specific sports field. No network connectivity is required. Locate a computer with an HDMI output for connectivity with the touchscreen for this outdoor kiosk located in a year-round sports complex. List the model number, basic description, and your fee for installing this system.

4. A 10-person purchasing department is going to a thin client environment. Select one desktop thin client computer model and one mobile thin client model from different manufacturers that can be used in the department. The models need to support dual displays. Detail any model numbers, basic parts descriptions, and costs.

5. A small company is expanding and is hiring an administrative assistant for the sales manager. Select a computer, monitor, keyboard, and an inkjet all-in-one printer for this assistant, who will be using Microsoft Office–type applications. The boss has put a $1,300 limit (not counting shipping) on the entire purchase. Provide a detailed list, description, and costs of parts chosen.

6. Select a CAD/CAM manufacturing design computer that uses 64-bit AutoCAD LT 2022 software. Research the AutoCAD LT application's video requirements. Provide a detailed list, description, and cost of parts chosen, including the video card and display. Assume that there is no price limit. (Note that AutoCAD LT requires a 1920×1080 display with True Color.)

____

____

____

____

____

7. You have an unlimited budget to build the best gaming rig possible. Choose two PC manufacturer sites at which you can select components, monitors, applications, and accessories for your new system.

____

____

____

____

8. You have an unlimited budget and need to build two systems from scratch. You will need cases, power supplies, motherboards, CPUs, RAM, hard drives, video cards, and more. List two websites at which you can compare and buy all the components you need to build the two systems.

____

____

____

Exercise 11.2 Understanding Design Components

Objective: To be able to recognize the unique components for a specific computer design scenario

Procedure: Using the list of components, identify which components would be used in the scenarios given. Note that any one component can be used multiple times.

Components

a. Multiple powerful processor cores
b. Maximum RAM
c. Lots of RAM
d. Multiple large-capacity hard drives
e. Large-capacity hard drive
f. RAID
g. Sound card and speakers
h. Powerful video card and RAM on the card
i. Multiple displays
j. Large display
k. DVR
l. TV tuner or cable card
m. 1 Gb/s NIC
n. Computer enclosure
o. KVM switch
p. SSD

Scenario 1

Identify the unique components from the provided list for a computer used for audio and video editing.

____

Scenario 2

You need to build a computer to test the Chrome operating system, along with your current Windows operating system. You have decided to do this in a virtual environment. Identify the unique components that would be in the computer.

____

Scenario 3

A customer wants to try out thin client workstations in one department. Identify one or more unique components that would be in one computer of this type.

____

Scenario 4

A tire shop would like to have a computer in the lobby where information about the latest and upcoming sales are displayed. The owner is concerned about theft. What unique component would be needed for this situation?

____

Scenario 5

A computer programmer works from home but likes to work from several types of computers—a mobile tablet, laptop, and desktop—and to be able to work on any mobile device when traveling. The programmer has decided to create a server to store and access everything from anyplace. The programmer does not want to have to buy another keyboard, mouse, or display for the server but wants to share these components connected to the desktop computer with the server. What unique components would be part of this system?

____

Exercise 11.3 Understanding Subsystem Design Components

Objective: To be able to design a subsystem of a computer, based on design requirements

Parts: Computer with internet access

Procedure: Use the internet to research specific computers, based on the given scenario.

Scenario 1

You have just ascertained that a customer's older ATX Pentium 4 motherboard in a home computer is bad. The customer wants a motherboard upgrade or replacement. The existing motherboard has a PCI sound card and VGA port that the user would like to continue using. The RAM on the existing motherboard has 512 MB of DDR2 memory. The hard drive and optical drive use PATA for connectivity, and the customer would like to continue using these devices and the current operating system. The customer does light computer work but likes listening to broadcasts and music on the computer. Locate suitable replacement upgraded components. The budget is $250, including labor. Detail each item, item description, and cost.

____

____

____

____

____

____

Scenario 2

A customer has been given a micro-ATX motherboard, an Intel Core i5 quad-core processor, and RAM. The customer has two 3.5-inch SATA drives and one 5.25-inch optical drive from other computers. The customer would like assistance getting a case and a power supply to handle all these devices. The customer does not have a lot of room but wants a tower case that provides good airflow through the computer. The customer has a budget of $200 for this. Locate a power supply and case for the customer. Detail the items, item descriptions, and costs.

___

___

___

Scenario 3

A retired naval officer has just gotten into classical music and now wants surround-sound in his office. Select an appropriate sound subsystem. The budget is $200. The office system has both PCI and PCIe expansion slots available. List the components, a description of each component, and the cost.

___

___

___

Scenario 4

A college graduate has started her own website design business. She wants a video card that supports two 18- to 20-inch displays. Recommend a video subsystem for her. The budget is $500 maximum. List the components, a description of each component, and the costs.

___

___

___

___

___

Scenario 5

Locate a motherboard, power supply, RAM, CPU, and midsized case that are compatible with one another for an administrative assistant. The budget is $600. List the components, a description of the components (ensure that you list the type of RAM the motherboard supports), and the costs.

___

___

___

___

___

___

___

___

___

Exercise 11.4 Determining the Troubleshooting Theory Step

Objective: To be able to determine which step of the troubleshooting process is occurring

Procedure: Match one of the six troubleshooting steps to the situation. Note that a particular step may be the answer for more than one situation.

Troubleshooting steps:

a. Identify the problem.

b. Establish a theory of probable cause.

c. Test the theory.

d. Establish a plan of action.

e. Verify full functionality.

f. Document findings.

Situation:

_____ A USB flash drive is not being recognized in a computer. You move the drive to a different USB slot.

_____ You provide the user with the registration/authentication code for the antivirus software that was installed into the computer after a virus was removed.

_____ You ask open-ended questions.

_____ The user explains what has happened in the past few days that was unusual.

_____ You phone the user to ask if the system appears to be running faster since the new memory module was installed.

_____ You order a new motherboard.

_____ You re-enable automatic Windows updates so they get applied in the future and prevent future issues.

_____ You believe that the problem is either the motherboard or the processor.

Activities

Internet Discovery

Objective: To become familiar with researching computer items used in designing systems or subsystems

Parts: Computer with internet access

Procedure: Use the internet to answer the following questions. Write the answers and the URL of the site where you found the information.

1. Locate the Bloom's Taxonomy chart that has been modified by Andrew Churches to include verbs for the digital age. Write at least five verbs that Andrew Churches recommends as being relative to the top level of the taxonomy—the creating level—and the URL where you found the chart.

____

____

____

____

____

2. Locate minimum requirements for either a student computer or a staff computer at a particular school. Write the requirements, school name, and the URL where you found this information.

3. What are the recommended video standards for use when playing Kerbal Space Program on a PC? Write the answer and the URL where you found this information. Then find a video card that meets those specifications. Document the video card and the price.

4. What are the minimum processor, RAM, and display resolution requirements for a client who wants to run AutoCAD 2019 software? Write the answer and the URL where you found the information.

5. Find a monitor that supports the minimum AutoCAD 2019 display resolution found for Question 4. List the monitor manufacturer, model number, and URL where you found the information.

6. Locate a website that has a troubleshooting flowchart. Write three things the flowchart provides that you find helpful or confusing. Write the URL where the chart was found.

7. Locate one website that lists at least two BIOS/UEFI error codes. Write the URL where this information was found.

8. Find a website that shows at least three recommendations for dealing with irate customers. Write three recommendations and the URL where you found this information.

Flip the CLASSROOM

Soft Skills

Objective: To become familiar with researching computer items used in designing systems or subsystems and to learn how to deal with difficult customers or situations

Activities:

1. Interview or email someone who works in your school to determine the school's minimum hardware requirements for its new computers. Document your findings.

2. In teams of two, find a video that shows how to deal with an irate customer. Document at least three observations from the video as well as the video URL.

3. In teams of two, three, or four, design a computer for a specific purpose. State the purpose and provide all the models, descriptions, and costs. Compete with other teams for the best design.

Flip the CLASSROOM

Critical Thinking Skills

Objective: To become familiar with researching computer items used in designing systems or subsystems

Activities:

1. Refer to Tables 11.1 through 11.4, which provide recommendations for hardware components. Find at least one type of computer configuration for which you disagree with the special hardware components; if you agree with them all, then think of one that should be added. List the component and the reason for your disagreement or addition.

2. Locate an image that shows a map of Bloom's Taxonomy, as modified by Andrew Churches. Explain why designing (in the creating stage) requires higher-level skills than working in the evaluating stage, which includes experimenting, judging, monitoring, and testing.

3. Do you think most technicians are good at designing computers for specific purposes? Explain your opinion.

12 Internet Connectivity, Virtualization, and Cloud Technologies

In this chapter you will learn:

- To describe dial-up networking
- About other internet connectivity options, such as satellite, cable, DSL, and fiber, as well as wireless options such as cellular, long-range fixed wireless, Wi-Fi, and wireless broadband
- To configure a browser and other basic issues related to a browser
- How cloud computing is used for personal and corporate purposes
- Terms associated with cloud computing
- The basics of virtualization, including terms and features associated with it
- The benefits of mentoring in the IT field

CompTIA Exam Objectives:

- ✓ 1101-2.2 Compare and contrast common networking hardware.
- ✓ 1101-2.3 Compare and contrast protocols for wireless networking.
- ✓ 1101-2.7 Compare and contrast internet connection types, network types, and their features.
- ✓ 1101-3.1 Explain basic cable types and their connectors, features, and purposes.
- ✓ 1101-4.1 Summarize cloud-computing concepts.
- ✓ 1101-4.2 Summarize aspects of client-side virtualization.
- ✓ 1101-5.7 Given a scenario, troubleshoot problems with wired and wireless networks.
- ✓ 1102-2.10 Given a scenario, install and configure browsers and relevant security settings.
- ✓ 1102-3.2 Given a scenario, troubleshoot common personal computer (PC) security issues.

Internet Connectivity Overview

Connecting to the internet can be done in a variety of ways: wirelessly or via analog modem, fixed wireless, cable modem, DSL modem, satellite modem, fiber, power line, or cellular network. These technologies have unique installation and configuration methods, but they all have in common the capability to connect a computer to an outside network. Each technology is a viable option for connectivity in a specific situation. By examining and understanding the technologies, you can offer customers connectivity options. More information about troubleshooting network connectivity is provided in Chapter 13, "Networking." Let's start with the oldest method: analog modems.

Dial-up Connectivity

One of the first devices still in operation that was used to connect to the internet is the modem. A modem (which stands for *modulator/demodulator*) connects a computer with the outside world through a phone line. This type of technology is frequently called a **dial-up network** or just dial-up because the analog modem uses the phone line to "dial up," or call, another modem. Modems can be internal or external peripheral devices. An internal modem is an adapter installed in an expansion slot. An external modem attaches to a USB port. A modem converts a signal transmitted over the phone line to digital 1s and 0s to be read by the computer. It also converts the digital 1s and 0s from the computer and modulates them onto the carrier signal and sends the data over the phone line. A modem normally connects to a remote modem through a phone line. Figure 12.1 shows two modems connecting two computers.

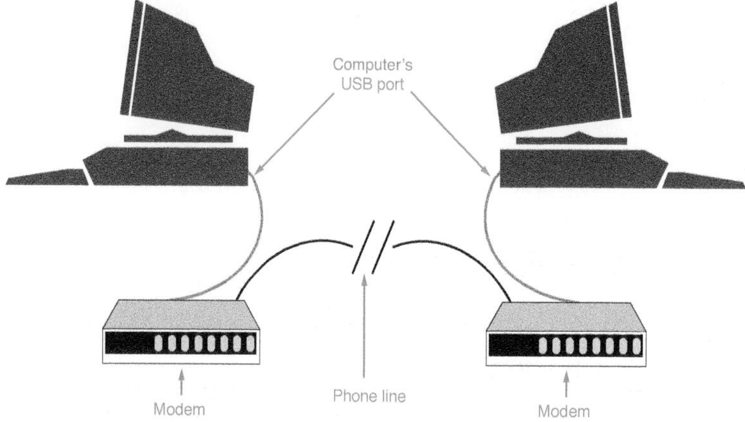

FIGURE 12.1 Sample modem connection

> **TECH TIP**
>
> **When connecting a modem to a phone line, be careful with the cabling**
>
> Some modems have two jacks on the back. The labeling varies, but one jack is usually labeled PHONE and the other LINE. The LINE jack is for the cable that goes from the modem to the phone wall jack. The modem's PHONE jack is an optional jack that connects a telephone to the modem. Figure 12.2 shows the ports on an internal modem.

Table 12.1 describes basic terminology associated with serial transmissions, such as transmissions that occur with a modem.

FIGURE 12.2 Internal modem ports

TABLE 12.1 Serial asynchronous transmission terminology

Term	Description
Baud	The number of times an analog signal changes in one second. Some use this term to speak of the modem speed. With modulation techniques, modems can send several bits in one cycle, so it is more accurate to specify modem speed in bits per second (bps or b/s).
Bits per second (bps)	A measurement used to describe the transmission speed of a serial device or port. Settings include 110, 300, 1,200, 2,400, 4,800, 9,600, 19,200, 38,400, 57,600, and 115,200. The application software must match the serial device's or serial port's bits per second rate.
Start/stop bit	A bit used in asynchronous transmission to signal the start or end of the data.

TECH TIP

Configuring transmission speeds

When configuring a serial port or using an application, the configured speed is the rate at which the serial port transmits. This is not the speed for an external serial device that connects to the port (such as a modem).

Serial ports and devices such as internal modems have three important configuration parameters: interrupt, input/output (I/O) address, and COM port number. An internal modem has all these parameters; an external modem uses these same parameters, but they are assigned to the serial port to which the external modem connects. Use *Device Manager* to identify these system resources. Other important settings associated with serial devices include what method of flow control they use, such as XON/XOFF (a software method) or RTS/CTS (a hardware method), the FIFO setting, and handshaking. Be sure both sides of a serial connection match.

To configure a dial-up connection using a 56 kbps modem, install the internal modem or connect the external modem to the computer. Ensure that the modem connects to a working phone outlet. In Windows access *Settings > Network & Internet > Dial-up > Set up a new connection* link unless the manufacturer's instructions say otherwise; some modems have their own installation software.

Cable Modems

One of the most popular ways to connect to the internet is through a **cable modem**, which connects a computer to a cable TV network and/or the internet. Cable modems can be internal or external devices but commonly are external. If a cable modem is external, two methods commonly exist for connectivity to a PC: (1) A NIC built into the motherboard is used or an adapter is installed, and a cable attaches between the NIC and the cable modem or (2) the cable modem connects to a USB port on the computer. Figure 12.3 shows the **coaxial** cable on the top for connection to the wall coax connector, both USB and RJ45 network connectors for connecting to a PC, and two additional RJ45 Ethernet network jacks for printers or additional devices.

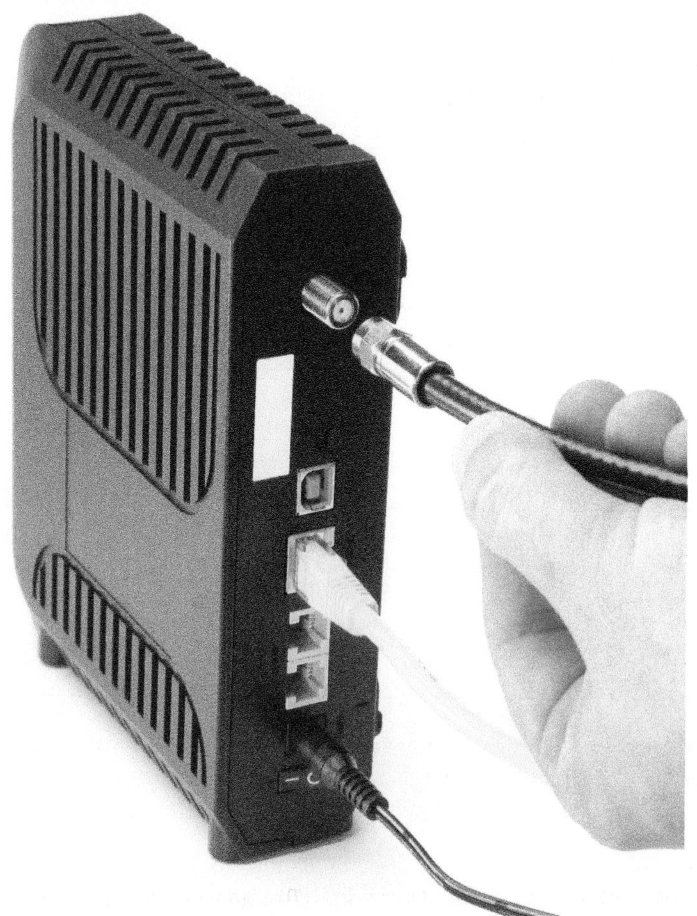

FIGURE 12.3 Cable modem coax, USB, and Ethernet LAN ports

Cable modem operation is not hard to understand. Internet data comes in through coax cable that plugs into the cable modem. The cable modem sends the information out its built-in Ethernet port. A network Ethernet cable connects from the cable modem to the computer. To send data to the internet, the reverse happens. Notice in Figure 12.3 that there are additional Ethernet ports below the yellow cable. If the cable modem needs to connect to a company or home router, one end of an Ethernet cable is attached to one of the cable modem Ethernet ports, and the other end is attached to the router.

Cable modem speeds vary by geographic location and vendor. Most people are interested in the downstream data (data coming from the internet into the home or business). Downstream speed can be from 40 Mb/s to 10 Gb/s, whereas upstream speeds are typically slower and can be in the range from 10 Mb/s to 10 Gb/s.

xDSL Modems

xDSL is another modem technology. The *x* in the term xDSL refers to the various types of digital subscriber line (**DSL**) that are on the market. The most common one is asymmetric DSL (**ADSL**), but there are many others. ADSL uses faster downstream speeds than upstream. This performance is fine for most home internet users. DSL uses traditional phone lines to send and transmit not only voice but also internet data. With DSL modems, bandwidth is not shared between people in the same geographic area. The bandwidth is exclusive to the user. DSL is not available in all areas. The DSLReports website (https://www.dslreports.com) lists major DSL vendors, other internet technology vendors, and geographic areas.

An internal or external DSL modem can be connected to a regular phone line. The phone line can be used for calls, faxes, and so on at the same time the modem is being used. An external modem can connect to a USB port or an Ethernet network card. Figure 12.4 shows DSL modem ports, including the DSL connector, which connects to the wall outlet and is labeled ADSL, and the multiple Ethernet LAN connections, which could be used to connect to one or more computers, printers, external network storage, or other wired network devices.

FIGURE 12.4 DSL modem ports

> **TECH TIP**
>
> **Corporate DSL, cable, or fiber**
>
> Corporate internet connectivity can use DSL, cable, or fiber connections. Chapter 2, "Connectivity," provides more information on fiber cabling.

A drawback to DSL is that the DSL signal needs to be separated from the normal phone traffic. DSL providers normally provide **phone filters** (see Figure 12.5) that must connect to each phone outlet, and a phone, fax machine, or voice recorder attaches to the filter. The connection from the DSL modem to the phone outlet does not have a filter on it, as you can see in Figure 12.5.

FIGURE 12.5 DSL phone line filter

VoIP

Traditionally, a company had separate networks for voice and data, with only computers and printers connected to the data network. Voice over IP (**VoIP**) uses a corporate data network and/or the internet for phone traffic rather than using the traditional public switched telephone network (PSTN). Free and purchased VoIP software can be used to enable a user to call someone using the internet. Figure 12.6 shows a VoIP phone that cables to a PC and into the corporate data network. Note that VoIP can also be implemented without a phone through PC-based software and using a speaker or headphones and an integrated or external microphone.

FIGURE 12.6 Corporate VoIP phone

A VoIP phone typically connects to an RJ45 data jack that is wired to a power over Ethernet (PoE) network switch that can provide power to the phone through the network cable. Most VoIP phones have a second RJ45 port so that a PC can connect directly to the phone instead of having a second RJ45 wall jack. Corporate VoIP phones commonly use PoE.

In the past, companies also used a separate network structure for the video network, but that has also now been moved onto the data network. **Convergence** is a term used to describe how these data, voice, and video technologies now use one network structure instead of multiple networks. Figure 12.7 shows a video conference in the corporate environment where people join using tablets, laptops, corporate conference rooms, and desktop computers.

FIGURE 12.7 Corporate video conference call

Through applications such as Skype, Zoom, and FaceTime, the video conferencing quality may not be as good as with a wired network. This is because guaranteed quality of service (**QoS**) is not provided. QoS prioritizes traffic so that important traffic—such as business transaction traffic and VoIP traffic—is sure to get through. Figure 12.8 shows this concept.

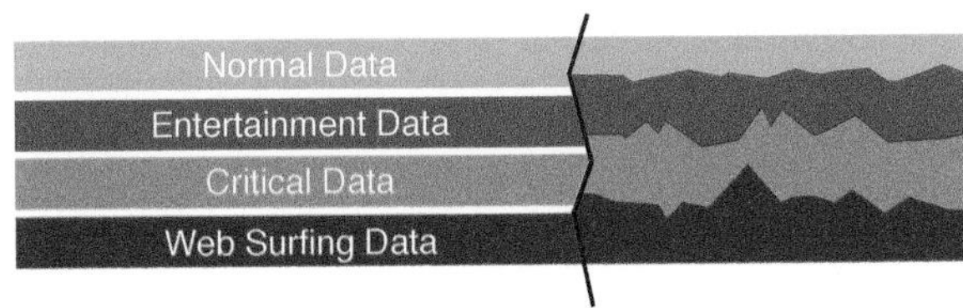

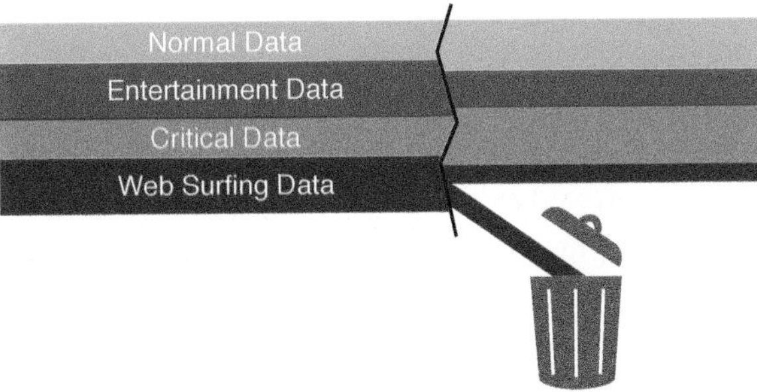

FIGURE 12.8 QoS

TECH TIP

What to do with poor VoIP quality

When QoS is not implemented or when it is not implemented properly, **poor VoIP quality** can occur (so that calls can be dropped or audio may not be clear), and the technician must report this to the network staff. Users may need help due to **jitter** (see Figure 12.9) and the helpdesk or senior technicians might ask for you to provide jitter statistics obtained from the phone.

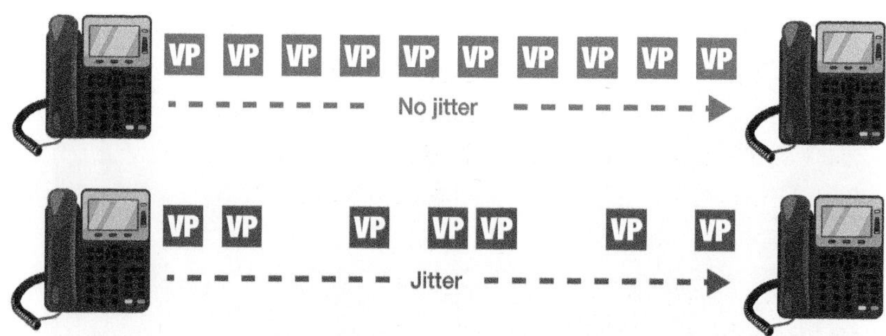

FIGURE 12.9 Jitter

In a network experiencing **latency**, packets get delayed. Latency is measured in milliseconds (ms) and can be caused by such things as too much traffic on a network, a server being overloaded with requests, long distance, or low bandwidth. Jitter is similar to latency except that it is inconsistent timing of the delivery of packets.

Technicians must be aware of VoIP for two reasons:

> A phone installed in a corporate office must be connected to the network in a similar fashion to a PC.
> A phone may be a software application (a soft phone) that has to be installed and configured on a computer.

A corporate environment will always need to be able to communicate with the outside world by using a PSTN connection to the traditional phone network and will especially need to be able to contact emergency services such as police, fire, and emergency responders.

Fiber Networks

A high-speed **fiber network** connection is commonly used to bring bundled technologies to subscribers. Such bundles may include phone, internet, and cable TV connectivity. In a fiber network, many fiber-optic cables are used to connect buildings, multiple companies, and home users. A single fiber carries voice, data, and video using three different optical wavelengths. This same type of connectivity is offered at higher speeds to small businesses. Whereas electrical pulses flow through copper cables, light flows through a fiber-optic cable. Instead of an electrical pulse being a 1, the light being on is a 1. A 0 is the light being turned off. Figure 12.10 shows the basic components of fiber-optic cable.

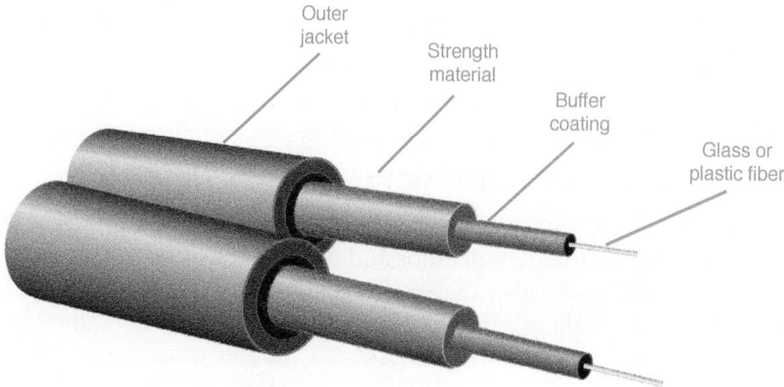

FIGURE 12.10 Fiber-optic cable

Fiber-optic cable has many advantages, including security, long-distance transmission, and bandwidth. Many government agencies use fiber-optic cable because it offers high security.

Unlike signals from other cable media, light signals that travel down fiber are impossible to detect remotely. Also, because light is used instead of electrical signals, fiber-optic cable is not susceptible to electromagnetic interference (EMI) or radio-frequency interference (RFI). Fiber-optic cable is the most expensive cable type, but it also handles the most data with the least amount of data loss. Figure 12.11 shows how fiber-optic cable is installed under a city street, along with electrical conduits.

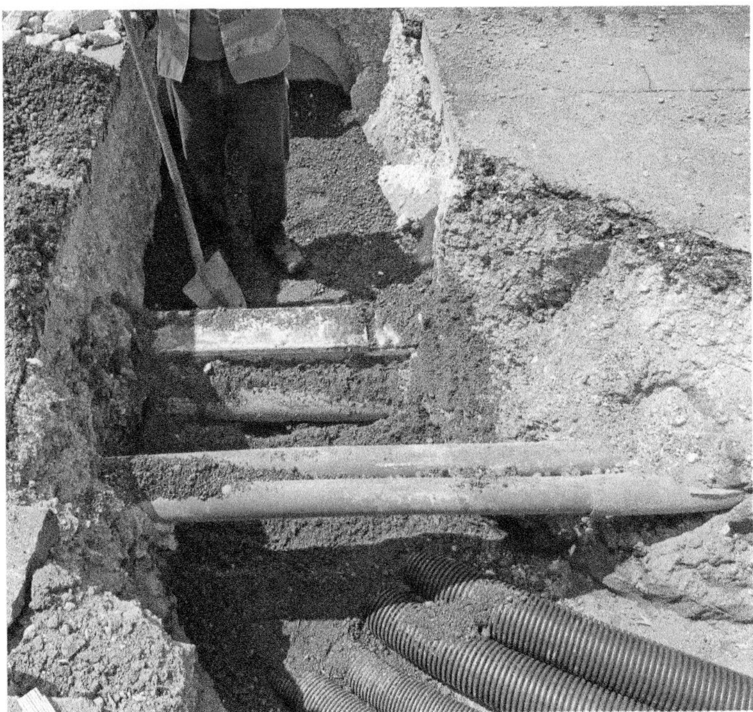

FIGURE 12.11 Laying fiber-optic cable

When a fiber connection is used, an optical network terminal (**ONT**) box is mounted on the wall that is near a wall jack near the router. This might be located in a home, basement, phone closet, or garage. The ONT converts the light taken from the fiber cable into electrical 1s and 0s transmitted into the internet modem. An Ethernet cable connects from the ONT to the port labeled broadband or ONT on a device that connects the home or business to the internet. Figure 12.12 shows an ONT box and the connection to the internet modem.

Two terms that are often associated with internet connectivity are upstream and downstream. **Upstream** refers to data sent from your home to the internet. **Downstream** refers to data pulled from the internet into your computer, as when you download a file or view a web page (see Figure 12.13). With cable modems, downstream (download) transfer rates are faster than upstream (upload) transfers. Downstream speeds can be as high as 5 Gbps for consumers and even higher for businesses. Upstream speeds vary; with an external cable modem, they tend to be between 384 kbps and 35 Mbps. Even though upstream speeds are slower, cable modems greatly improve speed over analog (dial-up) modems.

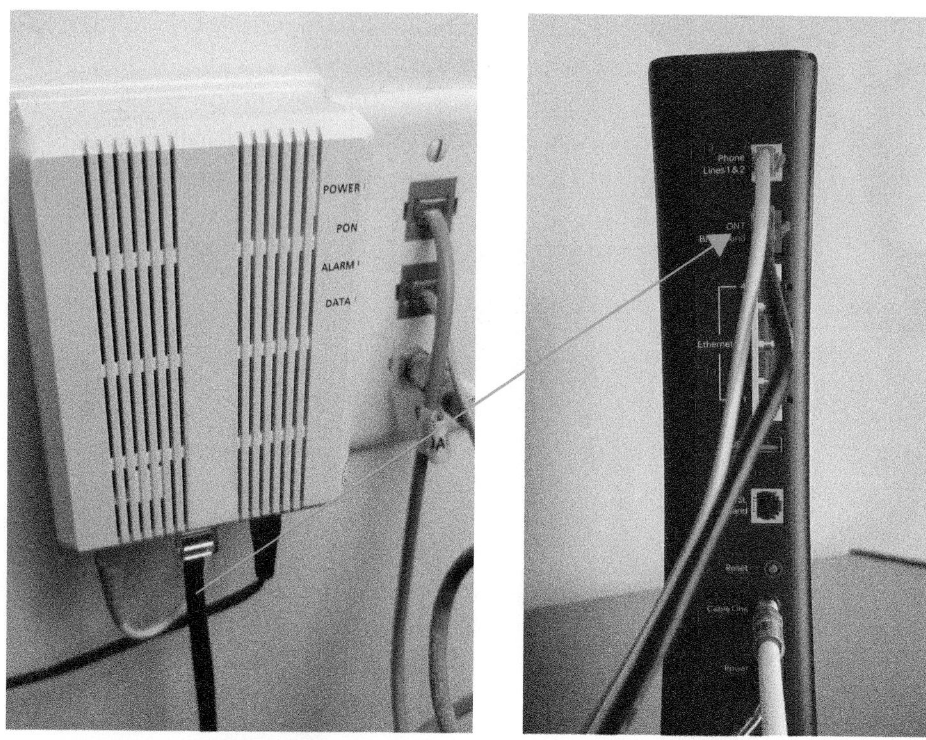

FIGURE 12.12 ONT box and connection to internet modem

Cable or ADSL Modem

FIGURE 12.13 Upstream and downstream

The speed of a cable modem connection depends on two things: the cable company and how many people in the area share the same cable TV provider. Each cable channel uses 6 MHz of the cable's bandwidth. **Bandwidth** is the capacity of the communications channel. Bandwidth is also known as *throughput* or *line speed.* The cable company designates one of the 6 MHz channels for internet access. Several homes can use the same channel, which reduces the amount of bandwidth each house has available. If you have three neighbors who all use the same cable vendor and they are internet warriors, you will have slower access than if you are the only person in the neighborhood connected.

Satellite Modems

An option available to areas that do not have cable or DSL service is satellite connectivity. The satellite relays communication back to receivers on Earth. Satellite connectivity requires, at a minimum, a satellite dish and a **satellite modem**. It may also require an analog modem and other equipment, depending on the satellite provider. With a satellite connection, the data goes from the computer to the satellite dish mounted outside the home or business (see Figure 12.14) to another satellite dish (and maybe more), up to the satellite orbiting Earth, down to the internet service provider (**ISP**), and from the ISP to the website requested; the web page returns via the same path. Satellite connectivity is not as fast as cable or DSL connectivity, but it can be five to seven times faster than dial-up. The downstream speeds can be from 9 kbps to 24 Mbps, but they are typically around 500 kbps. Some providers offer the same upstream speeds.

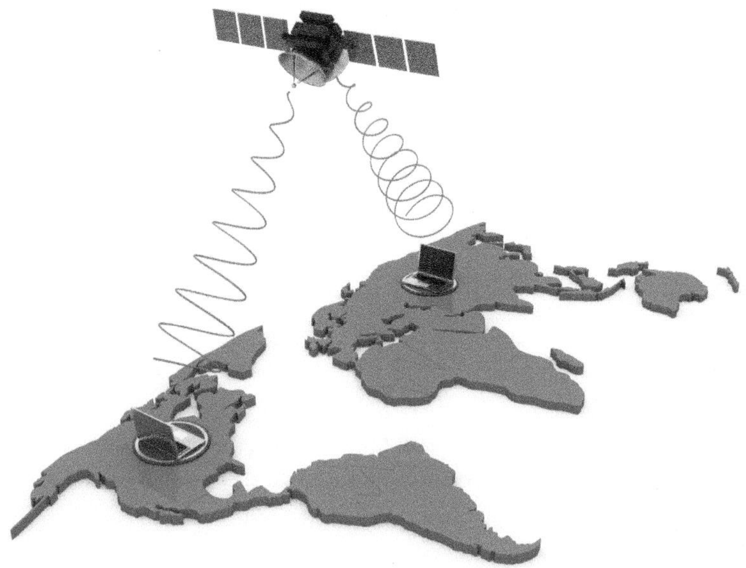

FIGURE 12.14 Satellite modem and dish

With a satellite modem, TV programs accessed via the satellite can be watched at the same time that web pages are downloaded from the internet. However, drawbacks to satellite modems are important to mention:

- The initial cost of installing a satellite modem can be high.
- If other people in the area subscribe to the same satellite service, speed is decreased during peak periods.
- Initial connections have a lag time associated with them, so playing multiplayer games is not very practical.
- Virtual private networks (VPNs) are not always supported.
- Weather elements, such as high winds, rain, and snow, affect performance and connectivity.

Mobile Connectivity Overview

Today's working environment is a mobile one featuring laptops, cell phones, and tablets. Connecting to the internet through an 802.11 wireless network is common, as introduced in Chapter 10, "Mobile Devices" (with even more information provided in Chapter 13). Smartphones, computers, and tablets can become **mobile hotspots**. Using a connection such as a USB port, Bluetooth wireless connectivity, or the cellular network, a device can provide wireless internet connectivity to others in the immediate vicinity. Some cell service providers offer this option as part of a cellular plan. The term *mobile hotspot* is also used to refer to an area of wireless connectivity (normally free), such as in a park, coffee shop, or museum. Another way of getting onto the internet is through the use of tethering. **Tethering** refers to the sharing of an internet connection with other mobile devices in the nearby area wirelessly through Bluetooth or Wi-Fi or through a wired USB connection.

Cellular Connectivity

Mobile devices use the cellular network to connect to the internet. Table 12.2 recaps the different cellular network types.

TABLE 12.2 Cellular network types

Cellular network type	Features
3G	Speeds of 200 kbps up to 2 Mbps
4G	Speeds up to 1 Gbps to support gaming, mobile TV, and video conferencing
LTE (Long Term Evolution)	An optimized version of 4G for video streaming and gaming
5G	Can support speeds up to 10 Gbps. 5G is used in corporate connectivity and Internet of Things (IoT) networks. Drones and balloons can be used in emergency situations to provide 5G connectivity.

Wireless Broadband

An increasingly popular feature with laptops and tablets is **wireless broadband**, with download speeds up to 45 Mbps. This technology is sometimes referred to as wireless WAN, mobile broadband, or cellular WAN. Cell phone companies and internet providers offer USB modems, mobile data cards, and integrated laptop connectivity to enable users to receive, create, and communicate internet information within a coverage area. For people who travel a lot, this option allows for connectivity in places where data connectivity has not previously been feasible. Mobile wireless broadband (**WiBro**) allows wireless connectivity for moving devices such as from a vehicle or train.

TECH TIP

Laptop wireless WAN connectivity

A laptop that ships with integrated wireless WAN capabilities does not need an additional adapter or antenna. However, the BIOS/UEFI must have the option enabled. Some laptops might have a key combination or a switch to enable the connection. The wireless application software is available through the Start button.

Long-Range Fixed Wireless

Fixed wireless is a very good internet connectivity solution for states with lots of rural areas like Vermont and Kansas. Fixed wireless is different from satellite, cellular, or Wi-Fi coverage and has been around for some time. Long-ranged fixed wireless can be used to connect buildings with one another, to connect homes and businesses in remote areas to the internet, and as a means to distribute data between remote locations, as shown in Figure 12.15.

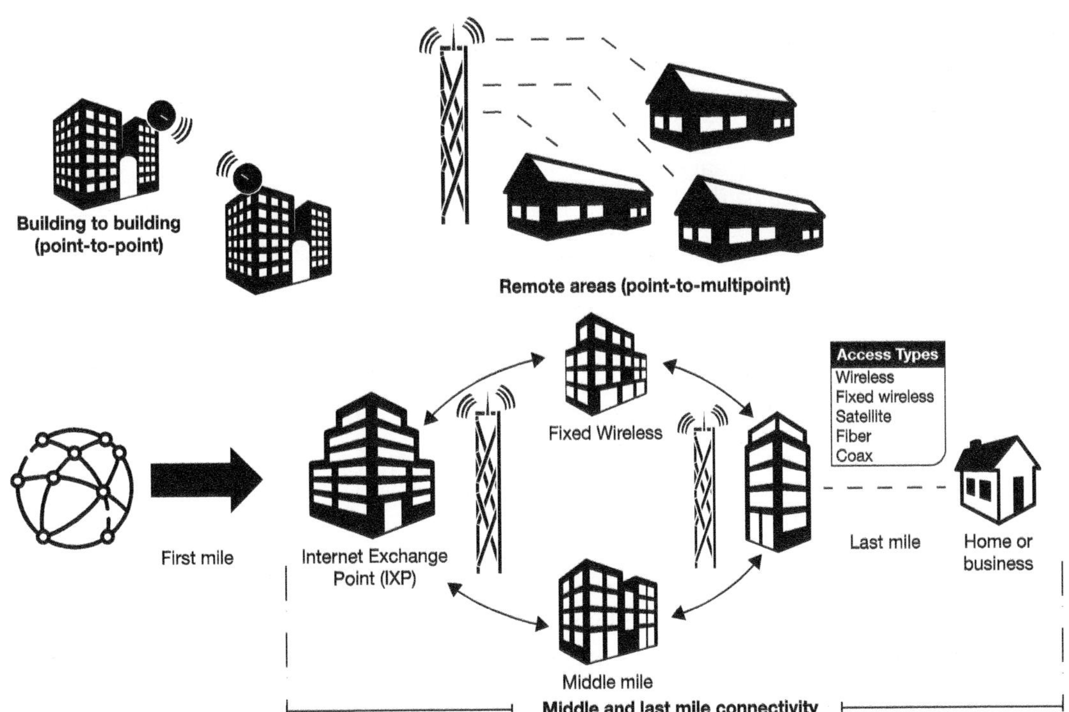

FIGURE 12.15 Long-range fixed wireless uses

Fixed wireless will become a more viable option for wireless internet service providers (**WISPs**) due to some changes in the wireless and communications standards. Compared to an unlicensed range, a **licensed range** of wireless spectrum frequencies provides better performance, reliability, and reduced interference from other devices. It also allows larger chunks of data to be transmitted. In the United States, the wireless spectrum is managed by the Federal Communications Commission (FCC), which assigns specific frequencies for a system or a range of frequencies for a particular service on a first-come, first-served basis in a geographic area. The geographic area is different for different industries; it may be an economic area, a cellular area, a basic trading area, and so on. There are auctions of blocks of frequencies, too, and vendors can obtain a frequency in a secondary market from someone who has obtained one of these blocks.

The **unlicensed range** of wireless frequencies can get very congested and may be subject to interference from all kinds of devices. Think of the current 2.4 and 5 GHz ranges for Wi-Fi. The FCC has opened up areas in the 6 GHz range and subdivided those areas into four Unlicensed National Information Infrastructure (U-NII) bands: U-NII-5, U-NII-6, U-NII-7, and U-NII-8.

There are rules about operating in the unlicensed 6 GHz wireless range. For example, rules specify the two categories of devices that may operate:

> Low-power indoor access points (APs) that cannot be battery operated and devices that connect to them
> Standard-power APs and devices that connect to them

Rules also specify the maximum amount of power that can be transmitted. Table 12.3 summarizes the power requirements for the devices operating in the 6 GHz range. Equivalent isotropic radiated power (EIRP) is a measurement of antenna output.

TABLE 12.3 6 GHz wireless power requirements

Wireless device	Operating band	Maximum EIRP
Standard-power AP	U-NII-5 and U-NII-7	36 dBm
Client that connects to standard-power AP	U-NII-5 and U-NII-7	30 dBm
Low-power indoor AP	U-NII-5, U-NII-6, U-NII-7, and U-NII-8	30 dBm
Client that connects to low-power AP	U-NII-5, U-NII-6, U-NII-7, and U-NII-8	24 dBm

You will learn more about wireless networks in Chapter 13. For now, let's consider the web browsers used to connect to the internet.

Web Browsers

Whether to work on information, data, or files from a server or surf the internet, a web browser is often used. A web browser is a graphical interface between a user and the internet. Common web browsers include Microsoft Edge, Mozilla Firefox, and Google Chrome. Edge is a browser that comes with Microsoft-based computers. Safari is the default browser on an Apple Mac or iPad. In addition, you can download and install other browsers. As with any app or software, be sure to download the browser from a **trusted source** directly from the company that makes the browser:

> *Mozilla Firefox:* mozilla.org
> *Google Chrome:* google.com/chrome
> *Brave:* brave.com

At the source (that is, the website of a company that makes a web browser), a **hash** is generated and sent with the installation file; at the receiving computer, the hash is used to verify that the file that was downloaded is the same as the original file and make sure no corruption occurred. It is best to choose a browser that is updated and in active development and not from a country known for hacking and security attacks or from an **untrusted source**, such as from an ad or an email link. Secure web connections use Hypertext Transfer Protocol Secure (HTTPS). You can see on the web address at the top of a browser that the URL includes https://www.whatever. HTTPS uses both HTTP and Secure Sockets Layer (SSL)/Transport Layer Security (TLS) to provide **secure connections**. Part of that process is to issue a security certificate, which ensures that the website address matches the web address on the security certificate as well as that the certificate is digitally signed by a trusted authority. A notification may appear that a certificate has expired or that an issue has occurred. You will see how to view a certificate in Table 12.5 and learn more about security certificates in Chapter 18, "Computer and Network Security."

Most browsers are similar to one another. Because Edge ships with Windows computers, we use it to explain browser concepts in this section. Figure 12.16 shows the menu that opens when you click on the three dots in the upper-right corner of Microsoft Edge. In other browsers, you might click a gear or three lines to access the *Settings* or *Tools* option. Figure 12.16 also shows the options available within *Settings*.

The *Internet Options* Control Panel is used to configure some options in non-Windows browsers. Table 12.4 explains the primary purposes of the main tabs.

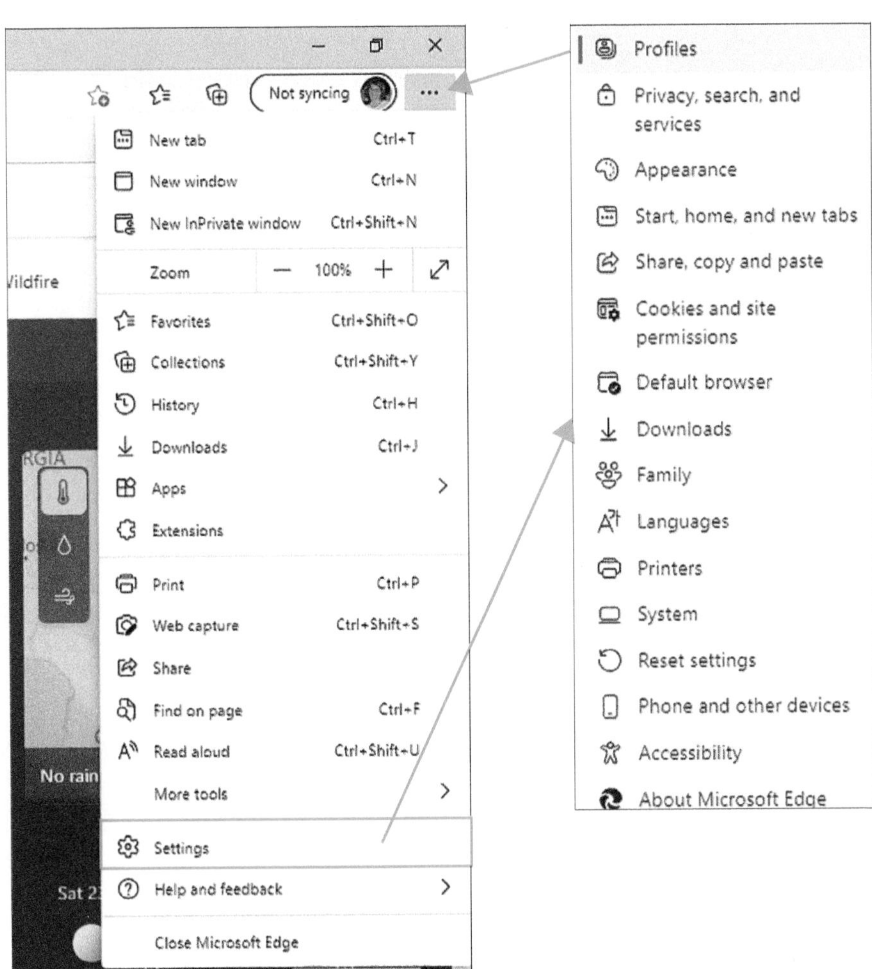

FIGURE 12.16 Settings within Microsoft Edge

TABLE 12.4 Purposes of the Internet Options Control Panel tabs

Tab	Purpose
General	Allows you to configure the home page (the page that opens every time Internet Explorer opens or the home icon is clicked), configure how long the browsing history (the websites visited) is kept, configure tab organization and behavior, and customize the font, language, and color scheme.
Security	Allows you to configure security options for sites that you trust and sites that you want blocked (see Chapter 18).
Privacy	Allows you to configure how your private information is handled, including cookies and pop-ups (see Chapter 18).
Content	Provides options for controlling security certificates, AutoComplete for ease of completing online forms, and Feeds and Web Slices for providing updated content directly into the browser.
Connections	Provides options for configuring an internet connection, dial-up (phone line) connection, proxy server, or VPN (virtual private network) information. (Proxy servers and VPNs are also covered in Chapters 13 and 18.)
Programs	Provides options for configuring email access, add-ons such as toolbars and extensions, and HTML-editing program options.
Advanced	Shows a list of options that might be set throughout the other tabs, also presented here in one easily configured list of checkboxes.

Most browsers can be customized. A **browser plug-in** is a downloaded executable that adds a specific feature to a browser. Closely related is a **browser extension**, which is downloadable code that enhances the browser such as easily capturing what's on the screen, removing ads, saving content to a file, or easily accessing an online meeting through a specific app. Many browsers no longer support plug-ins. Because extensions change browser settings and sometimes track user information, malware has been included in browser extension development. Malware is covered in Chapter 18. Research any extension downloaded and make sure you download only from trusted sources.

Some of the common basic web browser configuration settings that you need to know are listed in Table 12.5.

TABLE 12.5 Common web browser configuration settings

Setting	Purpose and how to configure
Default browser	Sets a particular browser as the default to be used when a web link is clicked. Can be set through OS Settings, too. Edge: *Settings > Default Browser > Make default* button Firefox: *Settings* General section > *Make default* button Chrome: *Settings > Default Browser > Make default* button
Clear browsing data	Removes cookies, websites visited history, and other data that is tracked based on the URLs used. Edge: *Settings > Privacy, search, and services > Clear browsing data* section Firefox: *Settings > Privacy & Security > Cookies and Site Data* section > *Clear Data...* Chrome: *Privacy and security > Clear browsing data*
Clear cache	Used when a particular website does not work or the web page is not formatted correctly. In the most common browsers, you can press Ctrl+Shift+Del to clear cache.
Private browsing	Does not keep browsing history, cookies, or data collected during a browsing session. Edge: *Three dots > New InPrivate window* Firefox: *Three lines > New Private Window* Chrome: *Three dots > New incognito window*
Browser synchronization	Browser settings and data such as bookmarks and passwords can be the same across multiple devices for a particular user if the user is logged into an account. Edge: Click on account picture > *Turn on sync* button Firefox: *Settings > Sync* Chrome: *Settings > Turn on sync* button
Security certificate verification of current website	Edge: Click lock icon in address bar to see the name of the certificate authority. Firefox: Click lock icon in address bar > *More Information* button > *Security > View Certificate* button. Chrome: Click lock in address bar > *Certificate (Valid)*
Additional security certificate information	Edge: *Settings > Privacy, search, and services > Security* section > *Manage certificates* Firefox: *Settings > Privacy & Security > Certificates* Chrome: *Settings > Privacy and security > Manage certificates*

You might determine that a browser extension or a plug-in is causing a browser issue. Here's how to view and potentially disable or remove a browser extension or plug-in:

> *Firefox:* Select *Open Application Menu* option from the upper-right corner > *Add-ons and themes > Extensions or Plugins*

> *Chrome:* From a browser tab in the address textbox type **`chrome://plugins`**. From the *Customize and control Google Chrome* option in the upper-right corner > *More tools* > *Extensions*
> *Edge:* Select *Settings and more* option from the upper-right corner > *Extensions*

Basic Web Browser Issues

Configuring a browser is one of the first steps in configuring security. Browsers are commonly upgraded to provide improved security options. Before upgrading an internet browser, you must determine the current web browser version. With many Windows-based applications, the version is determined by starting the application, clicking *Help* > *About x* (where *x* is the name of the application), or clicking the question mark menu item.

TECH TIP

Why keep your Windows and web browser current?

Internet hackers frequently target browsers, and constant updates are provided to counter these attacks.

One issue with browsers is that they can be hijacked (see Figure 12.17). A hijacked browser either replaces the home page with another one or directs whatever web page is being used to a different one. This is called a **browser redirection**. Besides sending you to another web page, a redirection can also be used to install a rootkit or install more malware ("bad software"), such as keystroke loggers (to record your keystrokes, including your typed usernames and passwords), perform DNS hijacking, or install a rogue HOSTS file. A **rootkit** can be used to act as a backdoor to your operating system and may be used to do things that require administrator access. Rootkits can also be downloaded and installed to a flash drive. The HOSTS file is a text file used to manually map a hostname to a particular IP address.

FIGURE 12.17 Web browser redirect

One security measure might be to use a **password manager**. This might make more sense after you review the concepts in Chapter 18, but it relates here. Make sure that the user researches password managers before making a choice about which one to use. The user should determine whether the software has any history of a security breach where data was compromised. Key factors include the following:

- What OS platforms the password manager supports, including mobile operating systems if users visit websites via phone. This would include having a browser extension on personal devices.
- Where the password information is saved (in the cloud or locally on the device).
- Whether the software can generate secure unique passwords.
- Whether the information is synced across all devices.
- Whether information is autofilled in accounts.
- Whether multifactor authentication is used, so that two pieces of information must be entered.

The following recommendations can help with hijacked browser issues:

- Change the home page URL to your normal home page and not the hijacked page. In any browser, go to the web page you want to be the home page and copy that web address. In Microsoft Edge, access *Settings* > *Start, home, and new tabs* > *Home button* section and enter the URL. For Chrome, access *Settings* > *Appearance* > enable *Show Home* > enter a URL in the *Enter custom web address* textbox. In Firefox, access *Settings* > *Home* option in left menu > type a URL in the *Homepage and new windows* textbox.
- Clear the browser history/cache. Refer to Table 12.4.
- If clearing the browser history/cache did not work, reset the browser settings. In Microsoft Edge, access *Settings* > in the *Clear browsing data* section, select *Choose what to clear* > enable all options > *Clear*. In Chrome, access *Settings* > expand *Advanced* and select *Reset and clean up*. In Firefox, select *Help* from the three lines menu > *More troubleshooting information* > *Refresh Firefox*.
- Try a different browser to see if the symptom remains. You could also uninstall the browser and reinstall it.
- If necessary, start the computer in *Safe Mode with Networking*. If the web browser works properly in this mode but not with normal booting straight to Windows, a DLL file might have been added to the computer. Run a scan with your anti-malware application.
- Start the browser with no add-ons to see if one of them is causing the problem. Then, if the browser starts working, turn on the add-ons one by one to determine which one caused the problem.
- Determine whether the HOSTS file has been modified and includes some rogue entries. The HOSTS file can be found in the `C:\Windows\system32\drivers\etc` folder.

If **pop-ups** (unwanted messages, screens, or windows) appear continuously, use *Task Manager* to stop the specific browser process. Reopen the browser and ensure that the pop-up blocker is turned on. In Microsoft Edge, access *Settings* > *Cookies and site permissions* > *Pop-ups and redirects* > enable *Block*. In Chrome, access *Settings* > *Privacy and security* > *Site Settings* > in the *Content* section select *Pop-ups and redirects* > *Don't allow sites to send pop-ups or use redirects*. In Firefox, access *Settings* > *Privacy & Security* > in the *Permissions* section enable *Block pop-up windows*. Otherwise, use a different browser. Install anti-malware software. You can later uninstall and reinstall a browser, too.

TECH TIP

Browser troubleshooting tools

Firefox has a *Troubleshoot Mode* link available through the *Help* menu option that you can use when you are experiencing issues. Chrome has its own Task Manager that can be used to stop specific processes: select *More tools* from the three dots > *Task manager*. Edge has something similar available from the three dots *More tools* option > *Browser task manager*.

Many websites include advertisements. With some browsers, private browsing (refer to Table 12.4) can help reduce or eliminate ads. Free software for **ad blockers** exists, but ensure that any ad blocker you use is legitimate, works on your favorite browser(s), and is downloaded from a legitimate source.

Slow Browser

If your browser seems like it is getting slower and slower, but the rest of the machine is running fine, there are a few things you can do:

> Disable unnecessary add-ons.
> Disable all add-ons and re-enable them one at a time.
> Disable extensions.
> Uninstall and reinstall the web browser.
> Clear the browser cache/history (refer to Table 12.4).
> Reset the browser settings.
> Use a different web browser.

Introduction to Virtualization

As a help desk technician or a PC technician, you will run into virtualization as this area of computers is becoming very popular. **Virtualization** uses software that allows a single computer to be made into multiple virtual computers. For example, with virtualization, one PC can run two operating systems that have no knowledge of each other (see Figure 12.18). You can also use virtualization to have a PC act like a different device (such as a router) and, for example, allow your gaming console to create a virtual private network (VPN) tunnel into your PC and connect to other networks. Another common use of virtualization is with servers, where a powerful machine can host multiple servers separated from one another (see Figure 12.19).

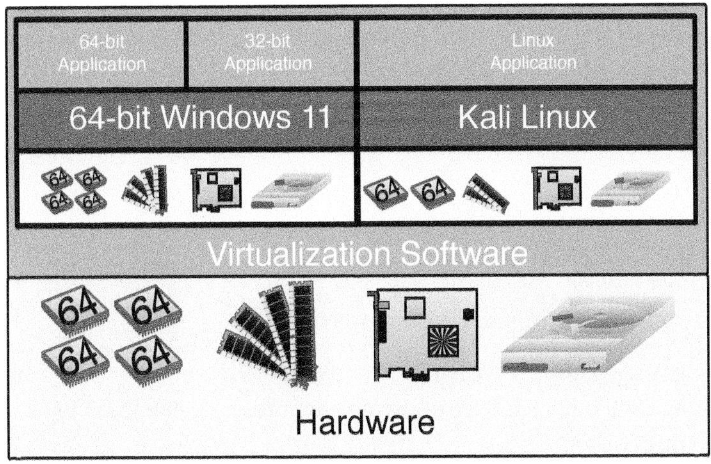

FIGURE 12.18 PC virtualization

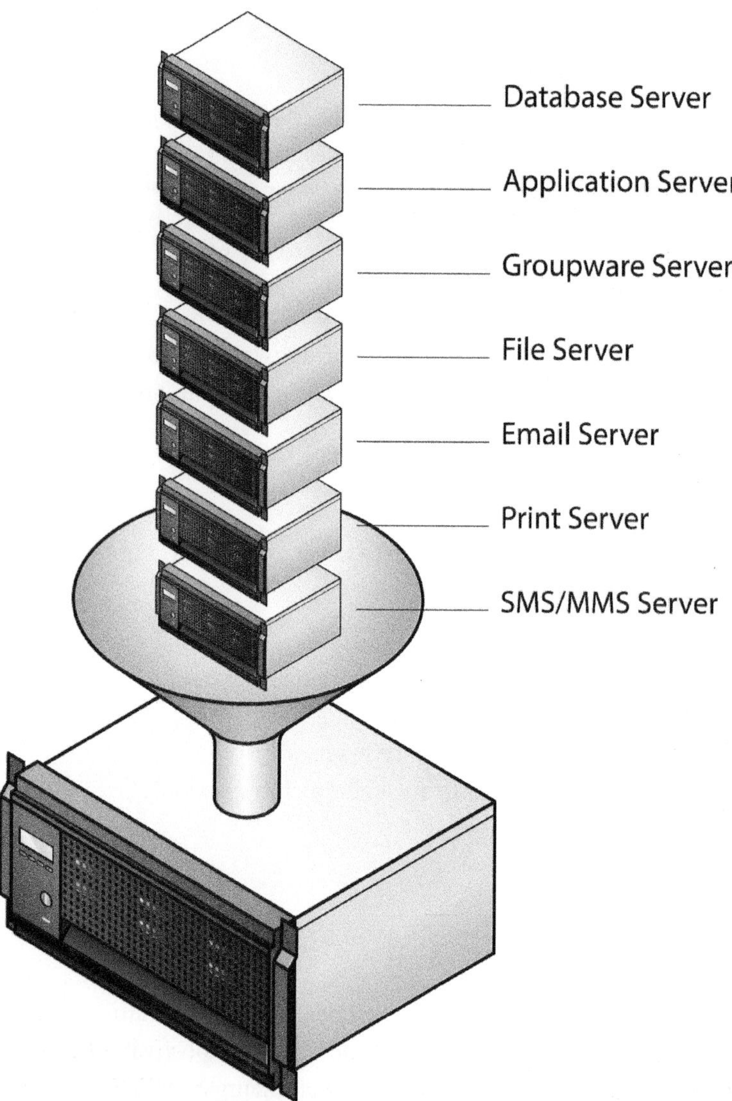

FIGURE 12.19 Server virtualization

So why is virtualization so popular? For one thing, virtualization enables **test development** as it provides a way to test things out in an environment that doesn't hurt anything else. Virtualization can provide a **sandbox** to do specific testing, such as opening suspicious software or files without allowing any malware to spread to other computers. In addition, virtualization can be used to run **legacy software** that is made for an older operating system or even to run that older OS. An example of **cross-platform virtualization** is running an additional OS on a computer, such as running Windows as well as macOS on a Mac.

Let's dive into how virtualization is used for desktop computers since that is our focus for a lot of this book.

Desktop Virtualization Basics

There are two ways to virtualize a desktop computer:

> You can use multiple operating systems on one computer. They can share hardware without affecting each other (or even knowing about each other). Look back at Figures 11.7 and 12.18 to see this concept.

> You can use a server to hold multiple virtualized desktop computers, as shown in Figure 12.20.

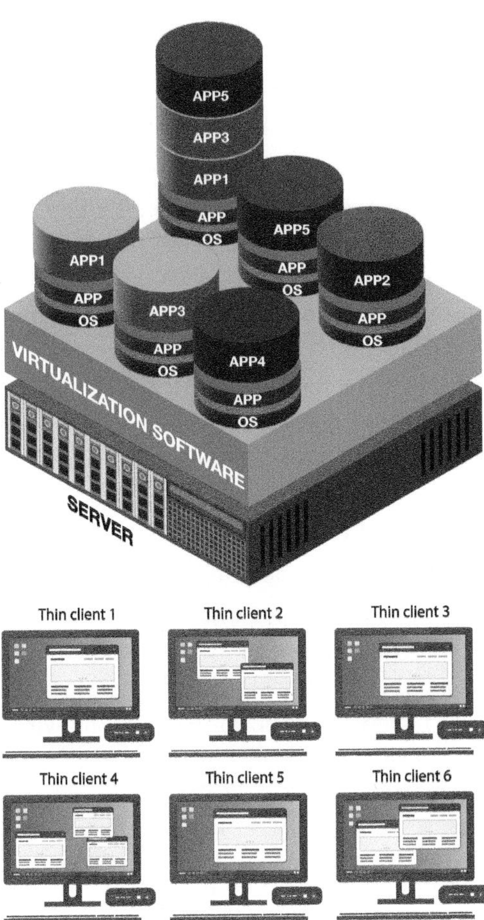

FIGURE 12.20 Desktop virtualization

A company may have servers, storage, and other infrastructure devices in its network operation center. Collectively this equipment is known as the virtual desktop infrastructure (**VDI**). When the equipment to do VDI is within the company, this is known as *VDI on premises*. The infrastructure equipment could also be at another site; this is known as *VDI in the cloud*. (More cloud concepts are coming in the next section.) The last option is to just get another company to handle these desktop images. This is known as *desktop as a service* (*DaaS*). If another company handles the virtualization, the users are more likely to have some customization regarding which apps are deployed to each user and more control over the data generated. With DaaS, new desktops can be provided to users quickly, and upgrades (as well as restoration when failures occur) tend to be quicker.

When you put more than one OS on a PC, the computer has to have a virtualization application such as a VMware Workstation, Oracle VirtualBox, or Microsoft Hyper-V to hold instances of one or more operating systems. Table 12.6 defines some terms commonly used with virtualization.

TABLE 12.6 Virtualization terms

Term	Description
Host machine	The real computer that holds multiple operating systems
Virtual machine	Also called a VM, a separate operating system from the host computer OS that has specifically chosen hardware components
Hypervisor	Also called virtual machine monitor or virtual machine manager, the software that can create a virtual machine and allocate resources to the virtual machine
Snapshot/ checkpoint	A copy or backup of the VM at a particular point in time, which can be used to revert the VM to that point in time (which is a similar concept to a Windows restore point)

The hypervisor is like an orchestra conductor for virtualization. The hypervisor is responsible for managing and overseeing the operation of the virtual machines (VMs). The hypervisor oversees RAM, hard drive space, and any processor(s) shared between the VMs.

There are two types of hypervisors: Type 1 and Type 2. A **Type 1 hypervisor** is also known as a native hypervisor because the operating system runs on top of the hypervisor. Examples of Type 1 hypervisors include VMware's ESXI and Microsoft's Hyper-V. A **Type 2 hypervisor**, also known as a hosted hypervisor, runs on top of a host operating system such as Windows 10. VMware Player, Oracle VirtualBox, and Windows Virtual PC are examples of Type 2 hypervisors.

In Figure 12.18, there are two CPUs and less RAM (two sticks) in the VM on the right than in the VM on the left, which uses four CPUs and four sticks of RAM. Within one virtual environment, you sometimes cannot "install" more hardware than is on the host machine (the real machine), even though some virtualization software allows you to do so. For example, say that the VM on the left in Figure 12.18 is assigned the full amount of RAM that is on the host machine, 64 GB, and the VM on the right is assigned 16 GB. The total is 80 GB, but the host machine has only 64 GB. This is allowed and common in the virtual environment. Some virtualization software (but not all) enables you to select 128 GB for the VM on the left, but doing so causes degradation in the virtual environment.

Working with VMs makes restoring an operating system (or a VM that holds an operating system) much easier than using the traditional operating system–based restoration methods. Technicians today are expected to know the basics of working in a virtual environment.

TECH TIP

You have to buy the OS license

A common misconception about virtualization is that you don't have to buy both operating systems when two operating systems are installed. This is not always true and depends on the virtualization software used. If you want to install Linux in one virtual machine, Windows 10 in another virtual machine, and Windows Server 2022 in a third virtual machine, you have to purchase any operating system that requires a license (Windows 10 and Windows Server in this example).

Each virtual machine can connect to a network using one of two basic options (and note that in Hyper-V, these options are configured through a virtual switch):

> *Internal network:* This option allows a particular VM access to other virtual machines that connect to the same network (though they may be on a different computer or in another VM on the same computer).

> *External network:* This option allows a particular VM access to a different (external) network from within the VM. In a college environment, for example, if a student computer can access the internet and that same computer is configured for virtualization, a VM on that student computer can be configured for the external network and have access to the internet.

Virtualization Resource and Emulator Requirements

Most Windows versions today have some type of emulation or virtualization included. An emulator is hardware or software that makes one operating system behave like an older or different one. Windows XP Mode is a program you can download from Microsoft.com that is designed to run Windows XP applications in a protected environment. Windows Virtual PC allows other Windows operating systems to run inside Virtual PC and provides one-click access to Windows XP Mode, which is integrated into Virtual PC.

Windows 8 and 10 Pro and higher versions have replaced Virtual PC with Hyper-V, which is a virtualization product. To enable Windows Hyper-V, access the *Programs and Features* Control Panel > *Turn Windows features on or off* > *enable Hyper-V* checkbox (see Figure 12.21).

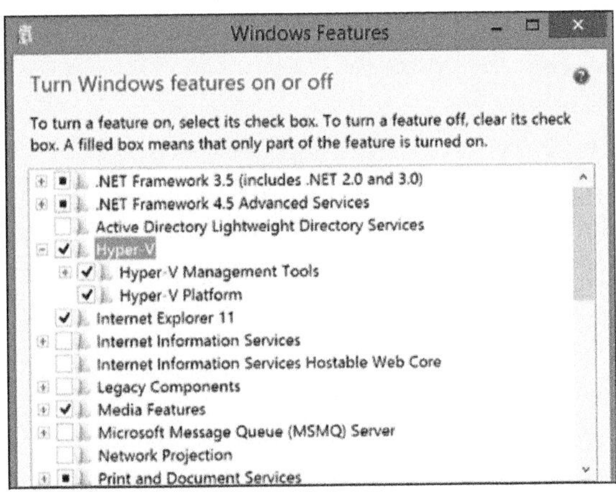

FIGURE 12.21 Enable Hyper-V in Windows

Virtualization Security

When using virtualization, each virtual machine needs the same protection as an individual computer. All security concepts apply not just to the host machine but to each virtual machine as well.

TECH TIP

A VM can get a virus

A common misconception about virtualization is that you don't have to worry about security because you are in a "protected" environment. This is not true. One operating system is indeed protected from the other operating system, but all virtual machines are susceptible to viruses and security attacks. It is important to install the appropriate protection. See Chapter 18 for more information on security.

Cloud Computing

Cloud computing was briefly introduced in Chapter 9, "Printers and Multifunction Devices," with printing to the cloud, and you have already heard how a desktop image might be provided by a remote company. You should learn a bit more about cloud computing because cloud technologies are prevalent in small, medium, and large businesses alike.

What does it mean to say that something is "in the cloud"? It simply means the network device, application, storage, connectivity, server, and more are not located within the company's physical location. Cloud technologies have been around for years. They might be used, for example, for a small business that doesn't have the resources or staff to create and maintain a web server. That web server can be hosted elsewhere, in which case it is considered "in the cloud"—that is, out on the internet somewhere (see Figure 12.22).

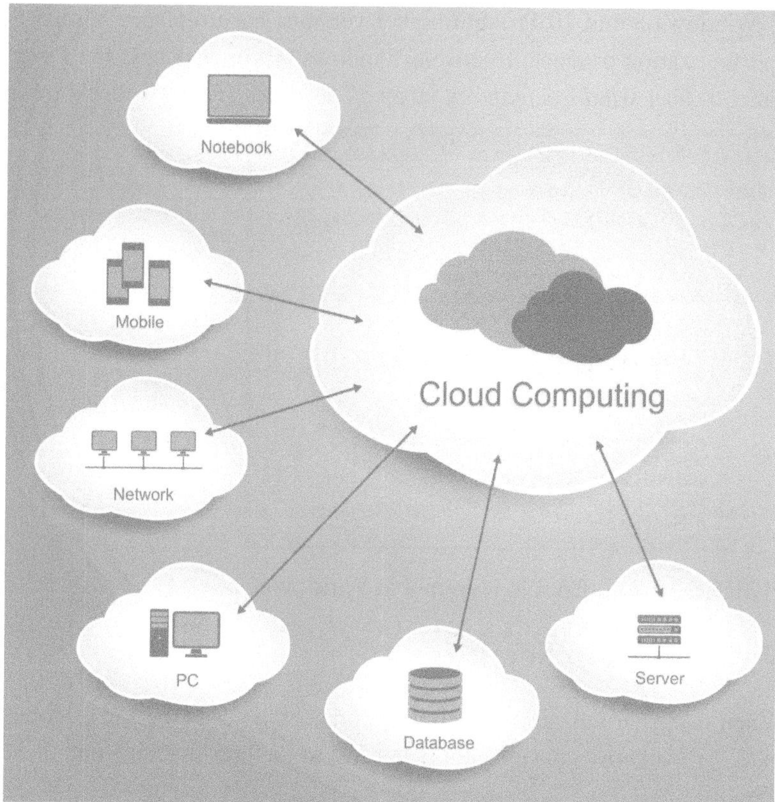

FIGURE 12.22 The concept of "in the cloud"

Cloud Services and Models

Different types of services are provided by cloud vendors, as outlined in Table 12.7.

TABLE 12.7 Cloud service types

Cloud service type	Description
Software as a service (**SaaS**)	Applications such as learning management, enterprise resource planning (ERP), human resources management (HRM), payroll, antivirus, and inventory management systems are hosted by another company. Cloud-based applications that you might be more familiar with—such as Microsoft Office 365, GitHub, a personal calendar, or a diet tracker—are also considered SaaS.
Desktop as a service (**DaaS**)	Users access a **virtual desktop** that is managed by another company or for which the equipment is located elsewhere. This would simply be the computer in a virtual environment so that the company that uses this service does not have to worry about software licenses, technicians to maintain operating system updates, and backups. A virtual desktop also includes a virtual network interface card (NIC), or **virtual NIC**, as discussed in more detail in Chapter 13.
Platform as a service (**PaaS**)	Servers, databases, operating system, storage, and development tools are provided in an outside environment to relieve the support burden on companies that need an environment to perform high-level programming and develop applications.
Infrastructure as a service (**IaaS**)	Routers, switches, servers, virtual machines, load balancers, access points, storage, and other infrastructure devices are provided through the online environment.

Cloud Technologies

Just about anything that is used within the corporate environment or personal computing environment can be offered as a cloud service. The most popular offerings for business include the following:

- *Off site email applications:* Instead of a company having to house its own email servers, email services are commonly housed in the cloud environment, either on the company's own servers located in a remote location or provided by a cloud-hosted email provider.
- *Cloud file storage services:* Many people use external storage, such as Microsoft OneDrive, Google Drive, Apple iCloud, Dropbox, SugarSync, Box, SpiderOak, or Tresorit. A popular feature of cloud-based storage is **file synchronization**, which allows for files and folders to be synced between devices and accessed from anywhere. It is important to have enough bandwidth when syncing to the cloud.
- *Virtual application streaming/cloud-based applications:* Applications can be virtualized so that each application doesn't have to be installed on individual devices. This prevents conflicts with other apps and provides better security controls. Some applications use streaming, which involves sending just some of the code needed to run the application and works well on mobile devices.
- *Cloud-based network controllers:* Vendors commonly have network controllers that control network devices (as discussed in Chapter 13). As shown in Figure 12.23, a cloud-based network controller might be used to monitor and control switches located at the main company and branch offices. Figure 12.24 shows a cloud-based network controller that is used to control and monitor access points.

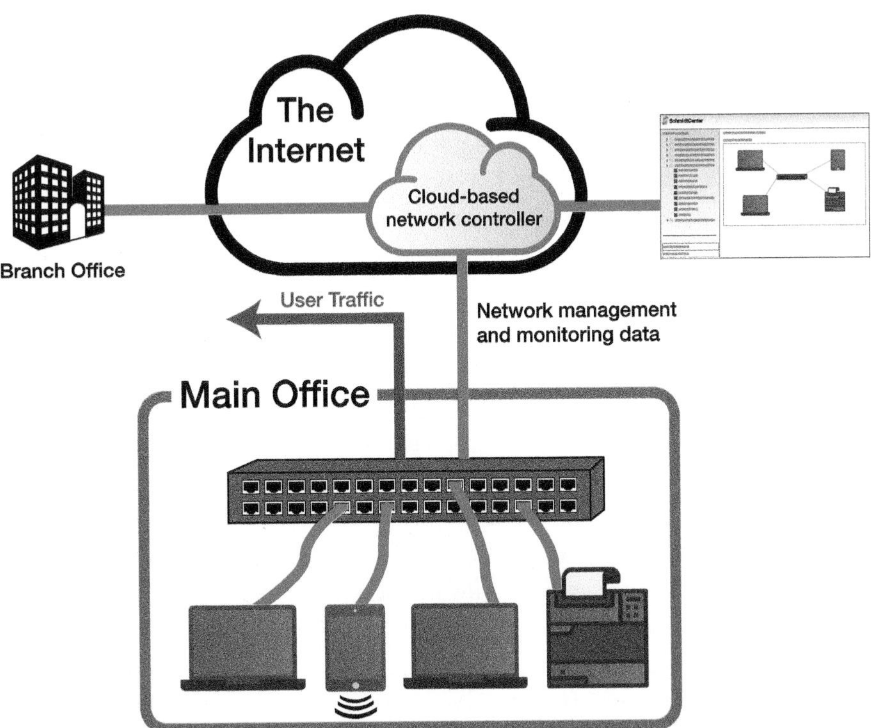

FIGURE 12.23 Cloud-based network controller for switch control

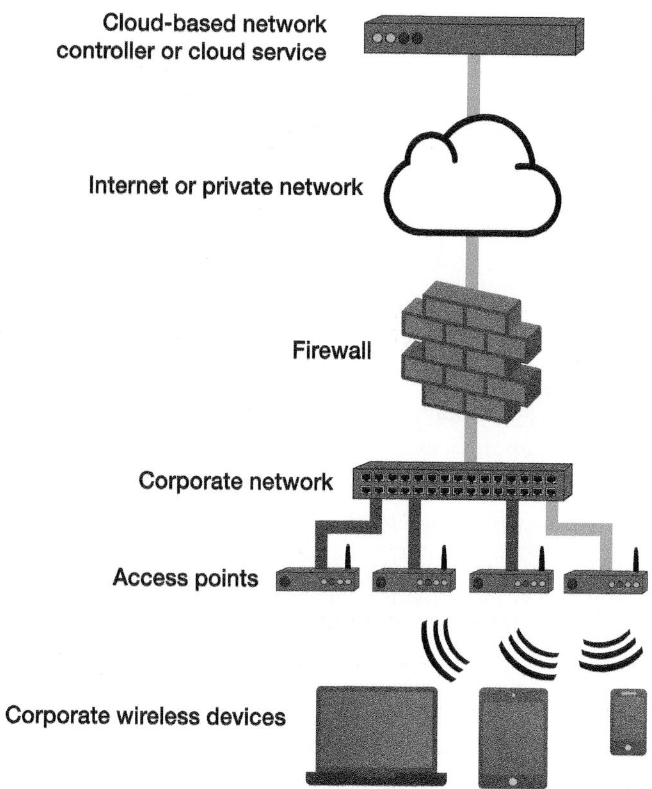

FIGURE 12.24 Cloud-based network controller for access point control

Cloud Service Deployment Methods

Cloud services can be deployed in a combination of ways: private, public, hybrid, and community (see Figure 12.25). A **private cloud** is part of a company's network infrastructure that is located outside the business in a remote location, but the company has responsibility for managing the software and/or hardware. For example, a college may purchase licenses for a learning management system (LMS) so that students can view grades and see assignments. The LMS could run on servers that are located in a remote vendor's location, but the college network administrators install, update, and maintain responsibility for supporting the LMS. Large businesses tend to be the biggest users of private clouds. With a private cloud deployment, the business doesn't have to worry about providing power, cooling, and space for the equipment and optionally can pay for redundant internet access and equipment and other features from the cloud provider.

A **public cloud** is an environment operated by a cloud provider. The cloud provider provides services to all business sizes for a cost. Again consider an LMS as an example; the servers and software for the LMS could be provided by the LMS vendor, who has the servers in a service provider's building. In a public cloud, the vendor or cloud provider has the responsibility for managing the software and/or hardware. In a public cloud deployment model, several companies pay for the services of the public cloud vendor. For an LMS, many colleges might purchase the public cloud option and allow another company to configure, monitor, and maintain the LMS.

A **hybrid cloud** is a combination of a private cloud and a public cloud. For example, a company using cloud services is responsible for the licensing and maintenance of the LMS in the private cloud but might need additional storage or servers during peak times. A hybrid cloud solution could be implemented as a failover solution as well. In such a case, the private cloud is used, but if a disaster occurs or during planned maintenance periods, the company uses the application in the public cloud instead.

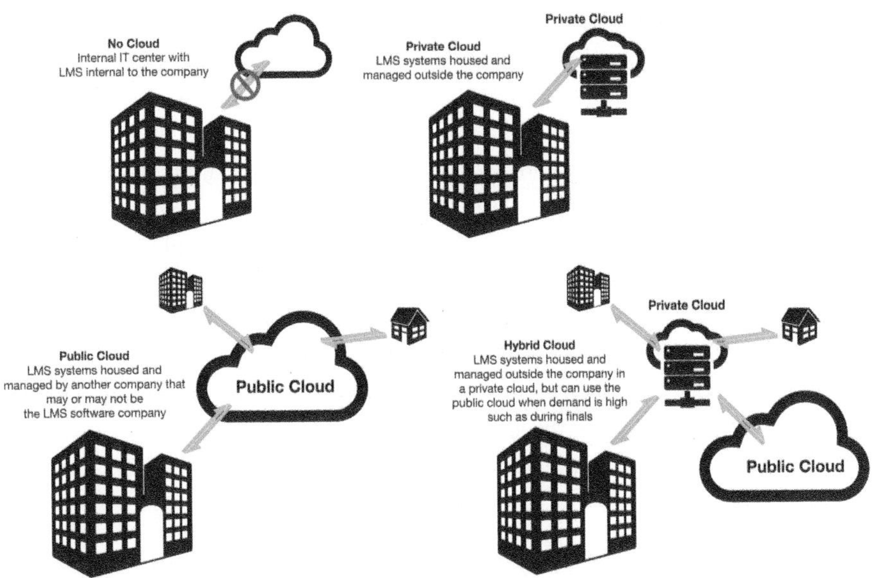

FIGURE 12.25 Cloud deployment models

With a **community cloud**, a number of organizations have access to IT resources that are in the community cloud. An example of this might be an IT system created by a consortium of colleges in one state that are co-developing the system. The system could be housed in the cloud and tested on systems in the cloud. The cost for the community cloud would be shared by all the colleges in the consortium.

Cloud Characteristics/Advantages

Cloud computing has many benefits to businesses, including reduced costs, increased flexibility, increased efficiency, and consistently applied software patches and upgrades. Costs related to network operations centers have increased due to the use of and reliance on technology throughout a business. Common network center costs and overhead include power, hardware, hardware redundancy, storage, fire protection system, licensing, cabling/interconnectivity, and backups.

Other advantages of using cloud technology include the following:

- *Corporate focus:* Cloud computing enables a company to focus on core IT services or the true function of the company, while an outside vendor focuses on its particular strengths (technical expertise on a particular product, staffing levels, quality of service, customer service, and so on).
- **High availability***:* Cloud computing supports continuous 24/7 access from anywhere and possibly any device. Access is on-demand, meaning that it is available when and where the customer needs it.
- **Rapid elasticity***:* Cloud computing facilitates quick expansion of services, software, and/or hardware. For example, if another server or more storage or more of anything else is needed, the outside vendor can access resources that allow expansion on demand. For some companies, such expansions might take several months for an internal system because of the time needed to requisition and obtain the resources.
- **Shared resources***:* A big part of cloud computing is taking advantage of resource pooling. Shared resources between companies or even within the same company can include servers, applications, hardware components like RAM and CPUs, data storage, internet connections, and network infrastructure equipment. Think back to virtualization, which is a big part of the cloud environment. Within one computer, the virtualized environment provides resource

pooling, such as sharing RAM or CPUs between the multiple operating systems loaded. The resources could be resources owned by the company but housed elsewhere (internal shared resources) or shared with other companies when hosted by an external vendor. By using an outside vendor's services, a company can pool resources with other companies that have the same need. A vendor might have access to hundreds of servers. Say that Company A needs just a few servers right now, but Company B has a high usage rate. The outside vendor can allocate servers to Company B to handle the load right now but later reallocate the additional servers to Company A, when its usage increases.

> *Service rates:* A provider can allocate resources easily by providing a **measured service**, which makes it possible to track (and charge for) cloud consumer usage and apply resources when needed. In contrast, a **metered service** requires that a company pay an amount based on how much of the service is used on an hourly or monthly basis. There is also a fee structure that involves a fixed charge and usually involves fixed resources or configurations.

SOFT SKILLS: MENTORING

Every great technician can tell you that he or she has had at least one mentor along the way. When you hear the word *mentor*, it probably conjures up other words and phrases in your head—coach, guidance, teacher, adviser, positive influence, leadership, setting an example, and so on. No technician can attain his or her ultimate level without being mentored. Also, no technician can learn everything from a book or from personal experience. Others helping us along the way enable us to learn faster and more efficiently.

When you enter your first (second, third, or fourth) job in the IT field, you should take a few days to look around the company. Find someone who appears to be very professional and knowledgeable—someone you want to emulate. Talk to that person and explain your goals. Ask if he or she will mentor you—whether to get help with problems you cannot solve or advice about office politics (see Figure 12.26).

FIGURE 12.26 Mentoring

Mentoring is an important part of life. Not only should you consider being mentored, you should consider mentoring others. Many technicians hoard information from other technicians and computer users. Knowledge is power, and by sharing information with others and helping them along the way, you cement and expand your own knowledge.

Chapter Summary

> Serial devices must be configured for the number of bits, parity, stop bits, FIFO setting, flow control such as XON/XOFF (software method) or RTS/CTS (hardware method), and handshaking. The two sides of a connection must match.

> Internet connectivity can be provided by an analog modem, satellite modem, cable modem, fiber, DSL modem, or wirelessly through the cell phone network, wireless broadband, long-range fixed wireless, a WISP, or a Wi-Fi network.

> Cable modem bandwidth is shared by the subscribers in an area. If the number of subscribers is too many and the cable bandwidth is unacceptable, a direct fiber connection might be an option.

> A DSL modem uses a phone line. ADSL has faster downstream speeds than upstream speeds.

> VoIP uses a corporate network and/or the internet for voice connectivity. Internet-based VoIP does not offer QoS.

> Wireless communications have both licensed and unlicensed frequency ranges. The licensed range has better performance due to reduced interference. Some of the unlicensed ranges still have rules associated with them.
> Technicians frequently have to configure web browsers. With most browsers, you use the *Settings* option to begin the configuration process.
> Keep a web browser current for security reasons.
> Private browsing prevents a web browser from storing browsing history information and passwords.
> A hijacked browser redirects a browser to a different web page. Pop-ups can be managed by using a pop-up blocker.
> Disable add-ons to prevent pop-ups and help with a hijacked browser.
> Virtualization can be used to test apps, operating systems, or code; as a sandbox to prevent other devices from being affected; or to run an older OS.
> Desktop virtualization can be done within a company on premises using a VDI or provided as a cloud service (DaaS).
> A computer that uses virtualization must have more hardware to run more than a single operating system environment.
> A virtual desktop is an operating system that is in a virtual machine and used within a corporate environment to more easily manage multiple computers.
> Cloud technology services are classified as SaaS, DaaS, IaaS, and PaaS. Cloud deployment models include private, public, hybrid, and community.
> Shared resources can be internal or external.
> Cloud services can be provided as measured services, as metered services, or for a flat fee.
> Mentoring is important when you get started as a technician and as you gain experience.

A+ CERTIFICATION EXAM TIPS

✓ Know cable modem, DSL, and ONT connectivity/hardware.

✓ Long-range fixed wireless was added for this certification so be aware of implications of a frequency range being licensed or unlicensed and the regulatory requirements for wireless power.

✓ Know the difference between and features of the following internet connection types: cable, DSL, cellular, WISP, satellite, and fiber.

✓ Know the differences between SaaS, PaaS, DaaS, and IaaS and between public, private, hybrid, and community cloud deployments.

✓ Be able to describe how desktops can be virtualized through a VDI on site (on premises) or from the cloud.

✓ Know the purpose of setting up a virtual machine, including using it as a sandbox, for test development, for application virtualization, when using legacy software or an OS, and for cross-platform virtualization. Also be aware of the resource and security requirements involved in using virtualization.

✓ Know the meanings of the following cloud-related terms: shared resources, rapid elasticity, on-demand, metered utilization, high availability, and file synchronization.

✓ When troubleshooting a network, be aware of jitter and how it might be used in determining issues with VoIP quality.

✓ Be able to install and configure browsers and know what a trusted or untrusted source is as well as how hashing is used. Be able to install and configure extensions and plug-ins. Settings include pop-up blockers, clearing cache and data, using private browsing, using ad blockers, and signing in with browser data synchronization.

✓ Be able to recommend, install, and configure a password manager. Be able to recognize a secure connection and know what a valid security certificate is.

Key Terms

3G 526
4G 526
5G 526
ad blocker 533
ADSL 519
bandwidth 524
baud 517
browser extension 530
browser plug-in 530
browser redirection 531
browser synchronization 530
cable modem 518
checkpoint 535
clear browsing data 530
clear cache 530
coaxial 518
community cloud 541
convergence 520
cross-platform virtualization 534
DaaS 538
dial-up network 516
downstream 523
DSL 519
fiber network 522
file synchronization 539
hash 528
high availability 541
host machine 535
hybrid cloud 540
hypervisor 535
IaaS 538
ISP 525
jitter 521
latency 522
legacy software 534
licensed range 527
LTE 526
measured service 542
metered service 542
mobile hotspot 525
ONT 523
PaaS 538
password manager 532
phone filter 519
poor VoIP quality 521
pop-up 532
private browsing 530
private cloud 540
public cloud 540
QoS 521
rapid elasticity 541
rootkit 531
SaaS 538
sandbox 534
satellite modem 524
secure connection 528
security certificate verification 530
shared resources 541
snapshot 535
test development 534
tethering 525
trusted source 528
Type 1 hypervisor 536
Type 2 hypervisor 536
unlicensed range 527
untrusted source 528
upstream 523
VDI 535
virtual desktop 538
virtual machine 535
virtual NIC 538
virtualization 533
VoIP 520
WiBro 526
wireless broadband 526
WISP 527
xDSL 519

Type	Two disadvantages	Two advantages
DSL modem		
Fiber		
Satellite modem		
Wireless broadband		

Exercise 12.2 Exploring the Internet Options Window

Objective: To explore the different tabs in the Internet Options window from Internet Explorer

Note: This exercise can be done with information found within the chapter, as an internet research exercise (which would require a device with internet access), or on a Windows computer.

Procedure: Indicate in Table 12.9 the *Internet Options* tab (General, Security, Privacy, Content, Connections, Programs, or Advanced) that would be used to perform each task.

TABLE 12.9 Internet Options tabs to use for specific tasks

Task	*Internet Options* tab
Enable pop-up blocker	
Specify the maximum amount of disk space for temporary internet files	
Configure security certificates	
Disable an add-on	
Designate which program opens sound files found in web pages	
Configure a proxy server	
Configure the version of HTTP supported	
Configure a VPN	
Designate the URL to be used as the home page	
Configure settings related to inside the corporate network (as opposed to the internet)	
Set the default font used for a web page	

Activities

Internet Discovery

Objective: To obtain specific information regarding a computer or its associated parts on the internet

Parts: Computer with internet access

Questions: Use the internet to answer the following questions.

1. Locate a cable modem website that explains how to increase speed on a cable modem. Write the URL where you found the answer as well as the recommendation.

   ____

   ____

2. Determine whether cable or DSL modems are supported in your area. If so, determine as many vendors as you can for these products.

   ____

   ____

3. Find one vendor of VDSL in the United States and write down the name of the vendor and the URL where you found the answer.

   ____

   ____

4. Find a website that provides cloud-based desktop virtualization. Write down pros and cons of services and URL of the vendor.

   ____

   ____

   ____

5. Determine how much a vendor charges to enable the mobile hotspot option or determine a phone/device that supports the mobile hotspot option. Document the price or phone model number and the URL where you found this information.

   ____

   ____

   ____

6. Find a vendor in your state that sells wireless broadband for a laptop. What type of technology does it use (USB, integrated, and so on)? Write the URL, the vendor name, the model number, and the cost.

   ____

   ____

Soft Skills

Objective: To enhance and fine-tune a future technician's ability to listen, communicate in both written and oral forms, and support people who use computers in a professional manner

Activities:

1. Divide the class into three groups—two groups that will be debating against one another and a third group of judges. The judges have 45 minutes to determine the rules and how the debate is to be conducted. During the same 45 minutes, the two debating groups should research material and plan a strategy for either cable modems or DSL modems. At the end of 45 minutes, the debate will start, and the judges will mediate with the rules they establish and present to the two teams before the debate begins. The judges, along with the instructor, determine which group proved its point the best.

2. Using whatever resources are available, research one of the following that has been assigned to you. Share the results with the class.

   What is the fastest DSL, cable, or analog connection within a 60-mile radius of your school?

   ___

   What is the most common type of internet connectivity for home users in your area?

   ___

   What is the most common type of internet connectivity among businesses in your area?

   ___

   What are the type and speed of the internet connectivity at your school?

   ___

   What are the type and speed of the internet connectivity at a college in your state?

   ___

   Which types of DSL services are available in your state?

   ___

   Which types of cable modem services are available in your state?

   ___

Critical Thinking Skills

Objective: To analyze and evaluate information as well as apply learned information to new or different situations

Activities:

1. In groups of three, research one of the following issues, as designated by the instructor. Share your findings with the other groups.
   > What are the pros and cons of changing the settings on a smartphone so that it can be a hotspot? Be prepared to share your findings.
   > What wireless broadband options are available from one of the most popular mobile phone providers in the area? Detail one option and its rate plan and cost. Be prepared to share your findings.
   > Determine the best internet connectivity rates for a small business in the area where your school is located. Share at least two competitors' rates, if possible. Detail the connectivity speeds and costs per vendor and be prepared to share your findings.
   > Find at least three VoIP solutions for home users. Prepare a chart that shows vendors, options, pros and cons of each option, costs, and customer ratings (and comments, if possible). Be prepared to share your findings.
2. In groups of two, write two problems that can affect analog/cable/DSL modems on two separate index cards. Give one problem to another class group and the other problem to a different class group. Your group will receive two index cards from two different groups as well. Solve the problems given to you, using any resource available. Share your group findings with the class.

13 Networking

In this chapter you will learn:

- To identify common network cables and connectors
- About Ethernet networks
- About the OSI and TCP/IP models, different networking protocols, differences between TCP and UDP, and important TCP or UDP port numbers
- To identify MAC, IPv4, and IPv6 addresses
- To set up wired and wireless networks
- Common network troubleshooting tools
- To configure and access a network printer
- Important network servers
- The basics of SDN
- To share data using a network
- How to be a proactive technician

CompTIA Exam Objectives:

- ✓1101-2.1 Compare and contrast Transmission Control Protocol (TCP) and User Datagram Protocol (UDP) ports, protocols, and their purposes.
- ✓1101-2.2 Compare and contrast common networking hardware.
- ✓1101-2.3 Compare and contrast protocols for wireless networking.
- ✓1101-2.4 Summarize the services provided by networked hosts.
- ✓1101-2.5 Given a scenario, install and configure basic wired/wireless small office/home office (SOHO) networks.
- ✓1101-2.6 Compare and contrast common network configuration concepts.
- ✓1101-2.7 Compare and contrast Internet connection types, network types, and their features.
- ✓1101-2.8 Given a scenario, use networking tools.
- ✓1101-3.1 Explain basic cable types and their connectors, features, and purposes.
- ✓1101-3.4 Given a scenario, install and configure motherboards, central processing units (CPUs), and add-on cards.
- ✓1101-3.6 Given a scenario, deploy and configure multifunction devices/printers and settings.
- ✓1101-5.5 Given a scenario, troubleshoot common issues with mobile devices.
- ✓1101-5.7 Given a scenario, troubleshoot problems with wired and wireless networks.
- ✓1102-1.1 Identify basic features of Microsoft Windows editions.
- ✓1102-1.2 Given a scenario, use the appropriate Microsoft command-line tool.
- ✓1102-1.4 Given a scenario, use the appropriate Microsoft Windows 10 Control Panel utility.
- ✓1102-1.5 Given a scenario, use the appropriate Windows settings.
- ✓1102-1.6 Given a scenario, configure Microsoft Windows networking features on a client/desktop.
- ✓1102-2.1 Summarize various security measures and their purposes.
- ✓1102-2.2 Compare and contrast wireless security protocols and authentication methods.
- ✓1102-2.9 Given a scenario, configure appropriate security settings on small office/home office (SOHO) wireless and wired networks.
- ✓1102-3.2 Given a scenario, troubleshoot common personal computer (PC) security issues.
- ✓1102-3.4 Given a scenario, troubleshoot common mobile OS and application issues.

Networking Overview

Networks are all around us. A few examples include the following:

> A network of roads and interstate highways
> A telephone network
> The electrical network that provides electricity to our homes
> The cellular network that allows cell phones/smartphones to connect to one another as well as to the wired telephone network and the internet
> The air traffic control network
> Your network of friends and family

A network as it relates to computers is two or more devices that can communicate with one another and share resources. A network allows computer users to share files; communicate via email; browse the internet; share a printer or scanner; and access applications and files. Networks can be divided into major categories based on the size and type of network. Table 13.1 describes these different networks.

TABLE 13.1 Types of networks

Network type	Description
Personal area network (**PAN**)	A PAN consists of personal devices such as keyboard, mouse, TV, cell phone, laptop, desktop, mobile device, and pocket video games that can communicate in close proximity through a wired or wireless network. A Bluetooth keyboard connected with a PC is an example of a PAN.
Local area network (**LAN**)	A LAN is a group of devices that can share resources in a single area, such as a room, home, or building. The most common LAN technology is Ethernet. The computers in a wired networked classroom are an example of a LAN.
Wireless LAN (**WLAN**)	A wireless network is used in home and business networks and includes devices such as laptops, tablets, smartphones, and smart home devices that transmit data through the air. A wireless bridge might be used to connect devices between two buildings.
Metropolitan area network (**MAN**)	A MAN provides connectivity between sites within the same city and multiple LANs. It can be wireless or use fiber cabling. For example, multiple college campuses connected within a city may be connected to form a MAN.
Wide area network (**WAN**)	A WAN provides connectivity between sites on a large geographic scale. Two remote locations that have connectivity between them as part of the company network are a WAN.
Wireless WAN (**WWAN**)	A WWAN provides wireless connectivity for a larger geographic area, using a mix of technologies, such as cellular or long-range fixed wireless.
Wireless mesh network (**WMN**)	A WMN provides wireless connectivity that is especially good in emergency situations because WMNs pass data between peer radio devices and can be used over large distances.
Storage area network (**SAN**)	A SAN is a collection of storage devices that are used by multiple servers/network devices and centrally managed.

Let's go into a few of these network types a little deeper so the acronyms can bring visuals to your mind.

Bluetooth PAN

A PAN is a network that has components that are in close proximity to one another. The most common type of PAN uses a technology called **Bluetooth**. Bluetooth devices include audio/visual products, automotive accessories, keyboards, mice, phones, game controllers, cameras, wireless cell phone headsets, sunglasses with radios and wireless speakers, and other small wireless devices.

Bluetooth works in the 2.4 GHz range, similarly to business wireless networks. Traditional Bluetooth has three classes of devices (1, 2, and 3) that have a range of less than 30 feet (less than 10 meters), 33 feet (10 meters), and 328 feet (100 meters), respectively, and a maximum transfer rate of 24 Mbps. Bluetooth version 5 introduced a second type of Bluetooth called Bluetooth Low Energy (BLE) that supports longer distances for speeds up to 2 Mbps. Vendors tout ranges of up to 800 feet (243 meters), although such distances are not defined in the standard. BLE is good for Internet of Things (IoT) devices such as sensors and controls for cameras, a stove, or lights within a home. The BLE standard is not compatible with the classic Bluetooth standard, but smartphones or other devices might have the capability of using both.

Up to eight Bluetooth devices can be connected in a piconet or PAN (a small network). Bluetooth has always had security features integrated into it, including 128-bit encryption (for scrambling of data). Figure 13.1 shows a Bluetooth connection between a cell phone mounted on a runner's arm and a fitness device on the wrist so that the phone app can be used to configure the device and download the activity data.

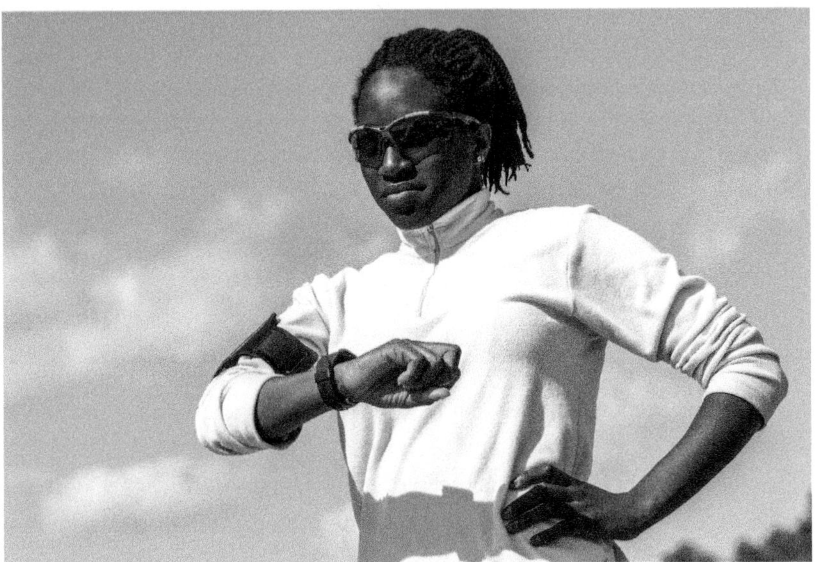

FIGURE 13.1 Bluetooth connectivity

A Bluetooth network provides computer-to-computer connectivity between Bluetooth devices. Each computer must support a PAN to join the network. In Windows, use *Settings > Devices > Bluetooth & other devices*. Review Chapter 10, "Mobile Devices," for complete installation steps.

LANs

LANs can be wired or wireless, but a LAN that is wireless is called a WLAN. Let's focus on the wired type first. A LAN is two or more devices connected via wiring. You can actually connect two devices with a cable between their NICs to form a LAN, but most LANs today are Ethernet LANs. An **Ethernet** LAN has a central device called a hub or a switch. An Ethernet cable connects an RJ45 port on the network device to the switch or hub, as shown in Figure 13.2. The hub or switch typically has 2 to 48 ports on the front.

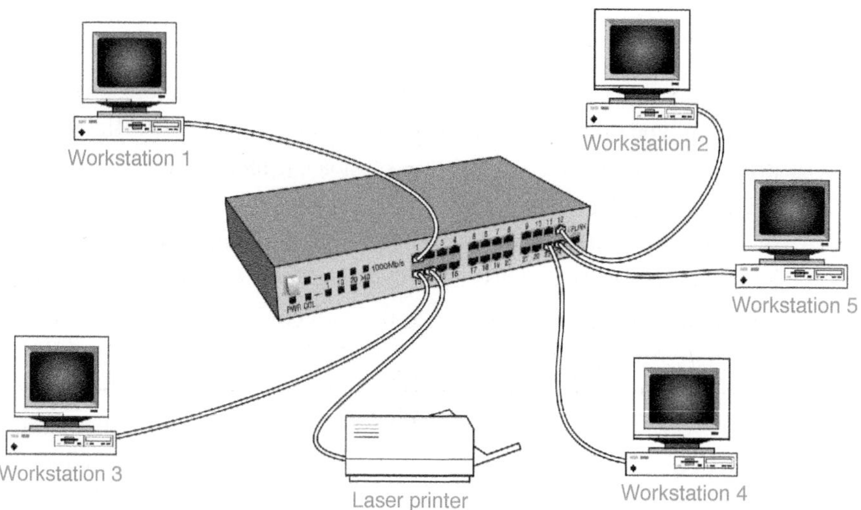

FIGURE 13.2 Ethernet LAN

A hub is not as intelligent as a switch. A switch examines each data frame as it comes through the switch. A hub cannot do this. You sometimes have to look at the model number/description to tell the difference between a hub and a switch because they are similar in appearance.

TECH TIP

Why a switch is better than a hub

When a workstation sends data to a hub, the **hub** broadcasts the data out all ports except for the port that received the original data (the port the data came in on). A better solution is a switch. A **switch** keeps a table of addresses. When a switch receives data, the switch looks up the destination MAC address (an address burned into a NIC) in the switch table and forwards the data out the port for which it is destined.

When a hub is used, collisions may occur because two devices can place data onto the network at the same time. Every device has to delay sending data for a period of time, and then transmissions can reoccur. This isn't an inefficient use of bandwidth. A switch eliminates collisions and is therefore a better network device to use.

Switches can be either managed or unmanaged. A **managed switch** has an IP address assigned and can be configured, modified, and monitored through a corporate network. An **unmanaged switch** simply connects devices so that they form a network. This would be like a switch you might have in a home or small business wired network.

TECH TIP

Ethernet networks are physically wired in a star

The most common network topology used today is the star topology, which is used with Ethernet networks.

In a star topology (refer to Figure 13.2), each network device has a cable that connects between the network interface card (NIC) on the device and the hub or switch. If one computer or cable fails, all other devices continue to function. However, if the hub or switch fails, the network goes down.

Star topologies are easy to troubleshoot. If one network device goes down, the problem is in the device, cable, or port on the hub/switch. If a group of network devices goes down, the problem is most likely in the device that connects them together (the hub or switch).

Table 13.2 lists the different types of Ethernet networks. In the term 100BaseT, the *100* means that the network runs at 100 Mbps. The *T* at the end of 100BaseT means that the computer uses twisted pair cable. The *1000* in 1000BaseT means that 1,000 Mbps is supported. *Base* means that the network uses baseband technology. Baseband describes data that is sent over a single channel on a single wire. In contrast, broadband is used in cable TV systems, and it allows multiple channels using different frequencies to be covered over a single wire.

TABLE 13.2 Ethernet standards

Ethernet type	Description
10BaseT	10 Mbps over Cat 3 or Cat 5 UTP cable
100BaseT	100 Mbps over Cat 5 or higher UTP cable
1000BaseT	Also known as Gigabit Ethernet; 1,000 Mbps or 1 Gbps over Cat 5 or higher UTP cable
1000BaseSX	1 Gbps using multi-mode fiber (a type of cable made of plastic or glass that carries data using light)
1000BaseLX	1 Gbps using single-mode fiber
2.5G/5GBaseT	2.5 or 5 Gbps over Cat 6 or higher cable
10GBaseSR	10 Gbps over multi-mode fiber
10GBaseLX4	10 Gbps over multi-mode or single-mode fiber
10GBaseLR	10 Gbps up to 6.2 miles (10 km) using single-mode fiber
10GBaseER	10 Gbps up to 24.85 miles (40 km) using single-mode fiber
10GBaseT	10 Gbps over UTP (Cat 6 or higher) or STP cable
25GBaseLR	25 Gbps over fiber up to 6.2 miles (10 km)
25GBaseER	25 Gbps over fiber up to 24.85 miles (40 km)
40 Gigabit Ethernet	40 Gbps over single-mode fiber or 23 feet (7 m) using copper
100 Gigabit Ethernet	100 Gbps over multi-mode or single-mode fiber

LANs typically are based on one of two models: a workgroup model or a domain model. A **workgroup** LAN is used in a wired home or small business network. A **domain** is used in a corporate environment and usually contains multiple networks. A domain typically contains servers, databases, and shared resources that are centrally managed. Table 13.3 compares the two types.

TABLE 13.3 Workgroup and domain network characteristics

Workgroup	Domain
Small number of devices (typically fewer than 20)	Typically more than 20 devices
All devices are usually on one network	Contains multiple networks
Each network device must have user accounts configured	User accounts are centrally managed
More of a security risk	Security is centrally managed with security policies applied

Workgroup	Domain
Might contain a web server, file server, or network-attached storage (NAS) but may have no servers	Storage is centralized, and multiple servers are usually involved
Easier to implement	Any change requires planning
Each PC uses a workstation OS	Each server requires a network operating system (NOS)
Requires fewer resources	Network resources are centralized, located in another location, cloud based, or a combination of these

Figure 13.3 shows the type of wired and wireless connectivity used in a workgroup. Figure 13.4 shows the kind of connectivity that can be used in a network domain.

FIGURE 13.3 Wired and wireless connectivity in a workgroup network

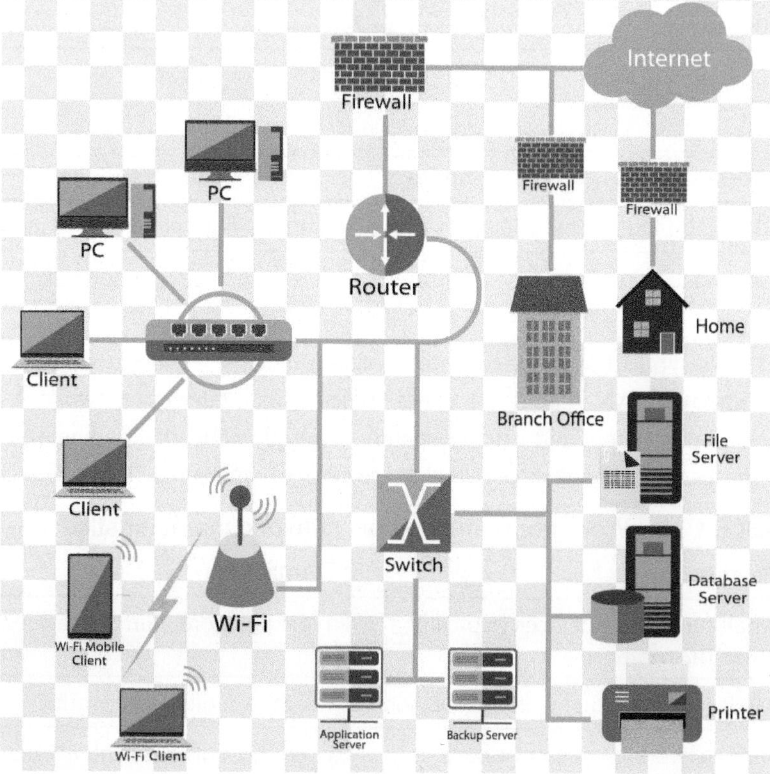

FIGURE 13.4 Domain network

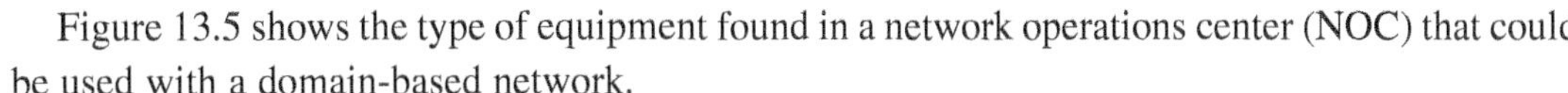

Figure 13.5 shows the type of equipment found in a network operations center (NOC) that could be used with a domain-based network.

FIGURE 13.5 Network operations center (NOC)

When you attach to a wired LAN and are using a Microsoft operating system, you are presented with three or four choices, depending on the OS you are using: workgroup network, guest network, public network, private network, or domain. A home or work environment is considered a **private network**, and private addresses are used. Characteristics of your computer can be seen or discovered by other devices. A **public network** is like when you are using a computer in the community library or at a hotel. With a public network, Windows does not allow discovery of the device even though it is connected to a network. The option chosen defines, to some extent, the type of network you could configure. Table 13.4 describes the basic choices.

TABLE 13.4 Windows network options

Network option	Description
Workgroup	Used to configure a device participating in a small home or business network. Use the System Control Panel to select this option.
Domain	Used to configure a device in an enterprise corporate environment where policies are enforced and deployed. Use the System Control Panel to select this option.
Private	Used when you are on a trusted network such as a home or corporate network. Use *Network & Internet* > *Ethernet* Settings option to select for a wired network or select the wireless network > *Properties* option.
Public	Used to configure a device on a network where the other devices are unknown. Network discovery is disabled. Use *Network & Internet* > *Ethernet* Settings option to select for a wired network or select the wireless network > *Properties* option.

WLANs

WLANs (sometimes called Wi-Fi networks) are popular in homes and businesses for connecting devices. WLANs connect wireless devices like phones, tablets, laptops, TVs, and smart speakers/devices, using a specific range of radio frequencies, as shown in Figure 13.6.

FIGURE 13.6 WLAN connectivity

SANs

A storage area network (SAN) has a large number of hard drives mounted in a unit that attaches to the network, and that storage is centrally managed. Figure 13.7 shows a person installing a server, and behind him is a SAN.

FIGURE 13.7 Storage area network (SAN)

If a PC needed to access data on a SAN, it could just do so through the normal LAN, but the PC might also contain a special NIC to connect to the SAN **iSCSI** or Fibre Channel (**FC**) connections (look back at Figure 2.40 in Chapter 2, "Connectivity," to see fiber connectors), as shown in Figure 13.8. Connectivity between a SAN and servers also is accomplished using these connectivity methods, as shown in Figure 13.9.

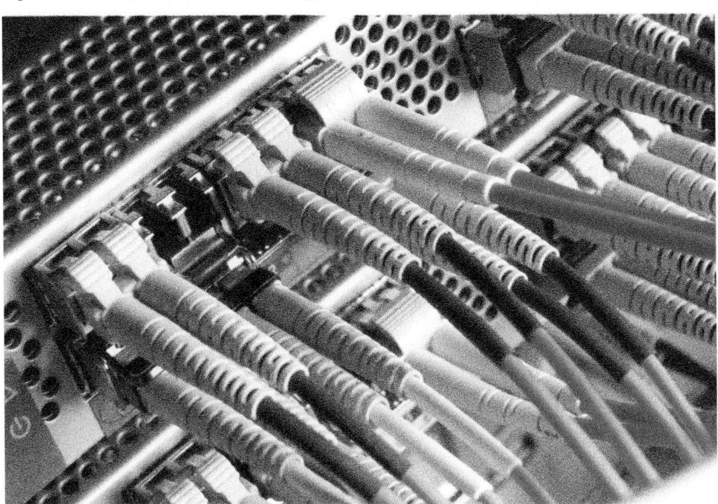

FIGURE 13.8 SAN fiber connectivity

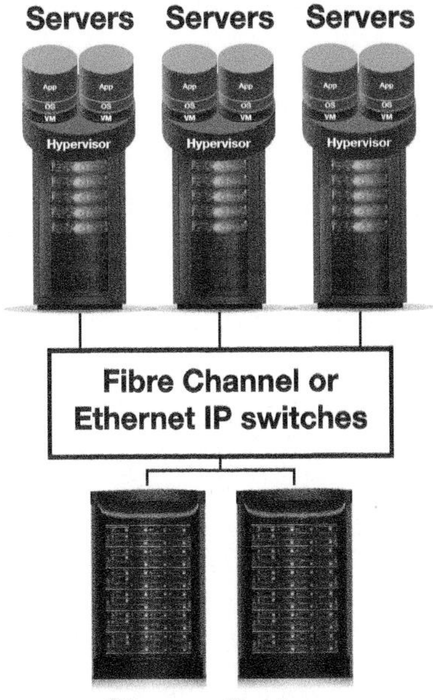

FIGURE 13.9 SAN connectivity to servers

Today, networks are vital to businesses. They can also be found in many homes. A technician must have a basic understanding of the devices that make up networks and their roles. No matter what IT position you are aspiring toward, you will have to deal with these concepts.

Network Media Overview

A network requires some type of medium to transmit data. This medium is normally some type of cable or air (wireless using radio, microwave, and electromagnetic signals). The most common types of cable are coax, twisted pair copper and fiber-optic cable. Air is used in wireless networking when data is sent over radio frequencies.

Copper Media

Copper media is the most common cabling used to connect devices to a network. Copper media comes in two major types: twisted pair and coaxial.

Twisted Pair Cable Overview

Twisted pair cable comes in two types: shielded and unshielded. The acronyms used with this type of cable are STP (shielded twisted pair) and UTP (unshielded twisted pair). The most common type of copper media used with computer networking and phone cabling is **UTP** cable. **Twisted pair cable** has four pairs of conductors entwined around each other—hence its name. Figure 13.10 shows the physical properties of an unshielded twisted pair cable.

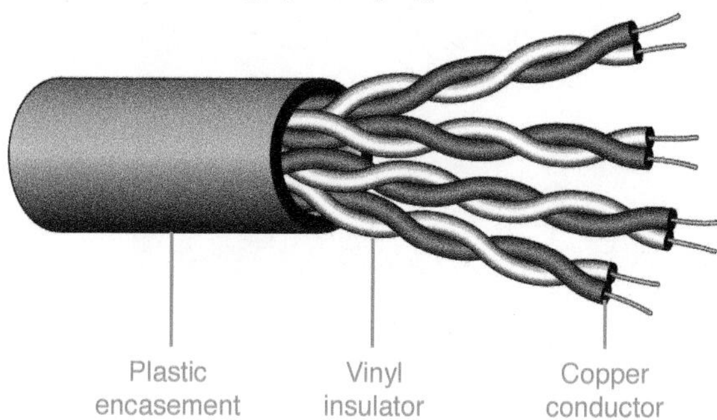

FIGURE 13.10 UTP cable

STP cable has extra foil that provides more shielding. Shielded twisted pair cable is used in industrial settings, such as factories, where extra shielding is needed to prevent outside interference from adversely affecting the data on the cable. It is also used with **direct burial cable** and underground outdoor cabling that has waterproofing and extra insulation so tubing or pipes are not required.

UTP cable is measured in gauges. The most common sizes of UTP cable are 22-, 23-, 24-, and 26-gauge cables. UTP cables come in different specifications called categories. The most common are Categories 5e, 6, 6a, and 7. People (and cable manufacturers) usually shorten the name *Category* to *Cat*, so Category 6 is spoken of as Cat 6. Table 13.5 shows some of the categories of UTP cable. You can also refer to Table 2.6 in Chapter 2 for a recap of the major Ethernet characteristics.

TABLE 13.5 UTP cable categories

Category	Description
Cat 5	No longer a recognized standard; replaced by Cat 5e.
Cat 5e	Known as Cat 5 enhanced. Can be used with 10BaseT, 100BaseT, and 1000BaseT (Gigabit) Ethernet networks. Cables are rated to a maximum of 328 feet (100 meters). Supports frequencies up to 100 MHz per pair (speeds up to 1 Gbps).
Cat 6	Supports Gigabit Ethernet better than Cat 5e but uses larger-gauge (thicker) cable. Supports frequencies up to 250 MHz per pair (speeds up to 1 Gbps). More stringent specifications to prevent crosstalk (signals from one wire going over into another wire). Commonly used in industry.
Cat 6a	Supports 10GBaseT Ethernet and frequencies up to 500 MHz (speeds up to 10 Gbps).
Cat 7	Backward compatible with Cat 5e and 6. Supports 10GBaseT Ethernet and frequencies up to 600 MHz (speeds up to 10 Gbps).
Cat 8	Allows speeds up to 40 Gbps using only STP at time of press.

A special type of UTP or STP cable is plenum cable. A *plenum* is a building's air circulation space for heating and air conditioning systems. **Plenum cable** is treated with Teflon or some other fire-retardant materials to reduce its fire risk. Plenum cable produces less smoke and is less toxic when burning than regular networking cable.

The alternative to plenum cable is polyvinyl chloride (**PVC**) cable, which has a plastic cable insulation or jacket. PVC is cheaper than plenum cable, and it can have flame retardant added to make the cable flame retardant if necessary for compliance with building codes. PVC is usually easier to install than plenum cable.

Terminating Twisted Pair Cable

Twisted pair network cable has an RJ45 connector that has a tang (a plastic clip) to securely insert the connector into an RJ45 jack, as shown in Figure 13.11. Tangs frequently get broken, and sometimes a technician must make an Ethernet cable. If a tang breaks off, the RJ45 connector is cut off and a new RJ45 connector attached. This is known as *terminating* a cable. To create a new cable, you purchase a spool of twisted pair cable, cut off a suitable length, and add an RJ45 connector to each end.

FIGURE 13.11 UTP connector with tang

Twisted pair cable uses either an **RJ45** (8 conductor) or **RJ11** (4 conductor) connector. RJ45 connectors are used with networks and RJ11 connectors with phone cabling. Twisted pair network cable has eight copper wires. The wires are grouped in colored pairs (see Figure 13.12). Each pair is twisted together to prevent crosstalk, which occurs when a signal on one wire interferes with the signal on an adjacent wire.

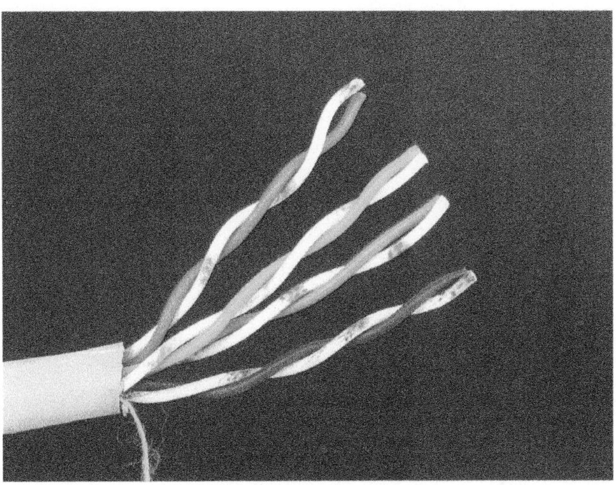

FIGURE 13.12 UTP color pairs

To connect a computer to a switch or network wall outlet, a **straight-through cable** (also known as a patch cable) is used. Both ends of the cable would be wired to the **T568A** standard, or both ends of the cable would be wired to the **T568B** standard (the more popular method). When connecting two computers (or two switches) together, a **crossover cable** is used. A crossover cable has one RJ45 connector created to the T568A standard and the other end created to the T568B standard. Figure 13.13 shows the color codes associated with the T568A and T568B standards. Figure 13.14 shows the location of pin 1 on an RJ45 port and on a connector. Notice in both figures how the tang is pointing down toward the floor.

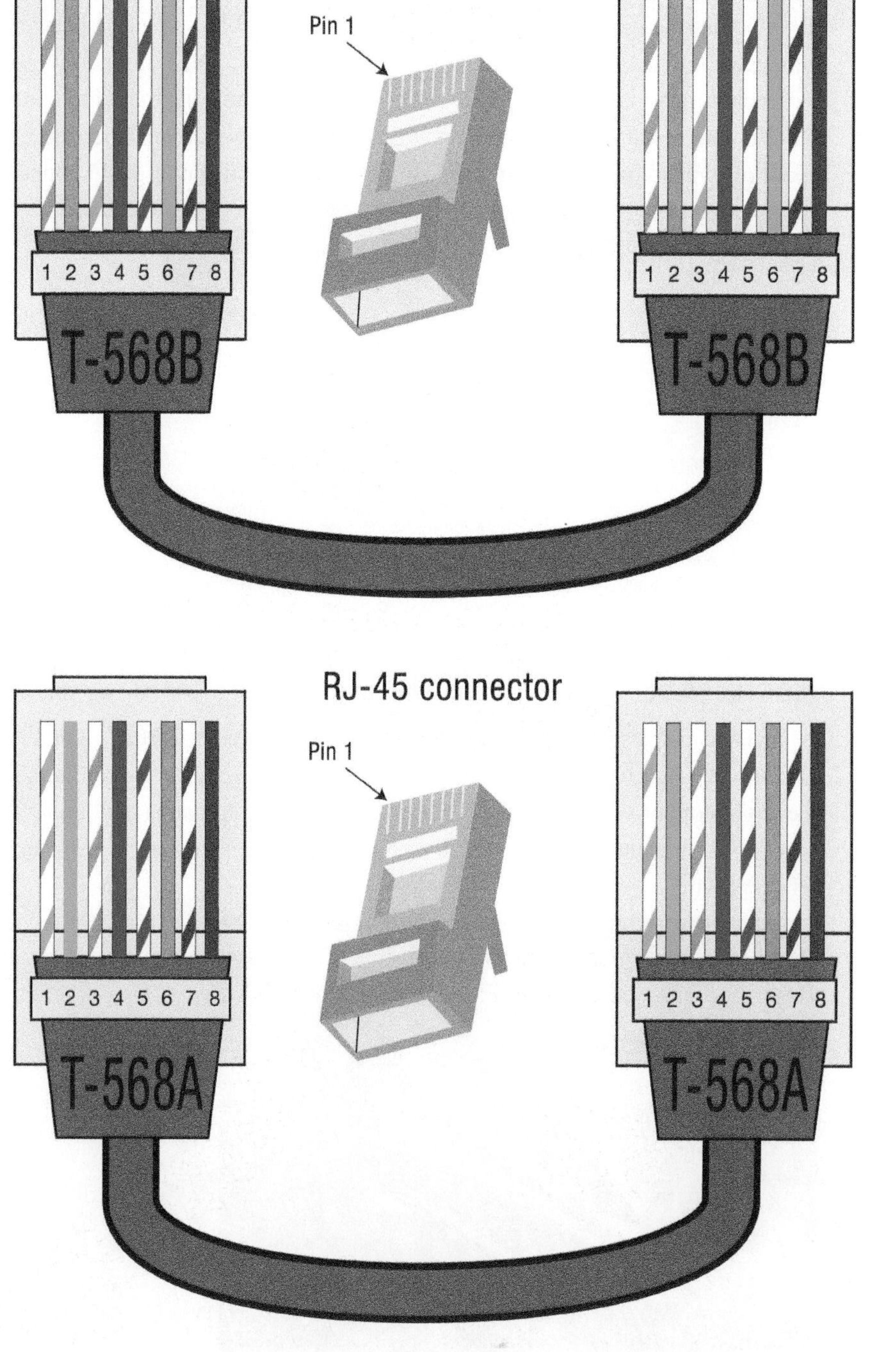

FIGURE 13.13 UTP cabling by color and wiring standards

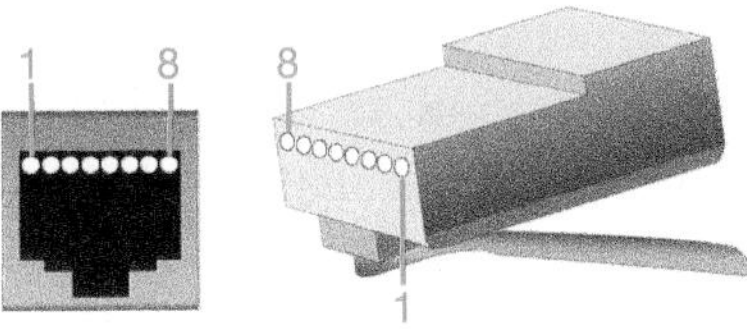

FIGURE 13.14 Pin 1 on an RJ45 port and connector

TECH TIP

Networking two PCs without a switch or hub

If you have two PCs with Ethernet NICs installed, you can connect them with a crossover cable attached to the RJ45 jack on each NIC.

To start creating your own cable, the plastic encasement must be stripped away with a **cable stripper** (also known as a wire stripper and shown in Figure 13.15) to expose approximately 1 inch (2 centimeters) of the vinyl insulator that covers the copper conductors. Look back to Figure 13.12 to see the exposed conductors after the insulator has been stripped.

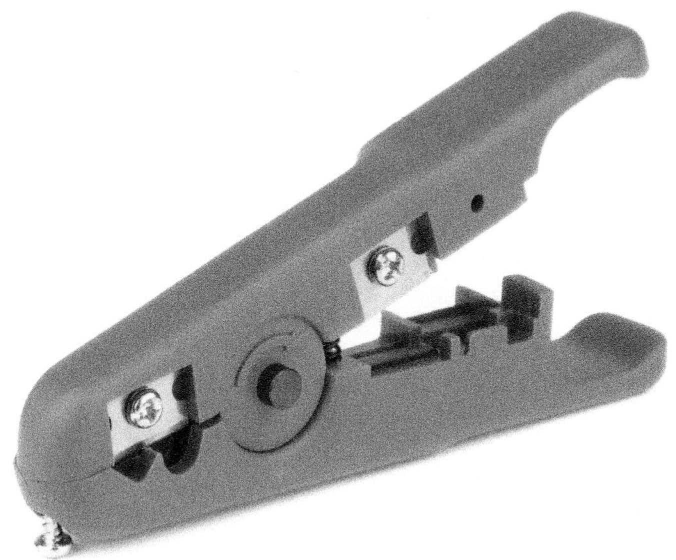

FIGURE 13.15 Cable stripper

A **crimper**, which is used to secure a cable to an RJ45 connector, may include a blade and/or a cable stripper. In the first photo in Figure 13.16, the cable is being stripped of the plastic encasement. The second photo in Figure 13.16 shows the vinyl insulator stripped away.

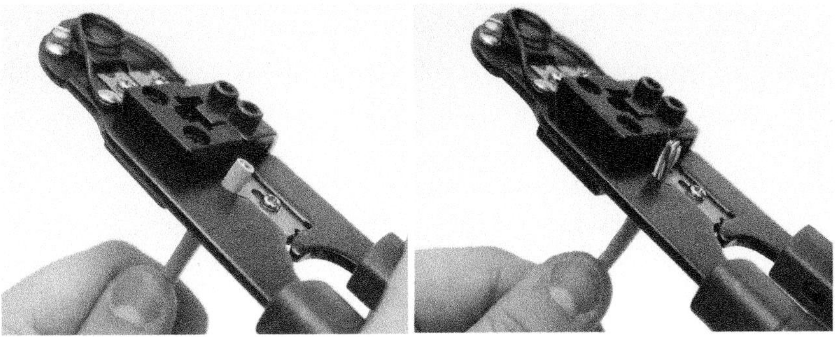

FIGURE 13.16 Crimper used as a wire stripper

After the plastic encasement is removed, untwist the cable pairs and place them in the proper color order. Wiggle each cable back and forth to make it more pliable. Cut the cables straight across, leaving 1/2 inch (1 centimeter) of cable. Insert the cables into the RJ45 connector in the correct color order. Ensure that the tang points toward the floor.

A common mistake when making a cable is not pushing the wires to the end of the RJ45 connector. Before crimping, look at the end of the RJ45 connector. You should see each wire jammed against the end of the RJ45 connector. You should see what looks like a set of eight gold dots staring at you when you turn the connector end toward you to verify that the conductors are pushed far enough into the connector before crimping.

Another check to do before crimping is ensure that the plastic encasement is inside the RJ45 connector. You do not want the vinyl insulator outside the connector, or data errors can occur. Notice in Figure 13.17 how the blue plastic encasement is in the wider part of the RJ45 connector. No unprotected wires are outside the RJ45 connector.

TECH TIP

Push the cable firmly into the jack

It is important to fully insert a UTP cable into an RJ45 jack and in the standardized order. A common mistake new technicians make is putting on the RJ45 connector upside down.

FIGURE 13.17 Crimping an RJ45 connector

When you have verified the color order, ensured that the eight gold connectors are pushed to the end, and verified the plastic encasement inside the RJ45 connector, you are ready to crimp. Crimping involves carefully inserting the RJ45 connector into the crimper (while keeping the wires pushed firmly into the connector) and pressing the crimper handles together firmly until the cable clicks and releases. Figure 13.17 shows a store-bought Ethernet cable that probably had a broken tang that required the RJ45 connector to be replaced. Notice how the cable has a protective sleeve that normally is positioned over the plastic part of the RJ45 connector. You must move the sleeve back before you can cut off the damaged RJ45 connector and replace it. You then slide the sleeve back over the RJ45 connector when crimping is complete.

After crimping, you must use a **cable tester** to ensure that the cable is ready for use. Figure 13.18 shows a cable tester. Plug one end of the cable into the RJ45 jack on the main tester piece (yellow case) and the other end into the RJ45 cap. Each cable tester is different, so review the instructions, if necessary.

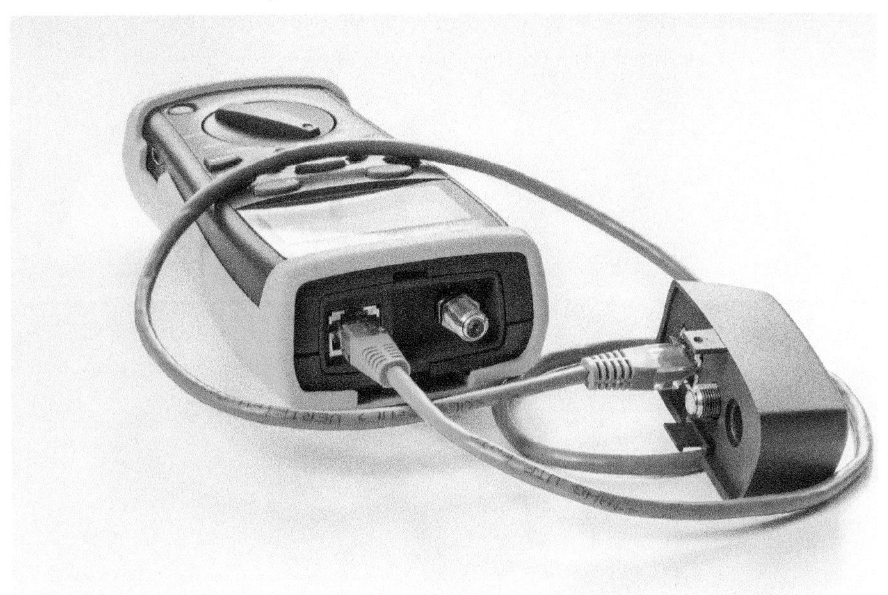

FIGURE 13.18 Cable tester

Twisted Pair Cable in the Corporate Environment

With twisted pair cable, all network devices connect to one central location, such as a patch panel, hub, or switch. Refer to Figure 13.2 to see how straight-through cables connect each network device to a switch. In a corporate environment, a patch panel is used. A **patch panel**, which mounts in a network wiring rack, has network ports on the front of it and wiring connected to the back of it to provide network connectivity. In Figure 13.19, the first photo shows the front of the patch panel, and the second photo shows the back.

A UTP cable connects from a network device to an RJ45 wall jack. That wall jack has UTP cabling (see Figure 13.20) that goes from the back of the wall jack to the back of a patch panel, as shown in Figure 13.21. A switch mounts in a wiring rack, along with a patch panel. A straight-through UTP patch cable connects from a port on the front of the patch panel to a switch located in the same network rack. Figure 13.21 also shows the cabling from PCs to a switch in a corporate environment.

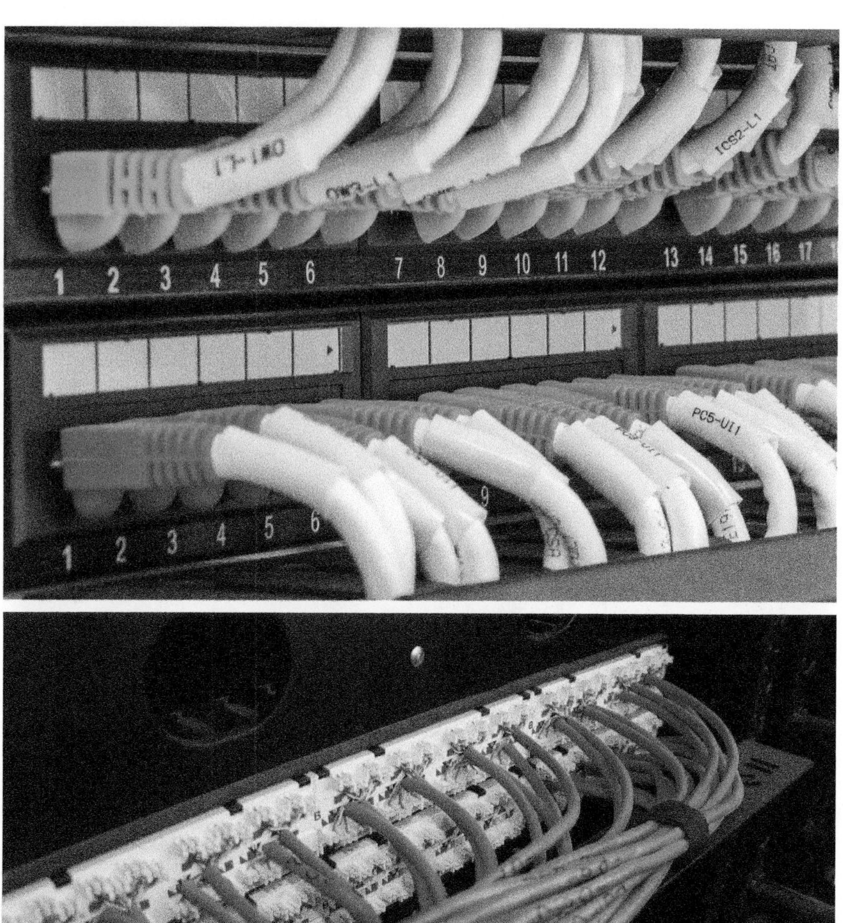

FIGURE 13.19 Front and back of a patch panel

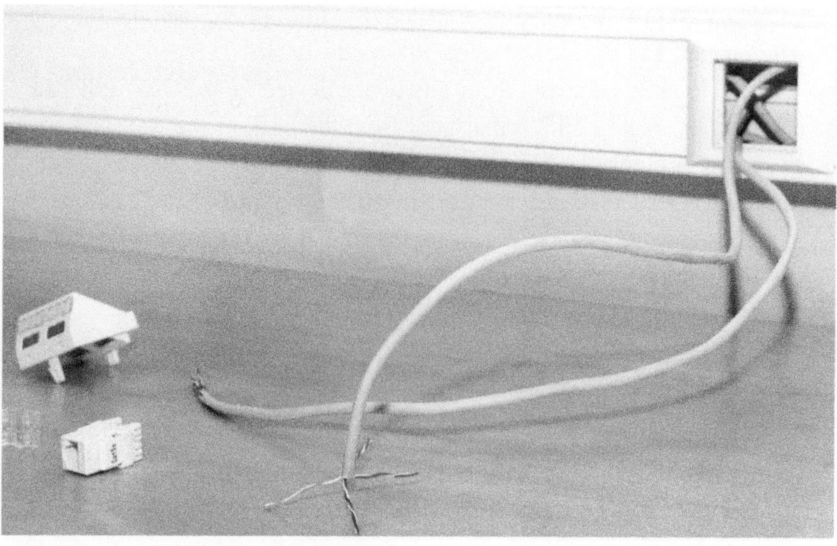

FIGURE 13.20 Network wall jack

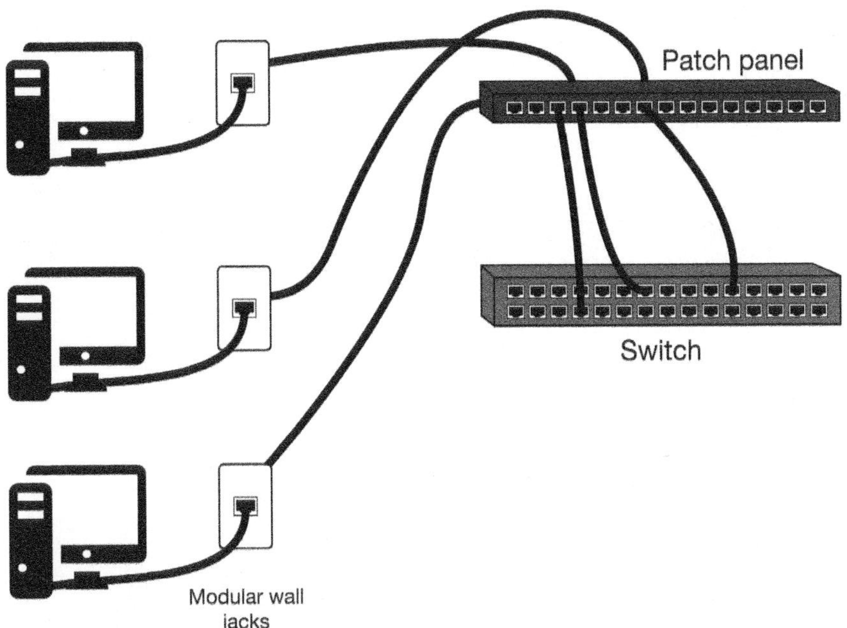

FIGURE 13.21 Corporate network connectivity from PCs to a switch

Ethernet cabling from the end device to the switch normally consists of three runs: (1) the cable from a patch panel to the wall at a maximum of 295 feet (90 meters), (2) the 16-foot (5 meter) maximum patch cable from the wall to a network device, and (3) a 16-foot (5 meter) maximum cable from a patch panel to a switch. The total length of cable from device to patch panel can be 328 feet (100 meters).

TECH TIP

Label both cable ends

When installing any type of network cable, you should label both ends with a unique identifier that normally includes the building and/or room number.

Power over Ethernet (PoE)

Corporate phones, IP cameras, projectors, wireless access points, and even audio systems or monitors can be powered through a technology called Power over Ethernet (**PoE**). There are different standards for PoE, and they are summarized in Table 13.6.

TABLE 13.6 PoE standards

Common name	IEEE standard	Description
PoE Standard (Type 1)	802.3af	2 pairs of UTP provide up to 15.4W of power to a port and 12.95W and 48V to power a device such as a voice over IP (VoIP) phone, wireless AP, or camera.
PoE Plus (PoE+ or Type 2)	802.3at	4 pairs of UTP provide up to 30W of power to a port and 25.5W and 50V to 57V to power a device such as an alarm system or a motion-tracking camera.

PoE++ (Type 3)	802.3bt	4 pairs of UTP provide up to 60W of power to the port and 51W and 50V to 57V to power a device such as a video phone or a door access reader.
PoE++ (Type 4)	802.3bt	4 pairs of UTP provide up to 100W of power to the port and 71W and 52V to 57V to power a device such as a monitor, laptop, or point-of-sale register.
POH (Power over HD-Base-T)	802.3at	4 pairs of UTP provide up to 100W of power to the port and 100W and 52V to 57V to power a device due to the end device being able to determine cable length and draw.

Power can be provided to a device via PoE through a switch that has PoE capability (called a **PoE switch**), a PoE patch panel, or a **PoE injector** (sometimes called a power injector) to inject DC voltage power. Figure 13.22 demonstrates these concepts.

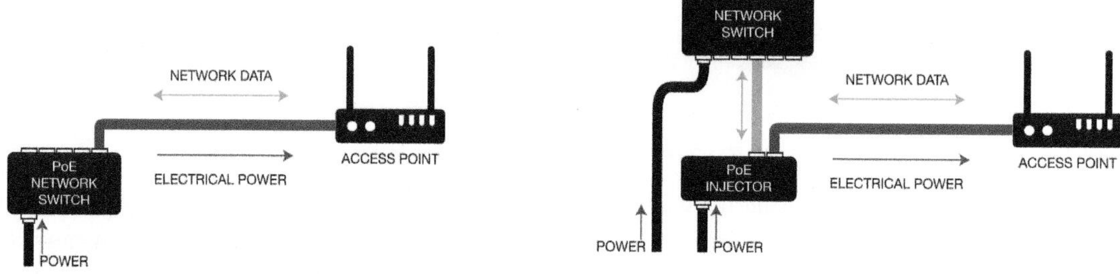

FIGURE 13.22 Access point with PoE and PoE injector

Ethernet over Power

One way to create an Ethernet network without switches, hubs, or a crossover cable between two PCs is to use electrical outlets. **Ethernet over Power** (EoP) (also known as *powerline communication*) sends network data to EoP modules plugged in to power outlets to extend an Ethernet network. Some EoP modules support wireless connectivity as well. To use EoP, you need a minimum of two EoP modules. One module plugs in to a power outlet near the internet modem/router. An Ethernet cable attaches from the internet modem/router to the EoP module. A second EoP module connects somewhere else in the home or business, near a device that has trouble connecting to the internet due to the absence of Ethernet wiring or weak wireless RF signal. Attach an Ethernet cable between the stranded device and the EoP module, and the device will have internet access. Figure 13.23 shows this concept.

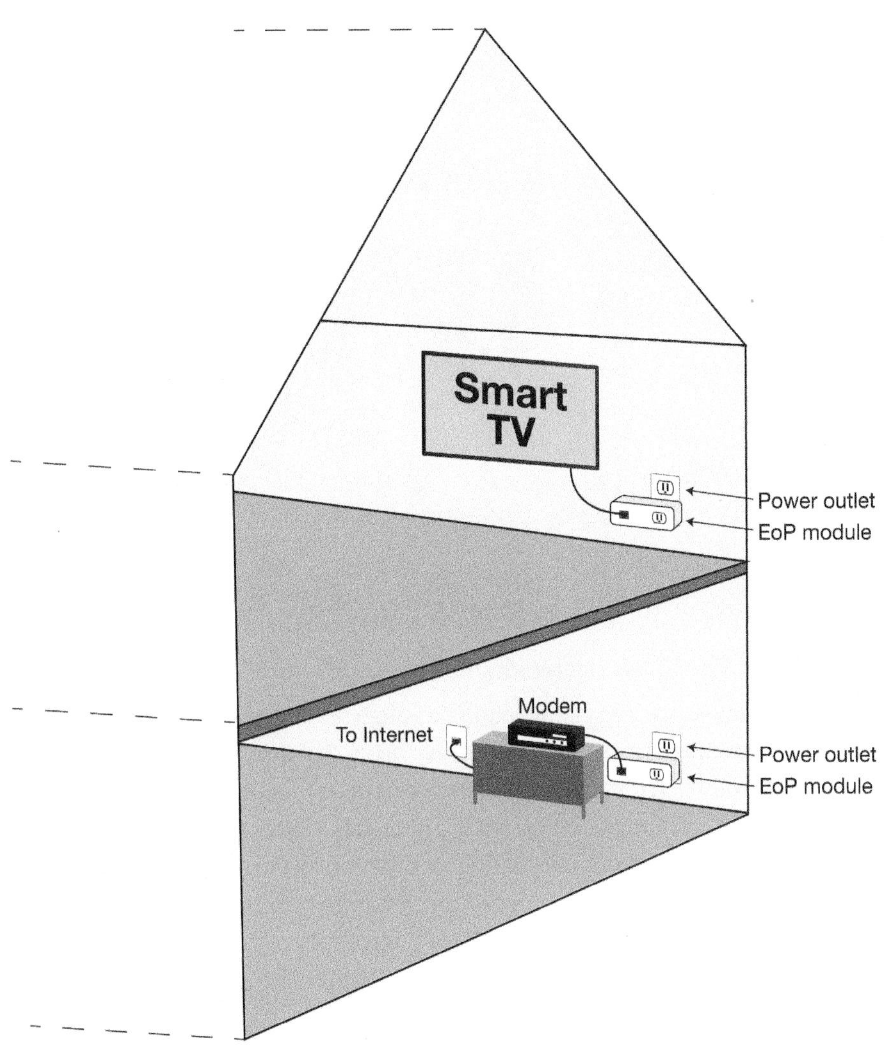

FIGURE 13.23 Ethernet over Power connectivity

Protecting Your Network and Cable Investment

IT professionals are charged with protecting cabling investments as well as ensuring that cabling does not cause personal safety risks. Network devices should be locked in a secure room or cabinet when possible. Figure 13.24 shows network cabinets that have network devices as well as cabling installed inside them.

Network racks, such as the one shown inside the cabinet in Figure 13.24, require grounding so that all of the equipment mounted to the rack is the same potential. Electrical codes indicating how this is to be done vary by country and state. On painted racks, it is important to remove the paint from a small section and attach a ground cable that connects from the rack to building ground or an electrical panel; electricians commonly do this. You might also see a ground wire connected to a UPS that provides backup power to network equipment.

FIGURE 13.24 Network cabinets

Network cable can be pulled through walls and over ceilings but should be installed in conduit or raceways (mesh racks or ladder racks that keep the cable away from other things), if possible. A professional **cable management system** can help keep network cables organized. Ensure that network cabling is not a trip or other safety hazard in any location. Of course, this increases the cost of the network installation, but it protects the network cabling and people. Figure 13.25 shows a network closet that is typical of the closets in many companies. Figure 13.26 shows a network wiring rack with a cable management system.

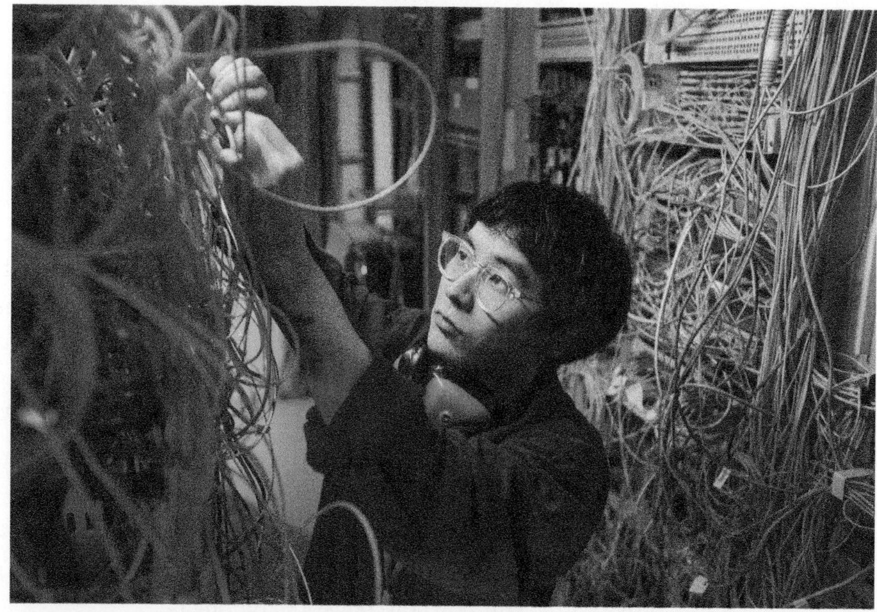

FIGURE 13.25 Messy network wiring rack

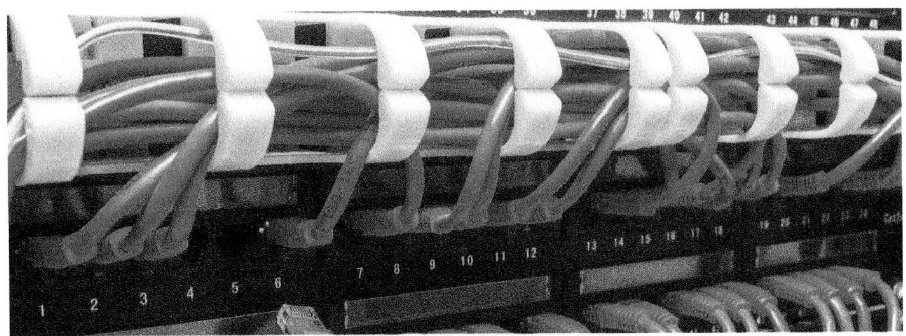

FIGURE 13.26 Cable management system

A ladder rack is a network cable accessory that holds multiple cables going across a room or from one side of a room to a network rack that is located away from the wall. Figure 13.27 shows a network cable ladder rack with bundles of cables.

FIGURE 13.27 Network cable ladder racks

Network Cabling and Troubleshooting Tools

Table 13.7 and Figure 13.28 describe and show network-related tools used in making cable and troubleshooting cable issues.

TABLE 13.7 Network cabling tools

Tool	Description
Cable stripper	Creates straight-through UTP patch cables or crossover cables. (Refer to Figures 13.15, 13.16, and 13.28.) Also called a wire stripper.
Cable tester	Checks coaxial and UTP cable (depending on the model). (Refer to Figures 13.18 and 13.28.)
Crimper	Permanently attaches an RJ45 or RJ11 connector to cable. (Refer to Figure 13.17.)
Loopback plug	Attaches to a specific port and tests the port or communications circuitry to see if a signal can be sent out and received. If the test succeeds, the port and communications circuits are good.
Multimeter	Takes voltage, resistance, and current readings. Can be used to check if data racks are grounded. (Refer to Figures 5.22, 5.23, and 5.24 in Chapter 5, "Disassembly and Power.")
Punchdown tool	Connects network cables to a patch panel (see Figure 13.28, 13.29, and 13.30) or phone cables to a punchdown block (see Figure 13.30).
Tone generator and probe	Used to identify cables when they are not labeled or are labeled incorrectly. A **tone generator** connects to a cable or is inserted into a network jack. The tone generator injects a tone down the cable. The **toner probe** (see Figure 13.28) is touched to the other end of a cable to identify it.
Network tap	Also known as a breakout tap, monitors/copies network data and can be a hardware device, done on some corporate switch models, or done through software. If hardware, think of a T-shaped device. The device typically has two ports that are used to allow the data to come in and then flow out. One or more additional ports are used to send the data that flowed through the first two ports out to a device that captures the data for further analysis.

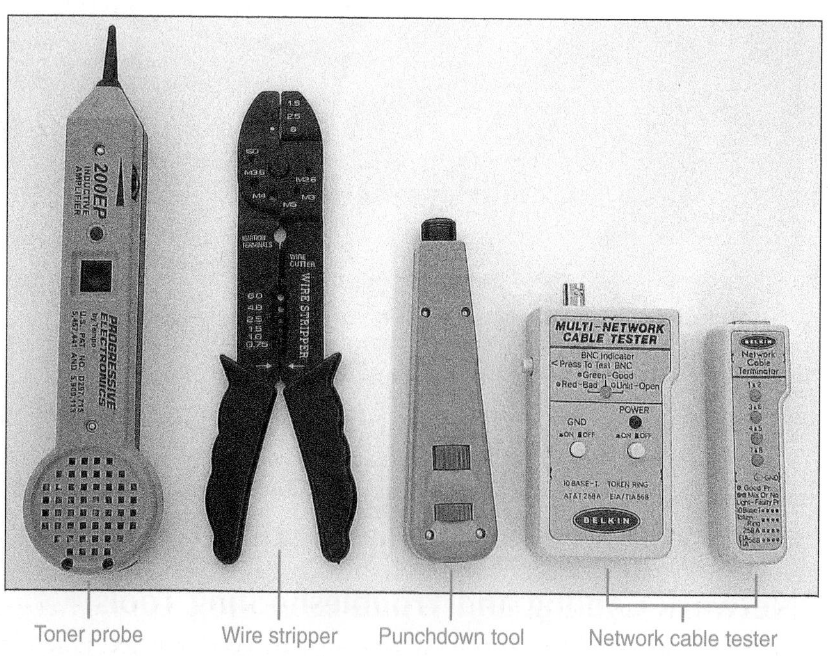

FIGURE 13.28 Network tools

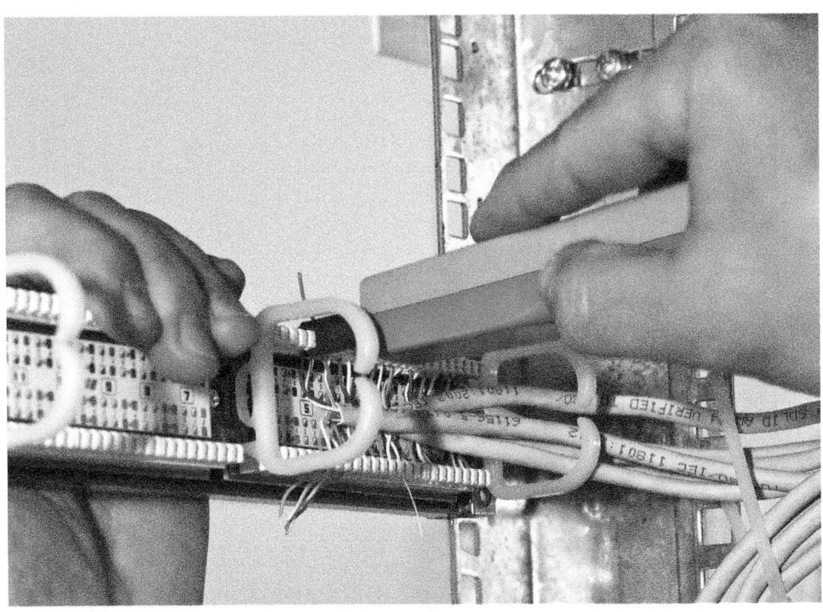

FIGURE 13.29 Punchdown tool with a network patch panel

FIGURE 13.30 Punchdown tool with a phone punchdown block

The OSI Model

The International Organization for Standardization (ISO) developed a model for network communications known as the OSI (Open Systems Interconnect) model. The **OSI model** is a standard for information transfer across the network. All network communication must be handled by a set of rules, and the OSI model provides a structure into which these rules fit.

Can you imagine a generic model for building a car? This model would state that you need some means of steering, a type of fuel to power the car, a place for the driver to sit, safety standards, and so forth. The model would not say what type of steering wheel to put in the car or what type of fuel the car must use but would just be a blueprint for making the car. The OSI model is a similar model in networking.

The OSI model divides networking into different layers so that it is easier to understand (and teach). Dividing the network into distinct layers also helps manufacturers. If a particular manufacturer wants to make a network device that works on Layer 3, the manufacturer has to be concerned only with Layer 3. This division helps networking technologies emerge much faster.

The layers of the OSI model (starting from the top and working down) are application, presentation, session, transport, network, data link, and physical (see Figure 13.31).

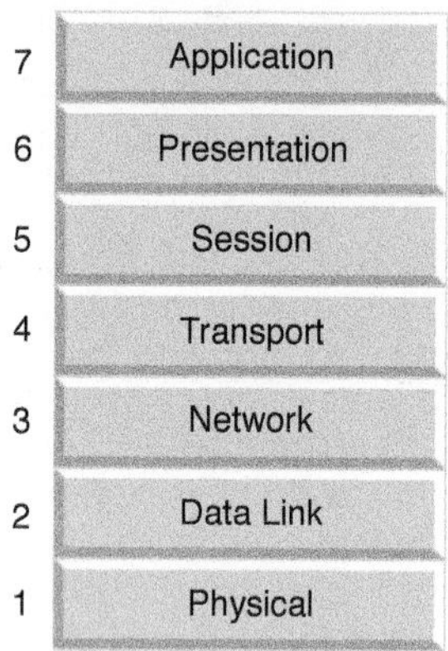

FIGURE 13.31 OSI model layers

Each layer of the OSI model uses the layer below it (except for the physical layer, which is at the bottom). Each layer provides some function to the layer above it. For example, the data link layer cannot be accessed without first going through the physical layer. If communication needs to be performed at Layer 3 (the network layer), the physical and data link layers must be used first.

> **TECH TIP**
>
> **OSI mnemonic**
>
> A mnemonic to help remember the OSI layers is Active People Seldom Take Naps During Parties. For example, A in Active reminds you of the application layer, P in People reminds you of the presentation layer, and so on.

Each layer of the OSI model from the top down (except for the physical layer) adds information to the data being sent across the network. Sometimes, this information is called a *header*. Figure 13.32 shows how a header is added as a packet travels down the OSI model. When the receiving computer receives the data, each layer removes the header information. Information at the physical layer is normally called *bits*. When referring to information at the data link layer, use the term *frame*. When referring to information at the network layer, use the term *packet*.

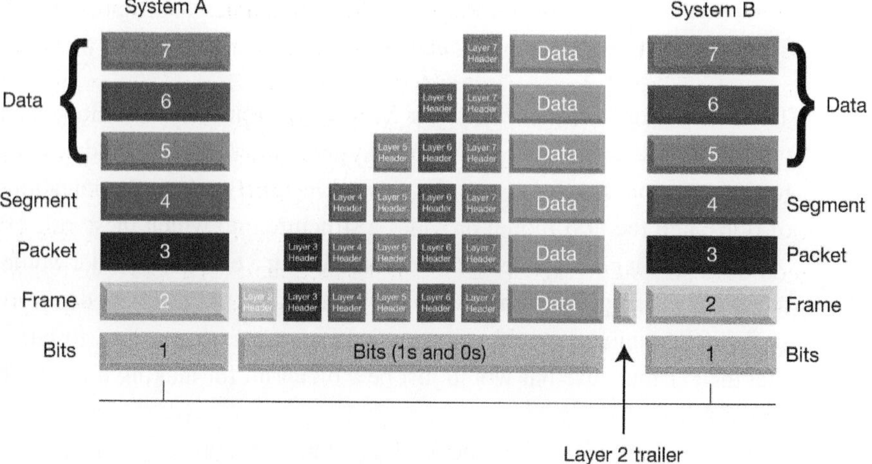

FIGURE 13.32 OSI peer communication

Each of the seven OSI model layers performs a unique function and interacts with surrounding it. The bottom three layers handle the physical delivery of data across the The top four layers handle the ins and outs of providing accurate data delivery between computers and their individual processes, especially in a multitasking operating system environment.

The OSI model can be confusing when you first learn about networking, but it is important. Understanding the model helps when troubleshooting a network. Knowing where a problem occurred narrows the field of possible solutions. Table 13.8 describes the layers of the OSI model.

TABLE 13.8 OSI model

OSI model layer	Description
Application	Provides network services (file, print, and messaging) to any software application running on the network. **Firewalls** (devices or software that inspect data for security purposes and filter traffic based on networking protocols and rules established by a network administrator) operate at this layer and can also inspect Layer 4, 3, and 2 data as well.
Presentation	Translates data from one character set to another.
Session	Manages communication and synchronization between network devices.
Transport	Provides mechanisms for how data is sent, such as reliability and error correction.
Network	Provides path selection between two networks. **Routers** reside at the network layer and send data from one network toward the destination network. Encapsulated data at this layer is called a *packet*. Multilayer switches can operate at this layer.
Data link	Encapsulates bits into frames. Can provide error control. A MAC address is at this layer. Layer 2 switches operate at this layer.
Physical	Defines how bits are transferred and received. Defines the network media, connectors, and voltage levels. Data at this level is called bits. Hubs, cables, and NICs operate at this level.

The TCP/IP Model

A **network protocol** is a data communication language. A protocol suite is a group of protocols that are designed to work together. Transmission Control Protocol/Internet Protocol (**TCP/IP**) is the protocol suite used in networks today. It is the most common network protocol suite and is required when accessing the internet. Most companies and homes use TCP/IP as their network standard. The TCP/IP protocol suite consists of many protocols, including Transmission Control Protocol (TCP), Internet Protocol (IP), Dynamic Host Configuration Protocol (DHCP), File Transfer Protocol (FTP), and Hypertext Transfer Protocol (HTTP), to name a few. These will be explained as we go along. The TCP/IP model describes how information flows through a computer when TCP/IP-based protocols are used. The TCP/IP model has only four layers, in contrast to the seven layers in the theoretical OSI model. Because there are fewer layers and because the TCP/IP model consists of protocols that are in production, it is easier to study and understand networking from the perspective of the TCP/IP model. Figure 13.33 shows the TCP/IP model and message formatting, and Table 13.9 describes the layers.

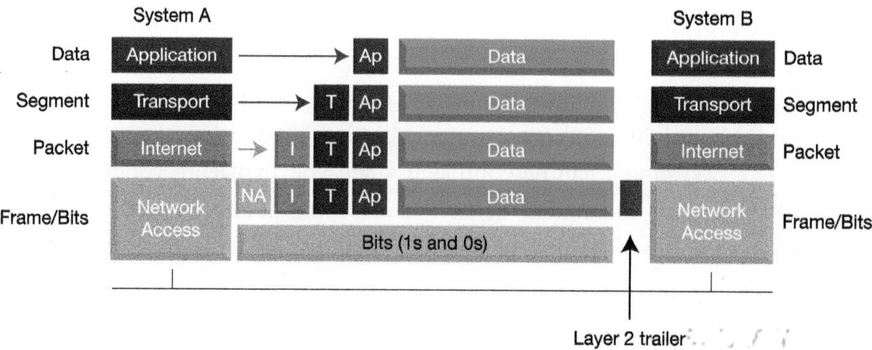

FIGURE 13.33 TCP/IP model and message formatting

TABLE 13.9 TCP/IP model layers

TCP/IP model layer	Description
Application	TCP/IP-based application layer protocols format data for specific purposes; equivalent to the application, presentation, and session layers of the OSI model. Protocols include HTTP, Telnet, DNS, HTTPS, FTP, TFTP, TLS, SSL, POP, SNMP, IMAP, NNTP, and SMTP.
Transport	Transport layer protocols add port numbers in the header, so a computer can identify which application sends the data. When data returns, this port number allows the computer to determine into which window on the screen to place the data. Protocols include TCP and UDP.
Internet	Sometimes called the internetwork layer, IP is the most common internet layer protocol. IP adds source and destination IP addresses to uniquely identify the source and destination network devices. An **IP address** is a unique 32- or 128-bit number assigned to a NIC.
Network access	This layer was called the link layer in the original RFC (request for comments). It defines how to format the data for the type of network used. For example, if Ethernet is used, an Ethernet header, including unique source and destination MAC addresses, will be added here. A **MAC address** is a unique 48-bit hexadecimal number burned into a chip on the NIC. The network access layer would define the type of connector used and put the data onto the network, whether it be voltage levels for 1s and 0s on the copper cable or pulses of light for fiber.

Table 13.10 shows what devices operate at the OSI and TCP/IP model layers. Wireless devices are covered later in this chapter.

TABLE 13.10 Devices and the OSI and TCP/IP models

Network devices	OSI layer	TCP/IP layer	Description
Router, wireless router	Network	Internet (internetwork)	A router connects two or more networks.
Switch, wireless access point, wireless bridge	Data link	Network access	A switch connects devices to a LAN and learns MAC addresses. An access point connects wireless devices to form a WLAN. A wireless bridge connects two networks.
Hub, wireless antenna, cable, connectors	Physical	Network access	A hub connects devices to a LAN. An antenna receives wireless signals. A cable connects a device to a wired network. A connector attaches to a cable.

Network Addressing

A network adapter normally has two types of addresses assigned to it: a MAC address and an IP address. A MAC address is a 48-bit unique hexadecimal number that is burned into a chip located on a NIC. A MAC address is unique for every computer on a network. The first 24 bits represent the manufacturer and the remaining 24 bits are unique. A MAC address is known as a Layer 2 address or a physical address. A MAC address is normally shown in one of the formats listed in Table 13.11.

TABLE 13.11 MAC address formats

Address format	Description
00-11-11-71-41-10	Groups of two hexadecimal digits are separated by hyphens.
01:11:11:71:41:10	Groups of two hexadecimal digits are separated by colons.
0111.1171.4110	Groups of four hexadecimal digits are separated by periods.

IP addressing provides a much more organized way of addressing a computer, and an IP address is sometimes known as a Layer 3 address, in reference to the OSI network layer. There are two types of IP addresses: IPv4 (IP version 4) and IPv6 (IP version 6). **IPv4** is the most common IP addressing used on LANs. An IPv4 address is a 32-bit number that is entered into a NIC's configuration parameters. This address is used when multiple networks are connected and when accessing the internet. An IPv4 address is shown using dotted decimal notation, such as 192.168.10.4.

TECH TIP

What is in an IPv4 address?

An IPv4 address is separated into four sections called octets. The octets are separated by periods, and each one represents 8 bits. The numbers 0 to 255can be represented by 8 bits.

IPv6 addresses are 128 bits in length and shown in hexadecimal format. IPv6 addresses are used by corporate devices and by most internet service providers. Today, a computer has both an IPv4 address and an IPv6 address assigned. An example of an IPv6 address is fe80::13e:4586:5807:95f7. Each set of four digits represents 16 bits. When an octet contains just three digits (for example, 13e), there is a "silent" zero in front that has been omitted from the octet (013e). A double colon (::) in an IPv6 address represents a string of zeros that has been omitted. Only one set of double colons is allowed in an IPv6 address. Many network cards are assigned IPv6 addresses, even when IPv6 is not used.

One IPv6 address assigned to a NIC is a link-local address. An IPv6 **link-local address** is used to communicate on a particular network. This address cannot be used to communicate with devices on a different network. A link-local address can be manually assigned or, more commonly, may be automatically assigned. Figure 13.34 shows a home computer that has an IPv6 link-local address that has been automatically assigned. You can also see the IPv4 address in this figure.

```
Ethernet adapter Local Area Connection:

   Connection-specific DNS Suffix  . : gateway.2wire.net
   Link-local IPv6 Address . . . . . : fe80::13e:4586:5807:95f7%10
   IPv4 Address. . . . . . . . . . . : 192.168.1.64
   Subnet Mask . . . . . . . . . . . : 255.255.255.0
   Default Gateway . . . . . . . . . : 192.168.1.254
```

FIGURE 13.34 IPv6 link-local address and IPv4 address

IPv4 addresses are grouped into five classes: A, B, C, D, and E. Class A, B, and C addresses are used by network devices. Class D addresses are used for multicasting (sending traffic to a group of devices such as in a distributed video or a web conference session), and Class E addresses are used for experimentation. It is easy to tell which type of IP address is used by a device: You just need to look at the first number shown in the dotted decimal notation. Table 13.12 shows the common classes of addresses.

TABLE 13.12 Classes of IPv4 addresses

Class	First octet (number) of the IP address
Class A	0 to 127
Class B	128 to 191
Class C	192 to 223

The IP address 12.150.172.39 is a Class A address because the first number is 12. The IP address 176.10.100.2 is a Class B address because the first number is 176. The IP address 200.1.1.1 is a Class C address because the first number of 200 is within the range of 192 to 223.

IP addresses are also classified as public addresses and private addresses. A **private IP address** is used inside a home or business. This address is not allowed to be transmitted across the internet. The service provider or company translates the address to a **public IP address** that is seen on the internet. Table 13.13 shows the private IP address ranges for the IPv4 classes.

TABLE 13.13 IPv4 private IP addresses

Class	First octet (number) of an IP address
Class A	10.*x*.*x*.*x* (where the *x* represents any number from 0 to 255), or 10.0.0.0 through 10.255.255.255
Class B	172.16.*x*.*x* through 172.31.*x*.*x*, or 172.16.0.0 through 172.31.255.255
Class C	192.168.*x*.*x*, or 192.168.0.0 through 192.168.255.255

More IPv4 Addressing

An IP address is broken into two sections: the network number and the host address. The **network number** is the portion of an IP address that represents which network the computer is on. All computers on the same network have the same network number. The **host address** (or host portion of the address) represents the specific computer on the network. All computers on the same network have unique host numbers; if they didn't, they could not communicate.

The number of bits that represent the network number and the host number depends on which class of IP address is used. With Class A IP addresses, the first 8 bits (the first number) represent the network portion, and the remaining 24 bits (the last three numbers) represent the host number. With Class B IP addresses, the first 16 bits (the first two numbers) represent the network portion, and the remaining 16 bits (the last two numbers) represent the host number. With Class C IP addresses, the first 24 bits (the first three numbers) represent the network portion, and the remaining 8 bits (the last number) represent the host number. Figure 13.35 illustrates this point.

	Network	Host	Host	Host
Class A	0-127	0-255	0-255	0-255
	Network	Network	Host	Host
Class B	128-191	0-255	0-255	0-255
	Network	Network	Network	Host
Class C	192-223	0-255	0-255	0-255

FIGURE 13.35 IP addressing (network and host portions)

To see how IP addressing works, say that a business has two networks connected with a router. On each network, there are computers and printers. Each of the two networks must have a unique network number. For this example, one network has the network number 192.168.151.0, and the other network has the network number 192.168.152.0. Notice that each network number is a Class C IP address because the first number is 192.

With a Class C IP address, the first three numbers represent the network number. The first network uses the numbers 192.168.151. to represent the network part of the IP address. The second network uses the numbers 192.168.152. in the network part of the address. Remember that each network must have a different network part of the IP address from any other network in the organization. This is part of the **IP addressing scheme** designed by a network engineer and implemented by technicians. Almost all organizations and home networks use private addresses (refer to Table 13.13) for their IP addressing scheme.

The last part of the IP address (the host portion) will be used to assign a number to each network device. On the first network, each device will have a number that starts with 192.168.151. because that is the network part of the number, and it stays the same for all devices on that network. Each device will then have a different number in the last portion of the IP address—for example, 192.168.151.1, 192.168.151.2, 192.168.151.3, 192.168.151.4, and so on (as shown in Figure 13.36).

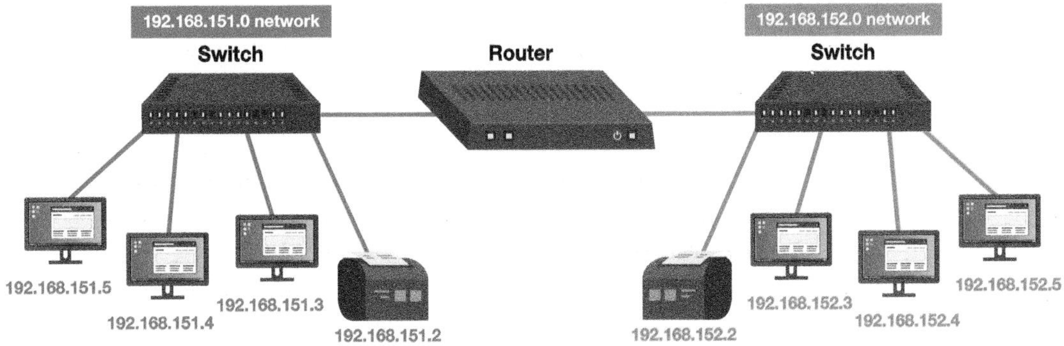

FIGURE 13.36 IP addressing (two networks example)

On the second network, each device will have a number that starts with 192.168.152. because that is the network part of the IP address. The last number in the IP address changes for each device. In this example, no device can have a host number that has 0 in the last octet because that number represents the network. In addition, no device can have an IP address where the last octet in the host portion of the address is 255 because that represents the **broadcast address**, which is the IP address used to communicate with all devices on a particular network.

In this example, no network device can be assigned the IP addresses 192.168.151.0 or 192.168.152.0 because these numbers represent the two networks. Furthermore, no network device can be assigned the IP addresses 192.168.151.255 or 192.168.152.255 because these numbers represent the broadcast address used with the 192.168.151.0 network and the 192.168.152.0 network. An example of a Class B broadcast address is 172.16.255.255. An example of a Class A broadcast address is 10.255.255.255.

VLANs

Another way of creating networks is by using VLANs. Creating a virtual local area network (**VLAN**) involves creating multiple networks within a switch. For example, IP phones, PCs, and printers typically connect to a switch, and companies that have switches that support VLANs tend to create separate networks for different types of devices or for devices in particular locations. For example, if you had two IP phones, three PCs, and a printer connected to the same switch, you might configure the switch ports that connect to the IP phones as VLAN 17, the switch ports that connect to the PCs as VLAN 18, and the port that connects to the printer as VLAN 19. The IP addressing schemes used within a company commonly include the VLAN number as part of the IP addressing. Notice in Figure 13.37 that the phones have IP addresses 192.168.17.*x* (where *x* is a unique number) and that the PCs have IP addresses 192.168.18.*x*. The printer has the IP address 192.168.19.3.

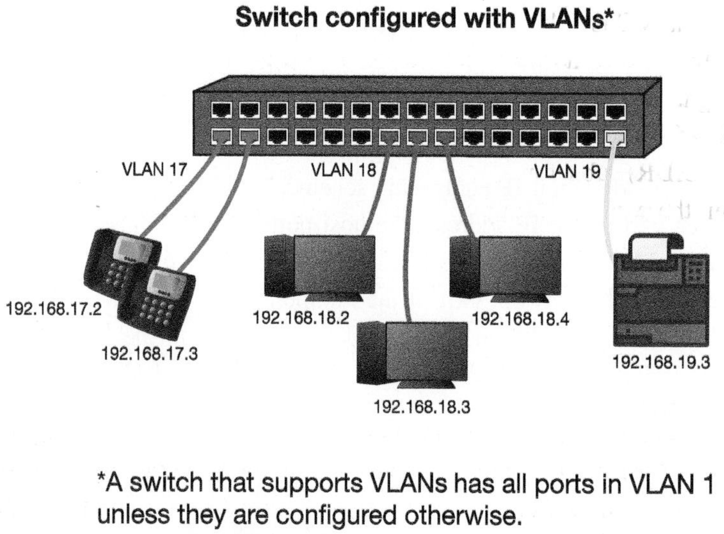

FIGURE 13.37 VLANs

Not all switches can be configured with VLANs, but on a switch that does support VLANs, all ports are assigned to VLAN 1 by default. If a switch does not support VLANs, then all ports need to be considered to be in the same network, and all devices connected to the switch will be in the same network.

Benefits of VLANs include the following:

- Separation of networks at Layer 2
- Reduced broadcast messages
- Ease of applying security
- Facilitates the use of quality of service (QoS)

Subnet Masks

In addition to assigning a computer an IP address, you must also assign a computer a subnet mask. A **subnet mask** (sometimes shortened to *mask*) is a number that a computer uses to determine which part of the IP address represents the network and which portion represents the host. The default subnet mask for a Class A IP address is 255.0.0.0, the default subnet mask for a Class B

IP address is 255.255.0.0, and the default subnet mask for a Class C IP address is 255.255.255.0. Table 13.14 recaps this important information.

TABLE 13.14 IP address information

Class	First number	Network/host number	Subnet mask
A	0–127	*N.H.H.H**	255.0.0.0
B	128–191	*N.N.H.H**	255.255.0.0
C	192–223	*N.N.N.H**	255.255.255.0

*N = network number; H = host number

Sometimes subnet masks are shown with a slash (/) followed by a number. The number represents how many consecutive 1s are in the subnet mask. For example, /8 indicates that there are eight consecutive 1s in the subnet mask, or 11111111.00000000.00000000.000000000. Notice that the subnet mask is all 0s after the eight 1s are shown. This is known as prefix notation format. A technician might have to refer to network documentation, and the subnet mask to use will be shown in prefix notation format. The prefix notation format for a Class A address is /8, Class B is /16, and Class C is /24.

A subnet mask does not always have to follow classful boundaries. Sometimes, a technician might see a subnet mask that looks like the following examples: 255.255.254.0 or /23, 255.255.255.192 or /26, and 255.255.255.240 or /28. These are known as classless inter-domain routing (CIDR) subnet masks. **CIDR** (pronounced "cider") is a method of allocating IP addresses based on the number of host addresses needed for a particular network. Because the subnet mask dictates where the network portion ends and where the host portion begins, CIDR subnet masks are different from the standard 255.0.0.0, 255.255.0.0, and 255.255.255.0 subnet masks.

To help you better understand the concept, let's look at how a /23 subnet mask becomes 255.255.254.0. The /23 means there are 23 1s in a row in the subnet mask, with the rest of the numbers being 0s; keep in mind that there are just eight 1s in each of the subnet mask sections where you enter the number. Write down the 23 1s with only eight digits in each section. Place 0s after the 1s for the remaining digits, keeping in mind that the subnet mask, like an IP address, has 32 bits. Then you perform simple binary-to-decimal conversion to get the subnet mask in dotted decimal notation, as it must be when you enter it on a network device:

11111111.11111111.11111110.00000000
255 . 255 . 254 . 0

Appendix A, "Subnetting Basics," goes into CIDR in a lot more detail.

Wireless Networks Overview

Even though wireless devices are covered elsewhere in the book, a networking chapter would not be complete without discussing wireless networking. Wireless data transfer occurs in both licensed and unlicensed ranges. In one of the licensed wireless ranges, a company or service provider has to obtain a specific frequency, possibly a frequency range, from the Federal Communications Commission (FCC) or its designee. Licensed wireless offers better performance than unlicensed, but it involves costs. Licensed wireless is used for radio and TV, military systems, and cellular communications.

Wireless networks in the home and corporate model are networks that transmit data over air using either unlicensed ranges such as infrared (1 THz to 400 THz range) for things like your TV remote or radio frequencies (the traditional **2.4 GHz** or **5 GHz** range, and the new **6 GHz** range) for wireless networks.

Wireless networks are popular and are great in places that are not conducive to running cabling, such as outdoor centers, convention centers, bookstores, coffee shops, and hotels, as well as between buildings and in between nonwired rooms in homes (as illustrated in Figure 13.38) or businesses. Wireless networks operate at Layers 1 and 2 of the OSI model and can be installed indoors or outdoors.

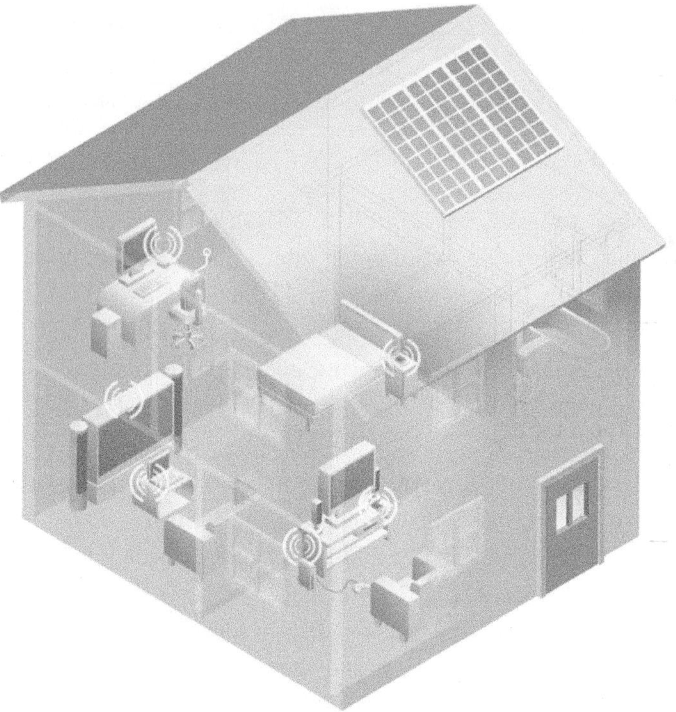

FIGURE 13.38 Wireless connectivity within a home

TECH TIP

What if I want wireless connectivity for my desktop computer?

Desktop workstations usually have integrated RJ45 Ethernet connections, but for wireless networking, a wireless NIC is required and may have to be added.

Laptops and portable devices are frequently used to connect to wireless networks and have wireless capabilities integrated into them. Laptops also normally have wired network connections. A technician must be familiar with installation, configuration, and troubleshooting of both wired and wireless technologies.

Wireless Network Standards

The IEEE 802.11 committees define standards for wireless networks, and these standards can be quite confusing. Table 13.15 shows the current and proposed wireless network standards.

TABLE 13.15 IEEE 802.11 standards

Standard	Purpose
802.11a	Came after the 802.11b standard. Has speeds up to 54 Mbps but is incompatible with 802.11b. Operates in the 5 GHz range.
802.11b	Operates in the 2.4000 and 2.4835 GHz radio frequency ranges, with speeds up to 11 Mbps.

Standard	Purpose
802.11e	Relates to quality of service.
802.11g	Operates in the 2.4 GHz range, with speeds up to 54 Mbps, and is backward compatible with 802.11b.
802.11i	Relates to wireless network security and includes Advanced Encryption Standard (AES) for protecting data.
802.11n	Operates in the 2.4 and 5 GHz ranges and is backward compatible with the older 802.11a, b, and g equipment. Offers speeds up to 600 Mbps using MIMO (multiple input/multiple output) antennas. Makes possible a maximum of four simultaneous data streams.
802.11ac (Wi-Fi 5)	Operates only in the 5 GHz range, which makes it backward compatible with 802.11n and 802.11a. Offers speeds up to 6.93 Gbps. Makes possible a maximum of eight simultaneous data streams using MU-MIMO (multi-user MIMO) antennas.
802.11ad	Also known as WiGig and works in the 60 GHz range. Offers speeds up to 6.76 Gbps.
802.11ax (**Wi-Fi 6**)	Operates in the 2.4, 5, and 6 GHz ranges and is backward compatible with 2.4 and 5 GHz devices. Supports multiple wireless devices more efficiently. Makes possible a maximum of eight simultaneous data streams using MU-MIMO antennas.

Wireless Network Components

The most common components of a wireless network are wireless NICs, access points, wireless bridges, and wireless routers. Table 13.16 describes the purposes of these devices.

TABLE 13.16 Common wireless devices

Wireless device	Description
Access point (AP)	The central connecting point for a wireless network. Coordinates wireless access for wireless devices. May connect to a wired network.
Wireless bridge	A physical device or software that connects two or more networks. Could connect a wireless network to a wired network. An example of a wireless bridge is a building where all devices connect wirelessly to the bridge. The bridge connects to the wired network, which eventually connects to the internet. Many access points or wireless routers can be placed in bridged mode.
Wireless NIC	Integrated into a wireless device, such as a laptop, smartphone, or tablet. Can also be a card or connect via USB.
Wireless router	An AP/router device that normally has both wireless capability and a few wired Ethernet ports. It is a router because it connects multiple networks.
Wireless printer/ multifunction device	Most common type of home/small office device today that can print, scan, and copy.

Major types of wireless NICs include integrated ports, USB, and PCIe. Figure 13.39 shows a wireless USB NIC with a detachable antenna.

FIGURE 13.39 Wireless USB NIC

To determine whether you have a wireless NIC installed on a Windows 10/11 device, access *Settings > Network & internet > Wi-Fi* appears in the window to the left if you have it installed and the adapter is not enabled. Use the *Change adapter options* from the *Advanced network settings* section to see all adapters and to see if any are disabled.

Figure 13.40 shows the Network Connections window of a computer that has virtualization enabled, a wired Ethernet port, Wi-Fi, and Bluetooth installed. Note that the wireless NIC is not being used, but it is enabled.

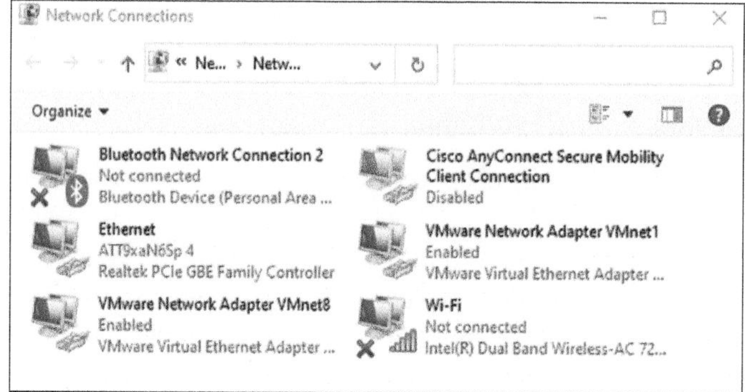

FIGURE 13.40 Wireless NIC in the Network Connections window

A wireless access point (AP) is a device that receives and transmits data from multiple computers that have wireless NICs installed. The AP can be a standalone unit or can be integrated into a router, as shown in Figure 13.41. It is the wireless AP part of the router that needs the three antennas shown in the figure.

Wireless routers commonly have switch ports built into them. This is referred to as having router/switch functionality. You might hear a wireless router referred to as a router/switch, but regardless of the name, such a device has switch ports integrated, as shown in Figure 13.42. Much like a wired router, a wireless router is used to connect devices between networks such as a home network and the internet. The switch part of the device is used to create a wired LAN, and each wired device has an Ethernet cable that runs between the device and the switch port on the wireless router.

FIGURE 13.41 Access point integrated with an ADSL router

FIGURE 13.42 Wireless router with integrated switch ports

Wireless Network Design

Think of an access point like a network hub, but instead of connecting wired devices and sharing bandwidth, the AP connects wireless devices that share bandwidth. Each access point can handle 1 to 100 wireless devices, depending on the wireless standard being used, vendor, environment (wood, drywall, brick, concrete, and so on), amount of usage, and type of data sent.

When designing a wireless network, you need to take into account several factors:

> Which standard you are going to use (802.11n, 802.11ac, 802.11ax, and so on).
> Which frequency range you are going use in a specific location and the type of devices to consider for a specific frequency. For example, you might want to use the 2.4 GHz range as a wireless network for guests and the 5 GHz range for company devices since the 5 GHz range is not as crowded with devices as the 2.4 GHz range is. Another idea would be to design based on the type of equipment, such as use the 2.4 GHz range for PC-based devices and the 5 GHz range for Apple and cellular devices.
> The location of the AP and what interference is around the area where the AP will be installed.

Let's take a look at some of the details involved with design.

Each AP is assigned a service set identifier (**SSID**). It is common for an AP to have a default SSID that can be changed. An SSID is a set of 32 alphanumeric characters used to differentiate between different wireless networks. It is common to have more than one SSID configured on a wireless router/AP, as illustrated in Figure 13.43. Figure 13.44 shows a screen capture of a sample wireless configuration for an 802.11ac TP-Link wireless router.

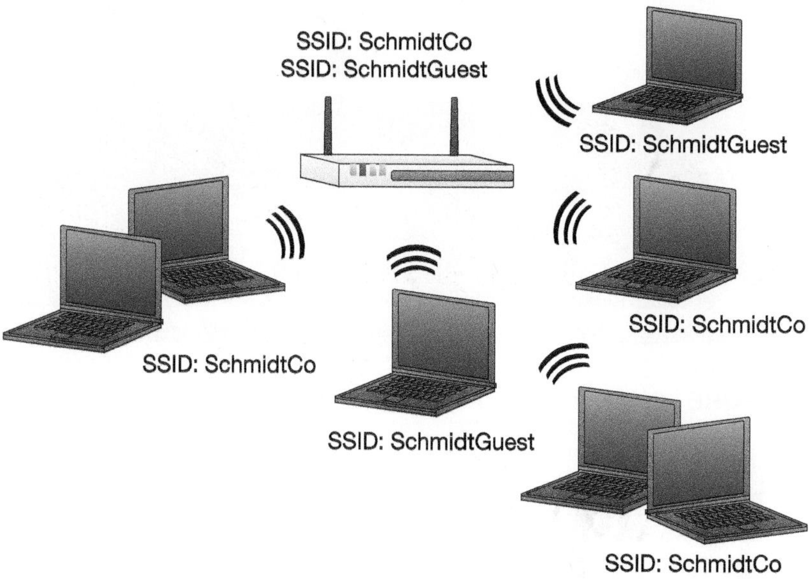

FIGURE 13.43 Each wireless network has its own SSID

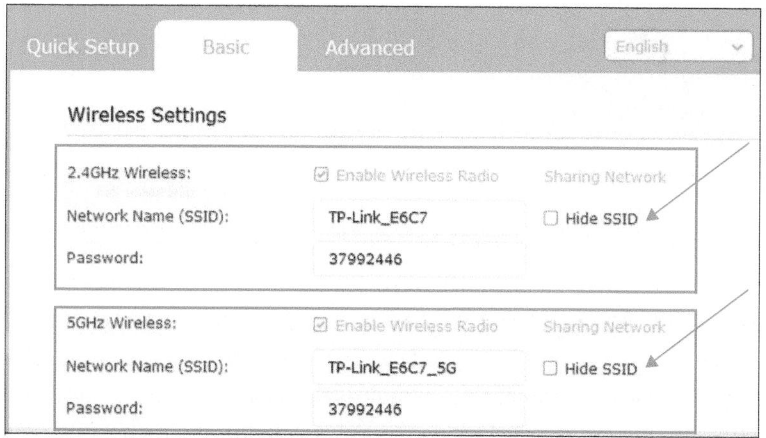

FIGURE 13.44 Configuring SSIDs and SSID broadcasting on a TP-Link wireless router

An AP broadcasts the SSID by default, but this setting can be changed. When the AP is broadcasting the SSID, wireless NICs can automatically detect that particular wireless network. When the AP is not broadcasting (that is, when the SSID cannot be found in the list of wireless networks), the SSID can be manually configured through the AP's configuration window. Look back at the 2.4 GHz and 5 GHz configurations shown in Figure 13.44. Beside each SSID is a *Hide SSID* checkbox that you can check to disable SSID broadcasting.

An access point can be wired to or can connect wirelessly to another AP, can have a wired or wireless connection to a wireless repeater (also called a **wireless extender**), or can connect to a wired network. The access point can then relay the transmission from a wireless device to another network or to the internet through the wired network. If two access points are used and they connect two different wireless networks, two different SSIDs are used (see Figure 13.45). If two access points connect to the same wireless network, the same SSID is used (see Figure 13.46).

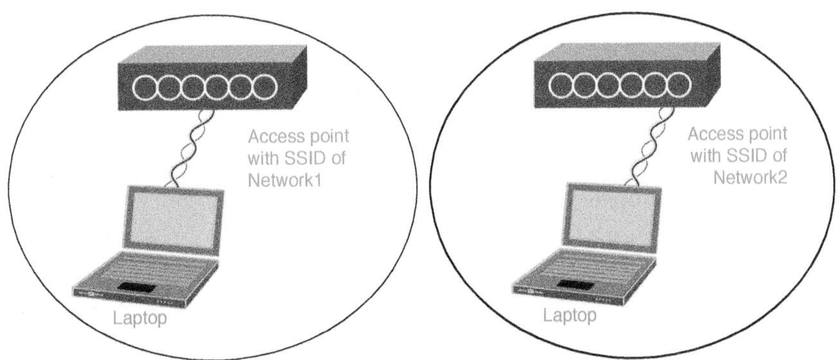

FIGURE 13.45 Two separate wireless networks with two SSIDs

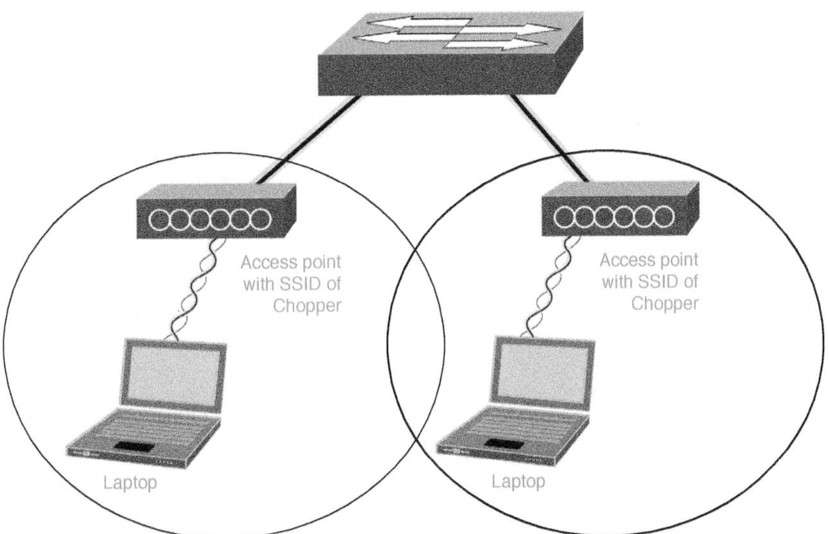

FIGURE 13.46 One extended wireless network with the same SSID on both APs

A home or small business network can expand its wireless network by using a wireless repeater (also known as a wireless range extender). In such a case, the access point cannot normally be connected to the wired LAN. Instead, the repeater access point attaches to a "root" access point. The repeater access point allows wireless devices to communicate with it and relays the data to the other access point. Both access points have the same SSID (see Figure 13.47)

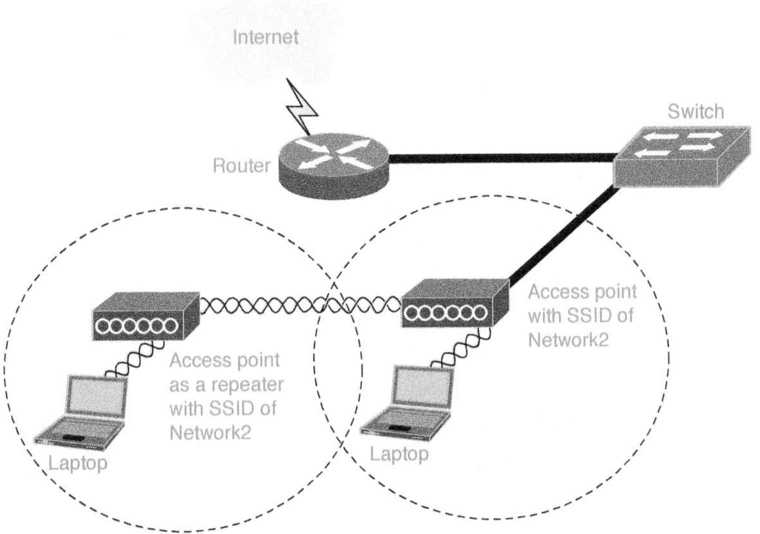

FIGURE 13.47 Access point as a repeater

Wireless Channel ID

In addition to having an SSID, an access point can be configured with a number known as a channel ID. The **channel**, sometimes called a channel ID, is a specific number that defines at what frequency the access point operates. With an AP that has a 2.4 GHz antenna, up to 14 channels are available, depending on where in the world the wireless network is deployed. In the United States, only 11 channels are used; they are listed in Table 13.17.

TABLE 13.17 Wireless frequency channels

Channel ID number	Frequency (in GHz)
1	2.412
2	2.417
3	2.422
4	2.427
5	2.432
6	2.437
7	2.442
8	2.447
9	2.452
10	2.457
11	2.462

The frequencies shown in Table 13.17 are center frequencies. The center frequencies are spaced 5 MHz apart. Each channel is actually a range of frequencies. For example, the channel 1 range is 2.401 to 2.423, with the center frequency being 2.412.

TECH TIP

Channel ID must match

The channel ID (frequency) must be the same between an access point and a wireless NIC for communication to occur between any wireless devices on the network. The wireless NIC can adjust to the same frequency as the AP so communication can occur.

The three commonly used nonoverlapping channel IDs are 1, 6, and 11. By using these three channel IDs, each of three access points mounted near one another does not experience interference from the other two. This is because each center frequency does not overlap with the adjacent frequency channels (see Figure 13.48).

Notice in Figure 13.48 that each center frequency is 5 MHz from the next center frequency. Also notice that each channel is actually a range of frequencies, as shown by the shaded ovals. Channels 1, 6, and 11 clearly do not overlap and do not interfere with each other. Other nonoverlapping channel combinations could be Channels 2 and 7, Channels 3 and 8, Channels 4 and 9, and Channels 5 and 10. The combination of Channels 1, 6, and 11 is preferred because it gives you three channels with which to work. Figure 13.49 shows a different way of looking at how Channels 1, 6, and 11 do not overlap.

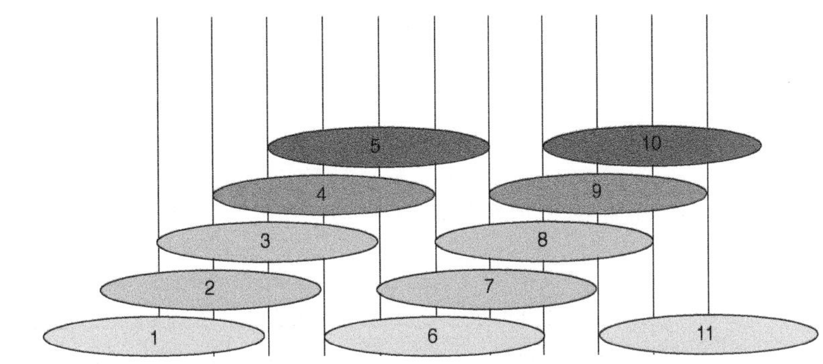

FIGURE 13.48 802.11b/g/n 2.4 GHz nonoverlapping channels

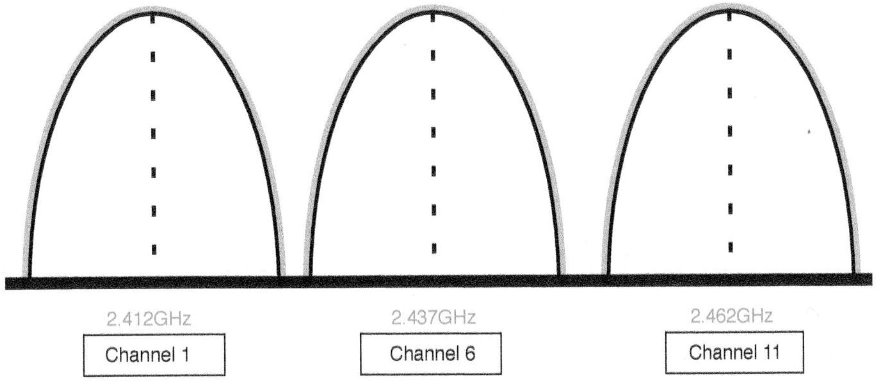

FIGURE 13.49 2.4 GHz channel IDs 1, 6, and 11

Figure 13.50 shows how the three nonoverlapping channels can be used to attain extended coverage even with multiple access points. Note that where there is blank space between the circles, no wireless coverage exists. The circles can be adjusted so that coverage is complete, but a slight overlap of channels will occur.

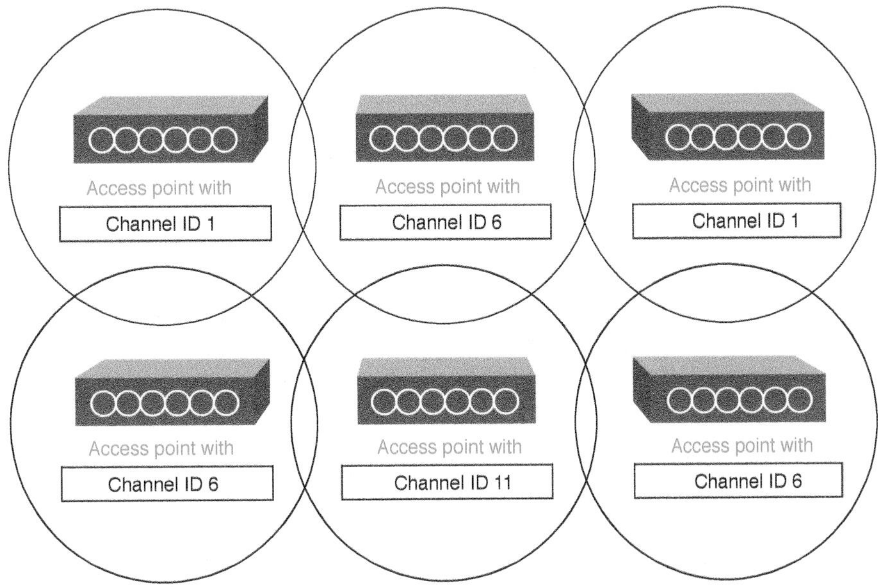

FIGURE 13.50 802.11b/g/n nonoverlapping channel IDs

With 802.11a, 12 20 MHz channels are available in the 5 GHz range. 802.11n supports 20 and 40 MHz channels. 802.11ac supports 20, 40, 80, and 160 MHz channels. The 5 GHz range has three subranges called Unlicensed National Information Infrastructure (UNII): UNII-1, UNII-2, and UNII-3. All bands can be used for indoor and outdoor usage. Figure 13.51 shows the 5 GHz channels.

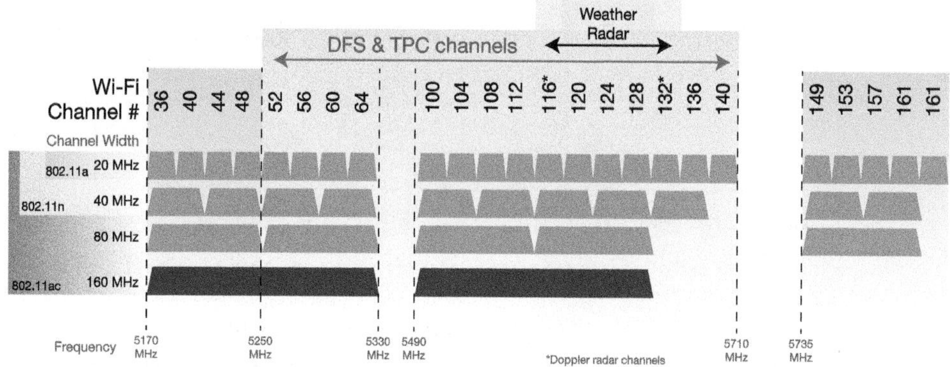

FIGURE 13.51 802.11 a/n/ac 5 GHz channel IDs

Devices that work in the UNII-2 frequency ranges must support dynamic frequency selection (DFS) and transmit power control (TPC) to avoid interference with military applications. These two terms are most often shortened to simply *DFS channels*. Channels 120, 124, and 128 are used for terminal Doppler weather radar (TDWR) systems. Channels 116 and 132 may optionally be used for Doppler radar. Most wireless routers can automatically configure themselves with the best channel, but if the surrounding area has interfering devices, this may need to be manually planned and configured. Figure 13.52 shows how you can select a specific 2.4 or 5 GHz channel on a TP-Link wireless router (and the transmit power is the option below that).

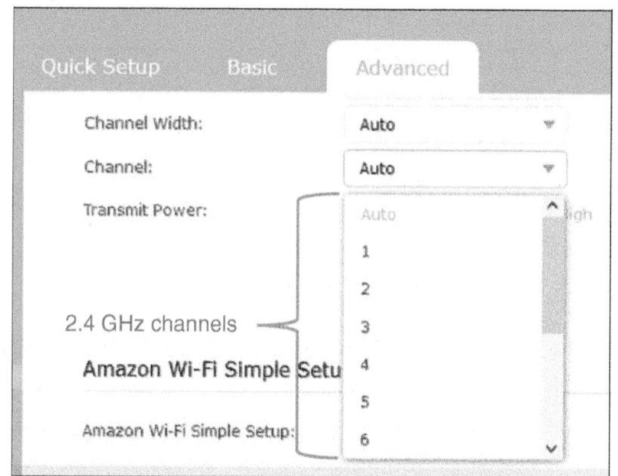

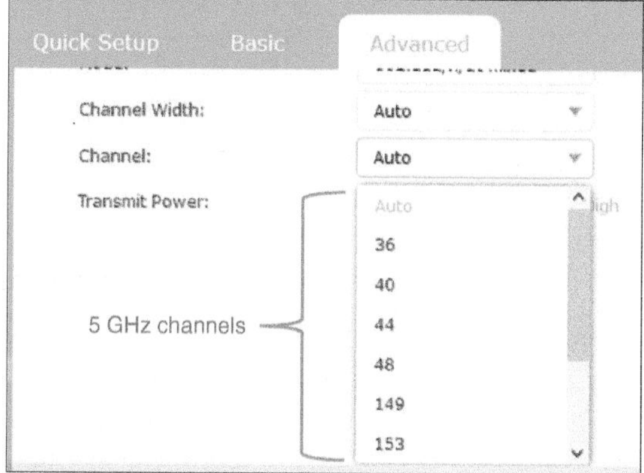

FIGURE 13.52 2.4 and 5 GHz channel selection

An important point to make is that the frequency ranges, channel ID, number of channels, sub-channel range, and so on must adhere to the **wireless regulations**. Most countries also regulate maximum wireless power levels that differ for indoor networks as well as outdoor networks and change often. The good news is there is some consistency in the 2.4 GHz and 5 GHz ranges so that a laptop used in the United States will work on the wireless networks in other countries.

Antenna Basics

Wireless cards and access points can have either external or built-in antennas. Some access points also have integrated antennas. Wireless NICs and access points can also have detachable antennas, depending on the make and model. An antenna radiates or receives radio waves. You can simply move an external antenna to a different angle to obtain a better connection. With some laptops, you must turn the laptop to a different angle to attach to an access point or get a stronger signal (and, therefore, faster transfers). Antenna placement is important in a wireless network.

TECH TIP

Where is the wireless antenna on a laptop?

For laptops with integrated wireless NICs, the wireless antenna is usually built in to the laptop display for best connectivity.

There are two major categories of antennas: omnidirectional and directional. An **omnidirectional antenna** radiates energy in all directions. Integrated wireless NICs use omnidirectional antennas. Refer to Figure 10.67 in Chapter 10 to see how the antenna wires attach to two posts on the wireless NIC. These wires connect the antenna to the wireless NIC. If a laptop always has low signal strength, ensure that these two wires are attached.

A **directional antenna** radiates energy in a specific direction. Directional antennas are frequently used to connect two buildings together or to limit wireless connectivity outside a building. Each antenna has a specific radiation pattern (sometimes called a propagation pattern), which is the direction(s) the radio frequency is sent or received. It is the coverage area for the antenna that is normally shown in a graphical representation in the antenna manufacturer's specifications. Figure 13.53 shows the difference in radiation patterns between omnidirectional and directional antennas.

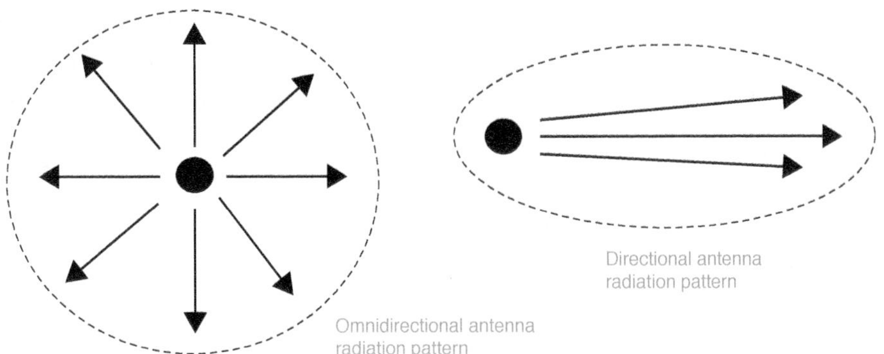

FIGURE 13.53 Basic antenna radiation patterns

A technician must be familiar with an antenna's radiation pattern so that the appropriate type of antenna can be chosen for the installation. As a signal is radiated from an antenna, some of the signal is lost. Attenuation, which is sometimes called path loss, is the amount of signal loss of a radio wave as it travels (that is, is propagated) through air. Attenuation is measured in decibels (dB), which are a measure of the ratio between two signal levels.

Factors that affect an antenna's attenuation are the distance between the transmitting antenna and the receiving antenna, any obstructions between the two antennas, and how high the antenna is mounted. Another factor that affects wireless transmission is interference, including radio frequencies being transmitted using the same frequency range and external noise. Other wireless devices, wireless networks, cordless phones, and microwave ovens are common sources of interference.

TECH TIP

What is the maximum distance of a wireless network?

The maximum distance of a wireless network depends on the wireless network standard used, the antenna attached to the AP, and the attenuation experienced.

An important concept related to antennas is gain, and to understand gain, isotropic antennas must be discussed. An isotropic antenna is not real; it is an imaginary antenna that is perfect in that it theoretically transmits an equal amount of power in all directions. The omnidirectional radiation pattern previously shown in Figure 13.53 would be the pattern of an isotropic antenna. A lot of ceiling-mounted APs have omnidirectional antennas. Figure 13.54 shows an AP that could be mounted on the ceiling and might have integrated omnidirectional antennas.

FIGURE 13.54 Ceiling-mounted AP

Antenna power levels are described as antenna gain. Gain is measured in dBi or dBd (dBd equals 2.14 dBi). More gain means more coverage in a particular direction. A technician must sometimes reduce the transmit power (that is, lower the signal strength) in order for multiple wireless access points to function in the same building or area.

TECH TIP

You might need to reduce power levels

If an open wireless network is being used by adjacent businesses, reduce the power level of the antenna to reduce the wireless network coverage area.

A **site survey** is an examination of an area to determine the best access point or antenna placement. To conduct such a survey, temporarily mount an access point (or use a telescoping pole to place the AP at different heights). With a laptop that has a wireless NIC and site survey software, walk around the wireless network area to see the coverage range. Some vendors provide site survey software with their wireless NICs.

A site survey can also be conducted by using a laptop and walking around and using the wireless network icon on the taskbar to see the signal strength. Radio waves are affected by obstructions such as walls, trees, rain, snow, fog, and buildings. Radio waves are also affected by **external interference** from other devices and other wireless networks operating in the same frequency range causing **intermittent wireless connectivity**. Figure 13.55 shows a wireless antenna signal strength display on a laptop.

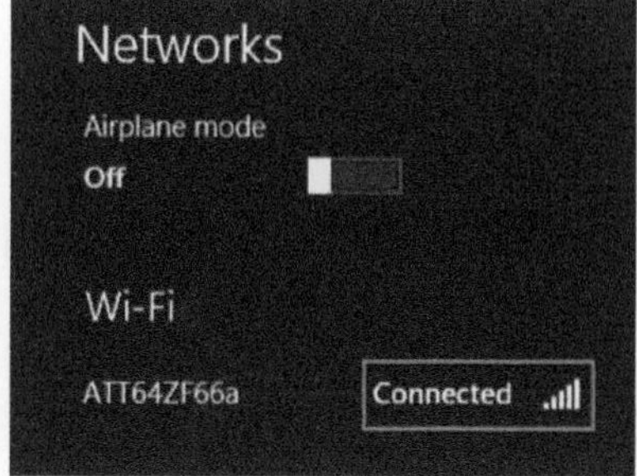

FIGURE 13.55 Signal strength

TECH TIP

The higher the decibel rating, the better the signal

The type of radio antenna and antenna gain affect the signal strength. However, no matter how good the antenna, as a wireless device is moved farther away from an access point or another wireless device, the more attenuation occurs. Walls, trees, obstacles, and other radio waves can cause attenuation.

A **Wi-Fi analyzer** or wireless locator can determine whether there are wireless networks or hotspots in the area. It can also locate wireless devices that can be attached to pets, people, keys, remotes, and so on. A phone or mobile device app can also locate a powered mobile device or locate a person who has a mobile device with this enabled.

Multiple input/multiple output (**MIMO**) uses multiple 2.4 GHz and 5 GHz antennas. Figure 13.56 shows an example of MIMO transmissions. Note that although each client that attaches to an AP using MIMO can have multiple data streams, the AP handles one client at a time.

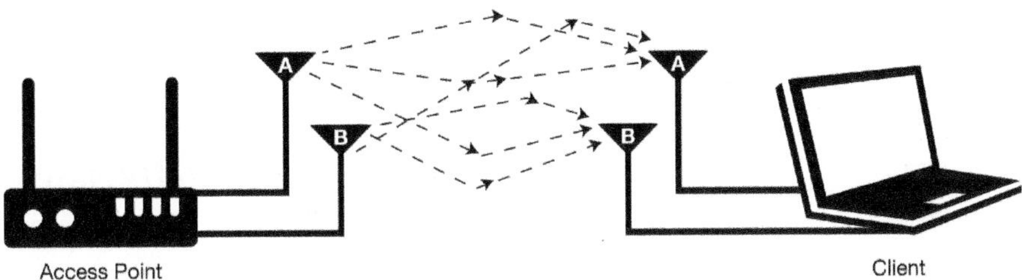

FIGURE 13.56 MIMO transmissions

MIMO antennas may be external or built in to a wireless device. Greater wireless speeds can be achieved by using multiple antennas. 802.11n, 802.11ac, and 802.11ax radios are defined by how many antennas can transmit and receive as well as the number of data streams supported. The documentation is commonly in a number formatted such as 2x2:1 or 4x4:4. The first number is the maximum number of antennas that can transmit. The second number is the number of antennas that can receive data. The last number is the number of data streams supported. 802.11ac and 802.11ax use multi-user MIMO (**MU-MIMO**) and allow up to eight simultaneous streams. MU-MIMO serves multiple devices simultaneously, whereas with pre-802.11ac implementations, an AP serves only one user at a time.

Wireless Data Transfer Speeds

The data transfer speed between a wireless NIC and an access point or another wireless device is automatically negotiated for the fastest transfer possible. The farther away from an access point a wireless device is located, the lower the speed. A low radio frequency signal (or **low RF signal**) could simply mean the device is too far from the access point and results in **slow network speeds** as well as intermittent wireless connectivity. Move closer or change the angle of the device to get a better signal. Figure 13.57 shows this concept.

External interference can also influence wireless connectivity and wireless transfer speeds. Check the area for devices or other wireless networks using the same frequency. Don't forget that walls, structures, and other objects also affect wireless reception/speeds.

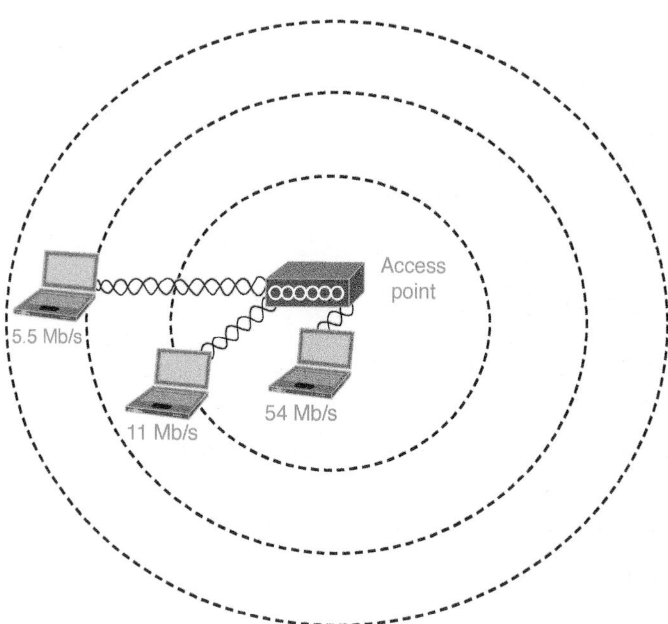

FIGURE 13.57 Wireless connectivity speed ranges

Wireless and Wired Client Device Configuration Overview

When you are connecting a device to a wired or wireless network, many things might have to be done, such as the following:

> Configure IP addressing.
> If the computer wants to share a printer or folders, file and print sharing might need to be enabled.
> If the device is on a corporate network, the device might have to be put on the domain with a unique name.
> If a wireless device is being configured, the SSID and possibly security parameters need to be entered.

TECH TIP

How to name a computer

In Windows, name a computer using the *System* section of the Control Panels or use the *Settings > System* option. Each device on the same network must be given a unique name.

Configuring an End Device: IP Addressing

No matter what device connects to a wired or wireless network, the device must have an IP address so that it is uniquely identified on the network. Every device on a wired or wireless network needs three important pieces of information: an IP address, subnet mask, and default gateway. The IP address and subnet mask are what make the network device unique and allow it to be reached by other devices. There are two ways to get IP addressing information: statically define the IP address and subnet mask or dynamically obtain the address/mask by using DHCP. The device also needs a default gateway IP address in order to communicate with other networks.

TECH TIP

My computer's IP address changes

A computer's IP address can change each time the computer boots because with DHCP, the DHCP server issues an IP address for a specific amount of time.

Statically Configuring an IP Address

When an IP address is statically defined, someone manually enters an IP address and mask into the computer as follows:

> *Windows 7/8/10/11:* Access *Network and Sharing Center* Control Panel > *Change Adapter Settings* link.

> *Windows 10/11:* Access *Settings* > *Network & Internet* > *Change adapter options* link.

Most support staff do not statically define IP addresses except for devices that are network infrastructure devices, such as web servers, database servers, other network servers, routers, or switches. Figure 13.58 shows the window that appears when you right-click a particular adapter and select *Properties* > *Internet Protocol Version 4 (TCP/IPv4)* > *Properties* button.

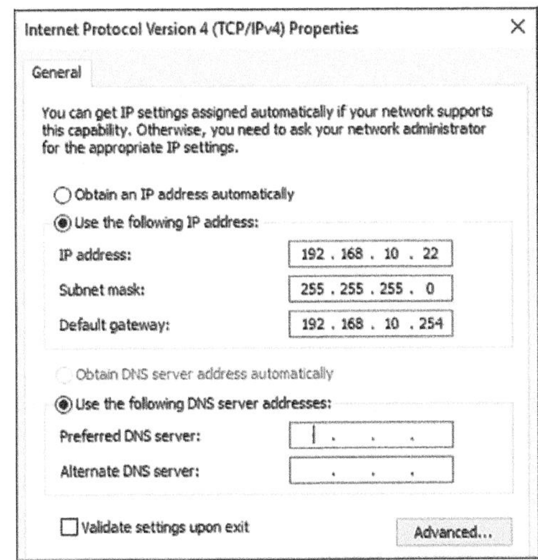

FIGURE 13.58 IP address configuration using a NIC's Properties

In Windows *Settings* > *Network & Internet*, you select either *Ethernet* from the left menu and then select the Ethernet connection shown in the pane on the right. Scroll to the *IP settings* section and select *Edit*. In the *Edit IP settings* dialog box, use the arrow to select *Manual* > and click on the *IPv4* slide option, as shown in Figure 13.59.

TECH TIP

What happens if you assign the same IP address to two devices?

Entering an IP address that is a duplicate of the address for another network device renders the new network device inoperable on the network and could affect the other device's traffic as well.

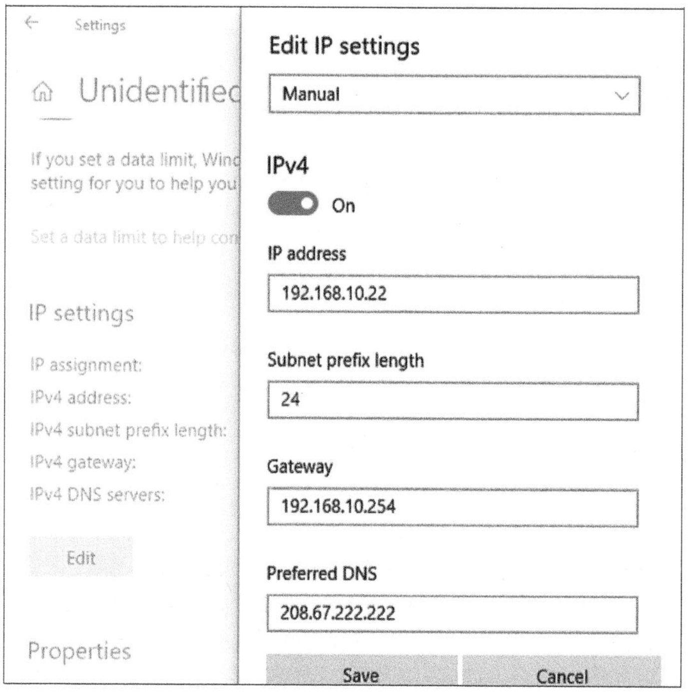

FIGURE 13.59 IP address configuration using Windows Settings

Another place that you might need to configure a static IP address is on a wireless router. Most of the time you automatically get an IP address when connecting a router to the internet, but sometimes if a router connects to another router or if you request a static address from the provider, you need to go into the wireless router's configuration and select a static WAN IP address. This is commonly done through the WAN or internet option and selecting *Static IP*, as shown on the TP-Link wireless router configuration screen in Figure 13.60. The *Dynamic IP* option is the default and is used when the address is sent from the internet provider.

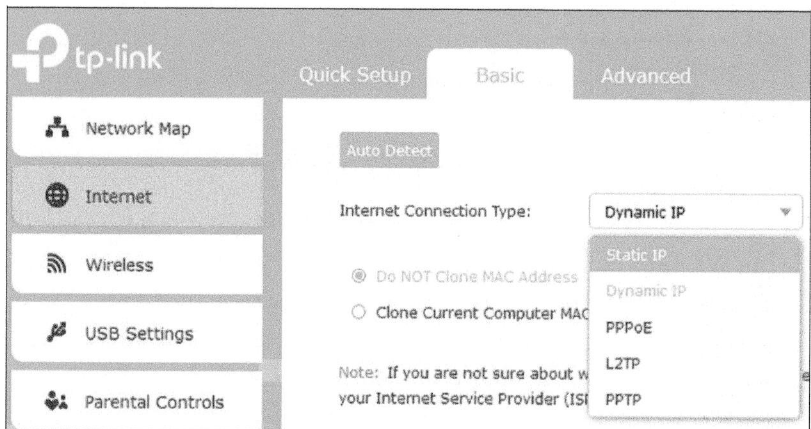

FIGURE 13.60 Static WAN IP address configuration on a wireless router using DHCP

Dynamic Host Configuration Protocol (**DHCP**) is a protocol used to assign IP addresses to network devices. A **DHCP server** (software configured on a network server, router, or wireless router) contains a pool of IP addresses known as a **DHCP scope** that defines the starting and ending IP addresses that can be issued to network devices. Commonly on servers or routers, you have to give the DHCP pool/scope a name before entering the range of IP addresses, but on a wireless router used for home or small business, you just enter the IP addresses and ensure that the DHCP server option is enabled, as shown in Figure 13.61.

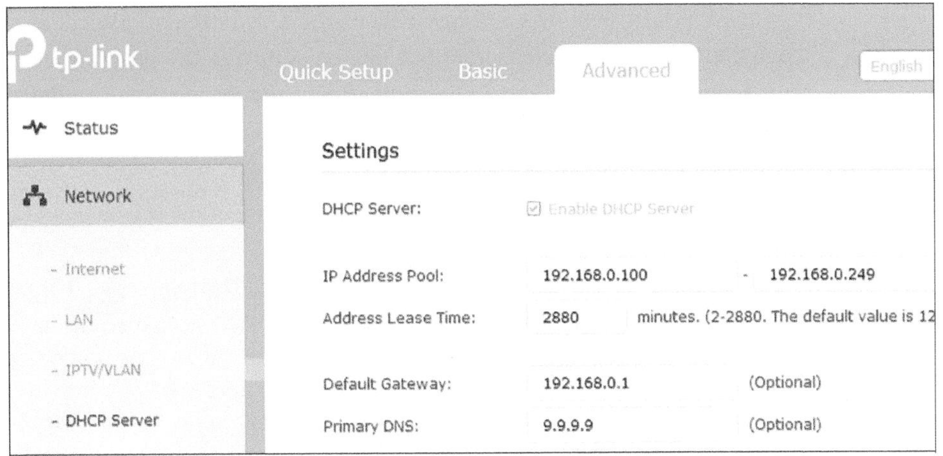

FIGURE 13.61 DHCP configuration on a wireless router

When a network device has been configured for DHCP and it boots, the device sends out a DHCP request for an IP address. A DHCP server responds to this request and issues an IP address to the network device that may be used for a specific period of time, such as a day or longer, depending on the **DHCP lease time** configured on the DHCP server. The default IP address lease time varies by vendor. For example, TP-Link has the lease time in minutes, with a max of 2880, or 2 days (refer to Figure 13.61). DHCP makes IP addressing easy and prevents network devices from being assigned duplicate IP addresses.

An important configuration on a DHCP server is a **DHCP reservation**, which is an IP address reserved for a particular device, such as a server or printer. Instead of statically assigning an IP address to a device, a technician enters the physical address (the MAC address) of the device, such as a network printer, into the DHCP server and the IP address to be assigned to the device. No other device will get that IP address, and the device will always get the reserved IP address. On the DHCP server, each network is configured with a starting IP address and an ending IP address. A technician can also create a range of reserved IP addresses that will not be issued to network devices by the DHCP server but that can be statically configured on the device as an alternative to making an individual reservation on the DHCP server for each device. Figure 13.62 shows this concept.

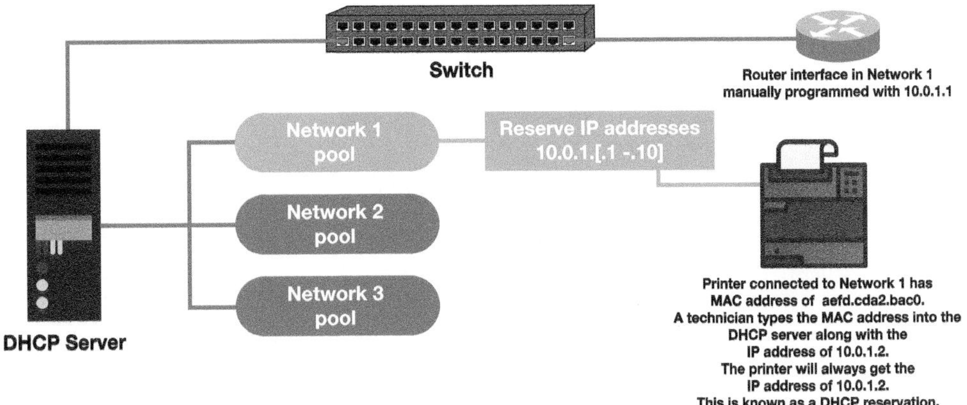

FIGURE 13.62 DHCP reservations

To configure client-side DHCP in Windows, access the *Network and Sharing Center* Control Panel > access the *Change adapter settings* link > right-click or tap and briefly hold on the wired and wireless NIC and select *Properties* > double-click on the *Internet Protocol Version 4 (TCP/IPv4)* option > ensure the *Obtain an IP address automatically* radio button is enabled (refer to

Figure 13.58). In Windows *Settings > Network & Internet*, you select either *Ethernet* from the left menu and then select the Ethernet connection shown in the pane on the right. Scroll to the *IP settings* section and select *Edit*. In the *Edit IP Settings* dialog box, use the arrow to select *Automatic (DHCP)*.

TECH TIP

Watch out for duplicate IP address messages

If a device displays a message relating to a duplicate IP address, check the device to see if a static IP address has been assigned (and to see if the DHCP server issued the same address to a different device or vice versa). If a computer cannot communicate on a network, use the `ipconfig` command to verify that the computer received an IP address. If a computer cannot communicate on a remote network, use the `ipconfig` command to verify that the computer received a default gateway.

APIPA

Windows computers support automatic private IP addressing (**APIPA**), which assigns an IP address and mask to the computer when a DHCP server is not available but continues trying to contact the server at five-minute intervals. The IP addresses assigned are 169.254.0.1 to 169.254.255.254. No two computers get the same IP address. If you can connect to other computers on your local network but cannot reach the internet or other networks, it is likely that the DHCP server is down and Windows has automatically used APIPA to assign an address. To determine if APIPA is configured, open a command prompt window and type **`ipconfig /all`**. If you see the words *Autoconfiguration Enabled Yes*, APIPA is turned on. If the last word is *No*, APIPA is disabled.

Configuring an Alternative IP Address

An alternative configuration is used when a DHCP server cannot assign an IP address, such as when there are network problems or the DHCP server is down. An alternative IP address could also be used on a laptop when DHCP is used at work, but addresses are statically assigned at home, for example. Figure 13.63 shows the *Alternate Configuration* tab settings. Note that this tab appears only if you have the *Obtain an IP address automatically* radio button enabled on the *General* tab of the *Internet Protocol Version 4 (TCP/IPv4) Properties* window.

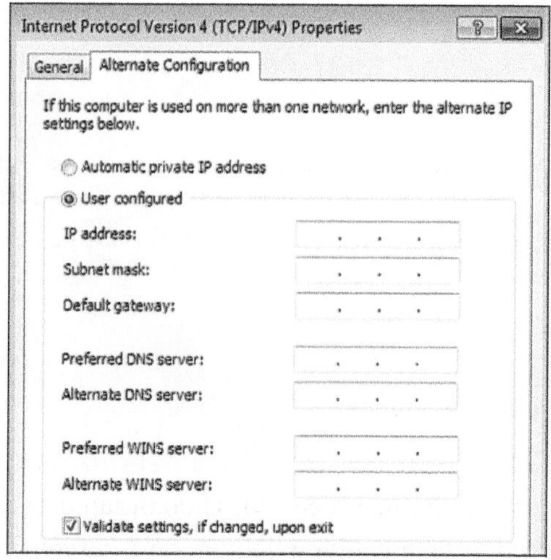

FIGURE 13.63 Alternate Configuration tab

Default Gateway

Another important concept that relates to IP addressing is a default gateway (sometimes called *gateway of last resort* or simply **gateway**). A **default gateway** is an IP address assigned to a network device that tells the device where to send a packet that is going to a remote network. Default gateway addresses are important for network devices to communicate with network devices on other networks. The default gateway address is the IP address of the router that is directly connected to that immediate network. Keep in mind that the primary job of a router is to find the best path to another network. Routers send traffic from one network to another throughout the internet. Your router at home might be used to get traffic from your wireless network and your wired network out to the internet. Consider Figure 13.64, which shows a router moving traffic from the network on the left to the network on the right (or vice versa).

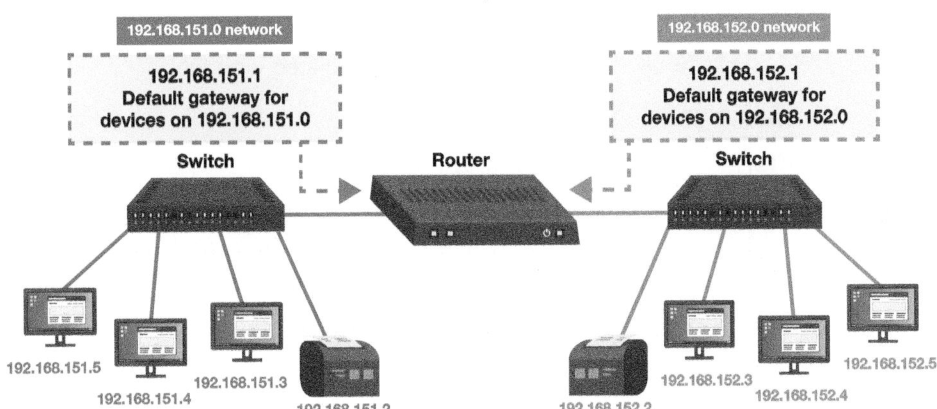

FIGURE 13.64 Default gateway addresses for two different networks

In the network shown in Figure 13.64, network devices on the 192.168.151.0 network use the router IP address 192.168.151.1 as a default gateway address. When a network device on the 192.168.151.0 network wants to send a packet to the other network, the device sends the packet to the default gateway, the router. The router, in turn, looks up the destination address in its routing table and sends the packet out the other router interface (192.168.152.1) to the device on the 192.168.152.0 network.

The default gateway address for all network devices on the 192.168.152.0 network is 192.168.152.1, the router's IP address on the same network. Any network device on 192.168.152.0 sending information to another network sends the packet to the default gateway address.

TECH TIP

How do I assign a default gateway?

If you are statically assigning an IP address, the default gateway address is configured using the *Network and Sharing Center* Control Panel or *Network & Internet* Settings link. Your computer can automatically receive a default gateway address through DHCP, just as it receives an IP address and mask.

DNS

One or more DNS server IP addresses may need to be configured or provided through DHCP. Domain Name Service (**DNS**) is an application that runs on a network server (sometimes called a domain name server, or **DNS server**) and translates internet names into IP addresses. DNS is used on the internet so that you do not have to remember the IP address of each site to which you connect. For example, DNS would be used to connect to Pearson Education, Inc. by translating the uniform resource locator (URL) https://www.pearson.com into the IP address 23.197.24.193. Figure 13.65 shows how DNS is organized. An organization can register a second-level domain, but all DNS web address lookups start at the root level.

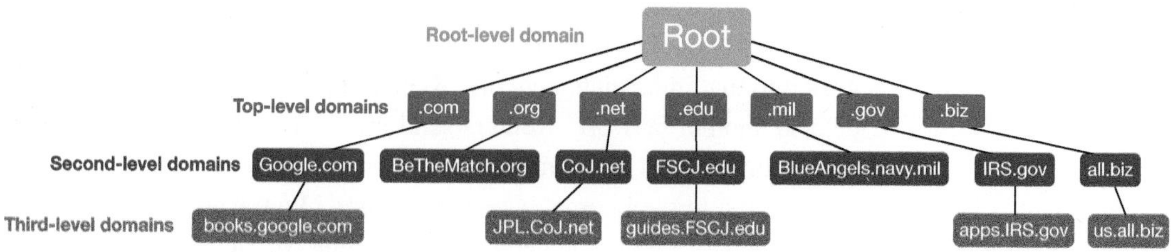

FIGURE 13.65 DNS address hierarchy

Table 13.18 shows common terms associated with DNS.

TABLE 13.18 DNS terminology

Term	Explanation
A record	An address record that holds the IPv4 address of a particular web address. When the A record contains an at (@) symbol, it means the record is for the root domain.
AAAA record	The DNS record that stores a domain's IPv6 address of a particular website.
MX record	A type of DNS record that forwards email to a mail server in another domain. MX stands for mail exchange.
TXT record	A text record used by administrators for documentation and security (such as email spam prevention and domain verification). Chapter 18, "Computer and Network Security," covers this in more detail.

TECH TIP

DNS servers provide name resolution

If a Windows computer is on an Active Directory domain, Active Directory automatically uses DNS to locate other hosts and services using assigned domain names.

If a DNS server does not know a domain name (that is, if it does not have the name in its database), the DNS server can contact another DNS server to get the translation information. Common codes used with DNS (three letters used at the end of a domain name) are `.com` (commercial sites), `.edu` (educational sites), `.gov` (government sites), `.net` (network-related sites), and `.org` (miscellaneous sites).

Client-side DNS involves configuring a computer to use one or more DNS servers. A computer can be programmed for one or more DNS server IP addresses by using DHCP. The DHCP server must be configured for this. Otherwise, a technician can manually configure the system for one or more DNS server IP addresses through the *Network and Sharing Center* Control Panel or *Network & Internet* Settings link. Refer to Figures 13.58 and 13.59 to see where to enter the information.

Wired and wireless adapters require IP addresses, default gateways, and DNS configuration, but before any wired or wireless adapters are installed or configured, the basic configuration parameters should be determined.

Adding a Computer to a Windows Domain

In a corporate environment, computers are in a network domain. This means that all the network devices are registered with (joined to) one or more network servers, called *domain controllers*, as shown in Figure 13.66.

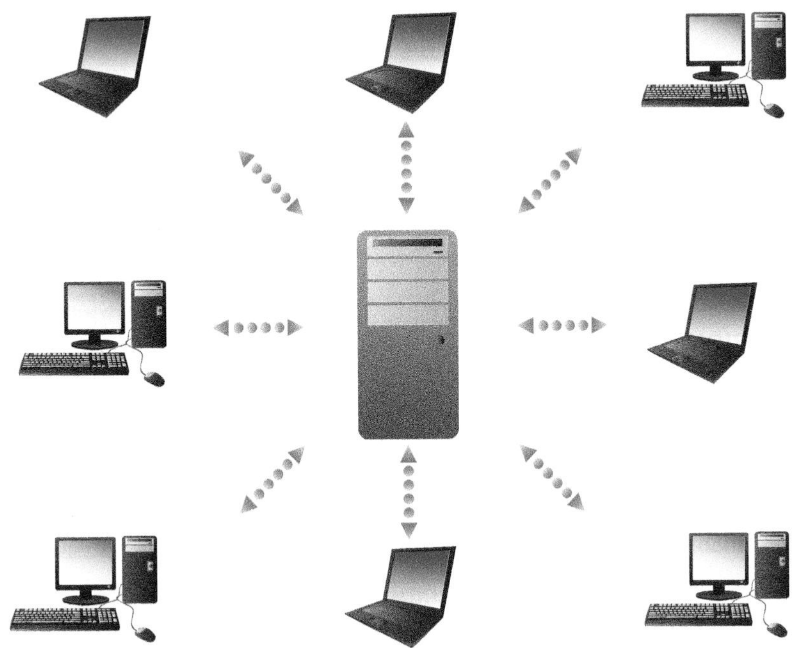

FIGURE 13.66 Corporate computers joined to a domain controller

A technician who has a domain user account that has the appropriate permission can add devices to the domain. On a Windows computer, use the *System* Control Panel to access the *Change settings* link from within the *Computer name, domain, and workgroup settings* section > *Computer Name* tab > select *Network ID* button > *This computer is part of a business network* radio button > *Next* > *My company uses a network with a domain* > *Next* > *Next* > enter a domain user account name that has permission to add a computer to the domain and password > enter a computer name and the domain name > *Next*. Restart the computer. You can also use the *Settings* > *System* link and click the *Join a domain* button.

With macOS, use the *System Preferences* option by clicking the *Apple* icon in the top-left corner > *Accounts* > select *Lock* > *Join* button > *Open Directory Utility* button > select *Lock* > highlight *Active Directory* and select the pencil icon > enter the domain name and a unique computer ID > *Bind* button > enter the domain user account name/password that has permission to add a computer to the domain.

Wireless NIC–Specific Settings

Not all computers in a wireless network need the same type of wireless NIC, but each NIC does require configuration to join a wireless network. After a wireless adapter is installed, SSID and security options can be entered. Specific security options are covered in Chapter 18. Wireless parameters can be configured through a utility provided by the wireless NIC manufacturer or through Windows by selecting the wireless network icon in the notification area, selecting the wireless network shown, and entering the required security information.

If the SSID is not being broadcast (that is, if you see **SSID not found** in the list of available wireless networks), a wireless network can be manually entered using the following procedure for

virtual NICs can be assigned. A physical network device has at least one NIC, but if the device is a server, it has more than one NIC.

Each virtual NIC has its own MAC address and can have an IP address assigned. If more than one virtual machine is installed, each can communicate with the other machine based on the NIC settings configured. Furthermore, the virtual NIC can go through the physical NIC and have internet access in the virtual environment. If the virtual machine doesn't have network connectivity, but the host workstation does, verify the virtual NIC settings. Figure 13.70 illustrates three virtual machines (one Linux, one Windows, and one Microsoft Server, for example) in one physical machine connecting to the one physical NIC even though each virtual machine has its own virtual NIC.

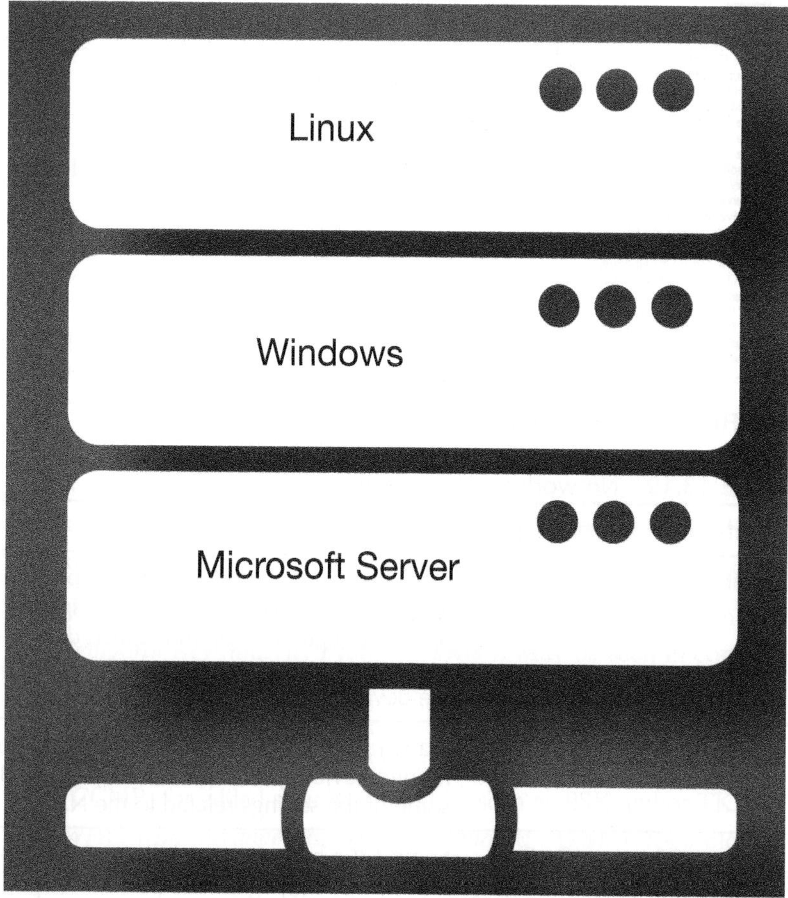

FIGURE 13.70 VMs connecting to a network

Rather than go into all of the different virtualization vendors' products, let's examine VMware Workstation's NIC settings. Other vendors have similar configurations. In VMware Workstation, a NIC can be configured for bridged, network address translation (NAT), host-only, or custom mode. Table 13.20 describes these modes.

TABLE 13.20 Virtualized NIC modes of operation

Mode	Description
Bridged	The NIC is normally manually configured and has access to the host machine's NIC (which normally is connected to the internet and provides internet access to the virtual machine).
Custom	Select the VM network that the NIC is assigned to.

Mode	Description
Host-only	Other virtual machines configured with an IP address on the same network can see and communicate with one another. DHCP is supported.
NAT (network address translation)	Cannot be seen by other virtual machines but can use the host machine's NIC for internet access. DHCP is also supported.

Thin or Thick Client Installation Overview

Thin client and *thick client* are terms used in the corporate environment. A business computer that is a tower under someone's desk is likely to be a thick client; thick clients are the most common. A thick client has software applications loaded on the local hard drive. In contrast, a thin client is an all-in-one unit or a small computer that usually mounts to the back of a monitor, as shown in Figure 13.71.

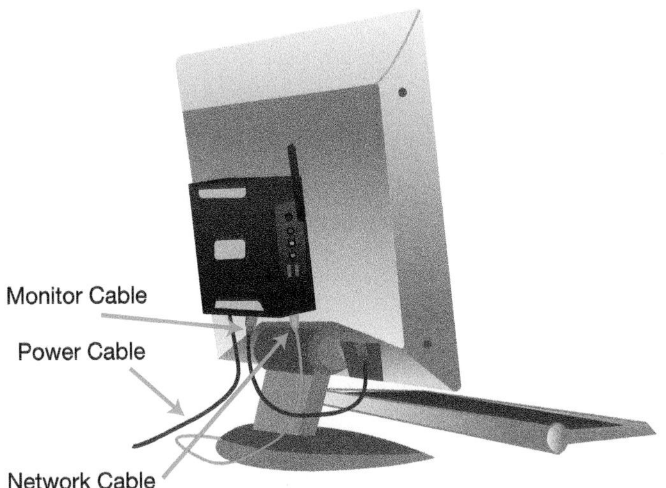

FIGURE 13.71 Thin client computer

A thin client does not have a hard drive, and it runs all the software from a network server. Thin clients have very few ports. Both thin and thick clients take advantage of and attach to the corporate network.

Thin Client Installation

Before installing a thin client, you need to ensure that the thin client hardware has the minimum hardware to run the server-based applications and a cable to connect to the network. Normally, companies that use thin clients have a system image already configured and stored somewhere. Image management software is used for creating, storing, modifying, and deploying an operating system image to the thin client. Some companies use a server and use Remote Desktop Services (previously called Terminal Services). **Remote Desktop Services** is software on a server that can be accessed by multiple client sessions running simultaneously. This is important when thin clients are used because you can deploy and manage Windows-based applications. Remote Desktop Services can also be used to access and control (manage) remote Windows-based computers and servers.

Settings that relate to thin client installation through the image management software or Remote Desktop Services include the following:

- MAC and/or IP address of the thin client
- Schedule settings, including what days and within which time periods the thin client can be used

> Monitor settings, such as resolution, color depth, and refresh rate
> Domain/username, such as the Windows network domain name and the username of the person(s) using the thin client computer
> Hardware drivers

To install a thin client computer, be sure to follow corporate guidelines. Here are the generic steps involved:

Step 1. The thin client may be an all-in-one unit that requires no assembly or a computer and a monitor (which might include a stand to attach both components). If using a computer, monitor, and stand, place the pieces into the stand and secure with screws as needed.

Step 2. Attach power to the thin client.

Step 3. Attach the Ethernet network cable from the wall outlet or cubicle outlet to the Ethernet port on the thin client.

Step 4. Attach the mouse and keyboard to the proper ports.

Step 5. If using a computer and monitor, attach the appropriate video cable from the computer video port to the monitor port.

Step 6. If using an external monitor, attach power to the monitor.

Step 7. Power on the computer and monitor and ensure that the device has network connectivity.

Step 8. If needed, set account settings such as language, time zone, display resolution, and network type.

Step 9. If required, use image management software or Remote Desktop Services to image the computer.

Step 10. Put the computer on the network domain.

Step 11. Ensure that the common applications work.

Step 12. Apply company-required settings or profile.

Thick Client Installation

Before installing a thick client, you need to ensure that the minimum hardware is available to run the applications that will be loaded. As with thin clients, medium to large companies tend to have a system image already configured, stored, and available somewhere on the network, and the same tools are used to get the image onto the computer as for a thin client. Smaller companies might have a technician load each application individually and then configure the account settings manually.

You can also use Remote Desktop Services, just as with a thin client, and push an image to the computer. In small companies, the applications are commonly installed by a technician one by one, or a standard image with the most common applications might be used. Then the technician would have to possibly configure the following settings:

> Network printer
> Local printer
> Application account settings
> Computer settings, such as wireless, display, and desktop icons

Wireless AP/Router Configuration

A wireless AP frequently has the capability to route. This type of device is made for a small office/home office (SOHO) environment. The screens used to configure a SOHO AP varies per vendor, but the process is common. Some of the specific configuration tasks have already been shown, such as DHCP configuration, but the generic steps for configuration follow:

Step 1. Connect an Ethernet cable between the wireless AP and another device that has a web browser.

Step 2. Open a web browser and in the address textbox, enter the default IP address of the AP, such as **`http://192.168.1.1`**.

Step 3. Enter the default username (if needed) and default password.

TECH TIP

Change the default username/password

When an access point or wireless router is purchased, sometimes a default username and/or password is assigned. Because default passwords are available on the internet, the password needs to be changed immediately so that unauthorized access is not permitted. Manufacturers recognized this weakness, and as a result, many newer devices enable you to create a password during the initial setup.

Typical AP configuration menu options are shown in Table 13.21.

TABLE 13.21 Common AP configuration options

Option	Description
Wireless	Used to configure basic wireless settings, such as the SSID. Also includes a link to security options such as MAC filtering, authentication, and encryption (covered in Chapter 18).
Security	Used to enable/disable a firewall and configure firewall features such as a VPN or allow particular network ports to be opened to allow certain types of traffic through.
Storage	Allows monitoring and control of an attached storage device and can even support a File Transfer Protocol (FTP) server.
Maintenance	Allows viewing the current status of the various components as well as access to any logging that is enabled.
Administration	Allows configuration of the device, such as password, IP address assignment, and event logging. Could also include configuration of features such as VoIP or QoS.

Wireless SOHO access points/routers frequently include network functions such as a demilitarized zone (DMZ), also known as a screened subnet, QoS, a DHCP server (sometimes seen as the DHCP on/off setting), a router, integrated switch ports, and a port to add a hard drive and support network-accessible storage. Chapter 18 provides explanations and configuration details related to wireless security, and Table 13.22 introduces some common configuration features.

TABLE 13.22 Common wireless network device configuration settings

Option	Description
Basic QoS	Used to enable QoS so that traffic such as gaming traffic or VoIP traffic is prioritized over other data types.
IP filtering	Uses lists to control which users, websites, IP addresses, protocols, and apps can be used on a device. A deny setting blocks, whereas an allow setting specifically permits network traffic.
Content filtering	Blocks access to specific web pages. Might also include a date/time range. Also called URL or web filtering.
Channel ID	Used to specify a particular 2.4 GHz or 5 GHz channel.
Demilitarized zone (**DMZ**)	Allows a PC or server to be accessed from a remote location. Also called DMZ host or **screened subnet**.
DHCP	Used to enable or disable DHCP as well as the specific network number, mask, and range of addresses to use.
Firmware	Used to update the embedded code within a device. Frequently contains security, performance, and software updates.
Network address translation (NAT)/ destination NAT (DNAT)	NAT, which is used to translate from private IP addresses to a public address, is enabled by default. DNAT maps a public IP address to a specific private IP address and is used in a home or small business network.
Port forwarding	Also called **port mapping** or port triggering, where specific port numbers, ranges of port numbers, and applications are allowed to be used instead of opening all ports. Port triggering allows data through on a limited basis when a specific/configured situation occurs.
SSID	Used to name a wireless network. An SSID cannot contain spaces. There is commonly an option to enable or disable SSID broadcasting.
Universal Plug and Play (**UPnP**)	Used as an alternative to port forwarding to allow peer-to-peer (P2P) gaming applications to function without further configuration. Could be a security risk for other devices on the network.

WWAN Cellular Configuration

Another type of wireless device that you might configure is a wireless broadband device or a WWAN (cellular) connection. A wireless broadband (WWAN cellular) device is normally a USB device, but this technology is integrated into some mobile devices. Software is normally installed either by using a disc or from the device. The device commonly has a phone number/account number associated with the broadband card. Figure 13.72 shows the type of information provided for a wireless broadband USB device.

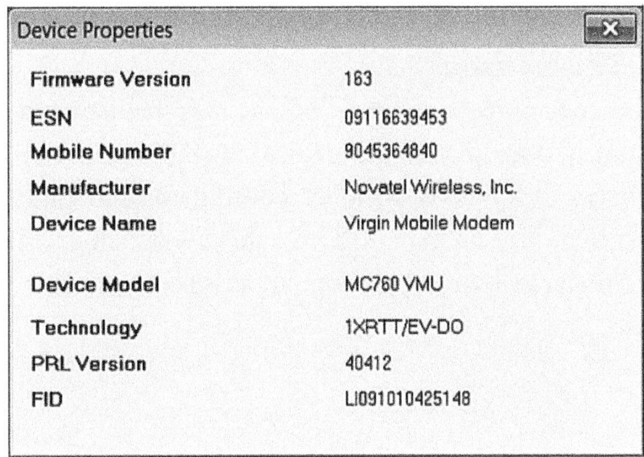

FIGURE 13.72 WWAN cellular properties

IoT and Smart Devices

Internet of Things (**IoT**) is a term that describes the interconnectivity of sensors and devices that connect to a network (usually a wireless one). The IoT has affected all industries, and home devices are particularly common. Smart homes (see Figure 13.73) are becoming popular, and even older existing homes can be made smart.

FIGURE 13.73 Smart home controls

Smart homes include devices that can monitor water consumption, air and heat, and electricity. In addition, it is possible to control locks, lights, thermostats, garage doors, computers, sound systems, TVs, and refrigerators—and the list just keeps growing. Smart devices are controlled through an app on a phone, tablet, laptop, or other computer. The smart devices can connect to a wired Ethernet network, an 802.11-based wireless network, or using two other standards that are common in smart homes: Zigbee and Z-Wave.

Zigbee is a standard managed by the Zigbee Alliance. Zigbee devices do not have a maximum number of hops (that is, a maximum number of devices the signal can go through to reach the destination). A Zigbee network includes a Zigbee coordinator and Zigbee devices. The network might include a Zigbee router, also called a Zigbee gateway, which extends the range of the wireless network. Figure 13.74 shows two sample topologies used with Zigbee: one without a Zigbee router and one with one.

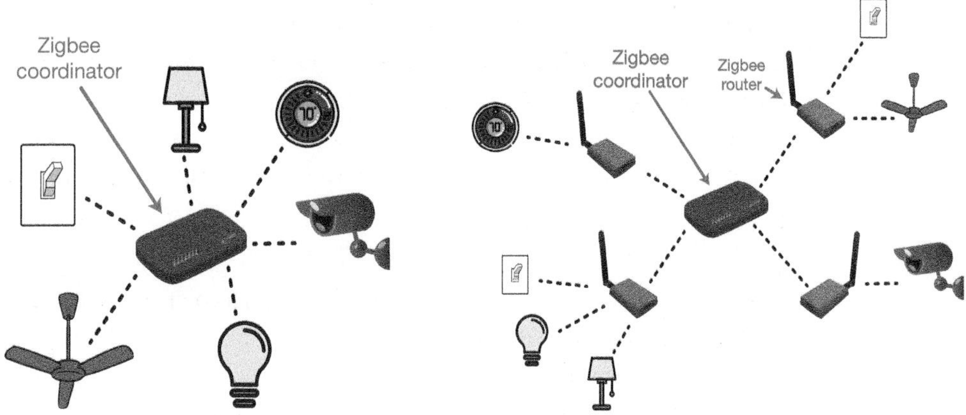

FIGURE 13.74 Zigbee topologies

Z-Wave is a wireless standard from Silicon Labs. Z-Wave supports only four hops between one particular device and the controller. If DeviceX has to go through Device1, Device2, and Device3 to get to the controller, all is good, but if DeviceX has to go through an additional device to get to the controller, DeviceX cannot be controlled.

Z-Wave has a limit of 232 devices in one network and is used to support thermostats, lights, locks, sensors, switches, and so on. Z-Wave, like Zigbee, requires a controller. The more devices you add to the network, the more repeaters you have because each device then boosts the signal as it transmits the data. Figure 13.75 shows a sample topology. Table 13.23 compares Zigbee and Z-Wave.

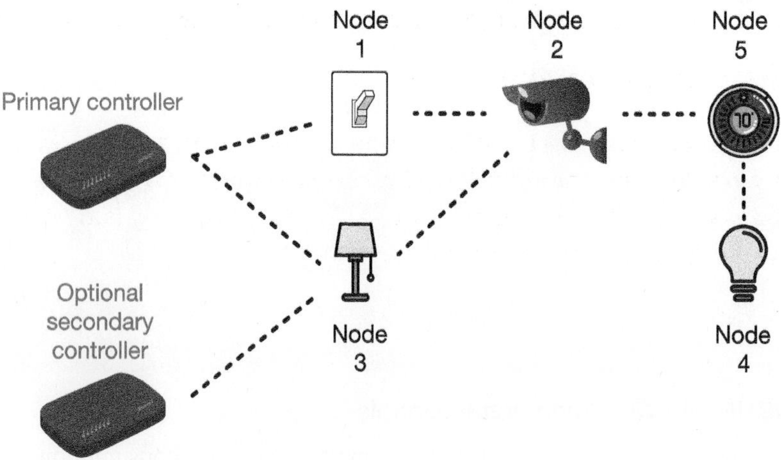

FIGURE 13.75 Z-Wave sample topology

TABLE 13.23 Common wireless network device configuration settings

Standard	Frequency	Data rate	Range	Security
Zigbee	915 MHz and 2.4 GHz	Up to 250 kbps	Up to 328 feet (100 meters)	128-bit AES encryption
Z-Wave	908.4, 908.42, and 916 MHz (United States, Canada, and Mexico)	Up to 250 kbps	Up to 328 feet (100 meters)	Proprietary and improved with Security2 (S2)

Both Zigbee and Z-Wave involve mesh networks. In a mesh network, wireless signals go from device to device, and a central hub/coordinator that commonly connects to the internet. Each device can connect to multiple other devices.

IoT devices are very susceptible to security breaches because of the lack of standardization within the industry; in addition, IoT devices are incapable of supporting security due to lack of hardware. They also provide an easy target if they connect to other networks like 802.11 or Ethernet networks. Here are some security suggestions for implementing IoT devices:

- Research the company and protocol(s) used to connect the devices. Make a selection based on a good security track record.
- Encrypt the IoT data sent between the devices and the systems that receive the data.
- Require user authentication to access the IoT devices.
- Secure the IoT network. Industry security leaders offer IoT solutions.
- Ensure that any communication between an IoT device and an app uses proven security methods.

Network Troubleshooting

One step in troubleshooting a network is to determine how many devices are affected by a problem. For example, if only one computer cannot communicate across a network, the issue will be handled differently than if several (or all) computers on a network cannot communicate. If a computer cannot get on a network at all, it might not have appropriate IP addressing information or may not be joined to a domain. If a network port is suspect, ensure that the interface is enabled, try another cable, or use a loopback plug to test the port. The easiest way to determine how many devices are having trouble is by using a simple test using the `ping` command.

The `ping` Command

The `ping` command can be used to check connectivity from one network device to another device (if you suspect **no connectivity, no internet connectivity,** or **intermittent connectivity/limited connectivity**). Figure 13.76 shows the sample network used here to illustrate how `ping` is used to check various network points.

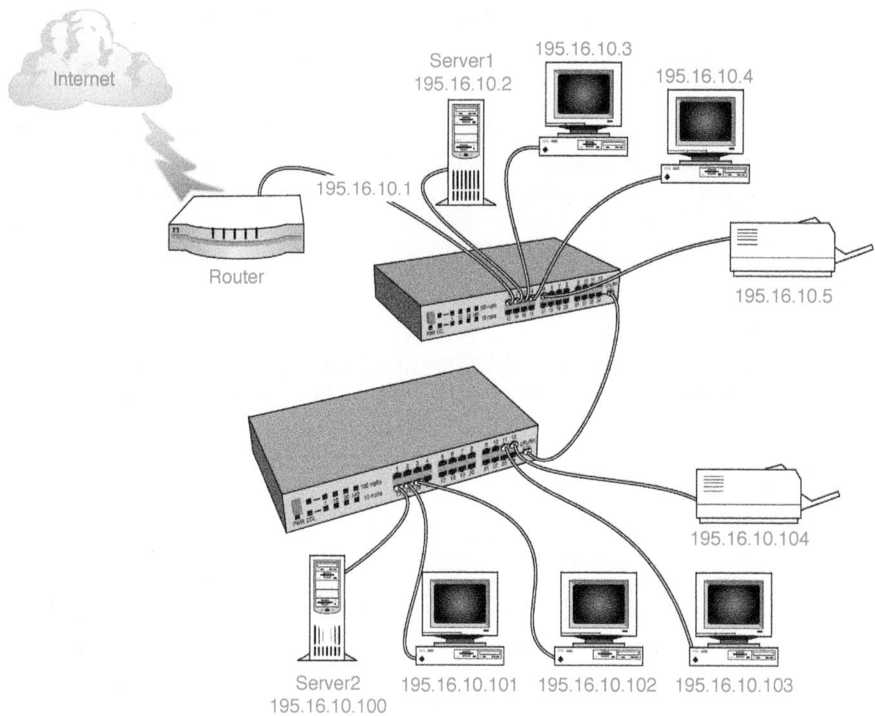

FIGURE 13.76 Sample network troubleshooting scenario

> **TECH TIP**
>
> **What does `ping` do?**
>
> The `ping` command can be used to determine whether a network path is available, whether there are delays along the path, and whether a remote network device is reachable. `ping` sends a packet to an IP destination (that you specify), and a reply is sent back from the destination device if everything works fine.

The network shown in Figure 13.76 consists of various network devices, including two servers and two laser printers. The devices connect to one of two switches that are connected using the uplink port via an Ethernet cable or a fiber cable. A router connects to the top switch, and the router connects to the internet.

If the 195.16.10.3 workstation cannot access a file on Server2 (195.16.10.100), the first step in troubleshooting is to ping Server2 from the workstation. If this ping is successful, you know the problem is with Server2 or the file located on the server.

If the ping is unsuccessful, you know there is a problem somewhere between the workstation and the server or on the server. To test this, ping another device that connects to the same switch; for example, from workstation 195.16.10.3, ping Server1 (195.16.10.2). A successful ping tells you the connection between the 195.16.10.3 workstation and the switch is good, the switch is working, the cable connecting to Server1 is fine, and Server1 is functioning. If the connectivity is intermittent (that is, if you get one or two out of numerous pings), this could be a result of **port flapping** (that is, a port going up and then down) due to faulty cabling or a faulty port.

What Resources Are Unavailable?

One of the first signs of network issues is a user complaining about **unavailable resources**. This might mean the user can't reach the internet or can't reach local resources within the company, such as network shares, printers, or email. The troubleshooting process helps you narrow down where you should ping and verify exactly what network resource(s) cannot be reached.

Pinging devices on the same network is a good check of local connectivity. The term *local connectivity* describes devices on the same network, including the default gateway. If a network device can ping other devices on the same network as well as the default gateway, the network device (and all its components and basic settings) are configured correctly.

> **TECH TIP**
>
> **Use `ping -t`**
>
> Use `ping x.x.x.x -t` (where you replace `x.x.x.x` with an IP address or a URL) to issue a continuous ping to a remote location. When you do, the ping does not stop until you press Ctrl+C.

Now ping workstation 195.16.10.101 (a device other than the server on the remote switch) by typing **`ping 195.16.10.101`**. If the ping is successful, you know that (1) the uplink cable is operational; (2) the second switch is operational; (3) the cable that connects workstation 195.16.10.101 to the switch is good; and (4) the 195.16.10.101 workstation has been successfully configured for TCP/IP. If the ping is unsuccessful, you know that one of these five items is faulty. The problems could be the (1) Server2 cable, (2) switch port to which the server connects, (3) server NIC, (4) server configuration, or (5) file on Server2.

> **TECH TIP**
>
> **How can I check the TCP/IP protocol stack on my own NIC?**
>
> The **`ping`** command can be used to test a network card as well as the TCP/IP protocol running on the NIC, with the command **`ping 127.0.0.1`** (IPv4), **`ping ::1`** (IPv6), or **`ping localhost`**, where *`localhost`* is a hostname that is translated to an IP address known as a private IP address, or loopback address, which means it cannot be used by the outside world.

You can use the **`ping`** command followed by the name of the device (or website) being tested (for example, **`ping www.pearson.com`**). A DNS server translates the name (pearsoned.com) to an IP address (23.197.24.193). If you can reach the site by pinging the IP address, but not the name, you know there is a problem with the DNS server.

> **TECH TIP**
>
> **What the `ping localhost` results mean**
>
> If a ping is successful (that is, if you get a message indicating that a reply was received from 127.0.0.1 or ::1), you know the TCP/IP protocol stack works correctly on the NIC. If the ping response is nothing (or appears to hang) or a 100% packet loss error, you know that TCP/IP is not properly installed or is not functioning correctly on that particular workstation.

The `ipconfig` Command

To see the current IP configuration on a Windows computer, use the `ipconfig` command from a Windows command prompt or the `ifconfig` command with Linux or macOS. The `ipconfig`

/all command can be used to see both wired and wireless NICs if both are installed, as shown in Figure 13.77. The ipconfig /all command also allows you to view MAC addresses.

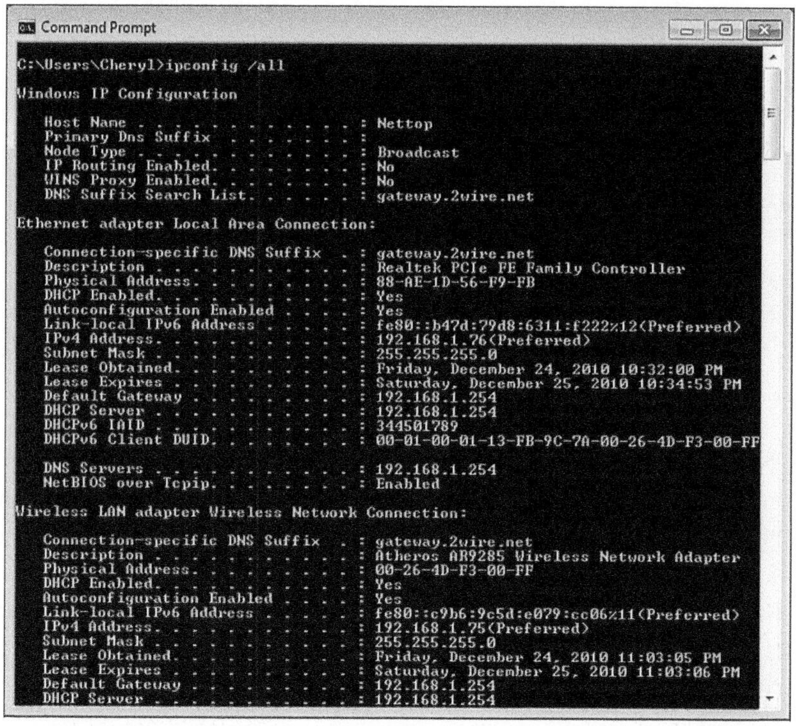

```
Command Prompt

C:\Users\Cheryl>ipconfig /all

Windows IP Configuration

   Host Name . . . . . . . . . . . . : Nettop
   Primary Dns Suffix  . . . . . . . :
   Node Type . . . . . . . . . . . . : Broadcast
   IP Routing Enabled. . . . . . . . : No
   WINS Proxy Enabled. . . . . . . . : No
   DNS Suffix Search List. . . . . . : gateway.2wire.net

Ethernet adapter Local Area Connection:

   Connection-specific DNS Suffix  . : gateway.2wire.net
   Description . . . . . . . . . . . : Realtek PCIe FE Family Controller
   Physical Address. . . . . . . . . : 88-AE-1D-56-F9-FB
   DHCP Enabled. . . . . . . . . . . : Yes
   Autoconfiguration Enabled . . . . : Yes
   Link-local IPv6 Address . . . . . : fe80::b47d:79d8:6311:f222%12(Preferred)
   IPv4 Address. . . . . . . . . . . : 192.168.1.76(Preferred)
   Subnet Mask . . . . . . . . . . . : 255.255.255.0
   Lease Obtained. . . . . . . . . . : Friday, December 24, 2010 10:32:00 PM
   Lease Expires . . . . . . . . . . : Saturday, December 25, 2010 10:34:53 PM
   Default Gateway . . . . . . . . . : 192.168.1.254
   DHCP Server . . . . . . . . . . . : 192.168.1.254
   DHCPv6 IAID . . . . . . . . . . . : 344501789
   DHCPv6 Client DUID. . . . . . . . : 00-01-00-01-13-FB-9C-7A-00-26-4D-F3-00-FF

   DNS Servers . . . . . . . . . . . : 192.168.1.254
   NetBIOS over Tcpip. . . . . . . . : Enabled

Wireless LAN adapter Wireless Network Connection:

   Connection-specific DNS Suffix  . : gateway.2wire.net
   Description . . . . . . . . . . . : Atheros AR9285 Wireless Network Adapter
   Physical Address. . . . . . . . . : 00-26-4D-F3-00-FF
   DHCP Enabled. . . . . . . . . . . : Yes
   Autoconfiguration Enabled . . . . : Yes
   Link-local IPv6 Address . . . . . : fe80::c9b6:9c5d:e079:cc06%11(Preferred)
   IPv4 Address. . . . . . . . . . . : 192.168.1.75(Preferred)
   Subnet Mask . . . . . . . . . . . : 255.255.255.0
   Lease Obtained. . . . . . . . . . : Friday, December 24, 2010 11:03:05 PM
   Lease Expires . . . . . . . . . . : Saturday, December 25, 2010 11:03:06 PM
   Default Gateway . . . . . . . . . : 192.168.1.254
   DHCP Server . . . . . . . . . . . : 192.168.1.254
```

FIGURE 13.77 ipconfig /all **command output**

A network device may not get an IP address from the DHCP server. A symptom of this problem is a device getting an APIPA (IPv4) or link-local (IPv6) address because a DHCP server is unavailable. When this occurs, use the ipconfig /release command and then issue the ipconfig /renew command. Also ensure that the device is actually configured for DHCP. A message appears on Windows-based devices when two devices have been manually assigned the same IP address. Note that not all operating systems and/or devices do this. Check any device that has a manually configured IP address for any duplicate IP addresses that are causing an IP address conflict.

The tracert and pathping Commands

The tracert command is a tool found in the Microsoft, macOS, and Linux environments. The tracert command is used to display the path a packet takes through the network. The benefit of using the tracert command is that you can see where a fault is occurring. It also allows you to see the network latency. Network latency is the delay measured from source to destination; **high latency** can mean slow network speeds. The tracert command is also useful when you have intermittent connectivity. An example of output from the tracert command is provided in Figure 13.78.

A similar command available in the Windows environment is pathping, which is a combination of the ping and tracert commands. Whereas the ping command checks for connectivity between one network device and another device and tracert displays the IP addresses of the routers between the source and destination addresses, pathping provides additional information, including the network latency and loss between the source and destination. pathping takes longer to execute than the ping or tracert commands. Sample output is provided in Figure 13.79.

```
C:\Users\Cheryl>tracert comptia.org
Tracing route to comptia.org [198.134.5.6] over a maximum of 30 hops:
 1 <1 ms <1 ms <1 ms vankman1 [192.168.1.1]
 2 8 ms 7 ms 8 ms 10.126.208.1
 3 10 ms 8 ms 7 ms 72-31-92-20.net.bhntampa.com [72.31.92.20]
 4 11 ms 14 ms 12 ms ten0-6-0-11.tamp27-car1.bhn.net [71.44.3.186]
 5 17 ms 16 ms 19 ms hun0-4-0-3.tamp20-car1.bhn.net [72.31.117.170]
 6 22 ms 19 ms 18 ms ten0-8-0-0.orld71-CAR1.bhn.net [71.44.1.211]
 7 17 ms 16 ms 19 ms 72-31-217-88.net.bhntampa.com [72.31.217.88]
 8 23 ms 19 ms 14 ms 10.bu-ether15.orldfljo00w-bcr00.tbone.rr.com
[66.109.6.98]
 9 36 ms 31 ms 31 ms bu-ether18.atlngamq47w-bcr01.tbone.rr.com [66.109.1.72]
 10 23 ms 23 ms 24 ms 0.ae2.pr1.atl20.tbone.rr.com [107.14.17.188]
 11 26 ms 29 ms 23 ms 67.106.215.89.ptr.us.xo.net [67.106.215.89]
 12 50 ms 51 ms 50 ms 207.88.13.54.ptr.us.xo.net [207.88.13.54]
 13 52 ms 56 ms 49 ms 207.88.12.174.ptr.us.xo.net [207.88.12.174]
 14 50 ms 51 ms 51 ms 207.88.12.31.ptr.us.xo.net [207.88.12.31]
 15 49 ms 57 ms 55 ms ae0d0.mcr1.chicago-il.us.xo.net [216.156.0.162]
 16 54 ms 52 ms 53 ms 216.55.11.62
 17 52 ms 60 ms 52 ms 198.134.5.6
Trace complete.
```

FIGURE 13.78 Sample output of `tracert`

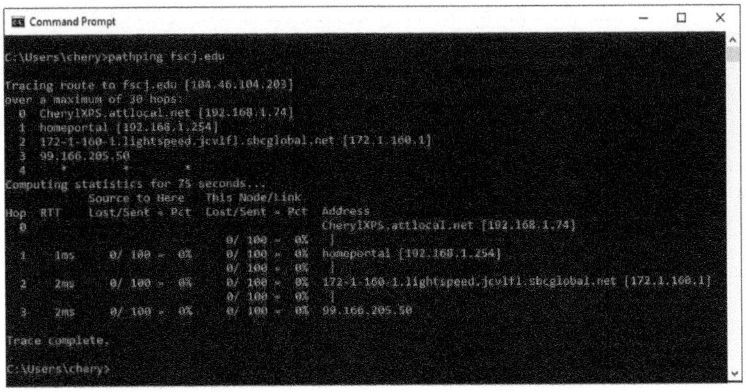

```
Command Prompt

C:\Users\chery>pathping fscj.edu

Tracing route to fscj.edu [104.46.104.203]
over a maximum of 30 hops:
  0  CherylXPS.attlocal.net [192.168.1.74]
  1  homeportal [192.168.1.254]
  2  172-1-160-1.lightspeed.jcvlfl.sbcglobal.net [172.1.160.1]
  3  99.166.205.50
  4     *        *        *
Computing statistics for 75 seconds...
            Source to Here   This Node/Link
Hop  RTT    Lost/Sent = Pct  Lost/Sent = Pct  Address
  0                                           CherylXPS.attlocal.net [192.168.1.74]
                                0/ 100 =  0%   |
  1    1ms     0/ 100 =  0%     0/ 100 =  0%  homeportal [192.168.1.254]
                                0/ 100 =  0%   |
  2    2ms     0/ 100 =  0%     0/ 100 =  0%  172-1-160-1.lightspeed.jcvlfl.sbcglobal.net [172.1.160.1]
                                0/ 100 =  0%   |
  3    2ms     0/ 100 =  0%     0/ 100 =  0%  99.166.205.50

Trace complete.

C:\Users\chery>
```

FIGURE 13.79 Sample output of `pathping`

High latency in wireless networks is caused by interference from devices operating in the same frequency range, obstacles such as walls and concrete, and distance from the access point. High latency in wired networks is typically caused by poor or faulty cabling and/or security issues.

The `nslookup` Command

The `nslookup` command is a tool that helps with DNS server troubleshooting. `nslookup` enables you to see domain names and their associated IP addresses. When an internet site (server) cannot be contacted by its name but can be contacted using its IP address, there is a DNS problem. The `nslookup` command can make troubleshooting these types of problems easier. To see this tool in action, bring up a command prompt, type **`nslookup pearson.com`**, and press ↵Enter. The IP address of the Pearson web server appears. Note that if the `nslookup` command shows a domain name such as a computer, but the domain name cannot be used to contact the device, the `ipconfig /flushdns` command can be used to clear the DNS cache.

The `net` Command

The `net` command is used to manage just about everything on a network from a command prompt. The `net` command is followed by other options, and each option has different parameters. Here is the command syntax:

```
net [ accounts | computer | config | continue | file | group
| help | helpmsg | localgroup | name | pause | print | send |
session | share | start | statistics | stop | time | use |user |
view ]
```

Table 13.24 lists some of the most commonly used `net` command options.

TABLE 13.24 `net` **command options and descriptions**

Command	Description
`net help`	Used to get help for the `net` commands. You can also use `net help` followed by the command (`net help computer`) or `net computer /help` or `net computer /?`.
`net computer`	Used to add or remove a computer in a Microsoft domain.
`net config`	Used to display information about a server or workstation service.
`net share`	Used to create, remove, or view network share resources.
`net start`	Used to start a network service.
`net stop`	Used to stop a network service.
`net use`	Used to map a drive letter to a network resource.
`net user`	Used to manage user accounts.
`net view`	Used to view network devices.

The `netdom` command

The `netdom` command, which is similar to `net`, is used to manage workstations in a domain environment. Use the `netdom /?` command to see all the options. Table 13.25 shows some of the most popular `netdom` command options.

TABLE 13.25 `netdom` **command options and descriptions**

Command	Description
`netdom add`	Used to add a workstation account to a domain
`netdom join`	Used to join a workstation to a domain
`netdom remove`	Used to remove a workstation from a domain
`netdom renamecomputer`	Used to rename a computer and its domain account
`netdom reset`	Used to reset the connection between a workstation and a network domain controller
`netdom resetpwd`	Used to reset the computer account password
`netdom verify`	Used to verify the connection between a workstation and a Microsoft domain controller

NIC Troubleshooting

The following methods can help with NIC troubleshooting:

- In a command prompt window, use `ping localhost` to test the NIC.
- Ping another device on the same network. If the ping is successful, you know the NICs, device, cable, switch or hub are all working.
- Ping the default gateway. If the ping is successful, you know connectivity and configuration of the device for communication on the local network work, and the device has the potential to communicate with other networks.
- Ping a device on a remote network. If the ping is successful, you know the Layer 3 device serving as the default gateway is working.
- Use the `tracert` command to determine the location of the fault (such as whether the problem is inside or outside the company).
- Check the status light(s) on the NIC (see Figure 13.80) to see if the physical connection is good. Different NICs have lights of different colors, but the two most common colors used with status lights to indicate a good connection are green and orange. Some status lights indicate the speed at which the NIC is operating (10 Mbps, 100 Mbps, or 1 Gbps).

FIGURE 13.80 NIC status lights

- Check the status light on the hub or switch (see Figure 13.81) that is used to connect the workstation NIC to the network. Green is a common color for a good connection on these devices.
- Check cabling. Even if the status lights indicate that the connection is good, the cabling may still be faulty.
- Update the device driver by obtaining a newer one from the NIC manufacturer's website.
- Check the IP addressing used. Use the `ipconfig` command from a prompt to ensure that the NIC has an IP address assigned. If you get a duplicate IP address error message, change the IP addressing to DHCP or another statically assigned address (that has not already been used).

FIGURE 13.81 Switch or hub status lights

> On a mobile device, ensure that wireless is enabled and that the wireless NIC is enabled. Look for a button or a keystroke combination that re-enables the wireless antenna and ensure that the NIC is not disabled in the *Network and Sharing Center* Control Panel.

> If your network connection on the desktop or from within the *Network and Sharing* section of the Control Panel shows limited connectivity (see Figure 13.82) or if you cannot reach the internet at all, try rebooting the PC (because of a 169.254.*x*.*x* address) or the router (if in a home or small business network). With a wireless connection, check security settings, the wireless button that controls the wireless antenna, or a wireless key that toggles the wireless NIC. If on a wired network, the cable could be an issue.

> If the network connection is intermittent or slow on a wireless connection, move closer to the AP, change the position of the wireless device, or add another AP in the area to extend the wireless network. On a wired connection, check cabling and duplex settings. Replace a hub with a switch.

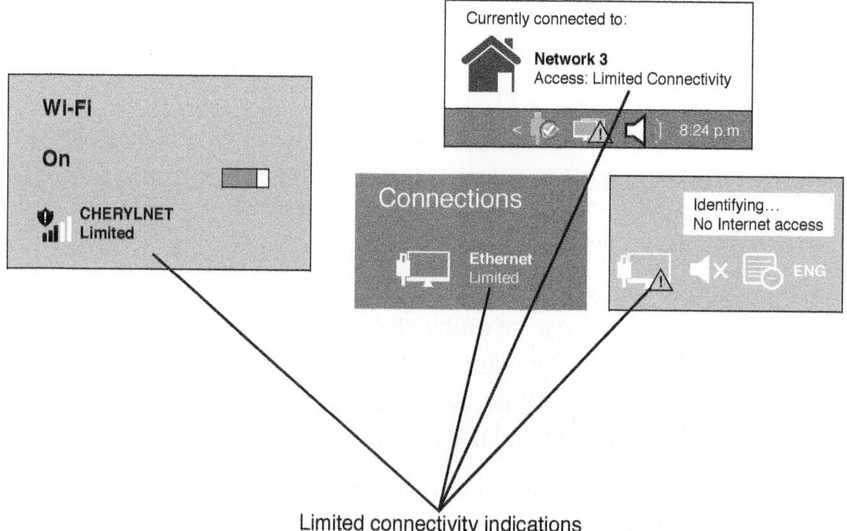

FIGURE 13.82 Windows limited connectivity network indications

Troubleshooting Cable and DSL Modems

Because most cable and DSL modems are external, the best tools for troubleshooting connectivity problems are the lights on the front of the modem (see Figure 13.83). The lights vary from vendor to vendor, but common ones are listed in Table 13.26.

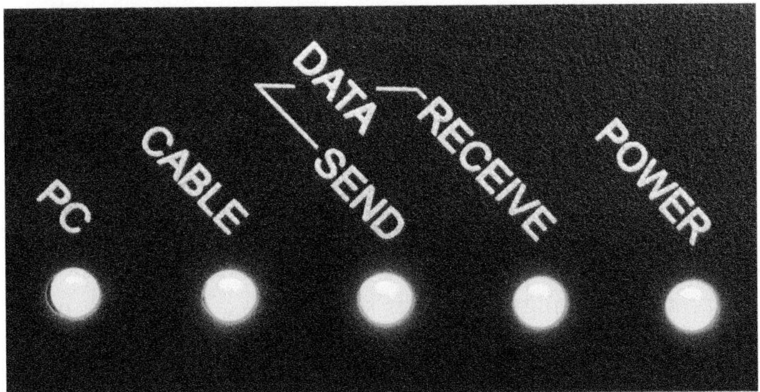

FIGURE 13.83 Cable/DSL modem lights for troubleshooting

TABLE 13.26 Cable/DSL modem lights and troubleshooting*

Light	Explanation
Cable, Data, or D/S	Usually blinks to indicate connectivity with internet provider
ENET, E, or Ethernet	Usually indicates connectivity between the PC and the modem; if unlit, ensure that you are using Ethernet (though if using USB, this will be unlit), check cabling, and check PC network card settings
Internet, Ready, or Rdy	Stays lit when the modem has established an internet connection
Link Status	Usually flashes when acquiring a connection with a provider and is steadily on when a link is established
PC	Used instead of Ethernet or USB lights to show the status of the connection between the modem and the PC
Power	Indicates power to the modem
USB or U	Usually indicates connectivity between the PC and the modem; if unlit, ensure that you are using USB (though if using a NIC, this light will be unlit), check cabling, and check *Device Manager* to see if the modem is recognized

* Refer to the modem documentation for the exact status of the lights.

After you have checked lights and possibly checked cables, if you still have a problem, power off the modem, wait two minutes, power the modem back on, and reboot the computer. Give the modem a couple minutes to initialize. Most modems have a reset button that can also be used, but powering off and powering back on works without having to wipe all the configuration information. If a modem is still not working after you take these steps, contact the service provider.

Networking Multifunction Devices

Chapter 9, "Printers and Multifunction Devices," outlines how to share a printer or multifunction devices across a network as well as how to access a wired or wireless network printer. Now that you know a bit more about networking, the processes outlined in Chapter 9 might be easier to understand. **Printer sharing** is commonly done in a home or small business environment. In a corporate environment, a print server is used, and printers are published or visible to users and devices on the network. A network printer will definitely have an IP address assigned. Users can perform network printer mapping, which enables network users to add a printer to their computer by using the domain printer name or printer IP address. To find printers by name in a corporate network domain, do the following:

> *Windows 7:* Use *Windows Explorer* to explore the network for printers.
> *Windows 8/10/11:* Use *File Explorer* to explore the network for printers.

You can also use a Control Panel or Windows Settings link to add a network printer:

> Access the *Add a device* Control Panel link > select *The printer that I want isn't listed* > enable the *Select a shared printer by name* radio button and enter the domain name (an example might be the domain name SchmidtCo, in this format: \\SchmidtCo\) and select from the printers that are listed.
> Add the printer by using the printer's IP address. A network printer commonly has a front panel that is used to access network configuration settings. A printer that connects directly to the network through a wired or wireless connection has a statically configured IP address, mask, and default gateway. Many times technical support staff attach a label to the printer that shows the IP address. You could access the network settings from the *Devices and Printers > Printers* section of the Control Panel to view the assigned IP address. Refer to Chapter 9 for how to connect using a printer's IP address.
> Use the *Printers & scanners* Settings link > *Add a printer or scanner* > *Add device* box. If you don't see the printer listed, select *Select a shared printer by name* and enter the network share name.

Network Printer/Scanner Services Configuration

Networked printers, copiers, scanners, and multifunction devices might include network services that provide the ability to copy/scan a document and email it to someone or to put a copied/scanned document in a network folder. Typically when configuring a device to be able to email a document, you must provide the following information:

> IP address of the email server (which might be listed as the Simple Mail Transfer Protocol [SMTP] gateway)
> The port number used for the server, obtained from the network administrator who manages the email server
> The email account created by the administrator for the printer
> On some devices, define a standard subject line for any documents emailed from the device

Devices might also be able to store a copied or stored document in a network folder. Make sure you know the network path to the shared folder and ensure that the folder permissions are set to allow new files to be placed into the folder. (Directions on how to share a folder are given later in this chapter.) An example of a network path is \\CherylXPS\ScannedDocs, where the first part is the network device name and the second part is the name of the shared folder. Configuration on the network device used to scan/copy the document typically requires the following:

> A name that appears in the device's address book. This name should be descriptive so that anyone wanting to store a document in the network folder will recognize it. An example is Shared Scanned Documents.
> The protocol used by the device to send the document to the folder. The most common one used is Server Message Block (**SMB**), though you might also see Common Internet File System (**CIFS**).
> The IP address of the SMB server or the device that holds the shared folder.

> The network path to the shared folder.
> The username/password used to put files in the shared folder. This may have to be obtained from the network administrator of the SMB server.

Network Printer/Scanner Troubleshooting

To begin troubleshooting a network printer, do all the things that are normally done when troubleshooting a local printer (refer to Chapter 9) and check the obvious things first. Does the printer have power? Is the printer online? Does the printer have paper? Are the printer's connectors secured tightly? Is the correct printer driver loaded? If all these normal troubleshooting steps check out correctly, try the following steps:

> Print a test page and see if the printer's IP address outputs or see if the printer is labeled with its IP address. If so, ping the printer's IP address to see if there is network connectivity between the computer and the printer. Use the `tracert` command to see if there is a complete network path to the printer.
> Check the printer's *Properties* page to see if the printer has been paused.
> Cancel any print jobs that are in the print queue and resubmit the print job.
> Reset the printer by powering it off and back on. If it connects to a print server device, reset that, too.
> Be sure the print job has been sent to the correct printer. Companies commonly have several network printers to use.
> If a network printer fails and a user has a USB-attached printer, share the USB printer. (Chapter 9 shows how to share a printer across a network.)
> If the printer has never worked, try a different version of the print driver.

Network Servers

Servers are an important part of networking and provide different functionality. One server could provide more than one function. For example, a corporate server might act as a web server as well as a DHCP server. Figure 13.84 shows several network servers mounted in a rack. Each physical box could contain several virtualized servers.

FIGURE 13.84 Network servers

Table 13.27 summarizes the most common servers on a network.

TABLE 13.27 Server types and descriptions

Server type	Description
Authentication server	Used to verify credentials (usually username and password), such as when someone logs in to a domain workstation. Sometimes called an authentication, authorization, and accounting server (**AAA server**).
DHCP server	Used to issue IP-related information, including IP address, subnet mask, default gateway, DNS server, and domain name. Commonly has a block of addresses that are in a pool to be assigned to common devices such as PCs and IP phones. A few addresses are reserved for statically assigned devices such as routers, switches, APs, and printers.
DNS server	Used to translate domain names to IP addresses.
Endpoint management server	Used as a centralized solution for discovering devices, distributing software, provisioning, updating, configuring, managing security, managing profile, imaging/re-imaging computers, and managing inventory.
File server	Used to store files that can be accessed and managed from a remote location. Sometimes called a **fileshare server**.
Mail server	Used to maintain a database of email accounts, store (email) messages sent and received, communicate with other mail servers, and use the DNS protocol to locate other servers. Also known as an email server.
Print server	Used to manage one or more network printers. See Chapter 9 for more information.
Proxy server	Used as a go-between between an application such as a web browser and a physical server. Details on how to configure a network device for a proxy server are provided in Chapter 18.
Syslog server	Used to receive information from multiple network devices and used as a historical record of events such as devices losing power, a particular interface going down, and logins or logouts on a particular device. Also called a logging server.
Web server	Used to provide web-based content that is accessed through a web browser that commonly requests the information through TCP port 80 or secure port 443.

Embedded, SCADA, and Legacy Systems

An **embedded system** is a computer that has a specific function within a larger system. Embedded systems have many of the same components as desktop or mobile computers: processor, RAM, flash memory, and ports. Embedded systems can be found in many places, including airports, manufacturing plants, medical equipment, electrical systems, mechanical systems, and telecommunication systems. Embedded systems tend to be self-contained, but they commonly attach to a wired or wireless network and may be part of an IT person's responsibility.

Closely related to an embedded system is a supervisory control and data acquisition (SCADA) system that is used in just about every industry you can think of, including power, water, manufacturing, oil/gas, mass transit, and food/beverage production. **SCADA** uses a wide variety of networks, servers, and software to handle industrial processes, provide 24/7 monitoring, and supply data in real time (see Figure 13.85). Frequently a SCADA system automates tasks in an attempt to eliminate human error, increase productivity, reduce risks, and improve management by providing real-time data and alerts. One concern about these types of systems is the security risk because of the complexity of hardware, software, protocols, and systems used.

FIGURE 13.85 SCADA example

A **legacy system** is an outdated computer system or piece of network equipment that in an ideal world would be replaced or updated with something new but is commonly kept because it might cost too much to replace it, it is used with a particular system that can't be replaced, or it provides a functionality that will not be needed much longer. A legacy system might contain ports that require converters to be attached to the newer equipment, outdated methods used for access, or proprietary cables that might not be easy to obtain or find. Legacy systems are challenging for technicians because of the lack of support and documentation, but they may still be part of the job requirements.

Software-Defined Networking

Traditional networking involves hardware and software to move information from one place to another. Software-defined networking (SDN) is like ramped-up virtualization. With SDN, network hardware can be virtualized and centrally controlled. Advantages of SDN include the following:

> Provides centralized management and control
> Makes applying security policies across the entire network easier
> Makes it possible to expand and contract the network by quickly and effortlessly adding or removing devices as needed
> Enables fine-tuning of the network for a specific application, time, or purpose

Two basic concepts associated with SDN are the control plane and data plane. The **control plane** is the part of SDN that is involved with getting the data ready to move, whether that means building a routing table for the routing function or a MAC address table for a switch. The **data plane** is where all the work is done to move or forward traffic from the source to the destination, such as sending the data out a specific router or switch port. By splitting up these areas, it is easy to virtualize network equipment.

Let's look at switches as an example. You may remember that switches build a MAC address table, and the network is therefore able to efficiently send data based on the destination MAC address out a specific port. The process of learning the MAC addresses, storing them, and deciding which port to send the data to could be handled by the control plane area, and the transmission of data could be handled by the data plane to allow for SDN switches to be used (see Figure 13.86).

of the most popular protocols and lists the TCP/IP port numbers that are commonly used for the various protocols. Table 13.30 lists some of the common protocols or network standards and the TCP/IP model layers at which they operate.

TABLE 13.29 TCP/IP protocols and port numbers

Protocol	Common port number(s)	Description
Dynamic Host Configuration Protocol (DHCP)	67/68	Issues IP addressing information, such as IP address, subnet mask, default gateway, and DNS server address to network devices.
Domain Name System (DNS)	53	Translates internet names and URLs into IP addresses.
File Transfer Protocol (**FTP**)	20/21	Sends/receives files from one computer to another network device; actually requires two port numbers: one to issue commands and the other one for data. Port 20 is sometimes but not always used for data. FTP sends data in cleartext and is not considered secure.
Hypertext Transfer Protocol (**HTTP**)	80	Provides browser-based internet communication. Not considered secure.
HTTP over SSL/TLS (Secure Sockets Layer/ Transport Layer Security) Protocol (**HTTPS**)	443	Provides encrypted HTTP communication through an SSL/TLS session.
Internet Message Access Protocol (**IMAP**)	143	Supports email retrieval. Allows synchronization from multiple devices. The latest version is IMAP4.
Lightweight Directory Access Protocol (**LDAP**)	389	Provides records related to directory services (any type of network resource, such as users, printers, phone numbers, files, access points, and so on).
NetBIOS over TCP/IP (**NetBT**)	137–139	Supports outdated applications that rely on the NetBIOS API to use a TCP/IP-based network. Also known as NBT.
Network Time Protocol (NTP)	123	Synchronizes time between network devices.
Post Office Protocol version 3 (**POP3**)	110	Supports email retrieval and stores email on a single network device. (Contrast with IMAP.)
Remote Desktop Protocol **(RDP**)	3389	Connects one Windows computer to a remote Windows computer.
Secure File Transfer Protocol (SFTP)	22	Supports file transfer using the SSH protocol suite.
Secure Shell (**SSH**)	22	Supports secure connectivity to a remote device and allows secure file transfer.
Server Message Block (SMB)/Common Internet File System (CIFS)	445	Provides access to shared network devices, files, and printers, especially in a mixed environment, such as a network consisting of Mac and Windows computers. CIFS is a version of SMB. SMB/CIFS can use TCP port 445, but when used with the NetBIOS API, UDP ports 137 and 138 as well as TCP ports 137 and 139 are used. (See NBT.)

Protocol	Common port number(s)	Description
Service Location Protocol (SLP)	427	Announces and discovers services in a LAN.
Simple Mail Transfer Protocol (**SMTP**)	25	Transmits email and is commonly used with MIME (Multipurpose Internet Mail Extensions) to include non-ASCII character sets and other rich media content within email.
Simple Network Management Protocol (**SNMP**)	161/162	Used to monitor, communicate with, and manage network devices.
Telnet	23	Supports connecting to a remote network device; is not secure.

TABLE 13.30 TCP/IP layers and associated protocols/standards

Layer	Protocols
Application	HTTP, HTTPS, Telnet, SSH, FTP, SFTP, DNS
Transport	TCP, UDP
Internet (internetwork)	IP, DHCP, ICMP
Network access	ARP, 802.3 (Ethernet), 802.11a, b, g, n, ac, and ax (wireless)

Networking protocols can seem a bit overwhelming at times, but remember that each one is just a set of rules for a specific purpose.

One more aspect of protocols that you need to understand is how TCP and UDP differ. What they have in common is that they both operate at the transport layer of the TCP/IP model, and they both work on port numbers. What is different is that TCP has a bigger header that contains features that let it do a lot more things, like make sure the destination connection is available and stay in constant contact with the destination during the data transfer. This is called being **connection-oriented**. Most of the TCP/IP protocols are connection-oriented, including HTTP, HTTPS, and SSH. Another feature of TCP is that if any data is lost along the way, it is re-sent.

In contrast, UDP is considered to be a **connectionless** protocol. I think of this as throwing a baseball (the data) and just hoping it gets to the destination. There are no "do overs," and data is not re-sent. UDP transfers are faster than TCP transfers. Some application layer protocols that use UDP are DHCP and TFTP. The voice data in VoIP calls is sent using UDP because VoIP cannot tolerate delay. DNS servers can actually use both TCP and UDP.

More Windows Network Settings

When you first configure a computer, you have to specify whether the computer is on a private network, such as your home or corporate network, or on a public network. This can be changed using the Windows *Network & Internet* Settings link, as shown in Figure 13.87. Once you select the *Properties* button from whatever type of network connection you are using, you can select whether the computer has a public or private network profile, as shown in Figure 13.88.

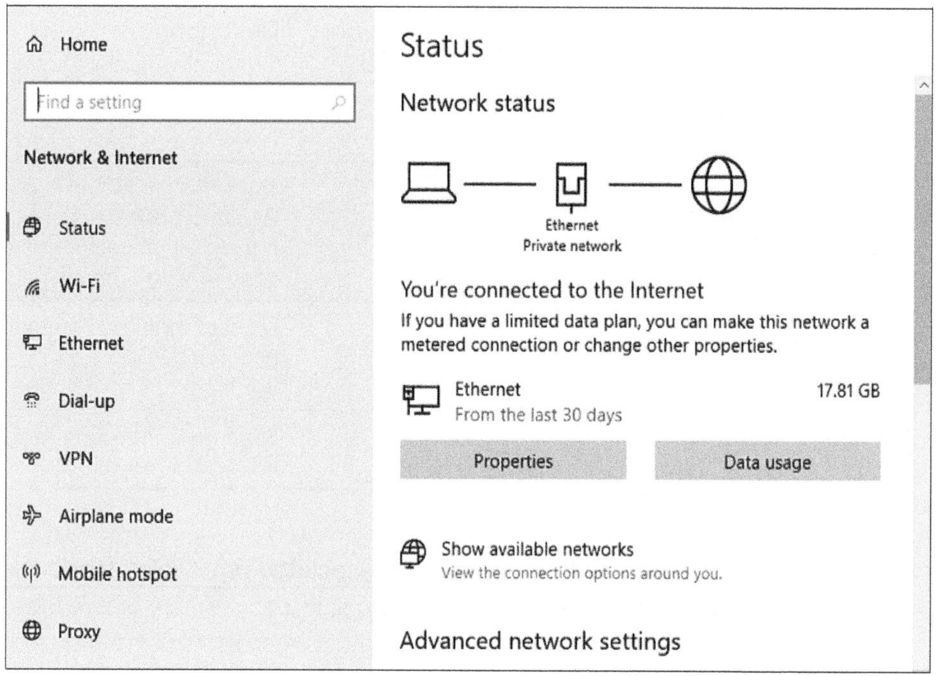

FIGURE 13.87 Windows Network & Internet options

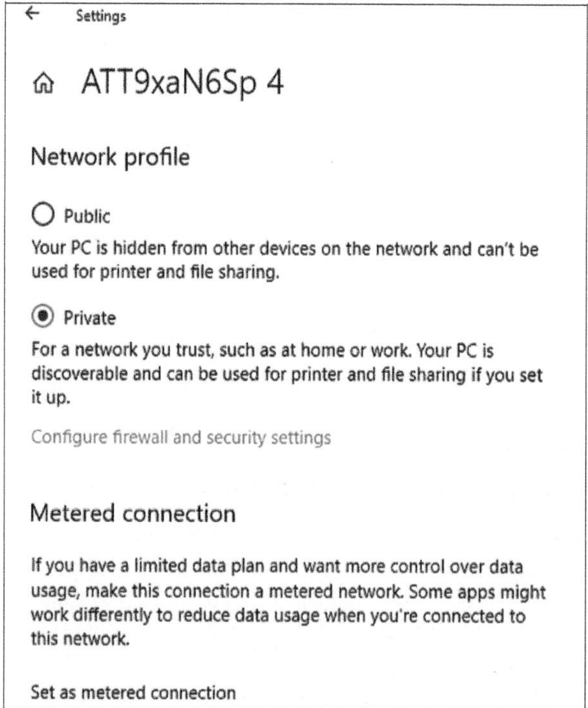

FIGURE 13.88 Windows public or private network profile

Notice at the bottom of Figure 13.88 the section for a metered connection. A **metered connection** is an internet connection that has a data limit imposed by the internet provider. You may be familiar with this because of your cell phone and cellular plan. Wi-Fi and Ethernet network connections can also be configured to be metered.

Even though you can control many things from the notification area or from some of the Settings options on Windows 8, 10, and 11, many network configuration settings are still done through the *Network and Sharing Center* Control Panel. The *Network and Sharing Center* Control

Panel has been used both in this chapter and in Chapter 12, "Internet Connectivity, Virtualization, and Cloud Technologies," but knowing the details and purpose of the options is important to IT personnel. Figure 13.89 shows the *Network and Sharing Center* window.

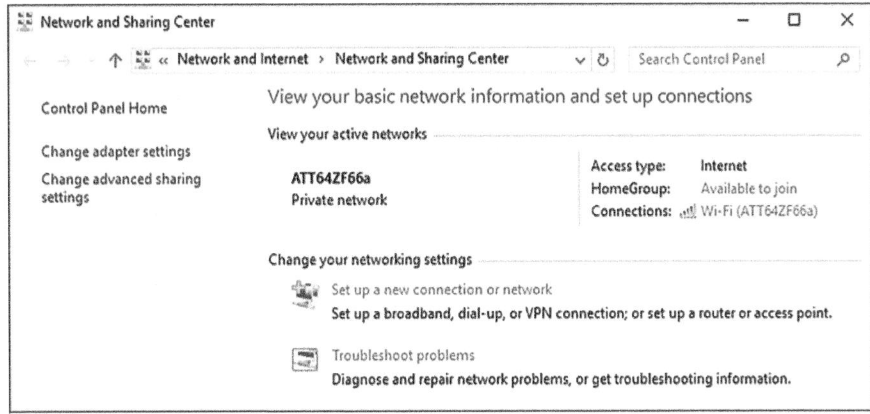

FIGURE 13.89 Windows Network and Sharing Center window

Notice in the main portion of the screen that you can see what network is currently being used. You can see whether the connection is wired or wireless and the name of the network. You can also tell in home or small business networks if the computer can share files with other devices (which is covered in the next section).

There are two important links in the left pane: *Change adapter settings* and *Change advanced sharing settings*. The *Change adapter settings* link enables you to access the network adapters that are installed, as shown in Figure 13.90. If a network adapter that is installed in the computer is not listed, use *Device Manager* to troubleshoot and ensure that the device is enabled through UEFI/system BIOS.

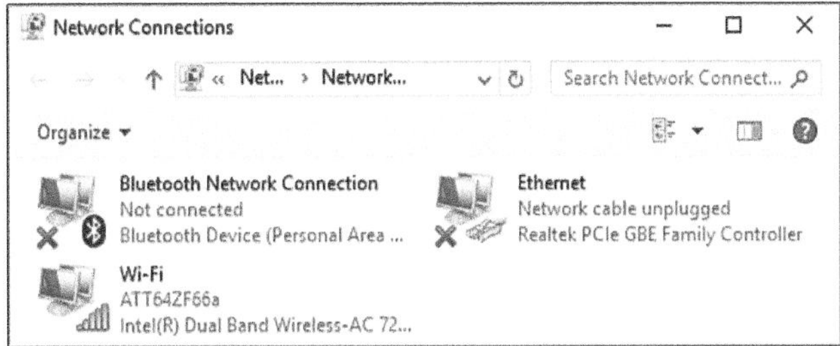

FIGURE 13.90 Windows 10 Network Connections window

The *Network Connections* window is important when configuring an adapter. In it you can perform some of the following tasks:

> Double-click the adapter icon to view device information. A wireless NIC shows wireless connectivity (see Figure 13.91), a wired NIC shows the wired network information (see Figure 13.92), and a Bluetooth adapter shows any Bluetooth pairs. At the bottom of each of the wired and wireless NIC windows, you can see the number of sent and received bytes.

> Select the *Details* button in the wireless or wired NIC windows (*Wi-Fi Status or Local Area Connection Status*) to see information similar to that provided with the `ipconfig /all` command (see Figure 13.93).

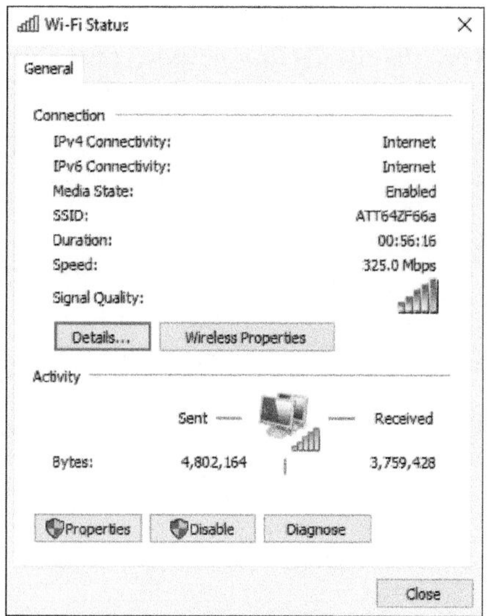

FIGURE 13.91 Wireless NIC window

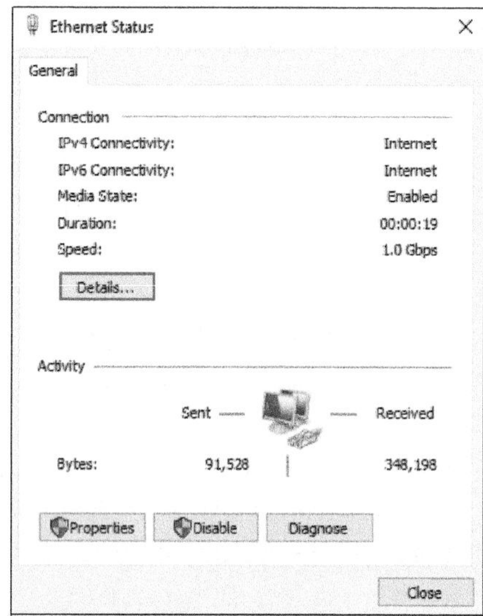

FIGURE 13.92 Wired NIC window

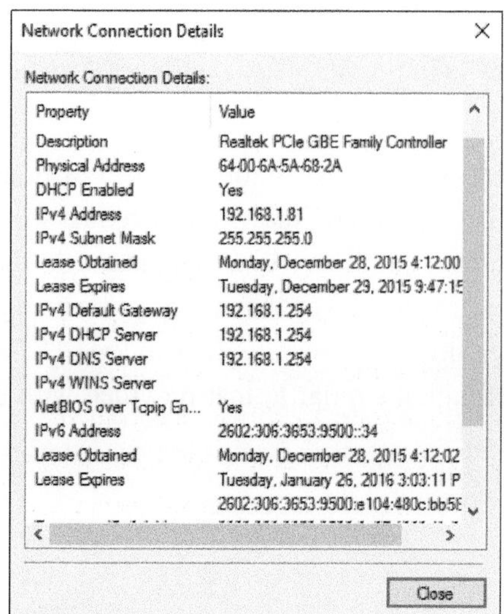

FIGURE 13.93 Wired or wireless NIC details

> Click the *Wireless Properties* button in the wireless NIC window (*Wi-Fi Status* window) to view information about the specific type of wireless network. Use the *Security* tab to view the type of security applied.

> In both the wireless and wired NIC windows, click the *Properties* button to manually configure the NIC properties or modify a connection, such as the TCP/IPv4 or TCP/IPv6 parameters (see Figure 13.94).

> Double-click the *Internet Protocol Version 4 (TCP/IPv4)* (or *TCP/IPv6*) link to configure the adapter for DHCP, statically assign an IP address (refer to Figure 13.58).

> Click or tap the *Configure* button to set wired or wireless NIC-related settings, such as speed and duplex.

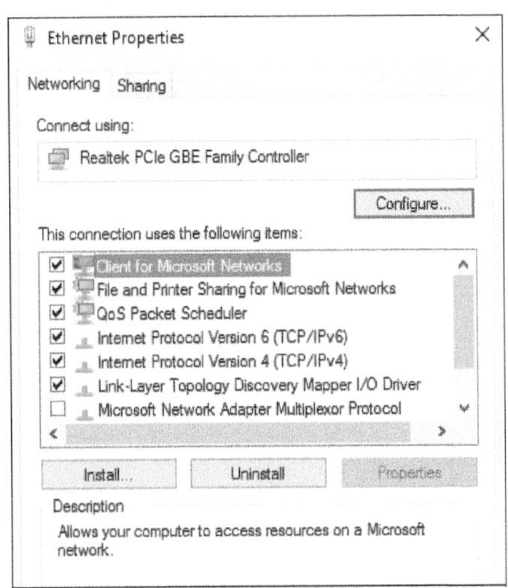

FIGURE 13.94 Wired or wireless networking properties window

> Manually configure the wireless NIC for a specific nonbroadcasting wireless network (refer to Figure 13.67).

> Set up a new Bluetooth connection. In Windows, access the *View Devices and Printers* Control Panel > *Add a Device* link. Ensure that the Bluetooth device is turned on and visible in the *Add a Device* window (see Figure 13.95). Select the device and click *Next*. Sometimes, a PIN or passcode must be verified in Windows and on the device.

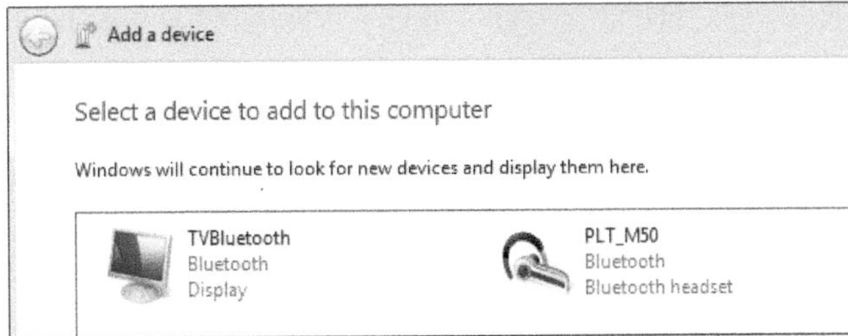

FIGURE 13.95 View Bluetooth devices in the Add a Device window

> Finally, from the *Network and Sharing Center* Control Panel, select *Change advanced sharing settings*. These settings relate to what the next section covers: sharing information across the networks you are now familiar with. Figure 13.96 shows the *Advanced sharing settings* window. Notice in the figure that there are three distinct and expandable sections: Private, Guest or Public, and All Networks. The Private section has been expanded so you can see the available options.

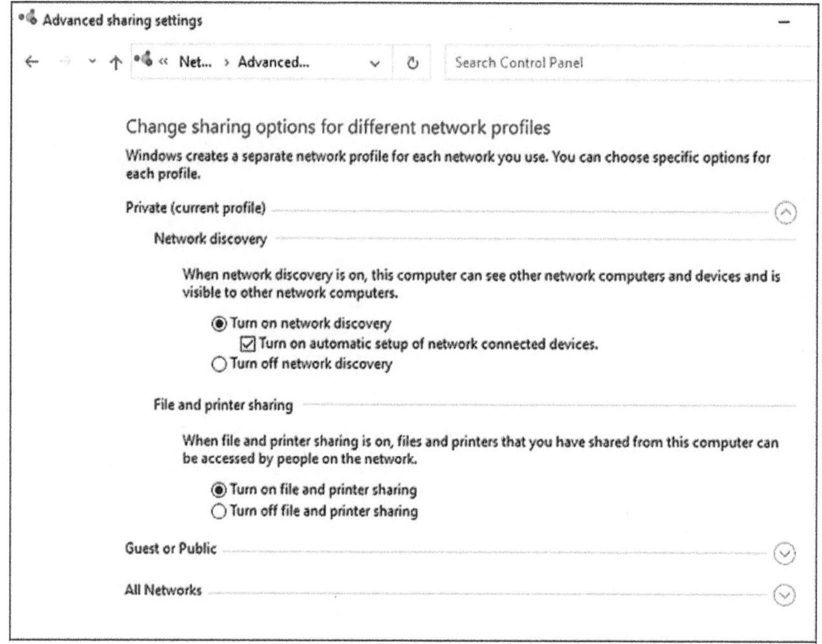

FIGURE 13.96 Advanced Sharing Settings window

Introduction to Shared Folders

When you double-click the *Network* option in Windows Explorer (Windows 7) or File Explorer (Windows 8/10/11), you can view other network devices by their assigned names. You can also view network device names by typing `nbtstat -n` at a command prompt. Knowing a network device name is important when accessing a network share across the network. A **network share** is a folder or device that has been shared and is accessible from a remote network device.

Using the Sharing Tab > Share Button

You can set up any Windows computer as a file server and share files with other network devices. If you right-click on any folder and select *Properties* > *Sharing* tab, you can share documents within a folder two different ways. The most common way is with the *Share* button (See Figure 13.97).

FIGURE 13.97 Sharing tab > Share button

Once you click on the Share button, you must choose the username to share the document with by clicking the down arrow, selecting a name or creating a new user, clicking the *Add* button > *Share* button (see Figure 13.98).

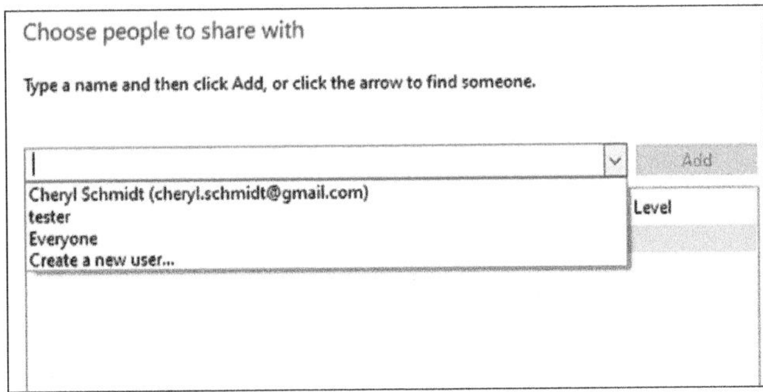

FIGURE 13.98 Adding a username to share the folder with

Once you click the *Share* button, the network path appears in the properties window, as shown in Figure 13.99.

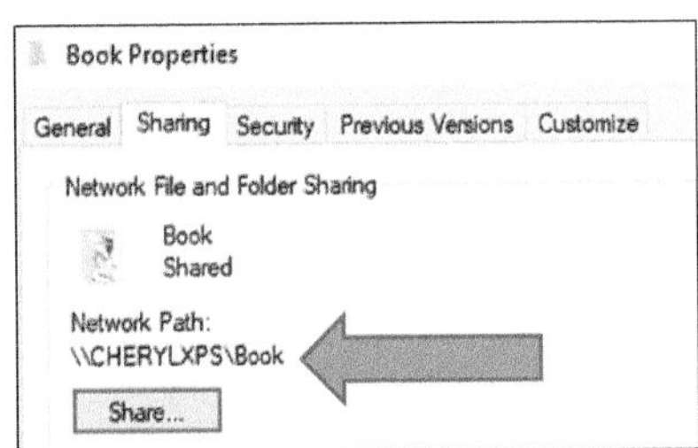

FIGURE 13.99 Network path

The network path is important to know when creating network shares. The **network path** is similar to driving locations to a restaurant except that it is how to get to something shared on the network from a remote device. The network path can be used from the command prompt or File Explorer to access the folder quickly. The network path can be the full path to get to the document or shown using the Universal Naming Convention (UNC). For example, say that a computer called *CSchmidt* has a network share called *TESTS*. By typing `\\CSchmidt\TESTS` at the command prompt, you can access the network share. Or you can type the IP address of the computer instead of the computer UNC. For example, if the CSchmidt computer had IP address 192.168.10.5, you could use `\\192.168.10.5\TESTS` from the command prompt instead. The problem with this method is that computer IP addresses are commonly provided by DHCP and could change. Next week, the CSchmidt computer could have the IP address 192.168.10.77, and the command would have to be adjusted. The *Advanced Sharing* button can also be used to create a network share (see Chapter 18).

Mapping to a Share

In a network, it is common to map a drive letter to a frequently used network share. To map a drive letter to a network share in Windows 7, click the *Start* button > *Computer* > *Map Network Drive* > select a drive letter in the *Drive* box > in the *Folder* textbox type the UNC for the network share or click the *Browse* button to select the network share. The *Reconnect at logon* checkbox allows you to connect to the mapped drive every time you log on.

In Windows 8/10/11, use File Explorer to locate and right-click *This PC* > *Map Network Drive* (though note that in Windows 11 you might have to select *Show more options* to see) > select a drive letter in the *Drive* box > in the *Folder* textbox type the UNC for the network share or click the *Browse* button to select the network share. The *Reconnect at sign-in* checkbox allows you to connect to the mapped drive every time you log on. Figure 13.100 shows the windows to map drive letter `Z:` to the shared folder on the computer called CHERYL-PC. Expand the CHERYL-PC option to see the shared folders on this computer.

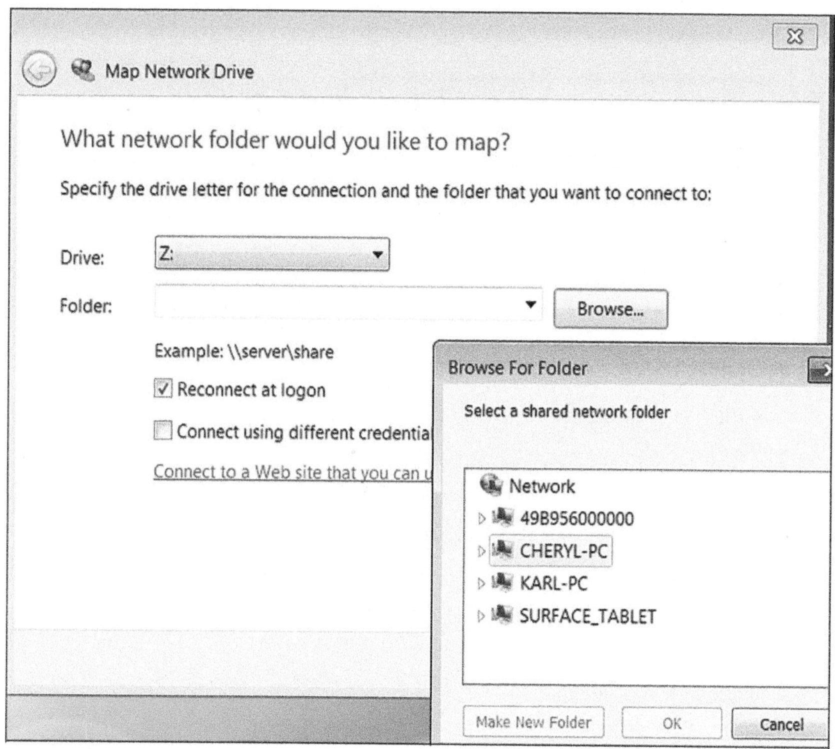

FIGURE 13.100 Windows Map Network Drive window

> **TECH TIP**
>
> **Seeing a mapped drive path in File Explorer**
>
> Select *This PC* and expand *Network locations*. Double-click the mapped drive to see the network path.

> **TECH TIP**
>
> **Mapping from a prompt**
>
> A drive can be mapped from a command prompt. Use the `net /?` command for more help. For example, say that a computer with the name *TECH01* has a share called *Cheryl*. The following command can be used to attach to it using the drive letter `M:`

```
net use m: /persistent:yes \\TECH01\Cheryl
```

Computer users commonly have frequently used network shares mapped to drive letters. It is faster to access a network share by drive letter than by searching around for the share through the *File Explorer Network* option.

SOFT SKILLS: BEING PROACTIVE

A good technician is **proactive**, which means the technician thinks of ways to improve a situation, anticipates problems, and fixes problems before being told to. A proactive technician follows up after a service call to ensure that a repair fixed the problem rather than waiting for another help desk ticket that states that the problem is unresolved. When something happens or a problem with a customer occurs, a proactive technician provides a list of recommended solutions or procedural changes to the supervisor rather than waiting for the supervisor to delineate what changes must occur.

For example, consider a technician at a college. The technician is responsible for any problems logged by computer users through the help desk. The technician is also responsible for maintaining the computer classrooms used by various departments. Each term, the technician reloads the computers with software updates and changes requested by the teachers. A proactive technician checks each machine and ensures that the computers boot properly and that the load is successful.

Another example involves checking new software. When the computers are reloaded each term, a faculty member is asked to check the load. A proactive technician has a list of "standard" software loaded on the computer, such as the operating system, service pack level, and any applications that are standard throughout the college. A separate list would include the changes that have been applied to the computer. Then the faculty member can simply look at the list and verify the load. Being proactive actually saves time for both the technician and the faculty member.

The opposite of proactive is *reactive*. A reactive technician responds to situations only when there is a problem reported. A reactive technician does not look for ways to avoid problems. For example, a proactive technician ensures that a computer is configured with automatic updates of virus scanning software. A reactive technician waits until a help desk ticket is created for a computer that exhibits unusual behavior (for example, it has a virus) even though the technician notices the unusual behavior when installing a second monitor.

As a student, practice being proactive. Start an assignment a day before you would normally start it. Talk to your teacher about your grade in advance (before the day preceding the final). Bring to school something to write with and paper. Finally, take this practice into your IT career: Be proactive as an IT professional and increase the level of service and professionalism in the field.

Chapter Summary

- Networks are created to share data and devices and connect to the internet. Types of networks include PANs, LANs, MANs, SANs, WANs, and WMNs.
- Networks can be wired or wireless.
- A workgroup network is composed of a small number of computers, whereas larger companies use a domain environment. A domain environment has a server that provides authentication to resources with a centralized user ID and password. A workgroup network manages the usernames on a computer-by-computer basis, which grows less secure and more difficult to manage as the network grows.
- An Ethernet LAN, which is the most common type of LAN, is wired in a star or extended star topology. A switch is used to connect the devices. Each network connects to a router for communication with other networks. The router's IP address is the default gateway for all network devices on a particular LAN.
- Computers must have IP addresses to participate in a TCP/IP-based network (and gain access to the internet). IPv4 is the most common addressing used on computers today, but IPv6 addresses are slowly being assigned and used by corporate devices and internet providers.

> IP addresses are grouped by classes, with a particular subnet mask for each class. Each default mask can be changed to further subdivide a network for more efficient and manageable addressing. DHCP can provide addresses to network devices, or a static address can be assigned. Public addresses are routable on the internet. Private addresses are used within homes and companies.
> TCP/IP is a suite that includes the following important protocols: FTP, Telnet, SMTP, DNS, DHCP, HTTP, HTTPS, POP3, IMAP, RDP, LDAP, SNMP, SSH, SFTP, SMB/CIFS, TCP, UDP, IP, and ICMP.
> The OSI model is a networking model that has seven layers: application, presentation, session, transport, network, data link, and physical. The TCP/IP model is a working model that contains four layers: application, transport, internet (internetwork), and network access. The devices and applications that work at Layer 3 (network or internet layers) include routers, IP, and ICMP. The devices and applications that work at Layer 2 (data link or network access) include switches, access points, and ARP. Keep in mind that Ethernet has Layer 2 specifications. This is why a MAC address is a Layer 2 address. The devices that work at Layer 1 (physical layer or network access layer) are cables, connectors, hubs, and wireless antennas.
> 802.11 and Bluetooth are wireless network technologies. Bluetooth is used in PANs, and 802.11 is used in wireless LANs. 802.11 wireless NICs include 802.11a, b, g, n, ac, and ax. 802.11a, n, ac, and ax work in the 5 GHz range; 802.11b, g, n, and ax work in the 2.4 GHz range. 802.11ax also functions in the 6 GHz range using Wi-Fi 6E. 802.11 antennas are either directional or omnidirectional.
> The key tools for troubleshooting a networked computer are the `ipconfig`, `ping`, `pathping`, `nslookup`, and `tracert` commands and a cable tester.
> A technician should be proactive as opposed to reactive and should prevent problems and situations whenever possible.

A+ CERTIFICATION EXAM TIPS

✓ This chapter provides information related to both the 220-1101 and 220-1102 exams. The information related to the 1102 exam includes the *Network and Sharing Center* Control Panel, *Network & Internet* settings, and network client configuration (including IP addressing scheme, DNS settings, subnet mask, gateway, static and dynamic addressing, wired network connection, wireless, wireless WWAN [cellular], network-related commands—`ipconfig`, `ifconfig`, `nslookup`, `tracert`, `netstat`, `net use`, `net user`, `pathping`, and `ping`—NIC properties, network shares, and drive mapping).

✓ Know the difference between a LAN, WAN, PAN, MAN, SAN, and WLAN.

✓ Know the purposes of these network devices: hubs, routers, access points, firewalls, patch panels, cable/DSL modems (see Chapter 12), repeaters, PoE devices (injectors and switches), and switches (both managed and unmanaged). Also be able to describe how software-defined networking (SDN) takes functions normally provided in hardware by dividing functions into the control and data planes.

✓ Know the purposes of key networking protocols, port numbers used by the protocols, and the differences between TCP and UDP.

✓ Know when to use a particular type of networking tool, whether it is a physical tool or a command. Physical tools include crimpers, cable strippers, Wi-Fi analyzers, toner probes, punchdown tools, cable testers, loopback plugs, and network taps.

✓ Describe how a hub and switch operate and the differences between the two. Know what a VLAN is and how it is configured on a switch.

- ✓ Know what to do when one or more computers cannot connect to the internet or when they have an IP address conflict. Be able to tell whether the problem is an internet connection problem or what specific network resources the device can't reach, such as network shares, printers, or email.
- ✓ Know how to manually configure an IP address on a network device such as a computer, an AP, or a printer.
- ✓ Know the different types of wireless networks and their compatibility with each other.
- ✓ Be able to configure a wireless network and 2.4 GHz and 5 GHz channels so multiple wireless APs can coexist as well as other parameters, such as an administrator password and DHCP.
- ✓ Know the purpose of an IP address, a default gateway, and a subnet mask.
- ✓ Know the difference between an IPv4 address and an IPv6 address.
- ✓ Recognize when an address is a private IP address and understand the difference between a public IP address and a private IP address.
- ✓ Be familiar with DHCP terminology such as leases, reservations, and scope.
- ✓ Know the different types of network cabling and connectors.
- ✓ Recognize when a computer gets assigned an IP address from APIPA.
- ✓ Know the port numbers and purposes of the following protocols as well as the differences between TCP and UDP: 20/21 (FTP), 22 (SSH), 23 (Telnet), 25 (SMTP), 53 (DNS), 67/68 (DHCP), 80 (HTTP), 110 (POP3), 143 (IMAP), 443 (HTTPS), 3389 (RDP), 137–139 (NetBIOS/NetBT), 161–162 (SNMP), 389 (LDAP), 445 (SMB/CIFS).
- ✓ Know the purposes of different servers: web, fileshare, print, DHCP, DNS, mail, syslog, and authentication (AAA).
- ✓ Review the section on troubleshooting network printer problems.
- ✓ If a wireless laptop cannot get on a wireless network, you might have to forget the network, reconnect, and provide credentials. You can also check to see if wireless has been disabled.
- ✓ Be able to recognize and troubleshoot problems with IP addressing information that comes from a DHCP server (including IP address, default gateway, subnet mask, and DNS server address).
- ✓ Be able to troubleshoot wireless problems. Move the device to a different location. Make sure that the wireless NIC is turned on.
- ✓ Be able to use the `ipconfig` command and review the options available (`ipconfig /?` to see).
- ✓ Know the difference between how a hub operates and how a switch operates.
- ✓ Review the different DNS message types: A, AAAA, MX, and TXT.
- ✓ Be able to describe the services provided by IoT devices and legacy/embedded systems like SCADA.

Key Terms

2.4 GHz 581
5 GHz 581
6 GHz 581
802.11a 582
802.11ac (Wi-Fi 5) 583
802.11ad 583
802.11ax (Wi-Fi 6) 583
802.11b 582
802.11e 583
802.11g 583
802.11i 583
802.11n 583
A record 600
AAA server 622
AAAA record 600
access point 583
AES 602
APIPA 598
Bluetooth 553
broadcast address 579
cable management system 570
cable stripper 563
cable tester 565
Cat 5 560
Cat 5e 560
Cat 6 560
Cat 6a 560
channel 588
CIDR 581
CIFS 620

client-side DNS 600
connection-oriented 627
connectionless 627
content filtering 608
control plane 623
crimper 563
crossover cable 562
data plane 623
default gateway 599
DHCP 596
DHCP lease time 597
DHCP reservation 597
DHCP scope 596
DHCP server 596
direct burial cable 560
directional antenna 591
DMZ 608
DNS 599
DNS server 599
domain 555
duplex 603
embedded system 622
Ethernet 553
Ethernet over Power 568
external interference 592
FC 559
fileshare server 622
firewall 575
firmware 608
FTP 626
gateway 599
high latency 614
host address 578
HTTP 626
HTTPS 626
hub 554
`ifconfig` 613
IMAP 626
intermittent connectivity 611
intermittent wireless connectivity 592
IoT 609
IP address 576
IP addressing scheme 579
IP filtering 608
`ipconfig` 613
IPv4 577
IPv6 577
iSCSI 559
LAN 552
LDAP 626
legacy system 623
limited connectivity 611
link-local address 577
loopback plug 572
low RF signal 593
MAC address 576
mail server 622
MAN 552
managed switch 554
metered connection 628
MIMO 593
MU-MIMO 593
MX record 600
`net` 616
`net use` 616
`net user` 616
NetBT 626
`netstat` 625
network number 578
network path 633
network protocol 575
network share 632
no connectivity 611
no internet connectivity 611
`nslookup` 615
omnidirectional antenna 591
OSI model 573
PAN 552
patch panel 565
`pathping` 614
`ping` 611
plenum cable 561
PoE 567
PoE injector 568
PoE switch 568
POP3 626
port flapping 612
port forwarding 608
port mapping 608
print server 622
printer sharing 619
private IP address 578
private network 557
proactive 635
proxy server 622
public IP address 578
public network 557
punchdown tool 572
PVC 561
QoS 603
RDP 626
Remote Desktop Services 605
RJ11 561
RJ45 561
router 575
SAN 552
SCADA 622
screened subnet 608
site survey 592
slow network speed 593
SMB 620
SMTP 627
SNMP 627
speed (NIC property) 603
SSH 626
SSID 585
SSID not found 601
STP 560
straight-through cable 562
subnet mask 580
switch 554
syslog server 622
T568A 562
T568B 562
TCP 625
TCP/IP 575
Telnet 627
TKIP 602
tone generator 572
toner probe 572
`tracert` 614
twisted pair cable 560
UDP 625
unavailable resources 612
unmanaged switch 554
UPnP 608
UTP 560
virtual NIC 603
VLAN 580
Wake on LAN 603
WAN 552
web server 622
WEP 602
Wi-Fi analyzer 593
wireless extender 586
wireless regulations 590
WLAN 552
WMN 552
workgroup 555
WPA 602
WPA2 602
WPA3 602
WWAN 552
Zigbee 610
Z-Wave 610

Review Questions

1. Match the network type on the left with the scenario on the right.

____ MAN	**a.** Home network of four PCs
____ SAN	**b.** City of Schmidtville networks
____ PAN	**c.** Hewlett-Packard corporate networks
____ WAN	**d.** Bluetooth network of two devices
____ LAN	**e.** Data storage for a company

2. Match the following. Note that even though an answer may be valid for more than one answer, only one answer will allow all answers to be used. No term is used twice.

a. Cat 8	____ Common type of LAN cable
b. Cat 6a UTP	____ 1 Gbps over UTP
c. 1000BaseT	____ Can only use STP
d. 1000BaseSX	____ 1 Gbps over fiber

3. Which network device would be best to use to connect wired devices, is common for this purpose, and can send data directly to the destination device without sending the data as a broadcast to every connected device?

   [Access point | Hub | Router | Switch]

4. Match each TCP/IP model layer to a description. Note that a layer can be used more than once.

a. Application	____ HTTP	____ a straight-through cable	____ a NIC
b. Transport	____ a router	____ UDP	____ DNS
c. Internet	____ a switch	____ IP	____ TCP
d. Network access	____ ICMP	____ MAC address	____ a wireless antenna

5. Some computers (both wired and wireless) in a specific area of the building are having problems connecting to printers, servers, and the internet. What should the technician do?

   a. Use a tone generator.

   b. Check the access point.

   c. Check the router that connects to the internet.

   d. Check problem computers for a DNS server address.

6. Software-defined networking splits tasks into which two major areas?

   a. Data plane and control plane

   b. 2.4 GHz and 5 GHz

   c. UTP and STP

   d. Network and transport

7. Which network device works at Layer 1 and sends received data out all its ports (except the port that received the data)?

   [Switch | Antenna | Router | Hub]

8. What is the most common network protocol suite and the protocol suite required to communicate on the internet?

   [LTE | TCP/IP | Bluetooth | ISO]

9. Which type of address is 48 bits long and is hard coded into a NIC?
   [IP | TCP | MAC | NAT]

10. Which type of address is called a Layer 3 address and needed to get to the internet?
    [IP | TCP | MAC | NAT]

11. Which type of IP address uses 128 bits? [IPv4 | IPv32 | IPv6 | IPv64]

12. Draw a vertical line between the network number and the host number for each of the following IP addresses (assuming the default subnet mask):

    130.5.15.177 130.5.| 15.177

    192.168.13.15 192.168.13.| 15

    10.12.17.18 10.| 12.17.18

13. What protocol could be used to issue an IP address and the IP address of the DNS server to network devices?

    [DNS | DHCP | ICMP | ARP]

14. What protocol is used to convert URLs to IP addresses?

    [HTTP | SSH | SSL | UDP | DNS]

15. Two access points connect and extend *the same* wireless network. List the SSIDs for each access point in the following chart.

Access point	SSID
Access Point 1	
Access Point 2	

16. Two access points (AP1 and AP2) operating in the 2.4 GHz range have overlapping coverage areas. List the two channel IDs to assign to each access point by filling in the following chart.

Access point	Channel ID
AP1	
AP2	

17. Which connectors are commonly used on network ports that connect to a SAN? (Choose two.)

    [RJ11 | RG-59 | FC | SATA | iSCSI]

18. A user has shared a folder with her corporate team. What information will the user need to give co-workers to enable them to easily access the shared documents across the network?

    [UNC | IP address of the computer that has the shared folder | MAC address of the computer with the shared folder | Network path for shared folder]

19. Match each technology to the appropriate definition. Note that not all of the definitions are used.

____ 802.11a	**a.** Operates in the 2.4 GHz range, with speeds up to 54 Mbps
____ 802.11b	**b.** Operates in the 2.4 GHz range, with speeds up to 2 Mbps
____ 802.11g	**c.** Operates in the 2.4 GHz range, with speeds up to 11 Mbps
____ 802.11i	**d.** Security specification
____ 802.11n	**e.** Operates in the 5 GHz range, with speeds up to 54 Mbps
____ 802.11ac	**f.** Specifies interoperability between access points
____ 802.11ax	**g.** Standard for quality of service
	h. Standard for wireless interference
	i. Backward compatible with 802.11a, b, and g
	j. Allows eight simultaneous data streams
	k. Allows access to 6 GHz range with Wi-Fi 6E

20. In Figure 13.101, what IP address is the default gateway for host 203.145.15.2?

____

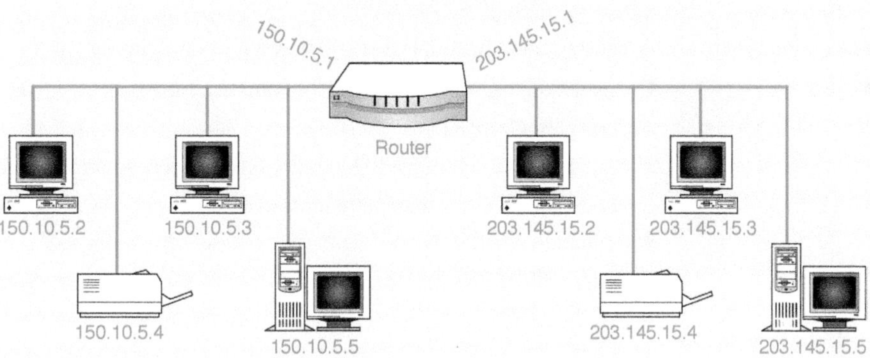

FIGURE 13.101 Review question network scenario

21. Which command determines whether another network device is reachable?

    [`ping` | `ipconfig` | `ipconfig /all` | `arp -a`]

22. On which network device would VLANs be configured?

    [Hub | Switch | Router | Firewall]

23. Which port numbers are used by a protocol whose purpose is to allow remote connectivity to a network device such as a server or router in order to make changes to the device? (Choose two.)

    [21 | 22 | 23 | 53 | 69 | 80 | 443]

24. What command can be used to see a computer's MAC address?

    [`netdom` | `net` | `netstat` | `ipconfig /all`]

25. A technician is setting up a new printer and notices that the computer is running unusually slowly. The technician decides to not only do the job that was logged (install the new printer) but also investigate the computer issue. Is the technician being reactive or proactive?

    [Proactive | Reactive]

Exercises

Exercise 13.1 Understanding Wireless AP Paper Configuration

Objective: To determine what menu items would be used for specific functions

Procedure: Use the given menu options to determine which one would be used to perform a common configuration task on a wireless AP.

Note: Many times an IT professional must deal with a device or a particular model that is unfamiliar. Many wireless AP menus are similar, so practicing which menu option might be the one chosen is a good activity.

Wireless AP sample menu and submenu options:

a. *Setup:* Language, Date/Time

b. *Wireless:* Basic Wireless Settings, Wireless Security, Wireless MAC Filter, Advanced Wireless Settings

c. *WAN/LAN:* Internet Setup and Network Setup

d. *Administration:* Management, Access, Security, Factory Defaults, Firmware Upgrade

e. *Status:* Access Point, Wireless Network, About

Select which menu option would be used to do each of the following tasks:

____ **1.** Change the password used to access the AP menu.

____ **2.** Configure UPnP.

____ **3.** Configure to only allow 802.11n 2.4 GHz devices to attach (not 802.11b or g).

____ **4.** Check connectivity with another device.

____ **5.** Change the SSID.

____ **6.** Disable SSID broadcasting.

____ **7.** Configure the device as a DHCP server for wireless clients.

____ **8.** Set the year.

____ **9.** Reset the device.

____ **10.** Determine how many wireless hosts are currently attached to the AP.

Exercise 13.2 Understanding T568B Color Sequence

Objective: To articulate the proper color order of a T568B straight-through cable

Procedure: Use the given graphic to denote which color of cable goes into the connector from left to right.

Use Figure 13.102 to designate which colors of vinyl insulator should go into making a T568B connector.

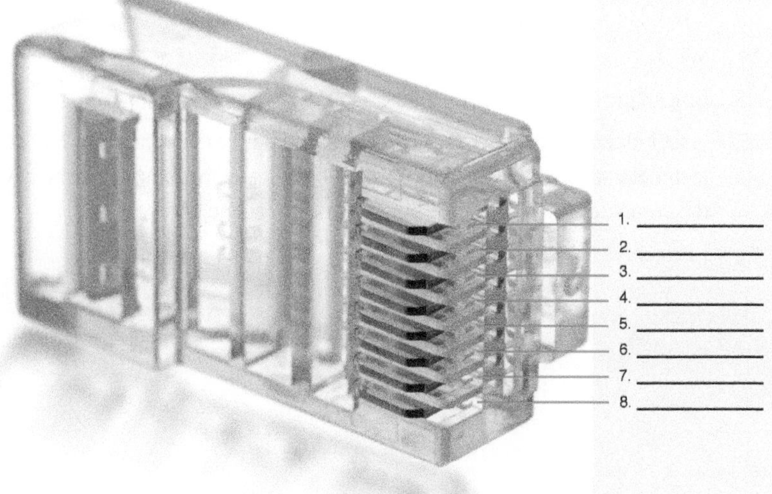

FIGURE 13.102 RJ45 connector/cabling exercise

Exercise 13.3 Recognizing Network Devices

Objective: To recognize a network device on sight

Procedure: Use Figure 13.103 to identify each network device.

Note: Possible answers could include the following. Note that not all devices are used. No device is shown twice.

Possible devices:

Internet router	Termination plate	Switch
Hub	Patch panel	Repeater
Bridge	Wireless router	Firewall

A

B

C

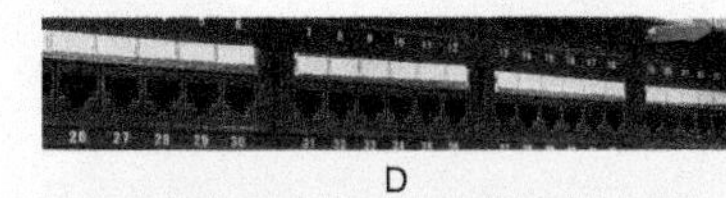
D

E

FIGURE 13.103 Network device identification

a. ____________________

b. ____________________

c. ____________________

d. ____________________

e. ____________________

Exercise 13.4 Identifying Basic Wireless Network Parts

Objective: To identify basic parts of a wireless network and determine the type of wireless network used

Procedure: Using Figure 13.104, identify the major parts of a wireless network. For the number 5 blank, document whether this network would most likely be for a home or a corporate network and explain why.

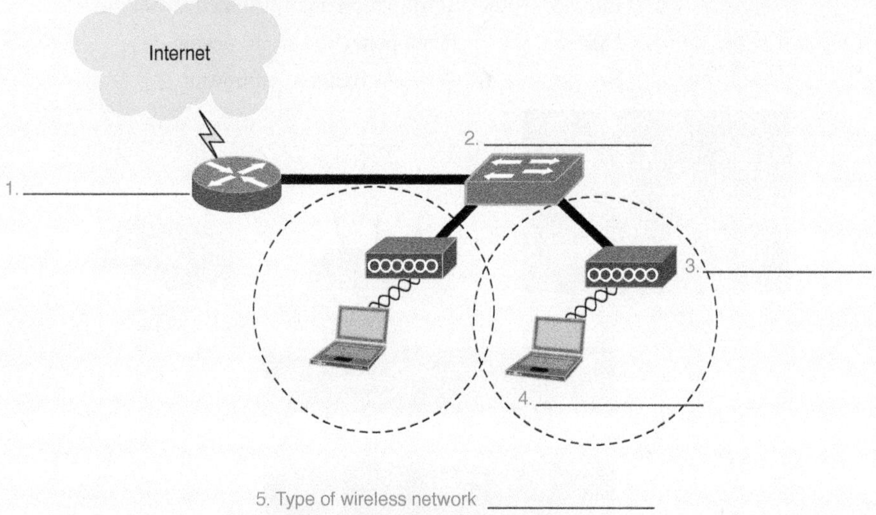

FIGURE 13.104 Wireless network components

1. ____________________
2. ____________________
3. ____________________
4. ____________________
5. ____________________

Exercise 13.5 Creating a Wireless Network

Objective: To design and price a wireless network based on the parameters given

Parts: Computer with internet access

Note: The instructor or lab assistant can speak on behalf of the faculty members if any design questions arise.

Scenario: A building has just been renovated to include corporate offices, as shown in Figure 13.105. The only wired network connections are the two stations in the reception area and the plotter in the leftmost office area. All other connections are wireless.

FIGURE 13.105 Building floor plan for wireless design

Tasks:

1. Design a 2.4 GHz wireless network plan that will cover the reception area and all office stations to the right. Draw a circle over each coverage area and label each circle with a 2.4 GHz channel ID.
2. Design a 5 GHz wireless network plan that will cover the conference room and all remaining office areas. Draw a circle over each coverage area and label each circle with a 5 GHz channel ID.
3. Provide a detailed list of wireless network parts, part numbers, and prices, as well as a web link where the prices were obtained. Be sure to include the antenna type, a printout of the wireless antenna radiation pattern, and antenna coverage range.
4. Provide the instructor with a typewritten list of policies and configuration settings for the wireless network you have designed. You are the designer and implementer, and what you decide goes.

Exercise 13.6 Practicing with Network Numbers and Broadcast Addresses

Objective: To determine the subnet numbers, broadcast addresses, and IP addresses that can be assigned to network devices

Procedure: Complete the following procedure and answer the accompanying questions.

1. Determine the network address for each of the following IP addresses, assuming that the default subnet mask is used.

   210.141.254.122 ____________________

   206.240.195.38 ____________________

   14.130.188.213 ____________________

   129.89.5.224 ____________________

   110.113.71.66 ____________________

2. Determine the broadcast address for each of the following IP addresses, assuming that the default subnet mask is used.

166.215.207.182 _______________

198.94.140.121 _______________

97.57.210.192 _______________

133.98.227.36 _______________

14.89.203.133 _______________

Exercise 13.7 Practicing with CIDR Notation

Objective: To determine the appropriate CIDR notation based on a given subnet mask

Procedure: Complete the following procedure and answer the accompanying questions.

For each subnet mask given in dotted decimal notation, determine the equivalent CIDR notation.

255.255.255.0 _______

255.255.255.224 _______

255.255.255.252 _______

255.255.254.0 _______

255.255.0.0 _______

255.255.255.128 _______

255.255.255.192 _______

255.0.0.0 _______

255.255.240.0 _______

255.255.255.240 _______

Exercise 13.8 Determining the Default Gateway

Objective: To determine the appropriate default gateway for a PC based on a given situation.

Procedure: Complete the following procedure and answer the accompanying questions.

1. Determine the appropriate IP address, subnet mask (in dotted decimal notation, x.x.x.x), and default gateway for PC 1 shown in Figure 13.106.

   IP address: _______________________________

   Subnet mask: _______________________________

   Default gateway: _______________________________

2. Determine the appropriate IP address, subnet mask (in dotted decimal notation, x.x.x.x), and default gateway for PC 2 shown in Figure 13.106.

   IP address: _______________________________

   Subnet mask: _______________________________

   Default gateway: _______________________________

3. Determine the appropriate IP address, subnet mask (in dotted decimal notation, x.x.x.x), and default gateway for PC 3 shown in Figure 13.106.

   IP address: _______________________________

   Subnet mask: _______________________________

   Default gateway: _______________________________

4. Determine the appropriate IP address, subnet mask (in dotted decimal notation, x.x.x.x), and default gateway for PC 4 shown in Figure 13.106.

   IP address: _______________________________

   Subnet mask: _______________________________

   Default gateway: _______________________________

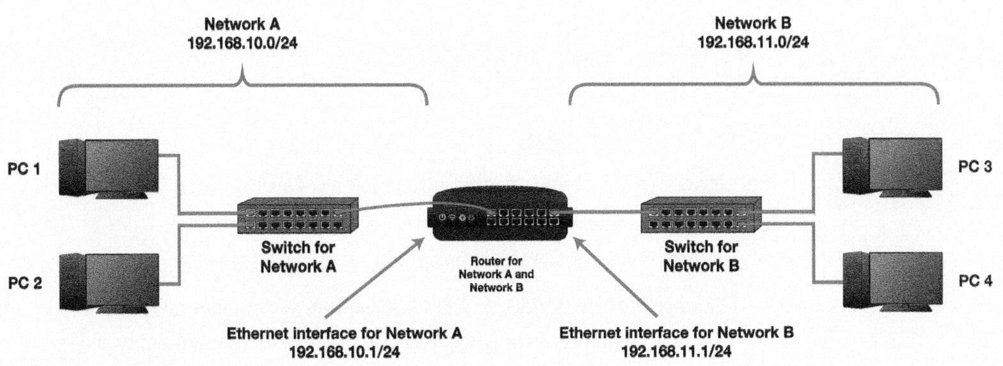

FIGURE 13.106 Network Topology 1

5. Determine the appropriate IP address, subnet mask (in dotted decimal notation, x.x.x.x), and default gateway for PC 1 shown in Figure 13.107.

   IP address: ______________________________

   Subnet mask: ______________________________

   Default gateway: ______________________________

6. Determine the appropriate IP address, subnet mask (in dotted decimal notation, x.x.x.x), and default gateway for PC 2 shown in Figure 13.107.

   IP address: ______________________________

   Subnet mask: ______________________________

   Default gateway: ______________________________

7. Determine the appropriate IP address, subnet mask (in dotted decimal notation, x.x.x.x), and default gateway for the printer shown in Figure 13.107.

   IP address: ______________________________

   Subnet mask: ______________________________

   Default gateway: ______________________________

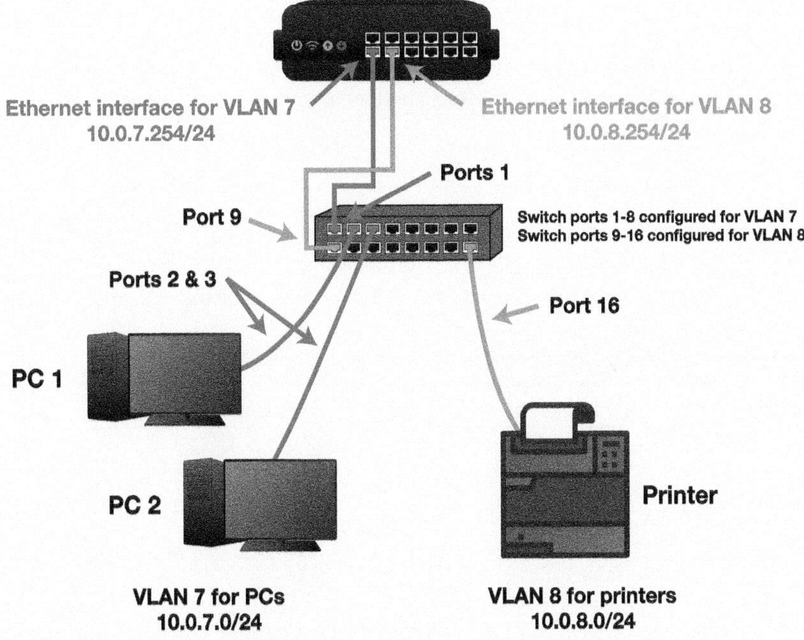

FIGURE 13.107 Network Topology 2

Activities

Internet Discovery

Objective: To obtain specific information regarding a computer or its associated parts on the internet

Parts: Computer with internet access

Procedure: Complete the following procedure and answer the accompanying questions.

1. On an HP ProBook 650 Windows 10 laptop, you cannot get the wireless NIC to attach to the wireless network. What are some steps you can take, as recommended by HP, to help in this situation?

   Write at least three solutions as well as the URL where you found the solution.

   ____

2. What does the term Wake on Wireless mean, and at what URL did you locate the answer?

   ____

3. Locate a website that describes how to reserve an IP address on a Netgear router. Write the one router model the answer applies to, the menu option used to configure it, and the URL where you found this information.

   ____

4. Find an internet forum that discusses Bluetooth and Windows 7 on Lenovo laptops. Write one key piece of information you found about configuring Bluetooth. Write the URL where you found the information.

   ____

5. Find a website that explains the differences between Cat 5e and Cat 6a UTP cable. Write which standard you would recommend to the CIO of your company and why. List the URL where you found this information.

   ____

Soft Skills

Objective: To enhance and fine-tune a technician's ability to listen, communicate in both written and oral forms, and support people who use computers in a professional manner

Activities:

1. Using the internet, find and access a utility that tests your soft skills. Compare your scores with those of others in the class and determine how you might improve in specific weak areas.
2. In groups of two, one person inserts a network problem in a computer while the other person is out of the room. When the other person comes back, they troubleshoot the problem by asking questions of the user (as if they were on the phone helping them). The person performing the troubleshooting cannot touch the computer. Discuss strategies for improving this troubleshooting process before swapping roles.
3. In groups of two or three, brainstorm three examples of a technician being reactive rather than proactive. List ways the technician could be more proactive for each example. Share your findings with other teams.

___

___

___

Critical Thinking Skills

Objective: To analyze and evaluate information as well as apply learned information to new or different situations

Activities:

1. A home user connects to the internet. The ISP provides hard drive space for the user's web page. Is this a network? Why or why not? Write your answer in a well-written paragraph using good grammar, capitalization, and punctuation.

   ___

   ___

   ___

   ___

   ___

2. Use the internet, magazines, newspapers, or books to find a network installation case study. Make a table of terms the case study uses that were introduced in this chapter. On the left side, list the term, and on the right side, define or describe how the term relates to the network installation. Analyze the installation and discuss with a team. Make a checklist of approved processes and of recommended changes to implemented processes. Share your team findings with the class.
3. In a team environment, design a wired and wireless network for a small business with 10 computers. Name the business, provide a design and implementation plan, and provide a list of items for which you should do more research. Share your plan with the class.

14 Introduction to Operating Systems

In this chapter you will learn:

- To identify the basic features and functions of an operating system
- To explain common types of operating systems and their uses: desktop, workstation, and mobile device operating systems
- To apply application installation and configuration concepts
- To identify end-of-life, compatibility, and updating operating system concerns
- To identify specific corporate needs
- To identify basic features of Microsoft Windows editions
- To identify and use common desktop icons in Windows
- To manage files and folders in Windows
- To use the appropriate Microsoft Windows Control Panel utility
- To work with the Windows registry
- To create backups and create a system image
- Techniques to stay current in the field

CompTIA Exam Objectives:

- ✓ 1102-1.1 Identify basic features of Microsoft Windows editions.
- ✓ 1102-1.3 Given a scenario, use features and tools of the Microsoft Windows 10 operating system (OS).
- ✓ 1102-1.4 Given a scenario, use the appropriate Microsoft Windows 10 Control Panel utility.
- ✓ 1102-1.7 Given a scenario, apply application installation and configuration concepts.
- ✓ 1102-1.8 Explain common OS types and their purposes.

Operating Systems Overview

The operating system (OS) is the most important piece of software on a computer because without it, no application can run and the hardware cannot work. While today's operating systems provide many services, the basic service of an **operating system** is to be the interface between the user and the hardware and software applications installed on or executed by the computer.

You might be wondering what kind of things an operating system can do. An operating system does many tasks, but some that really affect you as a student are recognizing what you type on the keyboard (or do using a mouse or a touchpad) and bringing that information into the computer as input. The operating system controls output to the display, keeps track of files and folders, manages and keeps track of open applications, and controls peripherals such as printers. Figure 14.1 shows that the operating system is the coordinator of all hardware and software. The operating system is the software that any computer device needs to function.

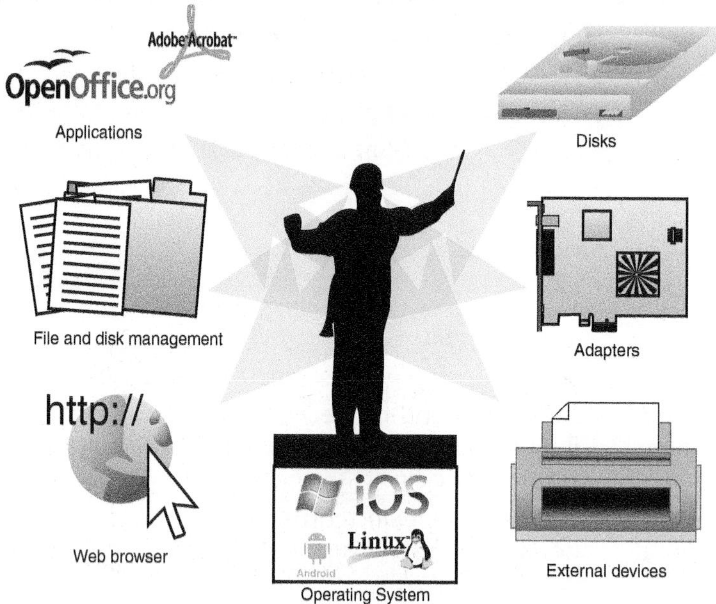

FIGURE 14.1 The operating system coordinates everything on a computer

The **boot process** is the steps a device goes through when a computer is first turned on. The central processing unit (CPU) initializes itself. It looks to the system's basic input/output system (BIOS or UEFI BIOS) for its first instruction. It runs the power-on self-test (POST), which makes sure the hardware is functioning properly. When this is complete, the BIOS looks for an operating system to load.

At this point, the operating system takes control of the boot process. The operating system loads the necessary device drivers to control devices such as a printer, CD/DVD drive, mouse, and keyboard. Once drivers are loaded, the user can access the system's applications and begin to work.

Virtually everything today's users do with their computers is done through an application, and every application must run through the operating system. The list of applications is endless, and new applications are being developed daily. The operating system allows a computer to communicate with almost anything—from the baby monitor installed by new parents, to the tablet a hospital nurse uses to enter patient information, to the digital music player a teenager uses to listen to their favorite tunes, to another computer a microbiologist is using to analyze data.

Each application must be written to communicate with a specific operating system because each operating system has its own specific code and syntax. Therefore, the choice of operating system largely determines the applications a computer can run. Many applications today are developed for multiple operating systems, and this requires that multiple versions of the application be created.

> **TECH TIP**
>
> **Buy an application for a particular operating system**
>
> When buying or installing an application, you must be careful to get the version created for your operating system.

User Interaction with Operating Systems

When you click on something or type something in a search box, you are interacting with the operating system. The operating system therefore has to be programmed with what to do based on what you do. At the most basic level, an operating system responds to a set of commands. The commands are accepted and processed by the operating system's command processor. Today's operating systems allow most commands to be entered by clicking on something through the graphical user interface (**GUI**) or by entering a command through the command-line interface. The **command-line interface** is not graphical and is only used to enter or view commands. For example, you can use the command-line interface to rename a file, as shown at the top of Figure 14.2, or you can use the GUI interface, as shown at the bottom of Figure 14.2. Through the GUI, simply right-click on the file in File Explorer and select the *Rename* option.

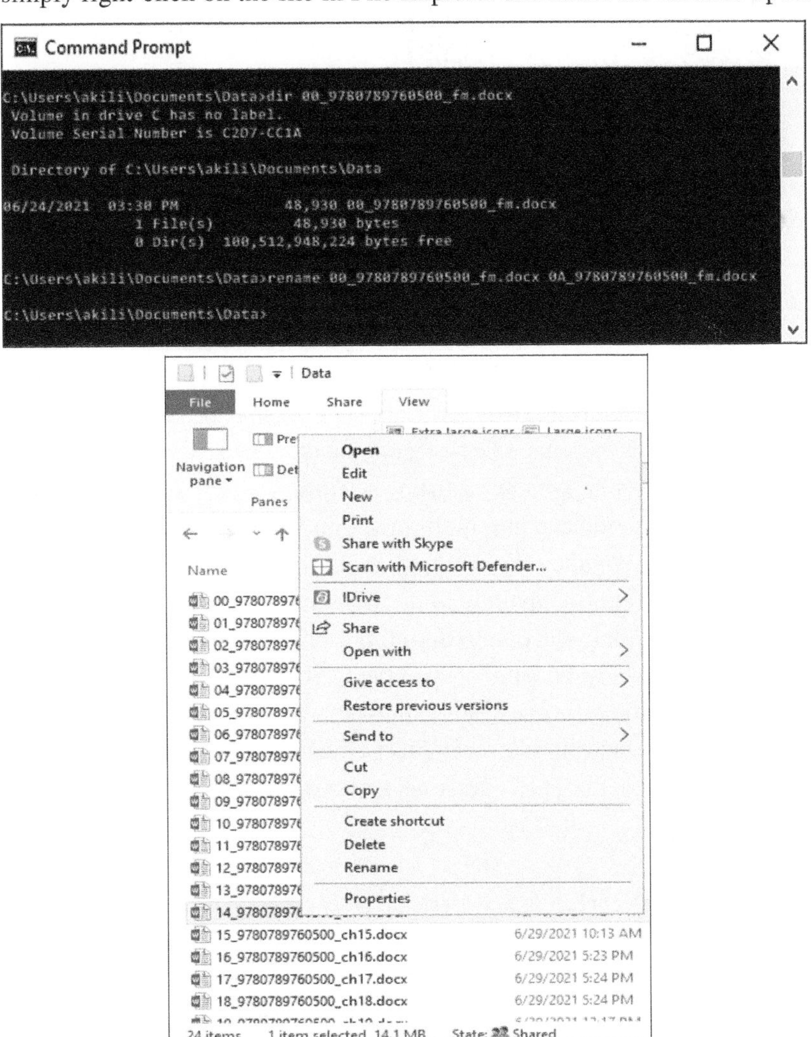

FIGURE 14.2 Command-line interface (top image) and GUI (bottom image)

The operating system is also responsible for handling file and disk management. That is why the File tools are part of the standard Windows operating system. Figure 14.3 shows File Explorer on a Windows 10 computer.

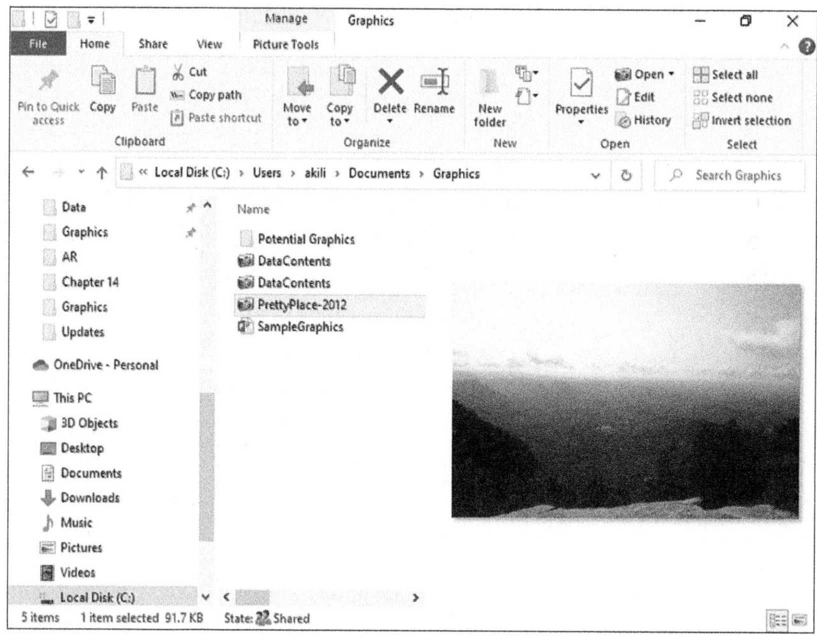

FIGURE 14.3 Windows 10 File Explorer

A **file** is an electronic container that holds computer code or data. Another way of looking at a file is to think of it as either a box of bits or an electronic piece of paper with information on it. A **folder** holds files and can also contain other folders. In Figure 14.3, *Potential Graphics* is a folder. With File Explorer, you can create, copy, or move files or folders.

An alternative environment used by technicians when there is a problem is the command prompt environment, also called the command-line interface. From a command prompt, you can enter commands that are specific to the operating system. For example, say that you type the word **`hop`** at the command prompt. The word "hop" is not a command that the computer has been programmed to understand, so an error message appears because the computer does not know what to do. However, if you type **`dir`** at a command prompt, the computer recognizes the command and displays a *directory*, which is a listing of files.

To access a command prompt from within Windows, you can right-click *Start* > select *Windows Powershell* or *Windows Powershell (Admin)*, but keep in mind that there are several ways of accomplishing almost anything in the Windows environment.

Chapter 15, "Introduction to Scripting," covers using the command prompt in greater depth.

Technicians must be familiar with the GUI environment and must also be able to function from a command prompt because sometimes the only way to execute a fix is by typing a command at a command prompt. Not only must technicians be familiar with the tools and environments, they must know multiple operating systems. This makes for a challenging and ever-changing environment.

Overview of Popular Operating Systems

Six of the most common operating systems today are Microsoft's Windows, Apple's macOS, Linux, Chrome OS, Android, and Apple's iOS and iPadOS. The last three are specifically used for mobile devices, such as cell phones and tablets.

As of early 2022, it was estimated that about 75% of all desktop personal computers use some version of Windows, and the remainder use Linux or macOS. It's important to remember that these numbers reflect worldwide usage.

The **Microsoft Windows** operating system dominates the personal computer world and remains the most popular operating system for home and office computers. Microsoft Windows was announced by Bill Gates in November 1983. Since then, there have been numerous versions and updates.

DOS 3.1 was used as the first operating system for Apple computers in 1978. The **Apple Macintosh OS** that might be more familiar to you was not introduced until 1997, as Mac OS 8. Mac OS 9 was introduced in 1999, the same year that Mac OS X Server was introduced. At the time of press, the latest version is macOS 12.3.1, also known as macOS Monterey. **macOS** is an example of a **proprietary operating system**. A proprietary system is generally designed and sold by one company (the proprietor). No other companies or individuals are expected to contribute to or alter the code, except under a business agreement with the proprietor.

In 1991 a Finnish student, Linus Torvalds, began work on a personal project: to build a new free operating system kernel known as **Linux**. The kernel is the core of a computer's operating system. People from all over the world continue to collaborate on the Linux **open source** code to submit tweaks to the central kernel. Open source systems are generally available for free; thus, they may or may not come with support. Open source systems such as Linux and Android (which is based on Linux) can be modified without permission from the creator.

The Windows operating system can be used on a wide variety of computers manufactured by many different companies. Apple computers, on the other hand, are the only computers that can use macOS. Linux has maintained its original goal of being a free and open source operating system. When you purchase an operating system license, there are several types available: (1) an open and free license such as when you download and install Linux, (2) a personal license such as when you buy the rights to use the operating system on one computer such as a home computer or for each small business computer, (3) a corporate license where you get a discount for a specific number of installations for Microsoft Windows, for example, and (4) an enterprise license, which might include more security, cloud, and virtualization options.

32-Bit vs. 64-Bit Operating Systems

Operating systems can use either a **32-bit architecture** or **64-bit architecture**. The number of bits is determined by the processor. Some versions of Windows and macOS are available in both 32-bit and 64-bit options.

The main difference between the two is the type of processors that can be supported. A 64-bit operating system supports 64-bit processors. A 64-bit processor features multiple cores, and the more cores, the more processing power a CPU has. This makes a 64-bit operating system better suited to handling tasks such as video editing and image rendering.

It is also significant to note that a 32-bit operating system can run only programs and use only drivers that are written specifically for a 32-bit operating system's instruction set. However, a 64-bit system supports software written for 64-bit architecture and also allows the computer to run 32-bit applications. Table 14.1 lists the differences between 32-bit and 64-bit Windows.

TABLE 14.1 32-bit and 64-bit Windows

32-bit Windows	64-bit Windows
32-bit or 64-bit processor	64-bit processor
4 GB **RAM limitation** (that is, the operating system can view no more than 4 GB, even if more RAM is installed)	Up to 2,048 GB RAM supported, depending on the version of Windows used

32-bit Windows	64-bit Windows
32 bits processed at a time	64 bits processed at a time
32-bit drivers required	64-bit device drivers required, and they must be digitally signed
32-bit applications and some support for older 16-bit applications	32- or 64-bit application support; 16-bit application support using the compatibility troubleshooter in Windows 10 or Windows 11
Use of DEP (Data Execution Prevention), which prevents a specific type of security attack by using both hardware and software technology	"Always-on" DEP support for 64-bit processes
N/A	Protection for the operating system kernel (the core of the operating system)
N/A	Better support for multiple processors

Windows 10 and Windows 11 Versions

The Microsoft Windows operating system was released in 1985. Since then, there have been several versions of Windows, including Windows 3.1, Windows 95, Windows 2000, and Windows XP. The most recent families of the Windows operating system are Windows 7, Windows 8, Windows 10, and the recently released Windows 11. Windows 7 was similar in look and operation to Windows XP, so people loved transitioning to it. Windows 8 had a different look and feel, which was modified in Windows 8.1 to have either a Windows 7 look or the tiled look of Windows 8.

Windows 10 is a mixture of both Windows 7 and Windows 8. **Windows 10**, and its successor **Windows 11**, were designed from the beginning to be used across all platforms: desktops, laptops, and mobile devices. Windows 11 includes several new features, such as a redesigned graphical interface, a centered taskbar, and compatibility with Android applications. Both Windows 10 and Windows 11 update device drivers automatically through Windows Update. Table 14.2 shows the various versions of Windows 10 and Windows 11 that can be purchased and briefly describes each one. Each version of Windows 10 can be 32- or 64-bit, except where noted. Windows 11 is only available for 64-bit systems.

TABLE 14.2 Windows 10/11 editions

Windows edition	Description
Home	Home is designed for home use on PCs and tablets; it comes with Microsoft Edge, Pen & Touch, and Cortana. It also features mobile and voice capabilities and a battery save mode. Some security features include device encryption, Internet protection, and Windows Defender antivirus. BitLocker and Windows Information Protection are not available in Home. Home supports peer-to-peer networks but not domain networks. Remote Desktop is not supported. By default, Group Policy Editor (`gpedit.msc`) is not available, but it can be installed to facilitate the configuration of local software, network, and security settings.

Windows edition	Description
Pro and Pro Education	Pro and Pro Education are designed for computers in the workplace. They include all features of Home, as well as features to support business networks. Local software, network, and security settings can be configured via Group Policy Editor (`gpedit.msc`), which is available by default. These editions include BitLocker and Windows Information Protection, which provide additional protection. Domain connectivity simplifies user and device administration. Remote Desktop facilitates configuration and troubleshooting. The Pro Education version provides additional management controls needed in schools.
Pro for Workstations	This edition is designed for people with advanced workloads or data needs, such as data scientists, CAD professionals, researchers, media production teams, graphic designers, and animators. Features include faster network file transfers, automatic repair of corrupted data, and persistent memory. Supports up to 4 CPUs and 6 terabytes (TB) of RAM.
Enterprise	Enterprise offers the same features as Pro, as well as additional security and management tools. Features include advanced credential protection and threat detection and response. This edition is not sold through retail centers but to corporate and educational institutions using bulk licensing.

The following links provide detailed comparisons of the different version of Windows 10 and Windows 11, respectively:

> https://www.microsoft.com/en-us/windowsforbusiness/compare
> https://www.microsoft.com/en-us/windows/business/compare-windows-11

Workstation Operating Systems

A workstation is a computer used by one or more users. It normally includes one or more high-resolution displays and a fast processor that is designed to handle complex manipulation of data such as data analysis, video editing, animations, or mathematical plots. Sometimes, however, the term is applied to any individual computer location that is hooked up to a mainframe.

Microsoft has Windows 10 Pro for Workstations and Windows 11 Pro for Workstations operating systems, which are higher-end versions of the Pro versions. They include features that were already available on Windows Server but were brought over to a desktop version of Windows. macOS and Linux are also operating systems used on workstations.

Operating Systems for Mobile Devices

A mobile operating system is an operating system for phones, tablets, smartwatches, and other mobile devices. Mobile operating systems tend to take less memory and combine features of a personal computer operating system with features needed on mobile devices, such as a touch screen, Bluetooth, GPS navigation, speech recognition, and more. Some specialized mobile devices need specialized operating systems. For example, drones use Robot Operating System (ROS).

Android OS, developed by Google, Inc., is based on the Linux kernel. Worldwide, Android dominates the field; in the last quarter of 2022, about 72% of the 329 million smartphones sold used Android OS. Android's early releases (before 2.0) were used exclusively on mobile phones. Android version 4.0 was the first version to be used by both smartphones and tablets.

Chrome OS is an operating system designed by Google that is also based on the Linux kernel. It was conceived as an operating system that would allow both applications and user data to reside in the cloud, and it uses the Chrome browser as its principal user interface. It is available only on hardware from Google manufacturing partners. Even though primarily used on laptops and tablets, Chrome OS can be used on desktops. Chromebooks (and other Chrome OS devices) are generally less expensive, lighter, and easier to transport than traditional laptops. In addition, they usually offer long battery life. Furthermore, viruses and malware pose less of a risk to Linux-based devices than to Windows devices.

The **iOS** mobile operating system was created and developed by Apple, Inc. to run only on Apple devices such as iPhones and iPads. It is the second-most-popular mobile operating system worldwide. Although it's gaining in popularity worldwide, iOS is still a distant second after Android, with only about 28% of the market (at the time of press).

As stated above, iOS was initially used on both iPhone and iPad devices. Over time, the version of iOS for the iPad required significant differences enabled by the larger screen, faster processor, increased memory, and optional devices such as keyboards. In 2019, Apple rebranded the variant of iOS for the iPad as iPadOS. **iPadOS** offers features such as improvements in the home screen, multitasking, and the Safari web browser. It also allows for use of external storage, mice, and trackpads. In addition, with iPadOS, an iPad can be used as a second monitor for a macOS computer via a feature called Sidecar.

End-of-Life (EOL) Concerns

Most IT departments replace their workstations, servers, and phones regularly in a replacement cycle. In other cases, users may be forced to move on when companies stop issuing OS updates or a warranty ends. There can be serious consequences associated with using software that has reached its **end-of-life (EOL)**, which can mean the end of support from the vendor or the end of the software's usefulness. Some of these consequences are listed here:

> **Security threats**: The operating system becomes far more vulnerable to security threats.
> **Software incompatibility**: Software vendors often cannot guarantee that new applications will be compatible with older operating systems.
> *Compliance issues:* Regulated industries, such as health care and e-commerce, deal with sensitive data. It is dangerous to entrust critical information to an outdated and possibly insecure system.
> *Operating costs:* It costs a lot to maintain and fix bugs in unsupported software. The expense of, for example, paying a company to patch an operating system that has reached its end-of-life can exceed the price of updating to a new system.
> *Performance and reliability:* Software, as it ages, can grow slow or fail to always perform as expected. Also, normally, old software is installed on old hardware, which is prone to breaking down.

Update Limitations

While there are many excellent reasons to update an operating system that has reached its EOL, the process of updating may cause problems. Those who have updated a system before often face the task of updating with anxiety and concern. Some potential problems are listed here, along with possible solutions or ways to avoid the problems:

> *Insufficient hardware:* Normally, a new operating system requires better hardware than the previous version. Hardware requirements should be checked before doing an upgrade. Insufficient hardware may cause a new operating system to run slowly. Often a faster processor and more memory are required, but other components may also need to be upgraded.

- *Setup errors and freezes:* Such problems could be caused by insufficient disk space, RAM, or drivers.
- *Drivers:* Drivers often cause trouble related to operating system upgrades. Unfortunately, sometimes vendors don't update their drivers to work with the newest systems, and this may mean you need to buy a new card or other component.
- *Application incompatibilities:* There are some workarounds that can be tried to get an older application to work with a new operating system, but sometimes the best course of action is to upgrade the application to a compatible version.
- *Data loss:* Data loss can be tragic, but it is the most preventable of all possible problems. User data should be stored on a different partition (if you have only one hard disk), on a different physical hard disk, on a different server, or in the cloud; data should be backed up regularly.

Compatibility Concerns

Computers are considered compatible if software that runs on one of the models can run on all other models of that family, even if that software differs in performance, reliability, or some other feature. Hardware compatibility means that some components, such as a RAM chip, can be used on various models.

One consideration is related to 32-bit vs. 64-bit systems. Most new systems today include processors based on a 64-bit architecture. These systems are compatible with 32-bit operating systems and 32-bit applications, but the converse is not true: 32-bit hardware cannot support 64-bit operating systems and applications. While there are many benefits to a 64-bit system and not many cons, it is important to understand that there are differences and to be aware of which system you are dealing with.

Software **compatibility** can refer to whether a particular application must be used with a specific CPU architecture, such as Intel. It can also refer to the ability of software to run on one or more operating systems or one or more versions of an operating system.

When purchasing software, it is important to consider compatibility. Sometimes even upgrading software you are already running can cause incompatibility issues. Software released for a newer version of an operating system may not work or may not work as expected on an older version of the same operating system.

Forward compatibility, also known as **upward compatibility**, is designed by the software manufacturer. It means that a system should be able to accept input intended for a later version and is meant to allow older devices to recognize when data has been generated for new devices. An application that has been designed with forward compatibility usually also has **backward compatibility**, which means the new system can still process data from the older software.

Software with both forward and backward compatibility is not the same as software that is extensible. A forward-compatible system only means that the software is able to process some of the data from a new version of itself, but an extensible system, or **extensible software**, can be upgraded easily.

Because of the nature of operating systems, software is never completely compatible between different operating systems. While there are rarely file type incompatibility issues between macOS and Windows, applications are not compatible across these operating systems. A **file type** is commonly defined by the application that created it or the type of application that can open the file. For example, a text file (a file that ends with `.txt`) is a file that doesn't have any special formatting and can be opened with Microsoft Word, WordPerfect, Notepad, WordPad, and a variety of other applications. The bottom line is that software must be chosen for a specific operating system.

Computers can have more than one OS installed. By dividing a hard drive into multiple sections, it is possible to use a dual-boot system. For example, when a Mac hard drive is partitioned, Windows can run on one partition and macOS on the other. With this type of setup, you would have to buy Windows-compatible software for the Windows partition and Apple-compatible software for the Apple partition.

One thing that must be considered when using a dual-boot system is what happens with the data. Luckily, most file types are compatible with both macOS and Windows. However, sharing folders may result in some issues since macOS and Windows deal with folders differently.

Corporate Operating System Needs

In a business environment, users have different needs than they would have at home, and corporate computers may have different operating systems than do computers used at home. The operating system in the corporate environment needs to be one that supports being on a corporate network, has rules imposed on it, and is controlled in a different way than a home computer. Let's take a look at some of these differences.

Business computers tend to be organized in either a domain or a workgroup. In Windows, the concept of a domain is different from that of a workgroup:

> *Domain:* Domains are used to create networks in medium to large companies. **Active Directory (AD)**, which is part of the Microsoft Windows Server operating system, provides centralized authentication and authorization for the network devices and people using the domain. Within AD, an organizational structure can be created to separate devices and people by location, department, or function. AD enables IT staff to implement security policies and provide support and changes easily and efficiently.

> *Workgroup:* In Windows, a workgroup is an alternative to a domain. Each computer has a user account, and if a user wants to use another computer, a separate user account must be created on the second computer. Software is usually installed on each computer that is part of a workgroup.

Windows workgroups are difficult to manage when there are more than a dozen clients, so they are more suitable for small businesses or home office networks. Active Directory, on the other hand, offers single sign-on, disaster recover functionality, and many security features that are lacking with workgroups. This makes Active Directory a better choice for larger businesses and organizations.

Domain Access

Computers in a business environment that has more than 10 computers commonly are registered with one or more domain controllers. A *domain controller* is a network server that has a network operating system installed. It has a centralized database that contains all the registered users and network devices. When a user logs into a company computer, the domain controller verifies the username and password to ensure that the user is allowed on the company network. A medium to large company is organized into one or more domains created on the domain controller. An authorized user who successfully logs into the domain is granted **domain access**.

BitLocker

BitLocker Drive Encryption is a Windows data protection feature that scrambles the data on internal drives. If a drive is removed from a computer, a password is required to access its data. This is of particular interest to companies because laptops are often lost, computers stolen, and drives removed/upgraded. BitLocker helps reduce the threat of unauthorized access by enhancing file and system protections. When computers are decommissioned or recycled, BitLocker protection helps render data inaccessible. **BitLocker To Go** provides the same data protection on removable drives such as USB flash drives, SD cards, and external hard disks. Both BitLocker and BitLocker to Go can optionally use Trusted Platform Module (TPM), which is a chip on the motherboard that stores security information such as encryption keys.

There are two additional tools that can be used to manage BitLocker: BitLocker Recovery Password Viewer and BitLocker Drive Encryption. A best practice is for technicians to back up BitLocker recovery passwords. The BitLocker Recovery Password Viewer allows a technician to see those passwords. BitLocker Drive Encryption, which is used from the command line, is used when scripts involving drive deployment or refreshes are created and deployed. Chapter 15 covers PowerShell cmdlets and scripting in more detail.

Encrypting File System (EFS)

Some corporate environments require that specific files and folders be encrypted, especially on a laptop that might be stolen or on a computer that contains sensitive data. Corporate versions of Windows include a feature called Encrypting File System (**EFS**) that allows you to encrypt a file or folder as easily as making a file or folder read-only. Whereas BitLocker encrypts an entire drive, EFS allows you to control the encryption on a file or folder basis.

To enable EFS, right-click on any file or folder and select *Properties* > click the *Advanced* button > enable the *Encrypt contents to secure data* checkbox > click *OK*. If you are encrypting a folder, you may be asked if you want the encryption for just this folder or all subfolders and files as well. Click *OK* again if necessary. When you are prompted to back up the file encryption certificate and key for security purposes, save the certificate to a separate drive. This file is very important for decrypting files and folders.

When you have a file or folder encrypted, you see what looks like a little lock over the file icon. To store and retrieve a file or folder, the user must request a key from a program that is built into Windows.

Basic Windows Usage Overview

If you have been using a Windows-based computer your entire life, you might find this first look at the Windows 10 and Windows 11 environments a little dry. It's the basics. However, little technical tricks and tips are among these basics, and even veteran technicians are likely to at some points say, "I didn't know that." So, look for those.

Windows Desktop/Start Screen

On a Windows computer, the user is initially presented with a logon screen. A user ID and password/PIN are entered as part of the operating system installation process or created as part of adding a new user, and those credentials are used thereafter. Windows 10 and Windows 11 can also be configured to allow access via facial recognition or fingerprint scan.

When in the Windows environment, the desktop appears. The **desktop** is the area on the screen of a GUI environment in which all work is performed. It is the interface between the computer user and files, applications, operating system settings, and installed hardware. The desktop contains **icons**, which are pictures that provide access to various devices, files, applications (apps), or other resources, such as a printer. The desktop can be customized so that the most commonly accessed applications or files are easily accessible. Figure 14.4 shows a Windows 10 desktop. Figure 14.5 shows a Windows 11 desktop.

FIGURE 14.4 Windows 10 desktop

FIGURE 14.5 Windows 11 desktop

Windows 8 introduced a **Start screen** in place of the traditional desktop. Windows 8.1 can have a Start screen or a traditional desktop. The Start screen contains tiles instead of icons. These **tiles** provide the same access to files and apps as the traditional icons. The Windows 10 desktop can use the Windows 8 Start screen look (tablet mode) or a combination of the traditional desktop and the Start screen. Figure 14.6 shows a Windows 10 Start screen. Notice that tiles are used instead of the traditional Windows icons. A scrollbar at the bottom enables you to see more desktop tiles. The tile labeled *Desktop* is used to access a more traditional desktop.

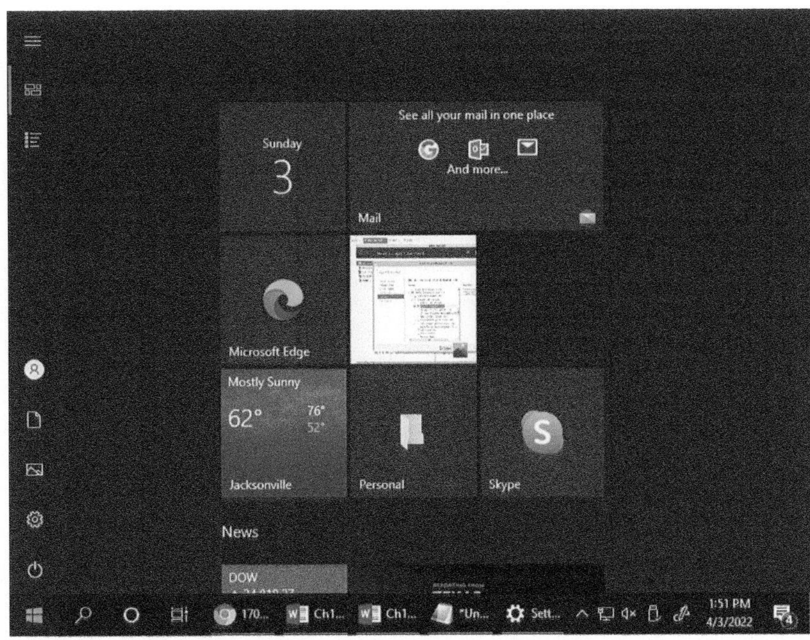

FIGURE 14.6 Windows 10 Start screen

Windows 10 and Windows 11 Desktop Components

The traditional Windows desktop has specific desktop components. Figures 14.7 and 14.8 show a Windows 10 desktop and a Windows 11 desktop, respectively, with the primary components labeled.

Taskbar

The **taskbar** is the bar that commonly runs across the bottom of the traditional desktop. The taskbar holds icons that allow quick launching of applications and icons that represent applications or files currently loaded into computer memory. The taskbar also holds icons that allow access to system utilities such as a clock for the date and time and a speaker symbol for access to volume control. Refer to Figure 14.7 (Windows 10) and Figure 14.8 (Windows 11) to ensure that you know the location of the taskbar. The basic Windows 10/11 taskbar consists of the five areas shown at the bottom of Figure 14.8: the Start button, the Search box or icon, the open or pinned applications area, the notification area, and the Show Desktop area.

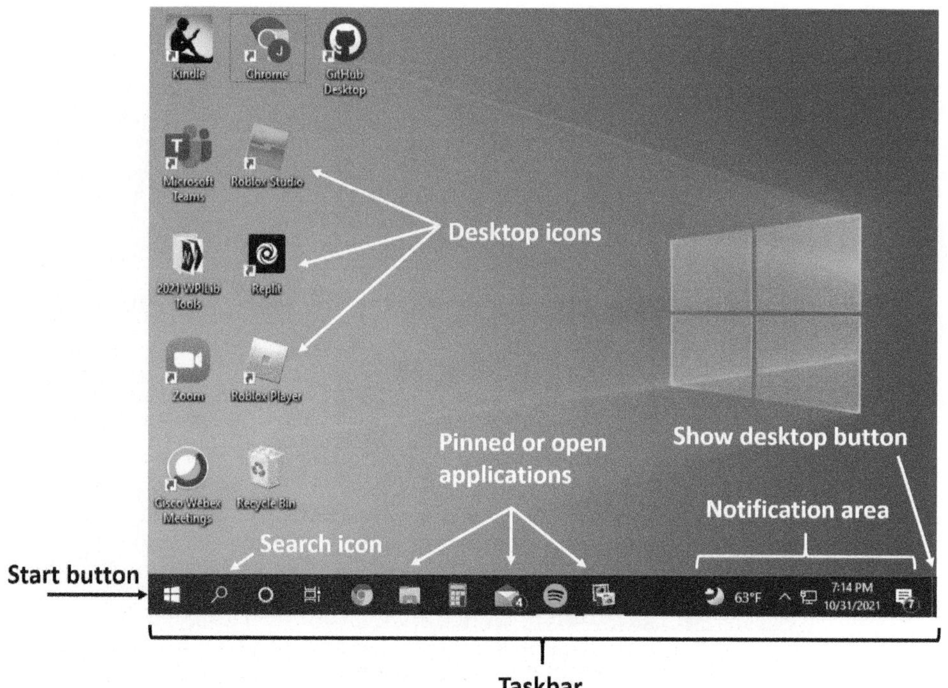

FIGURE 14.7 Windows 10 desktop components

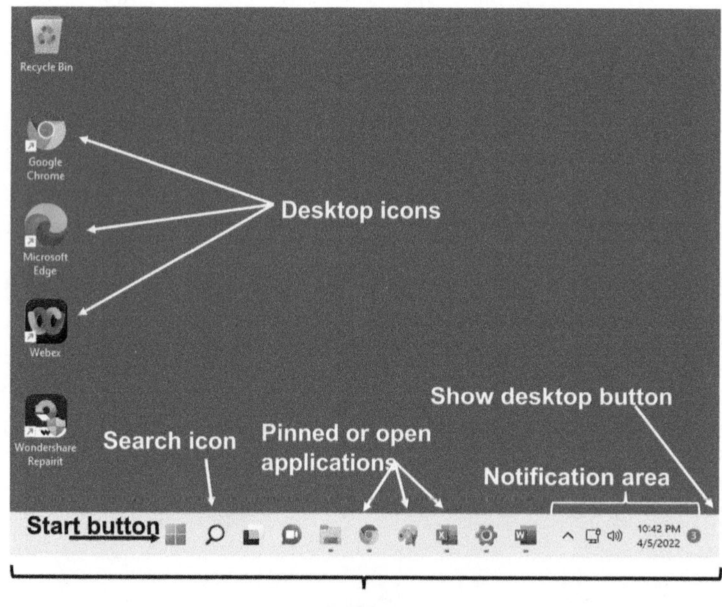

FIGURE 14.8 Windows 11 desktop components

Start Button

The **Start button** is used to launch applications and utilities, search for files and other computers, obtain help, and add and remove hardware and software. The Windows 10 Start button by default is located in the desktop's lower-left corner on the taskbar, as in previous versions of Windows. The Windows 10 Start button can be configured to show some tiles (see Figure 14.9) or the Start screen (all tiles, as in Figure 14.6). When viewing the Start screen, use the icons on the top and bottom left to re-access the Start button menu, access the power options, or view the apps in alphabetical order. Scroll down to see the rest of the tiles. The Start screen appears by default when a device is in tablet mode. Tablet mode optimizes the system for touch on devices like tablets and touch screen kiosks. When tablet mode is on, apps open full screen, and taskbar and desktop icons are reduced.

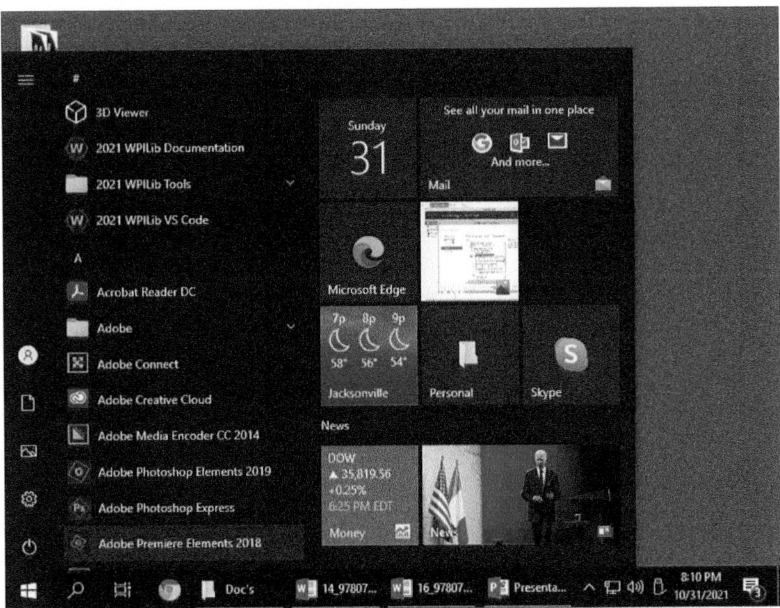

FIGURE 14.9 Windows 10 Start button with some tiles

As shown in Figure 14.8, the Windows 11 Start button is at the left of a group of icons that are centered on the taskbar. To return the Windows 11 Start button to the lower-left corner, right-click the taskbar > *Taskbar settings* > *Taskbar behaviors* > select *Left* for *Taskbar alignment.*

The Windows 11 Start menu consists of three sections: Pinned, All apps, and Recommended (see Figure 14.10). The pinned apps are a subset of all the applications available on the computer. Microsoft and/or the computer manufacturer configures the initial pinned apps and the apps that appear in Recommended. To view all the apps on the computer, click the *All apps* button. You can configure the contents of the Pinned section via *All apps* > right-click an app > click *Pin to Start* or *Unpin from Start.*

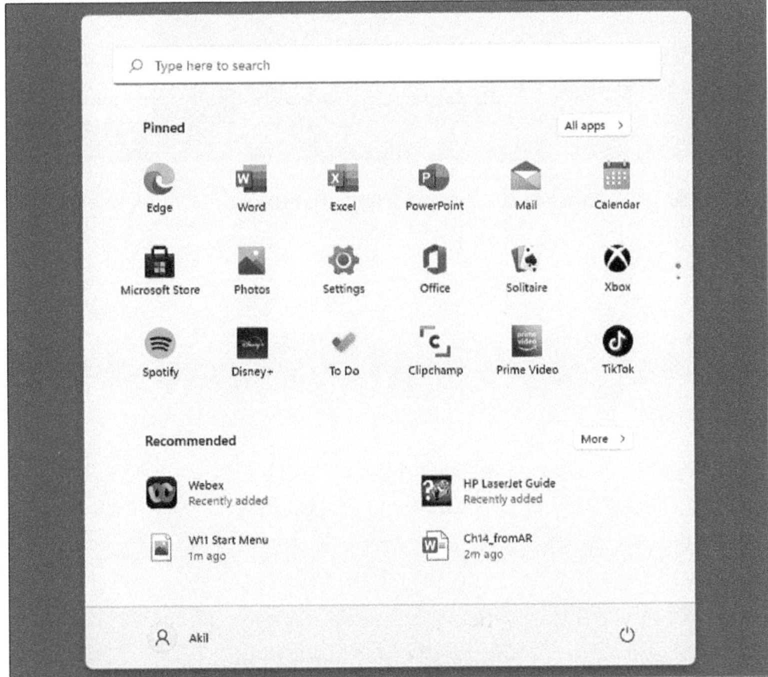

FIGURE 14.10 Windows 11 Start menu

TECH TIP

Start button missing?

The Start button (along with all other items on the taskbar) will not be visible if you turn on *Automatically hide the taskbar in desktop mode*. You can press the ⊞ key to show the Start menu or the Start screen.

Shutdown Options

Shutdown options appear in the Start menu. In Windows 10, click *Start* > *Power*. The options *Shut down* and *Restart* appear, as shown in Figure 14.11. The option *Sleep* also appears if your computer can be configured for Sleep mode. Some Windows updates need to be applied while the computer is booting up. If such updates are available, additional options appear (*Update and shut down* and *Update and restart*). In Windows 11, click *Start* > ⏻ (power icon). See Figure 14.12. The same options (*Shut down*, *Restart*, *Sleep*, *Update and restart*, and *Update and shut down*) may be available, depending on your computer and the status of your updates.

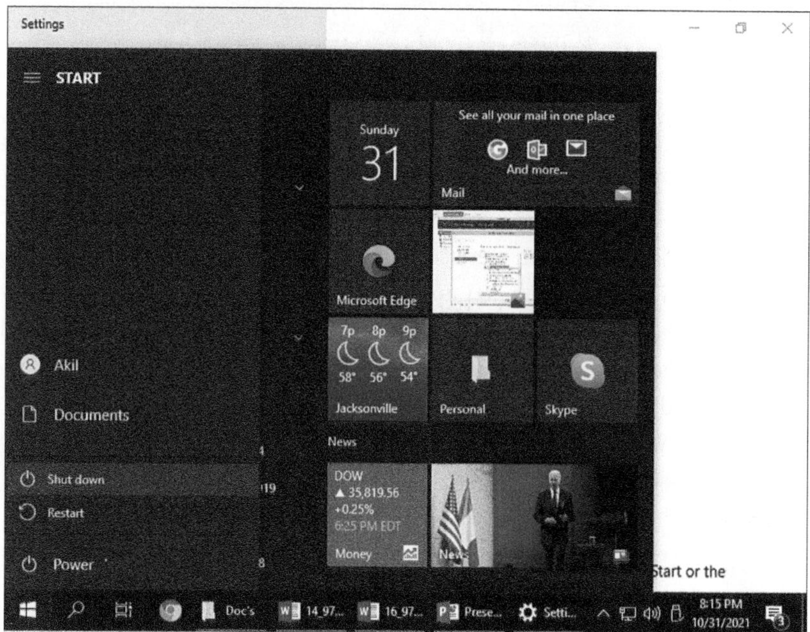

FIGURE 14.11 Windows 10 shutdown options

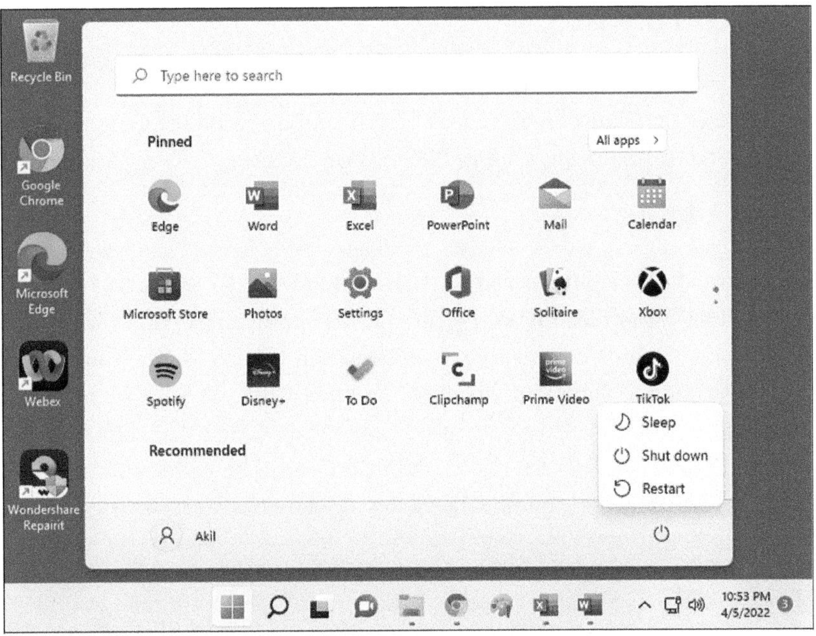

FIGURE 14.12 Windows 11 shutdown options

Pinning Applications

In Figure 14.7, the red, blue, yellow, and green Google Chrome icon, the File Explorer icon, and the Calculator icon are *pinned* to the taskbar; that is, they are always on the taskbar. When a pinned application icon is clicked, the corresponding application is launched. In Figure 14.7, the green circle icon for Spotify and the icon to the right of it, for Microsoft PictureIt!, are open applications, as indicated by the blue line under them.

TECH TIP

How to modify the buttons shown on the taskbar

To pin an application to the taskbar, launch the application, locate the application icon on the taskbar, right-click it, and select *Pin to taskbar*.

Notification Area

On the far right of the taskbar is the **notification area**, where you can find information about an application or a tool. In Figure 14.7, for example, the icons from left to right are the current weather and temperature, the *Show hidden icons* icon (up arrow), the *Network* icon, and the *Notifications* icon. Other icons are available by clicking the *Show hidden icons* icon.

Show Desktop Area

The space to the far right, immediately after the date/time, is the Show Desktop area. In Windows 10, there is a thin vertical line separating the Show Desktop area from the rest of the taskbar. A shorter vertical line appears in Windows 11 when the cursor is in the Show Desktop area. Click this area to instantly minimize all open windows and show the desktop. Click the area again, and whatever windows you were working with reappear. In Windows 10, the *Show the desktop* option is also available by simply right-clicking an empty space on the taskbar.

Search Function

The search function is built into the taskbar and can appear as a search icon, the Cortana search textbox, or the *Type here to search* search textbox. With the Cortana feature, you can type or speak a question or statement, such as "What's on TV tonight?" or "Show me the latest news."

Task View

The Task View icon was introduced in Windows 10 (refer to Figure 14.13). Windows 11 also offers Task View (see Figure 14.14). **Task View** enables you to view thumbnails of open apps and easily select which one to access, as shown in Figure 14.14. You may be familiar with using the Alt+Tab key combination to select an open window; Task View does the same thing but more efficiently. You can also create more than one desktop by selecting the *New desktop* option in Task View. Figure 14.14 shows two desktops created. The windows open in Desktop 1 (selected at the bottom) are shown as thumbnails in the top window.

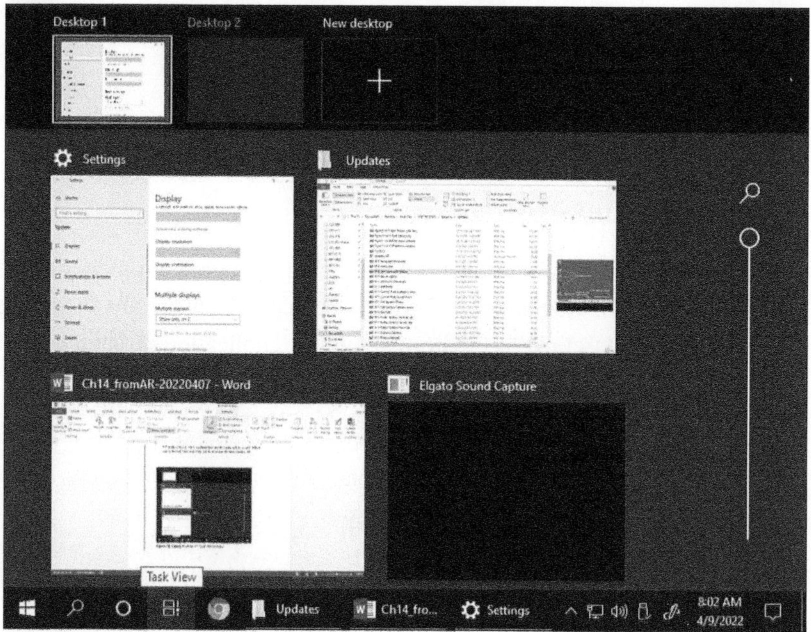

FIGURE 14.13 Windows 10 Task View window

> **TECH TIP**
>
> **Keeping the desktop organized**
>
> The desktop may become cluttered with icons the user puts on it. To organize the desktop nicely, right-click an empty desktop space, point to *View* > select *Auto arrange icons*.

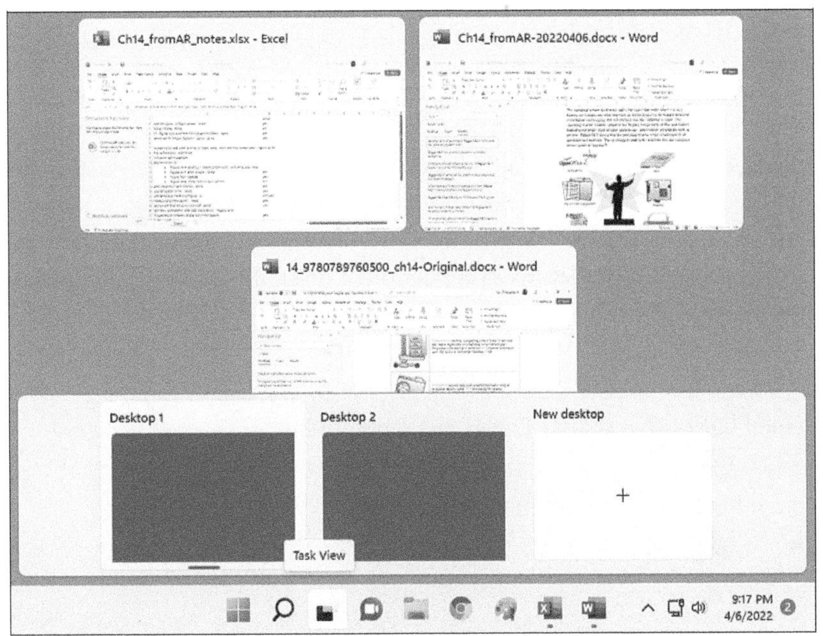

FIGURE 14.14 Windows 11 Task View window

Shortcuts and Tiles

Each of the tiles in the Windows 10 tablet mode is a shortcut. A **shortcut** represents a **path** (a location on a drive) to a file, folder, or program. It is a link (pointer) to where the file or application resides on a disk. On the traditional desktop, a shortcut has a small arrow in the left corner. When a shortcut icon is double-clicked, Windows knows where to find the specific file the icon represents based on the associated path. Users and technicians frequently place shortcuts or tiles on the desktop, and it is important to know how to create, remove, modify, and troubleshoot them.

By default, the Windows 10/11 desktop displays the Recycle Bin icon only. However, some people like to have other Windows icons displayed. Common desktop icons or tiles are listed in Table 14.3.

TABLE 14.3 Common Windows desktop icons or tiles

Icon	Purpose
Documents	Maps to a folder located on the hard drive that is the default storage location for files
This PC	Allows access to hardware, software, and files
Network	Allows access to network resources, such as computers, printers, scanners, fax machines, and files
Recycle Bin	Holds files and folders that have been deleted
Edge	Starts the Microsoft browser used to access the Internet

To discover the path to the original file used to create a shortcut, right-click the shortcut icon and select *Properties*. Click the *Shortcut* tab and look in the *Target* textbox for the path to the original file. The *Open File Location* button can be used to locate the original file. In tablet mode, right-click (or tap and hold briefly) a tile and select *Open File Location*. Note that you may have to point to the *More* option to access *Open File Location*.

Recycle Bin

An important Windows desktop icon is the one for the Recycle Bin, which holds files and folders that the user deletes. When a file or folder is deleted, it is not actually gone. Instead, it goes into the Recycle Bin, which is a folder on the hard drive. A deleted file or folder can be removed from the Recycle Bin just as a piece of trash can be removed from a physical trash can. Deleted files and folders in the Recycle Bin use hard drive space. To change how much space is reserved for the Recycle Bin or the drive on which the deleted files in the Recycle Bin are stored, right-click the *Recycle Bin* and select *Properties*.

TECH TIP

Need hard drive space? Empty the Recycle Bin

A technician must remember that some users do not empty the Recycle Bin. Emptying the Recycle Bin frees up space on the hard drive.

TECH TIP

How to delete a file permanently

If you hold down the Shift key when deleting a file, the file is permanently deleted without going into the Recycle Bin.

TECH TIP

Removable media files are permanently deleted

When deleting a file or folder from an optical disc, a memory card, an MP3 player, a digital camera, a remote computer, or a flash drive, the file or folder is permanently deleted. It does not go into the Recycle Bin, as is the case when a file is deleted from a hard drive.

Interactions Within a Window

Whenever anything is double-clicked in Windows, a window appears. A **window** is a square or rectangular section on the screen. Common options can appear within a window. A dialog box is one type of window. Technicians frequently interact with the Windows operating system through dialog boxes. Dialog boxes allow a technician to configure applications and operating system preferences. The most common features found in a dialog box are checkboxes, textboxes, tabs, drop-down menus, a Close button, an OK button, a Cancel button, and an Apply button. Figure 14.15 shows a sample dialog box.

A *textbox* is an area in which you can type a specific parameter. When the inside of a textbox is clicked, a vertical line or an entire default word appears. Any typed text is placed to the left of the insertion point. If you highlight any of the text in a textbox and then type, the original text is replaced with the text that you type. Textboxes sometimes have up and down arrows that can be used to select an option or enable a user to type in a new parameter.

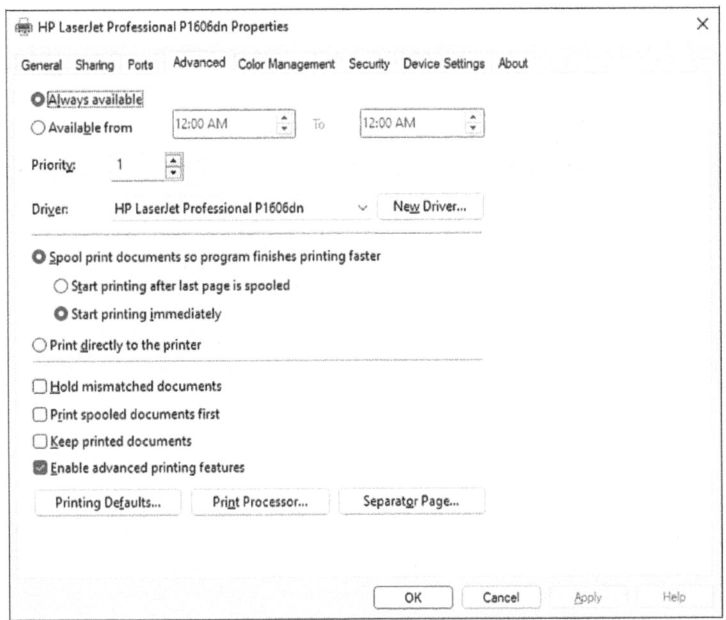

FIGURE 14.15 HP printing preferences dialog box

Tabs frequently appear across the top of a dialog box. Each tab holds a group of related options. Click a tab once to bring that particular major section to the window's forefront. The tabs in Figure 14.15 are General, Sharing, Ports, Advanced, Color Management, Security, Device Settings, and About.

The **Apply button** saves changes immediately. The dialog box remains open after you click the Apply button. When you click the OK button, all options selected or changed are saved, and the dialog box is closed. The Close button, which is an X in the upper-right corner of the dialog box, closes the dialog box. Clicking the Close button discards updates to the dialog box since the last time the Apply button was clicked; the same is true for the Cancel button.

TECH TIP

Click *OK* or *Apply* to make it work

To apply a change, inexperienced technicians often make the mistake of clicking the *Close* button (the red X button in the top right of a dialog box) instead of the *OK* or *Apply* button. When the *Close* button is used, changes in the dialog box made after the last Apply are neither saved nor applied.

When a checkbox option is checked, it is enabled or turned on. Clicking inside a checkbox option places a check mark inside the checkbox, such as the one for *Enable advanced printing features* in Figure 14.15. If you click again inside the checkbox, the check is removed, and the option is not enabled.

A similar dialog box option is a radio button. A radio button is a circle that, when enabled, has a solid dot inside it. Only one option within a group of radio buttons can be enabled. For example, in Figure 14.15, the *Always available* radio button is enabled, and the *Available from* radio button is disabled. Clicking *Available from* would enable that option and disable the *Always available* option.

A drop-down menu is presented when you click a down arrow to see the options. For example, in Figure 14.15, the *Driver* drop-down menu has the *HP LaserJet Professional P1606dn* option selected. When a drop-down menu is clicked, all the drop-down options are shown.

Within a dialog box, help is commonly provided as context-sensitive help. Simply hold the pointer over a particular item, and one or more words appear.

Another popular type of interaction is with a **context menu**, which appears when you right-click an item. The context menu that appears is different in every application but usually includes options that are available from the main menu or from a Windows Settings or Control Panel option. Context menus frequently save time and are commonly used by technicians.

Managing Windows Files and Folders

Technicians often create, delete, and move files and folders. You need to do these tasks quickly and without error. It is important to think about what file and folder you want to work with, where the files and folders are located now, and where you want the files or folders to be eventually.

Each drive in a Windows computer is represented by a drive letter followed by a colon. For example, the first hard drive partition is represented by `C:`. The optical drive, flash drive, and any external drives are each represented by a drive letter followed by a colon. File Explorer is used to manage files and folders. Figure 14.16 shows drive letters within File Explorer on a Windows 11 computer.

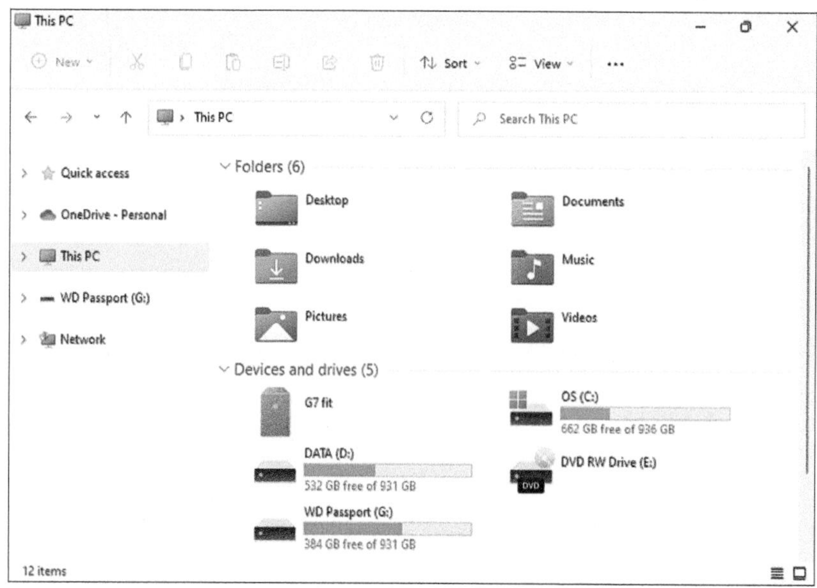

FIGURE 14.16 Windows 11 File Explorer drive letters

Folders, Filenames, and Extensions

Discs or drives hold files and folders. Files are usually organized in folders. In older operating systems, a folder was called a *directory*, and you still see this term today, especially when using the command-line interface. A folder within a folder is called a **subfolder** or **subdirectory**. Windows 7 and higher have automatic groupings, each one called a **library**, for saving files. The Windows 10 libraries, for example, include the following: *Documents*, *Downloads*, *Music*, *Pictures*, and *Videos*. By default, applications save files in these libraries. You can also create additional libraries, as needed.

Each file is given a name that includes two parts: the **filename** and the **extension**, separated by a dot. For example, in the filename `WIN8CHAP.DOCX`, the name of the file is `WIN8CHAP`, and the extension is `DOCX`. Regardless of whether you use lowercase or uppercase letters, Windows remembers the case; however, it does not require you to remember. Case does not matter when searching for a file or typing the name of a file to open. Some operating systems, like Linux, are case-sensitive with respect to filenames.

TECH TIP

Characters you cannot use in filenames and folder names

Folder names and filenames can include all keyboard characters, numbers, letters, and spaces *except* the following: / (forward slash), " (quotation mark), \ (backslash), | (vertical bar), ? (question mark), : (colon), and * (asterisk).

Normally with Windows, the application used to create a file automatically adds an extension to the end of the filename. In most views, Windows does not automatically show the extensions.

To view file extensions in Windows 10 File Explorer, select the *View* tab, as shown in Figure 14.17 > enable (select) the *File name extensions* checkbox. As shown in Figure 14.17, the context-sensitive help appears when the pointer is hovered over the *File name extensions* option. The checkbox has a check inside it if the option is enabled. To view file extensions in Windows 11, click *View* > *Show* > *File name extensions* (see Figure 14.18).

When Windows recognizes an extension, the operating system associates the extension with a particular application. Filename extensions can tell you a lot about a file, such as what application created the file or what its purpose is. Table 14.4 lists some common file extensions and their purposes and the applications that create particular extensions.

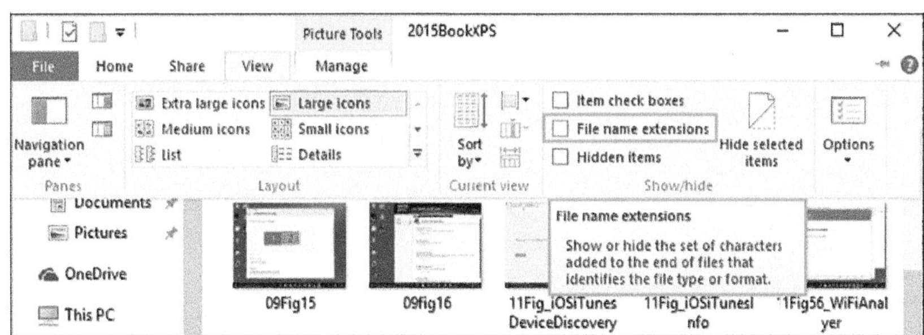

FIGURE 14.17 Selecting to view file extensions in Windows 10

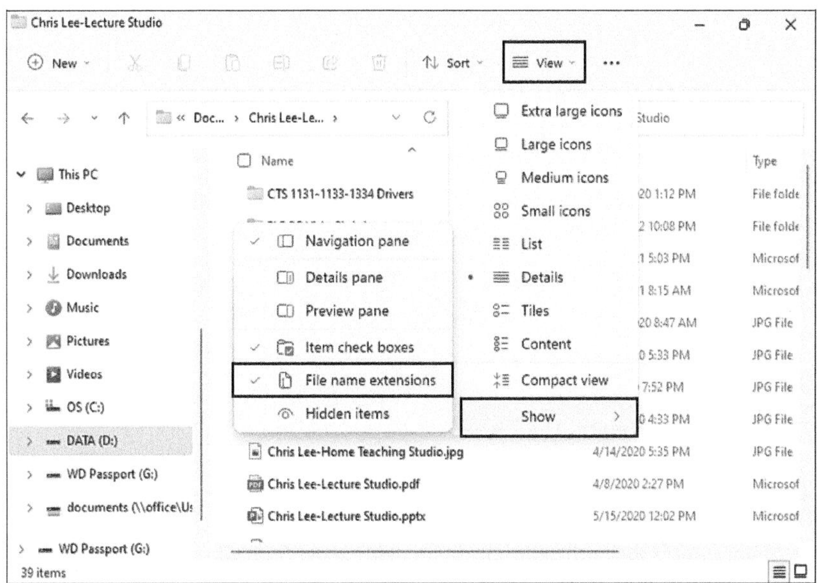

FIGURE 14.18 Selecting to view file extensions in Windows 11

TABLE 14.4 Common file extensions

Extension	Purpose or application	Extension	Purpose or application
AAX	Audible enhanced audio file	JPG or JPEG	Joint Photographic Experts Group graphics file
AI	Adobe Illustrator or Corel Trace file	MPG or MPEG	Movie clip file
BAT	Batch file, for executing commands from one file	ONE	Microsoft OneNote file
BMP	Bitmap file	PCX	Microsoft Paintbrush file
CAB	Cabinet file, a compressed file that holds operating system or application files	PDF	Adobe Acrobat portable document format file
COM	Command file, an executable file that opens an application or a tool	PNG	Microsoft Paint or Snipping Tool graphics file
DLL	Dynamic link library file, which contains executable code that can be used by more than one application and is called upon from other code that is already running	PPT or PPTX	Microsoft PowerPoint file
DOC or DOCX	Microsoft Word file	RTF	Rich text format file
DRV	Device driver, a piece of software that enables an operating system to recognize a hardware device	TIF or TIFF	Tag image file
EPS	Encapsulated PostScript file	TXT	Text file
EXE	Executable file, a file that opens an application	VXD	Virtual device driver
GIF	Graphics interchange file	WPS	Microsoft Works text file
HLP	Windows-based help file	WRI	Microsoft WordPad file
INF	Information or setup file	XLS or XLSX	Microsoft Excel file
INI	Initialization file, used in older Windows environments	ZIP	Compressed file

When you save a file in a Windows application, the application automatically saves the file to a specific folder or library unless the user specifies a different folder. This is known as the *default folder* or *default library*. With many applications, this folder is the *Documents* folder, Microsoft's OneDrive, or another cloud-based storage solution.

File Explorer Path

In documentation and installation instructions, and when writing the exact location of a file, the full path is used. A file's path is like a road map to the file. It includes the drive letter plus all folders and subfolders that must be navigated to get to that file's filename and extension. For example, if the `webgl_sharing` file is in the *Krazy Karts* folder, which is in the *Documents* folder on the `D:` hard drive partition, and the author, Akil, is logged on, the full path is as follows:

```
D:\Users\Akil\Documents\Krazy Karts\webgl_sharing
```

The first part is the drive letter where the file is stored: `D:` represents a hard drive partition. There is a *Users* folder on the `D:` drive. The name of the file is always at the end of the path. In the example given, `webgl_sharing` is the name of the file. Everything in between the drive letter and the filename is the name of one or more folders to get to where the `webgl_sharing` file is located. The top-level folder in this example is `Users`. In the *Users* folder is the *Akil* subfolder. In the *Akil* subfolder is another subfolder called *Documents*, which contains another subfolder, *Krazy Karts*. Finally, within that *Krazy Karts* subfolder is the `webgl_sharing` file. Figure 14.19 shows how this looks in Windows File Explorer.

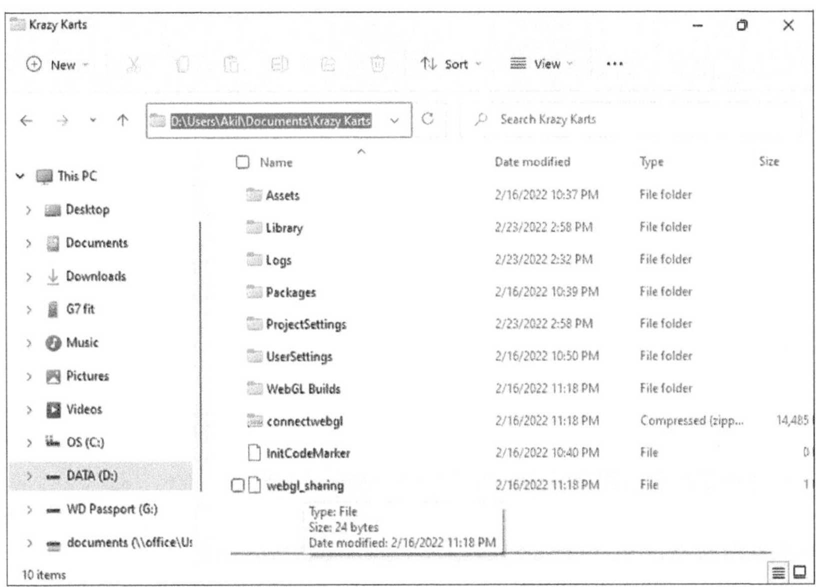

FIGURE 14.19 Windows File Explorer full path

Notice that the path appears at the top of the File Explorer window, and the filename appears within the *Krazy Karts* folder. Note that this was done intentionally to show you the full path. However, when you open File Explorer, expand *This PC* on the left, and navigate to *Documents*, the *Users* or *Akil* folder is not shown. The path simply shows as `This PC > Documents`. That's because the *Documents* library has been associated with the full path `D:\Users\Akil\Documents`.

The full path contains the drive letter and a list of folders. When you click a file or folder in File Explorer, the greater than sign (>) is used to separate folders in the address box. As shown in Figure 14.19, if you click to the right of the words in the address box, the full path appears with backslashes (the keyboard key above the ENTER key). Note that if you are viewing a library, only the name of the library appears. When writing a complete path to a file, a backslash is always used to separate the drive letter from the first folder name, to separate the folder names from each other, and to separate the last folder name from the filename. To display the full path at the top of File Explorer (title bar) in Windows 10, open File Explorer > select the *View* tab > access the *Options* down arrow on the far right > select *Change folder and search options* > select the *View* tab > enable the *Display the full path in the title bar* option. To open this same dialog box in Windows 11, open File Explorer > click the three dots beside the *View* menu > select *Options* > select the *View* tab (see Figure 14.20).

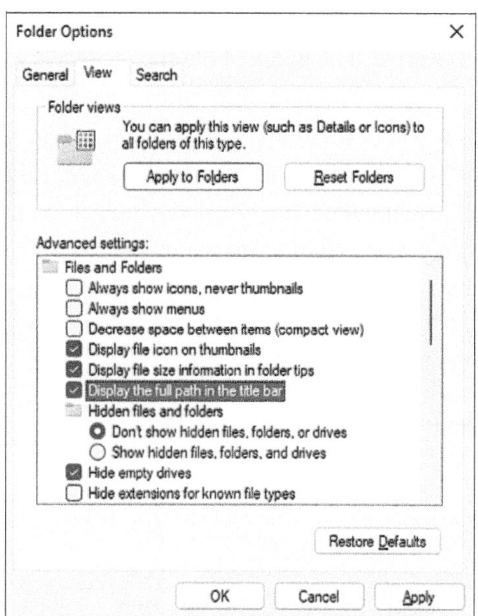

FIGURE 14.20 Windows 11 *Display the full path in the title bar* option

File Explorer View Options

It is important for a technician to be able to control how files and folders are displayed in File Explorer. Table 14.5 explains the available options.

TABLE 14.5 File Explorer display options

Windows 10 option	Explanation
List	File/folder name shown
Details	File/folder shown with size, extension, and modification date
Small Icons	Small graphics with the filename or folder name shown under the icon
Content	Reduced-size icons with file/folder contents shown
Tiles	Multiple columns of file/folder icons with name, application, and size shown
Medium Icons, Large Icons, Extra Large Icons	Varying-size file/folder icons

To see the *View* options that can be used to change how files, folders, images, and so on display in Windows 10 and Windows 11 in File Explorer, refer to Figure 14.20.

These options (and many others settings) are available in *Folder Options*, which contains all the folder and search options. In Windows 10, open File Explorer > select the *View* menu option > access the *Options* down arrow on the far right > select *Change folder and search options*. To access Folder Options in Windows 11, open File Explorer > click the three dots beside the *View* menu > select *Options* (see Figure 14.21). The *File Explorer Options* window contains the same settings as *Folder Options*. It can also be accessed using the *File Explorer Options* Control Panel. Control Panels are covered later in this chapter.

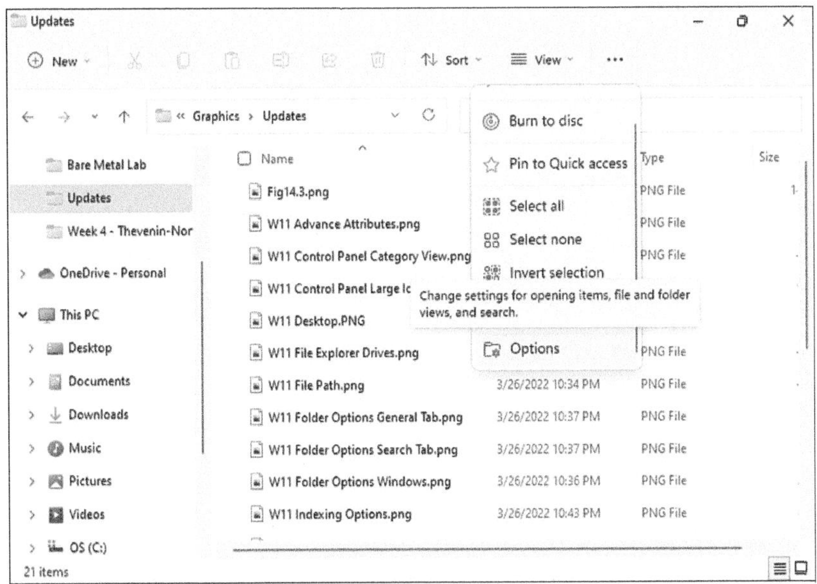

FIGURE 14.21 Windows 11 File Explorer Options button

Figure 14.22 shows the options that are available in the *General* tab of the *Folder Options* dialog. The *General* tab has three main sections: *Browse folders*, *Click items as follows*, and *Privacy*. Each section has either radio buttons or checkboxes to enable various items.

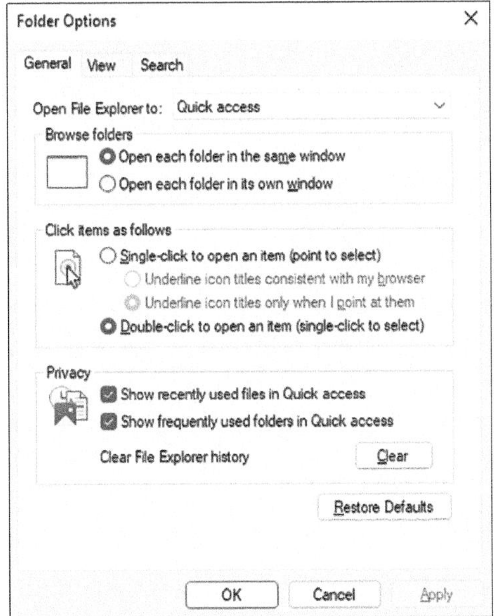

FIGURE 14.22 Windows 11 *File Explorer* Options > *General* tab

Figure 14.20 shows some of the options available in the *View* tab of the *Folder Options* dialog. A technician should be able to set the following important options through this window:

> View hidden files by using the *Hidden files and folders* option of the *View* tab

> Hide file extensions by using the *Hide extensions for known file types* checkbox on the *View* tab

> Use other options on the *View* tab to reset the settings or to apply settings to subfolders and display the full path

Searches and Indexing

You can perform a search from within File Explorer by typing a filename or phrase within the search textbox (refer to Figure 14.19). You can also search using the textbox on the taskbar or the Cortana search feature. Windows 10 and 11 always include filenames and data within the files in searches. They also search the links in your web search history.

The *Folder Options* window has a *Search* tab that has some technical significance. Figure 14.23 shows the contents of this tab.

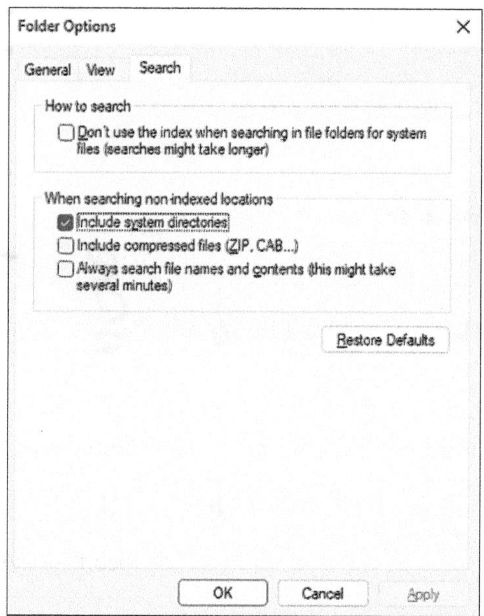

FIGURE 14.23 Windows 11 Folder Options > *Search* tab

The Windows index feature affects searches within the operating system. **Indexing** is the process used in Windows to quickly search common locations for files and folders, including all libraries, the Start button menu, and Edge browsing history. In Windows 10/11, the index is used for all files by default. The *How to search* section allows you to ignore the Windows index when searching for system files. This means that all the files and folders in the drive, folder, or subfolder will be searched, so searches might take longer. Files and folders to search outside the indexed locations can be specified in the *When searching non-indexed locations* section.

Modifying Index Locations

To modify what locations get indexed, use a search function and type `indexing` > select *Indexing Options* from the resulting list. Use the *Modify* or *Advanced* buttons to change the settings. For example, if you want to exclude a particular folder and its contents from the index, click *Modify* > navigate to the folder > uncheck the folder. Note that you cannot exclude individual filenames from being indexed. Figure 14.24 shows the Indexing Options window as well as the window that appears if you click the *Advanced* button.

If you don't want a file's contents to be indexed and easily found, in File Explorer, you can right-click the filename, select *Properties* > *Advanced* button > disable (uncheck) the *Allow this file to have contents indexed in addition to file properties* option.

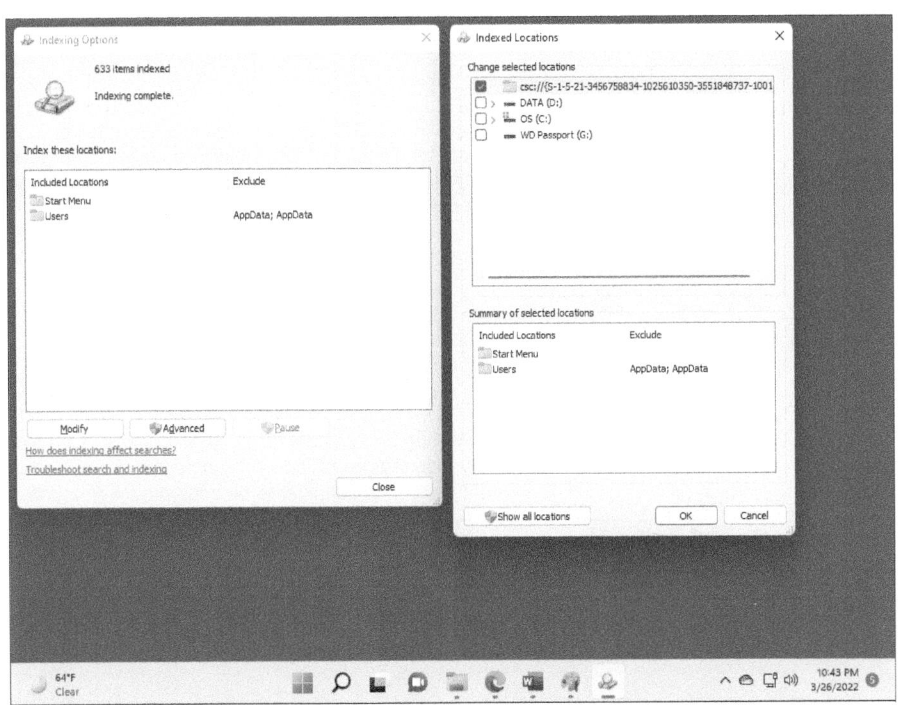

FIGURE 14.24 Windows 11 *Indexing Options* > *Advanced* button

Attributes, Compression, and Encryption

File Explorer can be used for setting attributes, which are specific qualities for a file or folder. The basic file and folder **attributes** are read-only, hidden, archive, and system (see Figure 14.25). Files and folders can also be compressed and encrypted (see Figure 14.26).

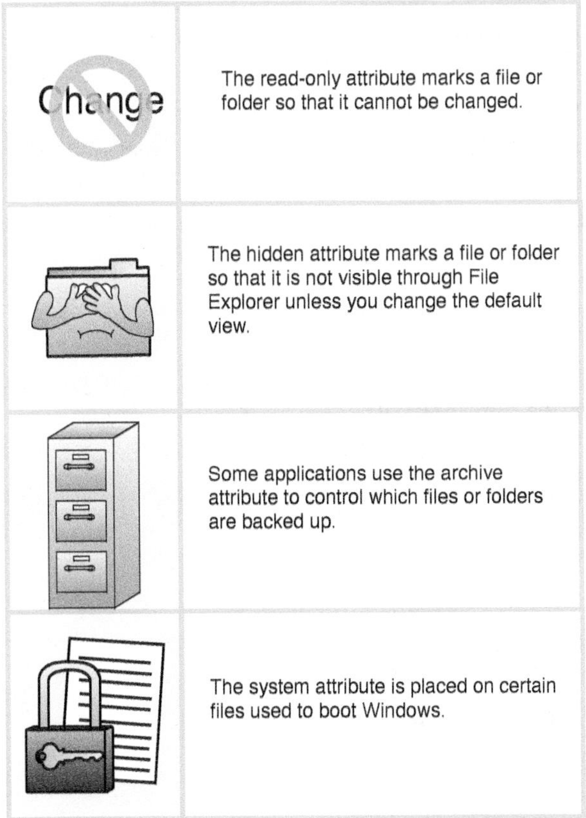

Change
The read-only attribute marks a file or folder so that it cannot be changed.
The hidden attribute marks a file or folder so that it is not visible through File Explorer unless you change the default view.
Some applications use the archive attribute to control which files or folders are backed up.
The system attribute is placed on certain files used to boot Windows.

FIGURE 14.25 Windows file/folder attributes

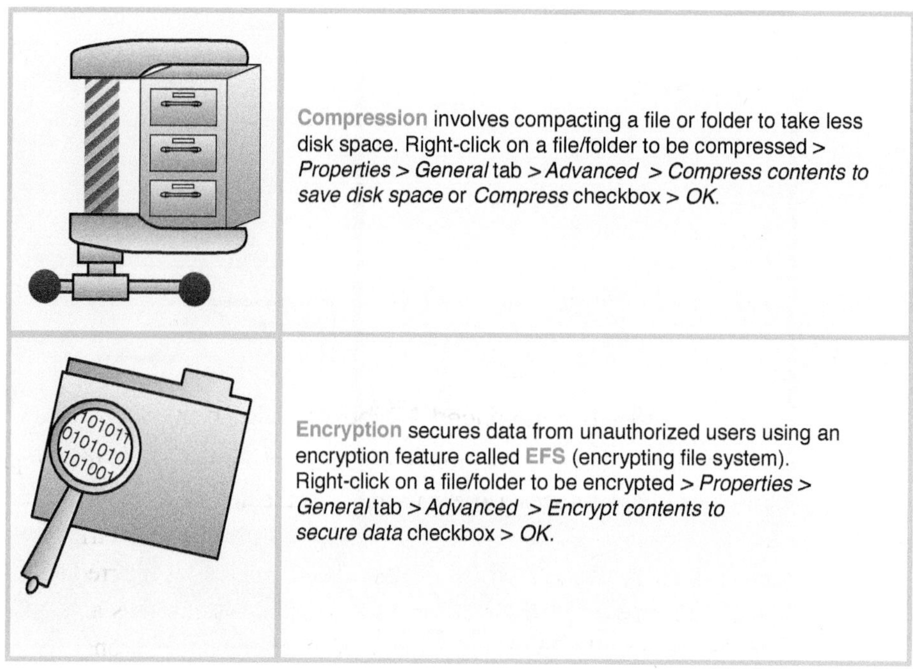

Compression involves compacting a file or folder to take less disk space. Right-click on a file/folder to be compressed > Properties > General tab > Advanced > Compress contents to save disk space or Compress checkbox > OK.
10101
0101010
101001
Encryption secures data from unauthorized users using an encryption feature called EFS (encrypting file system). Right-click on a file/folder to be encrypted > Properties > General tab > Advanced > Encrypt contents to secure data checkbox > OK.

FIGURE 14.26 Windows compression and encryption

> **TECH TIP**
>
> **How to change a file or folder's attributes**
>
> To change a file or folder's attributes, right-click the filename or folder name > *Properties*. The *Read-only* and *Hidden* attributes appear at the bottom of the dialog box (see Figure 14.27). Click *Advanced* to see the archive, indexing, compression, and encryption attributes (see Figure 14.28). Click the appropriate attribute checkboxes to enable or disable them. If a file is a system file, the *System* attribute is also available. Click *Apply*.

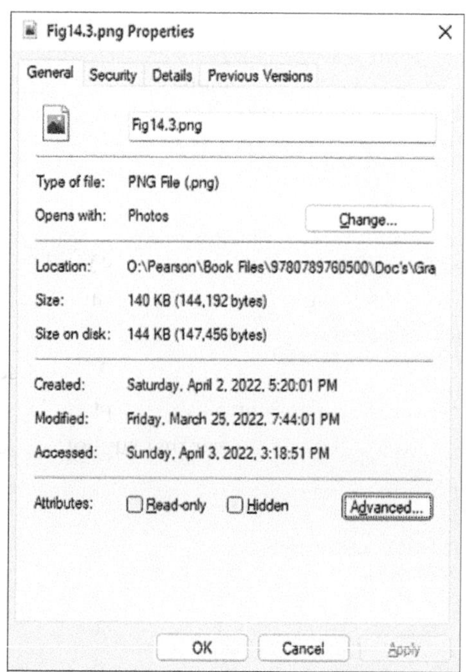

FIGURE 14.27 File Properties View tab

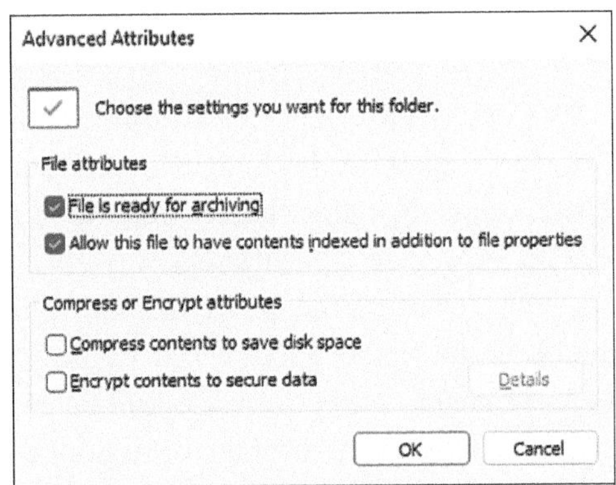

FIGURE 14.28 The Advanced Attributes dialog box

All Windows-based applications can read from and write to compressed files. The operating system decompresses a file, the file is available to the application, and the operating system recompresses the file when that file is saved. For the archive attribute, Windows files and folders have the archive attribute set by default. This is sometimes referred to as having the archive bit set.

If a hard drive is partitioned for the NTFS file system, files and folders can be compressed or encrypted. Figure 14.26 provides more information on these concepts.

> **TECH TIP**
>
> **Compression causes a computer to slow down**
>
> When **compression** is enabled, the computer's performance can degrade because when a compressed file is opened, the file must be uncompressed, and then it must be recompressed in order to be saved or closed. Degradation can also occur if a compressed file is transferred across a network because the file must be uncompressed before it is transferred.

> **TECH TIP**
>
> **What happens when a compressed file is moved or copied?**
>
> Moving or copying a compressed file or folder can alter the compression. When you move a compressed file or folder, the file or folder remains compressed. When you copy a compressed file or folder, it is compressed only if the destination folder (the folder you are moving it to) is already compressed.

When a file or folder is encrypted with EFS (Encrypting File System), only authorized users can view or change the file. Administrators designated as recovery agents have the ability to recover encrypted files when necessary.

Windows Home does not support file encryption, but the Pro, Enterprise, and Education editions do. The `cipher` command can be used at the command prompt to decrypt, modify, and copy an encrypted file obtained from another computer or server that supports it. Compressed files, system files, and read-only files cannot be encrypted.

> **TECH TIP**
>
> **Copying and moving**
>
> To copy a file or folder, use the *Copy* and *Paste* functions from the File Explorer *Edit* menu option. To move a file or folder, use the *Cut* and *Paste* functions.

Introduction to Windows Control Panel Utilities

Control Panels (also known as Control Panel applets or utilities) enable you to configure all aspects of Windows and can be accessed from the Start button. You have actually been using some of the Windows Control Panels already in this chapter (refer to the section "Modifying Index Locations"). Control Panels can be viewed in two different ways: using the older views, where all Control Panels are shown as icons, or using the newer method, where the Control Panels are displayed by categories. Figure 14.29 shows the Windows 11 Control Panel in icons view (large icons), and Figure 14.30 shows it in category view. Some Control Panel functionality is also available in the *Settings* app, which can be accessed by clicking or right-clicking the Start button. Note that since Windows 10, Microsoft has been incrementally moving Control Panel utilities to the Settings app. For example, clicking *System* in *Control Panel* now takes you to *Settings* > *System* > *About*. Be sure to look in Settings if you don't find what you expect to see in Control Panel. Figures 14.31 and 14.32 show the home pages for the Settings app in Windows 10 and Windows 11, respectively.

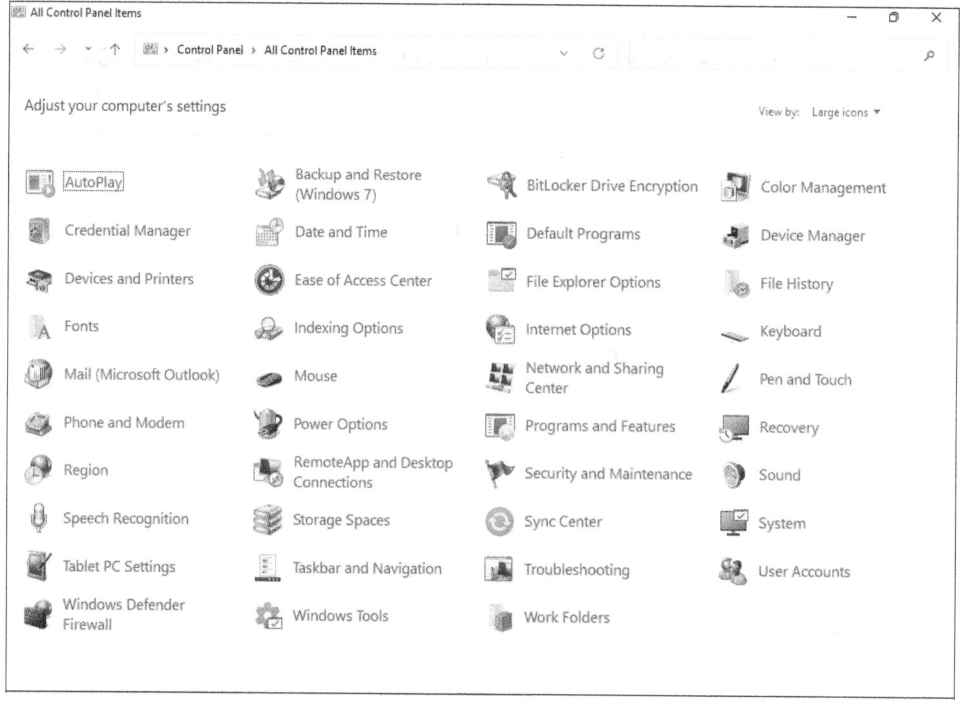

FIGURE 14.29 Windows 11 Control Panel utilities—icon view

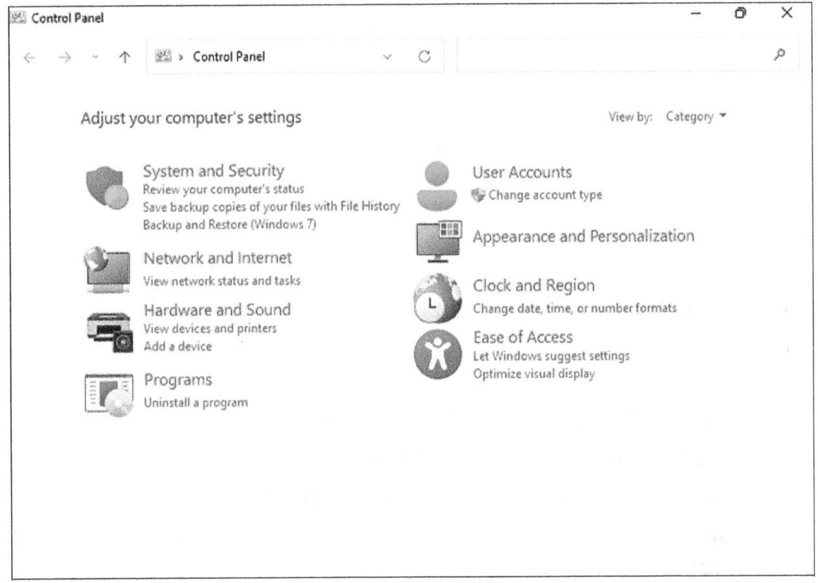

FIGURE 14.30 Windows 11 Control Panel utilities—category view

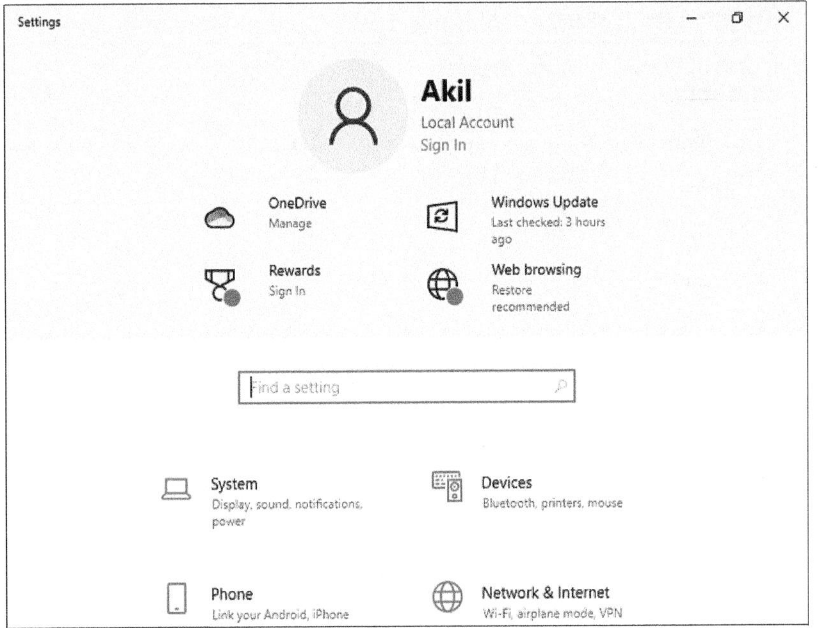

FIGURE 14.31 Windows 10 Settings app—home page

Table 14.6 shows all the Windows 10/11 Control Panel categories and subcategories. Control Panel utilities are similar across Windows versions, and in Windows 10/11 you configure some things through Settings. Keep in mind that a particular Control Panel utility might be accessible through two or more Control Panel categories.

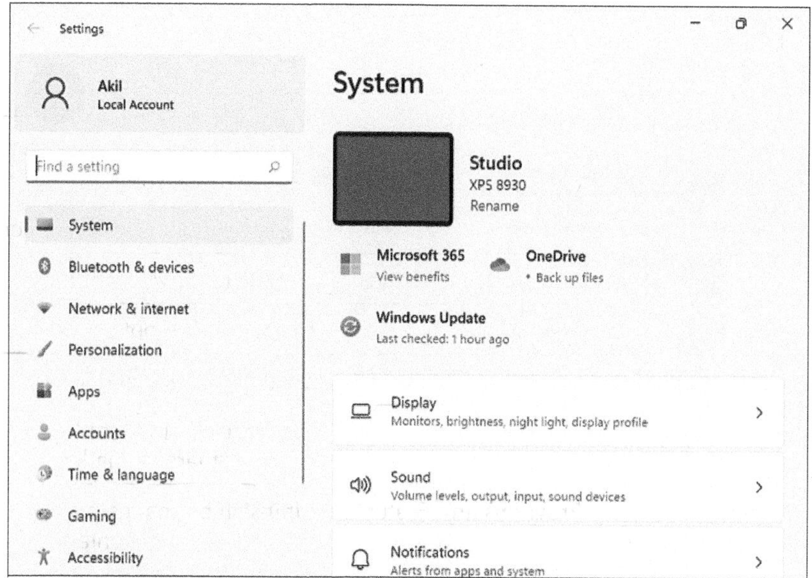

FIGURE 14.32 Windows 11 Settings app—home page

TABLE 14.6 Common Windows 10/11 Control Panel categories

Control Panel category	Subcategory	Function
System and Security	Security and Maintenance	Review computer's status and resolve issues; scan for viruses.
	Windows Defender Firewall	Prevent access to computer through the internet or a network.
	System	View basic computer properties, such as RAM, processor type, and computer name.
	Power Options	Configure power saving modes.
	File History	Automatically save backup copies of files.
	Backup and Restore (Windows 7)	Save or restore files and folders to or from a different location.
	BitLocker Drive Encryption	Change or use encryption options.
	Storage Spaces	Save files to two or more drives to help protect against a single drive failure.
	Work Folders	Make files available on all devices, even when offline.
	Administrative Tools	Free up hard disk space, manage hard drive partitions, schedule tasks, and view event logs.
Network and Internet	Network and Sharing Center	Check the status and modify network-related settings as well as share files, folders, and devices on the network.
	Internet Options	Customize settings for internet browsers.
Hardware and Sound	Devices and Printers	Add/remove/configure devices, scanners, cameras, printers, and mice and access Device Manager.

Control Panel category	Subcategory	Function
	AutoPlay	Change how media is automatically handled when a disc, flash drive, or type of file is added or inserted.
	Sound	Manage audio devices and change sound schemes.
	Power Options	Configure power saving modes.
	Pen and Touch	Configure pen options for tablet devices.
	Tablet PC Settings	Configure tablet and screen settings on a tablet PC.
	Display	Adjust resolution, configure an external display, or make text larger/smaller.
Programs	Programs and Features	Uninstall or change programs and turn Windows features such as Containers, Hyper-V, and TFTP Client on or off.
	Default Programs	Remove a startup program, associate a file extension with a particular application, or select the program used with a particular type of file.
Appearance and Personalization	Taskbar and Navigation	Select items that appear on the taskbar and control the behavior of the taskbar.
	Ease of Access Center	Make the computer easier to use, especially for those with physical or visual limitations.
	File Explorer Options	Control the appearance and behavior of folders, files, shortcuts, and links. Also configure search options.
	Fonts	Preview, install, delete, and configure fonts.
User Accounts	User Accounts	Add, remove, or modify accounts on the computer.
	Credential Manager	Manage saved logon information for websites, connected applications, and networks.
	Mail	Configure email accounts and email storage directories.
Clock and Region	Date and Time	Configure the primary time, date, and time zone for the computer. Add additional clocks for other time zones.
	Region	Configure the format for date, time, currency, and other region-specific options. Customize keyboard settings.
Ease of Access	Ease of Access Center	Make the computer easier to use, especially for those with physical or visual limitations.
	Speech Recognition	Configure built-in speech recognition system.

CHAPTER 14

Determining the Windows Version

The *Settings > System > About* option allows you to determine the amount of RAM installed, processor installed, and Windows version. Note that prior to Windows 10, the *System* Control Panel provided this information. The version of an operating system is important when troubleshooting because it is one more piece of information that can be placed within a search parameter. You can also access the *About* option by using *File Explorer* > right-click or tap and briefly hold *This PC* > *Properties*. Figure 14.33 shows the *About* option in Windows 11.

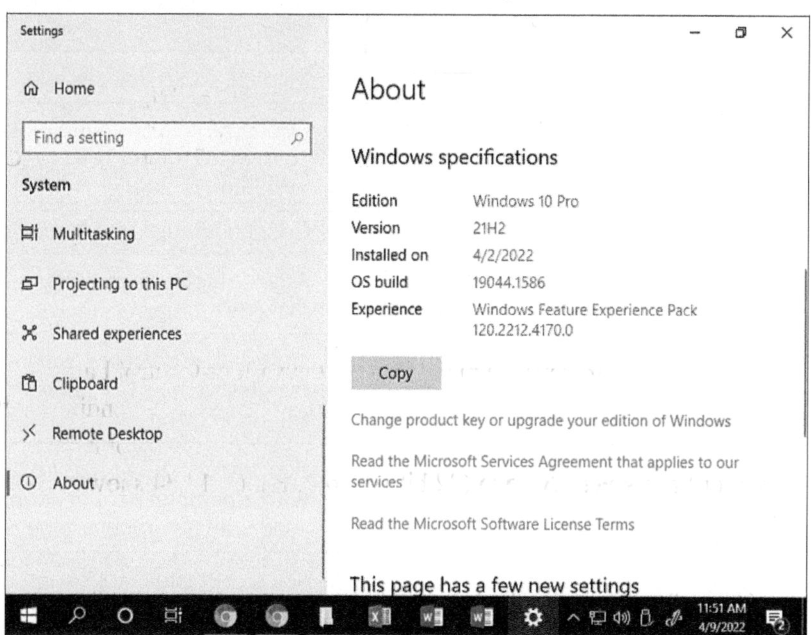

FIGURE 14.33 Windows 11 *Settings* > *System* > *About* option

Windows Registry

Every software and hardware configuration is stored in a database called the **registry**. The registry contains such things as folder and file property settings, port configuration, application preferences, and user profiles. A **user profile** contains specific configuration settings such as which applications the user can access, desktop settings, and each user's network configuration. The profile is different for each person who has an account on the computer. The registry is loaded into RAM (memory) during the boot process. When in memory, the registry is updated continuously based on changes made to software, hardware, and user preferences.

The registry data is organized in a tree format. Each node of the tree is called a key. The top-level keys are subtrees. Subtrees are also sometimes called *branches* or *hives*. The five standard subtrees are `Hkey_Local_Machine`, `Hkey_Users`, `Hkey_Current_User`, `Hkey_Current_Config`, and `Hkey_Classes_Root`. Each of these subtrees has keys and subkeys that contain values related to hardware and software settings. Table 14.7 lists the five subtrees and their functions. The registry can contain other subtrees that are user defined or system defined, depending on what hardware or software is installed on the computer.

TABLE 14.7 Windows registry subtrees

Registry subtree	Description
`Hkey_Local_Machine`	Holds global hardware configuration. Includes a list of hardware components installed in the computer, the software drivers that handle each component, and the settings for each device. This information is not user specific.
`Hkey_Users`	Keeps track of individual users and their preferences.

Registry subtree	Description
`Hkey_Current_User`	Holds a specific user's configuration, such as software settings, how the desktop appears, and what folders the user has created.
`Hkey_Current_Config`	Holds information about the hardware profile that is used when the computer first boots.
`Hkey_Classes_Root`	Holds file associations and file links. The information held here is what allows the correct application to start when you double-click a filename in File Explorer or This PC (provided that the file extension is registered).

Editing the Windows Registry

Most changes to Windows are made through the various Control Panel utilities, but sometimes the only way to make a change is to edit the registry directly. Depending on the Windows operating system used, one or two registry editors are available from a command prompt: **regedit.exe** (64 bit version) and **regedt32.exe** (32 bit version). Figure 14.34 shows the Windows 11 `regedit.exe` utility.

Notice in Figure 14.34 that subtrees such as `Hkey_Classes_Root` and `Hkey_Current_User` appear in the left window. If you click the arrow beside a subtree, keys appear under it. After several layers, when you click a folder in the left window (a key), values appear in the right window. These values are the ones you must sometimes change in order to fix a problem.

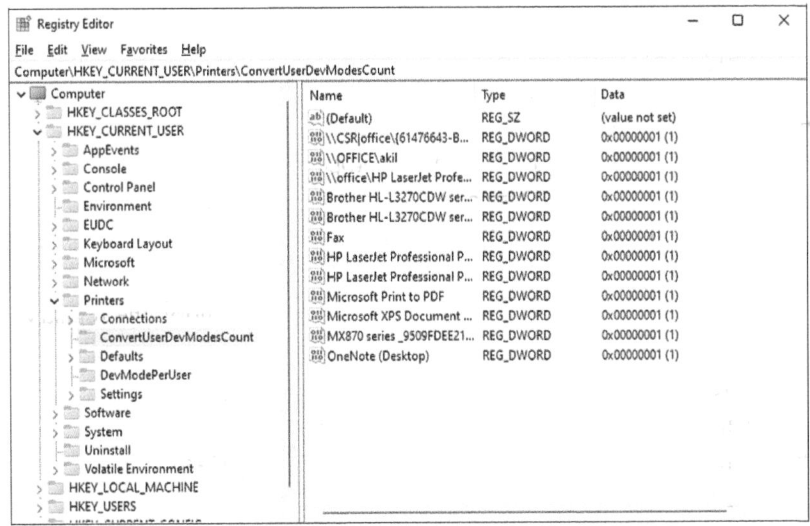

FIGURE 14.34 `regedit.exe` **in Windows 11**

> **TECH TIP**
>
> **Make a backup of the registry before you change it**
>
> Before making any change to the registry, you should make a backup of it. This way, if the change does not work properly, it can be easily reversed.

For 64-bit versions of Windows, the registry is divided into 32- and 64-bit keys. The 32-bit keys are kept in a subfolder called *Wow6432Node*, located within the `Hkey_Local_Machine\Software` subfolder. On some machines, the vendor may have a subfolder under *Software*; it is this vendor subfolder that contains the *Wow6432Node* folder. Just do a search for *Wow6432Node* to find it. 64-bit software keys are kept directly in the `Hkey_Local_Machine\Software` subfolder.

Backing Up Data

Having a data **backup**, or a copy of that data, is important. Many people store their data in a remote location, using cloud storage. Those who have accounts with Google (Gmail or another Google product) have access to Google Drive, Microsoft users have OneDrive, and Apple users have iCloud; there are also other cloud storage vendors, such as Dropbox and SugarSync. Windows 10 and Windows 11 allow backing up the entire system and files/folders by using the *Backup and Restore (Windows 7)* Control Panel. They also use *File History*, which saves files that are contained in the libraries (and you can create new libraries), contacts, desktop files, and favorites to external media or a network storage location.

WinRE

Windows Recovery Environment (**WinRE**) can be used when Windows 10/11 does not boot and other tools and startup options do not solve a problem. WinRE has a list of recovery options, including a command prompt–only environment. The WinRE environment provides access to tools to troubleshoot the operating system when the tools within the operating system cannot be accessed or don't work properly. You can access WinRE via *Settings* > *Update & Security* (*System* in Windows 11) > *Recovery* > *Advanced startup* section > *Restart now*. WinRE is also available via the original Windows installation disc (select *Repair your computer* > *Troubleshoot*). Some of the recovery methods in the next section require WinRE. Chapter 16, "Advanced Windows," discusses WinRE in detail, including other methods to access the environment.

Recovering the Windows OS

When a computer starts performing poorly and the operating system tools do not seem to help, you may need to repair, replace (**reload OS**), or uninstall/reinstall the operating system. A virus could also cause extensive damage, resulting in the need for an operating system recovery. How you do this depends on what measures have been taken (or have not been taken, in some cases) and the type of environment in which the computer is located (home or work). The following list describes some of the common methods used to recover an operating system:

- Before you start using your computer, create a Windows **recovery drive**. The recovery drive will contain the operating system, but it will not contain any user files, applications, or settings. In Windows 10/11, search for **`recovery`** and select *Create a Recovery Drive*. The system recovery drive can boot the system when you don't have an original Windows disc or flash drive, and then you can restore the computer from a previously saved system image.
- Periodically create a Windows 10/11 **system image** using the *Backup and Restore (Windows 7)* Control Panel > *Create a System Image* link, especially after installing new programs. The system image contains the operating system, settings, installed programs, and all user files. If the computer starts performing poorly, you can recover all or part of the image. The image can be saved to one of several locations:
  - Optical discs
  - Flash drive
  - Hard drive (but not on the same hard drive as the operating system)

  - Network location (Keep in mind that you have to get to the network location to get the image. This might be difficult if the computer is not working. You could burn the image from another computer that works.)
- When you boot the system from the Windows 10/11 original disc or flash drive, you can select the *Repair your computer > Troubleshoot > Advanced options* (if present) *System Image Recovery* option and then select the storage device that contains the system image.
- Before making a major change like installing an update or a driver, create a restore point. A restore point is a snapshot of the operating system settings but not the operating system itself. Furthermore, it does not contain applications or user files. If the operating system starts misbehaving, the settings can be restored to the previous values from *System > About > System protection > System Restore* or from *Windows Recovery Environment > Troubleshoot > Advanced options* (if present) > *System Restore*. Chapter 16 discusses *System Restore* in detail, including how to enable the tool and how to create a restore point.
- A recovery partition or section of the hard drive (sometimes called the HPA, or host protected area) is created by the computer manufacturer and commonly accessed through *Windows Recovery Environment > Troubleshoot > Reset this PC* in Windows 10/11. The *Reset this PC* tool reinstalls the operating system and removes all apps and settings. It offers the option of keeping the user's personal files.
- Use a recovery disc provided by the computer manufacturer to restore the computer to the original "as sold" condition. *Caution:* With this option, none of the user's applications or data will be restored.
- You can use imaging software. Companies frequently have a standard image stored on a server that can replace a failing operating system or that can be used on a new computer. The image will contain the pre-selected settings, files, and folders, as determined by the company. User-specific files and settings can be recovered via other means.
- Note that using an old operating system disc or image (such as the original one) is risky because it does not contain the latest service packs. Download **updates** and copy them to an optical disc, hard drive, flash drive, or network drive *before* reinstalling the operating system. Research the update requirements before installing. After the operating system is reinstalled, apply the updates before accessing any other data on a network.
- Backup/restore software may be provided by an external hard drive manufacturer.

SOFT SKILLS: STAYING CURRENT

Technicians must stay current in the rapidly changing field of computers. Benefits of staying current include understanding and being able to troubleshoot the latest technologies, being able to recommend upgrades or solutions to customers, saving time (and therefore money) on troubleshooting, and being considered for a promotion. Technicians use a variety of methods to stay current, including the following:

- Subscribe to a magazine or an online magazine.
- Subscribe to a news list that gives you email updates.
- Join or attend association meetings.
- Register for and attend a seminar.
- Attend an online webinar.
- Take a class.
- Read books.
- Talk to your department peers and supervisor.

Staying current on technology in the past few years has been challenging for all, but the rapidly changing environment is what draws many to the field.

Chapter Summary

- An operating system performs all the basic tasks to communicate between hardware and software, to communicate between hardware and users, and to facilitate communication between software and users.
- The user communicates with the operating system through a command prompt or a GUI interface.
- The most popular desktop/laptop operating systems are Microsoft's Windows, Apple's macOS, Chrome OS, and Linux. The most popular mobile operating systems are Android, iOS, and iPadOS.
- Operating systems use either 32-bit or 64-bit architecture. A 64-bit system has more processing power than a 32-bit system.
- When replacing or upgrading an operating system, end-of-life (EOL) concerns must be addressed. Concerns include security threats, software incompatibility, compliance issues, performance, reliability, and cost.
- Computers are considered compatible if software that runs on one model can run on all other models in that family, even if this results in performance issues. Forward and backward compatibility as well as extensibility are considerations.
- While specifics may differ, all Windows 10 and 11 editions offer the user a desktop or Start screen that consists of icons, the taskbar, shortcuts, and the Recycle Bin.
- Right-click a shortcut or tile and select *Properties* to see the path to the original file.
- File Explorer is commonly used to manipulate files and folders. Windows libraries (*Documents*, *Music*, *Pictures*, and *Videos*) are commonly part of the path to stored documents and subfolders.
- Deleted files are stored on the hard drive in a folder called Recycle Bin. The Recycle Bin must be emptied to release hard drive space. This is relevant only to files stored on hard drives.
- Windows supports encryption and compression. When a file or folder is encrypted with EFS, only authorized users can view or change the file. Encrypted files that are moved or copied on NTFS volumes remain encrypted. Compressed files, system files, and read-only files cannot be encrypted. When a file or folder is encrypted with EFS, only authorized users can view or change the file.
- Technicians commonly use the Control Panel to modify how the hardware, software, and operating system environment functions and appears. The *System* section of the Control Panel can be used to determine the Windows version and to modify the registry. Other uses for the important Control Panel utilities are covered in Chapter 16.

> The Windows registry is a database of everything within the Windows environment. Configuring Control Panel settings modifies the registry. Use `regedit.exe` or `regedt32.exe` to manually modify the registry.
> You can recover the operating system in various ways: using a Windows or manufacturer-provided recovery disc, a recovery partition, a previously created image, a reload of the operating system and service packs, or the System Restore tool.
> Technicians must stay current in the IT field to move up or maintain their current job status. Methods used to stay current include joining associations, reading relevant magazines, taking classes, reading current books, and interacting with peers.

A+ CERTIFICATION EXAM TIPS

✓ Know the differences between 32-bit and 64-bit architecture.

✓ Know the types and uses of operating systems, including Microsoft Windows, Apple macOS, and Linux. Know the different types of licenses for operating systems: open, personal, corporate, and enterprise.

✓ Know the types and uses of cell phone/tablet operating systems, including Microsoft Windows, Android, iOS, and Chrome OS.

✓ Describe the differences and similarities among Windows 10/11 editions, including Home, Pro, Pro for Workstations, and Enterprise. Pay special attention to the availability of security, networking, and remote access features.

✓ Describe how the following are addressed in a corporate environment and on a personal computer: workgroup vs. domain access, BitLocker, BitLocker To Go, and EFS.

✓ Be able to set various folder options, including hiding file extensions, viewing hidden files, view options, and the options available through the *Folder Options* Control Panel > *View* tab.

Key Terms

32-bit architecture 655
64-bit architecture 655
Active Directory (AD) 660
Android OS 657
Apple Macintosh OS 655
Apply button 671
attribute 679
backup 688
backward compatibility 659
BitLocker 660
BitLocker To Go 661
boot process 652
Chrome OS 657
command-line interface 653
compatibility 659
compression 681
context menu 672
Control Panel 682
desktop 661
Documents 669
domain access 660
Edge 669
EFS 661
end-of-life (EOL) 658
extensible software 659
extension 672
file 654
file type 659
filename 672
folder 654
forward compatibility 659
GUI 653
icon 661
indexing 678
iOS 658
iPadOS 658
library 672
Linux 655
macOS 655
Microsoft Windows 655
Network 669
notification area 667
open source 655
operating system 652
path 669
proprietary operating system 655
RAM limitation 655
recovery drive 688
Recycle Bin 669
regedit.exe 687
regedt32.exe 687
registry 686
reload OS 688
security threat 658
service pack 689
shortcut 669
software incompatibility 658
Start button 664
Start screen 662
subdirectory 672
subfolder 672
system image 688
Task View 668
taskbar 663
This PC 669
tile 662
updates 689
upward compatibility 659
user profile 686
window 670
Windows 10 656
Windows 11 656
WinRE 688

Review Questions

1. The key piece of software that provides an interface between the user and installed hardware is a(n) _____.

   [application | time machine | operating system | registry]

2. What is the core of a computer's operating system?

   [CPU | kernel | RAM | commands]

3. [T | F] Programs and drivers written for 64-bit systems can always run on 32-bit systems.

4. Two methods of interacting with the operating system are through a(n) ____ or a(n) _____. (Choose two.)

   [tunnel | GUI | OS cache | command line | core | workstation]

5. Name two features commonly needed on a mobile device's operating system.

6. Name three possible consequences associated with using software that has reached its end-of-life (EOL).

7. Name two potential problems associated with updating an operating system.

8. [T | F] Backward compatibility means that a new application can still process data from older software.

9. [T | F] A folder and a directory are the same thing.

10. A file's name consists of a filename and a(n) ___________.

    [path | size | folder | extension]

11. Describe how to show a file's extension if it is not displayed in File Explorer, using either Windows 10 or 11.

12. Name the subfolder(s) in the following path.

    `C:\Users\Cheryl\NewFiles\review.docx`

13. [T | F] Deleted files stored on a hard drive can be recovered from the Recycle Bin.

14. What Windows option can access various icons or links that can be used to configure the computer?

    [Control Panel | Time Machine | registry | Quick Launch]

15. What is the maximum memory that can be recognized by a Windows 32-bit operating system?

    [1 GB | 2 GB | 4 GB | 16 GB | 64 GB]

16. In the filename `Opsys_Quiz 4.docx`, what is the extension?

    [`Opsys_Quiz 4.docx` | `Opsys` | `4` | `docx`]

17. A user is working in Microsoft Word. She saves the document called `Ltr1.docx` to a folder called *Homedocs*. The *Homedocs* folder is a subfolder of the *Work* folder located on the `D:` hard drive volume. Write the complete path for the `Ltr1.docx` file.

    `D:\Work\Homedocs\Ltr1.docx`

18. [T | F] File and folder compression can degrade computer performance.

19. List three methods that can be used to recover an operating system.

    recovery drive, original disc (installation) recovery disc

20. Which of the following is the name of a registry editor?

    [registry | regedit.exe | edit | nano]

21. Describe or explain two common methods used to recover an operating system.

    recovery partition and system image

22. List two methods that you think you will use to stay current in the IT field.

    Join an association, stay up to date via the news, magazines, books, stay up to date with latest certs

Exercises

Exercise 14.1

Objective: To recognize common Windows Control Panel categories

Procedure: Match each task to the appropriate Windows Control Panel category. Note that a category can be used more than once.

Control Panel Category:

a. System and Security

b. Network and Internet

c. Hardware and Sound

d. Programs

e. User Accounts

f. Appearance and Personalization

g. Clock and Region

h. Ease of Access

Task:

A 1. Require a password to be entered when the computer comes out of sleep mode.

H 2. Enable screen reading for any text shown on the screen.

B 3. Determine whether a computer is on a domain or workgroup.

C 4. Access Device Manager.

D 5. Configure whether hidden files are shown.

H 6. Configure power saving options.

F 7. Disable the showing of Microsoft-provided games.

A 8. Back up the system.

D 9. Configure the home page for the default Microsoft browser.

G 10. Set the proper time zone.

E 11. Change the Windows password for a home computer.

C 12. Verify that a camera appears as being attached.

B 13. Configure the Ethernet NIC for DHCP.

Exercise 14.2

Objective: To differentiate between operating systems used today

Procedure: Match each OS to a description. Note that an operating system can be used more than once.

Operating System:

a. Windows
b. Android
c. Linux
d. iOS
e. macOS
f. iPadOS
g. Chrome OS

Description:

______ **1.** Microsoft's operating system
______ **2.** The operating system most commonly used for office computers
______ **3.** An open source operating system
______ **4.** A mobile operating system
______ **5.** Apple's operating system for iPhones
______ **6.** A proprietary operating system
______ **7.** An operating system designed for cloud-based apps
______ **8.** Torvalds worked on the kernel
______ **9.** Runs on Apple desktop computers
______ **10.** Has the Control Panel
______ **11.** Has worldwide development efforts
______ **12.** Operating system developed by Google
______ **13.** iPads use this operating system

Exercise 14.3

Objective: To differentiate between when a command-line environment is used and when a graphical user interface is used

Procedure: Determine whether each action is using a (a) GUI environment or (b) command-line interface. Note that an option can be used more than once. You may have to do some research on your own to determine the answers.

______ **1.** Working with File Explorer
______ **2.** Typing `dir` to see a list of files
______ **3.** Running a batch file
______ **4.** Writing a research paper in Microsoft Word
______ **5.** Setting a configuration by using *Settings > System*
______ **6.** Using `regedit.exe`
______ **7.** Running a script
______ **8.** Trying to fix a system on which the Windows operating system does not load

Activities

Internet Discovery

Objective: Access the internet to obtain specific information regarding a computer or its associated parts

Parts: A computer with internet access

Procedure: Complete the following procedure and answer the accompanying questions.

1. Locate an internet site that has a tutorial for Windows 10 troubleshooting or usage. Document the site and one thing you learned from the tutorial.

 ____

 ____

2. Find a web-based article on the differences between Windows 10 Pro and Windows 10 Home editions. List the name of the article, three important differences, and the URL.

 ____

 ____

 ____

3. Locate a website that demonstrates how to edit the Windows registry for any version of the Windows 10 operating system. Describe the registry hack using at least one complete sentence. State whether you would deploy such a hack and explain why or why not.

 ____

 ____

4. Locate a website that describes three things to do if Windows 10 (any version) will not boot. Briefly describe the three things and document the URL.

 ____

 ____

 ____

 ____

 ____

 ____

 ____

Soft Skills

Objective: To enhance and fine-tune a technician's ability to listen, communicate in both written and oral forms, and support people who use computers in a professional manner

Activities:

1. Access a monitor's settings in *Settings > Display*. Make a list of some of the settings that would be helpful to a computer user. Include in your list a description of each function. Document this in such a way that it could be given to users as a how-to guide.
2. On an index card, write a paragraph describing a problem and how a technician might look at the problem differently than a user would. Exchange cards with one classmate and discuss your paragraphs. Comment on anything you find unclear in the classmate's paragraph, listen to suggestions from your classmate, and rewrite your paragraph, if necessary.

Critical Thinking Skills

Objective: To enhance and fine-tune a technician's ability to listen, communicate in both written and oral forms, and support people who use computers in a professional manner

Activities:

1. In a group environment, on a piece of paper or an index card, list two topics you would like to hear about if you were to attend a local association such as a PC users' group meeting. Share your ideas with your group. Consolidate ideas and present five of the best ideas to the class.
2. In a group environment, select one of the five ideas presented in Activity 1 to research. Every group member should present something about a new technology to the rest of the class. The class will vote on the best presented topic and the most interesting topic.
3. On an index card, document a question that several students have asked the teacher about how to do a particular task. Exchange cards with a classmate. Correct each other's grammar, punctuation, and capitalization. When you have your original card back, exchange cards with a different classmate and perform the same task. Rewrite your index card based on the recommendations of your classmates. Keep in mind that all their suggestions are just that—suggestions. You do not have to accept any of them. A complaint in the industry is that technicians do not write well. Practice helps with this issue.

15 Introduction to Scripting

In this chapter you will learn:

> How to work from a command prompt
> How to use specific commands
> The basics of shell scripting and scripting in Python, JavaScript, VBScript, batch files, and PowerShell
> The most common use cases for scripting
> How to avoid unintended consequences of scripting
> How to define environment variables and distinguish between system and user environment variables
> How to view and modify environment variables
> The building blocks of scripting: variables and data types
> The three programming constructs used to build all scripts: sequence, selection, and repetition
> How to use relational and logical operators in a script
> The pros and cons of each of six scripting languages
> Changing your perspective when troubleshooting

CompTIA Exam Objectives

✓ 1102-1.2 Given a scenario, use the appropriate Microsoft command-line tool.

✓ 1102-1.3 Given a scenario, use features and tools of the Microsoft Windows 10 operating system (OS).

✓ 1102-4.8 Identify the basics of scripting.

Scripting Overview

While the Windows operating system offers technicians many dialog boxes that provide assistance in fixing problems and accessing various settings, sometimes technicians need to do things that cannot be done through a dialog box. In such cases, the command prompt environment can be used. From a command prompt, a technician can type commands that are specific to the operating system and to the required task. However, to do this, you must know the commands that a computer understands as well as the appropriate syntax to get commands to work. *Syntax* refers to the rules that specify the correct sequence of symbols or words. For example, in English, the phrase "table on this is book the" is meaningless, but the same words in a different order make perfect sense: "this book is on the table." In English, the correct syntax must be followed for the words to be understandable. Similarly, typing **`/p dir w/`** at a command prompt will give you an error, but typing **`dir /p /w`** will display the list of files and folders in a directory one page at a time in wide format. The same characters and symbols must be used in correct order—with correct syntax—for a command at the command prompt to work.

Access the command prompt from within Windows as follows: Access the *Search* function > type **`command`** in the textbox > select *Command Prompt* from the search result.

Remember that there are always several ways to accomplish almost anything in the Windows environment.

Some actions performed from the command prompt can only be done as an administrator of the machine. To open the command prompt window with administrator rights, right-click the *Command Prompt* option and select *Run as administrator*. Figure 15.1 shows a command prompt environment with administrator rights. This is also called an elevated command prompt.

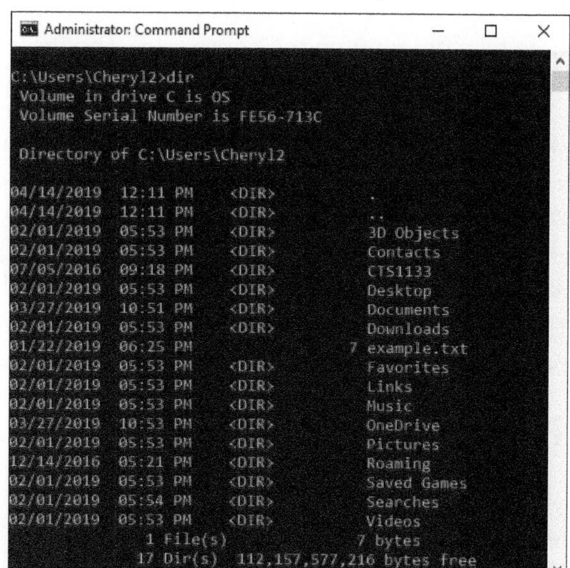

FIGURE 15.1 Windows command prompt

Network technicians can use scripts to automate tasks, to save time when completing complex procedures, to ensure consistency in tasks that must be executed over multiple servers in different locations, and to reduce human error. A *script* is a program that is designed to do a specific task. You can often find scripts written by others that you can use, and you can also create your own. Scripts are created in a text editor and are run from the command prompt. In this chapter you will learn the basics of scripting in some of the many scripting languages, including PowerShell, VBScript, Python, JavaScript, as well as shell scripts for Unix and batch files for Windows.

Command Prompt Overview

Even with the advent of newer and more powerful operating systems, a technician still must enter basic commands into computers while troubleshooting, when deploying computers, and when updating computers in a corporate environment. Functioning from a command prompt is a skill that a technician still must use sometimes.

Following are two ways to access a command prompt when a computer is functional:

> Access the *Search* function > type **`command`** and press ↵Enter.

> Access the *Search* function > type **`cmd`** and press ↵Enter.

TECH TIP

Use the command prompt with administrative privileges

When issuing commands from a prompt, you might need to log in or provide credentials that allow you to execute a particular command with administrative privileges. Right-click or tap and briefly hold the *Command Prompt* option > select *Run as administrator*. This option is also called an elevated command prompt.

You can close the command prompt window in several ways:

> Use the *Close* button in the upper-right corner.

> Click or tap the little black box in the upper-left corner > select *Close*.

> Type the **`exit`** command.

Command Prompt Basics

Drive letters are assigned to disk partitions when a computer boots. For example, the first hard drive partition gets the drive letter `C:`. The colon is part of the device drive letter. The devices detected by the operating system can use and be assigned drive letters `A:` through `Z:`.

All communication using typed commands begins at the **command prompt**, also called simply a *prompt*. A command prompt might look like `F:\>` or `C:\>` or `C:\Windows>`. Notice the backslash (\) that follows the colon and the greater-than sign (>) at the end of the prompt. Commands can be typed using a keyboard or entered through a touchscreen. Capitalization of commands does not matter when using a Windows command prompt (though this is not true for all operating systems), but commands *must* be typed in a specific format and in a specific order. Practicing using commands from a command prompt is the best way to become proficient at using them.

Files can be organized like chapters in a book; however, on a computer, a file grouping is called a folder in a GUI environment or a **directory** in a command prompt environment. The starting point for all directories is the **root directory**. From the root directory, other directories can be created or accessed. The root directory can hold only a limited number of files, and the quantity depends on the file system used. The root directory of a drive is shown as a backslash after the driver letter: `C:\` or `E:\`. In the command prompt environment, when you are at the root directory, a greater-than sign (>) follows the letter and the backslash: `C:\>` and `E:\>`.

Each filename or directory name within a directory must be unique, but multiple directories can contain the same file. For example, assume that the *Cheryl.txt* file exists in the *Documents* directory. A different *Cheryl.txt* file can exist in the *Lotus* or *Utility* directory. In fact, the file called

Cheryl.txt that contains the same information could also exist in all three folders. However, a second *Cheryl.txt* file cannot exist in the same folder (directory).

Files are kept in the root directory or within directories (folders) that reside within the root directory. A **subdirectory** can be created beneath another directory. For example, if a directory (folder) has the name *Book*, below the directory can be subdirectories titled *Chap1*, *Chap2*, *Chap3*, and so on. Since the word *root* identifies the start of the directory structure, many people describe the directory structure as a tree. Figure 15.2 illustrates this concept.

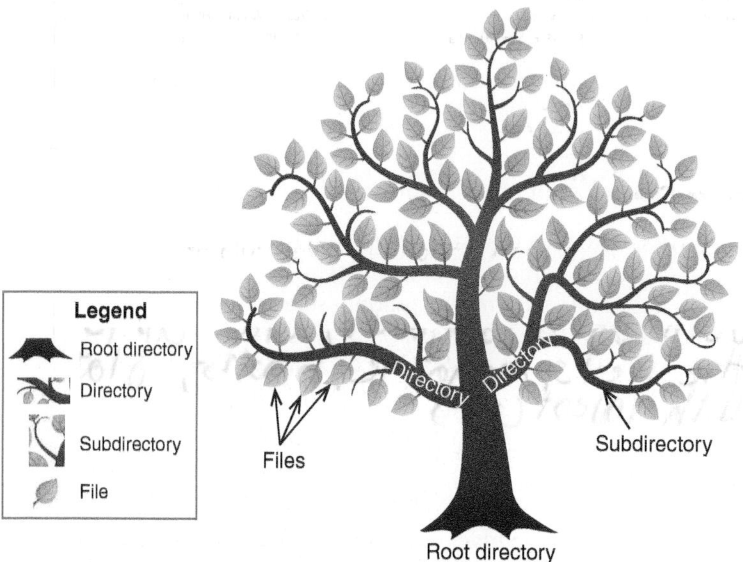

FIGURE 15.2 Tree structure concepts

Sometimes it's easier to see the file structure concepts from File Explorer than from the command prompt. Figure 15.3 shows the *Documents* directory of the `C:` drive for the user *Cheryl*. Notice that the path is listed at the top of the File Explorer window because that option has been enabled through the *Folder Options* window. Also notice the address bar, which shows part of the path (<< Users > Cheryl > Documents). The File Explorer window shows several types of items:

- *Folders: 2015BookWin8Laptop*, *Custom Office Templates*, *Outlook Files*, and *SugarSync Shared Folders*.
- *Shortcuts to the folders: My Music*, *My Pictures*, and *My Videos*.
- *Files (unhidden): Chap1.docx*, *kara's books.docx*, *My class books.docx*, and *Spectre.docx*.
- *Hidden file: desktop.ini.* Settings in the *Folder Options* section of the Control Panel allow you to determine whether filename extensions and hidden files are seen.

Now let's view this same structure from the command prompt by using the `tree` command. Figure 15.4 shows this perspective from the command prompt.

In Figure 15.4 notice that two commands have actually been given. The first one, `tree`, asks the computer to display a "tree," or the structure starting from `C:\Users\Cheryl\Documents`. The second command uses a `/f` at the end, causing files to be shown.

Every folder along the path is shown, starting with the root directory, `C:\`. The subfolders are separated by backslashes (\). The path tells you exactly how to reach the file. When something goes wrong in a particular application and Microsoft or another vendor posts a solution online, the solution commonly shows the complete path. This is the only way to clearly tell you where to find, put, delete, or replace a file.

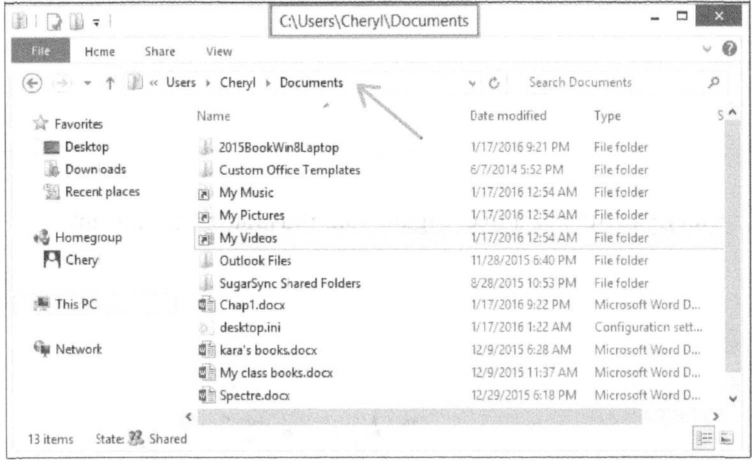

FIGURE 15.3 Sample file structure in File Explorer

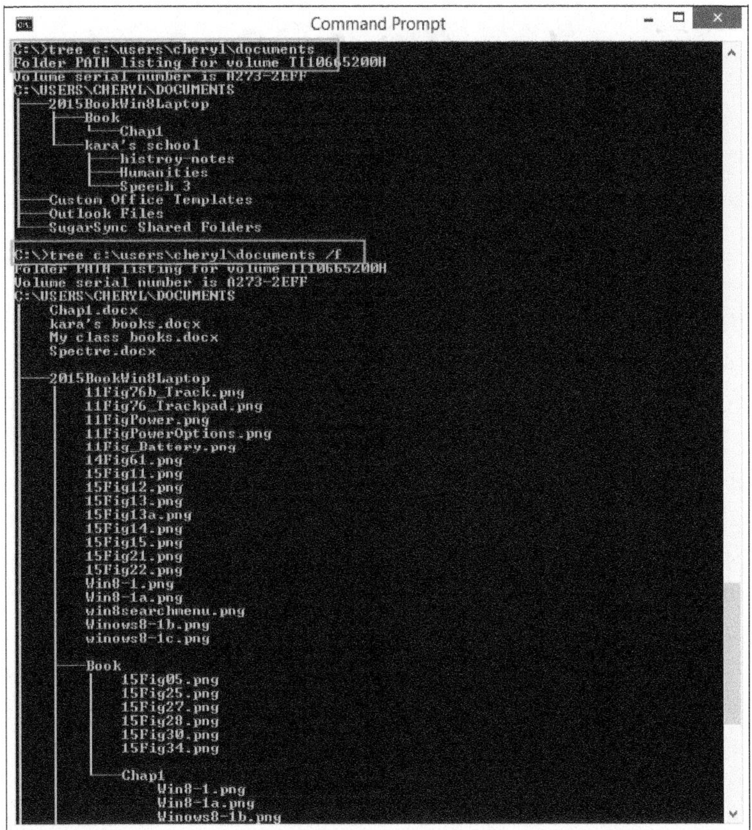

FIGURE 15.4 Tree structure from a command prompt

Moving Around from a Command Prompt

One of the most important skills when working in the command-line environment is to be able to move around within that environment. The `cd`, `md`, `rd`, and `dir` commands are the four most popular commands used within the Windows environment to move around the directory structure. Let's take a look at each one.

The `cd` Command

The most frequently used command for moving around in the cumbersome tree structure is `cd` (for *change directory*). The `cd` command enables you to "change" to a different directory so that the prompt changes to where you are within the directory (tree) structure. For example, say you have a flash drive with a *Test1* directory that has subdirectories called *Sub1*, *Sub2*, and *Sub3*, as shown in Figure 15.5.

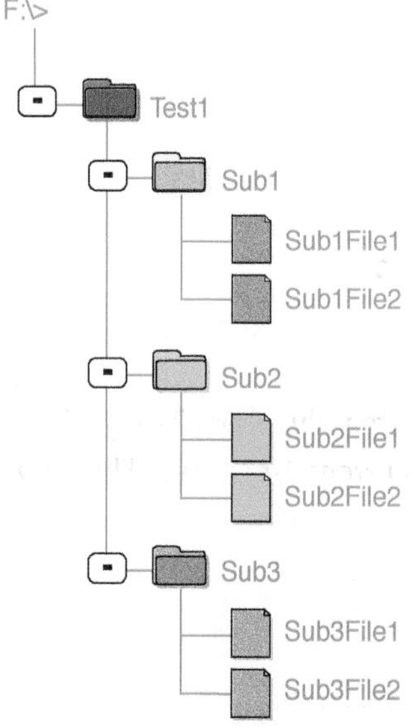

FIGURE 15.5 Sample tree structure

Assume that the prompt is at `F:\>`. To get to this prompt, you simply type the drive letter of your flash drive and press Enter. To move to the *Sub2* subdirectory (subfolder), type the command **`cd Test1\Sub2`**. The prompt changes to `F:\Test1\Sub2>`. Another command that does the same thing is `cd F:\Test1\Sub2`. The difference is that with the second command, the full path is given. The F:\ is not required because the prompt is already at the root directory of F: (F:\>).

Two subdirectories are said to be at the same level if they reside immediately within the same directory. To move to a subdirectory that is on the same level as the *Sub2* directory (such as *Sub1* or *Sub3*), several commands are possible. For example, you can type **`cd..`** (you must type the two periods after **`cd`**) to move back one level and then type **`cd Sub1`**. Notice that there is no backslash (\) between `cd` and `Sub1`. You omit the backslash only when moving one level down the tree structure, as shown in Figure 15.5.

From the `F:\Test1>` prompt, you can type **`cd Sub1`**, **`cd \Test1\Sub1`**, or **`cd F:\Test1\Sub1`** to get to the *Sub1* subfolder. However, if the prompt shows that you are at the root directory (`F:\>`), you must use either **`cd F:\Test1\Sub1`** or **`cd Test1\Sub1`**. The command **`cd Sub1`** does not operate properly because of the current location within the tree structure (as shown by the prompt F:\>). Practice is the best way to master moving around from a prompt.

The `dir` Command

The `dir` command lists all the files and directories from wherever you are at the prompt. Figure 15.6 shows the `dir` command issued from the root directory of a flash drive (`G:\>`).

Notice in Figure 15.6 that directories are shown with `<DIR>`. There is nothing listed in that column to identify a file. Directories in the root directory of `G:` are *Chip*, *Dale*, *cotlong*, *Photos*, and *classes*. Files in the root directory of the same flash drive are *Dinfo.txt* and *Ninfo.txt*.

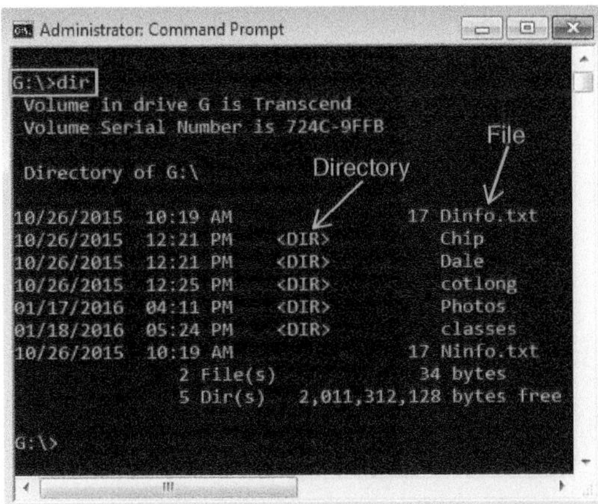

FIGURE 15.6 `dir` **command from a prompt**

When you use the `dir` command on a hard drive, you might notice a directory for `.` and `..` (see Figure 15.7). The `.` and `..` are used with commands like `cd` to move around the directory structure. A single period (`.`) represents the current directory. Two periods (`..`) represents the parent directory (the directory that contains the current directory). That is why the command `cd..` moves you back one directory level. In Figure 15.7, if someone were to type the command `cd..` from the `C:\Users\Cheryl2>` prompt, the prompt would change to `C:\Users>`. If the `cd \` command were issued from the `C:\Users\Cheryl2>` prompt, the prompt would change to `C:\`.

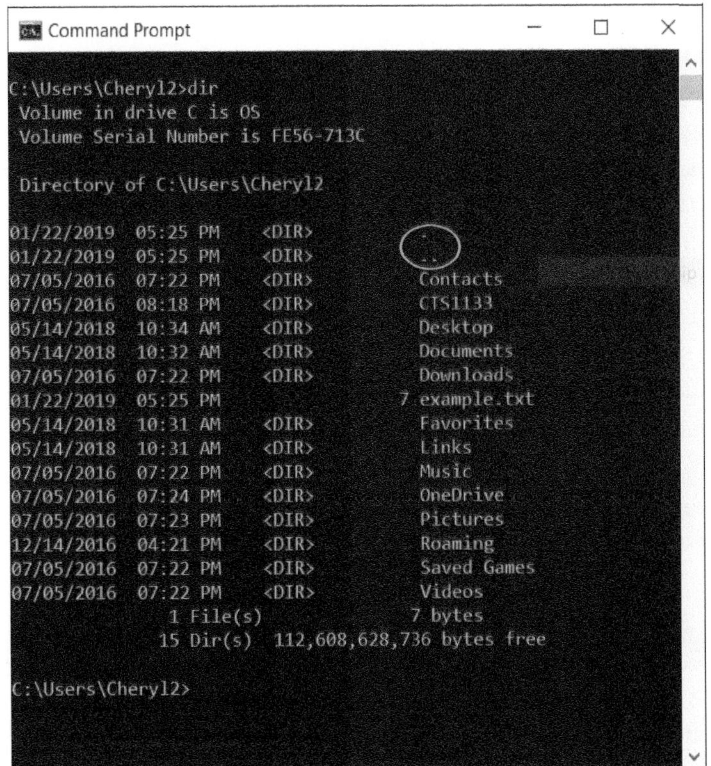

FIGURE 15.7 `dir` **command showing the** `.` **and** `..` **directories**

Each command commonly has one or more optional **command switches** that change how the command operates. To determine what switches are available with any command, type the following:

`command_name /?`

where *command_name* is any one command. For example, the command `dir /?` shows all the possible options that can be used with the `dir` command (see Figure 15.8). Notice how `dir` is the *command_name*, and `/?` is how to get help for the `dir` command. In the third and fourth lines from the top of Figure 15.8, you can see that there is an order to the listing of the switches. Normally, they are shown in alphabetical order.

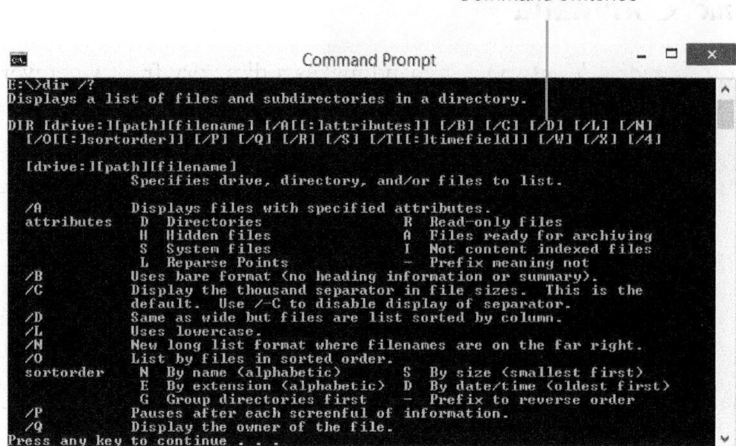

FIGURE 15.8 `dir` **command switches**

Notice in the output shown in Figure 15.8 that there are optional parameters such as `drive:` and `path`. Each optional parameter and switch has brackets ([ ]) around it. A switch is preceded by a / (forward slash). There is no space between the / and the switch. For example, with the `dir` command, you could simply type `dir` and press Enter. You could also type `dir /p` to display things one page at a time or `dir /w` to display the output in a wide format. You can use multiple switches together, such as `dir /p /w`. While it is not necessary to put a space after each switch, you must put a space between the command and a switch. The command `dir /p/w` works exactly the same way as `dir /p /w`.

Figure 15.8 shows that each command switch is described below the options. Also notice in this figure that when some commands list more than one page of output, you get a `Press any key to continue...` message at the bottom of the screen.

TECH TIP

Make a command output one page at a time

If a command outputs more than one page at a time, you can use the `| more` option after the command to make it show only one page at a time. Note that the | (pipe) symbol is created by holding down the Shift key and pressing the \ key located directly above the Enter key.

TECH TIP

Limited commands in WinRE

Not all command parameters or switches shown may be available when using the Windows Recovery Environment (WinRE), which is discussed in Chapter 14, "Introduction to Operating Systems" and Chapter 16, "Advanced Windows." WinRE has a limited number of commands. Type the **`help`** command to see a list of available commands.

The md and rd Commands

Sometimes as an IT staff person, you might be required to create or remove a directory from a command prompt to install software or as part of a repair. The md and rd commands are used to perform these tasks.

The md Command

The md (for *make directory*) command makes a directory from wherever you are in the directory structure (as shown from the prompt on the screen). Consider the following command: F:\>md CTS1133. The *CTS1133* directory would be made in the root directory of the F: drive. Now consider the following set of commands:

```
F:\>
F:\>cd classes
F:\Classes>md CTS1133
F:\Classes>
```

What is different about this set of commands is that before the md CTS1133 command was issued, the cd classes command was issued. The cd classes command changed the prompt to F:\Classes> (the *Classes* folder on the F: drive). Then the md CTS1133 command was issued, thus creating a subdirectory called *CTS1133* under the *Classes* folder.

An alternative way of doing the same thing is to issue the full path with the command, as shown here:

```
F:\>md \classes\CTS1133
```

or:

```
F:\>md F:\classes\CTS1133
```

Note that the second command would work from any prompt, including the C:\> prompt, because it includes the full path as part of the command.

TECH TIP

The full path works from everywhere

If you begin learning the command prompt by typing the full path no matter where you are in the directory structure, you will be better prepared for working in this environment.

CHAPTER 15

The rd Command

The rd command removes a directory or subdirectory. Note that if the directory has files in it, this message will appear: The directory is not empty. You can only use the rd command on an empty directory. The examples here show how to remove a directory from the different prompts:

```
F:\>rd F:\classes\cts1133
F:\>rd \classes\cts1133
F:\Classes>rd cts1133
```

Note that the first example here works from any prompt, even if it is another drive letter.

Two Useful Commands: del and type

When problems occur and a technician is working at a command prompt, two tasks that might need to be accomplished are to delete a particular file or to read the contents of a text file such as a log file. The `del` and `type` commands can be used to do this, so let's look at them next.

The del Command

Sometimes a file has to be deleted as part of the repair process. The `del` (for *delete*) command removes a file. It cannot be used to remove a directory. That is an important point to remember. To issue the command, simply type the `del` command followed by the name of the file you want to delete. You must be in the correct directory (as shown by the prompt) to use this method, and you must include the file extension as part of the filename. In the commands shown below, the user is in the root directory of the `F:` drive and wants to delete a file named `homework1.docx` that is in the `cts1133` subdirectory of the `classes` directory. Before issuing the `del` command, the user must change directories to be in the `cts1133` subdirectory:

```
F:\>
F:\>cd F:\classes\cts1133
F:\Classes\CTS1133>del homework1.docx
F:\Classes\CTS1133>
```

An alternative method can work from any prompt. This method requires that you type the full path of the file to be deleted, as shown here:

```
F:\>del F:\classes\cts1133\homework1.docx
```

The type Command

Another useful command is the `type` command, which displays text (`.txt`) or batch (`.bat`) files on the screen. Many times *Readme.txt* files are included with software applications and utilities. The `type` command allows you to view these files from the command-line interface; however, most of the time, these files occupy more than one screen. So, using the `| more` parameter after the `type` command permits viewing the file one screen at a time. After viewing each screen, press the Spacebar key to see the next screenful of content. For example, `type readme.txt | more` allows you to view the text file called *readme.txt* one page at a time.

Copying Files

Commands that can copy files are `copy`, `xcopy`, and `robocopy`. The `copy` command is used to make a duplicate of a file. The `xcopy` command is used to copy and back up files and directories. The `robocopy` command enables you to copy a directory, its contents, all its subdirectories (and their subdirectories), and each attribute.

We focus on the `copy` command because it is the command you can use in any environment. The `copy` command is an internal command, meaning it cannot be found as an executable file on the hard drive or Windows disc. The operating system can always find an internal command no matter where in the directory structure the command is located. The command enables you to copy a file to a different disk, copy a file from one directory to another, copy a group of files using wildcards, or rename a file as it is being copied. A **wildcard** replaces one or more characters. ? and * are examples of wildcards; ? represents a single character, and * represents any number of characters.

The `copy` command has three parts, separated by spaces:

> The command itself (`copy` or `xcopy`)
> The source (the file being copied)
> The destination (where the file is being copied to)

In technical documentation, this would be shown using the syntax `copy` *`source destination`*. *`destination`* is optional if the file is being copied into the current directory. For example, if you are working from the `E:\>` command prompt and copying a file called *Document.txt* from the hard drive's root directory, the command could be `copy C:\Document.txt`. The destination is omitted because the file automatically copies to the current drive and directory (which is `E:\`). The same function can be accomplished by typing `copy C:\Document.txt E:\`, which has all three parts: the `copy` command, the *`source`* (a file called *Document.txt* located on the hard drive or `C:\Document.txt`), and the *`destination`* (the root directory of `E:`, or `E:\`).

The command requires all three parts if the destination is *not* the current drive and directory. For example, consider the situation of being at the `C:\>` command prompt. To copy the *format.com* file from the hard drive (the *System32* subfolder of the *Windows* folder) to a disk shown as `E:`, type the following command:

```
C:\> copy C:\Windows\System32\format.com E:\
```

Note that the `copy` command is first. Then you use the source, location, and name of the file being copied: `C:\Windows\System32\format.com`. Finally, you include the destination, `E:\`, or the root directory of the flash drive where the file is to be placed. If the current directory is the `C:\Windows\System32` hard drive directory, then the source path does not have to be typed. Instead, the command would look like the following:

```
C:\Windows\System32>copy format.com E:\
```

The backslash (\) after the `E:` is not necessary if the flash drive does not have directories (folders). The `copy` command does not need the entire path in front of the command because `copy` is an internal command.

CHAPTER 15

TECH TIP

Getting the command straight in your head

Before using any command, consider the following questions:

> What command do you want to issue?
> Where in the directory structure are you currently working? Look at the prompt to determine where you are.
> If you are copying a file or moving a file, what is the name of the file, and what is the full path to it? This is the source file.
> If you are copying a file or moving a file, in what directory does the file need to be placed? This is the destination file.

The `attrib` Command

The `attrib` command sets, removes, or shows the attribute(s) of a file or a directory. Attributes change how a file or directory is displayed on the screen or what can be done with the file or directory. Possible attributes are read-only, archive, system, and hidden:

> The read-only attribute protects files so that they cannot be accidentally changed or deleted.
> The archive attribute marks files that have changed since they were last backed up by a backup program.
> The system attribute designates a file as a system file; by default, files with this attribute do not appear in directory listings.
> The hidden attribute allows you to hide files and even directories.

Set each attribute using the `+x` switch, where `x` is `r` for read-only, `a` for archive, `h` for hidden, or `s` for system. Remove each attribute by using the `-r`, `-s`, `-h`, or `-a` switch with the `attrib` command. One command can set more than one attribute on a file or directory. For example, to make the *Cheryl.txt* file hidden and read-only, type **`attrib +r +h Cheryl.txt`**.

Why Learn Commands?

With many Windows problems, some solutions involve working from a command prompt until a Windows update fixes the problem. Other problems simply involve using a command from a prompt. Commands can also be used in a script. A *script* is a group of commands in a file that together automate a particular task. For example, say that you want to write a script to stop a computer print spooler and delete all spooled files that are in the queue to be printed. The following commands could be written in Notepad and saved to a file called *DeletePrint.cmd*:

```
net stop spooler
del %systemroot%\system32\spool\printers\*.shd
del %systemroot%\system32\spool\printers\*.spl
net start spooler
```

After the file is saved, you could copy this file to a hard drive, type **`DeletePrint`**, and press Enter, and the four commands would execute.

TECH TIP

Start your favorite tool by using a command

For example, from a command prompt or from the *Search* textbox, type **`mmc devmgmt.msc`** to start Device Manager. Note that you can access the Microsoft Management Console and still get to Device Manager by simply typing **`mmc`**.

PowerShell

In today's computing environment, a technician frequently has to do things to hundreds, or even thousands, of computers. Scripts and Windows PowerShell can help. Windows PowerShell is a tool that helps technicians and network administrators automate support functions through the use of scripts and snippets. Windows10 and Windows 11 ship with PowerShell. Every command that you can type from a command window (and a lot more) can be executed from within PowerShell.

TECH TIP

How do you open PowerShell?

There are several ways to access PowerShell in Windows 10 and Windows 11:

> Type **`powershell`** in the search window, right-click on the resulting Windows PowerShell app, and selecting *Run as administrator*.

> In File Explorer, type **`powershell`** in the address bar and press Enter.

> In Task Manager, use *File* menu > *Run new Task* and then type **`powershell`** and click *OK*.

> If you're already at the command prompt, type **`powershell`** and press Enter. The letters `PS` will be added to the front of the prompt to indicate that you're in PowerShell instead of the command prompt.

Other Commands You Should Look Over

Some commonly used commands are discussed in other chapters of this book or are beyond the basics of learning how to function from a command prompt. When you understand how to work from a prompt, you can execute any command fairly easily. In the "Command Format" section that follows, commands shown as key terms (boldfaced and purple) are objectives for the certification exam.

The following are the most common and perhaps most important commands that you as a technician should be familiar with:

> `[command name] /?`
> Current directory and parent directory `(. and ..)`
> Drive navigation inputs `(C:` or `D:` or `x:)`
> `bootrec`
> `cd`
> `chkdsk`
> `command`
> `copy`
> `defrag`
> `del`
> `dir`
> `diskpart`
> `dism`
> `dxdiag`
> `exit`
> `expand`
> `explorer`
> `format`
> `gpresult`
> `gpupdate`
> `help`
> `hostname`
> `ipconfig`
> `md`
> `mmc`

- msconfig
- msinfo32
- mstsc
- nbtstat
- net
- net use
- net user
- netdom
- netstat
- notepad
- nslookup
- pathping
- ping
- rd/rmdir
- regedit
- regsvr32
- robocopy
- services.msc
- sfc
- shutdown
- taskkill
- tasklist
- tracert
- xcopy
- winver

Command Format

When Windows does not boot, a technician must work from a command prompt. Some of the most frequently used commands are outlined in detail on the following pages. Items enclosed by brackets ([ ]) are optional. Items in italics are command-specific values that you must enter. When the items are separated by a | (called a pipe, or bar), one of the items must be typed.

The following pages provide a command reference. Some of these commands are used elsewhere in this chapter or in others. This list is by no means comprehensive. You can expect to see the key terms (boldfaced and purple) on the CompTIA A+ Core 2 (220-1102) certification exam. Visit the microsoft.com website for a complete list of Windows commands; the Documentation area is a good asset.

TECH TIP

How to get help when working from a prompt

To get help while working from a prompt, type **`help command_name`** or type **`command_name /?`**. For example, to get help for the `attrib` command, type **`help attrib`** or **`attrib /?`**.

[command name] /?

The [**command name**] /? command displays help information about a specific command.

Syntax: [*command_name*] /?

Explanation: [*command_name*] is the name of the command for which you want help.

Example: dir /?

Notes: If you do not specify the *command_name* parameter when using this command, no commands are listed, and an error appears, saying that /? is not recognized as an internal or external command, operable program, or batch file.

Current Directory and Parent Directory (. and ..)

The special folder . refers to the current folder in which a file or folder is located. The special folder .. refers to the parent of the current folder. These special folders can be used when specifying filepaths.

Example: C:\Windows>cd..

This command changes the prompt to the C:\ prompt because C:\ is the parent of the Windows folder.

Drive Navigation Inputs (C: or D: or x:)

To change the active drive, type the new drive letter and a colon and then press ENTER.

Example: C:\Windows>D:

This command changes the active drive to D:. The new prompt will be D:\.

attrib

The attrib command controls the attributes for a file or folder.

Syntax: attrib [+|-h] [+|-r] [+|-a] [+|-s] [*drive*:] [*path*] *filename* [/S] [/D]

Explanation: + adds an attribute.

- takes away an attribute.

h is the hidden attribute.

r is the read-only attribute.

a is the archive file attribute.

s is the system attribute.

[*drive*:] is the drive where the file is located.

[*path*] is the directory/subdirectory where the file is located.

filename is the name of the file.

[/S] includes subfolders.

[/D] includes folders

Example: attrib +h c:\cheryl.bat

This command sets the hidden attribute for a file called *Cheryl.bat* located on the hard drive.

Notes: The dir command (typed without any switches) is used to see what attributes are currently set. You may set more than one attribute at a time.

bcdedit

The `bcdedit` command is used at the command prompt or in the System Recovery environment to modify and control settings contained in the BCD (boot configuration data) store, which controls how the operating system boots.

Syntax: `bcdedit [/createstore] [/copy] [/create] [/delete] [/deletevalue] [/set] [/enum] [/bootsequence] [/default] [/displayorder] [/timeout]`

Explanation: `[/createstore]` creates a new empty BCD store that is not a system store.

`[/copy]` makes a copy of a specific boot entry contained in the BCD store.

`[/create]` creates a new entry in the BCD store.

`[/delete]` deletes an element from a specific entry in the BCD store.

`[/deletevalue]` deletes a specific element from a boot entry.

`[/set]` sets a specific entry's option value.

`[/enum]` lists entries in a store.

`[/bootsequence]` specifies a display order that is used one time only. The next time the computer boots, the original display order is shown.

`[/default]` selects the entry used by the boot manager when the timeout expires.

`[/displayorder]` specifies a display order that is used each time the computer boots.

`[/timeout]` specifies, in seconds, the amount of time before the boot manager boots using the default entry.

Example: `bcdedit / set Default debug on`

This command troubleshoots a new operating system installation for the operating system. It is the default option that appears in the Boot Manager menu.

Notes: Use the `bcdedit /? types` command to see a list of data types. Use the `bcd /? formats` command to see a list of valid data formats. To get detailed information on any of the options, type `bcdedit /?` followed by the option. For example, to see information on how to export the BCD, type `bcd /? export`.

bootrec

The `bootrec` command is used in the System Recovery environment to repair and recover from hard drive problems.

Syntax: `bootrec [/FixMbr] [/FixBoot] [/ScanOs] [/RebuildBcd]`

Explanation: `[/FixMbr]` repairs the hard drive MBR (master boot record) by copying a new MBR to the system partition. The existing partition table is not altered.

`[/FixBoot]` repairs the hard drive boot sector if it has been corrupted and replaces it with a higher boot sector or if an earlier version of Windows has been installed after Windows 10 or Windows 11.

[/ScanOs] looks for compatible operating system installations that do not currently appear on the Boot Manager list.

[/RebuildBcd] scans all disks for operating systems compatible with Windows Vista or higher and optionally rebuilds the BCD (boot configuration data) store. The BCD store provides structured storage for boot settings that is especially helpful in multiple operating system environments. Discovered operating systems can be added to the BCD store.

Example: `bootrec /fixmbr`

This command could be used if a virus has destroyed the master boot record.

Notes: If you receive an `Element not Found` error when using the `bootrec` command, the hard drive partition might not be active. Use the Windows Recovery Environment command prompt and the `diskpart` command to select the drive disk number. (If you only have one and it has one partition, it will be the command `select disk 0`, as an example). Then type the command **`active`**. Exit the `diskpart` utility and reboot the computer. Re-access the System Recovery environment and rerun the `bootrec` command.

If the system needs a new BCD and rebuilding it does not help, you can export the existing BCD and then delete the current BCD. To export the BCD, type **`bcdedit /export`** ***`x:\folder`*** (where *`x:\folder`* is the location where you want the BCD store exported). Then type **`c:, cd boot, attrib bcd -s -h -r, ren c:\boot\bcd bcd.old, bootrec /RebuildBcd`** to create a backup copy of the BCD store, make it so it is not hidden and can be deleted, and then rebuild it.

cd

The `cd` command is used to navigate through the directory structure.

Syntax: `cd [`*`drive`*`:] [`*`path`*`] [..]`

Explanation: `[`*`drive`*`:]` specifies the drive (if it is different from the current drive) to which you want to change.

`[`*`path`*`]` is the directory/subdirectory to reach the folder.

`[..]` changes to the parent directory (moves you back one directory in the tree structure).

Examples:

```
C:\Windows>cd..
C:\>
```

This command moves you from the *Windows* directory (folder) to the parent directory, which is the root directory (`C:\`).

```
C:\>cd \Windows
```

This command moves you from the root directory to the *Windows* directory on the `C:` drive.

CHAPTER 15

chkdsk

The `chkdsk` command checks a disk for physical problems, lost clusters, cross-linked files, and directory errors. If necessary, the `chkdsk` command repairs the disk, marks bad sectors, recovers information, and displays the status of the disk.

Syntax: `chkdsk [drive:] [/r] [/f] [/i] [/b]`

Explanation: `[drive:]` specifies the drive to check.

`[/r]` locates bad sectors and attempts recovery of a sector's information.

`[/f]` fixes drive errors.

`[/i]` checks only index entries on NTFS volumes.

`[/b]` re-evaluates bad clusters.

Example: `chkdsk d:`

This command checks the disk structure on the `D:` drive.

Notes: This command can be used without switches. For the `chkdsk` command to work, the file *Autochk.exe* must be loaded in the *System32* folder or used with the correct path and run from the Windows disc. If one or more files are open on the drive being checked, `chkdsk` prompts you to schedule the disk to be checked the next time the computer is restarted.

chkntfs

The `chkntfs` command can display whether a particular disk volume is scheduled for automatic disk checking the next time the computer is started, or it can be used to modify automatic disk checking.

Syntax: `chkntfs volume: [/D] [/X] [/C]`

Explanation: `volume:` specifies the drive volume to display or modify.

`[/D]` places the computer back to default behavior. (All drives are checked at boot time, and `chkdsk` is run on those that are dirty.)

`[/X]` excludes a particular volume from the default boot-time check.

`[/C]` schedules a drive to be checked at boot time. The `chkdsk` command will be run if the drive is dirty.

Example: `chkntfs c:`

This command displays whether the drive is dirty or scheduled to be checked on the next computer reboot.

cipher

The `cipher` command displays or alters file or folder encryption.

Syntax: `cipher [/e] [/d] [/f] [/q] [/k] [/u] [/n] [path]`

Explanation: `[/e]` encrypts the specified folder, including files that are added in the future.

`[/d]` decrypts the specified folder.

`[/f]` forces encryption or decryption because, by default, files that have already been encrypted or decrypted are skipped.

`[/q]` reports essential information about the encryption or decryption.

[/k] creates a new file encryption key.

[/u] updates the encryption key to the current one for all encrypted files if the keys have been changed. /u works only with the /n option.

[/n] finds all encrypted files. It prevents keys from being updated. It is used only with /u.

[*path*] is a pattern, file, or folder.

Examples: `cipher /e Book\Chap1`

This command encrypts a subfolder called *Chap1* that is located in a folder called *Book*.

`cipher /e /s:Book`

This command encrypts all subfolders in the folder called *Book*.

`cipher Book`

This command displays whether the *Book* folder is encrypted.

`cipher Book\Chap 1\*`

This command displays whether any files in the *Chap1* subfolder of the *Book* folder are encrypted.

Notes: Multiple parameters are separated with spaces. Read-only files and folders cannot be encrypted.

cls

The cls command clears the screen of any previously typed commands.

Example: `C:\Windows>cls`

command

The command command is executed from the *Search* textbox by simply typing command and pressing Enter. A command prompt window appears. Type exit to close the window.

Syntax: `command`

Explanation: When command is entered, a command prompt window opens.

copy

The copy command is used to copy one or more files to the specified destination.

Syntax: `copy [/a] [/y] [/-y] source [destination]`

Explanation: [/a] indicates an ASCII text file.

[/y] suppresses the prompt to overwrite an existing file.

[/-y] prompts to overwrite an existing file.

source is the file that you want to copy, and it includes the drive letter and the path if it is different from your current location.

[*destination*] is the location in which you want to put the file and includes the drive letter and path if it is different from your current location.

Example: `copy c:\cheryl.bat f:\`

This command copies a file called *cheryl.bat* that is located in the root directory of the hard drive to a flash drive.

Notes: You do not have to include a target if the file is going to the current location specified by the command prompt. If a file already exists, you will be prompted whether to overwrite the file. Compressed files that are copied from the Windows media are automatically uncompressed to the hard drive as they are copied.

defrag

The `defrag` command is used to locate and reorder files so that they are contiguous (not fragmented) to improve system performance.

Syntax: `defrag [drive:] [/a] [/c] [/x]`

Explanation: `[drive:]` is the drive letter where the files are located.

`[/a]` analyzes the drive volume specified.

`[/c]` includes all volumes.

`[/x]` consolidates free space on the specified volume.

Example: `defrag c: d: /a`

This command defragments the `C:` and `D:` drives and analyzes them.

Notes: Multiple switches can be used, as long as spaces appear between them. Multiple drive letters (volumes) can be used with a single command.

del

The `del` command is used to delete a file.

Syntax: `del name [/p][/f][/s]`

Explanation: `name` is the file or directory (folder) that you want to delete, and it includes the drive letter and the path if it is different from your current location.

`[/p]` prompts for confirmation before deleting.

`[/f]` forces read-only files to be deleted.

`[/s]` deletes files from all subdirectories.

Example: `C:\Windows>del c:\cheryl.bat`

This command deletes a file called *cheryl.bat* that is located in the *Windows* directory on the hard drive.

dir

The `dir` command lists files and folders and their attributes.

Syntax: `dir [drive:] [path] [filename] [/a:attribute] [/o] [/p] [/s] [/w]`

Explanation: `[drive:]` is the letter of the drive where the files are located.

`[path]` is the directory/subdirectory to reach the folder.

`[filename]` is the name of a specific file.

`[/a:attribute]` displays files that have specific attributes, where the attributes are `D`, `R`, `H`, `A`, and `S`. `D` is for directories; `R` is for read-only, `H` is for hidden, `A` is for archive, and `S` is for system files.

[/o] displays the listing in sorted order. Options you can use after o are E, D, G, N, and S. E is used to sort by alphabetic file extension; D is used to sort by date and time, with the oldest listing shown first; G shows the directories listed first; N displays by alphabetic name; and S displays by size, from smallest to largest.

[/p] displays the information one page at a time.

[/s] includes subdirectories in the listing.

[/w] shows the listing in wide format.

Example: dir c:\windows

This command shows all the files and folders (and their associated attributes) for the *windows* folder that is located on the C: drive.

disable

The disable command disables a system service or hardware driver.

Syntax: disable *name*

Explanation: *name* is the name of the service or driver that you want to disable.

Notes: You can use the listsvc command to show all services and drivers that are available to disable. Make sure that you write down the previous *START_TYPE* before you disable a service in case you need to restart the service.

diskpart

The diskpart command is used to manage and manipulate the hard drive partitions.

Syntax: diskpart [/*add*|/*delete*] [*devicename*] [*drivename* | *partitionname*] [*size*]

Explanation: [/*add* |/*delete*] creates a new partition or deletes an existing partition.

[*devicename*] is the name given to the device when creating a new partition, such as \Device\HardDisk0.

[*drivename*] is the drive letter used when deleting an existing partition, such as E:.

[*partitionname*] is the name used when deleting an existing partition and can be used instead of the *drivename* option. An example of a *partitionname* is Device\HardDisk0\Partition2.

[*size*] is used when creating a new partition and is the size of the partition, in megabytes.

Notes: You can just type the diskpart command without any options, and a user interface appears that helps when managing hard drive partitions.

dism

The dism command is a Windows utility, Deployment Image Servicing and Management, which can be used to repair and prepare Windows images.

Syntax: dism /Online /Cleanup-Image /[/CheckHealth] [/ScanHealth] [/RestoreHealth]

Explanation: [/CheckHealth] checks whether the image has been flagged as corrupted and whether the corruption can be repaired.

`[/ScanHealth]` scans the image for component store corruption and records that corruption to the log file.

`[/RestoreHealth]` scans the image for component store corruption, performs repair operations automatically, and records that corruption to the log file.

dxdiag

The `dxdiag` command is used to perform DirectX diagnostics.

Syntax: `dxdiag [/dontskip] [whql:on|/whql:off] [/64bit target] [/x filename] [/t filename]`

Explanation: `[/dontskip]` causes all diagnostics to be performed, even if a previous crash in `dxdiag` has occurred.

`[/whql:on]` checks for WHQL digital signatures.

`[/whql:off]` prevents checking for WHQL digital signatures.

`[/64bit target]` uses 64-bit DirectX diagnostics.

`[/x filename]` saves XML information to the specified filename and quits.

`[/t filename]` saves TXT information to the specified filename and quits.

Notes: When DirectX diagnostics checks for WHQL digital signatures, the internet may be used.

enable

The `enable` command is used to enable a system service or hardware driver.

Syntax: `enable name [start-type]`

Explanation: `name` is the name of the service or driver that you want to disable.

`[start-type]` is used when you want the service or driver scheduled to begin. Valid options are as follows:

`SERVICE_BOOT_START`

`SERVICE_SYSTEM_START`

`SERVICE_AUTO_START`

`SERVICE_DEMAND_START`

Example: `enable DHCP client service_auto_start`

Notes: You can use the `listsvc` command to show all services and drivers that are available to enable. Make sure that you write down the previous value before you enable a service in case you need to restart the old service or driver.

exit

The `exit` command closes the command prompt environment window.

Example: `C:\Windows>exit`

expand

The `expand` command uncompresses a file from a CAB (short for *cabinet*) file. A CAB file holds multiple files or drivers that are compressed into a single file. Technicians sometimes copy the CAB files onto the local hard drive so that when hardware and/or software is installed, removed, or reinstalled, the application disc does not have to be inserted.

Syntax: `expand [-i] source [destination]`

Explanation: `[-i]` renames files but ignores the directory structure.

`source` is the name of the file, including the path that you want to uncompress.

`[destination]` is the path where you want to place the uncompressed file.

Example: `expand d:\i386\access.cp_ c:\windows\system32\access.cpl`

This command expands (uncompresses) the compressed file *Access.cp_* and puts it into the *C:\Windows\System32* folder with the name *Access.cpl*.

Notes: You may not use wildcard characters with the `source` parameter.

explorer

The `explorer` command is used to start File Explorer from a command prompt.

Syntax: `explorer`

format

The `format` command is used to format a disk or drive and can format it for a particular file system.

Syntax: `format [driveletter:] [/q] [/fs:filesystem] [/v:label] [/x]`

Explanation: `[driveletter:]` is the drive letter for the disk or hard drive volume that you want to format.

`[/q]` is the parameter used if you want to perform a quick format.

`[/fs:filesystem]` is the parameter used if you want to specify a file system. Valid values are FAT, FAT32, exFAT, and NTFS.

`[/v:label]` `/v:` must be part of the command, followed by the name of the volume assigned.

`[/x]` dismounts the volume first, if necessary.

Example: `format c: /fs:ntfs`

Notes: If no `/fs:filesystem` parameter is specified, the NTFS file system is used. FAT is FAT16. FAT16 hard drive volumes cannot be more than 4 GB in size.

gpresult

The `gpresult` command is used to display Group Policy settings. Group Policy determines how a computer is configured for both system and user (or a group of users) settings.

Syntax: `gpresult [/s computer] [/u domain\user] [/p password] [/user target_user] [ /r] [/v] [/z]`

Explanation: `[/s computer]` is an optional parameter that specifies a remote computer using the computer name or IP address; otherwise, the local computer is selected by default.

`[/u domain\user]` specifies authentication for the remote computer.

`[/p password]` specifies a password for the remote computer user ID.

`[/user target_user]` specifies to display a user's Group Policy settings.

`[/v]` outputs data in verbose mode.

`[/z]` displays all available data about the Group Policy.

Examples: `gpresult /r`

`gpresult /s 10.3.207.15 /u pearson\cschmidt /p G#t0Ut0fH3R3`

gpupdate

The `gpupdate` command refreshes local- and Active Directory–based Group Policy settings.

Syntax: `gpupdate [/target:{computer | user}] [/force] [/wait:value] [/logoff] [/boot]`

Explanation: `[/target:{computer | user}]` is an optional parameter used to specify whether either the *computer* settings or the current *user* settings are used. When neither is specified, both *computer* and *user* settings are processed.

`[/force]` reapplies all settings.

`[/wait:value]` specifies the number of seconds policy processing waits to finish. The default is 600 seconds. A `0` wait value processes immediately. A `-1` value places the wait time at indefinitely.

`[/logoff]` forces a logoff after the refresh completes.

`[/boot]` forces the computer to restart after the refresh completes.

Example: `gpupdate /force /boot`

help

The `help` command displays information about specific commands.

Syntax: `help [command]`

Explanation: `[command]` is the name of the command for which you want help.

Example: `help expand`

Notes: If you do not specify the *command* parameter when using the `help` command, all commands are listed.

hostname

The `hostname` command displays the name of current host.

Syntax: `hostname`

ipconfig

The `ipconfig` command is used to view and control information related to a network adapter.

Syntax: `ipconfig [/allcompartments] [/all|/renew [adapter] | /release [adapter]|/renew6 [adapter]|/release6 [adapter]| /flushdns|displaydns|/registerdns|/showclassid [adapter]| /setclassid adapter [classid]|/showclassid6 [adapter]| /setclassid6 adapter [classid]]`

Explanation: `[/allcompartments]` displays information regarding all compartments and, when used with the `/all` option, shows detailed information about all compartments.

`[/all]` displays all configuration information, including IP and MAC addresses.

`[/renew]` renews the IPv4 address for a specific adapter.

`[/release]` releases the IPv4 address for a specific adapter.

`[/renew6]` renews the IPv6 address for a specific adapter.

`[/release6]` releases the IPv6 address for a specific adapter.

`[/flushdns]` removes all entries from the DNS resolver cache.

`[/displaydns]` shows the contents of the DNS resolver cache.

`[/registerdns]` refreshes DHCP leases and re-registers recently used DNS names.

`[/show classid]` displays all configured IPv4 DHCP class IDs allowed for a specific adapter.

`[/setclassid adapter]` configures an adapter for a specific IPv4 DHCP class ID. A class ID is used to have two or more user classes that are configured as different DHCP scopes on a server. One class could be for laptops, and a different class could be for desktop computers in an organization.

`[/showclassid6 adapter]` displays all configured IPv6 DHCP class IDs allowed for a specific adapter.

`[/setclassid6 adapter]` configures an adapter for a specific IPv6 DHCP class ID.

Examples: `ipconfig /all`

This command verifies whether an IP address has been configured or received from a DHCP server.

`ipconfig /release`

This command releases a DHCP-sent IP address.

`ipconfig /renew`

This command starts the DHCP request process.

md

The `md` command is used to create a directory (folder).

Syntax: `md [driveletter:] [dirname]`

Explanation: `[driveletter:]` is the drive letter for the disk or volume on which you want to create a directory (folder). It can also include the path.

`[dirname]` is the parameter used to name the directory (folder).

Example: `md c:\test`

Notes: You cannot use wildcard characters with this command.

mmc

The `mmc` command is used to open the Microsoft Management Console in Windows.

Syntax: `mmc [path\filename.msc] [/a] [/64] [/32]`

Explanation: `[path\filename.msc]` is an option to specify where to locate a saved console.

`[/a]` opens the console in author mode.

`[/64]` opens the 64-bit console.

`[/32]` opens the 32-bit console.

Notes: Use the `/32` parameter if you are in a 64-bit operating system and want to run 32-bit snap-ins.

more

The `more` command is used to display a text file.

Syntax: `more filename`

Explanation: `filename` is the path and name of the text file you want to display on the screen.

Example: `more c:\boot.ini`

Notes: The Spacebar enables you to view the next page of a text file. The ↵Enter key enables you to scroll through the text file one line at a time. The Esc key enables you to quit viewing the text file.

msconfig

The `msconfig` command starts the System Configuration utility from a command prompt instead of from a Control Panel. The System Configuration utility is commonly used to troubleshoot boot issues specifically related to software and services. The Startup tab lists software that is loaded when the computer boots, and a checkbox enables you to disable and enable the particular application. The same concept is used with the Services tab, which contains checkboxes next to services that are started when the computer boots.

Syntax: `msconfig`

msinfo32

The msinfo32 command brings up the System Information window from a command prompt. The System Information window contains details about hardware and hardware configurations as well as software and software drivers.

Syntax: msinfo32 [/computer *computer_name*]

Explanation: [/computer *computer_name*] starts the System Information utility for a remote computer.

Examples:
```
msinfo
msinfo /computer Cheryl_Dell
```

mstsc

The mstsc command starts the Remote Desktop Connection utility.

Syntax: mstsc [/v:*computer*[:*port*]]

Explanation: [/v:*computer*[:*port*]] specifies the specific remote computer—by name or IP address and port number—to which you want to connect.

Example: mstsc /v:Cheryl-PC

Notes: The default port number for Remote Desktop is 3389, but if a different port has been specified, then you can specify a port by using this command.

nbtstat

The nbtstat command is used to display statistics related to current TCP/IP connections on the local computer or a remote computer using NBT (NetBIOS over TCP/IP).

Syntax: nbtstat [-a *remotename*] [-A *IPaddress*] [-c] [-S]

Explanation: [-a *remotename*] shows the NetBIOS name table for a remote computer designated by *remotename*.

[-A *IPaddress*] shows the NetBIOS name table for a remote computer designated by *IPaddress*.

[-c] shows the NetBIOS name cache, names, and resolved IP addresses.

[-S] shows NetBIOS client and server sessions.

Examples:
```
nbtstat -S
nbtstat -A 10.5.8.133
```


net

The net command has many options, and each of those options has specific parameters. A few options are shown. Use the net /? command to see all options.

Syntax: net [computer] [group] [localgroup] [print] [session] [share] [use] [user] [view]

Explanation: [computer] adds or removes a computer from the network domain.

[group] adds, views, or modifies domain groups.

[localgroup] adds, views, or modifies local groups.

[print] displays or controls a specific network printer queue.

[share] manages share resources.

[session] manages sessions with remote devices.

[use] attaches to a remote network device.

[user] adds, modifies, or views a network user account.

[view] lists resources or computers shared by the computer this is used on.

net use

The net use command attaches to a remote network device.

Syntax: net use [*drive_letter*] [*server_name**share_name* / user:*domain_name**user_name* [*password*]]

Explanation: *drive_letter* is the letter (followed by a colon) that net use assigns to the network device connection.

server_name is the name of the network device to which to connect.

share_name is the name of the share.

domain_name is the domain used to validate the user.

user_name is the user to be validated.

[*password*] is an optional entry, so the system does not prompt for a password. If this option is not entered, a password prompt appears, and the system automatically assigns a drive letter once a connection is made.

Example: net use \\ATC227-01\cisco /user:cisco\student

net user

The net user command is used to add, delete, and make changes to a user on a Windows domain.

Syntax: net user [*username [password* | *] [*options*]] [/domain]

Explanation: *username* is the domain username assigned to the person in the company.

password is used to change a password or assign one to a particular user.

* is used instead of the *password* option to force the password to be entered after the net user command is entered.

options include things like /add, /delete, /times, and /active.

/*domain* executes the command on the Microsoft domain controller instead of on the local computer.

Examples: net user cschmidt

This command allows you to see account information related to the cschmidt account.

net user cschmidt /active:no

This command allows you to disable the cschmidt account.

net user cschmidt /delete

This command allows you to delete the cschmidt account; note that common practice is to disable, not delete, an account.

netdom

The netdom command manages Active Directory domains and trust relationships. This command has many operations.

Syntax: netdom {add | computername | join | move | query | remove | renamecomputer | reset | resetpwd | verify} [<Computer>] [{/d: | /domain:} <*Domain*>] [<Options>]

Explanation: add adds a workstation to the domain.

[computername] manages the primary and alternative names for a domain controller.

[join] joins a computer to the domain.

[move] moves a computer to a new domain.

[query] presents information about the domain membership, trust, and so on.

[remove] deletes a computer form the domain.

[renamecomputer] renames a domain workstation.

[reset] resets the connection between a domain workstation and the domain controller.

[resetpwd] resets a computer account password for a domain controller.

[verify] verifies the connection between a domain workstation and the domain controller.

netstat

The netstat command attaches to a remote network device.

Syntax: netstat [-a] [-e] [-n] [-o] [-p *protocol*] [-r] [-s]

Explanation: [-a] shows all connections and listening port numbers.

[-e] shows Ethernet statistics and can be used with the -s option.

[-n] shows addresses and port numbers.

[-o] shows active TCP connections.

[-p *protocol*] shows specific connections that use a specific protocol. The *protocol* parameter can be one of the following: IP, IPv6, ICMP, ICMPv6, TCP, TCPv6, UDP, or UDPv6.

[-r] shows the routing table.

[-s] shows statistics for a particular protocol.

Examples:

```
netstat
netstat -a
netstat -p TCP
```

Note: The parameters used with this command must be preceded by a dash rather than the / (slash) used by most commands.

notepad

The notepad command starts the Windows Notepad accessory.

Syntax: `notepad`

nslookup

The nslookup command is used to troubleshoot DNS issues.

Syntax: nslookup [-*option*] [*hostname*] [*server*]

Explanation: [-*option*] has a variety of options that can be used, such as exit, finger, help, ls, lserver, root, server, and set. See Microsoft TechNet for a complete list.

[*hostname*] is the name of a host, such as the computer name for a specific computer in an organization.

[*server*] is the URL of a specific server, such as www.pearsoned.com.

Examples: `nslookup www.pearsoned.com`

`nslookup -querytype=hinfo -timeout=10`

The second example changes the default query type to a host and the timeout to 10 seconds.

Notes: You must have at least one DNS server IP address configured on a network adapter (which you can view with the ipconfig /all command) to use the nslookup command. There are two modes of operation: non-interactive and interactive. The non-interactive mode has more commands than are shown in the examples given. The interactive mode is started by simply typing nslookup and pressing Enter.

pathping

The pathping command sends multiple ping requests (see the following section on the **ping** command) to each router between the source computer and the target device over a period of time. Based on results from each device, the command provides information about network latency and network loss at the intermediate hops.

Syntax: pathping [-g host-list] [-h maximum_hops] [-i address] [-n] [-p period] [-q num_queries] [-w timeout] [-4] [-6] target_name

Explanation: [-g host-list] forces use of loose source routing along *host-list*. In other words, *host-list* is the set of routers that must be pinged along the path to *target*. *host-list* is a series of (a maximum of nine) IP addresses separated by commas.

[-h maximum_hops] specifies the maximum number of hops to search for the target.

[-i *address*] forces the use of the specified source address.

[-n] suppresses resolution of router IP addresses to hostnames, potentially speeding up the pathping process.

[-p *period*] defines the wait period, in milliseconds, between pings.

[-q num_queries] indicates the number of queries per hop.

`[-w timeout]` dictates the wait timeout, in milliseconds, for each reply.

`[-4]` forces the use of IPv4.

`[-6]` forces the use of IPv6.

`target` is the destination IP address.

Examples: `pathping -4 -n www.pearson.com`

This example generates network latency and loss statistics for the www.pearson.com website, using IPv4 and suppressing the resolution of intermediate router IP addresses to hostnames.

ping

The `ping` command tests connectivity to a remote network device.

Syntax: `ping [-t] [-a] [-n count] [-l size] [-i ttl] [-S source_addr] [-4] [-6] target`

Explanation: `[-t]` pings the destination until stopped with Ctrl+C keystrokes. To see the statistics and continue, use the Ctrl+Break keys.

`[-a]` resolves IP addresses to hostnames.

`[-n count]` defines how many pings (echo requests) are sent to the destination.

`[-l size]` defines the buffer size (the length of the packet).

`[-i ttl]` defines a Time to Live value from 0 through 255.

`[-S source_addr]` defines the source IP address to use.

`[-4]` forces the use of IPv4.

`[-6]` forces the use of IPv6.

`target` is the destination IP address.

Examples: `ping -t www.pearsoned.com`

This example pings the Pearson Technology Education website indefinitely until the Ctrl+C key combination is used.

`ping -n 2 -l 1450 165.193.130.107`

This example sends two echo requests (pings) that are 1,450 bytes to the Pearson Technology Education website.

rd or rmdir

The `rd` command and the `rmdir` command perform the same function. They are used to remove a directory (folder).

Syntax: `rd [driveletter:][path] name`

Explanation: `[driveletter:]` is the drive letter for the disk or hard drive volume from which you want to remove a directory (folder).

`[path]` is the optional path and name of the directory (folder) you want to remove.

`name` is the name of the folder/directory to remove.

CHAPTER 15

Example: `rd c:\Test\Junkdata`

This command removes a directory (folder) called *Junkdata* that is a subdirectory under a directory (folder) called *Test*. This directory is located on the hard drive (`C:`).

Notes: You do not have to use the *`driveletter:`* parameter if the default drive letter is the same as the one that contains the directory to be deleted.

regedit

The `regedit` command accesses the Windows registry editor.

Syntax: `regedit`

Explanation: All the Windows configuration information is stored in a hierarchical database. The registry editor can modify specific registry keys, back up the registry, or set specific values to the defaults.

Notes: The `regedt32` command brings up the same registry editor window as `regedit`.

regsvr32

The `regsvr32` command registers `.dll` files in the Windows registry.

Syntax: `regsvr32 [/u] name`

Explanation: *`name`* is the name of the `.dll` file that will be registered.

`[/u]` is an optional switch used to unregister a `.dll` file.

Example: `regsvr32 wuapi.dll`

This command registers a Windows update DLL file.

Notes: There is a 64-bit version of this file in the *SysWow64* folder.

ren

The `ren` command renames a file or directory (folder).

Syntax: `ren [driveletter:] [path] name1 name2`

Explanation: `[driveletter:]` is the drive letter for the disk or hard drive volume where you want to rename a file or a directory (folder).

`[path]` is an optional parameter that tells the operating system the path of the file or directory (folder) you want to rename.

`name1` is the old name of the file or directory (folder) that you want to rename.

`name2` is the new name of the file or directory (folder).

Example: `ren c:\cheryl.bat c:\newcheryl.bat`

Notes: The renamed file cannot be placed in a new location with this command. Move or copy the file after you rename it if that is what you want to do. The * and ? wildcard characters are not supported.

robocopy

The robocopy command is used to copy files but has a lot more parameters than copy or xcopy.

Syntax: robocopy [*source*] [*destination*] [*file* [*file*]...] [*options*]

Explanation: [*source*] specifies the source directory in the *drive*:| path format or the *server**share* path format.

[*destination*] specifies the destination directory in the drive:\path format or the *server**share* path format.

[*file*] is the files to copy, including wildcards. The default is *.*.

[*options*] includes various options, such as /s to copy subdirectories (but not empty ones), /e to copy subdirectories (including empty ones), /mov to move files and delete the source, /move to move files and directories and delete the source, /a to copy files with the archive attribute set, and /m to copy files with the archive attribute set and to reset the archive bit.

Examples: robocopy c:\users\cschmidt\My Documents\Book d:\ /e

This command copies the contents of the *Book* subfolder to the D: drive and includes any empty directories.

robocopy \\CSchmidt\Book \\RLD\SchmidtBook

This command copies all files from the *CSchmidt* computer share called *Book* to the *RLD* computer network share called *SchmidtBook*.

services.mmc

The services.msc command is used to open the Microsoft Management Console and display the Services window.

Syntax: services.msc

Notes: The Services window shows the applications that run as background applications. Some services are manually started by the user or a technician, some start automatically, and some start automatically but delay starting to allow faster booting. This window is commonly used to start a service or to verify that a service such as the print service is still started.

set

The set command is used to display and view different variables.

Syntax: set [*variable* = *value*]

Explanation: *variable* is one of the following:

AllowWildCards is the variable used to enable wildcard support for the commands that normally do not support wildcards.

AllowAllPaths is the variable that allows access to all the computer's files and folders.

AllowRemovableMedia is the variable that allows files to be copied to removable media.

[/f] forcefully terminates the process.

[/t] is a "tree kill" that kills all child processes associated with the process ID.

Examples: `taskkill /pid 1230 /pid 1231 /pid 1242`

`taskkill /im iexplore.exe`

`tasklist`

The `tasklist` command is used to list process IDs (PIDs) for active applications and services.

Syntax: `tasklist [/s computer] [/u domain\user] [/p password] [/fo {table|list|csv}] [/v]`

Explanation: `[/s computer]` is an optional parameter that designates a specific remote computer using the computer name or IP address; if no computer is specified, the local computer is selected by default.

`[/u domain\user]` specifies authentication for the remote computer.

`[/p password]` specifies a password for the remote computer user ID.

`[/fo {table|list|csv]` specifies the output format (table, which is the default, list, or CSV).

`[/v]` displays output in a verbose format.

Example: `tasklist /fo csv`

Notes: This command should be used before the `taskkill` command.

`telnet`

The `telnet` command is used to access a remote network device.

Syntax: `telnet [destination]`

Explanation: `[destination]` is the name or IP address of the remote network device.

Notes: The Telnet client must be enabled through the *Programs and Features* section of the Control Panel > *Turn Windows Features On or Off*. SSH is a better and more secure tool to use.

`tracert`

The `tracert` command verifies the path taken by a packet from a source device to a destination.

Syntax: `tracert [-d] [destination]`

Explanation: `[-d]` speeds up the `tracert` process by not attempting to resolve intermediate router IP addresses to names.

`[destination]` is the targeted end device, listed by IP address or name.

Example: `tracert -d www.pearsoned.com`

`type`

The `type` command displays the contents of a text file.

Syntax: `type filename`

Explanation: `filename` is the path and name of the text file you want to display on the screen.

Example: `type c:\byteme.txt`

Notes: The Spacebar key enables you to view the next page of a text file. The Enter key enables you to scroll through the text file one line at a time. The Esc key enables you to quit viewing the text file.

wbadmin

The `wbadmin` command is used to perform backups and restores.

Syntax: `wbadmin [start backup] [stop job] [get versions] [get items]`

Notes: Each parameter listed for `wbadmin` has options (settings) that follow. Use the `/?` after each parameter to see these options; for example, `wbadmin start backup /?`.

Explanation: `[start backup]` begins the backup process.

`[stop job]` halts the currently running backup.

`[get versions]` provides a list of available backups from the local computer or from a remote computer.

`[get items]` provides a list of items included in a particular backup.

Example: `wbadmin start backup`

If no parameters are specified after `wbadmin start backup`, the settings within the daily backup schedule are used.

Note: You cannot recover backups that were made with `ntbackup` using the `wbadmin` command, but you can download the `ntbackup` command/application from Microsoft.

winver

The `winver` command shows the Windows version that is currently running, in addition to the build number. The results are displayed in a graphical window, not the command prompt.

Syntax: `winver`

Example: `winver`

wscript

`wscript` is the command that brings up a Windows-based script property sheet. This property sheet sets script properties. The command-line version is `cscript.exe`.

xcopy

The `xcopy` command copies and backs up files and directories.

Syntax: `xcopy` *`source`* `[`*`destination`*`] [/e] [/h]`

Explanation: *`source`* is the full path from where the files are copied.

`[`*`destination`*`]` is the optional destination path. If the destination is not given, the current directory is used.

`[/e]` copies all directories and subdirectories, including empty ones.

`[/h]` copies hidden and system files.

Example: `xcopy c:\users\cheryl\Documents\Chap1\Chap1.docx e:\Book\Chap1`

This command copies a file called *Chap1.docx* (which is located in a folder called *Chap1* that is a subfolder of the *Documents* folder, which is a subfolder of the *cheryl* folder, which is a subfolder of the *users* folder) to the `E:` drive and places it in the *Chap1* subfolder that is contained in the *Book* folder.

Notes: The `xcopy` command normally resets read-only attributes when copying.

TECH TIP

Operation requires elevation

Some commands can be executed from a command prompt with **standard privileges** (user privileges). However, if a message within the command prompt window indicates that the requested operation requires elevation, you need to run the operation with **administrative privileges**. In such a case, close the command prompt window. Right-click the *Command Prompt* Windows accessory. Select *Run As Administrator* and re-execute the command from the prompt. This is also called an elevated command prompt.

Introduction to Scripting

A **script** is a little program that is designed to do a specific task. There are many scripts available for networking professionals to use, and you can also create your own. While you don't need to become a code monkey to write useful scripts, you'll find that being able to create short scripts yourself will not only help your career but make many of your tasks easier. This section will help you understand the basics of scripting and introduce you to various script languages, including Python, JavaScript, shell scripts for Unix-based systems; and PowerShell, VBScript, and batch files for Windows-based systems.

What Is Scripting?

A script is a small program that carries out a task or a series of tasks based on specific conditions. Whereas programs written in programming languages you may have heard of (such as C++ or Java) are compiled, scripts are interpreted. The difference is in how the code is executed. A **compiled program** is turned into machine language before it can be run. An **interpreted program** is carried out one line at a time as the computer encounters each line of code. This makes it ideal for use by IT professionals.

A script is a **text file**. This means it can be created in any text editor, like Notepad in Windows. However, each scripting language has its own specific syntax and commands that you need to learn before you can create your own scripts. Running a script is easy. From a command prompt or command line, simply type the name of the script and press Enter.

Scripting allows you to automate some network administration tasks. For example, every time a user logs into a network, that user must be assigned various network drives based on certain conditions. A script can automate this process. This type of script would run each time a user logs on. In other cases, a script may only need to run once, but it might be able to be written to be applied in different situations. For example, a script may be able to modify the registry under one specific condition. If many servers on a network need to do this task, the script can be distributed and can run that one task on all the servers.

A network administrator gains many advantages by being able to create and use scripts. The following are some of them:

- Scripts save time. They can be written to carry out complex tasks that would take you a lot of time if done by hand. While a script runs, you are free to concentrate on other things.
- Scripts ensure consistent operation. Once a script is written, each time it is run, you can be sure it will be completed exactly as before. Using scripts to complete a task is less likely to cause errors than if the task were done manually at various times.
- Scripts can be flexible. Since scripts use the basic logical constructs of all programming languages, they can be created to respond in different ways to different conditions.

Script File Types

There are many scripting languages that you can choose from, although some must be used with specific operating systems, and some are more suited to certain tasks than others. Table 15.1 shows the most common and easily learned scripting languages.

TABLE 15.1 Common scripting languages

Language	File extension	Description
Shell script	`.sh`	A shell script is a set of commands within a text file for a Unix- or Linux-based system. Shell scripts may not run correctly on a Windows system.
Batch file	`.bat`	A batch file is a script file that is strictly Windows based. It contains a series of commands to execute one after another. The instructions in a batch file can only be interpreted by the Windows operating system.
Python	`.py`	Python is a good language for writing scripts because it is relatively easy to learn, and Python scripts can run on most operating systems.
VBScript	`.vbs`	VBScript is a Microsoft scripting language that has some commands that are part of the Visual Basic programming language. It was designed specifically for use with Microsoft's Internet Explorer. Unless you are certain you will only use a script on a Windows machine, it is probably better to use a more versatile language.
JavaScript	`.js`	JavaScript is a programming language that has many uses. In some ways, it is valuable for creating script files because it can be run on any operating system. However, it may be more difficult to learn than Python, which also has the benefit of being platform independent. Creating and running command-line JavaScript requires that Node.js be installed.
PowerShell	`.ps1`	PowerShell is a Windows environment that was created to help in IT task automation and configuration management. It is an interface that allows you to use small programs called cmdlets that run consecutively from a single file that you can use repeatedly and share with others. PowerShell files with the `.ps1` extension can be opened, edited, and run in the PowerShell Script pane.

TECH TIP

Scripts are just text files

Scripts contain only text with no special formatting. Each byte of a text file represents one character of ASCII code. Text files must be created in a text editor such as Notepad. Files that have been created with Microsoft Word or OpenOffice's Writer are stored as binary files, which do not have a one-to-one mapping between bytes and characters. If you attempt to copy and paste code from any source that is not a text file, you may get in trouble, even if you see no visible difference between your file and the text that you copied. This is because formatting commands are automatically included in the copy process.

Use Cases for Scripting

As indicated above, scripting is available in many operating systems and application environments. Thus, scripts can be used for a wide variety of purposes, from automating a simple process to configuring an entire virtual network. The following are some of the most common use cases for scripting available in most operating systems:

- *Basic automation:* A task that needs to be completed at a particular time with specific requirements can be automated with scripting. In the Windows environment, Task Scheduler can execute a script according to the prescribed schedule. The `crontab` command is used to schedule automated jobs in Unix/Linux.
- *Restarting machines:* Sometimes, computers need to be restarted for maintenance purposes at particular times during the day or after they have been running for a specified amount of time. A script can be used to calculate the uptime, perform the required maintenance, and then send a restart command to the operating system. Additional tasks can be completed after the system boots up again.
- *Remapping network drives:* As discussed in Chapter 18, "Computer and Network Security," folders can be shared across a network so data can be centrally stored and accessed. If one or more shared drives are always needed on a computer, a script can connect (or mount) the required folders when the computer boots up or when specific users log in. The shared folders can also be mapped to drive letters; for example, the `T:` drive can represent the shared *contracts* folder on the *ATCDOC1* server.
- *Installation of applications:* Applications must be installed with the correct options in order to work properly. Most installation processes prompt the technician for settings as the application is installed. To minimize installation mistakes, a script can be configured to automatically provide the required information for the program.
- *Automated backups:* The backup schedule for a computer depends on the device's role and the type of information stored on the device. In addition, backups might need to be spaced out due to restraints on backup resources. A script can be used to back up a computer to a designated storage device (local, network, or cloud) according to a prescribed schedule.
- *Initiating updates:* Timely updates for applications, devices, and operating systems are important for the health and security of computers. As with backups, scripts can download and install the required updates from a specified location and on a predetermined schedule.
- *Gathering of information/data:* The health, security, utilization, and efficiency of network devices change over time. Network technicians and engineers need to collect information from devices to make decisions regarding issues such as deployments, maintenance, updates, and

replacements. Scripts can be used to automatically send various data points (disk utilization, failed logins, ping response times, and so on) to a central location for analysis. The collections can be scheduled or on-demand.

Note that some of these tasks are used in conjunction with each other; for example, a restart script can be used to back up a computer, download updates, and then restart the computer.

Mitigating Consequences of Scripting

Scripts must be carefully designed and thoroughly tested before they are deployed. Scripts can configure multiple system settings on several devices on a network. Therefore, any mistakes can potentially affect thousands of computers, even more internal users, and millions of customers. One seemingly small mistake could have a significant impact on a company's operations, finances, or reputation.

Furthermore, while scripts are intended to increase operational efficiency, a poorly written script can have the opposite effect and mishandle system or network resources. For example, a script can mount the wrong network drives, allocate excessive or insufficient memory space for a particular application, establish the wrong user rights or permissions, or create an infinite loop. These and other mistakes can cause browser or system crashes, create network delays, or render resources inaccessible.

Finally, since scripts are usually intended to run unattended, any issues that they cause might go undetected for days or months. For example, a threat actor could have unfettered access to a few machines or an entire network if a script accidentally introduces malware or creates some other security vulnerability.

The following practices can help you avoid these and other unintended consequences of scripting:

- *Team programming and peer review:* Whenever possible, at least two people should synchronously work on a script together, especially if the script is complicated. Team programming (also called pair programming) takes advantage of the fact that everyone brings their own perspective to a problem. This blending of ideas helps in developing solutions more quickly because everyone compensates for each other's deficiencies. For the same reason, a finished script should be reviewed by a qualified peer before it is deployed, especially if team programming is not feasible.
- *Establishing a test regimen:* All scripts should be thoroughly tested before they are deployed. In a corporate environment, any changes to a system (including script changes) should be tested in a development environment (DEV) and then in a user acceptance test environment (UAT) before they are deployed to the full live production environment (PROD). Because end users or customers do not access the DEV systems, technicians and engineers should use the DEV devices to perform the initial troubleshooting and testing. They can then coordinate with a small group of end users in UAT to validate the new code. Any issues discovered in UAT should be resolved and then retested in DEV and UAT. Only after the new code successfully passes DEV and UAT testing should it be deployed to PROD.
- *Testing multiple scenarios:* If a script is targeted for multiple devices, the unique characteristics of the devices must be considered during the testing phases because these differences can affect the script's performance across the network. Test units should account for variances in parameters such as memory and hard drive space, CPU type and speed, location, operating system version, internal network equipment, broadband connection, active directory domain, and so on.

Environment Variables

As in traditional programming languages, variables allow scripts to adapt to changing conditions. An **environment variable** is a variable that describes the environment in which a program runs. For example, environment variables can tell the computer where to find a specific program and can be used to answer questions such as, "Where are saved files stored?" or "Where are the temporary files stored for this particular application?" Environment variables can also describe parameters such as the number of processors or the processor architecture.

In Windows, an environment variable has a name and a value. For example, the variable that stores the location of the Windows operating system files is `windir` (short for *Windows directory*), and the value associated with that variable is normally `C:\Windows`. This means that the Windows program is located in the `C:\` drive in a folder called *Windows*. In this case, the value of the environment variable is the path to the program identified by the variable name.

Another important variable is `PATH`. The `PATH` **variable** tells a program where to find the files it may need. Programs that need specific files to run look for the `PATH` variable automatically. The value of the `PATH` variable is set by a program when it is installed.

Two types of environment variables are system and user. System environment variables are global and cannot be changed by any user. They refer to critical system resources, such as the location of Windows or where program files are stored on a computer. They are set by specific programs and drivers. System environment variable values are the same for all user accounts.

User environment variables, however, have values that differ from user to user. They store the location of such things as a user's profile, where that user stores temporary files, and so on. These variables can be set by the user, by Windows, or by various programs that work with user-specific locations.

To access environment variables in Windows, you can type **`environment`** into the search box and then click or select *Edit the system environment variables*. The System Properties window opens (see Figure 15.9), and you can click on *Environment Variables* to open the Environment Variables window (see Figure 15.10). There are some minor visual differences between various versions of Windows, but the options and buttons are the same, regardless of which version of Windows you are using.

You can also access the Environment Variables window by accessing the *System and Security* Control Panel > *System* > *Advanced system settings*. This takes you to the *System Properties* window, where you see the *Environment Variables* button. Clicking this button opens the *Environment Variables* window.

To edit an environment variable, to add a new environment variable, or to reorder the current environment variables, you can click the *Edit* button in the *Environment Variables* window.

You can also access the *System Properties* window by pressing ⊞+r to open the *Run* dialog box and then enter the command **`systempropertiesadvanced.exe`**, as shown in Figure 15.11.

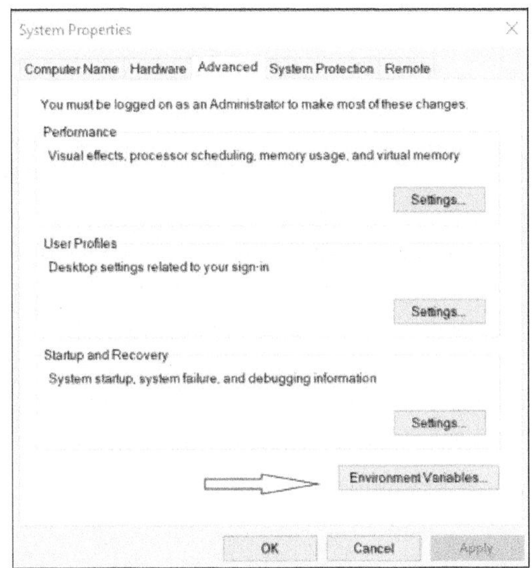

FIGURE 15.9 Accessing Windows environment variables

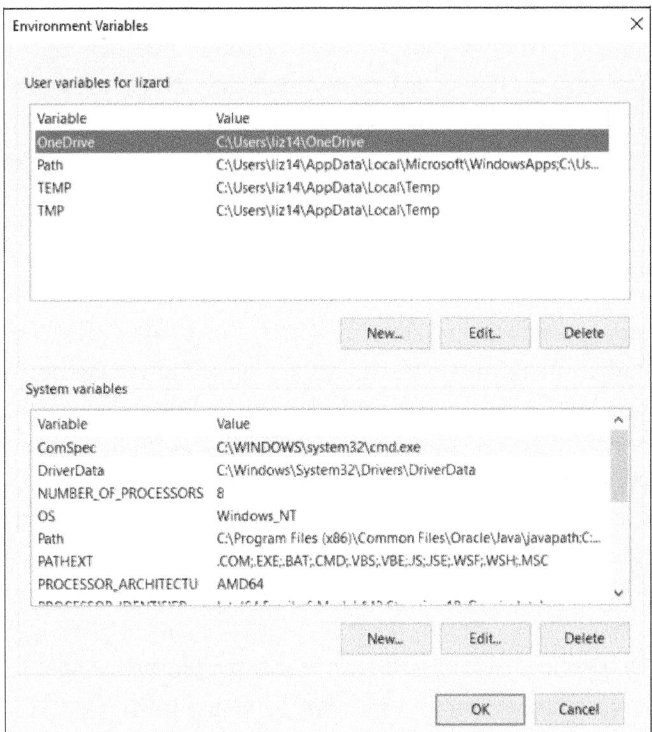

FIGURE 15.10 Environment Variables window

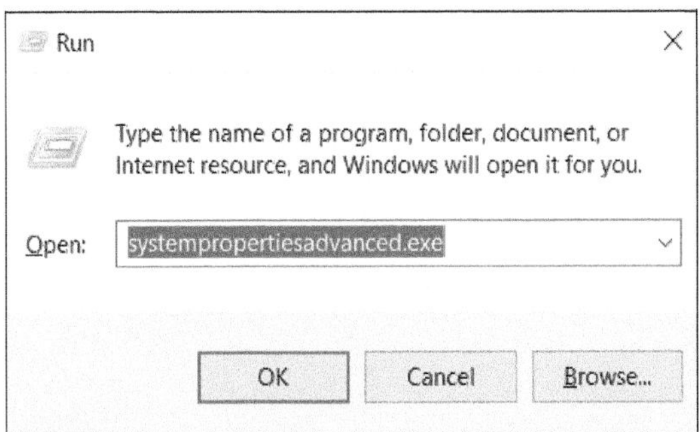

FIGURE 15.11 Accessing the System Properties window through the Run dialog box

From the command prompt, you can enter **`set`** to see all the environment variables, as shown in Figure 15.12.

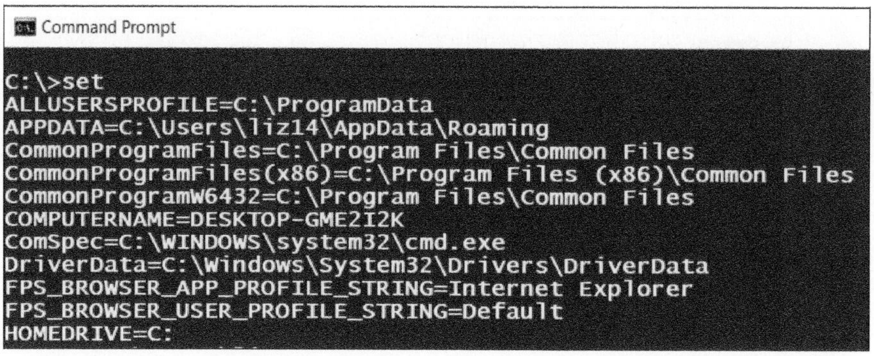

```
Command Prompt

C:\>set
ALLUSERSPROFILE=C:\ProgramData
APPDATA=C:\Users\liz14\AppData\Roaming
CommonProgramFiles=C:\Program Files\Common Files
CommonProgramFiles(x86)=C:\Program Files (x86)\Common Files
CommonProgramW6432=C:\Program Files\Common Files
COMPUTERNAME=DESKTOP-GME2I2K
ComSpec=C:\WINDOWS\system32\cmd.exe
DriverData=C:\Windows\System32\Drivers\DriverData
FPS_BROWSER_APP_PROFILE_STRING=Internet Explorer
FPS_BROWSER_USER_PROFILE_STRING=Default
HOMEDRIVE=C:
```

FIGURE 15.12 Viewing environment variables by using the `set` command

There may be times when you need to create an environment variable to tell a computer how to find the program needed to run a script. PowerShell (`.ps1` files) and VBScript (`.vbs` files) both run on the .NET framework, which is installed with Windows. Batch files (`.bat`) are run from the command line. Running Python, however, requires a little more work. The Python engine is not preinstalled on Windows, even though Windows installers have been included with every release. Still, you may need to create an environment variable to run Python. The same is true for JavaScript, for which you need to install Node.js. Node.js is a free, open source environment where you can run JavaScript code without a browser. Node.js is also very flexible in that it can run on most operating systems, including Windows, Linux, and macOS.

Script Syntax

Every programming language has its own syntax. The **syntax** of a language is the set of symbols and rules used to create instructions. Understanding and using correct syntax is the only way you can get a script to work because a computer cannot understand the context of an instruction otherwise. If an instruction is not composed in the exact syntax for that language, it will not be executed and, worse, may cause the whole script to crash.

Syntax refers to more than using the correct words in a command. It includes the correct symbols and punctuation. For example, if a language requires an instruction to terminate with a semicolon, leaving off the semicolon invalidates the entire instruction and usually causes serious errors. Each scripting language has its own specific syntax, which you must learn in order to write a script in that language. However, it isn't as hard as it sounds. Most languages have similar syntax. And all scripting and programming languages use the same logical constructs to write instructions. Once you understand the logic behind programming instructions and commands, learning a language's specific syntax is pretty easy.

For example, the syntax to display a sentence such as `Hello, my friend!` on the console uses the following syntax in these four scripting languages:

- *Python:* `print("Hello, my friend!")`
- *JavaScript:* `console.log("Hello, my friend!");`
- *Batch file:* `ECHO Hello, my friend!`
- *Shell script:* `echo "Hello, my friend!"`

Introduction to Script Programming

In the 1960s, scientists proved that all programming code can be done using three constructs: sequence, selection, and repetition. **Sequence** refers to how a computer executes code one line at a time, from top to bottom. **Selection** refers to how specific lines of code are run if a specific condition is met. **Repetition** (sometimes called iteration) refers to how a computer can execute specific lines of code repeatedly. Everything you see and do with any computer or any device that uses a computer runs on programming code, and all of that code is based on the simple logic described here. This is incredible.

A program is a list of instructions written by a programmer to perform a task or tasks. The instructions are executed one line at a time, in the order in which they are written. A script is simply a type of program. The difference between a scripting language and other types of programming languages lies in how the code executes, not in how the code is written.

Programming languages such as C++ or Java are compiled languages. A compiled language uses a compiler to translate the source code to machine code. Machine code is code specific to a given processor and operating system. Once a program has been translated to machine code, the computer runs the machine code on its own. Before a compiled program can be run, it must be completely error free.

In an interpreted implementation of a language, the computer does not execute the source code directly but uses an interpreter to execute each line of code. If an error is found, the program stops and sends feedback to the programmer. This allows the programmer to see the error immediately and make necessary changes. Interpreted languages are often called *scripting languages*. They are used by networking professionals because they are relatively easy to learn and use, they are easy to debug, and they are portable across various hardware and network platforms.

All programs rely on input, processing, and output. A program performs a task based on some type of input. The **input** may come from a user typing information at the program's request, from values sent by other parts of the program, or from the computer itself. Then the program processes the information and returns some output (the **processing**). The **output** can be results shown on the screen or console or may be changes sent to other parts of the program or to the computer itself.

Together, the input–processing–output sequence and the three programming constructs form the basis for all programs. Before learning about those constructs, it is important to understand two basic concepts: variables and data types.

Variables

A program **variable** is a named memory location that stores data of a specific type (integer, floating point number, or text). The *value* of that variable is the data contents at that memory location. It is called a variable because its value can change (vary) as the program runs. You can think of a location in the computer's memory as a mailbox. The variable is the name printed on that mailbox, and the value of the variable is the contents of that box. For example, if you have a variable named `myNumber` and you set its value to `23` using an instruction in the syntax of the language you are using, the memory location named `myNumber` stores the number `23`:

myNumber
23

However, as soon as you write another instruction to change the value of `myNumber` to, for example, `584`, the value `23` is lost forever, and the new value takes its place:

myNumber
584

From now on, every time `myNumber` is referenced in a program, it means `584`—at least until that value is changed by a different instruction.

Previously you saw how to display some text on the screen using the syntax of several different scripting languages. The text that was displayed was hard-coded, which means the programmer wrote the exact words to be displayed. But if the programmer had, instead, used a variable to store that text, the text could be changed every time the program runs, depending on different conditions.

For example, the program could display `Good morning` if the current time is between 5:00 a.m. and 11:59 a.m., `Good afternoon` if the current time is between noon and 5:00 p.m., `Good evening` if the current time is between 5:01 p.m. and 9:00 p.m., and so on. The instructions in this code would include a check of the system for the current time and would assign the correct greeting to the variable, depending on the result of the time check. Then the display would greet the user with a message that is appropriate for the time of day.

For example, if a variable is named `myGreeting`, the command to display the correct greeting would then be:

- *Python:* `print(myGreeting)`
- *JavaScript:* `console.log(myGreeting);`
- *Batch file:* `ECHO myGreeting`
- *Shell script:* `echo $myGreeting`

You can see that, while the specific command to have output displayed on the screen differs for each language, the logic for this instruction is the same for all languages: Use the correct command for outputting something on the screen, followed by the variable name that represents the value to be displayed.

A programmer must follow certain rules in selecting variable names. While not every language has exactly the same rules for naming variables, there are some universal rules:

- A variable name cannot begin with a number but may contain numbers. For example, `1stNumber` is not acceptable, but `Number1` is fine.
- A variable name may not include any spaces and, except for the underscore and sometimes the hyphen (_ and -), should not include any punctuation. For example, `my Greeting` is not acceptable, nor is `my&Greeting`, but `my_Greeting` is fine.
- Variables are case sensitive. For example, `Username` is not the same variable as `username` or `userName`.
- A variable name cannot begin with a language's keyword. A **keyword** is a set of characters that is an instruction in that language. In the Python language, for example, `try` is a keyword. Therefore, `tryIt` is not an acceptable variable name in Python; however, `attemptIt` is fine.
- Variable names can be long, but each language has a restriction on how many characters are allowed.
- A variable name should indicate what the content is about without being too long. Since you will probably have to type a variable name many times in a script, you want to keep your variable names as short as possible while still indicating what the variable represents. For example, `gt` is an acceptable variable name but would be confusing to someone who had to work with your code at a later date. Also, `the_greeting_to_be_displayed_to_the_user` is an acceptable variable name, but do you really want to type it 20 times in a script? A better option would be `greeting`.

In order to create a variable, a programmer must declare the variable. This means the programmer writes a line of code to tell the computer that there will be a variable with a specific name and type. (The concept of data types is explained more fully later in this chapter.) Each language has its own way to declare variables, but the concept of a variable **declaration** is consistent across languages: The computer must be told that a variable with a given name will exist, and the computer then assigns a memory location to hold the value of that variable.

When a variable is declared, if it is set to a beginning value, this is known as **initialization**. If no value is given when the variable is declared, the computer may leave the memory location empty or may place a default value in that location. The syntax for declaring a variable named `myVarName` and setting its initial value to `0` is, in four scripting languages, as follows:

> *Python:* `myVarName = 0`
> *JavaScript:* `var myVarName = 0;`
> *Batch file:* `set myVarName=0`
> *Shell script:* `myVarName=0`

Notice that JavaScript and `.bat` files require a keyword before the variable name (`var` in JavaScript and `set` in a batch file), but Python and shell scripts don't. In Python and JavaScript, the spaces before and after the = symbol are optional, while in a `.bat` file or a `.sh` file, putting spaces before and after this symbol will not work. JavaScript requires a semicolon at the end of the variable declaration, while the other languages shown here do not. You can see why learning the syntax of each language is important.

Data Types

The value of a variable is stored in computer memory as a specific type of data. Some languages have a long list of possible data types, while others have only a few. However, all languages distinguish between numbers, types of numbers, and characters or strings of characters (which could be numbers that are dealt with as text), sometimes simply called **strings**.

The data type of a variable determines how much space is allotted in memory to store that value and also determines what operations can be performed with that data. For example, numeric data can be multiplied, but you cannot multiply two alphanumeric characters. **Alphanumeric characters** include all the letters of the alphabet, both upper and lowercase, as well as the digits 0 through 9 plus the punctuation marks and symbols available on a normal keyboard (for example, @, #). If you try to perform an unsupported operation on data stored as a particular data type, your program will either not work at all or will work incorrectly.

There are two basic types of numbers that a computer program normally deals with: integers and floating-point numbers. **Integers** are whole numbers, including zero and negative numbers. **Floating-point numbers** are numbers that can be written in the form $x \div y$, where x and y are integers. A floating-point number can be thought of as a number that includes a decimal value, even if that value is 0. For example, the number 6 is an integer, but the number 6.0 is a floating-point number. Floating-point numbers are handled very differently from integers but, because they are rarely used in scripts, for the purposes of this book, we do not need to concern ourselves with them. When referring to numeric data, we will only consider integers.

In the previous examples, all the variables named `myVarName` would be stored as numeric data because they were initially given integer values (in this case, `0`). In some languages you must specify what data type a variable will be. In others, such as Python and JavaScript, the data type of a variable is set by the computer based on the variable's initial value. Once set, a variable's data type cannot be changed while the variable is in use.

Examples of Using Variables

The following examples demonstrate how variables can be used in several scripting languages. In each of the first set of examples, two numeric variables, named `num1` and `num2`, are declared and initialized to integer values and then added together. The result is stored in a third variable, named `numResult`, and then output to the console. The output in all cases would be `7`.

> *Python:*

```
num1 = 3
num2 = 4
numResult = num1 + num2
print(numResult)
```

> *JavaScript:*

```
var num1 = 3;
var num2 = 4;
var numResult = num1 + num2;
console.log(numResult);
```

> *Batch files:*

```
set /A num1=3
set /A num2=4
set /A numResult=%num1%+%num2%
Echo %numResult%
```

> *Shell scripts:*

```
num1=3
num2=4
numResult=$num1+$num2
echo $numResult
```

The following script snippets demonstrate how to join two string variables (variables that hold alphanumeric data) to output a result. In each case, one string variable named `username` is joined with the value of a second string variable named `message`, and the resulting string is output to the console. In these examples, it may be assumed that the name of this computer's user, to be stored in `username`, is Joey Jones. The output in all cases would be `Welcome Joey Jones`.

> *Python:*

```
username = "Joey Jones"
message = "Welcome "
result = message + username
print(result)
```

> *JavaScript:*

```
var username = "Joey Jones";
var message = "Welcome ";
var result = message + username;
console.log(result);
```

> *Batch files:*

```
set username=Joey Jones
set message=Welcome
set result=message+" "+username
Echo %result%
```

> *Shell scripts:*

```
username="Joey Jones"
message="Welcome "
result=$message$username
echo $result
```

You have now seen how to join variables of the same data type (integer and integer, string and string). But it is also possible to join a string variable with an integer variable; however, each language handles this situation differently.

Comments Within Scripts

When a script runs, the computer processes each instruction and does what that instruction says to do. In the examples shown in the previous section, you can see that a script works as follows:

> The first line declares a variable and initializes it with a value.

> The second line declares a second variable and initializes it with a value.

> The third line declares a third variable on the left-hand side of the instruction. Then it joins the values of the first and second variables on the right-hand side of the instruction. Finally, it puts that value into the third variable.

> The last line outputs the value of the third variable to the screen or console.

The purpose of each of these short snippets is clear and easy to see. But you can also see that some of the syntax may be confusing as, for example, when variable names are enclosed in symbols like `%` (batch files) or have a required symbol like `$` before the variable name (shell scripts). As a script becomes longer, the purpose of some parts of it may not be immediately clear. As you continue to write scripts, you will see that there may be more than one way to write code to do a specific task. And you may be asked to use or edit a script written by someone else who may no longer even be working with you.

For these reasons, it is always a good idea to include **comments** when you write scripts. Comments are put into a script to explain what the script or part of the script is supposed to do. They are meant to be read by the person who is using the script, and they are ignored by the computer when the script runs. Each language has its own syntax for writing comments:

> *Python:* A comment can be on one line or can span multiple lines. A comment that is on one line starts with a hash character (#). A comment may be placed on a new line or following a space at the end of a coded instruction. A multi-line comment begins and ends with three double quotes (`"""`). Consider these examples of Python comments:

```
# This is a single line comment in Python.
Print(result)  # Here's another comment.
""" This begins a multi-line comment. Everything
until the end of the comment is ignored by the
processor. The comment will end here. """
```

> *JavaScript:* A comment starts with two slashes (`//`) and goes to the end of the line. A comment may be placed on separate lines or following a line of code. If you want to include several lines in a single comment, open the comment with `/*` and end the comment with `*/`. Consider these examples of JavaScript comments:

```
// This is a single line comment in JavaScript.
Console.log(result)   // Here is another comment.
/* This begins a multi-line comment. Everything
until the end of the comment is ignored by the
processor. The comment will end here. */
```

> *Batch files:* A comment in a batch file begins with the keyword `REM` or can also begin with two colons (`::`). There is a slight danger in using the `REM` command. If `ECHO` (the command to output to the screen) is on, then the comment itself will be displayed. Consider these examples of batch file comments:

```
REM This is a comment in a batch file.
:: This is also a comment in a batch file.
```

> *Shell scripts:* The hash symbol (#) is used to identify a comment in a `.sh` file. It can be placed on a separate line or after the first space following a line of code, as in these examples:

```
# This is a comment in a shell script file.
echo $result  # This is another comment.
```

Basic Script Constructs

As mentioned earlier, all scripts—in fact, all computer programs—are built around three basic **constructs**: sequence, decision (or selection), and repetition (or iteration). Instructions in a script file are executed by the computer in the order in which they are written. Executing instructions in the order in which they appear in the code is known as the *sequence structure*. However, the code may instruct the computer to follow one sequence of instructions under certain conditions and a different sequence of instructions under different conditions. Without this ability to make decisions, a script could only do a very limited number of tasks.

Take, for example, a script that displays a greeting to the user based on the time of day. The computer must be told to check the time and, depending on the result of that check, do only one thing and skip the remaining options. This is known as a selection structure, or a **decision structure**.

A script may also require that a task or part of a task be repeated 2 or 3 or even 1,000 times. Rewriting an instruction many times is tedious and unnecessary. For example, if you want to check a directory to see if it includes a specific file, you need to compare the filename you're searching for with each file in that directory. Instead of writing separate instructions to check the first file, the second file, the third file, and so on, you can write a single structure that says to check a file in that directory and, if it is not the filename you seek, do the same thing again with the next file, and the next, and so on until the list of files in that directory ends or until you have found the file you want. This is known as a repetition structure, or a **loop structure**.

Decisions: The Selection Structure

A *selection structure* is also referred to as a *decision structure*. It consists of a test condition together with one or more groups (or blocks) of statements. The result of the test condition determines which block of statements will be executed. This means that, for any selection structure, some statements will never be executed. For example, if you wrote a script to display a greeting based on the time of day, and it is 10:00 a.m., you only want the block of statements that display `Good morning!` to be executed. The blocks that display `Good afternoon!` or `Good evening!` should be—and are—skipped.

Three main types of selection/decision structures are used in programming: single alternative, dual alternative, and multiple alternative. Before we discuss these three types of selection structures, we need to define the operators used in these structures.

Relational Operators

Operators that compare two expressions are known as **relational operators**. In most programming languages, the symbol >= means "greater than or equal to," the symbol <= means "less than or equal to," and the symbol `!=` means "is not equal to." The > and < symbols mean "greater than" and "less than," but in batch files, the > symbol is a redirection operator and cannot be used to compare values. Batch files and shell scripts use other commands to compare two expressions. Table 15.2 shows the various relational operators and their meanings in most languages.

TABLE 15.2 Relational operators

Meaning	Most common	Batch file command	Shell operator
Equal to	==	EQU	-eq
Not equal to	!=	NEQ	-ne
Less than	<	LSS	-lt
Less than or equal to	<=	LEQ	-le
Greater than	>	GTR	-gt
Greater than or equal to	>=	GEQ	-ge

Three Types of Selection Structures

As mentioned earlier, there are three types of programming structures: sequence, decision (or selection), and repetition (or iteration). In addition, there are three different types of the decision/selection structures: single alternative, dual alternative, and multiple alternative. It is also possible to nest a selection structure inside another selection structure. Let's take a look at each one of these.

Single Alternative

With the single-alternative structure, a test is performed. If the outcome of the test is true, a block of statements is executed, and then program control moves to the next instruction after the selection structure. If the outcome of the test is not true, nothing is executed, and the program control proceeds to the next instruction. For example, imagine a script that is written to check whether the current user is named `Jonas`. If it is, the program displays `user found`, and if it is not, it does nothing. The current user's name is stored in a variable named `name`. The single-alternative logic for this script in Python would be:

```
if name == "Jonas":
    print("user found!")
continue...
```

If `name` is anything other than `"Jonas"`, the program continues, and nothing happens. This is known as an `if` structure.

Notice the double equals sign (==) in the `if` statement shown in the preceding example. It is called the **comparison operator** or, sometimes, the **equals operator** or the **equality operator**. In most programming languages, a single equals sign (=) sets the value on the right side of the expression to the variable name on the left side. But a double equals sign *compares* the two values. This statement says, basically, "Is the value stored in the variable named `name` *the same as* `"Jonas"`?" This distinction is very important; using a single equals sign when trying to compare values is an error that often causes a lot of trouble.

Dual Alternative

With the dual-alternative structure, a test is also performed, but one of two possible blocks of statements will always execute. If the outcome of the test is true, one block of statements is executed, and then program control moves to the next instruction after the selection structure. If the outcome of the test is not true, a different block of statements is performed, and the program control proceeds to the next instruction. In a dual-alternative structure, the example shown above might look like this in Python:

```
if name == "Jonas":
    print("user found!")
else:
    print("user not found!")
continue...
```

In this case, one of the two statements (`user found!` or `user not found!`) would always be displayed, and the other would be skipped. This type of structure is called an `if-else` structure.

Multiple Alternative

Sometimes you need more than two options in a selection structure. For example, a script might assign a student's letter grade based on the numeric result of an exam score. Every language has the ability to create a multiple-alternative structure, but each has its own syntax for doing so. In Python, such a structure is known as an `if-elif-else` structure. The code to assign a letter grade in Python is as follows:

```
1.  if score >= 90:
2.      print("Congratulations! You have a grade of A.")
3.  elif score >= 80:
4.      print("You have a grade of B.")
5.  elif score >= 70:
6.      print("You have a grade of C.")
7.  elif score >= 60:
8.      print("You have a grade of D.")
9.  else:
10.     print("You have a grade of F.")
11. continue...
```

It is assumed that a variable named `score` already holds a student's numeric score on the exam. In this code, the value of `score` is checked against a test condition. If it matches, the block of statements that follows that test condition is executed, and all the other code up to the end of the `if-elif-else` structure is skipped. If the first condition is not true, the second condition is tested. If that one is also not true, the third condition is tested, and so on. As soon as one condition is found to be true, that block of statements is executed, and any remaining conditions are skipped. In a multiple-alternative structure, only one block of statements is executed and all the others are skipped.

Note: The line numbers shown above and referenced in the information that follows are for clarity only. In a real program, there would be no line numbers.

Note: In Python, the indentation of various statements is important. Proper indentation tells the computer which statements are part of the various blocks of code. Other languages use other syntax to define blocks of statements in control structures.

You might wonder how this program works for a score of 96 or 78 or why it is not necessary to specify that a score of 84 must be less than 90 as well as greater than 80. Consider the logic of the program. Line 1 checks to see if `score` is greater than or equal to 90. This includes everything from 90 and above, including 96. If, however, `score` is less than 90, line 2 is skipped, and the value of `score` is tested on line 3. The only way the program can execute line 3 is if the test on line 1 fails. And that means `score` is less than 90, so there is no need to specify it in the code. All that is needed is to check whether `score` is greater than or equal to 80. If `score` is 62, the only way line 8 can be executed is if the tests on lines 1, 3, and 5 have failed, which means `score` is already known to be less than 70. If `score` is anything greater than or equal to 60, line 8 is executed. If it is not greater than or equal to 60, then `score` must be less than 60, and there is no need to specify that in the code. No matter what value `score` holds, only one block of statements will be executed and, regardless of what that block is, the program will continue on line 11.

Selection Structure Examples

Following are examples of how a multiple-alternative selection structure would be coded in several scripting languages. In each case, it is assumed that one variable (`num1`) holds the value of a number, and a second variable (`num2`) holds the value of another number. If the first number is greater than the second number, one message is displayed. If the second number is greater than the first, a different message is displayed. If the two numbers are the same, a third message is displayed:

> *Python:*

```
if (num1 > num2):
    print(num1," is greater than ",num2)
elif (num1 < num2):
     print(num1," is less than ",num2)
else:
     print(num1," and ", num2," are the same")
```

> *JavaScript:*

```
if (num1 > num2){
       console.log(num1 + " is greater than " + num2);
   }
   else if (num1 < num2)    {
       console.log(num1 + " is less than " + num2);
   }
     else
       console.log(num1 + " and " + num2 + " are equal");
```

> *Batch files:*

```
IF  %num1% GTR %num2% (
    ECHO %num1% is greater than %num2%
         ) ELSE IF %num1% LSS %num2% (
       ECHO %num1% is less than %num2%
       ) ELSE (
         ECHO %num1% and %num2% are the same
       )
```

> *Shell scripts:*

```
if [ $num1 -gt $num2 ]
 then
   set str="$num1 is greater than $num2"
   echo $str
```

```
SET /A x=5
SET /A count=1
SET /A limit=11
:while
   if !count! LSS !limit! (
      SET /A product = !x!*!count!
      ECHO|set /p=!product!
      SET /A count=count + 1
      Goto :while
       )
```

Note: `setlocal EnableDelayedExpansion` and the use of ! instead of % accounts for the way that batch files handle variables within loops.

Note: `/A` is a switch that is used if a value needs to be numeric.

Note: Batch files do not have a `while` loop, but you can use other batch commands to write a script that closely mimics the logic of a `while` loop, as shown.

Note: `ECHO|set /p` prints the result without a linefeed. You need to add a space after the last ! to put spaces between the numbers.

The `for` Loop

Most often a loop is used to repeat a block of instructions a given number of times. For example, in the `while` loop shown earlier in this chapter, you know you want the loop to repeat 10 times. However, you may not always know how many times the loop should repeat. For example, imagine that you want to check each file in various directories to see how many files are over a certain size. The number of files in each directory to be checked would probably not be known. Most scripting languages have a type of loop known as a `for` loop to handle such situations.

A traditional `for` loop is, in effect, a shorthand way to write a `while` loop. The general syntax is as follows:

```
for variable=value; test condition; variable increment/decrement
{
        Several statements in a block to execute
}
```

In this type of loop, you initialize a variable first—a statement that is generally done before entering the `while` loop. Then you set up a test condition, as you would in a `while` loop. Finally, you increment or decrement the value of the variable; in a `while` loop, this is done within the block of statements. The JavaScript `for` loop version of the `while` loop shown above is as follows:

```
var x = 5;
    for (count = 1; count < 11; count++)    {
        console.log(count * x + "  ");
    }
```

A `for` loop is sometimes referred to as a *collection-controlled loop*. In such a loop, you identify the item to be tested, the collection of items, and, at the same time, the initial value, the ending value, and how much to increment or decrement the item. The general syntax for this type of `for` loop is as follows:

```
for variable in range(start, step, end) list do:
        Block of statements to execute
end loop
```

In most languages, one or more of the `start`, `step`, and `end` values are optional. If they are not specified, the computer will normally default to a value of `0` or `1` (depending on the type of collection) for `start` and a value of `+1` for `step`, and it will end at the end of the collection of items.

There are some variations on the `for` loop in most scripting languages that allow for more flexibility. The batch file example shown in the following section demonstrates how the `forfiles` loop, specific to batch files, makes solving the problem of checking all files in a directory easier than using a traditional `for` loop.

Examples of `for` Loops

Each of the following examples shows a loop that searches through a list of filenames in a directory and returns the date each file was last modified. Each of the scripting languages has specific functions that deal with the properties of files and directories, and some of them have other ways to automate this process. Note that "directory" represents the file path to a directory on the computer running the script.

- *Python:*

```
import time
import os
directory = 'C:\\users'
for file in os.listdir(directory):
    full_file_path = os.path.join(directory, file)
    print("modified: %s " %
        time.ctime(os.path.getmtime(full_file_path)))
```

- *Batch files:*

```
forfiles /C "cmd /c echo @file @fdate @ftime"
```

Note: Batch files also have a `for` command, but for this particular situation, the `forfiles` command works better.

- *Shell scripts:*

```
for entry in "$directory"/*
do
modDate=$(stat-c%y "$entry")
modDate=${modDate%%*}
echo $entry:$modDate
```

- *JavaScript:*

```
for(var i = 0; i < files.length; i++)
{
  console.log(files[i] + "<br>");
}
```

Note: This program is a little trickier in JavaScript. The example here is intended to show how a `for` loop is coded in JavaScript and will only display the names of the files without all the files' properties, including the date modified. As with many other scripting tasks, JavaScript is not the best language to use.

A Brief Look at VBScript and PowerShell

The examples in the preceding sections demonstrate how scripts are written in Python, JavaScript, batch files, and shell scripting. Two other scripting tools are VBScript and PowerShell. While VBScript is used exclusively with the Windows operating system, PowerShell can be used with Windows, Linux, Unix, and macOS.

VBScript

VBScript is a Microsoft scripting language that has some commands that are part of the Visual Basic programming language. It allows Windows system administrators to manage error handling, subroutines, and other processes managed by scripting languages. VBScript files have the extension `.vbs`.

However, VBScript is mainly used to allow functionality and interaction on web pages, and it is not supported by any modern browser. For use on web pages, JavaScript has usurped VBScript. For use in managing system administration tasks, any of the other cross-platform languages or batch files are preferable.

PowerShell

PowerShell was originally created in 2006 by Microsoft as a task automation and configuration management framework for the Windows operating system. A decade later, in 2016, Microsoft released an open source cross-platform version of PowerShell. Windows PowerShell runs on the full .NET Framework, and the cross-platform version runs on the **.NET Core**. PowerShell script files are identified by the `.ps1` file extension.

In PowerShell, administrative tasks are generally performed by specialized .NET classes called **cmdlets**. There are more than 200 basic cmdlets. Each cmdlet implements a particular operation and has help that includes an example of how to use the cmdlet.

Some of the core cmdlets are `Get-Location` to get the current directory, `Move-item` to move a file to a different location, and `New-item` to create a new file. You can also create PowerShell scripts to do tasks not covered by a cmdlet. A PowerShell script includes a combination of cmdlets and associated logic.

To get help with PowerShell, the `man` command is used. Figure 15.13 shows the `man Get-Location` command output and syntax for the `Get-Location` cmdlet.

```
Windows PowerShell
Copyright (C) Microsoft Corporation. All rights reserved.

PS C:\Users\chery> man Get-Location

NAME
    Get-Location

SYNTAX
    Get-Location [-PSProvider <string[]>] [-PSDrive <string[]>] [-UseTransaction]
[<CommonParameters>]

    Get-Location [-Stack] [-StackName <string[]>] [-UseTransaction]  [<CommonParame
ters>]
```

FIGURE 15.13 `Get-Location` **cmdlet syntax**

SOFT SKILLS: CHANGING PERSPECTIVE WHEN TROUBLESHOOTING

Troubleshooting is a hard topic to teach. Experience is the best way to learn how to tackle device problems, including problems with displays. In the classroom, teachers often rely on things going wrong during installation to teach troubleshooting. Also, broken machines can be used to encourage students to jump in and attempt repair. One troubleshooting technique that is seldom practiced in the classroom but that is great to do is to change your perspective.

When troubleshooting a problem, your perspective is that of a trained technician: You look at what is going wrong and determine what you know about that particular area that can cause the problem. Nothing is wrong with this perspective because it is a normal progression for a technician. But what happens when you are stuck or when you are faced with something you have never seen before?

One of the ways you can change your perspective is to put yourself in the mindset of the user. Through talking with a user just a bit, you can get an idea of how the person thinks and works. Then you can try imagining the problem from that person's perspective. First, this may give you troubleshooting ideas that you haven't thought of before. Second, it will make you more empathetic and a better technician. See Figure 15.14.

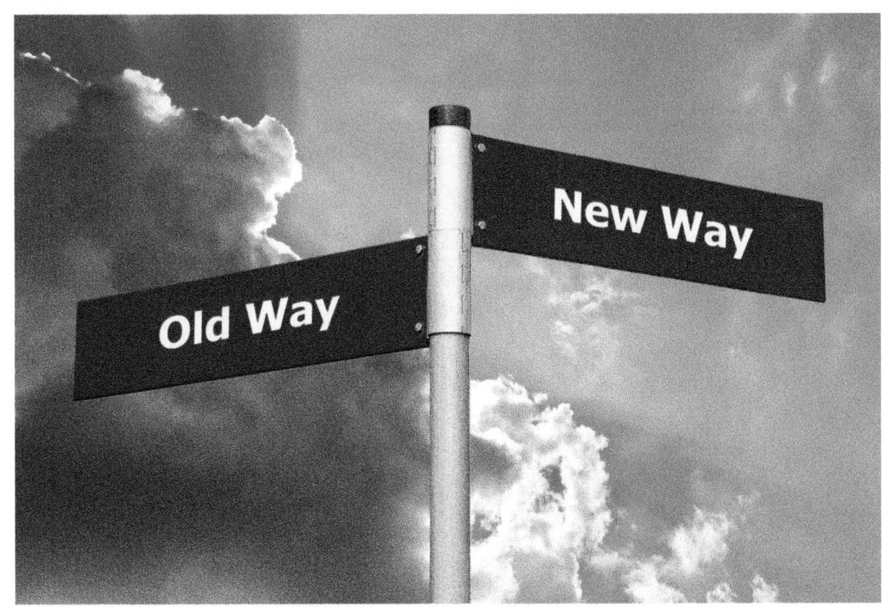

FIGURE 15.14 See things from a new perspective

Another way to look at things from a different perspective is to imagine a great technician you know. Put yourself in that person's shoes. What would that technician try that you haven't thought of yet? What tricks have you seen tried in the past?

Perspective shapes how we approach problems. By changing our perspective, we change how we troubleshoot problems and how we approach the troubleshooting task. As technicians, we must constantly update and refine our skills because most of our day is spent troubleshooting (see Figure 15.15).

FIGURE 15.15 Changing perspectives

Chapter Summary

- Commands are used in two environments: (1) in a command prompt environment when the GUI tools do not or cannot correct a problem and (2) when using a scripting environment to deploy the operating system and/or updates to multiple computers.
- Command switches alter the way a command performs or outputs information. Use *`command`* `/?` or `help` to receive help on any particular command.
- Important commands to know are `dir`, `cd`, `..`, `ipconfig`, `ping`, `tracert`, `netstat`, `nslookup`, `shutdown`, `dism`, `sfc`, `chkdsk`, `diskpart`, `taskkill`, `gpupdate`, `gpresult`, `format`, `copy`, `xcopy`, `robocopy`, `net use`, `net user`, `[command name] /?`, `msconfig`, `regedit`, `command`, `services.msc`, `mmc`, `mstsc`, `msinfo32`, and `dxdiag`.
- Environment variables describe the environment in which a program runs. In Windows, each environment variable has a name and a value. For example, the value can be the path to the program that is identified by the variable name.
- A script, as referred to in this text, is a small computer program designed to do a specific task. Common automation and configuration tasks include restarting machines, remapping network drives, installing applications, managing backups and updates, and gathering information. The ability to create and use scripts is valuable because scripts save time, ensure consistency in the execution of tasks, and allow for flexibility in responding to various conditions.
- Scripts can be written in many scripting languages. Some are designed for use on a single operating system, and others are cross-platform. While all scripting languages use the same logic to write a script for a given task, each language has its own unique and specific syntax. Scripting languages discussed in this chapter include batch files, shell scripts, VBScript, PowerShell, Python, and JavaScript.
- The building blocks of scripting include variables and data types. All scripts are written using three basic programming constructs: sequence, selection, and repetition.
- Looking at the problem from a different perspective can help a technician during troubleshooting.

A+ CERTIFICATION EXAM TIPS

- ✓ Be familiar with the commands and how to work in the command prompt environment. The following commands are on the certification exam: navigation commands (`dir`, `cd` `md`, `rmdir`, and `..`) as well as commands such as `chkdsk`, `copy`, `diskpart`, `dism`, `explorer`, `format`, `gpresult`, `gpupdate`, `hostname`, `ipconfig`, `mmc`, `msinfo32`, `mstsc`, `net use`, `net user`, `netstat`, `notepad`, `nslookup`, `pathping`, `ping`, `regedit`, `robocopy`, `services.msc`, `sfc`, `shutdown`, `taskkill`, `tracert`, `winver`, `xcopy`, and `[command name] /?`. You should also be familiar with commands available to someone with standard privileges vs. those that are available with administrative privileges. Practice these commands (and the various switches used with them) the week before taking the exam. Know when to use them. Consider what would be wrong that would force you to use a particular command.
- ✓ Be able to identify the program and file extension for each of the following script file types: batch files (`.bat`), PowerShell (`.ps1`), VBScript (`.vbs`), shell scripting (`.sh`), Python (`.py`), and JavaScript (`.js`).
- ✓ Understand and identify use cases for scripting. These include restarting machines, remapping network drives, installing applications, managing backups and updates, and gathering information.
- ✓ Understand unintended consequences of scripting.

Key Terms

`..` (navigation command) 703
`.bat` 735
`.js` 735
.NET Core 734
`.ps1` 735
`.py` 735
`.sh` 735
`.vbs` 735
administrative privileges 734
alphanumeric character 743
AND operator 750
`attrib` 708
batch file 735
`cd` 702
`chkdsk` 714
cmdlet 754
`command` 715
command prompt 699
command switch 703
comment 745
comparison operator 747
compiled program 734
compound condition 750
construct 746
`copy` 715
decision structure 746
declaration 743
`defrag` 716
`del` 716
`dir` 716
directory 699
`diskpart` 717
`dism` 717
`dxdiag` 718
environment variable 738
equality operator 747
equals operator 747
`explorer` 719
floating-point number 743
`for` loop 751
`format` 719
`gpresult` 720
`gpupdate` 720
`help` 720
initialization 743
input 741
integer 743
interpreted program 734
`ipconfig` 721
iteration 743
JavaScript 735
keyword 742
logical operator 750
loop 751
loop structure 746
`md` 722
`mmc` 722
`msconfig` 722
`msinfo32` 723
`mstsc` 723
`net` 723
`net use` 724
`net user` 724
`netstat` 725
NOT operator 750
`notepad` 725
`nslookup` 726
OR operator 750
output 741
`pathping` 726
PATH variable 738
`ping` 727
PowerShell 735
processing 741
Python 735
`rd` 727
`regedit` 728
relational operator 746
repetition 741
repetition structure 751
`rmdir` 727
`robocopy` 729
root directory 699
script 734
selection 741
sequence 741
`services.msc` 729
`sfc` 730
shell script 735
`shutdown` 730
standard privileges 734
string 743
subdirectory 699
syntax 740
`taskkill` 731
text file 734
`tracert` 732
`type` 732
variable 741
VBScript 735
`while` loop 751
wildcard 706
`winver` 733
`xcopy` 733

Review Questions

1. What command is used to create a directory? [`CD` | `MD` | `DIR` | `MAD`]
2. What command is used to list the contents of a directory? ____________________
3. Consider the following directory structure from the `C:` drive root directory:

   2019_Term (directory)

   CompRepair (subdirectory)

   Opsys (subdirectory)

   Cisco8 (subdirectory)

   VoIP (subdirectory)

   If the prompt is `C:\2019_Term>`, and you want to move into the VoIP subdirectory, what command do you type?

   a. `CD VoIP`

   b. `CD..`

   c. `CD C:\`

   d. `CD C:\VoIP`
4. The __________ and __________ file extensions are used with Windows executable files that are used to start applications. (Choose two.)
   [`.app` | `.com` | `.exe` | `.js` | `.ps1`]
5. What command would be used on a computer where a specific application has stopped?
   [`quit` | `net stop` | `taskkill` | `stop`]
6. List one example of where you think a technician might see or use a batch file or a script file.

   ____

   ____
7. A script is created as a __________ file. [Word | csv | text | HTML]
8. A(n) ____________________ tells the computer where to find a specific program.
   [batch file | environment variable | value variable | scripting language]
9. The two types of environment variables are __________ and __________ variables. (Choose two.)
   [experimental | external | internal | system | test | user]
10. The set of symbols and rules used to create instructions in a scripting language is its _________.
    [variable name | keywords | value | syntax]
11. What command would a technician use to apply a change to the security policy?
    [`gpupdate` | `mstsc` | `regedit` | `bootrec`]
12. The value of a variable is stored in the computer's memory as a specific __________.
    [integer | string | data type | ASCII code]
13. __________ are included in a script to explain what the script or a portion of the script does but are ignored by the computer when the script runs.
    [Comments | Variables | Commands | Syntax lines]

14. Which type of file would include the command `format d: /fs:ntfs /v:Corp /p:2`?

    [`.py` | `.vbs` | `.js` | `.bat`]

15. To compare two expressions in a selection structure, you use ________ operators.

    [>= | logic | equals | relational]

16. The ________ operator returns `false` only if both sides of the expression are false.

    [`AND` | `OR` | `NOT` | `equals`]

17. A ________ structure contains a block of statements that is executed repeatedly.

    [decision | selection | repetition | sequence]

18. Two types of loops are ________ and ________ loops. (Choose two.)

    [`continuous` | `decision` | `else` | `for` | `one-time` | `while`]

19. The scripting languages that were developed by Microsoft are ________ and ________. (Choose two.)

    [Basic | C | Java | PowerShell | VBScript]

20. A script that has the `.sh` extension is a ________ script and works on ________-based systems.

    ____

21. The `.py` extension indicates that a script is written in the ________ language.

    [PowerShell | JavaScript | batch | Python]

Exercises

Exercise 15.1 Identifying command-line commands

Objective: To recognize which command to use for a specific task

Procedure: Match the command to the task by writing the letter of the command beside the task that would use this command. Note that not all commands will be used.

Commands:

a. `dir`	**f.** `robocopy`	**k.** `attrib`
b. `rd`	**g.** `md`	**l.** `sfc`
c. `del`	**h.** `gpresult`	**m.** `regedit`
d. `cd`	**i.** `type`	**n.** `tasklist`
e. `gpupdate`	**j.** `copy`	

Task:

_____ Copy a directory, its contents, all subdirectories, and attributes.

_____ Create a folder.

_____ Remove a file.

_____ Copy a file from one place to another.

_____ List all files in a particular directory.

_____ Delete a directory.

_____ Display the contents of a test or batch file.

_____ Verify and optionally repair operating system files.

_____ Move to a different directory.

Exercise 15.2 Scripting Concepts

Objective: To recognize terms related to scripting.

Procedure: Match the item to its description.

a. .sh
b. .py
c. .bat
d. loop
e. shell script
f. PowerShell
g. string
h. environment variable

Item: Description:

____ A variable that describes the environment in which a program runs
____ A control structure used by a scripting language to write scripts
____ The extension used by the Python language
____ A data type consisting of alphanumeric characters
____ The extension that identifies a batch file
____ A script written for a Unix-based system
____ The extension that identifies a shell script
____ A Windows shell that was created to help in task automation and configuration management

Activities

Flip the CLASSROOM

Internet Discovery

Objective: Access the internet to obtain specific information regarding a computer or its associated parts

Parts: Access to the internet

Procedure: Complete the following procedure and answer the accompanying questions.

1. Locate an internet site that has a specific usage for the `chkdsk` command.

____

2. List three things that you think would be useful from Microsoft's Customizing the Out-of-Box Experience for IT Pros website and explain why you think they would help the technician.

____
____
____

3. Locate a website that provides a VBScript sample that could be used by a computer technician. Provide a basic description of what the script does and the URL where you found the answer.

____
____

4. You have been asked to add some user accounts to a domain, and the supervisor wants you to get some practice from the command line. Find a website that provides the command and specific instructions on how to use that command. Provide the command, one recommendation found on the website, and the URL of the website.

____
____
____
____
____

5. Six scripting languages are described in the chapter. Locate a website that compares and contrasts the use of at least two of these languages. Document the URL. Briefly describe which language you would choose and explain why you made this choice.

____

____

Soft Skills

Objective: To enhance and fine-tune a technician's ability to listen, communicate in both written and oral form, and support people who use computers in a professional manner

Activities:

1. In a group environment, have each group member use a piece of paper or an index card to list two commands to learn how to use in specific situations. Use the internet to find reports from other technicians who have used these commands. Write what you have learned, paying special attention to any issues that were brought up. Share this information with your group. Consolidate ideas and present five of the best ideas to the class.
2. In a team environment, select two of the five ideas presented in Activity 1 to research further. Every team member should present a problem and its solution to the rest of the class. The class votes on the presentation that includes the most interesting and useful topic.
3. In a team environment, assign one scripting language to each member of the team. Each member should research the pros and cons of that language and present the findings to the group. Make a list of when each language should be used and its restrictions to present to the class.

Critical Thinking Skills

Objective: To analyze and evaluate information and to apply learned information to new or different situations

Activities:

1. Write a four-line batch file that does the following tasks:
   - Removes the path (`C:\Whatever`) shown on the screen
   - Clears the screen
   - Puts a message on the screen about what the batch file is doing
   - Starts a particular application or opens a specific web browser

____

____

____

____

____

____

2. Describe what you would do if you were hired for an IT position and asked to create a script.

____

____

____

3. Describe what you would do if you were hired for an IT position and asked to display and modify the environment variable on a given system for a user-installed program.

____

____

____

16 Advanced Windows

In this chapter you will learn:

- > To install, configure, and troubleshoot Windows
- > To install hardware and software in the Windows environment
- > To use various tools and features, such as System Restore, driver rollback, and WinRE
- > To use basic security settings in the Windows environment
- > To use the Control Panel utilities
- > To implement the Windows boot process and troubleshoot boot problems
- > To use the Computer Management console, Task Manager, and Event Viewer
- > To backup and recover a Windows workstation
- > How to avoid burnout in the IT field

CompTIA Exam Objectives:

- ✓ 1102-1.3 Given a scenario, use features and tools of the Microsoft Windows 10 operating system (OS)
- ✓ 1102-1.4 Given a scenario, use the appropriate Microsoft Windows 10 Control Panel utility.
- ✓ 1102-1.5 Given a scenario, use the appropriate Windows settings.
- ✓ 1102-1.6 Given a scenario, configure Microsoft Windows networking features on a client/desktop.
- ✓ 1102-1.7 Given a scenario, apply application installation and configuration concepts.
- ✓ 1102-1.9 Given a scenario, perform OS installations and upgrades in a diverse OS environment.
- ✓ 1102-2.5 Given a scenario, manage and configure basic security settings in the Microsoft Windows OS.
- ✓ 1102-3.1 Given a scenario, troubleshoot Microsoft Windows OS problems.
- ✓ 1102-3.2 Given a scenario, troubleshoot common personal computer (PC) security issues.
- ✓ 1102-4.3 Given a scenario, implement workstation backup and recovery methods.

Advanced Windows Overview

Before we get into more technical issues related to Windows, let's go over some of the features you might not have heard of in Windows. Windows 10 comes in 32- and 64-bit versions, but Windows 11 is only available for 64-bit systems. Windows 10 and 11 have different tiers available: Home, Professional (Pro), Pro for Workstations, Education, and Enterprise. Enhanced features, which depend on the version, include the following:

- *Side-by-side apps or windows:* It is possible to drag the top of a window to one side of the screen (until an outline of the window appears) to view windows or apps side by side. An alternative is to be in an active window and use ⊞+← or ⊞+→, depending on whether you want the active window pinned to the left or right side. Open another window and do the same for the opposite side, and the windows or apps are automatically equally sized.
- *OneDrive:* Microsoft's cloud storage allows files to be synced from multiple devices and accessible from a browser.
- *UAC (User Account Control):* You can get notifications of potential security issues before anything is added to or removed from the system.
- *Microsoft Store:* You can purchase and download apps from this store.
- *Multi-monitor taskbar:* To modify this feature, right-click on the taskbar (or tap and briefly hold on an empty spot) > select *Taskbar Settings* > locate the *Multiple Displays* section > select whether the taskbar shows on all displays and which display buttons should be displayed on.
- *WinRE (***Windows Recovery Environment***):* You can use WinRE when things go wrong with Windows, such as when a system will not boot or operate properly.
- *Hyper-V:* This hypervisor runs virtual machines in Windows.
- *Cortana:* This is the Windows virtual assistant.

Preinstallation of Windows

Windows can be installed from either a central location using a network or locally using an optical disc or external drive. The preinstallation of any operating system is more important than the installation. Technicians who grab a disc or just download and load a new operating system without going through a preparation process are asking for trouble. The operating system is a complex piece of software that is critical to the operation of all hardware and other software.

It is important to follow these steps before installing Windows:

Step 1. Decide whether the installation will be an upgrade or a clean install and which version of the operating system is to be loaded. Take into account software application compatibility.

Step 2. Decide whether the computer will have more than one operating system installed.

Step 3. Plan the partition/volume size and select the file system.

Step 4. Determine whether or not the hardware is compatible.

Step 5. Obtain any drivers, upgrades, or hardware replacements.

Step 6. Back up any data files.

Step 7. Scan for viruses and then disable the virus protection during the installation process.

Step 8. Temporarily disable any power management or disk management tools.

Types of Installations

Windows can be installed for a variety of reasons, such as to have the latest features, to have a different operating system, to repair a system that doesn't boot, or to speed up a slow-performing operating system. Table 16.1 summarizes the various types of installations.

TABLE 16.1 Windows installation types

Installation type	Description
Clean install	An installation of an operating system when no other operating system is present.
Reset/**restore**	A reinstallation (reset) of Windows that gives you the option to keep your personal files (apps and settings are removed) or a restoration (restore) that brings Windows back to a previous state, such as to a time before a recent update was applied.
In-place upgrade	An upgrade of an existing operating system where the user keeps settings and files, such as moving from Windows 10 to 11.
Repair installation	Replacement of the Windows operating system when files have been corrupted or the system won't boot properly.
Recovery partition	Sometimes called a **factory recovery partition**, an area that contains the operating system and applications that came with the system when it was purchased.
Multiboot	Two or more operating systems on the same system; make sure you load the oldest operating system first.
Unattended installation	An installation in which a script or an answer file (usually a custom-prepared one for the company) is used; sometimes called zero-touch installation (ZTI).
Image deployment	Installation using a file that contains an image that can be deployed with little interaction. Windows operating system, software, drivers, and updates are added to a network share, and configuration files are created. Burn the boot images to optical media or an external drive. Boot the destination computer with the boot image, and the installation occurs without further intervention.
Remote network installation	An installation in which a server or network share containing a created image is accessed, and the image is deployed to a computer on a remote network. Network bandwidth is affected, and this may interfere with normal business operations. For this reason, remote installations are commonly done during light network usage time or during off hours.

In-Place Upgrade or Clean Install

The first decision to make when planning to install an operating system is whether to upgrade from another operating system or to perform a clean install. An upgrade or in-place upgrade occurs when a computer already has an older operating system on it, and a newer operating system is being installed. A clean install involves putting an operating system on a system that does not have one or removing the existing operating system in order to install a new one. There are three reasons to perform a clean install:

- The computer does not already have an operating system installed.
- The current operating system is not upgradable to the desired Windows version.
- The current operating system is upgradable to a specific Windows version, but the existing files and applications are going to be reloaded.

Microsoft describes an in-place upgrade as an installation that requires no movement of files. Although an in-place installation can usually be accomplished to upgrade from one version of Windows to another, this isn't always an option. For example, it is possible to do an in-place upgrade from Windows 7 or Window 8.1 to Windows 10, but not to Windows 11. Going from Windows 7/8.1 to Windows 11 requires a clean install. To make sure an upgrade is possible, consult the documentation for the version of Windows you want to upgrade to and know which version of Windows you currently have installed. Figure 16.1 shows how to use the *Settings > About* option to see what version is currently installed. The System Information window (`msinfo32.exe`) also provides this data, along with other details about software and hardware configuration. Table 16.2 shows the upgrade paths for Windows 8.1 to Windows 10. Upgrading from Windows 10 to Windows 11 is discussed in the next section.

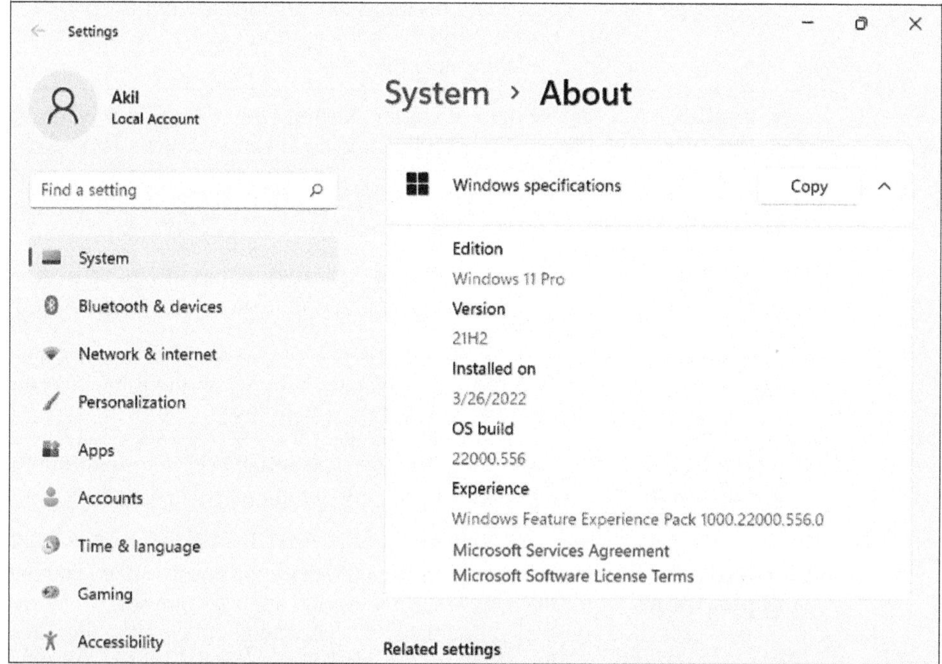

FIGURE 16.1 Windows About section of Settings: current Windows version

TABLE 16.2 Windows 10/11 upgrade paths

Original operating system	Upgrade possibilities
Windows 8.1 Home	Windows 10 Home, Pro, Pro Education, and Education
Windows 8.1 Pro	Windows 10 Pro, Pro Education, Education, and Enterprise
Windows 8.1 Enterprise	Windows 10 Education and Enterprise
Windows 10/11 Home	Windows 10/11 Education, Pro for Workstations, Enterprise, Pro Education
Windows 10/11 Pro	Windows 10/11 Pro, Education, Pro for Workstations, Enterprise, Pro Education
Windows 10/11 Enterprise/Pro Education	Windows 10/11 Education

When you decide to upgrade, you must take into account which operating system is installed, what hardware is installed, what applications are being used, and whether or not those applications are compatible with the new operating system (see Figure 16.2). When Windows is installed as an upgrade, the user's applications and data are preserved if the operating system is installed in the same folder as the original operating system (normally `C:\Windows`). If Windows is installed in a different folder than the original operating system, then all applications must be reloaded.

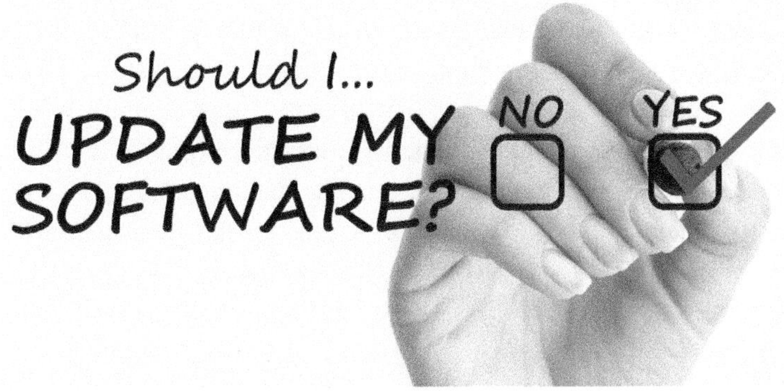

FIGURE 16.2 Applications are affected by an OS upgrade

Windows Update Assistant/Installation Assistant

The Windows Update Assistant application should always be used before upgrading a version of Windows 8.1 or Windows 10. Update Assistant can be downloaded, installed, and executed to see whether a Windows 8.1 or 10 computer can function well with a higher version of Windows 10. At the time of this writing, the Update Assistant was available at https://www.microsoft.com/en-us/software-download/windows10. The Windows Installation Assistant (https://www.microsoft.com/software-download/windows11) performs the same check for Windows 11. Update Assistant/Installation Assistant checks hardware, connected devices, and existing applications, and it makes recommendations before an upgrade. You will want to make sure you have all hardware peripherals that are commonly used with the system connected when you run the Update Assistant/Installation Assistant.

In order to take advantage of Windows reliability, enhancements, and security features, sometimes a clean installation is the best choice. Because a clean installation involves formatting the hard drive, the user's data must be backed up, and all applications should be reinstalled when the Windows installation is complete. Also, all user-defined settings are lost.

TECH TIP

OEM OS cannot go to another computer

An original equipment manufacturer (OEM) version of Windows that is sold as part of a computer sale is not transferable to another computer.

Even when Microsoft states that an in-place upgrade *can* be done, there is no guarantee that all applications and settings will work after the upgrade. In a corporate environment, if custom software is involved, contact the software developer for any known issues or test the software in a test environment before deploying corporatewide. The information may be posted on the software developer's website. Also, the Windows Compatibility Cookbook (currently available at https://docs.microsoft.com/en-us/windows/compatibility/windows-10-introduction) contains detailed information regarding hardware and software compatibility for the latest versions of Windows.

USMT and PCmover Express

The User State Migration Tool (**USMT**) and PCmover Express are two options for migrating data when an in-place Windows upgrade is not supported. See Figure 16.3 for an example of data migration. IT staff use USMT to perform large deployments of Windows as it can perform automated copying of user accounts, user files, operating system settings, and application settings. This tool is used from a command line for more control and customized settings, including registry changes. The `scanstate.exe` and `loadstate.exe` commands are used to transfer file and user settings. The USMT is freely available from Microsoft.

You can use PCmover Express for smaller deployments. The application was created by Microsoft's partner Laplink. It is not free. It can transfer files, settings, user profiles, and applications from an old PC to a new one. The application must be installed on both computers. Previously, the Easy Transfer program was available for free from Microsoft; it performed the same functions for Windows operating systems up to Windows 8.

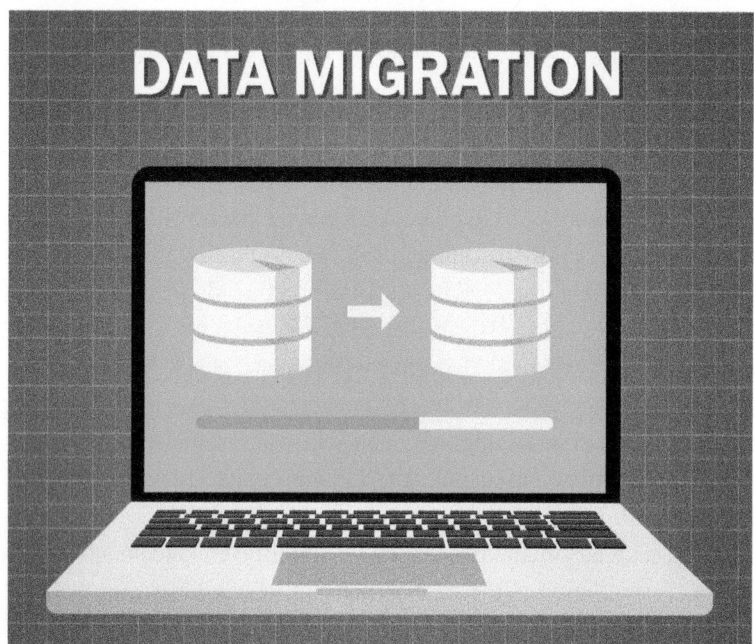

FIGURE 16.3 Local data migration

Compatibility Mode

Keep in mind while upgrading that not all 16- or 32-bit applications can be used in the 64-bit Windows environment. If a program is proving to be incompatible, try the **compatibility mode** available using the **Program Compatibility Wizard**: Open the Control Panel and then locate the *Programs* section> *Programs and Features* section > *Run programs made for previous versions of windows* link.

The *Compatibility* tab on the *Properties* dialogue allows you to manually assign a particular application that was made to be compatible with an older (selectable) Windows version. First, find the executable via this process: click the *Start* button > right-click the application icon > *More* > *Open file location*. A window will open that shows the executable file. Next, right-click the application file and select *Properties* > *Compatibility* tab > enable (check) the *Run this program in compatibility mode* checkbox > use the drop-down menu to select the specific operating system > use the specific video and administrator options available in the *Settings* and *Change settings for all user* sections > click *Apply* > click *OK*.

TECH TIP

Running a troublesome app in Windows 10/11

Windows 10/11 includes Hyper-V for virtualization. You can use Hyper-V to install and run older applications.

Types of Partitions

Before a drive can be used by the operating system, it has to be partitioned and formatted. Partitioning allows you to divide a drive into multiple sections called partitions, or you can select the entire drive to be used as a single partition. The operating system recognizes each partition as a separate area in which to store data.

As part of partitioning, you assign a drive letter to each drive section. You are already familiar with the `C:` drive, where the operating system normally resides. Once a drive is partitioned, that section must be formatted for a particular type of file system, such as NTFS, exFAT, or FAT32. The file system determines how the operating system will save and retrieve data from the partitions. Table 16.3 reviews the types of partitions found in the Windows environment. When Windows is being installed, you have the option of a quick format or a full format. A **full format** identifies and marks bad sectors so they will not be used for data storage. A **quick format** skips this analysis.

TABLE 16.3 Windows partition types

Partition type	Description
Basic disk	The most common type of partition, which can contain primary partitions, extended partitions, and logical drives. Each primary partition and logical drive must be formatted for a specific file system.
Primary partition	A partition that can hold an operating system. If the operating system is used to boot the system, it must be on a primary partition that is configured as an active partition. A primary partition is assigned a drive letter and formatted for a specific file system.
Extended partition	A type of partition that allows hard drive subdivisions called **logical partitions**. Each logical partition (also called a logical drive) is assigned a drive letter and formatted for a specific file system. Extended partitions can only be used with basic disks. They cannot be used to boot the computer.
MBR (master boot record partition table)	The traditional type of partition that uses primary and extended partitions.
Dynamic disk	A more advanced type of disk volume that supports simple, spanned, striped, and RAID drive configuration.
GPT (GUID partition table)	A more advanced type of partition that requires a UEFI BIOS and allows partition sizes larger than 2 TB, improved protection of the partition table, and more partitions.
Swap partition	The Linux equivalent of a Windows paging file. Paging uses hard drive space as RAM so that programs that exceed the size of available physical memory can operate.

Planning Drive Space

The third step when planning to install Windows is to determine how large to make the **drive partition** (also called the volume) and select the file system to be used. By default, an entire drive is used to create a partition; however, drives can be partitioned during the Windows installation process. One option is to place the operating system in one partition and data in a separate partition to make it easier to back up the data. Figure 16.4 shows this concept.

FIGURE 16.4 Partitioning (dividing) drive space during OS installation concept

The file system should be NTFS for the following reasons:

> Provides security (because individual files can be protected using encryption and permissions)
> Makes more efficient use of cluster space
> Supports file compression
> Supports larger hard drive partition sizes
> Includes journaling, which helps in rebuilding the file system after a crash or power failure

An issue that is relevant only when upgrading is whether to convert an old FAT16 or FAT32 hard drive partition to NTFS. Once a partition is converted to NTFS, the partition cannot be changed back to FAT16 or FAT32. If you are unsure whether to convert a partition, you can leave it unchanged and later use the `convert` command to upgrade (without losing any data).

TECH TIP

Using the `convert` command

The `convert` command can be used to change a FAT16 or FAT32 partition to NTFS and keep the data from the old partition. Use `convert x: /fs:ntfs` (where `x:` is the drive to be converted to NTFS). Remember that once you go to a higher file system, you cannot go back.

TECH TIP

Use the Disk Management tool

Partitions are created and managed using the Disk Management tool, accessed through the *System and Security* > *Administrative Tools* (*Windows Tools* in Windows 11) > *Computer Management* > *Disk Management* section of the Control Panel. You can also right-click the *Start* button and select *Disk Management*. Another method to access the tool is to type **`diskmgmt.msc`** at a prompt or in a search window. The Disk Management tool is covered in more detail later in this chapter.

File System Types

A file system determines how the operating system will save and retrieve data from the partitions. The most common Windows file systems are FAT16, FAT32, exFAT, and NTFS. The file system that can be used depends on what operating system is installed, whether the device is an internal or external device, and whether files are to be shared across a network. Table 16.4 lists file systems used with Windows and other operating systems.

TABLE 16.4 File system types

File system type	Description
Compact Disk File System (**CDFS**)	A file system for optical media.
FAT	Also called FAT16. Used with all versions of Windows. 2 GB partition limitation with old operating systems. 4 GB partition limitation with XP and higher versions of Windows.
FAT32	Supported with all versions of Windows. Commonly used with removable flash drives. Supports drives up to 2 TB. Can recognize volumes greater than 32 GB.
exFAT	Commonly called FAT64. A file system made for removable media (such as flash drives and SD cards) that extends drive size support up to 64 ZB in theory, although 512 TB is the recommended max. Made for copying large files such as disk images and media files. Supported by all versions of Windows.
NTFS	Used with Windows 7, 8, 10, and 11. Supports drives up to 16 EB (16 exabytes, which equals 16 billion gigabytes) but in practice is only 16 TB. Supports file compression and file security (encryption). NTFS allows faster file access and uses hard drive space more efficiently. Supports individual file compression and has the best Windows file security.
Hierarchical File System (**HFS**)	Used with Apple computers that have been upgraded to HFS+ and then later upgraded to Apple File System (APFS) in 2017.
Network File System (**NFS**)	An open source file system developed by Sun Microsystems that is found in Linux-based systems. Allows access to remote files over a network.
ext3	Also known as third extended file system. Used in Linux-based operating systems, it is a journaling file system, which means it tracks changes in case the operating system crashes, allowing it to be restarted without reloading.
ext4	An update to ext3 that allows for larger volumes and file sizes in Linux-based operating systems.

Hardware

The fourth step when planning to install Windows is to determine what computer hardware is installed. Table 16.5 lists the requirements for most Windows 10 installations. One thing that might influence your choice of Windows version is the amount of memory supported by the different versions.

TABLE 16.5 Windows 10 hardware requirements

Component	Minimum
Processor	1 GHz
RAM	1 GB (32-bit)/2 GB (64-bit)
Graphics	Support for DirectX9 or higher with 1.0 WDDM driver
Hard drive space	16 GB (32-bit)/20 GB (64-bit)

Windows 11 has stricter hardware requirements than previous versions of Windows. For example, it only runs on 64-bit systems with two or more cores. See Table 16.6 for the other requirements. You can download the PC Health Check App to determine whether a computer meets the requirements. At the time of this writing, it's available at https://www.microsoft.com/en-us/windows/windows-11.

TABLE 16.6 Windows 11 hardware requirements

Parameter	Minimum Requirement
Processor	1 GHz or faster with two or more cores on a compatible 64-bit processor or System on a Chip (SoC)
RAM	4 GB
Storage	64 GB or larger storage device
System firmware	UEFI, Secure Boot capable
TPM	Trusted Platform Module (TPM) version 2.0
Graphics card	Compatible with DirectX 12 or later with WDDM 2.0 driver
Display	High-definition (720p) display that is greater than 9 inches diagonally, with 8 bits per color channel
Internet connection and Microsoft account	Windows 11 Home edition requires internet connectivity and a Microsoft account

Drivers

Once hardware has been verified, you have to obtain hardware device drivers specific to the operating system from the hardware manufacturer's website so that you can **load alternate third-party drivers**, when necessary. A hardware device may have to be upgraded or replaced. Sometimes, older operating system drivers do work, but many times older drivers do not work or do not work properly. This is the cost of going to a more powerful operating system. The customer may also decide at this point not to upgrade but rather to buy a computer with the desired version of Windows already installed instead.

The Microsoft Update Assistant tool may recommend getting updated third-party drivers for specific pieces of hardware. Drivers related to hard drives—for example, drivers for hardware RAID, motherboard AHCI mode, SATA hard drives, and hard drives over 2 TB—are especially critical to the installation process. Obtain any of these hard drive–related drivers *before* the installation, or you will not be able to install the operating system to that hard drive.

TECH TIP

If upgrading, ensure that Windows updates are current

If upgrading to a new version of Windows, ensure that the current version has the latest Windows updates.

Backing Up Before an OS Installation

The next step in planning to install Windows is one of the most important: In any upgrade, hardware change, or software change, you *must* back up the user data. Whether you do a clean install or an upgrade, if the user has data on the computer, it must be backed up before the installation process starts. Also, before backing up the data, remove any unwanted files and/or applications in order to free up hard drive space. Right-click on the drive letter in File Explorer. From the General tab, use the *Disk Cleanup* button to check and defragment the hard drive. Once the data is backed up from a Windows system, create a system image backup and system repair disc.

Security Scan

The next step in planning for a Windows installation is to scan the system for viruses and malware (see Figure 16.5).

FIGURE 16.5 Do a security scan before an OS upgrade

TECH TIP

Antivirus software causes issues

Whether doing a clean install or an upgrade, disable the antivirus protection until after the installation. If possible, disconnect the computer from the network before disabling the antivirus software.

Disabling Interfering Software

The last step in the preinstallation checklist is to disable any power- or disk-management tools that are loaded. They can interfere with the new tools provided with Windows and can prevent an operating system from installing. Some security applications, including anti-malware and firewalls, can interfere with an operating system upgrade as well. Disable these utilities and applications before attempting an operating system installation or upgrade.

Installation/Upgrade of Windows

After completing all the preinstallation steps, you are ready to install Windows. The installation process is easy if you performed the preinstallation steps. The number-one piece of advice to heed is to do your installation/upgrade research first. Doing so will greatly reduce the number of possible problems.

Basically, an installation involves three phases.

- In the first phase of an installation (sometimes called the Windows Preinstallation Environment, or Windows PE), the system requests a product key, the user selects a specific Windows edition and accepts the license terms, the user selects whether to upgrade or perform a clean installation, and the user selects a partition on which to install the operating system.
- After the user selects a partition, the second phase begins. During this process, setup files are copied to the partition. The computer might reboot several times as the system detects hardware devices and installs the appropriate drivers.
- After the final reboot, the Windows Out of Box Experience (OOBE) begins. This phase is similar to what a user would see if they bought a new computer and started it for the first time. The user configures settings such as region, keyboard layout, and privacy settings. If the computer is already connected to the internet, the system prompts the user to create a new Microsoft account or log in to an existing account to access the computer. If the computer is not connected to the internet, the user will create a local account, password, and security questions. After the user answers all the questions, the computer saves the configurations and opens the Desktop; this might take several minutes.

You will probably have to set aside some time to allow the computer to receive and install updates issued since the operating system image/version you just installed was created. You may also have to install additional drivers and software apps that may not be part of the backup or image that was installed.

Part of the installation process is to select the type of network: public or private. Note that you can bypass the network configuration at this point during the installation of the operating system and configure it later. With a public network, a computer attaches to an unsecured network, as in a restaurant or bookstore. Your computer is not visible to other computers by default when the public network option is chosen.

Computers on private networks usually share information with each other, so they are normally visible to each other. There are two basic private types: workgroup or domain. (Table 16.7 describes the network types.) Large networks are usually organized as domains, in which all the user attributes (accounts, rights, and permissions) and computer settings are stored on a central server called a domain controller (or on multiple replicated domain controllers). Home networks and small business networks are usually organized as workgroups. Each user's account and rights must be configured on each individual computer.

TABLE 16.7 Network types

Network type	Description
Public	The computer is hidden from other devices on the network, and sharing of resources is not permitted. This is the recommended network type for devices on unsecured networks, as in restaurants and coffee shops.
Workgroup	User accounts, rights, and permissions (such as file and printer permissions) must be configured on each individual computer. This type of network is usually suitable for home networks and small business networks (with 10 or fewer users or computers).
Domain	A domain is used in a corporate environment in which users authenticate with a centralized user ID and password stored on a domain controller. Whatever machine the user goes to, the user ID and password would be the same if the computer has been configured to be on the domain. Likewise, the individual computers' settings can be centrally stored. Every time a computer boots or restarts, it receives its settings from the domain controller.

Corporate Windows Deployment

Corporate computer installations are much more involved than any other type of deployment. Computers are installed in bulk instead of one at a time, as in a home or small business. The computers are frequently the same model and have the same software installed.

Disk imaging is common in the corporate environment. Disk imaging software makes an exact copy (a binary copy) of the files loaded on the hard drive. The copy is then pressed to an optical disc or an external drive, or it is put on a network drive to be copied and deployed onto other computers. When a computer has an issue, it is faster to just **reimage** the computer than to troubleshoot the Windows problem.

Companies need automated installation tools to help with the corporate Windows deployment process. Tools that can help with this are the Windows Assessment and Deployment Kit (Windows ADK), Windows System Preparation (Sysprep) tool, imaging software such as Symantec Corporation's Ghost program, Microsoft's Setup Manager, and Windows System Image Manager (SIM). An image can be created and deployed to multiple computers. Table 16.8 describes some of these tools.

TABLE 16.8 Corporate computer deployment tools

Tool	Description
Windows Assessment and Deployment Kit (Windows ADK)	The Windows ADK contains several components to customize Windows images for deployment to large networks. It also provides tools for testing systems prior to deployment.
Sysprep	When a prototype computer has Windows, Windows updates, all drivers, and applications installed, Sysprep can remove the security identifier (SID)—a unique number assigned to a computer by a network domain controller—as well as other unique information, such as the computer name or network domain. The computer is then imaged, and the image is deployed to other computers. A third-party utility such as Symantec Ghost Walker or Microsoft's `newsid.exe` can be used to reassign the SIDs after the drive image has been deployed.

Tool	Description
SIM (System Image Manager)	SIM is used to create and configure answer files, install applications, apply service packs and updates to an image, and add device drivers. After the Windows `unattend.xml` answer file is created, you can use this file to answer the installation questions as the files are downloaded from a share or server on the network. SIM is part of the Windows ADK download.
WDS (Windows Deployment Services)	WDS is a server role that uses the corporate network(s) to deploy Windows-based operating systems, drivers, updates, and applications using a network-based installation.
MDT (Microsoft Deployment Toolkit)	MTD is a GUI shell that makes Windows deployment easier. Tools such as USMT, Application Compatibility Toolkit (ACT), Microsoft Assessment and Planning Toolkit (MAP), and the volume licensing application are inside the MDT shell.

When making a Windows image, you have to remove the unique identifiers from the computer—that is, computer name, security identifier (SID), a network domain, and so on—before deploying the image to other computers. You must also reset or re-arm the Windows **activation clock** if a single activation key is used. If you do not do this, you are prompted for the Windows product key as soon as the computer boots. Re-arming the activation clock gives you a 90-day grace period before you have to re-enter the product key.

TECH TIP

Three re-arms with Windows

There is no limit to the number of times a computer can be reimaged, but there is a limit to how many times a computer can be re-armed or have the Windows activation clock reset. You can use the Sysprep tool or the `slmgr -rearm` command to reset the re-arm count. To see how many times a computer has been re-armed, use the `slmgr /dlv` command.

When deploying Windows in an enterprise, licensing is handled a bit differently. Larger businesses buy a volume license key (VLK). Two other choices are MAK and KMS. With Multiple Activation Key (MAK), the internet or a phone call must be used to register one or more computers. This method has a limited number of activations, but more licenses can be purchased. The Key Management Service (**KMS**) method is used in companies with 25 or more computers to deploy.

TECH TIP

Be responsible

A technician is responsible for ensuring that any computer deployed has an antivirus application installed and that the application is configured to receive virus signature updates. Educate users about viruses and what to do if a computer gets one.

Verifying the Installation

In any upgrade or installation, verification that the upgrade is successful is critical in both home and business environments. After an upgrade has been done, verify that all applications still function. After a new installation has been completed, ensure that all installed hardware is detected by Device Manager (covered in the "Adding Devices" section, later in this chapter).

TECH TIP

Reinitialize antivirus software

If antivirus/anti-malware software was disabled through BIOS/UEFI and through an application, re-enable it after the operating system installation is complete. Verify that all settings are in accordance with the user requirements and departmental/organizational standards.

When you are satisfied that the installation is successful, don't forget to **apply updates** to the operating system, applications, and anti-malware software. You might also want to update device drivers to ensure the most up-to-date security and features for the installed hardware.

Troubleshooting a Windows Installation

Installation problems can be caused by a number of factors. The following are the most common causes of problems and their solutions:

> *No boot device available:* Access BIOS/UEFI settings and **update the boot order** so that the device that contains the operating system is listed first.
> *Incompatible hardware drivers:* Obtain drivers for the appropriate Windows version from the hardware manufacturer, if not Microsoft.
> *Incompatible applications:* Obtain upgrades from the software manufacturer, use the Program Compatibility Wizard, configure a multiboot environment, or use virtualization.
> *Minimum hardware requirements have not been met:* Upgrade the hardware. The most likely things to check are the CPU and RAM.
> *A virus is present:* Run an antivirus program and remove the virus.
> *Antivirus software is installed and active and is halting the installation/upgrade:* Disable the antivirus software through BIOS/UEFI and through the application. Restart the Windows installation and re-enable the antivirus software when the operating system installation is complete.
> *Preinstallation steps have not been completed:* Go back through the list of steps.
> *The installation disc/USB drive or download is corrupt (not as likely as the other causes):* Try the disc/drive in another machine and see if you can see the contents. If using an optical disc, check to see if a scratch or dirt is on the disc surface and clean the disc as necessary. Try another disc or drive. Redownload the operating system.
> *Incorrect registration key:* Type in the correct key to complete the installation. The key is located on the disc or disc case or in an email.
> *The Windows installation process cannot find a hard drive:* This is most likely due to a SATA drive being used and a driver not being available for the controller. Download the driver, put it on a flash drive, or use a software program such as NTLite to create a custom installation disc that includes the downloaded driver.
> *A STOP message occurs when installing a multiboot system:* Boot from the Windows installation disc rather than the other operating system.
> *The computer locks up during setup and shows a blue screen of death (BSOD):* Check the BIOS/UEFI and hardware compatibility. Also, if an error message appears, research the error on the internet.

> *Incompatible BIOS:* Obtain and upgrade to compatible BIOS/UEFI, replace the motherboard with one that has a compatible BIOS, or do not upgrade or install the higher Windows version.

> *BIOS needs to be upgraded:* Upgrade the BIOS/UEFI.

> *You get an "NTLDR Is Missing" error:* If you get an **NTLDR Is Missing** error on a Windows computer during the installation process, try the clean install process over again.

TECH TIP

Installation halts

If an installation stops, try removing any nonessential hardware, such as network cards, modems, and USB devices and start the installation again. Reinstall the hardware after Windows is properly installed.

> *A message appears during setup that a device driver was unable to load:* Obtain the latest device drivers that are compatible and restart the setup program.

> *After upgrading Windows, the computer freezes:* Boot to Safe Mode and check Device Manager (covered in the "Adding Devices" section, later in this chapter) for errors. **Safe Mode** is a boot option that starts the computer with a minimal set of drivers. If no errors are present within Device Manager, disable the following devices, if present: video adapter, sound card, network card, USB devices and controller (unless using a USB keyboard/mouse), optical drive, modem, and unused ports. Enable each disabled device one at a time until the blue screen appears. When the problematic device is known, obtain the appropriate replacement driver. Another option is to try the tools in the Windows Recovery Environment (WinRE), which is discussed in detail later in this chapter.

During the Windows installation, there are log files created that can be helpful for resolving installation issues. Table 16.9 outlines important log files for each version of Windows and briefly describes what they contain.

TABLE 16.9 Windows setup log files

Log file location	Description
`X:\Windows\setupapi.log`	Device and driver changes, **service pack**, and **hotfix** installations
`X:\$Windows.~BT\Sources\Panther\setupact.log`	Setup actions performed during the install
`X:\$Windows.~BT\Sources\Panther\setuperr.log`	Setup installation errors
`X:\$Windows.~BT\Sources\Panther\PreGatherPnPList.log`	Initial capture of devices information
`X:\$Windows.~BT\Sources\Panther\miglog.xml`	User directory structure and SID information
`X:\Windows\Inf\setupapi*.log`	Plug-and-play devices and driver information
`X:\Windows\Inf\setupapi.app.log`	Application installation information
`X:\Windows\Panther\PostGatherPnPList.log`	Device information after the online configuration

Reloading Windows

Chapter 14, "Introduction to Operating Systems," has a section called "Recovering the Windows OS" that helps in a **no OS found** situation. This section provides a few more technical suggestions for such situations.

Sometimes it's necessary to do a *repair installation* (sometimes called an *in-place upgrade* or a *reinstallation*) of Windows, such as when Windows does not start normally or in Safe Mode, or when it has a registry corruption that cannot be solved with System Restore (covered later in this chapter). Hopefully the user has backed up existing data. The installation process should not disturb the data, but there is always a chance that it could.

Windows Resource Protection (**WRP**) protects operating system files, folders, and important registry keys, using access control lists (**ACLs**) or code that permits or denies changes to the operating system. Changes made to a monitored file or folder cannot be changed even by an administrator unless the administrator takes ownership and adds the appropriate access control entities (ACEs) within an ACL. Use the process described below to identify files that cannot be repaired by **System File Checker** (`sfc`) and replace them:

Step 1. *Find the corrupted files:* From an elevated command prompt, run the command `findstr /C:"[SR] Cannot repair member file" %windir%\logs\cbs\cbs. log>sfcdetails.txt`

Step 2. *Read the list of files:* Use Notepad or use the `edit` command to open the `sfcdetails.txt` file (normally located in the `C:\Windows\System32` folder). **Notepad**, as you learned in Chapter 15, "Introduction to Scripting," is a text editor that is handy for creating scripts and opening `.txt` or log files.

Step 3. *Take ownership of a file:* For each of the files listed in `sfcdetails.txt`, execute the command `takeown /f` *`filename_including_path`* (where *`filename_including_path`* is the full path and filename of the problematic file).

Step 4. *Change file permissions:* Run the command `icacls` *`filename_including_path`* `/grant administrators:m`.

Step 5. *Replace the file:* Use the `copy` command to replace the corrupted file with a known good one: `copy` *`source_filename destination_filename`* (where *`source_filename`* and *`destination_filename`* are the full path and file).

CHAPTER 16

TECH TIP

Use `sfc` to solve system file problems

Use the `sfc /scannow` command as an administrator to replace any protected system files that have problems.

Modern Windows computers are likely to allow booting from a flash drive. The operating system image can be copied or downloaded and placed on the flash drive. Change the BIOS/UEFI settings to boot from the flash drive, and the installation process starts. Windows has great tools that help with startup problems such as a corrupt registry and missing or corrupt boot configuration files. These tools are covered later in this chapter.

TECH TIP

All existing system restore points are removed when Windows is reinstalled

The System Restore utility (covered later in this chapter) creates restore points that can be used to revert a Windows computer to a prior configuration. When Windows is reinstalled, no preexisting restore points are kept. Therefore, you should ensure that the System Restore utility is enabled and back up your data after Windows is reinstalled. You should also apply any service packs and patches after the reinstallation is complete.

Windows Updates

Almost daily, new vulnerabilities are found in every operating system. Windows makes available **Windows Update** or **Automatic Updates** for upgrading the operating system. Windows 10/11 does automatic updates by default. Microsoft provides updates according to a product's lifecycle. The Microsoft website provides lifecycle support dates for the various Microsoft products.

In Windows 10/11 the update settings have been moved out of the Control Panel to the *Settings* menu. To access the update settings in Windows 10/11, access *Settings* > *Update & Security* (only in Windows 10) > *Windows Update* (see Figure 16.6). Use these settings to pause updates, adjust active hours (times during which the system will not automatically restart after updates are applied), see your update history, and configure advanced options.

TECH TIP

Roll back Windows updates

When a Windows update causes the computer to not work properly, **roll back Windows updates** to at least one previous version. Note that you might have to do this from Safe Mode. In Windows 10/11, access *Settings* > *Update & Security* (Windows 10 only) > *Windows Update* > *View update history* or *Update history* link > *Uninstall update* to perform this task. You can also use the System Restore tool (covered later in this chapter) if the tool was enabled prior to the updates.

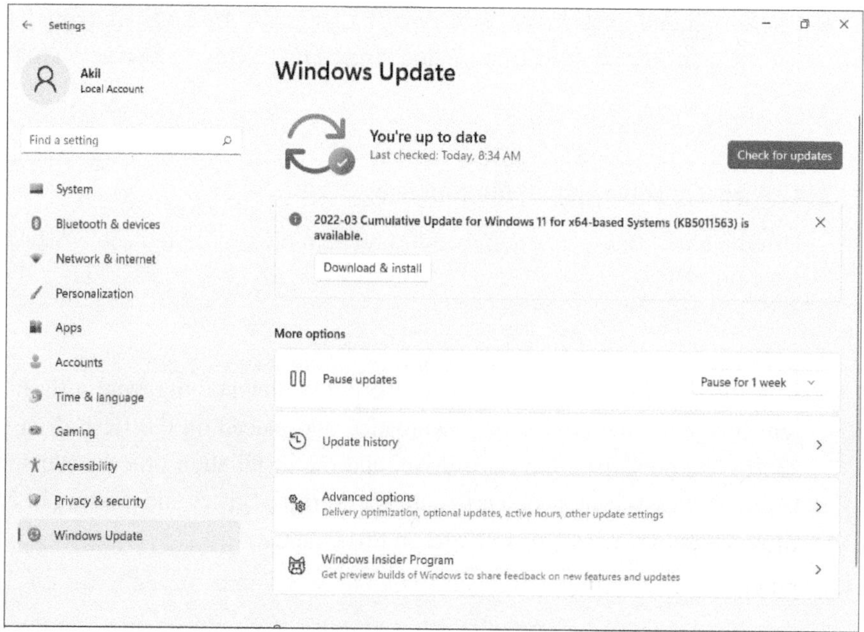

FIGURE 16.6 Windows Update options

The options to disable checking for updates and installing updates has been removed from the Windows Update utility. However, updates can be disabled via the registry or group policy. Automatic updates are often disabled in corporate environments so the system engineers have more control over which updates are applied and when they are applied. Also, in large environments, updates are normally verified on test (development) computers before they are applied to the employees' (production) computers.

Figure 16.7 shows the advanced update options available, including whether to receive updates for other Microsoft products (such as the Microsoft browser) at the same time as receiving operating system updates and the ability to download over a metered connection. By default, a Windows 10/11 device does not restart when the user is using the computer; however, the advanced options allows for restarting the computer as soon as possible (with a notice displayed prior to the restart). There are also options to show a notification when the computer needs to be restarted to finish updating and to pause updates for up to 35 days.

TECH TIP

You must be an administrator to change Automatic Updates settings

You must be logged in as the administrator or a user that is a member of the Administrators group to modify Automatic Updates settings.

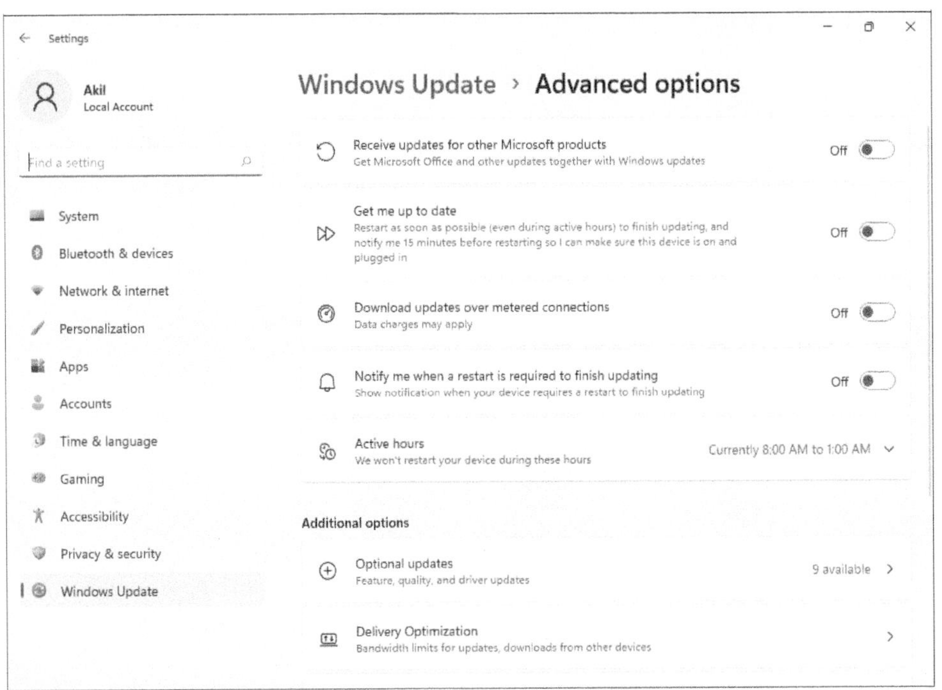

FIGURE 16.7 Advanced options for Windows Update

Backing Up the Windows Registry and Data

The **registry** is a database that contains information about the Windows environment, including installed hardware, installed software, and users. The registry should be backed up when the computer is fully functional and before and after any software or hardware changes are made.

TECH TIP

Back up the registry

The registry should be backed up and restored on a working computer *before* disaster hits. The time to learn how to restore the registry is not when the computer is down.

The registry can be backed up and restored several different ways:

> Using the `regedit.exe` program
> Using the System Restore tool (covered later in this chapter)

The `regedit.exe` program enables you to export the registry to a file that has the extension `.reg`. The file can be imported back into the computer if the computer fails.

Windows 10/11 uses **File History** backups (see Figure 16.8). File History enables you to back up only a specific user's libraries instead of the entire system. File History also allows you to schedule these backups. The feature can be accessed by opening *Control Panel > System and Security > File History*. In addition, the *Settings > Backup* app can back up the entire system or individual user profiles (files and preferences).

A user would be best served by backing up the entire system to an external drive or backing up the data and using one of the methods described in Chapter 14 to reinstall the operating system as well as user preferences.

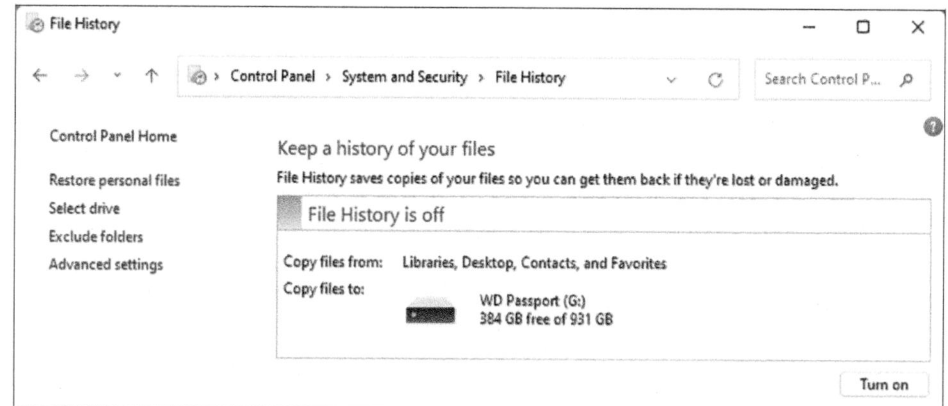

FIGURE 16.8 File History in Windows

TECH TIP

Who can use the Backup program?

To use the Backup program, you must be an administrator or have group rights to perform the backup.

To correct a problem with the system files, registry, or boot failure, you may restore from a **restore point**. A restore point is created by the **System Restore** utility (covered later in this chapter) any time a change happens to the system, such as when a program or driver is installed or a Windows update occurs. It is possible to revert to a restore point by opening the System Restore application when a change causes Windows to not operate properly or when a change causes Windows to fail to boot. Note that System Restore must be enabled for restore points to be created.

Configuring Windows Overview

One of the windows that technicians use most commonly is the *Control Panel* window. A Control Panel allows you to configure various components. Each Control Panel icon represents a Windows utility that customizes a particular part of the Windows environment. The number of Control Panels displayed depends on the type of computer and the components contained within the computer. Control Panels have been discussed throughout the book, but this chapter explores more in-depth tasks with them. Windows has various Control Panel views, depending on the operating system: *category*, *large icons*, and *small icons*.

In Windows you can also use *Settings* to configure a computer. See Figure 16.9 for the Windows 10 *Settings* home page and Figure 16.10 for the Windows 11 *Settings* home page (bottom). The options within each category contain much of what is in Control Panel utilities. Technicians must know which Control Panel category to use to change a computer's configuration. Windows has some configuration options that are unique to particular versions of the operating system. Several key Control Panel utilities are explained in the following sections.

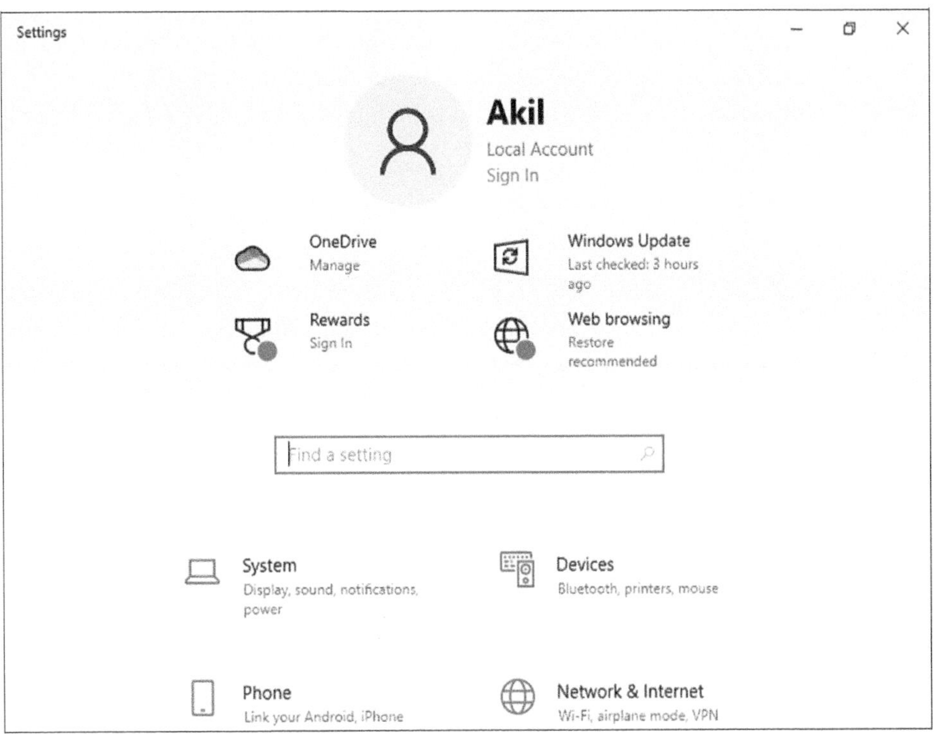

FIGURE 16.9 Settings in Windows 10

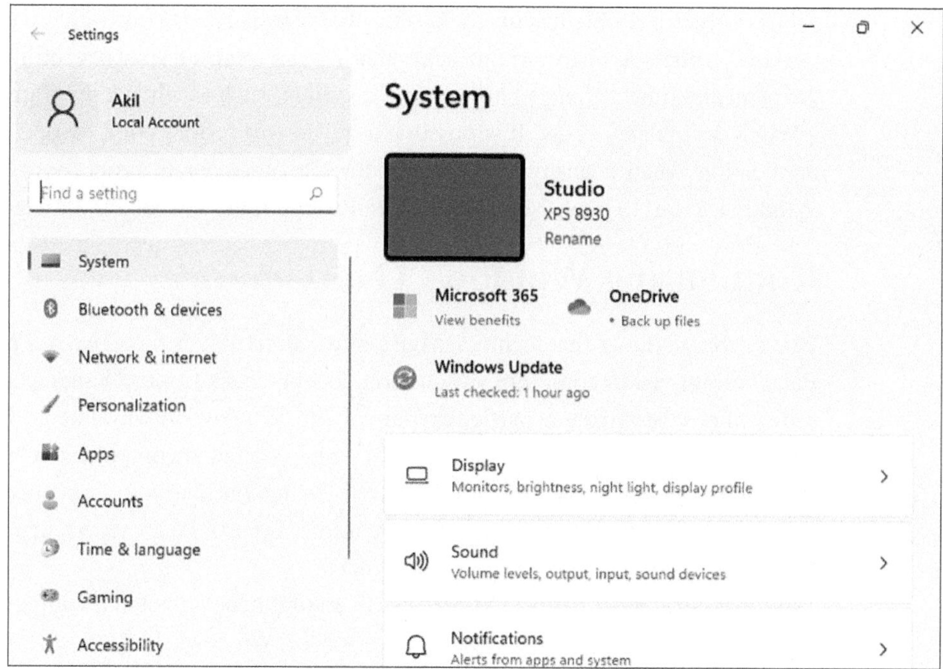

FIGURE 16.10 Settings in Windows 11

Configuring Windows

Technicians must frequently interact with the operating system when adding new hardware and software. Windows has specific tools for these functions. Using the correct procedure is essential for success. The following sections highlight tasks a technician commonly performs:

- Adding devices
- Removing hardware components
- Adding a printer
- Installing/removing software

Hardware devices are physical components that connect to a computer. A **device driver** is a piece of software that enables hardware to work with a specific operating system. Device drivers are operating system dependent. For example, a printer driver that works with Windows 10 may not work with Windows 11. Not all manufacturers provide updates for the newer operating systems. Some device drivers are automatically included with Windows and are updated continuously through Windows Updates. A technician must be aware of what hardware is installed on a system so that the latest compatible drivers can be downloaded and installed.

Adding Devices

Technicians are constantly adding devices to computers. Many devices today are plug-and-play devices that are designed to be automatically recognized by the operating system. Devices that use USB and Thunderbolt can be added or removed with power applied. Adapters are installed and removed with the computer powered off and the power cord removed. Let's look into some of the Windows tools used when adding devices.

Devices and Printers Control Panel Utility

The *Devices and Printers* Control Panel utility is used to view, install, remove, and manage wired and wireless devices such as mice, multimedia devices, printers, and speakers. When a device is added, Windows 10/11 searches the Microsoft Store to see if there is an app from the device manufacturer. If an installed device isn't detected, use the *Add a device* link to initiate the process.

Device Manager

Devices that are recognized or at least sensed by the OS are shown in the **Device Manager** utility (see Figure 16.11). Device Manager (`devmgmt.msc`) is a technician's best friend when it comes to adding and troubleshooting devices on a Windows computer. Device Manager is used after installing a new hardware device to verify that Windows recognizes the device. Device Manager is also used to change or view hardware configuration settings, view and install device drivers, return (roll back) to a previous device driver version, disable/enable/uninstall devices, and print a summary of all hardware installed.

Once you expand a particular category, such as *Network adapters* (see Figure 16.11), you can look for symbols that indicate trouble. A down arrow beside an icon means the device is disabled. An exclamation point indicates a problem that is usually a resource conflict or driver issue. An "I" beside a device means that the resources for the device were manually configured.

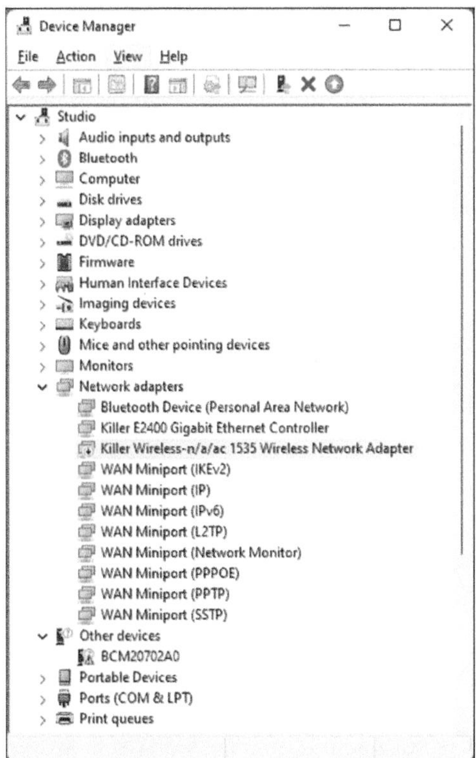

FIGURE 16.11 Device Manager in Windows

To verify that a device is working properly, expand a Device Manager section. Double-click or double-tap a device, and its *Properties* window appears. The *General* tab displays a message saying whether the device is working, according to Windows. The number of tabs a device has depends on the device. Figure 16.12 shows the *General* tab as well as the *Driver* tab for a USB mouse. The *Driver* tab is used to roll back the driver if an updated driver is installed and does not function properly. It also shows the current driver version. The *Driver* tab can be used to disable the device and uninstall the device driver.

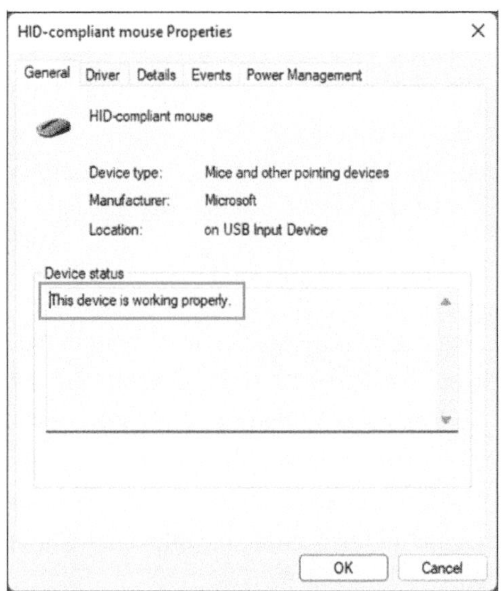

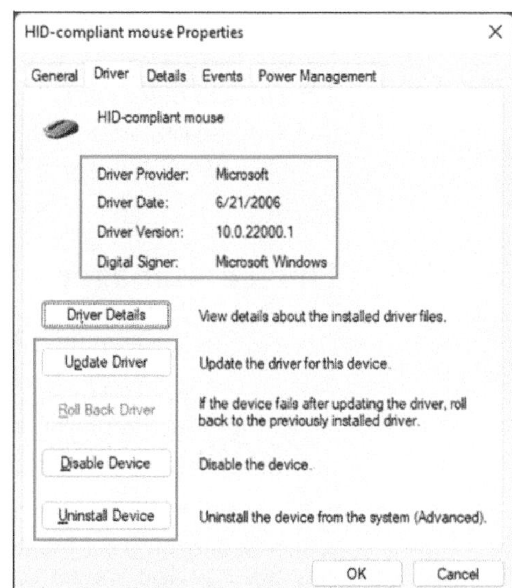

FIGURE 16.12 *Device Manager > General* and *Driver* tabs

The keys to a successful device installation follow:

> Possessing the most up-to-date device driver for the specific installed operating system
> Following the directions provided by the device manufacturer

Windows autodetects when a new device is installed or connected and attempts to find the appropriate driver. Windows searches driver packages that are stored in an indexed database. The drivers are stored in the `Windows\System32\DriverStore\FileRepository` folder. All driver files that are not part of the operating system must be imported into this folder before the driver package can be installed. Drivers created for earlier Windows versions may need to be updated.

TECH TIP

Installing a device driver requires Administrator rights

Remember that if the operating system cannot configure a device and prompts for a device driver, you must have Administrator rights to install the driver.

Some Windows device drivers use **digital signatures**; this is sometimes called driver signing or requiring a signed driver. The digital signature confirms that the device driver for a particular piece of hardware has met certain criteria for WHQL (Windows Hardware Quality Labs) tests and is compatible with Windows. Digital signatures are required for 64-bit kernel mode drivers in Windows. Figure 16.13 illustrates this concept, and Figure 16.14 shows a signed driver in Device Manager. Notice the little certificate icon to the left of the driver.

If you suspect that Windows is not booting because a driver is unsigned, access the *Windows Recovery Environment (WinRE)* > *Troubleshoot* > *Advanced options* > *Startup Settings* > *Restart* > select the *Disable driver signature enforcement* option. The computer boots normally and not in Safe Mode.

To control the downloading of manufacturers' apps and custom icons, use the *System and Security* section of the Control Panel > *System* > *Advanced system settings* link > *Hardware* tab > *Device Installation Settings* button. The options available follow:

> Yes (recommended)
> No (your device might not work as expected)

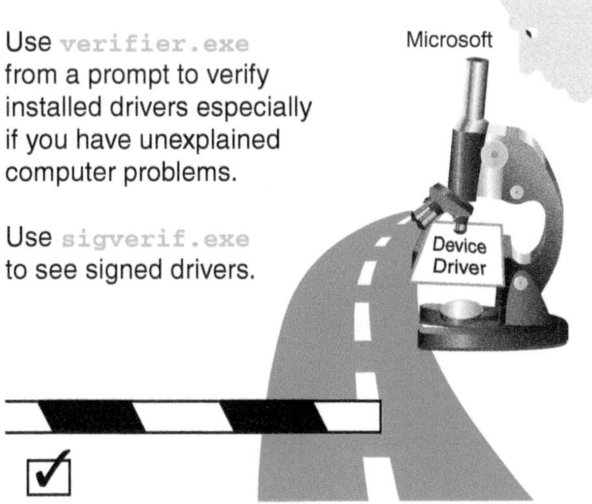

Use verifier.exe from a prompt to verify installed drivers especially if you have unexplained computer problems.
Use sigverif.exe to see signed drivers.
Microsoft
Device Driver
A signed device driver has not been altered and cannot be overwritten by another program's installation process.

FIGURE 16.13 Signed drivers

FIGURE 16.14 Signed driver in Device Manager

Audio Devices

Device Manager can also help when troubleshooting sound. Locate and expand the *Sound, Video and Game Controllers* category. Verify that a sound card or integrated sound processor is shown; look for the words "audio device." Right-click or tap and briefly hold on the sound card > select *Properties*. Verify the device status on the *General* tab.

The *Sound* Control Panel is used to adjust volume output and manage sound-related devices, including speakers, headsets, microphones, and integrated audio devices. In the *Category View* of the Control Panel, select *Hardware Sound* > *Sound.* In either icons view, just select *Sound.* From the *Sound* Control Panel, select the *Playback* tab to configure and manage headsets and speakers. Use the *Recording* tab to view the properties of and manage microphones and headset microphones. The *Sounds* tab can be used to select a sound scheme and test particular sounds. The *Recording* tab can be used to configure sound input devices. The *Communications* tab can be used to filter unwanted sounds. Refer to Chapter 8, "Video and Multimedia Devices," for sound troubleshooting tips.

Display/Display Settings

The *Display* section of the Control Panel is used to adjust the size of text on the screen (without changing resolution), to control and configure multiple monitors, to adjust the resolution if someone has set it to a suboptimal setting, and to configure the refresh rate. To access the *Display* section, you can open *Settings > Display* or you right-click a blank area of the desktop and then click *Display settings.*

Let's look at the most common settings:

> *Rearrange your displays*: If multiple displays are connected to the computer, the *Rearrange your displays* panel appears at the top of the *Displays* window. The panel contains numbered rectangles. You might need to click *Detect* to force the system to recognize older displays. When you click *Identify*, a number appears on each physical monitor so you can associate the rectangles with the displays. You can then drag the rectangles to match the physical layout of the actual displays. Click *Apply* after you rearrange the displays.

TECH TIP

Some displays don't appear in the *Displays* section

If multiple displays are connected to the computer, but they don't appear in the *Displays* section, make sure the correct drivers are installed for the display adapters and confirm that the adapters are enabled in Device Manager. Also, a motherboard may have a BIOS/UEFI setting that must be enabled for the motherboard to recognize multiple displays.

Note: If you have multiple displays, you must select one in the *Rearrange your displays* section to adjust the settings described below.

> *Display resolution:* **Resolution** is the number of pixels shown as a *horizontal* × *vertical* number, such as 1,920×1,080. A display's native resolution is the best resolution that it could be set to. Ensure that the correct display is chosen in *Rearrange your displays* if multiple displays are used.

> *Display orientation:* Orientation is the direction in which the display is rotated: landscape (horizontal) or portrait (vertical). Most displays are in the landscape orientation. There are also landscape/portrait (flipped) options that are for displays that can be turned upside down for others to view or displays that are suspended from a ceiling.

> *Multiple displays:* If multiple displays are connected to a computer, a drop-down allows you to show video output on only one display, duplicate video on multiple displays, or extend the output across multiple displays. If the *Extend these displays* option is chosen, the system treats the individual displays as one big monitor (based on the layout in *Rearrange your displays*), and different output can appear on the different monitors. For example, if Monitor 2 is to the right of Monitor 1, the cursor goes from Monitor 1 to Monitor 2 as the user moves the mouse from left to right. If Monitor 3 is above Monitor 1, the cursor travels from Monitor 3 to Monitor 1 as the user moves the mouse down. Select a monitor in *Rearrange your displays* and then click *Make this my main display* to choose the monitor where the taskbar will appear.

TECH TIP

Show taskbar on all displays

By default, the taskbar appears on only one display if the *Extend these displays* option is chosen. To show the taskbar on all displays, right-click the taskbar > *Taskbar settings* > *Multiple Displays* section (*Taskbar behaviors* in Windows 11) > *Show taskbar on all displays*.

> *Advanced display settings:* This option is used to view the properties, memory, **refresh rate** (a value shown in hertz [Hz] that describes how many times a screen is redrawn in one second; note that the higher the refresh rate, the smaller the pixel/icon appears on the screen), and color settings such as the bit depth (the number of bits that control color, thus determining the maximum number of colors that can be displayed). Click *Display adapter properties for Display...* to access additional information and configure some settings.

Troubleshooting a Device That Does Not Work or Is Not Detected

Use Device Manager to view installed hardware devices, to enable or disable devices, to troubleshoot a device, to view and/or change system resources such as IRQs and I/O addresses (see Chapter 4, "Introduction to Configuration"), to update drivers, and to access the *Roll Back Driver* option. The *Roll Back Driver* option is available in all versions of Windows. When you roll back a device driver, the older driver can be reinstalled if you suspect that the new driver causes the device to not start, not be detected, or not work properly.

TECH TIP

Driver rollback requires Administrator rights

You must have Administrator rights to access or use the *Roll Back Driver* option in Device Manager.

To **roll back the device driver**, access Device Manager > expand the appropriate category > right-click on the hardware device > *Properties* > *Driver* tab > *Roll Back Driver* button > *OK*.

If the device driver has not been updated, driver rollback is not possible, so the *Roll Back Driver* button in Device Manager is disabled.

Sometimes, Windows installs the wrong driver for an older device or adapter. The solution to this is to disable the device and then manually install it. To disable the driver in Device Manager, right-click or tap and briefly hold the device icon and select *Disable*.

Drivers can be manually installed by running an installation program or by installing a driver installation package. A driver installation package usually includes a setup information file, which has the `.inf` extension. The setup information file contains the information needed to install a driver package on the computer. Follow these steps to manually install a device driver package through Device Manager:

Step 1. Obtain the driver package files and save them to a folder on your computer.

Step 2. Open the Device Manager utility.

Step 3. Expand categories as needed to locate the device for which the driver is to be installed. To display hidden devices in Device Manager, select *Show Hidden Devices* from the *View* menu option.

Step 4. Right-click the device name > *Update driver*.

Step 5. Select *Browse my computer for drivers > Let me pick from a list of available drivers on my computer > Have Disk.* Click the *Browse* button to locate the driver files that you saved in step 1. Click the `.inf` file that is designed to work with the device.

Step 6. Follow the dialogs that appear to update the driver. If you are prompted with a warning about driver compatibility, you can click *No* and continue installing the driver. You can later remove it or roll back the driver if it does not install correctly or if it does not work.

If an `.inf` file cannot be found in a folder from your driver download, look in subfolders or other folders for the file. You could later download the driver again and pay attention to the folder name in which the driver is stored. If there are multiple `.inf` files in the folder, you may have to try them one at a time until you find the one that works with your hardware. Always **reboot** Windows after a driver installation, even if the system does not prompt for a reboot.

Driver installation programs usually have the extension `.exe.` They do not require Device Manager. When a driver installation program runs, it usually installs additional software or operating system features, in addition to the base driver files. For example, the driver installation program for a display adapter might install a custom feature to configure the adapter.

If you cannot install a device driver by using its installation program, you can try running the installation program in compatibility mode (using Administrator credentials) or by manually installing it using Device Manager.

To run the driver installation program in compatibility mode, locate and right-click or tap and briefly hold the executable file for the driver installation program. Select *Properties > Compatibility* tab > enable the *Run this program in compatibility mode for* checkbox > select a version of Windows that it is known to work on (see Figure 16.15) > click *OK.*

To use Administrator credentials, locate the executable file used to start the driver installation process. Right-click its filename and select *Properties > Compatibility* tab > enable the *Run this program as an administrator* checkbox > click *OK.* After configuring the file to run in compatibility mode and to run with Administrator credentials, double-click or double-tap the executable file icon to start the installation process. Provide the Administrator password, if required. Click *Continue.* Follow the normal installation instructions.

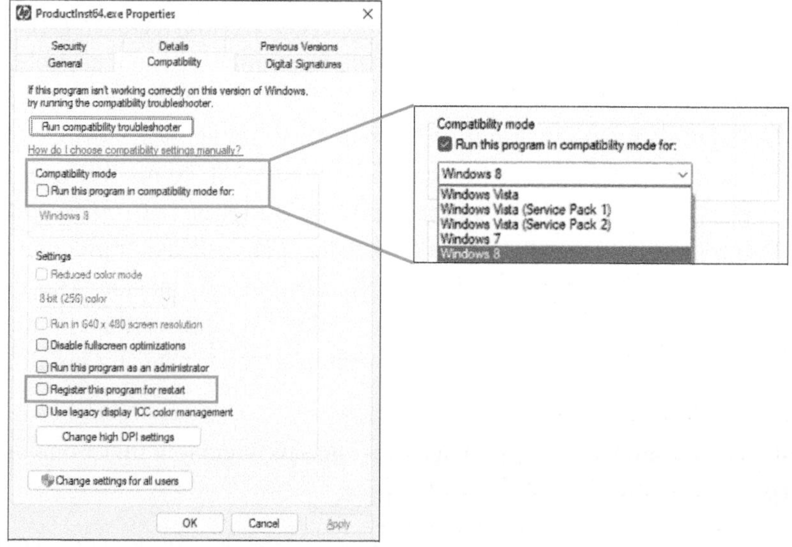

FIGURE 16.15 Installing a driver/application in compatibility mode

TECH TIP

Too many tray icons

If any icons in the notification area are not used, remove them. Right-click or tap and briefly hold on an empty space in the taskbar > *Taskbar settings* > *Select which icons appear on the taskbar* link. Alternatively, *Turn system icons on or off* link > select *On* or *Off* as needed.

Not Enough USB Controller Resources

If you get the message "Not enough USB controller resources," you've probably exceeded the maximum number of endpoints for a USB controller or a specific port. USB endpoints are similar to lanes of data in PCIe. While USB 3.2 and USB4 are faster than USB 2.0, a USB 2.0 controller actually has twice as many endpoints. To resolve the error, try one of these solutions:

> Use USB 2.0 ports as much as possible, reserving USB 3.2 and USB4 ports for devices that benefit from the increased speed.
> Connect USB hubs to USB 2.0 ports instead of the faster ports, since the USB 2.0 controller offers more endpoints to the hub's ports.
> Use Device Manager to uninstall and then reinstall the USB controller. Consider obtaining updated drivers.
> Disable the *xHCI Mode* option in UEFI/BIOS to turn off USB 3.2 or USB4.
> Run the *Hardware and Devices* troubleshooter: Run `msdt -id DeviceDiagnostic` from a command prompt > check *Advanced* > click *Next*.

Correcting Clock Drift

Synchronization, authentication, subscription, and logging issues can occur if a system's time is not correct. The system might even stop working altogether. Check these items to correct clock drift:

> Replace the CMOS/RTC battery on the motherboard.
> See the time manually by right-clicking the time in the taskbar > *Adjust date/time or Adjust date and time* > turn off *Set time automatically* > *Change* (or *Sync now* if you have access to a time server).
> If using automatic synchronization, confirm the following:
  > Local network access or internet access to a time service is available.
  > *Set time automatically* is on (see the second bullet above).
  > *Set time zone automatically* is on or the correct time zone is selected.
  > *Adjust for daylight saving time automatically* is set appropriately for the computer's location.
  > The Windows Time Service is running in **Services**.

More Troubleshooting: Using Wizards and Troubleshooting Links

Whenever a yellow warning icon appears next to a device in the **Devices and Printers** section of the Control Panel, right-click on the device and select *Troubleshoot* to open the Windows Troubleshooting Wizard. You can also configure troubleshooters to run automatically, and you can control the level of notification. Go to *Settings* > *Update and Security* (*System* in Windows 11) > *Troubleshoot* (or type **`troubleshoot`** in the *Search* textbox; the troubleshooting tool appears first in the output list) > select the appropriate option in *Recommended troubleshooting* (*Recommended troubleshooter preferences* in Windows 11). Click *Additional troubleshooters* to resolve common hardware and system issues.

Installing/Removing Software

Software makes a computer useful. One thing you should know about the newer Windows versions is that they may not support some of the older 16-bit software. Use the Compatibility tab in the Control Panel if you have issues when running older applications. Another option is to use the Hyper-V virtual environment to run older applications on older operating systems.

Most software today comes on a flash drive or is downloaded from the internet. An installation file often has the extension `.exe` or `.msi`. When the program is run, an installation wizard steps you through the process of installing the software. While most software today is 64-bit, older applications might be 32-bit. Table 16.10 shows common locations for 32- and 64-bit applications.

TABLE 16.10 Default locations for 32- and 64-bit files

Folder	Description
`System32`	Used for 64-bit Windows system files
`Program Files`	Used for 64-bit application files
`SysWOW64`	Used for 32-bit Windows system files (Note that the WOW in the folder name stands for Windows 32-bit on Windows 64-bit.)
`Program Files (x86)`	Used for 32-bit application files

The *Programs* section of the Control Panel is used to add and remove applications. This Control Panel utility is also used to configure which programs are the default programs, such as for email or a web browser.

TECH TIP

Launch an application

After an application is installed, launch the application by clicking the *Start* button > locate the application name and click it.

Before installing an application, you need to make sure the application meets all **system requirements** (the minimum hardware and software). You should look out for the following, keeping in mind that these concepts relate to all operating systems, including Windows, Linux, and macOS:

- *Compatibility:* Is the application compatible with the type of computer it is being installed on? Does it require a Windows, Mac, or Linux machine?
- *OS requirements:* Is the application 32-bit or 64-bit? If 64-bit, is the computer the application is being installed to 64-bit? If not, the application will not run.
- *Central processing unit (CPU) requirements:* In addition to system type (32-bit or 64-bit), some applications require specific levels of CPU features, such as clock speed, cache, threading, and number of cores.
- *RAM:* Does the computer have enough RAM for the application? Keep in mind that the minimum RAM might not provide the performance the customer wants.
- *Drive space:* Does the storage device that will be used to hold the application and files generated by the application have enough room? Do you need to remove some applications first, back up old files and delete them, or delete unwanted files?

- *Dedicated graphics card vs. integrated:* An integrated graphics processor (GPU) within the CPU handles video data quickly, with reduced power consumption. However, a dedicated graphics card is required for most intensive graphical applications like CAD/CAM, video editing, and gaming. Furthermore, an integrated GPU shares RAM with the overall system, thus reducing the memory available for the operating system, applications, and documents.
- *Video random-access memory (VRAM) requirements:* VRAM is physical memory dedicated to graphics data. It can be located on a CPU or on a dedicated graphics card. Generally, the more VRAM available in a system, the more graphics data can be stored, especially 2-D and 3-D images.
- *External hardware tokens:* External hardware tokens (also called dongles) are often used to enhance system security. For example, a token can display a unique number that changes over time. A VPN application may require the user to enter that number along with their username and password in order to log in. Another type of token is a read-only USB device with an encrypted security certificate. The user must insert the device in the computer in order to log in.

An application can be installed to a computer using a local method of installation, such as by using a USB/CD/DVD/Blu-ray disc or an application downloaded from the internet and then installed. Otherwise, a network-based method can be used; in this case, the application is installed from a network server or from a shared folder on the network.

One common type of downloaded software installation file is an ISO image. An ISO image is a single file that contains an exact copy of an optical disc such as a CD. After the file is downloaded, you can double-click it to give it a drive letter and access the contents as if you inserted an optical disc into the optical disc drive. This process is call *mounting*.

When installing an application, other considerations also have to be taken into account:

- What local security permissions need to be assigned? Chapter 18, "Computer and Network Security," covers how to make these assignments.
- Which files or folders are needed to install the application? Do the users need access to do it themselves, or does just the technician who will install it need access?
- What other security considerations are important? What impact does the application have on the computer or network?
- What other devices might be needed as a result of having access to this application? Is a printer, plotter, digitizer, second monitor, or some other device needed?
- What additional financial or personnel resources will be required to support the application? For example, will users contact the in-house IT department to address issues, or will they contact the vendor? How much does vendor support cost, and how long will it last?

Synchronization

Synchronization is the process of keeping things together or the same. Windows 10/11 has a **Sync Center** Control Panel utility that can be used to synchronize files, for example. If a file on one computer has been changed and the same file is on another computer, then the latest version of the file is put on whichever computer needs it. Even if a computer is not connected to the network, you can work on a file and then, when the computer connects, the file is updated (as long as it is not open). If the file is open on one machine and another computer is modifying the file, a conflict might occur. There is a *Resolve* option to help with this situation. Today, file synchronization is often done with a cloud solution such as Microsoft OneDrive.

Windows 10 also has a system synchronization feature configured through *Settings > Accounts > Sync your settings*. In Windows 11, go to *Settings > Accounts > Windows backup > Remember my preferences*. This synchronization affects the look and feel of your Windows working environment and having it the same on all devices you use. You can sync things like the computer theme, language preferences, and Ease of Access settings.

Programs and Features and Apps & Features

The *Programs and Features* Control Panel utility is the most commonly used subcategory under *Programs* because it is used to change a program's installation options, uninstall an application, and view the installation date, size (disk space consumption), and version of a particular application. The *Turn Features On or Off* link also resides in *Programs and Features*. It is used to enable or disable Windows features such as Hyper-V, PowerShell, Microsoft Print to PDF, Games, Telnet, TFTP server, or TFTP client. Use the *View installed updates* link to see when any applications or Windows updates were installed and to see the specific update number.

Figure 16.16 shows the *Uninstall or change a program* link and displays all the currently installed applications on a Windows 10 computer. Select an application, and up to three options appear at the top of the column as actions that can be taken: *Uninstall*, *Change*, or *Repair*. The options available depend on the program. You can use the *Change* link to change the program's installation option. The *Uninstall* link guides you through the process of removing the program from the computer. Use the *Repair* link if you suspect that the installation has been corrupted. Not all programs have *Change* and *Repair* links.

anel ▸ Programs ▸ Programs and Features   Search Programs and Featu

Uninstall or change a program

To uninstall a program, select it from the list and then click Uninstall, Change, or Repair.

Organize ▾   Uninstall   Change   Repair

Name	Publisher	Installed On	Size	Version
Adobe Reader XI MUI	Adobe Systems Incorporated	4/28/2013	570 MB	11.0.00
Adobe Reader XI (11.0.07)	Adobe Systems Incorporated	6/6/2014	183 MB	11.0.07
Adobe Shockwave Player 12.0	Adobe Systems, Inc.	1/17/2016		12.0.3.133
AMD Catalyst Install Manager	Advanced Micro Devices, Inc.	6/27/2013	26.3 MB	8.0.911.0
AMD Quick Stream	AppEx Networks	6/27/2013	9.69 MB	3.4.2.0
Apple Application Support	Apple Inc.	6/6/2014	94.4 MB	3.0.3
Apple Mobile Device Support	Apple Inc.	6/6/2014	22.7 MB	7.1.1.3
Apple Software Update	Apple Inc.	8/7/2013	2.38 MB	2.1.3.127
Bonjour	Apple Inc.	6/6/2014	2.00 MB	3.0.0.10
Canon MX880 series MP Drivers		1/17/2016		
Cisco EAP-FAST Module	Cisco Systems, Inc.	6/27/2013	1.53 MB	2.2.14
Cisco LEAP Module	Cisco Systems, Inc.	6/27/2013	632 KB	1.0.19
Cisco PEAP Module	Cisco Systems, Inc.	6/27/2013	1.22 MB	1.1.6
Conexant HD Audio	Conexant	1/17/2016		8.64.51.51
DTS Sound	DTS, Inc.	6/27/2013	3.92 MB	1.00.0064
ETDWare PS/2_SMBus-X64 11.8.3.2_WHQL	ELAN Microelectronic Corp.	1/17/2016		11.8.3.2
Genesys Logic USB2.0 Card Reader	Genesys Logic	6/27/2013		4.3.0.3
Google Chrome	Google Inc.	8/6/2013		48.0.2564.103
iTunes	Apple Inc.	6/6/2014	219 MB	11.2.2.3
Java 8 Update 40	Oracle Corporation	3/13/2015	76.9 MB	8.0.400

FIGURE 16.16 *Programs and Features* section of the Control Panel > *Uninstall or Change a Program* window

Similar actions are available in *Apps & features* (*Settings > Apps*). See Figure 16.17. Click on an app and select the appropriate option; use the *Advanced options* link to see the program's version information and to configure additional settings. Not all programs have the *Advanced features* option.

TECH TIP

Handling application misbehavior

To **repair an application** that is not working or that is not working properly, select the application in the *Programs and Features* section of the Control Panel > select *Repair*.

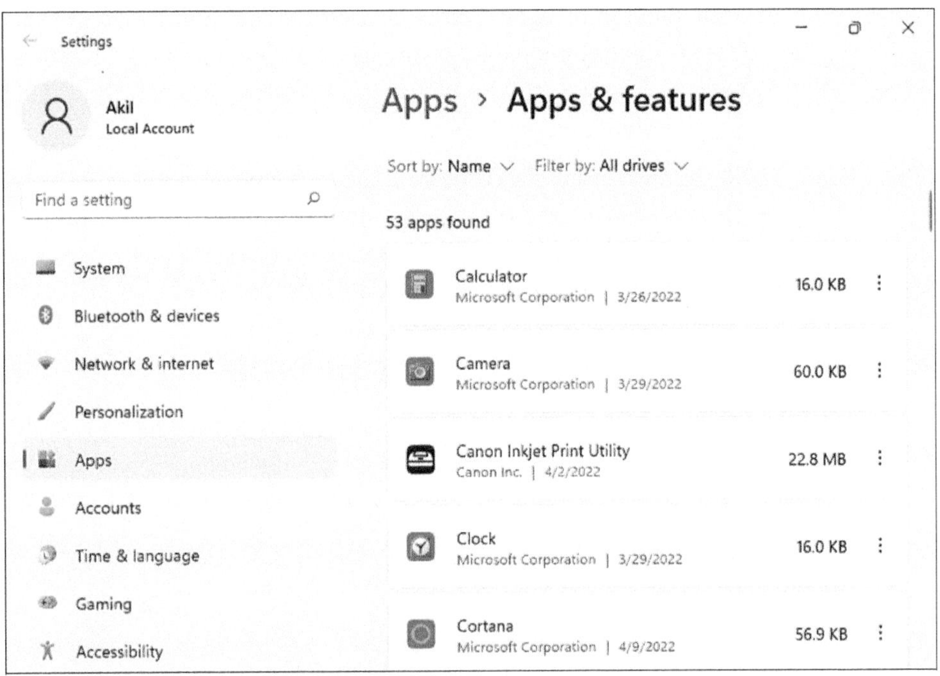

FIGURE 16.17 *Apps & features* section of Settings

Figure 16.18 shows the *Turn windows features on or off* window. A check in a feature's checkbox means that feature is enabled. An unchecked checkbox means that option is not turned on.

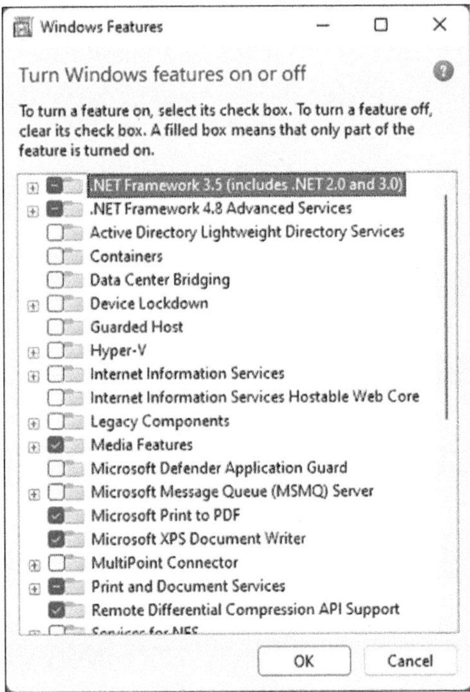

FIGURE 16.18 *Programs and Features* section of the Control Panel > *Turn Windows Features On or Off* window

Another software-related issue involves dynamic link libraries (DLLs). DLL files contain reusable code that can be used by multiple applications. A DLL must be registered with the Windows registry in order to function. Sometimes, DLL registry links get broken, and the links must be re-established. You can use the following techniques to resolve DLL errors:

> Run the built-in System File Checker (`sfc`) to replace missing or corrupted operating system files.
> Repair or reinstall the software if an application reports a DLL error.
> Download Windows 10/11 operating system files from Microsoft.
> Copy the DLL file from another system and restore it on your PC. Then re-register the DLL file with the **regsvr32.exe** command.

Computer Management Console

The **Microsoft Management Console** holds snap-ins, which are tools that are used to maintain a computer. Open this tool by using the `mmc` command or searching for **`mmc`** in the search textbox. You can then add snap-ins via *File* > *Add/Remove Snap-in*. After you add the snap-ins you need, you can save the customized console. Later, you can start the Microsoft Management Console and open a saved console by using the `mmc` *`path\filename`*`.msc` command.

The **Computer Management** console is a preconfigured snap-in that provides a number of technical tools for an IT technician. The Computer Management console allows a technician to manage shared folders and drives, start and stop services, look at performance logs and system alerts, and access Device Manager to troubleshoot hardware problems. Access the Computer Management console by using one of the following methods:

> Right-click *Start* button > *Computer Management.*
> Use the search textbox to search for **`computer management`** or **`compmgmt`**.
> In Windows 10, *System and Security* section of the Control Panel > *Administrative Tools* > *Computer Management.*
> In Windows 11, *System and Security* section of the Control Panel > *Windows Tools* > *Computer Management.*

Figure 16.19 shows the Computer Management console. The three major tool categories in this console are System Tools, Storage, and Services and Applications. Expand the *System Tools* section to see some of the most technical utilities available to a technician. Expand the *Storage* section to find the Disk Management utility. The expanded *Services and Applications* section shows access to Internet Information Services (IIS) Manager, Services, WMI Control, and Message Queuing.

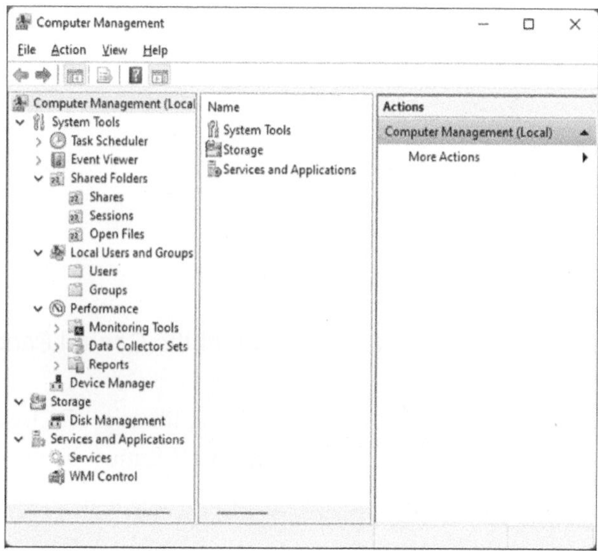

FIGURE 16.19 Computer Management console

TECH TIP

Using Component Services?

You can use a particular snap-in called **Component Services** to view, configure, and administer the Component Object Model (COM) components, COM+ applications, and Distribution Transaction Coordinator (DTC). COM applications are a group of components within applications that were designed to work together. When deployed, Component Services can be used to track services and assess performance measures.

System Tools

The System Tools section of the Computer Management console includes Task Scheduler, Event Viewer, Shared Folders, Local Users and Groups, Performance, and Device Manager. Each of these tools is important when supporting Windows computers. Let's dive into each one.

Task Scheduler

Task Scheduler (`taskschd.msc`) enables you to plan and execute apps, scripts, and utilities on a regular basis. Use the *Actions* pane to create a new task, show what tasks are running, and import a task from another machine (see Figure 16.20). If a company has an executable it wants to run at 2 a.m. every week on Wednesday or every time a user logs on, Task Scheduler is the tool to use.

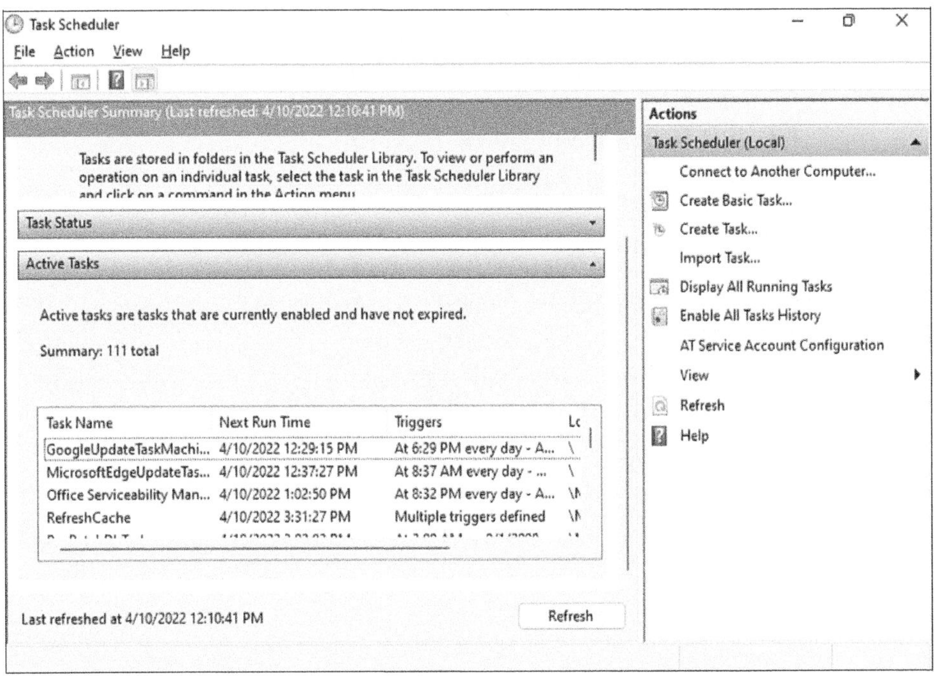

FIGURE 16.20 Task Scheduler

Event Viewer

Logs are created every time something happens in a Windows system, and Event Viewer is what you use to see the logs (see Figure 16.21). **Event Viewer** (`eventvwr.msc`) is a Windows tool used to monitor various events on a computer such as when a driver or service does not start properly. The Windows Event Log service starts automatically every time a computer boots to Windows. This service allows the events to be logged, and then Event Viewer is used to see the log.

CHAPTER 16

Windows Event Viewer has two types of logs: Windows logs and applications and services logs. In the Windows Logs section, there are the application, setup, security, system, and forwarded events logs, along with two new ones: setup and forwarded events. Also, there is an Applications and Services Logs section. Table 16.11 summarizes the types of things you might see in these logs. Event Viewer can display five different types of events. The events and related symbols are shown in Table 16.12.

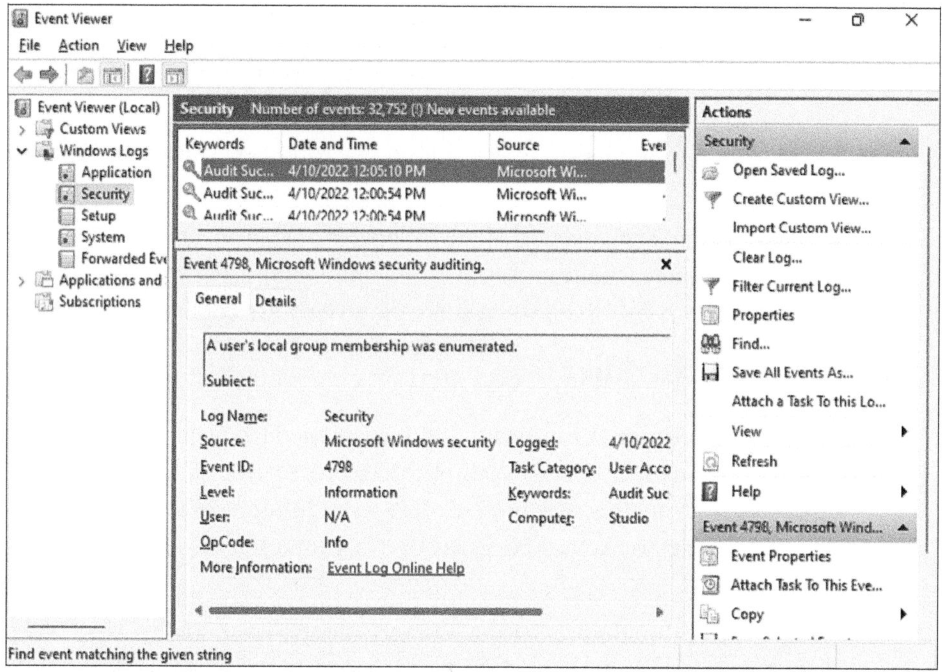

FIGURE 16.21 Event Viewer

TABLE 16.11 Windows Event Viewer logs

Major log category	Log	Description
Windows Logs	Application	Contains events logged by software applications. The company that writes the software applications decides what to log.
	Security	Contains events specified by administrators, such as valid and invalid logon attempts and network share usage.
	Setup	Contains setup events logged by software applications.
	System	Contains Windows system events such as when a driver or service fails to load or start.
	Forwarded events	Contains events from remote computers.
Applications and Services Logs	Vendor specific	Contains logs from a specific application or Windows component. The logs can be one of four types: admin, operational, analytic, and debug. The admin log is for normal users and technical support staff. The operational log is used by technical staff to analyze a problem. The analytic and debug logs would likely be used by the application developer; both of these logs create a large number of entries and should be used for a short period of time only.

TABLE 16.12 Event Viewer symbols

Symbol	Type of event	Description
Lowercase "i"	Information	Normal system operations, such as the system being initialized or shut down.
Exclamation point (!)	Warning	An event that is not critical but that you might want to take a look at. The system can still function, but some features may not be available.
X	Error	A specific event failed, such as a service or device failing to initialize properly.
Yellow key	Audit success	You can audit a specific event. This symbol indicates a successful audit.
Yellow lock	Audit failure	When you specify a specific event to audit and the event fails, the yellow lock appears. For example, if you are auditing a system login and someone tries to log in without having a valid username or password, the system creates an audit failure event.

The Application log displays events associated with a specific program. The programmers who design software decide which events to display in Event Viewer's application log.

TECH TIP

Application hangs, crashes, or doesn't respond

If an application hangs, crashes, or shows a "not responding" message, take a look at the Event Viewer application log. Research any messages or error codes found. Ensure that the application does not need to be updated. Any proprietary crash screens should be researched in Event Viewer.

The security log displays events such as when different users log in to the computer, including both valid and invalid logins. A technician can pick which events display in the security log. All users can view the system log and the application log, but only a member of the Administrators group can enable security log information. Event Viewer logs can be saved as files and viewed later. This is especially useful with intermittent problems. Use the *Actions* section to save and retrieve Event Viewer log files.

TECH TIP

What to do with a blue screen

Sometimes when Windows crashes, a **blue screen** with an error code and numbers appears. Check the Event Viewer for a system event. Try to reboot with the power button; this may require you to remove the computer's power cord, re-insert the power cord, and once again power on the computer. When the computer has been restarted, you can research the error message and problem on the internet.

The most commonly used log is the system log. The system log displays events that deal with various system components, such as drivers or services that load during startup. The type of system log events cannot be changed or deleted.

Access **system log** errors whenever you want detailed information about Windows-controlled events; look at the **application log** errors when troubleshooting a particular program. Figure 16.22 shows the filters applied to see only system error events. Figure 16.23 shows the results. Notice in Figure 16.23 that you can select a particular event. The *General* tab shows the gist of the error. Select the *Details* tab for even more details.

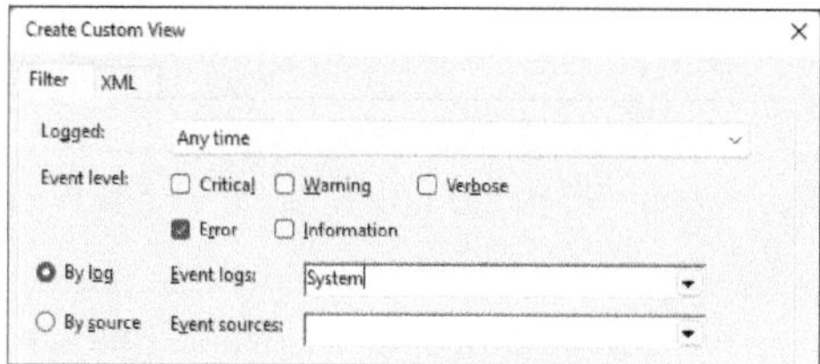

FIGURE 16.22 Event Viewer filter

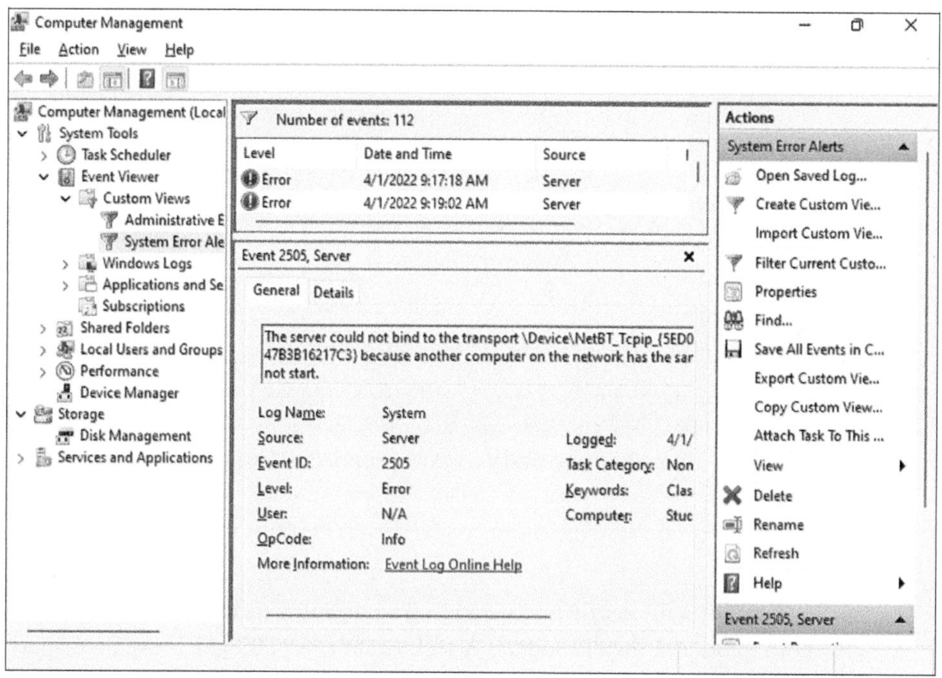

FIGURE 16.23 Event Viewer filter results

> **TECH TIP**
>
> **What to do if the Event Viewer log is full**
>
> You can clear the log or adjust the log settings. To clear the log, start *Event Viewer* > select a log > *Action* menu option > *Properties* > *General* tab > *Clear Log* button. Some settings that might need to be adjusted include *Maximum Log Size* and *When maximum event log size is needed.*

Shared Folders

The **Shared Folders** tool is used to view shares, sessions, and open files. **Shares** can be folders that have been shared on the computer, printers, or a network resource such as a scanner. Sessions are network users who are currently connected to the computer as well as the network users' computer names, the network connection type (Windows or Mac, for example), how many resources have been opened by the network user, how long the user has been connected, and whether this user is connected using the Guest user account. Open files are files that are currently open by network users.

In the left Computer Management pane, expand the *Shared Folders* option and click the *Shares* option. The network shares appear in the right pane. Double-click any of the shares to view its *Properties* window. From this window, using the *Share Permissions* or *Security* tabs, permissions can be set for shared resources. Permissions are covered later in this chapter.

User Account Management

User account management in Windows is an important function for a technician and involves creating accounts, managing accounts, and putting people into groups that are used in different situations. Windows 10 stores information credentials for Windows and web accounts. You can make configuration changes by using the *User Accounts* Control Panel.

Credential Manager

Have you ever gone to a website or accessed a remote computer and been asked if you want your username and password saved? If you agree to such a request while using a Windows computer, your information is saved using Credential Manager. **Credential Manager** is where Windows stores login credentials. You can back up Windows credentials to protect yourself in the event that the computer crashes, and you can view or remove forgotten or old credentials. Information stored in Credential Manager can be used by Windows and other applications and can be of several varieties:

- *Windows credentials:* Windows services use Windows credentials when you access a specific computer or server with a username and password.
- *Certificate-based credentials:* Certificate-based credentials are mainly used in complex business network environments with smart cards.
- *Generic credentials:* Apps such as Microsoft Office, Microsoft Live products, OneDrive, and Xbox Live use generic credentials. Websites that require usernames and password also use generic credentials.
- *Web credentials:* Web credentials include username and password information stored by Windows for specific websites. Your machine might store your web credentials for logging in to the main portal where you work, a gaming website, email, and shopping sites. Web credentials are also used for password reset links.

TECH TIP

Stored credentials pose a security risk

Storing usernames and passwords saves all of us time. If someone gains access to your computer, however, he or she can quickly use *Back up Credentials* to save all your Windows credentials to the cloud or removable media and then use that information from another computer to access accounts.

To open Credential Manager, use the *User Accounts* Control Panel and select *Credential Manager*, as shown in Figure 16.24. You can also locate Credential Manager by using *Search*. Notice in Figure 16.25 that there are two sections: Web Credentials and Windows Credentials.

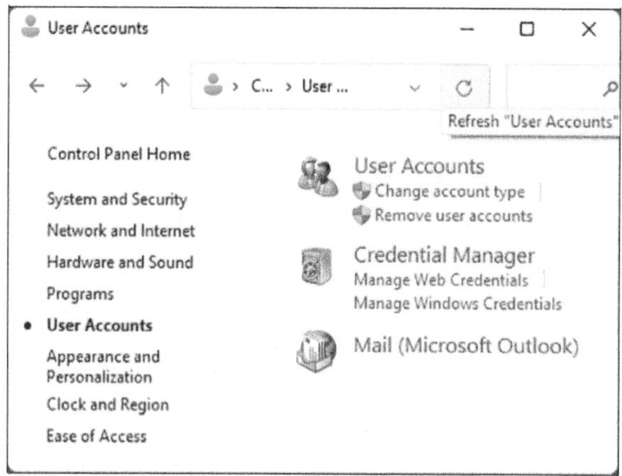

FIGURE 16.24 Opening Credential Manager

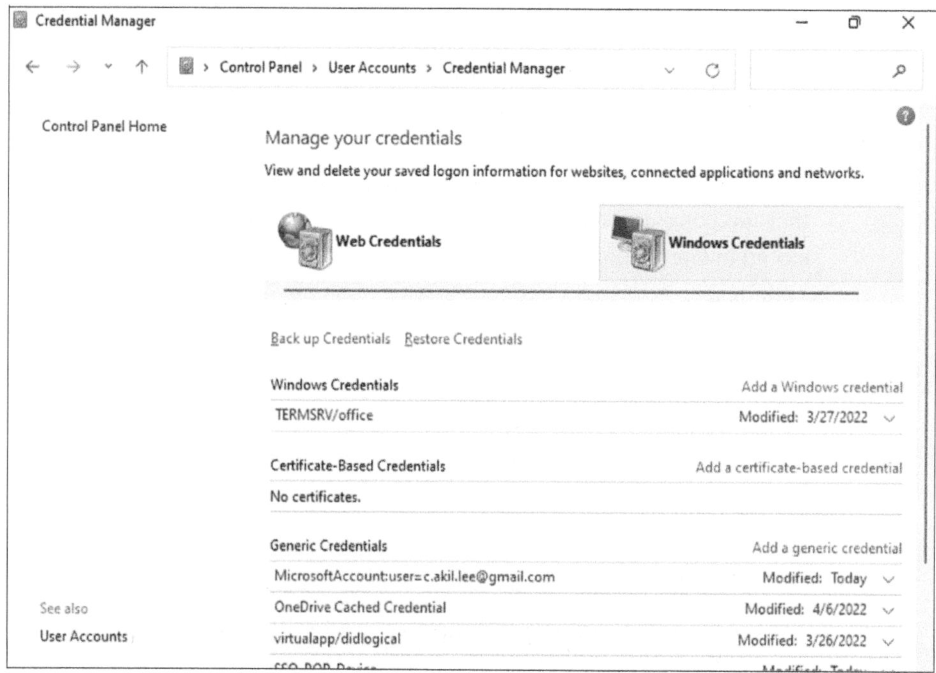

FIGURE 16.25 Credential Manager

How to Add a Windows Credential

As a technician, you might need to manually add credentials for Windows to use. To do this, access *Windows Credential* > locate the area that contains the specific type of credential > click *Add a Windows credential*, *Add a certificate-based credential*, or *Add a generic credential*. For example, Figure 16.26 shows the link to use if you want to add a Windows credential.

Before adding the information to Credential Manager, you should access the server, network device, network share, or website and verify the username and password. Then you can enter that information into the appropriate textboxes, as shown in Figure 16.27.

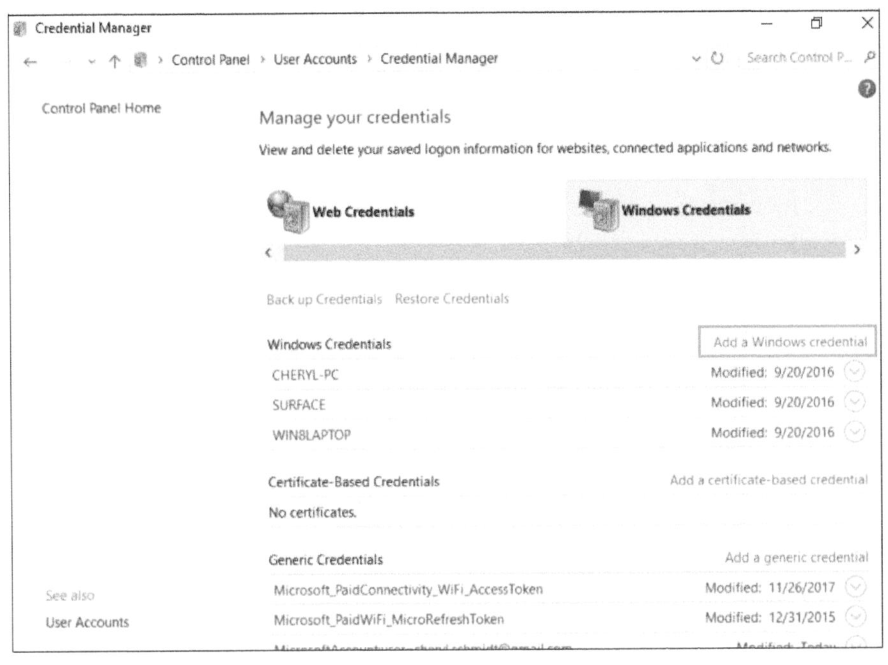

FIGURE 16.26 Adding a Windows credential, step 1

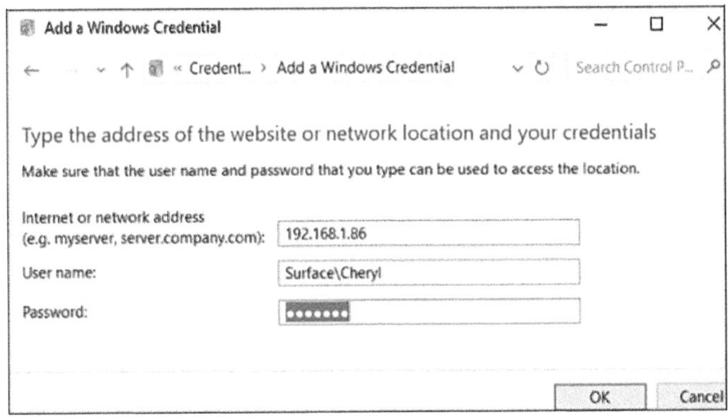

FIGURE 16.27 Adding a Windows credential, step 2

How to Remove a Windows Credential

If you want to remove a specific credential, such as when you see one that you do not recognize or that you no longer use, click the arrow associated with that credential to expand the section. Then click the *Remove* link, as shown in Figure 16.28.

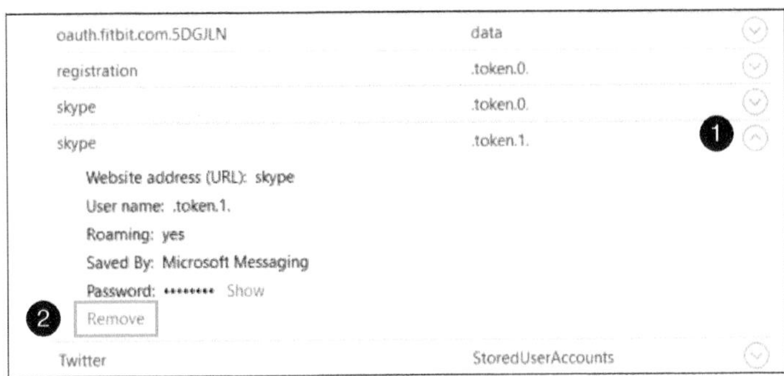

FIGURE 16.28 Deleting a credential

How to Edit an Existing Credential

In some cases, you might be required to change a password. When doing so, if you decline the dialog that asks if you want to update the password, you will then have to type the credentials each time rather than have them prepopulated for you. You can edit credentials in Credential Manager by using the arrow to the right of the credential to expand the section and then clicking the *Edit* link (see Figure 16.29).

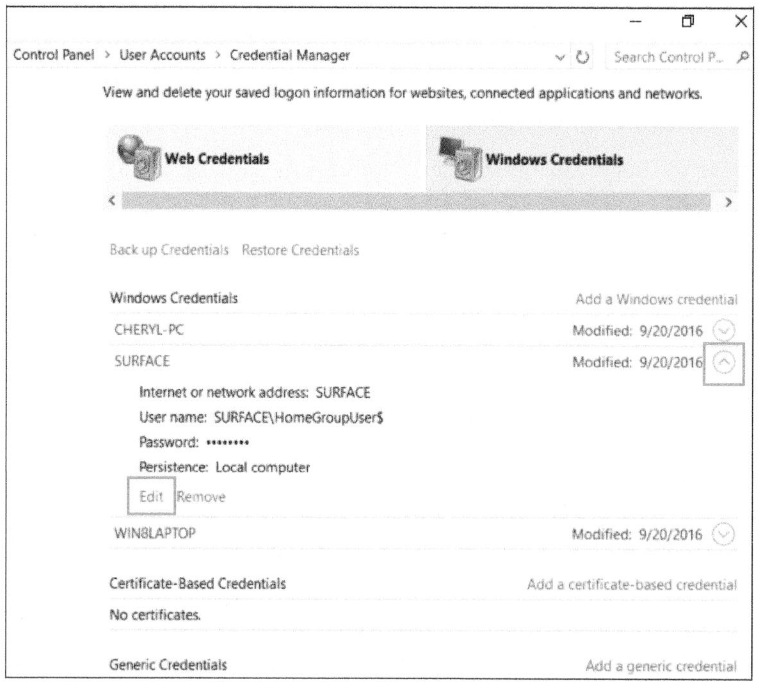

FIGURE 16.29 Editing a credential, step 1

> **TECH TIP**
>
> **Use the specific application to change the credentials**
>
> Not all applications respond well to editing credentials within Credential Manager. Be especially cautious when editing credentials used to access virtual machines.

Local Users and Groups

The **Local Users and Groups** tool (`lusrmgr.msc`) is located in the Computer Management console. It is available only in Windows Pro versions and above. It is used to create and manage accounts for those who use the computer or those who use the computer resources from a remote network computer. These accounts are considered local users or local groups and are managed from the computer being worked on. In contrast, domain or global users and groups are administered by a network administrator on a network server. Permissions are granted or denied to files, folders, and network resources such as a shared printer or scanner. Rights can also be assigned. **Rights** allow different users to execute certain computer actions such as performing a backup or shutting down the computer.

Open the *Local Users and Groups* option by expanding the *Local Users and Groups* selection in the *Computer Management* window. Click on the *Users* option, and a list of current users appears in the right pane. Figure 16.30 shows an example of local users. To create a new user, click the *Action* menu option and select *New User*.

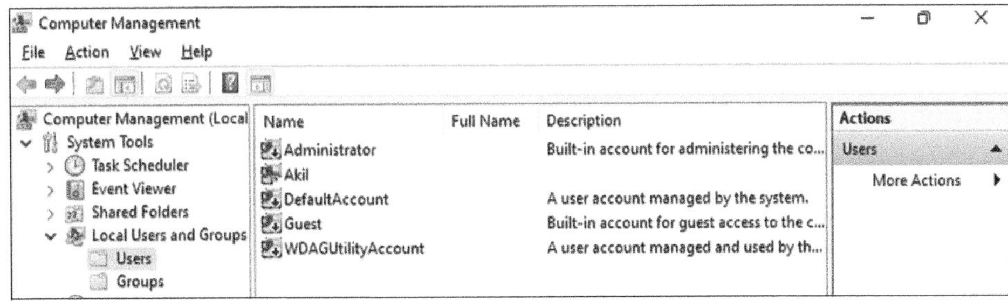

FIGURE 16.30 Local users and groups

Notice in Figure 16.30 that the Guest account has a small down arrow in the lower-right corner of its icon. This means the account has been disabled. Double-click the *Guest* icon. Look at the *Account is disabled* checkbox to see if the account is disabled. The box is checked by default, meaning that the Guest account is not available for use.

TECH TIP

Where are the local user settings?

Windows local user settings are found in the following folder: `%userprofile%\AppData\Local` (for example, `C:\Users\Cheryl\AppData\Local`). You might have to enable *Show Hidden Files* in File Explorer to see the *AppData* folder.

Windows has two basic types of user accounts available in the different Windows editions: Standard user and Administrator. The **Administrator** account has full control over the system, as it always has in Windows. By default, a **Standard user** account cannot install most applications or change system settings. Each user on a computer should have a Standard user account that is used for everyday use. Any account designated as an Administrator account should be used only to log on to the system to make system changes and install new software.

In Windows Pro and higher versions, additional types of user accounts can be used for various security levels. These user groups are covered elsewhere, but one user group that should be mentioned here is Power Users. In older Windows versions (Windows XP and earlier), users who were in the Power Users group had elevated permissions to perform common configuration tasks such as changing user-related Control Panel settings and changing the time zone. Today, the Standard user group has most of those permissions.

Account Recovery Options: Local Account

Windows 10/11 supports use of an online Microsoft account as a login or a local account. Windows **account recovery options** are limited for security reasons. You should always have a backup account that is an Administrator account on a local (workgroup) computer. Here are some other ways that you can recover a Windows user account:

- Use the Windows password reset disk that was previously created.
- Have someone who has an Administrator account log in to Windows and reset your password for you.
- If you use your Microsoft account, go online and use Microsoft tools to reset that password.
- Boot from a Windows installation disk, boot to a command prompt, and use the `net user` command to create an Administrator account. You will have to do research on this one.

> If there are accidentally no users with Administrator rights, boot the computer into Safe Mode and change one of the accounts to an Administrator account type.
> Use the *Reset Password* link and take the necessary steps to reset the password.
> Reload Windows. Use this option as a last resort as it causes you to lose everything that is stored on the hard disk or SSD.

UAC

The Administrator and Standard user accounts are affected by a feature in Windows called User Account Control (**UAC**). UAC works with Internet Explorer/Edge, Windows Defender, and Parental Controls to provide heightened awareness of security issues. A UAC message appears any time something occurs that normally would require an administrator-level decision to make changes to the system. An application that has a security shield icon overlay displays a UAC prompt when executed. If a Standard user is logged in, a message appears, stating that the task is prohibited, access is denied, or Administrator credentials must be provided in order to proceed (see Figure 16.31). UAC is meant to protect users from themselves as well as from software that tries to change the system. Even if a person is logged in with an Administrator account, the UAC prompt appears to confirm the action that is about to be performed.

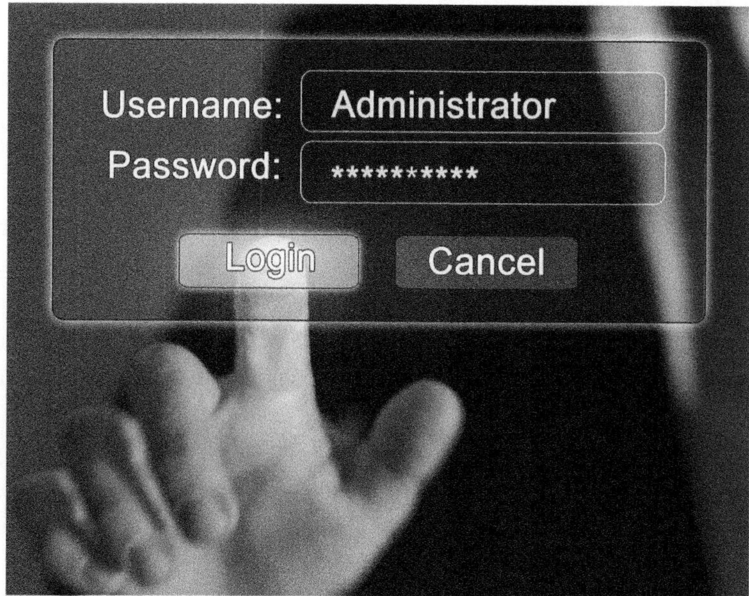

FIGURE 16.31 Administrator credentials required

The following configurations help with UAC:

> To configure a specific application to run in an elevated mode—meaning it has the Administrator access token given to it or permission given to it to run—right-click the application and select *Properties* > *Compatibility* tab > under Privilege Level select *Run This Program as Administrator* > *OK*.
> If a user demands that UAC be disabled, use the System Configuration window (`msconfig`) *Tools* tab. Select *Change UAC Settings* and click *Launch*. The *User Account Control Settings* dialog opens (see Figure 16.32). The dialog box is also available through Control Panel > *User Accounts* > *User Accounts* > *Change User Account Control settings*.

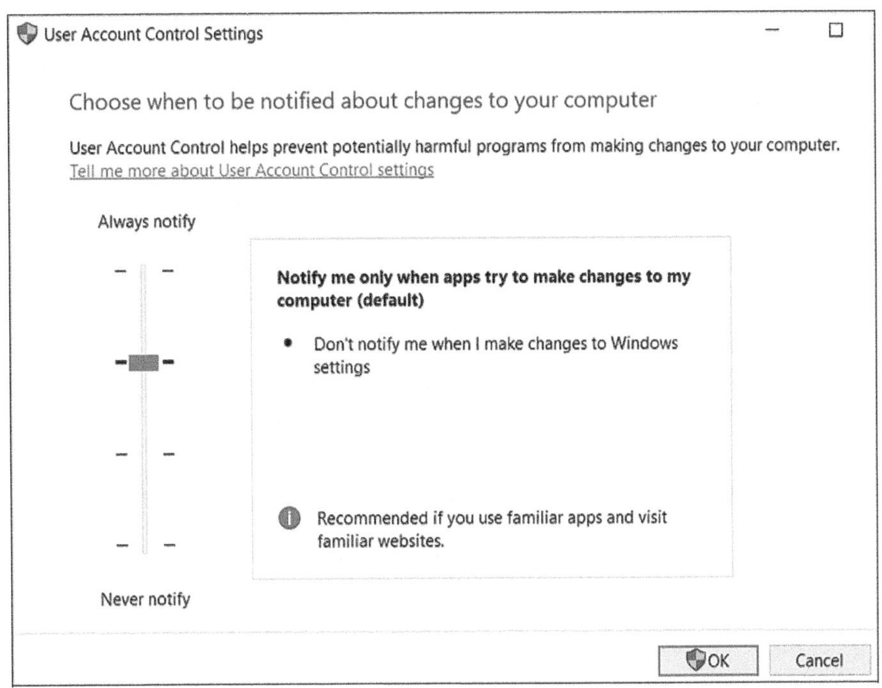

FIGURE 16.32 UAC configuration in Windows

Managing Storage

Mechanical hard drives and SSDs can be managed using the *Storage* Computer Management console option, which includes the Disk Management tool. The **Disk Management** tool (`diskmgmt.msc`) is used to manage hard drives, including volumes or partitions. With it you can initialize drives; create volumes; format volumes for FAT, FAT32, and NTFS; configure RAID; and manage remote drives. You must be a member of the Administrators group to perform any tasks using Disk Management.

Chapter 7, "Storage Devices," introduced Disk Management, but let's review the basics again. Figure 16.33 shows the Disk Management utility. Disks are numbered starting with 0 (Disk 0), and a disk can be segmented into separate volumes. Notice that the drive volumes display in the top window as well as at the bottom. The volumes' attributes are listed in the top window. Each volume appears as a section of a disk in the bottom window.

Figure 16.34 shows the options available if you right-click or tap and briefly hold inside the unallocated space in Disk 2. Because the disk is currently a basic disk, only a simple volume can be created. When you create a volume, you are prompted to select a file system as well as assign a drive letter. See Chapter 7 for more information on volumes and partitions.

Figure 16.35 shows that you can right-click or tap and briefly hold on a particular disk on the far left to control the disk via a context menu. The menu shown is for a drive that is already in use and online. If a drive shows a **drive status** other than online, appropriate actions can be taken from the context menu.

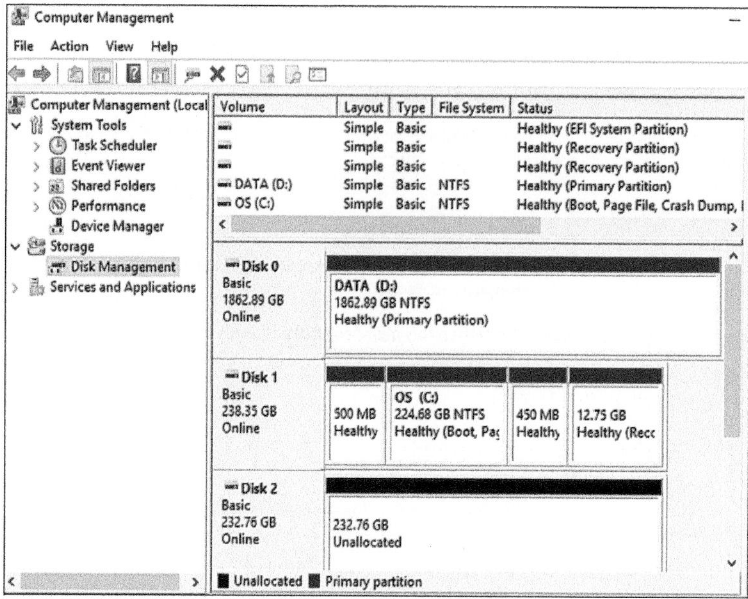

FIGURE 16.33 Disk Management utility

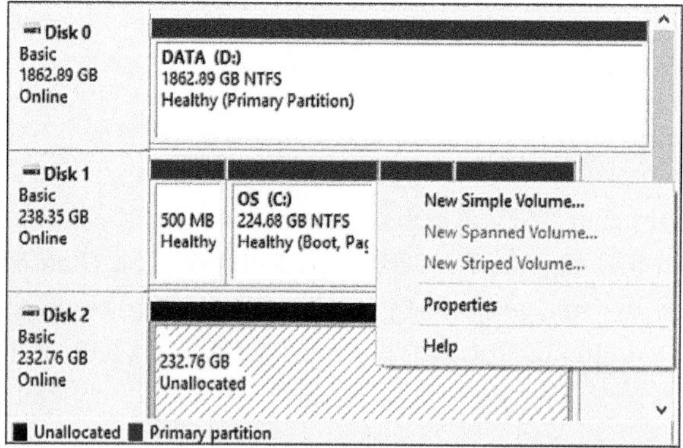

FIGURE 16.34 Managing drive space on a new drive

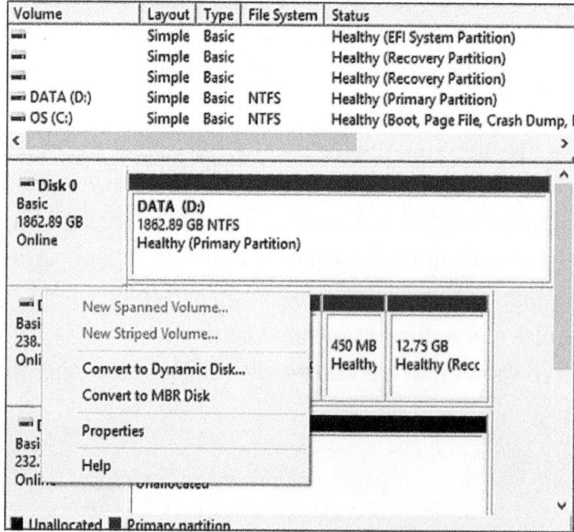

FIGURE 16.35 Controlling a particular disk

Figure 16.36 shows the context menu that appears if you right-click or tap and briefly hold within a disk volume, such as within the slanted lines of the `D:` drive (Drive 0). Notice that you can delete, extend, or shrink a volume. You can also change the drive letter. Table 16.13 describes the tasks that are commonly accomplished within the Disk Management tool.

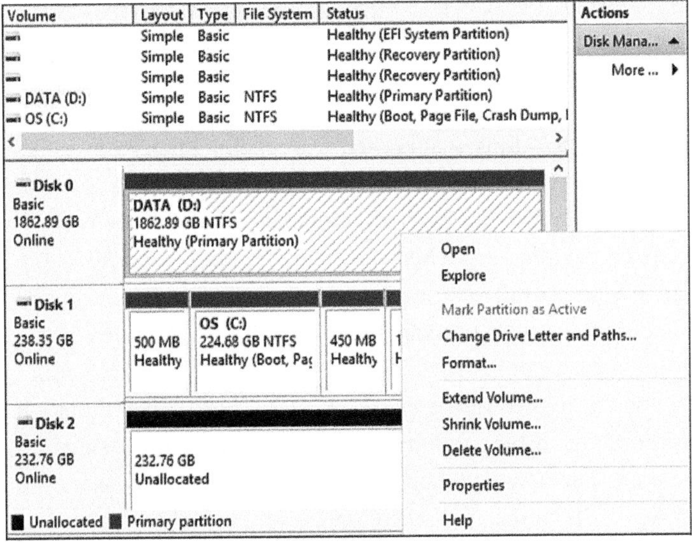

FIGURE 16.36 Controlling a particular volume

TABLE 16.13 Disk Management tasks

Task	Description
Initializing	Make a new disk available to be used by right-clicking a drive > *Initialize Disk*.
Adding a volume	Ensure that the drive is recognized by the BIOS/UEFI and then create a partition and format it for a particular file system.
Assigning/ changing drive letter	Right-click on a drive volume > *Change Drive Letter and Paths*.
Mounting	Map an empty folder on an NTFS volume by right-clicking on a partition or volume > *Change Drive Letter and Paths* > *Add* > *Mount in the Following Empty NTFS Folder* and either type the path or browse to an empty folder > *OK* > *OK*.
Extending partition	Increase the size of a partition by right-clicking on the drive letter > *Extend Volume*. Some volumes cannot be extended.
Shrinking partition	Decrease the size of the partition by right-clicking on the drive letter > *Shrink Volume*. Some volumes cannot be shrunk.
Splitting partition	To divide space on a hard drive or make one partition smaller, right-click the drive > *Shrink Volume*. Then create a new partition with the relinquished drive space.
Adding array	Right-click inside unallocated space of a drive > *New Spanned Volume, New Mirrored Volume, New Striped Volume*, or *New RAID 5 volume*. Then select another drive(s) to be added and select a drive letter and file system.

TECH TIP

All Windows disk management tools require Administrator rights

You must be a member of the Administrators group to perform any disk management tasks.

Storage Spaces

Another Control Panel utility that is used with disk management is Storage Spaces (Control Panel > *System and Security* > *Storage Spaces*). The **Storage Spaces** Control Panel is used for data storage using two or more drives that the operating system sees as one drive; this combination of drives is called a *storage pool*. The unusual thing about Windows Storage Spaces is that the drives can be different types of drives; for example, an eSATA drive and a USB flash drive can be used to create a virtual disk that is seen as one drive. A logical drive (pool) created through Storage Spaces is formatted for either the NTFS or ReFS file system. Note that if you use drives in a logical drive created through Storage Spaces, each of those drives cannot be given an individual drive letter. In addition, the drives no longer appear in Disk Management, and they can only be used for the storage pool. The new pool appears in Disk Management as a disk.

Use the steps below to create a new pool:

Step 1. From the *Storage Spaces* Control Panel, select the *Create a new pool and storage space* link.

Step 2. Ensure that at least two drives that you want to use for the virtual drive created using Storage Spaces are attached. Select the drives by clicking in the checkbox beside each drive that is to be used. Note that any existing files on a selected drive will be erased and cannot be recovered.

Step 3. Click the *Create Pool* button.

Step 4. Name the storage space and select the drive letter, file system, resiliency type, and pool size > select *Create storage space*.

Use the *Change Settings* button within the *Storage Spaces* Control Panel to manage or modify a logical drive.

Disk Maintenance

Mechanical hard drives get sluggish over time. The good news is that disk management and maintenance are now done for you automatically in Windows 10/11. Let's look at the tools that are available to keep mechanical drives running smoothly.

Right-click or tap and briefly hold a drive letter in File Explorer > select *Properties*. On the *General* tab, you can access the **Disk Cleanup** tool (`cleanmgr /d` *`drive`*, for example), which scans the drive volume to see what files could potentially be deleted.

The *Tools* tab provides access to two additional tools: *Error checking* and *Optimize and defragment drive*. The **Error checking** tool is extremely important to Windows. The tool checks the drive for file system errors, bad hard drive sectors, and lost clusters. Using *Error checking* is the equivalent of running the `chkdsk` command.

Windows 10 and 11 do not need to have the drive checked as often as earlier versions because certain disk errors are fixed immediately and do not need a utility executed to make that happen. Microsoft integrated some of the new features of the Resilient File System (ReFS). **ReFS** is expected to eventually replace NTFS as the file system used on Microsoft Windows systems, but at the time of press, ReFS volumes cannot be used to boot a system.

Files and folders become fragmented due to file creation and deletion over a period of time. That is, the bits that comprise a file can be located in non-contiguous locations on the disk. A defragmented volume provides better performance than a volume with files and folders located throughout the drive. With a mechanical drive, **defragment the hard drive** to get better drive performance after you have used the Error Checking tool or the `chkdsk` command. The **Optimize and defragment** tool (*Optimize* button, `dfrgui` command, or `defrag` command) is used to place files in contiguous clusters on the hard drive. Microsoft automatically runs a defragment operation once a week, but you can defragment the drive volume manually.

TECH TIP

Defragmentation requires Administrator rights

Note that only a member of the Administrators group can defragment a hard drive.

If you want to implement your own defragmentation schedule, search for **`defragment`** and select the *Defragment and Optimize Drives* option. Select *Change settings* and choose the option that fits the computer user best:

> *Run on a schedule:* Select how often the drive optimization executes.
> *Frequency:* Choose daily, weekly, or monthly. (The default is weekly and runs during automatic maintenance.)
> *Drives:* Click the *Choose* button to select drives. Note that SSDs are not supposed to be defragmented using the drive optimization routine and should be deselected by default.

Managing Services and Applications

The *Services and Applications* section of the Computer Management console can contain a multitude of options, depending on the computer and what is loaded. Common options include Telephony, WMI Control, Services, and Indexing Service. A frequently used option is *Services*. A **service** is an application that can be started using this window or configured so that it starts when the computer boots. It runs in the background and is often a vital component of the operating system. When you click the *Services* option, a list of services installed on the computer displays in the right window. Double-click or double-tap any service, and the service's *Properties* window appears. In this window, you can use the *General* tab to start, stop, pause, resume, or disable a service on the local computer or on a remote computer, but you must be logged on as a member of the Administrators group to change a service. Figure 16.37 shows the Computer Management console Services window and some examples of installed services.

If you double-click a service, you can use the *Recovery* tab to select what should happen when a service fails a first time, a second time, and even a third time. For example, if the print service fails the first time, a restart of the service occurs. After the print service fails a second time, the print server can be restarted automatically. The third time the print service fails, an executable file that pages a technician can be executed.

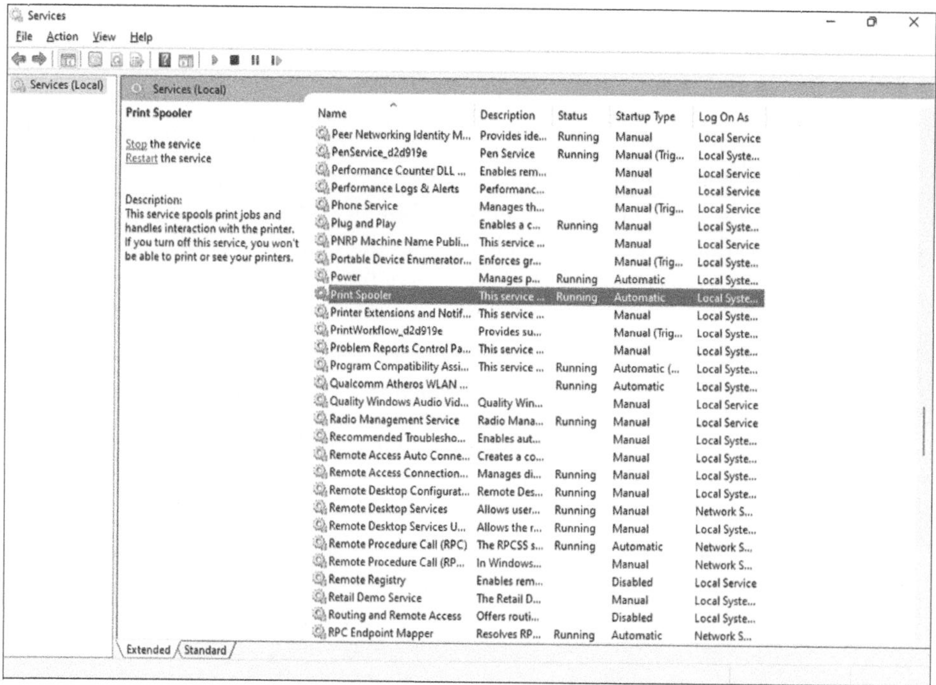

FIGURE 16.37 Computer Management console: Services window

Data Sources (ODBC)

Open database connectivity (ODBC) is a programming interface that enables applications to access data from a database. Use the ODBC **Data Sources** administrative tool to select which particular database application is associated with a particular type of file. Access the *ODBC Data Sources* section of the Control Panel by searching for the *Administrative Tools* (*Windows Tools* in Windows 11) section of the Control Panel > double-click on *ODBC Data Sources (32-bit)* or *ODBC Data Sources (64-bit)*. Figure 16.38 shows the User DSN (where DSN stands for *data source name*) tab of the *ODBC Data Sources (64-bit)* window. Figure 16.39 shows the *Tracing* tab, which can be used to create logs that help when applications misbehave.

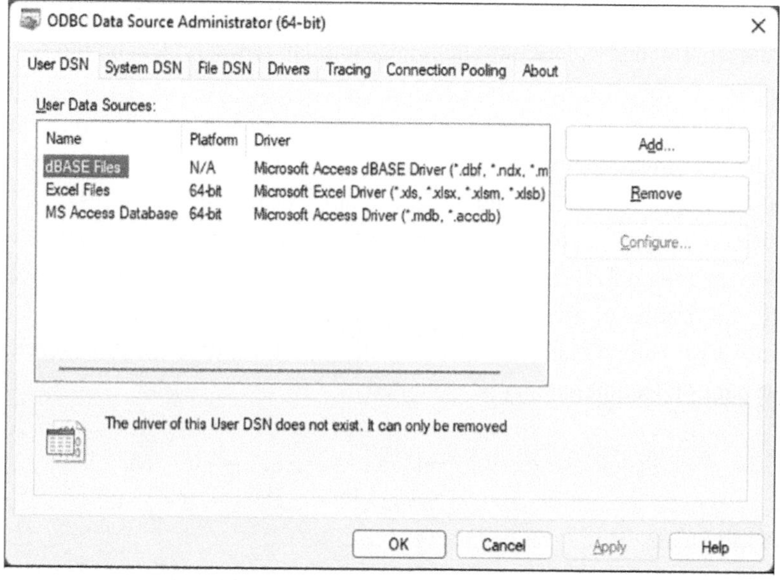

FIGURE 16.38 Data Sources (ODBC) section of the Control Panel

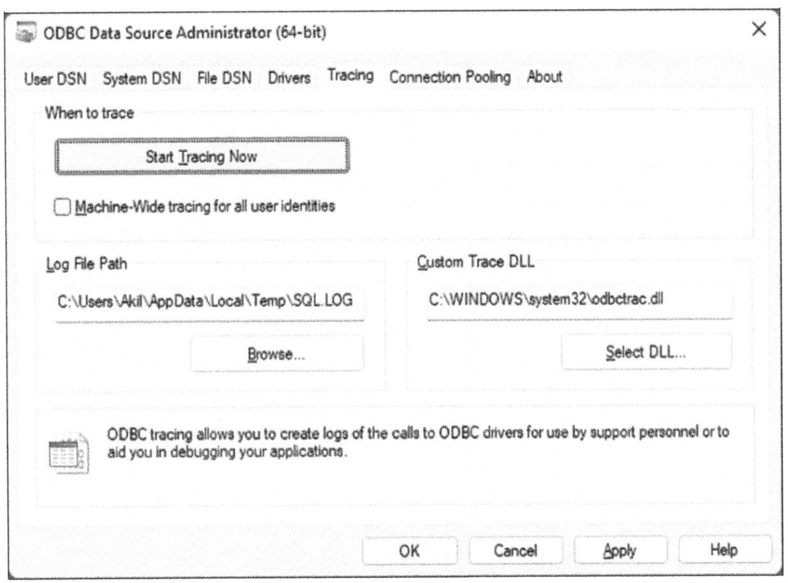

FIGURE 16.39 Data Sources (ODBC) Tracing tab

Print Management Console

The **Print Management** console is used to manage printers on Windows 10/11 Pro and higher versions. To access the console, use one of the following methods:

> Access the *System and Security* section of the Control Panel > select *Administrative Tools* (*Window Tools* in Windows 11) > double-click or double-tap *Print Management*.

> Use the `printmanagement.msc` command.

Figure 16.40 shows the Print Management console window. On the left, expand *Custom Filters* to see all the printers, all drivers, the printers that show a not ready status, and printers that currently have print jobs. In the center of the screen is a list of printers in a home or small business environment. In the corporate environment, there would be more; plus you could use the *Print Servers* option in the left pane.

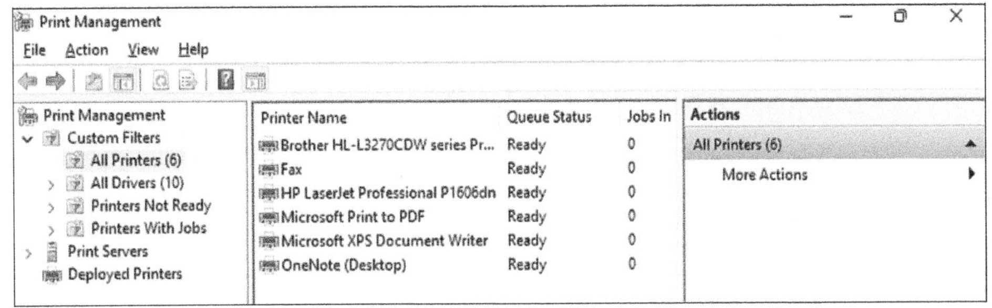

FIGURE 16.40 Print Management console

Printing Issues

Chapter 9, "Printers and Multifunction Devices," is an entire chapter devoted to printers of all types, with a section on troubleshooting for each type. Here are some recommendations specifically related to Windows **printing issues**:

> Try printing a test page from an application. If that doesn't work, use the printer's *Properties* or *Printer Properties* window (*General* tab) to print a test page.

- Use the Windows troubleshooting tool. In Windows 10 or 11, use the *Search* text box to locate *Settings > Update & Security (System* in Windows 11) > *Troubleshoot.* For Windows 10 computers, click *Additional troubleshooters > Printer > Run the troubleshooter.* In Windows 11, click *Other troubleshooters > Printer > Run.*
- Ensure that the user is printing to the correct printer. Companies commonly have multiple network printers.
- Clear the print spooler (queue) files and restart the print spooler service from the printer's *Properties* or *Printer Properties* window.

Overview of the Windows Boot Process

When a computer boots and after executing the power-on self-test, the computer looks for an operating system. The Windows operating system can be loaded using several boot methods, and you might have to use an alternative boot method to solve a problem. Here are the most common boot methods, but remember that the boot order set within BIOS/UEFI affects which methods the operating system looks for first, second, and so on:

- An **internal hard drive partition** on an **internal fixed disk** that could be a hard disk drive (HDD), solid-state drive (SSD), or M.2 SSD. Note that the partition must be a bootable partition.
- An **optical disc** such as a CD, DVD, or Blu-ray disc. Note that this will work only if the BIOS/UEFI boot option is configured correctly and listed before a hard drive.
- An **external hard drive** such as a USB or eSATA drive. Check BIOS/UEFI boot options.
- **Network boot**, sometimes called pre-boot execution environment (**PXE**) boot, where the system boots from an image shared on the network from a server. Configure BIOS/UEFI for the appropriate setting, which might be listed as PXE, PXE Boot, Boot to Network, or LAN Boot ROM Enabled, as well as the network boot option, which might be placed before any of the other options.
- Internet-based booting, which is similar to network booting except that the image is retrieved from the internet.

The **system volume** is the active drive partition that has the files needed to load the operating system. The **boot volume** is the partition or logical drive where the operating system files are located. One thing that people sometimes forget is that the system volume and the boot volume can be on the same partition. These partitions are where certain boot files are located.

Every operating system needs specific files that allow the computer to boot. These files are known as **system files**, or startup files. Windows goes through four basic phases to get started:

1. *Preboot*: BIOS/UEFI controls the process of looking for, finding, and allowing an operating system to load.
2. *Windows boot manager* (`bootmgr.exe`): Windows locates and executes the Windows loader (`winload.exe`) from the boot partition/volume.
3. *Windows operating system loader*: Some drivers that are needed by the Windows kernel are loaded.
4. *Windows OS kernel* (`ntoskrnl.exe`): More drivers are loaded, services start, group and local policies are applied, and the logon screen is shown.

Table 16.14 shows the system files and their specific locations on the hard drive.

The Windows installation media usually contains drivers for the most common types of hardware. Some devices (such RAID controllers) require specialized drivers that are not included on the media. During the installation process, the system prompts the user to supply the required drivers. Alternatively, the location of the drivers must be included in an automated installation process.

TABLE 16.14 Windows system files

Startup filename	File location
`bootmgr.exe`	Root directory of system partition
`hal.dll`	`%systemroot%\System32*`
`ntoskrnl.exe`	`%systemroot%\System32*`
`winload.exe`	`%systemroot%\System32*`
`winresume.exe`	Root directory of system partition
`bcd` (boot configuration data)	`%systemroot%\Boot`
`system` (registry file)	`%systemroot%\System32\Config\System`
`winlogon.exe`	`%systemroot%\System32`

* `%systemroot%` is the boot partition and the name of the folder where Windows is installed (normally `C:\Winnt` or `C:\Windows`).

Reading about Windows files can be confusing because the file locations frequently have the entries `%systemroot%` and `%systemdrive%`. This is because computers can be partitioned differently. If you install Windows onto a drive letter (a partition or logical drive) other than the active partition (normally `C:`), the startup files can be on two different drive letters. Also, you do not have to use the default folder name *Windows* to install Windows. To account for these different scenarios, Microsoft uses `%systemroot%` to represent the **boot partition**—the partition and folder that contains the majority of the Windows files. `%systemdrive%` represents the root directory. On a computer with a single operating system, this would be `C:\`.

If a computer shows *Invalid Boot Disk*, ensure that the BIOS/UEFI boot order settings are correct, ensure that no virus is installed, and make sure the first boot device has a valid installed operating system or has a valid installation image. Depending on the installed version, you can also use `bootrec /fixmbr` or `bootrec /fixboot`. Use other `bootrec` command options if multiple operating systems are installed. Following is a breakdown of the commands you should try after using the Startup Repair option:

> `bootrec /fixmbr`*:* Used to resolve MBR issues; writes a Windows-compatible MBR to the system partition.

> `bootrec /fixboot`*:* Used if the boot sector has been replaced with a non-Windows boot sector, if the boot sector has become corrupt, or if an earlier Windows version has been installed *after* Windows was installed and the computer was started with `ntldr` instead of `bootmgr.exe`.

> `bootrec /scanos`*:* Used when any Windows operating system has been installed and is not listed on the Boot Manager menu; scans all disks for any and all versions of Windows.

System Restore

Any hardware or software installation can cause a system not to boot or to operate correctly. You can use the System Restore utility to return the system to an operable state so that you can try the installation again or determine a better method. The System Restore program makes a snapshot image of the registry and backs up certain dynamic system files. The program does not affect your email or personal data files. Each snapshot is called a *restore point*, and multiple restore points can be created on a computer; when restoring the machine, you can select which one to use.

System Restore requires the NTFS file system. Windows uses **Shadow Copy** technology, which employs a block-level image instead of monitoring certain files for file changes. Backup media can be optical discs, flash devices, other hard drives, and server storage (but not tape).

In Windows 10/11, System Restore is disabled by default. The **Settings > System > About > System protection** link is used to set up and configure System Restore, manage restore points, and manage the amount of disk space used for System Restore. You can manually create a restore point at any time. It is a good idea to create a restore point before performing an important upgrade or installation. A fixed amount of disk space is used for restore points. When a new restore point is created, the oldest one is removed automatically. System Restore is your number-one tool for solving problems within the operating system and registry.

To verify whether System Restore is on or not, use the following steps:

Step 1. Access the *Settings > System > About > System protection* link. The *System Protection* tab of the *System Properties* window opens.

Step 2. Look in the *Protection Settings* section to see if the system drive (`C:`) shows *On* in the *Protection* column.

If System Restore is turned off, you can use the following steps to turn it on:

Step 1. Access the *Settings > System > About > System protection* link. The *System Protection* tab of the *System Properties* window will open.

Step 2. In the *Protection Settings* section, locate and select the system drive (`C:`).

Step 3. Click *Configure* > enable the *Turn on system protection* radio button > set the amount of disk space to be used > *OK*.

Windows Recovery Environment (WinRE)

Windows Recovery Environment (**WinRE**) is used when Windows 10 does not boot and other tools and startup options do not solve a problem. Figure 16.41 shows the initial screen of Windows Recovery Environment. WinRE has a list of recovery options, including a command prompt–only environment. The WinRE environment provides access to tools to troubleshoot the operating system when the tools within the operating system cannot be accessed or don't work properly. The tools are stored on a special recovery partition when the operating system is installed. Some of the troubleshooting options mentioned in this section are available in WinRE. You can launch WinRE via a variety of means:

Option 1. At the login screen, press and hold the Shift key > click the *Power* icon > *Restart.*

Option 2. While logged into Windows, do either of the following:

- **a.** Access *Settings > Update & Security (System* in Windows 11) > *Recovery* > locate the *Advanced Startup* section and click the *Restart now* button.
- **b.** Click *Start* button > press and hold the Shift key > click *Restart.*

Option 3. If you can't get to the login screen or to the desktop, boot from the original Windows installation media, select *Repair your computer.*

Option 4. There also two command-line methods (which must be used by an Administrator account):

```
> reagentc /boottore
> shutdown /r /o
```

Table 16.15 summarizes the initial WinRE options.

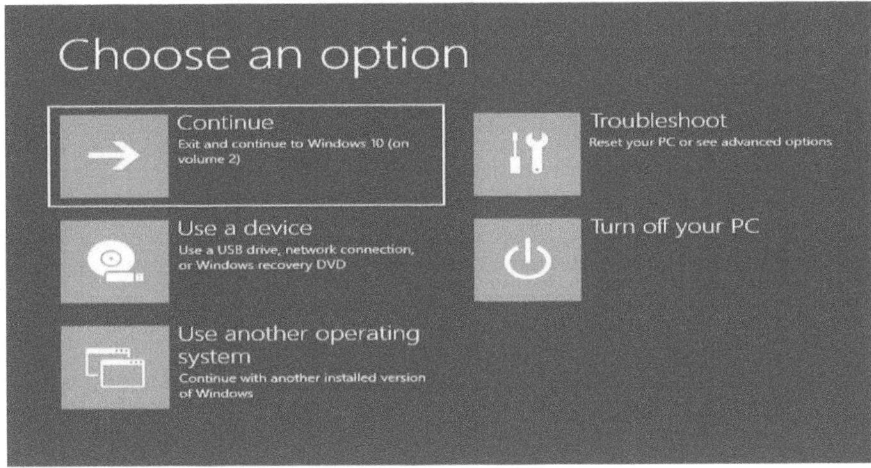

FIGURE 16.41 Windows Recovery Environment

TABLE 16.15 WinRE initial options

Option	Description
Continue	This option exits WinRE and attempts to boot the computer as normal.
Use a device	This option allows you to boot from another device, such as a USB drive, an optical disc, or a network share. You can then use tools from the external device to troubleshoot or repair the computer.
Use another operating system	This option appears if more than one operating system is installed on the hard drive (dual booting, not virtualization).
Troubleshoot	This option opens another screen that gives you options to reset the PC or launch advanced options.
Turn off your PC	This option shuts down the computer.

As mentioned in Table 16.15, the Troubleshoot option allows you to reset the PC or launch advanced options:

- Resetting the PC reinstalls Windows and gives you the choice of whether to keep the user files, remove everything, or, on some computers, restore to factory settings (including Windows and the apps that came with the computer when you bought it).
- The advanced options are the primary tools used to troubleshoot, repair, and recover a Windows installation, including a command prompt. You must be careful when using these tools because you can permanently misconfigure, delete, or overwrite important files (the operating system, applications, user documents, drivers, and so on). Some of the Windows 10 advanced options are shown in Figure 16.42 and explained in Table 16.16. Note that *UEFI Firmware Settings* appears only if the motherboard uses UEFI (not legacy BIOS) and the disks use the GPT partitioning style. The other tools available vary by Windows edition and PC manufacturer.

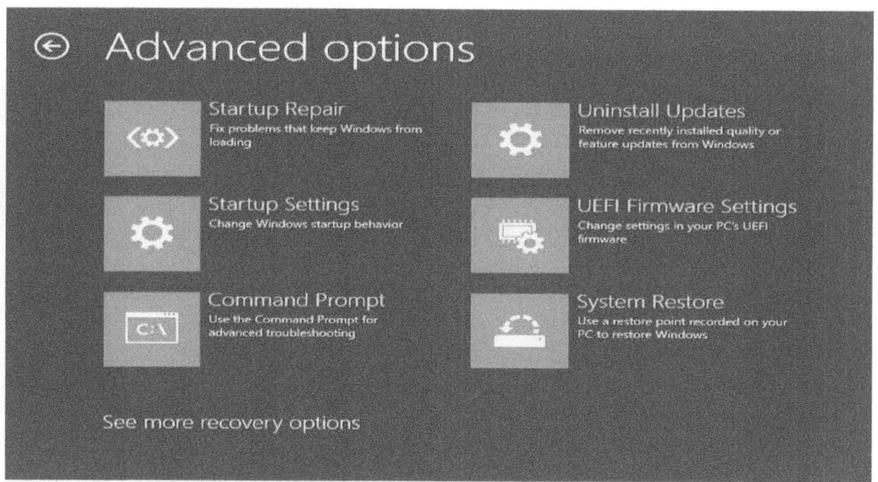

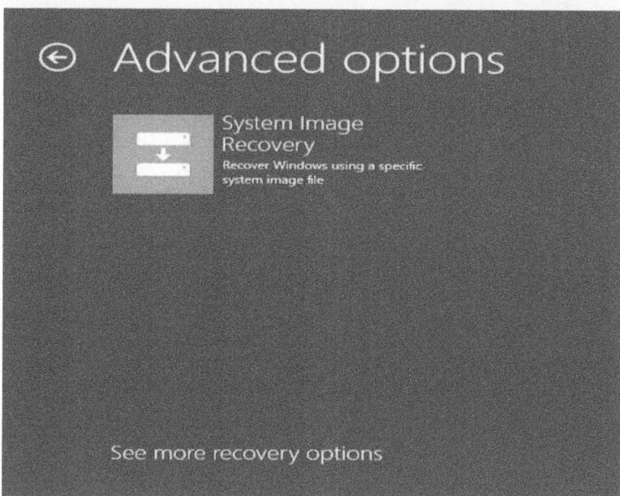

FIGURE 16.42 Windows 10 Advanced Options tools, first screen (top) and second screen (bottom)

TABLE 16.16 *WinRE > Troubleshoot > Advanced Options* **tools**

Tool	Description
Startup Repair	Startup Repair analyzes a computer and tries to fix any missing or damaged system files or Boot Configuration Data (BCD) files. This tool can be run multiple times. After a single repair and system reboot, try the tool again (and again). The system could have multiple problems.
Startup Settings	This option eventually takes you to the *Startup Settings* menu, a non-GUI menu that includes options like Safe Mode, Low-Resolution Video, and Disable Driver Signature Enforcement.
Command Prompt	This option allows execution of any command-line program.
Uninstall Updates	This option makes it possible to uninstall the latest quality update or the latest feature update. Use this option if you suspect that an update is preventing the computer from booting.
UEFI Firmware Settings	This option launches the motherboard's UEFI configuration system. This option is useful if you don't have time to press the designated UEFI hotkey while the computer is starting up, especially when booting from an SSD.

Tool	Description
System Restore	This option returns the system to an earlier time, such as before a service pack or update was installed and the system stopped booting.
System Image Recovery	This option is available in all versions of Windows 10 and higher to restore the contents of the hard drive from some type of backup media, such as another hard drive or DVDs.

Startup Settings Menu

When Windows does not boot properly, you can use the Windows **Advanced Boot Options** menu to select special modes to diagnose the issue. The menu is accessible via *WinRE* > *Troubleshoot* > *Advanced Options* > *Startup Settings* > *Restart*. The Advanced Boot Options menu appears when the computer reboots. Table 16.17 briefly describes these options. Note that the options available vary depending on the version of Windows used.

TECH TIP

Press F8 during startup

When Windows is booting, press F8 to access the Windows Advanced Boot Options menu. Note that this feature is disabled by default in Windows 10/11. To enable it, run this command from an elevated command prompt: **`bcdedit /set {default} bootmenupolicy legacy`**. Disabling the feature speeds up the boot process. To disable it, run this command from an elevated command prompt: **`bcdedit /set {default} bootmenupolicy standard`**.

TABLE 16.17 Windows Advanced Boot Options window

Boot option	Description
Repair Your Computer	This option launches WinRE if system recovery tools are installed on the hard disk. Otherwise, these tools are available when booting from the Windows installation media.
Safe Mode	This option uses a minimal set of drivers and services to start Windows; it is a commonly used option.
Safe Mode with Networking	This option is the same as Safe Mode but includes a NIC driver.
Safe Mode with Command Prompt	This option is the same as Safe Mode except that Windows Explorer (GUI mode) is not used; instead, a command prompt appears. This option is not used often.
Enable Boot Logging	This option enables logging for startup options. The logging file is `ntbtlog.txt`.
Enable Low-Resolution Video (640×480)	This option is used when Safe Mode does not work and you suspect that the default video driver is not working.
Debugging Mode	This option enables debugging information to be sent through the serial port to another computer running a debugger program. This option is not used often.

Boot option	Description
Disable Automatic Restart on System Failure	This option prevents Windows from automatically rebooting after a system crash.
Disable Driver Signature Enforcement	This option allows drivers that are not properly signed to load during startup.
Disable Early Launch Anti-malware Driver	This option disables anti-malware protection for booting. Sometimes driver files might be flagged as malware, causing the system not to boot; disable this feature to boot the system to fix it.
Start Windows Normally	This option restarts Windows and attempts to boot normally.

Safe Mode enables you to access configuration files and make necessary changes, troubleshoot installed software and hardware, disable software and services, and adjust hardware and software settings that may be causing problems. In other words, Safe Mode puts the computer in a "bare-bones" mode so that you can troubleshoot problems. As it is a reduced environment, most applications will not work in Safe Mode.

System Configuration Utility

The **System Configuration utility** (`msconfig.exe`) is used to troubleshoot Windows startup problems by disabling startup programs and services one at a time or several at once. This graphical utility reduces the chances of typing errors, file deletions, and other misfortunes that occur when technicians work from a command prompt. Only an administrator or a member of the Administrators group can use the System Configuration utility.

To start the System Configuration utility, type **`msconfig`** in the search textbox.

The first System Configuration utility tab is *General* (see Figure 16.43). The *General* tab has three radio buttons: Normal Startup, Diagnostic Startup, and Selective Startup. *Normal Startup* is the default option, and all device drivers and services load normally when this radio button is selected. Select the *Diagnostic Startup* radio button when you want to create a clean environment for troubleshooting. When *Diagnostic Startup* is chosen and Windows is restarted, the system boots to Safe Mode, and only the most basic device drivers and services are active.

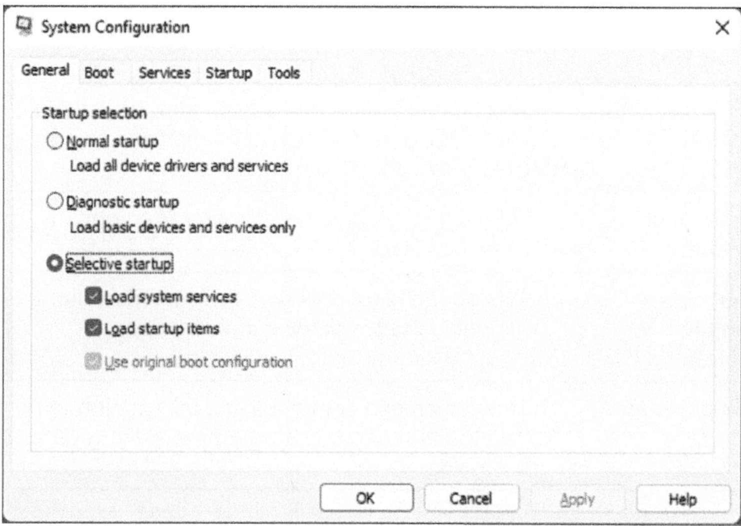

FIGURE 16.43 System Configuration utility: *General* tab

The *Selective Startup* radio button is the most commonly used troubleshooting option on the General tab. When you choose *Selective Startup*, you can pick which startup options load. Use the divide-and-conquer method of troubleshooting to find the startup file that is causing boot problems. Start with the first checkbox, *Load System Services*: Deselect it > *OK* and restart the computer. When you determine which file is causing the problem (that is, when the problem reappears), select the System Configuration utility tab that corresponds to the problem file and deselect files until the exact problem file is located.

TECH TIP

File fails to open

If a file does not open, check the System Configuration utility to verify if *Selective Startup* is used and a file has been left unchecked. Otherwise, ensure that the application is still installed and other files from this application open properly. Finally, change folder options so that extensions can be seen and verify that the file's extension has not been altered.

The *Boot* tab of the System Configuration utility (see Figure 16.44) enables you to control and modify the Windows boot environment. The functions available on this tab include selecting the default operating system and the time allotted to wait for the default operating system to load if no other operating system is chosen from the boot menu in a multiple–operating system situation. Notice that **Safe Boot** and other options are available at the bottom of the window. Table 16.18 describes the *Safe Boot* options on the *Boot* tab.

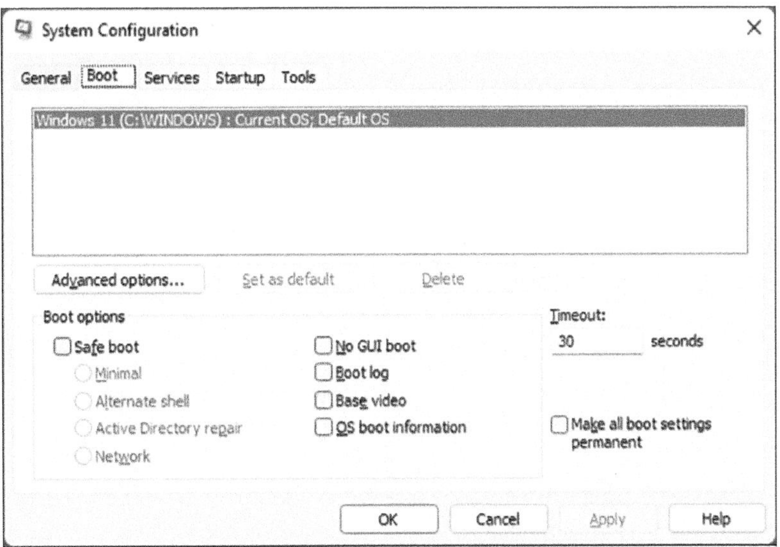

FIGURE 16.44 System Configuration utility: *Boot* tab

TABLE 16.18 *System Configuration Boot* tab > *Safe Boot options*

Safe Boot option	Description
Minimal	Boots in Safe Mode with only critical system services operational (no networking)
Alternate Shell	Boots into a command prompt without a GUI or networking
Active Directory Repair	Boots into Safe Mode, running critical system services and Active Directory
Network	Boots in Safe Mode GUI with networking enabled

Safe Boot option	Description
No GUI	Does not display the Windows welcome screen
Boot Log	Stores information about the startup process in the `ntbtlog.txt` file
Base Video	Starts in low-resolution VGA mode
OS Boot Information	Displays driver names during the boot process
Timeout	Controls how long the boot menu shows before the default boot entry executes

TECH TIP

Computer boots into Safe Mode for no obvious reason

Check the *System Configuration* utility *Boot* tab to see if some form of *Safe Boot* is enabled.

Click the *Advanced Options* button on the *Boot* tab to define the number of processors and maximum memory used to boot the system if you want fewer than the maximum (see Figure 16.45). When the *PCI Lock* option is enabled, it prevents Windows from changing I/O and IRQ assignments from those set by the system BIOS/UEFI.

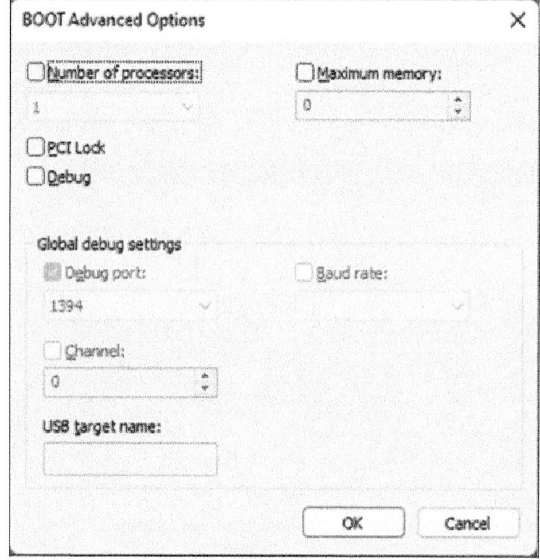

FIGURE 16.45 Windows System Configuration utility: *BOOT Advanced Options*

The *Services* and *Startup* tabs in the System Configuration utility window are also quite useful when troubleshooting boot problems. Certain applications, such as an antivirus program or printer software, run as services, meaning they run in the background and usually do not require user interaction. Many of these services are started during the boot process. Use the *Services* tab (see Figure 16.46) to disable and enable these boot services. Enable the *Hide All Microsoft Services* option to view and manipulate third-party (non-Microsoft) services.

Prior to Windows 8, the *Startup* tab allowed you to enable and **disable Windows applications** that start automatically when Windows boots. This function is now available in the *Startup* tab of Task Manager. When you click *Startup* in the System Configuration utility, you can click *Open Task Manager* to reach the startup settings (see Figure 16.47). Task Manager is covered in the next section.

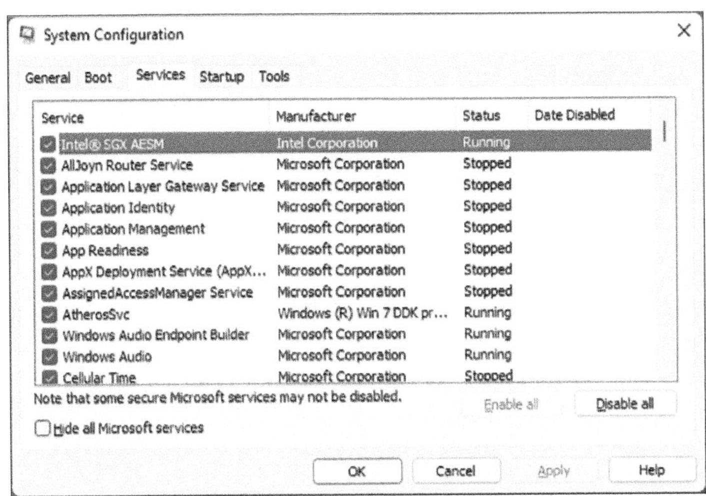

FIGURE 16.46 Windows System Configuration utility: *Services* tab

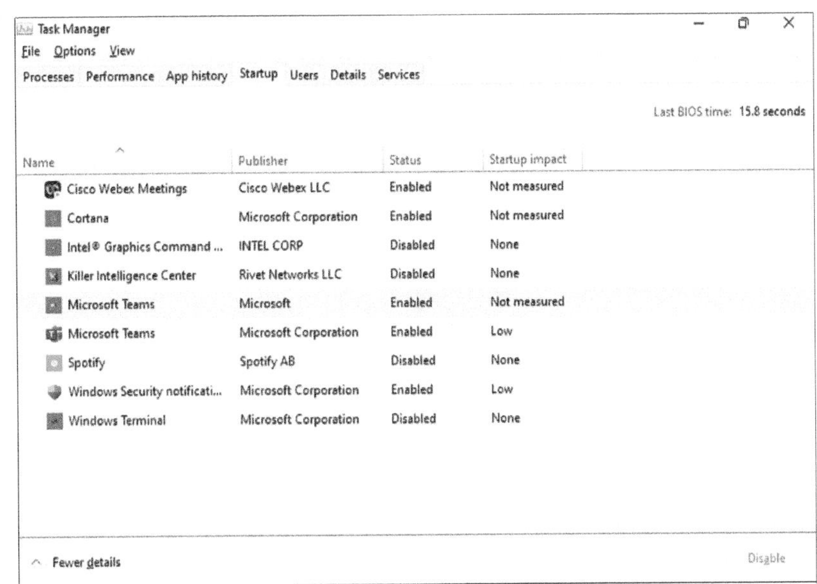

FIGURE 16.47 Windows System Configuration utility: *Startup* tab (top); Windows Task Manager: *Startup* tab (bottom)

TECH TIP

The *Tools* tab is useful

The System Configuration utility *Tools* tab allows you to launch options—such as Task Manager, Performance Monitor, and Internet Options from Internet Explorer—that might need to be changed as a result of a startup issue.

The System Configuration *Tools* tab allows you to launch the majority of the Windows utilities, such as Task Manager, About Windows, Computer Management, System Information, Event Viewer, Programs, Performance Monitor, Registry Editor, System Restore, Command Prompt, and so on, as shown in Figure 16.48.

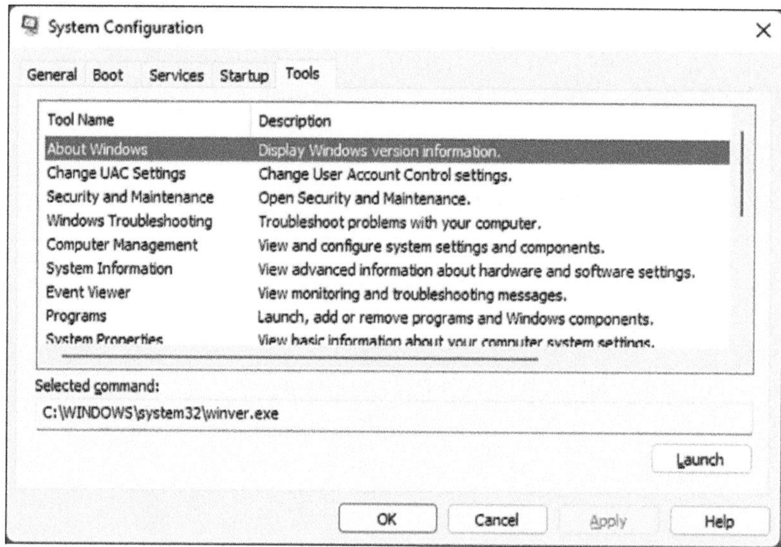

FIGURE 16.48 Windows System Configuration utility: *Tools* tab

Task Manager

Task Manager is a Windows-based utility that displays applications that are currently loaded into memory, processes that are currently running, processor usage, and memory details. To activate Task Manager, right-click or tap and briefly hold an empty spot on the taskbar and select *Task Manager*. Task Manager is commonly used when an **application crashes**. Access Task Manager to **kill task** (stop) one or more programs that have stopped responding. Using Task Manager is also a great way to get a graphical overview of how the system performs or which programs use a lot of memory. Windows Task Manager has the following tabs: Processes, Performance, App History, Startup, Users, Details, and Services.

Figure 16.49 shows the Task Manager *Processes* tab, which lists the applications currently running on a computer. Notice in the figure that there is a green leaf by two of the apps. If you went over to the *Details* tab, you would see that the applications that have the green leaf beside them would show the status *suspended.* Suspended apps are apps that are running as background apps; for example, if you have the Calculator app minimized and haven't used it in a while, the app is suspended. A suspended app isn't using a lot of system resources.

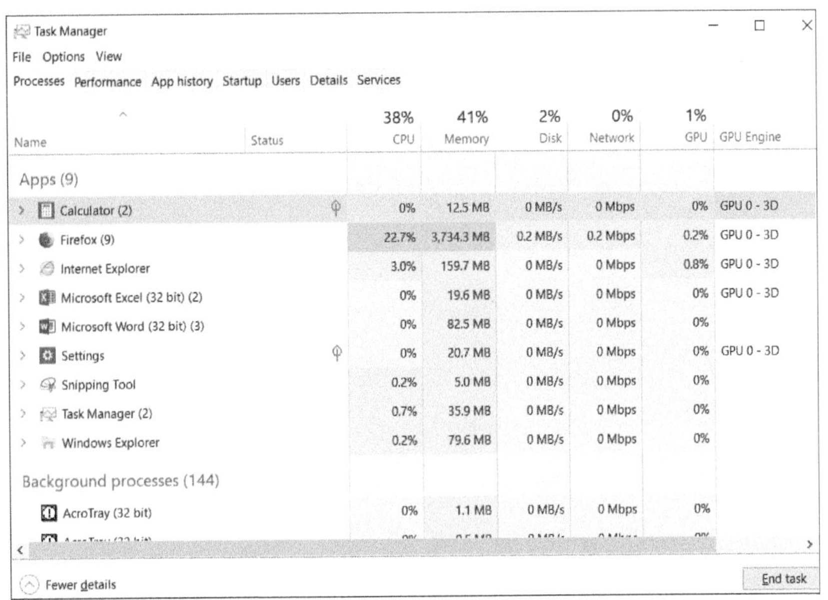

FIGURE 16.49 Windows Task Manager: *Processes* tab

Notice in Figure 16.49 that the Calculator app has a green leaf next to it. You can highlight an app and then click the *End task* button to stop an application.

> **TECH TIP**
>
> **Task Manager tabs are missing**
>
> If Task Manager is missing the menu bar and tabs, it is in Tiny Footprint mode. Double-click an empty space in the top border to make the menu and tabs reappear.

The Task Manager *Performance tab* (see Figure 16.50) shows performance indicators for key computer components, including the CPU, disk, Ethernet and Wi-Fi for network connectivity, Bluetooth, and GPU. When a user complains about a computer being slow, this is one of the first places for a technician to look.

The Task Manager *App history* tab shows resource usage for individual applications, including CPU time, network utilization, metered network utilization, and the amount of network utilization for any live tile updates. This is helpful with mobile devices to identify which applications are using resources so that you can disable them to conserve battery power.

The Task Manager *Startup* tab is used to see any app that executes as part of the Windows startup routine. If the tab is missing, select the *More details* option. The *Startup impact* column lets a technician know how much the application impacts the startup time. By right-clicking on a particular application, you can disable, enable, view properties, and open the `.exe` file or script file location.

> **TECH TIP**
>
> **Windows 10/11: Start an application during startup**
>
> In Windows 10/11, you can use the *Settings > Apps > Startup* option to turn on any app that you would like to start automatically as part of the Windows boot process.

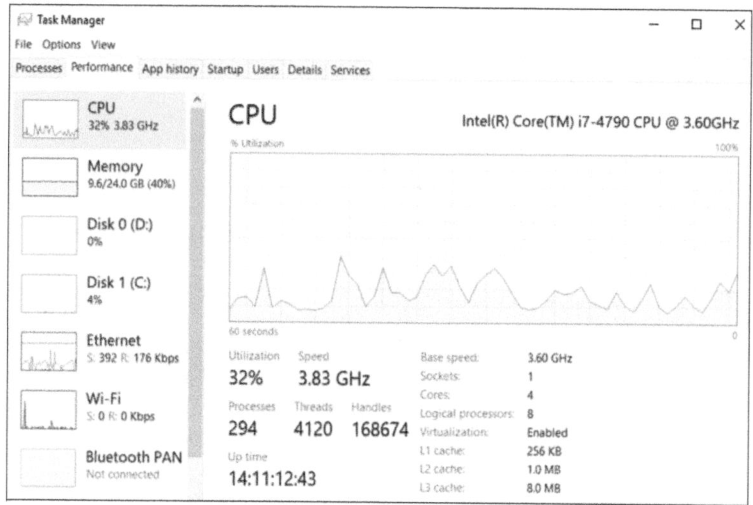

FIGURE 16.50 Windows Task Manager: *Performance* tab

The Task Manager *Users* tab shows which users are logged on. You can also use this tab to disconnect another user who is logged on, such as when a work cubicle is shared by two people and the other person forgot to log out. The *Users* tab shows what resources that particular user is using in a table format.

The Task Manager *Details* tab shows more information on the processes that are running. Note that the processes that appear here may not be shown in the *Processes* tab or *Performance* tab. The process ID (PID) is also shown here.

The Task Manager *Services* tab is a handy place to see what services are currently running or stopped. You can also start, stop, and restart services from this tab. Note that not all services are shown here, and services cannot be fully configured here. The *Open Services* link provides access to *Services*, where you can see services that were started but that have a delayed start startup type, as well as a list of all services available on the computer.

TECH TIP

What to do if a system appears to lock up or is slow

If a system appears to lock up or is slow, allow the system time to try to respond. If you get no response, access Task Manager by pressing Ctrl+Alt+Del. Keep in mind that it might take a bit of time for Task Manager to open. Access the *Processes* tab > locate and select the troublesome application > *End task* button. Normally, if an application is causing a problem, the status shows the application as "not responding." If Task Manager never appears, power down the computer and reboot.

Speeding Up the Windows Boot Process

Windows can seem to take forever to boot (especially if you do not have an SSD), but there are things a technical person can do to help speed up the OS boot process (see Figure 16.51).

FIGURE 16.51 Fine-tuning the startup process

The following tips can help reduce the time it takes Windows to become operational:

> Configure BIOS/UEFI boot options so that the drive used to boot Windows is listed as the first option.
> Configure BIOS/UEFI for the fast boot option or disable hardware checks.
> Enable *Turn on fast startup* in *Power Options > Define power buttons > Choose what the power buttons do*. See the section "Power Options," later in this chapter.
> If multiple operating systems are installed, use the `msconfig` utility *Boot* tab to reduce the boot menu timeout value.
> Remove unnecessary startup applications by using the `msconfig` utility. Use the *Startup* tab in *Device Manager.*
> Ensure that you have hard disk space available and keep the drive defragmented. Note that Windows is automatically configured to defragment the hard drive at 1:00 a.m. on Wednesday. If the computer is powered off at that time, defragmentation occurs when the computer next boots.
> Disable unused or unnecessary hardware by using Device Manager.
> Use Windows **ReadyBoost** to cache some startup files to a 256 MB+ flash drive, SD card, or CF card. Right-click the storage device to access the *Properties* option and select the *ReadyBoost* tab. Note that ReadyBoost does not increase performance on a system that boots from an SSD, so Windows disables ReadyBoost as an option when an SSD is in use.
> Use the *Administrative Tools* Control Panel > access *Services*. Change services that are not needed the moment Windows boots to use the *Automatic (Delayed Start)* option instead of *Automatic*.

Troubleshooting the Windows Boot Process

Troubleshooting the boot process when Windows will not load (**failure to boot**) is sometimes easier than troubleshooting other types of problems that can occur within the operating system. You can try several tools but keep in mind that you may need to reload the operating system.

TECH TIP

Troubleshooting, repair, and recovery

There is risk associated with all troubleshooting, repair, and recovery options. Therefore, you should be sure to back up any critical files, software, drivers, and operating system installation media.

If a computer locks, has a BSOD, becomes unstable, or will not start, try the following:

> If Windows fails to load the login prompt two consecutive times, it automatically runs Automatic Repair on the third boot attempt. Automatic Repair gives you two options: (1) Restart the system immediately (which might fix the problem) or (2) enter the Windows Recovery Environment.
> Check the BIOS/UEFI setting to ensure that the boot order is correct.
> Remove the power cord and leave the computer powered down for one to two minutes. Then re-insert the power cord and power on the computer again. Make note of any beeps or error codes. Use these symptoms to start your troubleshooting process.
> Determine the last thing that was done before the computer refused to boot. If possible, boot the computer to Safe Mode. Use the System Restore utility to bring the computer back to a date before the issue occurred. The following are some questions to ask the user:
  > Did a Windows Update just occur?
  > Was an application recently installed?
  > Was any hardware added recently?
  > Did any type of application update just occur?
> Examine the list of startup items. Use the *Startup* tab in *Device Manager* to remove unfamiliar or unexpected entries.
> Disconnect any unnecessary peripherals from the computer, leaving just the power and monitor connected. If the computer starts, connect peripherals one by one while restarting to see which item is causing a boot to fail.
> Boot to Safe Mode and run the System File Checker (`sfc`) to replace missing or corrupt operating system files or load an appropriate graphics driver.
> Use the **Reset this PC** option, which reinstalls Windows and gives you the choice of whether you keep the files, remove everything, or, on some computers, restore to factory settings (including Windows and the apps that came with the computer when you bought it).
> Use the *System Image Recovery* option that is available in the Windows Recovery Environment. This option reloads a specific Windows image file. If the image is loaded onto the same volume as an existing Windows installation, all files (operating system, software installations, drivers, user documents, and so on) are deleted.

Quite a few things can cause Windows to fail to boot into the graphical interface properly. For example, a nonbootable disk listed as the first boot device or nonbootable media inserted into an optical drive (and listed as a boot device) can cause Windows not to boot. If none of the hard drives contains an active partition or if the hard drive's boot sector information is missing or corrupt, any of the following messages or events could appear:

> *Invalid Partition Table*
> *Error Loading Operating System*
> *Missing Operating System*
> `BOOTMGR` *Is Missing*
> *Windows Has Blocked Some Startup Programs*
> *The Windows Boot Configuration Data File Is Missing Required Information*
> *No OS found*
> *Windows Could Not Start Because the Following File Is Missing or Corrupt*

Also, if you receive a message indicating that you have an invalid boot disk, a disk read error, or an inaccessible boot device, troubleshoot your hard drive and/or BIOS/UEFI settings.

TECH TIP

How to stop programs that automatically load at startup from running

To disable startup programs, go to *Task Manager* > *Startup* > select a program > click *Disable*. You can also go to *Settings* > *Apps* > *Startup*. Locate the program that you don't want to load at startup and slide the switch to *Off*.

If a startup problem occurs before the Starting Windows logo appears (**graphical interface fails to load**), the cause is typically missing startup files, corrupt files, or hardware problems. You can use the Windows command `bootsect /nt60 all` (or a drive letter instead of `all` if multiple operating systems are installed) to manually repair the boot sector. The `bootsect.exe` file is available from the *Boot* folder of the Windows installation media and can be executed from within WinRE, covered earlier in this chapter, or from within Windows.

If the Windows logo appears but there is a problem before the logon prompt appears, the problem is usually with misconfigured drivers and/or services. If problems occur after the logon window appears, then (1) investigate the startup applications or (2) see if the `userinit.exe` file has issues. Use the *Advanced Boot Options* startup menu, and from a command prompt, use the `sfc /scannow` command to fix the `userinit` file.

Black Screen/Video Issues

Windows is not supposed to hang during the boot process because of video driver incompatibility. Instead, the operating system loads a default video driver. If video is a problem while working in Windows (that is, if you get a **black screen** or a blank screen), check your video power and cabling and try booting to Safe Mode or restoring a restore point and then load the correct driver. You could also perform a driver rollback if a new driver has just been installed.

To save time booting into Safe Mode, you could use the *System Configuration* (`msconfig`) tool > *Boot* tab > enable the *Base Video* checkbox > *OK* (see Figure 16.52).

FIGURE 16.52 *System Configuration* > *Boot* tab

If multiple monitors are installed, another option is to verify that each monitor has power and the data cable attaches securely. Check the monitor settings to verify that the monitor detection is accurate. In Windows 10, use the *Settings* > *System* > *Display* link. You can also right-click on an empty space on the Desktop and click *Display settings*.

CHAPTER 16

TECH TIP

Display is dark

If the display is dark, check to see whether the computer is in sleep mode or won't come out of sleep mode. Check the video cable. Hold down the power button and try restarting. Check the power management settings.

TECH TIP

BSOD after a Windows update

Always research the error code associated with a failed update. Windows updates include device driver updates. If the computer fails to boot after a Windows update, reboot the computer to WinRE Safe Mode and use the System Restore tool to restore the registry to an earlier time so that the problem can be researched. If multiple updates were installed, try loading the updates one at a time.

Use System Restore if you suspect that the registry is corrupt. For example, if an application worked fine yesterday but today displays a message that the application cannot be found, you may have a virus, a corrupt application executable file, or a corrupt registry. Run an antivirus check first with updated virus definitions. If free of viruses, use the System Restore utility to roll back the system to yesterday or the day before this problem occurred. Sometimes System Restore works best if executed from Safe Mode. If System Restore does not fix the problem, reinstall the application.

Access the window to configure System Restore via *Settings > System > About > System Protection* link > *System Protection* tab. Figure 16.53 shows how you can select a specific date during the System Restore process. You can also select the *Show more restore points* checkbox at the bottom of the window to see more restore points.

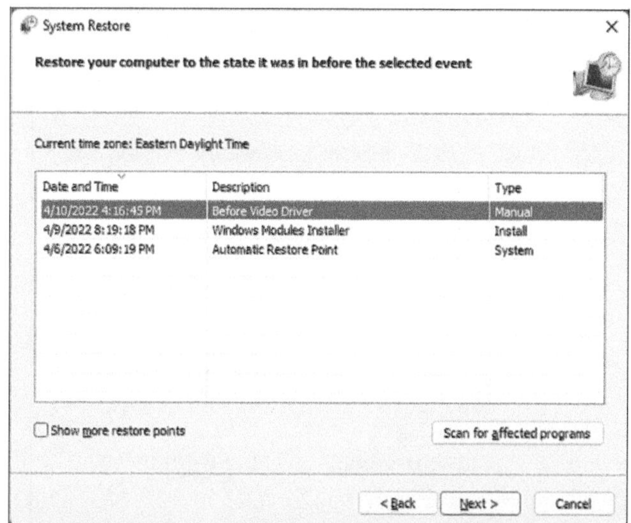

FIGURE 16.53 Windows System Restore

TECH TIP

You can run System Restore from a command prompt

If Windows does not load properly, you can execute System Restore from a command prompt with the command `%systemroot%\system32\rstrui.exe`.

Troubleshooting a Service That Does Not Start

Some Windows services start automatically each time the computer boots. If one of these services has a problem or if a particular **service fails to start**, normally an error message appears during the boot sequence. You can use the System Configuration utility (`msconfig`) discussed previously to enable and disable services or **restart services**. You can also use Event Viewer to see if the service loaded properly.

Another program that you can use is the Services snap-in. It can be used from the Computer Management tool, or, at a command prompt, type **`services.msc`** and press Enter. The *Services* tool allows you to fully configure and monitor the services, including what services have started and stopped and, if desired, enables you to **disable a service**. In the *Services* snap-in (see Figure 16.54), the services are listed in alphabetical order.

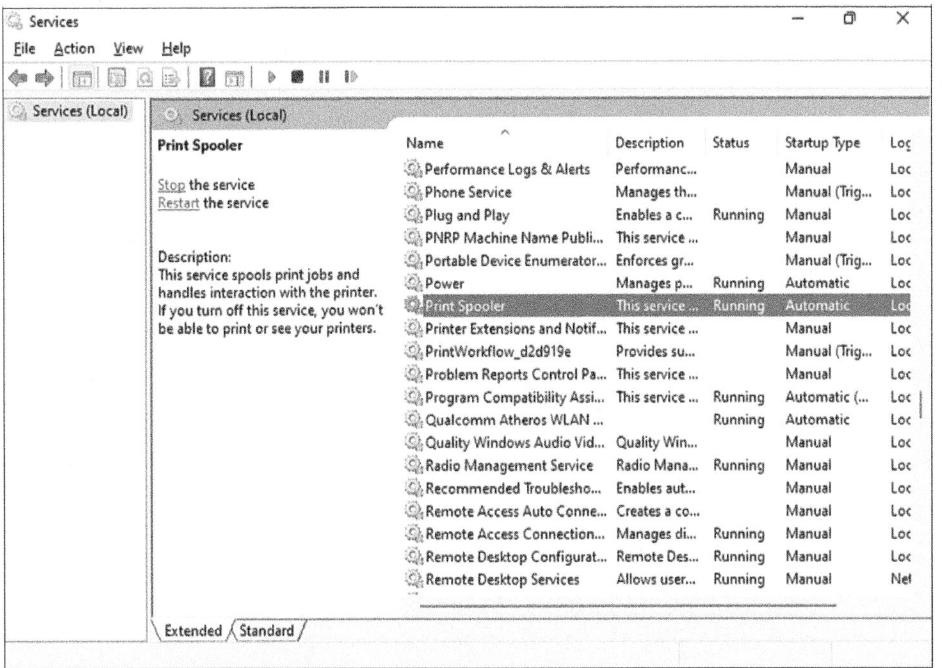

FIGURE 16.54 Windows Services

Double-click or double-tap any particular service to learn more about that service. Through the window that appears, as shown in Figure 16.55, you can control whether the service starts automatically, starts manually, or is disabled. Notice in Figure 16.55 that, because the Print Spooler service is already running, the only action that can be performed is to stop the service.

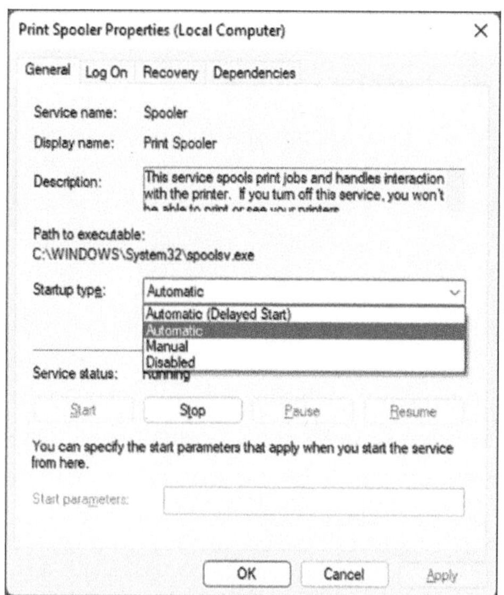

FIGURE 16.55 Controlling a Windows service

Slow Boot

Whenever the problem of a **slow boot** is reported to you, several issues could be the culprit. The operating system could be running slowly, the hard drive could be lacking free hard drive space, there might be too many startup applications or services running, or there might be too many startup login scripts. If you recently installed an app, restore the system from a system restore point. If you just received a Windows update or an application update, remove that update.

If you suspect that the operating system is the problem, use Safe Mode when the computer stalls, slows down, or does not work correctly or when there are problems caused by improper video, intermittent errors, or new hardware/software installation. Safe Mode can start Windows with minimal device drivers and services. Software that automatically loads during startup is disabled in Safe Mode, and user profiles are not loaded.

The other tools that are really helpful with a slow boot are the System Configuration utility and the *Services* Computer Management tool, which are both covered earlier in this chapter. In the System Configuration utility, use the *Startup* tab to determine which applications are having to load as part of the startup process. See if some of them can be disabled (unchecked). One application in particular might also be causing the slowness. With the *Services* Computer Management tool, look in the *Startup Type* column to see if any of the services that automatically start can be changed from *Automatic* to *Automatic (Delayed Start)*. To change any service, right-click on it > *Properties* > use the *Startup Type* drop-down menu.

You can also use the *Reset this PC* option and reinstall the operating system. If you have a recovery drive, you could use it to restore or reset the PC. Taking care of the problem as soon as you can and not letting it get worse is the best approach.

Slow Profile Load or Profile Problems

Companies make use of login scripts that run every time a user logs on to a computer. Such a script can reference a local profile, a domain profile, or both. (Profiles are covered in detail in Chapter 18.) A problem that might be reported to you as a slow boot problem may actually relate to a **slow profile load**. A large profile or multiple profiles (for example, a personal one, one that is part of a group, and/or a local one) can cause the user to have to wait a long time for the computer to execute.

The operating system might also display a message that the user profile cannot be loaded. The user profile could be corrupt; in this case, you have to **rebuild a Windows profile**. One way to fix this is to create a new account and copy the files from the old user account. Otherwise, you will have to make changes to the registry, as described in the following steps:

Step 1. Log in to the computer in Safe Mode with an account that has Administrator rights.

Step 2. From a command prompt, use the `set` command to look for `USERPROFILE=` to see the problematic user profile.

Step 3. Rename the folder associated with the user profile, such as `C:\Users\CSchmidt`, to something like `Cschmidt.old folder`.

Step 4. Look to see if a temporary profile was created in the `C:\Users\TEMP` folder. Delete the profile if there is one.

Step 5. Access the registry and export it to an external drive as a backup.

Step 6. Locate the key `Hkey_Local_Machine\Software\Microsoft\Windows NT|CurrentVersion\ProfileList`.

Step 7. Click on each SID key (folder) under `ProfileList` and find the `ProfileImage-Path` that matches the user that has the profile issue.

Step 8. Delete or rename the SID registry key with the matching path. For example, if the SID S-1-5-21-3423371916-2792405005-1110847961-1008 contains a `ProfileImage-Path` value `C:\Users\CSchmidt`, you delete that SID.

Step 9. Restart the computer and log in with the user profile that had the problem. You will have to copy the user's data from the `.old profile` folder.

Troubleshooting Windows Network Settings

Remember that most corporate devices connect to the wired or wireless network. (Troubleshooting network settings is covered in detail in Chapter 13, "Networking.") If a user cannot access the network, be sure to check the Windows network settings and keep in mind that you might have to **update network settings** to fix the problem. Check the following:

- For a wired network, confirm that the network cable is securely connected to the computer and the network jack. If the link lights on the computer don't come on, check the connections from the network jack to the switch and make sure the switch is working properly.
- If the device is a wireless one, see if the device is connected to the appropriate wireless network.
- Use the *Network and Sharing Center* to see if the network is connected to the internet.
- See if the device has the appropriate IP address, subnet mask, and default gateway. Remember that without a default gateway, the device cannot access any resource outside its own network (where most servers and connectivity are needed today). Use the `ipconfig` command to verify the IP address and default gateway.
- If the device has an IP address that starts with 169, use the `ipconfig /release` and `ipconfig /renew` commands to get a proper DHCP IP address.
- Another way to force the computer to request a new DHCP address is to configure the computer for static addressing and then switch to dynamic addressing. Use this procedure:
  1. Right-click on the wired or wireless NIC in the *Network Connections* section of the Control Panel > *Properties* > select *Internet Protocol Version 4 (TCP/IPv4)* > *Properties* > *Use the following IP address* radio button.

2. Input any IP address and mask > *OK* > *OK*.
3. Re-access the same TCP/IPv4 settings and enable the *Obtain an IP address automatically* radio button to receive IP address settings from a DHCP server > *OK* > *OK* (see Figure 16.56).
4. Use the **`ipconfig`** command to verify that the appropriate adapter received, at a minimum, an IP address, subnet mask, and default gateway, as shown in Figure 16.57.

> If the device is supposed to use static addressing, obtain the appropriate IP settings from the system administrator and use this procedure:

1. Right-click on the wired or wireless NIC in the *Network Connections* section of the Control Panel > *Properties* > select *Internet Protocol Version 4 (TCP/IPv4)* > *Properties* > *Use the following IP address* radio button.
2. Input the appropriate settings > *OK* > *OK*.
3. Use the **`ipconfig`** command to verify that the settings were applied to the appropriate adapter.

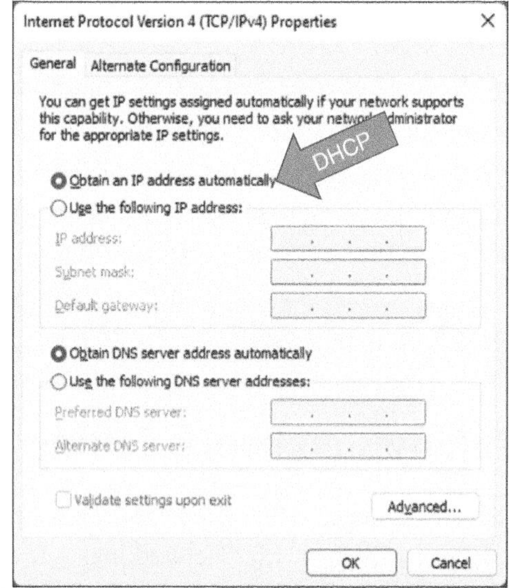

FIGURE 16.56 Configuring a Windows PC for DHCP services

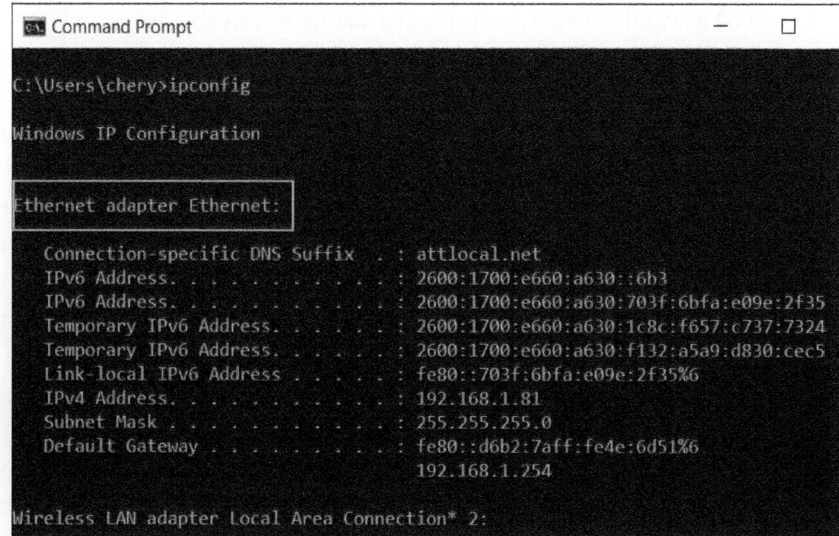

FIGURE 16.57 Verifying IP addressing information by using `ipconfig`

Windows Reboots/System Instability

Intermittent problems are some of the hardest problems to solve. When Windows reboots or shuts down unexpectedly, a lot of different things could be the cause. Spontaneous reboots could be caused by a newly installed Windows update, newly installed application, or newly updated driver. A corrupt device driver could also be the culprit, but that is hard to find. An internet search on your specific hardware device might speed up the troubleshooting process.

A spontaneous reboot can also be caused by a virus or malware. See Chapter 18 for more on those security issues. Other hardware issues could be the RAM, processor, video card, and hard drive. You can quickly see why the cause of spontaneous reboots is one of the hardest problems to narrow down.

However, spontaneous reboots are different from spontaneous shutdowns. Spontaneous shutdowns tend to be heat-related problems. Check the CPU and case fans. Some BIOS/UEFI menus have options that display internal temperatures. Start noting temperature readings. A failing CPU, overloaded power supply, or failing power supply could also cause a spontaneous shutdown.

Shutdown Problems

Windows should be shut down properly when all work is finished. Before Windows can shut down, the operating system sends a message to all devices, services, and applications. Each device or system service that is running sends back a message, saying it is okay to shut down now. Any active application saves data that has not been previously saved. If the application cannot save the data automatically, the user is given the opportunity to do so. After the data has been saved, the application sends a message back to the operating system indicating that it is okay to shut down.

If the system has trouble shutting down, it may be due to devices, services, or applications. The most common problem is an application that does not respond. When this happens, open Task Manager. Manually stop any applications that show a status of not responding. You may also click any other applications and stop them to see if they are causing the problem. Sometimes, a program does not show a status of not responding until you try to manually stop the application from within Task Manager. If a single application continually prevents Windows from shutting down, contact the software manufacturer to see if there is a fix or check online.

TECH TIP

Try the restart option instead of the shutdown option

If you cannot stop a problematic application or determine whether the problem is a service or hardware issue, try restarting the computer instead of shutting down. After the computer restarts, try shutting down again. As a last resort, use the computer power button to power off the computer. If even this does not work in a laptop, remove the battery (if possible).

For problems that deal with Windows services, boot the computer into Safe Mode and then shut down the computer. Notice whether the computer had any problems shutting down. If the process works, use the System Configuration window *General* tab *Selective Startup* radio button with the *Services* tab to selectively disable services. Because there are so many services loaded, you might try the divide-and-conquer method: Disable one-half of the services to narrow the list.

Devices do not frequently cause shutdown problems, so eliminate services and applications first. Then, while working on the computer, notice what devices you are using. Common devices are video, hard drive, optical drive, keyboard, and mouse. Access the Advanced Boot Options menu in *WinRE > Troubleshoot > Advanced options > Startup Settings* and select *Enable boot logging*. When the system boots, locate the `ntbtlog.txt` file in the Windows folder. You may have to set folder options in File Explorer to list the file and access it. Verify that all your devices have the most up-to-date drivers loaded and that the drivers are compatible with the installed version of Windows.

Sometimes USB or IEEE 1394 FireWire ports can stop a computer from shutting down or powering off. Check the event logs to see if any device did not enter a suspend state. A feature called *USB Selective Suspend* allows the Windows hub driver to suspend a particular USB port and not affect the other USB ports. This is particularly important with laptops, netbooks, and Ultrabooks because of power consumption. Suspending USB devices when a device is not in use conserves power. If USB device suspension is causing the problem, this default behavior can be modified using the *Power Options* section of the Control Panel link: click *Change plan settings* for the active plan > *Change advanced power settings* > *USB Settings* > *USB selective suspend setting* > *Disabled* > *OK*.

Summary of Troubleshooting Steps

The previous sections offer troubleshooting advice specific to a variety of topics. Use troubleshooting steps in the order listed below to minimize the impact on a system's operating system, configurations, applications, and data:

Step 1. Save and close any open applications.

Step 2. Verify hardware, OS, and application requirements. Add resources (RAM, disk space, upgraded hardware) as needed and when convenient to the user and overall operation.

Step 3. Confirm that a recent backup is available or create a new one.

Step 4. Run a system file check.

Step 5. Restart services.

Step 6. Reboot the system.

Step 7. Rebuild Windows profiles.

Step 8. Run appropriate troubleshooting wizards.

Step 9. Update, reinstall, or uninstall applications.

Step 10. Use System Restore to remove recent configuration changes and/or roll back updates in Windows Update.

Step 11. Reboot into Windows Recovery Console and run Startup Repair.

Step 12. Reimage the entire system using a backup image or do a clean install and then apply updates.

Power Options

Windows has three customizable power plans available. You can access the *Power Options* Control Panel via *Control Panel* > *System and Security* > *Power Options* (see Figure 16.58). Use the *Change plan settings* link followed by the *Change advanced power settings* link to expand a section, such as the *Multimedia Settings* option. There are three main power plans:

- *Balanced:* This is the most common plan. It provides full power when you need it and saves power when the computer is not being used.
- *Power Saver:* This plan saves power by running the CPU more slowly and reducing screen brightness.

> *High performance:* This plan provides the maximum performance possible, but the computer might consume more energy.

Additional plans might be available from the computer manufacturer. Depending on the version of Windows and the manufacturer, you might need to select the *Show additional plans* link.

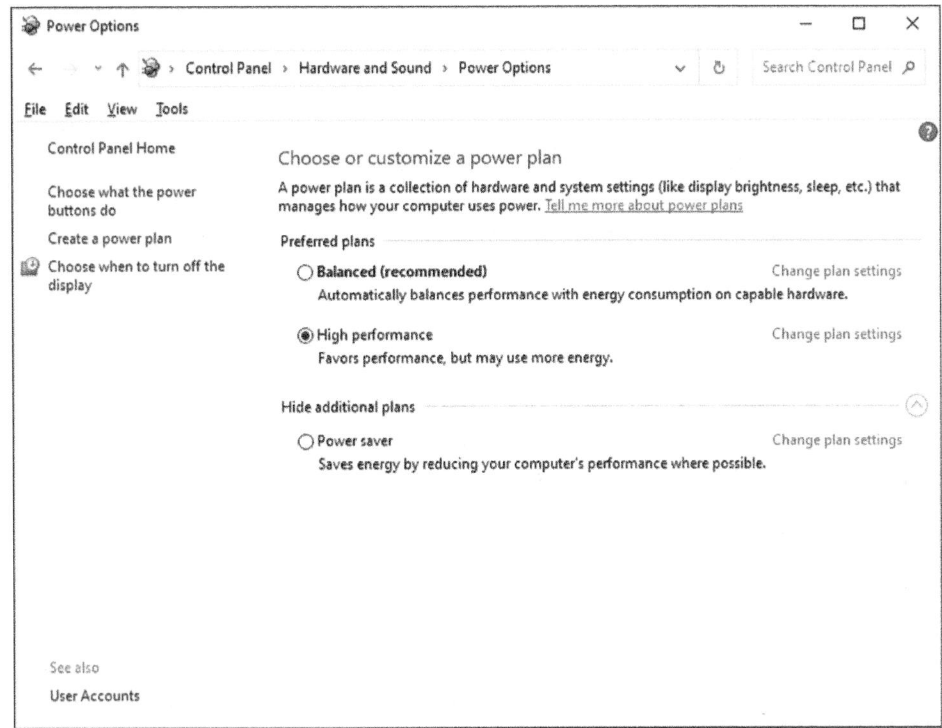

FIGURE 16.58 ***Power Options*** **section of the Control Panel in Windows 10**

The *Power Options* Control Panel also includes the *Choose what the power buttons do* option. As shown in Figure 16.59, you can control how the computer responds when the power and sleep buttons are pressed. Possible selections include *Do Nothing*, *Sleep* (maintain system state in RAM in a low power mode), *Hibernate* (save system state to hard drive and turn off computer), *Shut Down*, and *Turn off the display*.

When the computer enters hibernation, the contents of RAM are copied to the hiberfile (`hiberfil.sys`), and then the computer shuts down. When the computer is turned back on, `hiberfil.sys` is copied back into RAM, restoring the previous state. Note that the Hibernate option appears only if the motherboard supports hibernation. If the motherboard has this feature but Hibernate does not appear, run the command `powercfg /hibernate on` from an elevated command prompt and then open *Power Options* again.

Choose what the power buttons do > Turn on fast startup (recommended) can be used to speed up the boot process. It is available only if hibernation is enabled. During a normal startup, the boot loader copies sections of the Windows kernel from the hard drive into RAM and links them, and then it loads required drivers in memory. When fast startup is enabled, the system saves an image of the Windows kernel and loaded drivers to the hiberfile every time the computer is shut down. When the computer is turned back on, the kernel and drivers are loaded directly to RAM.

Laptop computers also have the *When I close the lid* option when you click *Choose what the power buttons do*. For example, if an external monitor is connected to a laptop, the computer can be configured to stay on when the lid is closed. Laptops also allow for separate settings based on power source (*On Battery* or *Plugged in*).

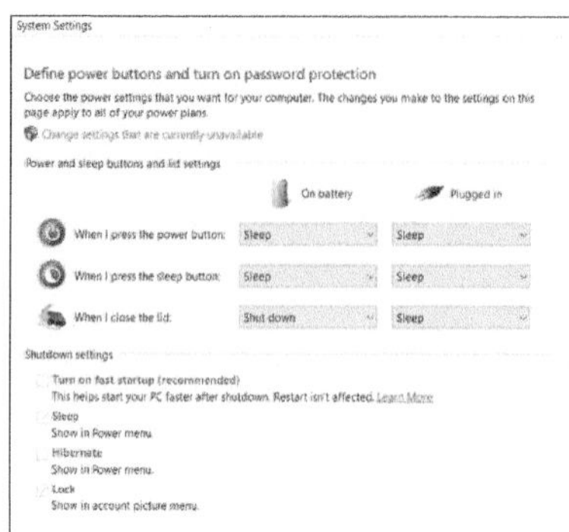

FIGURE 16.59 *Define power buttons* section of the Control Panel (laptop version)

Monitoring System Performance

It is important for a technician to understand how a computer is performing and to analyze why a computer might have **slow performance** (see Figure 16.60). A technician must know what applications are running on the computer and their effects on the computer resources. A technician must also monitor the computer's resource usage when problems occur, change the configuration as needed, and observe the results of configuration changes. Utilities commonly used to monitor system performance include Task Manager, Performance Logs and Alerts, Reliability Monitor, and Performance Monitor.

FIGURE 16.60 Slow performance

Sometimes computers seem sluggish. The most common causes of a slowdown are that the computer's resources are insufficient or an application is monopolizing a particular resource, such as memory. Other causes of slowdowns include a resource such as a hard drive not functioning properly or being outdated, a resource not being configured for maximum performance and needing to be adjusted, or resources such as hard drive space and memory not sharing workloads properly and needing adjustment.

Viewing system performance when a problem occurs is good, but it is easier to figure out what is happening if the normal performance is already known. A baseline can help with this. A

baseline is a snapshot of computer performance during normal operations (before the computer has problems). Task Manager can give you an idea of what normal performance is. The Windows Performance Monitor and Reliability Monitor tools are better suited to capturing and analyzing specific computer resource data.

TECH TIP

When do I need to do a baseline of a computer?

A baseline report is needed before a computer slowdown occurs.

Using Task Manager to Measure Performance

Although Task Manager is discussed earlier in this chapter, how to use it to monitor computer performance has not yet been discussed. Using Task Manager is the easiest and quickest way for anyone to quickly and visually see how a computer is performing. Access *Task Manager* and select the *Performance* tab. Task Manager immediately starts gathering CPU and memory usage statistics and displays them in graph form in the window. You can see graphs for CPU performance (refer to Figure 16.50), memory, disk drives, Ethernet, and Wi-Fi performance.

TECH TIP

What to do if you think memory is the problem

To address a memory problem, you can add RAM, create multiple paging files when multiple hard drives are installed in the system, manually set the paging file size, run one application at a time, close unnecessary windows, upgrade or add another hard drive, delete unused files, and defragment the hard drive.

CPU shows the processor usage percentage—that is, what percentage of time the processor is working. Actually, it is more accurate to say that *CPU* shows the percentage of time the processor is running a thread. A *thread* is a type of Windows object that runs application instructions. The window on the right in the Task Manager is a graph of how busy the processor is over a period of time.

Memory is frequently a bottleneck for computer performance issues. When available memory is extremely low, you might get the error message "Your computer is running low on memory." You can use Task Manager to see the total amount of RAM installed, how much RAM is available, and statistics regarding memory. Use the *Memory* option on the left side of the *Performance* tab. The amount of physical RAM installed appears in the upper-right corner. The information at the bottom shows the physical RAM and virtual memory (hard drive space called a paging file that is used as if it were RAM). Note that this might be referred to in articles, documentation, or the CompTIA certification as system **performance (virtual memory)** because any computer's virtual memory affects performance. If you think the page file for virtual memory is too small, you can adjust it with the following steps:

Step 1. Access *Settings* > *System* > *About* > *System protection* > *Advanced* tab > *Performance* section *Settings* button.

Step 2. Select the *Advanced* tab.

Step 3. In the *Virtual memory* section, look at the total size of the paging file. Click the *Change* button, deselect the *Automatically Manage Paging File Size for All Drives* checkbox, and you can make adjustments, as shown in Figure 16.61.

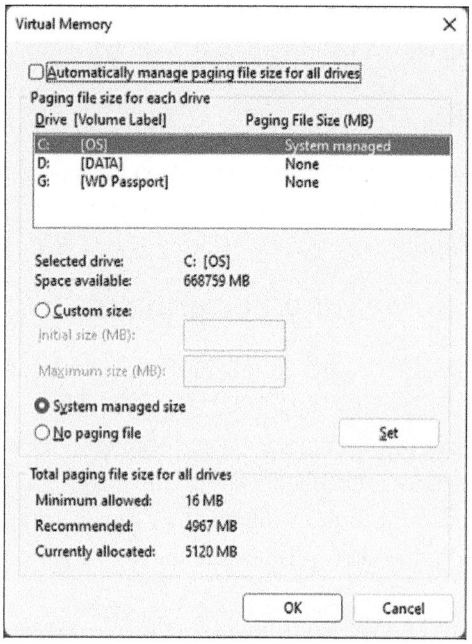

FIGURE 16.61 Manually configuring page file (virtual memory) size

To see how much memory an individual process is using, use the *Processes* tab and locate the program executable file. The CPU and memory usage are shown in separate columns on the *Processes* tab. Windows 10 and 11 offer disk and network columns as well.

Click on a particular network card on the left side of the *Performance* tab to see a graph of network performance for that interface, including Bluetooth. Figure 16.62 shows the Task Manager *Performance* option for an Ethernet card.

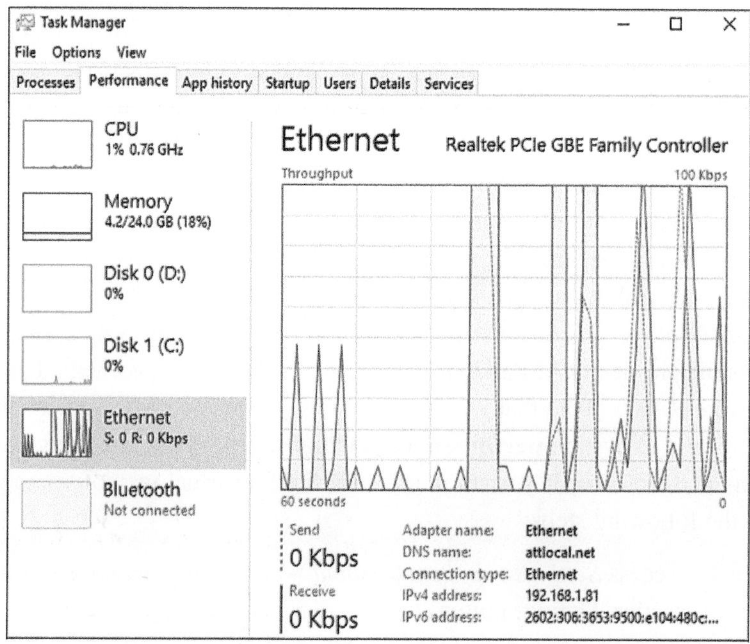

FIGURE 16.62 Task Manager: *Performance* tab, *Ethernet*

The Task Manager *Users* tab shows users that are logged on to the computer and the specific performance statistics regarding CPU, memory, disk, and network for each particular user. This is probably one of the least used Task Manager tabs in either the corporate environment or at home. However, if multiple people are logged on, one of them might have a particular application or service running that is causing the machine to slow down.

Performance Monitor

Performance Monitor (`perfmon.msc`) is a visual graph in real time or from data saved in a log file that provides information on specific computer components. Use the *System and Security* section of the Control Panel > *Administrative Tools* > double-click *Performance Monitor.* After the Performance Monitor window opens, click *Performance Monitor* under *Monitoring Tools.* Performance Monitor shows counters, which provide specific measurements for objects. Common objects include cache, memory, paging file, physical disk, processor, network interface, system, and thread. Use the green + (plus sign) in Performance Monitor to select various counters. At the bottom of the window is a legend for interpreting the graph, including what color is used for each of the performance measures and what counter is used. Table 16.19 shows common counters used in Performance Monitor, and Figure 16.63 shows an example of Performance Monitor.

TABLE 16.19 Performance Monitor counters

Computer component	Object name	Counters
Memory	Memory	Available Bytes and Cache Bytes
Hard disk	Physical disk	Disk Reads/sec and Disk Writes/sec
Hard disk	Logical disk	% Free Space
Processor	Processor	% Processor Time (All Instances)

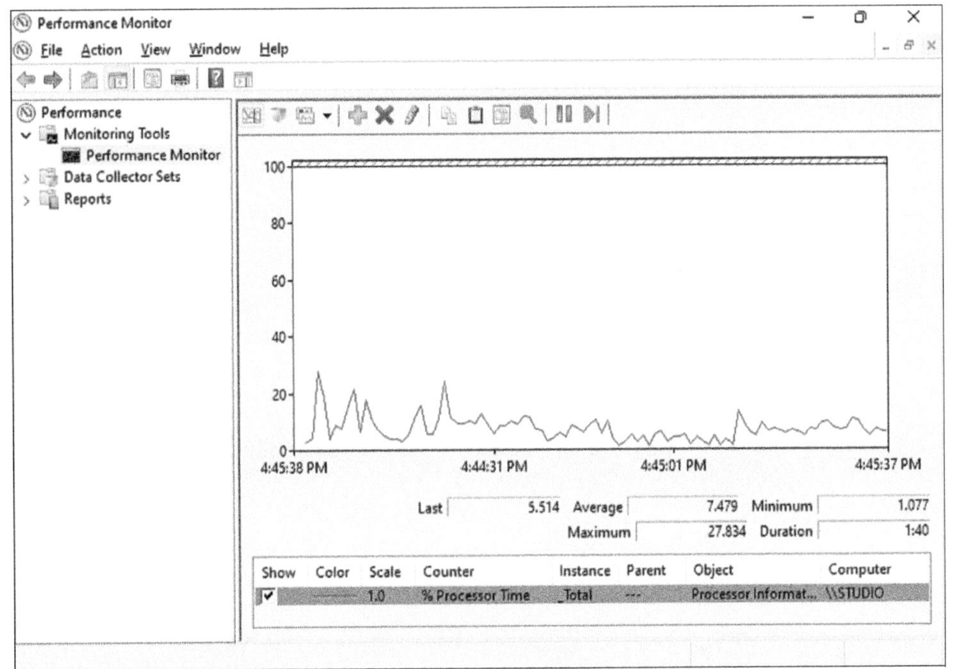

FIGURE 16.63 Windows Performance Monitor

Resource Monitor

The Windows **Resource Monitor** (`resmon.msc`) is a nice graphical tool that requires little work and shows the main components of a system. Access the tool by selecting the *Open Resource Monitor* link from within the Performance Monitor window or access the *System and Security* section of the Control Panel > *Administrative Tools* > double-click *Resource Monitor*. Figure 16.64 shows Resource Monitor.

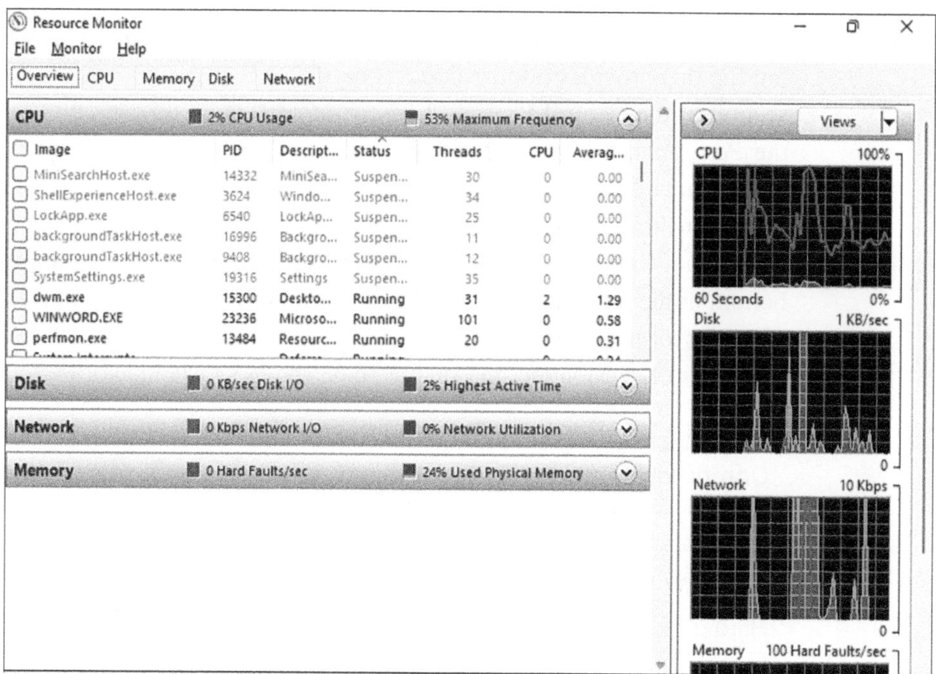

FIGURE 16.64 Windows Resource Monitor

Running any performance monitoring tool affects a computer's performance, especially when using the Graph view and sampling large amounts of data. The following recommendations help when running any performance monitoring tool:

- Turn off any screen saver.
- Use Report view instead of Graph view to save on resources.
- Minimize the number of counters monitored.
- Sample at longer intervals, such as 10 to 15 minutes, rather than at short intervals such as a few seconds or minutes.

Windows **Reliability Monitor** provides a visual graph and detailed report of system stability and details on events that might have affected the computer's reliability. The details can help technicians troubleshoot what has caused the system to become unreliable. Reliability Monitor is found by typing **`reliability monitor`** in the *Search* box on the taskbar. Figure 16.65 shows this tool.

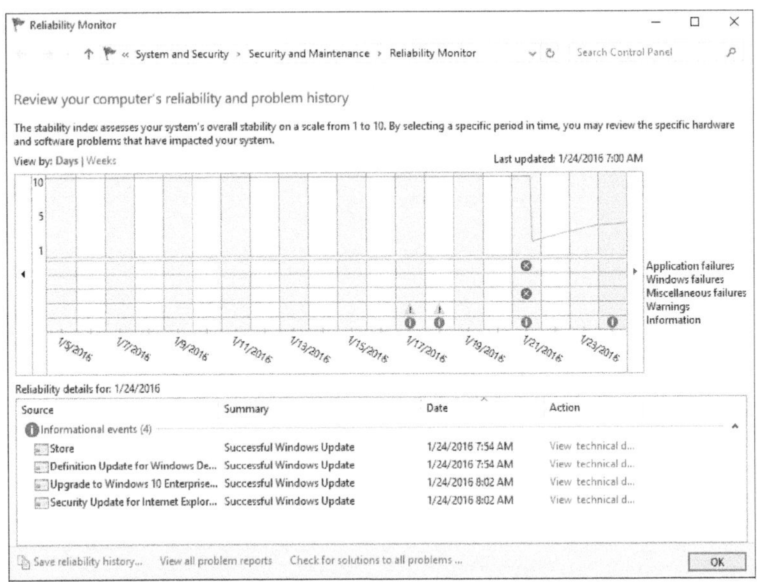

FIGURE 16.65 Windows Reliability Monitor

Supporting Windows Computers Remotely

Windows provides two products for accessing a PC remotely: **Remote Desktop Connection** and **Remote Assistance**. Both products are useful for those working at a help desk and for technicians who must support computers in other locations. There are some key differences between these two products:

> Remote Desktop Connection allows full control of the remote desktop, whereas Remote Assistance only allows viewing of the remote desktop.

> Remote Desktop Connection requires network connectivity between the controlling computer and the remote computer (or a VPN connection through the internet).

> Remote Assistance displays a prompt at the remote computer, asking permission to allow the computer to be viewed remotely, and Remote Desktop Connection does not display this prompt.

Using Remote Desktop Connection (the `mstsc` command) requires the following elements:

> The local computer that the technician is using and the remote computer must have some type of network connectivity with each other.

> The computer used to access the remote computer must run Windows 7 Professional or higher, Windows 8/10 Pro or higher, or Windows Server or must have some type of terminal services running.

> Any firewalls between the two computers must allow port 3389 to be open.

> The remote PC must have the Remote Desktop Connection application installed and enabled. Remote Desktop Connection is disabled by default in Windows. To enable/configure it, open *File Explorer* and right-click *This PC* > *Properties* > *Remote desktop* link from left panel > toggle *Enable Remote Desktop* (simply *Remote Desktop* in Windows 11) to *On* (see Figure 16.66).

> You need to know the computer name or IP address of the remote PC. For example, the local network name of the remote PC in Figure 16.66 is *Office*.

> You need to have a user account with a password on the remote PC, and that account must be permitted to use Remote Desktop Connection. By default, accounts with administrator rights are permitted to use Remote Desktop Connection. Use the *Select users that can remotely*

access this PC link in Windows 10 or the *Remote Desktop users* link in Windows 11 to admit additional users.

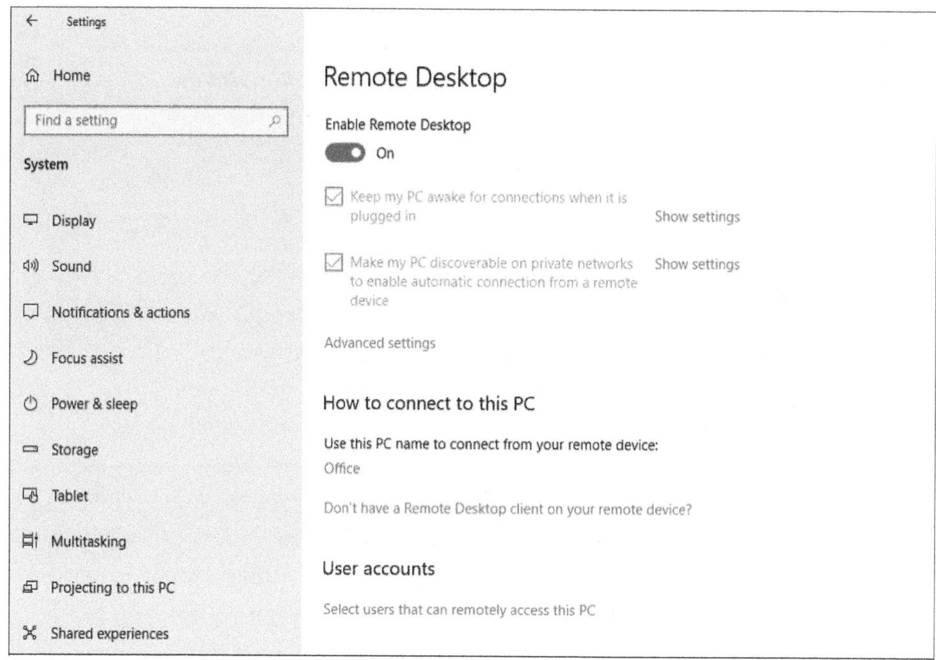

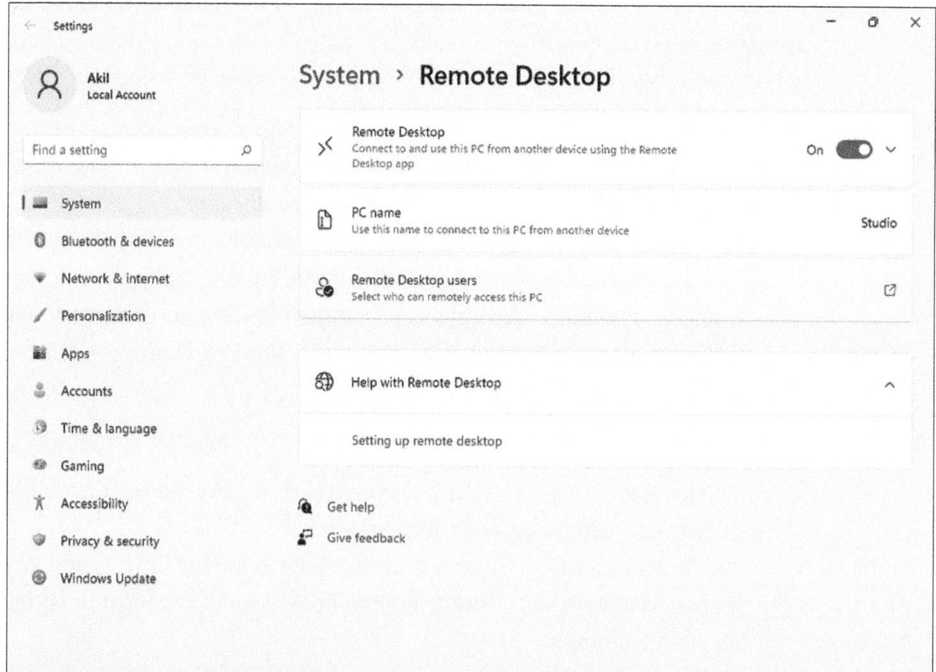

FIGURE 16.66 Windows Remote Desktop configuration for Windows 10 (top) and Windows 11 (bottom)

To initiate a remote connection, search for **`Remote Desktop Connection`**, enter the hostname or IP address of the remote computer, and then click *Connect.* If a connection is available, you are prompted for the username and password of a valid user (see Figure 16.67).

When you are on a computer that is remotely accessing another computer via Remote Desktop Connection, there is a bar across the top of the screen that contains the remote computer name. This is how you know that you are on another computer. The user on the remote computer is logged off and cannot see what the remote technician is doing.

FIGURE 16.67 Windows Remote Desktop Connection login

With Remote Assistance, one computer user (known as the expert) views another computer user's (the novice's) desktop using a secure connection. The novice controls the computer, and the expert can only see what the novice is doing and cannot control the novice's computer.

Remote Assistance sessions can be established over the internet without a VPN connection. On computers that use network address translation (NAT), you may have to go into the Windows Defender Firewall application and, in the left panel, select *Allow an app or feature through the Windows Defender Firewall*. Click the *Change settings* button and enable *Remote Assistance*. You must also set up a password for the guest user and manually send the password to the person invited to take over the computer.

To initiate a Remote Assistance session, follow these steps:

Step 1. Run the `msra` command or search for *Remote Assistance*.

Step 2. Choose an invitation method:

- *Save this invitation as a file:* This method creates an invitation file that the novice can send through web-based email or Windows Messenger service.
- *Use email to send an invitation:* This method starts the default email program on the novice's computer and attaches the invitation to an email message.
- *Use Easy Connect:* This option is available if Easy Connect is installed and enabled on the novice's computer. Easy Connect must also be available on the Expert's computer.

Figure 16.68 shows the available options.

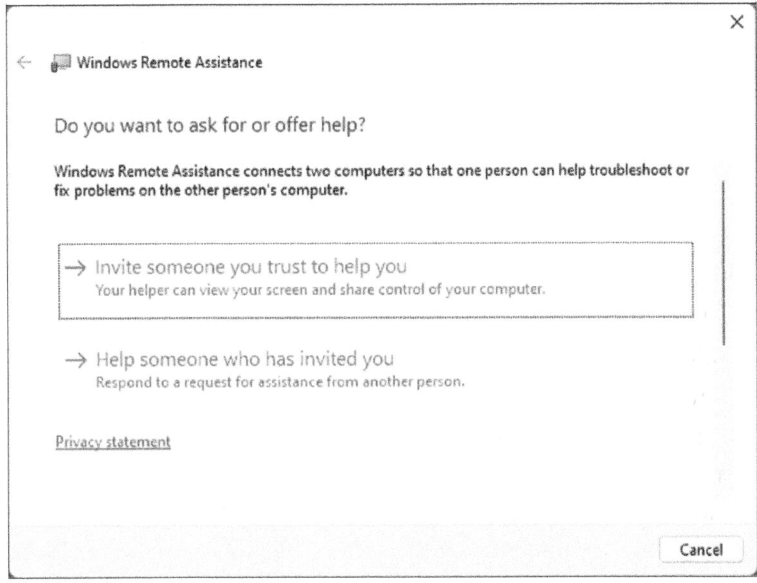

FIGURE 16.68 Windows Remote Assistance

Preventive Maintenance for Your Operating System

Your operating system is a key component of a working system. Properly applied preventive maintenance can help avoid issues and reduce downtime. No application or hardware can work without an operating system. It is important that you keep your operating system healthy. The following suggestions can help:

- Be sure an antivirus software program that has current virus definitions is installed.
- Have a backup of your operating system. Many external hard drives include backup software.
- Make frequent data backups.
- Ensure that the System Restore utility is enabled.
- Update the operating system with service packs and **patches**.
- Use the Task Scheduler tool to automate some of the preventive maintenance tasks. You can use the `at` command to create a script file or have an application run at a specific time. (Type **`at /?`** at a command prompt to see the options.)

SOFT SKILLS: AVOIDING BURNOUT

Burnout—commonly caused by too much work and stress—is a mental state that can also affect emotional and physical capabilities. Many technicians tire of the fast pace of technology (see Figure 16.69). One attraction of technology for many students is that technology is always changing; however, it is the speed of change that also provides a challenge—even to seasoned veterans. As a person matures, it seems to take more effort to stay current in the skills required for business. After being in the same job for multiple years, a technician may show signs of burnout. Technicians should monitor their own attitude and mental state constantly and watch for warning signs associated with burnout:

- Overreaction to common situations
- Constant tiredness
- Reduced productivity
- Poor attitude
- Lack of patience with customers or peers
- Feeling of a loss of control
- Use of food, drink, or drugs as coping mechanisms

FIGURE 16.69 Burnout affects your performance

Burnout can be prevented and dealt with if you recognize the symptoms. Working too much, having too many responsibilities, and expecting too much of yourself can lead to burnout. The following list can help you recognize and cope with burnout:

> Take vacations during which you do not stay in contact with work.
> Set reachable goals, even on a daily basis.
> Take a couple breaks during the day to do something nontechnical.
> Learn something new that is not related to technology.
> Have good eating, sleeping, and exercising routines.
> Subscribe to a positive saying or joke of the day.
> Participate in a fun or relaxing hobby or activity.

Chapter Summary

> Windows operating systems come in different editions that have various features and tools and can be 32-bit or 64-bit. The 32-bit versions are limited to a maximum of 4 GB of RAM; 32-bit operating systems or applications are sometimes referred to as x86 instead of 32-bit.
> Before installing Windows, you should complete the eight preinstallation steps to ensure a smooth, error-free installation.
> The installation of Windows includes three phases: determining whether to upgrade or perform a clean installation, choosing a partition system, and completing the installation.
> Corporate computer installations are more complex than other types of installations. Automated tools and disk imaging software can help with corporate computer installations.
> Many installation problems are addressed in the chapter, along with possible causes and solutions.
> Updates to Windows may be configured manually, but Windows 10 does automatic updates by default.
> The registry should be backed up whenever the computer is fully functional and immediately before any software or hardware changes are made.
> The System Configuration Utility (`msconfig`) is used to troubleshoot startup issues, set boot conditions, and access services and quick links to Windows tools.
> Tasks that a technician commonly performs to configure Windows include adding devices, removing hardware components, adding a printer, and installing or removing software.
> The Computer Management console can access three categories: System Tools (Task Scheduler, Event Viewer, Shared Folders, Local Users and Groups, Performance, and Device Manager), Storage (Disk Management), and Services and Applications.
> Managing accounts for those who use computers or computer resources from remote network computers is an important function of a technician or administrator.
> The Storage Computer Management category includes just the Disk Management tool, which is used to manage hard drives, including volumes or partitions.
> A service is an application that can be started using the Services option or configured to start when the computer boots.
> The Data Sources administrative tool can be used to select which database application is associated with a particular type of file.
> The Print Management console is used to manage printers.

> There are various methods to speed up and troubleshoot the boot process. The Windows Recovery Environment (WinRE) is accessed by booting from Windows installation media or from within Windows. It includes many diagnostic and other helpful tools.
> Task Manager can be used to perform preventive maintenance on a regular basis. Preventive maintenance can reduce downtime and includes keeping the operating system and applications patched, keeping the antivirus definitions current, keeping the hard drive defragmented, and ensuring ample space on the hard drive.
> Technicians should understand how to determine how a computer is performing by using Task Manager and comparing current performance to a baseline that was taken at a time when the computer was running optimally. Other tools, such as Performance Monitor or Resource Monitor, are also very helpful.
> Technicians may be required to access computers remotely, and this can be done using the Remote Desktop or Remote Assistance products.
> Technicians can do positive things to avoid burnout, including getting good rest, avoiding drugs and alcohol, doing nontechnical things, and having good time-management skills.

A+ CERTIFICATION EXAM TIPS

- ✓ Know the minimum hardware requirements for installing 32- and 64-bit Windows 8.1 and Windows 10. Know that Windows 11 can only be installed on 64-bit systems.
- ✓ Use all Windows tools before taking the certification exams. Ensure that you pay attention to the purpose of each tool and consider why (or in what situation) you would use each Windows tool.
- ✓ Review all symptoms and resolutions for a system that is running slowly or is slow to boot.
- ✓ Know the various boot methods.
- ✓ Review the various types of installations, such as an unattended installation, in-place upgrade, clean install, repair installation, remote network install, image deployment, recovery partition, and reset/restore. Review Table 16.1.
- ✓ Know the various types of partitions and what they are best used for.
- ✓ Be familiar with different user/group accounts and Credential Manager.
- ✓ Be familiar with common symptoms/troubleshooting of software problems. Common symptoms include slow performance, failure to boot, and application crashes.
- ✓ Be familiar with the following features: Computer Management, Print Management, Device Manager (which can be used to disable a device), Local Users and Groups, Performance Monitor, Services, System Configuration, Task Scheduler, Component Services, Data Sources, Windows Memory Diagnostic Tool, Task Manager, Disk Management (including knowing how to install a drive, create an MBR, create a dynamic disk, convert an MBR to a dynamic disk, partition, select files system, and format), Upgrade Advisor, System Restore, and Windows Update.
- ✓ Interact with and use for troubleshooting the following Windows Control Panel utilities: Display/Display Settings, User Accounts, System, Power Options, Programs and Features, Devices and Printers, Sound, and Troubleshooting.

Key Terms

account recovery options 805
ACL 779
activation clock 776
adding array (Disk Management) 809
Administrator 805
Advanced Boot Options 819
application crash 824
application log 800
apply update 777
assigning/changing drive letter 809
Automatic Updates 780
baseline 839
basic disk 769
black screen 829
blue screen 799
boot partition 815
boot volume 814
CDFS 771
clean install 765
compatibility mode 768
Component Services 797
Computer Management 796
`convert` 770
Credential Manager 801
Data Sources 812
defragment the hard drive 811
device driver 784
Device Manager 785
Devices and Printers 791
digital signature 786
disable a service 831
disable Windows applications 822
Disk Cleanup 810
Disk Management 807
domain 775
drive partition 770
drive status 807
dynamic disk 769
Error Checking 810
Event Viewer 797
exFAT 771
ext3 771
ext4 771
extended partition 769
extending partition (Disk Management) 809
external hard drive (boot option) 814
factory recovery partition 765
failure to boot 827
FAT 771
FAT32 771
File History 782
full format 769
GPT 769
graphical interface fails to load 829
HFS 771
hotfix 778
image deployment 765
in-place upgrade 765
initializing (Disk Management) 809
internal fixed disk (boot option) 814
internal hard drive partition (boot option) 814
kill task 824
KMS 776
load alternate third-party driver 772
Local Users and Groups 804
logical partition 769
MBR 769
Microsoft Management Console 796
`mmc` 796
mounting (Disk Management) 809
`msconfig` 820
`mstsc` 843
multiboot 765
network boot 814
NFS 771
no OS found 779
Notepad 779
NTFS 771
NTLDR Is Missing 778
optical disc (boot option) 814
Optimize and Defragment 811
patch 846
performance (virtual memory) 839
Performance Monitor 841
primary partition 769
Print Management 813
printing issue 813
Program Compatibility Wizard 768
PXE 814
quick format 769
ReadyBoost 827
reboot 790
rebuild a Windows profile 833
recovery partition 765
refresh rate 789
ReFS 810
registry 781
`regsvr32.exe` 796
reimage 775
Reliability Monitor 842
Remote Assistance 843
Remote Desktop Connection 843
remote network installation 765
repair an application 794
repair installation 794
Reset This PC 828
resolution 788
Resource Monitor 842
restart service 831
restore (installation method) 765
restore point 783
rights 804
roll back the device driver 789
roll back Windows update 780
Safe Boot 821
Safe Mode 778
service 811
service fails to start 831
service pack 778
Services 791
`services.msc` 831
`sfc` 779
Shadow Copy 816
share 800
Shared Folders 800
shrinking partition (Disk Management) 809
slow boot 832
slow performance 838
slow profile load 832
splitting partition (Disk Management) 809
Standard user 805
Storage Spaces 810
swap partition 769
Sync Center 793
Sysprep 775
System Configuration utility 820
system file 814
System File Checker 779
system log 800
System Protection 816
system requirements 792
System Restore 783
system volume 814
Task Manager 824
Task Scheduler 797
UAC 806
unattended installation 765
update network settings 833
update the boot order 777
user account management 801
USMT 768
Windows Recovery Environment 764
Windows Update 780
WinRE 816
workgroup 775
WRP 779

Review Questions

1. What is the maximum amount of RAM that can be recognized by any version of 32-bit Windows?

2. A customer has an older 16-bit game as well as some 32- and 64-bit games. The customer is considering upgrading to 64-bit Windows 10. Will there be any issues with this? If so, what are they, and how might they be resolved?

3. List three steps to be taken before installing Windows.

4. Which tool can limit and control the number of applications used to boot the computer?

   [`taskmgr` | `regedit` | `msconfig` | `diskpart`]

5. Which Windows setting would be used to enable Windows PowerShell, Hyper-V, or Microsoft's Print to PDF option?

   [Turn Windows Features On or Off | Task Manager | System Configuration | Performance Monitor]

6. Which performance tool would a technician use first to see if a computer has enough hardware resources when a particular application executes?

   [Performance Monitor | Task Manager | Reliability Monitor | Device Manager]

7. How could you have both Windows 10 and Windows 11 operating systems installed on one computer?

8. [T | F] Existing restore points are deleted if Windows is reinstalled.

9. [T | F] Device drivers are specific to a particular Windows operating system version.

10. Which System Configuration tab is used to configure a computer to boot in diagnostic startup mode?

    [Boot | Services | Startup | General | Tools]

11. What user group is allowed to perform driver rollback? (Select all that apply.)

    [Standard User | Guest | Administrator | Backup Operators]

12. What is the purpose of the System Restore utility?

13. When Windows boots, nothing appears on the screen. If the display is powered on and attached, which Windows tool would be best to try first?

    [System Restore | Safe Mode | Command Prompt | Reset Your PC]

14. When would a technician use Event Viewer?

15. Detail specifically how Task Manager can monitor computer performance?

____

____

____

16. Which disk management option would be used to create a flexible data storage option from a USB drive and an eSATA drive that is seen as one drive letter?

    [RAID 0 | RAID 1 | RAID 5 | Storage Spaces]

17. Where does Windows store passwords and login details for a particular user?

    [Storage Spaces | Credential Manager | BIOS/UEFI | C:\Windows\System32\Configuration]

18. Which type of Windows installation setup is used for a corporate environment?

    [workgroup | homegroup | domain | peer-to-peer]

19. Which type of Windows boot process is used in conjunction with the PXE BIOS/UEFI option?

    [in-place upgrade | multiboot | network | recovery]

20. List three things a student can do to avoid burnout in school.

____

____

Exercises

Exercise 16.1 Windows Tools

Objective: To determine which Windows tool to use, based on the task

Procedure: Match each scenario to the best Windows tool to use for the given situation. Note that one tool is used twice.

Tools:

a. Event Viewer

b. System Restore

c. System Repair

d. `msconfig`

e. Device Manager

f. Folder Options

g. System Properties

h. Devices and Printers

i. Disk Management

j. Task Scheduler

k. Services

l. Performance Monitor

m. Task Manager

n. Computer Management console

o. Windows Memory Diagnostics Tool

p. Safe Mode

q. `regsvr32`

r. safe boot

s. Print Management

Scenarios:

_____ **1.** Configure two drives in a RAID configuration.

_____ **2.** Determine when a user logged into a computer yesterday.

_____ **3.** Restart the program that allows the print spooler to function.

_____ **4.** You suspect one of the DDR4 modules has an issue.

_____ **5.** Quickest way to see the default printer.

_____ **6.** Disable a computer vendor app that keeps running every time the computer boots, trying to get the user to buy storage space.

____ 7. Configure a specific number of processors the computer uses to boot.

____ 8. Run a test of hard drive reads per second and writes per second to see if the drive is causing slowdown issues.

____ 9. Bring the system back to before a particular Windows update was installed.

____ 10. Instruct the system to perform disk maintenance twice a week instead of just once.

____ 11. Have the ability to access Device Manager and the Disk Management tool from one window.

____ 12. View system files through Windows Explorer/File Explorer.

____ 13. Testing mode with limited drivers loaded.

____ 14. Unregister a DLL.

____ 15. Disable a piece of hardware.

____ 16. Adjust virtual memory.

____ 17. View all print servers.

____ 18. Halt a misbehaving app.

____ 19. Control the Safe Mode boot type the next time the computer restarts.

____ 20. Let the OS try to figure out why Windows won't boot.

Exercise 16.2 Task Manager Tabs

Objective: To determine which Task Manager tab to use, based on the task

Procedure: Match each scenario to the best Task Manager tab to use in Windows 10. You might want to review figures throughout the chapter. Each tab is used only once.

Tabs:

a. Processes

b. Performance

c. App history

d. Startup

e. Users

f. Details

g. Services

Scenarios:

____ 1. See a graph of how quickly the SSD used to boot the system is responding to requests for information.

____ 2. Determine what applications a person has used today and how much memory each of them has used.

____ 3. Document how much bandwidth a particular application used on a metered network.

____ 4. Stop and restart Wlansvc.

____ 5. Learn which apps are considered to be actively used on the computer right now.

____ 6. Look up the specific process ID (PID) for the firefox.exe application.

____ 7. Research which applications launched automatically when the computer booted.

Exercise 16.3 System Configuration Tabs

Objective: To determine which System Configuration tab to use, based on the task

Procedure: Match each scenario to the best System Configuration tab to use for the given situation. You might want to review figures throughout the chapter. Each tab is used only once.

Tabs:

a. General

b. Boot

c. Services

d. Startup

e. Tools

Scenarios:

____ **1.** Determine what applications began as part of the Windows boot process.

____ **2.** Allow a technician to choose either a normal, diagnostic, or selective startup.

____ **3.** Quickly access Event Viewer.

____ **4.** Create a log file of the boot process for a computer that doesn't boot properly.

____ **5.** Select only three Windows apps that enable specific Windows features that start as part of the boot process.

Activities

Internet Discovery

Objective: To access the Internet to obtain specific information regarding a computer or its associated parts

Parts: Access to the Internet

Procedure: Use the Internet to answer the following questions.

1. Find a website that offers Windows freeware tools. Write the name of the website and the URL where this information was found.

____

____

2. What is the latest update available from Microsoft for Windows 11? Write the answer and the URL where you found the answer.

____

3. Find a website that details what to do if a Windows 10 upgrade results in a black screen. Detail what the website recommends and the URL where you found it.

____

____

____

4. Microsoft always has a planned lifecycle for any of its operating systems. Find a website that tells you what the planned retirement date is for Windows 11 Pro (Version 21H2). Write the mainstream support end date as well as the URL.

____

____

5. You get the error code 0x80072EE7 on a Windows 10 computer. Find a website that describes this error. Write at least one thing that could cause this error, one solution, and URL where the answer can be found.

____

____

____

6. Find a technical certification related to a Microsoft operating system. List the certification. List all URLs used to find this information.

____

____

Soft Skills

Objective: To enhance and fine-tune a future technician's ability to listen, communicate in both written and oral forms, and professionally support people who use computers

Activities:

1. In groups of two or three students, one student inserts a problem related to Windows on the computer. The other student or students use the Remote Desktop Connection utility to find the problem and then repair it. Document each problem, along with the solution provided. Exchange roles so that each student practices the repair and documentation.
2. Divide into five groups. Five questions about operating systems follow:

   (1) What should you do before installing an operating system?

   (2) What are alternatives to Windows 10 or 11 as an operating system, and what are pros and cons of these alternatives?

   (3) What is the difference between an active partition, a system partition, and a boot partition in regard to Windows?

   (4) What operating systems can be upgraded to Windows 10 or 11? What is the difference between a clean install and an upgrade, and what determines which one you do?

   (5) What differences can be seen for a Windows hard drive that has a FAT32 partition and one that has an NTFS partition?

   Each group is assigned one of these five areas or another set of five questions related to Windows. Each group is allowed 20 minutes (and some whiteboard space or poster-sized paper) to write their ideas. All group members help to present their findings to the class.
3. Find a magazine article related to a Windows solution or feature. Share your findings with the class.
4. Using any research method and resource, determine the pros and cons of upgrading to Windows 11 from Windows 10. Make a list of things to check before upgrading.

17 macOS and Linux Operating Systems

In this chapter you will learn:

- > What operating systems are available besides Windows
- > How to navigate the user interfaces of macOS and Ubuntu Linux
- > How to manipulate files and folders in the graphical and command-line interfaces
- > How to create system backups
- > How to find Unix/Linux software
- > How to work from a Linux-based command line
- > Reasons to be humble in the IT field

CompTIA Exam Objectives:

- ✓ 1102-1.8 Explain common OS types and their purposes.
- ✓ 1102-1.9 Given a scenario, perform OS installations and upgrades in a diverse OS environment.
- ✓ 1102-1.10 Identify common features and tools of the macOS/desktop OS.
- ✓ 1102-1.11 Identify common features and tools of the Linux client/desktop OS.
- ✓ 1102-3.2 Given a scenario, troubleshoot common personal computer (PC) security issues.
- ✓ 1102-3.3 Given a scenario, use best practice procedures for malware removal.

Introduction to macOS

macOS is a Unix-based operating system that was developed by Apple, Inc., for its Macintosh (or Mac) line of computers. This Apple operating system is the second most commonly used desktop operating system, after Windows, and it is the most commonly used type of Unix/Linux-based desktop operating system.

Like most other Unix/Linux operating systems, macOS utilizes many open source projects to make up the core and functionality of the operating system, along with a touch of Apple's own customization. **Open source** software is software that is made freely available and that is open to outside contributions. Although many parts of macOS are open source, the operating system is not. macOS is unique to Apple-released hardware (see Figure 17.1) because it comes preinstalled only on Mac systems and is not sold or distributed to run on other hardware, as Windows and most other Unix/Linux distributions are.

FIGURE 17.1 Apple computer running OS X

The predecessor to macOS was **OS X**. The desktop OS X releases were named after felines, and macOS versions are named after California landmarks. Table 17.1 lists macOS operating system distributions by release number and name. The information in this chapter is based on macOS Monterey Version 12.2.

TABLE 17.1 macOS releases since 2016 by name and number

Release number	Name	Release date
10.12	Sierra	September 2016
10.13	High Sierra	September 2017
10.14	Mojave	September 2018
10.15	Catalina	October 2019
11	Big Sur	November 2020
12	Monterey	October 2021

macOS is a Portable Operating System Interface (**POSIX**)–compliant operating system, which means it meets the specifications for a standardized operating system outlined by the IEEE Computer Society and contains a Bourne shell and other standard programs and services that are found in all POSIX-compliant operating systems. A **shell** is a user interface that is used to interact with an operating system. POSIX standardization makes it easier for end users, IT professionals, and developers to use different operating systems that are POSIX compliant and have familiar tools available. Because of this standardization, many skills that you learn with macOS can be applied to other operating systems.

Navigating the User Interface

macOS is renowned for its intuitive and easy-to-learn graphical user interface (GUI); there are multiple ways to interact with this GUI, including using the standard mouse and keyboard and using the more modern trackpad multitouch gestures. The macOS GUI is called Aqua. Steve Jobs, co-founder of Apple Inc., famously said, "One of the design goals was when you saw it you wanted to lick it." He was referring to the original water-like theme of the GUI, which made heavy use of translucent and reflective design elements. Now the GUI is a flatter, toned-down interface that more resembles Apple's mobile operating system iOS than earlier versions of the operating system.

There are four basic elements to the macOS GUI (see Figure 17.2). The one that sticks out first on the desktop is known simply as the Dock. The **Dock** is the shortcut organizational bar used for launching, switching, and managing applications. You can easily customize the Dock by dragging and dropping applications and folder shortcuts to it. By default, the Dock is at the bottom of the screen, but its position can be changed so it is located on the side of the screen.

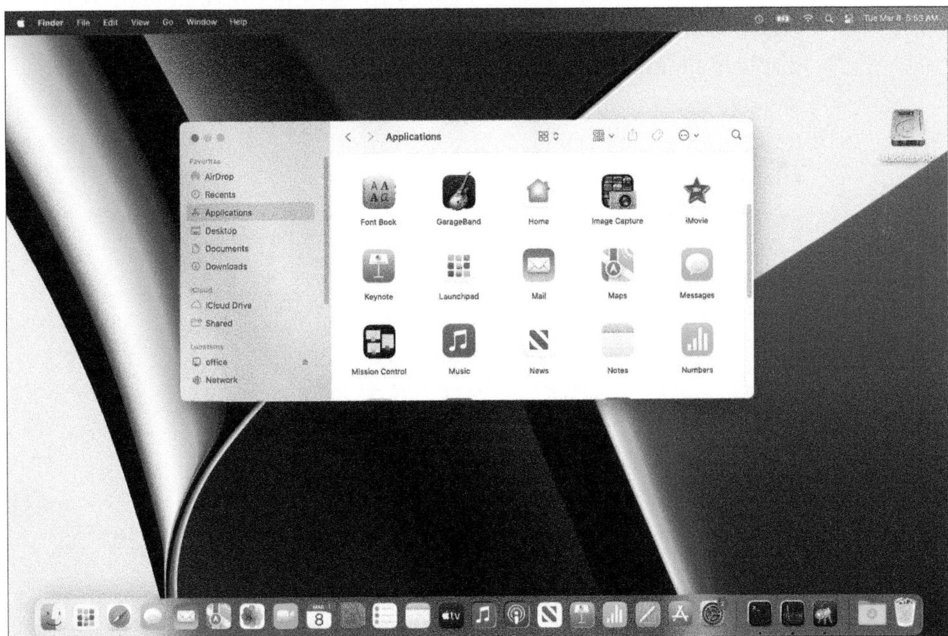

FIGURE 17.2 macOS desktop

The **Finder**, which is the file manager included in macOS, is used for navigating and managing files or folders in the file system. The Finder is similar to the Microsoft Windows File Explorer. You can open the Finder by clicking the iconic Finder icon, known for its smiling face, which is always located on the Dock.

The **menu bar**, which is anchored to the top of the screen, is a dynamically changing bar that presents contextual drop-down menu options on the left side, depending on what window is active. On the right side, the menu bar provides shortcuts for actions such as connecting to a Wi-Fi network or changing volume. The menu bar is also informative, displaying information such as battery life on MacBooks and the time of day.

Another important element of the macOS GUI is the desktop, which can hold anything the end user wants to save to it, such as documents, pictures, or mounted drives, for quick access.

Notice in Figure 17.2 the three colored dots on the upper-left corner of the Finder window. The red dot on the far left is used to close the window. The middle yellow dot is used to minimize the open window down to the Dock. The green dot (the rightmost one) is used to expand the window to full screen mode. These three dots are universal across all windows in macOS. When a window is in full screen mode, the menu bar disappears. It reappears when you move the mouse to the top of the screen. The green dot can then be used to reduce the window to its previous size.

TECH TIP

What to do if the Dock is missing

If the Dock is not present, try hovering the pointer toward the bottom or sides of the screen. Many macOS users hide the Dock to gain more screen space so that the Dock pops up only when the pointer is nearby.

On top of the core GUI elements are a few built-in utilities that make using the GUI easier. macOS supports multiple desktops, much as Microsoft Windows 10 does with Task View. **Mission Control** is a feature that gives an overview for managing all application windows and virtual desktops. It can be invoked by pressing the F3 key (or the F9 key on older Mac keyboards), by clicking the *Mission Control* icon (located in the *Applications* folder), or by swiping up on a trackpad with three or four fingers at once (depending on the trackpad settings). Mission Control displays all the running applications (see Figure 17.3), their respective windows grouped together, and any extra virtual desktops. From this view, you can create, delete, or rearrange virtual desktops; switch which application windows reside on each virtual desktop; and easily explore all the open application windows.

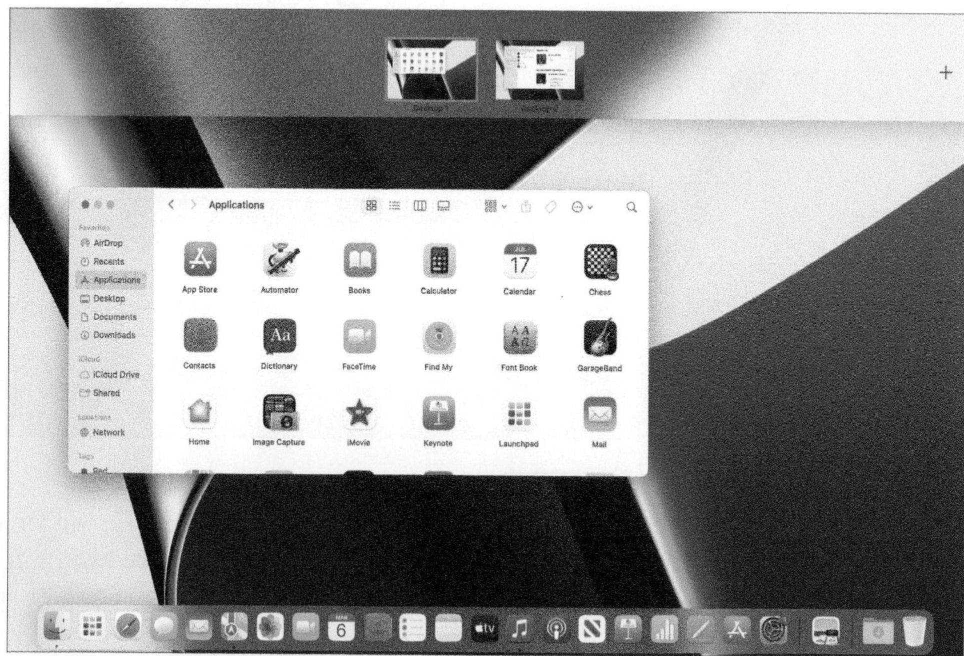

FIGURE 17.3 macOS Mission Control

Although Mission Control is great for managing applications, it cannot launch them. **Launchpad** is an application launcher shortcut. It can be invoked by pressing the F4 key, clicking the *Launchpad* icon, or using a thumb + three-fingers pinch gesture on a trackpad. This view is a grid-like display of all installed applications that you can click to launch (see Figure 17.4). This grid interface can be searched with the search bar at the top of the Launchpad interface. Applications can also be sorted into folders and multiple pages in this view for easy organization.

FIGURE 17.4 macOS Launchpad

Finder is used for navigating the file system, but it can be cumbersome, and it can take a long time to find something, especially if you are not sure where that something is located. For searching the system, you can use Spotlight. **Spotlight** is a universal search tool that can search every file and directory, as well as contacts, email, music, and even the web (see Figure 17.5). It is invoked by holding down ⌘ and pressing the Spacebar or by clicking the magnifying glass icon on the right side of the menu bar. A large search bar appears in the middle of the screen, allowing you to type in your search. The results are then presented to you underneath the search bar.

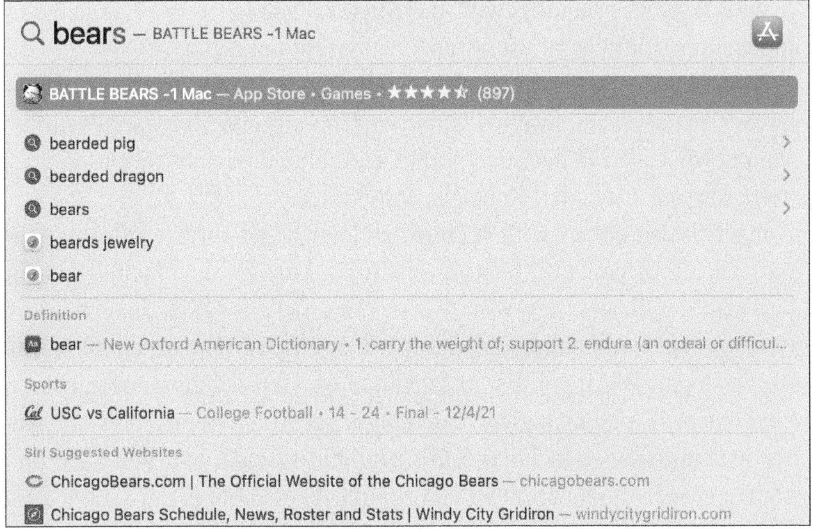

FIGURE 17.5 macOS Spotlight

You may have noticed that many of these shortcuts have their own dedicated gestures that can be triggered using a trackpad. Apple introduced the idea of finger-based **gestures** (use of fingers to make motions that provide input) in its mobile operating system, iOS. These gestures and functionality were later brought to MacBook laptops. To easily use these gestures, a user could purchase a Magic Mouse, which is a multitouch mouse sold by Apple, or a Bluetooth trackpad known as a Magic Trackpad. Table 17.2 lists the most commonly used trackpad gestures and the actions they trigger. Keep in mind that other gestures can be enabled, and many of them can be changed to have different effects, depending on the user's preference.

TABLE 17.2 Commonly used macOS gestures

Gesture	Action
Swipe left or right with two fingers	Swipe between pages
Swipe left or right with three fingers	Swipe between full-screen applications
Swipe left or right with four fingers	Swipe between desktops
Swipe up with three or four fingers	Open Mission Control
Pinch in with the thumb and three fingers	Open Launchpad
Spread apart the thumb and three fingers	Show the desktop
Pinch in or out with two fingers	Zoom in or out
Tap with two fingers at the same time	Right-click
Tap and hold down with three fingers	Take control of a window in order to drag it around the screen

Basic System Usage, Updates, and Backups

When macOS starts, you may be presented with a login screen if the user accounts have passwords enabled. You can log in with a previously created user account or, if it is enabled, you can use the guest login selection. If you log in as a guest, any changes you make or items you save will be deleted from the system when you log out. Every time you are logged in as a guest user, you are presented with a fresh desktop experience, as if it has never been used before.

macOS comes bundled with the software shown in the Launchpad in Figure 17.4, including applications for general use as well as system upkeep. macOS's office productivity suite, known as **iWork**, includes a word processor called Pages, a presentation application called Keynote, and a spreadsheet application called Numbers. These productivity applications are Apple's answer to the popular Microsoft Office suite. Other useful bundled applications include Mail, Safari (the default web browser), Calendar, Contacts, and Photos.

macOS also comes with **iCloud**, a cloud-based service offering storage, application support, and syncing of contacts, photos, email, bookmarks, documents, and more between multiple OS X, macOS, iOS, and even Windows devices. On any OS X, macOS, or iOS device, you can create an iCloud account, either generating a new iCloud domain email or using another email address as your login. When you log in to iCloud on your machine, which can be done inside the *System Preferences* iCloud menu, you can then select which items you want synced between devices. The free syncing service includes 5 GB of cloud storage, and you have the option to purchase more storage space with a monthly subscription. The whole iCloud service is optional to use but worth looking into for easy syncing to all devices.

One unique feature of iCloud that sets it apart from other cloud services is that it has built-in remote connectivity. If you log in to iCloud, have Internet access, and enable the *Sharing* feature in the *System Preferences* menu, you can browse that Mac from another macOS device. The remote

Mac appears as a shared device in Finder, enabling you to browse the file system. You can click the *Share Screen* button to start a remote desktop session.

> **TECH TIP**
>
> **iCloud screen-sharing requirements**
>
> An iCloud screen-sharing session needs at least 300 Kbps of full-duplex bandwidth. You might need to edit firewall settings to allow a connection to go through.

App Store

macOS comes with a wide range of bundled software, and there is also a software marketplace. The **App Store** is a centralized marketplace where developers can list and sell software (see Figure 17.6). You can find a wide range of software, from simple utilities to advanced 3D games. The App Store allows for easy management of purchases, as they are tied to a user's Apple ID, and a user can install the software on multiple systems or re-download past purchases by logging in with their account. The App Store also allows for easy application updates because developers can push out updates through this centralized repository to end users. This also provides a layer of security: Users know the applications found in the App Store have been vetted by Apple and most likely include no harmful or malicious code.

> **TECH TIP**
>
> **Apple ID**
>
> To use the App Store and other Apple cloud services, you need an Apple ID. This login is used for tracking software purchases through all of Apple's stores. You can create one in the App Store, through iTunes (an Apple media player, radio app, and media library), or by going to https://appleid.apple.com/account.

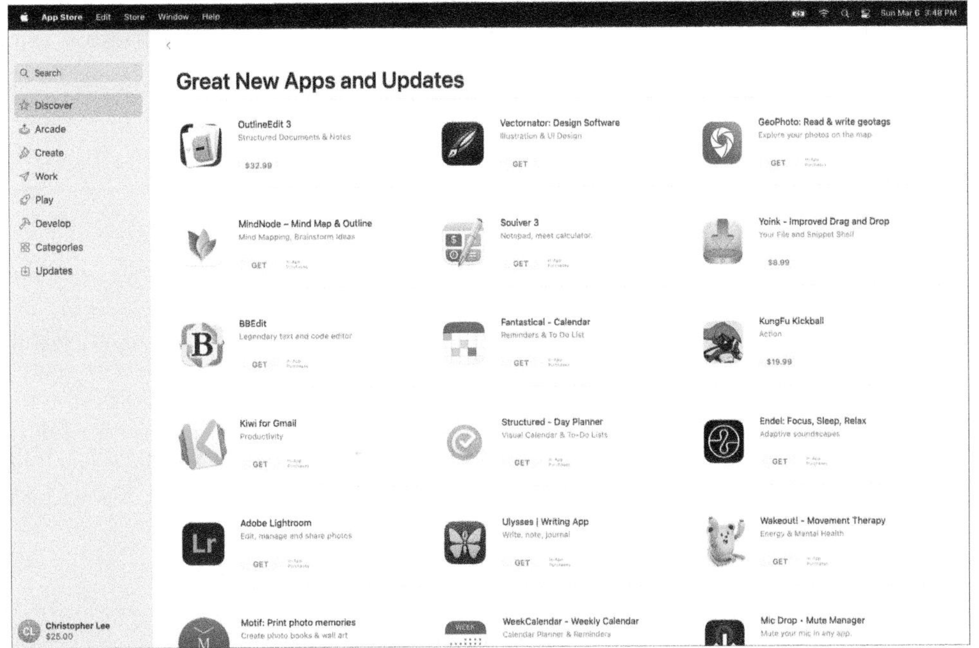

FIGURE 17.6 App Store

Share a Mac Screen

If you have **screen sharing** turned on, another Mac user who is on the same network can view and even control the display of your Apple computer. To view another computer's display remotely, open *Finder > Network*. Then double-click the Mac that you want to share and click *Share Screen*. Screen sharing is especially helpful to technicians supporting remote users.

System Updates

Apple uses the App Store to release patches and updates for macOS. It is important to check the Updates tab in the App Store from time to time to get the latest operating system and application updates. You can also have the number of updates available dynamically display on the App Store icon as a reminder that you have updates to perform.

Time Machine

It is easy to recover your previously purchased applications through the App Store, but the App Store is not a backup system. For that you need to set up Time Machine. **Time Machine** is a bundled application in macOS that enables you to do full and incremental system backups to an external hard drive. It gets its clever naming from the capability to navigate your past backups as if you were traveling through time. Notice in Figure 17.7 that the current Finder is on top. The stacked windows behind it are previous snapshots shown in time order from present to further in the past.

To use Time Machine, you need to connect an external hard drive to the system, typically through a USB or Thunderbolt connection. You can also do the backups to a disk over your network by using Time Capsule, a remote backup system sold by Apple. When an external drive is connected, you simply go into the Time Machine settings, which are located in the *System Preferences* menu, select the disk you want to use, and turn it on. Also while in the settings, you can click *Show Time Machine in menu bar* for a quick way to access Time Machine.

From there, Time Machine performs a full system backup and then continues to do a new incremental backup every hour. It retains the past 24 hours of backups, a daily backup for each day in the past month, and a weekly backup for all prior months. It deletes the oldest backups when the disk gets too full for the next backup. It keeps as many backups as possible following those rules. After Time Machine is set up, all these backups are done in the background, without user intervention.

TECH TIP

Requirements for using a disk for backups

When selecting a drive to use for backups, you need to use a drive with a partition that is APFS (Case-sensitive) formatted. APFS (Case-sensitive) is a variant of the APFS file system, which is discussed later in this chapter. By default, macOS cannot write to an NTFS-partitioned drive. If you choose such a drive, the disk will be reformatted, and all data on the disk will be erased. The number of backups possible depends on the size of the external drive. At a minimum, you want the drive to have at least as much disk space as your internal Mac hard drive so that you can always fit at least one full backup set on it. The larger the drive, the better. But remember: Creating a single backup is not a reliable way to back up important data. Always have multiple backup options for data that you cannot risk losing (for example, a local backup such as Time Machine as well as a remote or cloud backup).

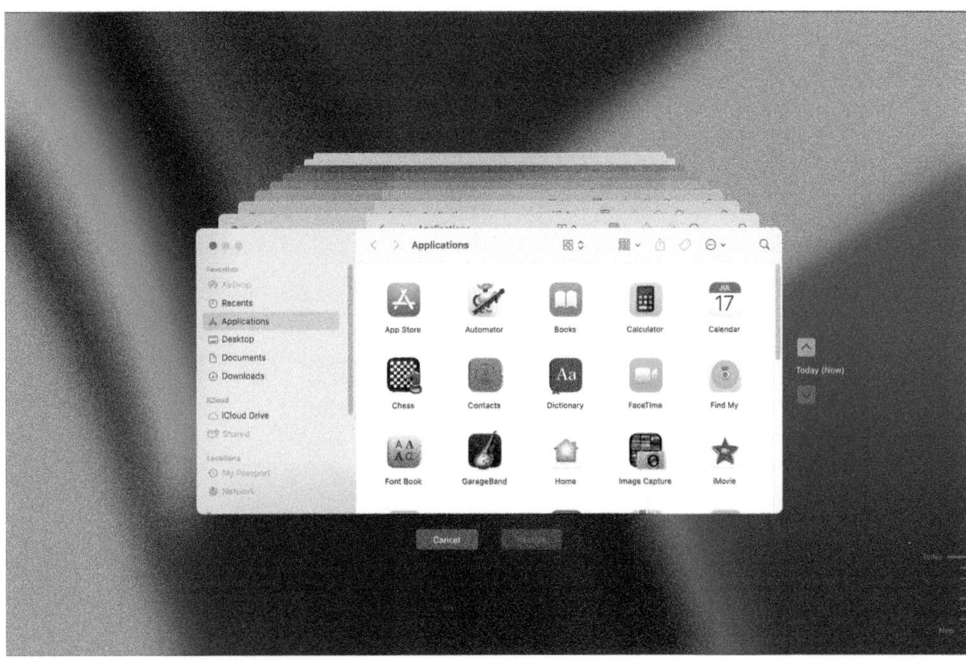

FIGURE 17.7 Time Machine

With the Time Machine interface, you can recover deleted files or even restore older versions of a file, as well as applications that were deleted. If a system failure occurs, you can even restore the entire backup from your Time Machine external drive onto a different Mac. You do this by booting the Mac you want to restore to into recovery mode. To enter recovery mode, make sure the computer is completely shut down. Then press and hold the power button until *Loading startup options* appears. Click *Options* > *Continue.* Select an administrator account and enter the password. Next, click *Continue*, and the Recovery menu appears.

When recovery mode boots, you see the option *Restore from a Time Machine Backup.* Make sure the external Time Machine drive is connected, select this option, and follow the prompts to restore the backup. If using a networked disk for Time Machine, you have the option to connect to the remote disk for the restore process.

You can restore an individual file or find an older version of the file while logged in to the normal mode. Simply select the file or navigate to the location where it was saved in Finder. Then open the Time Machine application from the Finder or from the Menu Bar icon to bring up a timeline view of that particular selected file or the files that have been in the selected location. You can navigate the backups available by scrolling through the timeline presented on the right side. When you find the file or version you want to restore, select it and click the *Restore* button.

If the Time Machine external drive is not connected, local snapshots are automatically created once a day. Figure 17.7 shows tick marks at the bottom-right of the screen. Each tick mark is a backup. When you position the pointer over a tick mark, you see that tick mark light up in a particular color. For macOS Yosemite and later, a bright red tick mark indicates that the particular backup can be used to restore the system (from a local snapshot or backup drive). A less bright tick mark indicates a backup that can only be restored from the backup drive.

Force Quit

macOS is a stable operating system that rarely crashes or requires you to use backups to recover anything, but applications can still run into issues in day-to-day use. When a program stops responding or working properly, you may need to use the **Force Quit** feature. To access the Force Quit menu, either click the *Apple* icon on the top left of the screen and then select *Force Quit* or hold down ⌘+Option+Esc at the same time. The window that appears allows you to choose which applications to quit (see Figure 17.8).

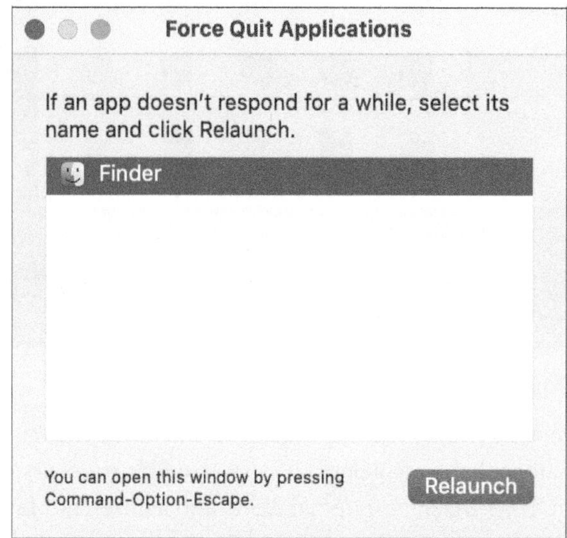

FIGURE 17.8 Force Quit Applications window

Another way of stopping an application is through the Terminal application, described later in this chapter. The Terminal program gives you access to a command prompt environment. Type **`top`** to see currently running processes. Locate the process ID associated with the problem application and press Ctrl+C to return to the command line. Next, type **`kill -9`** ***`process_id`*** (replacing *`process_id`* with the process ID number associated with the problem application).

Management and Troubleshooting Tools

macOS comes with a robust set of tools to keep the system running smoothly. But as with many other things in technology, macOS computers eventually break. As an IT professional, you need to understand what tools are at your disposal for fixing a system.

The most basic tool is the System Preferences menu (see Figure 17.9). **System Preferences** is equivalent to the Control Panels in Windows. System Preferences contains most of the system settings, from desktop backgrounds and screen savers to more advanced settings such as user accounts and file sharing. Third-party applications can also insert their own preferences menus into the System Preferences menu.

The System Preferences shortcut is, by default, located on the Dock, listed in Launchpad. It can also be opened from within Finder. Select the *Applications* menu on the left sidebar and then click the *System Preferences* icon. Table 17.3 lists all the default options in System Preferences and provides a brief description of each option.

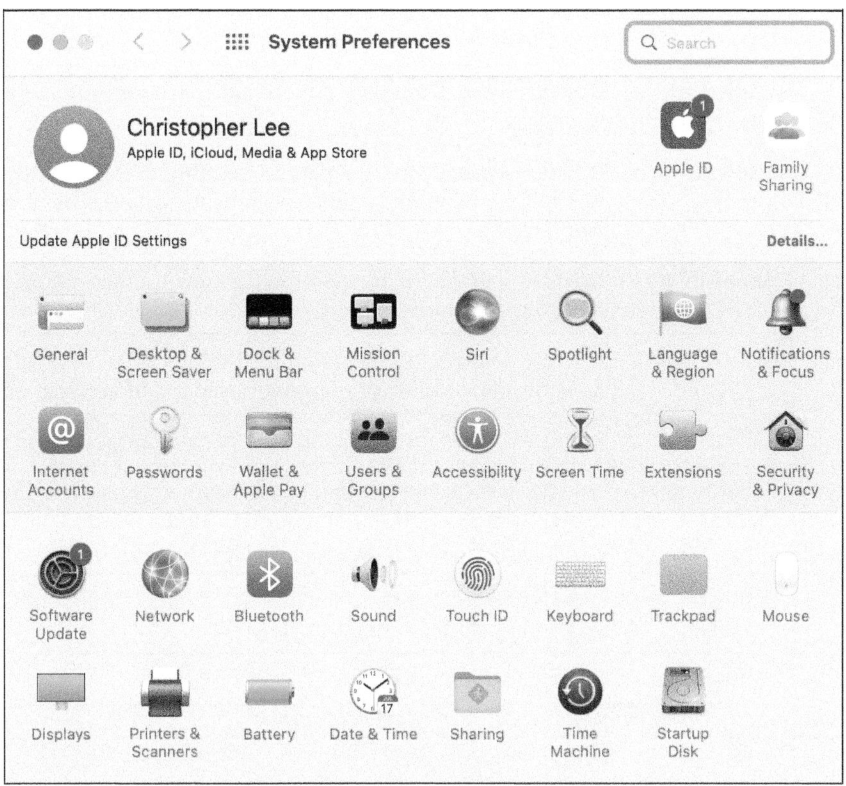

FIGURE 17.9 System Preferences window

TABLE 17.3 System Preferences settings

Option	Description
iCloud/ Apple ID	Allows you to use your Apple ID to sign in for access to iCloud, the App Store, and other services.
General	Provides settings for button, menu, and window colors, scrollbar behavior, default web browser choice, default actions for closing/opening documents and windows, and the option to enable handoff.
Desktop & Screen Saver	Provides settings for desktop backgrounds as well as for screen savers, such as the image to use, and when to turn on the screen saver.
Dock & Menu Bar	Provides settings for the size of the Dock and how the shortcuts behave. Also contains settings for the contents of the Menu Bar.
Mission Control	Provides settings for shortcuts that can be used inside Mission Control as well as grouping settings.
Siri	Provides an option to enable and configure Siri, a virtual personal assistant that responds to voice commands.
Spotlight	Provides settings for what is and isn't allowed to be searched.
Language & Region	Provides settings for adding and removing language options as well as setting the local region, calendar used, and date/number formatting.
Notifications & Focus	Provides settings for what apps can display notifications and how they are displayed. The Focus tabs provides settings to help minimize distractions from notifications.
Internet Accounts	Provides settings for management of email, contacts, calendars, messages, and other accounts.
Passwords	Provides settings to manage passwords for websites.

Option	Description
Wallet & Apple Play	Provides settings to add payment cards and use Apple Pay to make online purchases.
Users & Groups	Provides settings for creating and deleting user accounts, as well as what groups they belong in. Also provides settings for what items open automatically when a user logs in.
Accessibility	Provides settings for accessibility options such as colors, zoom, voiceover, captions, and more.
Screen Time	Provides settings for managing restrictions for accounts, such as restricted websites, time limits for computer usage, and application usage.
Extensions	Provides settings for managing third-party extensions used for customizing macOS.
Security & Privacy	Provides settings for general security, such as password requirements to unlock the screen from sleep, disk encryption using FileVault, general firewall settings, and privacy settings (such as using location-based services).
Software Update	Provides settings updates for macOS software and configures automatic checking and downloading of updates.
Network	Contains all network settings.
Bluetooth	Provides settings for toggling Bluetooth on and off and pairing devices such as Bluetooth headsets.
Sound	Provides settings for which audio output/input to use, volume, balancing the sound between speakers, and system sounds for alerts.
Touch ID	Provides settings for use of your fingerprint to unlock the computer and make purchases.
Keyboard	Provides settings for functions, shortcuts, and auto-correct.
Trackpad	Provides settings for multitouch gestures.
Mouse	Provides settings for mouse speed, scroll direction, and primary mouse button side.
Displays	Provides settings for managing resolution, brightness, and multiple display settings.
Printers & Scanners	Provides settings for adding and removing printers and scanning devices.
Battery (mobile)/ Energy Saver (desktop)	Provides settings to configure power options for the display and the computer. On laptops, allows users to monitor battery and power usage.
Date & Time	Provides settings for adjusting the time zone and the date and setting the clock.
Sharing	Provides settings for external access, such as enabling remote login and remote file sharing. Also provides settings for sharing of devices such as printers and setting the computer name.
Parental Controls	Provides settings for managing restrictions for kids' accounts, such as restricted websites, time limits for computer usage, and application usage.
Time Machine	Provides settings for toggling Time Machine backups on or off, selecting which external disk to use, and setting how to handle backups.
Startup Disk	Provides settings for selecting a different bootup disk, such as an external drive or Boot Camp partition (and allows Windows to be loaded as well).

Safe Mode

Safe mode (sometimes called safe boot) allows a Mac computer to be booted with a slimmed-down version of the operating system. Some of the software that is normally loaded automatically is not loaded; user-installed fonts are not installed; and font caches, kernel cache, and other system cache files are deleted. One really important function of safe mode is that the startup disk is checked and repaired, if possible, when issues are detected. Safe mode can also be used when removing malware.

> **TECH TIP**
>
> **How to start a Mac in safe mode**
>
> Make sure the computer is completely shut down. Next, press and hold the power button until *Loading startup options* appears. Click your startup drive and press and hold the ⇧Shift key. Then click *Continue in Safe Mode*. Select an administrator account and enter the password. The computer boots into safe mode, with *Safe Boot* in red letters near the upper-right corner.

Utilities

For more advanced system management, maintenance, and troubleshooting, use the tools located in the *Utilities* directory (see Figure 17.10). This is found by opening *Finder*, selecting the *Applications* section on the left side of the bar, and going into the *Utilities* folder.

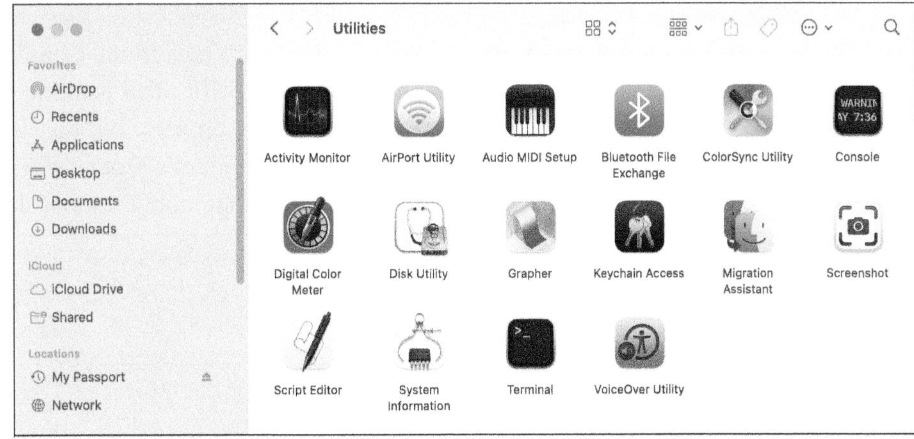

FIGURE 17.10 Utilities window

Activity Monitor

You need to be familiar with a few key utilities to properly troubleshoot a macOS system. **Activity Monitor** is a tool used to see what processes and services are running, as well as what system resources are being used. It is extremely useful in discovering why a system is running slowly (such as when an application appears to be frozen or when the system presents a constantly spinning **pin wheel**). You can look at the *CPU* tab, shown in Figure 17.11, to see what is consuming most of the CPU processing power. The *Memory* tab shows how much RAM each process is using, and the *Disk* tab provides a breakdown of how much disk read/write I/O is occurring. macOS automatically reserves some hard drive space to use as RAM. This is known as swap space. A good rule of thumb is to keep about 15% of the hard drive (and more, if possible) unused at all times. All these statistics are great tools for pinpointing poor system performance due to errant processes or lack of resources available for what the system is trying to do.

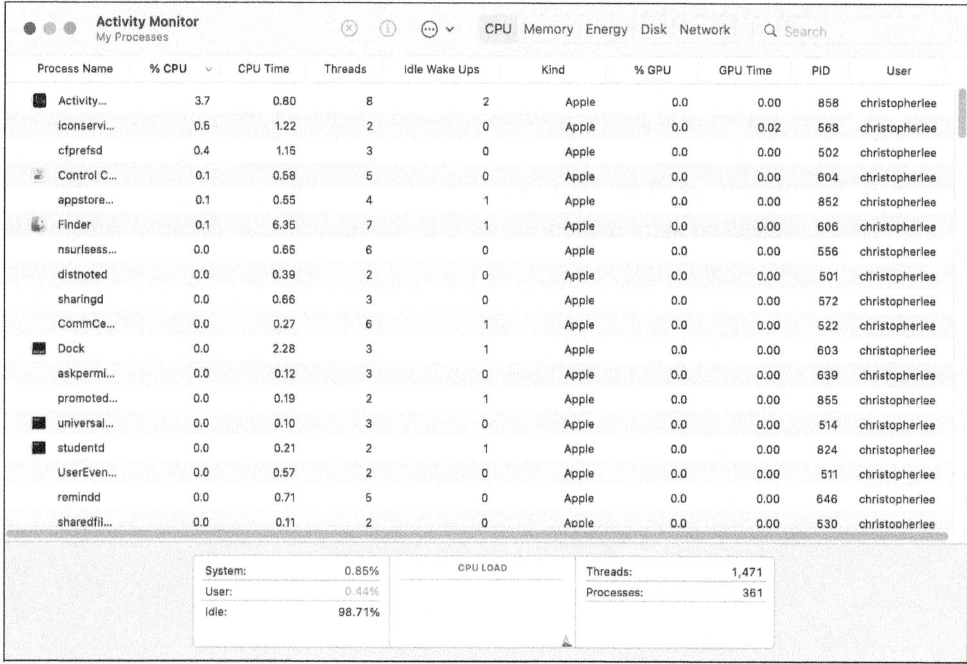

FIGURE 17.11 *Activity Monitor > CPU* tab

Console

The **Console** is a centralized place to find system and application logs and messages. macOS and the applications running on it constantly send activity logs to the Console, which lets you parse these logs manually or by searching for something specific. This is particularly helpful if you have an application or system service that is not behaving properly but that is not presenting an error message in the user interface. Most likely, if something has a problem, you can find a log explaining why in the Console. Figure 17.12 shows sample output in the Console.

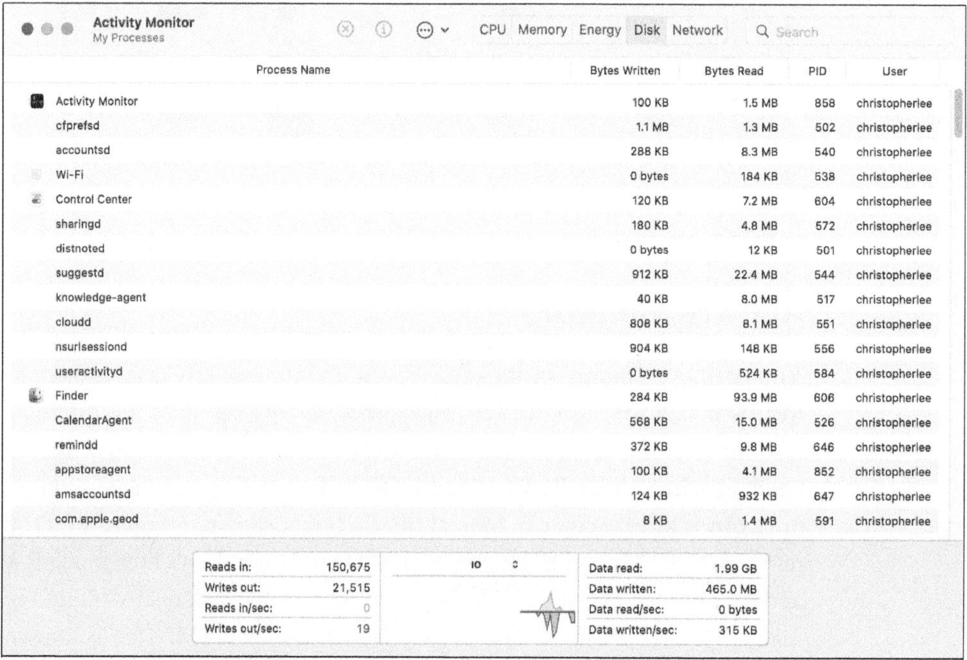

FIGURE 17.12 Console messages

Kernel Panic

The Console is good for troubleshooting **kernel panic**, which is a critical system error that the operating system cannot recover from. When this happens in macOS, the Mac reboots to return to a stable state. Trying to find the cause of kernel panic can be difficult because a wide array of issues can cause it, such as a hardware failure, operating system failure, or a faulty application. If kernel panic happens only once, it is typically fine to ignore it. But if problems continue to occur, the logs in the Console can be helpful for determining the cause. The kernel panic logs are saved in the `/Library/Logs/DiagnosticReports` directory, which can be viewed from inside the Console.

System Information

System Information is a utility that provides an overview of the Mac, including basic diagnostic information such as installed hardware, software, and network settings. If you need to find information about what is installed, such as the name of a graphics card, or the firmware version used for the network card, this is the place to look. System Information can be accessed from the *Utilities* directory or by clicking the *Apple* icon in the upper-left corner of the menu bar, selecting *About This Mac* from the drop-down menu, and then selecting *System Report* from the System Information menu that appears. Figure 17.13 shows sample output for hardware found from the System Information utility.

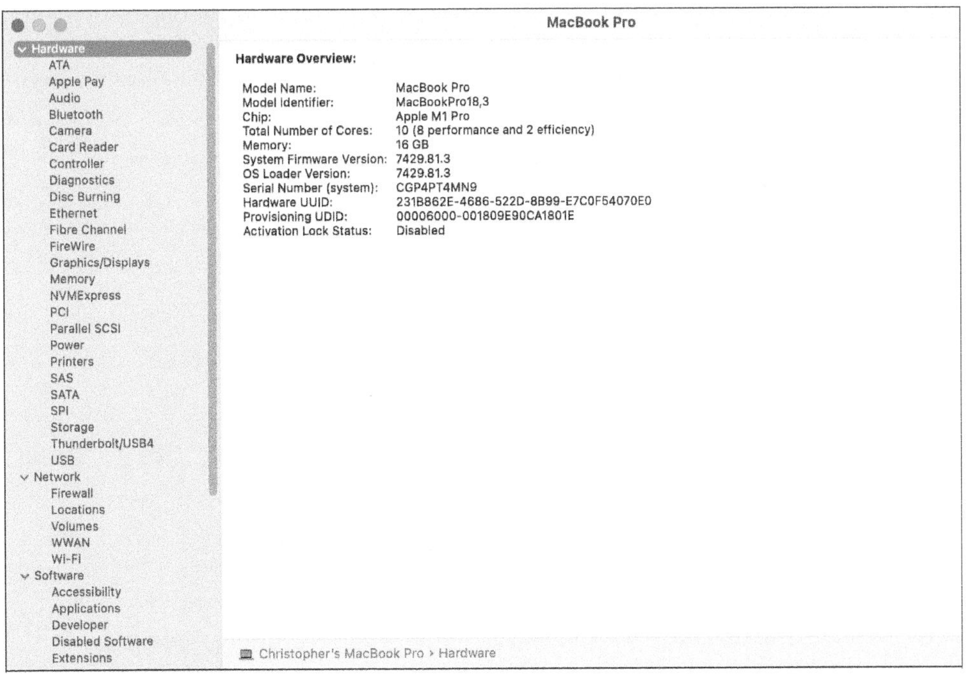

FIGURE 17.13 *System Information > Hardware*

Keychain Access

Keychain Access is a utility for securely managing saved passwords so users do not have to remember so many passwords saved on the system, whether for a Wi-Fi network or a web page login. These passwords are encrypted by default. A keychain file can be unlocked using the login password; however, you can set up a different password for the keychain, thus providing additional security.

A common problem occurs when a user updates their password when logging on, and then Keychain Access asks for the keychain password. This happens if someone uses a network-based account and updates their account on the server (which does not update the keychain password) or if they use the reset password feature in macOS recovery mode. Not all users are aware of what Keychain Access is or that they even have a keychain password because the password is created automatically. To remedy this, open the *Keychain Access* utility > select the appropriate keychain > from the menu bar select *Edit* > choose *Change Password for Keychain* > enter the previous password > click *OK*. A window opens, allowing you to update the password to the new login password.

A useful feature of the Keychain Access utility is the ability to see saved passwords. It is easy to forget passwords. If you were in a situation in which you were already connected to a Wi-Fi network but did not know the password, you could open the *Keychain Access* utility > select *Local Items* > double-click or double-tap the entry for the Wi-Fi network > enable the *Show password* option. You are then prompted to authenticate with your keychain password. You then see the saved password, unencrypted, as shown in Figure 17.14.

TECH TIP

What to do if users cannot remember their keychain password

A user who cannot remember his or her old keychain password needs to start a new keychain. This is done by selecting the Keychain Access *Preferences* drop-down menu > *Reset My Default Keychain*. The user can either delete the old keychain or opt to keep it in case they later remember the password.

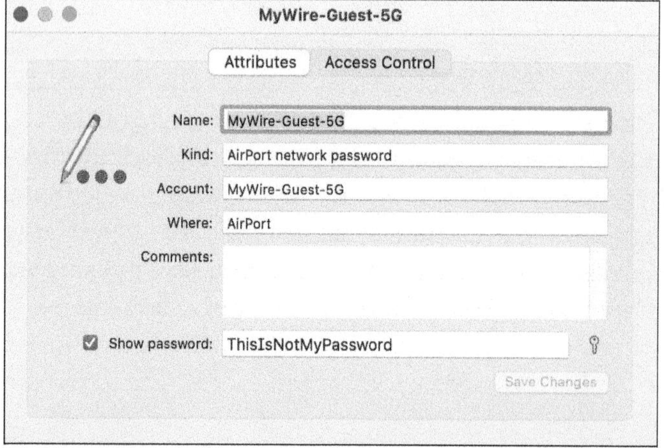

FIGURE 17.14 Viewing a password in Keychain Access

Disk Utility

Disk Utility is an application that handles the management of disks and disk images in macOS (see Figure 17.15). This utility can be used to rename, reformat, erase, repair, and restore disks. It is a powerful tool and should be used with caution because it is easy to delete all data on a system or on an external disk attached to the system.

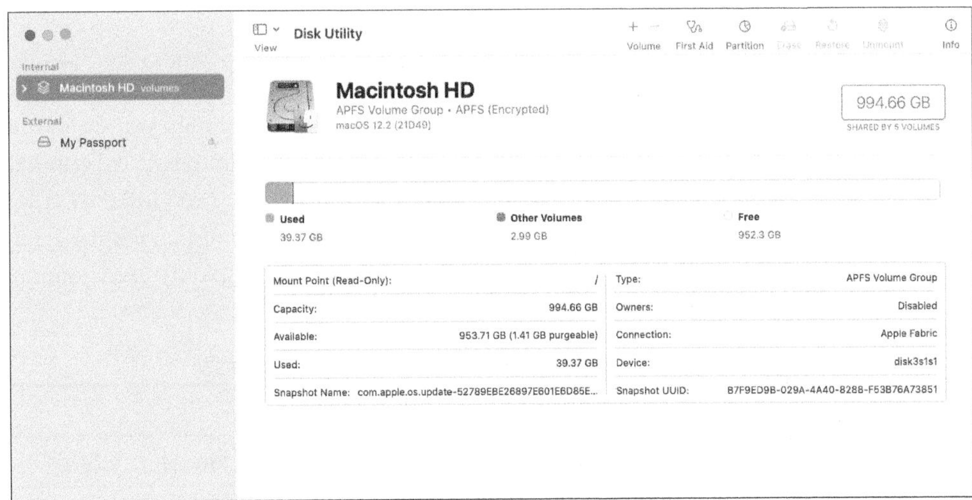

FIGURE 17.15 macOS Disk Utility

When a drive is connected to a Mac, it is mounted and shows up on the left side of the Disk Utility window. Selecting the drive gives you a handful of options: First Aid, Erase, Partition, Restore, Unmount, and Info. The First Aid disk option is similar to `fsck` or `chkdsk` in windows. It checks the file system integrity on a system and repairs issues it finds. It is highly advisable not to repair the disk unless you have a system backup and have a reason to run it, such as when a system boots only into safe mode or into recovery mode.

The *Erase* option allows you to wipe a disk, choose the format for the disk, and name the partition. You may also perform a secure erase by going into the security options on the menu. Secure erase has a few options, all of which write 0s or random data over the previous data on the disk to make it unrecoverable. You can choose no passes of zeros to quickly wipe out the disk, one pass of zeros, three passes of various types of data that is Department of Energy (DOE) compliant, or a seven-pass erase that meets the Department of Defense (DOD) standard for safely deleting data. Keep in mind that the more passes you do, the longer it takes to erase the disk.

The *Partition* tab enables you to manage the addition and deletion of partitions on a disk. An interactive chart shows the physical partition layout. You can adjust the chart with your mouse cursor to resize partitions, free up space to add new partitions, or free up space to expand a partition. As with all other disk modifications, you need to make sure you have any data backed up on a disk that you are repartitioning. Even if this is done properly, there is a risk of corruption and data loss.

macOS supports Hierarchical File System Plus (HFS+), also known as macOS Extended, as well as Apple File System (APFS), which supports SSDs and allows drive volumes to be reduced or increased as needed. To view the type of file system being used on a drive, select the drive in Disk Utility, and the file system type displays under the name of the disk.

Boot Camp

Boot Camp is a boot-loading utility designed to assist with partitioning, installation, and support in running Windows on a Mac. Installation requires a USB flash drive with at least 16 GB of space, a Windows installation ISO file or DVD installer, and a minimum of 30 GB of free space on the hard drive. The Boot Camp application guides you through the process of repartitioning your hard drive to make a partition labeled *BOOTCAMP*. It also copies the Windows ISO or DVD installer to the USB flash drive and copies the appropriate Mac drivers to it. After Boot Camp sets up the partition and copies everything you need to the flash drive, it reboots the system into the Windows installer, allowing you to complete the installation. As always, make sure you back up a system before doing anything involving partitioning. Boot Camp can also be used to remove a Windows partition.

Terminal

Terminal is the terminal emulator for macOS. It allows the command-line interface (CLI) access to the operating system. Although the majority of things you do in macOS can be performed in the GUI, there are times when using the CLI is required. The Terminal application can be found in the *Applications* folder > *Utilities* subfolder. You need to know at least a few basic commands and how to use them in case you run into a situation that can be fixed only by using Terminal. Table 17.4 outlines some of the most basic and commonly used commands. (More commands are provided later in the chapter.)

TABLE 17.4 Commonly used macOS commands

Command	Description
`c`	Lists the contents of the current working directory
`pwd`	Shows the current working directory path
`cd`	Moves between directories
`touch`	Creates a file
`mkdir`	Creates a directory
`cp`	Copies a file
`mv`	Moves a file
`rm`	Deletes a file or directory
`ls`	Shows the contents of a directory
`chown`	Changes ownership
`chmod`	Changes file permissions
`sudo`	Temporarily allows root privileges
`kill`	Stops a process ID associated with a particular application
`nano`	Opens an easy-to-use text editor
`vi`	Opens a text editor used by more experienced Linux users
`less`	Shows the contents of a file
`grep`	Searches output for a specified search term
`man`	When followed by another command, brings up a manual for using that command

The basic commands in Table 17.4 are enough to navigate the file system, create and remove files and directories, and do some basic troubleshooting. Keep in mind that for all these commands, you can use a variety of flags. It is best to reference the `man` page to discover what a command can do if you are unfamiliar with it. For example, the `ls` command run by itself shows the contents of the current working directory, but you can also specify a directory that is not the one where you are working so you can see its contents, as shown here:

```
testmac:~ testuser$ ls
Applications Desktop Documents Downloads Dropbox Library Movies Music
Pictures Public
testmac:~ testuser$ ls Public
Drop Box
```

As you can see here, by using `ls` and specifying another directory (in this case *Public*), the contents of the *Public* folder can be seen instead of the user's home folder. The following paragraphs provide brief examples of using the commands listed in Table 17.4.

`ls` lists the contents of a directory, including any directories located inside the current path in the file system. Here is an example:

```
testmac:~ testuser$ ls
Applications Desktop Documents Downloads Dropbox Library Movies Music
Pictures Public
```

`pwd` identifies the current working path, as shown in this example:

```
testmac:~ testuser$ pwd
/Users/testuser
```

`cd`, which is short for *change directory*, does exactly what its name indicates. Typing `cd` followed by a directory takes you to that directory. Notice that the working path is updated on the command line to help the user keep track of the current location:

```
testmac:~ testuser$ cd Applications
testmac:Applications testuser$
```

`touch` creates a blank file with the specified name. This command is not limited to text files. For example, you could make a file with the extension `html` if you wanted to work on creating a web page. Notice in the following example that the modifier `-l` and the filename `test.txt` are added to the `ls` command when showing the file created with the `touch` command:

```
testmac:~ testuser$ touch test.txt
testmac:~ testuser$ ls -l test.txt
-rw-r--r-- 1 testuser Editors 0 Sep 29 13:56 test.txt
```

The `-l` modifier is a flag for what is called *long listing*, which includes the normal output of the `ls` command plus add-ins. From left to right, the add-ins are as follows: file permission, number of file links, owner name, owner group, file size, time of last modification, and filename. In this example, instead of seeing all contents of the directory, you see only the file specifics.

`cp` is short for *copy*. The syntax of this command is `cp` followed by the source file and then the destination of the copy. You can also rename a file while copying it. Consider this example:

```
testmac:~ testuser$ cp test.txt testcopy.txt
testmac:~ testuser$ ls
Applications Documents Dropbox Movies Public
test.txt Desktop Downloads Library Music Pictures testcopy.txt
```

`mv` is short for *move*. It works similarly to `cp`, except it does not keep the original file in place. It actually modifies the file by moving it in the file system. During this process, you have the option to rename the file. In the following example, the `testcopy.txt` file is moved to `testmove.txt`:

```
testmac:~ testuser$ mv testcopy.txt testmove.txt
testmac:~ testuser$ ls
Applications Documents Dropbox Movies Public
test.txt Desktop Downloads Library Music Pictures testmove.txt
```

As shown above, `testcopy.txt` no longer exists because it is now named `testmove.txt`.

`rm` is short for *remove*. By using the `rm` command, you can designate which file or files to remove, as in this example:

```
testmac:~ testuser$ rm test.txt testmove.txt
testmac:~ testuser$ ls
Applications Desktop Documents Downloads Dropbox Library Movies Music Public
```

`sudo` is a command used to gain superuser (also known as root) privileges. In Unix/Linux, the administrator account is known as **root**. The root user has absolute power on a system, including within macOS. However, by default, this user account is disabled. It is advised that you not log in directly using root because if you were to accidentally run something malicious, the system could be degraded or compromised. However, administrative access is occasionally needed to perform certain tasks, such as running a script or installing an application. When you need such access at the command-line level, use the `sudo` command, which invokes a temporary root session to complete the command you are running.

In the following example, the file `importantdocument.txt` is created.

```
testmac:~ testuser$ touch importantdocument.txt
```

When you run `ls -l` for the file, you can see that you are the owner of it.

```
testmac:~ testuser$ ls -l importantdocument.txt
-rw-r--r-- 1 testuser Editors 0 Sep 30 10:39 importantdocument.txt
```

Then you want to make root the owner of the file, so you attempt to use the command `chown`, which changes file ownership. When `chown` is run, the message `Operation not permitted` appears, indicating that you do not have permission to do this.

```
testmac:~ testuser$ chown root importantdocument.txt
chown: importantdocument.txt: Operation not permitted
```

To fix this, you add `sudo` to the start of the command. When prompted, you enter your account password for verification. The command runs as the root user.

```
testmac:~ testuser$ sudo chown root importantdocument.txt
Password:
```

When you use `ls -l` again, you can see that the file owner changes from testuser to root.

```
testmac:~ testuser$ ls -l importantdocument.txt
-rw-r--r-- 1 root Editors 0 Sep 30 10:39 importantdocument.txt
```

To understand how to use the `chmod` command, you have to understand Unix/Linux file permissions. There are three types of permissions a user or group can have for a file: read, write, and execute. Permissions are indicated using the `-rwxrwxrwx` notation, with `r` being read, `w` being write, and `x` being execute. Notice the three sets of `rwx` entries. The first set, starting from the left, represents the owner's permissions. The second set represents the group's permissions. The last set represents everyone else (otherwise known as others). In the following example, look at the leftmost entries:

```
testmac:~ testuser$ ls -l importantdocument.txt
-rw-rw-r-- 1 root Editors 0 Sep 30 10:39 importantdocument.txt
```

The root owner of the file can read and write to the file, as designated by the first set of letters, `rw`. The users belonging to the Editors group can also read and write to the file, as shown by the second set of letters, `rw`. Everyone else can only read the file and is not allowed to modify it in any way, as designated by the last `r`.

To use chmod to change these permissions, there are various syntax options. The easiest to visualize uses letters. For instance, to add a write permission to the importantdocument.txt file for those known as others, use o+w, as shown in the following example:

```
testmac:~ testuser$ sudo chmod o+w importantdocument.txt
Password:
testmac:~ testuser$ ls -l importantdocument.txt
-rw-rw-rw- 1 root Editors 0 Sep 30 10:39 importantdocument.txt
```

This syntax can be used with the letters u (user), g (group), o (other), and a (all). The letters r, w, and x are then used to signify what permissions to either add or subtract for the subject specified. Then you specify the file for which permissions are to be changed.

There is another way of specifying permissions that involves using numbers to represent the permissions. The syntax for this is a three-digit number string, with the first number starting from the left representing the owner, the second number representing the group, and the final number representing others. The numbers range from 0 to 7, and they are translated into binary numbers to represent the permissions value, but an easy thing to do is remember that read permission equals 4, write permission equals 2, and execute permission equals 1. All the permissions you want to assign are added together. For example, if you want to give the root user read (4), write (2), and execute (1) permissions, the group read (4) permissions, and others no (0) permissions, you end up with 740. You can then use the command chmod followed by this number and then the file that is changed. The following example shows what this looks like:

```
testmac:~ testuser$ ls -l importantdocument.txt
-rw-rw-rw- 1 root Editors 0 Sep 30 10:39 importantdocument.txt
testmac:~ testuser$ sudo chmod 740 importantdocument.txt
Password:
testmac:~ testuser$ ls -l importantdocument.txt
-rwxr----- 1 root Editors 0 Sep 30 10:39 importantdocument.txt
```

nano is a text editor. When using the command line, it is common to need to use a text editor to fix files. Instead of going through the slow process of using a graphical text editor and navigating to the file to open it, you can quickly edit a file at the command line.

There are a few command-line text editors available to use in macOS and Linux, including vi, emacs, and nano. nano is an easy-to-use command-line text editor. You launch it by typing nano followed by the name of the file you want to edit. If the file does not exist, nano creates it. Entering the command q cancels the editing session. What makes nano so convenient to use is that it is a powerful editor with many options, such as search and replace, line numbers, and quick navigation with page up/page down. It also has a set of quick controls displayed in its interface, which is helpful for occasional users who have not memorized all the shortcuts.

less is a tool you can use to quickly view the contents of a file. It presents a window of the contents that you can scroll through by using the b key to scroll up and Spacebar to scroll down; you can also page to the bottom by holding down Shift and pressing the g key. less becomes a powerful tool when combined with a search utility known as grep and the | (pipe) function. The | key is used for passing output from one command to another. You can use less to see the content of a file and then pipe it to grep to search for something inside it. For example, you can add the following text to the importantdocument.txt file with which you have been working:

```
OS X 10.8 Mountain Lion
OS X 10.9 Mavericks
OS X 10.10 Yosemite
OS X 10.11 El Capitan
```

CHAPTER 17

If you want to find this information somewhere within a few hundred pages, it will be difficult to find it by just reading the document. Using `nano` to search could also take a long time because you would have to run the search over and over to find all the multiple entries. A better command to use in this case is `less` to get the output of the file and send it to `grep` to search for the wanted file:

```
testmac:~ testuser$ less importantdocument.txt | grep Yosemite
OS X 10.10     Yosemite
```

You can see that `grep` works by taking the input it receives and using it as a search source. It then outputs every line of the input (`importantdocument.txt`) that contains the search term.

TECH TIP

Use the manual!

You need to know your commands and their options, but it is easy to forget the ones that you do not use often. When you cannot remember how to use a command, use the command `man`, which is short for manual. `man` brings up directions on how to use any command for which there is a manual page entry. The syntax is simply the command `man` followed by the command you want to know more about.

Introduction to Linux

Linux, released in 1991 by developer Linus Torvalds, is a widely used operating system platform that is similar to trademarked UNIX, a group of operating systems that grew from the AT&T-developed UNIX. It is meant to be a free, open source operating system that everyone can use, contribute to, and modify as needed. Because of this, it is widely used in many different areas of technology, such as servers, desktops, embedded systems, and smartphones. It is also mostly POSIX compliant, so some of the concepts you have already learned in this chapter about macOS also apply to most Linux systems.

The terminology of Linux can be confusing for someone who is new to it. The name *Linux* refers to an operating system kernel. A **kernel** is the heart of an operating system. It acts as the controller and interpreter for nearly everything in a system, so hardware and software can interface and work together. It controls things such as memory management, peripherals, and allocation of other system resources to processes.

The Linux kernel is repackaged into different operating system distributions (distros for short). There are hundreds of different distros. Table 17.5 lists the most popular ones and where to find more information about them. Although these distros are all different from one another in some ways, they are all Linux operating systems because they use the Linux kernel.

TABLE 17.5 Linux distros

Distro name	Website
Ubuntu	http://www.ubuntu.com
Debian	http://www.debian.org
Mint	http://linuxmint.com
SUSE	https://www.suse.com
Red Hat	http://www.redhat.com
Fedora	https://getfedora.org

Distro name	Website
CentOS	https://www.centos.org
Gentoo	https://www.gentoo.org
Arch	https://www.archlinux.org
Kali	https://www.kali.org

Anyone going into IT should explore the different Linux distros to see the differences and similarities between them. Ubuntu is the most widely used home desktop distribution, and it also has a server version. Although you probably will not find Ubuntu in an enterprise environment, you are likely to encounter it with end users, developers, and simple servers. And a lot of the skills you learn for Ubuntu are useful with other distros.

You do not have to install Ubuntu onto a computer to experiment with it. Unlike with Windows or macOS, you can use a live DVD or flash drive, which is simply a disc you can boot to or run from a flash drive. By booting from a DVD or flash drive, you can run the operating system as if it were installed on the computer. This makes it much easier to try different distributions without having to dedicate a computer solely to running Linux. If you do launch Linux from a DVD or flash drive, however, you need to be careful because you can still modify the local file system on the computer and cause harm to the installed operating system.

TECH TIP

Downloading Ubuntu

Download Ubuntu's latest release from http://www.ubuntu.com/download/desktop. It will be needed to complete some of the labs.

Navigating the GNOME User Interface

There are many types of graphical user interfaces for Linux, such as GNOME, KDE, Xfce, and Cinnamon. Each has unique interface operation and tools. GNOME is the name of the graphical user interface in Ubuntu. It has some similarities to the user interface of macOS, but it is drastically different from Windows.

The **dash** is the shortcut bar on the left side of the screen. It is reminiscent of the macOS Dock, but it doesn't work completely the same. It has the functionality of being an application launcher shortcut as well as having a universal search feature built in to it. Clicking a shortcut in the dash opens its application. If you right-click or control-click the icon, a context window will appear. The *Show Applications* button at the bottom reveals several other applications. When you click the *Activities* button at the top of the dash, you open the Activities Overview. The Activities Overview shows all open windows and applications, as well as a menu for a local search tool that can get results for applications, files, and folders.

The bar at the top of the screen contains contextual information on the left side and static information on the right side; it is a lot like the menu bar in macOS. **Nautilus** is the file manager for Ubuntu (see Figure 17.16). You can quickly access it by clicking the *Files* icon on the **Launcher**. Nautilus is the default file manager, but because Linux is so modular and customizable, it can be replaced with an alternative file manager. Like all other GUI operating systems, Linux has a standard desktop.

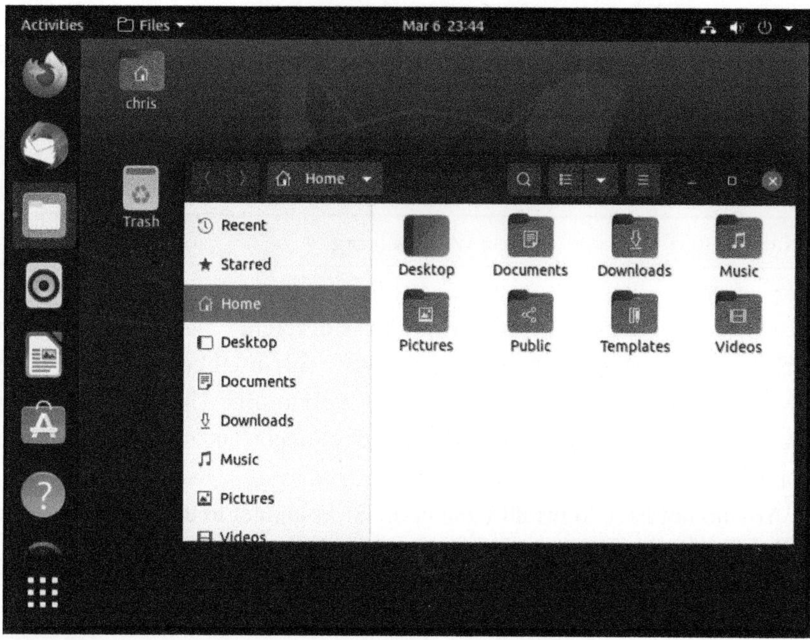

FIGURE 17.16 Nautilus file manager window

The universal search tool that is built into the Launcher searches local content. Search locations can be enabled or disabled in *dash > Show Applications > Settings > Search*. Search results appear in subcategories at the bottom of the search interface, called lenses (see Figure 17.17).

The Ubuntu user interface is straightforward, which makes it convenient for home use. A Linux system in an enterprise environment is not accessed through the GUI. Most of the Linux systems in the corporate environment do not even have a GUI installed. However, a few GUI tools should be mentioned, and they are covered in the following sections.

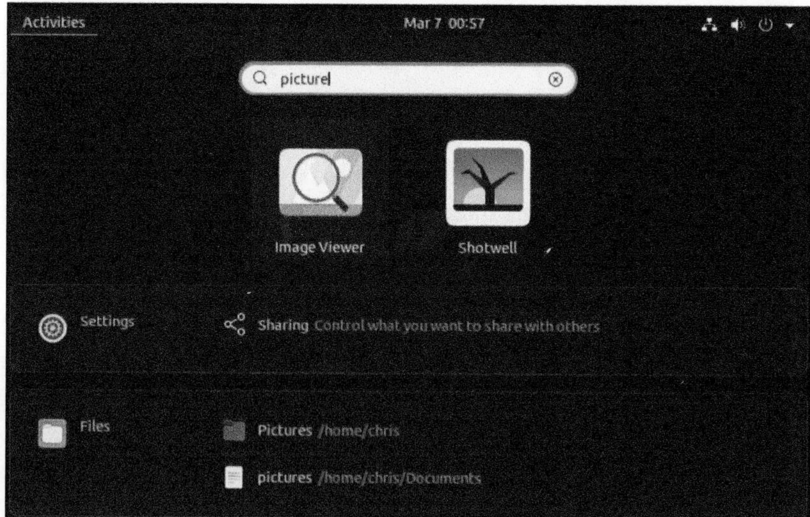

FIGURE 17.17 Launcher's search tool

Basic System Usage, Updates, and Backups

Numerous useful tools for managing the system come bundled with Ubuntu. Some of them are best used through the GUI. Although everything can be done through the command-line interface, some tools are much easier to use on the desktop.

The best example of this is **Disks**, a disk management tool that allows for the creation, deletion, and resizing of partitions on a physical disk (see Figure 17.18). Disks has an easy-to-use drag-and-drop interface for partition management that is far easier to visualize and understand than the command line. If you experiment with Disks, be mindful that you can wipe out your system if you are unsure of the correct procedures.

Whereas Windows mostly uses NTFS, and macOS uses HFS+ or APFS, there are many more file system options to choose from on Linux. When installing Linux or partitioning with Disks, you need to be aware of these options. Table 17.6 lists and describes the most common file systems. Most distros, including Ubuntu, default to using a file system known as ext4 (fourth extended file system), an improvement on **ext3** (third extended file system), which was the most widely used file system for many years.

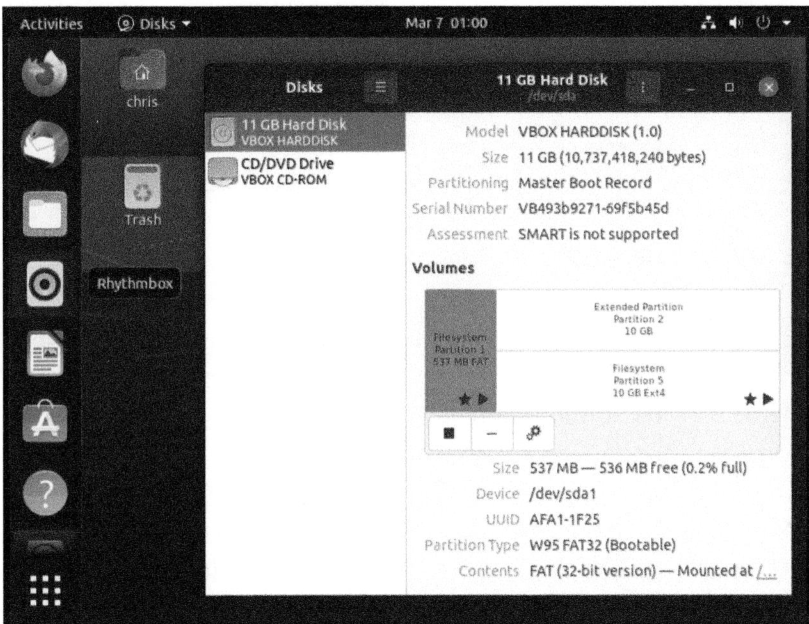

FIGURE 17.18 Disks window

TABLE 17.6 Linux file systems

File system name	Description
ext4	Fourth generation of the extended file system, which contains features such as journaling, volume support up to 1 exbibyte (EiB), and file sizes up to 16 tebibytes (TiB). It is a common file system choice.
ZFS	File system that focuses on data integrity and that can do integrity checks on mounted disks (unlike ext4). You would not use ZFS on a machine that is using RAID. It is recommended for use on a single drive or just a bunch of disks (JBOD).
Btrfs	Pronounced "butter F S," adds features absent in ext4, such as snapshots, volume spanning, live resizing of file systems, and live addition/removal of disks to live file systems. It can support volumes and file sizes up to 16 EiB.

Ubuntu comes with a fair amount of software installed, but one of the great things about using Linux is the amount of free, open source software available. It isn't always easy to find software, especially if you are new to Linux and are unfamiliar with the tools that are available. **Ubuntu Software Center** is a software manager that lets you access software from Ubuntu's repositories.

With Ubuntu Software, shown in Figure 17.19, you can uninstall existing applications and install new ones, many of which are available for free. Although Ubuntu Software Center is useful for finding new software, you need to use the **Software Updater** tool to update your operating system and applications.

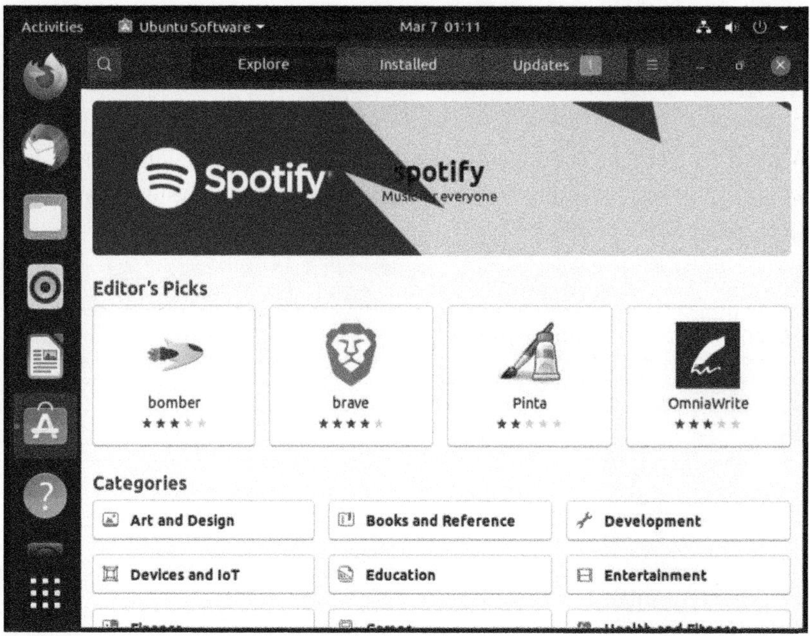

FIGURE 17.19 Ubuntu Software app

Ubuntu comes bundled with Backups, a built-in backup application (see Figure 17.20) that supports local and remote backups, encryption, and scheduling; in addition, it can run seamlessly in the background. The Backups application can be found by searching for `backups` in the GNOME search tool. However, a wide array of other backup software is available for Linux. Many companies have their own backup procedure that involves using custom scripts and various utilities, such as `rsync`, to save on resources compared to doing a full system backup, as experienced in most Windows environments.

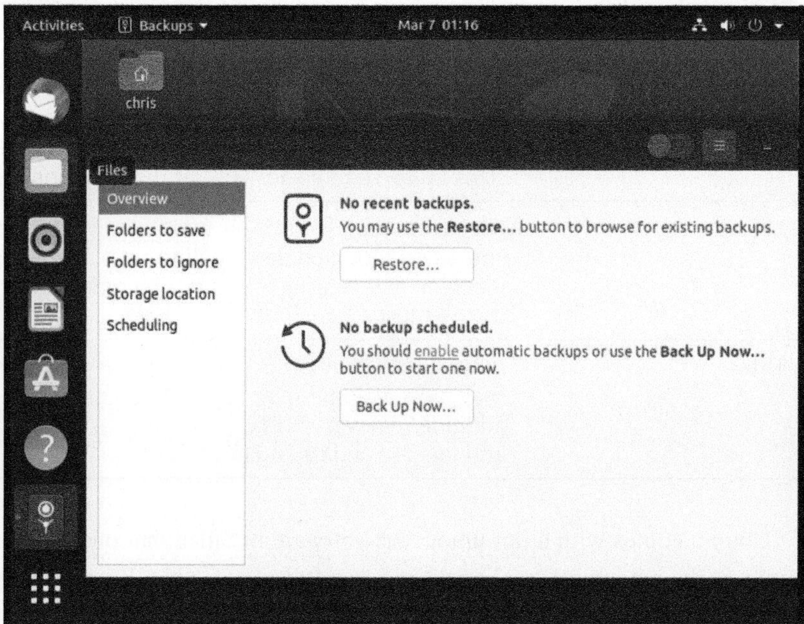

FIGURE 17.20 Ubuntu's Backups application

Command-Line Interface

The **command-line interface** (CLI) is where most system management takes place for Linux and Unix systems. The CLI for most Linux systems uses a terminal language known as bash. bash is simply the command language used in the CLI, but there are a few other notable shells, such as Dash, fish, zsh, and tcsh. Ubuntu uses bash, as do most other distros, so we focus on using that for the rest of this chapter.

You may want to refer to Table 17.4 to review basic command-line usage in macOS. Because macOS is based on Unix (and so is Linux), those commands also work in Linux. There are also more advanced commands that everyone who supports Linux systems should know. Table 17.7 lists and briefly describes these commands.

TABLE 17.7 Advanced CLI commands

Command	Description
`shutdown`	Shuts down or restarts the system, depending on the options used
`passwd`	Sets the password for a user
`su`	Switches from one user account to another
`ifconfig`	Shows network interface information for Ethernet ports
`iwconfig`	Shows network interface information for wireless adapters
`ps`	Shows a list of all currently running processes
`apt-get`	Allows management of packages
`dd`	Copies and converts files
`locate`	Searches the system for a file
`updatedb`	Updates the file database of the system for the `locate` command

To use the CLI on Ubuntu, click the *Activities* button and search for *Terminal*. If a few options appear, you might want to use the one specifically labeled *Terminal*. This interface is similar to the macOS interface in that the command line shows the username and computer name.

Shutting Down the System

The `shutdown` command is straightforward: It shuts down the system. Here is an example:

```
ubuntu@ubuntu:~$ sudo shutdown
Shutdown scheduled for Sun 2019-10-25 16:13:07 UTC, use 'shutdown -c' to
cancel.
Broadcast message from root@ubuntu (Sun 2019-10-25 16:12:07 UTC):
The system is going down for power-off at Sun 2019-10-25 16:13:07 UTC!
```

When you run the `shutdown` command, you must have superuser permissions; this is why `sudo` is used before the `shutdown` command. By default, running `shutdown` schedules a shutdown one minute into the future, which gives you an opportunity to cancel it. There are also options to schedule the shutdown for a different time, to have the shutdown happen immediately, or to restart instead of powering off. You can also have a shutdown message broadcast to warn anyone else who might be logged in to the system.

passwd vs. pwd

The passwd command, not to be confused with pwd, is used to change a user's password. Remember that the pwd command is used to view the current working directory. To change the logged-in user's password, just run the passwd command by itself. A prompt appears, where you can enter the current password and then enter the new password twice, as shown here.

```
ubuntu@ubuntu:~$ passwd
Changing password for ubuntu.
Current password:
New password:
Retype new password:
passwd: password updated successfully
```

If you want to change the password of a different user, enter the command followed by the username, as shown here:

```
ubuntu@ubuntu:~$ sudo passwd test
New password:
Retype new password:
passwd: password updated successfully
```

Note that you must have superuser permissions to change another user's password. To modify an account, you either need to be logged in to that account or have administrative (root) privileges.

Performing Network Configuration

The command ifconfig is an essential Linux command that all Linux administrators and users need to be familiar with. The basic output shows the current network settings, such as IP address, subnet mask, interfaces used, MAC address, and interface statistics, as you can see in the following example:

```
ubuntu@ubuntu:~$ ifconfig
eth0 Link encap:Ethernet HWaddr b8:27:eb:43:c3:ad
 inet addr:10.0.0.250 Bcast:10.0.0.255 Mask:255.255.255.0
 UP BROADCAST RUNNING MULTICAST MTU:1500 Metric:1
 RX packets:5633010 errors:0 dropped:6300 overruns:0 frame:0
 TX packets:9370432 errors:0 dropped:0 overruns:0 carrier:0
 collisions:0 txqueuelen:1000
 RX bytes:429577586 (409.6 MiB) TX bytes:3680672251 (3.4 GiB)
lo Link encap:Local Loopback
 inet addr:127.0.0.1 Mask:255.0.0.0
 UP LOOPBACK RUNNING MTU:65536 Metric:1
 RX packets:0 errors:0 dropped:0 overruns:0 frame:0
 TX packets:0 errors:0 dropped:0 overruns:0 carrier:0
 collisions:0 txqueuelen:0
 RX bytes:0 (0.0 B) TX bytes:0 (0.0 B)

wlan0 Link encap:Ethernet HWaddr 80:1f:02:bb:ee:fa
 UP BROADCAST MULTICAST MTU:1500 Metric:1
 RX packets:0 errors:0 dropped:0 overruns:0 frame:0
 TX packets:0 errors:0 dropped:0 overruns:0 carrier:0
 collisions:0 txqueuelen:1000
 RX bytes:0 (0.0 B) TX bytes:0 (0.0 B)
```

As you can see in this output, you are presented with three different interfaces. `eth0` is an abbreviation for ethernet 0, the wired Ethernet connection. `lo` is an abbreviation for localhost, a loopback interface that is used for testing and routing information inside the operating system. Finally, `wlan0` represents wireless LAN interface 0. In this example, only `eth0` and `lo` have IP addresses assigned, and `wlan0` is yet to be configured.

More advanced use of `ifconfig` allows you to change interface settings. If you want to set an address for `wlan0`, you can use `ifconfig` followed by the interface name `wlan0` and then the appropriate settings, as shown in the following example:

```
ubuntu@ubuntu:~$ sudo ifconfig wlan0 10.0.0.200 netmask 255.255.255.0
broadcast 10.0.0.255
ubuntu@ubuntu:~$ ifconfig
eth0 Link encap:Ethernet HWaddr b8:27:eb:43:c3:ad
 inet addr:10.0.0.250 Bcast:10.0.0.255 Mask:255.255.255.0
 UP BROADCAST RUNNING MULTICAST MTU:1500 Metric:1
 RX packets:5668535 errors:0 dropped:6327 overruns:0 frame:0
 TX packets:9430245 errors:0 dropped:0 overruns:0 carrier:0
 collisions:0 txqueuelen:1000
 RX bytes:432348412 (412.3 MiB) TX bytes:3758820467 (3.5 GiB)

lo Link encap:Local Loopback
 inet addr:127.0.0.1 Mask:255.0.0.0
 UP LOOPBACK RUNNING MTU:65536 Metric:1
 RX packets:0 errors:0 dropped:0 overruns:0 frame:0
 TX packets:0 errors:0 dropped:0 overruns:0 carrier:0
 collisions:0 txqueuelen:0
 RX bytes:0 (0.0 B) TX bytes:0 (0.0 B)

wlan0 Link encap:Ethernet HWaddr 80:1f:02:bb:ee:fa
 inet addr:10.0.0.200 Bcast:10.0.0.255 Mask:255.255.255.0
 UP BROADCAST MULTICAST MTU:1500 Metric:1
 RX packets:0 errors:0 dropped:0 overruns:0 frame:0
 TX packets:0 errors:0 dropped:0 overruns:0 carrier:0
 collisions:0 txqueuelen:1000
 RX bytes:0 (0.0 B) TX bytes:0 (0.0 B)
```

In this example, even though an appropriate address has been assigned to `wlan0` for the wireless network, `wlan0` is not a working wireless interface. Other wireless settings, such as the wireless network SSID as well as any authentication settings, must be configured. That is where the command `iwconfig` comes into play. Although `ifconfig` can edit IP settings, it cannot do the wireless-specific settings that `iwconfig` provides.

Say that you have a Linux computer connected to a wireless network named Test that uses the WEP encryption key 1234567890. You would enter the following command:

```
ubuntu@ubuntu:~$ sudo iwconfig wlan0 essid Test key restricted 1234567890
```


TECH TIP

`iwconfig` supports only WEP authentication

It is important to realize that `iwconfig` supports only WEP authentication. For more advanced authentication, such as WPA or WPA2, you need to use `wpa_supplicant`. It is recommended not to use WEP if you can use higher-level encryption because WEP is an older standard that is easily cracked.

Viewing Processes

ps is another command to have in your toolbox for administering a Linux system. ps shows all active processes running on a system. This important information tells you what is running, how long things have been running, and how many resources are being used. Here is an example:

```
ubuntu@ubuntu:~$ ps
 PID TTY TIME CMD
 4093 pts/0 00:00:01 bash
14766 pts/0 00:00:00 ps
```

By default, ps shows only processes being run by the current user and from the current login session. Generally, you use ps along with other modifiers to get useful information. The most common version of ps is ps aux. The a modifier lists all processes from other users, u shows the user who is running the process, and x shows processes from all sessions. The ps command effectively shows everything that is running on the system. Here is an example:

```
ubuntu@ubuntu:~$ ps aux
USER PID %CPU %MEM VSZ RSS TTY STAT START TIME COMMAND
root 1 0.0 0.1 2148 1348 ? Ss Oct23 0:10 init [2]
root 2 0.0 0.0 0 0 ? S Oct23 0:00 [kthreadd]
root 3 0.0 0.0 0 0 ? S Oct23 0:16 [ksoftirqd/0]
root 5 0.0 0.0 0 0 ? S< Oct23 0:00 [kworker/0:0H]
root 7 0.0 0.0 0 0 ? S Oct23 1:53 [rcu_preempt]
root 8 0.0 0.0 0 0 ? S Oct23 0:00 [rcu_sched]
root 9 0.0 0.0 0 0 ? S Oct23 0:00 [rcu_bh]
```

A lesser-known option is to add the f modifier, so the command is ps faux. This shows everything from ps aux and also organizes the processes in a tree format so you can see what processes are the parent and the child. In the following example, a screen session is running for a script being run by the program supervisor. Some of the command output has been omitted here to make it easier to read:

```
root 2316 0.0 0.3 4816 2372 ? Ss Oct23 1:02 SCREEN
root 2317 0.0 0.5 5680 4088 pts/1 Ss Oct23 0:00 \_ /bin/bash
root 2325 0.0 0.3 4592 2660 pts/1 S+ Oct23 0:00 \_ sudo supervise /etc/
init.d/
```

Obtaining Software via the CLI

Earlier in this chapter you read about using the Ubuntu Software tool to obtain software. apt-get is the command-line interface tool that is the equivalent of the Ubuntu Software tool. There is another common command-line package manager, named rpm, short for Red Hat Package Manager. Despite its name, it is used on more distros than just Red Hat. There is another lesser-used manager called yum, short for Yellowdog Updater, Modified, that builds on rpm.

To use apt-get, start by refreshing the list of available software. Systems that use apt-get have a file located at /etc/apt/sources.list, which lists the software repositories that should be checked for available software. It is common to edit this list to add different sources to get different applications. To update the list of available software from your sources list, you use the command apt-get followed by the modifier update. Only the first few lines of the following example are shown because the complete output can take up a lot of screen space, depending on the number of sources:

```
ubuntu@ubuntu:~$ sudo apt-get update
Get:1 http://archive.ubuntu.com vivid InRelease [218 kB]
Get:2 http://security.ubuntu.com vivid-security InRelease [64.4 kB]
```

After updating the sources, use the `apt-get` command followed by `install` and then the name of the package to install the software. Say that you want to obtain software called `install screen`, which is a tool that enables you to use multiple screens. At the CLI, execute the command `apt-get install screen`.

It is recommended that you always simulate a software installation first by using the `-s` modifier to make sure the installation will not affect something important on the system. Here is an example:

```
ubuntu@ubuntu:~$ sudo apt-get install screen -s
Reading package lists... Done
Building dependency tree
Reading state information... Done
Suggested packages:
 select screen byobu
The following NEW packages will be installed:
 screen
0 upgraded, 1 newly installed, 0 to remove and 282 not upgraded.
Inst screen (4.2.1.-3 Ubuntu:15.04/vivid [amd64])
Conf screen (4.2.1.-3 Ubuntu:15.04/vivid [amd64])
```

This simulation shows what would happen if you actually installed the screen. Once you determine that the installation would be correct, you can rerun the command without the `-s` modifier to install the software.

TECH TIP

Always predownload packages

When working with systems that need high uptime, it is always advisable to predownload the packages you plan to install ahead of time to avoid downtime while waiting for a download to occur. This can be done by running the `apt-get install` command with the `-d` flag.

Copying Data

The command `dd` is a versatile command you can use to copy and convert data. Some common uses include copying the contents of a DVD or flash drive to an ISO file, cloning a partition to another one, creating a backup, erasing a disk, converting a file or its content, and benchmarking. The general syntax is the command `dd` followed by the input file and then the output file. You can also use many other modifiers, such as `conv` for conversions, `bs` for maximum byte per read or write, and `count` for the number of blocks to copy.

We'll use Figure 17.21 to show the capabilities of `dd` in an environment with two partitions. The partitions were created using the application `Disks`. They are equal in size, are virtually empty, and are named `/dev/sdb1` and `/dev/sdb2`.

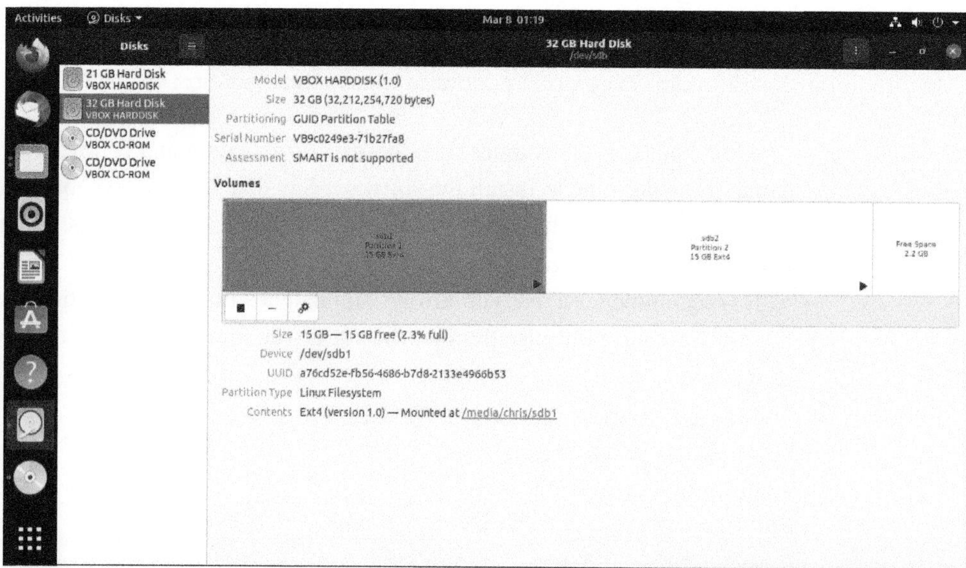

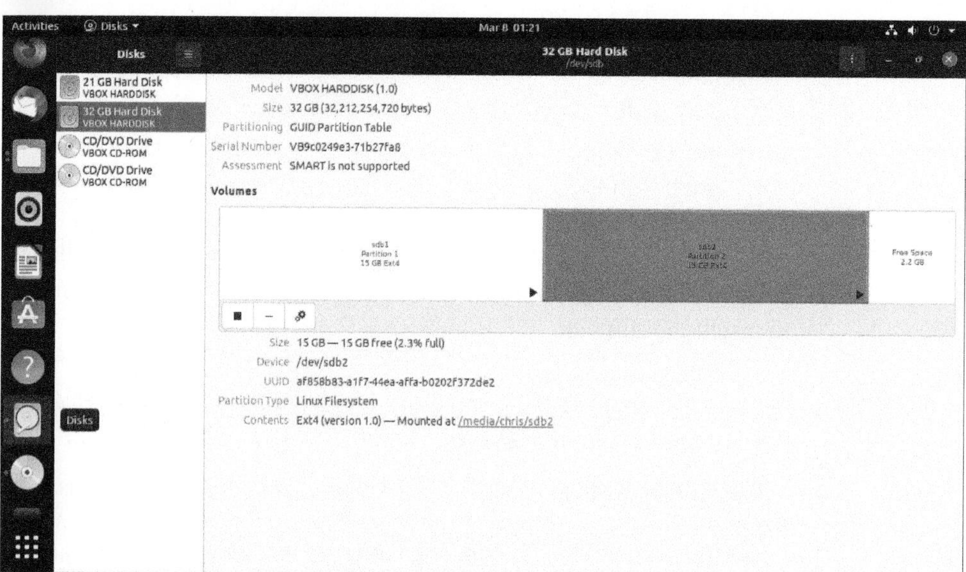

FIGURE 17.21 Disk partitions in Disks

To copy the contents of a DVD onto `/dev/sdb1`, the syntax is `dd` followed by the input file (the DVD) and the output file, which is `/dev/sdb1/test.iso`. Here is an example:

```
chris@ubuntulee:~$ sudo dd if=/dev/sr1 of=/media/chris/sdb1/test.iso
6599744+0 records in
6599744+0 records out
3379068928 bytes (3.4 GB, 3.1 GiB) copied, 36.0662 s, 93.7 MB/s
```

The output in this example shows 3.4 GB of data copied, the size of the data on the DVD. The command took 36 seconds, and it copied at almost 94 MB/s. Look at the partitions with Disks in Figure 17.22. The `sdb1` partition now has more space used.

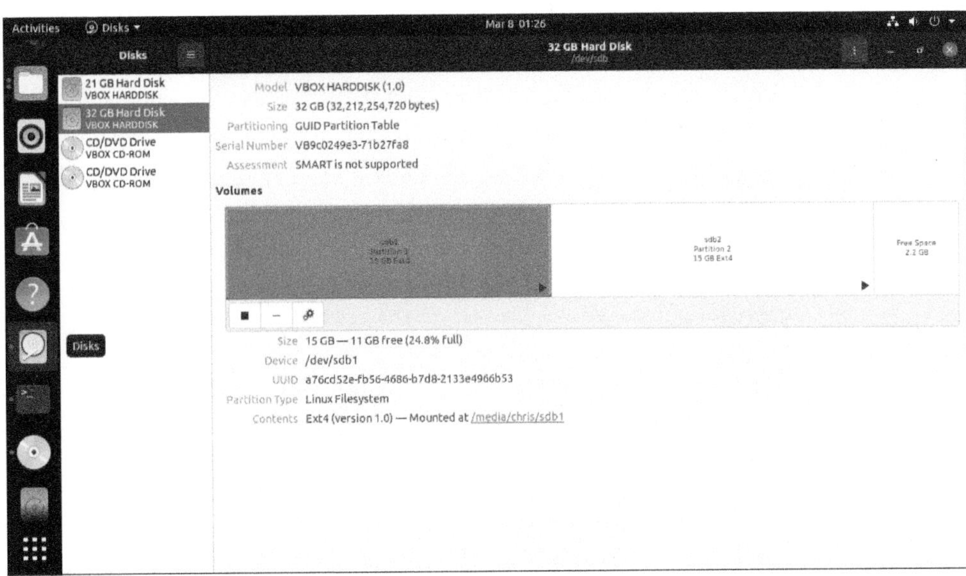

FIGURE 17.22 DVD copied onto the `sdb1` partition

Now use `dd` to clone `sdb1` to `sdb2`. The syntax is virtually the same as before; the only difference is that when you copy one partition to another partition, you use the full device name of the partition rather than the folder to which it is mounted. The following example shows this command and its output, and Figure 17.23 shows the results in Disks:

```
chris@ubuntulee:~$ sudo dd if=/dev/sdb1 of=/dev/sdb2
29298688+0 records in
29298688+0 records out
15000928256 bytes (15 GB, 14 GiB) copied, 722.424 s, 20.8 MB/s
```

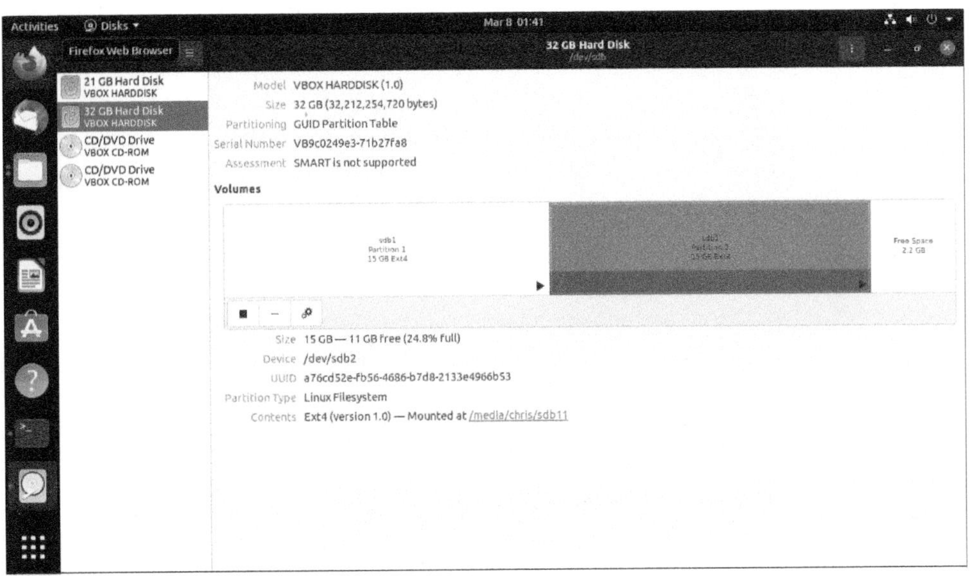

FIGURE 17.23 Cloned partition in Disks

Figure 17.23 shows that you can verify in Disks that the dd command cloned sdb1 to sdb2. They are exact clones. Comparing Figure 17.23 to Figure 17.22, notice that even the device label copied over to sdb2. And now both partitions use the same amount of disk space. Compare the mounted partitions, and you see that they both contain the same file—the ISO previously created:

```
chris@ubuntulee:~$ ls -l /media/chris/sdb1
total 3299892
drwx------ 2 root root       16384 Mar  7 17:00 lost+found
-rw-r--r-- 1 root root 3379068928 Mar  7 18:57 test.iso
chris@ubuntulee:~$ ls -l /media/chris/sdb2
total 3299892
drwx------ 2 root root       16384 Mar  7 17:00 lost+found
-rw-r--r-- 1 root root 3379068928 Mar  7 18:57 test.iso
```

In the next example, the dd command is used to convert a file, and the cat command is used to show the content of one or more files. A file has been created on /sdb1 that contains only the word test in all lowercase. This example shows how to use dd to copy the file to sdb2 and the conv option to convert the contents of the file to uppercase characters:

```
chris@ubuntulee:/media/chris/sdb1$ cat test.txt
test
chris@ubuntulee:/media/chris/sdb1$ sudo dd if=test.txt of=/media/chris/sdb2/
test.txt conv=ucase
0+1 records in
0+1 records out
8 bytes copied, 0.000114985 s, 69.6 kB/s
chris@ubuntulee:/media/chris/sdb1$ cat /media/chris/sdb2/test.txt
TEST
```

The dd command can also be used to erase the sdb2 partition. One option is to write all zeros to the partition. You do this by using the /dev/zero device, which is a software device that is used specifically for outputting just zeros. It is used as the input file and is sent to the output device sdb2, using block sizes of 4 kB. This process, shown in the following example, is called zeroing out a drive:

```
chris@ubuntulee:/media/chris/sdb1$ sudo dd if=/dev/zero of=/dev/sdb2 bs=4k
dd: error writing '/dev/sdb2': No space left on device
3662337+0 records in
3662336+0 records out
15000928256 bytes (15 GB, 14 GiB) copied, 81.0878 s, 185 MB/s
```

Zeroing out a device is a secure method of erasing data, as the whole drive is filled with zeros until it runs out of space. This makes typical data recovery methods impossible to use and renders the partition useless until it is repartitioned.

In Figure 17.24 you can see that sdb2 now has an error. This is because Ubuntu cannot find a file system for the device; it has been rendered unusable until it is repartitioned.

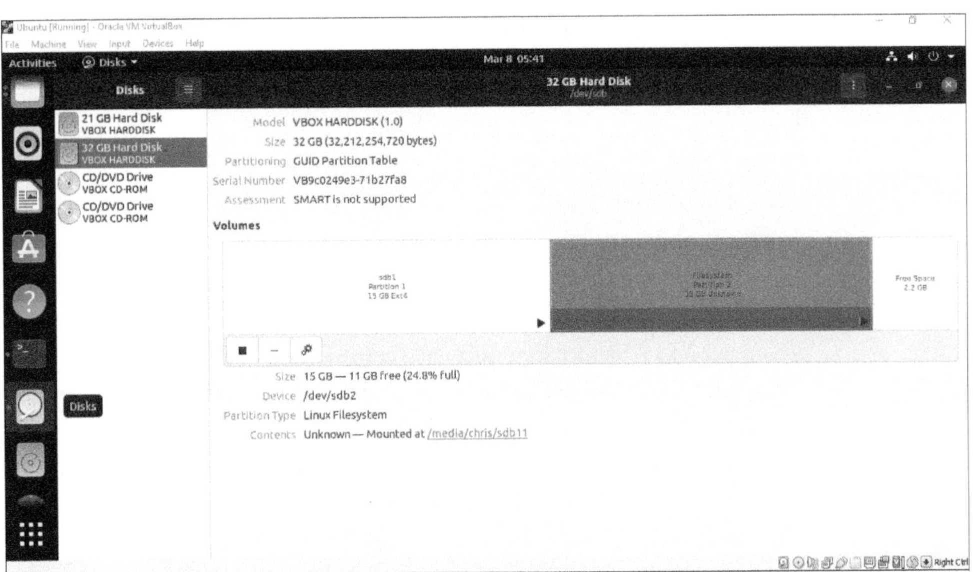

FIGURE 17.24 Unusable partition in Disks

Finding Files

Sometimes, when managing a system (especially an unfamiliar system) at the command line, it is difficult to find the locations of files. This is where two commands called `updatedb` and `locate` come into use. `updatedb` is a command you can run to update a local database on the system that contains the full pathname of each file. You can then use the command `locate` to search for a file in this database of paths.

This is a much quicker way to search for a file than searching the system itself, but there are limitations to this search method. The database of paths has to be updated regularly to be accurate. Usually, this is done via a scheduled task through the `cron` service. If you are searching for a file that was recently added, you may need to run the `updatedb` command and press Enter to manually refresh the database. Because this command looks at the entire file system, you need to run it with superuser permissions to ensure that it can read all file paths. Here is an example:

```
ubuntu@ubuntu:~$ sudo updatedb
```

You can now search the system. Say that someone left an important file called `testdocument.txt` that you need to retrieve, but the person didn't tell you where the file is located. You could use `locate` to find the path to the file, as in this example:

```
ubuntu@ubuntu:~$ locate testdocument.txt
/home/test/testdocument.txt
```

You can see from this example that `testdocument.txt` was left in the `test` user's home directory.

CHAPTER 17

TECH TIP

User forums

Usually, a quick internet search is enough to find a command to accomplish a task, but some deeper questions might require the advice of those more familiar with using Linux. There are many Linux user forums, and the Ubuntu-specific ones are especially good places for beginners to seek help. They are located at https://ubuntuforums.org.

Missing GRUB/LILO

The bootloader contains all the information about how the disk is organized, such as the size and layout of partitions. Linux distros typically install one of two bootloaders: Grand Unified Boot Loader (GRUB) or Linux Loader (LILO). LILO used to be the more predominant bootloader, but GRUB is now the default because it supports more modern features; the current version is GRUB 2. LILO, which has been marked as discontinued, is an older and more basic bootloader; it is missing some features, such as network boot and a command-line interface, that GRUB supports. The majority of the time you should keep whatever default bootloader your distro comes with unless you need a key feature that only another bootloader offers.

If you have problems booting into a Linux system, there is a chance that the bootloader has been overwritten or corrupted. This problem might happen, for example, if a PC technician decides to install a Windows operating system on the same disk that has Linux installed. When the technician does the installation, the Windows installation could overwrite the bootloader with its own MBR. After that, Linux cannot be loaded because the boot information created by GRUB or LILO no longer exists. To fix this issue, it is necessary to re-create the bootloader for the system. To fix the broken bootloader in this situation, you would boot to an Ubuntu live DVD or flash drive and run a few commands to fix it.

To use LILO to replace the MBR, you would open a command prompt and first install LILO with `sudo apt-get install lilo`. You would then run the command `sudo lilo -M /dev/`*`XXX`*` /mbr` (replacing *XXX* with the device name, such as `sda`), which references the name of the disk device where you installed Linux (or, in a more advanced partition setup, where the boot partition is, which is usually the device containing a /boot partition).

To fix this problem with GRUB, you would install GRUB2 with `sudo apt-get install grub2` and then run the command `sudo grub-install /dev/`*`XXX`* (replacing *XXX* with the device name, such as `sda`).

A missing bootloader scenario could require a slightly different fix, depending on the partition layout and the operating systems installed. It is important to read the documentation for either bootloader that you intend to use to make sure you are using a solution that fits the problem.

macOS and Linux Best Practices

Apple macOS and any flavor of Linux, like other operating systems, should be maintained using best practices. Key best practices are as follows:

- *Perform scheduled backups:* Back up the operating system and important data on a regular basis. As an IT staff member, you should gently remind users to do this, too.
- *Schedule disk maintenance:* Drives become fragmented over time. For best system performance, perform disk maintenance on a regular basis.
- *Perform system updates:* Be sure to install the latest operating system updates to prevent security and performance problems.
- *Perform driver/firmware updates:* Ensure that the latest hardware drivers and firmware updates are installed.
- *Perform patch management:* A patch is code changes that fix a particular problem in an operating system or application. Patch management is the process of downloading, testing, installing, retesting, and documenting these changes. Patch management helps with security issues, too. See Chapter 18, "Computer and Network Security," for more information.
- *Install and update antivirus/anti-malware:* Many people believe that Apple computers and Linux-based computers do not need antivirus or anti-malware software. This is not true. Not only should this software be installed, but it needs to be updated regularly.

SOFT SKILLS: BE HUMBLE

As an IT staff member, you have to be confident that you can repair almost anything and figure things out. However, that confidence sometimes comes across to others as arrogance. Anyone who has worked in IT knows that you cannot know everything. You might know a little bit about a lot of things. You may know a lot about a specific side of IT. But no one can be an expert in it all. Show a little humility and be humble about your knowledge. Do not lord your knowledge and expertise over those you support. Showing empathy for the people you support and interact with goes a long way. See Figure 17.25.

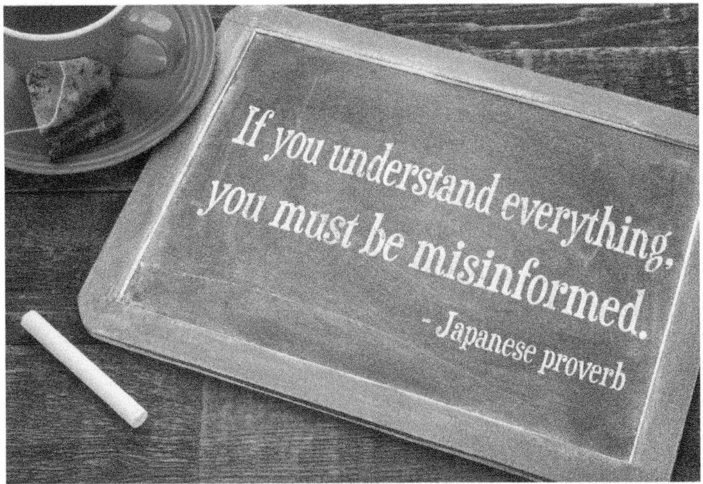

FIGURE 17.25 No technician knows everything

Chapter Summary

> macOS is a Unix-based operating system developed by Apple.
> Open source software is made freely available and is open for modification.
> macOS can only run on Apple hardware, even in virtual machines.
> The macOS user interface, known as Aqua, contains the Dock, Finder, and menu bar.
> Spotlight can be used to quickly search a macOS system to find files, emails, applications, and even web search results.
> iCloud is Apple's online service that provides online storage and syncing.
> To get the most out of using macOS, end users should have an Apple ID to use with iCloud and the App Store.
> Time Machine is the tool used for automated macOS backups.
> Most system settings can be found and managed in the System Preferences menu, which is equivalent to the Control Panel in Windows.
> Boot Camp, an application that comes bundled with macOS, guides you through the installation of Windows on a separate partition on a Mac.
> Basic macOS troubleshooting can be done using the Console and Activity Monitor. The Console allows you to see detailed logs of macOS, applications, and services. Activity Monitor allows you to see what is running on the system and what resources processes are using.
> Keychain Access is a utility for storing passwords, and users tend not to understand it. Be prepared to show users how to update their keychain password when they update their passwords.
> System administrators may need to use the Terminal application to access the command-line interface of macOS.

> Linux is an open operating system platform built on the principles of Unix.
> Most Linux administration happens at the command-line level, not in the graphical user interface.
> You must learn the basics of using the command line to properly administer Linux/Unix systems. Be familiar with the commands in Tables 17.4 and 17.7.
> Be prepared to spend many hours researching how to use Linux/Unix systems; it can take years to master understanding how they work and how to properly administer them. If you aren't sure about something, use online resources or ask a colleague to get a better understanding.

A+ CERTIFICATION EXAM TIPS

✓ This chapter and the objectives contained within account for only a small percentage of the exam.

✓ Be familiar with the following Mac features: multiple desktops/Mission Control, Keychain, Spotlight, iCloud, gestures, Finder, the Dock, and Boot Camp.

✓ Know the purpose of the shell/Terminal application and review commands such as `su`/`sudo`, `ls`, `cd`, `shutdown`, `mv`, `cp`, `rm`, `grep`, `pwd`, `passwd`, `chmod`, `chown`, `iwconfig`, `ifconfig`, `ps`, `vi`, `dd`, `kill`, and `apt-get`. Know that you need to use the `sudo` command to be able to modify settings within the operating system.

✓ Know macOS and Linux client best practices, including those related to scheduled backups, scheduled disk maintenance, system updates, App Store for macOS, patch management, driver and firmware updates, and antivirus/anti-malware updates.

✓ Be able to use (and know why you would use) the following tools in a macOS or Linux client: Time Machine backups, snapshot restores, image recovery, disk maintenance utilities, the Terminal application/shell, screen sharing, and Force Quit.

✓ Know that the Time Machine tool and iCloud can be used to back up/restore Mac images.

✓ Be familiar with the file systems associated with macOS and Linux: ext3, ext4, HFS+, and APFS.

Key Terms

Activity Monitor 869
App Store 863
`apt-get` 883
Boot Camp 873
`c` 874
`cd` 874
`chmod` 874
`chown` 874
command-line interface 883
Console 870
`cp` 874
dash 879
`dd` 883
Disk Utility 872
Disks 881
Dock 859
ext3 881
ext4 881
Finder 859
Force Quit 866
gestures 860
`grep` 874
iCloud 862
`ifconfig` 883
`iwconfig` 883
iWork 862
kernel 878
kernel panic 871
Keychain Access 871
`kill` 874
Launcher 879
Launchpad 860
`less` 874
Linux 878
`locate` 883
`ls` 874
macOS 858
`man` 874
menu bar 859
Mission Control 860
`mkdir` 874
`mv` 874
`nano` 874
Nautilus 879
open source 858
OS X 858
`passwd` 883
pin wheel 869
POSIX 858
`ps` 883
`pwd` 874
`rm` 874
root 876
safe mode 869
screen sharing 864
shell 859
`shutdown` 883
Software Updater 882
Spotlight 860
`su` 883
`sudo` 874
System Information 871
System Preferences 866
Terminal 874
Time Machine 864
`touch` 874
Ubuntu Software Center 881
`updatedb` 883
`vi` 874

Review Questions

1. What are the four main parts of the macOS graphical user interface? (Choose four.)

   [Desktop | Finder | Time Machine | Console | Spotlight | Dock | Menu Bar]
2. [T | F] Ubuntu 22.04 uses the GNOME user interface.
3. What wireless encryption does `iwconfig` support, and what is an alternative to using `iwconfig`? (Choose one answer from each set below.)

   Choose one of these: [WEP | WPA | WPA2 | AES]

   Choose one of these: [ipconfig | ipconfig /all | WPA supplicant | TSA]
4. In what ways could you quickly launch an application in macOS?

   ____
5. What type of account do you need to create to purchase software through the Apple App Store?

   ____
6. Write out the steps you would take to create a file with the Terminal application in macOS or Linux.

   ____
7. What `dd` command would you use to copy the contents of a partition named `/dev/drive1` to another partition, called `/dev/backup`?

   ____
8. What command is used to look for the word mouse in a filename?

   [`sudo` | `apt-get` | `grep` | `rd`]
9. The _________ command lists the contents of the current directory.

   [`apt-get` | `grep` | `ls` | `sudo`]
10. Which macOS tool is used to display and modify the main system settings?

    [Launchpad | Activity Monitor | Safari | System Preferences]
11. How would you create a file from the command-line interface?

    ____
12. What steps would you take in Ubuntu, from the command line, to install a new package named lynx?

    ____

    ____

    ____

    ____
13. If an application is not starting properly on macOS, what steps could you take to resolve this?

    ____

    ____
14. If a Mac is running slowly, what utility could you use to identify the cause of the slowdown?

    [Activity Monitor | Dash | Launchpad | Mission Control]
15. What is the difference between `passwd` and `pwd`?

    ____
16. How large should a Time Machine backup drive be?

    ____
17. If you wanted to use `chmod` to give a file owner read, write, and execute permissions, what command would you use?

    ____

18. Which command grants temporary superuser permissions? [`ls` | `less` | `root` | `sudo` | `app-get`]
19. [T | F] The `locate` command searches the Linux file system.
20. How would you find out more information about a Linux command?

____

Exercises

Exercise 17.1

Objective: To become familiar with macOS tools

Procedure: Match each tool to the correct description.

a. Time Machine	____ Stop a non-responsive application
b. Screen sharing	____ Configure file sharing
c. App Store	____ Get system updates
d. Force Quit	____ Use an optical disc on another computer
e. Remote Disc	____ Troubleshoot kernel panic
f. System Preferences	____ View processes and used system resources
g. Activity Monitor	____ View a remote Mac
h. Console	____ Create a system backup

Exercise 17.2

Objective: To become familiar with Mac/Linux commands

Procedure: Match each command to the correct description.

a. `cd`	____ Delete a file
b. `rm`	____ Gain root privilege
c. `touch`	____ Move a file
d. `chown`	____ Move to a different directory
e. `mv`	____ Change the owner of a directory
f. `grep`	____ Get help for a particular command
g. `man`	____ Create a file
h. `sudo`	____ Search output for a specific value

Activities

Internet Discovery

Objective: Access the Internet to obtain specific information regarding a computer or its associated parts

Parts: A computer with Internet access

Procedure: Complete the following procedure and answer the accompanying questions.

1. Search online to find a Linux distro besides Ubuntu. Document the website and give a brief description of the distro.

   ____

2. What are some of the common business uses of the distro you found?

   ____

3. Research why Linux servers usually do not have a graphical user interface installed. Write down the URL of the website you used to help come to your conclusion and explain your reasoning for not installing a GUI.

   ____

   ____

4. Linux is a stable platform but still has issues and can crash. Research to determine what log files are useful in Linux for troubleshooting.

   ____

5. Find a website that describes how to troubleshoot a Linux system that will not boot. Write the URL you used and one thing you learned from the site.

   ____

   ____

Soft Skills

Objective: To enhance and fine-tune a future technician's ability to listen, communicate in oral form, work together in a group on technical problems, and support people who use computers in a professional manner.

Activities: Complete the following questions in a group of three and share your opinions.

1. Write down two things you find confusing about using macOS or Linux and share them with your group. See which areas are the most common problems for everyone.

   ____

2. With your group, do more research on your group's list of the most common confusing items from step 1; as a group, try to come to a better understanding of each issue. For any topics that you cannot get a better grasp on, create a plan to better understand them and describe your plan.
3. Working with Unix or Linux requires the ability to do independent research to discover and understand new technologies in the field. You need to know how to properly search on the internet to effectively find information, especially when troubleshooting an issue you are unfamiliar with. Have everyone in the group search to find what is the most popular web server application used to run on Linux. Compare answers to see if everyone got the same results. Also compare what terms each person used to search for the answer. Some searches will be more precise at finding the answer than others. It is important to take a look at how you search to get results as quickly as possible. List the most common answer for the most popular web server to run on Linux, as well as what was the most concise search phrase or term used.

   ____

   ____

✓ 1102-2.7 Explain common methods for securing mobile and embedded devices.

✓ 1102-2.8 Given a scenario, use common data destruction and disposal methods.

✓ 1102-2.9 Given a scenario, configure appropriate security settings on small office/home office (SOHO) wireless and wired networks.

✓ 1102-2.10 Given a scenario, install and configure browsers and relevant security settings.

✓ 1102-3.2 Given a scenario, troubleshoot common personal computer (PC) security issues.

✓ 1102-3.3 Given a scenario, use best practice procedures for malware removal.

✓ 1102-4.1 Given a scenario, implement best practices associated with documentation and support systems information management.

✓ 1102-4.3 Given a scenario, implement workstation backup and recovery methods.

✓ 1102-4.6 Explain the importance of prohibited content/activity and privacy, licensing, and policy concepts.

✓ 1102.-4.7 Given a scenario, use proper communication techniques and professionalism.

✓ 1102.-4.9 Given a scenario, use remote access technologies.

Security Overview

Computer and network security relates to the hardware, software, and data protection of PCs and mobile devices. Security should be of concern to everyone in a business or a home—including, of course, the people who repair and support PCs: the technicians. A technician must be able to implement and explain security concepts. Every technician has the responsibility to promote security consciousness and to train users to be good stewards of equipment and data.

Security Policy

The corporate security landscape has become complicated today because people bring their own electronic devices to work. This is commonly referred to as *bring your own device*, or **BYOD**. Management must define and make clear what devices may be put on corporate wired or wireless networks and also what devices are unacceptable, along with the consequences of attaching unapproved devices.

A **security policy** is one or more documents that provide rules and guidelines related to computer and network security. Every company, no matter its size, should have a security policy. Small businesses tend to have general operating procedures that are passed verbally from one employee to another, but it is best to have these processes documented in detail. **Non-compliant systems**, or systems that do not meet security policy guidelines, are some of the biggest threats to companies today. Some sectors, such as education, health care, and government, require IT security policies.

Common elements of a security policy are listed in Table 18.1.

TABLE 18.1 Security policy elements

Security policy element	Description
Physical access	Describes who is allowed into a building, to what part of the building they have access, and badge/key control. Delineates what type of security log is kept when a person is allowed access to a space.
Anti-malware	States whether anti-malware software is required on every system, possibly what product is used, how updates are obtained, and steps taken when a machine is not compliant or if a person refuses to be compliant.

Security policy element	Description
Acceptable use policy (AUP)	Defines who has access to, and what level of usage is appropriate for, company-provided information resources such as email and internet usage. Sometimes, an AUP defines what data can be taken from the company or data storage limitations. The details might include defining what web browser and hardware platforms are supported. It might include the process for assigning folder and file rights and what to do if an account has been disabled.
Password policy	Spells out guidelines for protecting passwords, such as not writing them down, a timeline for changing passwords, the number and types of characters required, and processes for forgotten passwords, such as whether a new password can be given by phone or by email only.
Email usage	Defines who owns email that resides on a company server, how long email is stored, proper usage of email, and when it is backed up. Lawsuits related to this area continue to be decided in favor of the company regarding email rights because the data is stored on company-owned and company-provided servers.
Regulatory compliance	Depending on the industry, a section of the policy may be devoted to industry-related regulations relating to data, equipment, and security requirements.
Remote access	Contains statements related to who is allowed remote access, the type(s) of remote access permitted, company resources that can be accessed remotely, the process to obtain desired rights and access, and the security level required.
Emergency procedures	Details what to do when something is missing and the steps to take if a natural disaster such as a hurricane occurs. Stipulates who overrides a security policy and authorizes access to someone.

Many corporate security policies are implemented based on user profiles. Within each profile, mandatory requirements such as password length and frequency of password changes are dictated and enforced. The profile also can enforce what network resources a particular user has access to. Even though not every company has a formal security policy, specific points related to a security policy are referenced throughout this chapter. Whether written or just commonly accepted guidelines, many implementations are based on a particular company's rules for computer and network security.

To ease into the topic of security, a good place to start is security methods that might prevent a security breach from occurring in the first place. Four methods of security methods are physical security, logical security, end-user education, and the principle of least privilege.

Physical Security

Typical physical security includes door locks, cipher locks, **keys**, guards, **bollards** (upright posts in front of a door, such as those shown in Figure 18.1), and fences, and can include more. A **door lock** can be a lock that requires a key or an electronic one used for equipment such as servers, firewalls, switches, and data storage devices. Even in a locked room, it is important to disable unused ports on devices in case the room is compromised. Companies commonly use electronic key cards, instead of keys, for physical access to rooms. Electronic key cards (see Figure 18.2) are part of an access control system, which includes the key cards, door readers, and software to control and monitor the system.

FIGURE 18.1 Bollards

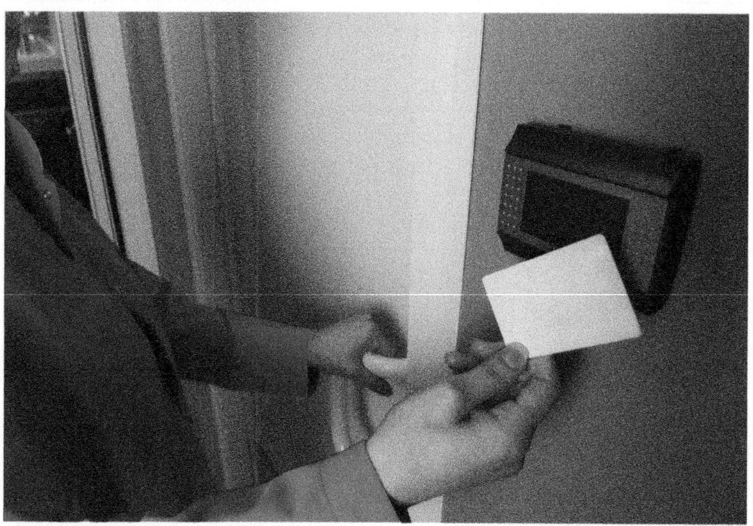

FIGURE 18.2 Electronic key card system

Electronic key cards have many benefits, including the following:

- They are easy to program and issue/revoke compared to issuing a key and getting it back from an employee who quits or is dismissed.
- Data is stored in a database instead of on a checkout form.
- Access to information, such as who entered a room and at what time, can be logged and monitored more easily than with a checkout sheet.
- More layers of control can be exercised with key cards. With metal keys, the usual process is to give a key for each room, issue a submaster key for an entire wing, or issue a master key for the entire building.
- When keys are issued and one is lost, the lock must be rekeyed and new keys issued. When an electronic key card is lost, the old card is deactivated, and a new one is issued.

Other electronic devices and technologies also provide access to computers and rooms—in other words, authenticate the user. **Authentication** is the process of determining whether a network device or person has permission to access a network.

Table 18.2 lists and describes security devices that help with the physical security of computers.

TABLE 18.2 Physical security devices

Device/ technology	Description
Smart card	A small ID-sized card that can store data, which can be encrypted, and that requires authorization in order to be changed. A smart card can be swiped through a card reader or may interact wirelessly with a card reader. Smart cards are used in government IDs (with information such as medical/dental records), mobile phones (as subscriber ID modules), driver's licenses, and employee badges (see Figure 18.3).
Key fob	A device used for keyless entry to a car, a building, or an interior door, such as a fitness room in an apartment complex.
Radio frequency ID (**RFID**)	A technology that allows automatic identification of people, objects, or animals in which an RFID tag is read wirelessly by an RFID reader. RFID is used in libraries and inventory systems and is used for computers, hospital equipment, and locating lost pets or people. An RFID badge can be used to access and track access to a locked area.
Badge reader	A device that can be contactless or that may require a swipe or insertion of an identification card to allow entry into a space.
Guard	A human who provides security by controlling access to a controlled space such as a network closet or server room.
Security token	A device—also called an authentication token, USB token, hardware/hard token, or software/soft token—that authorizes access to something. A **hard token** (see Figure 18.4), for example, is a physical device used to gain access to a resource such as a file or company. Examples of hard tokens are smart cards, one-time passwords, and Bluetooth tokens.
Lighting	Illumination that makes it easier to record and provide better security. Some network equipment areas have automatic lights that trigger camera recording when activated.
Trusted Platform Module (**TPM**)	A USB device or a chip on a motherboard (refer to Figure 3.35 in Chapter 3, "On the Motherboard"), smartphone, or network equipment used for hardware/software authentication. A TPM stores information such as security certificates, passwords, and encryption keys. **Encryption** is the process of converting data into an unreadable format. A TPM can also authenticate hardware devices. Applications can use TPM for file and folder encryption, local passwords, email, VPN/PKI authentication, and wireless authentication.
Hardware security module (**HSM**)	A module that is similar to a TPM except that it is specialized hardware that can be added as a USB device or a device on the network and used for digital key management, storage/protection of cryptographic keys, encryption, and authentication.
Cable lock	A physical lock used with devices in common areas such as libraries or lobby areas. Also used to secure laptops. Refer to Figure 10.78 in Chapter 10, "Mobile Devices."
Equipment lock	A physical or electronic lock on a cabinet that can provide monitoring and security for individual cabinet doors. It might also include a special cable attached to a device that cannot be removed without a specialized tool.

Device/ technology	Description
USB lock	A device that prevents USB storage devices from being used in USB ports in order to prevent moving, transferring, and copying files.
Access control vestibule	An area, also known as a **mantrap** or an air lock, that separates a nonsecure area from a secured area (see Figure 18.5). An access control vestibule is useful in preventing unauthorized access and **tailgating** (in which an unauthorized person enters directly behind an authorized person).
Privacy screen	A device, also called a privacy filter, that prevents **shoulder surfing**, in which someone looks over a user's shoulder to gain information by looking at the person's screen. A privacy screen allows a user to view the screen clearly only if sitting directly in front of the monitor (see Figure 18.6).
Video surveillance	The use of security cameras for equipment and personnel safety as well as data in the event of a security breach.
Alarm system/ motion sensor	A system that can send out an audible or silent alarm that triggers video or calls to security, police, or fire personnel.
Magnetometer	A device that is used to scan for firearms and weapons and might also be used in location tracking.

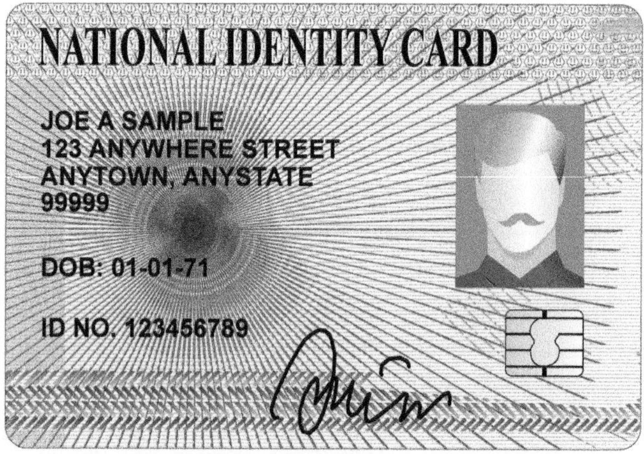

FIGURE 18.3 Smart card

FIGURE 18.4 Hard token

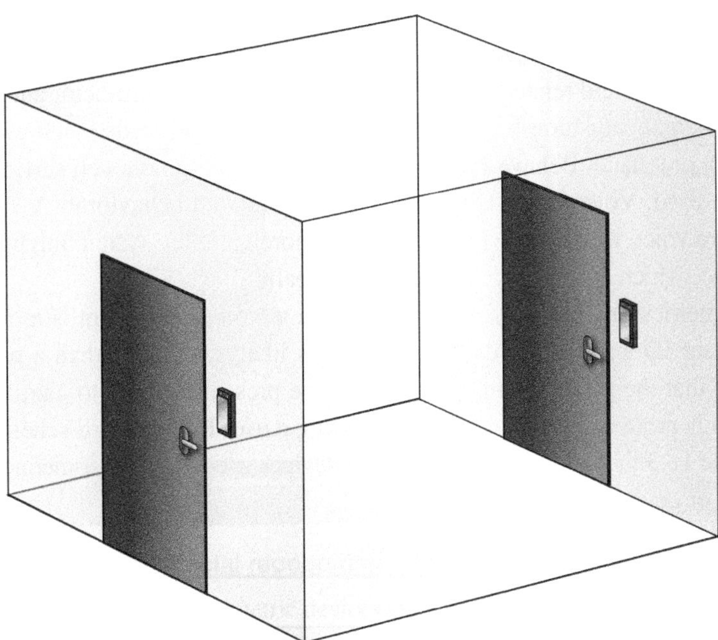

FIGURE 18.5 Access control vestibule

FIGURE 18.6 Shoulder surfing

Logical Security

Logical security involves protection through the use of software. A number of devices and techniques can help in this area. The types of logical security methods on the CompTIA A+ certification exam are briefly outlined here, and some of them are explained in more detail later in the chapter:

> **Antivirus/anti-malware***:* This type of software is used to protect an operating system and applications from small programs that wreak havoc on the system, even causing it not to work at all.

> **Firewall***:* A **software firewall** is a tool provided with a device or an application that can be configured on a PC, router, or other device. A firewall can also be a hardware device that protects an organization. A company may have more than one firewall, depending on the network design (see Figure 18.10).

FIGURE 18.10 Corporate firewall design

> *Directory permissions:* When data is shared across a network or stored in one or more folders on a server, permissions can be assigned to differentiate between people who just need to see the data and those who need to change or even delete the data.

> *Virtual private network (VPN):* A **VPN** enables secure connectivity across an unsecure network such as the internet to a remote location; an example of someone who would need to use a VPN is a mobile user who must connect to the corporate network to upload data weekly or to access corporate data stored in folders on a server. See the section "VPN Configuration," later in this chapter, for more information on how to configure a VPN.

> *Disabling unused ports:* In highly sensitive areas, ports such as Ethernet, USB, IEEE 1394 FireWire, eSATA, Thunderbolt, and more are disabled so that an external device cannot be attached to gain access to corporate or government-sensitive data. It is also important to disable unused ports on routers, switches, and firewalls.

- *Access control list (**ACL**):* ACLs are security rules that permit or deny the types of traffic flowing into a device, out of a device, or toward a particular network or that specify the type of traffic, such as HTTP or HTTPS packets.
- *Port security:* When people bring their own devices to work, they sometimes attach those devices to the physical network. Port security is used on a corporate switch to allow only a device with a particular MAC address to attach. Whenever someone unplugs the specified device and attaches a different one, port security settings shut down the switch or firewall port because a device with a different MAC address has been attached.
- **Trusted sources** *vs.* **untrusted sources**: Windows and mobile device users commonly have security software that tells them whether a website or a downloaded file is a trusted or untrusted software source. All users, no matter the operating system, should be aware of untrusted software sources when downloading files.
- **Email filtering**: Security rules can be used to process incoming email messages before putting them into specific users' inboxes. These rules search for and remove suspicious and harmful emails, and they may potentially scan outgoing emails to ensure security or legal compliance (see Figure 18.11).

Let's dive a little more deeply into some of these security items.

FIGURE 18.11 Email filtering

Authentication

Authentication involves proving who a particular person or device is by using something someone has, something a person knows, something a person is, or somewhere a person is located. For example, when you are logging into your bank account, you might have a short message service (**SMS**) text message sent to you that has a code that you enter into an app or online or to get a voice call where you get that authentication code.

Smart cards or security tokens are often described as two-factor authentication, sometimes referred to as 2FA or **multifactor authentication**. With this type of authentication, you need something you possess, such as your ATM card, your current location, or a security token device, and something you know, such as a PIN, in order to gain access to something (such as a room, a bank account, a shared folder, or data stored in the cloud). This is more secure than single-factor authentication, which uses only one means of authentication, such as a username/password combination.

Multifactor authentication is used to gain access to a computer, network room, or other shared media. Mobile devices sometimes enable additional multifactor authentication measures, such as a touch pattern. Biometrics also add one more security layer to authentication.

Soft tokens (or software tokens) and authenticator apps can be used as part of multifactor authentication. A **soft token** is a code generated through software. It could be a code provided through a text message, an email, a phone call, and so on. An **authenticator app** provides a one-time password and is used in addition to the commonly required user ID and password.

Two other technologies used with authentication are RADIUS and TACACS+. The Remote Authentication Dial-in User Service (**RADIUS**) protocol is used to centralize authentication, authorization, and accounting (AAA). A RADIUS server can provide a way to authenticate wired and wireless users as well as devices before they are allowed to communicate on the network. Terminal Access Controller Access-Control System (**TACACS+**) also supports AAA, and it also makes it possible to separate the pieces of AAA so you don't have to do all three on the same server. You could do authentication on a different server but still support authorization and accounting on a TACACS+ server, for example.

An important protocol used in conjunction with an authentication server is Kerberos, which can also be used as an alternative to the SSH, POP, and SMTP protocols. **Kerberos** prevents transmitted packets from being changed or read.

BIOS/UEFI

Most computers have BIOS/UEFI options that prevent others from altering the settings. A BIOS/UEFI password can also be assigned to require a password before the operating system loads. Table 18.4 shows some BIOS/UEFI options related to security.

TABLE 18.4 BIOS/UEFI security options

Option	Description
Supervisor/ Administrator	Unrestricted access to all BIOS/UEFI options.
User	Enables a limited number of configuration changes, such as changes to time and boot sequence.
Trusted Platform Module (TPM)	Allows initialization and viewing of a password for the TPM motherboard chip that generates and stores cryptographic keys.
LoJack	Locates a mobile device and displays a message on the lost device.
Secure boot	Prevents an unauthorized operating system from loading.
Boot password or power-on password	Required before BIOS/UEFI looks for an operating system. This is not the Windows user password.

In a corporate environment, the supervisor password is commonly configured. Other options that may affect the corporate environment include the following:

> Enabling/disabling device options
> Enabling/disabling ports
> Encrypting a drive
> Enabling TPM
> Enabling LoJack (which allows a mobile device to be located, remotely locked, and made to display an "if found" message)
> Viewing/changing security levels/passwords
> Restoring security settings to the default values

Laptops and other mobile devices sometimes have an additional password configured through the BIOS/UEFI for their internal storage drive. That way, if the device is stolen, the drive cannot be inserted into another device and used without the password.

Login OS Security Options

Getting into any device usually requires some form of login or authentication. Here are some common login options used by devices today:

> **Username and password**: A name associated with a person that is stored on the local computer or on an authentication server along with a unique code used for access
> **PIN** *(personal identification number):* A unique set of numbers defined by the user as a quick means to access a computer such as a home computer
> *Fingerprint:* Common in mobile devices
> *Facial recognition:* One of the most secure methods available
> **Single sign-on** *(SSO):* Enables a user to authenticate to multiple systems/servers, printers/copiers, and networked-based applications with a minimum of a user ID and password

Table 18.5 lists some password guidelines.

TABLE 18.5 Computer/network password guidelines

Guideline	Description
Reminders	Do not write down your passwords. Do not put your passwords in a document stored on the same computer. Passwords can be kept digitally through an app or an encrypted file.
Number of characters/ complexity	Passwords can use uppercase letters, lowercase letters, numbers, and special characters like @, ~, !, #, %, &, (, _, and -. Many companies now are requiring a passphrase that requires special characters, numerals, and a large number of characters.
Format	Do not use consecutive letters or numbers on the keyboard, such as *asd* or *123*. Do not use passwords that are words such as *children* or *happiness* because password-cracking programs use **dictionary attacks** to hack passwords including foreign words and names.
Expiration	On servers, this is known as the minimum password age and the maximum password age. The minimum password age is how long a user must keep a password before changing it. Microsoft recommends 3 to 7 days. The maximum is the amount of time before the user is required to change it. Common values are 30, 60, and 90 days.

Guideline	Description
Reuse	Authentication servers often have a setting that dictates the number of times you have to change to new passwords before an old password can be used again. It is best practice to not allow users to reuse passwords.
Log off when not in use	Use a screen saver or lock the computer with the ⊞+L key combination. Use the *Personalization* Settings link to configure the screen saver and require login credentials to re-access the computer.
Failed attempts	A common setting for the number of times a person is allowed to try a password that is wrong before being locked out is three failed attempts.
Social	If someone is standing near enough to you that he or she could be shoulder surfing when you log in, ensure that the person's eyes are averted or wait until the person moves away to type your password into the system. Obtain a privacy filter.

Research is ongoing into the effectiveness of requiring frequent password changes since many people write passwords down, use weaker passwords, or use passwords that are easily modified. One solution people are turning to is using a **password manager**, an application that is on a computer or a USB drive, mobile app, or web browser plug-in that locally or remotely stores passwords used to access accounts. When stored remotely, the passwords and associated data (site, device, and so on) should be encrypted.

Considering the End User

End-user education is a great way to prevent security events and issues. New hires should be presented with the acceptable use policy (AUP) during the onboarding process. Some companies present this policy every time a user logs in to the network. Companies also might require annual security training for all employees to update them on common threats.

Humans are the weakest security link. Technicians must take care to not record users' personally identifiable information (PII) or passwords and to remind users to secure their passwords and any printed material if they leave the area. Users should be reminded that if their computer is remotely accessed by a technician, they should close windows that contain corporate or personal information prior to agreeing to the remote connection. Corporate mobile devices must be kept secure and protected. Any time a technician removes a virus or malware from a user device, training should be part of the solution. Violations of security best practices are a common security threat and make a company more vulnerable to other security problems. Let's explore some of the common areas that apply to users.

Licensing

An ethical problem technicians often face is being asked to install software or other content that is not legitimate. Digital rights management (**DRM**) involves the use of technology to implement controls placed on digital media (software, hardware, songs, videos, and more). Users often request that technicians share with them methods to break copyright laws or work around copy protection controls. Technicians must maintain their professionalism and ethics to ensure that corporate interests are protected.

Instances like these provide great opportunities to talk to users about different software sources:

- **Open source**: Software for which the original software code is provided.
- *Freeware:* Software that doesn't cost anything but that could include some harmful code within the software.

> *Shareware:* Software that might be free at first but that may require later payment; may include only part of a particular software package with the option to buy an upgrade.
> *Commercial license:* Purchased software for a specific number of users and/or machines. Even when commercial licensing is obtained, there is an end-user licensing agreement (**EULA**) that specifies what can be done with that particular license.
> *Personal license:* Purchased software for a specific number of users and/or machines. Commonly used for home or small business environments and also covered by a EULA.
> *Valid license:* Software bought for a specific machine.
> *Non-expired license:* Software that is still updated and supported by the originating company.

A Business Software Alliance (BSA) global software piracy survey found that 37% of PC software did not have a legitimate license. **Piracy** (see Figure 18.12) is defined by the BSA as follows:

> Copying or distribution of copyrighted software that is not authorized
> Purchasing a copy of a particular application or software and putting it on more than one computer
> Installing, sharing, selling, copying, downloading, or uploading stolen software to another site
> Installing company software on or permitting access to unauthorized devices

FIGURE 18.12 Software pirate

Software companies have different pricing structures for individual or personal licenses and corporate or enterprise licenses. An enterprise license gives a company permission to load the software on unlimited or a maximum number of devices. A personal license is more limiting (usually to one device).

People use software piracy websites to obtain illegal software. These sites are riddled with security threats that are downloaded along with the desired software. The current penalty in the United States for software piracy is $100,000 per program copied. If prosecuted for copyright infringement, fines can be up to $250,000 and/or up to five years in jail. Don't be persuaded to risk your personal life and professional future for software piracy.

Regulated Data

As ever-increasing computing power has made the mining, collection, and storage of private data more efficient and invasive, so too have the world's standards for privacy protection increased. Inadvertently disclosing regulated data embarrasses you and your employer, and it could subject you both to civil and/or criminal penalties.

Regulated data is defined by federal law or regulation according to its purpose, such as in the areas of education, health care, financial institutions, arms trafficking, exports administration, and online children's privacy. There are four specific types to give you an overall framework for privacy protections:

> *PII:* Personally identifiable information
> *PCI:* Payment card information
> *GDPR:* European General Data Protection Regulation
> *PHI:* Protected health information

Personally identifiable information (**PII**) is information that uniquely identifies someone, such as a Social Security number, an employee ID, a patient number, a passport number, or a user ID. Any type of personal government-issued information is protected. There are two broad types of PII: nonsensitive and sensitive. Nonsensitive PII is information that can be found publicly, such as a person's name, telephone number, and email address. Nonsensitive information can be transmitted unencrypted (unscrambled and with no security) without causing harm to an individual. Sensitive PII should be encrypted if transmitted or stored.

All members of the credit card/debit card industry, such as financial institutions, credit card companies, and merchant services, must comply with standards related to payment card industry (**PCI**) information. The Payment Card Industry Data Security Standard (PCI DSS) was developed to encourage and enhance the security of personally identifiable information and payment data. As a technician, you may have exposure to PII and PCI data that must be kept on a separate network than other types of data. You are obligated to protect the privacy of this data.

The General Data Protection Regulation (**GDPR**) was adopted in 2016 by the European Union (EU). The GDPR unifies protection for the personal data of EU residents and sets forth restrictions on processing and transferring personal data outside the EU. Any entity that offers goods or services to, or monitors the behavior of, residents in the EU must comply with the GDPR. Violations of GDPR provisions subject organizations to financial penalties of up to 4% of the organization's global annual turnover.

The Health Insurance Portability and Accountability Act (HIPAA) of 1996 required the U.S. Department of Health and Human Services (HHS) to develop privacy and security regulations for certain health information. HHS developed the HIPAA Privacy Rule, which defines protected health information (**PHI**) as "individually identifiable health information," including demographic data, that relates to an individual's past, present, or future physical or mental health or condition; the provision of health care to the individual; past, present, or future payment for providing health care; and the individual's identity. Common identifiers are name, Social Security number, birth date, and address. Each state in the United States has laws regarding how long medical records are to be kept, but the HIPAA rules do state that privacy-related documents like notices of privacy practice, PHI logs, and IT security reviews must be retained for at least six years.

Security Threats and Vulnerabilities

Several types of security threats and vulnerabilities exist. Many of them fall into multiple categories because there might be multiple threats. They all do bad and weird things to devices. Malware is a good place to start.

Malware

Malware is software code that is designed to damage a computer system (causing lockups, slowness, applications crashing or failing to run or running incorrectly, operating system update failures, random and frequent browser pop-ups, and so on). In most cases, allowing more users to bring their own devices to work increases the risk of introducing malware into the network. Table 18.6 lists common types of malware.

TABLE 18.6 Types of malware

Type	Description
Spyware	Collects personal information without consent through logging keystrokes, accessing saved documents, and recording internet browsing. Results in unsolicited pop-ups and identity theft.
Virus	Does something harmful to a computer (for example, displays a message, prevents the computer from booting, makes it run slowly, changes file or application permissions, or logs keystrokes). A virus commonly attaches itself to an installed program.
Boot sector virus	Installs into a storage device's boot sector code used to boot the computer and can spread to drives and other network devices.
Trojan	Disguises itself as a legitimate program to gain unauthorized access to a device. Also known as a Trojan horse (see Figure 18.13).
Rootkit	Gains administrator access (known as root access in Linux) to the operating system. It is important to check for unknown processes running to see if a rootkit is installed.
Ransomware	Restricts access to a device until a user pays money to regain access (see Figure 18.14).
Keylogger	Records every keystroke entered in an attempt to collect user IDs and passwords.
Botnet	Software that spreads from hacked device to hacked device and that is under control of someone else (called zombie computers, or zombies; see Figure 18.15).
Cryptojacking	Embedded malicious code that acts as a **cryptominer**, using a computer's processing power in order to do cryptomining of digital currencies like bitcoin.

"Sure, bring her in. I've always wanted to work on one of these babies."

FIGURE 18.13 Trojan (disguising itself)

FIGURE 18.14 Ransomware

FIGURE 18.15 Zombies and botnets

The following are common symptoms of a virus/malware:

> Computer does not boot.
> Computer hard drive space is reduced.
> Applications do not load.
> An application takes longer to load or function than it used to.
> Hard drive activity increases (especially when no work is being done by the user and the antivirus software is not currently scanning).
> An antivirus software message appears.
> The number of hard drive sectors marked as bad steadily increases.
> Unusual graphics or messages appear on the screen.
> Someone notices **missing files** or altered/renamed system/personal files.
> A message indicates that the hard drive cannot be detected or recognized.
> Strange sounds come from the computer.

Antivirus applications can be configured to run in manual mode (on demand) or as scheduled scans. When you have an infected computer, you should quarantine it. This means you should disconnect the computer from the network until the computer is virus free. Some antivirus programs can quarantine a computer automatically if the computer has a virus. Many antivirus software programs have the capability to quarantine files—files that appear to the antivirus program as possible virus-infected or suspicious files that might be dangerous. A message or **desktop alert** normally appears with a list of files that have been quarantined, and each one must be identified as a valid file or to be left in the quarantine (unusable) until a new version of the antivirus signature files has been updated and can identify the file.

Social Engineering

All technicians (and employees) should be aware of social engineering. **Social engineering** involves tricking people into divulging information, including their own personal information or corporate knowledge. Social engineering does not happen just through email and internet links but can be done over the phone or through mail surveys. A common social engineering technique is **impersonation**, in which someone pretends to be from a trusted bank or company, such as Microsoft.

Shoulder surfing—looking at someone's computer screen while standing behind them—is a type of social engineering. Another type is dumpster diving, where someone looks in a trash bin inside or outside the office to gather information. No auditing or network security applications and devices can help with such deviousness.

TECH TIP

Watch out for tailgating

Tailgating (also known as piggybacking) is a type of social engineering in which an unauthorized person enters a building or an area of a building behind an authorized person. Prevention of tailgating requires training and diligence by all employees.

Phishing

Closely related to social engineering is the concept of phishing. **Phishing** (pronounced "fishing") is a type of social engineering that involves attempting to get personal information by using email messages from a company that appears to be legitimate. Most browsers include a phishing filter, which proactively warns computer users when they go to a site that is a known phishing site or when a site contains characteristics common to phishing sites.

Three variants of phishing are spear phishing, whaling, and vishing. With spear phishing, the attacker knows some information about you, and the subject line or first part of a spear phishing message may include your name; the body of the message may reference someone you know or may appear to be from a legitimate company with which you do business (see Figure 18.16). **Whaling** targets senior executives with well-crafted messages to get them to select a link, transfer funds, or provide information about the company. **Vishing** involves using a voice call to obtain information from a target.

FIGURE 18.16 Spear phishing

Companies frequently have yearly training on security, with a specific focus on phishing because it can be so damaging to the corporate network environment. Here's how to recognize phishing:

> Look closely at the address line and specifically the name after the @ symbol. Look up that domain name and see if it belongs to a legitimate company.
> Look for transposed letters in what at first glance would seem to be the name of a company you know but that is spelled incorrectly.
> Be suspicious of emails coming from an IT department or that have "IT department" (or another department that you would trust) in the subject line.
> Be suspicious of emails that use poor grammar.
> Hover your cursor over a link to see if the link address is suspect.
> Consider and review any email that seems to want to give you a sense of urgency.

A similar problem is **scareware**, where you get a message that appears to be about a virus or a problem with your computer and the link redirects you to a fake antivirus application, repair application, or company. The link might disable your own security software. Do not click within the message but use the close button to close the message and use a legitimate malware detection program to scan your system.

Security Attacks

Security attacks can come from outside or from within a corporate network. Table 18.7 lists various types of network attacks.

TABLE 18.7 Types of network attacks

Type of attack	Description
Access	A type of attack that frequently uses multiple dictionaries to gain entry to accounts, databases, servers, and/or network devices. Types of access attacks include man-in-the-middle, port redirection, buffer overflow, and password.
Backdoor	Also known as a trapdoor, a planted program that executes to bypass security and/or authentication.
Botnet	Software that spreads from hacked device to hacked device (called zombie computers or zombies) and that is under control of someone else (refer to Figure 18.15).
Brute force	Repeated attempts to check all possible key combinations to gain access to a network device or stored material.
Dictionary	A brute-force attack to try to determine a password or decryption key by trying different words found in a dictionary.
DoS	A denial of service (DoS) is a string of data/messages sent to overload a particular firewall, router, switch, server, access point, or computer in an attempt to deny service to other network devices.
DDoS	A distributed denial of service (DDOS) is a group of infected computers attacking a single network device by flooding the network with traffic.
Evil twin	An attack in which the threat actor has a rogue AP and broadcasts the same SSID as is in the same general area in order to capture packets from unsuspecting users.
Insider	An attacker that either works for the company being attacked or is using a corporate network device to do the attack.

Type of attack	Description
Man-in-the-middle (MITM) or **on-path**	A technique in which a hacker inserts a device between a sender and a receiver so the device can receive the intended traffic. Breaches may affect data or email communications and may potentially change information that is being transmitted. Access points, DHCP servers, and default gateways are commonly simulated in this type of attack.
Password spraying	An attack in which the attacker uses a commonly used password on a few accounts to avoid triggering password lockout or a firewall reaction.
Rainbow table	A method of obtaining a password in a short amount of time by using a table that contains previously discovered hash values that are used to encrypt a password.
Reconnaissance	A technique that involves attempting to gather information about a network before launching another type of attack. Tools used include port scanners, pings, and packet-sniffing programs.
Replay	A technique in which a valid network message or certificate is re-sent, usually in an attempt to obtain login information.
Smurf	A technique that involves using ICMP to ping a large amount of network traffic at a specific device to deny that device network access, ping a nonexistent device to generate network traffic, or ping all network devices to generate traffic in ICMP replies.
Spoofing	A technique that involves sending an Ethernet frame with a fake source MAC address to trick other devices into sending traffic to a rogue device. Can be used in conjunction with a man-in-the-middle attack.
SQL injection	An attack in which Structured Query Language (SQL) is used to access, query, and change databases as well as build data views for users. An SQL injection attack is used to acquire data, access data, cause data errors to display, or destroy data.
TCP/IP hijacking	A technique in which a stolen IP address is used to gain access and/or authorization information from a network.
Vulnerability scanner	A software program used to assess network devices to identify weaknesses such as unpatched operating systems, open ports, or missing/outdated virus-scanning software.
XSS	Cross-site scripting (XSS) involves inserting code into a legitimate website that can result in stealing data, inserting Trojan horse programs, or redirecting to a rogue website.
Zero day	A type of attack that takes advantage of a vulnerability in a particular software application that is found by hackers before it is known/fixed by the software developer.
Zombie	A device that has been hacked and is controlled by someone else or that carries out malicious tasks. Refer to Figure 18.15.

Protecting Access to Local and Network Resources

Several techniques exist to protect computer access, and some of them have already been considered in this chapter as part of physical access. Authentication is used to determine what network resources can be used. **Authorization** involves an operating system or a network granting access to specific resources, such as files, folders, printers, video conferencing equipment, scanners, and so on, on a computer system or network.

TECH TIP

Prevent a computer from being seen through the network

Search and access the *Network and Sharing Center* Control Panel > *Change advanced sharing settings* > select the *Turn off network discovery* option.

User Management

In a corporate environment, each domain user inputs a username as well as a password to authenticate to a centralized server. In a home or small company, local accounts are used, and they can be either Microsoft accounts or local accounts. A local account is a traditional user account, but by having a Microsoft account, your account settings are synced across all Microsoft devices, including OneDrive, Messenger, Xbox, Outlook, and Hotmail. With a Microsoft account, if you are locked out, you are locked out of all of those accounts, and you have to take steps to reset your Microsoft account, which could take a little bit of time.

Users can be added and placed into groups for ease of management. Table 18.8 shows the default local users/groups for Windows. Note that in Windows Home versions, local groups are not supported.

TABLE 18.8 Windows default users/groups

User or group	Description
Administrator (user)	Has total control of the computer; best practice is to rename the account and password protect it and create another user account that belongs to the administrator group and has a complex password.
Administrators (group)	A user account that has been created and placed in this group that has total control of the computer.
Guest (user)	A member of the Guest group; disabled by default; no default user rights.
Guests (group)	Used by those who do not have an account on the computer; normally does not require a password; best practice is to disable it.
Standard Account (user)	Default type of account created when you create a common corporate staff worker; the user is required to request an administrator to make changes to software, hardware, or security settings.
Backup Operators (group)	Can back up and restore files and folders, regardless of permissions assigned; cannot change security settings; can access the computer from a remote location.
Power Users (group)	Same as a Standard user account (and can change things like time zone or date/time). This group is meant for backward compatibility.
Users (group)	Can perform common tasks and create local groups but cannot share folders or printers.
Remote Desktop Users (group)	Can log on to the computer from a remote location.
Remote Management Users (group)	Can use the Remote Assistance program to help a computer user.
Network Configuration Operators (group)	Can make TCP/IP changes and release/renew IP addresses.
Performance Log Users (group)	Can manage local or remote performance logs and alerts.

TECH TIP

Always change the default admin password

Whether it is a Windows computer, a router, or any other electronic device, always **change the default admin user account password** or create an account that has administrator access and disable the default account.

Windows 10 and 11 do not allow you to disable the Administrator account, but you can add a user that has administrator access. In Windows 10/11, access the *User Accounts* Control Panel. Select the *Manage another account* link > select the *Add a new user in PC settings* link > in the *Other users* section, select the *Add someone else to this PC* option > if you don't want to use a Microsoft, Xbox, or other type of email or phone number and account information, select the *I don't have this person's sign-in information* link > select the *Add a user without a Microsoft account* link. Select the newly created user and select the *Change account type* button > change the account type to *Administrator > OK.*

TECH TIP

Lock your computer when away from the desk

When away from your desk, lock the PC by pressing Ctrl+Alt+Del and selecting *Lock* or *Lock this computer*.

Basic Active Directory Functions

Technicians sometimes have to use a Windows server and specifically the **Active Directory** (AD) service on the server to manage users and devices on the network as part of security best practices in the corporate environment. You can use Active Directory to define domains. Remember that a domain makes it possible to organize user accounts and devices such as computers and printers.

Within Active Directory, users can be placed in groups so that administration (for example, assigning security rights) is easier. Figure 18.17 shows a corporate structure in which one group of users is the Information Technology Services group. By expanding the group, you can see the users listed there.

Groups can further be combined into a domain group for even more centralized administration. When you create a domain group, you must choose between one of two types: security or distribution. A **security group** makes it possible to apply group policy settings or permissions to any shared resource. Distribution groups are merely email distribution lists.

Organizational units (OUs) are useful when you apply policies such as security policies or other corporate Windows rules to a part of an organization. OUs can contain groups, users, computer accounts, and even other OUs. OUs are useful when you want to delegate or let one or more administrators have control over a specific area of users, computers, and groups.

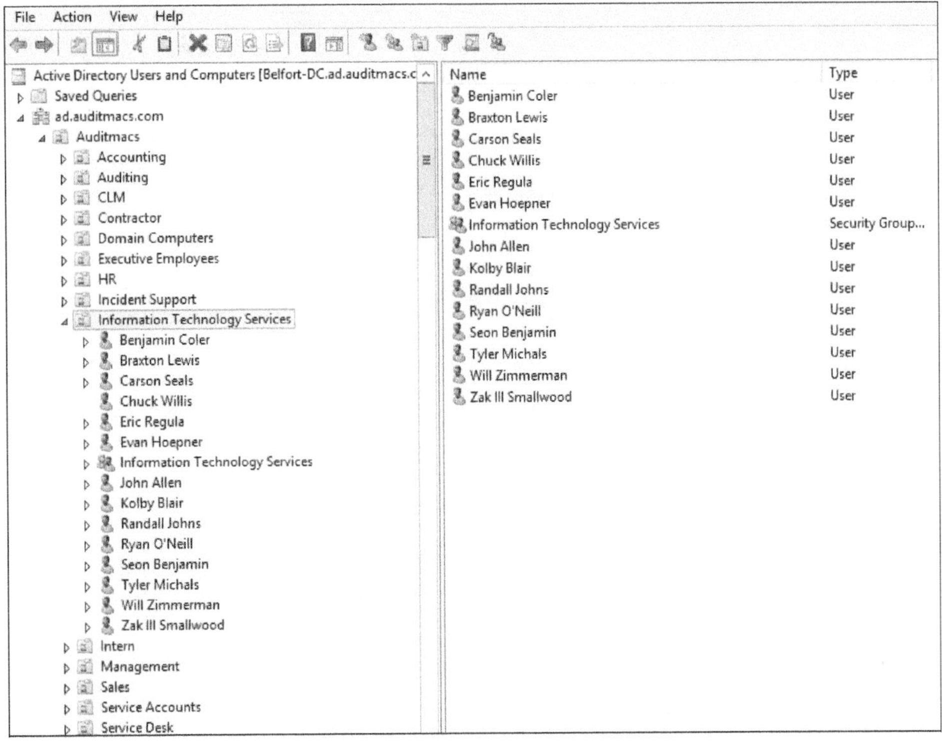

FIGURE 18.17 Active Directory Groups

To do account creation in AD (that is, add a user to a particular group), open the User Manager by going to the *Start* button > *Programs* > *Administrative Tools* > *Active Directory Users and Computers*. Expand the domain (the section that starts with "ad.xxx") until you see the group you want; click on that group. From the menu bar, select *Action* > *New* > *User*. In the dialog box shown in Figure 18.18, enter the user information and click *Next*. Enter the password and select any appropriate security settings, such as *User must change password at next logon*, as shown in Figure 18.19. Figure 18.20 shows the user account properties screen, where you click *OK*.

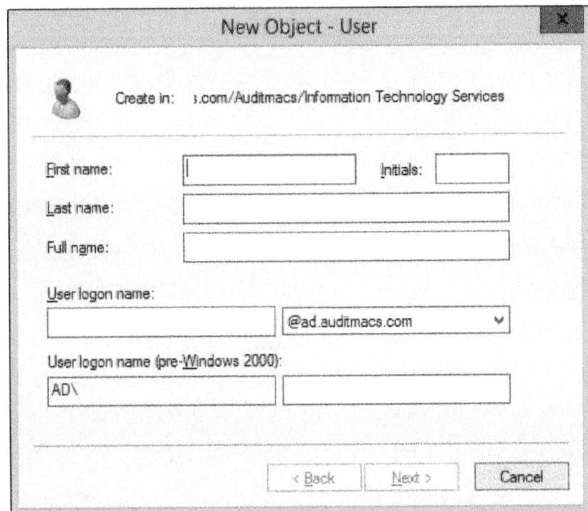

FIGURE 18.18 Active Directory > creating a new user

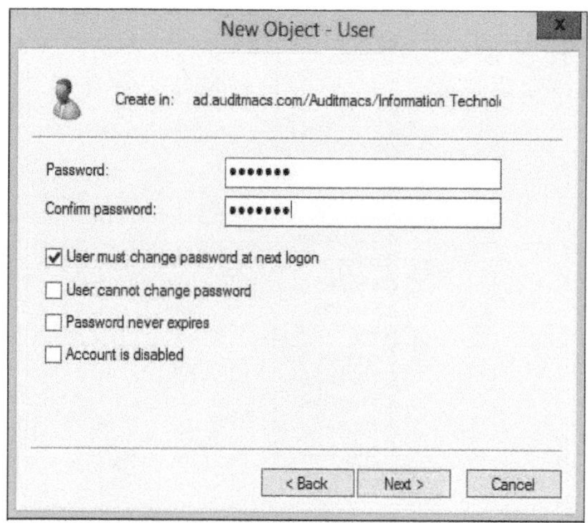

FIGURE 18.19 Active Directory > setting a new user password

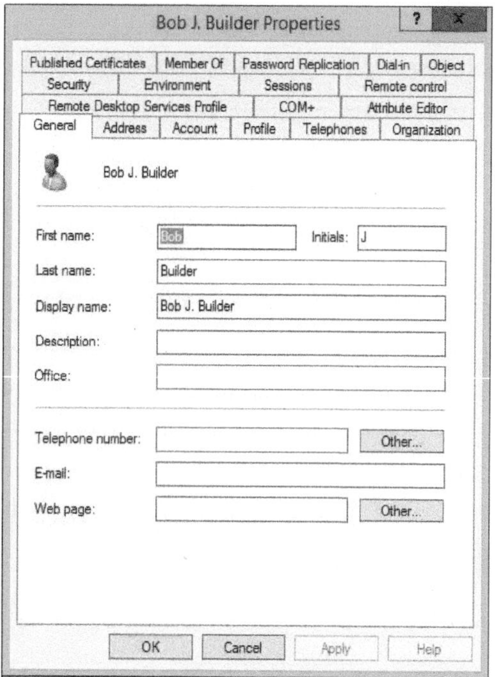

FIGURE 18.20 Active Directory > viewing properties of a new user

Users are commonly placed in groups so that they can be managed more easily. To place a user in a group, expand the particular group the user is currently in or just select the *Users* folder > locate the user that has been added previously and right-click on the name > *Add to a group*. Note that you can also add a user to a group from the user's *Properties* window (refer to Figure 18.20) and select the *Member Of* tab > *Add* button. Either way, you are presented with the Select Groups window, as shown in Figure 18.21.

At the bottom of the textbox, type the name of the group you want the user to be in. Look at the groups within the domain shown to the left of this window (refer to Figure 18.17), such as HR or Information Technology Services. A user can be a member of multiple groups, and those groups are shown on the *Members Of* tab.

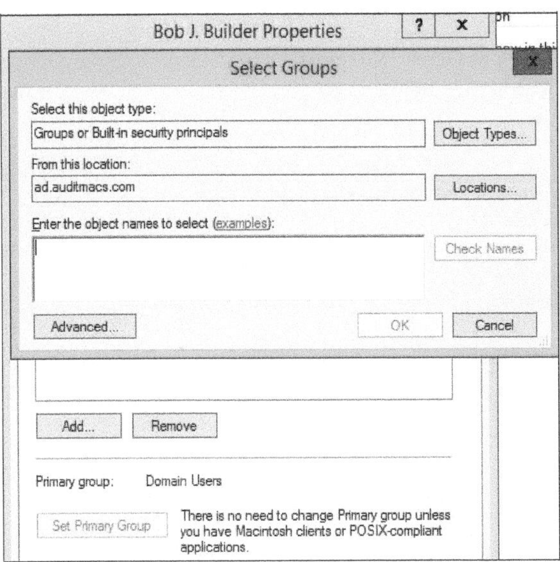

FIGURE 18.21 Active Directory > adding a user to a group

Other functions within the user account properties that might need to be set by a technician are the logon script, home folder, and folder redirection. A logon script (sometimes referred to as a **login script**) is a set of tasks configured in one file that run when a user logs in, such as running a specific application, performing an operating system function on the local computer, or setting system environment variables. The logon script can be defined as part of a group policy (covered in the next section) or through the *Properties* window > *Profile* tab, as shown in Figure 18.22.

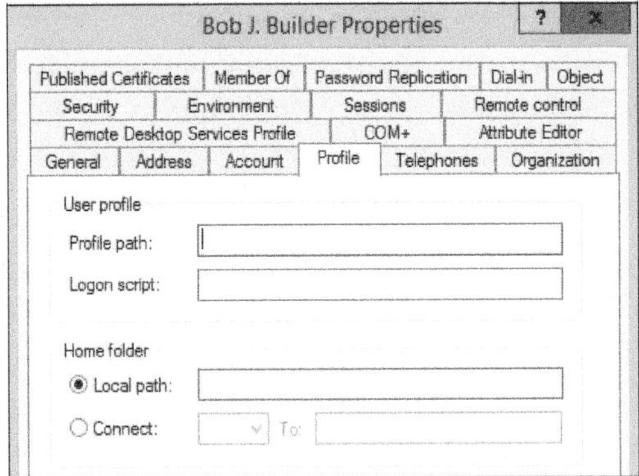

FIGURE 18.22 Active Directory > using the *Profile* tab

Notice in Figure 18.22 the Home Folder section. A **home folder** is a network folder that allows users to store their files and have access to them from any device that they log onto within the same domain. Commonly the *Connect* radio button is used to assign a drive letter in the first drop-down menu, and then the network path where the files are stored is provided (for example, \\ServerName\FolderName\%username%).

Another technique used for user data storage is folder redirection. **Folder redirection** involves mapping a folder on the local machine to a network location such as a server. The user then has access to the files within that folder from any device on the network domain.

To delete an account, right-click on someone's name (see Figure 18.23) and select the *Delete* option. Some companies have a policy of not deleting user accounts in case users come back or in case you might for some other reason need to access accounts. Instead, some managers disable an account and put that disabled account into a group with all the other disabled accounts. To manually disable an account, locate and right-click on the user account and select *Disable Account*.

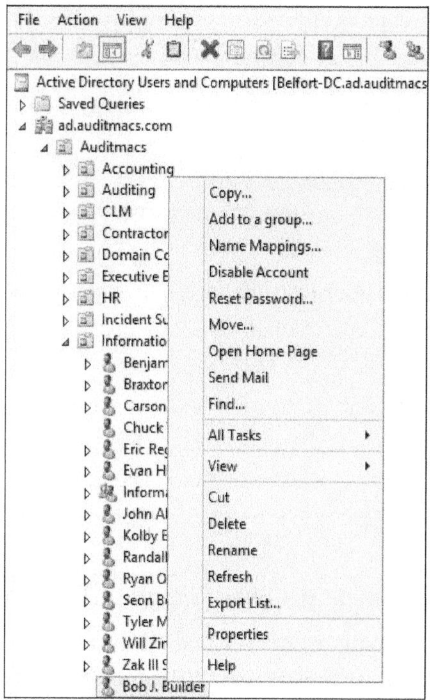

FIGURE 18.23 Active Directory > right-clicking on user account

Local and Group Policies

Another method of controlling login passwords is through a local- or domain-based group account policy. Policies do more than just define password requirements. They can define the desktop, what applications are available to users, what options are available through the *Start* menu, whether users are allowed to save files to external media, and so on. A domain policy, or **group policy**, can be created, updated, and applied to every computer on the domain. This practice is common in Microsoft Active Directory (AD) domain networks.

A **local security policy** is created on a computer, and it could be used to disable auto-playing of media such as USB thumb drives and optical discs, prevent users from shutting down or restarting a computer, turn off personalized menus, or prevent someone from changing the Internet Explorer or Microsoft Edge home page. A local security policy might be implemented in a workgroup setting. A group policy is more common in a corporate environment, and a group policy can overwrite a local policy. If any computer settings on a networked computer in a corporate environment are grayed out, the settings are probably locked out due to the policy deployed throughout the domain.

TECH TIP

Accessing the local security policy and group policy

Access the Local Group Policy Editor window by typing **`gpedit.msc`** at a command prompt or in the *Search* textbox. Use the **`gpresult`** command to display group policy settings. Use the **`gpupdate`** command to update all domain users with a newly deployed group policy. Use the **`secedit`** command to configure or analyze a security policy.

The following list describes some best practices for securing a workstation in a corporate environment:

> **Restrict login times.** If someone works during the daytime Monday through Friday, then restrict Saturday and Sunday or evenings.

> Set expiration requirements. Require the user to change their password after 60 or 90 days unless a long, complex passphrase is required. Then, only require changing the password if a security breach is suspected.

> **Disable guest account.** Use the Computer Management Console > expand *System Tools* > expand *Local Users and Groups* > double-click on the *Guest* account > select the *Account is disabled* checkbox.

> Enable the failed attempts lockout feature to lock out users after a specific number of failed login attempts. In the **group policy editor**, expand *Security Settings* > *Account Lockout Policy* to access how long someone is locked out and how many failed attempts are allowed.

> Configure a **timeout/screen lock** for when users are away from their workstations to automatically lock their screens after a period of nonuse.

> Restrict user permissions and apply the principle of least privilege (which is covered later in this chapter).

Through the defined policy, criteria for auditing can also be set. Auditing, sometimes called *event logging* or just *logging*, is the process of tracking events that occur on the network, such as someone logging in to the network. In a business environment, a server with special auditing software is sometimes devoted to this task because it is very important to security. Figure 18.24 shows the Local Group Policy Editor window.

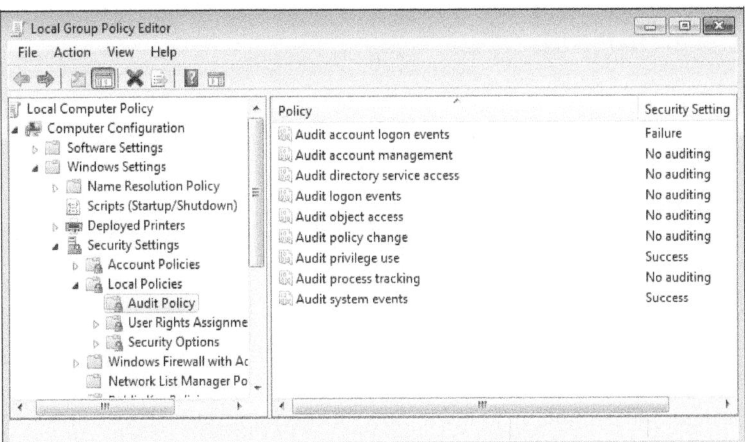

FIGURE 18.24 Local Group Policy Editor window

TECH TIP

Requiring password protection

You can enable or disable password protection through the Network and Sharing Center on a workgroup computer. If password protection is enabled, a person accessing a shared folder from a remote location must have a user account and password on the computer that holds the network share.

Permissions

Monitoring users and groups as well as the devices, data, and applications they have access to is important. Permissions control what can or cannot be done (permit or deny access) to files, folders, and devices from a remote connection. (This is similar to file attributes, covered in Chapter 15, "Introduction to Scripting.") By sharing files and folders, each computer can act as a file server. A security best practice is to restrict user permissions, but permissions can cause havoc. Network administrators and end users can set permissions on folders, and these permissions may affect another user's access to files and folders. Technicians need to be familiar with permissions.

Two types of permissions can be assigned in Windows: share permissions and NTFS permissions. **Share permissions** provide and/or limit access to data across a network. Using share permissions is the only way to secure network resources on FAT16 or FAT32 drives. **NTFS permissions** provide tighter control than shared folder permissions. NTFS permissions can be used only on NTFS drives.

TECH TIP

If file permissions change

If you ever notice that file permissions change (for example, you can no longer access an application or a file that you once could), check for a virus. Note that in the case of some viruses that change file permissions, you may need to repartition the hard drive and reinstall the operating system to remove the virus.

Share Permissions

To share a folder other than the Public folder, use *File Explorer* > right-click on the folder name > *Give access to* > type the name of the person > *Add*. You can do one of the following at this point:

> If the computer is attached to a network domain, select the arrow to the right of the textbox > *Find* > type the name of the person with whom you want to share the folder > *Check names* > *OK*.

> If the computer is on a workgroup, click the arrow to the right of the textbox, select the appropriate name, and click *Add*. If the name does not appear, click the arrow to the right of the textbox and click *Create a new user to create the user account.*

> An alternative method is to locate the folder using *File Explorer* > right-click or tap and briefly hold on the folder icon > *Properties* > *Sharing* tab > click the *Share* button. Figure 18.25 shows this window.

TECH TIP

Share permissions are only applicable across a network

Notice that shared folder permissions are applicable only across a network. This type of share does not prevent someone sitting at the computer from accessing files and folders. For best protection across a network and at the computer, use NTFS file and folder permissions.

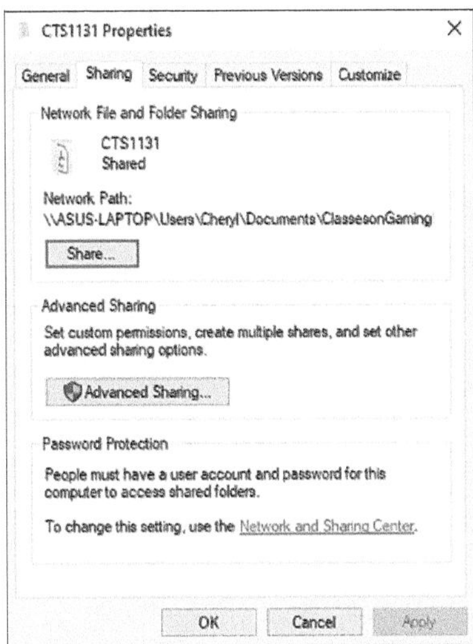

FIGURE 18.25 Using the Sharing tab to share a folder

Permissions are set by clicking the *Advanced Sharing* button (see Figure 18.26). Notice that you can limit the number of simultaneous users who can connect to this folder from a remote location. Click the *Permissions* button. Notice in Figure 18.27 that you can select the Allow or Deny checkboxes for the individual permissions.

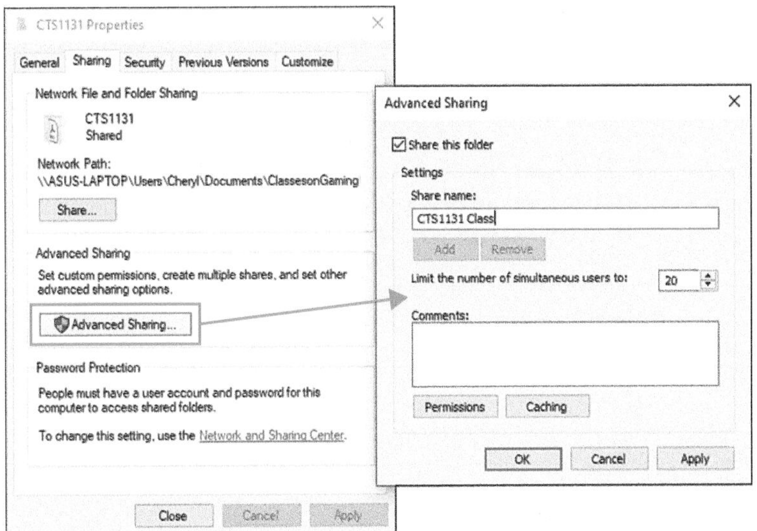

FIGURE 18.26 Folder Sharing tab > *Advanced Sharing* options

TECH TIP

What is the maximum number of concurrent users?

A maximum of 20 users can simultaneously use the same shared folder.

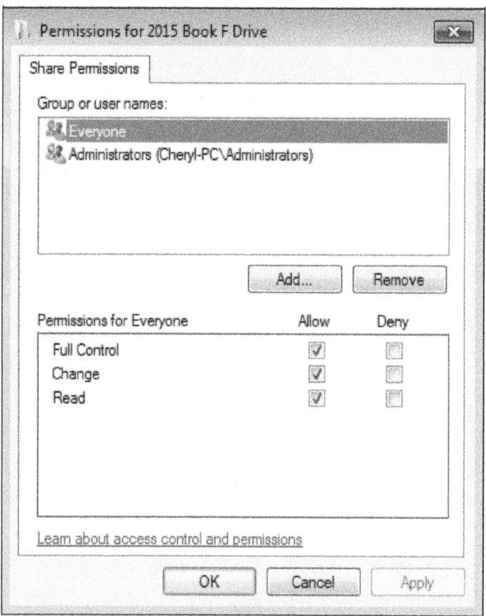

FIGURE 18.27 *Sharing* tab > *Advanced Sharing* button > setting *Permissions* button window

Notice in Figure 18.27 that you can select Allow or Deny for specific types of permissions (Full Control, Change, and Read). Table 18.9 shows the effects of setting each of these permissions to Allow.

TABLE 18.9 Share permissions

Permission	Description
Full Control	Users can do everything, such as change the file permissions, take ownership of files, and perform everything that can be done with the *Change* permission.
Change	Users can add new subfolders, add files to a folder, change the data in a file, add data to files, change file attributes, delete folders and files, and do all the tasks that are possible with the Read permission.
Read	Users can look at file and folder names and attributes and can open files and execute scripts.

TECH TIP

Principle of least privilege

When determining access to a folder or to a server room, you should give access to only what is needed and only to the people who need access (and no more). Giving people access to an entire drive or building when they just need access to a particular folder or room puts the entire hard drive or company at risk. The **principle of least privilege** as it relates to computer and network security is that the maximum rights you give people are limited to only the rights they need to do their job.

File and folder security protection is a concern. A subfolder and any files created within that subfolder all inherit security permissions from the parent folder or the folder that contains the subfolder. This feature can be disabled when necessary.

Local and Administrative Shares

Files and folders can be shared in a network workgroup or a domain. A **local share** is something—a printer, folder, or media device—that is shared on a specific computer. **Administrative**

shares are shares created by Microsoft for drive volumes and the folder that contains the majority of Window files. An example of an administrative share is a drive volume letter (such as **C:**) followed by the dollar sign (**$**) symbol (**C$**). The **admin$** administrative share is used to provide access to the folder that contains the Windows operating system files.

Windows automatically creates administrative shares, but by default Windows prevents local accounts from accessing administrative shares through the network. If this feature is desired, a registry edit must be made. A better solution is to disable a particular administrative share through a group policy.

Any local share can be made a **hidden share**, which is a share that is not visible by default throughout the network. To make a share a hidden share, add the dollar sign ($) to the share name. This might be beneficial for computer users who want to access something from their remote computer without making it visible to other network users.

TECH TIP

Access denied message

If a user or technician ever receives an access denied message on a shared folder or hidden share, ensure that the user login is one that has administrative privileges or check the assigned permissions on the shared folder.

Public Folder

Another way to share files is through using the Public folder. The default path for the Public folder is `C:\Users\Public`. You can copy or move any file to the Public folder. Note that when files are copied into this folder, twice as much storage space is used because there are copies of the same material in two folders.

If sharing is enabled for the Public folder, anyone who has a user account and password on the computer can access the data. In addition, any user on the network can see all files and folders in the Public folder by selecting *Network* from File Explorer, accessing the appropriate computer, browsing to the *Users* folder, and opening the *Public* folder. You can set permissions so that this folder is inaccessible or can restrict anyone from changing files or creating new files. However, you cannot pick and choose what files can be seen by individuals.

Here's how to use the *Public* folder: Access the *Network and Sharing Center* Control Panel > *Change advanced sharing settings* > expand the *All Networks* section by selecting the down arrow if it is not showing any information below it > locate the *Public Folder Sharing* area > select the *Turn on sharing so anyone with network access can read and write files in the public folders* radio button. Note that you must also turn on network discovery and file and print sharing to see shared files across the network.

NTFS Permissions

On an NTFS partition, additional security protection is available. Locate the folder in File Explorer. Right-click on the folder name and select *Properties* > select the *Security* tab (see Figure 18.28). Table 18.10 defines these permissions.

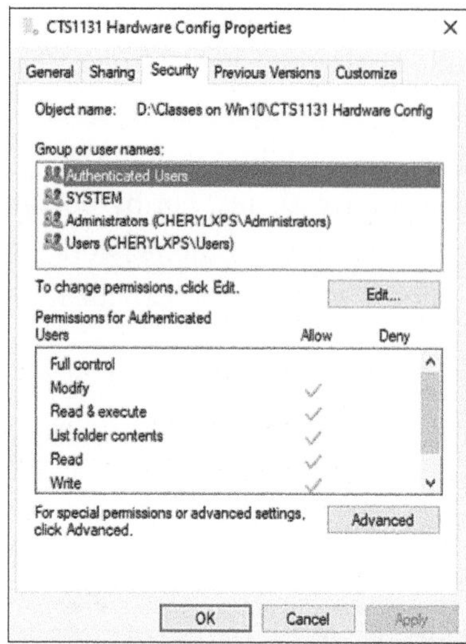

FIGURE 18.28 Windows NTFS permissions—using the *Security* tab

TABLE 18.10 NTFS permissions

Permission	Description
Full Control	Users can do anything in the files and folder, including delete, add, modify, and create files and folders.
Modify	Users can list items in a folder, read data, and write data, but they cannot delete subfolders and files and cannot take ownership.
Read & Execute	Users can list items in a folder and read a file, but they cannot change or delete a file or create new files. Users can execute applications contained within the folder.
List Folder Contents	Users can only look inside a folder.
Read	Users can display folder and subfolder attributes and permissions as well as look at a particular file.
Write	Users can add files or folders, change attributes for the folder, and add or append data in a file.

Inherited permissions are propagated from what Microsoft calls a *parent object*. For example, if a folder is given the Read permission, then all files within that folder cannot be changed (they are read-only). If a subfolder is created, it inherits that permission. If the Allow or Deny checkboxes for any object are selected, the current permissions have been inherited.

There may also be issues when copying or moving is performed on objects that have NTFS permissions set. Consider these guidelines for copying and moving:

> When you copy a file/folder on the same or different NTFS drive letter, the copy inherits the destination folder's permissions.

> When you move a file/folder on the same NTFS drive letter, the original permissions of the object are retained.

> When you move a file/folder to a different NTFS drive letter, the moved object inherits the destination folder permissions.

> When you copy or move a file/folder to a drive that uses a different file system (like FAT), the object loses all its permissions.

> If you change permissions on a folder that has content, only the new content inherits the changed permissions.

Effective permissions are the final permissions granted to a person for a particular resource. Effective permissions are important when you combine shared folder permissions given to an individual, shared folder permissions given to a group, and individual permissions. The following are some helpful tips when sharing folders and files across a network:

> Folder permissions are cumulative: When you grant folder permission to a group and then grant an individual permission to that same folder, the effective permission for that person is the combination of what the group gets and what the person gets. For example, if the group gets the Write permission and the person gets only the Read permission (and the person is a member of the group that has the Write permission), the person can both read and write files to the folder.

> Deny overrides any allowed permissions that have been set for a user or a group. For example, if a group is denied access to a folder, but a person is specifically allowed access to the folder, the person is not allowed to access the folder.

> When NTFS and shared folder permissions are both used, the most restrictive of the two is the effective permissions level.

Windows provides help in determining effective permissions. Right-click on a file or folder > *Properties* > *Security* tab > *Advanced* button > *Effective Access*. Note that what is shown is only for NTFS permissions. Share permissions are not part of the Windows calculation for this window. Permissions-related issues are a common problem. A technician must be familiar with the results of misconfiguring permissions. If users have files stored in a mapped drive share and those files are moved to a different server, then the mapped drive will need to be redone and point to the new server, and permissions will need to be applied on the new server.

TECH TIP

All subfolders are shared when a folder is shared

When you share a folder, all subfolders are automatically shared unless you make the subfolders private.

File and Folder Attributes

File and folder attributes are covered in Chapters 14, "Introduction to Operating Systems," and 15, "Introduction to Scripting," but need to be reviewed here as well. From the beginning, there have always been four main attributes:

> *Read-only:* Information cannot be changed.

> *Archive:* Used in backup operations to tell when a file folder has been backed up.

> *Hidden:* File or folder doesn't show by default in File Explorer.

> *System:* The file isn't visible in File Explorer by default and is a file used by the operating system.

With a drive that has been formatted with NTFS, additional attributes are available:

> *Compressed:* Indicates reduced storage size.

> *Encrypted:* Indicates that the data within is scrambled.

> *Indexed:* Is not included in searches by default.

> *Offline:* Used by remote storage options.

When a folder is shared across the network, the permissions given specify what a user is allowed to do with a particular folder. By default, all subfolders and files contained within a shared folder or subfolder inherit the same permissions. For example, if you select read-only as the shared folder permission, then someone can open a file but cannot modify and save it. If you right-click the name of a file within a shared folder that has read-only permissions assigned, you can then select *Properties* in order to access attributes, and you will see that the file has the read-only attribute already marked.

Getting the Job Done with the Correct Permissions

When working on a staff member's computer, remember that when you are logged on as that user, you may not be able to use specific utilities. Commonly used utilities or commands executed from a command prompt may not be available to you unless you **run as administrator**. Search for `command prompt`. In the resulting list, right-click on the *Command Prompt* option > select *Run as administrator*.

To see some problems, you may need the user to be logged in. Logging in with an account that has administrator access may not allow you to see the same issues the user sees. Always ensure that users log on and test whatever you fix to ensure that it works for their own account and permissions.

Another adjustment that might need to be done is through User Account Control (**UAC**), which can prevent users from installing apps that might contain malware or using system tools that could cause harm to the system if used improperly. Windows 10 has four options to choose from:

- *Always notify:* Requires an administrator account in order to make changes.
- *Notify me only when apps try to make changes to my computer* (default)*:* Provides feedback if any app or program tries to make changes on the computer or install software. It will not let any other tasks be performed until a response is made and it does not provide notification if any Windows settings are modified.
- *Notify me only when apps try to make changes to my computer (do not dim my desktop):* Helps if the computer takes a long time to dim the desktop (the computer is slow).
- *Never notify:* Does not provide any notifications if a program tries to make changes to the computer or install software.

Folder Options

Because of quarantined files or the need to check system files, a technician needs to be familiar with File Explorer display options. Access the *View* menu option > *Options* > *Change folder and search options* > *View* tab. Use the *Layout* section or *File Explorer Options* Control Panel to configure how folders/files display and what information is included with that display.

A technician often has to work with system files and folders that are not visible by default. Table 18.11 summarizes the security-related *View* tab options. A technician must remember to set the settings to the way they were previously so that users do not see them by default. The *View* tab has a *Restore Defaults* button that resets all settings.

TABLE 18.11 View tab options

Function	Options to select
View hidden files	*Hidden files and folders* section > enable *Show hidden files, folders, and drives*
View file extensions	*Files and Folders* section > uncheck *Hide extensions for known file types*
View system files	*Files and Folders* section > uncheck *Hide protected operating system files (Recommended)*
Sharing menu/options	*Files and Folders* section > enable *Use Sharing Wizard (Recommended)*

Protecting the Operating System and Data

Several chapters have contained important security-related tips, steps, and information related to protecting the operating system and data. In this section, let's review some tips that pertain specifically to the security of the operating system and data:

- Use the NTFS file system.
- Conduct good **patch/update management**. Ensure that operating system and application service packs and updates are applied regularly. If a Windows update fails, a message usually appears when the machine reboots. Try the update again; sometimes an update might fail when being installed with other updates. Successfully install as many as you can and then reinstall the failed updates one by one. Note that in Windows 8 and higher, updates come as a package, but they can be uninstalled individually by update number. Note that mobile devices also need **patching/OS updates**, including updates to the phone's radio firmware.
- Ensure that the OS has not reached **end-of-life** (EOL) and is no longer able to be updated or receive security patches.
- Have an alternative boot source (such as an optical disc, a flash drive, another hard drive, or an operating system disc).
- Watch out for **unprotected systems**. Check for missing antivirus/anti-malware software and make sure the firewall is not disabled. Install antivirus/anti-malware software with the latest updates and enable the firewall, if necessary.
- Encrypt data that needs to be protected.
- Optionally, place operating system files and data files on separate hard drive partitions.
- Some firmware or driver versions may cause security issues. Keep the versions updated.
- Notifications may appear from an icon in the bottom-right corner of the display. Any **unwanted notifications** can be controlled by using the *Notifications & actions* Windows Settings link, as shown in Figure 18.29. Scroll down to see configurable actions for specific apps.
- Virtual machines need the same security software as host machines.
- If the computer you use does not need to share files or a printer with others on the network, use the *Network and Sharing Center* Control Panel and disable *File and Print Sharing*.
- To create a shared folder that is not seen by any others across the network, add a `$` (dollar sign) to the end of the share name. An example of a hidden shared folder is `Book$`.
- Use the System Restore program to control restore points before installing new software or hardware. Use the *System* Control Panel > *System Protection* link to access the restore points.
- Disable ports through the system BIOS/UEFI settings. Password protect the BIOS to prevent use of external devices that might be infected with viruses.

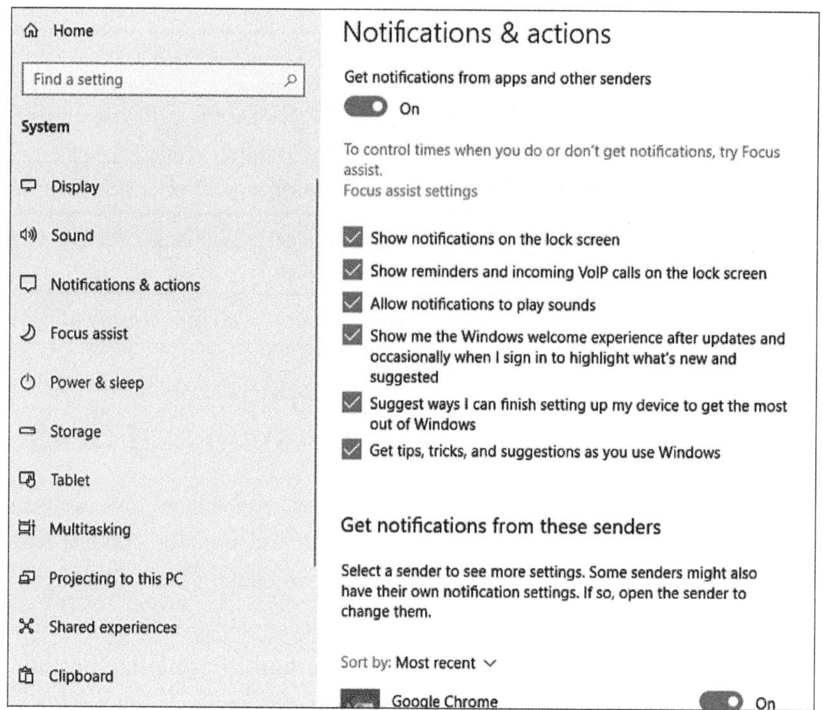

FIGURE 18.29 Windows Notifications & actions options

Backup/Restore

One preventive maintenance procedure that is commonly overlooked is performing a backup of the data and operating system. Backup and restoration should be part of any disaster prevention plan. Most people do not realize that the most important part of any computer is the data that resides within it. Data cannot be replaced as easily as hardware can be.

Back up data routinely. Also make a backup of critical applications—applications that are critical to the family or business. The sensitivity and importance of the data determine how frequently backups are performed.

> **TECH TIP**
>
> **Backup testing**
>
> Ensure that you test a backup to ensure that your method works and the time required to restore is as expected. **Backup testing** should be part of an implementation plan as well as a disaster prevention/recovery plan and should be done on a scheduled basis.

Traditionally, backups were saved to magnetic tape—quarter-inch cartridge, linear tape-open (LTO), or digital linear tape (DLT) being the most common types—but optical discs, thumb drives, and external drives are viable **on site storage** alternatives today. Cloud storage (shown in Figure 18.30) or **off site storage** is also an important part of a backup plan.

Advantages of local storage include the ability to control the security of that data and the cost of the media used. A disadvantage is that you have to store and maintain that media. Cloud storage can be free for an individual or for a charge, but security is a concern. In addition, restoration requires connectivity to the cloud storage.

TECH TIP

A second hard drive makes an excellent backup device

Storage devices are inexpensive and easy to install. Install a second one to back up your data. Another alternative is to put your operating system and applications on an SSD and use a mechanical drive for your data for easier backups.

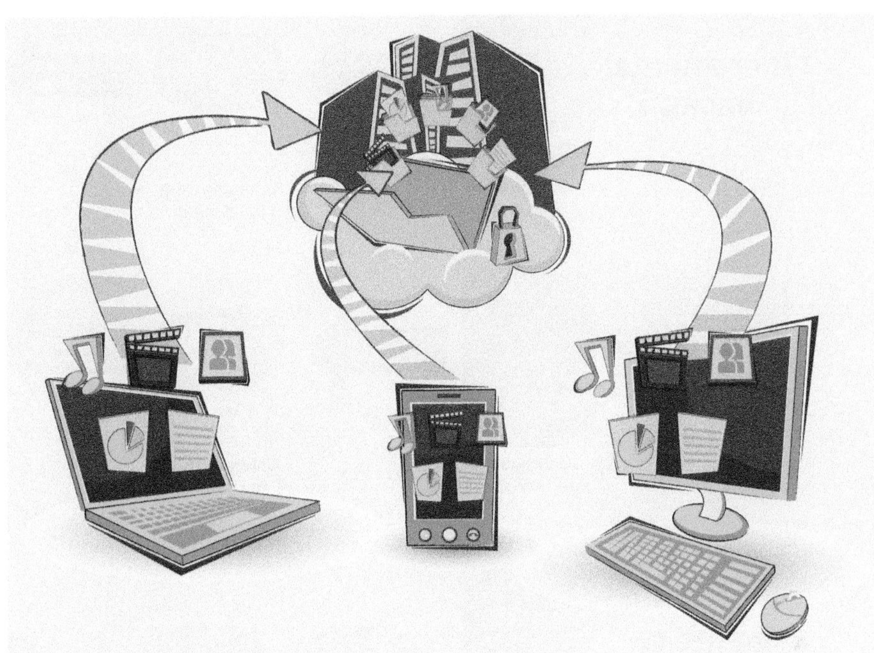

FIGURE 18.30 Cloud storage for backups

Backups use the file archive bit. A **full backup** backs up all selected files and sets the archive bit to off. An **incremental backup** backs up all files that have changed since the last backup. The files selected are the ones that have the archive bit set to on. The backup software resets those archive bits to off. In contrast, a **differential backup** backs up files that have changed since the last full backup (files that have the archive bit set to on), but the backup software does not reset the archive bit, as an incremental backup does. A **synthetic backup** makes use of a full backup and incremental backup, as shown in Figure 18.31.

All of these backup types are known as file-level backups. Another type of backup is an image-level backup, which backs up an entire drive to one file (called an image). The drawbacks to this type of backup are the size of the image and the time involved. A company may have a computer image of an operating system and standard applications that is pushed onto the machine, and then users back up their data by using a file-level backup technique.

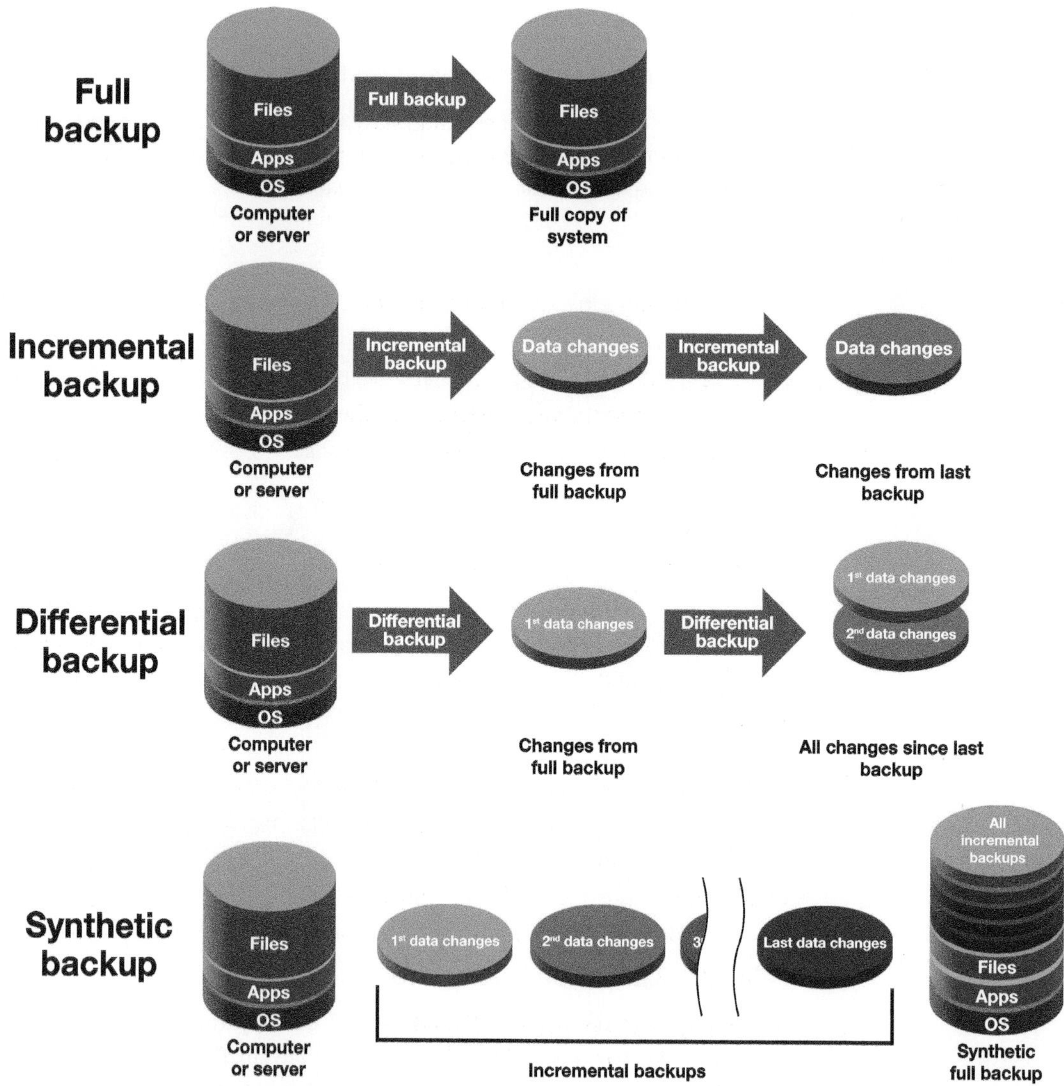

FIGURE 18.31 Backup types

There are several backup rotation techniques, but all of them should include off site storage in case of disaster, and every company should have a plan for how often backups are done. Here are two popular ones:

- **Grandfather-father-son** (GFS) **backup**: A full (grandfather) backup is done on a schedule of perhaps once every two weeks or once a month and stored (potentially off site). Then another full backup (father) backup is done (potentially to faster storage) more frequently, such as once a week. Then incremental (son) backups are performed daily until another full father backup is done.
- **3-2-1 backup**: Three copies (one primary and two copies) of the data are made to two different media types, and one of the backups is kept off site.

Windows has the File History utility. Many external hard drives come with their own software that is easier to use, has more features, and allows easy and selective data backup scheduling. Some vendors have a backup and recovery option that is part of BIOS/UEFI, part of the Windows System Recovery Options, or accessed in another manner. No matter what method of backup you use, test your backup for restoration. Install it to a different drive, if necessary.

TECH TIP

Don't use the same hard drive as a backup device

Backing up data to a different partition on a drive is *not* a good idea. The drive is a physical device that may have moving parts—motor, heads, and so on. Mechanical failure is always a possibility.

Probably the most asked question of those with drive failures or failing/failed sectors is regarding file recovery. Windows does not have file recovery software beyond being able to locate and repair lost clusters. However, there are third-party file recovery utilities that you can use. Many times files cannot be recovered unless the file recovery utility was installed prior to the loss. Many companies also provide data recovery services for a fee.

TECH TIP

For critical data, keep backups in a different location

Offsite storage, or cloud storage, for critical data is important even for home users—to prepare for the possibility of disasters such as flooding, fire, theft, hurricane, or tornado. A company may even have redundant systems or servers located in a distant location (hot site) in case of disaster.

Even though much data is stored locally, many companies favor centralized storage, even for individual users. This protects the company's interest and also ensures that backups are done on a regular and reliable basis. Another option in business is a thin-client environment, in which no hard drives are included with the systems. Storage is provided across the network to a central location. This reduces hardware and software costs and PC maintenance staffing costs, and it makes data security easier to manage as well.

Account Recovery Options

Whenever disaster occurs and backups/restores have to be done, there may also be a need to recover accounts from various vendors, including Microsoft, to aid in local account password recovery. This can be very time-consuming. Document critical information such as the following *before* disaster occurs:

- Computer/laptop/device make, model, year purchased, and warranty length
- Names, IP addresses, and backup configurations of network infrastructure devices
- Firewall rules
- Domain settings
- Account names and passwords for network infrastructure devices, network administrators, email, and internet provider settings
- BIOS passwords
- Software license keys, information, applications, versions, and purchasing agreements

BitLocker

BitLocker encrypts an entire disk volume, including the operating system, user files, page files (also known as paging files or swap files), and hibernation files. It is available on Windows 8 Pro and Enterprise; Windows 10 Pro, Enterprise, Education, Mobile, and Mobile Enterprise; and Windows 11 Pro, Enterprise, Education versions. BitLocker requires two NTFS disk partitions. **BitLocker To Go** is used to encrypt and password protect external drives and removable media

128 MB and larger. BitLocker can optionally use Trusted Platform Module (TPM), which is a chip that stores security information such as encryption keys.

TECH TIP

What does it take to unlock a drive encrypted with BitLocker?

You will need the BitLocker recovery key or the BitLocker password in order to unlock or decrypt a drive that has been encrypted using BitLocker.

Device Encryption

Mobile devices support **full device encryption**, which involves scrambling or encoding all user data. Once full device encryption is enabled, any new data created is automatically encrypted. A drawback to full device encryption is slower performance; in addition, disabling the option might require resetting the option back to factory defaults, which means you would lose any data and customization.

On an Android device, use the *Security* or *Lock Screen and Security* settings option. Apple iPhones have encryption enabled by default, and the option cannot be disabled.

Encryption Options

Data at rest is data that is not being used but that is stored somewhere such as on a local drive, in the cloud, within a spreadsheet, on an external drive, and so on. To protect this type of data, you can put a password on the file/folder or encrypt it using Advanced Encryption Standard (AES) or Rivest-Shamir-Adleman (RSA) (see Figure 18.32). **AES** is an encryption standard with key sizes of 128, 192, or 256 bits. AES has been used in wireless government networks for some time and is now common in almost all wireless network implementations that use WPA2 or WPA3 (covered later in the chapter). RSA is a slower algorithm and is not used as commonly as AES.

FIGURE 18.32 Encrypt data files and folders

NTFS volumes can have files, folders, and subfolders encrypted using Encrypting File System (**EFS**). The EFS algorithm originally used Data Encryption Standard (DES), which used 56- or 128-bit encryption, but now the EFS algorithm uses Advanced Encryption Standard (AES), Secure

Hash Algorithm (SHA), smart card–based encryption, and in Windows 7, 8, and 10, Elliptical Curve Cryptography (ECC).

When a folder or subfolder is encrypted, all newly created files within the folder or subfolder are automatically encrypted. If any files are copied or moved into an encrypted folder or subfolder, those files are automatically encrypted. System files cannot be encrypted. EFS can use a certificate from a certificate authority (CA), such as one issued from a server, or a self-signed certificate.

TECH TIP

Can you encrypt someone else's files?

The answer is "yes" if you have the write attribute, create files/write data, and list folder/read data permissions for the file.

AutoRun and AutoPlay

Disable AutoRun to prevent software or programs that are executables from automatically starting from an optical disc, flash drive, or external drive. An executable may not be a safe program and may pose a security threat. In contrast, AutoPlay is a setting related to what happens when media is attached or inserted. As an example of AutoPlay, when you insert a music CD, the music may automatically start playing, or you may be prompted for the default action. To **disable AutoPlay** and control what happens when you insert each type of media device, use the *Devices* section of *Settings > Auto Play* link. You can also do this through the security policy. Use the following steps to disable AutoPlay and AutoRun so that the action will not occur and the user will not be prompted:

Step 1. At a command prompt or in the *Search* textbox, type **`gpedit.msc`** and press Enter.

Step 2. Expand *Administrative Templates* > expand *Windows Components*.

Step 3. Select *Autoplay Policies* > double-click *Turn off autoplay* > select *Enabled* > select *All Drives* > restart the computer.

Note that specific Windows security updates are also required; see https://support.microsoft.com for more details.

Storage Drive Security

When donating a computer or replacing a hard drive, data on the drive needs to be removed after the data has been transferred to the new drive or is not needed any longer. Furthermore, the hard drive partitions need to be deleted and re-created. Some hard drive manufacturers offer utilities that rewrite (sometimes called drive overwrite) the drive with all 1s or all 0s to prevent data remnants from being recovered. Another option is a **drive wipe**, which may use a number of techniques (not all guaranteed to be 100% effective on highly sensitive data) to remove data from the drive. A hard drive manufacturer may have a **low-level format** utility that is different from the **standard format** done through the drive installation/preparation process. You can use the SDelete utility, which can be downloaded from Microsoft (see http://technet.microsoft.com/en-us/sysinternals/bb897443.aspx).

Another option is to use the `format` and `cipher` commands. First use `format x: /p:n` (where `x:` is the drive letter and *n* is the number of passes) to format a disk volume with a 0 in every sector. Then use the `cipher /w x:` command, where `x:` is the hard drive volume letter. The `cipher` command writes all unused sectors with 0s, then 1s, and then a random number.

Because this command is performed on unused sectors, it is important to remember to use the `format` command first.

A company that has extremely sensitive data stored on a hard drive should destroy the hard drive by doing the following:

> Securely erasing the drive, which requires special software
> **Degaussing** the drive (using electromagnets to change the drive's magnetic fields, or 1s and 0s, which can be expensive and requires drive disassembly)
> Drilling through the drive platters (see Figure 18.33) and then destroying the pieces with a hammer or using a machine designed for this purpose (see Figure 18.34)

Specific requirements such as the HIPAA Privacy Rule and Security Rule might need to be examined. For example, if non-sensitive protected health information (PHI) is on a drive, then securely erasing the data is fine, but if sensitive information is on there, the drive has to be degaussed.

FIGURE 18.33 Drilled hard drive platter

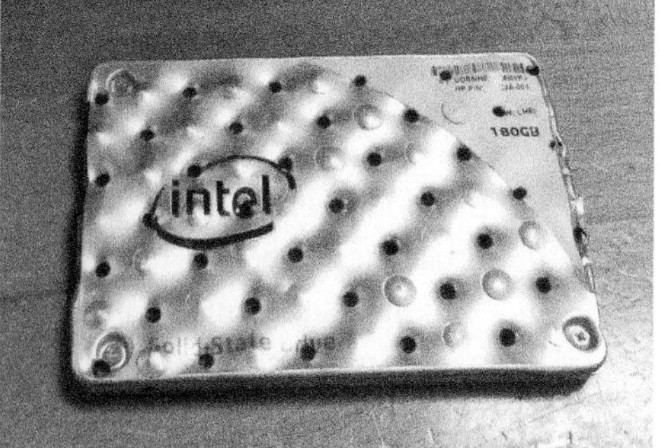

FIGURE 18.34 Hard drive/SSD destroying machine with destroyed drive

Internet Security

Internet security basics are covered in Chapter 12, "Internet Connectivity, Virtualization, and Cloud Technologies," in the "Basic Web Browser Issues" section. This section goes into more technical detail. First, no system should connect to the internet without antivirus and anti-malware software installed. These applications are your first line of defense for internet security, but they are not foolproof.

Second, pay attention to the security alerts provided by antivirus and anti-malware software, browser applications, and the operating system! If you see a message that you haven't seen before, write it down, take a screenshot of it, and research it. Even if you have seen it before, it's a good idea to research and ensure that nothing new is the problem.

Lack of money is not an excuse for not having antivirus software. Microsoft Defender (formerly Windows Defender) is included in Windows 8.1/10/11 and has virus scanning (**Microsoft Defender Antivirus** that is compatible with other antivirus products), or another free antivirus program can be downloaded. To activate Microsoft Defender Antivirus, use the *Windows Security* link from within *Settings* > *Update & Security* > *Open Windows Security* button > *Virus & threat protection* > scroll down to the *Microsoft Defender Antivirus options* link > ensure the *Periodic scanning* option is set to *on*, as shown in Figure 18.35. You can use the setting *Check for updates* to check for updated definitions.

FIGURE 18.35 Microsoft Defender Antivirus activation

If you use a free antivirus program, ensure that you obtain it from a reputable download site. Beware of **rogue antivirus** applications that pretend to be legitimate software to help you with a computer problem but are actually viruses.

Windows comes with **Microsoft Defender**, which works with Internet Explorer/Microsoft Edge to warn users about spyware. The Microsoft Baseline Security Analyzer (MBSA) identifies security misconfigurations on computers. Configure your browser to display a security warning or to ask or warn you about potential security threats.

Digital Security Certificates

A digital certificate authenticates and secures information. The certificate authority (CA) is the sender (the device or person who originated the communication). A digital certificate typically contains a public key (a key used with a private key so that messages can be unencrypted), sender information, and the length of time the certificate is to be considered valid. Browsers sometimes present security warnings related to certificates. The following are sample messages:

- The security certificate presented by this website was not issued by a trusted certificate authority.
- www.hacker.com uses an invalid security certificate. The certificate is not trusted because the issuer certificate is unknown.

> The security certificate has expired or is not yet valid. The certificate for the particular website has expired, the time/date on the server is incorrect, or the time/date on the client computer is incorrect.

> www.watchout.com uses an invalid security certificate. The certificate is not trusted because it is self-signed.

Use the Microsoft **Certificate Manager** (`certmgr.msc`) to see details about certificates. There you can view, modify, import, export, or delete a security certificate. Use the arrows on the left to expand a category. Right-click on any specific certificate to see options, as shown in Figure 18.36.

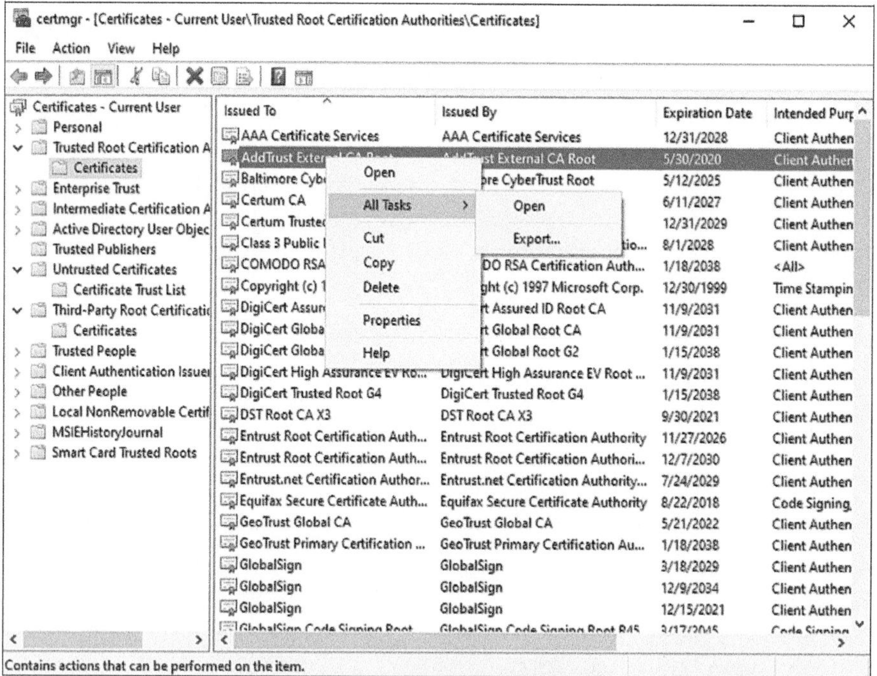

FIGURE 18.36 Microsoft Certificate Manager

If a user visited a website that should have been avoided, close the browser. Reopen the browser and use the security settings within the browser to delete a certificate that was trusted but shouldn't have been.

Malware Removal

Malware symptoms are numerous. A device may run slowly, crash, or lock; applications might behave abnormally or not at all; you might experience disappearing or missing files; you might see file attribute or file permission changes; there might be constant storage device activity or constant (greater-than-normal) network activity; your email might be hijacked (in which case you should change your password to something totally different as soon as you notice); you might get access denied messages or security messages; and you might experience removed, corrupted, or renamed system files. (Note that access denied messages are sometimes normal if a user account does not have administrative permissions to do a particular task.)

If malware has infected a system's boot sector, you may have to use the Windows Advanced Startup Options to access Safe mode, use a boot disk to run anti-malware, or even reinstall the operating system. For anti-malware, Microsoft provides the Malicious Software Removal Tool for free. Other vendors provide free anti-malware software, too. It is easier to deal with such issues with security software installed than without it. The following steps are best practice procedures for malware removal:

Step 1. Investigate and verify malware symptoms. Do not act based only a customer's word that he has a virus or malware. An application could be the culprit, or something else entirely might be happening. Be sure to log all actions performed.

Step 2. Quarantine the infected system. Disconnect the system from the network or disable the wireless NIC. Do not power off the computer or reboot it.

Step 3. For Windows machines, disable *System Restore.*

Step 4. Remediate the infected system. You might need to update the anti-malware software or might have to use another system to research your support options from your antivirus/anti-malware software vendor. Rescan the system for security issues using the updated software. Some antivirus software vendors have images that can be downloaded and used to create bootable antivirus discs or flash drives.

If the system still performs strangely, boot into Safe Mode and run the virus checker from there. Use the `msconfig` utility to isolate a startup application or service that might be causing the issue. If you purchased an antivirus disc, run the software from the optical disc. Boot from an alternative boot source (flash drive, external hard drive, or operating system disc).

With some worms and Trojan horse viruses, files must be manually deleted because they cannot be repaired, but the antivirus software will quarantine such files so they cannot be dangerous and affect other files. If it an executable file is quarantined, you may have to reinstall one or more apps. A hijacked web browser—which may occur, for example, when the requested web page is redirected to a different web page—may require browser configuration, different DNS settings, or a new or updated HOSTS file applied after removal. You might be required to use the `SFC /scannow` command to replace/repair operating system files after removing a virus. Test all applications to ensure that they operate. Then manually delete any files that are quarantined (see Figure 18.37).

Step 5. Schedule antivirus/anti-malware scans and run updates.

Step 6. For Windows-based computers, re-enable *System Restore.* Create a new restore point.

Step 7. Educate the user on security best practices.

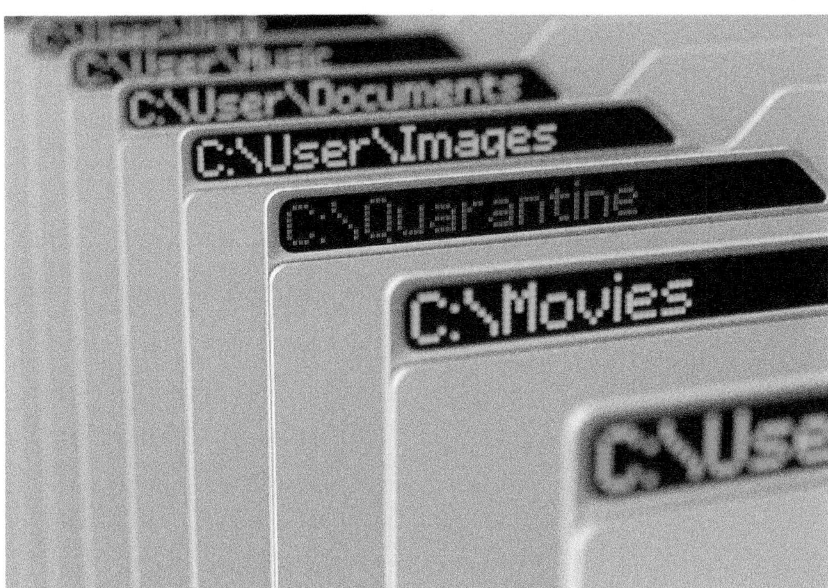

FIGURE 18.37 Quarantined files

TECH TIP

Manually delete files, if necessary

If antivirus software or other preventive software applications state that a particular file cannot be deleted, make a note of the file and its location. File Explorer *View* options may have to be adjusted before viewing/deletion can occur.

DNS Issues

Domain Name System (DNS) is used to translate a URL to an IP address. Homes and small businesses almost always use the DNS server of the internet provider. Medium to large companies may have their own DNS server, might use the internet provider's, or might pay for another company to host the DNS server. DNS is a common security target because an attacker can use it to redirect a web browser to another website under control of the attacker.

If you suspect that the DNS server has been compromised because your browser is redirecting you to unusual websites, you can't access the internet, or URLs don't look quite right, you can change your DNS configuration setting to another DNS server just to see if the symptoms change. In a router, the setting is commonly found in the Setup or Basic Settings section. In Windows, use the *Network & Internet* Setting to access *Properties* for the NIC being used > *Edit* button in the *IP settings* section > select the *Manual* setting and ensure that *IPv4* is turned on > configure the *Preferred DNS* and *Alternate DNS* sections, as shown in Figure 18.38.

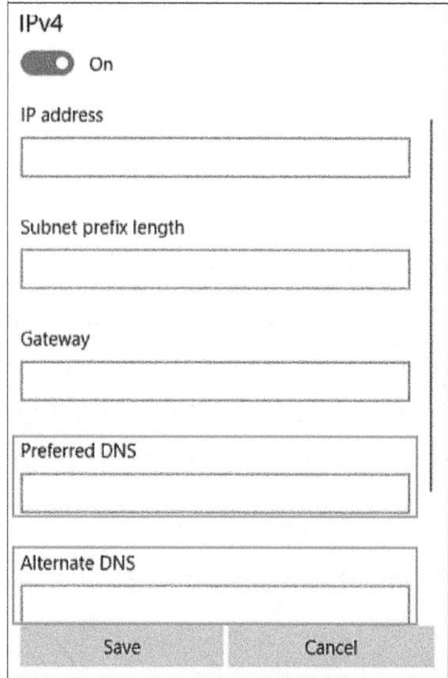

FIGURE 18.38 Manual DNS IP address configuration

OpenDNS offers free and fee-based configurations. The following IPv4 and IPv6 addresses can be used:

IPv4 OpenDNS addresses:

> 208.67.222.222
> 208.67.220.220
> 208.67.222.220
> 208.67.220.222

IPv6 OpenDNS addresses:

> 2620:119:35::35
> 2620:119:53::53

In addition, OpenDNS FamilyShield uses two addresses to automatically prevent adult websites from being accessed:

> 208.67.222.123
> 208.67.220.123

If you suspect DNS server issues, clear the browser history/cache using the directions below or by researching the browser being used:

> *Edge: Settings* (gear) icon > *Internet Options* > *General* tab *Browsing history* section > *Delete* button
> *Firefox: Open menu* icon in top-right corner > *Options* > *Privacy & Security* in the *History* section > *Clear History*
> *Chrome: Customize* (three vertical dots in the top-right corner) > *Settings* > *Settings* menu on left > *Privacy and Security* > *Clear Browsing Data* link > *Clear Data*

You should also clear the DNS cache on the computer. On a PC, access a command prompt and, as an administrator, type **`ipconfig /flushdns`**. On a Mac version 10.9 or higher, access *Terminal* and type the following two commands:

```
sudo dscacheutil -flushcache
sudo killall -HUP mDNSResponder
```

Email Issues

Email has its own section in this chapter because it is something most people deal with on a daily basis. Avoid checking email on a public computer or on an unsecure network as doing so may lead to your email account being hijacked; if this happens, you will not be able to log in using normal procedures, you may get an automated message from an unknown person as if it were an automated response to your own email, people in your contacts might send you a note about constant emails or spam from the hijacked account, or your account might have a lot of undeliverable emails. For an account that has been hijacked, perform the following steps:

Step 1. Contact the email account company to report the problem.

Step 2. Ensure that Windows, antivirus, and anti-malware updates have been applied.

Step 3. Ensure that you have an alternative email account available for when you have to register with sites, such as for online shopping.

Step 4. Try logging in to the account from a different computer to see if the email settings have been changed. *Note:* If you can get to the account, change the password.

Step 5. Create rules in your email account to delete files from specific nontrusted sources.

Spam is unsolicited email from a company or person previously unknown. People who send this type of email are known as spammers. Most email applications have spam filters, but they do not catch all spam. Most email applications also enable you to create a rule to block messages from particular sources or with specific subject lines. Figure 18.39 demonstrates the concept of a spam filter.

FIGURE 18.39 Spam filtering

Email apps use **DNS TXT** messages to try to determine if a message is from a trusted domain. Spammers often use false domains to send emails. Several authentication methods can be used to authenticate email messages:

> *Domain Keys Identified Mail (DKIM):* Used by email providers like Gmail, AOL, and Yahoo! to electronically sign emails so the receiving server knows that they are legitimate messages.
> *Sender Policy Framework (SPF):* Designates authorized mail servers that legitimately send email for a specific domain.
> *Domain-based Message Authentication, Reporting, and Conformance (DMARC):* Used if an email message does not pass SPF or DKIM to ensure that the sender of the email matches and determine what to do with messages from unknown or unauthorized senders.

Another email problem is email messages sent in clear text. If such a message is intercepted, it is easy to read. Pretty Good Privacy (PGP) and Secure Multipurpose Internet Mail Extensions (S/MIME) are frequently used to provide encryption and authentication for email messages.

Some companies make use of a spam gateway (also called a gateway spam filter or a spam filter) that attempts to get rid of spam emails before they are processed by the email server. A spam gateway might also be used for outbound email to prevent a business from being blocklisted (or blacklisted) due to having a high level of spam being sent from the business.

Proxy Servers

A company may use a **proxy server** to protect its network. This server acts as an agent (a go-between) between an application such as a web browser and a remote server. A proxy server can also cache frequently accessed web pages and provide them when requested from a client instead of accessing the web server. A proxy server is commonly located with other network servers in a corporate network design, as shown in Figure 18.40.

All traffic from corporate wired and wireless devices that is being sent to the internet will be directed to the proxy server. The proxy server will then change the source IP address to its own address and send that traffic to the internet. When the traffic returns from the internet, the traffic will be sent to the proxy server (not the original device); the proxy server then forwards the traffic to the original network device.

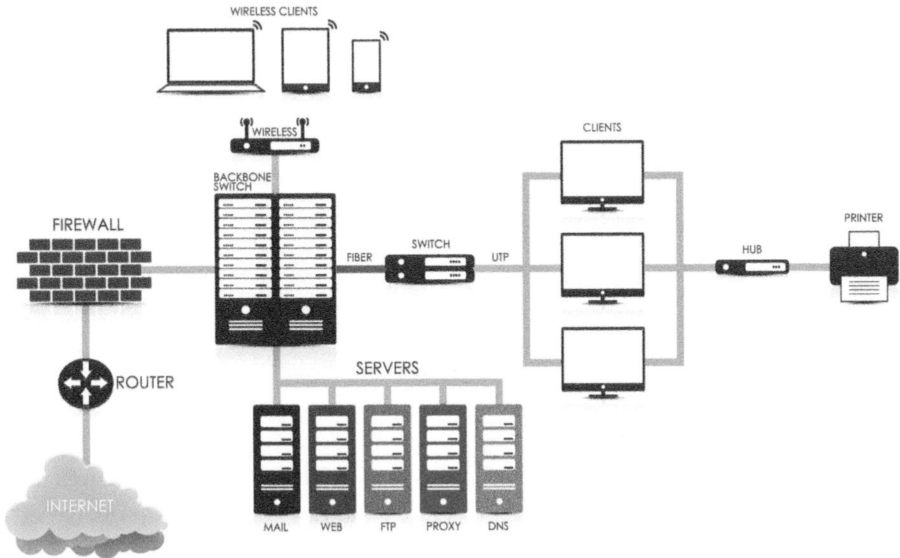

FIGURE 18.40 Proxy server

To configure any device or application to use a proxy server, obtain the following information from the company's network administrator or through the Web Proxy Auto-Discovery protocol:

- IP address of the proxy server
- Port number of the proxy server
- Optionally a username and password (although some organizations use server-based authentication)

Use the *Network & Internet* Windows *Settings* link > *Proxy* and locate the *Manual proxy setup* section. Improperly configured proxy settings may cause a computer to be redirected to an invalid website with no internet connectivity.

Firewalls

If a computer connects to the internet, it should be connected behind a firewall. No computer should be unprotected and missing a firewall as this is software that comes with the operating system. A firewall protects one or more computers from outside attacks and is used to implement security policies. The concept of a firewall is similar to the concept of a moat with a drawbridge protecting a castle. The castle is the inside network, the moat with the drawbridge is the firewall, and everyone outside the castle is an "attacker." The drawbridge controls access to and from the castle.

TECH TIP

Antivirus and anti-malware applications are needed even when a firewall is installed

A computer protected by a firewall still needs antivirus and anti-malware applications for protection. Having a firewall on each computer as well as on a router or modem that connects to the internet (or a device dedicated to providing firewall services) is common in both home and business environments.

A firewall can be either a software application or hardware, and it should be implemented for any computer that connects to another network, especially a computer that connects to the internet. A firewall keeps hackers from accessing a computer that connects to the internet. A software firewall is a Windows tool or software application that is a good security solution for individual computers. A hardware firewall is a good solution for home and business networks. Both types of firewall can be used concurrently. Look back at Figure 18.40 to see the concept of a firewall.

Allow Lists and Deny Lists

A security concept related to firewalls is allow lists and deny lists. Security measures are commonly implemented based on one of these two methods. An allow list implementation is based on a list of who is allowed in (through the firewall to use a VPN, use an application, enter a secured network closet, and so on). An easy way to remember the allow list method is to think of your front door at home. Anyone who has a key to the door is allowed in; each person with a key is on the allow list.

On the other hand, a deny list details what users or websites are not allowed. Anyone or any site that is not on the deny list is allowed in. To remember the deny list method, think of a college's list of people not allowed on campus or the list of blocked calls on your cell phone.

DMZ

In a corporate environment, a firewall, router, or wireless router can be used to create an area called a demilitarized zone (**DMZ**), or a **screened subnet**, that might be in a home or in a small office/home office (SOHO) router configuration. Servers such as web servers or application servers can reside in the DMZ. Customers can use a server within the DMZ without having to be let into the part of the network where the sensitive corporate data resides. A DMZ might also be used to separate IoT devices from the rest of the network.

A DMZ can also be created by using two firewalls, with one firewall connected to the router, as shown in Figure 18.41, and the DMZ connected to that firewall and to a second firewall. The second firewall also connects to the internal corporate network (see Figure 18.41), so the setup looks like this: internet | firewall | DMZ | firewall | internal corporate network.

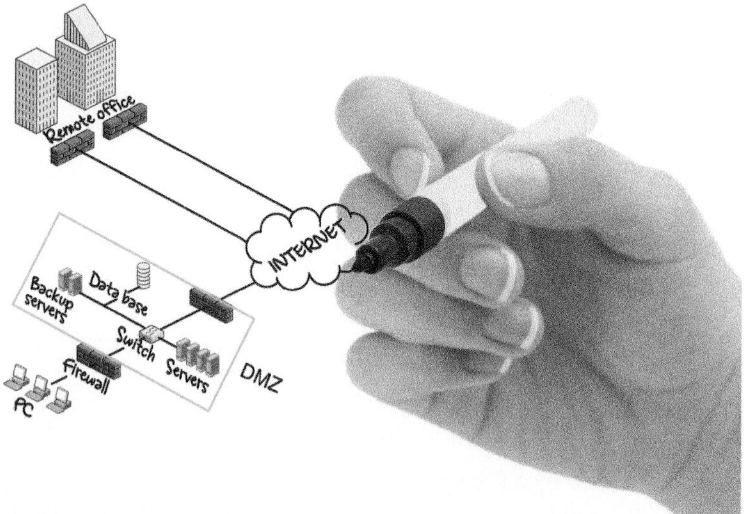

FIGURE 18.41 DMZ

Universal Plug and Play

Universal plug and play (**UPnP**) is used to set up a network with very little configuration, such as a home network. Devices such as a home router, printers, PCs, and mobile devices can all be configured for UPnP, and the devices discover each other. Note that this setting is commonly found in an Administration or Advanced tab or section and might be enabled by default. On a Windows computer, when you enable *Turn on network discovery* in the *Network and Sharing Center* Control Panel > *Change advanced sharing settings* option, you are enabling UPnP.

Windows Firewall and Advanced Security

Windows displays messages and warnings related to security and maintenance. To control the types of messages seen, access *Settings > System > Notifications & actions > Get notifications from these senders* section and ensure that the *Security and Maintenance* option is set to *On*.

Part of the Windows Security app is the **Windows Defender Firewall**, which is a local or host-based firewall that is just for the one system. The firewall allows or blocks inbound/outbound traffic based on rules that have been configured automatically for the network profile (domain, public, or private) being used currently by the system and viewable using the *Update & Security* Settings link > *Windows Security* app > *Firewall & network protection* Windows Security app link. For example, if a corporate laptop connects to the organization domain through a wired Ethernet connection, the domain security settings might be less restrictive than if the laptop wireless is being used at an airport and the public security settings are in effect and are more restrictive. The following are the types of profiles you see in Windows:

- The *Private (Home or Work)* network location setting turns on file sharing and network discovery through the firewall, so communication will be easier at work or in a private home network.
- The *Guest* or *Public* setting configures these settings to be off through the firewall to help protect your computer when on a public network such as when you are in an airport.
- With the *Domain* setting, the computer participates in a Windows Active Directory domain environment.
- The *All Networks* setting includes private folder sharing, media streaming, file sharing, and password-protected sharing options that can apply to all types of network connections.

Settings can also be accessed/configured through the *Windows Defender Firewall* Control Panel, as shown in Figure 18.42, which shows the expanded network profiles.

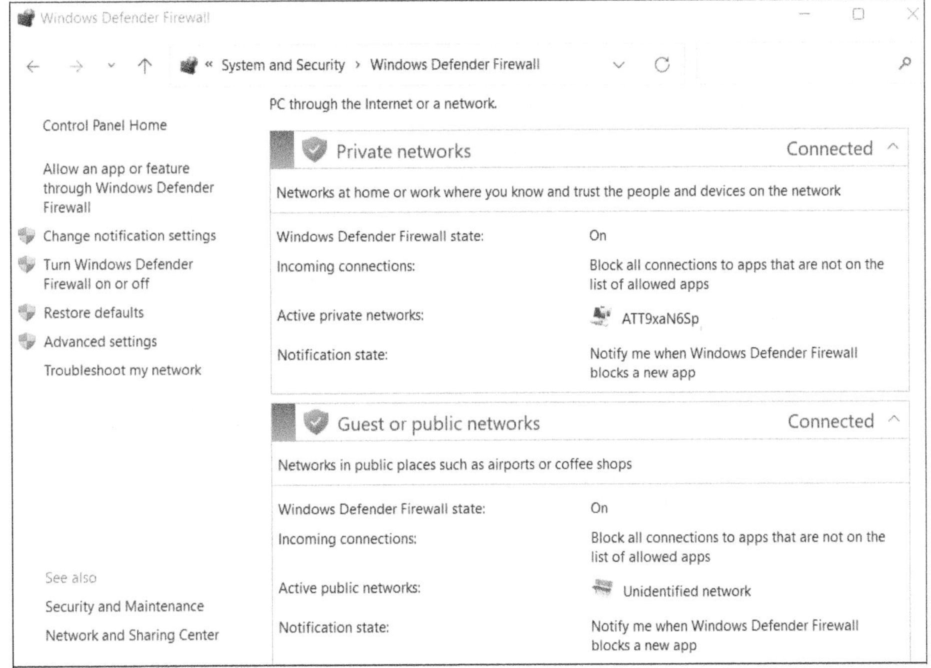

FIGURE 18.42 Windows Defender Firewall profile settings

Notice how each of the profiles shown in Figure 18.42 appears with a green checkmark. This means the firewall is activated or active. A red background with an X over it indicates that the firewall is deactivated. Use the *Turn Windows Defender Firewall on or off* link on the left to change the state.

TECH TIP

Be sure you work with the correct profile

If you cannot access devices and resources that are normally available through a wireless NIC, ensure that the correct location profile is used. Access the *Change advanced sharing settings* link from the *Network and Sharing Center* Control Panel. The profile used will have the following words after the profile name: *(current profile)*.

When Windows Firewall is installed and enabled and another computer or application tries to connect, Windows Firewall blocks the connection and prompts with a security alert to allow a choice of *Unblock*, *Keep Blocking*, or *Ask Me Later*. Table 18.12 describes these options.

TABLE 18.12 Windows Firewall security alert options

Option	Description
Unblock This Program	The program is allowed to execute, and the program is automatically added to the Windows Firewall exceptions list (allow list).
Keep Blocking This Program	The program is not allowed to execute or listen. Use this option whenever you do not know the source of the alert.
Keep Blocking This Program, but Ask Me Again Later	Does not allow the program to execute or listen, but the next time you access the site, the security alert prompts you again.

TECH TIP

Allowing an application through Windows Firewall

Open the *Windows Defender Firewall* section of the Control Panel > select the *Allow an app or feature through Windows Defender Firewall* > *Change Settings* > enable the checkbox beside the app you want to allow and select the network types this applies to > *OK*.

Port forwarding is a term used for a packet allowed through the firewall based on a particular port number/protocol. Port triggering is a similar concept. **Port triggering** allows data into a computer temporarily, based on a configured situation. To configure the firewall to allow inbound traffic for a specific TCP/UDP port number (that is, to configure **port security**), use the *Advanced settings* link > *Inbound Rules* > in the *Action* column select *New Rule* (see Figure 18.43) > select the *Port* radio button. The *Outbound Rules* link can be used in the same manner for a specific port.

Table 18.13 shows Windows Defender Firewall issues and solutions to help with troubleshooting.

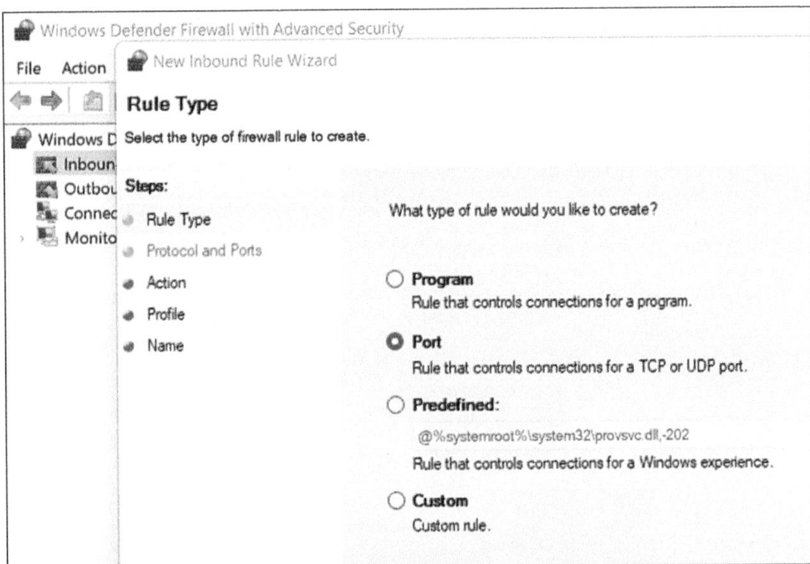

FIGURE 18.43 Configuring Windows Defender Firewall rule for a specific port number

TABLE 18.13 Windows Defender Firewall and advanced security troubleshooting

Windows firewall issue	Resolutions
The firewall is blocking all connections.	Disable the *Block All Incoming Connections* checkbox.
The firewall is blocking a specific application.	If a dialog box appears, select the *Unblock* option to allow it through. If the dialog box does not appear, use the *Exceptions* tab to create a rule that allows the application through the firewall.
No one can ping a Windows computer.	Ensure that *File and Print Sharing* is enabled through the *Network and Sharing Center* Control Panel. Access the *Administrative Tools* link and select *Windows Defender Firewall with advanced security*. Select *Inbound Rules* in the left pane. Select *New Rule* in the *Actions* column. Select the *Custom* radio button and *Next*. Select the *All programs* radio button and click *Next*. Select *ICMPv4* from the *Protocol Type* drop-down box. Select the IP addresses to which this rule will apply and name the rule.
Windows Firewall is turned off every time the computer restarts.	Another security firewall is installed.
No one can access local files and/or a shared printer.	File and Print Sharing has not been enabled.

Freeware programs are available as well as full security suites, such as the ones from McAfee or Symantec that include software firewalls and components to prevent malicious types of software applications from executing.

NAT/PAT

Companies use private IP addresses (192.168.x.x, 172.16.x.x through 172.31.x.x, 10.x.x.x) on devices inside the company, but these addresses cannot be routed on the internet. A network device such as a router or firewall performs network address translation (**NAT**), which means it translates private IP addresses to public addresses that can be routed over the internet. If NAT/PAT is not working, internet access is unavailable.

One public address can be used for multiple internal company connections due to port mapping. **Port mapping** allows the combination of one public address and a specific port number to represent one internal company host. The same public address and a different port number represent a second internal company host. Some people also call this concept port forwarding or port address translation (PAT). Figure 18.44 shows this concept.

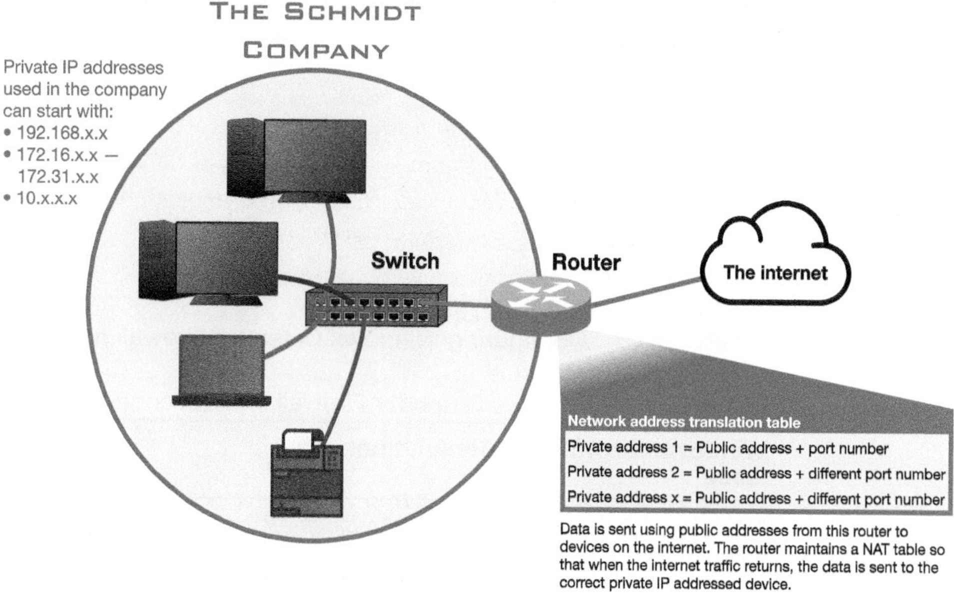

FIGURE 18.44 Network/port address translation

VPN Configuration

A popular business solution for security is a VPN. A virtual private network (VPN) is a special type of secure network created over the internet from one network device to another. One example is a home PC that connects to a corporate server and has access to company resources that cannot otherwise be accessed except by being on a computer on the inside network. The VPN connection makes it appear as if the home computer is on the inside corporate network. Another example is a branch office network device connecting to a corporate server, VPN concentrator, firewall, or other network device. When connected, the branch office network device connects as if it were directly connected to the network. Figure 18.45 illustrates the concept of a VPN.

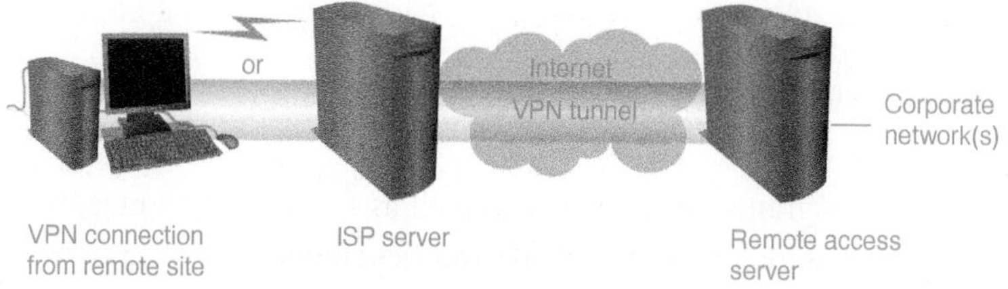

FIGURE 18.45 VPN connectivity

Users also use a VPN to browse the internet anonymously, bypass restrictions set by a network administrator or service provider, watch shows/listen to music that is unavailable in a particular country, protect a computer that is connecting to the internet through free WiFi, encrypt data, or download files anonymously. VPN services are available. You can also set up a computer to serve as a VPN server. Before configuring a VPN, you should know which protocol you will be using on both sides of the connection: PPTP, L2TP/IPsec, SSTP, or OpenVPN.

TECH TIP

Both sides of the VPN tunnel must match

The two devices used to create a VPN tunnel must have identical VPN settings, or the VPN tunnel will not be formed.

To configure a VPN in Windows, you must have a VPN profile configured through Control Panels or Settings:

- Use the *Network and Sharing Center* Control Panel > select the *Set up a new connection or network* link > *Connect to a workplace* > *Next* > *Use my Internet connection (VPN)* > enter the IP address or fully qualified domain name of the network device on the other end of the VPN connection > *Next* > enter the required credentials > click *Connect.*
- An alternative is to use *Settings* to access the *Network & Internet* link > *VPN* > *Add a VPN connection* > use *VPN provider* to select *Windows (built-in)* > type a name in the *Connection name* textbox > type the IP address or name of the other end of the VPN connection in the *Server name or address* textbox.

Remote Access to Network Devices

Corporate users commonly work from home or travel as part of the job and need to access printers, servers, and other devices within the company. Technicians commonly use remote desktop or third-party tools in order to perform troubleshooting and repairs. Let's explore the protocols used to do remote access, the methods used, and how security is handled.

Remote Access Techniques

Several techniques, protocols, and apps are used to remotely access devices. With any technology used to remotely access a network device, there are risks in that someone may pose as a legitimate company or department and gain access or even convince users to provide specific company files. Most companies limit the use of remotely accessing devices on the corporate network. Remote access technologies are described in Table 18.14, along with security concerns.

TABLE 18.14 Remote access technologies and security concerns

Remote access technology	Description	Security concerns
MSRA (Microsoft Remote Assistance)	Creates a secure connection to a Windows computer.	It may be necessary to configure the firewall to allow access through.
Quick Assist	Windows 10/11 app that allows a user to view or remotely control another computer. May have to enable in *Apps > Optional features*.	An internet connection is required. The invitation could be from a threat actor that includes a modified invitation file that infiltrates the target computer, if accepted.
RDP (Remote Desktop Protocol)	Creates a peer-to-peer remote desktop connection from one computer to a remote computer. You might have to enable port forwarding (see Chapter 13, "Networking") and allow port 3389 in order to connect to the remote device.	Reported security issues should be taken into consideration before using RDP.

Remote access technology	Description	Security concerns
SSH (Secure Shell)	Uses port 22 to securely log in to a remote network device. Is an alternative to Telnet that includes strong encryption within the secure channel created between devices.	There are security vulnerabilities with version 1. Use SSH version 2.
Telnet	Uses port 23 to access a remote device on the network, such as a router, a server, an access point, or a switch.	Telnet uses clear text to send data and passwords. Telnet should not be used unless the network device supports no other remote access protocol.
VNC (virtual network computing)	Uses one computer as a "server" and another computer as a "viewer" to access the other computer.	The viewer and server software must be downloaded. Some versions cost money. It is important to ensure that the firewall is configured to allow this connection through.

Because of the security shortcomings of RDP, companies use third-party remote monitoring and management (**RMM**) tools to share a screen with a user in order to troubleshoot a specific problem or share files. Examples of such software include LogMeIn Rescue, TeamViewer, AnyPlace Control, ConnectWise Control, GoToMyPC, AnyDesk, Bomgar, ShowMyPC, LiteManager, Splashtop, Radmin, BeamYourScreen, RealVNC, join.me, and Highfive. Furthermore, a company may use a specific desktop management software/server that makes supporting and controlling corporate PCs easier in terms of remote imaging/re-imaging, OS/app updating, inventory control, and security.

Internet Appliances

An important strategy for servers, apps, and network traffic is the use of a load balancer. A **load balancer** is used when you have redundancy in the network. For example, if you have multiple servers for the same app, the load balancer can direct traffic so that one particular server doesn't get overloaded. A load balancer can be a piece of hardware, deployed as a virtual appliance, or a cloud technology. A load balancer can work using different types of algorithms. Here are some of the more common algorithms:

- *Least connections:* Tracks how many active connections are used on a particular device and sends traffic onward to the one that has the smallest number of connections.
- *Least response time:* Tracks the number of connections as well as the average response time in order to forward traffic onward.
- *Round robin:* Similar to a card dealer in that traffic is sent to each device, one after another. This is a good method to use if all the receiving devices are equal in their capabilities.
- *Weighted round robin:* Similar to round robin except weighting values can be given so that a particular device that has more capabilities is sent more traffic.

Other devices that an IT staff member should be familiar with include the UTM, IDS, and IPS. A unified threat management (**UTM**) system is a single device that commonly provides multiple security functions such as content filtering, antivirus, antispyware, anti-malware, firewall, and intrusion detection and prevention. The device might also have the capability to route, accept VPN connections, and provide NAT. **Content filtering** involves using a device or security software to screen data for specific web addresses, websites, web domains, emails, or files that are defined as being suspect. This is similar to applying parental controls on a home Windows computer.

An intrusion detection system (**IDS**) can be hardware or software that constantly monitors and scans network traffic for malicious traffic or violations of defined security policies. An IDS is considered a passive system; it doesn't take action but just detects and sends data, reports, and alerts to the network management team (see Figure 18.46). It is like a babysitter whose job is to just tend to the kids (the network data). If there is a fight (a security threat), the babysitter notifies the parents (the network personnel), who deal with the problem.

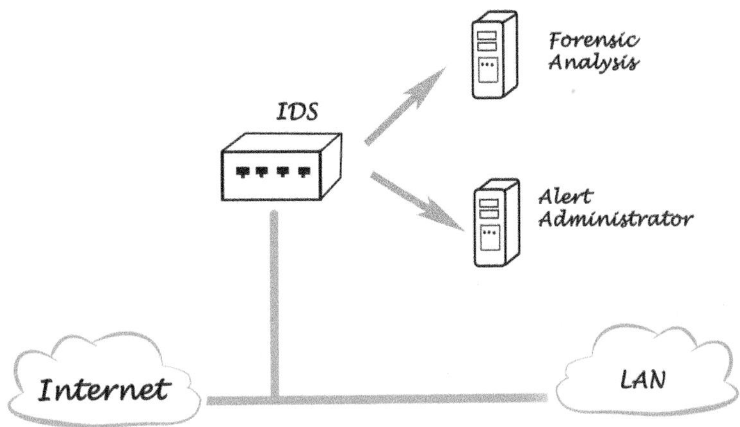

FIGURE 18.46 IDS

A device that is similar to an IDS is an intrusion prevention system (**IPS**). An IPS is an active system; it constantly monitors and scans network traffic for malicious traffic and violations of security policies, and it takes appropriate action. An IPS can send an alarm, reset connections, block traffic, disable ports, and drop packets. An IPS is like a school hall monitor who can issue detentions, break up fights, and restore order to the hallway. Sometimes, an IDS and an IPS are both used in a network design, with the IDS inspecting the network traffic and reporting the information and the IPS taking preventive action.

Wireless Network Security Overview

Traditionally security has been a concern when installing wireless networks because originally security was disabled by default and there was lack of knowledge about default passwords and misconfigured wireless settings. Wireless LANs (WLANs) are much more secure today than when they first began to be used.

Wireless access points (APs) are an integral part of a wireless LAN and are normally mounted on the ceiling or on a wall where they are inconspicuous. Sometimes, they are mounted in or above the ceiling tile in a special enclosure.

Data transmitted over air can be in clear text, which means that with special frame capturing software (packet sniffers or analyzers) on a computer with a wireless NIC installed, the data can be captured and viewed. Negotiation between the wireless devices and the AP can be in clear text so that information can be captured. Every frame includes a source MAC address. Someone with a wireless device and free hacking software can capture the frame to use the MAC address to gain access to other resources. (But note that the hackers are not this obvious!) (This is known as session hijacking or MAC spoofing.) By default, most APs transmit their SSIDs in clear text. All these issues must be considered when installing a wireless network.

TECH TIP

How a firewall helps a wireless computer

A firewall can protect a computer connected to a wireless network; however, the firewall cannot prevent the outgoing wireless data from being hijacked. The firewall simply protects a hacker from accessing the computer.

Mobile Device Management

Mobile device management (**MDM**) can help with security by enabling a technician to view and manage mobile devices, as shown in Figure 18.47. MDM software can be used to push application updates, enforce security policies, track, or remotely wipe data or the operating system from a device. A tracking module is available on some mobile devices and is used to track the device and provide recovery/wiping options that can be used in the event that the device is lost or stolen.

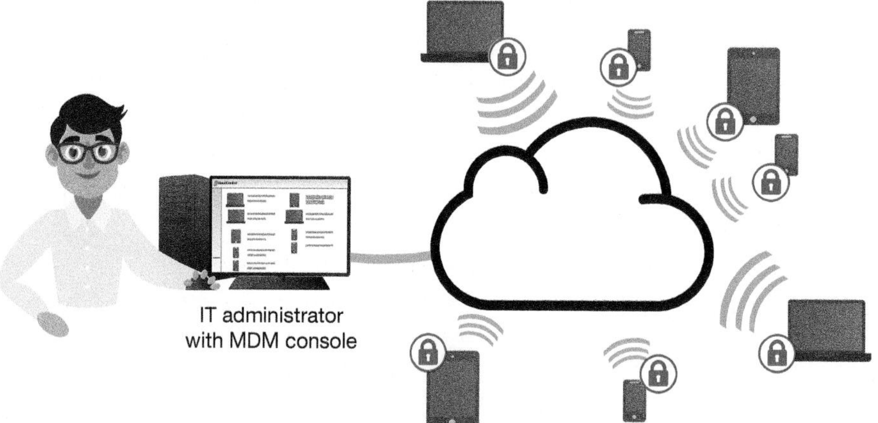

FIGURE 18.47 Mobile device management (MDM)

MDM policies vary from one company to another, but they commonly define operating systems supported as well as password and security requirements. Optional policies might include the following:

- Password storage
- Software/firmware installation
- System updates
- Backup process
- VPN connectivity
- How to report lost or stolen devices
- Steps involved when a security breach occurs
- Data storage

Wireless Security

Security on wireless devices has always been a concern, and several options can be used. Here are the most common ones:

- WEP
- WPA
- WPA2

> WPA3
> TKIP
> AES

TECH TIP

Mobile device security options must match AP settings

Whatever security is configured on an access point must be used on any mobile device that uses the wireless network.

Wired Equivalent Privacy (**WEP**) encrypts data being transmitted. WEP commonly has two versions: 64-bit and 128-bit. With WEP enabled, the shared "secret" key is entered into the wireless NIC configuration window usually in either hexadecimal or ASCII characters. WEP can be hacked but may have to be used because one device on the network cannot do any higher-level security.

An improvement on WEP is Wi-Fi Protected Access (WPA), which has been enhanced with newer versions called WPA2 and WPA3. **WPA2** uses Temporal Key Integrity Protocol (**TKIP**) or Advanced Encryption Standard (AES) to improve security. TKIP is an improvement on WEP in that the encryption keys change, and AES is even better than TKIP. WPA2 includes dynamic negotiation between the AP and the client for authentication and encryption algorithms (see Figure 18.48). WPA2 is a common choice for securing wireless networks until all the devices can support WPA3.

WPA3 uses Simultaneous Authentication of Equals (SAE) encryption instead of pre-shared keys, which prevents attackers from using dictionary attacks to gain access to the wireless network. WPA3 also has features that help with on-path (man-in-the-middle) and evil twin attacks.

Figure 18.48 shows the security options available if you are manually adding a wireless network. Figure 18.49 shows the process for manually adding a WPA2 wireless network that has security applied for a Windows 10 computer. Figure 18.50 shows an example of where security encryption is selected on a wireless router.

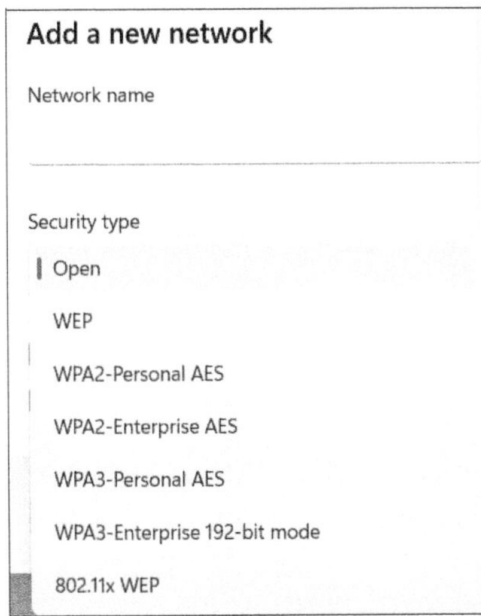

FIGURE 18.48 Windows 11 wireless security options

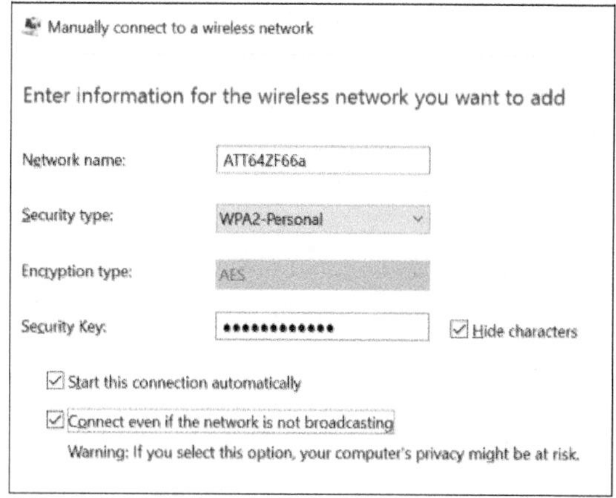

FIGURE 18.49 Windows 10 wireless security window

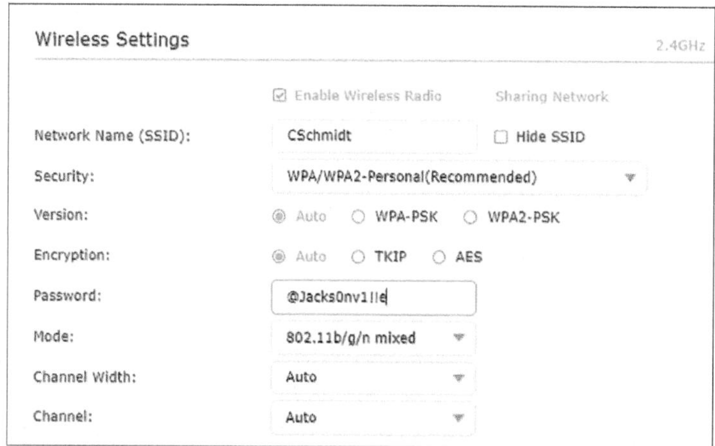

FIGURE 18.50 Sample security window on a wireless router

You can commonly set up a wireless router as a firewall and configure security settings. Some routers allow configuration of a screened subnet, also known as a DMZ, and you need to enable this, as shown in Figure 18.51, and also provide the IP address of the server or computer that will be in the DMZ.

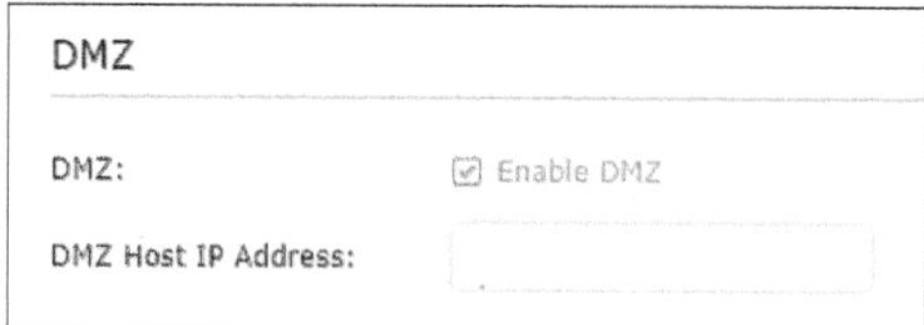

FIGURE 18.51 DMZ configuration on a wireless router

On wireless networks, **MAC address filtering** (also known as MAC filtering) allows only the devices that have been manually entered into the access point. MAC filtering is used with a limited number of wireless devices and when those devices' MAC addresses are known by the person who configured the access point. Any new personnel or wireless devices have to be added to the access point manually to use the wireless network.

TECH TIP

Who would use MAC filtering?

Most access points have a limited number of MAC addresses (20 to 50), so MAC address filtering tends to be used only by small companies that want to have strict control of who gets onto the wireless network.

Some wireless routers can be configured for content filtering (which might be called web filtering, domain filtering, or parental controls), which involves entering websites to block. You can also configure **IP filtering** by either selecting IP addresses that are not allowed or selecting IP addresses that are allowed, as shown in Figure 18.52.

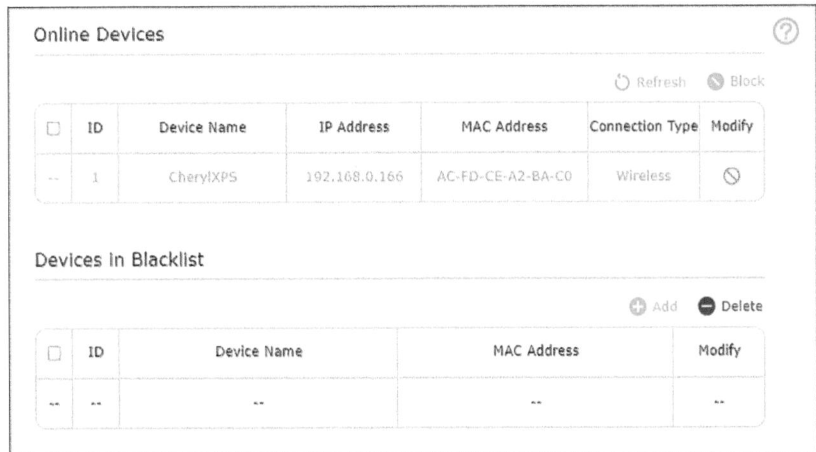

FIGURE 18.52 Wireless router IP filtering

Wireless routers also have security settings related to TCP and UDP ports. These are usually in the advanced security link. Look for SPI (Stateful Packet Inspection) or DoS protection settings. Note that all ports that are not being used should be disabled.

WPS

Wi-Fi Protected Setup (**WPS**) is configured based on the SSID and WPA2 wireless security key for an AP or a client's devices. It supports 802.11a, b, g, n, and ac devices, including computers, access points, consumer electronics, and phones. There are four ways to configure a wireless network using WPS:

> A personal identification number (PIN) is entered. This PIN is sometimes found on a sticker or displayed on the wireless product.
> A USB device attaches to the AP or wireless device to provide configuration information.
> A button is pushed or clicked. This method is known as push button configuration (PBC).
> With near field communication (NFC), the wireless device is brought close to the AP (or a device known as the registrar), and the configuration is applied. RFID tags are suited for this method.

TECH TIP

Avoid WPS

Because of security issues with WPS, disable this mode if possible and do not use it.

AP Default Settings

All wireless networks have security features. A SOHO AP/router can come with a default password and SSID, but many such devices ask you to change the password the first time you access the AP/router. Change both of these settings as soon as the access point is powered on. Default passwords are posted on the internet, and a hacker could use that information to lock out access from the access point. Be careful when using older APs that might have no security or the default administrator user ID and password.

TECH TIP

Never leave an access point password set to the default

After powering up an access point and connecting to it, one of the first things to do is change the default password.

Firmware

Firmware is software that is embedded into a piece of hardware. Firmware can be upgraded in network routers, switches, access points, firewalls, and so on. Companies update firmware as security issues become known, when enhancements become available, or to support new technology. In a corporate environment, it is critical that firmware updates be applied. The process for obtaining and applying firmware updates varies per vendor but is commonly done through a web browser window used to access the network device.

SSID Broadcasting

As mentioned in Chapter 13, the service set identifier (SSID) announces to wireless devices that a particular wireless network is in the area. With **SSID broadcasting**, the access point periodically sends out a beacon frame that includes the SSID. This should be changed to a descriptive setting if it is being broadcast so users can easily select from the list of wireless networks in the area. SSID broadcasting can be disabled as a preventive measure so that the wireless network is not announced in the area. Look back at Figure 13.44 to see how that might be configured on a wireless router.

TECH TIP

Reduce transmit power

If adjacent companies or people nearby are using the guest wireless network, reduce the signal power to reduce the size of the wireless network.

Some wireless APs/routers can be configured with a guest wireless network. Disable it if you do not need it.

Wireless AP/Router Installation Checklist

Many wireless access points have the capability to route. A router, whether standalone or integrated with a wireless access point, connects wired and wireless networks together. A router also enables DHCP to service both wired and wireless networks and provides a firewall for network security.

Many of the parameters needed for wireless NIC configuration are also needed for access point installation. However, installing an access point is more involved because the access point is the central device of the wireless network. Answer the following questions *before* an access point is installed to help with the installation:

> What SSID is to be used?

> What static IP address will be assigned to the device?

- Is WEP, WPA, WPA-PSK, WPA2-PSK, WPA3, TKIP, AES, or any other security option enabled?
- What security key lengths, security keys, or passphrases are used?
- Is MAC filtering enabled?
- Is there power available for the access point? Note that some access points can receive power through a Power over Ethernet (PoE) switch.
- How will the access point be mounted or placed? Is mounting hardware provided with the access point, or does extra equipment have to be purchased? If out in the open, could a disgruntled employee access it and change the settings?
- Where should the access point be mounted for best coverage of the wireless network area? Where should the antenna be placed, or how should it be angled? Perform a site survey to determine how to achieve the best performance. Temporarily mount the access point. With a laptop that has a wireless NIC and site survey software, walk around the wireless network area to see the coverage range. The site survey can also be conducted by double-clicking the network icon on the taskbar; the signal strength is shown in the window that appears. Move the access point as necessary to avoid attenuation and obtain the largest possible area coverage.
- What channel ID will be used?
- Will the access point connect to the wired network and, if so, is there connectivity available where the access point will be mounted?

Wireless networking is an important and popular technology. Technicians today must be familiar with wireless devices as corporations and home users install these types of products.

Wireless Security Conclusion

Wireless security is an important issue. The following list recaps some of the important issues and provides recommendations along with a few suggestions for securing a wireless network:

- Change the default SSID and password. Make the password as long as possible and include non-alphanumeric characters.
- Enable encryption on the access point to the highest level possible while still allowing wireless NIC access. Use authentication when possible.
- Put the wireless network on its own subnetwork and place it behind a firewall, if possible.
- In a small company, consider enabling MAC authentication (MAC filtering) for company devices.
- If supported, authenticate using an authentication server.
- If the SSID is manually configured, periodically change the SSID.
- Assign a static IP address to the access point rather than use DHCP for it.
- Disable remote management on the access point.
- Place the access point in the center of the wireless network and not next to an outside window.
- Use wireless network scanning software to test the network security.
- Require that wireless clients use a virtual private network (VPN) tunnel to access the access point.
- When using a wireless network such as a hotspot, use a VPN to access a corporate network. When viewing private or financial data, make sure the website uses the HTTPS protocol so that it encrypts the data using Transport Layer Security (TLS) or the older Security Socket Layer (SSL) protocol.
- If a rogue access point (an unauthorized AP) is found on the network, disconnect the device and confiscate it. Try to determine who owns the device and report the owner to IT security personnel.

Wireless networks have a strong presence today and will continue to do so in the future. The 802.1x and 802.11 standards are constantly being improved to tighten security for wireless networks so that they rival wired solutions.

IoT Device Security

IoT devices are rapidly being integrated into our homes and corporate devices, but they are a source of security breaches. Put smart devices on a separate network, make sure they are configured for automatic updates, use strong passwords on them, and secure the router that allows connectivity to the internet for them.

Wireless Network Troubleshooting

Troubleshooting wireless networks is sometimes easier than troubleshooting wired networks because of the mobility factor. A wireless device can be used to troubleshoot connectivity, configuration, security, and so on. Most wireless network problems stem from inconsistent configuration. The standards deployed must be for the lowest common denominator, although some routers now have combination settings such as WPA/WPA2 or WPA2/WPA3.

The following list includes questions about wireless networking that are designed to steer a technician in the right direction. Most of these issues have been discussed in previous sections, but it is nice to have the following troubleshooting list in one spot:

- Is the SSID correct?
- Is the wireless NIC seen by the operating system? (Use Device Manager to check.) Check the mobile device for a wireless disable button or use a key to disable/enable the wireless NIC.
- Is the correct security level enabled?
- Can any devices attach to the access point? If not, check the access point.
- Is anything causing interference or attenuation? Check antenna placement.
- Is there a channel ID overlap problem?
- If a wireless printer is to be shared across the network, ensure that the printer attaches to the company protected wireless network and not the open (guest) wireless network unless you want customers to use the printer.
- A program from the wireless NIC manufacturer can be installed and used instead of using Windows to control the wireless NIC. If the customer wants to use Windows instead of the software provided, access a command prompt with elevated privileges. At the prompt, type **`netsh wlan show settings`**. From the output, determine whether the Windows automatic wireless configuration is disabled. You may have to disable the wireless NIC and uninstall the vendor software to use Windows to control the NIC.

Security Incident Response

Many companies define what to do when a security incident has occurred. However, in some businesses or for an incident that occurs on a home network, people are not always sure what to do. Following are the steps to take:

Step 1. Identify the issue. (See Table 18.15 for issues and best practices.)

Step 2. Report the issue through the proper channels (refer to Table 18.15).

Step 3. Preserve the data/device by documenting the incident and securing any storage device, if possible. Note that in some cases, preservation of the storage device and copying of it must be done on a machine that ensures that no data has been modified. Ensure that the documentation includes everything, including any changes or moves. Use a chain-of-custody form that travels with the data/device as more people get involved. Chain-of-custody forms commonly include the following information:

- What is the issue (with data, a device, or something else)?
- How did you get involved with the evidence?
- When did you see the issue?
- What did you do to handle the issue?
- To what person did you turn over the issue, data, device, and so on?

TABLE 18.15 Incident reporting and actions

Type of event	Action to take
Virus	Disconnect the computer from the internet and log all actions. Do not power off the computer or reboot it. Run a full antivirus scan. Notify the appropriate personnel, as outlined in the security policy. Do not forget that other IT personnel may need to be notified, such as network personnel who may need to block connections to contain the spread of the virus or personnel responsible for corporate messaging, for example. You may also need to contact legal or public relations personnel. You can also notify your internet provider and file a complaint with the FBI Internet Crime Complaint Center.
Spyware	Use a freeware or other software application to remove the application. Many of the security suites have a method of reporting found incidents. Submit a report using the FTC Consumer Complaint Form.
Phishing	Notify the agency from which the contact was received. Report the incident to the U.S. Computer Emergency Readiness Team (CERT).
Child exploitation	Use parental control software to prevent this. Log off immediately and notify your local police department and/or the nearest FBI field office. You can also report the event to the National Center for Exploited and Missing Children.
Software piracy	Report incidents of organized software piracy to the Software and Information Industry Association (SIIA) and the Business Software Alliance (BSA).

If a security incident occurs and you do not know what to do, talk to your supervisor (see Figure 18.53). She should have the experience to guide you or know to whom she should go to resolve the issue. If you feel uncomfortable talking to your supervisor about this, consider going to the human resources department or a higher administrator. The BSA and other organizations allow anonymous reporting. Reporting and documenting security violations is important, especially in the business environment. It is every person's responsibility to be security aware and responsible.

FIGURE 18.53 Report security violations

A Final Word About Security

Whether for a wired or wireless connection, standalone PC or networked PC, or full desktop computer, laptop, tablet, or smartphone, data and device security are important. Security measures must always be taken. Technicians must be aware of the latest threats, take proactive measures to implement security, and share their knowledge with users so the users can take proactive steps. Security risks and threats cause technicians a lot of work and time. These threats and attacks cost billions in lost data and time to businesses. Because most technicians do not see themselves as a dollar figure on a spreadsheet, they don't realize that if the business loses money as a result of security threats, the business has to cut costs, and one of those costs could be the technical position. Think about it and be proactive in guarding against security threats.

TECH TIP

Follow all policies and security best practices

It is very important for technicians to follow corporate policies and security best practices. If in doubt, ask your supervisor or ask for a copy of them.

SOFT SKILLS: BUILDING CUSTOMER TRUST

It is fitting in the security chapter to discuss building a trust relationship with the customer. Trust begins with professionalism. Be professional in your attire, attitude, written communication, and oral communication. Trust also includes being honest with the customer. If you are going to be late, let the customer know that. If you need to do more research, explain the situation. No one can be expected to know all technical information.

Trust also involves being honest if you find confidential material. Do not use or discuss any material you see while in a customer area. If you see confidential material, let the customers know you have seen the material. If the material is a password, let the customer know and recommend that he or she change the password immediately.

Do not touch or move things or papers in a customer's area. Also do not try to work around a mess. Instead, ask the customer to move or put things away to clear the area you need. Simply explain that you need space to determine and/or repair the problem.

Trust involves giving customers documentation related to the product just installed or replaced. Trust involves doing what you say you will do. If you say you will call back to check on the situation in the next 24 hours, do so. If you say you will drop off the documentation the following week, do that. Be true to your word.

Trust also involves being honest about billing. Do not overcharge customers. When presenting customers with an invoice or a work order, explain the details with patience. Do not allow customers to argue with you over facts or time. Your time is valuable, too.

You never know where you are going to meet your next boss. Every time you step into a customer's area or talk to a customer, it might lead to a professional reference, a job recommendation, a job lead, or a promotion. Part of building the customer relationship is building trust. Be professional in all that you do. See Figure 18.54.

FIGURE 18.54 Building customer trust

Chapter Summary

> A security policy guides a company in security matters. The policy defines things such as physical access, antivirus, acceptable usage of devices and data, password policies, email usage guidelines, remote access strategies, and emergency procedures.

> Physical security can include door access, key control, authentication methods including the use of smart cards, locks, key fobs, RFID, biometric devices, access control vestibule, physical protection of network devices such as servers, APs, switches, and routers, video surveillance, alarm systems, motion sensors, bollards, fences, lighting, magnetometer, and privacy filters.

> Document shredding can help with corporate data security. If a third party should provide this service, ensure that the company provides a certificate of destruction.

> Authentication involves proving you are the person gaining access to a system or a network. Multifactor authentication requires multiple means of proof to be more secure. Authentication servers such as RADIUS or TACACS+ can be used, and they might use the Kerberos in order to prevent packets from being altered or read.

> BIOS/UEFI security options include configuring a supervisor/user password, using a TPM, disabling unused ports, disabling USB ports, and disabling device options.

> To protect the operating system, use NTFS and have a plan for updating the operating system, web browser, antivirus, anti-malware, and antispyware. Encrypt files and folders as necessary. Use BitLocker and TPM technologies, implement a firewall, and disable AutoRun and AutoPlay.

> If a computer with sensitive data on the hard drive is to be donated, moved, or sold, perform the following: secure erasing, degaussing, and drilling through drive platters and then destroying the pieces with a hammer.

> If virtualization is used, ensure that each virtual machine has adequate protection (firewall, antivirus, anti-malware, and antispyware).

> After a security scan, any virus or malware files that are quarantined must be manually deleted.

> The Windows Guest account should be disabled; the administrator account should be renamed and have a strong password. User accounts should limit rights to only the rights the person requires to do his or her job; this is known as the principle of least privilege.

> Ensure that data is backed up routinely on site or in the cloud. Backup strategies include full, incremental, differential, and synthetic.

> Permissions should be assigned appropriately to remotely accessed files and folders. Use either share permissions or NTFS permissions (for more control) but not both on the same network share. If a file is placed in a folder that has permissions, the file inherits the folder permissions. Effective permissions are the bottom-line permissions someone has when group permissions and individual permissions have been granted.

> A hijacked browser can cause a different home page to appear, a particular web page to be displayed, a rootkit or other malware to be installed, different DNS settings to be applied, or a new or updated HOSTS file to be applied.

> Email applications now protect against spam, but you can also create rules to block messages from a particular source or subject line.

> On a wireless network, implement encryption and authentication. Change default SSIDs and passwords.

> When a security incident occurs, identify the issue, report it through the proper channels and to the appropriate authorities, and preserve the data by using a chain-of-custody form.

> When dealing with a customer, a coworker, or your boss, maintain your professionalism and do everything you can to build trust.

A+ CERTIFICATION EXAM TIPS

- ✓ This chapter includes information related to both the CompTIA A+ Core 1 (220-1101) and CompTIA A+ Core 2 (220-1102) exams. It is the most complex chapter in the book because many security issues need to be experienced to know exactly what things to try when problems arise.
- ✓ Be familiar with wireless configuration on both the client and router/AP: default username, firmware update, SSID, channels, encryption, SSID broadcasting, IP and content filtering, firewall, disabling guest access, port forwarding/mapping, turning off TCP/UDP ports that aren't used, DHCP reservations, WAN IP address, UPnP, and screened subnet.
- ✓ Know login options, including SSO, fingerprint, username/password, PIN, facial recognition, and multifactor authentication. Be familiar with these security concepts: ACLs, principle of least privilege, email security (including how DKIM, SPF, and DMARC are used for spam management as part of DNS and how TXT messages are used), hard tokens, soft tokens, SMS, voice calls, and authenticator apps.
- ✓ Acquaint yourself with these security items: TPM, VPN (and be able to configure a VPN on a Windows computer), UTM, proxy server, and load balancer.
- ✓ Know what to do if you find prohibited content/data and what PII is.
- ✓ Review hard drive security, including BitLocker and what to do with a hard drive when moving it to another device or simply removing it.
- ✓ Practice security measures that a technician must implement, such as viewing hidden files, using an administrator account/rights, assigning Windows user roles, or adjusting browsers.
- ✓ Practice manually configuring a wireless router/AP with security settings and a wireless NIC.
- ✓ Review what to do with security problems such as computer slowdowns, certificate warnings, browser redirection, desktop alerts, false antivirus alerts, and altered files. Know the steps to take to remove malware. Be able to configure Windows Defender Firewall and Windows Defender Antivirus, and understand how to use the Windows Privacy settings.
- ✓ Be able to implement backup and recovery. Know the difference between full, incremental, differential, and synthetic backups.
- ✓ Configure basic firewall settings, including screened subnet (DMZ), port forwarding, NAT, UPnP, allow lists/deny lists, and MAC filtering.
- ✓ Explain the purpose of MDM, port security, and the following Active Directory concepts: login script, domain, group policy/updates, organizational units, home folder, folder redirection, and security groups.
- ✓ Configure BIOS/UEFI security settings including passwords, drive encryption, TPM, and HSM.
- ✓ Describe Windows users and groups, including administrator, power user, guest, and standard user. Review NTFS permissions, administrative shares vs. local shares, permission propagation, and inheritance factors.

Key Terms

3-2-1 backup 938
acceptable use policy 901
access control vestibule 904
ACL 909
Active Directory 922
administrative share 930
AES 940
anti-malware 908
antivirus 908
authentication 903
authenticator app 910
authorization 920
backup testing 936
badge reader 903
biometrics 906
BitLocker 939
BitLocker To Go 939
bollard 901
boot password 910
boot sector virus 915
brute force 919
BYOD 900
Certificate Manager 944
certificate of destruction 907
change the default admin user account password 922
content filtering 956
cryptominer 915
data at rest 940
DDoS 919

degaussing 942
desktop alert 917
dictionary attack 911
differential backup 937
disable AutoPlay 941
disable AutoRun 941
disable guest account 927
DMZ 950
DNS TXT 948
door lock 901
DoS 919
drive wipe 941
DRM 912
dumpster diving 907
effective permissions 933
EFS 940
email filtering 909
encryption 903
end-of-life 935
end-user education 912
equipment lock 903
EULA 913
evil twin 919
failed attempts 912
fingerprint scanner 906
firewall 908
folder redirection 925
full backup 937
full device encryption 940
GDPR 914
`gpedit.msc` 926
grandfather-father-son backup 938
group policy 926
group policy editor 927
hard token 903
hidden share 951
home folder 925
HSM 903
IDS 957
impersonation 918
incineration 907
incremental backup 937
inherited permissions 932
IP filtering 961
IPS 957
Kerberos 910
key 901
key fob 903
keylogger 915
load balancer 956
local security policy 926
local share 930
log off when not in use 912
login script 925
low-level format 941
MAC address filtering 960
magnetometer 904
malware 915
man-in-the-middle 920
mantrap 904
MDM 958
Microsoft Defender 943
Microsoft Defender Antivirus 943
missing files 917
MSRA 955
multifactor authentication 910
NAT 953
non-compliant system 900
NTFS permissions 928
off site storage 936
on site storage 936
on-path [attack] 920
open source 912
organizational unit 922
palmprint scanner 906
password manager 912
patch/update management 935
patching/OS updates 935
PCI 914
PHI 914
phishing 918
PII 914
PIN 911
piracy 913
port forwarding 952
port mapping 954
port security 952
port triggering 952
principle of least privilege 930
proxy server 948
RADIUS 910
ransomware 915
RDP 955
restrict login time 927
retinal scanner 906
RFID 903
RMM 956
rogue antivirus 943
rootkit 915
run as administrator 934
scareware 919
screened subnet 950
secure boot 910
security group 922
security policy 900
share permissions 928
shoulder surfing 904
shredding 907
single sign-on 911
smart card 903
SMS 910
social engineering 917
soft token 910
software firewall 908
spam 947
spoofing 920
spyware 915
SQL injection 920
SSH 956
SSID broadcasting 962
standard format 941
synthetic backup 937
TACACS+ 910
tailgating 904
Telnet 956
third-party vendor 907
timeout/screen lock 927
TKIP 959
TPM 903
Trojan 915
trusted source 909
UAC 934
unprotected system 935
untrusted source 909
unwanted notification 935
UPnP 950
USB lock 904
username and password 911
UTM 956
virus 915
vishing 918
VNC 956
VPN 908
WEP 959
whaling 918
Windows Defender Firewall 951
WPA2 959
WPA3 959
WPS 961
XSS scripting 920
zero day [attack] 920

Review Questions

1. Match each of these security policy components with a definition in the list that follows.

   ____ physical access

   ____ acceptable use

   ____ remote access

   ____ password

   a. The specific web browser that is allowed to be installed

   b. Defines whether you can send the code used to access an account (such as shared network storage) via email

   c. The type of security required for a remote VPN connection

   d. The time, day, and year someone entered a network server room

2. Describe two-factor authentication.

   ____

   ____

3. In what situation would an access control vestibule be used?

   a. When multiple people share the same area and each screen can be seen by one of the other people

   b. For physical security

   c. When the access server is unavailable or busy with other requests

   d. When a SAN is being used

4. Which wireless security feature would be most likely to be used in a small company where the staff are the only individuals using the wireless network and a couple of the laptops are older ones?

   a. VPN

   b. IDS

   c. WPA3

   d. WPA2

5. List five recommendations for protecting the operating system.

   ____

   ____

   ____

   ____

   ____

6. What is BitLocker?

   a. A wireless security setting

   b. A method used to secure passwords for websites, users, and files using TPM

   c. Online secure storage

   d. A utility that encrypts an entire disk volume, including operating system files, user files, and page files

7. [T | F] A new file is created and stored in an encrypted folder. The file must be manually encrypted because it was added after the folder was encrypted.
8. Describe the security rights for a subfolder when the parent folder is shared.

____

9. List three password guidelines you would recommend that a company use.

____

____

____

____

____

10. Where are domain user passwords stored?

    [local database | registry | network server | the cloud]
11. A network administrator in a large corporation goes to a popular network vendor site to research security settings, but a message appears, saying that this particular site cannot be accessed and is blocked. What security measure most likely caused this message?
    - **a.** BitLocker
    - **b.** Magnetometer
    - **c.** Port security
    - **d.** Content filtering
12. Describe the difference between a local security policy and a domain policy.

____

____

____

13. What two things are needed to configure a computer for a proxy server? (Choose two.)

    [IP address of the proxy server | MAC address of the proxy server | administrator name on the proxy server | IP address of the local computer | MAC address of the local computer | port number on the proxy server | administrator password on the local computer]
14. What is the purpose of a screened subnet (DMZ)?

____

____

____

15. [T | F] A virtual machine used in a small company should have anti-malware installed.
16. In which security situation would Kerberos most likely be used?

    [OS recovery | authentication | web filtering | content filtering | OS security]
17. No one can ping a specific Windows computer. What administrative tool can change this default behavior?

    [Windows Firewall | Local Security Policy | Internet Explorer > Internet options | Windows Defender]
18. What type of unsolicited internet message records the URLs visited and keystrokes used?

    [virus | grayware | spam | spyware]
19. An unofficial email is sent from your bank, asking you to click a link to verify your account information. What type of social engineering is this?

    [phishing | grayware | spyware | VPN]

20. Match the incident on the left with the action on the right. Even though some of the incidents might have multiple answers, each answer is used only once.

____ virus	a. BSA
____ child exploitation	b. police department
____ software piracy	c. CERT
____ phishing	d. FBI Internet Crime Complaint Center

Exercises

Exercise 18.1 Examining the Security Incident Response

Objective: To become familiar with security incident response

Procedure: Answer the following questions.

1. Place the security incident response tasks in the appropriate order.

   ____ First

   ____ Second

   ____ Third

   a. Report the incident through the proper channels.

   b. Preserve the data/device(s) involved.

   c. Identify the threat.

2. A college requires that each employee use the last four digits of his or her Social Security number to access the copier. Which type of security threat is this? Describe how you would respond to the incident if you were an IT security person for this college.

   a. Malware

   b. Sensitive PII

   c. Security policy

   d. Licensing

   ____

   ____

3. Your neighbor asks if she can borrow your application DVD and code. She promises she will not register the application. How will you respond to this, given that it is a personal request and not a professional one? To whom would you report this, if anyone?

   ____

   ____

4. You work as an IT support person for a company. The user complains of slowness when opening files. A security scan shows evidence of malware. Place the steps in the order in which they will be carried out.

   Step _____: Remediate the infected system.

   Step _____: Investigate and verify the symptoms.

   Step _____: Quarantine the infected system.

Exercise 18.2 Wireless Security

Objective: To become familiar with wireless security options

Procedure: Match the scenario to the correct term. Each answer is used only once.

Scenario:

a. Manually type Layer 2 addresses into a table.

b. Commonly used channels are 1, 6, and 11.

c. The most common corporate wireless security protocol is used.

d. Don't broadcast the name of the network.

e. Nearby companies get a stronger wireless signal than employees.

f. SAE encryption

g. Someone can easily get into the AP settings.

h. Easy to configure but has security risks.

i. Someone can get into the AP settings using hacking tools.

Term:

____ WPA2

____ WPA3

____ MAC filtering

____ Move AP and/or antenna

____ 2.4 GHz

____ WPS

____ Disable SSID broadcasting

____ Default settings

____ Update firmware

Exercise 18.3 Data Security

Objective: To become familiar with regulated data

Procedure: Answer the questions.

1. Match each description with the correct term related to regulated data.

Description:

a. U.S. companies are subject to this rule when engaging in trade in the European Union.

b. This sensitive data should be encrypted when in storage or in transit.

c. The 1996 HIPAA law prompted regulations related to this.

d. Banks, businesses, colleges, airlines, and railroads are subject to these standards if credit cards are accepted as a payment method.

Term:

____ PHI

____ PCI

____ GDPR

____ PII

2. [T | F] Personally identifiable information must be encrypted.
3. [T | F] A U.S. citizen who retires to Italy is not subject to the GDPR but is only subject to U.S. federal laws.
4. Which information would be considered nonsensitive PII? (Choose all that apply.)

   [name | user ID | password | email address | passport number | Social Security number]
5. Of the four types of regulated data, which two are most likely to be encountered by a PC technician who works at a college? (Choose two.)

   [PII | PCI | GDPR | PHI]

Activities

Internet Discovery

Objective: To become familiar with researching computer security concepts using the internet

Parts: A computer with internet access

Questions: Use the internet to answer the following questions.

1. Access the Internet Crime Complaint Center to answer the following questions. At the time of writing, the URL is https://www.ic3.gov.

   What are three recommendations for dealing with spam?

   ____

   ____

   ____

   ____

   What is internet crime, according to this website? Write the answer and the URL at which you found the answer.

   ____

   ____

   ____

   ____

2. Access the U.S. Computer Emergency Readiness Team website and access the technical user link to answer the following questions. At this writing, the URL is https://www.us-cert.gov.

   What are the three highest-rated vulnerabilities for the past week?

   ____

   ____

   ____

   List three recommendations made by this site for a new computer being connected to a network.

   ____

   ____

   ____

   ____

   ____

3. Access the National Institute of Standards and Technology Computer Security Resource Center (CSRC) website to answer the following questions.

   Access the glossary of security terms. Windows allows programming of ACLs (access control lists). What are ACLs, and how do they relate to computer security?

   ____

   ____

   ____

   Select the CSRC site map link. List one security section that you find interesting and define one term from that section that is not in this chapter.

   ____

   ____

4. Using a browser, answer the following questions and provide the website where you found each answer.

   What percentage of software installed is pirated?

   ____

   What is the current maximum fine for software pirated in the United States?

   ____

   ____

   ____

Soft Skills

Objective: To enhance and fine-tune a future technician's ability to listen, communicate in both written and oral forms, and support people who use computers in a professional manner

Activities:

1. Prepare a presentation on any topic related to network security. The topic can relate to wired or wireless security. Share your presentation with the class.
2. In small groups, find a security policy on the internet or use any of your school's computer policies. Critique the policy and make recommendations for how the policy can provide for stronger security.

Critical Thinking Skills

Objective: To analyze and evaluate information as well as apply learned information to new or different situations

Activities:

1. Create a wired workgroup network. Before users are created, determine what security policies will be enforced. Document the security policy. Also determine what activities are logged. Share folders between the computers with security implemented. Document the network shares and policies. View and capture activities logged and include those captures with the documentation. Present your design, implementation, and monitoring to the class.
2. In teams, build a wired and wireless network with security in place. Document the security as if you were presenting it to a home network customer who hired you to build and implement it.

19 Operational Procedures

In this chapter you will learn:

- Proper personal safety precautions and equipment
- Workplace safety precautions, procedures, and equipment
- How to protect computer equipment from airborne pollutants
- How to dispose of waste (computers, mobile devices, batteries, laser printer toner cartridges, monitors)
- Types of IT documentation
- Change management processes
- Proper communication skills

CompTIA Exam Objectives:

✓ 1102-4.1 Given a scenario, implement best practices associated with documentation and support systems information management.

✓ 1102-4.2 Explain basic change-management best practices.

✓ 1102-4.4 Given a scenario, use common safety procedures.

✓ 1102-4.5 Summarize environmental impacts and local environmental controls.

✓ 1102-4.7 Given a scenario, use proper communication techniques and professionalism.

Operational Procedures Overview

Being up-to-date on the latest safety precautions and procedures regarding both personal and workplace safety is beneficial to all involved. This chapter reviews the role that federal, state, and local governments play in protecting human health and the environment by operating regulated recycling and disposal sites for electronics. Also covered are the dangers of damaged batteries that leak acid and how to handle those situations. We review why and how:

- Electronics need to be protected from moisture, dust, extreme temperature fluctuations, and weight-bearing loads.
- Toxic fumes can cause degradation of components.
- Electronic waste (computers, mobile devices, batteries, laser printer toner cartridges, and monitors) is considered toxic waste.
- It is important to protect computer equipment with surge (power) suppressors, personal enclosures, and clean rooms.
- Personal protective equipment and personal safety techniques are necessary.
- It is important to properly handle and store electronics using antistatic bags, ESD straps, and ESD mats.
- Equipment grounding, self-grounding, and fire safety knowledge are important.

Paperwork is a part of any job, but it is especially critical in IT, where systems cross all parts of the business. Technicians use IT documentation as reference material and as a historical record of IT devices. Change is also a constant in IT, and change management is therefore important. This chapter covers the type of documentation commonly used and created within the IT department as well as the change management process. Finally, we discuss why looking, acting, and *thinking* like a professional, along with having good communications skills, are necessary for an IT professional.

Workplace Safety Precautions and Procedures

All companies are required to have workplace safety precautions and procedures posted and in effect, as mandated by the federal government. Most employers provide education and training on those procedures. Some precautions and procedures are a matter of common sense. Be sure to remove the power cord and/or battery before working on a PC or mobile device. Most people will not walk on a slippery floor if a "Wet Floor" sign is posted. As a technician, you will want to keep your work area relatively neat so as not to hamper other workers or potentially cause an accident. Determine where you can safely install your computer and network equipment. You want to make sure to practice good cable management, ensuring that no cables cause a trip hazard. (Chapter 13, "Networking," further discusses good network cable management techniques.) If an accident does occur, do the following:

- Immediately notify medical personnel, if needed.
- Report the incident to a supervisor.

The supervisor must then complete an incident report (see Figure 19.1).

TECH TIP

Always comply with local government regulations

There are many government regulations regarding workplace safety, and there are also local government regulations related to disposal requirements. Check with your supervisor if you are unsure about an unsafe environment or have questions about processes.

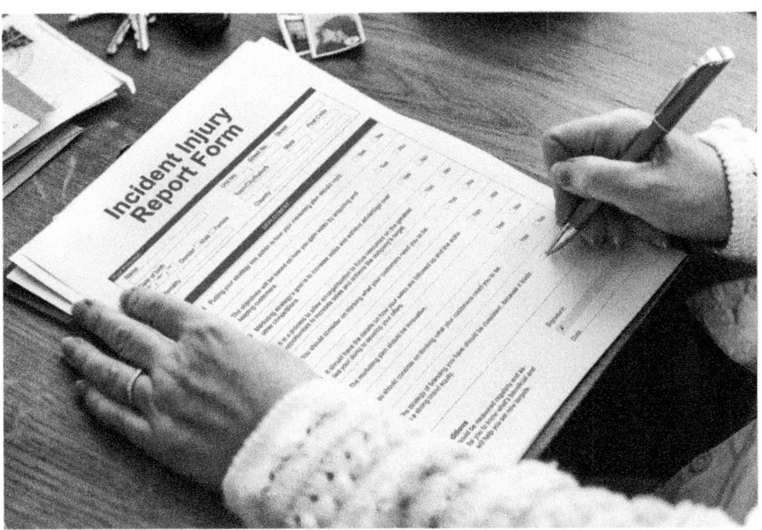

FIGURE 19.1 Incident report

OSHA

The Occupational Safety and Health Administration (**OSHA**) is a division of the U.S. Department of Labor. OSHA promotes safe and healthy working conditions by enforcing standards and providing workplace safety training. In addition, Environmental Protection Agency (EPA) standards and local government regulations specify that workplace environments should be free of harmful and/or hazardous chemicals or situations.

An important form required by OSHA is the material safety data sheet (**MSDS**), which outlines handling, storage procedures, disposal, and first aid on all potentially harmful or hazardous substances that you may come in contact with while working. Because MSDSs are available to employees, anyone working with these substances should review this important information. A similar form is the safety data sheet (SDS), which outlines similar information regarding chemicals.

Fire Safety

It is rare for electrical fires to occur in computers, but it is important to have **electrical fire safety** knowledge in case a fire does happen. If a fire occurs inside a computer or peripheral, evacuate everyone and unplug the equipment, if possible. Do not put yourself in harm's way in attempting to do this. A Type C or Type A-B-C fire extinguisher can be used to put out the fire. **Type C fire extinguishers** are made specifically for electrical (Type C) fires. **Type A-B-C fire extinguishers** can be used for Class A, Class B, and Class C fires.

Here's some quick information about classes of fires:

> Class A fires involve paper, wood, cloth, or other normal combustibles.
> Class B fires involve flammable liquids and gases.
> Class C fires involve electrical or electronic equipment.

In order to use a Type A-B-C or a Type C fire extinguisher, follow these steps:

Step 1. Pull the fire alarm.

Step 2. Pull out the fire extinguisher pin (see Figure 19.2).

Step 3. Aim the fire extinguisher nozzle at the base (bottom) of the fire.

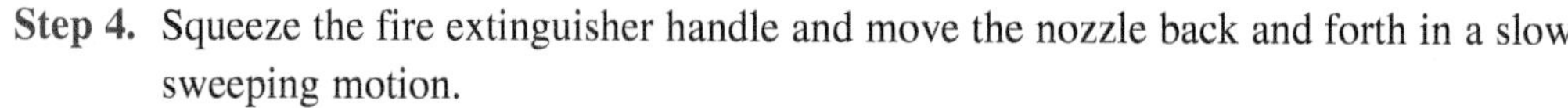

Step 4. Squeeze the fire extinguisher handle and move the nozzle back and forth in a slow sweeping motion.

FIGURE 19.2 Pull the fire extinguisher pin

A Review of Safety Equipment in the Technical Field Kit

Let us examine three simple and inexpensive products that are essential parts of a technical field kit. Your personal protective equipment (PPE) should consist of safety goggles or glasses, gloves, and a dust mask/air filter mask. All of these items can be purchased at most hardware, drug, and grocery stores.

Safety goggles or glasses (see Figure 19.3) protect precious eyes from injury or irritation due to dust, airborne particles, debris, or any liquids or contaminants that might be in the working environment. Even though prescription eyeglasses provide some protection, it is wise to have a pair of safety glasses or goggles that fit over eyeglasses.

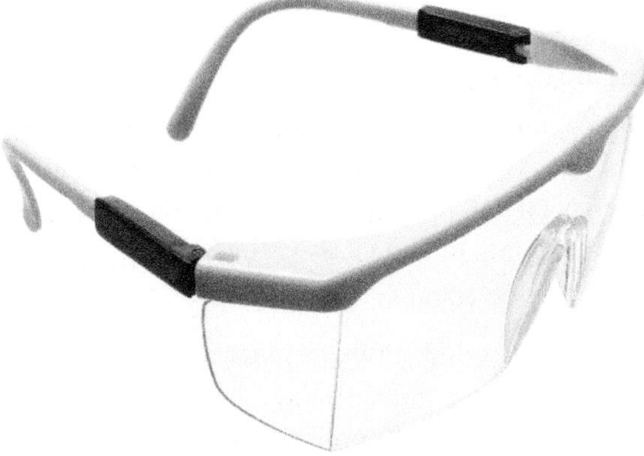

FIGURE 19.3 Safety goggles

For some situations, such as when working with laser toner, it is important to wear gloves and a dust mask or an **air filtration mask** to prevent inhalation of harmful airborne particulates, smoke, perfumes, odors, and fumes. When you use **compressed air**, dust and debris are an issue. Simply removing the cover from something that needs to be vacuumed poses a hazard. Use a **vacuum**, when possible, to remove dust and debris, but if in doubt, wear a mask. Dust masks like the one shown in Figure 19.4 are available in many hardware, grocery, drug, and discount stores.

FIGURE 19.4 Dust mask

Personal Safety

Personal and equipment safety are paramount in IT. Having proper personal safety precautions and equipment will facilitate a smoother repair task by getting you into a routine of automatically putting on safety glasses or goggles, gloves, and a dust mask (when applicable). It will lessen the chance of electrostatic discharge, of forgetting a repair step, or of a careless mishap because your safety procedures will become second nature to you. Other important things to remember follow:

- Remove jewelry, watches, dangling necklaces/earrings, or ID lanyards that could get caught, hooked, or entangled in the equipment.
- Disconnect power cords.
- Be sure that the work area is clear of liquids (coffee, soda, water bottles) and foods that may spill or otherwise contaminate the equipment.
- Remember to use good **lifting techniques** (such as using your legs, not your back) and get help when lifting more than 50 pounds.
- Be familiar with the location of the nearest fire extinguisher and the nearest fire exit.

Environmental Impacts

Awareness has been raised in the past few decades about "going green," and the "reduce, reuse, recycle" movement is practiced in many communities. Collectively, as a society, we can make a huge impact. Individually, we can make a difference by being good stewards of our resources. Every state and many cities have specific guidelines about how to dispose of electronics or e-waste (see Figure 19.5). These rules must be followed by technicians who replace broken computer equipment. If you are unsure about how to get rid of any piece of broken electronic equipment, contact your direct supervisor for instructions.

FIGURE 19.5 E-waste

The following list provides alternatives and suggestions for being environmentally conscious about discarding electronics:

> Donate equipment that is operational to schools and charities so that those who do not have access to technology can get some exposure. If the operating system is not transferred to another system, leave the operating system on the machine and provide proof of purchase along with documentation. Also, do not forget to erase all data stored on the computer before donating it.
> Recycle outdated electronics. If devices are so outdated that a school or charity cannot use them, consider recycling. Many companies accept old electronics and have found ways to reuse some of their parts.
> Remove parts that do work and donate or recycle them.
> Buy electronics that are designed to save resources and are easy to upgrade. Extend their usefulness by ensuring that they are energy efficient. They will also be more useful if they contain fewer toxins, use recycled materials, and have leasing or recycling programs.
> Check with the computer or component manufacturer to see if it has a recycling program. Most of them do.

Electronic Disposal/Recycling

Computers and other electronic devices contain materials such as beryllium, chromium, cadmium, lead, mercury, nickel, and zinc. The levels of these materials in landfills increase dramatically every year and can pose a threat to our environment. Each city/state has its own laws about disposing of electronics. Important disposal and handling measures should be taken with old heavy monitors that contain cathode ray tubes (CRTs), cell phones, tablets, batteries, and laser printer toner cartridges.

Cell phones and tablets are now classified as toxic waste in the United States because of the lead they contain. Lead-free phones do not solve the problem because of the zinc, nickel, copper, and antimony within them. Manufacturers have not always been willing to take back old phones because extracting the gold, copper, silver, and other metals can be expensive.

Currently, the best advice is to follow local guidelines on disposal, look to see if the manufacturer of your new device has a trade-in program; donate to an organization that helps victims of violence, soldiers, or charities; or use a responsible recycler. The website e-stewards.org can help you find responsible e-waste recycling locations.

Don't forget to erase your data and remove the SIM card and any memory storage before donating or recycling a cell phone or tablet. If you have broken parts, wear a mask and gloves while handling them. Place parts in a plastic bag and seal it before disposing of it properly.

A battery produces DC voltage through a chemical reaction that occurs within the battery. Batteries contain acids that can potentially burn or hurt body parts. Batteries can introduce lead and acid into the environment; thus, they need to be recycled (see Figure 19.6). Use protective equipment such as gloves when handling batteries.

Lithium-ion (Li-ion) batteries used in mobile devices and laptops may need to be replaced in the following cases:

> If the device has been subjected to extreme temperature changes
> If the device was dropped, crushed, or flooded with liquid
> If the device has sustained up to 500 cycles of discharge and recharge

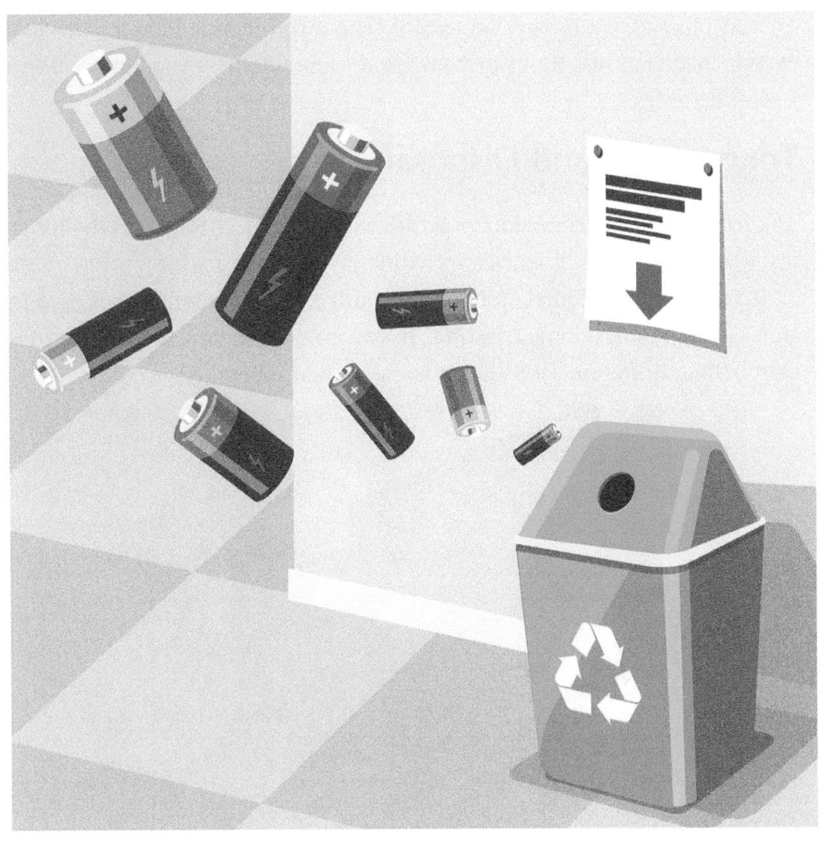

FIGURE 19.6 Battery recycling

The contents of a lithium-ion battery are under pressure; thus, Li-ion batteries can explode or catch on fire (see Figure 19.7) if subjected to high temperatures. If you see a bulging Li-ion battery, hear one hiss, or feel one that is overheated, immediately move the device away from anything that might catch on fire. If possible, remove the battery and put it in a safe fireproof place. If it catches on fire, use a foam or A-B-C fire extinguisher. If on a train or plane, you might see the attendant use water to douse a battery fire because a Li-ion battery has very little lithium metal that would react with water.

FIGURE 19.7 Li-ion battery on fire

Recycling all batteries is important. The recommended method of disposal is to recycle batteries at regulated stations. Refer to your local municipality's regulations for recycling and disposing of Li-ion batteries.

Toner Safety and Disposal

The **toner** in laser printer toner cartridges is not earth friendly as the toner is made up of plastic, toxins, and heavy metal. It takes approximately 1,000 years for a printer cartridge to fully decompose.

If you accidently inhale toner, you could experience headaches, eye irritation, itching, and other side effects that are longer lasting. If you come into contact with it, toner can cause itchiness and skin irritation. Figure 19.8 shows some spilled toner.

FIGURE 19.8 Spilled toner

Here are some points to remember about toner safety:

> Remember to wear some type of rubber or nitrile gloves and a dust mask when handling toner cartridges. Inhalation of toner particles can cause respiratory damage equivalent to that of smoking.

> Do not attempt to clean up any loose toner particles with a regular vacuum sweeper as the toner particles may seep into the vacuum's motor and melt. Use a vacuum with a high-efficiency particulate air (HEPA) vacuum bag.

> Allow the printer (and cartridge) to cool before repairing or replacing the cartridge. The fusing assembly and heated toner can cause severe burns. You should wait after copying or printing before doing any service or removing a toner cartridge.

Component Handling and Storage

Proper handling and storage of electronic parts and equipment reduces the chance of electrostatic discharge (ESD). ESD is sneaky. It damages, weakens, and destroys electronic equipment—often without the technician being aware that it has happened. Atmospheric conditions play a part in ESD in that the potential for ESD is greater when the **humidity** (moisture in the air) is low. Make sure to place or store electronic equipment in a well-ventilated, cool, low-humidity space. Antistatic bags for storage, ESD straps and mats for repair jobs, and self-grounding knowledge and techniques are all discussed in Chapter 5, "Disassembly and Power." The following is a brief review:

> Remember to use **antistatic bags** (see Figure 19.9) for storing adapters, RAM, and motherboards when not in use for an extended period of time. Date the bags as a reminder to change them out after a few years as their protective quality diminishes.

> When repairing a computer, wear an antistatic strap, **ESD strap**, antistatic gloves, and/or antistatic heel strap to prevent ESD (see Chapter 5). Caution: The voltages are very high on a CRT monitor (even unplugged) and within a high-voltage power supply of a laser printer. Do not attempt to work on either one unless you have special training.

> Place a computer that is being repaired on an **ESD mat**. Some mats have a snap to which you can fasten an antistatic wrist strap.

> If antistatic devices are not available, it is recommended that you rest an arm on a metal part. This **self-grounding** method is an effective way of keeping you and the computer at the same voltage potential.

FIGURE 19.9 Antistatic bag

Electronic Safety: Equipment Grounding

Homes and businesses have a consistent shared (or panel) ground on all electrical outlets (see Figure 19.10). Businesses have a similar ground system but might also include additional independent grounding by using ground plates, ground bars, and a ground bus. As a technician, you don't have to design this, but you do have to be aware of it.

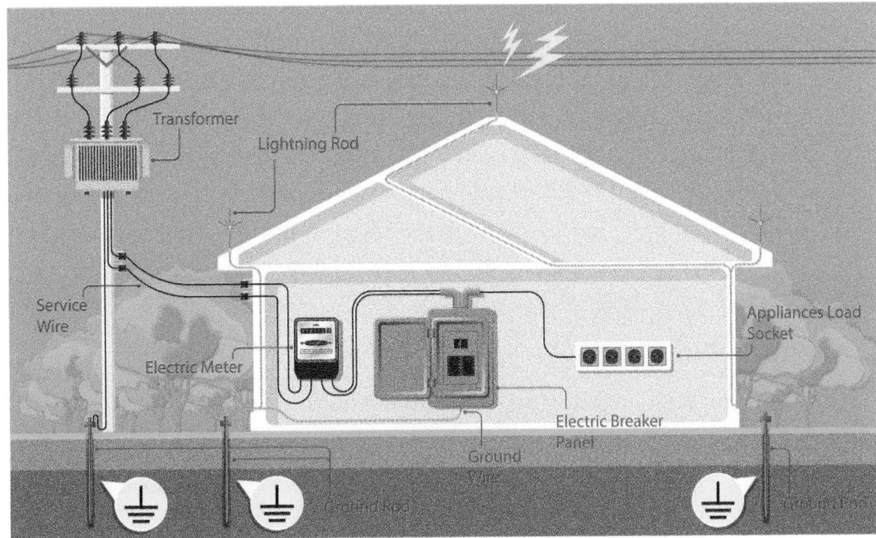

FIGURE 19.10 Equipment grounding

Equipment grounding means that the components in a device such as a computer are at the same voltage potential. Grounding is important to personal safety because consistent grounding minimizes the potential for voltage to be applied to places where it shouldn't be applied. For example, if a piece of equipment is not grounded, someone could receive a shock or be electrocuted simply by touching it (see Figure 19.11). As a technician, you might see a grounding wire connect to a network rack or battery backup system. Review Chapter 5 for more information about power and grounding.

FIGURE 19.11 Electrical shock

Proper Power Handling and Adverse Power Conditions

Disconnect power before working on/inside equipment. Ground yourself and try to keep humidity between 45% and 55% to prevent or reduce the threat of ESD. Use an ESD strap or antistatic gloves to prevent ESD.

There are two adverse AC power conditions that can damage or adversely affect a computer: overvoltage and undervoltage. **Overvoltage** occurs when the output voltage from the wall outlet (the AC voltage) is over the rated amount. Normally, the output of a wall outlet is 110 to 130 volts AC. When the voltage rises above 130 volts, an overvoltage condition exists. An overvoltage condition is harmful to components because too much DC voltage destroys electronic circuits. An overvoltage condition can be a surge or a spike (see Table 19.1).

When the voltage falls below 110 volts AC, an **undervoltage** condition exists. If the voltage is too low, a computer power supply cannot provide enough power to all the components. Under such conditions, the power supply draws too much current, causing it to overheat and weakening or damaging the components. An undervoltage condition may be a brownout or sag that is also explained in Table 19.1.

TABLE 19.1 Adverse power conditions

Major type	Subtype	Explanation
Overvoltage	Spike	A spike lasts 1 to 2 nanoseconds. A spike is harder to guard against than a surge because it has such short duration and high intensity.
	Surge	A **power surge** lasts longer than a spike. A surge is also called transient voltage. Causes of surges include lightning, poorly regulated electricity, faulty wiring, and devices that turn on periodically, such as elevators, air conditioners, and refrigerators.

Major type	Subtype	Explanation
Undervoltage	**Brownout**	In a brownout, power circuits become overloaded. Occasionally, an electric company intentionally causes a brownout to reduce the power drawn by customers during peak periods.
	Sag	A sag occurs when the voltage from the wall outlet drops momentarily.
	Blackout	A blackout is a total loss of power.

Surge Protectors

A **surge suppressor**, also known as a surge strip or surge protector, is commonly a multi-outlet strip that offers built-in protection against overvoltage. Surge protectors do not protect against undervoltage; they protect against voltage increases. Figure 19.12 shows a surge suppressor.

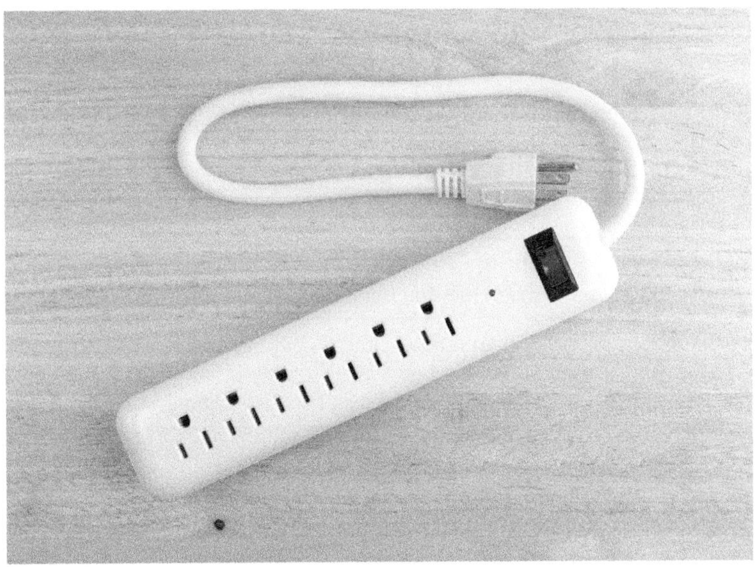

FIGURE 19.12 Surge suppressor

A surge protector commonly has an electronic component called a metal oxide varistor (**MOV**), which protects the computer or device that plugs into one of the outlets on the surge strip. When a surge occurs, the MOV prevents the extra voltage from passing to the outlets. If a large surge occurs, the MOV will take the hit and be destroyed, which is better than damaging the computer. However, with small overvoltages, each small surge weakens the MOV. A weakened MOV might not give the proper protection to the computer in the event of a bigger surge. Also, there is no simple check for an MOV's condition. Some MOVs have indicator lamps attached, but they indicate only when the MOV has been destroyed, not when it is weakened. Some surge protectors also have replaceable fuses and/or indicator lamps for fuses. A fuse works only once and then is destroyed during a surge in order to protect devices plugged into surge protector outlets. Figure 19.13 shows a surge protector that has done its job.

TECH TIP

Do not create a trip hazard with a surge strip

When installing a surge protector, install it in such a manner that it does not cause a trip hazard due to the cord lying in an area where people walk.

FIGURE 19.13 Blown surge protector

Several surge protector features deserve consideration. Table 19.2 outlines some of them.

TABLE 19.2 Surge protector features

Feature	Explanation
Clamping voltage	The level at which a surge protector starts protecting the computer. The lower the value, the better the protection.
Clamping speed	The amount of time that elapses before protection begins. The lower the value, the better the protection. Surge protectors cannot normally protect against power spikes because of their rated clamping speed.
Energy absorption/ dissipation	The ability of a surge protector to absorb or dissipate energy. The greater the number of joules (a unit of energy) that can be dissipated, the more effective and durable a surge protector is.
TVS (transient voltage suppressing) rating	This is also known as response time. The lower the rating, the better. For example, a 330 TVS-rated surge protector is better than a 400 TVS-rated one.
UL rating	UL (Underwriters Laboratories) developed the 1449 VPR (voltage protection rating) standard to measure the maximum amount of voltage a surge protector will let through to the attached devices.

The federal government designates surge suppressor grades—A, B, and C. Suppressors are evaluated on the basis of 1,000 surges at a specific number of volts and amps. A Class A rating is the best.

Electric companies offer surge protection for homes. Frequently, there are two choices. A basic package protects large appliances that allows no more than 800 volts to enter the electrical system. A premium package protects more sensitive devices (TVs, stereos, and computers) and reduces the amount of voltage allowed to 323 volts or less. The exterior surge arrestor does not protect against voltage increases that originate inside the building, such as those caused by faulty wiring.

TECH TIP

Which surge strip to buy?

When purchasing or recommending a surge protector, be sure it conforms to the UL 1449 standard and has an MOV status lamp. Also, check to see if the vendor offers to repair or replace any surge-protected equipment that is damaged during a surge.

Common criteria used when buying a surge suppressor include the following:

> Cable length
> Number of outlets
> Room to connect peripheral power connectors that may take additional space
> Diagnostic LED(s)
> Integrated circuit breaker
> Outlets that power off when not in use for nonessential electronics such as lamps, speakers, or printers
> Outlets that are always on for devices such as cordless phone handset cradles, modems, and external hard drives
> Insurance to cover damaged devices attached to the surge suppressor
> UL 1449 compliance

Surge protectors do not provide the best protection for a computer system because most provide very little protection against adverse power conditions other than surges. Even the good ones protect only against overvoltage conditions. Those with the UL 1449 rating and an MOV status lamp are usually more expensive.

Line Conditioners

An alternative for computer protection is a line conditioner. **Line conditioners**, sometimes known as power conditioners, are more expensive than surge protectors, but they protect a computer from overvoltages, undervoltages, and adverse noise conditions over electrical lines. A line conditioner monitors AC electricity. If the voltage is too low, the line conditioner boosts the voltage to the proper range. If the voltage level is too high, the line conditioner clamps down the voltage and sends the proper amount to the computer.

Power Failures

A **battery backup** provides AC power when power from the wall outlet fails, such as during a brownout or blackout. The power is provided by a battery within a unit. Two different types of battery backups are available for home and business computers and devices: uninterruptible power supplies (UPSs) and standby power supplies (SPSs).

UPS

A **UPS**, sometimes called an online, true, or line-interactive UPS, provides power to a computer or other device for a limited amount of time when there is a power outage. A UPS provides enough time to save work and safely shut down the computer. A network server is a great candidate for a UPS. Some UPS units have USB and/or network connections as well. Figure 19.14 shows the front and back of a UPS.

A UPS also provides power conditioning for the devices attached to it. The AC power is used to charge a battery inside the UPS. The battery inside the UPS supplies power to an inverter. The inverter makes AC for the computer. When AC power from the outlet fails, the battery inside the UPS continues to supply power to the computer. The battery inside the UPS outputs DC power, and the computer accepts (and expects) AC power. Therefore, the DC power from the battery must be converted to AC voltage. AC voltage looks like a sine wave when it is in its correct form, but cheaper UPSs produce a square wave that is not as effective. Figure 19.15 illustrates a sine wave and a square wave.

FIGURE 19.14 Front and back of a UPS

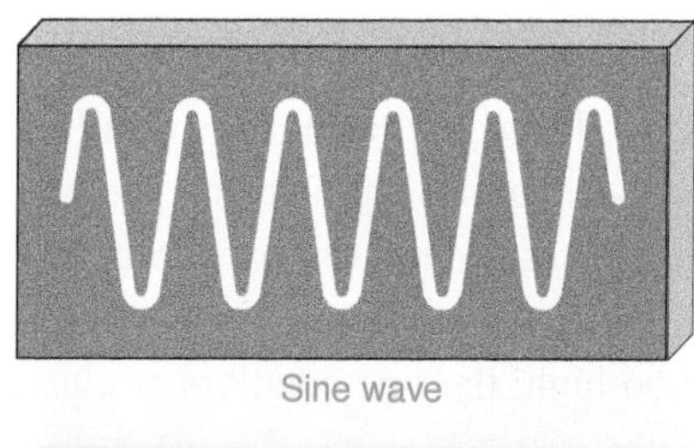

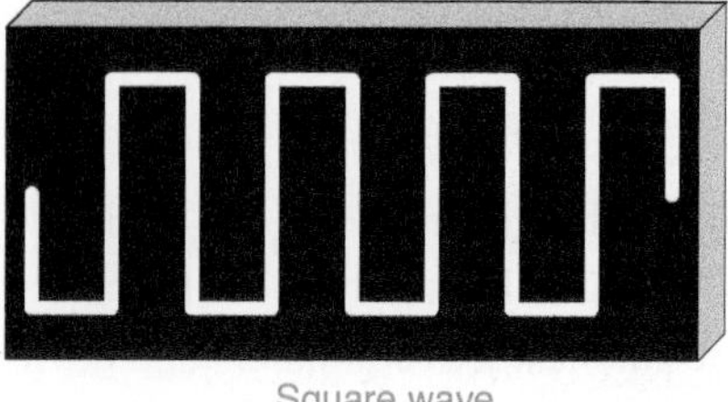

FIGURE 19.15 Sine wave and square wave

TECH TIP

Do not plug a laser printer into a UPS unless it has a rating less than 1400VA

Most UPSs cannot handle the very high current requirements of a laser printer. Other devices to avoid attaching to a UPS include space heaters, vacuums, curling irons, paper shredders, and copiers.

A UPS can provide the best protection against adverse power conditions because it protects against overvoltage and undervoltage conditions, and it provides power so a system can be shut down properly. When purchasing a UPS, be sure that the amount of battery time is sufficient; the amount of current the UPS produces is sufficient; and the output waveform is a sine wave.

A UPS has a battery inside that is similar to a car battery (except that the UPS battery is sealed). Because this battery contains acid, you should never drop a UPS or throw it in the trash. Research your state's requirements for recycling batteries. All batteries fail after some time, and most UPSs have replaceable batteries.

Standby Power Supply (SPS)

A device similar to a UPS is a standby power supply (SPS). Much like a UPS, an **SPS** contains a battery, but an SPS battery provides power to the computer only when it loses AC power. It might not provide constant power, as a UPS does. It might use a simulated sine wave. An SPS is not as effective as a UPS because the SPS must detect a power-out condition first and then switch over to the battery to supply power to the computer. As a result, SPS switching time is important. Any time under 5 milliseconds is fine for most systems. Figure 19.16 shows a CyberPower UPS that produces a simulated sine wave (which would be fine for a home system).

FIGURE 19.16 CyberPower UPS (simulated sine wave output)

Comparison of UPSs and SPSs

Sometimes it is difficult to discern between UPS and SPS products. Figures 19.17 and 19.18 show the differences between how some SPSs and UPSs work.

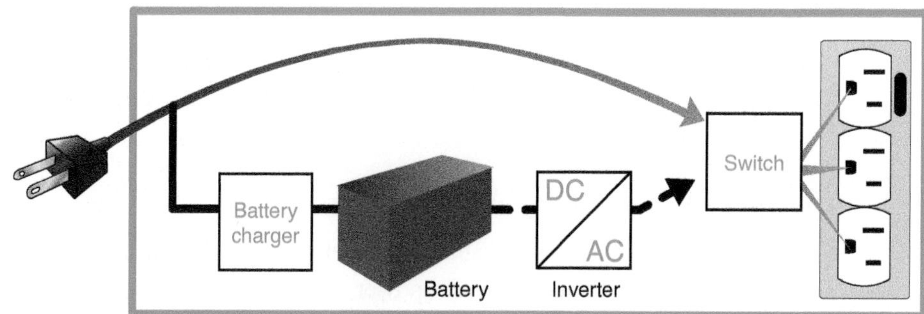

SPS/Line interactive UPS normal operation (solid line)

1. AC power is brought through the UPS.
2. The battery is charged simultaneously.
3. With some units, small over- or undervoltages are evened out before sending through the UPS.

SPS/Line interactive UPS abnormal power operation (dashed line)

1. When high voltage or large undervoltage for some units and with loss of power present in all units, DC power from the battery is sent to the inverter for as long as the battery lasts.
2. The DC power is converted to AC and provided to the attached devices.

FIGURE 19.17 SPS/line-interactive UPS operation

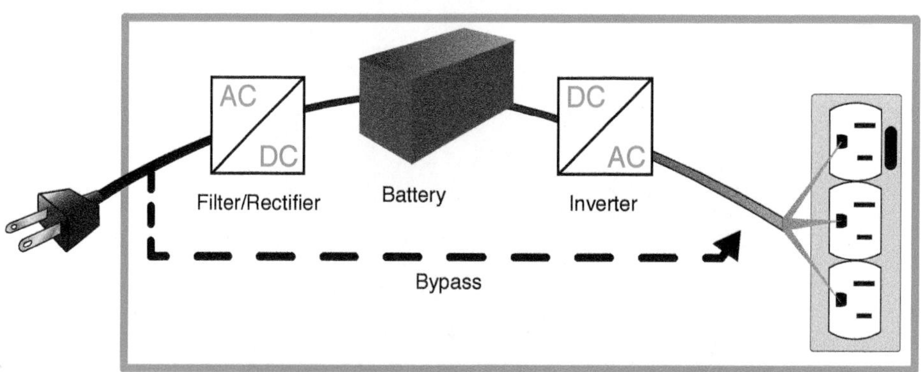

Online UPS normal operation (solid line)

1. AC power is brought into the UPS and cleaned up by the filter and converted to DC by the rectifier.
2. The battery is charged and outputs DC to the inverter.
3. The DC is converted to AC and provided to the attached devices.

Online UPS abnormal power operation (dashed line)

1. When the battery has died, the attached devices still receive power through the bypass circuit.

FIGURE 19.18 Online UPS operation

Protection Measures

Particulate matter (PM)—or airborne particle pollution—can be extremely detrimental to humans, causing respiratory problems. Make sure you always wear an air filter or mask when working in any environment where harmful airborne particles such as dust and debris are present. For **dust cleanup**, use a vacuum to remove PM where possible.

Some companies utilize an enclosure assembly for desktops or laptops to protect parts from PM or other hazardous conditions. Some vendors target the civilian market with similar "rugged" models or enclosures designed for youngsters. Figure 19.19 shows a computer case designed for a rugged environment.

Computer enclosures can also be purchased to protect equipment against impact or weather conditions. One or more air filters may be needed for a non-traditional computer area such as at a construction site. A kiosk (see Figure 19.20) is likely to contain a lockable area for the computer contained within.

FIGURE 19.19 Rugged industrial computer enclosure

FIGURE 19.20 Kiosk

Temperature and Humidity Control

Computers generate heat. It is best to look at the location for any computer or network equipment installation to ensure that it is safe and well ventilated. Computers and network equipment operate best in **temperatures** between 60 and 75 degrees. If you leave a laptop in a car and then bring it inside, allow the laptop time to adjust to the inside temperatures.

TECH TIP

A temperature that is comfortable for you is good for a computer, too

A good rule of thumb related to computer temperatures is that if you are comfortable in the room, the room is probably an appropriate temperature for the computer.

High levels of humidity can cause computer equipment to short-circuit because the moisture corrodes the contact points and interrupts connectivity. Low humidity increases the chance of a technician causing ESD and causing damage to electronics when handling them. Dust and debris abrade, plug, and smother connection points and retard or interrupt flow of electricity.

Proper **ventilation** is important for any electronic device. Check to make sure that a unit's fan is not blocked. Heat generated from an electronic device, if not properly ventilated, can cause overheating and damage to the unit. Refer to Chapter 5 for more information on temperature and humidity control.

IT Documentation

For IT personnel, technical skills are important, but written and oral communications skills are just as important. Although being able to write clearly is important when documenting what has been done in the IT department, it is not everyone's favorite thing to do (see Figure 19.21).

"Know what I call a technician
that doesn't document?
......unemployed"
BOB DOVER

FIGURE 19.21 Documentation is required of IT personnel

Every IT job requires documentation, and frequently this documentation is part of a standard operating procedure (**SOP**) that details what to do to complete a specific task such as the procedures and approvals that must be done for custom software to be installed. Here are some examples of IT documentation:

- Help desk personnel must log problems.
- PC repair technicians must document what was done for billing and historical purposes.
- Technicians of any type are required to close help desk problems with a written explanation of what was done.
- Updates to IT departmental documentation must be made in some instances.
- If an incident occurs, regulations or corporate policies may require documentation.

In order to understand common operational procedures related to documentation, let's look at the practices associated with several types of documentation:

> Network topology diagrams
> New user setup checklist
> Knowledge base/articles
> Incident documentation
> Regulatory and compliance policy
> Acceptable use policy
> Password policy
> Inventory management

Network Topology Diagrams

In addition to creating documentation, IT personnel must often update documentation. This might include using and updating **network topology diagrams** when moves, adds, or changes (MACs) are done, such as when someone changes cubicles or new personnel are due to arrive. A network topology diagram might be a high-level one, as shown in Figure 19.22, or a more granular drawing, as shown in Figure 19.23. Some network drawings are even more detailed and include port numbers, IP addresses, VLAN numbers, rooms and locations of access points, and so on.

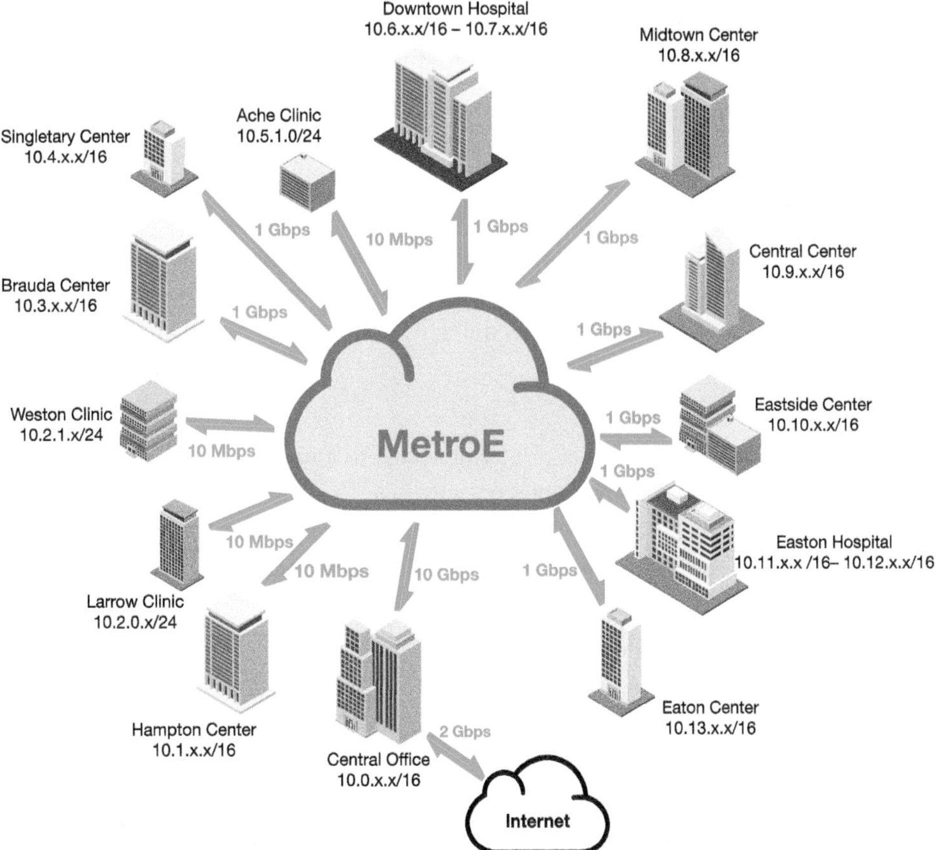

FIGURE 19.22 High-level network topology diagram example

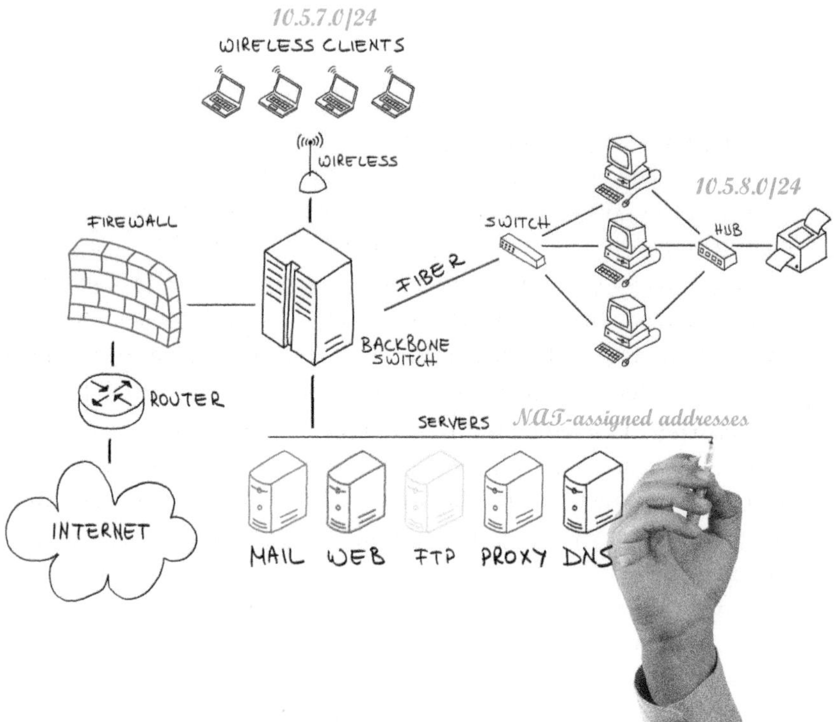

FIGURE 19.23 Detailed network topology diagram example

New User/Exiting User Checklist

Many companies have specific IT-related tasks that are completed for a new employee, for an employee who is leaving, or for an existing employee who is moving. These tasks might include delivering a newly imaged machine, receiving any previously issued equipment, or adding/removing a person's name and ID from the company directory, printers/copiers, phone directory, authentication database, and email server. When a new employee is assigned, a typical checklist includes the following:

> Office location
> Need for a local printer or access to a network one
> Need for any mobile devices
> Specialized software needed or customization of software
> Access to shared mailboxes, drives, or folders

Knowledge Base/Articles

A knowledge base is extremely helpful to a technician when solving a problem. A **knowledge base** is collection of documents with answers to commonly asked questions and solutions to common problems. Examples of information in a knowledge base include the following:

> How to reset an IP phone password
> How to request a wireless guest account
> How to report a spam or phishing incident
> How to configure a mobile device for email
> How to configure email with an out-of-office message
> How to do a web conference
> How to find and print to a network printer

A technician might copy information from a knowledge base document to send to a user or might directly send them a link to a document. Apple, Microsoft, and other IT vendors also have their own knowledge bases to support their hardware, operating systems, or applications.

Incident Documentation

Incident documentation is used when an IT problem is reported. Most companies use an incident management system, a help desk, or some type of ticketing software for this. It is critical for technicians to clearly and succinctly document a problem, update the problem with progress notes, and then document what was done to solve the problem for historical and billing purposes, and to help other technicians deal with the same problem or a similar problem at a later date. Ticketing systems commonly require user information, device information including location, and a description of the problem. Some companies use categories, such as servers or PC repair, so that problems get directed to the correct IT division. The software might also allow users to assign severity levels, and a technician might need to become familiar with how to escalate a problem and the different escalation levels. Common information contained in incident documentation is shown in Figure 19.24.

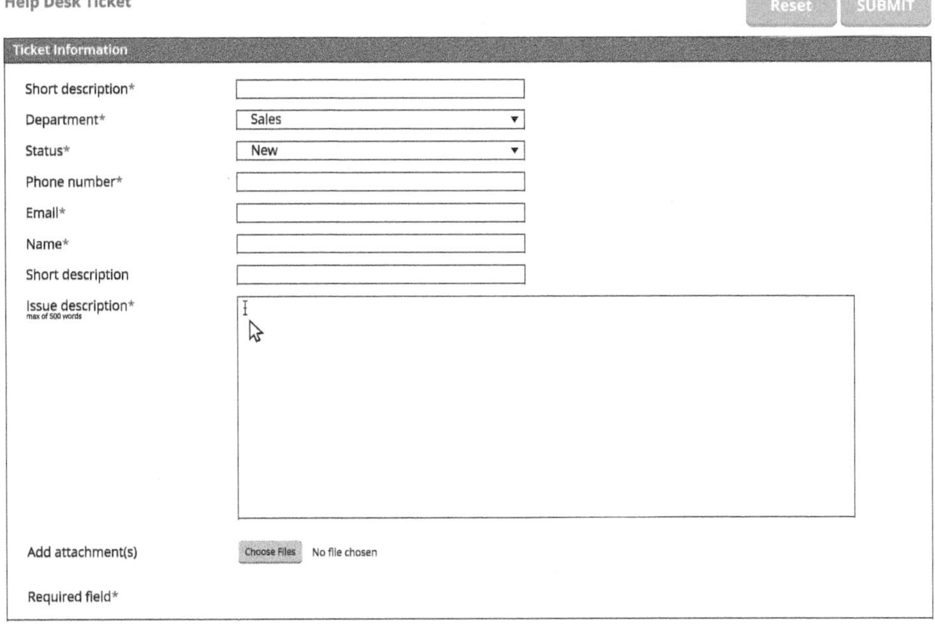

FIGURE 19.24 Help desk ticket example

At the end of a service call, a technician should provide the proper documentation on the services provided. This could include the following:

- Manuals
- Software or hardware boxes and materials that include proof of purchase, UPC codes, activation codes, registration numbers, and warranty information
- Invoice
- Research or information used in the repair that might benefit the customer
- Service ticket with details of work performed

Asset Management

IT personnel have to deal with new parts, computers, printers, and network devices all the time. It is important that you at least know what goes into getting those IT assets through the

procurement life cycle. It all starts with the planning process and defining what features are needed in a particular asset. That takes research. Then you set up a process for how you are going to evaluate and select a specific product, and a lot of times this is done in conjunction with the purchasing department. In medium-size to large companies, the purchasing department sends out quotation requests, and then a particular vendor is chosen and awarded a contract. Then comes the receiving/storage process, followed by delivery and implementation.

Many technicians do not like dealing with inventory management, but it is a fact of life in the IT department. Whenever any piece of hardware is moved, the move is commonly documented through an inventory management system. Some help desk software or a **database system** includes inventory management that allows printing or viewing of an **inventory list.** Whenever a technician moves or installs a new piece of gear, the technician must commonly enter an **asset tag** number, which is a unique ID or an asset ID, and the relevant technical details, such as a model number, serial number, and possibly a MAC address on a wireless device or printer. The system commonly shows the employee assigned and responsible for the hardware/software. It is also important to track **licensing** and **warranty** information as part of this process.

Inventory must be done regularly, typically once a year. Technicians are commonly asked to use a scanner to scan the barcode located on any item over a specified dollar amount, as shown in Figure 19.25. Items that cannot be found during the inventory period must be searched for and accounted for. Unfound items are placed on a report given to the executive leaders and board of directors; the report affects assets shown on the company balance sheet as well as net income on the income statement, and these write-offs can negatively affect both current employee bonuses and future capital budgets.

FIGURE 19.25 Technician doing inventory

Policies

Technicians may have to refer to specific policies in the normal course of their job or when issues arise. Four policies commonly relate to computer technicians. A technician does not need to know these policies verbatim but does need to know the gist of them and where to find them easily (see also Chapter 18, "Computer and Network Security"):

> **Password policy**: Even though users are presented with the information regarding the password policy when resetting a password, they commonly request technical assistance with the process.
> **Acceptable use policy** *(AUP)*: Any service or app used today will have an AUP, but businesses also have their own AUPs that define what is allowed to be used or done when connected to the corporate network or using company-owned hardware/software. Technicians need to be familiar with the AUP and should refer users to it when necessary.
> **Regulatory and compliance policy**: Every industry (for example, health care, manufacturing) has unique regulations and compliance policies. For example, you may see a **splash screen** that states the criteria for accessing a device, a service, or a website. A technician must be familiar with such policies because IT systems cross all departments within a company.
> **Security policy**: A security policy should outline what to do when a breach or an incident occurs, and it may include the AUP and password policy. Security policies are constantly being updated, and technicians should review them on a regular basis.

Change Management

The IT department, whether in-house or outsourced, is a key part of any business. It is very important that an IT department use **documented business processes** and continue to update the documentation related to those processes. The IT department is a constant source of change. The IT department should always plan for change instead of being reactive to situations. For example, servers that are on old hardware or that have outdated network operating systems are vulnerable to attacks and/or failure. Planning and executing their replacements is better than waiting for each piece of equipment to die.

Change management is an organized way of systematically choosing and implementing IT changes. A business may have a very complex system that includes software that helps the company stay informed about, document, and implement changes. A large company is likely to have a formal board that is known as a **change board**, change advisory board, software change control board, or change control board (CCB); whatever its name, this group makes decisions about which proposed changes are approved and implemented. Alternatively, a company may implement a basic system that involves just a formal check of the changes before they are implemented. One of the most important things to remember about change management is that everything feasible should be done to minimize the negative impact on the users, whether regarding time, system unavailability/reduced capabilities, security, or consequences that are avoidable.

The management cycle of any IT project commonly involves four steps (see Figure 19.26):

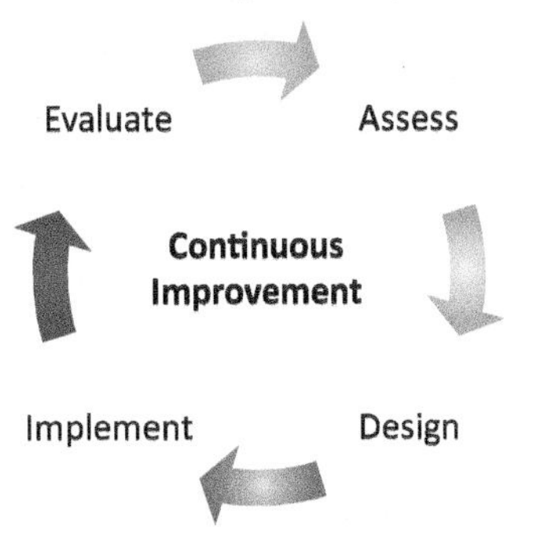

FIGURE 19.26 Management cycle

Step 1. *Assess:* Determine the **purpose of the change**. Why is the change needed? Which corporate strategic goal(s) does the plan align with? The change management process typically starts with a request form and a **risk analysis** to determine the risks involved and whether the benefits outweigh the risks.

IT risks are varied. Here are a few to consider:

- Costs associated with implementation compared to the benefits or potential gain/profits made
- Skills provided by outside vendors or internal staff
- Legal or compliance requirements
- Length of time an upgrade would prolong the life of a system or application vs. a new platform
- The amount of training and adjustment to new processes and procedures needed
- The amount of downtime

The output of a risk analysis is a **risk level** that can be a designation such as low, medium, or high or a numerical value with the lowest and highest values provided as a reference. Figure 19.27 shows a risk analysis where the value 1 is a proposed change that shows a low likelihood level, which means the risk is not very likely to occur often or to occur at all over a specific period of time, and the severity of the risk or the consequences of the risk are low. Compare this to a value of 25, which means the risk is most likely to occur often or constantly and have some painful consequences for the company.

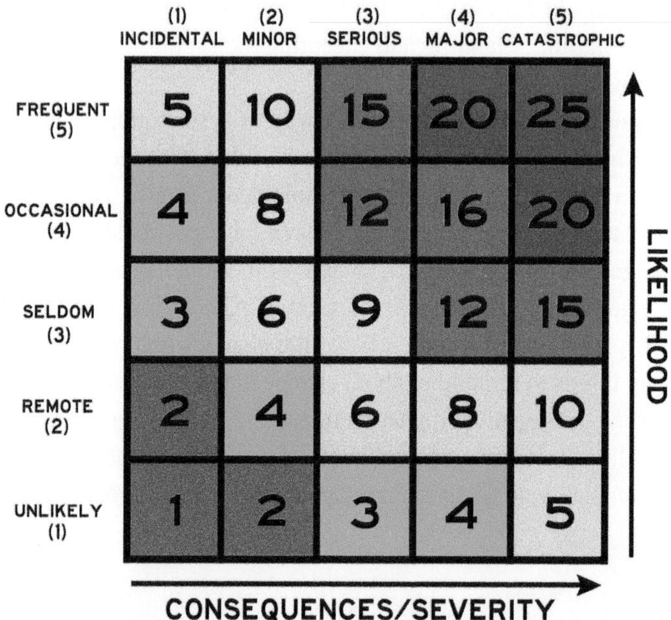

FIGURE 19.27 Sample risk analysis

Step 2. *Design:* Make a plan for the change and share that plan. What is the timeline? What resources are needed? Who will do what? Who is the responsible staff member or manager? Are parts needed? Which systems are affected? When will the change occur? What is the **scope of the change**? Defining limits of a project prevents project creep (that is, the tendency of a project to increase in complexity and depth). Project scopes include time, resources, money, deliverables, and acceptance criteria. Are other departments involved? If so, who is the contact person? Can the change be tested in a non-production environment (**sandbox testing**)? Can the change be piloted so it doesn't impact the company so much? Can **IT automation** help by delivering modifications to devices or applications without a human doing repetitive changes to multiple systems? What is the **rollback plan**, or at what step do things get reversed if the changes are not working? This might include testing backups in advance to ensure that they work before needing the backup. A rollback (sometimes called a backout) plan might be part of a document called a statement of work (SOW) that outlines all activities, deliverables, timelines, reporting structure, and quality checks.

Step 3. *Implement:* Execute the plan. Have meetings or establish an online method to share progress. **Document changes**. Correct any issues that are discovered. Have an **end-user acceptance** process in which the person who will be using the IT system verifies that it works appropriately.

Step 4. *Evaluate:* Ensure that each part of the plan was done properly. Document findings.

IT projects tend to be repetitive in nature in that a project that has been finished will have to be done again in the future; documentation and lessons learned are therefore very important. Part of the fun of being in IT is this constant change and the projects that need to be done. Many who go into the field of IT thrive on change.

SOFT SKILLS: SKILLS TO SUCCEED

The importance of good work habits cannot be stressed enough, no matter where you are or what situation you are in. Good communication skills are priceless. Let's explore some areas in which your job as a computer technician will involve good communication skills.

Customer Service

What comes to mind when you hear the two words *customer service*? Being of service to others is very rewarding, educational, and fun! You have the skills and training to be tops! Let Figure 19.28 inspire you as a computer technician.

FIGURE 19.28 Customer service inspiration

You can set the tone and instill assurance by being the confident, caring professional that you've trained to become. You know more about computer problems than the customers, and they are looking to you to solve their problems. You have many avenues of tracking down solutions. Don't be shy about tackling new things. Stretch yourself. Allow new situations to be learning opportunities. Step out of your comfort zone, as illustrated in Figure 19.29.

FIGURE 19.29 Comfort zone/opportunity

When you have been called in to fix a company's computer, have your ID badge visible. Introduce yourself and state your business. Some customers like to hover. Don't let that bother you. Reassure your customers that you are working diligently on their problem and taking care of them. Other clients will disappear, and you won't have any interaction with them the entire time you're working. Focus on the task at hand.

Proper Language

Always address customers by their title: Dr. Schmidt, Mr. Schmidt, Director Durrence, Miss Hannah, Your Honor, Officer Young, Professor Brauda, and so on. Most dictionaries have a section in the back that lists titles and proper forms of address. Mind your manners.

Grooming

Be neat, clean, and well groomed. Wear clean clothes and professional shoes. Wear properly fitting attire that will allow you to get in hard-to-reach places when needed (see Figure 19.30). If you are new to IT and unsure about attire, look again at the "Soft Skills" section of Chapter 10, "Mobile Devices," on appearance. Be sure to match your attire to the environment. Three common environments are formal (such as a board meeting), business casual (for everyday work), and casual (for dirty work, such as cleaning out a wiring closet).

Employ good hygiene. Wash your hands and brush your teeth. Carry breath mints. Do you have dandruff? Do you smoke? Did you just enjoy a spicy lunch? Do a self-check before meeting a customer to avoid offending anyone or embarrassing yourself or the customer (see Figure 19.31).

FIGURE 19.30 Dress appropriately

You are your most valuable asset. Take care of your body, mind, and spirit. Always have clean hands when handling someone else's property. If you use cologne, hair spray, perfume, or scented lotion or cosmetics, avoid using too much as some people have reactions to the smells.

FIGURE 19.31 Bad breath

Be Organized

Be able to flip open your case and pull out exactly the tool or paperwork that you need. Not only does being organized save time, frustration and, ultimately, money, it instills confidence in both your client and you. Rate yourself on organization skills (see Figure 19.32) and make organization a goal. Before going on a service call or calling a customer, have all the relevant parts, paperwork, tools, and so on organized and easy to locate. Pick up after yourself and leave the area at least as clean as it was before you arrived.

FIGURE 19.32 Organization measure

Use Proper Language

Use no slang, profanity, or jargon. Avoid acronyms. (An acronym is a group of words describing something, such as SATA.) Every profession/industry has its own vernacular, and you need to be conscious of using "geek speak" (see Figure 19.33). Be careful not to confuse or intimidate your customers.

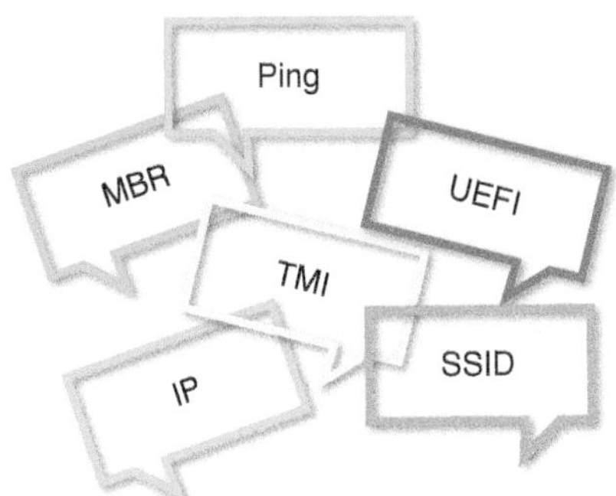

FIGURE 19.33 Avoid "geek speak"

Write your reports in complete sentences. Pay attention to the grammar suggestions within software. For software that doesn't provide corrections, type your message in a word processing application. Then, paste the text into the original software application.

Maintain a Positive Attitude and Project Confidence

Walk through the door with a purpose and a smile! Emphasize your customer's value with kindness, respect, and gratitude. Project confidence. The customer will be relieved to see you.

In many IT jobs, there is more work than time to do it. Technicians must constantly juggle to keep up with it all. Make sure you take allowed breaks and do non-technical things. Use a phone or a tablet to keep reminders for the day. If you are going to be late, call and let the customer know. Customers are often happy to rearrange their schedule and tasks to be available when a technician is coming. Courteous promptness will be rewarded.

Actively Listen

Listen attentively and maintain good eye contact. Avoid interrupting the customer. Don't assume anything (see Figure 19.34). Avoid finishing your customer's sentences to avoid seeming like you are rushing the customer. Make sure you are clear in what you are asking the user. Clarify their statements by asking open-ended questions to narrow the problem area, restate the issue, or further question them to verify you understand the issue. Open-ended questions such as "What were you doing on the computer when the problem occurred?" or "What made you think there was a problem? How did the computer act differently?" After the customer has explained the problem, repeat it back to him or her to make it clear that you both understand the situation.

"The hospital computer system has a virus.
Ironic, isn't it?"

FIGURE 19.34 Hatchet in monitor

Be Culturally Sensitive

Take the time to know your customers. Understand and accept that there will be differences among all people (see Figure 19.35), and it is not your place to judge. Be aware of things that you do that might be offensive to others. Be aware of any facial expressions, hand gestures, or body movements you tend to make that may be deemed offensive or insulting. If the customer is doing something that you find offensive, you can politely ask him or her to stop. For example, if someone feels compelled to tell you a joke or an anecdote that is degrading, belittling, or humiliating to another person, immediately and politely ask that person to stop. If the behavior continues, you could say, "I'm trying to do a professional job here, and I am offended by that."

FIGURE 19.35 Diversity

Be on Time

It is better to be 10 minutes early than 5 minutes late. If something causes you to be late in reaching your next appointment at the agreed time, call that customer as soon as possible. Customers commonly get angry when techs are late, so by calling ahead, you can give them time to adjust. If you have kept your customer waiting—whether on the phone or in person—apologize, ask if you may go ahead with the work, and thank the customer. Be gracious.

Time Management

Time management is how much time you budget and then actually spend on doing each task throughout the workday. IT personnel tend to have busy schedules (see Figure 19.36). Be aware of how you might improve your time management and the things that contribute to time management.

FIGURE 19.36 Time management

Always remember that you are a paid employee, and time is money to the company. If you encounter a chatty person, steer the customer toward talking about the problem at hand in a constructive way.

Avoid Distractions

Give your customer your undivided attention. Be in the moment. Here are some best practices:

- Turn off your cell phone or switch to vibrate mode so that you are not interrupted with personal or professional calls.

> Avoid looking at social media sites and doing any texting until you have finished with your customer.
> Avoid talking to coworkers while interacting with a client.
> Avoid gossiping.
> Avoid personal interruptions.
> Avoid checking your watch, drumming your fingers, yawning, rolling your eyes, sighing, and so on.

The most common customer complaints are that they feel ignored, not listened to or taken seriously, passed over or put aside, or kept waiting. Do what you can to ensure that you don't have any of these effects on your customers. Be pleasant and avoid being condescending. Avoid regaling your customers with stories of your personal life. This doesn't mean that small talk is off-limits. Just remember to keep it appropriate and professional. Remember that the customer is concerned about the immediate problem.

Don't Make Commitments You Can't Keep

Part of being professional is having integrity. Be business-like with clients and ensure that the subjects you talk about are relevant to the job. Even though the tone is light in Figure 19.37, the point is to be professional and take your job seriously. Do not be flippant.

"The computer repair people
take their job very seriously."

FIGURE 19.37 Be professional

It is much better to say, "I am not sure how long this will take [or cost]" or "I am not sure, but I can check on that for you and get back to you." Don't be afraid to call someone else for help. If you do not have time or abilities to fix a particular problem, ask another technician for help. Many companies have tiers of technical support.

Dealing with a Difficult Customer or Situation

When you are faced with an uncomfortable situation, above all remember to breathe deeply and slowly. It will give you a moment to think and compose yourself before you answer. Here are some suggestions for dealing with difficult customers:

> Let the customer talk.
> Make good eye contact and give physical affirmation cues (for example, nodding your head "yes").
> Do not ever tell someone to "calm down." That is akin to scoffing and saying, "You don't have a legitimate complaint." Telling someone to "calm down" is likely to increase the person's anger.
> Do not argue with a customer or be defensive. Remember that the customer has been stewing and fuming about this particular problem and wants to tell you every last detail about it. Listen to him or her and don't interrupt or try to finish sentences.
> Remind yourself that you have been trained in this field and are the expert. Don't dismiss the customer's problems. Acknowledge that he is understandably upset, frustrated, angry, and so on, and reassure him in a calm, steady voice that you are there to help.
> Avoid being judgmental.
> Be personable yet professional. Replies such as "I'll do my absolute best to help you" or "I'm sorry that this glitch has been so upsetting to you" or "Let's see what I can do for you" can go a long way toward defusing the situation. Let the client know that you have a hearty interest in her well-being—that you are genuinely concerned with helping.
> Be careful not to giggle or laugh inappropriately, or the customer may mistakenly think you are making fun of, belittling, or dismissing the problem.
> Avoid laughing constantly while talking. Some people do this—whether out of nervousness or habit—when engaged in conversation. Constant laughing could cause the other person to wonder what is so humorous about the situation.
> Always keep in mind what your customers want, need, and/or expect from you (or your company). Offer different repair/replacement options.
> Utilize resources that are available to you from which you can pull answers to solve the problem.
> Don't post work-related frustrations or experiences to social media sites.
> Go over and above the expected service.
> Pay attention to detail.

In order to keep the customer focused on the problem at hand, clarify customer statements by asking open-ended questions to narrow the scope of the problem; if necessary, restate the issue or ask questions to verify your understanding of the problem. Do not frustrate a customer who seems to have some technical skills. Feedback keeps the lines of communication open and flowing between you and nurtures the active work relationship that is so vital to good customer service (see Figure 19.38).

If someone is invading your space (getting too close for comfort), try stepping back a step. If the person steps in, raise a palm to give the indication to stop. If this does not work, stop what you are doing, look the person in the eyes, and politely ask him or her to give you more room. If someone is verbally abusive to you or even physically abusive, step back and raise a palm (refer to Figure 19.39). Prevent the situation from escalating by keeping your voice in an even, professional tone. You can always ask the person to take a short break or excuse yourself to take a moment. You have the right to a safe work environment.

FIGURE 19.38 Feedback

FIGURE 19.39 Stop what you are doing; stay back

Set and Meet Expectations

A customer usually wants to know when his computer will be fixed. If you must give an estimated repair time, estimate a little longer than you anticipate. That way, if you finish earlier than you expected, you'll both be happy! Discuss and offer different repair or replacement options, if applicable. Keep your customer informed of your progress. A small morsel of information from time to time helps quell the anxiety about an unknown situation ("Here's where we're at now…" or "Just checking in to let you know that…"). This type of response reassures the customer that you are actively working to fix the problem.

Deal Appropriately with Confidential and Private Materials

Discretion is another integral part of professionalism. Keep information private; for example, hard copies and faxed materials should be secured in folders—not spread around on a table for any passerby to read. Keep your own personal information private.

When working for a client, if you notice what seems to be sensitive information (for example, passwords taped somewhere, documents left in a printer, employee evaluations), it is best practice to ask the client to remove that information. Also, it is prudent to notify the client if you might have inadvertently seen sensitive information so that the client can take any necessary measures (for example, change the password). If you spot a bad security practice such as a password taped somewhere, take the opportunity to talk about security in today's environment.

Never discuss a customer's business or your professional matters with anyone—at a public venue, on social media, or even in off-hand conversation (see Figure 19.40).

FIGURE 19.40 Social network

Closing Remarks

No IT person is perfect. All you can do is strive to be the best professional possible. Try to do the right thing, be professional, be honest, and apologize if you are in the wrong, and people will recognize that you are doing the best you can. Keep learning. Even if you remain in the same job for some time, there will be new technologies and areas that you can improve upon.

Good luck to you in your IT profession! It is a wonderful field, and there are always opportunities to slide into something new. An inspiring quotation to leave you with comes from Vincent van Gogh: "Your profession is not what brings home your weekly paycheck. Your profession is what you're put here on earth to do with such passion and such intensity that it becomes spiritual in calling."

Chapter Summary

- Important safety items you should have in your technician kit are safety goggles, gloves, and a dust mask/air filter mask.
- Power issues include overvoltage conditions such as a surge or spike that can be managed with surge protectors, power conditioners, and UPSs. Power conditioners and UPSs help with undervoltage conditions such as sags. A UPS is the only device that powers a computer when a blackout occurs.
- Ensure that a surge protector has a Class A rating and adheres to the UL 1449 standard.
- Two types of battery backup are UPS and SPS.
- You have the right to expect a safe working environment. Federal government agencies such as OSHA and the EPA work hand in hand with state and local governments to regulate, enforce, and promote safe work practices—both for individuals and for the environment.
- A good computer technician knows how to recycle and/or dispose of electronic waste (specifically how to handle batteries, toner cartridges, CRT monitors, PCs, cell phones, and tablets) and understands the importance this makes to the health of humans and to the environment.
- Federal government agencies, such as OSHA and the EPA, work in tandem with state municipalities and local governments to monitor environmental impacts of toxic waste. Batteries, mobile devices, computers, and printers all contain toxic heavy metals. Most municipalities have electronic waste recycling/disposal toxic waste handling sites. Never attempt to dispose of any toxic electronic waste by burning it. Never crush or puncture any device that contains a battery as doing so can cause leakage of heavy metals or chemicals.
- IT documentation is an important part of any IT staff member's job and is used for reference and sometimes requires updating.
- Change management is a requirement for documented business processes within IT. A risk analysis should be done as part of the change management process to determine if the change is worth the risk of implementation. A rollback plan should also be part of any IT project.
- Proper communication and positive interaction with customers are required of IT professionals. Use no profanity, street-talk, or slang. Address a customer by using their title and surname.
- Attentiveness to customers means making good eye contact, listening actively, avoiding interrupting or finishing the customer's sentences, and taking detailed notes.
- Keep personal business and activities out of the workplace.
- Hygiene, appearance, manners, and confidence are important traits to possess.
- Look, act, dress, and think like a professional, and you will be a professional.

A+ CERTIFICATION EXAM TIPS

- ✓ Be cognizant of personal safety techniques and issues, including removing power before working on a PC, being careful while lifting and minding weight limitations, taking measures to promote and know electrical fire safety, and using an air filter mask and/or safety goggles when appropriate. Be sure to comply with all local government regulations.
- ✓ Know the purpose of MSDS and the documentation associated with handling or disposal of materials. Also be familiar with temperature, humidity, and ventilation requirements for electronic equipment. Be cognizant of where to place equipment with these requirements in mind. Clean up dust and used compressed air and a vacuum when needed.
- ✓ Compare equipment needed for power surges, brownouts, and blackouts, including battery backup options and surge suppressors.
- ✓ Explain equipment grounding and be familiar with proper component and power handling, including the use of self-grounding techniques, antistatic bags, ESD straps, and ESD mats. Be familiar with government safety regulations.
- ✓ Describe environmental impacts and local environmental controls specifically for batteries, toner, and other devices/assets such as PC hardware, CRTs, cell phones, and tablets.
- ✓ Be familiar with and know when to use the following types of documentation: network topology diagrams, knowledge base articles, incident documentation, regulatory and compliance policy, acceptable use policy, regulatory compliance requirements that may include splash screens, incident reports, and standard operating procedures (which may also include standard things, such as a new user or user termination setup list, and things that are not so standard, such as the requirements for a custom software package installation).
- ✓ Be familiar with how asset management and the procurement life cycle relate to IT, including inventory lists, a database system, asset tags/IDs, barcodes, assigned users, and warranty and licensing information.
- ✓ Be familiar with IT ticketing systems and the information that is entered or provided to IT staff: user, device, problem description, category, severity, and escalation levels. Be sure to use clear and concise information when documenting a problem, including progress notes and the resolution.
- ✓ Be able to describe best practices related to documentation and change management. As part of the change management process, describe the purpose of the change, the scope of the change, and a plan for the change. Include a risk analysis and provide a risk level to determine whether the change is worth the business risk. The change implementation might include sandbox testing to lower the risk factor. Include end-user acceptance testing as part of the plan. Documentation should include a rollback plan and information on the changes implemented.
- ✓ The change management process may include a change board that determines whether an IT change is approved. A document that might be created in the change management process is a SOW, which outlines the purpose and scope of the plan, affected systems and impact on the company, responsibilities, responsible staff member, due dates, and a rollback plan.
- ✓ Communication techniques and key areas of professionalism include the following: dress appropriately for the job and situation (whether in formal or business casual attire); use proper language; maintain a positive attitude; project confidence; actively listen; avoid interrupting the customer; be culturally sensitive; use appropriate titles; be on time; avoid distractions; be able to deal with a difficult customer or situation (don't argue or be defensive, don't be dismissive regarding the problem, avoid being judgmental); clarify customer statements with open-ended questions; set and meet expectations; communicate the status with the customer; and deal appropriately with customers' confidential and private information.
- ✓ At this point, you've learned every topic that is covered on the CompTIA A+ exams. Now you should take time to specifically prepare for the certification exams and get the professional credentials you have earned. Refer to the Introduction to this book for details on the 220-1101 and 220-1102 CompTIA A+ exams, including how to sign up for them. And note that Pearson, the publisher of this book, is offering you an exclusive deep discount on several types of certification exam preparation resources. See the Introduction to this book and the advertisement inserts in the back for more details. Take a look at what Pearson has to offer and figure out which resource(s) would work best for your study style. Good luck!

Key Terms

acceptable use policy 999
air filtration mask 980
antistatic bag 984
asset tag 998
battery backup 989
blackout 987
brownout 987
change board 999
change management 999
compressed air 980
database system 998
document changes 1001
documented business processes 999
dust cleanup 992
electrical fire safety 979
end-user acceptance 1001
equipment grounding 986
ESD mat 985
ESD strap 985
humidity 984
incident documentation 997
inventory list 998
IT automation 1001
knowledge base 996
licensing 998
lifting technique 981
line conditioner 989
MOV 987
MSDS 979
network topology diagram 995
OSHA 979
overvoltage 986
password policy 999
power surge 986
procurement life cycle 998
purpose of the change 1000
regulatory and compliance policy 999
risk analysis 1000
risk level 1000
rollback plan 1001
safety goggles 980
sandbox testing 1001
scope of the change 1000
security policy 999
self-grounding 985
SOP 994
splash screen 999
SPS 991
surge suppressor 987
temperature 993
time management 1007
toner 984
Type A-B-C fire extinguisher 979
Type C fire extinguisher 979
undervoltage 986
UPS 989
vacuum 980
ventilation 994
warranty 998

Review Questions

1. You are working in an area that has multiple cubicles with multiple PCs. You see smoke coming from the laser printer in the area where you are working. You pull the fire alarm, tell everyone to leave (and they do), and grab the fire extinguisher. Now what do you do?
   a. Push the lever to engage or activate the pump inside the extinguisher.
   b. Pull out the fire extinguisher pin.
   c. Aim the nozzle at the printer.
   d. Squeeze the handle and slowly move the nozzle back and forth.
2. Which IT documentation would a technician need to refer to when connecting a redundant link between two switches?
   [incident documentation | regulatory and compliance policy | security policy | network topology drawing]
3. On which piece of device would a PC technician most likely see a grounding wire?
   [patch panel | air vent | wiring rack | laser printer]
4. A company is implementing new payroll software. The project manager has outlined the scope of the project, responsibilities, due dates, and quality assurance checkpoints. What is missing from this plan?
   [end-user acceptance | network topology diagrams | backup testing | backout plan]
5. A computer technician's repair kit should always include which of the following?
   a. Pen, paper, ID badge
   b. Soap, toothbrush, toothpaste
   c. Surge suppressor, laptop enclosure case, resealable antistatic bags
   d. Safety glasses/goggles, gloves, dust mask/air filtration mask
6. Which UL rating and surge suppressor grade would be best when ordering new surge strips for a small business? (Choose two.)
   [UL 497 | UL 1283 | UL 1449 | Class A | Class B | Class C]
7. Which part of the change management cycle would include an evaluation of whether a particular IT change is worth implementing?
   a. Plan scope
   b. Risk analysis
   c. Backup plan
   d. Plan purpose
8. What is a safety risk related to old or damaged batteries?
   a. They can leak acid.
   b. They can contain lead.
   c. They can contain water.
   d. All sizes are interchangeable.
9. Equipment grounding means which of the following?
   a. The equipment is tethered to a desk.
   b. The components in a computer are all the same voltage potential.
   c. The technician wears a tether device.
   d. Someone could receive a shock or be electrocuted from simply touching the case.

10. Which method is best for cleaning up scattered laser toner particles?
    a. Use a hair dryer to blow away the residue.
    b. Use moist paper towels to wipe up particles.
    c. Use your shirt sleeve to make them disappear.
    d. Use a vacuum cleaner equipped with a HEPA filter.
11. In what two situations would it be most appropriate for an IT technician to wear business casual attire instead of formal attire? (Choose two.)
    a. When going to a business to repair a PC
    b. When meeting with the chief information officer (CIO) regarding an idea you had for saving money in the department
    c. When presenting the latest departmental statistics on downtime and escalations to the VP of business affairs
    d. When attending a virtual meeting of the change management board regarding an upcoming project
    e. When representing the company at a local business event
12. What is the best way to dispose of mobile devices, PCs, monitors, toner, and batteries?
    a. Burn them in bonfires.
    b. Dump them in landfills.
    c. Deposit them in a local municipality-approved receptacle.
    d. Call 911.
13. In the event of an electrical fire, which two fire extinguishers would be best? (Choose two.)
    a. Type A fire extinguisher
    b. Type B fire extinguisher
    c. Type C fire extinguisher
    d. Type D fire extinguisher
    e. Type A-B-C fire extinguisher
14. A device that protects electronic equipment from an increase in power but not a decrease or outage is a _____.

    [battery backup | surge suppressor | CRT | UPS]
15. When encountering a difficult or confrontational customer, the best thing to do initially is which of the following?
    a. Step back and take a few deep breaths before responding.
    b. Call a supervisor.
    c. Suggest a short break.
    d. Reschedule the appointment.
16. [T | F] Federal, state, and local governments do not interact with one another concerning toxic waste issues.
17. Which safety measure would be helpful in a network wiring closet that is filled with particulate matter (PM) and that is being cleaned for the first time in years as the cabling is reorganized?
    a. air filtration mask
    b. HEPA vacuum
    c. compressed air
    d. UL 1449 device

18. Laser toner cartridges _____.
    a. are easily recycled anywhere
    b. can be donated to charities
    c. can be refilled many times
    d. must be disposed of in approved regulated waste receptacles
19. A user has requested help converting a Word document to PDF. Which of the following IT documentation types would a technician use in this case?
    [security policy | inventory management | article | network topology diagram | acceptable use policy]
20. Which two items would be used as part of inventory management? (Choose two.)
    [asset tag | flatbed scanner | incident documentation | barcode | AUP]

Exercises

Exercise 19.1 Determining a Power Solution

Objective: To be able to determine the proper power solution for a particular situation

Procedure: Match one of the power solutions to each situation. Note that a particular solution may be the answer for more than one situation.

Power solutions

a. Surge suppressor
b. Power conditioner
c. UPS
d. SPS

Situations

____ A company has a very old building that has one corporate division. The company suspects a power issue in the lowest room because the three PCs located there continually reset.

____ A particular network rack has a switch that is used to connect to every executive on a single floor. The president of the company has requested that these executives' computers remain powered as long as possible, even when power to the building is lost.

____ A home tower computer has two monitors, powered speakers, and a printer attached, and it needs to be protected from an overvoltage condition.

____ A cubicle in a company has only two outlets. The cubicle contains a thin client computer, a monitor, and an IP phone.

____ An entrepreneur has a home office with a server that stores all company data, a PC, three monitors, and a printer. The owner wants to be protected in over- and undervoltage situations with clean power to all devices.

____ A gamer would like to have power provided even when power to the house is lost but does not want the cost of a UPS.

Exercise 19.2 Determining the Type of Documentation Needed

Objective: To be able to determine which type of documentation is needed in a particular situation

Procedure: Match one of the documentation types to each situation. Note that only one documentation type matches each situation.

Documentation types

a. Network topology diagram

b. Knowledge base/articles

c. Incident documentation

d. Regulatory and compliance policy

e. Security policy

f. Inventory management

Situations

____ A technician has solved a problem that required reloading a computer due to a virus infection.

____ A technician has moved a barcoded network printer to a newly created divisional copy room.

____ A technician is responding to a complaint about wireless connectivity in a particular area. The technician needs to know how many access points are in the area and the coverage area.

____ A technician working in a hospital notices that a computer is displaying private patient health information.

____ A person calls the help desk because of a problem with changing the domain password. The technician needs to know the company's exact password requirements.

____ A technician needs to connect an IP phone and needs to know which switch port has been programmed for the appropriate phone VLAN.

Activities

Internet Discovery

Objective: To obtain specific information on the internet regarding administrative procedures

Parts: Computer with internet access

Questions: Use the internet to answer the following questions.

1. Research how to dress professionally for your job. Write three things that impressed you the most about the advice given and whether you found the website helpful or confusing. Write the URL where the information was found.

   ____

   ____

2. Locate at least two videos of poor technician interaction/service with customers. Compare with the lessons in this book and write how the techs in the videos could improve their skills.

   ____

   ____

   ____

   ____

   ____

3. Research at least two local municipalities that have approved regulated sites for recycling and disposal of computer and electronic equipment. List what they advise for their communities. Describe differences in their regulations. List the URL for each municipality.

4. Research electrical fire safety videos. Combine the information from this book with what you learn from the fire safety videos. Document what new things were shown. How confident are you that you could extinguish an electrical fire? List the URL where your information was found.

5. Research at least five healthy things you could do for yourself every day. Decide which ones you'd like to implement. List the URLs where your information was found.

Flip the CLASSROOM

Soft Skills

Objective: To enhance and fine-tune a future technician's ability to listen, communicate in both written and oral forms, and support people who use computers in a professional manner.

Activities:

1. Refine your customer skills by play-acting situations with another student. One student should take the role of the technician, and the other should take the role of the customer. Instead of asking "Did you do _________?" ask "When did you do _________?" "What happened when you did ________?" or "When did you first notice _______?" Rate each other, using positive words. You can give negative feedback but do it in a positive manner. For example, if the person spoke in a low tone, but the words were good, you might give the following feedback: "Your explanation was very good, but I had a hard time hearing you. You might want to speak up just a bit louder."
2. Hone your job interviewing skills by practicing with another student. Be prepared with questions about the company with which you are seeking employment. Think ahead to what questions a prospective employer might ask you.

3. In a group with other students, inspect the fire extinguisher in the room and then research electrical fire safety. After becoming familiar with fire safety signs and exit routes for the classroom, create a scenario to demonstrate fire safety. Produce an escape route, act out the scenario, and present an escape route drawing to the rest of the class.
4. Build a virtual wardrobe appropriate for your future job. Research websites and record in a professionally formatted document descriptions of the garments you would choose. Don't forget accessories such as shoes, hats, purses/briefcases, computer bags, and so on. Share and discuss with other students why you chose specific items. Provide feedback to other students on their choices. Optionally place your findings in a presentation to be shared with others.

Critical Thinking Skills

Objective: To analyze and evaluate information as well as apply learned information to new and different situations.

Activities:

1. Break into groups of three students. Each group receives a box containing a laser toner, an old cell phone, and a battery. Research local municipality regulations regarding recycling and/or disposal of electronic waste. Present findings to the class. Aggregate all groups' findings in table form. Offer to share with the school.
2. Engage in conversation the number of friends/acquaintances specified by your instructor. Ask about and record specific problems they encounter with their mobile devices and laptops. What problem occurs most? What new problems were presented that were unfamiliar to you? What solutions would you offer to these people? Record all your data in table form and present it to the class.
3. Divide into groups of three or four students. As a group, consider the following information: A local veterans' home has 100 computers and 10 printers; 96 computers and 8 printers are used by the staff, 4 computers and 2 printers are used by the veterans. The computers and printers used by the veterans experience a high rate of downtime. Think of different reasons the veterans' computers and printers might be frequently nonfunctional. Offer at least three solutions to improve the situation.

____
____
____
____
____
____
____
____

4. Prepare a change management plan for any of the solutions proposed in Question 3.
5. Use the internet to locate a video that features a technician using poor communication skills. List things that were recommended in this chapter that were not addressed in the video or that the technician could have handled differently.

____
____
____

6. Find current news stories that feature safety issues related to technology.

____
____

A Subnetting Basics

In business, the subnet mask assigned to a device commonly is not the default mask based on the class of IP address being used. For example, at a college, the IP address 10.104.10.88 and subnet mask 255.255.255.0 are assigned to a computer. The 10 in the first octet shows that this is a class A IP address. A class A IP address has a default mask of 255.0.0.0. The 255 in the subnet mask is made up of eight 1s in binary in the first octet (11111111) followed by all 0s in the remaining octets (00000000.00000000.00000000).

The purpose of a subnet mask is to tell you (and the network devices) which portion of the IP address is the network part. The rest of the address is the host portion of the address. The network part of any IP address is the same 1s and 0s for all computers on the network. The rest of the 1s and 0s can change and be unique addresses for the network devices on the same network. The following important rules relate to subnetting:

- The network number *cannot* be assigned to any device on the network.
- The network number contains all 0s in the host portion of the address. Note that this does not mean that the number will be 0 in decimal (as explained next).
- The broadcast address (the number used to send a message to all devices on the network) *cannot* be assigned to any device on the network.
- The broadcast address contains all 1s in the host portion of the address. Note that this does not mean that the number will be 255 in decimal.

Consider the IP address and mask used in the earlier example: 10.104.10.88 and 255.255.255.0. Put these numbers in binary, one number on top of the other, to see the effects of the subnet mask:

```
   10         104        10         88
00001010.01101000.00001010.01011000
11111111.11111111.11111111.00000000
```

The 1s in the subnet mask show which bits in the top row are the network part of the address. The subnet mask is always a row of consecutive 1s. Where the 1s stop is where the network portion of the address stops. Keep in mind that this does not have to be where an octet stops, as in this example. A good technique is to draw a line where the 1s in the subnet mask stop, as shown in the example that follows:

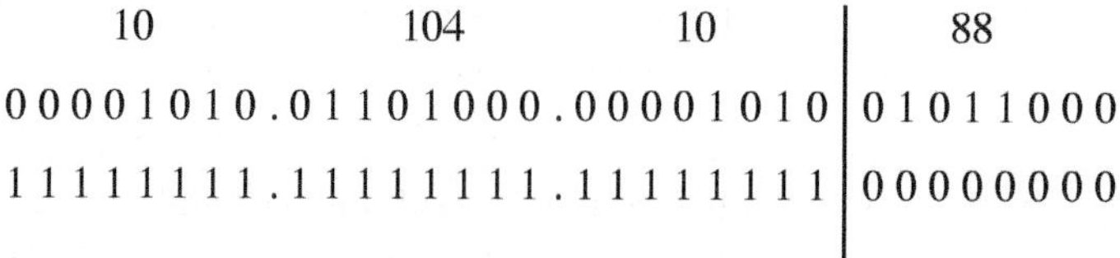

TECH TIP

Subnet mask in prefix notation

Subnet masks in network documentation are commonly shown in prefix notation, using a slash with the number of consecutive 1s found in the subnet mask. For example, 10.104.10.88 255.255.255.0 can be shown as 10.104.10.88/24, and 192.168.10.213/27 is the same as a 255.255.255.224 subnet mask.

At this point, there is no other purpose for the subnet mask. You can get rid of it, as shown in the example that follows:

10 104 10 | 88
00001010.01101000.00001010 | 01011000

All 1s and 0s to the left of the drawn line are the network portion of the IP address. All devices on the same network will have this same combination of 1s and 0s up to the line. All 1s and 0s to the right of the drawn line are in the host portion of the IP address:

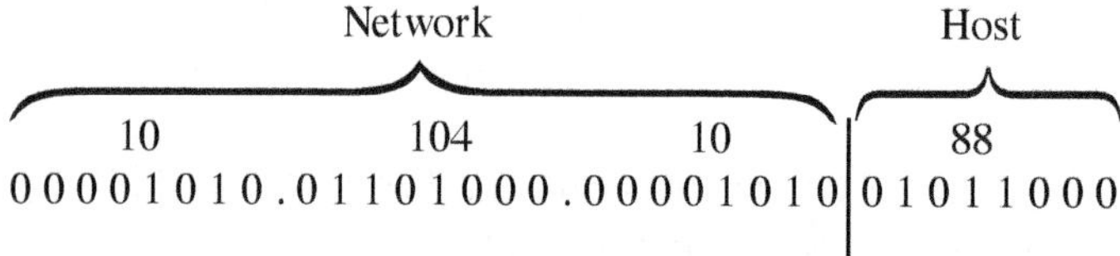

The network number—the IP address used to represent an entire single network—is found by setting all host bits to 0. The resulting number is the network number:

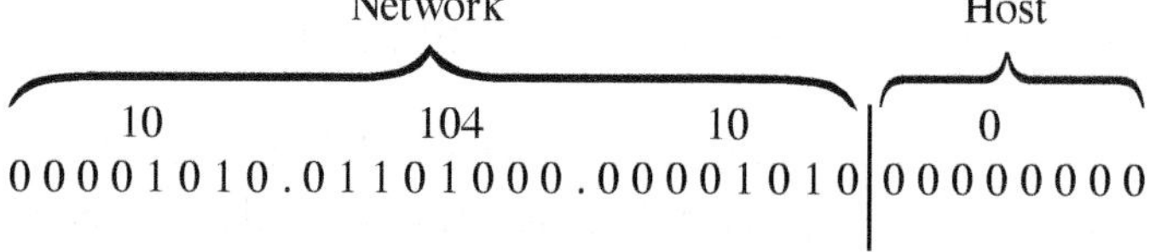

The network number for the network device that has the IP address 10.104.10.88 is 10.104.10.0. To find the broadcast address, the IP address used to send a message to all devices on the 10.104.10.0 network, set all the host bits to 1:

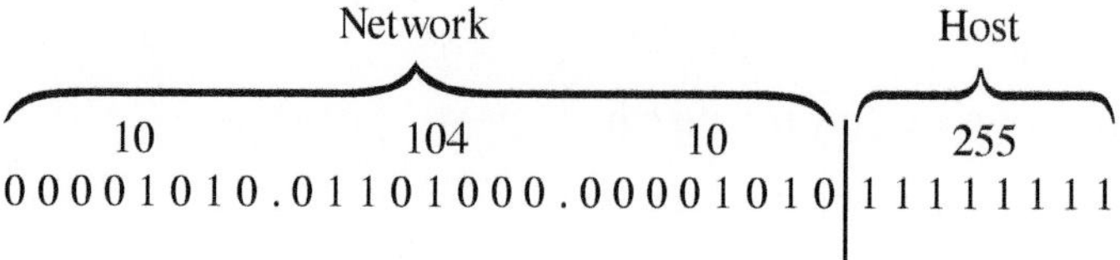

The broadcast IP address is 10.104.10.255 for the 10.104.10.0 network. This means that hosts can be assigned any addresses between the network number 10.104.10.0 and the broadcast address 10.104.10.255. Another way of stating this is that IP addresses 10.104.10.1 through 10.104.10.254 are usable IP addresses on the 10.104.10.0 network.

Consider the IP address 192.168.10.213 and the subnet mask 255.255.255.224 assigned to a computer in a college. What would be the network number and broadcast address for this computer? To find the answer, write 192.168.10.213 in binary octets. Write the subnet mask in binary under the IP address:

```
   192        168        10        213
11000000.10101000.00001010.11010101
11111111.11111111.11111111.11100000
```

Now draw a line where the 1s in the subnet mask stop:

```
   192        168        10        213
11000000.10101000.00001010.110|10101
11111111.11111111.11111111.111|00000
```

Remove the subnet mask because it is not needed anymore:

```
   192        168        10        213
11000000.10101000.00001010.110|10101
```

Set all host bits to 0 to find the network number:

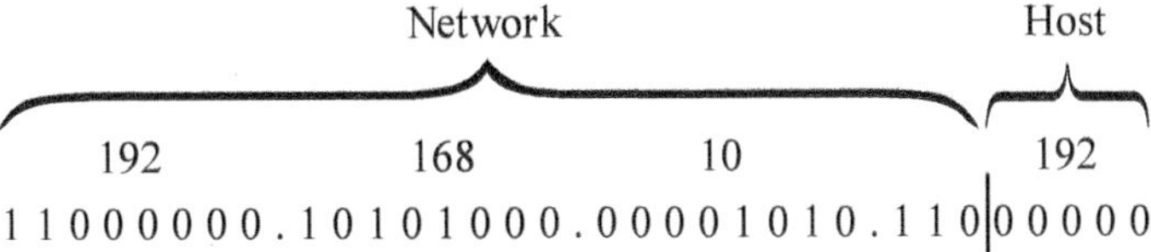

The network number for the network device that has IP address 192.168.10.213 is 192.168.10.192. To find the broadcast address, set all host bits to 1:

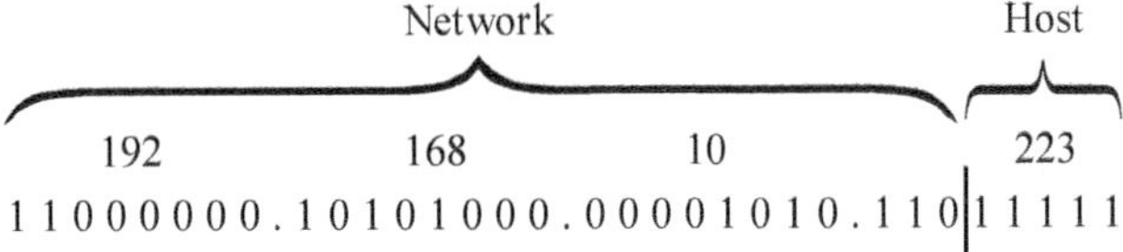

The broadcast address for the network device that has the IP address 192.168.10.213 is 192.168.10.223. Notice how all eight bits are used to calculate the number 223 in the last octet. Valid IP addresses are any numbers between the network number 192.168.10.192 and the broadcast IP address 192.168.10.223. In other words, the range of usable IP addresses is from 192.168.10.193 (one number larger than the network address) through 192.168.10.222 (one number less than the broadcast address). Practice problems in the following exercise help you explore this concept.

Exercise

Exercise A.1 Subnet Practice Exercise

Objective: To be able to determine the subnet number, broadcast address, and IP addresses that can be assigned to network devices

Procedure: Complete the following procedures and answer the accompanying questions.

1. Determine the network address for each of the following IP address and subnet mask combinations.

   210.141.254.122 255.255.255.192

   ___

   206.240.195.38 255.255.255.224

   ___

   104.130.188.213 255.255.192.0

   ___

   69.89.5.224 255.240.0.0

   ___

   10.113.71.66 255.128.0.0

   ___

2. Determine the broadcast address for the following IP address and subnet mask combinations.

   166.215.207.182 255.255.255.240

   ___

   198.94.140.121 255.255.255.224

   ___

   97.57.210.192 255.255.224.0

   ___

   133.98.227.36 255.255.192.0

   ___

   14.89.203.133 255.128.0.0

   ___

3. Determine the valid IP addresses on the networks that contain the following IP address and subnet mask combinations.

   131.107.200.34 255.255.248.0

   ___

   146.197.221.238 255.255.255.192

   ___

   52.15.111.33 255.255.248.0

   ___

   192.168.10.245/30

   ___

   209.218.235.117 255.255.255.128

   ___

Glossary

Numerals and Symbols

.. (navigation command) At a Windows command prompt, a representation of the parent directory.

+12V A voltage level from the power supply that is used for drive motors, CPU, internal cooling fans, and the graphics card.

+5V A voltage level from the power supply that is used for electronics, the motherboard, adapters, ports, and peripherals.

1.8-inch drive A storage device form factor.

115V vs. 220V input voltage The voltage level accepted from an electrical outlet. Some power supplies accept 120V (listed as 115V on the certification), and others accept 220V power from an electrical outlet.

10,000 RPM A hard drive speed. The faster the drive RPM, the faster the transfer rate.

15,000 RPM A hard drive speed. The faster the drive RPM, the faster the transfer rate.

2G/3G/4G/5G Types of cellular networks shown by generation, with 5G being the latest generation type.

2.4 GHz A frequency commonly used for 802.11 wireless networks.

2.5-inch drive A storage device form factor.

20-pin to24-pin motherboard adapter A device that connects an older power supply to an ATX motherboard.

24-pin motherboard connector The main ATX motherboard power connector.

3.3V A common desktop power supply output voltage.

3.5-inch drive A storage device form factor.

3-2-1 backup A type of backup that involves creating three copies of the data (one primary and two copies) using two different types of media and keeping at least one copy off site.

3-D printer A type of printer used to create 3-D solid objects out of various materials, including plastic, metal, clay, and ceramics.

32-bit architecture A standard that supports CPU processing or the movement of data up to 32 bits at one time.

3G The third generation of wireless cellular technology, which allowed mobile devices to have faster internet connectivity.

4-pin 12V A power supply connector that is sometimes labeled AUX or 12V and used to provide extra power to the processor.

4G The fourth generation of cellular technology, which supports IP telephony, gaming services, mobile TV, and video conferencing at speeds up to 1 Gb/s.

5 GHz A frequency commonly used for 802.11 wireless networks.

5,400 RPM A hard drive speed. The faster the drive RPM, the faster the transfer rate.

568A/B An ANSI/TIA/EIA Ethernet network cabling standard.

5G The fifth generation of cellular network technology that supports speeds up to 10 Gb/s.

6-pin PCIe A power supply connector used to provide power to a video adapter.

64-bit architecture A standard that allows CPU processing or the movement of data up to 64 bits at one time.

7,200 RPM A hard drive speed. The faster the drive RPM, the faster the transfer rate.

8-pin PCIe A power supply connector used to provide power to a video adapter.

802.11a An IEEE wireless standard that used the 5 GHz range and had speeds up to 54 Mb/s.

802.11ac (Wi-Fi 5) An IEEE wireless standard that uses the 5 GHz range and supports speeds up to 4.9 Gb/s.

802.11ad A wireless standard that works in the 60 GHz range and is also known as WiGig.

802.11ax (WiFi 6) A wireless standard that uses the 2.4, 5, and 6 GHz ranges, improves wireless connectivity and throughput, and is backward compatible with older 2.4 and 5 GHz devices.

802.11b The first IEEE wireless standard to hit the market; used the 2.4 GHz range and supported speeds up to 11 Mb/s.

802.11e A wireless quality of service standard.

802.11g An IEEE wireless standard that was an upgrade to 802.11b and was backward compatible with it; used the 2.4 GHz range and had speeds up to 54 Mb/s.

802.11i A wireless security standard.

802.11n An IEEE wireless standard that uses both the 2.4 and 5 GHz ranges and that supports speeds up to 600 Mb/s.

A

A record A DNS address record, which holds the IPv4 address of a particular web address.

AAA server A server used in a corporate environment that is used to verify credentials such as a username and password.

AAAA record A DNS record that holds the IPv6 address of a particular website.

A/V (audio/video) A reference to sound and visual data, such as movies or stills.

AC (alternating current) The type of electrical power from a wall outlet.

AC circuit tester A device that checks a wall outlet's wiring.

acceptable use policy (AUP) A policy that defines rules regarding using a company network, data, and a specific application.

access control list (ACL) A list of the permissions for a specific object (such as a file or directory), such as what is allowed to be done to the object by particular users or operating system processes. An ACL provides a security filter where traffic is allowed or denied based on configured parameters.

access control vestibule A method of separating a nonsecure area from a secure area to prevent unauthorized access and tailgating. Also known as a mantrap.

access point (AP) A component of a wireless network that accepts associations from wireless network cards.

account recovery option An option used when a Microsoft account or password has been forgotten.

account settings Settings required when putting a thick client or thin client onto a network.

ACL See *access control list.*

ACPI (Advanced Configuration and Power Interface) Technology that allows the motherboard and operating system to control the power needs and operation modes of various devices.

activation clock A timer for the Windows operating system. When creating an image, a technician must reset or re-arm the activation clock if a single activation key is used. This gives a 30-day (Windows 7) or 90-day (Windows 8/10) grace period before the product key must be re-entered.

Active Directory (AD) A service used on Microsoft Windows Server to manage network accounts and devices.

active listening An effective communication technique that ensures what the speaker says is accurately received.

ActiveSync A Microsoft product that allows data including contacts, email, and calendar synchronization between a mobile device and a Windows desktop computer.

Activity Monitor A troubleshooting tool in a macOS system that sees what processes and services are running, as well as what system resources are used.

ad blocker Software that is made specifically to not show advertisements that appear in certain websites.

ad hoc mode A type of wireless configuration in which two 802.11 wireless devices can make a wireless network without the use of an access point.

adapter An electronic circuit card that can be inserted into an expansion slot. Also called a controller, card, controller card, circuit card, circuit board, or adapter board.

adding array (Disk Management) Right-click inside unallocated space of a drive > *New Spanned Volume* or *New Striped Volume* > select another drive to be added > select a drive letter and file system.

ADF (automatic document feeder) A feature on a printer or multifunction device that allows paper to be fed into the device to be copied, scanned, or faxed, depending on the model and task.

ADF scanner A scanner that has the added feature of having an automatic document feeder (ADF) to allow multiple pages to be fed or input into the scanner.

administrative privileges A security function in Windows that requires elevated security rights in order to execute specific commands. Use the *Run as administrator* option if blocked.

administrative share A share created by Microsoft for drive volumes and the folder that contains the majority of Windows files. An administrative share has a dollar sign at the end of its name.

administrator A person responsible for setting up and maintaining a system, such as a Windows computer. Logging in as an administrator allows settings to be changed that may not be allowed for other users.

Administrator Password A BIOS/UEFI Setup option used to prevent access and changes made to BIOS.

ADSL (Asymmetrical DSL) A type of digital subscriber line (DSL) that provides speeds up to 150 Mb/s; it provides faster downloads than uploads.

Advanced Boot Options A Windows boot menu used to access tools used for troubleshooting. Press F8 when the computer is booting (and before Windows loads) to access the Advanced Boot Options menu.

Advanced Technology eXtended (ATX) A form factor for motherboards, cases, and power supplies.

AES (Advanced Encryption Standard) A specification for encryption used in wireless networks that uses 128-bit, 192-bit, and 256-bit encryption keys.

AFP (Apple Filing Protocol) A set of rules for file services on an Apple device that uses macOS. AFP uses port 548.

AGP (accelerated graphics port) An extension of the PCI bus (a port) that provides a dedicated communication path between the expansion slot and the processor. AGP is used for video adapters.

air filter/mask Personal protective equipment that should be used whenever dust, airborne particles, or debris could cause personal issues. An air filter might also be used in an area where the air quality is not appropriate for a computer or networking equipment.

Airplane Mode A mode on smartphones and tablets that enables users to disable all wireless communication but still view a movie or play a game that does not require internet connectivity.

AirPrint An Apple print server.

alphanumeric character A character that can be a letter of the alphabet (uppercase or lowercase), a digit from 0 through 9, or a punctuation mark or symbol, such as @, #, or !.

AMD (Advanced Micro Devices) A company that makes processors, graphics processors, and chipsets. AMD is the largest rival of Intel for PC processors.

amp Short for ampere, a measurement of electrical current.

analog signal A type of signal used mainly by older video ports, modems, and sound devices; its signal strength varies in amplitude.

AND operator An operator used with two or more conditions that returns true only if all expressions are true.

Android A mobile device operating system.

Android OS A mobile device operating system.

antenna A component that attaches to a wireless device or is integrated into it. An antenna radiates or receives radio waves.

anti-malware Software used to protect the operating system and applications.

antistatic bag A plastic enclosure that protects electronic gear from being affected by static charges if the equipment is left exposed.

antistatic wrist strap A strap that connects a technician to a computer that equalizes the voltage potential between the two to prevent electrostatic discharge (ESD).

antivirus Software that protects the operating system and applications from malware.

AP (access point) See *access point* and *wireless access point*.

APFS (Apple File System) An operating system developed and owned by Apple that is used on desktop computers and iPads. It uses GPT partitions and allows disk cloning.

APIPA (automatic private IP addressing) A Windows option that enables a computer to automatically receive an IP address from the range 169.254.0.1 to 169.254.255.254.

APK A file format that can be used to distribute and install Android apps.

app fails to close The process to go through on a mobile device to manually stop an app. May require rebooting the device.

App Store A site or app where Apple users shop for various applications to download on a device.

Apple Macintosh OS Any operating system on an Apple device, including OS X, iOS, and macOS.

application crash A situation in which a specific program quits working. In the Windows environment, use Task Manager to quit a crashed application.

application log A record of an application's crashes and failures to operating properly. In Windows, use Event Viewer to see such information.

application spoofing The act of masquerading a mobile app as being from a trusted source.

Apply button An option within the Windows OS that makes any changes take effect immediately.

apply update After an operating system installation, do not forget to download and install the operating system and application updates as well as check for newer device drivers.

`apt-get` The Linux command-line interface tool that is the equivalent of Ubuntu Software Center; a utility to manage software.

APU (accelerated processing unit) A processor that combines a central processing unit (CPU) with a graphics processing unit (GPU).

ARM (Acorn RISC Machine) A type of processor used in mobile devices that requires low power, is fast, and is low cost.

ARM processor A type of processor used in mobile devices, servers, and microcontrollers that runs cooler, takes less power, and is cheaper than Intel and AMD processors.

asset tag A method of IT inventory used on hardware and network items.

assigning/changing drive letter In Disk Management, right-click on a drive volume > *Change Drive Letter and Paths.*

attitude A person's behavior and/or mindset toward another person or a thing.

attribute An operating system condition used to hide, archive, make a file read-only, or designate a file as a system file.

`attrib` A command that designates a file as hidden, archived, read-only, or a system file.

audio/video editing workstation A computer used to create and modify sound or video files. The computer commonly has multiple powerful multicore processors, maximum system RAM, specialized video and audio cards, one or more fast and large-capacity hard drives, good speakers, a high-quality mouse, dual displays, and possibly a digital tablet and scanner.

audio issue A problem with sound output, including on a projector. Check muting, volume settings, and cabling.

audit log Information saved on servers and printers that can be used when troubleshooting problems. On a printer or print server, this might be called a print log.

auditing Tracking network events such as logging onto the network domain. Auditing is sometimes called event logging or simply logging.

AUP See *acceptable use policy (AUP).*

authentication The process of determining whether a network device or person has permission to access a network.

authenticator app An app that can be downloaded and, if a site is configured to use it, provides an additional level of security for mobile devices.

authorization Controls what network resources—such as files, folders, printers, video conferencing equipment, fax machines, scanners, and so on—can be accessed and used by a legitimate network user or device.

Automatic Updates A method for getting newer Windows operating system files.

B

`.bat` A file extension used with a batch file (a file that has multiple commands that, when executed, run one after another). See also *batch file.*

b/s (bits per second) The number of 1s and 0s transmitted per second.

Back to My Mac A feature in the *System Preferences* iCloud menu that enables you to browse a Mac from another macOS device. The remote Mac appears as a shared device in Finder, enabling you to browse the file system.

back up data Before making changes to a system, back up the data.

backlight A fluorescent lamp or LEDs that are always on for an LCD.

backup A precautionary technique used to have a secondary piece of hardware or backup software/files.

backward compatibility In software, the ability of an application to run on older operating systems.

badge reader A security device that allows entry into a space.

Balanced Technology eXtended (BTX) A motherboard form factor that is larger than ATX.

bandwidth The width of a communications channel, which defines the channel's capacity for carrying data.

barcode A series of lines used to uniquely identify an item. In IT, barcodes are commonly used on asset tags for PC hardware and network items.

baseline A snapshot of a computer's performance (memory, CPU usage, and so on) during normal operations (before a problem or slowdown is apparent).

basic disk A Windows term for a drive that has been partitioned and formatted.

basic storage A Windows term for a partition. Contrast with *dynamic storage.*

batch file A Windows-based script that can only be interpreted by the Windows operating system. A batch file has the extension `.bat`.
battery A small self-contained unit used to power a device without using an AC outlet.
battery backup A device that provides power to a computer when a brownout or a blackout occurs.
battery not charging In this situation, inspect the battery compartment. Try to charge with a different connector, such as a car adapter.
baud The number of times an analog signal changes in 1 second. If a signal that is sent changes 600 times in 1 second, the device communicates at 600 baud. Today's signaling methods (modulation techniques, to be technically accurate) allow modems to send several bits in one cycle, so it is more accurate to speak of bits per second than baud.
be on time A good work habit to have. If you are going to be late for work, contact your supervisor. If you are going to be late for a customer appointment, notify the customer.
biometrics The use of one or more devices that can authenticate someone based on one or more physical traits, such as a fingerprint, an eyeball (retina), or a hand, or a behavioral trait such as voice or signature.
BIOS (basic input/output system) A chip that contains computer software that locates the operating system, POST, and important hardware configuration parameters. Also called ROM BIOS, Flash BIOS, or system BIOS. Replaced with UEFI BIOS.
bit An electrically charged 1 or 0.
BitLocker A Microsoft utility that encrypts an entire disk volume, including operating system files, user files, and paging files. The utility requires two disk partitions at a minimum.
BitLocker To Go A Microsoft application that can encrypt and password protect external drives and removable media that are 128 MB or larger.
black screen A problem with power (no power, bad power supply) or a CPU, no power to the monitor, disconnected video cable, faculty monitor, turned off monitor, bad motherboard, or a failed CPU cooling system. For video issues, use the *Safe Mode* or *Last Known Good Configuration* boot option.
blackout A total loss of AC power.
blue screen *or* blue screen of death See *BSOD*.
Bluetooth A wireless technology for personal area networks (PANs).
BNC connector (Bayonet Neill–Concelman connector) A connector used on coaxial cable.
bollard An upright post that tends to be set in front of a door and is used as a security deterrent.
boot The process of a computer coming to a usable condition.
bootable device not found An error message indicating you should check the boot order. If the boot order is correct, the operating system needs to be installed or reloaded.
Boot Camp A boot loading utility designed to assist with partitioning, installation, and support in running Windows on a Mac.
Boot Options A BIOS configuration setting that prioritizes devices in the order in which the computer looks for boot files, known as the boot drive order, boot sequence, or boot menu.
boot partition A type of partition in Windows that contains the operating system. The boot partition can be in the same partition as the system partition, which is the part of the hard drive that holds hardware-specific files.
Boot Password A BIOS/UEFI setup option used to access the computer before the operating system loads.
boot process The specific order a device goes through to power up, locate an operating system, and automatically load services and applications.
boot sector Previously called DBR or DOS boot record, a section of a disk that contains information about the system files (the files used to boot the operating system).
boot sector virus A virus program placed in a computer's boot sector code, which can then load into memory. When in RAM, the virus takes control of computer operations. The virus can spread to installed drives and drives located on a network.
boot volume A Windows term describing the storage space that holds the majority of the Windows operating system files. Can be the same volume as the system volume (which holds the Windows boot files).
bootleg app Software that is pirated (has not been paid for).
`bootrec` A Windows command used to repair and recover from hard drive problems.
bps (bits per second) A measurement of speed.
broadcast address An IP address that communicates with all devices on a particular network.

broken screen A mobile device part that might have to be replaced. Replacing a screen might require removing the keyboard, drive, memory, and motherboard.
brownout A loss of AC power due to overloaded electrical circuits.
browser extension Downloadable code that provides an enhanced browser feature or functionality.
browser plug-in An executable file downloaded to provide an enhanced browser feature or functionality.
browser synchronization The process of coordinating settings such as bookmarks and passwords across multiple devices when the user is signed into the account.
brute force A type of attack in which repeated attempts are made to try to gain access to a network device or stored material.
BSOD (blue screen of death) In Windows, an error in which the monitor screen displays all blue, and the computer locks or is nonfunctional.
buffered memory A type of memory in which the modules have extra chips (registers) that delay data transfers to ensure accuracy.
burn-in An image imprint, or ghost image on a display screen when an LCD or plasma display has been left on too long.
burned out bulb A possible issue when a projector does not display anything.
burning smell A symptom that there is something wrong with a power supply.
BYOD (bring your own device) A situation in which personal mobile devices are brought to the work environment and used on the wired or wireless network.
byte 8 bits grouped together as a basic unit.

C

`c` A Linux command used to list the contents of the current working directory.
cable management system A system that helps keep network cables neat and organized. A ladder rack is a type of cable management system.
cable modem A modem that connects to the cable TV network.
cable stripper A tool used to cut away the sheathing over a cable's copper wire. Also called a wire stripper.
cable tester A tester that checks coaxial and UTP cable ends (depending on the model) to determine if cable terminals are suitable for use.
cache memory Fast memory designed to increase processor operations.
calibrate (inkjet) A print head alignment process that must be performed when installing the printer and when replacing the print head.
calibrate (laser printer) A maintenance task that involves adjusting for print density.
capacitor swelling A bulging end or top of a capacitor that indicates it is time to change it or the component of which it is a part, including the motherboard.
carriage belt An internal inkjet printer part that moves the printhead.
Cat 5 Another name for Category 5 twisted pair cable, which has a bandwidth maximum of 100 MHz, a maximum transmission speed of 100 Mb/s, and a 100-meter (328-foot) maximum cable distance.
Cat 5e Another name for Category 5e twisted pair cable, which has a bandwidth maximum of 100 MHz, a maximum transmission speed of 1,000 Mb/s, and a 100-meter (328-foot) maximum cable distance. This type of cable reduces crosstalk found in Cat 5 cable.
Cat 6 Another name for Category 6 twisted pair cable, which, with the Cat 6a specification, has a bandwidth maximum of 500 MHz, a maximum transmission speed of 10,000 Mb/s, and a 100-meter (328-foot) maximum cable distance.
Cat 6a A type of Ethernet cabling in which the wires are twisted together more closely than in Cat 6 so that speeds up to 10 Gb/s can be achieved over a 100-meter (328-foot) maximum cable distance. This type of cabling sometimes has a thick conductor and jacket.
CCFL (cold cathode fluorescent lamp) The older flat-panel backlight technology used before LED backlights were used.
`cd` The same as the `chdir` command in Windows. Used from a Windows or a Linux/macOS command prompt to move into a different directory.
CDMA (Carrier Detect Multiple Access) A protocol used on older 2G/3G mobile networks.
cellular card A device that is used to connect a laptop to a cell phone network.
cellular location service Software used to pinpoint where a mobile device is located.

Certificate Manager A Windows tool used to view, modify, import, export, or delete a digital security certificate.
certificate of destruction A security measure that provides proof that printed material or stored data has been destroyed.
change board A group of individuals who approve IT projects within an organization.
change default admin user account password A security best practice is to change the default administrator user account password or create an account that has administrator access and disable the default account.
change management The formal process of systematically choosing and implementing business changes.
channel A specific number that signifies the frequency used by a wireless device to transmit and receive. Also called a channel ID.
charging A laser printing imaging process that can also be known as conditioning. This process gets the drum ready for use by applying a uniform voltage on the drum surface by using a primary/main corona or a conditioning roller.
charging USB port A port that can provide power to charge and run an unpowered attached device such as a flash drive.
checkpoint In a virtualization environment, a copy or backup of the virtual machine (VM) at a particular point in time that is used to revert the VM to that point in time.
`chkdsk` A program that locates clusters that are disassociated from the appropriate data file.
`chmod` A Linux command that gives the file owner read, write, and execute permissions.
`chown` A Linux command that changes ownership.
Chrome OS An operating system supported by Google and Google partners that is used on laptops.
CIDR (classless interdomain routing) A type of subnet mask that does not have a classful boundary. CIDR is a method of allocating IP addresses based on the number of host addresses needed for a particular network.
CIFS (Common Internet File System) A version of Server Message Block (SMB) that can provide access to shared network devices, files, and printers, especially in a mixed environment of Mac and Windows computers. SMB/CIFS uses port 445.
`cipher` A Windows command used to decrypt, modify, or copy an encrypted file.
CL rating (column address strobe [CAS] latency rating) The amount of time (number of clock cycles) that passes before the processor moves on to the next memory address. Chips with lower access times (CL rating) are faster than those with higher access times (larger numbers).
clarify customer statement A technique in which a technician asks open-ended questions that provide more information than questions that result in just yes or no answers.
clean a laser printer A maintenance task that involves vacuuming inside a laser printer using a special vacuum bag.
clean install The process of loading an operating system on a computer that does not already have one installed.
clean the heating element A maintenance process task for a thermal printer.
clean the printhead A task done through the printer software or manually by using a clean lint-free cloth to softly wipe the print head.
cleaning A laser printing imaging process that involves removing residual toner from the drum by using a wiper blade or brush.
clear a jam A process that involves checking the printer paper path for obstructions or creased paper.
clear browsing data The process of removing all cookies, browsing history, and other data tracked by a web browser.
clear cache A process used to troubleshoot browser issues such as a page not displaying correctly or not formatted properly.
client-side DNS A form of Domain Name System (DNS) in which individuals or businesses configure their computer to use one or more DNS servers to translate uniform resource locators (URLs) into IP addresses.
clock An electronic component that provides timing signals to all motherboard components. A PC's clock speed is normally measured in MHz.
clock speed The rate at which timing signals are sent to motherboard components (normally measured in MHz).

cloud services Functions provided through a network on devices that are either remote or local but managed and configured through remote applications. Examples of cloud services include wireless networking, network switches, servers, printing, scanning, and file storage.

cluster The minimum amount of space that one saved file occupies.

cmdlet A function used and associated with a particular operation when creating tasks within PowerShell.

CMOS (complementary metal oxide semiconductor) A special type of memory on a motherboard in which Setup configuration is saved.

CMOS battery A small, coin-shaped lithium battery that provides power to CMOS memory.

coaxial A type of cabling used in video connections that has a copper core surrounded by insulation and shielding to protect against EMI.

collate To print complete copies of documents in numerical order, one set at a time.

`command` A command issued from the Run utility in Windows to bring up a command prompt window.

`command /?` A command issued from the Run utility in Windows to list commands and options that are available for that particular command. Replace *command* with a particular command, such as `dir /?`.

command-line interface An operating environment that is not graphical and in which only typed commands are available.

command prompt Otherwise known as a prompt or command-line interface (CLI), a text-based environment in which commands are entered.

command switch An option used when working from a command prompt that allows a command to be controlled or operated on differently.

comment In a script, an explanation of what some part of the code does that is ignored by the computer when running the script.

community cloud A type of cloud deployment model that is a combination of a private cloud and a public cloud.

comparison operator A function used in scripting to evaluate two values.

compatibility A feature of hardware or software that allows functionality on multiple models.

Compatibility Mode A Microsoft Windows mode used to emulate older operating systems so that older applications or hardware can be used on a newer operating system.

compiled program Software that must be turned into machine language before it can execute.

component/RGB video Three RCA jacks commonly found on TVs, DVD players, and projectors. One connection is for luminescence (or brightness), and two jacks are for color difference signals.

compound condition A situation in scripting in which two test conditions are contained in a single statement.

compressed air A can of air whose top can be pressed to direct high-powered air to remove dust from hard-to-reach places such as under keys, under motherboards, and inside power supplies and devices.

compression Compaction of a file or folder to take up less disk drive space.

Computer Management A Windows tool that displays a large group of tools on one screen.

computer reboot A symptom that something is wrong with the power supply, CPU, or motherboard.

connection oriented A feature of TCP that creates a connection to a destination before data is sent and allows for packets to be re-sent. Examples of application layer protocols that are connection oriented are HTTP, HTTPS, and SSH.

connectionless A feature of UDP protocols that makes data transfers faster but that allows packets to be dropped and not re-sent. Examples of application layer protocols that are connectionless are DHCP and TFTP.

Console In macOS, a centralized place to find system and application logs and messages. It allows parsing manually or by searching for something specific.

construct One of the three elements scientists in the 1960s showed are common to all programming code: sequence, selection (or decision), and repetition (or loops).

content filtering The process of using a device or software to screen data for suspected security risks.

context menu A menu of options usually available from the main menu that is brought up by right-clicking an item.

continuity An electrical resistance measurement that indicates whether a wire is good or broken.

continuous ink system A method of providing extra ink for heavily used inkjet printers.
continuous reboot A symptom of a CPU, motherboard, or power supply problem.
Control Panel A traditional Windows utility that allows computer configuration such as adding or removing software, adding or removing hardware, configuring a screen saver, adjusting a monitor, configuring a mouse, installing networking components, and so on. Many of these functions have moved over to a Windows Settings link.
control plane The part of software-defined networking that is involved with the "brains" of whatever network device is being virtualized, such as a routing table being built in preparation for routing data to a remote destination or MAC address table being built in order to do switching of the data to a specific port to get the data to a specific device. Contrast with *data plane*.
convergence The use of a traditional data network for another type of traffic, such as voice and video traffic (which used to have networks of their own).
`convert` A command issued from a command prompt that changes an older file system into NTFS.
copper cabling A type of cabling used to bring video channels into and throughout a home; with home and business wired networks, it uses electrical pulses to represent data (in contrast to the light pulses used in fiber-optic cabling).
`copy` A command used from a command prompt to transfer one or more files from one place to another.
`cp` A Linux command for copying a file. Short for *copy*.
CPU (central processing unit) See *processor*.
CPU socket The motherboard part where a processor inserts.
CPU speed The rate at which a CPU operates. It is the speed of the front side bus multiplied by the multiplier. Normally measured in GHz.
CPU throttling The process of reducing the clock frequency to reduce power consumption.
Credential Manager The location where Windows stores login credentials such as usernames, passwords, and addresses.
crimper A tool that permanently attaches an RJ45 or RJ11 connector to a copper core cable.
cross-platform virtualization The process of using virtualization to run a different OS than was intended for the machine, such as Windows on a Mac computer.
crossover cable Cabling that connects two like devices (for example, two computers, two switches, two routers).
cryptominer Malicious software code that uses a computer's processing power in order to do cryptomining of digital currency.
cursor drift A situation in which the mouse pointer moves across the screen even if no one is touching the input device. Commonly caused by improper touchpad sensitivity settings, outdated drivers, or malware.

D

DaaS (data as a service) A type of cloud service that provides data to a company.
DaaS (desktop as a service) A type of cloud service in which an outside company provides the OS and apps to multiple computers.
dash The universal search tool built in the macOS Launcher bar. It searches local content as well as internet sources, all of which can be enabled or disabled simply by opening up Dash.
data at rest Data that is stored in some location. Data at rest should be encrypted or password protected.
data cap A data limit imposed by an internet service provider, usually based on a contract.
data plane A part of software-defined networking that is involved with moving data from one location to another. Contrast with *control plane*.
Data Sources Also called Data Sources ODBC (open database connectivity), a programming interface that allows applications to access data from a database.
database system A computer or server that has software on it that provides for a structured way of collecting, analyzing, sorting, and displaying data.
DB9 A male port on older motherboards, networking equipment, and projectors. Also known as a serial or RS-232 port.
DBR (DOS boot record) An area of a disk that contains system files.
DC (direct current) The type of power a computer needs to operate.
DC jack A part on a laptop where the external power brick attaches.
`dd` In Linux, an advanced command-line interface command that copies and converts files.

DDoS (distributed denial of service) A type of security attack in which several computer systems are used to attack a network or device with the intention of preventing access, such as to a web server.

DDR3 (Double Data Rate 3) A memory module that is an upgrade from DDR2 for speeds up to 1,600 MHz that better supports dual-core and quad-core processor-based systems.

DDR4 (Double Data Rate 4) A memory module that operates at a lower voltage and faster speeds than DDR3 and lower modules.

DDR5 (Double Data Rate 5) A lower-voltage memory module that requires a DDR5 motherboard memory expansion slot.

dead pixel A pixel on an LCD monitor that does not illuminate. Displays commonly have one or more dead pixels.

decision structure A selection structure consisting of a test condition together with one or more groups (or blocks) of statements. The result of the test condition determines which block of statements will be executed.

declaration The process of creating a variable in a script. The exact syntax to do this is known as a variable declaration.

default gateway The IP address of a Layer 3 device, such as a router, that is directly connected to its immediate network. It tells a device on its network where to send a packet destined for a remote network.

default printer When a computer can use multiple printers, the one printer that all applications use by default. A computer user can change the printer to a different one through the Print dialog window. To mark a printer as default, right-click the printer icon and click the *Set as Default* option.

`defrag` The Windows command that starts the defragmentation process of reordering and placing files in contiguous sectors for better performance.

defragmentation The process of reordering and placing files in contiguous sectors.

degaussing The process of using a strong electromagnet (sometimes called a degausser or degaussing coil) to change a drive's magnetic field and erase the drive as a security measure.

`del` A command issued from a command prompt that deletes a file or folder.

desktop The part of a graphical user interface that is between the user and the applications, files, and hardware. It is the area in which all work is performed.

desktop alert A message that appears relating to the system or notifications chosen by the user or a security-related message regarding a problem or potential threat.

developer mode A mode on a mobile device that allows for the device to be customized or apps to be developed. App customization and development can pose a security risk and/or the device operating system to be unstable so be careful using this mode.

developing A laser printer process in which toner is attracted to the laser printer drum.

device driver Special software that allows an operating system to access a piece of hardware.

Device Manager A Windows program that is used to view and configure hardware.

Devices and Printers A Windows Control Panel that is used to view, install, remove, and manage wired and wireless devices. Current version of Windows can use the Devices settings link.

DHCP (Dynamic Host Configuration Protocol) A protocol that is involved in automatically assigning IP addresses to network devices from a pool of IP addresses. DHCP uses ports 67 and 68.

DHCP lease time The amount of time in minutes, days, or hours that a device that receives an IP address from a DHCP server gets to keep the address.

DHCP reservation An IP address set aside for a specific network device like a router, switch, or printer that needs an IP address that does not change.

DHCP scope The starting IP address and ending IP address for a pool of addresses to be issued to network end devices.

DHCP server Software configured on a network server or router that issues IP addresses from its pool of numbers upon request to a network device.

dial-up network A network formed by using a modem that connects to the traditional phone network. The modem connects to a remote network device.

dictionary [attack] A brute-force security attack that tries to determine a password by using words in a dictionary in order to gain access to data.

differential backup A backup that backs up files that have changed since the last full backup (files that have the archive bit set to on) but in which the backup software does not reset the archive bit, as an incremental backup does.

digital signal A signal using 1s and 0s to represent data.

digital signature A type of electronic signature that confirms that the hardware or updated driver being installed is compatible with Windows. Sometimes called a driver signing.

digitizer A device that provides input into documents such as architectural drawings, technical plans, and photos. It can also be used to draw electronic pictures.

dim display An indication to check display settings and the battery level. The display could require calibration.

DIMM (dual inline memory module) A style of 168-pin, 184-pin, 240-pin, or 288-pin memory chip normally used for RAM on Pentium and higher motherboards.

`dir` A command used from a command prompt to display the contents of a directory.

direct burial cable A type of cable that has extra insulation, cover, and waterproofing added so it can be used underground without any additional protection.

directional antenna A type of antenna that radiates energy in a specific direction.

directory In older operating systems, an electronic container that holds files and even other directories. Today's operating systems use the term *folder*.

DirectX A Microsoft technology that integrates multimedia drivers, application code, and 3-D support for audio and video.

disable a service In Windows, use the *Services* option from within the Computer Management console in order to disable a service that might be causing issues.

disable AutoPlay A best practice for security is to disable this option, which is used to control what happens when you insert media.

disable AutoRun A best practice for security is to disable this option, which dictates whether software or programs start automatically from discs, USB, or other drives.

Disable Execute Bit A setting that, when enabled in BIOS/UEFI, prevents executable code such as that found in viruses or other malware from loading into memory locations where operating system code resides.

disable guest account A Windows security best practice.

disable Windows application A best practice is to use the System Configuration utility *Startup* tab to disable applications that start automatically.

disappearing files A symptom of malware.

disk cache A portion of RAM set aside for hard drive data that speeds up hard drive operations. A cache on a hard drive controller is also known as a data buffer.

Disk Cleanup A Windows utility that helps free up hard drive space by emptying the Recycle Bin, removing temporary files, removing temporary internet files, removing offline files, and so on.

Disk Management A Windows tool used to partition and manage hard drives.

disk mirroring A process that protects against hard drive failure by using two or more hard drives and one disk controller. The same data is written to both drives. If one hard drive fails, the other hard drive continues to function. Disk mirroring is considered to be RAID level 1.

disk striping Another name for RAID 0, in which data is alternately written on two or more hard drives, thus providing increased system performance.

Disk Utility A powerful application that manages disks and images in macOS. The utility can rename, reformat, erase, repair, and restore disks. It should be approached with caution because the wrong usage could delete all data on the system or on an attached external disk.

`diskpart` A command-based utility used in preparing hard disk partitions and volumes for use.

`dism` (Deployment Image Servicing and Management) A Windows utility used to repair and prepare Windows images.

DisplayPort A port, developed by Video Electronics Standards Association (VESA), that can send and receive audio and video signals. Used primarily for display devices and can connect to a single-link DVI or HDMI port with the use of a converter.

DMZ (demilitarized zone) A network area that is separate from the corporate network but contains servers that are accessible to outside devices. Also known as a screened subnet.

DNS (Domain Name System) A naming system that translates internet names into IP addresses. DNS uses port 53.

DNS server A network server that is used to translate internet names into IP addresses.

DNS TXT A type of DNS message used by email apps to try to determine if a message is from a trusted source/domain.

Dock The shortcut organizational bar used for launching, switching, and managing applications in the macOS graphical user interface (usually the bar at the bottom of the screen).

docking station A hardware device that has connections for a monitor, printer, keyboard, and mouse that allows a laptop computer to be more like a desktop system. Sometimes called a mobile docking station or a laptop docking station.

document changes The part of change management that creates a historical record of what changes occurred.

documented business processes A set of business documents that relate to how things are supposed to be done or have been done in the past.

Documents A default Windows folder where files are saved.

does not autorotate A problem with the device settings, another app, outdated OS, G-sensor, or accelerometer on a mobile device.

domain A term used in Windows server-based networks for an area where users are required to have logins, and file storage, email, and web-based services are commonly provided. Domains are used to organize user accounts and network devices in Microsoft's Active Directory service.

domain access Access to an account or a device onto a Microsoft corporate network.

door lock A keyless entry option for a smart home that allows keyless entry. It is also important to have a door lock of any type on a room that holds network infrastructure equipment such as routers and switches.

DoS (denial of service) A type of security attack in which the intent is to make a machine or a network unusable.

dot matrix printer See *impact printer.*

double image A burn-in; an image seen on a display screen when an LCD or a plasma display has been left on too long.

downstream Describes information pulled from the internet, such as when viewing web pages or downloading a file.

DRAM (dynamic random-access memory) One of two major RAM types, which is less expensive but also slower than SRAM. DRAM requires periodic refreshing of the stored 1s and 0s.

drawing pad A device used to draw, annotate an existing document or drawing, type, or write. Also known as a drawing tablet or graphics tablet. Commonly used by teachers, graphic artists, space planners, and engineers.

drive activity LED A light on the front of a hard drive that blinks when data is being retrieved or written.

Drive Encryption (BIOS) A BIOS/UEFI setting that scrambles all the data on the hard drive as a security measure.

drive not recognized A storage device error condition that indicates a problem with physical settings, BIOS/UEFI settings, cabling, or a lack of power.

drive partition A division of space on a hard drive that is recognizable by the operating system.

drive status A storage device state that can be viewed in Windows Disk Management.

drive wipe A technique that can be used to eradicate personal or corporate data from a hard drive before donating or reusing a computer.

driver See *device driver.*

DRM (digital rights management) Technology used to implement controls placed on digital media.

DSL (digital subscriber line) A type of internet connection that uses a traditional phone line. A filter is needed on each phone outlet that has a normal analog device attached to separate the analog sound from the internet data.

dual-channel A system in which the motherboard memory controller chip handles processing of memory requests more efficiently by handling two memory paths simultaneously.

dual-rail power supply A power supply that has two +12 volt lines available.

dual-voltage memory Motherboard memory modules that use less power and produce less heat if the motherboard supports this feature. Not all installed modules must support the lower voltage for the system to take advantage of the modules that do support the lower voltage.

Dumpster diving A social engineering threat in which someone digs through trash in or out of the office as a way to get information.

duplex An assembly option that allows a printer to print on both sides of a paper without intervention. Duplex is also a NIC setting to choose between half (transmitting in one direction at a time), full (transmitting and receiving simultaneously), or auto.

duplexing assembly An option available on some printers to allow two-sided printing.

dust cleanup An unsafe condition for technicians to work in without an air filter or mask.

DVI (Digital Visual Interface) A standard for a digital video adapter.

DVI port A port on a video adapter that connects a flat panel monitor to a computer.

DVI-D A type of video connector used with digital monitors.

DVI-I The most common type of DVI video connector that is used with both analog and digital monitors.

DVI-to-HDMI adapter A video connector with a DVI connector on one end and an HDMI connector on the other.

`dxdiag` A Windows command to access DirectX software that helps resolve DirectX display and sound driver problems.

dynamic disk A Windows term for a volume that can be resized and managed without rebooting.

dynamic storage A disk that has been configured for the Windows operating system that can be resized and managed without rebooting and that contains primary partitions, extended partitions, logical drives, and dynamic volumes.

E

ECC (error correcting code) A technique that uses a mathematical algorithm to verify data accuracy. ECC is more expensive than parity, and the motherboard or memory controllers must also have additional circuitry to process ECC.

echo image See *double image*.

`echo off` A command used from a command prompt to prevent characters from displaying on the screen.

effective permissions The final permissions granted for a particular resource. Folder permissions are cumulative—the combination of the group and the person's permissions. The deny permission overrides any allowed permission set for a user or a group. When NTFS and shared folder permissions are both used, the more restrictive permissions become the effective permissions.

EFS (Encrypting File System) A Windows encryption feature in which only the authorized user may view or change a file encrypted with EFS.

electrical fire safety Knowledge of how to extinguish an electrical fire using a Type A-B-C or Type C fire extinguisher.

email filtering The use of security rules specific to email that process incoming messages before forwarding on to a specific user.

embedded system A computer that has a specific function within a larger system, such as in medical, manufacturing, or airport industries.

EMI (electromagnetic interference) Electronic noise generated by electrical devices.

encryption A method of securing data from unauthorized users in which data is converted into an unreadable format.

end-of-life A term used with hardware or software that typically means the vendor no longer supports the product.

end-user acceptance A part of change management in which the person who will use an IT system tests the changes to ensure that the deliverables or outcomes have been met.

end-user education A great security method to use because by educating users, security issues get reported and dealt with earlier and with less damage to a company. Part of a technician's job might be to teach a user how to do something to avoid technical issues or to prevent security issues.

ENERGY STAR A set of energy-efficiency standards including those related to total energy requirements and low power mode(s) and an efficiency standard that a product must meet to achieve this standard.

environment variable A variable that describes the environment in which a program runs. It contains a name and a value, where the value is the path to the program identified by the variable name.

EPEAT rating system A rating system of gold, silver or bronze to identify products that have an environmental (green electronics) design.
equality operator A method in scripting that is used to compare two values. Another name for comparison operator or equals operator.
equals operator A method in scripting that is used to compare two values. Another name for comparison operator or equality operator.
equipment grounding The process of ensuring that the components in a device like a PC or rack are at the same voltage potential. Grounding is important to personal safety because consistent grounding minimizes the possibility of voltages being applied to places they shouldn't be applied, such as the case. If a piece of equipment is not grounded, someone could receive a shock or be electrocuted simply by touching it.
equipment lock A physical or electronic lock, a special cable that cannot be removed without a tool, or a lock-in device for a port.
Error Checking A Windows tool that checks a drive for file system errors, bad hard drive sectors, and lost clusters.
error message An indication provided by a system or an application that should be noted to help in troubleshooting.
eSATA (External Serial ATA) A port used to connect external SATA devices to a computer.
eSATA bracket A part that installs into an empty expansion slot that has one or more eSATA ports. Each port on the bracket has a SATA cable that attaches to an available motherboard SATA port.
eSATA cable A cable that attaches to an eSATA port located on the outside of a device such as on a motherboard or card. The maximum length of such a cable is 6 feet (2 meters).
eSATA card An adapter used to add external SATA ports so that external storage devices can be used. It may include ports for internal SATA devices.
eSATAp port A port that accepts both eSATA and USB connectors and can provide power when necessary. Also known as eSATA/USB or power over eSATA.
ESCD (Extended System Configuration Data) A specification that provides the BIOS and operating system a means for communicating with plug-and-play devices. As the computer boots, the BIOS records legacy device configuration information. Plug-and-play devices use this information to configure themselves and avoid conflicts. When an adapter has resources assigned and the resources are saved in ESCD, the resources do not have to be recalculated unless a new device is added to the computer.
ESD (electrostatic discharge) A sudden flow of electric current that occurs when stored-up static electricity is discharged in an instantaneous surge of voltage. Cumulative effects of ESD weaken or destroy electronic components.
ESD mat A pad that is placed on a surface to prevent electrostatic discharge events. Such a mat commonly has a place to attach an antistatic wrist strap.
ESD strap An item that fits around a technician's wrist and connects to an electronic component so that the technician and the component are at the same voltage potential, thus preventing an electrostatic discharge event, which can cause damage to electronic components.
Ethernet A network system that carries computer data along with audio and video information. Ethernet adapters are the most common network cards.
Ethernet over Power (EoP) A technology, also called powerline communication, in which network data is sent to EoP modules that are plugged into power outlets to extend Ethernet networks.
Ethernet port An RJ45 port that connects a device to a wired network.
EULA (end-user license agreement) Legal language that specifies what can and cannot be done with a particular software application or operating system.
Event Viewer A Windows tool that monitors various events in a computer.
evil twin A rogue AP that broadcasts the same SSID as a legitimate AP in the area to intercept wireless traffic.
exabyte (EB) 1 billion times 1 billion bytes, or 2^{60} (1,152,921,504,606,800) bytes.
executable file A file with a `.bat`, `.exe`, or `.com` extension that starts an application, a utility, or a command. It is a file on which the operating system can take action.

exFAT A file system type that improves upon FAT32 by having a theoretical maximum file size of 16 EB, maximum volume size of 64 ZB (but 512 TB is the current limit), smaller cluster sizes than FAT32, and an increased number of files allowed in a directory. Created for external storage media such as flash drives and hard drives for saving images/video.
expansion slot A motherboard socket to which adapters are connected.
`explorer` A command used on a Windows device to bring up File Explorer.
exposing A laser printer imaging process in which light is directed toward the drum to put 1s and 0s on the drum surface. Light hitting the drum changes the drum surface voltage.
ext3 (Third Extended File System) A file system type used in Linux-based operating systems that introduced journaling.
ext4 (Fourth Extended File System) A file system type used in Linux-based operating systems that supports larger volumes and file sizes than ext3.
extended partition A hard drive division.
extended read/write time An indication that a storage device is nearly full or in need of replacement because it takes longer than normal to retrieve and/or save data.
extending partition (Disk Management) Increasing the size of a partition by right-clicking on the drive letter and selecting *Extend Volume*.
extensible software Software that is easily upgraded.
extension In operating systems, the three or more characters at the end of a filename, after a period (.). The extension associates a file with a particular application that executes the file.
external data bus The electronic lines that allow a processor to communicate with external devices. Also known as an external data path or external data lines.
external hard drive (boot option) An operating system boot option when a USB or eSATA drive is used.
external interference Problems that wireless devices and other networks can cause with wireless network connectivity and reception when using the same unlicensed frequency range.
external shared resources In cloud computing, resources such as servers, applications, hardware (for example, CPUs and RAM), data storage, and network infrastructure equipment shared between organizations through an external vendor.
external storage device A peripheral that attaches to a computer that is used for saving data.
extremely short battery life An indication that it may be time to replace the battery and also close apps and services that are not being used.

F

F type A type of connector used with coaxial cable that screws onto the cable.
facial recognition lock A type of security lock on a mobile device or computer that uses the integrated camera and stored data to determine whether someone is granted access to the computer.
factory recovery partition A drive partition that contains files and folders including the operating system, drivers, and preinstalled programs that is used when a system must be rebuilt, restored, or re-created or when troubleshooting Windows problems.
factory reset An option to reset a computing device back to original settings.
faded print A condition that arises due to inadequate ribbon, ink level, or toner. Check quality settings. In a thermal printer, reduce the print head energy or print head pressure setting.
fail to boot An error condition that occurs when a boot device such as a hard drive is not responding.
failed attempts A Windows feature that locks out a user after a specific number of failed login attempts.
failure to boot A Windows condition that may require operating system repair or reloading.
fake security warning An illegitimate warning that may come through the operating system or a web browser. Do not tap, call, or reply to one of these.
fan A mechanical cooling device attached to or beside a processor or in a computer case.
Fan Control A BIOS/UEFI Setup option used to control the configuration of case and/or CPU fans, including the ability to place the fans in silent mode and/or control speed.
FAT (File Allocation Table) A method of organizing a computer's file system.
FAT file system A file system type also known as FAT16.

FAT16 A file system supported by DOS and all Windows versions since DOS. DOS and Windows 9x have a 2 GB limit. Newer Windows operating systems have a 4 GB FAT16 partition size limit. Also known as FAT.

FAT32 A file system that supports hard drives up to 2 TB in size.

FC (Fibre Channel) A standard used to connect a storage area network (SAN) to the other network devices.

feed assembly The part of a printer responsible for taking the paper through the printer.

feeder On a printer, a device that rolls the paper through the paper tray.

fiber cable An expensive network cabling made of plastic or glass fibers that carries data in the form of light pulses. It handles the greatest amount of data with least amount of data loss, and it comes in single mode and multi-mode. Also known as optical cable and fiber-optic cable.

fiber network A high-speed, high-capacity computer network composed of fiber-optic cables.

filament A supply that a 3-D printer needs for printing instead of using ink or toner.

File History A Windows tool that backs up a specific user's libraries instead of the entire system and supports scheduling these backups.

file recovery software An application used to recover data from a storage device.

file synchronization An option sometimes available with cloud file storage or a program that you can download that allows you to access files that have been placed in a special folder.

file system A data structure that defines how data is stored on a drive. Examples of file systems include FAT16, FAT32, exFAT, and NTFS.

file type A specific type of file based on the application that created it. For example, a `.txt` file created in Word is a different file type than an Acrobat reader `.pdf` file.

filename The name of a file. In older operating systems, the filename was limited to 8 characters plus a 3-character extension. Today's operating systems allow filenames up to 255 characters.

fileshare server A high-end computer configured to store files that can be accessed and managed from a remote location.

Finder A Mac application that is used for navigating and managing files or folders in the file system. It is similar to Microsoft's Windows Explorer/File Explorer.

fingerprint lock A type of security lock on mobile devices and computers that requires a valid stored fingerprint to be matched with the fingerprint of the person trying to gain access.

fingerprint scanner A biometric security device that requires a finger to be placed on a reader and compared against a stored image.

firewall Software or a hardware device that protects one or more computers from being electronically attacked. It inspects data for security purposes and filters traffic based on network protocols and rules established by a network administrator. Firewalls operate at the application layer of the OSI model.

firmware A combination of hardware and software attributes. An example is a BIOS chip that has instructions (software) written into it.

firmware update The process of obtaining and installing updates to the BIOS/UEFI so that the latest options or security patches are applied. Updating firmware is also known as flashing the BIOS.

flash BIOS A type of motherboard memory that allows updates by disk or by downloading internet files.

flash drive A type of memory that holds data even when the power to the device is removed.

flash memory A type of nonvolatile memory that holds data when the power is off.

flashing screen A display issue that could be caused by cabling not being inserted fully or having bent/broken pins.

flatbed scanner A peripheral used to digitize photos and texts.

floating-point number A number that can be written in the form $x \div y$, which means it includes a decimal value, even if that value is 0. For example, the number 7 is an integer, but the number 7.0 is a floating-point number.

folder In Windows-based operating systems, an electronic container that holds files as well as other folders. It is also called a directory.

folder redirection A feature of Microsoft Active Directory that maps a folder on the local machine to a network location such as a server so the user has access to the folder from any device on the network domain.

`for` loop A shorthand way to write a `while` loop.
Force Quit An option used on an Apple device to close an unresponsive app.
form factor The shape and size (height, width, and depth) of a motherboard, adapter, memory chip, power supply, and so on. Before building or upgrading, make sure the device's form factor fits the computer case.
`format` A command that prepares a disk for use.
formatted (disk) A disk that has been prepared to accept data.
forward compatibility A design feature in software that enables a system to accept input intended for a later version.
frequency response range The range of sounds a speaker can reproduce.
front panel connector A connector found on the motherboard that can have a cable that attaches from the motherboard to the front panel of the computer.
FSB (front side bus) Part of the dual independent bus that connects the CPU to the motherboard components.
FTP (File Transfer Protocol) A standard used for transferring files from one computer to another across a network.
fTPM (firmware trusted platform module) A module used to store security data such as passwords, digital certificates, and encryption keys using protected space and the CPU instead of a separate TPM chip.
full backup A method of backing up a hard drive in which the archive attribute is used. The backup software backs up all selected files and sets the archive bit to off.
full device encryption A security measure on mobile devices that supports encoding or scrambling of all user data.
full format During an installation process to partition a hard drive, an option that identifies and marks bad sectors on the drive so they will not be used for data storage. Contrast with *quick format*.
function key A function (Fn) key that, when used with another key, provides a specific function such as turning up speakers, connecting to an external monitor, or turning on the wireless adapter. This key is commonly found on laptops.
fuser assembly The part of a laser printer that melts the toner onto the paper.
fusing A laser printing process in which toner is melted into the paper.
fuzzy image A display issue that can be caused by faulty electronics or broken/bent pins on a cable.

G

gaming PC A computer design that includes a powerful processor, high-end video or specialized GPU, an SSD, a good sound card, and high-end cooling due to the demands placed on hardware when playing computer-based games.
garbled print A printed output indication that the printer cable is not securely attached or a print driver problem exists.
gateway An IP address assigned to a network device that tells the device where to send a packet that is going to a remote network. Also known as a default gateway or a gateway of last resort.
Gb An abbreviation for gigabit.
GB See *gigabyte*.
GDPR (General Data Protection Regulation) A European Union (EU) security standard developed to protect individuals and firms within the EU.
gestures On a touch device, finger motions (swipe, pinch, tap, spread, and so on) used to manipulate applications or features.
gigabyte Approximately 1 billion bytes of information (exactly 1,073,741,824 bytes); abbreviated GB.
GParted A disk management tool bundled with Ubuntu that allows the creation, deletion, and resizing of partitions on a physical disk.
`gpedit.msc` A command that brings up the group policy editor, which is used to control various Windows functions, apps, and what specific groups are allowed to do.
`gpresult` A command that displays Group Policy settings. A group policy determines how a computer is configured for both system and user (or user group) settings.
GPS (Global Positioning System) A satellite-based navigation system that transmits location information to receivers in mobile devices. Most mobile devices have GPS capability.
GPT (GUID [globally unique identifier] partition table) A type of partition table available in 64-bit Windows editions. GPTs can have up to 128 partitions and volumes up to 18 EB.

GPU (graphics processing unit) A video adapter processor that assists in video communication between a video adapter and a system processor. Also known as video processor, video coprocessor, or video accelerator.

`gpupdate` A command used to refresh local and Active Directory–based Group Policy settings.

grandfather-father-son backup A backup method in which a full backup (grandfather) is done relatively infrequently, such as once a month. Then another full backup (father) is done once a week followed by incremental backups (son) daily.

graphic/CAD/CAM design workstation A powerful computer system utilized by design engineers or graphic designers. It usually has multicore processors, high-end video cards with maximum GPU and video RAM, large displays, a large-capacity hard drive and SSD, and maximum system RAM. It uses output devices such as a scanner, plotter, or 3-D printer.

graphical interface fails to load A Windows startup problem in which startup files are missing or corrupt or there are hardware problems.

`grep` A common Linux utility that searches output for a specified term.

grinding noise The sound that a fan on a motherboard, case fan, hard drive, optical drive, or printer could make due to something getting caught in it, lack of oil, improperly inserted disc, or starting to fail. For a printer, check gears, torn paper, paper clips, staples, or labels along the paper path.

grounding See *equipment grounding*.

group policy A type of security policy applied in a network domain environment. The policy dictates what a set of users can do.

group policy editor A Microsoft snap-in that is used to control various Windows functions, apps, and what specific groups are allowed to do and deploy security settings.

GRUB (Grand Unified Boot Loader) A Linux boot loader that generally replaces the earlier LILO boot loader. It contains all information about how a disk is organized, such as the size and layout of partitions. The latest version is called GRUB2.

GSM (Global System for Mobile Communications) An older worldwide cellular network standard previously used in Europe and other places (and still used in some countries).

GUI (graphical user interface) In operating systems, an interface in which the user selects files, programs, and commands by clicking pictorial representations (icons) rather than typing commands at a command prompt.

H

hard drive A sealed data storage medium on which information is stored. Also called a hard disk.

hard reset The process of turning a device off and back on or a factory reset of a mobile device.

hard token A physical device used to gain access to a resource such as a file or company.

hardware A tangible, physical item, such as a keyboard or monitor.

hash A function used in security encryption and for file transfers to ensure that a file did not get changed during the download.

HDMI (high-definition multimedia interface) An upgraded digital interface that carries audio and video over the same cable.

head crash A problem that occurs when a read/write head touches a platter in a mechanical hard drive, causing damage to the heads or the platter.

header A set of motherboard pins that allows the addition of a specific function such as USB 2 or 3.x ports, UCB-C ports, SATA/eSATA ports, RGP LEDs, and a Trusted Platform Module (TPM).

headset A mobile wearable device that commonly includes a microphone and headphones.

heat sink A metal device for cooling a processor by conducting heat to its fins or bars. Convection then transfers the heat away by flowing air through the case.

heat spreader Aluminum or copper fittings on memory modules used to dissipate heat.

heating element The part on a thermal printer that is a component of the print head.

`help` A command used to list all of the available commands.

HFS (Hierarchical File System) A type of file system used with Apple computers that was upgraded to HFS+ and then later upgraded to Apple File System (APFS).

hidden share A share that has a dollar sign ($) added to the share name so that the share is not shown to a remote networked computer.

high-level formatting A process that sets up a file system for use by the computer. It is the third and last step in preparing a hard drive for use.
high availability A desired network feature where the network is available to be used 99.999% of the time.
high latency An undesired network characteristic where packets are dropped frequently and network systems respond slowly to network requests.
high network traffic An issue on a mobile device that may prompt you to try moving to a different location and getting closer to the access point or using a different cellular area to get better performance.
high number of ads A situation that can affect a mobile device data plan. Use OS, browser, and app privacy and location settings to block ads.
high sensitivity of thermal paper Thermal paper is affected by heat and requires special handling. Store thermal paper in a cool setting as it is highly sensitive to heat.
hole punch A device or feature on a printer that puts holes in paper. Check if paper that has been hole punched is being misfed or if the chaff from hole-punched paper is causing an issue.
home folder A network folder that allows users to store their files and have access to them from any device that they log onto within the same domain.
home server A server commonly used to act as a web server and print server, control home devices, manage backups, and be accessed from outside the home. A home server commonly includes the capability to stream sound or video, share files, have a Gigabit NIC, or have a RAID hard drive array.
host address A portion of an IP address that represents a specific network device.
host machine In a virtualization environment, a real computer.
hot fix Software used to fix a particular software problem. Contrast with *patch* and *service pack*.
hotspot A wireless network that provides free internet access. Security is a concern because no encryption or authentication is commonly required.
HPA (Host Protected Area) A hidden part of the hard drive that is used to reinstall the operating system. It sometimes contains applications installed when the computer was sold. Using an HPA reduces the amount of hard drive space available to the operating system.
HSM (hardware security module) Specialized hardware that can be a USB device or a device on a network used for digital key management, storage/protection of cryptographic keys, encryption, and authentication that operates much like a TPM.
HT See *Hyperthreading (HT)*.
HTTP (Hypertext Transfer Protocol) A standard for internet data communication.
HTTPS (HTTP over SSL) HTTP communication encrypted through an SSL session. With HTTPS, web pages are encrypted and decrypted.
hub A device used with Universal Serial Bus or in a star network topology that allows multiple device connections. A network hub cannot look at each data frame coming through its ports as a switch does. It forwards data frames (packets) to all ports.
humidity The amount of moisture in the air. The potential for an electrostatic discharge (ESD) event is higher when the humidity is low.
hybrid cloud A type of cloud technology in which a company has some cloud services maintained by internal staff (private cloud) and some cloud services that are outsourced (public cloud).
Hyperthreading (HT) A technology created by Intel that is an alternative to using two processors. HT allows a single processor to handle two separate sets of instructions simultaneously.
HyperTransport AMD's I/O architecture in which a serial-link design allows devices to communicate in daisy-chain fashion without interfering with any other communication. Thus, I/O bottlenecks are mitigated.
hypervisor In a virtualization environment, the software that creates the virtual machine (VM) and allocates resources to the VM. Also called a virtual machine monitor or virtual machine manager (VMM).

I

I/O address (input/output address) A port address that allows an external device to communicate with the microprocessor. It is analogous to a mailbox number.
I/O shield A part that allows for optimum air flow and grounding for the motherboard ports.
IaaS (infrastructure as a service) A type of cloud technology service in which routers, switches, servers, virtual machines, load balancers, access points, storage, and other infrastructure devices are provided through an online environment.

iCloud (offsite data storage and email option) An Apple cloud-based service that comes with macOS, offering storage, application support, and syncing of contacts, photos, email, bookmarks, documents, and more between multiple macOS, iOS, and even Windows devices.

ICMP (Internet Control Message Protocol) A Layer 3 protocol used for troubleshooting network connectivity. Commands that use ICMP include `ping`, `pathping`, and `tracert`.

icon An operating system graphic that represents a file, an application, hardware, or shared network resources.

IDE (Integrated Drive Electronics) An interface that evolved into the ATA (now PATA) standard and supports internal storage devices.

IDE cable Another name for a PATA cable, an older 40-pin parallel cable that could have two devices attached to the same cable that connects to the motherboard.

IDS (intrusion detection system) Software or hardware that is designed to detect potential security issues that could allow illegal entry to the computer or network. The IDS could log the incident and contact someone in order to prevent invasion.

`ifconfig` In Linux/Unix environments, a command that shows network interface information for Ethernet ports.

image deployment An operating system installation method in which a system image is taken from an external drive, disc, or server and put on a computer.

imaging drum A photosensitive drum inside a toner cartridge that attracts laser toner particles.

imaging process The stages a laser printer goes through to get an image on the page: processing, charging, exposing, developing, transferring, fusing, and cleaning.

IMAP (Internet Mail Access Protocol) A protocol used to receive email through the internet. Uses port 143 by default.

impact paper Special paper designed to withstand the pressure of images struck upon it in an impact printer printhead.

impact print head A component of an impact printer that holds tiny wires called print wires.

impact printer Sometimes called a dot matrix printer, a type of printer that physically impacts a ribbon in order to place images on the paper.

impersonation A social engineering security threat in which someone pretends to be from a user's bank or a company such as Microsoft to get the user to divulge information or to allow the attacker access to the user's account.

improper charging A situation in which a phone is inconsistent in how it charges. To solve such an issue, inspect the phone connection, clean the battery and pins with compressed air, and check the charger.

in-place upgrade A method of upgrading Windows when an older Windows version is already installed.

inaccurate system date/time A symptom of the CMOS battery failing or being dead.

incident documentation The process of providing details on what a technician has done about a particular problem.

incineration Destruction by fire.

incorrect chroma A problem that can be remedied by checking printer ink levels, running color calibration, and checking whether the manufacturer has a chroma optimizer.

incorrect color A problem caused by bent or broken video pins on a monitor's cable ends.

incorrect data source A problem that can be remedied by checking the input source and ensuring that it is correct for the project output.

incorrect orientation A problem that can be remedied by checking the printer page setup when the printed page does not come out the correct way.

incorrect paper size A problem that can be remedied by using the printer properties to select the correct size and orientation of the paper before printing.

incremental backup A backup method in which only files that have changed since the last backup are backed up. This type of backup is therefore faster than a full backup.

indexing A Microsoft Windows configurable feature that allows quick searches for files and folders.

inherited permissions Windows NTFS permissions that are propagated from what Microsoft calls a parent object. For example, if a folder is given the permission Read, then all files within that folder inherit the read-only attribute.

initialization A process in which a variable in a script is given an initial value.

initialize disk A disk option available through the Windows Disk Management tool that enables a disk so that data may be stored on it.

initializing (Disk Management) Making a drive available to be used by right-clicking on a drive > *Initialize Disk.*

ink cartridge A container that holds the ink and the nozzles for an inkjet printer. Also known as a print cartridge.

inkjet print head The part of an inkjet printer that holds the ink reservoir and the spray nozzles and is easily replaced.

inkjet printer A type of printer that squirts ink through tiny nozzles to produce print. Inkjet printers produce high-quality, high-resolution color output.

input To put data into a device or program.

integer A whole number, including zero and negative numbers.

integrated GPU (graphics processing unit) A video adapter processor that speeds up video processing and reduces power consumption.

Intel Corporation The largest processor manufacturer in the world. Intel also makes chipsets, motherboards, network cards, microcontrollers, and other electronic chips and components.

intermittent connectivity A symptom of poor or faulty connections with devices on the same network. To remedy this issue, use the `ping` command to check connections all around the network.

intermittent device failure A symptom of a faulty device that involves sporadic or irregular problems occurring with that device.

intermittent projector shutdown A common safety precaution for a projector when it has been used for a long period of time and needs to cool. If this occurs when the projector has only been powered a short period of time, check the filter.

intermittent shutdown A problem that can be caused by a bad power supply, motherboard, RAM, or CPU.

intermittent wireless A problem that can be remedied by turning off Wi-Fi and turning it back on again and moving the device to find a higher signal strength (as shown on the display on a laptop).

intermittent wireless connectivity A problem in which a wireless device's connection to a wireless network is affected by obstructions such as walls, trees, concrete columns, rain, snow, fog, other buildings, microwave ovens, and other wireless networks operating in the same unlicensed frequency range.

internal data bus The electronic lines inside a processor.

internal fixed disk (boot option) An operating system boot option to boot from a partition on an internal hard drive.

internal hard drive partition (boot option) An operating system boot option to boot from a bootable partition.

internet calling Communicating using the internet and an app such as Skype, Google Hangouts, or WhatsApp.

Internet Explorer An older Microsoft browser that is being replaced by Edge.

interpreted program Code that is carried out one line at a time.

interrupt See *IRQ (interrupt request).*

Intrusion Detection/Notification A BIOS/UEFI setting, also known as Chassis Intrusion, that allows for notification when the computer cover is removed.

inventory list A list of assets input into an inventory management system or database that can be viewed or printed to see specific details on hardware and/or software maintained by a company.

inverter A device that converts low DC voltage to high AC voltage for the backlight bulb in an LED display.

IOPS (input/output operations per second) A measurement of hard drive speed for both magnetic drives and SSDs that takes into account sequential reads/writes and random reads/writes.

iOS An Apple operating system for mobile devices.

IoT (Internet of Things) Connected technology including sensors and smart devices that provides data, information, warnings, and control of things like lights, cameras, appliances, thermostats, and locks.

IP (Internet Protocol) A Layer 3 protocol that is part of the TCP/IP protocol suite.

IP address A type of network adapter address used when multiple networks are linked. Known as a Layer 3 address, in IPv4 it is a 32-bit binary number with groups of 8 bits separated by a dot. This numbering scheme is also known as dotted-decimal notation. Each 8-bit group represents numbers from 0 to 255. An example of an IPv4 IP address is 113.19.12.102. See also *IPv4 (Internet Protocol version 4)* and *IPv6 (Internet Protocol version 6).*

IP addressing scheme A methodical way of setting up network numbers within an organization. Within a company, the IP addressing scheme tends to be private IP addresses.

IP filtering A process that permits or denies specific network traffic based on websites, users, IP addresses, protocols, or apps.

iPadOS The operating system used on a Macintosh tablet (an iPad).

`ipconfig` A command used from a command prompt in Windows to view the current IP configuration settings.

IPS (intrusion prevention system) A security device that actively monitors and scans network traffic for malicious traffic and violations of security policies and that takes appropriate action.

IPS (in-plane switching) A type of LCD display that is best to use when viewing from an angle and needing good quality and color.

IPv4 (Internet Protocol version 4) A standard that includes a type of IP address that uses 32 bits (four groups of 8 bits each) shown as decimal numbers in dotted-decimal format. An example of an IPv4 address is 192.168.10.1.

IPv6 (Internet Protocol version 6) A standard that includes a type of IP address that uses 128 bits represented by hexadecimal numbers. An example of an IPv6 address is fe80::13e:4586:5807:95f7. Each set of four digits represents 16 bits.

IR (infrared) A technology used for wireless input/output that is useful only over short distances.

IRQ (interrupt request) A microprocessor priority system that assigns a number to each expansion adapter or port to facilitate orderly communication.

iSCSI A fiber standard used to connect a storage area network (SAN) to the other network devices.

ISP (internet service provider) A vendor that provides a connection to the internet.

IT automation A method of implementing change where changes to devices or applications can occur without a human making repetitive changes to multiple systems.

iteration A programming loop that consists of a block of statements that are executed repeatedly for a specific number of times or until a specific condition is met.

iTunes An Apple program that allows users to play and manage music, books, movies, and lectures.

ITX (Information Technology eXtended) A motherboard form factor size that is smaller than ATX which is the most common form factor. Comes in mini-ITX, nano-ITX, and pico-ITX sizes.

`iwconfig` In Linux/Unix systems, a command that shows network interface information for wireless adapters.

iWork A macOS office productivity suite that includes a word processor, a spreadsheet, and presentation applications.

J

`.js` A file extension used with JavaScript files.

jailbreak To compromise the operating system of an iOS mobile device so the user has an increased level of privilege.

JavaScript A programming language that can be run on any operating system. Creating and running JavaScript commands requires installing `Node.js`. The extension that identifies a JavaScript file is `.js`.

JBOD (just a bunch of disks or just a bunch of drives) A term that refers to combining multiple drives, with the combination recognized as a single drive letter or a single virtual disk. This is similar in concept to RAID but is not one of the RAID levels.

jitter Irregular receipt of voice packets that is measured in seconds and can cause poor VoIP quality.

jumper A plastic cover for two metal pins on a jumper block.

K

Kb Abbreviation for kilobit.

KB See *kilobyte*.

Kerberos A protocol used in conjunction with an authentication server to prevent transmitted packets from being altered or read.

kernel The heart of an operating system, which acts as the controller and interpreter for nearly everything in a system so that hardware and software can interface and work together. It controls memory management, peripherals, and allocating other system resources to processes.

kernel panic A critical system error that the operating system cannot recover from. When this happens in macOS, the Mac reboots to return to a stable state.

key A physical security measure that can be a physical metal key or an electronic key.
key fob A device used for keyless entry.
keyboard A device that allows a user to provide input to a computer.
keyboard port A DIN connector on the motherboard into which only the keyboard cable must connect.
Keychain Access A macOS utility for managing saved passwords securely.
keylogger Software designed to capture keystrokes in an effort to collect user IDs and passwords.
keyword A set of characters that is an instruction in a particular programming or scripting language.
`kill` A command used through the Terminal application on a Mac or in Linux to halt a program that has frozen or is not responding. An example is `kill -9`, where `9` is the *process_id*.
kill task A step to take if an application has frozen or has quit responding.
kilobyte Approximately 1,000 bytes of information (exactly 1,024 bytes).
KMS (Key Management Service) A software application used in companies that have 25 or more Windows computers to deploy. All newly installed computers register with the computer that has KMS installed. Every 180 days, the computer is re-activated for the license. Each KMS key can be used on two computers up to 10 times.
knowledge base A collection of documents used to answer commonly asked IT questions or describe IT procedures.

L

L1 cache Fast memory located inside the processor.
L2 cache Fast memory located inside the processor housing but not inside the processor.
L3 cache Any fast cache memory installed on the motherboard when both L1 and L2 cache are on the processor. Could also be located inside the processor housing.
LAN (local area network) A group of devices sharing resources in a single area, such as a room or a building.
laptop docking station A device used to provide increased connectivity, such as to one or more displays, full-sized keyboard, mouse, and so on, as well as wired network connectivity.
laptop RAM A memory module that is normally in the SODIMM form factor.
laser printer A type of printer that produces output using an imaging process similar to a copier. Laser printers are the most expensive type of printer.
laser printer maintenance kit A kit that may include a separation pad, pickup roller, transfer roller, charge roller, and fuser assembly, depending on the vendor.
latency The amount of time a packet takes to travel from source to destination. Use the `tracert` command to see the amount of latency.
launcher A dock-like shortcut bar that allows manipulation of the graphical user interface (GUI) so that multiple apps and/or commands are easily deployed. It has the functionality of being an application launcher shortcut as well as having a universal search feature built in to it.
Launchpad A macOS application launcher shortcut.
LCD (liquid crystal display) A video technology used with laptops and flat screen monitors. The two basic types of LCD are passive matrix and active matrix.
LDAP (Lightweight Directory Access Protocol) A networking protocol that is used to access, maintain, and distribute directory and database-type information. LDAP uses port 389.
LED (light-emitting diode) A video output technology that is a low-power, low-heat, long-lasting electronic device using liquid crystals.
legacy software An older software program that might require an older OS to run or that does not run properly under a newer OS.
legacy system An outdated computer system or piece of network equipment that needs to be replaced or updated.
`less` A common macOS and Linux command that shows the contents of a file.
library Windows storage that is similar to a folder but that is automatically indexed for faster searching.
licensed range A set of wireless frequencies that are managed by the FCC for a specific geographic region.
licensing Legitimately using a particular software package after purchasing or registering with the software provider.
lifting technique The proper method to use when lifting equipment, involving using your legs and not your back.

Lightning port An Apple port used to connect displays and external drives. Commonly used to connect Apple mobile devices like iPhones and iPads to host computers and USB battery chargers.
limited connectivity An error condition in which internet connectivity is lost.
line conditioner A device that protects a computer from overvoltage and undervoltage conditions as well as adverse noise conditions. Also known as a power conditioner.
link-local address A type of IPv6 address assigned to a NIC. It is used to communicate on a particular network and cannot be used to communicate with devices on a different network.
Linux A widely used operating system platform, released in 1991 by developer Linus Torvalds, that is similar to Unix. It is a free open source operating system that anyone can use, contribute to, and modify. It is widely used in many different areas of technology, such as servers, desktops, embedded systems, and smartphones.
liquid cooling An alternative to a fan or heat sink for processor cooling in which liquid is circulated through the system, and heat from the processor is transferred to the cooler liquid.
liquid damage A common hazard of mobile devices.
live tile A Windows 8/8.1/10 feature that allows the content within to change, such as a news headline feed.
load alternate third-party driver The part of the Windows installation process in which a technician downloads drivers for hardware such as a RAID controller before continuing the installation process.
load balancer A technology used with redundancy, such as multiple paths through the network or multiple servers for a particular app or purpose such as DNS.
local security policy Security rules that can be applied to a computer.
local share Something such as a printer, folder, or disc that has been made available across a network.
Local Users and Groups A Windows tool used to create and manage accounts for those who use the computer or computer resources from a remote network computer. These accounts are considered local users or local groups and are managed from the computer being worked on. In contrast, domain or global users and groups are administered by a network administrator on a network server.
`locate` A macOS command that searches for a file in a database of paths. Commonly used subsequently to `update`, which is a command used to update a local database on the system that contains the full pathname of each file.
locator application Software used to pinpoint where a mobile device can be found.
log off when not in use A best practice when not using a computer, which involves configuring a screen saver to appear or locking the computer after a period of non-use.
logical drive A division of an extended partition into a separate unit, which appears as a separate drive letter.
logical operator An operator used in scripting to allow for two or more conditions to be tested in one statement. Examples of logical operators include `AND`, `NOT`, and `OR`.
logical partition A division of an extended partition. A logical partition can be assigned a drive letter, formatted, and used for storage.
login script A set of tasks that run when a user logs in when the device is part of a Windows domain. Also known as a logon script.
logon script See *login script*.
LoJack (BIOS option) A BIOS setting option that controls locating the device, remotely locking the device, remotely deleting data, and displaying an "if lost" message.
loop In scripting, a method of repeating something.
loop structure A repetition structure that uses loops, which contains blocks of statements that are executed repeatedly.
loopback plug A troubleshooting device used for port testing.
lost cluster A sector on a disk that the file allocation table cannot associate with any file or directory.
low RF signal A problem caused by a wireless device being too far away from a wireless access point/router or obstructions such as walls.
low-level format Use of a utility that formats a drive; note that this is different from the high-level format done on a newly installed drive or during an operating system installation.
`ls` A Linux command that lists the contents of the current directory.
LTE (Long Term Evolution) A version of the 4G cellular network generation that optimized the network for video streaming and online games.

Lucent connector (LC) A type of fiber-optic connector that snaps into a connector.

lumens A measure of light output or brightness; how much visible light is coming out of equipment such as lamps, lighting equipment, or projectors.

M

M.2 A type of connector that allows attachment of modules of varying size. First found in mobile devices and used for SSDs but now found on desktop motherboards.

MAC address (Media Access Control address) One of two types of addresses assigned to network adapters, used when two devices on the same network communicate. Also known as a Layer 2 address.

MAC address filtering A security feature on an access point that allows MAC addresses to be entered to limit the number of wireless devices allowed on the wireless network.

macOS A Unix-based operating system that was developed by Apple, Inc., for its Macintosh line of computers, called Mac for short. macOS is the second-most-commonly used desktop operating system behind Windows and is the most-used type of Unix/Linux-based desktop operating systems.

magnetometer A device used to scan for firearms/weapons that might also be used for location tracking.

mail server An application that is used to maintain a database of email accounts, store email that has been sent and received, and communicate with other mail servers. Also known as an email server.

maintain a positive attitude A great idea for professionalism and good rapport with customers.

maintenance counter An option on a laser printer that counts the number of pages until the message to apply the maintenance kit appears again.

maintenance kit A collection of items commonly used for technical support that includes a portable vacuum, toner vacuum, compressed air, swabs, monitor wipes, lint-free cloths, general-purpose cloths, general-purpose cleanser, denatured alcohol, antistatic brush, optical drive cleaning kit, gold contact cleaner, safety goggles, and an air filter or mask.

malicious app An illegitimate piece of software that could install a virus or ransomware, that could be spyware, and that could disrupt normal usage.

malware Software code designed to damage an electronic device (that is, cause lockups or slowness, crash an app, cause the device not to run or boot, and more).

MAM (mobile application management) A platform used to manage apps on mobile devices so that new apps can be pushed out, older apps updated, and new features or security measures added.

`man` A Linux command, short for *manual*, that can be used with another command to bring up an instruction manual for using the other command.

MAN (metropolitan area network) In a networking environment, a network that spans a city or town.

man-in-the-middle (MITM) See *on-path [attack]*.

managed switch A type of switch used in a corporate network that has an IP address assigned and can be remotely accessed, configured, and monitored by an administrator.

mantrap See *access control vestibule*.

mATX See *micro-ATX*.

Mb An abbreviation for megabit.

MB See *megabyte*.

MBR (master boot record) A program that reads the partition table to find the primary partition used to boot the system.

`md` A command issued from a command prompt that creates a directory (folder) or subdirectory.

MDM (mobile device management) The capability to view and manage multiple mobile devices.

measured service The capability to track cloud consumer usage and apply resources as needed, based on usage.

megabyte Approximately 1 million bytes of data (exactly 1,048,576 bytes). Abbreviated MB.

memory The part of a computer that temporarily stores applications, user documents, and system operating information.

memory address A unique address for memory chips.

memory card reader A device that accepts varied types of memory cards so that data can be copied or read.

Memory Diagnostic Tool A tool accessed by booting from the Advanced Boot Options menu in Windows to thoroughly test RAM.

menu bar A component of the macOS GUI that is anchored to the top of a screen and is a dynamically changing bar that presents contextual drop-down menu options on the left side, depending on which window is active. On the right side, it provides shortcuts such as for connecting to a Wi-Fi network or changing volume. It is also informative, displaying information such as battery life on laptops and the time.
metered connection A type of internet connection that has a data limit imposed by the service provider.
metered service A cloud computing service for which a company pays an amount based on how much of the service is used on an hourly or monthly basis.
micro-ATX A smaller version of a standard ATX-sized motherboard form factor. Also known as mATX.
microphone An audio input device that can be integrated into a mobile device or that can be added externally, as with a wireless Bluetooth device; controlled with an app.
microprocessor See *processor.*
Microsoft Defender Antivirus Security software that is compatible with other antivirus products and is available in Windows.
Microsoft Management Console See *MMC (Microsoft Management Console) or* `mmc`.
Microsoft Windows An operating system used on PCs, tablets, and laptops.
microUSB A standard interface port on mobile devices and smartphones.
MIMO (multiple input/multiple output) An 802.11n wireless technology in which multiple antennas operate cooperatively to increase throughput on a wireless network.
miniPCIe A 52-pin expansion slot or card used in mobile devices.
miniUSB A port on mobile devices that is a miniaturized version of the Universal Serial Bus (USB) interface created for connecting smartphones, GPS devices, printers, and digital cameras.
mini-DIN A motherboard connector, sometimes called a PS/2 connector, that connects keyboards and mice.
missing drive in OS A problem in which the BIOS/UEFI recognizes the storage device, but the OS does not. To handle this issue, use the Disk Management tool to initialize and/or partition the drive.
Mission Control A macOS utility that gives an overview for managing all application windows and virtual desktops.
missing files A symptom of malware.
`mkdir` A Linux (and Windows) command used to make a directory.
MMC (Microsoft Management Console) or `mmc` A Windows container for management tools. Also known as the Computer Management console. It holds tools such as Device Manager, Disk Management, Local Users and Groups, Event Viewer, Task Scheduler, Performance, Shared Folders, and Services. `mmc` is also the command used from a command prompt to open the Microsoft Management Console.
mobile device motherboard A motherboard that tends to be proprietary and must be replaced with one from the same manufacturer.
mobile docking station A recharging station that provides a stable environment for mobile devices. A mobile docking station may be able to charge more than one device at a time.
modem (modulator/demodulator) A device that connects a computer to a phone line or that connects computers and mobile devices to broadband, wireless, Wi-Fi, Bluetooth, or satellite networks.
modular power supply A type of power supply that allows the customization of the number and type of power connections plugged into the power supply.
Molex A type of power connector that extends from a computer's power supply to various devices.
monitor A device that displays information from a computer to a user.
motherboard The main circuit board of a computer. Also known as the mainboard, planar, or system board.
motherboard LED A light on a motherboard that is used in troubleshooting. Common LEDs include those for the CPU, boot or drive, VGA or video, and RAM or DRAM.
mount To make a drive available and recognizable to the operating system through use of the `diskpart` command utility.
mounting (Disk Management) Mapping an empty folder on an NTFS volume by right-clicking on a partition or volume > *Change Drive Letter and Paths* > *Add* > *Mount in the Following Empty NTFS Folder* and either type the path or browse to an empty folder > *OK* > *OK*.
mouse A data input device that moves the cursor or selects menus and options.

mouse port A DIN connector on the motherboard that should accept only a mouse cable.
MOV (metal oxide varistor) An electronic component built in to some surge protectors to absorb overvoltage spikes or surges.
mSATA A connector type used for SSDs on desktop motherboards, laptops, and mobile devices.
`msconfig` A system configuration utility command that allows an administrator to enable or disable services, access Control Panel links, and control applications.
MSDS (material safety data sheet) A safety-related document that contains information about a product, including its toxicity and recommendations for storage/disposal.
`msinfo32` A Windows command used to bring up the System Information window from a command prompt. The System Information window contains details about hardware and hardware configurations as well as software and software drivers.
MSRA (Microsoft Remote Assistance) See *Remote Assistance*.
`mstsc` A Windows command used to control and use a remote computer that brings up the Remote Desktop Connection utility.
MTBF (mean time between failures) The average number of hours before a device fails.
MU-MIMO (multi-user multiple input/multiple output) A wireless technology used with 802.11ac that allows up to eight simultaneous streams from multiple devices.
multi-mode fiber A type of fiber-optic cabling that allows multiple light signals to be sent along the same cable.
multiboot A situation in which a computer can boot from two or more operating systems.
multicore A term used to indicate multiple processor cores in the same housing.
multifactor authentication Use of two or more factors to provide access. The factors can be something you possess, such as a card, current location, security token–provided code, PIN, fingerprint, facial recognition, palm print, or password.
multifunction device A device that can print, copy, scan, and sometimes act as a facsimile (fax) machine.
multipage misfeed A printer problem that requires checking the rollers through the paper path, crooked paper, or the alignment guides.
multiple print jobs pending A printer problem that requires checking for paper, ink/toner, and device error message. Repair the problem and clear the print job or restart the printing.
multisocket A feature on a motherboard that allows more than one processor to be installed.
multithreading A method of processing that allows an operating system to be more efficient as it can perform multiple tasks to keep the processor busy.
`mv` A Linux command that moves a file.
MX record (mail exchange record) A type of DNS record that forwards email to a server in another domain.

N

.NET Core An open source managed computer software framework used for the cross-platform version of Windows PowerShell.
`nano` An easy-to-use Linux text editor.
NAS (network-attached storage) Hardware that contains multiple drives that can be accessed by networked computers and devices.
NAS drive A drive used in a network-attached storage device that costs more than a drive of the same capacity used in a PC, for example, because a NAS drive is built to run 24/7.
NAT (network address translation) A method of conserving public IP addresses. NAT uses private IP addresses that become translated to public IP addresses.
native resolution The number of pixels going across and down a flat panel monitor. This resolution is the specification for which the monitor was made and is the optimum resolution.
Nautilus The default file manager for the GNOME desktop in Linux systems.
`net` A command that manages almost everything on a network. It can be followed by a number of options, each of which has different parameters.
`net use` A command that is used to map a network share to a drive letter or to view mapped drives on a Microsoft-based machine.
`net user` A command that is used to create, delete, or make changes to user accounts from a command prompt on a Microsoft-based machine.

NetBT (NetBIOS over TCP/IP) A protocol that uses TCP ports 137–139 to support outdated applications that rely on the NetBIOS API to use a TCP/IP-based network. Also known as NBT.

`netdom` A command that is used to manage workstations in a domain environment.

`netstat` A command that is used to view current network connections and the local routing table for a PC.

network Two or more devices that can communicate and share resources with each other.

Network A Windows File Explorer link found in the left panel that allows access to other network devices.

network boot Sometimes called a Preboot Execution Environment (PXE) boot, where the system boots from a server that deploys an operating system image to a computer.

network interface card See *NIC (network interface card).*

network number The portion of an IP address that represents which network the computer is on.

network path An address that can be used from a command prompt or File Explorer that can be used to go to a shared resource such as a folder.

network port A port that connects a computer to a wired network.

network protocol A data communication language.

network share A folder or network device that has been shared and is accessible from a remote computer.

network topology diagram A type of IT documentation that shows how wired and wireless devices connect.

NFC (near field communication) A technology that connects nearby devices without a cord.

NFS (Network File System) An open standard protocol used for sharing files across a network.

NIC (network interface card) A port on a device that allows connectivity to a network. A NIC can connect to a wired or wireless network.

no Bluetooth connectivity An issue that could be helped by turning the device off and back on, checking for interference, ensuring that Bluetooth is enabled, and entering passkeys/PINs.

no connectivity An error condition that exists if the self-test issued from a computer fails.

no display A problem on a mobile device that can be solved by attaching an external display, or, if attached to a projector, checking the output port chosen. Other options are to check the lid close detector, turn the device off and back on, and charge the device fully.

no internet connectivity See *no connectivity.*

no OS found An error that indicates that the operating system is corrupt, there is a problem with the boot device such as the hard drive, or the BIOS/UEFI settings are incorrect.

no power A problem with a computer that can be remedied by checking that the power cord is attached, the power button is pushed, the surge strip is turned on, and the monitor is turned on; the problem could be an indication of a faulty power supply. On a mobile device, check brightness, the lid close sensor, and the battery. On any computer, check for malware.

no wireless connectivity A problem with a computer that can be remedied by checking whether Wi-Fi is enabled and ensuring that the device is not in Airplane Mode. Turn off Wi-Fi and turn it back on again. Move the device to see if you have a higher signal strength (display on a laptop). Ensure that the correct wireless network is chosen.

non-compliant system A machine that does not meet security policy requirements and that could be a potential security threat.

non-parity A less expensive type of memory chip that does not perform error checking.

`NOT` operator A scripting operator that flips the result of an expression so that if an expression is true, it will return false and vice versa; if the expression is false, it will return true.

Notepad An accessory text editor program in Windows.

`notepad` **[command]** A command that opens the Windows Notepad text editor app.

notification area (Windows) The far-right area of the taskbar, which contains information about an application or a tool, such as security, network access, speaker control, and date and time.

`nslookup` A Windows troubleshooting command that displays network domain names and their associated IP addresses.

NTFS (New Technology File System) The file system used with Microsoft operating systems today (starting with Windows NT). It enables encryption, compression, larger file sizes, and longer filenames.

NTFS permissions A security measure that can dictate what a specific user or group can do with a file or folder.

NTLDR is missing A Windows boot error condition in which the operating system needs to be reinstalled.
NTP (Network Time Protocol) A protocol that synchronizes time between network devices.
NVMe (Non-Volatile Memory Express) A technology used with SSDs that provides fast performance when accessing NAND flash memory.

O

off site storage Storage of data and backups at a remote location or in the cloud.
ohm A measurement of electrical resistance.
OLED (organic LED) A display screen technology used in many monitors, TVs, and mobile devices today. It does not require a backlight like LCDs but has a film of organic compounds placed in rows and columns that can emit light. It is lightweight and has a fast response time, low power usage, and a wide viewing angle.
omnidirectional antenna A type of antenna that has a radiation pattern in all directions.
on site storage Storage of data and backups kept within a business.
on-path [attack] An attack in which a threat actor collects or even changes data between a user and the device providing the service (such as a web server). The attacker inserts a device that mimics being an AP, DHCP server, or router/Layer 3 switch that is the default gateway for a network. Formerly referred to as a man-in-the-middle attack.
OneDrive Microsoft's cloud storage solution.
ONT (Optical Network Terminal) A device that converts light signals from a fiber connection into electrical for a copper connection.
open source Software that allows vendors to use the core source code and gives them the ability to customize the software. Examples include Google Android and Linux.
open-ended question A soft skills technique that results in more information about a problem than questions that have just yes or no answers.
operating system (OS) A piece of software that loads a computer and makes it operational.
optical cable See *fiber cable.*
optical disc (boot option) A boot method that uses a CD, DVD, or Blu-ray disc that has an operating system on it.
optical drive A storage device that accepts optical discs such as CDs, DVDs, or BDs that hold data, music, video, or software applications.
Optimize and Defragment A Windows tool accessed with the Defragment button or by using the `defrag` command. It is used to put files in contiguous clusters on the hard drive for better performance.
`OR` operator A scripting operator that returns false if and only if both sides of the expression are false.
organizational unit (OU) An Active Directory container that groups users, groups, accounts, or even other OUs in order to subdivide administrative duties.
orientation The way in which a document or screen is presented: portrait vs. landscape.
OS See *operating system (OS).*
OS fails to update [mobile] An issue that requires a technician to be sure device is powered on and connected to Wi-Fi or a wired network; free up space; ensure that the device is still supported; turn off Bluetooth; reset the device and clear the cache and storage space; and restart the device or perform a factory reset.
OS not found An issue that occurs when the boot order in the BIOS/UEFI is incorrect, when the hard drive does not contain an operating system, or when there is an issue with the drive that contains the operating system being recognized by the computer.
OS update [mobile] An upgrade to an operating system that is important on mobile devices because the update commonly contains security patches; a device should be connected to power if possible during an update.
OS X An older Apple operating system family that has been replaced by macOS.
OSHA (Occupational Safety and Health Administration) A division of the U.S. Department of Labor that promotes safe and healthy working conditions by enforcing standards and providing workplace safety training.
OSI model (Open Systems Interconnection model) A standard for information transfer across a network that was developed by the International Organization for Standardization. The model has seven layers; each layer uses the layer below it, and each layer provides some function to the one above it.
output In programming or scripting, the result, which could be a screen, a value, a computation, a printed document, and so on.

overclocking Manually changing the front side bus speed and/or multiplier to increase CPU and system speed, but at the cost of increasing the CPU operating temperature. Overclocking a CPU may void the manufacturer's warranty.
overheating An issue with a device getting too hot. For a mobile device, power off the device and let it cool. See if you can determine if a specific spot is getting hotter than other places. Check the battery and replace it, if necessary.
overvoltage A condition in which the AC voltage is above the rated amount of voltage.

P

`.ps1` A file extension used for a PowerShell script.
`.py` A file extension used for a Python script.
PaaS (platform as a service) A type of cloud service in which servers, databases, operating system, storage, and development tools are provided in an outside environment to relieve the support burden on companies that need an environment to perform high-level programming and develop applications.
paging file A temporary file in hard disk space used by Windows that varies in size depending on the amount of RAM installed, the available hard drive space, and the amount of memory needed to run the application. Also known as a swap file.
palmprint scanner A biometric security device that is more secure than a fingerprint reader and scans the hand and possibly provides vein analysis.
PAN (personal area network) A network of personal devices such as cell phones, laptop computers, and other mobile devices that can communicate in close proximity through a wired network or wirelessly. A Bluetooth wireless keyboard and mouse form a PAN.
Panel A part of a Linux GUI and similar to macOS, Panel is a menu bar at the top of the screen containing contextual information on the left side and static information on the right side.
paper jam A problem that occurs when paper gets stuck along the printer paper pathway.
paper not feeding A problem that may be due to poor-paper quality or to the inefficiency of the rubber rollers that move the paper.
partition A process that can divide a hard drive so that the computer sees more than one drive.
`passwd` A Linux/Unix command to set or change a user password.
password manager Software that can potentially fill in web forms and that manages passwords for various websites.
password policy A policy that may be contained within a security policy that defines password requirements (length and types of characters) as well as the password change process.
password security The act of being conscientious about where passwords are written and stored.
Passwords [BIOS] A BIOS/UEFI setting that provides protection of the BIOS menu option by storing one or more passwords to access the Setup program.
patch A piece of software that fixes a specific problem in an application or operating system.
patch panel With twisted pair cable, a central location to which network cables terminate. It mounts in a network wiring rack, has network ports on the front, and has wiring connected to the back to provide network connectivity.
patch/update management A security best practice in which the operating system, drivers, and BIOS/UEFI are kept up to date so that known security issues are addressed.
patching/OS updates A security best practice for mobile devices in which the operating system (OS) and radio firmware for devices such as cell phones are updated.
path A reference that tells where a file is located among drives and folders (directories).
PATH variable A variable that is used in programming and scripting to tell a program where to find the files that it may need.
`pathping` A command that provides output similar to the `ping` and `tracert` commands and that includes network latency and loss information between source and destination IP addresses.
PC (personal computer) A common name for a computer, derived from the IBM PC brand.
PCI (payment card industry) A generic term for the entities surrounding businesses using payment cards, such as debit and credit cards, for transactions.
PCI (payment card information) A type of regulated data related to a credit card, debit card, and the finance industry.

PCI (Peripheral Component Interconnect) An older 32-bit and 64-bit, 66 MHz local bus standard used in computers.

PCIe A point-to-point serial bus used for motherboard adapters. Each bit can travel over a lane, and each lane allows transfers up to 250 MB/s, with a maximum of 32 lanes (which gives a total of an 8 GB/s transfer rate).

PCL (Printer Control Language) A language that uses printer hardware to do the translation between the printer and the computer.

PD (Power Delivery) A USB standard that allows up to 20V at 5A for 100 watts of power. The standard has five levels of power: 10W, 18W, 36W, 60W, and 100W.

PDL (Page Description Language) A language unique to a printer that allows communication between the computer and printer and handles the overall page look of a document.

performance (virtual memory) The level of operation of a computer, which is affected by the virtual memory settings that allocate specific hard drive space to be used when more applications and data are loaded than the amount of RAM installed.

Performance Monitor A Windows tool that monitors resources such as memory and CPU usage and that allows the creation of graphs, bar charts, and text reports.

Performance utility A utility that monitors memory and usage of other hardware parameters.

PHI (protected health information) Certain types of private health-related information that are protected by the Health Insurance Portability and Accountability Act (HIPAA).

phishing A type of social engineering in which the attacker attempts to get personal information by sending emails that appear to be from legitimate companies.

phone filter A part used with DSL internet connectivity that must be attached to every phone outlet and used to connect a traditional analog device.

phone skills An important skill set for technicians when talking to users and supporting them over the phone.

physical cabling issue [projector] Inability of a projector to output from a particular source. This issue can be solved by checking all physical connections on both ends of the cable.

physically damaged port A problem that leads to a device failing to charge after changing the cable. This issue can be solved by closely inspecting a mobile device port.

pickup rollers Printer feed rollers.

PII (personally identifiable information) Any personal data or method of identifying, locating, or contacting a particular person.

PIN (personal identification number) A unique identifier used to access an account or a device such as a mobile tablet.

PIN code A security option commonly available on mobile devices.

`ping` A network troubleshooting command used to test TCP/IP communications and determine whether a network path is available, whether any delays exist along the path, and whether a remote network device is reachable.

pinwheel A spinning wheel, often seen in macOS, generated by the operating system to indicate possible problems such as a nonresponsive application.

pipe symbol A character (|) used at the command prompt that allows control of where or how the output of the command is processed.

piracy The act of copying or distributing copyrighted software.

plastic filament A consumable supply that a 3-D printer needs for printing.

plenum cable A type of cable that is treated with fire-retardant materials so that it poses reduced fire risk.

PoE (Power over Ethernet) A method of powering a remote device through an Ethernet switch or a patch panel.

PoE injector A method of providing power to a remote device using an injector when a PoE switch or patch panel is not available.

PoE switch A switch that has the ability to provide power to devices such as access points or IP phones through the Power over Ethernet standard.

poor battery health A problem that can be solved by closing any apps and services that are not being used and replacing the battery.

poor VoIP quality A problem that results in dropped calls or unintelligible audio that is solved by implementing QoS. Key measurements of VoIP quality are latency and jitter.

poor wireless connectivity See *intermittent wireless*.
POP3 (Post Office Protocol) A protocol used to retrieve email from a mail server. It uses port 110.
pop-up A small window that appears (pops up) to display a message, a warning, or advice. Pop-ups often are a nuisance but can be managed through the browser's pop-up blocker feature.
port A connector located on a motherboard or on a separate adapter.
port flapping A situation in which a port is continuously going up and down.
port forwarding The process of sending data through a firewall, based on a particular port number or protocol.
port mapping The combination of one public address and a port number that represents one internal company host; also called port address translation (PAT).
port replicator A part that is similar to a docking station that attaches to a laptop computer and allows more devices, such as a monitor, keyboard, and mouse, to be connected.
port security A security feature on a corporate switch that detects whether someone has swapped one corporate device for another one.
port security [firewall] An advanced setting that can allow inbound or outbound traffic based on a specific TCP or UDP port number.
port triggering Temporarily sending data through a firewall, based on a preconfigured condition.
POSIX (Portable Operating System Interface) A designation that meets the specifications of a standardized operating system outlined by the IEEE Computer Society, containing a Bourne shell and other standard programs and services.
POST (power-on self-test) Startup software contained in the BIOS/UEFI that tests individual hardware components.
POST beep An indication that a hardware error exists, such as an error in the CPU, motherboard, RAM, or or a stuck key. Look up the code for more information.
POST card An adapter or a USB attached card that performs diagnostics and displays the results as a series of codes on an LED display.
PostScript A popular page description language from Adobe Systems Inc.
power A measurement, expressed in watts, that represents how much work is being done.
power rating A measurement, expressed in watts per channel, that represents how loud the speaker volume can go without distorting the sound.
power supply A device that converts AC voltage into DC voltage that the computer can use to power all internal and some external devices.
power supply tester A tool that checks DC voltages sourced from the power supply.
power surge An overvoltage condition that is like a spike but that has a longer duration.
PowerShell A Windows technology that helps technicians and network administrators automate support functions through the use of scripts and snippets.
prefix notation A method used to describe a subnet mask. It includes a forward slash followed by a number, such as /24. The number is how many consecutive bits are set in the subnet mask.
preventive maintenance Maintenance that is done to prolong the life of a device.
primary partition The first detected drive partition on a hard drive that has been configured with a basic disk.
principle of least privilege A security measure in which a user receives only enough security permissions (on devices, files, network resources, and so on) to do his or her job.
print bed The part of a 3-D printer where an object is built.
print driver A piece of software that coordinates between the operating system and the printer.
Print Management A Windows administrative tool used to manage printers. Use the Print Management administrative tool from the System and Security Control Panel or use the `printmanagement.msc` command.
print ribbon A ribbon in an impact printer that is struck by the print head to leave images on paper.
print server A device (a computer or a separate device) that connects to a printer used by multiple people through a network.
print spooler Also known as a print manager, a software program that intercepts a request to print and sends print information to the hard drive, from which it is then sent to the printer whenever the processor is not busy with other tasks. A print spooler allows multiple print jobs to be queued inside the computer so that other work can be performed.

printer A peripheral used to output text and/or graphics onto paper.
printer sharing The process of allowing multiple users on the same printer. It is commonly used in home and small business environments. Contrast with a printer server, used in corporate environments.
printhead The part of an impact printer that holds the print wires and impacts the ribbon.
printing issue A problem that occurs when trying to send output to a printer. In Windows, try to print a test page from the printer's *Properties > General* tab. Use the Windows Troubleshooting tool.
private browsing A privacy feature that prevents browsing history, cookies, and data from being collected and kept.
private cloud Part of a company's network infrastructure located outside the business in a remote location. The company has responsibility for managing the software and hardware involved in a private cloud.
private IP address An IP address used inside a home or business that is not allowed to be transmitted across the internet. Contrast to a public IP address.
private network A home or corporate network that uses private IP addresses that are not allowed to be routed on the internet but that are translated at the network border into public addresses using a process called NAT.
PRL (preferred roaming list) The default roaming list created by a cell network provider.
PRL update A software configuration changed pushed out to a smartphone by a service provider.
proactive A good trait to have as a technician that involves implementing measures to avoid problems rather than waiting for problems to occur before implementing measures.
processing [laser printing] A laser printing process in which data is converted from the printer language into a bitmap image. This process is also known as raster image processing.
processing [scripting] The part of a program involved in performing work or a task. Input and output are the other two parts of a program.
processor A central 32-bit or 64-bit electronic chip that determines the processing power of a computer. Also known as a microprocessor or central processing unit (CPU).
procurement life cycle Company processes that are performed in order to obtain equipment or applications.
Program Compatibility Wizard A program that can check for software application compatibility with a newer Windows version.
project confidence A skill needed in IT personnel.
projector A device that takes input from a device such as a computer, laptop, camera, and so on and sends an image to a screen or wall.
`prompt` A command that changes how the command prompt appears. See also *command prompt*.
proprietary crash screen An error condition on a particular computer or application that is unique to the manufacturer.
proprietary operating system A type of computer that only allows a particular operating system or has hardware that is incompatible with other vendors. For example, macOS is used only on Apple devices and is a proprietary system.
proprietary vendor-specific ports Ports primarily for power connections or used as communication options.
proxy server A server that acts as a go-between for an application and another server.
`ps` A Linux/Unix command that lists all current processes.
PS/2 port Common name for a keyboard and mouse connector, which is an example of a miniDIN-6 connector.
public cloud A service or an environment operated by an external vendor to provide an IT service such as storage or an application to a company.
public IP address A private IP address that a service provider or company translates to a public IP address that is seen on the internet.
punchdown block A part of a network or phone cabling system that allows a wire to be attached and firmly secured into the block using a punchdown tool.
punchdown tool An implement that is used to terminate cable on a patch panel.
purpose of the change In change management, the part of the planning process that involves documenting why a change is needed.
PVC (polyvinyl chloride) Cable that has a plastic insulation or jacket that is cheaper and easier to install than plenum cable. It can have flame retardant added.

pwd In the Linux environment, a command that identifies the current working path.
PXE (Preboot Execution Environment) boot An option some computers have that can be modified to search for the network device that holds the computer image.
Python A good language for writing scripts because it is easy to learn and can be run on most operating systems. The extension .py is used for Python files.

Q

QoS (quality of service) A collection of techniques that ensure that the most important corporate data, voice, and/or video is sent before other noncritical data that may get dropped as a result.
quad-channel A memory type in which a motherboard can access four memory modules simultaneously.
quick format During an installation process, a function used to prepare a hard drive partition but not identify and mark bad sectors so that they will not be used for data storage.

R

radio A wireless input/output technology that has a longer range than infrared.
RADIUS (Remote Authentication Dial-in User Service) A secure method of authentication using a server.
RAID (redundant array of independent [or inexpensive] disks) A redundancy method that writes to multiple hard drives for larger storage areas, better performance, and fault tolerance.
RAID 0 Also called disk striping without parity, a type of RAID that enables data to be alternatively written on two or more hard drives but be seen by the system as one logical drive. RAID level 0 does not protect data if a hard drive fails; it only increases system performance.
RAID 1 Also called disk mirroring or disk duplexing, a type of RAID that protects against hard drive failure. See also *disk mirroring*. It requires two drives at a minimum.
RAID 10 A type of RAID in which a mirrored set and a striped set are combined. It requires four hard drives as a minimum.
RAID 5 A type of RAID in which data is put on three or more hard drives, with one of the three drives used for parity.
RAID failure An error condition that requires use of the Windows Disk Management tool to verify the status of the drives used in RAID.
RAID not found An error condition that sometimes occurs with a power failure or surge, misconfiguration in BIOS/UEFI, system upgrade, application upgrade, or new application installation.
RAM (random-access memory) A volatile type of memory that loses its data when power to the computer is shut off.
RAM limitation The maximum amount of memory that an operating system can recognize. Even if a system has more RAM installed, the operating system will not be able to use that extra memory.
random reboot A problem that could be caused by overheating, a power issue, a particular app, or the OS.
ransomware A security situation in which a hacker restricts a user's access to a device, and pressures the user to pay money to regain access to the device.
rapid elasticity The ability for a provider to expand software and hardware quickly, in response to a customer's needs.
RAW volume A part of a hard drive that has been set aside as a volume but has never been high-level formatted and does not contain a specific type of file system.
RCA A type of connector used with coaxial cable.
rd A Windows command used to remove a directory (folder).
RDP (Remote Desktop Protocol) A Microsoft protocol used for accessing and controlling networked computers and mobile devices. RDP uses port 3389.
read/write failure An error condition that indicates a hard drive has a defective area.
ReadyBoost A utility that can speed up the Windows boot process by caching some startup files to a 256 MB+ flash drive, SD card, or CF card.
reboot A restart of an operating system, also known as a warm start.
rebuild a Windows profile To make a copy of the user profile folder, rename the registry key, and have the user log in again. This should be done if a message appears, saying that a user profile cannot be loaded.

recovery drive A storage location for a backup of only the operating system (and not user files, applications, or current settings).

recovery partition An optional partition provided by some vendors that contains the operating system, files, and applications installed on the system when purchased.

Recycle Bin A location in Windows-based operating systems in which user-deleted files and folders are held. This data is not discarded from the computer until the user empties the Recycle Bin.

redundant power supply A device that has two or more power supplies that provide power in the event that one power supply fails.

refresh (installation method) A Windows 8/8.1 tool that reinstalls the operating system but keeps user data and settings. Windows 10 uses Reset This PC for this purpose.

refresh rate The amount of time it takes a screen to be drawn in 1 second, measured in hertz (Hz) or milliseconds (ms). In LCDs, the refresh rate is also called temporal resolution. LCD refresh rates are traditionally 60 Hz.

ReFS (Resilient File System) The Microsoft replacement file system for NTFS.

`regedit.exe` A Windows utility that can modify and back up the registry.

`regedt32.exe` One of two Windows registry editors. See also *registry* and *regedit*.

region code A setting on a DVD or Blu-ray drive or disc that specifies a geographic region. The drive's region code must match the disc's region code.

registry A central Windows database file that holds hardware and software configuration information.

`regsvr32.exe` A command used to register `.dll` files in the Windows registry.

regulatory and compliance policy A policy that is specific to an industry such as health care or manufacturing.

reimage A process of putting a new image (operating system, applications, and settings) on a corporate computer.

relational operator An operator that compares one side of an expression to another and that is used in scripts.

Reliability Monitor A tool that provides a visual graph in Windows Vista or 7 of how stable the system is and shows details on events that might have affected system reliability.

reload OS A repair option that installs a new copy of the operating system when other repair options haven't been successful in fixing the problem.

Remote Assistance A Windows tool used to remotely access a Windows device. The remote computer displays a prompt requesting permission for remote access. Contrast with Remote Desktop, which does not request permission.

remote backup An option on a mobile device to allow the device or specific data—such as personal contacts, videos, pictures, and/or music—to be backed up to remote storage.

Remote Desktop Connection A Windows tool used to remotely access a Windows-based device that does not require someone to be at that computer and does not prompt for permission.

Remote Desktop Services Previously known as Terminal Services, software on a server that can be used to deploy images to computers and to access, control, and manage remote computers and servers.

remote network installation The process of pulling an image from a server or network share in order to load an operating system.

remote wipe The process of using software to send a command to a mobile device to delete data, perform a factory reset, remove everything from the device so that it cannot be used, and overwrite data storage to prevent forensic data recovery.

remove debris A maintenance process task for a thermal printer.

repair an application A process that involves selecting the application in the *Windows Programs and Features* section of the Control Panel and selecting *Repair*.

repair installation A process used when you have to reload the Windows operating system. Sometimes called an in-place upgrade or a reinstallation.

repeater A network device that boosts the network signal. Network switches are repeaters. Wireless repeaters boost the wireless signal to extend the wireless network.

repetition A loop structure, in which a loop contains a block of statements that is executed repeatedly.

repetition structure In scripting, a block of statements that are used repeatedly.
replace an ink cartridge A maintenance or repair process for an inkjet printer.
replace paper [impact] A maintenance process in which paper is inserted into the paper tray, threaded into the printer, or threaded onto a sheet feeder for fanfold paper.
replace paper [thermal] A maintenance process in which the technician must ensure that the proper size and type of thermal paper are used and thread the paper through the rollers as directed by the manual or an image on/inside the printer.
replace the print head [impact] A maintenance process in which the part that holds all the pins used to press against the ribbon is replaced.
replace the ribbon A maintenance or repair process for an impact printer.
replace the toner cartridge A maintenance or repair process for a laser printer.
Reset This PC A recovery option that reinstalls Windows and deletes users' files, apps, and settings.
resin An alternative to 3-D filament printing that produces better-quality objects.
resistance A measurement, in ohms, of how much opposition is applied to an electrical circuit.
resolution The number of pixels shown on a monitor or the output of a printer.
Resource Monitor A Windows graphic tool that shows performance for the main system components.
restart service In Windows, to use the *Services* Computer Management tool to restart a service that has stopped responding.
restore (installation method) A Windows installation method that takes the operating system back to a previous point in time.
restore point A snapshot image of the registry and some of the dynamic system files that have been saved previously by the System Restore utility. This is used when a Windows computer has a problem.
restrict login time A security measure in which user or group accounts can be restricted to specific days and times through Windows account management.
retinal scanner A biometric security device that scans the eye for authentication and access.
RFI (radio frequency interference) A specific type of EMI noise that occurs in the radio frequency range. It often results from operation of nearby electrical appliances or devices.
RFID (radio frequency identification) A technology that allows automatic identification of people, objects, or animals.
rights Permissions granted or denied to files, folders, and network resources.
risk analysis A part of change management in which the risks of the proposed changes are weighed against the benefits.
risk level A rating such as low, medium, or high or a numerical value representing the level of risk an IT change brings if implemented.
RJ11 A type of connector used with analog modems and traditional phone jacks.
RJ45 A type of connector used on Ethernet network cards and ports to connect a device to a wired network.
`rm` Short for remove, a Linux command that deletes a file or directory.
RMM (remote monitoring and management) A process used to share a screen with a user or remotely access a computer to troubleshoot a specific problem, share files, share a remote image, update apps or the OS, handle inventory control, and deploy security solutions.
`robocopy` A command used to copy files. It has more parameters than `COPY` or `XCOPY`.
rogue antivirus A downloaded application that appears to help someone with a problem but that is, in reality, a virus.
roll back the device driver Use *Device Manager* and right-click on a particular piece of hardware > *Properties* > *Driver* tab > *Roll Back Driver* button to take a device driver back to a previous version.
roll back Windows update A process used when a Windows update causes a system to have issues that involves rolling back the update to at least one previous version and then applying the updates one at a time.
rollback plan A documented business process that outlines what to do when an IT change isn't going as planned.
roller A printer part that is part of the system used to move paper through the printer.
root In Unix/Linux, the administrator account. The root user has absolute power on a system, including within macOS.
root access An administrative level in Unix/Linux that has the greatest amount of ability to modify the operating system.

root directory The starting place for all files on a disk. A hard drive is limited to 512 entries. The designation for a hard drive's root directory is `C:\`.

router A network device that determines the best path for sending a packet. A router works at Layer 3 of the OSI model.

run as administrator An elevated level of security access that may be needed to execute specific commands from the command prompt or to access administrative tools or utilities.

S

.sh An extension used with a shell script or a text file that has a sequence of commands for a Unix-based system.

S/PDIF (Sony/Phillips Digital Interface Format) An audio transfer format interface that defines how audio signals are carried between audio devices and stereo components. It can also be used to connect the output of a DVD player in a PC to a home theater or some other external device.

S-video port A composite video port, coded yellow, that uses a 7-pin mini-DIN connector.

SaaS (software as a service) A type of cloud service that describes hosted applications such as a learning management system, enterprise resource planning (ERP), human resources management (HRM), payroll, antivirus, and inventory management that are hosted by another company and accessible from anywhere.

Safe boot A Windows System Configuration option available on the Boot tab.

safe mode (Mac) A way to start a Mac so that the startup disk is checked and repaired if possible. To use this mode, hold down Shift while starting the computer.

Safe Mode (Windows) A Windows option used when a computer stalls, slows down, does not work properly, or has improper video settings or intermittent errors or when a new hardware/software installation causes problems. In Safe Mode, Windows starts with minimal device drivers and services.

safety goggles A form of personal protection that should be worn when working on equipment to protect the eyes from debris, chemicals, and liquids.

SAN (storage area network) A collection of storage media that is centrally managed and available to a multitude of network devices, such as servers, network-based applications, virtual machines, and users.

sandbox A method of using virtualization or non-production equipment to test code or app changes before deployment.

sandbox testing Implementing a proposed change in a non-production environment.

SAS (Serial Attached SCSI) A type of device that connects in a point-to-point bus. Used in an enterprise environment where high reliability and high mean time between failures are important.

SATA (Serial ATA) A point-to-point architecture for IDE devices that provides faster access for attached devices.

SATA cable A cable used to connect a SATA device to a motherboard SATA port.

SATA connector A motherboard connector used to attach a cable between the motherboard and a SATA device. This connector can also be used to connect an adapter that contains one or more additional external SATA ports.

satellite modem A type of modem that can provide internet access at speeds faster than an analog modem but slower than cable or DSL access.

scareware A fake message that warns of a virus or computer problem.

scope of the change Within a project plan, a scope of change describes the implications of the IT modifications and specifies affected systems.

screen lock A feature on a mobile device that requires a PIN, fingerprint, facial features, security pattern, voice, or something else to unlock the screen of the device so the device can be used.

screen sharing A macOS feature that allows one user to view and even control the display of another Apple computer that is on the network.

screened subnet See *DMZ (demilitarized zone).*

scribe A plastic tool that helps with prying plastic parts or covers off laptop and mobile devices.

script A small program written in one of several scripting languages that is designed to do a specific task.

SCSI (Small Computer System Interface) cable A Serial Attached SCSI (SAS) drive cable that attaches from the SAS drive to a SATA controller that is capable of supporting a SAS drive.

SD (Secure Digital) A storage device with non-volatile flash memory used for mobile devices.

GLOSSARY

SDS (safety data sheet) A document that describes a product, including its toxicity, storage, and disposal procedures, as well as information regarding health or safety concerns.

secure boot A BIOS/UEFI setting option that prevents unauthorized software from loading during the boot process.

secure connection A website connection that uses HTTPS and security certificates through a browser.

Secure Sockets Layer See *SSL.*

secured print An option available on some printers that requires a passcode in order to send/retrieve a print job.

security certificate verification The process of verifying that the address in a certificate matches the web address and is digitally signed by a "trusted" authority.

security group An Active Directory type that makes it possible to apply group policy settings or permissions to any shared resource.

security pattern A security option that requires tracing a specific set of dots to access a mobile device.

security policy One or more documents that provide rules and guidelines related to computer and network security.

security settings A section of BIOS/UEFI Setup options that allows configuration of specific security, such as power-on password, chassis intrusion detection, TPM, LoJack, and so on.

security threat A risk to a business, such as an operating system that is no longer supported by a vendor and that becomes a risk to the business due to lack of security updates.

selection A decision structure that consists of a test condition together with one or more groups (or blocks) of statements. The result of the test condition determines which block of statements will be executed.

self-grounding The act of placing a part of your body in contact with an electronic device to prevent an electrostatic discharge (ESD) event.

separation pad A bar or pad in a laser printer that can have a rubber or cork surface that rubs against the paper as it is picked up.

sequence One of the three basic programming constructs, which means that code executes one instruction at a time, in the sequence the code is written.

Serial ATA See *SATA (Serial ATA).*

serial cable A type of cable that connects to an RS-232 or DB9 port.

server motherboard A motherboard that tends to be proprietary and that cannot be replaced with a desktop motherboard.

server-based network A basic type of LAN in which users log in to a controlling computer, called a server, that knows who is authorized to connect to the LAN and what resources the user is authorized to access. This type of network is usually used in businesses that have 10 or more computers.

service A Windows process that provides a specific function to the computer.

service fails to start A situation in which a technician should use the *Services* Computer Management tool to investigate and possibly manually start the service.

service pack A group of upgrades or patches provided by Microsoft for an operating system.

service release Software available from a manufacturer to fix a known problem (bug) in its applications program.

Services A tool that can be accessed through the Windows Computer Management console or by typing `services.msc` from a command prompt. You can also control it from *System Configuration* utility > *Services* tab.

`services.msc` A command that brings up the *Services* snap-in Computer Management tool so that you can start and stop services.

session layer Layer 5 of the OSI model, which manages communication and administrative functions between two network devices.

Setup Software that tells a computer about itself and the hardware it supports, such as the amount of RAM memory, type of hard drive installed, current date and time, and so on.

setup location An appropriate place to install a new printer.

`sfc` A command used to start the System File Checker utility, which verifies operating system files.

Shadow Copy A Windows technology used with the System Restore program that uses a block-level image instead of monitoring certain files for file changes.

share A folder that has been set so that others can use it. This can be on a computer, printer, or network resource such as a scanner.

share permissions A security measure that can dictate what a specific user or group can do with a file or folder that can be accessed across a network.
Shared Folders A Windows tool used to view shares and sessions and to open files.
shared resources In cloud computing, resources such as servers, applications, hardware (such as CPUs and RAM), data storage, and network infrastructure equipment shared among people within an organization or between organizations.
shell A standardized user interface to interact with the operating system.
shell script A text file that contains a sequence of commands for a Linux/Unix-based system. Shell scripts may not run correctly on a Windows system. A shell script has the file extension `.sh`.
shielded twisted pair (STP) See *STP (shielded twisted pair).*
shortcut A desktop icon with a bent arrow in the lower-left corner. It is a link to a file, a folder, or a program on a disk. If the file is a document, it opens the application used to create the document.
shoulder surfing An attack in which someone sits or stands behind a user and looks at what the user is typing or at what is on the screen to glean information in an unauthorized way.
shredding A method of destroying documents for security reasons.
shrink (partition) Making a hard drive section smaller. In the *Disk Management* tool, right-click the drive letter > *Shrink Volume.*
`shutdown` A Linux/Unix and Windows command to shut down or restart the system, depending on the options used.
SIM (subscriber identification module) A small card used in mobile devices and phones that stores personal contacts, numbers, and phone services.
simple volume A Windows term for the storage unit that contains the files needed to load the operating system. The system volume and the boot volume can be the same unit.
single-core processor A processor that has only one core CPU.
single-mode fiber A type of fiber-optic cabling that sends one light beam down the cable.
single sign-on An authentication technique that allows a user to authenticate to multiple systems, servers, printers, and other network devices with a minimum of a user ID and password.
site survey A process used in wireless network design to determine the best wireless hardware placement for the optimum coverage area.
sleep-and-charge USB port A computer port that provides power to an attached device (power to charge the device) even when the computer is powered off.
SLI (Scalable Link Interface) A technology used with video cards that allows two cards to work together.
slow boot A situation in which a computer is slow to start up that could be caused by the operating system, startup applications, services, or too many startup login scripts.
slow network speed Increased time to transmit data from source to destination, resulting from network latency. For wireless networks, this is caused by obstructions such as objects, walls, weather, microwave, ovens, and devices/other wireless networks operating in the same unlicensed frequency range. For wired networks, it is typically caused by poor or faulty cabling or security issues.
slow performance An indication that a computer system is operating in a less-than-efficient manner. It could be caused by lack of hard drive space, inadequate memory, a poorly performing application, malware, or insufficient CPU cores/speed. For mobile devices, check battery power level, close apps that aren't being used, close services that aren't being used, connect to a Wi-Fi network, and move closer to the AP.
slow profile load A slow startup/login process that results when too many profiles are required at startup or the company makes use of local or domain policies including user and group profiles.
sluggish performance See *slow performance.*
S.M.A.R.T. (Self-Monitoring, Analysis, and Reporting Technology) A feature that allows a storage device to send messages about possible failures or data loss. This configuration setting is located in the BIOS/UEFI.
smart card A small ID-size card that can store data, be encrypted, and swiped through and/or interact wirelessly with a smart card reader. Examples of smart cards are identification, medical, credit, and access cards.
smart card reader A device that can read flash media. Also called a multi-card reader. It can also be a device used to read the embedded chips in smart cards.

smart watch A wristwatch that is capable of functions such as syncing with a smartphone, downloading apps, and using GPS.

smartphone A device that has more capabilities than a cell phone, such as internet connectivity, GPS tracking, apps, camera functions, music options, and wireless connectivity to other devices.

SMB (Server Message Block) A means of providing access to shared network devices and files. SMB uses port 445.

smoke An indication of a power supply problem.

SMS (Short Message Service) Text messaging, which can be used to provide a security code for authentication.

SMTP (Simple Mail Transfer Protocol) A standard used for email or for transferring messages across a network from one device to another. SMTP uses port 25.

snapshot In a virtualization environment, a copy or backup of the virtual machine (VM) at a particular point in time that is used to revert the VM to that point in time. It is similar in concept to a restore point.

SNMP (Simple Network Management Protocol) A standard that supports network monitoring and management. SNMP uses ports 161/162.

social engineering A technique used to trick people into divulging information, including their own personal information or corporate knowledge.

SODIMM (small outline DIMM) A special small DIMM used in laptops and printers.

soft reset Simply restarting a device. Contrast this to a hard reset, which is also called a factory reset.

soft token A security technique in which a code that is required in addition to the user ID and password is delivered via text, phone call, or email.

software An application or operating system consisting of a set of instructions that makes the hardware work.

software firewall A software application or tool provided with a computer or device like an access point that can be configured to permit or block specific types of traffic.

software incompatibility Failure of a new application to work with an older operating system.

Software Updater An Ubuntu tool used to update Linux operating systems and applications.

SOP (standard operating procedure) A documented set of instructions on how to do a specific task.

sound card An adapter, also known as an audio card, that has several ports that convert digital signals to audible sound and also the reverse. Common devices that connect to the ports include microphones and speakers.

spam Email that is unsolicited and comes from unknown people or businesses.

spanned volume A Windows term that describes hard drive space created from multiple hard drives.

SPD (serial presence detect) An extra EEPROM feature that allows the system BIOS to read the EEPROM (which contains memory information such as capacity, voltage, error detection, refresh rates, and data width) and adjusts motherboard timing for the best CPU-to-RAM performance.

SPDIF (Sony-Phillips Digital Interface Format) See *S/PDIF*.

speaker A mechanical device that produces acoustic sound and that may be internal or external to a computer or mobile device.

special function key One of the uppermost keys on a keyboard, which activate specific functions. Labeled F1, F2, and so on, these keys control things like sound level, screen brightness, and more.

special thermal paper Paper sensitive to heat that is used with thermal printers, typically in retail establishments.

speed (NIC property) A network card configuration property that is normally configured automatically, but manual options include 10 Gb/s, 1 Gb/s, 100 Mb/s, and 10 Mb/s.

spinning pinwheel A macOS error indication that can indicate a lack of response from the hard drive and/or a particular application.

splash screen An introductory screen that appears on a device that may be required and that states the criteria for accessing the device or a particular service or website.

splitting partition (Disk Management) A way of dividing space on a hard drive or making one partition smaller (right-click the drive > *Shrink Volume*) and then creating a new partition with the relinquished drive space.

spoofing Sending an Ethernet frame with a fake source MAC address to trick other devices into sending traffic to a rogue device.

Spotlight A macOS universal search tool that can locate every file and directory and also search email, contacts, music, and even the web.

SPS (standby power supply) A device that provides power to a computer only after it first detects an AC voltage power-out condition.

spyware Software that collects information without user consent, using keystroke logging, gaining access to saved documents, and recording internet activity. It results in unsolicited pop-ups and identity theft.

SQL (Structured Query Language) injection An attack that targets a database to either collect, delete, display, or modify data.

SRAM (static random-access memory) Memory that is faster but more expensive than DRAM. SRAM is also known as cache memory, or L1, L2, or L3 cache.

SSD (solid-state drive) A drive that uses non-volatile flash memory and no moving parts to store data. It is faster but more expensive than a mechanical hard drive.

SSH (Secure Shell) A means of securing data communication, including remote connectivity of devices and file transfers. SSH uses port 22.

SSHD (solid-state hybrid drive) A drive that contains both a mechanical hard drive and flash memory used as an SSD.

SSID (service set identifier) A set of up to 32 alphanumeric characters used in wireless networks to differentiate between networks.

SSID broadcasting A process used with wireless network access points to periodically send out a beacon frame that includes the SSID. Wireless devices can automatically detect the SSID from this beacon.

SSID not found A particular SSID not being found in the list of wireless networks, which could be because the wireless router/AP has been configured to not broadcast the SSID, and it has to be entered. Alternatively, the device might be out of range of the wireless network.

SSL (Secure Sockets Layer) A protocol within the TCP/IP protocol stack that is used to create a connection between two network devices such as when you use a website that begins with https:// in the address bar.

standard format The type of drive formatting done through the drive installation process. Contrast with a low-level format.

standard privileges A security function in Windows that allows people using a Standard user account to execute specific commands from a CLI.

Standard user One of the two basic types of Windows user accounts. By default, a Standard user cannot install most applications or change system settings. Contrast with an Administrator account, which has full control over a system.

standoff A plastic connector on the bottom side of a motherboard.

Start button A button, located in the lower-left corner of the Windows desktop, that is used to access and launch applications, files, utilities, and help, as well as to add/remove hardware and software.

Start screen The standard look of Windows 8 that has tiles instead of icons, like the traditional Windows desktop. Windows 8.1 has both the traditional desktop and a Start screen.

Storage Spaces A Windows 8/10 technology that makes it possible to combine different types of storage devices into one writable space.

STP (shielded twisted pair) Network cable with extra foil to prevent outside noise from interfering with data on the cable.

straight tip (ST) connector A type of fiber connector that attaches like a BNC connector and requires the user to turn the metal part of the connector in order to make a secure attachment.

straight-through cable A network cable that uses twisted pair copper wires and RJ45 connectors at each end. The cable uses the same pinout at each end and is also known as a patch cable.

streak A paper issue in a printer caused by the drum, toner cartridge, dirty or damaged fusing assembly, or the paper.

string A basic data type that is simply a string of characters.

striped volume A term describing how data is written across 2 to 32 hard drives. Each drive is used alternately instead of filling the first hard drive before going to the second hard drive. Related terms include striping and RAID 0.

`su` A Linux command that switches from one user account to another.

subdirectory A directory contained within another directory. Subdirectories are also called subfolders.

subfolder A folder contained within another folder that might also be called a subdirectory.

subnet A portion of a network number that has been subdivided so that multiple networks can use separate parts of that single network number. Subnets allow more efficient use of IP addresses. Also called a subnetwork or a subnetwork number.
subnet mask A number a computer uses to determine which part of an IP address represents the network and which portion represents the host.
subscriber connector (SC) An older type of fiber-optic connector that is square and doesn't have a push lever as part of the connector like the LC type, but it does snap into a socket.
sudo A Linux command that gives a user temporary root privileges.
surge suppressor/protector A device that helps protect power supplies from overvoltage conditions. Also known as a surge strip.
suspend mode Another name for sleep mode, used to conserve power in a computing device.
swap partition A file, also known as a paging file, that acts as a memory overflow and allows secondary storage to let programs exceed the size of available physical memory by using hard drive space as memory.
swipe lock A type of mobile device locking/unlocking mechanism that involves a finger sweep movement.
switch In star networks, a Layer 2 central controlling device that looks at each data frame as it comes through each port.
swollen battery A bulging battery, which requires immediate replacement as it may not hold a charge and could soon leak.
Sync Center A Windows Control Panel area used to synchronize files between computers.
syntax A set of symbols and rules used to create instructions. Every scripting language has its own syntax.
synthetic backup A backup method that uses a full backup and incremental backups.
syslog server A device used to receive information from multiple network devices and that provides a historical record of events such as devices losing power, a particular interface going down, or access (login/logout) to the device.
Sysprep A tool used to deploy Windows in a corporate environment. Also known as Windows System Preparation.
system attempts to boot to an incorrect device In this situation, change the boot order in BIOS/UEFI.
System Configuration utility A Windows utility that allows boot files and settings to be enabled/disabled for troubleshooting purposes. The command that brings up this utility is `msconfig.exe`.
System Control Panel A window that is used to view details about a computer, including the name, amount of RAM, and processor speed; it also allows for remote access/assistance. Similar options are not available through the System Settings link.
system file A file that is needed to allow a computer to boot. Also known as a startup file.
System File Checker (SFC) A Windows tool used to verify operating system files.
system image A saved copy of the operating system and all user files that can be used to restore a damaged or corrupted computer.
System Information A macOS utility that provides an overview of the Mac, including basic diagnostic information such as installed hardware, software, and network settings.
system lockout A configuration setting used to prevent unauthorized access when a security method is not successful (for example, incorrectly entering a password three times).
system lockup A symptom of a motherboard, CPU, RAM, or power supply problem.
system log An operating system log that can be viewed when things go wrong. In Windows, Event Viewer is used to view system logs.
system partition A type of active hard drive partition that contains the hardware-specific files needed to load the operating system.
System Preferences A macOS basic management and troubleshooting tool, equivalent to Control Panel/Settings utilities in Windows. It contains most of the system settings, such as desktop backgrounds and screen savers, as well as more advanced settings, such as user accounts and file sharing. Third-party applications can also insert their own preferences menu into the System Preferences menu.
system protection The *System* section of the Control Panel > *System Protection* tab, which is used to set up and configure System Restore, manage restore points, and manage the amount of disk space used by System Restore.

system requirements (application) The hardware and software required for an application to be installed.
system resources The collective set of interrupt, I/O address, and DMA configuration parameters.
System Restore A utility that makes a snapshot of the registry and backs up certain dynamic system files. When a problem occurs, a technician can use this utility to take the system back to a time before the error started.
system volume A Windows term describing the storage space that holds Windows operating system files used to boot the computer.

T

T568A An ANSI/TIA/EIA Ethernet network cabling standard.
T568B An ANSI/TIA/EIA Ethernet network cabling standard.
tablet A mobile device with a touch screen, camera(s), microphone, and possibly one or more ports.
TACACS (Terminal Access Controller Access-Control System) A secure method of authentication using a server.
tailgating A breach of physical security that occurs when an unauthorized person enters a secure space behind an authorized person. Training and diligence by all employees are the only ways to stop tailgating. Also known as piggybacking.
taskbar On a Windows program, the bar that runs across the bottom of the desktop and holds buttons that represent files and applications currently loaded into RAM. It also holds icons representing direct access to system tools.
`taskkill` A command used to halt a process or task.
Task Manager A Windows-based utility that displays memory and processor usage data and also displays currently loaded applications as well as currently running processes.
Task Scheduler A Windows-based utility that allows applications or tasks to be executed periodically or at a specific date and time. This can include a systemwide message.
Task View A Windows icon that allows a user to create multiple desktops and switch between them.
TCP (Transmission Control Protocol) An OSI model Layer 4 standard that ensures reliable communication between two devices.
TCP printing Also known as TCP/IP printing, the ability to connect to and print to a printer that has been assigned an IP address.
TCP/IP (Transmission Control Protocol/Internet Protocol) The most widely used network protocol stack for connecting to the internet. Developed by the Defense Advanced Research Projects Agency in the 1970s, it is the basis of the internet.
teamwork The ability to work with others toward a common goal.
Telnet A nonsecure application protocol that allows connection to a remote network device. Telnet uses port 23. Commonly replaced by the more secure SSH.
temperature Computers should operate at temperatures between 60 and 75 degrees.
terabyte (TB) Approximately 1 trillion bytes of information, or 2^{40} (1,099,511,627,776) bytes.
Terminal The terminal emulator for macOS and Linux that allows command-line interface (CLI) access to the operating system. Certain tasks or functions are not GUI-friendly, and CLI commands are required.
test development A safe way to use virtualization or other means when trying out new software without hurting any other device.
tethering A means of sharing internet connectivity among mobile devices in the area. It is a form of hotspot.
text file A file in which each byte represents one character of ASCII code. Scripts are all text files.
thermal pad A part applied between a processor and a heat sink to provide consistent heat dispersion.
thermal paste A substance applied between a processor and its heat sink to provide a thermal pad that disperses heat more evenly.
thermal printer A printer commonly used in retail that uses heat and special thermal paper to create printed images.
thick client Another name for a computer that contains storage and some applications are installed locally.
thin client A type of computer that does not have all the ports and components (such as a hard drive) of a traditional PC. It includes basic applications, meets minimum requirements for the selected OS, and has network connectivity.

third-party vendor [security] A business commonly used for security measures such as shredding corporate documents or destroying data on storage devices.

This PC A category shown in Microsoft Windows that contains local drives and quick access to the desktop, documents, music, and downloads.

thread A unit of programming code that receives a slice of time from Windows, so it can run concurrently with other units of code or threads.

throttle management The process of controlling processor speed by slowing down the processor when it is not used heavily or when it is running too hot.

Thunderbolt A type of video port on PCIe adapters or on Apple computers.

tile A square block on a Windows 8/10 Start screen with a picture of the function it performs when activated.

Time Machine A bundled application in macOS that performs full and incremental system backups to an external hard drive. It gets its clever naming from the capability to navigate past backups as if traveling backward through time.

time management Budgeting and then actually spending time well on doing tasks throughout the workday.

timeout/screen lock A security feature in which, after a period of non-use, the computer requires a username and password to again access the computer.

TKIP (Temporal Key Integrity Protocol) A method of encryption that is an improvement over WEP because the encryption keys periodically change.

TN (twisted nematic) A technology used with LCDs.

tone generator A tool used with a toner probe to identify cables when they are unlabeled or incorrectly labeled.

toner The combined particles in a laser toner cartridge that produce an image when fused onto paper. Toner is harmful if inhaled and messy if spilled.

toner is not fused A problem that may occur with a laser printer. The culprit is commonly in the fuser assembly.

toner probe A tool used with a tone generator to locate and identify cables.

toner vacuum A vacuum that can be safely used inside a laser printer.

TOSLINK A type of fiber S/PDIF connection.

`touch` A Linux command used to create a file.

touch pen An input device that may be known as a stylus and that is used to provide input on a mobile device.

touch screen non-responsive A problem that can be fixed by closing apps, checking whether the problem is app specific, restarting the device (by turning off the device, removing the battery, allowing the device to dry or cool, reinstalling the battery, and turning on the device), removing the screen protector, calibrating the screen, and doing a factory reset.

TPM (Trusted Platform Module) A motherboard chip used for hardware and software authentication. TPM increases security by generating and storing cryptographic keys, passwords, and other authentication information, as well as digital certificates. TPM can authenticate hardware devices. Applications can use TPM for file and folder encryption, local passwords, email, VPN/PKI authentication, and wireless authentication.

`tracert` A Windows network troubleshooting command that displays the path a data packet takes through a network, thus allowing you to see where a fault occurs in a network. A similar command, `traceroute`, is used in macOS and Linux.

trackpad A part of a laptop or keyboard that allows cursor control.

tractor feed A part of an impact printer used to move fanfold paper through the printer; the paper has holes on each side.

transfer belt A part located at the bottom of a laser printer used to move paper through the printer.

transfer corona A wire inside a laser printer that applies a positive charge to the back of the paper so that the toner is attracted to the paper as it moves through the printer.

transfer roller A roller inside a laser printer that replaces the transfer corona. The roller applies a positive charge to the back of the paper so that the toner is attracted to the paper as it moves through the printer.

transferring A laser printer imaging process in which the toner (image) moves from the drum to the paper.

transport layer Layer 4 of the OSI model, which determines the details of how data is sent, supervises the validity of the transmission, and defines the protocol for structuring messages.

tree A Windows command that shows a directory and file structure, depending on the option used.
tri-channel A type of memory execution in which motherboards access three memory modules simultaneously.
Trojan A virus program that appears to be a normal application but that, when executed, changes something. It does not replicate but could gather information that could later be used to hack into someone's computer.
trusted source A security measure that is built in to some browsers and security software that indicates whether a website or downloaded file is a trusted or untrusted software source.
twisted pair cable Network cable made of eight copper wires twisted into four pairs. Can be shielded or unshielded.
two-factor authentication A security process where two key pieces of information are required such as your username/password and pressing a message on a cellphone in order to authorize access.
`type` A command that displays a file's contents on the screen.
Type 1 hypervisor In a virtualization environment, a hypervisor that has the operating system running on top of the hypervisor. Also known as a native hypervisor.
Type 2 hypervisor In a virtualization environment, a hypervisor that runs on top of a host operating system to manage and oversee the virtual machine. Also known as a hosted hypervisor.
Type A-B-C fire extinguisher A fire extinguisher that can be used on either Type A, Type B, or Type C fires.
Type C fire extinguisher A fire extinguisher that can be used only on electrical fires.

U

UAC (User Account Control) A Windows dialog box that asks permission to do something that might be harmful or change the operating system environment. Some changes require an administrator password to continue.
Ubuntu Software Center A software manager to access Ubuntu's repositories of open source software. It can install new applications and uninstall existing ones, many of which are available for free.
UDP (User Datagram Protocol) A Layer 4 connectionless standard that applications use to communicate with a remote device.
UEFI (Unified Extensible Firmware Interface) The replacement for the traditional BIOS that has a boot manager instead of the BIOS controlling the boot process. The UEFI environment allows for a graphical interface, the use of a mouse, antivirus software to be used before the operating system loads, and internet access.
unattended installation A method of installing Windows in which the remote computer does not have to be touched. It can be conducted using Microsoft Deployment Toolkit with Configuration Manager or another imaging product.
unavailable resources A symptom of a network problem in which the network device cannot access the internet, a network printer, a network share, a particular server, email, and/or other resources.
unbuffered memory Memory that does not delay all data transfers by one clock tick to ensure accuracy as registered memory does. Used in low- to medium-powered computers.
undervoltage A condition that occurs when AC power drops below 100 volts, which may cause the computer's power supply to draw too much current and overheat.
unexpected app behavior Strange behavior that could be caused by a free app, the OS version, a malicious app, or poorly written software.
unexpected shutdowns A symptom of an issue with the processor, motherboard, or power supply.
unlicensed range Wireless frequencies that any manufacturer can use.
unmanaged switch A type of switch that cannot be remotely accessed and is commonly found in home and small business wired networks.
unprotected system A computer that has no antivirus/anti-malware software installed and/or that has the firewall disabled.
unshielded twisted pair See *UTP (unshielded twisted pair)* and see also *twisted pair cable*.
untrusted source A security measure that is built in to some browsers and security software that indicates whether a website or downloaded file is a trusted or untrusted software source.

unwanted notifications Windows notifications that can be controlled on a per-app basis using the *Notifications & actions* link through Windows Settings.
`updatedb` A Linux command that updates the file database.
update boot order A process used when a Windows computer does not boot due to the boot order in the BIOS/UEFI settings.
update network settings The process of updating network settings in order to get onto a wired or wireless network. This could involve using the `ipconfig /release` and `ipconfig /renew` commands or changing the IP address to a manually assigned one.
UPnP (universal plug and play) An alternative to port forwarding that allows peer-to-peer (P2P) gaming applications to function without further configuration.
UPS (uninterruptible power supply) A device that provides power for a limited time to a computer or device during a power outage.
upstream Describes information that is sent to the internet, such as sending email or uploading a file to a server.
upward compatibility Design of a software product such that it can accept input intended for a future version. Another name for forward compatibility.
USB (Universal Serial Bus) A bus that allows 127 devices to be connected to a single computer port.
USB 2.0 A standardized port that supported speeds up to 480 Mb/s, a maximum of 0.5 amps, 5VDC, and Type A and Type B connectors.
USB 3.0 A standardized port that supports speeds up to 5 Gb/s, a maximum of .9 amps, and 5VDC.
USB 3.1 A standardized port that supports speeds up to 10 Gb/s and supports the Type C connector.
USB expansion card A metal plate that has one or more USB ports and a cable that connects to the motherboard. The metal plate fits in a slot that a normal card in an expansion slot would take.
USB lock A security device that prevents USB storage devices from being inserted into a USB port.
USB Permissions A BIOS/UEFI Setup option used to modify parameters such as USB speed options and the number of ports to enable/disable.
USB Type-A An upstream male connector on a USB cable that connects to an upstream Type-A port on a host computer or other hub.
USB Type-B A downstream male connector on a USB cable that connects to a Type-B connector on the downstream device.
USB Type-C A reversible plug connector for USB devices and hosts that will eventually replace USB Type-A/Type-B plugs.
USB-C See *USB Type-C.*
USB-PD A USB power delivery standard that allows up to 20V at 5A for 100 watts of power. The standard has five levels of power: 10W, 18W, 36W, 60W, and 100W.
USB-to-Ethernet converter A connector cable with a USB plug and an Ethernet end.
User Account Control See *UAC (User Account Control).*
user account management The process of creating a user, adding that user to a group, and managing those functions.
user authentication/strong passwords A security method used to ensure that a person accessing a device, network, or resource is allowed to do so.
user profile All settings associated with a specific user, including desktop settings, network configurations, and applications that the user has access to. A user profile is part of the registry.
User State Migration Tool See *USMT (User State Migration Tool).*
username and password A form of security in which a device or an authentication server has a specific unique identifier and associated characters to allow access.
USMT (User State Migration Tool) A Windows tool used when deploying a large number of Windows computers.
UTM (unified threat management) A security device that provides multiple functions, such as content filtering, antivirus, antispyware, anti-malware, firewall, and intrusion detection and prevention.
UTP (unshielded twisted pair) The most common type of network cable, which comes in different categories for different uses. See also *twisted pair cable.*

`.vbs` The file extension for VBScript files.
VA (vertical alignment) An LCD panel technology that provides wide viewing angles, good color, and high contrast.

vacuum A device used to suction dust and debris from computers and wiring closets.
variable In scripting, the name of a storage location in the computer's internal memory. The value of the variable is the contents at that memory location. It is called a variable because the value can change (vary) as the program runs.
VBScript A scripting language designed specifically for use with Microsoft Internet Explorer. A VBScript file has the extension `.vbs`.
VDI (virtual desktop infrastructure) An environment in which the PC's operating system and apps reside on a server.
ventilation Airflow, which is crucial for computers. Never block air vents, especially on a laptop.
vertical lines Lines that appear on printer paper that may be caused by debris on the corona wires or in the developer unit in the cartridge. When vertical lines appear, replace the toner cartridge.
VGA port A type of 15-pin three-row video port that normally has a CRT monitor attached.
`vi` A command-line text editor used on macOS and Linux.
video capture card An adapter that makes it possible to bring in video from an external source such as a video camera.
video card An adapter used to output video to a display.
virtual desktop An environment in which the client computer operating system and applications are hosted remotely in the cloud.
virtual machine A virtualized computer, which enables an operating system to appear as a separate computer to each application. A virtual machine, or VM, is a computer that has two or more operating systems installed that are unaware of each other due to virtualization software.
virtual NIC A network interface card used in a virtual environment. Each virtual NIC has its own MAC address and can have an IP address assigned.
virtual printing Printing to somewhere other than to the directly connected printer and to a specific file so that the information can be viewed, saved, emailed, or sent to another printer.
virtual RAM A method of using storage space on the hard drive as if it were memory.
virtualization A process that allows a computer to run multiple operating systems without affecting each other. It allows the different operating systems to share hardware, and it provides a test environment for software that may not be compatible on a specific platform.
virtualization support A BIOS/UEFI option that allows virtualization to be enabled on a computer that has the hardware and an operating system that supports virtualization.
virtualization workstation A computer that has multiple operating systems in a virtual environment in which one operating system has no interaction with the other operating system; they are independent of one another.
virus A program designed to change the way a computer originally operated.
vishing A form of phishing that uses a voice call in order to obtain personal information.
VLAN (virtual local area network) A switch technology that allows assignment of ports to a specific VLAN number, thus creating separate networks so that the devices that connect to ports assigned to one VLAN number cannot see devices that connect to switch ports assigned to a different VLAN number.
VM (virtual machine) See *virtual machine*.
VNC (virtual network computing) A situation in which a computer can be controlled from a remote network.
VoIP (Voice over IP) A technology for sending phone calls over the internet or over networks that traditionally transmitted only data.
volt The measurement for voltage.
voltage An electronic measurement of the pressure pushing electrons through a circuit. Voltage is measured in volts.
volume A section of a storage device that receives a drive letter and to which data can be written.
VPN (virtual private network) A remote computer connection to a remote network that involves "tunneling" over an intermediate network, such as the internet or a LAN.

W

Wake on LAN A BIOS and adapter feature that allows a network administrator to remotely control power to a workstation and allows a computer to come out of the sleep mode.

Wake on Ring A BIOS and adapter feature that allows a computer to come out of sleep mode when the telephone rings, so the computer can accept faxes, emails, and so on when the user is absent.

WAN (wide area network) Two or more LANs communicating, often across large distances. The most famous WAN is the internet.

WAP (wireless access point) See *wireless access point.*

warm boot The process of restarting a computer by pressing Ctrl+Alt+Del, using the restart function, or by clicking the Windows Restart option. A warm boot puts less strain on a computer than a cold boot.

warranty The time during which a particular piece of hardware is guaranteed by the manufacturer.

watt The electrical measure in which computer power supplies are rated.

wattage rating A measure used to determine whether a power supply is powerful enough to support the devices within a computer.

web server A computer configured to provide web-based content that is accessed through a web browser.

webcam Short for web camera, a small camera used for communicating via video across the internet.

weight limitation A specification included in a job advertisement that describes expectations for lifting. As a general rule, do not lift anything that weighs over 40 pounds by yourself.

WEP (Wired Equivalent Privacy) A type of encryption that is sometimes used in wireless networks.

whaling A form of phishing attack that targets senior executives.

`while` loop In scripting, a type of loop that begins with the keyword `while` along with a test condition. If the condition is true, the loop begins, and the block of statements in the loop repeats until the condition is no longer true.

WiBro (mobile Wireless Broadband) A technology, also known as mobile WiMAX, that allows wireless connectivity for moving devices, such as those on a bus or train.

Wi-Fi (Wireless Fidelity) A type of network in which no wires are needed to connect to the network.

Wi-Fi analyzer A tool used to identify what wireless networks are in the area, determine what frequencies (channels) are used, and find a less crowded channel for any wireless installations, hotspots, or tethering that may be needed in a particular area. Also known as a wireless locator.

Wi-Fi antenna A device that attaches to a WLAN card to receive or transmit wireless signals.

Wi-Fi calling A common mobile device capability used to make phone calls using a Wi-Fi connection rather than a cell phone network.

wildcard A special character used at the command prompt when typing commands. The `?` character is used to designate "any" for a single character place, whereas the `*` character denotes any characters from that place forward.

window A specific area of the screen that contains information.

Windows 10 A Microsoft operating system that was released after Windows 8/8.1.

Windows 11 A Microsoft operating system that has a centered taskbar, integrated Android apps, widgets, and better security than prior OSes.

Windows Defender A Windows application that detects spyware.

Windows Defender Antivirus See *Microsoft Defender Antivirus.*

Windows Defender Firewall Security software provided with Microsoft Windows that is used to allow or block network traffic based on rules.

Windows domain A type of computer network in which all user accounts, computers, printers, and other network devices are registered with a central database located on one or more clusters of central computers known as domain controllers.

Windows Explorer An older Windows application used to view and manipulate files and folders that has been replaced with File Explorer.

Windows Memory Diagnostic tool A tool used to thoroughly test RAM. It is accessed from a command prompt using the `mdsched` command or using the *Administrative Tools* section of the Control Panel > *Diagnose Your Computer's Memory Problems* link.

Windows Recovery Environment See *WinRE (Windows Recovery Environment).*

Windows Resource Protection See *WRP (Windows Resource Protection).*

Windows Storage Spaces A Windows 8/10 technology that allows the combination of different types of storage devices into one writable space.

Windows Update A Microsoft tool that initiates a connection to Microsoft and download/install modified files to revise the current operating system.

WinRE (Windows Recovery Environment) A tool available on the Windows installation disc and also in Windows that includes multiple tools that can be used to troubleshoot Windows when it does not work properly.

wireless access point A device that receives and transmits data from multiple computers that have wireless NICs installed. The access point can be a standalone unit or can be integrated into an ADSL router.

wireless broadband A feature available from service providers that allows USB modems, mobile data cards, or integrated laptop connectivity to have the capability to receive, create, and communicate internet information within a specific coverage area.

wireless card Also known as a wireless NIC, an electronic device that allows wireless network connectivity.

wireless extender Another name for a wireless repeater that increases the size of a wireless network.

wireless regulations Wireless frequency rules that include licensed and unlicensed ranges, but even in the unlicensed ranges there are rules that must be followed regarding maximum power, subchannels, and so on.

WISP (wireless internet service provider) A vendor that provides internet access.

WLAN (wireless LAN) A wireless network that consists of an access point and some wireless devices, including laptops, tablets, and smartphones.

WMN (wireless mesh network) A type of wireless network that does not require access points. Peer radio devices allow connectivity over distances, which is especially good in emergency situations. Data is passed from one device to another to reach its final destination.

workgroup A term given to a peer-to-peer Windows network. A workgroup does not use a server to authenticate users during the login process.

WPA (Wireless Protected Access) A data encryption program that uses Temporal Key Integrity Protocol (TKIP) or Advanced Encryption Standard (AES) to improve security.

WPA2 (Wireless Protected Access 2) An improvement over WPA that includes dynamic negotiation between the AP and the client for authentication and encryption algorithms. It is a common choice for securing wireless networks.

WPA3 (Wireless Protected Access 3) A wireless security standard that makes use of Simultaneous Authentication of Equals (SAE) encryption.

WPS (WiFi Protected Settings) A method used to easily configure a wireless device for SSID and WPA2 security.

written communication An important skill for a person in IT to have, especially when communicating with others and documenting IT issues/processes.

WRP (Windows Resource Protection) A tool that protects system files and registry keys in Windows.

WWAN (wireless wide area network) A wireless network that extends across more than one county, such as when WiMAX is used.

x64 A term that refers to the architecture and commands used originally with the Intel 8086 CPU that have been updated to a 64-bit version.

x86 A term that refers to the architecture and commands used with the Intel 8086 CPU.

`xcopy` A command that transfers files from one place to another in the command prompt environment.

xDSL A term used to describe the various types of digital subscriber lines (DSLs) available for connecting to the internet. Examples include ADSL, CDSL, DSL Lite, HDSL, RADSL, SDSL, VDSL, and x2/DSL.

XSS (cross-site scripting) An attack in which a threat actor collects and even changes data between a user and a device providing a service (such as a web server).

Z

Z-Wave A wireless standard used in smart homes that allows a wireless mesh topology where devices can talk to another device until the controller is reached.

zero day [attack] A vulnerability in a particular software application that is found by hackers before it is known or fixed by the developer of the application.

ZIF socket (zero insertion force socket) A common CPU socket that has a lever that provides easy access for CPU removal.

Zigbee A wireless standard managed by the Zigbee Alliance that is used in low-power, low-distance devices such as sensors and devices in smart homes, like lights, thermostats, security, cameras, door locks, garage doors, and digital assistants.

zombie A device that has been hacked and is controlled by someone else or that carries out malicious tasks.

Index

Symbols

[command name] /? command, 711
\error messages, 490

Numbers

1s and 0s
  binary bits, 18
  bytes, 19
  EB (exabytes), 21
  frequencies, 21
  GB (gigabytes), 20-21
  kB (kilobytes), 19-21
  MB (megabytes), 19-21
  PB (petabytes), 21
  TB (terabytes), 20-21
  YB (yottabytes), 21
  ZB (zettabytes), 21
2G cellular networks, 385
2.4 GHz frequencies, 395, 581
3-2-1 backups, 938
3.3V output voltage, 163
3-D printers, 319
  filaments, 330-331
  print beds, 329
  resin printing, 330
3G cellular networks, 385, 526
3-pin ATX power supply connectors, 164
4G cellular networks, 385, 526
4-pin 12V ATX power supply connectors, 164
4-pin Berg power supply connectors, 164
4-pin Molex power supply connectors, 164
5 GHz frequencies, 395, 581
5G cellular networks, 385, 526
5V output voltage, 163
6 GHz frequencies, 581
6-pin ATX power supply connectors, 164
6-pin PCIe ATX power supply connectors, 164
8-pin 12V ATX power supply connectors, 163
8-pin PCIe ATX power supply connectors, 164
12V output voltage, 163
15-pin SATA power ATX power supply connectors, 163
16-bit sampling, 292
24-pin main power ATX power supply connectors, 163
24-pin motherboard connectors, 164
32-bit OS, 655-656
64-bit OS, 655-656
80 PLUS efficiency ratings, power supplies, 171
110V vs. 220V input voltage, 163
802.11 wireless standard, 395
802.11a wireless standard, 395
802.11ac (Wi-Fi 5) wireless standard, 395, 583
802.11ad (WiGig) wireless standard, 583
802.11ax (Wi-Fi 6) wireless standard, 395, 583
802.11b wireless standard, 395, 582
802.11e wireless standard, 583
802.11g wireless standard, 395, 583
802.11i wireless standard, 583
802.11n wireless standard, 395, 583
5,400 RPM (Revolutions Per Minute), magnetic hard drives, 226
7,200 RPM (Revolutions Per Minute), magnetic hard drives, 226
10,000 RPM (Revolutions Per Minute), magnetic hard drives, 226
15,000 RPM (Revolutions Per Minute), magnetic hard drives, 226

A

A records, DNS, 600
AAA servers, 622
AAAA records, DNS, 600
.AAX file extensions, 674
AC (Alternating Current), 159-160, 174
acceptance of changes, 1001
access
  ACL, 909
  attacks, 919
  Bluetooth printers, 353
  command prompt, 698-699
  Device Manager, 121
  environment variables, 738-739
  IMAP, 626
  Keychain Access, macOS, 871-872
  LDAP, 626
  local access, security, 920-923, 926-927
  network access
    security, 920-923, 926-927
    user management, 921
  Network Access layer, TCP/IP, 627
  network printers, 353
  physical access, security policies, 900
  remote access
    MSRA, 955
    Quick Assist, 955
    RDP, 955
    RMM, 956
    security policies, 901
    SSH, 956
    Telnet, 956
    VNC, 956
  remote networks, 732
  root access, unauthorized, 445
  Setup programs, 111
  TACACS+, 910
  unauthorized account access, 443
  wireless printers, 353
  WPA, 602
  WPA2, 602, 959
  WPA3, 602, 959

access control vestibules (mantraps), physical security, 904
"access denied" messages, share permissions, 931
accessories, mobile devices
  drawing (track) pads, 381
  headsets, 381
  mobile docking stations, 381-382
  speakers, 381
  touch pens (styluses), 381
  track (drawing) pads, 381
  webcams, 381
accounts
  AD accounts
    creating, 923
    deleting, 925
  administrator accounts, 805
  group accounts
    administrators, 921-922
    backup operators, 921
    guests, 921
    network configuration operators, 921
    performance log users, 921
    power users, 921
    remote desktop users, 921
    remote management users, 921
    users, 921
  guest accounts, disabling, 927
  recovery, 805, 939
  root user accounts, 876
  standard user accounts, 805
  unauthorized access, 443
  user accounts
    adding credentials, 802-803
    administrators, 921-922
    certificate-based credentials, 801
    Credential Manager, 801-804
    editing credentials, 804
    generic credentials, 801
    guests, 921
    Local Users and Groups tool, 804-805
    network configuration operators, 921
    performance log users, 921
    recovering accounts, 805
    remote desktop users, 921
    remote management users, 921
    removing credentials, 803
    rights, 804
    root user accounts, 876
    standard users, 921
    storing credentials, 801
    UAC, 764, 806, 934
    web credentials, 801
ACL (Access Control Lists), 779, 909
ACPI (Advanced Configuration and Power Interface), 115, 168-169
action plans (troubleshooting process), 497
activation clocks, 776
active listening (soft skills), 2, 98-99, 1005
Active status messages, 265
ActiveSync, 401-402
Activity Monitor, macOS, 869
AD (Active Directory)
  accounts
    creating, 923
    deleting, 925
  basic functions, 922-923
  folders
    home folders, 925
    redirecting, 925
  login scripts, 925
  OU, 922
  security groups, 922
ad blockers, 533
adapters, 13
  advantages of, 54
  AGP video adapters, power requirements, 171
  DVI-to-HDMI adapters, 36
  functions, identifying, 13
  installing, 13-14
  nonvideo adapters, power requirements, 171
  PCIe adapters, removing, 91
  removing, 152
  video adapters, 36
  Wake on LAN, 169
  Wake on Ring, 169
adding
  arrays, 809
  computers to domains, 601
  credentials, 802-803
  devices, Windows, 784
    audio devices, 787
    clock drift, 791
    Device Manager, 785-786, 789-790
    Devices and Printers Control Panel utility, 785, 791
    display settings, 788-789
    "Not enough USB controller resources" error messages, 791
    Sound Control Panel, 787
    USB endpoints, 791
  snap-ins, 796
  volumes to hard drives, 809
addressing
  ARP, 624
  broadcast addresses, 1023
  I/O addresses, 120-122
  IP addresses, 961, 1021-1023
  IPv4 addressing
    CIDR, 581
    classes of, 578
    examples of, 579
    host addresses, 578
    network numbers, 578
    octets, 577
    private IP addresses, 578
    public IP addresses, 578
    subnet masks, 580
    VLAN, 580
  IPv6 addressing, 577
  link-local addressing, 577
  MAC addressing, 957
    filtering, 960
    formats of, 577
  memory addresses, 120-122
  NAT, 624, 953
  PAT, 624, 954
ADF (Automatic Document Feeder) scanners, 302
Administration option, AP configurations, 607
administrative privileges, commands, 734
administrative shares, 930
administrator accounts, 805, 921-922
Administrator Password setting (BIOS/UEFI), 114

administrators
- BIOS/UEFI security, 910
- command prompt privileges, 699
- defragmentation rights, 811
- permissions, 934
- rootkits, 915

ads
- blocking, 399
- high number of ads, 445

ADSL (Asymmetric DSL), 519
Advanced BIOS setting (BIOS), 115
Advanced Boot Options menu, Windows, 819-820
adverse power conditions, 986-987
advertisements
- memory, 198-199
- SODIMM, 425

aerosol cans, disposal laws, 158
AES (Advanced Encryption Standard), 602, 940
AGP (Accelerated Graphics Ports), 88
AGP buses, speeds, 72
AGP video adapters, power requirements, 171
AHCI (Advanced Host Controller Interface) mode, SATA, 241
.AI file extensions, 674
air, compressed, 157-158, 980
air filtration masks, 158, 980
airborne particle pollution, safety, 992
AirDrop, troubleshooting, 452
airflow, cases, 167
Airplane mode, 396
alarm systems, physical security, 904
alcohol, denatured, 157
alerts, 917
algorithms, search engines, 6-7
all-in-one computers, disassembly, 155
all-in-one (multifunction) devices. *See also* printers
- installing, 343
- overview, 318
- sensitive material, 318

allow/deny lists, 950
alphanumeric characters, 743
alternative IP addresses, configuring, 598
ALU (Arithmetic Logic Units), 70
AMD
- APU, 76
- Direct Connect, 74
- HyperTransport, 74
- processors, 68, 79, 281
- sockets, 80
- video cards, 281

amplification, speakers, 295
amps, 161-162
analog signals, video ports, 33
analysis
- cell tower analyzers, 410
- risks, 1000
- Wi-Fi analyzers, 409, 593

AND operators, 750
Android OS, 378
- Android Backup Service, 405
- Android Device Manager, 444
- APK, 390
- developer mode, 390
- email configuration, 400
- factory resets, 406
- mobile devices
  - backups, 405-406
  - synchronization, 403
- NFC, 399
- Recovery Mode, 449

antennas, 590
- attenuation, 591
- directional antennas, 591
- gain, 591-592
- MIMO, 593
- networks, 576
- omnidirectional antennas, 591
- path loss, 591
- radiation patterns, 591
- ranges, 591
- signal strength, 592
- Wi-Fi, 436
- wireless laptops, 431

anti-malware, 908
- mobile devices, 409
- reinitializing, 777
- security policies, 900

antistatic bags, 146, 984
antistatic brushes, 157
antistatic gloves, 145
antistatic mats, 146
antistatic wrist straps, 144-145
antivirus software, 908
- Microsoft Defender Antivirus, 943
- mobile devices, 409
- reinitializing, 777
- rogue antivirus apps, 943
- Windows installations, 773

AP (Access Points), 576, 583-584
- default settings, 961
- firmware, 962
- installing, 962-963
- passwords, 962
- rogue AP, 963
- security, 959-960
- SSID, 585-586, 962
- wireless AP, 607-608
- wireless networks, 957-960
- as wireless repeaters, 587

APFS (Apple File Systems), 244
APIPA (Automatic Private IP Addressing), 598
APK (Android Application Packages), 390
app scanners, 409
App Store, macOS, 863
appearance (soft skills), 461-462
Apple
- Apple ID, 863
- iCloud, mobile device backups, 407
- iOS, 378
  - AirDrop, troubleshooting, 452
  - email configuration, 401
  - mobile device backups, 407
  - mobile device synchronization, 404
- iTunes
  - mobile device backups, 407
  - mobile device synchronization, 405
- Lightning
  - cabling, 43
  - ports, 43, 391
- macOS, 858
  - Activity Monitor, 869
  - Apple ID, 863
  - App Store, 863
  - best practices, 892
  - Boot Camp, 873

c command, 874
cd command, 874-875
chmod command, 874-876
chown command, 874-876
Console, 870-871
cp command, 874-875
desktop, 859-860
Disk Utility, 872-873
Dock, 859-860
Finder, 859-860
Force Quit, 866
gestures, 861-862
grep command, 874, 878
GUI, 859-862
iCloud, 862
iWork, 862
kernel panic, troubleshooting, 871
Keychain Access, 871-872
kill command, 874
Launchpad, 860
less command, 874, 877
ls command, 874-875
man command, 874, 878
menu bar, 859
Mission Control, 860
mkdir command, 874
mv command, 874-875
nano command, 874, 877
POSIX, 858
pwd command, 874-875
releases, 858
rm command, 874-876
root user accounts, 876
Safe mode, 869
screen-sharing, 862-864
Spotlight, 861
sudo command, 874-876
System Information, 871
System Preferences, 866-868
system updates, 864
Terminal, 874
Time Machine, 864-865
touch command, 874-875
troubleshooting, 869
troubleshooting, kernel panic, 871
utilities, 869-874
vi command, 874

OS X, 858

Application layer
OSI model, 575
TCP/IP model, 576, 627

application logs, troubleshooting, 800

Apply button, Windows, 671

Apps & features (Settings > Apps), Windows, 794-795

apps (applications)
antivirus apps, rogue, 943
APK, 390
App Store, macOS, 863
authenticator apps, 442, 910
bootleg apps, 441
closing, 390, 451
cloud computing, 539
common apps, 387
crashes, 205, 799, 824
deleting, 390, 451
disabling, 822
DRM, 912
email
off-site apps, 539
troubleshooting decryption failures, 452
force quitting, 390
hanging apps, troubleshooting, 799
installing, 390, 451, 736, 792-793
launching, 792
Launchpad, macOS, 860
loading failures, troubleshooting, 452
locator apps, 388
logs, 798
malicious apps, 441
MAM, 408
Microsoft Store, 764
Mission Control, macOS, 860
moving app icons, 390
"not responding" error messages, troubleshooting, 799
off-site email apps, 539
older apps, Windows compatibility, 204-205
opening, 384
organizing apps, folders, 390
OS-specific apps, 652
pinning to Windows 10/11 taskbars, 667
quitting, Force Quit, macOS, 866
recovery, Time Machine, macOS, 864-865
repairing, 794-795
rogue antivirus apps, 943
SDK, 390
Services and Applications, Windows, 811
side-by-side apps, Windows, 764
spoofing, 441
streaming virtual apps, 539
system requirements, 792-793
Time Machine, macOS, 864-865
troubleshooting
closure failures, 451
email decryption failures, 452
installation failures, 451
load failures, 452
unexpected behavior, 450
update failures, 451
uninstalling, 794
updating failures, troubleshooting, 451
virtual apps, streaming, 539
Windows Installation Assistant, 767
Windows Update Assistant, 767

apt-get command, Linux, 883, 886-887

APU (Accelerated Processing Units), 76

ARM processors, 68

ARP (Address Resolution Protocol), 624

arrays
adding, 809
RAID
BIOS/UEFI settings, 255
concepts, 254
configuring, 253
failures, 266
fault tolerance, 253-254
FCM, 253
hardware RAID, 254
hot swappable RAID drives, 254
levels of, 253-254
RAID 0, 254
RAID 0+1, 254
RAID 1, 254
RAID 5, 254

RAID 10, 254
"RAID not found" error messages, 266
software RAID, 253
troubleshooting, 266
articles/knowledge bases, 996-997
aspect ratios, displays, 484
asset management, 998
asset tags, 998
assigning hard drive letters, 809
assistants (virtual), 389
ATA (Advanced Technology Attachments)
PATA
connectivity, 231
IDE cabling, 231
installing devices, 235
motherboard connectors, 231
SATA, 229
AHCI mode, 241
BIOS/UEFI settings, 241
cabling, 231
connectivity, 231-233, 236
eSATA, 233, 238-239
installing devices, 236
Legacy mode, 241
motherboard connectors, 231
mSATA, 232, 237, 241
ports, enabling in BIOS/UEFI, 237
RAID BIOS/UEFI configuration settings, 255
RAID mode, 241
attacks, security
access attacks, 919
backdoor attacks, 919
boot sector viruses, 915
botnets, 915, 919
brute force attacks, 919
cryptojacking/cryptomining, 915
DDOS attacks, 919
dictionary attacks, 911, 919
DoS attacks, 919
dumpster diving, 907
evil twin attacks, 919
impersonation attacks, 918
inside attacks, 919
keyloggers, 915
malware, 915-917
MITM attacks, 920
password spraying attacks, 920
phishing, 918-919
piggybacking, 918
ransomware, 915
reconnaissance attacks, 920
replay attacks, 920
rootkits, 915
scareware, 919
shoulder surfing, 904, 918
Smurf attacks, 920
social engineering attacks, 912, 917
spear phishing, 918
spoofing attacks, 920
spyware, 915
SQL injection attacks, 920
tailgating, 904, 918
TCP/IP hijacking attacks, 920
Trojans, 915
viruses, 915-917
vishing, 918
vulnerability scanners, 920
whaling, 918
XSS attacks, 920
zero day attacks, 920
zombie attacks, 920
attenuation, antennas, 591
attitude (soft skill), 308-309
attrib command, 708, 711
attributes
files/directories, handling, 708
Windows files/folders, 679-680
ATX (Advanced Technology Extended)
motherboards, 94
power connectors, 166
power supplies, 163
audio
BIOS/UEFI beeps, 489
cards, 44
devices, adding with Sound Control Panel (Windows), 787
digitized sound, 292
editing workstations, system design, 476
headsets, 381
microphones
laptops, 436
replacing, 439-440
system design, 484
unauthorized activation, 444
Windows operations, 293-294
microphones, choosing, 293-294
motherboards
ports, 290
speakers, 289
ports, 44, 290-291
POST codes, 489
projectors, 289
S/PDIF in/out ports, 44
sound cards, 290
16-bit sampling, 292
installing, 292
muting, 293
system design, 484
theory of operation, 292
Windows operations, 293
speakers
amplification, 295
choosing, 296
frequency response ranges, 295
mobile devices, 381
motherboards, 289
power ratings, 295
shielding, 295
system design, 483
troubleshooting, 296
USB speakers, 295
volume control, 295-296
subsystem design, 483-484
troubleshooting, 289, 296
voice recognition, physical security, 906
AUP (Acceptable Use Policies), 901, 999
authentication, 903, 909, 920
apps, 910
authenticator apps, 442
DMARC, 948
Kerberos 910
multifactor authentication, 910
printers, 355
RADIUS, 910
SAE, 959
scanners, 355
servers, 622
soft tokens, 910
SSO authentication, 911
TACACS+, 910

INDEX

two-factor authentication, 398
WEP, iwconfig command, Linux, 885
authorization, 920
Automatic Updates, 780
automating
backups, 736
IT, 1001
processes, 734-736
automobiles, mobile device synchronization, 402
AutoPlay, disabling, 941
autorotating screens, troubleshooting, 454
AutoRun, disabling, 941
auto-switching power supplies, 163
auxiliary fans
cases, 167
power requirements, 171
availability (HA), cloud computing, 541
avoiding
burnout (soft skills), 847-848
distractions (soft skills), 1007-1008

B

back side buses, 72
backdoor attacks, 919
backlights (screens), 434, 454
backup operators accounts, 921
backups, 486
3-2-1 backups, 938
Android Backup Service, 405
automating, 736
Backups, Ubuntu, 882
batteries, 989
before
OS installations, 773
troubleshooting, 485
credentials, 801
data backups, Windows, 781-782
differential backups, 937
File History backups, 782
full backups, 937
GFS backups, 938
incremental backups, 937
mobile devices
Android OS, 405-406
iCloud, 407
iOS, 407
iTunes, 407
OneDrive, 408
multiple hard drives as backups, 937
offsite backups, 939
OS security, 936-939
remote backups. *See* synchronization
restore points, 783
synthetic backups, 937
testing, 936
Ubuntu, 882
wbadmin command, 733
Windows, 688
Windows registry, 781-782
badge readers, physical security, 903
bags, antistatic, 146
balanced power, Windows, 836
bandwidth, 524, 624
barcode scanners, 302-304
baselines, 839
basic disks, 251, 769
Basic QoS, wireless networks, 608
basic skills
Internet searches, 6-7
screen captures, 7
text files, creating, 7
basic storage, 251
.bat files, 674, 706, 735
batteries
backups, 989
charging, 456
CMOS, 119
electronics disposal/recycling, 982
failing batteries, signs of, 118
laptop batteries
optimizing performance, 417-418
removing, 416
Li-ion batteries, 416, 982-983
motherboard batteries, 118
poor battery health, 456
recycling, 118
swollen batteries, 456
troubleshooting, 456
bauds, 517
bcdedit command, 712
BD (Blu-ray Discs), preventive maintenance, 301-302
be humble (soft skills), 893
beeps, POST, 96, 205
being on time (soft skills), 210, 1007
being proactive (soft skills), 635
best practices
Linux, 892
macOS, 892
security, 966
binary bits, 18
biometric security
facial recognition, 906
fingerprint scanners, 906
mobile devices, 398, 442
palmprint scanners, 906
retinal scanners, 906
voice recognition, 906
BIOS (Basic Input/Output Systems). *See also* UEFI
beeps, troubleshooting, 489
boot process, 488
bootstrap programs, 110
configuration change options, 116
configuration settings, 113
ACPI, 115
Administrator Password, 114
Advanced BIOS, 115
Boot Options, 114
Boot Password, 114
Built-in Diagnostics, 116
CPU Configuration, 114
Devices, 115
Disable Execute Bit, 115
Drive Encryption, 115
Fan Control, 114
fTPM, 116
General Optimization, 114
Hardware Monitor, 115
Hyper-Threading, 114
IDE configuration, 115
iGPU, 116
Integrated Peripherals, 114
Interface Configuration, 115
Intrusion Detection/Notification, 115
LoJack, 115
Numlock On/Off, 114
Onboard Device Configuration, 114

passwords, 114
PCIe Configuration, 115
PCI/PnP Configuration, 115
SATA Configuration, 115
Secure Boot, 115
System Information, 114
TPM, 116
USB Permissions, 114
Video Options, 114
Virtualization Support, 115
Virus Protection, 114
downgrading, 112
Flash BIOS, 112
flashing, 118-120
functions, 110
M.2 SSD settings, 241
mSATA settings, 241
NVMe SSD settings, 241
on-board NIC, 603
overview, 110
POST, 110
POST error messages, troubleshooting, 490-491
RAID configuration settings, 255
resetting, 119
resource conflicts, 121
SATA
ports, 237
settings, 241
security, 910-911
Setup programs, 110-111
storage devices, configuring, 241
system boots from the wrong device, troubleshooting, 116
TPM considerations, 117
troubleshooting, 131
upgrading, 112
viruses, 119
BitLocker, 939-940
BitLocker To Go, 939
bits, 18, 574
blackouts, 987
blank/black screens, troubleshooting, 96, 173, 829-831
blocking ads, 399, 533
Bloom's Taxonomy, 474, 486
Bluetooth
Bluetooth cards, replacing, 430-431
connectivity, 56, 393-394, 459-460, 553
installing, 394
mobile device connectivity, 393-394
PAN, 553
printers
access, 353
connectivity, 342, 352
Blu-ray disc drives. *See* optical drives
Blu-ray region codes, 299
.BMP file extensions, 674
BNC connectors, 49
bollards, physical security, 901
"bootable device not found" error messages, 263
Boot Camp, macOS, 873
Boot Options setting (BIOS/UEFI), 114
boot orders, updating, 777
boot partitions, 248, 815
Boot Password setting (BIOS/UEFI), 114
boot process, 652
boot volumes, 251, 814
bootleg apps, 441
bootrec command, 263, 712
bootrec /fixboot command, 815
bootrec /fixmbr command, 815
bootrec /scanos command, 815
boot sector viruses, 915
bootstrap programs, 110
bootup
Advanced Boot Options menu, Window, 819-820
blank/black screens, troubleshooting, 96
Boot Camp, macOS, 873
boot partitions, 815
continuous reboots, troubleshooting, 96
failures
troubleshooting, 262
Windows, 827-828
finding missing bootloaders, 892
GRUB, finding, 892
"Invalid Boot Disk" error messages, 815
LILO, 892
multiboots, Windows, 765
network boots/PXE, 814
passwords, 910
preventive maintenance, 157
process, 487
PXE, 814
reboots, troubleshooting, 96
Safe Boot, 821
Secure Boot setting (BIOS/UEFI), 115
security, 910
system boots from the wrong device, troubleshooting, 116
System Configuration utility, Windows, 820-824
Task Manager, Windows, 824-826
troubleshooting
blank/black screens, 96
continuous reboots, 96
failures to boot, 827-828
finding missing bootloaders, 892
graphical interfaces, 829
resetting PC, 828
slow boot, 832
system boots from the wrong device, 116
warm bootups, 111, 494
Windows boot process
overview, 814-815
reboots, 835
speeding up, 826-827
troubleshooting, 827-829
botnets, 915, 919
bps (bits per second), 517
breakout (network) tabs, 572
Bridged mode, virtual NIC, 604
bridges, wireless, 583
brightness, monitors/projectors, 288
broadband, 624
broadband (WiBro), wireless, 526
broadcast addresses, finding, 1023
broken LCD displays, 435
brownouts, 987
browsers
ad blockers, 533
clearing caches/data, 530
configuration settings, 530
default browsers, 530

Edge, 532
Edge tile, Windows Start screen, 669
Internet Options Control Panel settings, 528-529
extensions, disabling/removing, 530-531
Firefox, 532
Google Chrome, 532
password managers, 532
performance, 533
plug-ins, disabling/removing, 530-531
pop-ups, 532
private browsing, 530
redirection, 531
rootkits, 531
security, 528-532
synchronizing, 530
troubleshooting
basic issues, 531-532
extensions, 530-531
plug-ins, 530-531
slow performance, 533
tools, 533
trusted sources, 528
untrusted sources, 528
updating, 531
verifying security certificates, 530
brushes, antistatic, 157
brute force attacks, 919
BSOD (Blue Screen of Death), 491, 799
troubleshooting, 261, 285
Windows updates, 830
Btrfs, 881
BTX (Balanced Technology eXtended), 94
bubble jet printers. *See* inkjet printers
buffered memory, 191
building customer trust (soft skills), 967
Built-in Diagnostics setting (BIOS/UEFI), 116
burn-in (screens), troubleshooting, 286
burned out bulbs (projectors), troubleshooting, 288
burning smells, troubleshooting, 96, 173
burnout (soft skills), avoiding, 847, 848
buses
AGP bus speeds, 72
back side buses, 72
external data buses, 69
FSB, 72
internal data buses, 69
PCI bus speeds, 72
PCIe bus speeds, 72
performance, 70
pipelines, 70
business process, documentation, 999
buying memory, 198-199
BYOD (Bring Your Own Device), 900
bytes, 19

C

c command, 874
.CAB file extensions, 674
cabinets, network, 569
cable connectors, 53, 576
cable locks, 440, 903
cable modems, 518, 619
cable testers, 565, 572
cable (wire) strippers, 563, 572
cabling
BNC connectors, 49
cable (wire) strippers, 563, 572
Cat 5 cables, 51, 560
Cat 5e cables, 51, 560
Cat 6a cables, 51, 560
Cat 6 cables, 51, 560
Cat 7 cables, 51, 560
Cat 8 cables, 51, 560
coaxial cables, 49-50, 518
connectors, 53, 576
copper media, 560
corporate networks, 565-567
crimpers, 563-565, 572
crossover cables, 562-563
crosstalk, 50, 561
direct burial cables, 51, 560
eSATA cables, 45
Ethernet cables, 50-51, 567
external cables, removing, 148
fiber cables, 52-53
fiber networks, 522-524
IDE cables, 150, 231
internal cables, removing, 149-151
Lightning cables, 43
loopback plugs, 572
management systems, 570
modems, 516
multimeters, 572
network (breakout) taps, 572
network cabinets, 569
network racks, 569-571
patch cables, 562
patch panels, 565
pin 1, 150
plenum cables, 52, 561
PoE, 567-568
power cables, removing, 148
power supplies, 481
punchdown tools, 51, 572-573
PVC cables, 52, 561
reassembling computers, 156
RJ45 connectors, 51
RJ45 wall jacks, 565
SAS cables, 234
SATA cables, 231
serial cables, 46
STP cables, 51, 560-561
straight through cables, 562
T568A wiring standard, 52, 562
T568B wiring standard, 52, 562
tangs, 561
testers, 565, 572
Thunderbolt cables, 43
tone generators, 572
toner probes, 572
twisted pair cables
corporate networks, 565-567
RJ11 connectors, 561-564
RJ45 connectors, 561-565
STP cables, 560-561
terminating, 561-565
UTP cables, 560-564
USB cables, 38
USB-to-serial port converters, 46
UTP cables, 50, 560-564
video cables, laptops, 436
video connections, troubleshooting, 284

caches
- clearing, 530
- disk caches, 256-257
- L1 caches, 73
- L2 caches, 73
- L3 caches, 73
- memory, 73, 188
- processors, 73

CAD/CAM/graphic workstations, system design, 475
calibrating
- inkjet printers, 338
- laser printers, 340
- touch, trackpads, 454

cameras
- digital cameras, 305
- smart cameras, 377
- unauthorized activation, 444
- video capture cards, 282
- webcams, 17, 306-307, 381, 436
  - facial recognition, physical security, 906
  - replacing, 439-440

capacitors, swelling, 96
capitalization, commands, 699
captures, screen, 7
cards
- Bluetooth cards, replacing, 430-431
- cellular cards, laptops, 413
- expansion cards, laptops, 413-414
- M.2 expansion cards, 414
- miniPCIe cards, 413
- NIC
  - advanced properties, 603
  - configuring, virtualization, 603-605
  - duplexing, 603
  - on-board NIC (BIOS/UEFI), 603
  - QoS, 603
  - speed, 603
  - troubleshooting, 617-618
  - virtual NIC, 603-605
  - Wake on LAN, 603
  - Windows network settings, 631
  - wireless NIC, 431, 583-584, 601-602
- NVMe cards, 414
- sound cards, system design, 484
- vCards, contact synchronization, 402
- video cards, replacing, 433
- wireless cards, 413, 430-431

carriage belts, inkjet printers, 322
carriages, inkjet printers, 322
cars, mobile device synchronization, 402
cartridges (ink), inkjet printers, 321-322, 338
cases, 9-10
- airflow, 167
- fans, 167
- form factors, 164
- motherboard form factors, 94
- opening (disassembly), 149
- standoffs, 154
- system design, 481-482
- types of, 164
- ventilation, 167

Cat 5 cabling, 51, 560
Cat 5e cabling, 51, 560
Cat 6 cabling, 51, 560
Cat 6a cabling, 560
Cat 6aa cabling, 51
Cat 7 cabling, 51, 560
Cat 8 cabling, 51, 560
CCFL (Cold Cathode Fluorescent Lamps), 434
cd command, 702, 713, 874-875
CD (Compact Discs), preventive maintenance, 301-302
CD drives. *See* optical drives
CDFS (Compact Disk File Systems), 771
CDMA (Code Division Multiple Access), 385
cell phones. *See* smartphones
cell tower analyzers, 410
cellular cards, laptops, 413
cellular data, mobile device connectivity, 399
cellular location services, 388
cellular networks
- 2G, 385
- 3G, 385, 526
- 4G, 385, 526
- 5G, 385, 526
- CDMA, 385
- connectivity, 526
- GSM, 385
- LTE, 385, 526

Certificate Manager, 944
certification
- CompTIA Core 1 (220-1101) A+ certification domains, 5
- CompTIA Core 2 (220-1102) A+ certification domains, 5
- credentials, 801
- destruction/incineration certificates, 907
- digital security certificates, 943-944

CF (CompactFlash) cards, 379
CFX12V power supplies, 163
change boards, 999
change management, 999-1001
Change permissions, 930
changing
- documenting changes, 132, 1001
- end user acceptance of changes, 1001
- hard drive letters, 809
- IP addresses, 595
- one thing at a time (soft skills), 132
- passwords, 922
- permissions, 928
- purpose of, 1000
- scope of change, 1000
- troubleshooting perspectives (soft skills), 755
- usernames/passwords, 607

channel ID, wireless networks, 588-589, 608
characters (passwords), number of, 911
charging
- batteries, troubleshooting, 456
- USB ports, 41

charging/conditioning phase, laser printer imaging process, 324
chassis, 9-10
checkboxes, Windows, 671
checking power supply voltages, 174
checkpoints/snapshots, VM, 535
child exploitation, security, 965
chipsets, system design, 481

INDEX

chkdsk command, 260, 714
chkntfs command, 714
chmod command, 874-876
choosing
  fiber cabling, 53
  microphones, 293-294
  power supplies, 171-172
  speakers, 296
chown command, 874-876
chroma displays (printing), troubleshooting, 363
Chrome, Google, 532
Chrome OS, 378
CIDR (Classless Inter-Domain Routing), IP addressing, 581
CIFS (Common Internet File System), 626
cipher command, 714-715
circuit testers, AC, 174
CIS (Continuous Ink Systems), 335-336
CL ratings, 199
clarifying customer statements, 2
classes, IPv4 addressing, 578
clean installations, 408, 765
cleaning
  blades, laser printers, 326
  kits, optical drives, 158
  laser printers, 326, 340-341
cleaning phase, laser printer imaging process, 325
cleansers, general-purpose, 157
clearing
  browser data, 530
  caches, 530
  Event Viewer logs, 800
  paper jams, 356
clicking sounds, troubleshooting, 262, 301
CLI (Command-Line Interface), 653, 883, 886-887
client-side DNS, 600
clocking processors, 72, 84
clocks
  activation clocks, 776
  drift, troubleshooting, 791
Close button, Windows, 671
closing
  apps, 390, 451
  command prompt, 699, 718
cloths
  general-purpose cloths, 157
  lint-free cloths, 157
cloud computing, 537
  advantages of, 541
  apps, 539
  corporate focus, 541
  DaaS, 538
  deploying services
    community clouds, 541
    hybrid clouds, 540
    private clouds, 540
    public clouds, 540
  files
    storage services, 539
    synchronizing, 539
  HA, 541
  IaaS, 538
  iCloud, 407, 862
  iTunes, mobile device backups, 407
  LMS, 540
  mobile device synchronization, 402
  network controllers, 539
  off-site email apps, 539
  OneDrive, 764
  PaaS, 538
  printing, 354
  rapid elasticity, 541
  SaaS, 538
  scanning, 354
  services, 354, 540-541
  shared resources, 541
  storage, 224
  streaming virtual apps, 539
cls command, 715
clusters, 244
  FAT (FAT16) file systems, 245
  lost clusters, 258
  NTFS file systems, 245
cmdlets, 754
CMOS (Complementary Metal-Oxide Semiconductors)
  batteries, 117
  error messages, 490-491
  ESCD, 123
  jumpers, 119
  memory, 117
coaxial cabling, 49-50, 518
collating pages, 347
collection-controlled loops. *See* for loops
color
  appearance (soft skills), 462
  audio ports, 291
  incorrect colors (screens), troubleshooting, 284
  inkjet printers, 323, 363
.COM file extensions, 674
command command, 715
command-line interface. *See* CLI
[command name] /? command, 711
command prompt
  accessing, 698-699
  administrative privileges, 699
  attrib command, 708, 711
  bcdedit command, 712
  bootrec command, 712
  cd command, 702, 713
  chkdsk command, 714
  chkntfs command, 714
  cipher command, 714-715
  closing, 699, 718
  cls command, 715
  command command, 715
  [command name] /? command, 711
  copy command, 706-707, 715
  defrag command, 716
  del command, 706, 716
  dir command, 702-704, 711, 716-717
  directories
    naming, 699
    navigating, 701-705
    root directories, 699
    subdirectories, 700
  disable command, 717
  diskpart command, 717
  dism command, 717-718
  drive navigation inputs, 711
  dxdiag command, 718
  enable command, 718
  exit command, 718
  expand command, 719
  explorer command, 719

files
naming, 699
organizing, 699
tree structure, 700-702
format command, 719
formatting commands, 699
gpresult command, 720
gpupdate command, 720
help command, 710, 720
hostname command, 721
ipconfig command, 721
md command, 705, 722
mmc command, 722
more command, 722
msconfig command, 722
msinfo32 command, 723
mstsc command, 723
nbtstat command, 723
net command, 723
netdom command, 725
netstat command, 725
net use command, 724
net user command, 724
notepad command, 726
nslookup command, 726
overview, 699
pathping command, 726
ping command, 727
PowerShell (.psl), opening, 709
rd command, 705, 727
regedit command, 728
regsvr32 command, 728
ren command, 728
rmdir command, 727
robocopy command, 706-707, 729
services.msc command, 729, 831
set command, 729, 740
sfc command, 730
shutdown command, 730-731
systeminfo command, 731
taskkill command, 731
tasklist command, 732
telnet command, 732
tools, starting with commands, 708
tracert command, 732
type command, 706, 732
wbadmin command, 733
Windows, 698
winver command, 733
wscript command, 733
xcopy command, 706-707, 733
commands
Linux commands
apt-get command, 883, 886-887
dd command, 883, 887-890
ifconfig command, 883-885
iwconfig command, 883-885
locate command, 883, 891
passwd command, 883-884
ps command, 883, 886
shutdown command, 883
su command, 883
updatedb command, 883, 891
macOS commands
c command, 874
cd command, 874-875
chmod command, 874-876
chown command, 874-876
cp command, 874-875
grep command, 874-878
kill command, 874
less command, 874-877
ls command, 874-875
man command, 874, 878
mkdir command, 874
mv command, 874-875
nano command, 874, 877
pwd command, 874-875
rm command, 874-876
sudo command, 874-876
touch command, 874-875
vi command, 874
Windows commands
administrative privileges, 734
attrib command, 708, 711
bcdedit command, 712
bootrec command, 712
bootrec /fixboot command, 815
bootrec /fixmbr command, 815
bootrec /scanos command, 815
capitalization, 699
cd command, 702, 713
chkdsk command, 714
chkntfs command, 714
cipher command, 714-715
cls command, 715
command command, 715
[command name] /? command, 711
common commands list, 709-710
convert command, 770
copy command, 706-707, 715
defrag command, 716
del command, 706, 716
dir command, 702-704, 711, 716-717
disable command, 717
diskpart command, 717
dism command, 717-718
drive navigation inputs, 711
dxdiag command, 718
enable command, 718
exit command, 718
expand command, 719
explorer command, 719
format command, 719
formats of, 699
formatting, 710
gpresult command, 720
gpupdate command, 720
help command, 710, 720
hostname command, 721
ipconfig command, 721
learning, 708
md command, 705, 722
mmc command, 722, 796
more command, 722
msconfig command, 722
mskinfo32 command, 723
mstsc command, 723, 843
nbtstat command, 723
net command, 723
netdom command, 725
netstat command, 725
net use command, 724
net user command, 724
notepad command, 726
nslookup command, 726
output, multiple pages, 704
pathping command, 726
ping command, 727
rd command, 705, 727
reasons for learning, 708
regedit command, 728
regsvr32 command, 728
regsvr32.exe command, 796

ren command, 728
rmdir command, 727
robocopy command, 706-707, 729
services.msc command, 729, 831
set command, 729, 740
sfc command, 730
shutdown command, 730-731
starting tools with, 708
switches, 703-704
systeminfo command, 731
taskkill command, 731
tasklist command, 732
telnet command, 732
tracert command, 732
type command, 706, 732
usage considerations, 707
user privileges, 734
wbadmin command, 733
wildcards, 706
WinRE limited commands, 704
winver command, 733
writing, 708
wscript command, 733
xcopy command, 706-707, 733

comments within scripts, 745-746
commercial licenses, 913
commitments (soft skills), making/keeping, 1008
communication skills (soft skills)
phone, 267-268
written, 176-177
community clouds, 541
comparison (equality) operators, 747
compatibility, Windows
Compatibility tab, 204-205, 768
older apps, 204-205
compiled programs, 734
complexity of passwords, 911
compliance policies, 901, 999
component handling/storage, safety, 984-986
Component Services, 797
Component/RGB video ports, 287
compound conditions, 750
compressed air, 157-158, 980
compression, files/folders (Windows), 681
CompTIA Core 1 (220-1101) A+ certification domains, 5
CompTIA Core 2 (220-1102) A+ certification domains, 5
Computer Management console, Windows, 796
disk maintenance, 810-811
Disk Management tool, 807-809
Local Users and Groups tool, 804-806
ODBC Data Sources, 812-813
Print Management console, 813-814
Services and Applications section, 811
Storage Spaces Control Panel, 810
System Tools section
Event Viewer, 798-800
Shared Folders tool, 800
Task Scheduler, 797
User Account Management section, 801-803
computers
adding to domains, 601
design
audio subsystems, 483-484
audio/video workstations, 476
Bloom's Taxonomy, 474
cases, 481-482
chipsets, 481
cooling systems, 481
CPU, 481
display subsystems, 484-485
environment concerns, 480
gaming PC, 475
graphic/CAD/CAM workstations, 475
home servers, 479
memory, 481
motherboards, 481
NAS devices, 477
overview, 474
power supplies, 481-482
processors, 481
recycling components, 480
storage subsystems, 483
thick client workstations, 479
thin client workstations, 478
virtualization workstations, 477
enclosures, 992
hiding from networks, 921
locking, 922
types of, 8
concurrent users (share permissions), maximum number of, 929
conditioning rollers, laser printers, 326
conditioning/charging phase, laser printer imaging process, 324
conferencing features, displays, 485
confidence (soft skills), projecting, 210, 1005
confidential/private materials (soft skills), dealing with, 1011
configuring
alternative IP addresses, 598
BIOS. *See also* UEFI
ACPI setting, 115
bootstrap programs, 110
configuration change options, 116
configuration settings, 113
CPU Configuration setting, 114
downgrading, 112
Exit Without Saving, 117
Flash BIOS, 112
flashing, 118-120
functions, 110
IDE Configuration setting, 115
Interface Configuration setting, 115
Load Fail Safe Defaults, 117
Load Optimized Defaults, 117
overview, 110
PCI/PnP Configuration setting, 115
PCIe Configuration setting, 115
POST, 110
resetting, 119
resource conflicts, 121
SATA Configuration setting, 115
Save & Exit Setup, 117
Setup programs, 110-111
storage devices, 241
troubleshooting, 131
upgrading, 112
viruses, 119

browsers, 530
change options, 117
CMOS, 117
DHCP
lease time, 597
reservations, 597
scope, 596
servers, 596
email, mobile devices, 399-400
end devices, IP addressing, 594
alternative IP address configurations, 598
APIPA, 598
default gateways, 599
DNS, 599-600
static configurations, 595-597
ESCD, 123
firmware, updating, 118-120
hardware, installing/updating drivers 123
IP addresses, alternative, 598
manufacturer's advice, ignoring, 124
mobile devices
email, 399-400
network configurations, 396
networks
configuration operators, 921
ifconfig command (Linux), 884-885
NIC, virtualization, 603-605
PnP, 115
RAID, 253-255
storage devices, overview, 235
System Configuration utility
msconfig command, 722
Windows, 820-824
system resources
I/O addresses, 120-122
IRQ, 120
memory addresses, 120-122
troubleshooting, 130
UEFI. *See also* BIOS
ACPI setting, 115
configuration change options, 116
configuration settings, 113
CPU Configuration setting, 114
Exit Without Saving, 117
flashing, 118-120
IDE Configuration setting, 115
Interface Configuration setting, 115
Load Fail Safe Defaults, 117
Load Optimized Defaults, 117
PCI/PnP Configuration setting, 115
PCIe Configuration setting (BIOS/UEFI), 115
resource conflicts, 121
SATA Configuration setting, 115
Save & Exit Setup, 117
storage devices, 241
troubleshooting, 131
viruses, 119
USB devices, installing, 124
USB expansion cards, 124-126
VPN, 954-955
Windows, 783-784
wireless AP, 607
WWAN, 608
connection-oriented protocols, TCP/IP, 627
connectionless protocols, UDP, 627
connectivity
24-pin motherboard connectors, 164
adapters, advantages of, 54
ATX power connectors, 166
ATX power supply connectors, 163
Bluetooth, 459-460, 553
BNC connectors, 49
cabling, 576
BNC connectors, 49
Cat 5 cables, 51
Cat 5e cables, 51
Cat 6a cables, 51
Cat 6 cables, 51
Cat 7 cables, 51
Cat 8 cables, 51
coaxial cables, 49-50
crosstalk, 50
direct burial cables, 51
Ethernet cables, 50-51
fiber cables, 52-53
LC, 53
MT-RJ connectors, 53
plenum cables, 52
punchdown tools, 51
PVC cables, 52
RJ45 connectors, 51
SC, 53
ST connectors, 53
STP cables, 51
T568A wiring standard, 52
T568B wiring standard, 52
UTP cables, 50
cellular networks, 526
copper media, 560
dial-up Internet connectivity, 516-518
direct burial cabling, 560
dual Molex-to-PCIe converters, 165
EoP, 568
front panel connectors, 151
intermittent/limited connectivity, troubleshooting, 611-612
intermittent wireless connectivity, 458-459, 592
internal connectors, removing, 149-151
Internet. *See also* mobile connectivity
cable modems, 518
dial-up connectivity, 516-518
fiber networks, 522-524
modems, cabling, 516
modems, dial-up connectivity, 516-518
overview, 516
satellite modems, 524-525
troubleshooting, 459, 611-612
VoIP, 520-522
xDSL modems, 519
IR, mobile devices, 399
limited/intermittent connectivity, troubleshooting, 611-612
local connectivity, 613
metered connections, 628
mobile connectivity. *See also* Internet, connectivity
cellular networks, 526
hotspots, 525
licensed ranges, 527
long-range fixed wireless, 526
overview, 525
power requirements, 527-528
synchronization, 403

tethering, 525
unlicensed ranges, 527
WAN, 526
WiBro, 526
wired connectivity, 390-392
wireless connectivity, 393-399
WISP, 527
Molex-to-SATA converters, 165
motherboards, 150
24-pin motherboard connectors, 164
ATX power connectors, 166
front panel connectors, 151
PATA connectors, 231
pins, 152
power supplies, 163
SATA connectors, 231
networks
cable management systems, 570
cabling cabinets, 569
cabling racks, 569-571
direct burial cables, 560
EoP, 568
PoE, 567-568
twisted pair cabling, 560-567
unintentional connections, troubleshooting, 459
ODBC Data Sources, 812-813
PATA, 231
PCI, 88-90
PCIe, 89-91
pin 1, cables, 150
ping command, 727
ports
audio ports, 44
common ports table, 54-55
eSATA ports, 45
eSATAp ports, 45
Ethernet ports, 47-48
integrated motherboard ports, 54
keyboard ports, 32
mini-DIN (PS/2) ports, 32
modem ports, 45-46
motherboard ports, 32
mouse (mice) ports, 32
network ports, 47-48
serial ports, 45-46
video ports, 33-43
power supplies, motherboards, 163
printers
Bluetooth, 342, 352
USB, 342-344, 359
Windows environments, 359-362
wired networks, 342
wireless networks, 342, 351-352
processors, 74
projectors, 288
reassembling computers, 156
RJ11 connectors, 561-564
RJ11 ports, 45-46
RJ45 connectors, 51, 561-565
SAN, 559
SATA, 150, 231-233, 236
scanners, 304
snug connectors, 150
sound cards, 290
SSH, 626
troubleshooting, 611-612
twisted pair cabling
corporate networks, 565-567
RJ45 connectors, 561
STP cables, 560
terminating, 561-565
UTP cables, 560-561
USB connectors, 38
video cabling, troubleshooting, 284
Wi-Fi connectivity, troubleshooting, 458-459
wired connectivity, 594
Ethernet connectivity, projectors, 288
mobile devices, 390-392
wireless connectivity, 594
Bluetooth, 56
desktop workstations, 582
IR, 56
mobile devices, 393-399
NFC, 56
projectors, 288
radio, 56
WiBro, 526
consequences of scripting, mitigating, 737
Console, macOS, 870-871
constructs, scripting, 746
contact cleaners, gold, 158
contacts, vCard synchronization, 402
content filtering, 608, 956
context menus, Windows, 672
context-sensitive help, Windows, 672
continuity checks, 161-162
continuous reboots, troubleshooting, 96
contrast ratios, displays, 485
Control Panel, Windows, 682-685
control panel assemblies, laser printers, 326
control plane, SDN, 623
controllers, cloud-based network, 539
convert command, 770
converters
dual Molex-to-PCIe converters, 165
Molex-to-SATA converters, 165
USB-to-Ethernet converters, 41
USB-to-serial port converters, 46
video converters, 36
converting
MBR to GPT, 249
partitions, 244
cooling systems
CPU, 81-82, 85-86
design, 481
fans, 80, 85-86, 114
auxiliary fans, 167
cases, 167
troubleshooting, 173
heat sinks, 80-82, 85-86
liquid cooling, 80
phase-change (vapor) cooling, 80
processors, 80-82
thermal pads, 80, 85-86
thermal paste, 80-82, 85-86
copper media, 560
copy command, 706-707, 715
copying
data, Linux, 887-890
directories, 706-707
files/directories, 706-707, 729, 733
in NTFS permissions, 932-933
Shadow Copy technology, 816
Windows files/folders, 681
Core i3 processors, 78
Core i5 processors, 78
Core i7 processors, 77

Core i9 processors, 77
Core X processors, 77
corporate focus, cloud computing, 541
corporate networks
- cabling, 565-567
- disk imaging, 775
- Windows deployments, 775-776

corruption/data loss, troubleshooting, 260
Cortana search feature, Windows, 678
Cortana virtual assistant, 764
covers (slot), replacing, 147
cp command, 874-875
CPU (Central Processing Units). *See also* processors
- cooling, 81-82, 85-86
- CPU Configuration setting (BIOS/UEFI), 114
- handling, 83
- installing, 85
- overclocking, 85
- photographing before installation, 85
- sockets, 79-80
- speeds, 72
- system design, 481
- throttle management, 84
- throttling, 72
- upgrading, 84

cracked/broken LCD displays, 435
crash screens, proprietary, 96, 491
crashing apps, 205, 799, 824
Credential Manager
- adding credentials, 802-803
- editing credentials, 804
- removing credentials, 803
- storing credentials, 801

credentials
- adding, 802-803
- backups, 801
- certificate-based credentials, 801
- editing, 804
- generic credentials, 801
- removing, 803
- storing, 801
- web credentials, 801

crimpers, 563-565, 572
cross platform virtualization, 534
cross-site scripting (XSS) attacks, 920
crossover cabling, 562-563
crosstalk, 50, 561
CRT monitors, safety, 21
cryptojacking/cryptomining, 915
cultural sensitivity (soft skills), 1006
current
- multimeters, 572
- voltage, 161-162

current directory (.), 711
current (soft skills), staying, 690
cursor drift, troubleshooting, 454
Custom mode, virtual NIC, 604
customers (soft skills)
- clarifying statements, 2
- difficult customers, 1009
- feedback, dealing with, 501-502, 1009
- service, 1002-1003
- trust, building, 967

cylinders, magnetic hard drives, 227

D

D89 serial ports, 46
DaaS (Desktop as a Service), 535, 538
damaged ports, troubleshooting, 448
dark displays, troubleshooting, 285, 830
dash, Linux, 879
data at rest, 940
data backups, Windows, 688, 781-782
data gathering, 736
Data Link layer (OSI model), 575
data loss/corruption, troubleshooting, 260
data packets, tracert command, 732
data plane, SDN, 623
data privacy, printers/scanners, 355
data security, 935
- account recovery, 939
- AES, 940
- AutoPlay, disabling, 941
- AutoRun, disabling, 941
- backups, 936-939
- BitLocker, 939-940
- BitLocker To Go, 939
- data at rest, 940
- device encryption, 940
- EFS, 940
- EOL, 935
- hard drives, storage, 941
- patch management, 935
- restores, 936-939
- unknown notifications, 935
- unprotected systems, 935
- update management, 935

data sources (projectors), troubleshooting, 288
data transfer speeds, wireless networks, 593
data types, 743
data-usage limit notifications, 445
databases
- ODBC Data Sources, 812-813
- systems, 998

dates/times, inaccurate system, 118
DC (Direct Current), 159-160
- jacks, replacing, 431
- power supplies, 166

dd command, Linux, 883, 887, 890
DDOS (Distributed DOS) attacks, 919
DDR (Double Data Rate) memory, 190
DDR2 memory, 190
DDR3 memory, 190
DDR4 memory, 190
DDR5 memory, 190
dead pixels (screens), troubleshooting, 285
dealing with difficult customers (soft skills), 501-502
decision (selection) structures
- dual-alternative structures, 748
- examples of, 749-750
- multiple alternative structures, 748-749
- relational operators, 746-747
- single-alternative structures, 747

declaring variables, 742-743
decrypting email, troubleshooting, 452
default browsers, 530
default gateways, 599
default printers, 345

defaults, BIOS/UEFI
  Load Fail Safe Defaults configuration change option, 117
  Load Optimized Defaults configuration change option, 117
defrag command, 716
defragmenting
  hard drives, 259-260, 811
  SSD, 260
degaussing hard drives, 942
del command, 706, 716
deleting. *See also* removing
  AD accounts, 925
  apps, 451
  apps, 390
  files, 670, 706, 716
  partitions, 248
  removable media files, 670
denatured alcohol, 157
density control blades, laser printers, 326
deny/allow lists, 950
DEP (Data Execution Prevention), 656
deploying
  tools
    MDT, 776
    SIM, 776
    Sysprep, 775
    WDS, 776
    Windows ADK, 775
  Windows
    corporate deployments, 775-776
    image deployments, 765
    licensing, 776
design
  computer design
    audio subsystems, 483-484
    audio/video workstations, 476
    Bloom's Taxonomy, 474
    cases, 481-482
    chipsets, 481
    cooling systems, 481
    CPU, 481
    display subsystems, 484-485
    environment concerns, 480
    gaming PC, 475
    graphic/CAD/CAM workstations, 475
    home servers, 479
    memory, 481
    motherboards, 481
    NAS devices, 477
    overview, 474
    power supplies, 481-482
    processors, 481
    recycling components, 480
    storage subsystems, 483
    thick client workstations, 479
    thin client workstations, 478
    virtualization workstations, 477
  wireless networks, 585
desk controllers, projectors, 288
Desktop tile, Windows Start screen, 669
desktops
  DaaS, 538
  macOS, 859-860
  malware alerts, 917
  mobile device synchronization, 402
  RDP, 626
  Remote Desktop Services
    thick client installations, 606
    thin client installations, 605-606
  virtual desktops, 538
  virtualization, 534-535
  Windows 10/11
    notification area, 667
    organizing, 668
    pinning apps to taskbar, 667
    Remote Assistance, 843-845
    Remote Desktop Connection, 843-844
    search function, 668
    Show Desktop area, 667
    shutdown options, 666-667
    Start button, 664-665
    Task View, 668-669
  workstations, wireless connectivity, 582
destroying hard drives, 942
destruction/incineration, certificates of, 907
developer mode, Android OS, 390
developing cylinders, laser printers, 326
developing phase, laser printer imaging process, 325
device drivers, 8
  installing, 786, 789
  rolling back, 789
  signed drivers, 786
  troubleshooting installations, 789
device encryption, 940
device failures (intermittent), troubleshooting, 493
Device Manager, 785-786
  accessing, 121
  hardware, verifying, 130-131
  troubleshooting with, 131, 789-790
  undetected/nonfunctioning devices, troubleshooting, 789-790
Devices and Printers Control Panel utility, Windows, 785, 791
Devices setting (BIOS/UEFI), 115
DHCP (Dynamic Host Configuration Protocol), 626
  lease time, 597
  reservations, 597
  scope, 596
  servers, 596, 622
  wireless networks, 608
diagnostics, Built-in Diagnostics setting (BIOS/UEFI), 116
diagonal cutters, 147
diagrams, network topology, 995
dial-up networks, 516-518
dialog boxes, Windows, 670-672
dictionary attacks, 911, 919
differential backups, 937
difficult customers (soft skills), dealing with, 501-502, 1009
digital cameras, 305
digital security certificates, 943-944
digital signals, video ports, 33
digital signatures, 786
digitized sound, 292
digitizers, 307
  laptops, 436-439
dim displays (screens), troubleshooting, 285, 454
DIMM (Dual In-line Memory Modules)
  advertisements, 199
  installing, 201
  models of, 190-191

physical packaging, 188
removing, 200
SODIMM, 188, 425
solutions, 197
dir command, 702-704, 711, 716-717
direct burial cabling, 51, 560
Direct Connect, 74
directional antennas, 591
directories
attributes, handling, 708
cd command, 713
copying, 706-707, 733
current directory (.), 711
LDAP, 626
making, 705
md command, 722
naming, 699, 728
navigating with command prompt, 701
cd command, 702
dir command, 702-704
md command, 705-706
rd command, 705
parent directory (..), 711
permissions, 908
removing, 705, 727
renaming, 728
root directories, 699
subdirectories, 700, 705
DirectX, optical drives, 301
disable command, 717
Disable Execute Bit setting (BIOS/UEFI), 115
disabling
apps, 822
AutoPlay, 941
AutoRun, 941
browser plug-ins/extensions, 530-531
guest accounts, 927
interfering software from OS installations, 774
motherboards, sound card installations, 293
ports, 908
services, 831
disassembly
adapters, removing, 152
all-in-one computers, 155
cases, opening, 149
EMI, 146
equipment grounding, 144
ESD
antistatic bags, 146
antistatic gloves, 145
antistatic mats, 146
antistatic wrist straps, 144-145
self-grounding, 146
SSD, 153
external cables, removing, 148
hard drives, removing, 153
internal cables/connectors, removing, 149-151
motherboards, removing, 154
overview, 144
power cables, removing, 148
power supplies, 174
process (overview), 148
RFI, 146
steps of (overview), 148
storage devices, removing, 153
tools, 147
disk caches, 256, 257
Disk Cleanup, 258, 810
disk imaging, 775
disk maintenance, 810-811
disk management
Disk Management tool, Windows, 242-245, 250-251, 771, 807-809
Disk Utility, macOS, 872-873
disk mirroring (RAID 1), 254
disk quotas, NTFS, 246
disk striping (RAID 0), 254
Disk Utility, macOS, 872-873
diskpart command, 717
diskpart utility, partitioning hard drives, 242-245
Disks, Linux, 881
dism command, 717-718
displaying
.bat files, 706
.txt files, 706
variables, 729, 740
DisplayPorts, 35-36
displays
aspect rations, 484
autorotating, 454
backlights, 434
black/blank screens, troubleshooting, 829-831
BSOD
troubleshooting, 799
Windows updates, 830
CCFL, 434
conferencing features, 485
contrast ratios, 485
dark displays, troubleshooting, 830
dim displays, troubleshooting, 454
flickering displays, troubleshooting, 455
inverters, 436, 440
laptops, 433-434, 157
LCD, 434-435
LED, 434
multiple displays, 788
no display, troubleshooting, 454
OLED, 434
orientation, 788
preventive maintenance, laptops, 157
private screens, physical security, 904
rearranging, 788
refresh rates, 789
replacing, 437
resolution, 437, 788
settings, 788-789
sharing, macOS, 862-864
subsystem design, 484-485
taskbars, viewing, 789
timeouts/screen locks, 927
touch screens, 436-439
troubleshooting
autorotation failures, 454
backlight failures, 454
black/blank screens, 829-831
dim displays, 454
flickering display, 455
no display, 454
video adapters, 485
disposal procedures
aerosol cans, 158
electronics, 982-983
e-waste, 982
monitors, 287
toner, 984

distractions (soft skills), avoiding, 1007-1008
distros (distributions), Linux, 878-879
DKIM (Domain Keys Identified Mail), 948
DLL (Dynamic Link Libraries), 674, 795
DMARC (Domain-based Message Authentication, Reporting, and Conformance), 948
DMZ (Demilitarized Zones), 607-608, 950, 960
DNAT (Destination NAT), wireless networks, 608
DNS (Domain Name Systems), 599, 626
  A records, 600
  AAAA records, 600
  client-side DNS, 600
  Internet security, 946-947
  MX records, 600
  name resolution, 600
  nslookup command, 726
  OpenDNS, 946-947
  servers, 622
  troubleshooting, 946-947
  TXT messages, 600, 948
.DOC (.DOCX) file extensions, 674
Dock, macOS, 859-860
docking stations, 381-382, 412
documentation, 995
  asset management, 998
  AUP, 999
  business processes, 999
  changes, 132, 1001
  digitizers, 307
  documenting outcomes, troubleshooting process, 497
  incident documentation, 997
  incident reports, 978
  inventory lists, 998
  knowledge bases/articles, 996-997
  MSDS, 158, 979
  network topology diagrams, 995
  new user/exiting user checklists, 996
  operational procedures, 978
  password policies, 999
  regulatory/compliance policies, 999
  rollback plans, 1001
  SDS, 158
  security
    certificates of destruction/incineration, 907
    policies, 999
    shredding documents, 907
  sensitive material, 318
  SOP, 994
  transferring with AirDrop, troubleshooting, 452
  written communication skills, 176-177
domain controllers, 601
domains, 555-557, 775
  adding computers to domains, 601
  CompTIA Core 1 (220-1101) A+ certification domains, 5
  CompTIA Core 2 (220-1102) A+ certification domains, 5
door locks, physical security, 901
DoS (Denial-of-Service) attacks, 919
dot matrix printers. *See* impact printers
double images (printing), troubleshooting, 364
double-sided printing (duplexing), 347
double-tap actions (mobile devices), 384
downgrading BIOS, 112
downloading
  software packages, 887
  Ubuntu, 879
downstream/upstream data, fiber networks, 523
DPI (optimized), inkjet printers, 321-323
draft mode, inkjet printers, 322
DRAM (dynamic RAM), 188-190
drawing pads, 376, 381
dress codes (soft skills), 461-462
drift, clock, 791
drilling hard drive platters, 942
drive activity LED, 261
drive arrays, RAID
  BIOS/UEFI configuration settings, 255
  concepts, 254
  configuring, 253
  failures, 266
  fault tolerance, 253-254
  FCM, 253
  hardware RAID, 254
  hot swappable RAID drives, 254
  levels of, 253-254
  RAID 0, 254
  RAID 0+1, 254
  RAID 1, 254
  RAID 5, 254
  RAID 10, 254
  "RAID not found" error messages, 266
  software RAID, 253
  troubleshooting, 266
Drive Encryption setting (BIOS/UEFI), 115
drive letters, 699
drive navigation inputs, 711
"drive not recognized" error messages, 261
drive partitions (volumes), 770
drive status, 807
drivers
  installing, 123
  load alternate third-party drivers, 772
  updating, 123
  Windows installations, 772-773
DRM (Digital Rights Management), 912
drop-down menus, Windows, 671
drums (photosensitive). *See* imaging drums
.DRV file extensions, 674
DSL (Digital Subscriber Lines), 519, 619
dual-alternative structures, 748
dual-channel memory, 195-197
dual Molex-to-PCIe converters, 165
dual-rail power supplies, 170
dual-voltage memory, 192, 426
dumpster diving, 907
duplexing
  assemblies, printers, 332
    inkjet printers, 322
    laser printers, 326

double-sided printing, 347
NIC, 603
duplicate IP address messages, 598
dust, preventive maintenance, 156, 992
DVD (Digital Versatile Discs)
preventive maintenance, 301-302
region codes, 299
DVD drives. *See* optical drives
DVI (Video Graphics Array) ports, 33, 36
DVI-to-HDMI adapters, 36
dxdiag command, 282, 718
dye sublimation printers, 323
dynamic disks, 251, 769
Dynamic status messages, 265
dynamic storage, 251

E

e-readers, 377
e-waste, 982
EB (exabytes), 21
ECC (Error Correction Codes), 191-192
ECP (Electronic Control Packages), laser printers, 326
Edge, Microsoft, 528-529, 532
Edge tile, Windows Start screen, 669
editing
credentials, 804
environment variables, 738
Windows registry, 687
workstations (audio/video), system design, 476
educating users, security, 912
effective permissions, 933
EFS (Encrypting File Systems), 681, 940
EIRP (Equivalent Isotropic Radiated Power), 527
elasticity (rapid), cloud computing, 541
electrical fire safety, 979
electricity, static
antistatic brushes, 157
EMI, 146
ESD
antistatic bags, 146
antistatic gloves, 145
antistatic mats, 146
antistatic wrist straps, 144-145
self-grounding, 146
SSD, 153
RFI, 146
electronic key cards, physical security, 902
electronics
AC, 159-160, 174
amps, 161-162
continuity checks, 161-162
current, 161-162
DC, 159-160
disposal/recycling, 982-983
multimeters, 160
ohms, 161-162
overview, 159
polarity, 160-162
resistance, 161-162
safety
equipment grounding, 986
ESD, 984-985
self-grounding, 985
terminology, 160-162
voltage, 160-163
watts, 161-162
email
decryption, troubleshooting, 452
DKIM, 948
DMARC, 948
DNS TXT messages, 600, 948
Exchange Online, 400
filtering, 909
IMAP, 400
mail servers, 622
MIME, 400
mobile device configuration, 399-400
off-site email apps, 539
POP3, 399, 626
security, 901, 909, 947-948
S/MIME, 400, 452
SMTP, 400, 627
spam, 947
SPF, 948
SSL/TLS, 400
troubleshooting, 947-948
embedded systems, 622
emergencies
notifications, 389
procedures, security policies, 901
EMI (Electromagnetic Interference), 146
emulators
Terminal, macOS, 874
virtualization, 536
enable command, 718
enclosures, computer, 992
encryption, 903
AES, 602, 940
AutoPlay, disabling, 941
AutoRun, disabling, 941
BitLocker, 939-940
BitLocker-To-Go, 939
cipher command, 714-715
data at rest, 940
device encryption, 940
Drive Encryption setting (BIOS/UEFI), 115
EFS, 681, 940
full device encryption, 940
other people's files, 941
SAE, 959
TKIP, 602
unlocking encrypted hard drives, 940
WEP, 602
Windows files/folders, 681
WPA, 602
WPA2, 602
WPA3, 602
end devices, IP addressing, 594
alternative IP address configurations, 598
APIPA, 598
default gateways, 599
DNS, 599-600
static configurations, 595-597
end user acceptance of changes, 1001
end-user education, security, 912
endpoint management servers, 622
endpoints, USB, 791
ENERGY STAR ratings, 480
enlarging screens/images, 384
Enterprise edition, Windows 10/11, 657

environmental concerns in system design, 480
environmental impacts, safety, 981-982
environment variables
  accessing, 738-739
  editing, 738
  system environment variables, 738
  user environment variables, 738
  viewing, 740
EOL (End of Life), OS security, 935
EPEAT rating system, 480
EPS12V power supplies, 163
EP (toner) cartridges, laser printers, 327, 339
.EPS file extensions, 674
equality (comparison) operators, 747
equipment grounding, 144, 986
equipment locks, physical security, 903
erasable-bond paper, 332
erase lamps, laser printers, 326
Error Checking tool, 810
error messages, 489
  \error messages, 490
  "bootable device not found" messages, 263
  CMOS, 490, 491
  "drive not recognized" messages, 261
  hard drive installations, 490
  intruder detection errors, 490
  "Invalid Boot Disk" error messages, 815
  memory, 491
  motherboards, 491
  "no OS found" messages, 263, 779
  "Not enough USB controller resources" messages, 791
  "not responding" messages, 799
  "NTLDR Is Missing" messages, 778
  "RASID not found" messages, 266
eSATA (external SATA), 233
  brackets, 128-129
  cabling, 45
  drives, troubleshooting, 264
  installing cards, 128-129
  mounting/unmounting drives, 238-239
  partitions, 246
  ports, 45
eSATAp ports, 45
ESCD (Extended System Configuration Data), 123
ESD (Electrostatic Discharge), 984
  antistatic bags, 146
  antistatic gloves, 145
  antistatic mats, 146
  antistatic wrist straps, 144-145
  mats, 985
  self-grounding, 146
  SSD, 153
  straps, 985
Ethernet
  cabling, 50-51, 567
  EoP, 568
  networks
    EoP, 568
    LAN, 553
    star topologies, 554
  NIC, installing, 129-130
  PoE
    injectors, 568
    standards, 567-568
    switches, 568
  ports
    RJ45 ports, 47-48
    symbols, 48
  standards, 555
  types of, 555
  USB-to-Ethernet converters, 41
  wired Ethernet connectivity, projectors, 288
  wireless connectivity, projectors, 288
ethics (soft skills), 365
EULA (End-User Licensing Agreements), 913
Event Viewer
  clearing logs, 800
  logs, 798
  symbols, 799
  troubleshooting apps, 799
events
  forwarded events, 798
  logging, 927
evil twin attacks, 919
exabytes (EB), 21
Exchange Online, 400
.EXE file extensions, 674
exFAT file systems, 243, 250, 771
exit command, 718
Exit Without Saving configuration change option (BIOS/UEFI), 117
exiting user checklists, 996
expand command, 719
expansion cards
  configuring, 124-126
  installing, 124-126
  laptops, 414
  M.2 expansion cards, 414
  miniPCIe cards, 413
  NVMe cards, 414
expansion slots, 13-14, 87-91
expectations (soft skills), setting/meeting, 1011
expired passwords, 911
explorer command, 719
exposing/writing phase, laser printer imaging process, 325
ext3 file systems, 244, 771, 881
ext4 file systems, 244, 771, 881
extended partitions, 246-247, 769
extended read/write times, troubleshooting, 259
extenders, wireless, 586
extending partitions, 809
extensions
  browser, 530-531
  Windows files, 672-674
external cables, removing, 148
external connectivity, motherboard ports, 32
external data buses, 69
external hard drives, 427, 814
external interference, wireless networks, 592-593
external laptop devices, 412
external networks, VM, 536
Extreme Memory Profiles (XMP), 192

F

facial recognition security, 911
  locks, mobile devices, 442
  physical security, 906

factory recovery partitions. *See* recovery partitions
factory resets, 406
faded print, troubleshooting, 358
failed login attempts, 443, 912
Failed status messages, 265
failing batteries, signs of, 118
failures to boot, troubleshooting, 262
fake security warnings, mobile devices, 441
fans, 80
- auxiliary fans, 167, 171
- cases, 167
- Fan Control setting (BIOS/UEFI), 114
- troubleshooting, 86, 173

FAT (FAT16) file systems, 243-245, 250, 771
FAT32 file systems, 243-245, 250, 771
FAT64 file systems, 243, 250, 771
fault tolerance, 253-254
FC (Fibre Channel), SAN connections, 559
FCM (Flash Cache Modules), RAID, 253
fdisk management, Disks (Linux), 881
feed assemblies, thermal printers, 328, 341
feed rollers. *See* pickup rollers
feedback, dealing with, 1009
feeders/paper trays, inkjet printers, 322
feeds, paper, 332-333, 356
fiber cabling, 52-53
fiber networks, 522-524
filaments, 3-D printers, 330-331
File Explorer, Windows, 654, 672
- copying files, 681
- display options, 676-677
- file attributes, 679-680
- file compression, 681
- file encryption, 681
- indexing, 678
- moving files, 681
- paths, 674-676
- searches, 678
- starting, 719
- troubleshooting, 455

File History backups, 782
file managers
- Linux, 879
- Nautilus, Ubuntu, 879

file recovery software, 260
file servers, 622
file systems
- APFS, 244
- Btrfs, 881
- CDFS, 771
- defined, 243
- EFS, 940
- exFAT, 243, 250
- ext3, 244, 771, 881
- ext4, 244, 771, 881
- FAT (FAT16), 243-245, 250, 771
- FAT32, 243-245, 250, 771
- FAT64, 243, 250, 771
- HFS, 771
- NFS, 771
- NTFS, 244, 770, 771
  - benefits of, 246
  - boot partitions, 248
  - clusters, 245
  - disk quotas, 246
  - partitioning, volume structures, 250
  - system partitions, 248
- types of, 771
- ZFS, 881

files, 654
- attributes, 679-680, 708
- .bat files, 706, 735
- cloud file storage services, 539
- compression, 681
- copying, 681, 706-707, 729, 733
- deleting, 670, 706, 716
- directories, 699, 705
- encryption, 681, 941
- finding, Linux, 891
- FTP, 626
- image files, Print to image (virtual printing), 334
- .inf files, 789-790
- ISO files/images, optical drives, 300
- JavaScript (.js), 735
- leaked personal files/data, 444
- missing files, viruses/malware attacks, 917
- moving, 681
- naming, 699, 728
- NTFS permissions, 933-934
- organizing, 699
- Print to PDF (virtual printing), 334
- Print to XPS (virtual printing), 334
- Python scripts (.py), 735
- ReFS, 810
- removable media files, deleting, 670
- renaming, 728
- sfc, 779
- SFTP, 626
- shell scripts (.sh), 735
- swap files, 257
- synchronizing, 539
- System File Checker, 260, 264, 730
- system files, 814-815
- text files, 734-736
  - creating, 7
  - more command, 722
  - type command, 732
- tree structure, 700-702
- .txt files, displaying, 70
- uncompressing, 719
- VBScript (.vbs), 735
- Windows files
  - extensions, 672-674
  - filenames, 672-673
  - paths, 674-676
  - saving, 674
- Windows setup log files, 778
- XPS files, 334

fileshare servers, 622
filtering
- content, 608, 956
- email, 909
- IP addresses, 961
- IP filtering, wireless networks, 608
- MAC addresses, 960

Finder, macOS, 859-860
finding
- files, Linux, 891
- GRUB, 892

INDEX

fingerprints, security, 911
  locks, mobile devices, 442
  scanners, physical security, 906
fire extinguishers, 979
fire safety, 979
Firefox web browser, 532
firewalls, 575, 908, 949-950
  port forwarding, 952
  Windows Defender Firewall, 951-953
  wireless networks, 958
FireWire ports, troubleshooting, 836
firmware
  AP, 962
  fTMP setting (BIOS/UEFI), 116
  updating, 118-120
  wireless networks, 608
fixed wireless connectivity, long-range, 526
flapping, ports, 612
Flash BIOS, 112
Flash Cache Modules (FCM), RAID, 253
flash drives, 207-208
flash memory, 207
  CF cards, 379
  digital cameras, 305
  memory card readers, 379
  SD cards, 378-379
  SSD, 427-429
  SSHD, 228
flashing BIOS/UEFI, 118-120
flashing screens, troubleshooting, 284
flatbed scanners, 17, 302-303
FlexATX power supplies, 163
flick/swipe actions (mobile devices), 384
flickering displays, troubleshooting, 455
floating point numbers, 743
flowcharts, troubleshooting, 498-500
fnas, 85-86
folders, 654
  attributes, 679-680
  compression, 681
  copying, 681
  encryption, 681
  home folders, AD, 925
  List Folder Contents permissions, 932
  moving, 681
  NTFS permissions, 933-934
  organizing apps, 390
  Public folders, share permissions, 931
  redirecting, 925
  security options, 934-935
  shared folders, 632-634
  Shared Folders tool, 800
  Windows folders
    naming, 673
    subfolders, 672
for loops, 751-753
Force Quit, macOS, 866
force quitting apps, 390
Foreign status messages, 265
form factors
  cases, 164
  hard drives, 225
  motherboards, 94, 164
  power supplies, 163-164
  SODIMM, 425
format command, 719
formatting
  commands, 699, 710
  full formatting, 250, 769
  hard drives, 719
    high-level formatting, 242, 249
    low level formatting, 941
    standard formatting, 941
  passwords, 911
  quick formatting, 250, 769
forwarded events, 798
forwarding, port, 608, 952
frames, OSI model, 574
freeing up disk space, 670
freeware, 912
frequencies, 21
  channel ID, 588-589
  response ranges, speakers, 295
  wireless networks, 581
Friend, Ernie, 495
front panel connectors, 151
frozen systems, troubleshooting, 456
FSB (Front Side Buses), 72
FTP (File Transfer Protocol), 626
fTPM (firmware Trusted Platform Module) setting (BIOS/UEFI), 116
full backups, 937
Full Control permissions, 930-932
full device encryption, 940
full formatting, 250, 769
full system functionality, verifying, 497
functionality (full system), verifying, 497
functions, adapter, 13
fused toner (printing), troubleshooting, 364
fuser assemblies, laser printers, 325-326
fusing phase, laser printer imaging process, 325
fusing rollers, laser printers, 326, 341
fuzzy images (screens), troubleshooting, 284

G

gain, antennas, 591-592
gaming
  P2P, 608
  PC system design, 475
garbled print, troubleshooting, 357
gateways, default, 599
gathering information/data, 485, 736
GB (gigabytes), 20-21
GDPR (General Data Protection Regulation), 914
General Optimization setting (BIOS/UEFI), 114
general-purpose cleansers, 157
general-purpose cloths, 157
generic credentials, 801
geotracking, 388
gestures, macOS, 861-862
GFS (Grandfather Father Son) backups, 938
.GIF file extensions, 674
gigabytes (GB), 20-21
gloves, antistatic, 145
glue, thermal paste as, 82
GNOME user interface, Linux, 879
goggles, safety, 158, 980
gold contact cleaners, 158
Google
  Chrome OS, 378, 532
  Cloud Print, 354
  mobile device synchronization, 403

government regulations, workplace safety, 978
gpresult command, 720
GPS (Global Positioning Systems), 376, 387, 459
GPT (GUID Partition Tables), 249, 769
GPU (Graphics Processing Units), 280
  GPGPU, 76
  iGPU setting (BIOS/UEFI), 116
gpupdate command, 720
graphic/CAD/CAM design workstations, system design, 475
graphical interfaces, troubleshooting, 829
grep command, 874, 878
grinding noises, troubleshooting, 86, 173, 262, 301
grooming (soft skills), 1003
grounding, electronic safety, 144, 985-986
group accounts, 921-922
group policies, 720, 926-927
groups
  Local Users and Groups tool, Windows, 804-805
  security groups, 922
GRUB (Grand Unified Boot Loader), finding, 892
GSM (Global System for Mobile Communications), 385
guards, physical security, 903
guest accounts, 921, 927
GUI (Graphical User Interfaces), 653
    Dock, 859-860
    Finder, 859-860
    gestures, 861-862
    Launchpad, 860
    menu bar, 859
    Mission Control, 860
    Spotlight, 861
GUID (Globally Unique Identifiers), GPT, 769
gun slinger technicians, 132

H

HA (High Availability), cloud computing, 541
halting installations, 778
handheld scanners, 302
handling
  CPU, 83
  motherboards, 96
hanging apps, troubleshooting, 799
hard drives (hard disks), 10
  arrays, adding, 809
  basic disks, 251
  clusters, 244
    FAT (FAT16) file systems, 245
    lost clusters, 258
    NTFS file systems, 245
  defragmenting, 259-260, 811
  degaussing, 942
  destroying, 942
  disk caches, 256-257
  disk mirroring (RAID 1), 254
  disk striping (RAID 0), 254
  drive activity LED, 261
  drive letters, assigning/changing, 809
  dynamic disks, 251
  encrypted hard drives, unlocking, 940
  external hard drives, 427, 814
  fault tolerance, 253-254
  formatting, 719
  form factors, 225
  freeing up space, 670
  HDI, 226
  head crashes, 226
  hibernation/sleep mode, 251
  high-level formatting, 242, 249
  HPA, 249
  hybrid drives, 427
  IDE, 229
  initializing disks, 809
  installing, 428, 490
  internal fixed drives, 814
  internal laptop drives, 427
  JSOD. *See* spanned volumes
  laptops, 426
    external hard drives, 412
    internal drives, 427
  letter assignments, 249
  logical drives, 246-247
  low level formatting, 941
  magnetic hard drives, 225-227
  maintenance, 810-811
  managing
    Disks, Linux, 881
    Disk Utility, macOS, 872-873
  mechanical hard drives, 427, 430
  mounting, 239, 809
  mSATA drives, 427
  MTBF, 226
  multiple hard drives as backups, 937
  noisy hard drives, troubleshooting, 262, 430
  overview, 225
  paging files, 202
  partitioning, 242-243
    basic disks, 769
    boot partitions, 248, 815
    converting, 244, 770
    deleting, 248
    disk part command, 717
    drive partitions (volumes), 770
    dynamic disks, 769
    extended partitions, 246-247, 769, 809
    FAT (FAT16) file systems, 245
    FAT32 file systems, 245
    GPT, 249, 769
    internal hard drive partitions, 814
    logical partitions, 769
    MBR, 247-249, 769
    planning drive space, 770
    primary partitions, 246, 769
    shrinking, 809
    splitting, 809
    swap partitions, 769
    system partitions, 248
  PATA IDE hard drives, power requirements, 171
  planning drive space, 770
  platters, 225, 942
  RAID
    BIOS/UEFI settings, 255
    concepts, 254
    configuring, 253
    failures, 266
    fault tolerance, 253-254
    FCM, 253
    hardware RAID, 254
    hot swappable RAID drives, 254

levels of, 253-254
RAID 0, 254
RAID 0+1, 254
RAID 1, 254
RAID 5, 254
RAID 10, 254
"RAID not found" error messages, 266
software RAID, 253
troubleshooting, 266
rails, 153-154
removing, 153
replacing, 428
SATA hard drives, power requirements, 171
SCSI, SAS drives, 229
security, storage, 941
SSHD, 427
standard formatting, 941
status, 265, 807
storage, security, 941
swap files, 257
troubleshooting
bootup failures, 262
data loss/corruption, 260
extended read/write times, 259
fragmented drives, 259-260
noises, 262
performance, 258-260, 264
read/write failures, 264
sticky hard drives, 263
types of, 225
volumes
adding, 809
boot volumes, 251, 814
RAW volumes, 251
resizing partitions, 252
simple volumes, 251
spanned volumes, 251
striped volumes, 251
system volumes, 251, 814
wiping, 941
hard resets, 449
hard tokens, physical security, 903
hardware
adapters, installing, 13-14
configuration, 123
device drivers, 8
hard drives (hard disks), 10
Hardware Monitor setting (BIOS/UEFI), 115
installing, 495
keyboards, 9, 14
maintenance, 15
ports, 32
troubleshooting, 16
laptops, 410
memory, 12
monitors, 9
motherboards, 11
expansion slots, 13-14
integrated motherboard ports, 54
ports, 32
mouse (mice), 14
maintenance, 15
ports, 32
troubleshooting, 16
optical drives, 10
power supplies, 10
RAID, 254
reinstalling, 495
sound (audio) cards, 44
troubleshooting, 493
verifying with Device Manager, 130-131
Windows installations, 772
HDI (Head-to-Disk Interference), 226
HDMI (High-Definition Multimedia Interface) ports, 35-36
head crashes, 226
headers, OSI model, 574
headphones, troubleshooting, 458
heads (printers)
impact printers, 319, 337
inkjet printers, 321-322, 339
headsets, 17, 381
health of batteries, 456
Healthy status messages, 265
heat sinks, 80-82, 85-86
heat spreaders, 190
heating elements, thermal printers, 328, 341
Hello, Windows, 442
help command, 710, 720
help, context-sensitive, 672
help desks, ticket systems, 997
HFS (Hierarchical Fire Systems), 771
hibernation/sleep mode
hard drives, 251
power supplies, 169
hidden shares, 931
hiding computers from networks, 921
high availability (HA), cloud computing, 541
high latency, 614-615
high-level formatting, hard drives, 242, 249
high network traffic, 458
high number of ads, 445
high performance plans, Windows, 837
hijacking attacks, TCP/IP, 920
HIPAA (Health Insurance Portability and Accountability Act), 914
Hkey_Classes_Root subtree, Windows registry, 687
Hkey_Current_Config subtree, Windows registry, 687
Hkey_Current_User subtree, Windows registry, 687
Hkey_Local_Machine subtree, Windows registry, 686
Hkey_Users subtree, Windows registry, 686
.HLP file extensions, 674
hole punched paper, 358
Home edition, Windows 10/11, 656
home folders, AD, 925
home servers, system design, 479
host addresses, IPv4 addressing, 578
host machines, 535
Host-only mode, virtual NIC, 605
hosted (Type 2) hypervisors, 536
hostname command, 721
hot swappable RAID drives, 254
hotfixes, 778
hotspots, 397, 525
HPA (Host Protected Areas), 249
HSM (Hardware Security Modules), 93, 903
HTTP (Hypertext Transfer Protocol), 626
HTTPS (HTTP over SSL/TLS), 626
hubs, 40, 553-554, 576

humidity
- ESD, 984
- paper, 332
- temperature control, safety, 993-994

humility (soft skills), 893
hybrid clouds, 540
hybrid drives, 427
hygiene (soft skills), 1003
hyperthreading, 73-74, 114
HyperTransport, 74
Hyper-V, 77, 537, 764, 769
hypervisors, 535-536

I

iCloud
- macOS, 862
- mobile device backups, 407

ICMP (Internet Control Message Protocol), 624
icons
- moving, 390
- moving on mobile devices, 384
- removing from notification area, 791

IDE (Integrated Drive Electronics), 229
- cabling, 150, 231
- IDE Configuration setting (BIOS/UEFI), 115

identification
- Apple ID, 863
- channel ID, wireless networks, 588-589, 608
- GDPR, 914
- PCI DSS, 914
- PID, listing, 732
- PII, 914
- PIN, 911
- RFID, physical security, 903
- SSID, 608, 962

identifying
- adapter functions, 13
- problems, troubleshooting process, 486

IDS (Intrusion Detection Systems), 957
IEEE 802.11 wireless standard, mobile devices, 395
IEEE 802.11a wireless standard, 395
IEEE 802.11ac (Wi-Fi 5) wireless standard, 395, 583
IEEE 802.11ad (WiGig) wireless standard, 583
IEEE 802.11ax (Wi-Fi 6) wireless standard, 395, 583
IEEE 802.11b wireless standard, 395, 582
IEEE 802.11e wireless standard, 583
IEEE 802.11g wireless standard, 395, 583
IEEE 802.11i wireless standard, 583
IEEE 802.11n wireless standard, 395, 583
IEEE 1394 FireWire ports, troubleshooting shutdowns, 836
ifconfig command, 613
ignoring manufacturer's advice, 124
IGP (Integrated Graphics Processors), 280
iGPU setting (BIOS/UEFI), 116
image deployments, Windows, 765
images
- burn-in(screens), troubleshooting, 286
- dim images (screens), troubleshooting, 285
- disk imaging, 775
- double images (printing), troubleshooting, 364
- enlarging, 384
- fuzzy images (screens), troubleshooting, 284
- ISO files/images, optical drives, 300
- moving through, 384
- Print to image (virtual printing), 334
- reimaging computers, 775-776
- System Image Recovery, 828
- system images, Windows recovery, 688

imaging, SIM, 776
imaging drums, laser printers, 326
imaging process, laser printers, 324-325
IMAP (Internet Message Access Protocol), 400, 626
IMEI (International Mobile Equipment Identities), 385
impact paper, 320, 337
impact printers, 318
- heads, 319, 337
- impact paper, 320, 337
- maintenance, 336-337
- print ribbons, 319, 336-337
- troubleshooting, 362-363

impersonation attacks, 918
improper charging, troubleshooting, 456
IMSI (International Mobile Subscriber Identities), 386
inaccurate system dates/times, troubleshooting, 118
incident reports, 978, 997
incident response, security, 964-965
incineration/destruction, certificates of, 907
inconfig command, Linux, 883-885
incorrect chroma displays (printing), troubleshooting, 363
incorrect colors (screens), troubleshooting, 284
incorrect data sources (projectors), troubleshooting, 288
incremental backups, 937
indexing, Windows, 678
indicator lights, printers, 356
.inf files, 674, 789-790
information/data, gathering, 485, 736
infrastructures, IaaS, 538
inherited permissions, 932
.INI file extensions, 674
Initialize Disk status messages, 265
initializing
- disks, 809
- TPM, 117
- variables, 743

initiating updates, 736
ink cartridges
- CIS, 335-336
- inkjet printers, 321-322, 338
- recycling, 336
- refilling, 335-336

inkjet printers, 318
- calibrating, 338
- carriage belts, 322
- carriages, 322
- color, 323, 363
- draft mode, 322

INDEX

- duplexing assemblies, 322
- heads, 321-322, 339
- ink cartridges, 321-322, 338
- maintenance, 337-339
- NLQ mode, 322
- optimized DPI, 321-323
- paper trays/feeders, 322
- parts of, 322
- power supplies, 322
- rollers, 322
- stepper motors, 322
- troubleshooting, 363

in-place upgrades, Windows, 765-767
input, programming, 741
input voltage selectors, 166
insider attacks, 919
instability in Windows systems, troubleshooting, 835
installing
- adapters, 13-14
- apps, 390, 451, 736, 792-793
- Bluetooth, 394
- clean installs, 408
- CPU, 85
- device drivers, 786, 789
- DIMM, 201
- drivers, 123
- eSATA cards, 128-129
- halting installations, 778
- hard drives, 428, 490
- hardware, 495
- manufacturer's advice, ignoring, 124
- memory, 201
  - laptops, 426
  - overview, 200
  - planning installations, 189
  - planning installations, how many of each memory type, 195-197
  - planning installations, how much memory to install, 192
  - planning installations, memory features, 191-192
  - planning installations, memory modules, 189-193
  - planning installations, researching/buying memory, 198-199
  - safety, 200
  - viewing amount of installed memory, 193
- mSATA, 237
- multifunction (all-in-one) devices, 343
- NIC, 129-130
- optical drives, 300
- OS, verifying installations, 776
- PATA devices, 235
- printers, connectivity, 342-344
- processors, 82-83
- routers, wireless, 962-963
- SATA devices, 236
- scanners, 304
- software, 495
  - ISO images, 793
  - system requirements, 792-793
- sound cards, 292
- SSD, 239-240, 429
- storage devices, troubleshooting, 260-264
- thick clients, 606
- thin clients, 605-606
- USB devices, 124
- USB expansion cards, 124-126
- USB ports (extra), 42
- verifying installations, 777
- video cards, 283
- Windows
  - antivirus software, 773
  - backups before OS installations, 773
  - clean installations, 765
  - compatibility mode, 768
  - corporate deployments, 775-776
  - disabling interfering software, 774
  - drivers, 772-773
  - file systems, 771
  - hardware, 772
  - image deployments, 765
  - in-place upgrades, 765-767
  - licenses, 776
  - multiboots, 765
  - PCmover Express, 768
  - phases of, 774
  - preinstalling, 708-709
  - recovery partitions, 765
  - remote network installations, 765
  - repair installations, 765, 779
  - resets/restores, 765
  - security scans, 773
  - selecting networks, 774-775
  - types of, 765
  - unattended installations, 765
  - USMT, 768
  - Windows Installation Assistant, 767
- wireless AP, 962, 963
- wireless routers, 962-963

"insufficient disk space" messages, 264
integers, 743
integrated motherboard ports, 54
Integrated Peripherals setting (BIOS/UEFI), 114
Intel
- processors, 68, 77
  - Core i3 processors, 78
  - Core i5 processors, 78
  - Core i7 processors, 77
  - Core i9 processors, 77
  - Core X processors, 77
  - Xeon processors, 77
- sockets, 80

interfaces
- ACPI, 115, 168-169
- AHCI mode, SATA, 241
- GNOME user interface, Linux, 879
- Interface Configuration setting (BIOS/UEFI), 115
- optical drives, 300
- Ubuntu, 880

interference
- EMI, 146
- interfering software, disabling from OS installations, 774
- RFI, 146
- wireless networks, 592-593

intermittent device failures, troubleshooting, 493
intermittent/limited connectivity, troubleshooting, 611-612
intermittent shutdowns
- memory, 205
- projectors, 289
- troubleshooting, 96, 173

intermittent wireless connectivity, 458-459, 592
internal cables/connectors, removing, 149-151
internal data buses, 69
internal fixed disks, 814
internal hard drive partitions, 814
internal laptop drives, 427
internal networks, VM, 536
Internet
  appliances, 956
  calling, 389
  connectivity. *See also* mobile connectivity
    cable modems, 518
    dial-up connectivity, 516-518
    fiber networks, 522-524
    modems, cabling, 516
    modems, dial-up connectivity, 516-518
    overview, 516
    satellite modems, 524-525
    tethering, 525
    troubleshooting, 459, 611-612
    VoIP, 520-522
    xDSL modems, 519
  IoT, 609-611
  ISP, 525
  metered connections, 628
  online resources, searches, 6-7
  security, 942
    allow/deny lists, 950
    digital security certificates, 943-944
    DMZ, 950, 960
    DNS, 946-947
    email, 947-948
    firewalls, 949-950
    malware removal, 944-946
    Microsoft Defender, 943
    Microsoft Defender Antivirus, 943
    NAT, 953
    PAT, 954
    proxy servers, 948-949
    rogue antivirus apps, 943
    screened subnets, 950
    UPnP, 950
    VPN, 954-955
    Windows Defender Firewall, 951-953
  WISP, 527
Internet layer (TCP/IP model), 576, 627
Internet Options Control Panel settings, Microsoft Edge, 528-529
interpreted programs, 734
intruder detection error messages, 490
Intrusion Detection/Notification setting (BIOS/UEFI), 115
"Invalid Boot Disk" error messages, 815
Invalid status messages, 265
inventory lists, 998
inverters, 436, 440
I/O (Input/Output) addresses, 120-122
I/O shields, 154
IOPS (Input/Output Operations per Second), 259
iOS, 378
  AirDrop, troubleshooting, 452
  email configuration, 401
  mobile devices
    backups, 407
    synchronization, 404
IoT (Internet of Things), 609-611, 964
IP (Internet Protocol)
  addressing, 576
    alternative IP addresses, configuring, 598
    assigning the same address on multiple devices, 595
    changing addresses, 595
    duplicate messages, 598
    end devices, 594-600
    filtering, 608, 961
    subnet masks, 1021-1023
  IPv4 addressing
    CIDR, 581
    classes of, 578
    examples of, 579
    host addresses, 578
    network numbers, 578
    octets, 577
    private IP addresses, 578
    public IP addresses, 578
    subnet masks, 580
    VLAN, 580
  IPv6 addressing, 577
  VoIP, 520-522
ipconfig command, 613, 721
IPS (In-Plane Switching) LCD displays, 434
IPS (Intrusion Prevention Systems), 957
IR (Infrared) connectivity
  mobile devices, 399
  wireless connectivity, 56
IRQ (Interrupt Requests), 120
iSCSI (Internet Small Computer Systems Interface), SAN connections, 559
ISO files/images
  optical drives, 300
  software installations, 793
isolating problems, troubleshooting process, 495-496
ISP (Internet Service Providers), 525-527
IT (Internet Technology)
  automation, 1001
  documentation, 995
    asset management, 998
    AUP, 999
    incident documentation, 997
    inventory lists, 998
    knowledge bases/articles, 996-997
    network topology diagrams, 995
    new user/exiting user checklists, 996
    password policies, 999
    regulatory/compliance policies, 999
    security policies, 999
    SOP, 994
iteration, loops, 751
iTunes
  clean installs, 408
  mobile device backups, 407
  mobile device synchronization, 405
ITX (Information Technology eXtended), 94
iwconfig command, Linux, 883-885
iWork, macOS, 862

J

jailbreaking/unauthorized root access, 445
jams, paper, 356
JavaScript (.js), 735
JBOD (Just a Bunch Of Disks). *See* spanned volumes
jitter, VoIP, 521
.JPG (.JPEG) file extensions, 674
jumpers, 119

K

kB (kilobytes), 19-21
keeping commitments (soft skills), 1008
Kerberos authentication servers, 910
kernels, 9
  Linux, 878
  panic, troubleshooting, 871
key cards, physical security, 902
key fobs, physical security, 903
keyboards, 9, 14
  error messages, 490
  maintenance, 15
  ports, 32
  repairing, 422
  special function keys, 424-425
  troubleshooting, 16
Keychain Access, macOS, 871-872
keyloggers, 915
keys, physical security, 901
keywords, variable names, 742
kill command, 874
kill tasks (stop), 824
kilobytes (kB), 19-21
kiosks, 992
KMS (Key Management Service), 776
knowledge bases/articles, 996-997

L

L1 caches, 73
L2 caches, 73
L3 caches, 73
ladder racks, 571
languages, printers, 348
LAN (Local Area Networks), 554
  Ethernet LAN, 553
  VLAN, 580
  Wake on LAN, 169
  Wake on LAN, NIC, 603
  WLAN, 552, 558, 957
  workgroups, 555-557
laptops
  apps
    deleting, 451
    troubleshooting, 450-452
  Bluetooth cards, replacing, 430-431
  cable locks, 440
  cellular cards, 413
  components, 410
  DC jacks, replacing, 431
  digitizers, 436-439
  displays, 433-434
    preventive maintenance, 157
    replacing, 437
  docking stations, 412
  expansion cards, 413-414
  external devices
    hard drives, 412, 427-428
    monitors, 412
    optical drives, 412
  hard drives, 426-428
  hardware, 410
  input voltage selectors, 166
  internal drives, 427
  inverters, 436, 440
  keyboards
    repairing, 422
    special function keys, 424-425
    troubleshooting, 453
  lid close detectors, 436
  M.2 expansion cards, 414
  memory
    dual-voltage memory, 426
    installing, 426
    RAM, 425
    removing, 426
    SODIMM, 425
    upgrading, 425-426
  microphones, 436, 439-440
  miniPCIe cards, 413
  motherboards, 95, 419
  NVMe cards, 414
  overview, 410
  performance, troubleshooting, 455
  port replicators, 412
  power supplies, 415
    optimizing battery performance, 417-418
    removing batteries, 416
    temperature changes, 416
  processors, repairing, 420
  repairing
    keyboards, 422
    motherboards, 419
    overview, 418
    processors, 420
    touchpads, 422
  rotating screens, 435
  screens
    orientation, 435
    replacing, 437
    resolution, 437
    troubleshooting, 454-455
    Wi-Fi antennas, 436
  security
    data-usage limit notifications, 445
    failed login attempts, 443
    jailbreaking, 445
    leaked personal files/data, 444
    system lockouts, 443
    unauthorized account access, 443
    unauthorized camera activation, 444
    unauthorized location tracking, 443-444
    unauthorized microphone activation, 444
    unauthorized root access, 445
    VPN, 446
  sound, 432
  SSD, 414, 429
  storage, 426, 447
  touchpads, repairing, 422
  touch screens, 436-439
  trackpads, troubleshooting, 454
  traveling with, 447
  troubleshooting
    app closure failures, 451-452
    app email decryption failures, 452

app installation failures, 451
app load failures, 452
app update failures, 451
autorotating screens, 454
backlight failures, 454
batteries, 456
Bluetooth connectivity, 459-460
damaged ports, 448
dim displays, 454
frozen systems, 456
GPS, 459
hard resets, 449
keyboards, 453
liquid damage, 448
network issues, 458-459
NFC, 460
no display, 454-455
no power, 456
OS update failures, 450
overheating, 457
performance, 455
soft resets, 448
sound issues, 458
trackpads, 454
unexpected app behavior, 450
Wi-Fi connectivity, 458-459
video cabling, 436
video cards, replacing, 433
WAN connectivity, 526
webcams, 436, 439-440
Wi-Fi antennas, 436
wireless cards, 413, 430-431
wireless connectivity
cellular networks, 526
hotspots, 525
long-range fixed wireless, 526
power requirements, 527-528
tethering, 525
WiBro, 526
wireless NIC, 431
large-format inkjet printers, 323
laser printers, 319, 323
calibrating, 340
cleaning, 340
cleaning blades, 326
cleaning pads, 326, 341
conditioning rollers, 326
control panel assemblies, 326
density control blades, 326
developing cylinders, 326
duplexing assemblies, 326
ECP, 326
erase lamps, 326
fuser assemblies, 325-326
fusing rollers, 326, 341
imaging drums, 326
imaging process, 324-325
main motors, 326
maintenance, 339-341
noises, 326
ozone gas, 341
parts of, 326-327
pickup rollers, 326
power supplies, 326
primary (main) coronas, 326
registration assemblies, 326
scanner units, 327
separation pads, 327
toner, 327, 339, 984
transfer belts, 325
transfer corona wires, 327, 341
transfer rollers, 325
troubleshooting, 363-364
latency
networks, 614-615
VoIP, 522
Launcher, Linux, 879
launching apps, 792
Launchpad, macOS, 860
lb (pounds), paper, 332
LC (Lucent Connectors), 53
LCD (Liquid Crystal Displays), 157, 434-435
LDAP (Lightweight Directory Access Protocol), 626
leaked personal files/data, 444
learning commands, 708
lease time, DHCP, 597
least privilege (share permissions), principle of, 930
LED (Light-Emitting Diode) displays
drive activity LED, 261
motherboards, 261, 492
OLED, 434
Legacy mode, SATA, 241
legacy software, 534
legacy systems, 623
less command, 874, 877
letter assignments, hard drives, 249
levels of risk, 1000
LFX12V power supplies, 163
libraries
DLL, 795
Windows, 672
licensed ranges, wireless connectivity, 527
licensing
asset management, 998
commercial licensing, 913
DRM, 912
EULA, 913
KMS, 776
non-expired licenses, 913
personal licenses, 913
piracy, 913
regulated data, 914
security, 913
valid licenses, 913
lid close detectors, laptops, 436
lifting techniques, safety, 21, 981
light printing, troubleshooting, 363
lighting, physical security, 903
Lightning
cabling, 43
ports, 43, 391
Li-ion batteries, 416, 982-983
LILO (Linux Loader), 892
limitations of memory, 193
limited/intermittent connectivity, troubleshooting, 611-612
limited Internet connectivity, troubleshooting, 459
limits, data-usage, 445
line conditioners, 989
line speed. *See* bandwidth
link-local addressing, IPv6, 577
links, troubleshooting, 791
lint-free cloths, 157
Linux, 655
apt-get command, 883, 886-887
backups, 882
best practices, 892
Btrfs, 881
CLI, 883, 886-887
copying data, 887, 890
dash, 879
dd command, 883, 887, 890
Disks, 881

INDEX

- distros (distributions), 878-879
- ext3 file systems, 881
- ext4 file systems, 881
- file managers, 879
- finding
  - files, 891
  - GRUB/LILO, 892
- GNOME user interface, 879
- GRUB, 892
- ifconfig command, 883-885
- iwconfig command, 883-885
- kernels, 878
- LILO, 892
- locate command, 883, 891
- memory recommendations, 193
- network configurations, 884-885
- passwd command, 883-884
- passwords, 884
- processes, viewing, 886
- ps command, 883, 886
- searches, 880
- shutdown command, 883
- software
  - downloading software packages, 887
  - obtaining, 886-887
- Software Updater, 882
- su command, 883
- Ubuntu
  - Backups, 882
  - downloading, 879
  - Nautilus file manager, 879
  - Ubuntu Software Center, 881
  - user interface, 880
- updatedb command, 883, 891
- user forums, 891
- WEP authentication, 885
- ZFS, 881

liquid cooling, 80

liquid damage, troubleshooting, 448

List Folder Contents permissions, 932

listening (soft skills), active, 2, 98-99, 1005

lists
- moving through, 384
- PID, 732
- PRL, updates, 387

LMS (Learning Management Systems), 540

load alternate third-party drivers, 772

load balancers, 956

Load Fail Safe Defaults configuration change option (BIOS/UEFI), 117

Load Optimized Defaults configuration change option (BIOS/UEFI), 117

loading apps, troubleshooting, 452

local access, security, 920
- AD functions, 922-923
- group policies, 926
- local security policies, 926-927
- user management, 921

local connectivity, 613

local security policies, 926-927

local shares, 930

Local Users and Groups tool, Windows, 804-805

locate command, Linux, 883, 891

location tracking, unauthorized, 443-444

locator apps, 388

locking computers, 922

lockouts, system, 443

locks
- cable locks, 440, 903
- equipment locks, 903
- facial recognition locks, mobile devices, 442
- fingerprint locks, mobile devices, 442
- physical security, 901
  - cable locks, 903
  - equipment locks, 903
  - USB locks, 904
- screen locks, mobile devices, 442
- swipe locks, mobile devices, 442
- USB locks, 904

lockups (system), troubleshooting, 96

logging off when not in use, 912

logical drives, 246-247

logical operators, testing conditions, 750

logical partitions, 769

logical processors, 76

logical security
- ACL, 909
- anti-malware, 908
- antivirus software, 908
- authentication, 909-910
- BIOS/UEFI, 910-911
- directory permissions, 908
- email filtering, 909
- firewalls, 908
- login OS security, 911-912
- ports, 909
- trusted/untrusted sources, 909
- unused ports, disabling, 908
- VPN, 908

logins
- Apple ID, 863
- failed attempts, 443
- failed login attempts, 912
- OS security, 911-912
- restricting login times, 927
- scripts, 925

logs
- application logs, 798-800
- clearing, 800
- event logs, 927
- Event Viewer, 798
- performance log user accounts, 921
- security logs, 798-799
- service logs, 798
- setup logs, 798
- system logs, 798-800

LoJacks, 115, 910

long-range fixed wireless connectivity, 526

long touch/touch and hold actions (mobile devices), 384

loopback plugs, 493, 572

loops, 746
- for loops, 751-753
- iteration, 751
- while loops, 751-752

loss of data/corruption, troubleshooting, 260

lost clusters, 258

low level formatting, hard drives, 941

ls command, 874-875

LTE (Long Term Evolution), 385, 526

lumens, monitors/projectors, 288

M

M.2
  BIOS/UEFI settings, 241
  devices, 230
  expansion cards, 414
MAC addressing, 957
  filtering, 960
  formats of, 577
macOS, 655
  Activity Monitor, 869
  Apple ID, 863
  App Store, 863
  best practices, 892
  Boot Camp, 873
  c command, 874
  cd command, 874-875
  chmod command, 874-876
  chown command, 874-876
  Console, 870-871
  cp command, 874-875
  desktop, 859-860
  Disk Utility, 872-873
  Dock, 859-861
  Finder, 859-860
  Force Quit, 866
  gestures, 861-862
  grep command, 874, 878
  GUI
    Dock, 859-861
    Finder, 859-860
    gestures, 861-862
    Launchpad, 860
    menu bar, 859
    Mission Control, 860
  iCloud, 862
  iWork, 862
  kernel panic, troubleshooting, 871
  Keychain Access, 871-872
  kill command, 874
  Launchpad, 860
  less command, 874, 877
  ls command, 874-875
  man command, 874, 878
  memory recommendations, 193
  menu bar, 859
  Mission Control, 860
  mkdir command, 874
  mv command, 874-875
  nano command, 874, 877
  POSIX, 858
  pwd command, 874-875
  releases, 858
  rm command, 874-876
  root user accounts, 876
  Safe mode, 869
  screen-sharing, 862-864
  Spotlight, 861
  sudo command, 874-876
  System Information, 871
  System Preferences, 866-868
  system updates, 864
  Terminal, 874
  Time Machine, 864-865
  touch command, 874-875
  troubleshooting, 869-871
  utilities
    Activity Monitor, 869
    Boot Camp, 873
    Console, 870-871
    Disk Utility, 872-873
    Keychain Access, 871-872
    System Information, 871
    Terminal, 874
  vi command, 874
magnetic hard drives, 225-227
magnetic screwdrivers, 147
magnetometers, physical security, 904
mail servers, 622
main motors, laser printers, 326
maintaining a positive attitude (soft skills), 210
maintenance
  aerosol cans, disposal laws, 158
  air filtration masks, 158
  antistatic brushes, 157
  BD, 301
  bootups, 157
  cameras, 305
  CD, 301-302
  compressed air, 157-158
  denatured alcohol, 157
  disk maintenance, 810-811
  dust, 156
  DVD, 301-302
  general-purpose cleansers, 157
  general-purpose cloths, 157
  gold contact cleaners, 158
  hard drives, 810-811
  inkjet printers, 337-339
  keyboards, 15
  laptop displays, 157
  laser printers, 339-341
  LCD monitors, 157
  lint-free cloths, 157
  maintenance counters, 340
  monitor wipes, 157
  mouse (mice), 15
  MSDS, 158
  optical drive cleaning kits, 158
  optical drives, 301-302
  OS, 846
  portable vacuums, 157
  printers, 336-337, 341
  projectors, 288
  safety goggles, 158
  scanners, 304
  SDS, 158
  thermal printers, 341
  toner vacuums, 157
  urethane swabs, 157
  vacuum bags, 157
  vacuuming, 158
Maintenance option, AP configurations, 607
making/keeping commitments (soft skills), 1008
malicious apps, 441
malware, 915-917
  anti-malware, 908
    initializing, 777
    mobile devices, 409
    security policies, 900
  mobile devices, 409
  removing, 944-946
MAM (Mobile Application Management), 408
man command, 874, 878
MAN (Metropolitan Area Networks), 552
managed/unmanaged switches, 554
managing
  assets, 998
  cable management systems, 570
  Certificate Manager, 944

INDEX

change management, 999-1001
Computer Management console, Windows, 796
  disk maintenance, 810-811
  Disk Management tool, 807-809
  Local Users and Groups tool, 804-806
  ODBC Data Sources, 812-813
  Print Management console, 813-814
  Services and Applications section, 811
  Storage Spaces Control Panel, 810
  System Tools section, 797-800
  User Account Management section, 801-803
Credential Manager
  adding credentials, 802-803
  editing credentials, 804
  removing credentials, 803
  storing credentials, 801
Device Manager, 785-786, 789-790
Disk Management tool, 771, 807-809
DRM, 912
files
  Linux, 879
  Nautilus file manager, Ubuntu, 879
hard drives
  Disks, Linux, 881
  Disk Utility, macOS, 872-873
macOS
  Safe mode, 869
  System Preferences, 866-868
MDM, 408, 958
MMC, 796
passwords, 532, 912
patches, 935
power, USB ports, 127
Print Management console, 813-814
remote management user accounts, 921
RMM, 956
storage, Disk Management tool, 807-809
Task Manager, Windows, 824-826
throttles, 84
time (soft skills), 1007
updates, 935
user accounts
  adding credentials, 802-803
  certificate-based credentials, 801
  Credential Manager, 801-805
  editing credentials, 804-805
  generic credentials, 801
  Local Users and Groups tool, 804-805
  recovering accounts, 805
  removing credentials, 803
  rights, 804
  storing credentials, 801
  UAC, 806
  web credentials, 801
users, 921
UTM systems, 956
mantraps (access control vestibules), physical security, 904
manual paper feeds, 333
manufacturer's advice, ignoring, 124
mapping
  network shares, 633-634
  ports, 608, 954
masks, air filtration, 158
mats, antistatic, 146
mATX. *See* micro-ATX
MB (megabytes), 19-21
MBR (Master Boot Records), 247
  converting to GPT, 249
  features of, 249
  partition tables, 769
md command, 705, 722
MDM (Mobile Device Management), 408, 958
MDT (Microsoft Deployment Toolkit), 776
mechanical hard drives, 427, 430
meeting expectations (soft skills), 1011
megabytes (MB), 19-21
memory
  addresses, 120-122
  advertisements, 198-199
  application crashes, 205
  buffered memory, 191
  buying, 198-199
  cache memory, 73, 188
  card readers, 208
  cards, 208
  CL ratings, 199
  CMOS, 117
  crashes, 205
  DDR memory, 190
  DDR2 memory, 190
  DDR3 memory, 190
  DDR4 memory, 190
  DDR5 memory, 190
  DIMM
    advertisements, 199
    installing, 201
    models of, 190-191
    physical packaging, 188
    removing, 200
    solutions, 197
  DRAM, 188
  dual-channel memory, 195-197
  dual-voltage memory, 192, 426
  ECC, 191-192
  error messages, 491
  flash memory, 207
    CF cards, 379
    digital cameras, 305
    memory card readers, 379
    SD cards, 378-379
    SSD, 427-429
    SSHD, 228
  heat spreaders, 190
  installing, 201
    laptops, 426
    overview, 200
    safety, 200
    viewing amount of installed memory, 193
  intermittent shutdowns, 205
  laptops, 425-426
  limitations, 193
  Memory Diagnostic tool (Windows), 206
  monitoring usage, 203-204
  motherboards
    limitations, 193
    slots, 196-197
  non-parity memory, 191
  NVMe, 231, 414

OS recommendations, 193
out of memory error messages, 205
overview, 188
performance, 206
physical packaging, 188
planning installations
how many of each memory type, 195-197
how much memory to install, 192
memory features, 191-192
memory modules, 189-193
researching/buying memory, 198-199
POST beeps, 205
POST error messages, 201
printers, 359
quad-channel memory, 197
RAM, 12, 188
disk caches, 257
laptops, 425
limitations, 655
power requirements, 171
replacement motherboards, 96
video RAM, 282
virtual memory, 256
registered memory, 191
removable storage, 207-208
removing, 200, 426
researching, 198-199
SDRAM, 190
shared system memory, 282
sluggish performance, 205-206
SODIMM, 188, 425
SPD, 192
speeds, 199
SRAM, 188
system design, 481
triple-channel memory, 197
troubleshooting, 205-206
unbuffered memory, 191
upgrading, 193, 206, 425-426
video memory, 282
virtual memory, 256, 839
VRAM, 202
Windows performance, 839
XMP, 192
memory card readers, 379
mentoring (soft skills), 543
menu bar, macOS, 859
metered connections, 628
micro-ATX
motherboards, 94
power supplies, 163
microphones, 17
choosing, 293-294
headsets, 381
laptops, 436
replacing, 439-440
system design, 484
unauthorized activation, 444
Windows operations, 293-294
microprocessors. *See* processors
Microsoft Defender, 943
Microsoft Defender Antivirus, 943
Microsoft Edge, 528-529, 532
Microsoft Store, 764
Microsoft Windows. *See* Windows
microUSB ports, 39, 391
migrating USMT, 768
MIME (Multipurpose Internet Mail Extensions), 400
MIMO (Multiple Input/Multiple Output), antennas, 593
mini-DIN (PS/2) ports, 32
miniPCIe cards, 413
miniUSB ports, 39, 391
mirroring (RAID 1), disk, 254
missing bootloaders, troubleshooting, 892
missing drives in the OS, 261
missing files, viruses/malware attacks, 917
Mission Control, macOS, 860
mitigating consequences of scripting, 737
MITM (Man-In-The-Middle) attacks, 920
mITXD. *See* ITX
mkdir command, 874
MMC (Microsoft Management Console), 796
mmc command, 722
opening, 729
Services window, 729
mmc command, 722, 796
mobile connectivity. *See also* Internet, connectivity
cellular networks, 526
hotspots, 525
licensed ranges, 527
long-range fixed wireless, 526
overview, 525
power requirements, 527-528
tethering, 525
unlicensed ranges, 527
WAN, 526
WiBro, 526
WISP, 527
mobile devices
accessories
drawing (track) pads, 381
headsets, 381
mobile docking stations, 381-382
speakers, 381
touch pens (styluses), 381
track (drawing) pads, 381
webcams, 381
Android OS, 378, 400
anti-malware, 409
antivirus software, 409
apps
APK, 390
closing apps, 390
common apps, 387
deleting, 390, 451
force quitting apps, 390
installing apps, 390
locator apps, 388
MAM, 408
moving app icons, 390
organizing apps, folders, 390
SDK, 390
troubleshooting, 450-452
app scanners, 409
backups
Android OS, 405-406
iCloud, 407
iOS, 407
iTunes, 407
OneDrive, 408
blocking ads, 399
bootleg apps, 441
cell tower analyzers, 410
cellular location services, 388
cellular networks, 385
Chrome OS, 378
connectivity, synchronization, 403
disposal/recycling, 982

double-tap actions, 384
drawing pads, 376
email configuration, 399-400
e-readers, 377
geotracking, 388
GPS, 376, 387
interacting with, 384
iOS, 378, 401
keyboards, troubleshooting, 453
long touch/touch and hold actions, 384
malicious apps, 441
malware, 409
MAM, 408
MDM, 408, 958
mobile OS
Android OS, 390, 403-406
emergency notifications, 389
features of, 388-389
Internet calling, 389
iOS, 404, 407
mobile payment services, 389
Recovery Mode, 449
updating, 441
virtual assistants, 389
Wi-Fi calling, 389
motherboards, 95
moving
between screens, 384
icons, 384, 390
multitouch techniques, 384
network configurations, 396
overview, 376-377
performance, troubleshooting, 455
phablets, 377
pinch open/close actions, 384
remote wipes, 441
screens, troubleshooting, 454-455
scrolling actions, 384
security, 958, 963
authenticator apps, 442
biometric security, 442
bootleg apps, 441
data-usage limit notifications, 445
DMZ, 960
facial recognition locks, 442
failed login attempts, 443
fake security warning, 441
fingerprint locks, 442
IP address filtering, 961
jailbreaking, 445
leaked personal files/data, 444
MAC address filtering, 960
malicious apps, 441
patterns, 442
PIN codes, 442
screen locks, 442
spoofing apps, 441
swipe locks, 442
system lockouts, 443
TKIP, 959
unauthorized account access, 443
unauthorized camera activation, 444
unauthorized location tracking, 443-444
unauthorized microphone activation, 444
unauthorized root access, 445
USS, 440
VPN, 446
WEP, 959
Windows Hello, 442
WPA2, 959
WPA3, 959
WPS, 961
sleep mode, 384
sluggish response times, 441
smart cameras, 377
smartphones, 376
cellular networks, 385
IMEI, 385
IMSI, 386
PRI updates, 387
PRL updates, 387
SIM cards, 386
sound, 432
speakers, 432
spoofing apps, 441
spreading/pinching open actions, 384
storage, 447
CF cards, 379
flash memory, 378
memory card readers, 379
SD cards, 378-379
swipe/flick actions, 384
synchronization
ActiveSync, 401-402
Android OS, 403
automobiles, 402
cloud computing, 402
connection types, 403
desktops, 402
Google, 403
iOS, 404
iTunes, 405
methods of, 401-403
vCards, 402
tablets, 376
touch/tap actions, 384
trackpads, troubleshooting, 454
traveling with, 447
troubleshooting
AirDrop failures, 452
app closure failures, 451
app installation failures, 451
app load failures, 452
app update failures, 451
autorotating screens, 454
backlight failures, 454
battery failures, 456
Bluetooth connectivity, 459-460
damaged ports, 448
dim displays, 454
email decryption failures, 452
flickering displays, 455
frozen systems, 456
GPS, 459
hard resets, 449
keyboards, 453
liquid damage, 448
network issues, 458-459
NFC, 460
no display, 454
no power, 456
OS update failures, 450
overheating, 457
performance, 455
soft resets, 448
sound issues, 458
touch screens, 455
trackpads, 454
unexpected app behavior, 450
Wi-Fi connectivity, 458-459
using, 382-384
viruses, 409

WAN connectivity, 526
Wi-Fi analyzers, 409
wired connectivity
Lightning ports, 391
microUSB ports, 391
miniUSB ports, 391
mobile serial ports, 392
proprietary vendor specific ports, 390
USB-C ports, 391
wireless connectivity
802.11 wireless standard, 395
Airplane mode, 396
biometric security, 398
Bluetooth, 393-394
cellular data, 399
cellular networks, 526
hotspots, 397, 525
IR, 399
long-range fixed wireless, 526
NFC, 398
power requirements, 527-528
RFID, 398
tethering, 397, 525
two-factor authentication, 398
WiBro, 526
zooming in/out of objects, 384
mobile docking stations, 381-382
mobile hotspots, 525
mobile motherboards, 419
mobile OS
Android OS
Android Backup Service, 405
Android Device Manager, 444
APK, 390
backups, 405-406
developer mode, 390
factory resets, 406
NFC, 399
Recovery Mode, 449
synchronization, 403
emergency notifications, 389
features of, 388-389
Internet calling, 389
iOS
backups, 407
synchronization, 404
mobile payment services, 389
updating, 441
virtual assistants, 389
Wi-Fi calling, 389
mobile payment services, 389
mobile serial ports, 392
modems
cable modems, 518, 619
cabling, 516
DSL modems, troubleshooting, 619
Internet connectivity, dial-up connectivity, 516-518
ports, 45-46, 516
satellite modems, 524-525
serial transmissions, 516-517
xDSL modems, 519
Modify permissions, 932
modular power supplies, 172
Molex-to-SATA converters, 165
monitoring
Hardware Monitor setting (BIOS/UEFI), 115
memory usage, 203-204
RMM, 956
Windows performance, 838
baselines, 839
Performance Monitor, 841
Reliability Monitor, 842
Resource Monitor, 842
Task Manager, 839-840
monitors, 9
brightness, 288
BSOD, troubleshooting, 799
CRT monitors, safety, 21
disposal procedures, 287
energy efficiency, 172
laptops and external monitors, 412
LCD monitors, preventive maintenance, 157
lumens, 288
multi-monitor taskbars, 764
resolution, 288
screen savers, 172
troubleshooting
BSOD, 285
burn-in, 286
dark displays, 285
dead pixels, 285
dim images, 285
flashing screens, 284
fuzzy images, 284
incorrect colors, 284
smoke/sparks, 286
wipes, 157
more command, 722
motherboards, 11
ATX, 94
audio ports, 290
batteries, 118
BIOS, 110
BTX, 94
capacitors, swelling, 96
cases and, 94
components, 68
connectivity, 150
24-pin motherboard connectors, 164
ATX power connectors, 166
front panel connectors, 151
pins, 152
CPU
cooling, 81-82, 85-86
handling, 83
installing, 85
overclocking, 85
photographing before installation, 85
throttle management, 84
upgrading, 84
disabling, 293
ED, boot/driver failures, 261
error messages, 491
expansion slots, 13-14, 87
AGP, 88
PCI, 88-90
PCIe, 89-91
form factors, 94, 164
handling, 96
integrated motherboard ports, 54
I/O shields, 154
ITX, 94
laptop motherboards, 95
LED, 492
memory
limitations, 193
slots, 196-197
micro-ATX, 94
mobile device motherboards, 95
mobile motherboards, 419
PATA connectors, 231
ports, 32

INDEX

POST, 96
power requirements, 171
power supply connectivity, 163
processors
ALU, 70
AMD, 79
AMD processors, 68
APU, 76
ARM processors, 68
buses, 69-72
caches, 73
clocking, 72, 84
connectivity, 74
cooling, 80-82
Core i3 processors, 78
Core i5 processors, 78
Core i7 processors, 77
Core i9 processors, 77
Core X processors, 77
CPU sockets, 79-80
GPU, 76
installing, 82-83
Intel, 77-78
Intel processors, 68
logical processors, 76
multicore processors, 74
multisocket motherboards, 79
overclocking, 84
overview, 68
performance, 70-72
pipelines, 70
power requirements, 171
Ryzen 3 processors, 79
Ryzen 5 processors, 79
Ryzen 7 processors, 79
Ryzen 9 processors, 79
Ryzen Threadripper processors, 79
single-core processors, 74
speeds, 70-72
threading, 73-74
troubleshooting, 86
upgrading, 84
virtualization, 76-77
x64 processors, 68
x86 processors, 68
Xeon processors, 77
reassembling computers, 156
removing, 154
replacing, 95-96
SATA connectors, 231
security, 93
server motherboards, 95
slots, memory, 196-197
sockets
AMD, 80
CPU sockets, 79-80
Intel, 80
multisocket motherboards, 79
ZIF sockets, 80
sound card installation, 293
speakers, 289
standoffs, 154
switches, 492
system design, 481
troubleshooting, 96
types of, 94, 164
upgrading, 95
motion sensors, physical security, 904
mounting, 793, 809
mounts, 239
mouse (mice), 14
maintenance, 15
ports, 32
troubleshooting, 16
MOV (Metal Oxide Varistors), 987
moving
around from command port, 701
cd command, 702
dir command, 702-704
md command, 705
rd command, 705
between screens, mobile devices, 384
icons, 384, 390
in NTFS permissions, 932-933
through lists/images, 384
Windows files/folders, 681
.MPG (.MPEG) file extensions, 674
mSATA (mini-Serial ATA), 232
BIOS/UEFI settings, 241
drives, 427
installing, 237
msconfig command, 722
MSDS (Material Safety Data Sheets), 158, 979
msinfo32 command, 723
MSRA (Microsoft Remote Assistance), 955
mstsc command, 723, 843
MT-RJ (Mechanical Transfer Registered Jack) connectors, 53
MTBF (Mean Time Between Failures), 226
mu. *See* micro-ATX
multiboots, Windows, 765
multicore processors, 74
multifactor authentication, 910
multifunction (all-in-one) devices. *See also* printers
installing, 343
overview, 318
sensitive material, 318
sharing, 619-621
troubleshooting, 621
wireless networks, 583
multimedia devices
audio
digitized sound, 292
microphones, 293-294
motherboard audio ports, 290
motherboard speakers, 289
ports, 291
sound cards, 290-293
speakers, 295-296
troubleshooting, 296
cameras
digital cameras, 305
webcams, 306-307
digitizers, 307
optical drives
connectivity, 300
DirectX, 301
DVD/Blu-ray region codes, 299
features of, 298-299
installing, 300
interfaces, 300
ISO files/images, 300
overview, 297-298
preventive maintenance, 301-302
reading Blu-ray discs, 298
symbols, 299
testing, 300
troubleshooting, 300-301
writable media, 298-299
overview, 280
projectors
audio, 289
brightness, 288
bulbs, 288
connectivity, 288

data sources, 288
desk controllers, 288
features of, 288
lumens, 288
maintenance, 288
ports, 287
remote control, 288
resolution, 288
shutdowns, 289
troubleshooting, 288-289
wired Ethernet connectivity, 288
wireless connectivity, 288
scanners
ADF scanners, 302
barcode scanners, 302-304
connectivity, 304
flatbed scanners, 302-303
handheld scanners, 302
installing, 304
preventive maintenance, 304
types of, 302-304
USB scanners, 304
video
GPU, 280
IGP, 280
memory, 282
overview, 280
subsystems, 280
troubleshooting, 284
video capture cards, 282
video cards, 280, 283
multimeters, 160, 572
multi-mode fiber cabling, 53
multi-monitor taskbars, 764
multiple alternative structures, 748-749
multiple-device ports, IRQ, 120
multiple displays, 788
multiple hard drives as backups, 937
multiple pending print jobs, 361
multipurpose ports, 37
multisocket motherboards, 79
multithreading, 73-74
multitouch techniques, mobile devices, 384
muting sound cards, 293
mv command, 874-875
MX records, DNS, 600

N

name resolution, DNS, 600
naming
directories, 699
files, 672-673, 699, 728
folders, Windows, 673
variables, 742
nano command, 874, 877
NAS (Network-Attached Storage) devices
drives, 229
system design, 477
NAT (Network Address Translation), 624, 953
DNAT, wireless networks, 608
NAT mode, virtual NIC, 605
wireless networks, 608
native (Type 1) hypervisors, 536
Nautilus file manager, Ubuntu, 879
navigating
directories, 701
cd command, 702
dir command, 702-704
md command, 705
rd command, 705
drive navigation inputs, 711
GNOME user interface, Linux, 879
macOS GUI
Dock, 859-860
Finder, 859-860
gestures, 861-862
Launchpad, 860
menu bar, 859
Mission Control, 860
Spotlight, 861
nbtstat command, 723
needle-nose pliers, 147
net command, 616, 723
net computer command, 616
net config command, 616
.NET Core, 754
net help command, 616
net share command, 616
net start command, 616
net stop command, 616
net use command, 616, 724
net user command, 616, 724
net view command, 616
NetBT (NetBIOSD over TCP/IP), 626
netdom command, 616, 725
netstat command, 725
Network Access layer, TCP/IP, 576, 627
network adapters, ipconfig command, 721
network boots/PXE, 814
network (breakout) taps, 572
Network layer (OSI model), 575
network numbers, IPv4 addressing, 578
network protocols, 575
Network tile, Windows Start screen, 669
networks
access
attacks, 919
security, 920-923, 926-927
user management, 921
antennas, 576, 590
attenuation, 591
directional antennas, 591
gain, 591-592
MIMO, 593
omnidirectional antennas, 591
path loss, 591
radiation patterns, 591
ranges, 591
signal strength, 592
AP, 576, 583-584
as wireless repeaters, 587
DMZ, 607-608
SSID, 585-586
wireless AP, 607
ARP, 624
backdoor attacks, 919
bandwidth, 624
botnets, 919
bridges, wireless, 583
broadband, 624
brute force attacks, 919
cabinets, 569
cable connectors, 576
cable modems, troubleshooting, 619
cabling
cabinets, 569
coaxial cables, 49-50
Ethernet cables, 50-51

management systems, 570
racks, 569-571
cabling, twisted pair, 560
corporate networks, 565-567
RJ11 connectors, 561-564
RJ45 connectors, 561-565
STP cables, 560-561
terminating, 561-565
UTP cables, 560-564
cellular networks
2G networks, 385
3G networks, 385, 526
4G networks, 385, 526
5G networks, 385, 526
CDMA, 385
connectivity, 526
GSM, 385
LTE, 385
LTE networks, 526
cloud-based network controllers, 539
configuration operators, 921
configuring, ifconfig command (Linux), 884-885
connectivity
cable management systems, 570
cabling cabinets, 569
cabling racks, 569-571
direct burial cables, 560
EoP, 568
local connectivity, 613
PoE, 567-568
twisted pair cabling, 560-567
unintentional connections, troubleshooting, 459
copper media, 560
corporate networks
cabling, 565-567
disk imaging, 775
Windows deployments, 775-776
DDOS attacks, 919
DHCP, 596-597
dial-up networks, 516-518
dictionary attacks, 919
domain controllers, 601
domains, 555-557, 601, 775
DoS attacks, 919
DSL modems, troubleshooting, 619
embedded systems, 622
end devices, IP addressing, 594
alternative IP address configurations, 598
APIPA, 598
default gateways, 599
DNS, 599-600
static configurations, 595-597
Ethernet networks
EoP, 568
LAN, 553
star topologies, 554
evil twin attacks, 919
extenders, wireless, 586
external networks, VM, 536
fiber networks, 522-524
hiding computers from, 921
high network traffic, 458
hubs, 553-554, 576
ICMP, 624
insider attacks, 919
internal networks, VM, 536
IPv4 addressing
CIDR, 581
classes of, 578
examples of, 579
host addresses, 578
network numbers, 578
octets, 577
private IP addresses, 578
public IP addresses, 578
subnet masks, 580
VLAN, 580
IPv6 addressing, 577
ladder racks, 571
LAN, 552-554
Ethernet LAN, 553
VLAN, 580
Wake on LAN, NIC, 603
WLAN, 552, 558, 957
workgroups, 555-557
latency, 522, 614-615
legacy systems, 623
MAC addressing, 577
MAN, 552
MITM attacks, 920
mobile device configurations, 396
multifunction devices
sharing, 619-621
troubleshooting, 621
NAS devices, system design, 477
NAT, 624, 953
NIC
advanced properties, 603
configuring, virtualization, 603-605
duplexing, 603
on-board NIC (BIOS/UEFI), 603
QoS, 603
speed, 603
virtual NIC, 603-605
Wake on LAN, 603
wireless NIC, 583-584, 601-602
NOC, 557
OSI model, 573-576
overview, 552
PAN, 552-553
password spraying attacks, 920
PAT, 624
patch panels, 565
paths, 633
PoE, 567-568
ports, 47-48
printers, 362
accessing, 353
sharing, 619-621
troubleshooting, 621
wireless printers, 583
private networks, 557, 774
public networks, 557, 774-775
racks, 569-571
reconnaissance attacks, 920
remapping drives, 736
remote access, 955-956
remote networks
accessing, 732
ping command, 727
Windows installations, 765
repeaters, wireless, 587
replay attacks, 920
RJ45 wall jacks, 565
routers, 575-576
DMZ, 607-608
wireless routers, 583-584, 607
SAN, 552, 558-559
SCADA systems, 622
scanners, 620-621
SDN, 623

selecting during OS installations, 774-775
servers, 621-622
shares (shared folders), 632-634
Smurf attacks, 920
SNMP, 627
spoofing attacks, 920
SQL injection attacks, 920
SSL, 625
star topologies, 554
subnet masks, 580, 1021-1023
switches, 553-554, 576
TCP, 625
TCP/IP model, 575
  Application layer, 576
  devices, 576
  example of, 625-627
  hijacking attacks, 920
  Internet layer, 576
  Network Access layer, 576
  Transport layer, 576
thick clients, 605-606
thin clients, 605-606
TLS, 625
topology diagrams, 995
troubleshooting
  Bluetooth connectivity, 459-460
  GPS, 459
  high traffic, 458
  ifconfig command, 613
  ipconfig command, 613
  net command, 616
  net computer command, 616
  net config command, 616
  netdom command, 616
  net help command, 616
  net share command, 616
  net start command, 616
  net stop command, 616
  net use command, 616
  net user command, 616
  net view command, 616
  NFC, 460
  nslookup command, 615
  pathping command, 614
  ping command, 611-613
  tracert command, 614
  unavailable resources, 612-613
  Wi-Fi connectivity, 458-459
types of, 552
UDP, 625
virtual networks, VNC, 956
VLAN, 580
VPN, 446, 908, 954-955
vulnerability scanners, 920
WAN, 552
  wireless broadband (WiBro) connectivity, 526
  WWAN, 608
WAP, 576
Windows network settings, 627-628, 631, 833-834
wired networks
  device connectivity, 594
  printer connectivity, 342
wireless antennas, 576
wireless networks
  802.11ac (Wi-Fi 5) wireless standard, 583
  802.11ad (WiGig) wireless standard, 583
  802.11ax (Wi-Fi 6) wireless standard, 583
  802.11b wireless standard, 582
  802.11e wireless standard, 583
  802.11g wireless standard, 583
  802.11i wireless standard, 583
  802.11n wireless standard, 583
  antennas, 590-593
  AP, 583-587, 957-963
  Basic QoS, 608
  bridges, 583
  channel ID, 588-589, 608
  content filtering, 608
  data transfer speeds, 593
  design, 585
  desktop workstations, 582
  device connectivity, 594
  DHCP, 608
  DMZ, 608
  DNAT, 608
  extenders, 586
  external interference, 592-593
  firewalls, 958
  firmware, 608
  frequencies, 581
  intermittent wireless connectivity, 592
  IoT, 609-611
  IP filtering, 608
  Mac addresses, 957
  MDM, 958
  multifunction devices, 583
  NAT, 608
  NIC, 583-584
  overview, 581
  port forwarding/mapping, 608
  printer connectivity, 342, 351-352
  repeaters, 587
  routers, 583-584, 962-963
  security, 958-963
  signal strength, 459
  site surveys, 592
  SSID, 608
  troubleshooting, 964
  UPNP, 608
  Wi-Fi analyzers, 593
  WLAN, 552, 558, 957
  WMN, 552
  WWAN, 552, 608
  Zigbee wireless standard, 610-611
  Z-Wave wireless standard, 610-611
wireless routers, 576
WLAN, 552, 558, 957
WMN, 552
workgroups, 555-557, 775
WWAN, 552, 608
XSS attacks, 920
zero day attacks, 920
zombie attacks, 920
new user/exiting user checklists, 996
NFC (Near Field Communication), 56, 398, 460
NFS (Network File Systems), 771
NIC (Network Interface Cards)
  advanced properties, 603
  configuring, virtualization, 603-605
  duplexing, 603
  installing, 129-130
  on-board NIC (BIOS/UEFI), 603
  QoS, 603
  speed, 603

TCP/IP protocol stacks, checking, 613
troubleshooting, 617-618
virtual NIC, 603-605
Wake on LAN, 603
Windows network settings, 631
wireless NIC, 396, 431, 583-584, 601-602
NLQ mode, inkjet printers, 322
no Bluetooth connectivity, troubleshooting, 459-460
no connectivity, troubleshooting, 611-612
no display, troubleshooting, 454
no Internet connectivity, troubleshooting, 459
"no OS found" error messages, 263, 779
no power, troubleshooting, 173, 456
NOC (Network Operations Centers), 557
noises, troubleshooting
hard drives, 430
laser printers, 326
POST beeps, 96
non-compliant systems, security, 900
nonfunctioning/undetected devices, troubleshooting with Device Manager, 789-790
non-parity memory, 191
nonvideo adapters, power requirements, 171
"Not enough USB controller resources" error messages, 791
Notepad, 360, 726, 779
not-expired licenses, 913
Not Initialized status messages, 265
NOT operators, 750
notification area
removing icons from, 791
Windows 10/11, 667
notifications
data-usage limit notifications, 445
emergency notifications, 389
fake security warnings, mobile devices, 441
Intrusion Detection/Notification setting (BIOS/UEFI), 115
unknown notifications, OS security, 935
"not responding" error messages, troubleshooting, 799
nslookup command, 615, 726
NTFS (New Technology File Systems), 244, 770-771
benefits of, 246
boot partitions, 248
clusters, 245
disk quotas, 246
partitioning, volume structures, 250
permissions, 928-931
copying in, 932-933
effective permissions, 933
files, 933-934
folders, 933-934
Full Control permissions, 932
inherited permissions, 932
List Folder Contents permissions, 932
Modify permissions, 932
moving in, 932-933
Read & Execute permissions, 932
Read permissions, 932
Write permissions, 932
system partitions, 248
"NTLDR Is Missing" error messages, 778
NTP (Network Time Protocol), 626
number of characters, passwords, 911
Numlock On/Off setting (BIOS/UEFI), 114
NVMe (Non-Volatile Memory Express), 231, 241, 414

O

octets, IPv4 addressing, 577
ODBC (Open Database Connectivity), Data Sources, 812-813
ODD. *See* optical drives
OEM (Original Equipment Manufacturer) versions of Windows, 767
off-site email apps, 539
off-site storage, 224, 936
office productivity, iWork (macOS), 862
Offline status messages, 265
offsite backups, 939
ohms, 161-162
older apps, Windows compatibility, 204-205
OLED (Organic LED) displays, 434
omnidirectional antennas, 591
on-board NIC (BIOS/UEFI), 603
on-site storage, 936
Onboard Device Configuration setting (BIOS/UEFI), 114
.ONE file extensions, 674
OneDrive, 408, 764
Online (errors) status messages, 265
online resources, searches, 6-7
ONT (Optical Network Terminal) boxes, 523
OOBE (Out of Box Experience), Windows, 774
OpenDNS, 946-947
open source software, 858, 912. *See also* Linux
open-ended questions, 2
opening
apps, 384
cases (disassembly), 149
MMC, 729
PowerShell (.psl), 708-709
System Information window, 723
operational procedures
business process documentation, 999
change management, 999-1001
component handling/storage, 984-986
documentation, 978
dust cleanup, 992
electronic disposal/recycling, 982-983
IT documentation
asset management, 998
AUP, 999
incident documentation, 997
inventory lists, 998
knowledge bases/articles, 996-997
network topology diagrams, 995
new user/exiting user checklists, 996
password policies, 999
regulatory/compliance policies, 999

security policies, 999
SOP, 994
overview, 978
PM/airborne particle pollution, 992
power handling
adverse power conditions, 986-987
battery backups, 989
line conditioners, 989
MOV, 987
SPS, 991
surge suppressors, 987-989
UPS, 989-991
temperature/humidity control, 993-994
toner safety/disposal, 984
ventilation, 994
workplace safety
environmental impacts, 981-982
equipment, 980
fire extinguishers, 979
fire safety, 979
government regulations, 978
lifting techniques, 981
MSDS, 979
OSHA, 979
personal safety, 981
optical cabling. *See* fiber cabling
optical discs, 814
optical drives, 10
cleaning kits, 158
connectivity, 300
DirectX, 301
DVD/Blu-ray region codes, 299
features of, 298-299
installing, 300
interfaces, 300
ISO files/images, 300
laptops and external optical drives, 412
overview, 297-298
power requirements, 171
preventive maintenance, 301-302
reading Blu-ray discs, 298
symbols, 299
testing, 300
troubleshooting, 300-301
writable media, 298-299
Optimize and defragment tool, 811
optimizing
battery performance, laptops, 417-418
DPI, inkjet printers, 321-323
General Optimization setting (BIOS/UEFI), 114
Options button, File Explorer (Windows 11), 677
OR operators, 750
organization (soft skills), 1004
organizing
apps, 390
desktop, Windows 10/11, 668
files, 699
orientation
page orientation (printers), 347, 361
screens, 435, 788
OS (Operating Systems), 8
32-bit OS, 655-656
64-bit OS, 655-656
Android OS, 378
Android Backup Service, 405
APK, 390
developer mode, 390
email configuration, 400
factory resets, 406
mobile device backups, 405-406
mobile device synchronization, 403
NFC, 399
Recovery Mode, 449
apps, 652
boot process, 652
Chrome OS, 378
clusters, 244-245
command-line interface, 653
files, 654
folders, 654
GUI, 653
iOS, 378
email configuration, 401
mobile device backups, 407
mobile device synchronization, 404
Linux, 655
apt-get command, 883, 886-887
backups, 882
best practices, 892
Btrfs, 881
CLI, 883
copying data, 887, 890
dash, 879
dd command, 883, 887, 890
Disks, 881
distros (distributions), 878-879
ext3 file systems, 881
ext4 file systems, 881
file managers, 879
finding files, 891
finding GRUB/LILO, 892
GNOME user interface, 879
GRUB, 892
ifconfig command, 883-885
iwconfig command, 883-885
kernels, 878
LILO, 892
locate command, 883, 891
network configurations, 884-885
passwd command, 883-884
passwords, 884
ps command, 883, 886
searches, 880
shutdown command, 883
software, downloading packages, 887
software, obtaining, 886-887
Software Updater, 882
su command, 883
Ubuntu, downloading, 879
updatedb command, 883, 891
user forums, 891
viewing processes, 886
WEP authentication, 885
ZFS, 881
macOS, 655
Activity Monitor, 869
Apple ID, 863
App Store, 863
best practices, 892
Boot Camp, 873
c command, 874
cd command, 874-875
chmod command, 874-876
chown command, 874-876
Console, 870-871
cp command, 874-875
desktop, 859-860

INDEX

Disk Utility, 872-873
Dock, 859-860
Finder, 859-860
Force Quit, 866
gestures, 861-862
grep command, 874, 878
GUI, 859-862
iCloud, 862
iWork, 862
kernel panic, troubleshooting, 871
Keychain Access, 871-872
kill command, 874
Launchpad, 860
less command, 874, 877
ls command, 874-875
man command, 874, 878
menu bar, 859
Mission Control, 860
mkdir command, 874
mv command, 874-875
nano command, 874, 877
POSIX, 858
pwd command, 874-875
releases, 858
rm command, 874-876
root user accounts, 876
Safe mode, 869
screen-sharing, 862-864
Spotlight, 861
sudo command, 874-876
System Information, 871
System Preferences, 866-868
system updates, 864
Terminal, 874
Time Machine, 864-865
touch command, 874-875
troubleshooting, 869-871
utilities, 869-874
vi command, 874
maintenance, 846
memory recommendations, 193
missing drives in the OS, 261
mobile OS
Android OS, 399-400, 444
emergency notifications, 389
features of, 388-389
Internet calling, 389
iOS, 378, 401
mobile payment services, 389
updating, 441
virtual assistants, 389
Wi-Fi calling, 389
"no OS found" error messages, 263
OS X, 858
overview, 652-654
popular OS, 655
POSIX, 858
proprietary OS, 655
security
account recovery, 939
AES, 940
backups, 936-939
BitLocker, 939-940
BitLocker To Go, 939
data at rest, 940
device encryption, 940
disabling AutoPlay, 941
disabling AutoRun, 941
EFS, 940
EOL, 935
hard drives, storage, 941
logins, 911-912
patch management, 935
restores, 936-939
unknown notifications, 935
unprotected systems, 935
update management, 935
shells, 859
sluggish performance, 206
updating, 450, 777
Windows (non-specific). *See also* Windows 10; Windows 11
32-bit OS, 655-656
64-bit OS, 655-656
Apply button, 671
backups, 688
checkboxes, 671
Close button, 671
command prompt, 698
context menus, 672
context-sensitive help, 672
Control Panel, 682-685
Cortana search feature, 678
determining version of, 685
dialog boxes, 670-672
drop-down menus, 671
enhanced features, 764
File Explorer, 674-681, 719
files, attributes, 679-680
files, compression, 681
files, copying, 681
files, encryption, 681
files, extensions, 672-674
files, filenames, 672-673
files, moving, 681
files, paths, 674-676
files, saving, 674
folders, attributes, 679-680
folders, compression, 681
folders, copying, 681
folders, encryption, 681
folders, moving, 681
folders, naming, 672-673
folders, subfolders, 672
Group Policy, 720
indexing, 678
libraries, 672
Notepad, 726
PowerShell (.psl), 708-709, 735, 754
preinstalling, 764. *See also* installing
radio buttons, 671
recovery, 688-689
registry, 686-687, 728
reload OS, 688
Remote Desktop, 723
subdirectories, 672
System Information window, 723
tabs, 671
textboxes, 670
UAC, 764
user profiles, 686
versions, 733
windows interactions, 670-671
WinRE, 688, 704
Windows 10
Control Panels, 683
desktop, notification area, 667
desktop, organizing, 668
desktop, pinning apps to taskbar, 667
desktop, search function, 668
desktop, Show Desktop area, 667
desktop, shutdown options, 666
desktop, Start button, 664-665
desktop, Task View, 668-669
Enterprise edition, 657

File Explorer, 654
Home edition, 656
Pro and Pro Education editions, 657
Pro for Workstations edition, 657
Recycle Bin, 669-670
shortcuts, 669
tiles, 669
Windows 11
Control Panels, 683
desktop, notification area, 667
desktop, organizing, 668
desktop, pinning apps to taskbar, 667
desktop, search function, 668
desktop, Show Desktop area, 667
desktop, shutdown options, 666-667
desktop, Start button, 664-665
desktop, Task View, 668-669
Enterprise edition, 657
File Explorer, 672
Home edition, 656
indexing options, 678
Pro and Pro Education editions, 657
Pro from Workstations edition, 657
Recycle Bin, 669-670
shortcuts, 669
tiles, 669
OS X, 858
OSHA (Occupational Safety and Health Administration), 979
OSI (Open Systems Interconnect) model, 573-576
OU (Organizational Units), 922
"out of memory" error messages, 205
output, programming, 741
overclocking
CPU, 85
processors, 84
overheating
printers, 321
troubleshooting, 96, 173, 457
overvoltage, 986
ozone gas, laser printers, 341

P

P2P (Peer-to-Peer) gaming, 608
PaaS (Platform as a Service), 538
passwd command, Linux, 883
packages
memory, 188
software packages, downloading, 887
packets
OSI model, 574
tracert command, 732
page orientation, printers, 347, 361
paging files, 202
palmprint scanners, physical security, 906
PAN (Personal Area Networks), 552-553
paper
collating pages, 347
erasable-bond paper, 332
feeds, 332-333, 356
hole punched paper, 358
humidity, 332
impact paper, 320, 337
incorrect paper sizes, troubleshooting printers, 357
jams, 356
page orientation, printers, 347, 361
pounds (lb), 332
printers, 332
printer trays, 333
ratings, 332
recycled paper, 332
sources (printing), 347
thermal paper, 328, 341
tractor feeds, 332
trays, 347
two-sided printing, 332
paper trays/feeders, inkjet printers, 322
parent directory (..), 711
partitioning
basic disks, 769
boot partitions, 248
convert command, 770
converting, 244
deleting, 248
drive partitions (volumes), 770
dynamic disks, 769
eSATA drives, 246
extended partitions, 246-247, 769
FAT32 file systems, 245
FAT (FAT16) file systems, 245
GPT, 249, 769
logical partitions, 769
MBR, 247
converting to GPT, 249
features of, 249
partition tables, 769
planning drive space, 770
primary partitions, 246, 769
swap partitions, 769
system partitions, 248
partitioning, 769
boot partitions, 815
diskpart command, 717
extending, 809
hard drives, 242-244
internal hard drive partitions, 814
recovery partitions, 765
resizing, 252
shrinking, 809
splitting, 809
passwd command, Linux, 884
passwords
AP, 962
BIOS/UEFI settings, 114
boot passwords, 910
changing, 922
complexity, 911
disabling password protection, 927
expired passwords, 911
failed login attacks, 912
formatting, 911
guidelines, 911
Keychain Access, macOS, 871-872
logging off when not in use, 912
managing, 532, 912
number of characters, 911
passwd command, Linux, 884
policies, 999
power-on passwords, 910
rainbow tables, 920

reminders, 911
reusing, 912
saving, macOS, 872
security policies, 901
social engineering attacks, 912, 917
special characters, 911
spraying attacks, 920
usernames, 911
wireless AP, 607
wireless routers, 607

PAT (Port Address Translation), 624, 954

PATA (Parallel ATA)
connectivity, 231
IDE cabling, 231
IDE hard drives, power requirements, 171
installing devices, 235
motherboard connectors, 231

patch panels, 565
patch (straight through) cabling, 562
patches, 846
managing, 935
software, 494

path loss, antennas, 591
PATH variables, 738
pathping command, 614, 726
paths
files, Windows, 674-676
networks, 633
shortcuts, 669

patterns, security, mobile devices, 442
payment services, mobile, 389
PB (petabytes), 21
PC (Personal Computers)
gaming PC, system design, 475
resetting, 828
This PC tile, Windows Start screen, 669
virtualization, 533

PCI (Peripheral Component Interconnect), 88-90
buses, speeds, 72
miniPCIe cards, 413
slots, PCI/PnP Configuration setting (BIOS/UEFI), 115

PCI DSS (Payment Card Industry Data Security Standard), 914
PCIe (PCI Express)
6-pin PCIe ATX power supply connectors, 164
8-pin PCIe ATX power supply connectors, 164
buses, speeds, 72
dual Molex-to-PCIe converters, 165
expansion slots, 89-91
PCIe Configuration setting (BIOS/UEFI), 115
video cards, 171, 280
power requirements, 171

PCL (Printer Control Language), 348
PCmover Express, 768
.PCX file extensions, 674
PD (Power Delivery), USB-PD, 38
.PDF file extensions, 334, 674
PDL (Page Description Language), 348
peer communication, OSI model, 575
peer reviews, 737
pending print jobs, 361
performance
baselines, 839
browsers, 533
buses, 70-72
CPU, 72
defrag command, 716
Disk Cleanup, 258
laptop batteries, optimizing, 417-418
memory
sluggish performance, 205-206
virtual memory, 839
Windows, 839
Performance Monitor, measuring Windows performance, 841
Performance utility (Windows, Task Manager), 203-204
processors, 70-72
sluggish performance, memory, 205-206
storage devices, 258-260, 264
troubleshooting, 455
virtual memory, 839
Windows
memory, 839
monitoring, 838-842

performance log user accounts, 921
peripherals
all-in-one printers, 17
cameras, 17
digital cameras, 305
unauthorized activation, 444
webcams, 306-307, 381
common peripherals, 17
digitizers, 307
flatbed scanners, 17
headphones, troubleshooting, 458
headsets, 17, 381
Integrated Peripherals setting (BIOS/UEFI), 114
keyboards, 9, 14
maintenance, 15
ports, 32
troubleshooting, 16
microphones, 17, 444
mobile docking stations, 381-382
monitors, 9
brightness, 288
CRT monitors, 21
disposal procedures, 287
lumens, 288
multi-monitor taskbars, 764
preventive maintenance, 157
resolution, 288
troubleshooting, 284-286
wipes, 157
mouse (mice), 14
maintenance, 15
ports, 32
troubleshooting, 16
multifunction (all-in-one) devices. *See also* printers
installing, 343
overview, 318
sensitive material, 318
sharing, 619-621
troubleshooting, 621
wireless networks, 583
optical drives
connectivity, 300
DirectX, 301
DVD/Blu-ray region codes, 299

features of, 298-299
installing, 300
interfaces, 300
ISO files/images, 300
overview, 297-298
preventive maintenance, 301-302
symbols, 299
testing, 300
troubleshooting, 300-301
writable media, 298-299

printers, 17. *See also* cloud computing, printing; multifunction (all-in-one) devices; virtual printing
3-D printers, 319, 329-331
adding printers, 785, 791
Bluetooth printers, 353
bubble jet printers. *See* inkjet printers
categories of, 318-319
CIS, 335-336
collating pages, 347
connectivity, 342-344, 359-362
data privacy, 355
default printers, 345
dot matrix printers. *See* impact printers
double images, 364
duplexing assemblies, 332
duplexing (double-sided printing), 347
dye sublimation printers, 323
feeds, 332-333
impact printers, 318-320, 336-337, 362-363
incorrect chroma displays, 363
indicator lights, 356
inkjet printers, 318, 321-323, 337-339, 363
installing, 342-344
languages, 348
large-format inkjet printers, 323
laser printers, 319, 323-327, 339-341, 363-364, 984
light printing, 363
maintenance, 336, 341
memory, 359
network printers, 353, 362
orientation (page), 347, 361
overheating, 321
overview, 318
paper, 332
paper feeds, 356
paper jams, 356
paper settings, 347
PCL, 348
PDL, 348
pending print jobs, 361
PostScript, 348
print drivers, 346-348
print preferences, 347, 361
print queues, 346
print spoolers, 348, 360
print trays, 347
quality, print, 347-348
recycling ink cartridges, 336
refilling ink cartridges, 335-336
resolution, 347-348
rollers, 358
secure print, 355
security, 318
sensitive material, 318
setup locations, 342
sharing, 349-353, 619-621
solid ink printers, 323
streaks, 363
testing, 346
thermal printers, 319, 328-329, 341
thermal wax transfer printers, 323
toner, 336, 364
toner spills, 327
toner vacuums, 157
tractor feeds, 332
trays, 333
troubleshooting, 355-362, 621, 813-814
two-sided printing, 332
upgrading, 336
user authentication, 355
vertical lines, 363
Windows environments, 344-350
wireless printers, 351-353, 583

projectors, 287-289

scanners
ADF scanners, 302
barcode scanners, 302-304
connectivity, 304
data privacy, 355
flatbed scanners, 302-303
handheld scanners, 302
installing, 304
preventive maintenance, 304
sharing, 620-621
troubleshooting, 621
types of, 302-304
USB scanners, 304
user authentication, 355

speakers
laptops, 432
mobile devices, 381

touch pens (styluses), 381

webcams/cameras, 17, 306-307, 381

permanently deleting files, 670

permissions
Change permissions, 930
directories, 908
effective permissions, 933
Full Control permissions, 930-932
inherited permissions, 932
List Folder Contents permissions, 932
Modify permissions, 932
Read permissions, 930-932
Read & Execute permissions, 932
USB Permissions setting (BIOS/UEFI), 114
Write permissions, 932

permissions, security
changing, 928
NTFS permissions, 928-931
copying in, 932-933
effective permissions, 933
files, 933-934
folders, 933-934
Full Control permissions, 932
inherited permissions, 932
List Folder Contents permissions, 932
Modify permissions, 932
moving in, 932-933
Read & Execute permissions, 932
Read permissions, 932
Write permissions, 932

running as administrators, 934
share permissions, 928
"access denied" messages, 931
administrative shares, 930
Change permissions, 930
concurrent users, maximum number of, 929
Full Control permissions, 930
hidden shares, 931
local shares, 930
principle of least privilege, 930
Public folders, 931
Read permissions, 930
UAC, 934
personal appearance (soft skills), 461-462
personal files/data, leaked, 444
personal grooming (soft skills), 1003
personal licenses, 913
personal safety, 981
perspectives on troubleshooting (soft skills), changing, 755
petabytes (PB), 21
phablets, 377. *See also* smartphones; tablets
phase-change (vapor) cooling, 80
PHI (Protected Health Information), 914
phishing, 918-919, 965
PHONE jacks, modem connectivity, 516
phones/smartphones. *See also* phablets; tablets
apps
deleting, 451
troubleshooting, 450-452
cellular networks, 385
communication skills (soft skills), 267-268
disposal/recycling, 982
filters, DSL lines, 519
IMEI, 385
IMSI, 386
performance, 455
PRI updates, 387
PRL updates, 387
screens, 454-455
security, 443-446
SIM cards, 386
storage, 447
traveling with, 447
troubleshooting
AirDrop failures, 452
app closure failures, 451
app installation failures, 451
app load failures, 452
app update failures, 451
autorotating screens, 454
backlight failures, 454
batteries, 456
Bluetooth connectivity, 459-460
damaged ports, 448
dim displays, 454
email decryption failures, 452
flickering displays, 455
frozen systems, 456
GPS, 459
hard resets, 449
liquid damage, 448
network issues, 458-459
NFC, 460
no display, 454
no power, 456
OS update failures, 450
overheating, 457
performance, 455
screens, 454-455
soft resets, 448
sound issues, 458
touch screens, 455
unexpected app behavior, 450
Wi-Fi connectivity, 458-459
VoIP, 520-522
physical access, security policies, 900
Physical layer (OSI model), 575
physical security
access control vestibules (mantraps), 904
alarm systems, 904
badge readers, 903
biometrics, 906-907
bollards, 901
cable locks, 903
door locks, 901
equipment locks, 903
guards, 903
hard tokens, 903
HSM, 903
key cards, 902
key fobs, 903
keys, 901
lighting, 903
magnetometers, 904
motion sensors, 904
private screens, 904
RFID, 903
smart cards, 903
tokens, 903
TPM, 903
USB locks, 904
video surveillance, 904
physically damaged ports, troubleshooting, 448
pickup rollers, laser printers, 326
PID (Process ID), listing, 732
piggybacking, 918
PII (Personally Identifiable Information), 914
PIN (Personal Identification Numbers), 442, 911
pin 1, cables, 150
pinch open/close actions (mobile devices), 384
ping command, 611-613, 727
pinning apps to Windows 10/11 taskbars, 667
pins, motherboard connectivity, 152
pinwheels (spinning), troubleshooting, 205, 265, 491
pipelines, 70
piracy, 913, 965
pixels (screens)
dead pixels, troubleshooting, 285
resolution, 288
planning
hard drive space, 770
memory installations
how many of each memory type, 195-197
how much memory to install, 192
memory features, 191-192
memory modules, 189-193
researching/buying memory, 198-199
plans of action (troubleshooting process), establishing, 497
plastic filaments, 3-D printers, 330-331

plate glass, scanners, 304
platforms, PaaS, 538
platters (hard drives), 225, 942
plenum cabling, 52, 561
plug-ins (browsers), disabling/removing, 530-531
plugs, loopback, 572
PM (Particulate Matter) pollution, safety, 992
.PNG file extensions, 674
PnP (Plug and Play), PCI/PnP Configuration setting (BIOS/UEFI), 115
PoE (Power over Ethernet)
- injectors, 568
- standards, 567-568
- switches, 568

polarity, voltage, 160-162
policies
- AUP, 999
- group policies, 926-927
- local security policies, 926-927
- password policies, 999
- regulatory/compliance policies, 999
- security policies, 900-901, 999

poor battery health, 456
poor VoIP quality, 521
POP3 (Post Office Protocol version 3), 399, 626
pop-ups, browsers, 532
portable vacuums, 157
port replicators, 412
ports
- audio ports
  - motherboards, 290
  - S/PDIF in/out ports, 44
- common ports table, 54-55
- Component/RGB video ports, 287
- damaged ports, troubleshooting, 448
- disabling, 908
- eSATA ports, 45
- eSATAp ports, 45
- Ethernet ports, 47-48
- FireWire ports, troubleshooting, 836
- flapping, 612
- forwarding, 608, 952
- integrated motherboard ports, 54
- keyboard ports, 32
- Lightning ports, 391
- mapping, 608, 954
- microUSB ports, 391
- mini-DIN (PS/2) ports, 32
- miniUSB ports, 391
- mobile serial ports, 392
- modem ports, 45-46, 516
- motherboard ports, 32
- mouse (mice) ports, 32
- multiple-device ports, IRQ, 120
- network ports, 47-48
- PAT, 624, 954
- projectors, 287
- proprietary vendor specific ports, 390
- RS232 serial ports, 392
- SATA ports, enabling in BIOS/UEFI, 237
- security, 908-909, 952
- serial ports, 45-46
- triggering, 952
- troubleshooting damaged ports, 448
- unused ports, disabling, 908
- USB ports
  - power management, 127
  - troubleshooting shutdowns, 836
- USB-C ports, 391
- video ports
  - adapters, 36
  - analog signals, 33
  - converters, 36
  - digital signals, 33
  - DisplayPorts, 35-36
  - DVI ports, 33, 36
  - HDMI ports, 35-36
  - Lightning ports, 43
  - multipurpose ports, 37
  - S-Video ports, 33, 36
  - Thunderbolt ports, 43
  - USB ports, 37-43, 46
  - VGA ports, 33, 36

positive attitude (soft skills), maintaining a, 210, 1005
POSIX (Portable Operating System Interface), 858
POST (Power-On Self-Tests), 96, 110
- audio POST codes, 489
- beeps, 205
- BIOS/UEFI POST error messages, 490-491
- error messages, 201
- setup errors, troubleshooting, 117

PostScript, 348
pounds (lb), paper, 332
power-on passwords, 910
power ratings, speakers, 295
power saver plans, Windows, 836
power supplies, 10
- 3.3V output voltage, 163
- 5V output voltage, 163
- 12V output voltage, 163
- 80 PLUS efficiency ratings, 171
- 110V vs. 220V input voltage, 163
- AC circuit testers, 174
- ACPI, 115, 168-169
- adverse power conditions, 986-987
- ATX connectors, 163
- auto-switching, 163
- batteries
  - backups, 989
  - charging, 456
  - CMOS, 117-119
  - electronics disposal/recycling, 982
  - laptop batteries, optimizing performance, 417-418
  - laptop batteries, removing, 416
  - Li-ion batteries, 416, 982-983
  - poor battery health, 456
  - swollen batteries, 456
  - troubleshooting, 456
- blackouts, 987
- brownouts, 987
- cabling, 148, 481
- CFX12V, 163
- choosing, 171-172
- CMOS batteries, 117-119
- component requirements, 171
- damaging, 163
- DC
  - jacks, replacing, 431
  - voltage, 166
- disassembly, 174
- dual-rail power supplies, 170

EPS12V, 163
failures, troubleshooting
battery backups, 989
SPS, 991
UPS, 989-991
FlexATX, 163
form factors, 163-164
frozen systems, troubleshooting, 456
hibernate mode, 169
inkjet printers, 322
input voltage selectors, 166
laptops, 415
optimizing battery performance, 417-418
removing batteries, 416
temperature changes, 416
laser printers, 326
LFX12V, 163
line conditioners, 989
micro-ATX, 163
modular power supplies, 172
motherboard connectivity, 163
MOV, 987
no power, troubleshooting, 456
overheating, troubleshooting, 457
overview, 163
overvoltage, 986
powering on, 163
purposes of, 166
recycling, 118
redundant power supplies, 171
replacing, 170
sags, 987
SFX12V, 163
signal checks, 175
spikes, 986
SPS, 991
standby mode, 169
surge protectors, 172
surges, 986
surge suppressors, 987-989
system design, 481-482
testing, 174
TFX12V, 163
troubleshooting, 173-175
types of, 163-164
undervoltage, 986-987
upgrading, 170
UPS, 989-991
USDB power management, 127
voltage, checking, 174
Wake on LAN, 169
Wake on Ring, 169
wattage ratings, 170
watts, 161-162
WFX12V, 163
Windows
power options, 836-837
power saver plans, 836
wireless requirements, 527-528
power user accounts, 921
PowerShell (.psl), 708-709, 735, 754
.PPT (.PPTX) file extensions, 674
prefix notation, subnet masks, 1022
preinstalling Windows, 764. *See also* installing
Presentation layer (OSI model), 575
preventive maintenance
aerosol cans, disposal laws, 158
air filtration masks, 158
antistatic brushes, 157
BD, 301-302
bootups, 157
cameras, 305
CD, 301-302
compressed air, 157-158
denatured alcohol, 157
dust, 156
DVD, 301-302
general-purpose cleansers, 157
general-purpose cloths, 157
gold contact cleaners, 158
inkjet printers, 337-339
keyboards, 15
laptop displays, 157
laser printers, 339-341
LCD monitors, 157
lint-free cloths, 157
monitor wipes, 157
mouse (mice), 15
MSDS, 158
optical drive cleaning kits, 158
optical drives, 301-302
OS, 846
portable vacuums, 157
printers, 336-337, 341
safety goggles, 158
scanners, 304
SDS, 158
thermal printers, 341
toner vacuums, 157
troubleshooting process, 497
urethane swabs, 157
vacuum bags, 157
vacuuming, 158
primary (main) coronas, laser printers, 326
primary partitions, 246, 769
principle of least privilege, share permissions, 930
print beds, 3-D printers, 329
print drivers, 346-348
Print Management console, 813-814
print ribbons, 319, 336-337
print servers, 352, 622
print spoolers, 348, 360
Print to File (virtual printing), 334
Print to image (virtual printing), 334
Print to PDF (virtual printing), 334
Print to XPS (virtual printing), 334
printers, 17 *See also* multifunction (all-in-one) devices
3-D printers, 319
filaments, 330-331
print beds, 329
resin printing, 330
adding, 785, 791
Bluetooth printers, access, 353
bubble jet printers. *See* inkjet printers
categories of, 318-319
CIS, 335-336
cloud printing, 354
collating pages, 347
connectivity
Bluetooth, 342, 352
USB, 342-344, 359
Windows environments, 359-362
wired networks, 342
wireless networks, 342, 351-352
data privacy, 355
default printers, 345

Devices and Printers Control Panel utility, Windows, 785, 791
dot matrix printers. *See* impact printers
duplexing assemblies, 332
duplexing (double-sided printing), 347
dye sublimation printers, 323
feeds, 332-333
Google Cloud Print, 354
impact printers, 318
  heads, 319, 337
  impact paper, 320, 337
  maintenance, 336-337
  print ribbons, 319, 336-337
  troubleshooting, 362-363
indicator lights, 356
ink cartridges, 335-336
inkjet printers, 318
  calibrating, 338
  carriage belts, 322
  carriages, 322
  color, 323, 363
  draft mode, 322
  duplexing assemblies, 322
  heads, 321-322, 339
  ink cartridges, 321-322, 338
  maintenance, 337-339
  NLQ mode, 322
  optimized DPI, 321-323
  paper trays/feeders, 322
  parts of, 322
  power supplies, 322
  rollers, 322
  stepper motors, 322
  troubleshooting, 363
installing, 342-344
languages, 348
large-format inkjet printers, 323
laser printers, 319, 323
  calibrating, 340
  cleaning, 340
  cleaning blades, 326
  cleaning pads, 326, 341
  conditioning rollers, 326
  control panel assemblies, 326
  density control blades, 326
  developing cylinders, 326
  duplexing assemblies, 326
  ECP, 326
  erase lamps, 326
  fuser assemblies, 325-326
  fusing rollers, 326, 341
  imaging drums, 326
  imaging process, 324-325
  main motors, 326
  maintenance, 339-341
  noises, 326
  ozone gas, 341
  parts of, 326-327
  pickup rollers, 326
  power supplies, 326
  primary (main) coronas, 326
  registration assemblies, 326
  scanner units, 327
  separation pads, 327
  toner, 327, 339, 984
  transfer belts, 325
  transfer corona wires, 327, 341
  transfer rollers, 325
  troubleshooting, 363-364
maintenance, 336, 341
memory, 359
network printers, 353, 362
Notepad, printing from, 360
orientation (page), 347, 361
overheating, 321
overview, 318
paper, 332
  jams, 356
  sources, 347
paper feeds, 356
PCL, 348
PDL, 348
pending print jobs, 361
PostScript, 348
print drivers, 346-348
print preferences, 347, 361
print queues, 346
print spoolers, 348, 360
print trays, 347
quality, print, 347-348
resolution, 347-348
rollers, troubleshooting, 358
secure print, 355
security, 318
sensitive material, 318
sharing, 349, 353, 619-621
  print servers, 352
  Windows environments, 350
  wireless printers, 351-352
solid ink printers, 323
testing, 346
thermal printers, 319, 329
  debris removal, 341
  feed assemblies, 328
  heating elements, 328, 341
  maintenance, 341
  thermal paper, 328, 341
thermal wax transfer printers, 323
toner
  handling, 336
  spills, 327
toner vacuums, 157
tractor feeds, 332
trays, 333
troubleshooting, 355, 621, 813-814
  faded print, 358
  garbled print, 357
  incorrect chroma displays, 363
  incorrect paper size, 357
  light printing, 363
  paper feeds, 356
  paper jams, 356
  slick rollers, 358
  USB-attached printers, 359
  vertical lines, 363
  Windows environments, 359-362
two-sided printing, 332
upgrading, 336
user authentication, 355
virtual printing, 334
Windows environments
  default printers, 345
  print drivers, 346-348
  printing in, 344
  print queues, 346
  sharing printers, 350
  testing, 346
wireless printers, 351-353, 583
PRI (Product Release Instruction) updates, 387

privacy
browsing, 530
cloud computing, 540
confidential/private materials (soft skills), dealing with, 1011
data, printers/scanners, 355
GDPR, 914
HIPAA, 914
impersonation attacks, 918
IP addresses, 578
networks, 557, 774
PCI DSS, 914
PHI, 914
PII, 914
screens, physical security, 904
WEP, 959
privilege (share permissions), principle of least, 930
privileges, administrative/user privileges, 734
PRL (Preferred Roaming List) updates, 387
Pro and Pro Education editions, Windows 10/11, 657
Pro for Workstations edition, Windows 10/11, 657
proactive technicians (soft skills), 635
probable cause (troubleshooting process), theories of, 487
BIOS/UEFI
beeps, 489
POST error messages, 490-491
bootup process, 487
error messages, 489-491
hardware errors, 493
intermittent device failures, 493
POST codes, 489
software errors, 494
testing, 495-496
UEFI diagnostics, 491
probes, toner, 572
problems
isolating, 495-496
troubleshooting process
identifying, 486
resolving, 497
procedures, operational
business process documentation, 999
change management, 999-1001
component handling/storage, 984-986
documentation, 978
dust cleanup, 992
electronic disposal/recycling, 982-983
IT documentation
asset management, 998
AUP, 999
incident documentation, 997
inventory lists, 998
knowledge bases/articles, 996-997
network topology diagrams, 995
new user/exiting user checklists, 996
password policies, 999
regulatory/compliance policies, 999
security policies, 999
SOP, 994
overview, 978
PM/airborne particle pollution, 992
power handling
adverse power conditions, 986-987
battery backups, 989
line conditioners, 989
MOV, 987
SPS, 991
surge suppressors, 987-989
UPS, 989-991
temperature/humidity control, 993-994
toner safety/disposal, 984
ventilation, 994
workplace safety
environmental impacts, 981-982
equipment, 980
fire extinguishers, 979
fire safety, 979
government regulations, 978
lifting techniques, 981
MSDS, 979
OSHA, 979
personal safety, 981
processes (Linux), viewing, 886
processing phase, laser printer imaging process, 324
processing, programming, 741
processors
ALU, 70
AMD
Ryzen 3 processors, 79
Ryzen 5 processors, 79
Ryzen 7 processors, 79
Ryzen 9 processors, 79
Ryzen Threadripper processors, 79
AMD processors, 68, 281
APU, 76
ARM processors, 68
buses, 69-72
caches, memory, 73
clocking, 72, 84
connectivity, 74
cooling, 80-82
GPU, 76
installing, 82-83
Intel processors, 68
Core i3 processors, 78
Core i5 processors, 78
Core i7 processors, 77
Core i9 processors, 77
Core X processors, 77
Xeon processors, 77
logical processors, 76
multicore processors, 74
overclocking, 84
overview, 68
performance, 70-72
pipelines, 70
power requirements, 171
single-core processors, 74
sockets
AMD, 80
CPU sockets, 79-80
Intel, 80
multisocket motherboards, 79
ZIF sockets, 80
speeds, 70-72
system design, 481
threading, 73-74
troubleshooting, 86
upgrading, 84
virtualization, 76-77
x64 processors, 68
x86 processors, 68
procurement life cycles, 998

profile loads, troubleshooting, 832-833
profiles, Windows
  rebuilding, 833
  troubleshooting, 832
Program Compatibility Wizard, 768
programming, 741
Programs and Features Control Panel utility, Windows, 794-795
projecting confidence (soft skills), 210, 1005
projectors, 287-289
promptness (soft skills), 1007
proper language (soft skills), using, 1003-1005
property sheets, 733
proprietary crash screens, 96, 491
proprietary OS, 655
proprietary vendor specific ports, 390
protocols
  network protocols, 575
  TCP/IP model, 575-576
proxy servers, 622, 948-949
ps command, Linux, 883, 886
PS/2 (mini-DIN) ports, 32
public clouds, 540
Public folders, share permissions, 931
public IP addresses, 578
public networks, 557, 774-775
punchdown blocks, 51
punchdown tools, 51, 572-573
purpose of change, 1000
PVC (Polyvinyl Chloride) cabling, 52, 561
pwd command, 874-875
PXE (Pre-Boot Execution Environment), 814
Python scripts (.py), 735

Q

QoS (Quality of Service)
  Basic QoS, wireless networks, 608
  NIC, 603
  VoIP, 521
quad-channel memory, 197
qualities of technicians, 2-3
quality, print, 347-348
questions, open-ended, 2
queues, print, 346
Quick Assist, 955
quick formatting, 250, 769
quitting apps, 390, 866
quotas, disk, 246

R

racks, network, 569-571
radiation patterns, antennas, 591
radio buttons, Windows, 671
radio connectivity, 56
RADIUS (Remote Authentication Dial-In User Service), 910
RAID (Redundant Array of Independent Disks)
  BIOS/UEFI configuration settings, 255
  concepts, 254
  configuring, 253
  failures, 266
  fault tolerance, 253-254
  FCM, 253
  hardware RAID, 254
  hot swappable RAID drives, 254
  levels of, 253-254
  RAID 0, 254
  RAID 0+1, 254
  RAID 1, 254
  RAID 5, 254
  RAID 10, 254
  "RAID not found" error messages, 266
  software RAID, 253
  troubleshooting, 266
RAID mode, SATA, 241
rails, hard drives, 153-154
rainbow tables, 920
RAM (Random Access Memory), 12
  disk caches, 257
  DRAM, 188
  laptops, 425
  limitations, 655
  power requirements, 171
  replacement motherboards, 96
  SRAM, 188
  video RAM, 282
  virtual memory, 256
  VRAM, 202
ranges
  antennas, 591
  licensed/unlicensed ranges, 527
ransomware, 915
rapid elasticity, cloud computing, 541
RAW volumes, 251
rd command, 705, 727
RDP (Remote Desktop Protocol), 626, 955
Read permissions, 930-932
Read & Execute permissions, 932
read/write failures, troubleshooting, 264
read/write times, troubleshooting, 259
reading devices. *See* e-readers
ReadyBoost, Windows, 827
rearranging displays, 788
reassembling computers, 156
reboots
  continuous reboots, troubleshooting, 96
  spontaneous reboots, 835
  troubleshooting, 173
  Windows, 790, 835
rebuilding Windows profiles, 833
reconnaissance attacks, 920
recovery, 264. *See also* troubleshooting
  accounts, 939
  file recovery software, 260
  System Image Recovery, 828
  Time Machine, macOS, 864-865
  user accounts, 805
  Windows
    recovery drives, 688
    reload OS, 688
    service packs, 689
    system images, 688
  WinRE, 264, 688, 704, 764, 816-819
Recovery Mode (Android OS), 449
recovery partitions, Windows, 765
Recycle Bin, Windows 10/11, 669-670
recycled paper, 332
recycling
  batteries, 118
  components, 480
  electronics, 982-983

INDEX

e-waste, 982
ink cartridges, 336
redirecting
browsers, 531
folders, 925
redundant power supplies, 171
refilling ink cartridges, 335-336
refresh rates, displays, 789
ReFS (Resilient File Systems), 810
regedit command, 728
regedit.exe command prompt, 687
regedt32.exe command prompt, 687
region codes, DVD/Blu-ray discs, 299
registered memory, 191
registration assemblies, laser printers, 326
registry, Windows, 123
backups, 781-782
editing, 687
regedit command, 728
regedit.exe command prompt, 687
regsvr32 command, 728
regedt32.exe command prompt, 687
subtrees, 686-687
troubleshooting, 830
user profiles, 686
regsvr32 command, 728
regsvr32.exe command, 796
regulated data, licensing, 914
regulatory/compliance policies, 901, 999
reimaging computers, 775-776
reinitializing anti-malware/antivirus software, 777
re-inking print ribbons, 336
reinstalling hardware/software, 495
relational operators, 746-747
reloading Windows, 688, 779-780
remapping network drives, 736
reminders, passwords, 911
remote access
MSRA, 955
Quick Assist, 955
RDP, 955
RMM, 956
security policies, 901
SSH, 956
Telnet, 956
VNC, 956
remote backups. *See* synchronization
remote control, projectors, 288
Remote Desktop Services
thick client installations, 606
thin client installations, 605-606
remote desktops
group accounts, 921
RDP, 955
starting, 723
Windows
Remote Assistance, 843-845
Remote Desktop Connection, 843-844
remote management user accounts, 921
remote networks
accessing, 732
installations, Windows, 765
ping command, 727
remote wipes, mobile devices, 441
removing. *See also* deleting
adapters, 152
browser plug-ins/extensions, 530-531
credentials, 803
DIMM, 200
directories, 705, 727
external cables, 148
hard drives, 153
icons from notification area, 791
internal cables, 149-151
laptop batteries, 416
malware, 944-946
media files, 670
memory, 200, 426
motherboards, 154
PCIe adapters, 91
power cables, 148
snap-ins, 796
software, 792
storage, 207-208
storage devices, 153
subdirectories, 705
USB ports, 41
ren command, 728
renaming files/directories, 728
repairing. *See also* troubleshooting
apps, 794-795
keyboards, 422
laptops
keyboards, 422
motherboards, 419
overview, 418
processors, 420
touchpads, 422
touchpads, 422
Windows installations, 765, 779
repeaters, wireless, 587
repetition, programming, 741
repetition structures. *See* loops
replacing
Bluetooth cards, 430-431
DC jacks, laptops, 431
digitizers, 438-439
displays, 437
hard drives, 428
inverters, 440
microphones, laptops, 439-440
motherboards, 95-96
power supplies, 170
screens, 437
slot covers, 147
touch screens, 438-439
video cards, 433
webcams, laptops, 439-440
wireless cards, 430-431
replay attacks, 920
requirements
power supplies, wireless networks, 527-528
system requirements, apps, 792-793
virtualization, 536
researching memory, 198-199
reservations, DHCP, 597
resetting
BIOS, 119
factory resets, 406
hard resets, 449
PC, 828
soft resets, 448
Windows, 765
resin printing, 330
resistance, voltage, 161-162, 572
resizing partitions, 252

resolution
- displays, 788
- monitors/projectors, 288
- printers, 347-348
- screens, 437

resolving
- names, DNS, 600
- problems, troubleshooting process, 497

resource conflicts, BIOS/UEFI, 121

resources
- online resources, searches, 6-7
- shared resources, cloud computing, 541
- unavailable resource, troubleshooting, 612-613
- virtualization, 536

responding to security incidents, 964-965

response times, mobile devices, 441

restarting
- computers, warm boots, 111
- machines, 736

rest, data at, 940

restore points, 783

restores
- OS security, 936-939
- System Restore, 815-816
- wbadmin command, 733
- Windows, 765

restricting login times, 927

retinal scanners, physical security, 906

reusing passwords, 912

RFI (Radio Frequency Interference), 146

RFID (Radio Frequency Identification), 398, 903

RG-6 cabling, 50

RG-59 cabling, 50

rights
- defragmentation rights, 811
- user accounts, 804

risk analysis, 1000

risk levels, 1000

RJ11 connectors, 561-564

RJ11 ports, 45-46

RJ45 connectors, 51, 561-565

RJ45 ports, 47-48

RJ45 wall jacks, 565

rm command, 874-876

rmdir command, 727

RMM (Remote Monitoring and Management), 956

robocopy command, 706-707, 729

rogue antivirus apps, 943

rogue AP, 963

roll back Windows updates, 780

rollback plans, 1001

rollers, printer, 322, 358

rolling back device drivers, 789

root access, unauthorized, 445

root directories, 699

root user accounts, 876

rootkits, 531, 915

rotating screens, laptops, 435

routers, wireless, 575-576, 583-584
- changing usernames/passwords, 607
- DMZ, 607-608
- installing, 962-963
- IP filtering, 961

RS-232 serial ports, 46, 392

.RTF file extensions, 674

run as administrator, permissions, 934

Ryzen 3 processors, 79

Ryzen 5 processors, 79

Ryzen 7 processors, 79

Ryzen 9 processors, 79

Ryzen Threadripper processors, 79

S

S-Video ports, 33, 36

SaaS (Software as a Service), 538

SAE (Simultaneous Authentication of Equals), 959

Safe Boot, 821

Safe mode, macOS, 869

safety
- aerosol cans, disposal laws, 158
- air filtration masks, 980
- antistatic bags, 984
- component handling/storage, 984-986
- compressed air, 980
- dust cleanup, 992
- electronic safety
  - equipment grounding, 986
  - ESD, 984-985
  - self-grounding, 985
- environmental impacts, 981-982
- equipment, 980
- equipment grounding, 986
- ESD, 984-985
- ESD mats, 985
- ESD straps, 985
- fire extinguishers, 979
- fire safety, 979
- goggles, 158, 980
- lifting techniques, 21, 981
- memory installations, 200
- monitors, 21
- MSDS, 158, 979
- OSHA, 979
- personal safety, 981
- power handling
  - battery backups, 989
  - line conditioners, 989
  - MOV, 987
  - SPS, 991
  - surge suppressors, 987-989
  - UPS, 989-991
- SDS, 158
- self-grounding, 985
- technical field kits, 980
- toner, 984
- trip hazards, 987
- vacuums, 980
- ventilation, 994
- workplace safety, 978
  - environmental impacts, 981-982
  - equipment, 980
  - fire extinguishers, 979
  - fire safety, 979
  - government regulations, 978
  - lifting techniques, 981
  - MSDS, 979
  - OSHA, 979
  - personal safety, 981

sags, voltage, 987

sandbox testing, 1001

sandboxes, virtualization, 534

SAN (Storage Area Networks), 552, 558-559

INDEX

SAS (Serial-Attached SCSI), 229, 234
SATA (Serial ATA), 229
- 15-pin SATA power ATX power supply connectors, 163
- AHCI mode, 241
- BIOS/UEFI settings, 241
- cabling, 231
- connectivity, 231-233, 236
- connectors, 150
- eSATA, 233
  - brackets, 128-129
  - drives, troubleshooting, 264
  - installing eSATA cards, 128-129
  - mounting/unmounting drives, 238-239
  - partitions, 246
- hard drives, power requirements, 171
- installing devices, 236
- Legacy mode, 241
- Molex-to-SATA converters, 165
- motherboard connectors, 231
- mSATA, 232
  - BIOS/UEFI settings, 241
  - drives, 427
  - installing, 237
- ports, enabling in BIOS/UEFI, 237
- RAID BIOS/UEFI configuration settings, 255
- RAID mode, 241
- SATA Configuration setting (BIOS/UEFI), 115

satellite modems, 524-525
saving
- Exit Without Saving configuration change option (BIOS/UEFI), 117
- files, Windows, 674
- passwords, macOS, 872
- Save & Exit Setup configuration change option (BIOS/UEFI), 117

SCADA (Supervisory Control and Data Acquisition) systems, 622
scanner units, laser printers, 327
scanners
- ADF scanners, 302
- app scanners, 409
- barcode scanners, 302-304
- cloud scanning, 354
- connectivity, 304
- data privacy, 355
- fingerprint scanners, physical security, 906
- flatbed scanners, 17, 302-303
- handheld scanners, 302
- installing, 304
- palmprint scanners, physical security, 906
- preventive maintenance, 304
- retinal scanners, physical security, 906
- sharing, 620-621
- troubleshooting, 621
- types of, 302-304
- USB scanners, 304
- user authentication, 355
- vulnerability scanners, 920

scareware, 919
scheduling tasks, 797
scope
- of change, 1000
- DHCP, 596

screened subnets. *See* DMZ
screen savers, energy efficiency, 172
screens
- aspect ratios, 484
- autorotating, 454
- backlights, 434
- blank/black screens, troubleshooting, 96, 173, 829-831
- BSOD, 491, 830
- captures, 7
- CCFL, 434
- conferencing features, 485
- contrast ratios, 485
- crash screens, proprietary, 96
- enlarging, 384
- flashing screens, troubleshooting, 284
- inverters, 436, 440
- laptops, Wi-Fi antennas, 436
- LCD, 434-435
- LED, 434
- locks, mobile devices, 442
- moving between screens, mobile devices, 384
- OLED, 434
- orientation, 435
- private screens, physical security, 904
- proprietary crash screens, 96, 491
- replacing, 437
- resolution, 288, 437
- rotating screens, laptops, 435
- sharing, macOS, 862-864
- splash screens, 999
- subsystem design, 484-485
- timeouts/screen locks, 927
- troubleshooting
  - autorotation failures, 454
  - backlight failures, 454
  - blank/black screens, 96, 173, 829-831
  - BSOD, 285
  - burn-in, 286
  - dark displays, 285
  - dead pixels, 285
  - dim displays, 454
  - dim images, 285
  - flashing screens, 284
  - flickering displays, 455
  - fuzzy images, 284
  - incorrect colors, 284
  - no display, 454
  - touch screens, 455
- video adapters, 485

screwdrivers, 147
scribes, 418
scripting
- advantages of, 735
- alphanumeric characters, 743
- AND operators, 750
- apps, installing, 736
- automating
  - backups, 736
  - processes, 734-736
- backups, automating, 736
- batch files (.bat), 735
- command prompt
  - accessing, 698-699
  - closing, 699, 718
  - naming directories, 699
  - naming files, 699
  - navigating directories, 701-705
  - PowerShell (.psl), 709

commands
- administrative privileges, 734
- attrib command, 708, 711
- bcdedit command, 712
- bootrec command, 712
- cd command, 702, 713
- chkdsk command, 714
- chkntfs command, 714
- cipher command, 714-715
- cls command, 715
- command command, 715
- [command name] /? command, 711
- command switches, 703-704
- common commands list, 709-710
- copy command, 706-707, 715
- defrag command, 716
- del command, 706, 716
- dir command, 702-704, 711, 716-717
- directories, 699
- disable command, 717
- diskpart command, 717
- dism command, 717-718
- drive navigation inputs, 711
- dxdiag command, 718
- enable command, 718
- exit command, 718
- expand command, 719
- explorer command, 719
- format command, 719
- formatting commands, 699
- gpresult command, 720
- gpupdate command, 720
- help command, 710, 720
- hostname command, 721
- ipconfig command, 721
- md command, 705, 722
- mmc command, 722
- more command, 722
- msconfig command, 722
- msinfo32 command, 723
- mstsc command, 723
- nbtstat command, 723
- net command, 723
- netdom command, 725
- netstat command, 725
- net use command, 724
- net user command, 724
- notepad command, 726
- nslookup command, 726
- organizing files, 699
- output, multiple pages, 704
- overview, 699
- pathping command, 726
- ping command, 727
- rd command, 705, 727
- regedit command, 728
- regsvr32 command, 728
- ren command, 728
- rmdir command, 727
- robocopy command, 706-707, 729
- services.msc command, 729, 831
- set command, 729, 740
- sfc command, 730
- shutdown command, 730-731
- starting tools with commands, 708
- subdirectories, 700
- systeminfo command, 731
- taskkill command, 731
- tasklist command, 732
- telnet command, 732
- tracert command, 732
- tree structure of files, 700-702
- type command, 706, 732
- user privileges, 734
- wbadmin command, 733
- wildcards, 706
- WinRE limited commands, 704
- winver command, 733
- writing, 708
- wscript command, 733
- xcopy command, 706-707, 733

comments within scripts, 745-746
comparison (equality) operators, 747
compiled programs, 734
compound conditions, 750
constructs, 746
decision (selection) structures
- dual-alternative structures, 748
- examples of, 749-750
- multiple alternative structures, 748-749
- relational operators, 746-747
- single-alternative structures, 747

defined, 734
environment variables
- accessing, 738-739
- editing, 738
- system environment variables, 738
- user environment variables, 738
- viewing, 740

floating point numbers, 743
information/data gathering, 736
initiating updates, 736
installing apps, 736
integers, 743
interpreted programs, 734
JavaScript (.js), 735
logical operators, 750
login scripts, 925
loops, 746, 751-753
mitigating consequences of scripting, 737
NOT operators, 750
OR operators, 750
overview, 698
PATH variables, 738
peer reviews, 737
PowerShell (.psl), 708-709, 735, 754
programming, 741
property sheets, 733
Python scripts (.py), 735
remapping network drives, 736
restarting machines, 736
shell scripts (.sh), 735
strings, 743
syntax, 740
system environment variables, 738
team programming, 737
testing, 737
text files, 734-736
updates, initiating, 736
use cases, 736-737
user environment variables, 738
variables, 741
- data types, 743
- declaring, 742-743
- environment variables, 738-740
- initializing, 743

INDEX

keywords, 742
naming, 742
PATH variables, 738
use cases, 744-745
VBScript (.vbs), 735, 754
wildcards, 706
XSS attacks, 920
scrolling actions (mobile devices), 384
SC (Subscriber Connectors), 53
SCSI (Small Computer System Interface)
SAS cabling, 234
SAS drives, 229
SD (Secure Device) cards, 378-379
SDK (Software Development Kits), 390
SDN (Software-Defined Networking), 623
SDRAM (Synchronous DRAM), 190
SDS (Safety Data Sheets), 158
search function, Windows 10/11, 668
searches
algorithms, 6-7
File Explorer (Windows), 678
Linux, 880
online resources, 6-7
search engines, 6-7
Spotlight, macOS, 861
sectors, magnetic hard drives, 227
security
administrators/supervisors, 910
ads
blockers, 533
high number of ads, 445
AES, 602
allow/deny lists, 950
anti-malware, 900, 908
antivirus software, 773, 908
AP, 959-960
configurations, 607
default settings, 961
firmware, 962
installing, 962-963
passwords, 962
SSID, 962
attacks
access attacks, 919
backdoor attacks, 919
boot sector viruses, 915
botnets, 915, 919
brute force attacks, 919
cryptojacking/cryptomining, 915
DDOS attacks, 919
dictionary attacks, 911, 919
DoS attacks, 919
dumpster diving, 907
evil twin attacks, 919
impersonation attacks, 918
insider attacks, 919
keyloggers, 915
malware, 915-917
MITM attacks, 920
password spraying attacks, 920
phishing, 918-919
piggybacking, 918
ransomware, 915
reconnaissance attacks, 920
replay attacks, 920
rootkits, 915
scareware, 919
shoulder surfing, 904, 918
Smurf attacks, 920
social engineering attacks, 912, 917
spear phishing, 918
spoofing attacks, 920
spyware, 915
SQL injection attacks, 920
tailgating, 904, 918
TCP/IP hijacking attacks, 920
Trojans, 915
viruses, 915-917
vishing, 918
vulnerability scanners, 920
whaling, 918
XSS attacks, 920
zero day attacks, 920
zombie attacks, 920
AUP, 901
authentication, 903, 909, 920
apps, 442, 910
DMARC, 948
Kerberos, 910
multifactor authentication, 910
RADIUS, 910
SAE, 959
soft tokens, 910
SSO authentication, 911
TACACS+, 910
two-factor authentication, 398
authorization, 920
best practices, 966
biometrics, 906
facial recognition, 906
fingerprint scanners, 906
mobile devices, 398, 442
palmprint scanners, 906
retinal scanners, 906
voice recognition, 906
BIOS, 910-911
boot sector viruses, 915
boots, 910
bootups, 910
botnets, 915
browsers, 530-531
BYOD, 900
cable locks, laptops, 440
certificates of destruction/incineration, 907
child exploitation, 965
content filtering, 956
credentials, storing, 801
data
account recovery, 939
AES, 940
backups, 936-939
BitLocker, 939-940
BitLocker To Go, 939
data at rest, 940
device encryption, 940
disabling AutoPlay, 941
disabling AutoRun, 941
EFS, 940
hard drive storage, 941
patch management, 935
restores, 936-939
unknown notifications, 935
unprotected systems, 935
update management, 935
deny/allow lists, 950
DEP, 656
desktop alerts, 917
digital security certificates, 943-944
Disable Execute Bit setting (BIOS/UEFI), 115
DMZ, 950, 960
DNS, 946-947
documentation, 907

DRM, 912
EFS, 681
email, 947-948
  filtering, 909
  S/MIME, 452
encryption, 903
  AES, 940
  BitLocker, 939-940
  BitLocker-To-Go, 939
  data at rest, 940
  device encryption, 940
  disabling AutoPlay, 941
  disabling AutoRun, 941
  Drive Encryption setting (BIOS/UEFI), 115
  EFS, 940
  full device encryption, 940
  other people's files, 941
  SAE, 959
end-user education, 912
event logs, 927
facial recognition, 442, 911
fake security warnings, mobile devices, 441
fingerprint locks, 442
fingerprints, 911
firewalls, 575, 908, 949-950
  port forwarding, 952
  Windows Defender Firewall, 951-953
  wireless networks, 958
folder options, 934-935
fTPM setting (BIOS/UEFI), 116
GDPR, 914
groups, 922
hard drives, 941-942
HIPAA, 914
HSM, 93
identification, PIN, 911
IDS, 957
incident response, 964-965
Internet appliances
  content filtering, 956
  IDS, 957
  IPS, 957
  load balancers, 956
  UTM systems, 956
Internet security, 942
  allow/deny lists, 950
  digital security certificates, 943-944
  DMZ, 950, 960
  DNS, 946-947
  email, 947-948
  firewalls, 949-950
  malware removal, 944-946
  Microsoft Defender, 943
  Microsoft Defender Antivirus, 943
  proxy servers, 948-949
  rogue antivirus apps, 943
  screened subnets, 950
  UPnP, 950
  VPN, 954-955
  Windows Defender Firewall, 951-953
Intrusion Detection/Notification setting (BIOS/UEFI), 115
IoT, 611, 964
IPS, 957
Keychain Access, macOS, 871-872
laptops
  cable locks, 440
  data-usage limit notifications, 445
  failed login attempts, 443
  jailbreaking, 445
  leaked personal files/data, 444
  system lockouts, 443
  unauthorized account access, 443
  unauthorized camera activation, 444
  unauthorized location tracking, 443-444
  unauthorized microphone activation, 444
  unauthorized root access, 445
  VPN, 446
licensing, 912-914
load balancers, 956
local access, 920
  AD functions, 922-923
  group policies, 926
  local security policies, 926-927
  user management, 921
logging off when not in use, 912
logical security
  ACL, 909
  anti-malware, 908
  antivirus software, 908
  authentication, 909-910
  BIOS/UEFI, 910-911
  directory permissions, 908
  disabling unused ports, 908
  email filtering, 909
  firewalls, 908
  login OS security, 911-912
  ports, 909
  trusted/untrusted sources, 909
  VPN, 908
logins, OS, 911-912
logs, 798-799
LoJacks, 115, 910
malware
  anti-malware, 908
  removing, 944-946
MDM, 958
mobile devices, 440, 958, 963
  authenticator apps, 442
  biometric security, 442
  bootleg apps, 441
  data-usage limit notifications, 445
  DMZ, 960
  facial recognition locks, 442
  failed login attempts, 443
  fake security warnings, 441
  fingerprint locks, 442
  IP address filtering, 961
  jailbreaking, 445
  leaked personal files/data, 444
  MAC address filtering, 960
  malicious apps, 441
  patterns, 442
  PIN codes, 442
  screen locks, 442
  spoofing apps, 441
  swipe locks, 442
  system lockouts, 443
  TKIP, 959
  unauthorized account access, 443
  unauthorized camera activation, 444
  unauthorized location tracking, 443-444
  unauthorized microphone activation, 444
  unauthorized root access, 445
  USS, 440
  VPN, 446
  WEP, 959

Windows Hello, 442
WPA2, 959
WPA3, 959
WPS, 961
motherboards, 93
multifunction (all-in-one) devices, 318
NAT, 953
network access, 920
AD functions, 922-923
attacks, 919-920
group policies, 926
local security policies, 926-927
remote access, 955-956
user management, 921
NIC, 602
non-compliant systems, 900
OS
account recovery, 939
AES, 940
backups, 936-939
BitLocker, 939-940
BitLocker To Go, 939
data at rest, 940
device encryption, 940
disabling AutoPlay, 941
disabling AutoRun, 941
EFS, 940
EOL, 935
hard drive storage security, 941
logins, 911-912
patch management, 935
restores, 936-939
unknown notifications, 935
unprotected systems, 935
update management, 935
overview, 900
passwords
AP, 607, 962
BIOS/UEFI settings, 114
boot passwords, 910
complexity, 911
disabling password protection, 927
expired passwords, 911
failed login attempts, 912
formatting, 911
guidelines, 911
Keychain Access, macOS, 871-872
logging off when not in use, 912
managing, 532, 912
number of characters, 911
passwd command, Linux, 884
policies, 901, 999
power-on passwords, 910
rainbow tables, 920
reminders, 911
reusing, 912
routers, 607
saving, macOS, 872
social engineering attacks, 912, 917
special characters, 911
spraying attacks, 920
usernames, 911
PAT, 954
patterns, mobile devices, 442
PCI DSS, 914
permissions
changing, 928
NTFS permissions, 928, 931-934
running as administrators, 934
share permissions, 928-931
UAC, 934
PHI, 914
phishing, incident response, 965
physical security
access control vestibules (mantraps), 904
alarm systems, 904
bade readers, 903
biometrics, 906-907
bollards, 901
cable locks, 903
door locks, 901
equipment locks, 903
guards, 903
hard tokens, 903
HSM, 903
key cards, 902
key fobs, 903
keys, 901
lighting, 903
magnetometers, 904
motion sensors, 904
private screens, 904
RFID, 903
smart cards, 903
tokens, 903
TPM, 903
USB locks, 904
video surveillance, 904
PII, 914
PIN, 911
piracy, 913
policies, 900-901, 999
ports, 908-909, 952
printers/multifunction (all-in-one) devices, 318, 355
private browsing, 530
ransomware, 915
regulated data, 914
remote access, 955-956
routers, 607, 961
scans, Windows installations, 773
screened subnets, 950
Secure Boot setting (BIOS/UEFI), 115
security certificates, verifying in browsers, 530
shredding documents, 907
smartphones, 443-446
spyware, incident response, 965
SSH, 956
SSID, 962
SSO authentication, 911
supervisors/administrators, 910
Telnet, 956
third-party vendors, 907
threats/vulnerabilities
access attacks, 919
backdoor attacks, 919
boot sector viruses, 915
botnets, 915, 919
brute force attacks, 919
cryptojacking/cryptomining, 915
DDOS attacks, 919
dictionary attacks, 911, 919
DoS attacks, 919
dumpster diving, 907
evil twin attacks, 919
impersonation attacks, 918
insider attacks, 919
keyloggers, 915
malware, 915-917
MITM attacks, 920
password spraying attacks, 920

phishing, 918-919
piggybacking, 918
ransomware, 915
reconnaissance attacks, 920
replay attacks, 920
rootkits, 915
scareware, 919
shoulder surfing, 904, 918
Smurf attacks, 920
social engineering attacks, 912, 917
spear phishing, 918
spoofing attacks, 920
spyware, 915
SQL injection attacks, 920
tailgating, 904, 918
TCP/IP hijacking attacks, 920
Trojans, 915
viruses, 915-917
vishing, 918
vulnerability scanners, 920
whaling, 918
XSS attacks, 920
zero day attacks, 920
zombie attacks, 920
TKIP, 602
TLS, 625
tokens, 903
TPM, 93, 116, 910
trusted/untrusted sources, 909
UEFI, 910-911
UPnP, 950
user management, 921
usernames and passwords, 911
users, 910
USS, 440
UTM systems, 956
virtualization, 537
viruses, 915-917
antivirus software, 908
BIOS/UEFI, 119
incident response, 965
Virus Protection setting (BIOS/UEFI), 114
VM, 537
VPN, 446, 908, 954-955
web browsers, 528
WEP, 602, 959
Windows
files/folders, 681
installations, scans, 773
Windows Firewall, 951-953
Windows Hello, 442
wireless networks, 958-963
wireless routers, 961-963
wireless security, 958-963
WPA, 602
WPA2, 602
WPA3, 602
selection (decision) structures
dual-alternative structures, 748
examples of, 749-750
multiple alternative structures, 748-749
relational operators, 746-747
single-alternative structures, 747
self-grounding, 146, 985
sensitive material, printers/multi-function (all-in-one) devices, 318
separation pads, laser printers, 327
sequences, programming, 741
serial cabling, 46
serial ports, 45-46, 392
serial transmissions, 516-517
servers
AAA servers, 622
authentication servers, 622
DHCP servers, 596, 622
DNS servers, 622
endpoint management servers, 622
file servers, 622
fileshare servers, 622
home servers, system design, 479
Kerberos authentication servers, 910
mail servers, 622
motherboards, 95
network servers, 621-622
print servers, 352, 622
proxy servers, 622, 948-949
SAN connectivity, 559
syslog servers, 622
virtualization, 533
web servers, 622
service packs, 494, 689, 778
services
cloud services, 354, 539
Component Services, 797
DaaS, 535, 538
defined, 811
deploying
community clouds, 541
hybrid clouds, 540
private clouds, 540
public clouds, 540
disabling, 831
DNS, 599-600, 622, 948
IaaS, 538
KMS, 776
learning about, 831
logs, 798
PaaS, 538
releases, software, 494
Remote Desktop Services, 605-606
SaaS, 538
Services and Applications, Windows, 811
services.msc command, 729, 831
SLP, 627
troubleshooting startup failures, 831
WDS, 776
Services and Applications, Windows, 811
services.msc command, 729, 831
Services window, MMC, 729
Session layer (OSI model), 575
set command, 729, 740
setting/meeting expectations (soft skills), 1011
Setup programs, 110-111
setups
logs, 778, 798
POST errors, troubleshooting, 117
printer installations, 342
Save & Exit Setup configuration change option (BIOS/UEFI), 117
sfc (System File Checker), 730, 779
SFTP (Secure File Transfer Protocol), 626
SFX12V power supplies, 163
Shadow Copy technology, 816
share permissions, 928
"access denied" messages, 931
administrative shares, 930

Change permissions, 930
concurrent users, maximum number of, 929
Full Control permissions, 930
hidden shares, 931
local shares, 930
principle of least privilege, 930
Public folders, 931
Read permissions, 930
Shared Folders tool, 800
shared resources, cloud computing, 541
shared system memory, 282
shares (shared folders), 632-634
shareware, 913
sharing
multifunction devices, 619-621
printers, 349-353, 619-621
scanners, 620-621
screens, 862-864
shell scripts (.sh), 735
shells, 859
shielding, speakers, 295
shortcuts, Windows 10/11, 669
shoulder surfing, 904, 918
Show Desktop area, Windows 10/11, 667
shredding documents, 907
shrinking partitions, 809
shutdown command
Linux, 883
Windows, 730-731
shutdowns
intermittent shutdowns
memory, 205
troubleshooting, 173
projectors, 289
troubleshooting, 96
Windows
options, 666-667
troubleshooting, 835
side-by-side apps, Windows, 764
signal strength
antennas, 592
wireless networks, 459
signatures, digital, 786
signed drivers, 786
SIM (Subscriber Identification Module) cards, 386, 982
SIM (System Image Manager), 776
simple volumes, 251
single-alternative structures, 747
single-core processors, 74
single-mode fiber cabling, 53
site surveys, 592
skills
basic skills
Internet searches, 6-7
screen captures, 7
text files, creating, 7
soft skills (technicians)
active listening, 98-99, 1005
appearance, 461-462
attitude, 308-309
avoiding burnout, 847-848
avoiding distractions, 1007-1008
be humble, 893
being on time, 210
being proactive, 635
changing one thing at a time, 132
confidence, projecting, 1005
confidential/private materials, dealing with, 1011
cultural sensitivity, 1006
customer service, 1002-1003
customer trust, building, 967
difficult customers, dealing with, 501-502, 1009
documenting changes, 132
expectations, setting/meeting, 1011
grooming, 1003
hygiene, 1003
maintaining a positive attitude, 210
making/keeping commitments, 1008
mentoring, 543
organization, 1004
phone communication skills, 267-268
positive attitude, maintaining a, 1005
projecting confidence, 210
proper language, 1003-1005
staying current, 690
teamwork, 210
timeliness, 1007
time management, 1007
troubleshooting, changing perspectives when, 755
work ethics, 365
written communication skills, 176-177
sleep-and-charge USB ports, 41
sleep/hibernation mode
hard drives, 251
mobile devices, 384
slick printer rollers, troubleshooting, 358
slots
covers, replacing, 147
motherboards, memory, 196-197
slow boot, troubleshooting, 832
slow performance, troubleshooting, 455
browsers, 533
storage devices, 258-260
Windows, 838
slow profile loads, troubleshooting, 832-833
SLP (Service Location Protocol), 627
sluggish performance, troubleshooting
hard drives, 264
memory, 205-206
response times, mobile devices, 441
smart cameras, 377
smart card readers, 379
smart cards, physical security, 903
smart devices, IoT, 609-611
smartphones, 376-377. *See also* phablets
apps
deleting, 451
troubleshooting, 450-452
cellular networks, 385
disposal/recycling, 982
IMEI, 385
IMSI, 386
performance, 455
PRI updates, 387
PRL updates, 387
screens, 454-455
security
data-usage limit notifications, 445
failed login attempts, 443

jailbreaking, 445
leaked personal files/data, 444
system lockouts, 443
unauthorized account access, 443
unauthorized camera activation, 444
unauthorized location tracking, 443-444
unauthorized microphone activation, 444
unauthorized root access, 445
VPN, 446
SIM cards, 386
storage, 447
traveling with, 447
troubleshooting
AirDrop failures, 452
app closure failures, 451
app installation failures, 451
app load failures, 452
app update failures, 451
autorotating screens, 454
backlight failures, 454
batteries, 456
Bluetooth connectivity, 459-460
damaged ports, 448
dim displays, 454
email decryption failures, 452
flickering displays, 455
frozen systems, 456
GPS, 459
hard resets, 449
liquid damage, 448
network issues, 458-459
NFC, 460
no display, 454
no power, 456
OS update failures, 450
overheating, 457
performance, 455
screens, 454-455
soft resets, 448
sound issues, 458
touch screens, 455
unexpected app behavior, 450
Wi-Fi connectivity, 458-459
S.M.A.R.T. (Self-Monitoring, Analysis and Reporting Technology), troubleshooting, 263-264
SMB (Server Message Blocks), 626
smells (burning), troubleshooting, 96
S/MIME (Secure MIME), 400, 452
smoke, troubleshooting, 173, 286
SMS (Short Message Service) text messages, 910
SMTP (Simple Mail Transfer Protocol), 400, 627
Smurf attacks, 920
snap-ins
adding/removing, 796
Component Services, 797
Computer Management Console, Windows, 796
MMC, 796
snapshots/checkpoints, VM, 535
SNMP (Simple Network Management Protocol), 627
snug connectors, 150
social engineering attacks, 912, 917
sockets
AMD, 80
CPU sockets, 79-80
Intel, 80
multisocket motherboards, 79
ZIF sockets, 80
SODIMM (Small-Outline DIMM), 188, 425
soft resets, 448
soft skills (technicians)
active listening, 98-99, 1005
appearance, 461-462
attitude, 308-309
avoiding burnout, 847-848
avoiding distractions, 1007-1008
be humble, 893
being on time, 210
being proactive, 635
changing one thing at a time, 132
confidence, projecting, 1005
confidential/private materials, dealing with, 1011
cultural sensitivity, 1006
customer service, 1002-1003
customer trust, building, 967
difficult customers, dealing with, 501-502, 1009
documenting changes, 132
expectations, setting/meeting, 1011
grooming, 1003
hygiene, 1003
maintaining a positive attitude, 210
making/keeping commitments, 1008
mentoring, 543
organization, 1004
phone communication skills, 267-268
positive attitude, maintaining a, 1005
projecting confidence, 210
proper language, 1003-1005
staying current, 690
teamwork, 210
timeliness, 1007
time management, 1007
troubleshooting, changing perspectives when, 755
work ethics, 365
written communication skills, 176-177
soft token authentication, 910
software
anti-malware, mobile devices, 409
antivirus software, 908
Microsoft Defender Antivirus, 943
mobile devices, 409
reinitializing, 777
rogue antivirus apps, 943
Windows installations, 773
botnets, 919
commercial licenses, 913
DaaS, 538
DLL, 795
downloading, 887
DRM, 912
file recovery software, 260
firewalls, 908, 949-950
port forwarding, 952
Windows Defender Firewall, 951-953
firmware, AP, 962
freeware, 912
IaaS, 538
installing, 495
ISO images, 793
system requirements, 792-793

INDEX

interfering software, disabling from OS installations, 774
legacy software, 534
malware, 915-917, 944-946
non-expired licenses, 913
obtaining with Linux CLI, 886-887
open source software, 858, 912
OS, 8
PaaS, 538
packages, downloading, 887
patches, 494
personal licenses, 913
piracy, 913, 965
RAID, 253
reinstalling, 495
removing, 792
SaaS, 538
scareware, 919
SDK, 390
SDN, 623
service releases, 494
shareware, 913
spyware, 915, 965
troubleshooting, 494
Ubuntu Software Center, 881
uninstalling, 794
updating, Software Updater (Linux), 882
valid licenses, 913
viruses, 915-917
vulnerability scanners, 920

Software Updater, Linux, 882
solid ink printers, 323
SOP (Standard Operating Procedures), 994
sound
BIOS/UEFI beeps, 489
cards, 44
headphones, troubleshooting, 458
headsets, 17
laptops, 432
microphones, 17, 484
mobile devices, 432
POST codes, 489
S/PDIF in/out ports, 44
sound cards, 290
16-bit sampling, 292
installing, 292
muting, 293
system design, 484
theory of operation, 292
Windows operations, 293
Sound Control Panel, Windows, 787
speakers
laptops, 432
mobile devices, 432
system design, 483
troubleshooting, mobile devices, 458
voice recognition, physical security, 906

spam, 947
spanned volumes, 251
sparks (monitors), troubleshooting, 286
SPD (Serial Presence Detect), memory, 192
S/PDIF (Sony/Phillips Digital Interface) in/out ports, 44
speakers
amplification, 295
choosing, 296
frequency response ranges, 295
laptops, 432
mobile devices, 381, 432
motherboards, 289
power ratings, 295
shielding, 295
system design, 483
troubleshooting, 296
USB speakers, 295
volume control, 295-296

spear phishing, 918
special characters
file/folder names, Windows, 673
passwords, 911
wildcards, 728

special function keys, 424-425
special thermal paper, 328, 341
speed (performance)
buses, 72
CPU, 72
data transfer speeds, wireless networks, 593
DSL, 519
memory, 199
NIC, 603
processors, 70-72
serial transmissions, modems, 517
Windows boot process, 826-827

SPF (Sender Policy Frameworks), 948
spikes, 986
spinning pinwheels, troubleshooting, 205, 265, 491
splash screens, 999
splitting partitions, 809
spontaneous reboots, 835
spoofing
apps, 441
attacks, 920

spoolers, print, 348, 360
Spotlight, macOS, 861
spreading/pinching open actions (mobile devices), 384
SPS (Standby Power Supplies), 991
spyware, 915, 965
SQL (Structured Query Language), injection attacks, 920
SRAM (static RAM), 188
SSD (Solid-State Drives), 414, 427-429
costs, 227
defragmenting, 260
ESD, 153
installing, 239-240
M.2 devices, 230
M.2 SSD, BIOS/UEFI settings, 241
NVMe, 231
NVMe SSD, BIOS/UEFI settings, 241
overview, 227
SSHD, flash memory, 228
static electricity, 240
troubleshooting, 266
upgrading, 241

SSH (Secure Shell), 626, 956
SSHD (Solid-State Hybrid Drives), 228, 427

SSID (Service Set Identifiers), 585-586, 962
- SSID not found messages, 601
- wireless networks, 608

SSL (Secure Sockets Layer), 625-626
SSL/TLS (Secure Sockets Layer/ Transport Layer Security), email, 400
SSO (Single Sign-On) authentication, 911
ST (Straight Tip) connectors, 53
standard formatting, 250, 941
standard privileges, commands, 734
standard user accounts, 805, 921
standby mode, power supplies, 169
standoffs, 154
star topologies, 554
Start button, Windows 10/11, 664-665
Start screen, Windows, 669
start/stop bits, 517
starting
- Remote Desktop, 723
- tools with commands, 708

Startup Settings menu, Windows, 819-820
statements (customer), clarifying, 2
static electricity
- antistatic brushes, 157
- EMI, 146
- ESD, 144-146 153
- RFI, 146
- SSD, 240

static IP address configurations, 595-597
status, hard drives, 265, 807
staying current (soft skills), 690
stepper motors, inkjet printers, 322
sticky hard drives, troubleshooting, 263
stop (kill tasks), 824
storage
- AP configurations, 607
- basic disks, 251
- basic storage, 251
- BIOS/UEFI configuration, 241
- boot volumes, 251
- CF cards, 379
- cloud storage, 224, 764
- component storage, safety, 984-986
- credentials, 801
- device configuration, overview, 235
- disk caches, 256-257
- Disk Management, 250-251, 807-809
- dynamic disks, 251
- dynamic storage, 251
- external hard drives, 427
- fault tolerance, 253-254
- files, cloud file storage services, 539
- flash memory, 378
- hard drives
  - basic disks, 251
  - boot volumes, 251
  - defragmenting, 259-260
  - disk caches, 256-257
  - disk mirroring (RAID 1), 254
  - disk striping (RAID 0), 254
  - drive activity LED, 261
  - dynamic disks, 251
  - fault tolerance, 253-254
  - form factors, 225
  - HDI, 226
  - head crashes, 226
  - hibernation/sleep mode, 251
  - IDE, 229
  - lost clusters, 258
  - magnetic hard drives, 225-227
  - mounts, 239
  - MTBF, 226
  - overview, 225
  - platters, 225
  - RAID, 253-255, 266
  - RAW volumes, 251
  - resizing partitions, 252
  - SCSI, 229
  - security, 941
  - simple volumes, 251
  - spanned volumes, 251
  - status messages, 265
  - striped volumes, 251
  - swap files, 257
  - system volumes, 251
  - troubleshooting, 258-264
  - types of, 225
  - volumes, 251
- hibernation/sleep mode and hard drives, 251
- hybrid drives, 427
- iCloud, macOS, 862
- installing devices, trouble-shooting, 260-264
- internal laptop drives, 427
- JSOD. *See* spanned volumes
- laptops, 426
- logical drives, 246-247
- M.2 devices, 230
- mechanical hard drives, 427, 430
- mobile devices, 378-379, 447
- mSATA drives, 427
- NAS devices
  - drives, 229
  - system design, 477
- offsite storage, 224, 936
- on site storage, 936
- OneDrive, 764
- optical drives, 814
  - connectivity, 300
  - DirectX, 301
  - DVD/Blu-ray region codes, 299
  - features of, 298-299
  - installing, 300
  - interfaces, 300
  - ISO files/images, 300
  - overview, 297-298
  - preventive maintenance, 301-302
  - reading Blu-ray discs, 298
  - symbols, 299
  - testing, 300
  - troubleshooting, 300-301
  - writable media, 298-299
- overview, 224
- partitions, resizing, 252
- PATA, installing devices, 235
- performance, 258-260, 264
- pools, 810
- RAID
  - BIOS/UEFI settings, 255
  - concepts, 254
  - configuring, 253
  - failures, 266
  - fault tolerance, 253-254
  - FCM, 253
  - hardware RAID, 254

INDEX

hot swappable RAID drives, 254
levels of, 253-254
RAID 0, 254
RAID 0+1, 254
RAID 1, 254
RAID 5, 254
RAID 10, 254
"RAID not found" error messages, 266
software RAID, 253
troubleshooting, 266
RAW volumes, 251
removable storage, 153, 207-208
SAN, 552, 558-559
SAS drives, 229
SATA, 236-237
SD cards, 378-379
simple volumes, 251
spanned volumes, 251
SSD, 414, 427-429
costs, 227
installing, 239-240
M.2 devices, 230
NVMe, 231
overview, 227
SSHD, 228
static electricity, 240
troubleshooting, 266
upgrading, 241
SSHD, 427
storage pools, 810
Storage Space Control Panel, 810
striped volumes, 251
subsystem design, 483
swap files, 257
system volumes, 251
troubleshooting
new device installations, 260-261
performance, 258-260, 264
previous installed devices, 262-264
virtual memory, 256
volumes, 251-252
Windows Storage Spaces, 255
STP (Shielded Twisted Pair) cabling, 51, 560-561
straight through (patch) cabling, 562
streaks (printing), troubleshooting, 363
streaming, virtual apps, 539
strings, 743
striped volumes, 251
striping (RAID 0), disk, 254
styluses (touch pens), 381
su command, Linux, 883
subdirectories, 672, 700, 705
subfolders, 672
subnet masks, 580, 1021-1023
subsystem design, 483-485
subtrees, Windows registry, 686-687
sudo command, 874-876
supervisors/administrators, BIOS/UEFI security, 910
support, virtualization, 77
surge protectors, 172
surge suppressors, 987-989
surges, 986
surveillance (video), physical security, 904
swabs, urethane, 157
swap files, 257
swap partitions, 769
swelling capacitors, 96
swipe/flick actions (mobile devices), 384
swipe locks, mobile devices, 442
switches, 553-554, 576
command switches, 703-704
managed/unmanaged switches, 554
motherboard switches, 492
PoE switches, 568
SDN, 623
swollen batteries, 456
symbols
Ethernet ports, 48
Event Viewer, 799
Sync Center Control Panel utility, Windows, 793
synchronizing
browsers, 530
files, 539
mobile devices, 401-403
Windows, 793
syntax, scripting, 740
synthetic backups, 937
syslog servers, 622
Sysprep, 775
system bootups, troubleshooting boots from the wrong device, 116
system buses. *See* internal data buses
System Configuration utility, Windows, 722, 820-824
system dates/times (inaccurate), troubleshooting, 118
system design
audio subsystems, 483-484
audio/video workstations, 476
cases, 481-482
chipsets, 481
cooling systems, 481
CPU, 481
display subsystems, 484-485
environmental concerns, 480
gaming PC, 475
graphic/CAD/CAM workstations, 475
home servers, 479
memory, 481
motherboards, 481
NAS devices, 477
power supplies, 481-482
processors, 481
recycling components, 480
storage subsystems, 483
thick client workstations, 479
thin client workstations, 478
virtualization workstations, 477
system environment variables, 738
System File Checker, 260, 264, 730
system files, 814-815
System Image Recovery, 688, 828
System Information, 723
BIOS/UEFI, 114
macOS, 871
system instability (Windows), troubleshooting, 835
system lockouts, 96, 443
system logs, 798-800
system partitions, 248
System Preferences, macOS, 866-868
system requirements, apps, 792-793
system resources, 120-122

System Restore, 780, 783, 815-816
- command prompt operation, 831
- corrupted registries, troubleshooting, 830

System Tools section, Computer Management console
- Event Viewer, 798-800
- Shared Folders tool, 800
- Task Scheduler, 797

system updates, macOS, 864
system volumes, 251, 814
systeminfo command, 731

T

T568A wiring standard, 52, 562
T568B wiring standard, 52, 562
tables, rainbow, 920
tablets, 376-377, 982. *See also* smartphones; phablets
tabs, Windows, 671
TACACS+ (Terminal Access Controller Access-Control System+), 910
tailgating, 904, 918
tangs, cabling, 561
tap/touch actions (mobile devices), 384
taskbars
- multi-monitor taskbars, 764
- viewing in displays, 789

taskkill command, 731
tasklist command, 732
Task Manager, Windows, 824-826
- measuring Windows performance, 839-840
- monitoring memory usage, 203-204

Task Scheduler, 797
Task View, Windows 10/11, 668-669
TB (terabytes), 20-21
TCP (Transmission Control Protocol), 625
TCP/IP (Transmission Control Protocol/Internet Protocol), 575
- Application layer, 576, 627
- CIFS, 626
- connection-oriented protocols, 627
- devices, 576
- DHCP, 626
- DNS, 626
- example of, 625-627
- FTP, 626
- hijacking attacks, 920
- HTTP, 626
- HTTPS, 626
- IMAP, 626
- Internet layer, 576, 627
- LDAP, 626
- NetBT, 626
- Network Access layer, 576, 627
- NTP, 626
- POP3, 626
- protocol stacks, checking on NIC, 613
- RDP, 626
- SFTP, 626
- SLP, 627
- SMB, 626
- SMTP, 627
- SNMP, 627
- SSH, 626
- telnet, 627
- Transport layer, 576, 627

team programming, 737
teamwork (soft skills), 210
technical field kits, 980
technicians
- gun slinger technicians, 132
- qualities of, 2-3
- soft skills
  - active listening, 98-99, 1005
  - appearance, 461-462
  - attitude, 308-309
  - avoiding burnout, 847-848
  - avoiding distractions, 1007-1008
  - be humble, 893
  - being on time, 210
  - being proactive, 635
  - changing one thing at a time, 132
  - confidence, projecting, 1005
  - confidential/private materials, dealing with, 1011
  - cultural sensitivity, 1006
  - customer service, 1002-1003
  - customer trust, building, 967
  - difficult customers, dealing with, 501-502, 1009
  - documenting changes, 132
  - expectations, setting/meeting, 1011
  - grooming, 1003
  - hygiene, 1003
  - maintaining a positive attitude, 210
  - making/keeping commitments, 1008
  - mentoring, 543
  - organization, 1004
  - phone communication skills, 267-268
  - positive attitude, maintaining a, 1005
  - projecting confidence, 210
  - proper language, 1003-1005
  - staying current, 690
  - teamwork, 210
  - timeliness, 1007
  - time management, 1007
  - troubleshooting, changing perspectives when, 755
  - work ethics, 365
  - written communication skills, 176-177
- tools, 147

Telnet, 627, 956
telnet command, 732
temperature/humidity control, safety, 993-994
terabytes (TB), 20-21
Terminal, macOS, 874
terminating twisted pair cabling, 561-565
testing
- cables, 565, 572
- conditions with logical operators, 750
- optical drives, 300
- POST, 96, 110
- power supplies, 174
- printers, 346
- sandbox testing, 1001
- scripts, 737
- test development, virtualization, 534
- theories of probable cause, troubleshooting process, 495-496

tethering, 397, 525

text files, 734-736
- creating, 7
- more command, 722
- type command, 732

text messages, SMS, 910
textboxes, Windows, 670
TFX12V power supplies, 163
theories of probable cause, troubleshooting process, 487
- BIOS/UEFI
  - beeps, 489
  - POST error messages, 490-491
- bootup process, 487
- error messages, 489-491
- hardware errors, 493
- intermittent device failures, 493
- POST codes, 489
- software errors, 494
- testing, 495-496
- UEFI diagnostics, 491

thermal pads, 80, 85-86
thermal paper, 328, 341
thermal paste, 80-82, 85-86
thermal printers, 319, 329
- debris removal, 341
- feed assemblies, 328
- heating elements, 328, 341
- maintenance, 341
- thermal paper, 328, 341

thermal wax transfer printers, 323
thick clients, 479, 605-606
thin clients, 478, 605-606
third-party vendors, security, 907
This PC tile, Windows Start screen, 669
threading, 839
- hyperthreading, 73-74, 114
- multithreading, 73-74

threats/vulnerabilities, security
- access attacks, 919
- backdoor attacks, 919
- boot sector viruses, 915
- botnets, 915-919
- brute force attacks, 919
- cryptojacking/cryptomining, 915
- DDOS attacks, 919
- dictionary attacks, 911, 919
- DoS attacks, 919
- dumpster diving, 907
- evil twin attacks, 919
- impersonation attacks, 918
- insider attacks, 919
- keyloggers, 915
- malware, 915-917
- MITM attacks, 920
- password spraying attacks, 920
- phishing, 918-919
- piggybacking, 918
- ransomware, 915
- reconnaissance attacks, 920
- replay attacks, 920
- rootkits, 915
- scareware, 919
- shoulder surfing, 904, 918
- Smurf attacks, 920
- social engineering attacks, 912, 917
- spear phishing, 918
- spoofing attacks, 920
- spyware, 915
- SQL injection attacks, 920
- tailgating, 904, 918
- TCP/IP hijacking attacks, 920
- Trojans, 915
- viruses, 915-917
- vishing, 918
- vulnerability scanners, 920
- whaling, 918
- XSS attacks, 920
- zero day attacks, 920
- zombie attacks, 920

throttling
- CPU, 72
- managing, 84

throughput. *See* bandwidth
Thunderbolt
- cabling, 43
- USB-C ports, 43

ticket systems, help desks, 997
.TIF (.TIFF) file extensions, 674
tiles, Windows Start screen, 669
time
- being on time (soft skills), 210
- inaccurate system dates/times, troubleshooting, 118
- managing (soft skills), 1007
- NTP, 626
- timeliness (soft skills), 1007

Time Machine, macOS, 864-865
timeouts/screen locks, 927
TKIP (Temporal Key Integrity Protocol), 602, 959
TLS (Transport Layer Security), 625-626
TN (Twisted Nematic) LCD displays, 434
tokens, physical security, 903
tone generators, 572
toner
- handling, 336
- laser printers, 327, 339
- safety/disposal, 984
- spills, 327
- unfused toner, troubleshooting, 364

toner probes, 572
toner vacuums, 157
tools
- AC circuit testers, 174
- air filtration masks, 980
- antistatic bags, 984
- browser troubleshooting tools, 533
- cable testers, 565, 572
- cable (wire) strippers, 563, 572
- change boards, 999
- compressed air, 980
- crimpers, 563-565, 572
- deployment tools
  - MDT, 776
  - SIM, 776
  - Sysprep, 775
  - WDS, 776
  - Windows ADK, 775
- diagonal cutters, 147
- disassembly tools, 147
- ESD mats, 985
- ESD straps, 985
- fire extinguishers, 979
- line conditioners, 989
- loopback plugs, 572
- multimeters, 160, 572
- needle-nose pliers, 147
- network (breakout) taps, 572
- power supply testers, 174
- punchdown tools, 51, 572-573
- safety goggles, 980
- screwdrivers, 147

scribes, 418
starting with commands, 708
surge suppressors, 987-989
System Tools section, Computer Management console
Event Viewer, 798-800
Shared Folders tool, 800
Task Scheduler, 797
technical field kits, 980
tone generators, 572
toner probes, 572
toner vacuums, 157
vacuums, 980
Wi-Fi analyzers, 593
topology diagrams, networks, 995
Torvalds, Linus, 655, 878
touch and hold/long touch actions (mobile devices), 384
touch calibration, trackpads, 454
touch command, 874-875
touch pens (styluses), 381
touch screens, 436
replacing, 438-439
troubleshooting, 455
touch/tap actions (mobile devices), 384
touchpads, repairing, 422
Tower cases, 9-10
TPM (Trusted Platform Modules), 93
BIOS/UEFI, 116, 910
initializing, 117
physical security, 903
versions of, 117
tracert command, 614, 732
track (drawing) pads, 381
tracking (location), unauthorized, 443-444
trackpads, 454
tracks, magnetic hard drives, 227
tractor feeds, 332
traffic (networks), troubleshooting, 458
transfer belts, laser printers, 325
transfer corona wires, laser printers, 327, 341
transfer rollers, laser printers, 325
transferring
documents (AirDrop), troubleshooting, 452
laser printer imaging process, 325
Transport layer
OSI model, 575
TCP/IP, 576, 627
traveling with mobile devices, 447
trays, paper/printer, 333, 347
tree structure, files, 700-702
triggering, port, 952
trip hazards, 987
triple-channel memory, 197
Trojans, 915
troubleshooting. *See also* recovery; repairing
AirDrop, 452
apps
closure failures, 451
crashes, 799
email decryption failures, 452
hanging apps, 799
installation failures, 451
load failures, 452
logs, 800
unexpected app behavior, 450
update failures, 451
audio, 289, 296
backups, 485-486
batteries, 456
BIOS issues, 131, 489
blank/black screens, 96, 173, 829-831
Bloom's Taxonomy, 486
Bluetooth connectivity, 459-460
bootups, 262, 487
blank/black screens, 96
failures to boot, 827-828
finding missing bootloaders, 892
graphical interfaces, 829
resetting PC, 828
slow bootups, 832
system boots from the wrong device, 116
Windows, 827-829
browsers
basic issues, 531-532
extensions, 530-531
plug-ins, 530-531
slow performance, 533
tools, 533
BSOD, 261, 491, 799, 830
burning smells, 96, 173
cable modems, 619
cabling, video connectivity, 284
capacitors, swelling, 96
changing perspectives (soft skills), 755
clicking sounds, 262, 301
clock drift, 791
configurations, 130
connectivity, 611-612
continuous reboots, 96
crash screens, 491
cursor drift, 454
dark displays, 830
data loss/corruption, 260
displays, 454-455
with Device Manager, 131
DNS, 946-947
documenting outcomes, 497
DSL modems, 619
email, 452, 947-948
error messages, 489-491
eSATA drives, 264
extended read/write times, 259
fans, 173
File Explorer, 455
FireWire ports, 836
flowcharts, 498-500
frozen systems, 456
full system functionality, verifying, 497
GPS, 459
graphical interfaces, 829
grinding noises, 86, 173, 262, 301
halting installations, 778
hard drives
bootup failures, 262
data loss/corruption, 260
extended read/write times, 259
fragmented drives, 259-260
noises, 262
performance, 258-260, 264
read/write failures, 264
hardware, 493
headphones, 458
identifying problems, 486
inaccurate system dates/times, 118
information gathering, 485
inkjet printers, 363

installations, halting, 778
intermittent device failures, 493
intermittent shutdowns, 96, 173
intermittent wireless connectivity, 458-459
Internet connectivity, 459, 611-612
isolating problems, 495-496
kernel panic, 871
keyboards, 16
laptops
AirDrop failures, 452
app closure failures, 451
app installation failures, 451
app load failures, 452
app update failures, 451
autorotating screens, 454
backlight failures, 454
battery failures, 456
Bluetooth connectivity, 459-460
damaged ports, 448
dim displays, 454
email decryption failures, 452
flickering displays, 455
frozen systems, 456
GPS, 459
hard resets, 449
keyboards, 453
liquid damage, 448
network issues, 458-459
NFC, 460
no display, 454
no power, 456
OS update failures, 450
overheating, 457
performance, 455
soft resets, 448
sound issues, 458
touch screens, 455
trackpads, 454
unexpected app behavior, 450
Wi-Fi connectivity, 458-459
laser printers, 363-364
links, 791
liquid damage, 448
macOS
kernel panic, 871
Safe mode, 869
memory, 205-206
missing
bootloaders, 892
drives in the OS, 261
mobile devices
AirDrop failures, 452
app closure failures, 451
app installation failures, 451
app load failures, 452
app update failures, 451
autorotating screens, 454
backlight failures, 454
battery failures, 456
Bluetooth connectivity, 459-460
damaged ports, 448
dim displays, 454
email decryption failures, 452
flickering displays, 455
frozen systems, 456
GPS, 459
hard resets, 449
keyboards, 453
liquid damage, 448
network issues, 458-459
NFC, 460
no display, 454
no power, 456
OS update failures, 450
overheating, 457
performance, 455
soft resets, 448
sound issues, 458
touch screens, 455
trackpads, 454
unexpected app behavior, 450
Wi-Fi connectivity, 458-459
motherboards, 96
mouse (mice), 16
multifunction devices, 621
networks, 611
Bluetooth connectivity, 459-460
GPS, 459
high traffic, 458
ifconfig command, 613
ipconfig command, 613
net command, 616
net computer command, 616
net config command, 616
netdom command, 616
net help command, 616
net share command, 616
net start command, 616
net stop command, 616
net use command, 616
net user command, 616
net view command, 616
NFC, 460
nslookup command, 615
pathping command, 614
ping command, 611-613
tracert command, 614
unavailable resources, 612-613
Wi-Fi connectivity, 458-459
Windows settings, 833-834
NFC, 460
NIC, 617-618
no connectivity, 611-612
nonfunctioning/undetected devices with Device Manager, 789-790
no power, 173, 456
optical drives, 300-301
OS
no OS found error messages, 779
update failures, 450
overheating, 96, 173, 457
overview, 485-486
performance
mobile devices, 455
storage devices, 258-260, 264
pinwheels, spinning, 491
plans of action, 497
port flapping, 612
POST
beeps, 96, 489
errors, 117
power failures, 989-991
power supplies, 173-175
preventive measures, 497
printers, 355, 621, 813-814
double images, 364
faded print, 358
garbled print, 357
impact printers, 362-363
incorrect chroma displays, 363
incorrect paper size, 357
light printing, 363
paper feeds, 356
paper jams, 356

slick rollers, 358
streaks, 363
toner, 364
USB-attached printers, 359
vertical lines, 363
Windows environments, 359-362
process overview, 486
processors, 86
profile loads, 832-833
projectors, 288-289
RAID, 266
read/write failures, 264
reboots, 96, 173
reimaging computers, 775-776
resolving problems, 497
resource conflicts, 121
scanners, 621
services, 831
setups
POST errors, 117
programs, 111
shutdowns, 96, 835
slow performance, 455
slow profile loads, 832-833
sluggish performance, 264
S.M.A.R.T. errors, 263-264
smartphones
AirDrop failures, 452
app closure failures, 451
app installation failures, 451
app load failures, 452
app update failures, 451
autorotating screens, 454
backlight failures, 454
battery failures, 456
Bluetooth connectivity, 459-460
damaged ports, 448
dim displays, 454
email decryption failures, 452
flickering displays, 455
frozen systems, 456
GPS, 459
hard resets, 449
liquid damage, 448
network issues, 458-459
NFC, 460
no display, 454
no power, 456
OS update failures, 450
overheating, 457
performance, 455
soft resets, 448
sound issues, 458
touch screens, 455
unexpected app behavior, 450
Wi-Fi connectivity, 458-459
smoke, 173
software, 494
sound
mobile devices, 458
speakers, 296
spinning pinwheels, 205, 265, 491
SSD, 266
storage
new device installations, 260-261
performance, 258-260, 264
previously installed devices, 262-264
swelling capacitors, 96
system boots from the wrong device, 116
system dates/times (inaccurate), 118
system instability, Windows, 835
system lockups, 96
system logs, 800
theories of probable cause
BIOS/UEFI beeps, 489
BIOS/UEFI POST error messages, 490-491
bootup process, 487
error messages, 489-491
hardware errors, 493
intermittent device failures, 493
POST codes, 489
software errors, 494
testing, 495-496
UEFI diagnostics, 491
trackpads, 454
UEFI, 131
beeps, 489
diagnostics, 491
unavailable resources, 612-613
undetected/nonfunctioning devices with Device Manager, 789-790
unexpected shutdowns, 96
unintentional network connections, 459
unplugging computers, 161
USB
devices, 126-128
ports, 836
verifying full system functionality, 497
video, 829-831
adapters, 493
BSOD, 285
burn-in, 286
cabling/connectivity, 284
dark displays, 285
dead pixels, 285
dim images, 285
flashing screens, 284
fuzzy images, 284
incorrect colors, 284
smoke/sparks, 286
web browsers, 455
Wi-Fi connectivity, 458-459
Windows
boot process, 828
installations, 777-778
network settings, 833-834
profiles, 832
shutdowns, 835
slow performance, 838
summary of steps, 836
system instability, 835
Windows Defender Firewall, 952-953
wireless networks, 964
wizards, 791
trust (soft skills), building, 967
trusted sources
security, 909
web browsers, 528
turning on/off Windows features, 795
tweaker screwdrivers, 147
twisted pair cabling
corporate networks, 565-567
RJ11 connectors, 561-564
RJ45 connectors, 561-565
STP cables, 560-561
terminating, 561-565
UTP cables, 560-564
two-factor authentication, 398
two-sided printing, 332

INDEX

.txt files, 674, 706
TXT messages, 600, 948
Type 1 (native) hypervisors, 536
Type 2 (hosted) hypervisors, 536
Type A-B-C fire extinguishers, 979
Type C fire extinguishers, 979
type command, 706, 732
types of
  cases, 164
  motherboards, 164
  power supplies, 163-164

U

UAC (User Account Control), 764, 806, 934
Ubuntu. *See also* Linux
  Backups, 882
  downloading, 879
  Nautilus file manager, 879
  Ubuntu Software Center, 881
  user interface, 880
UDP (User Datagram Protocol), 625-627
UEFI (Unified Extensible Firmware Interface). *See also* BIOS
  beeps, troubleshooting, 489
  boot process, 488
  configuring
    change options, 116
    settings, 113-116
  diagnostics, 491
  flashing, 118-120
  M.2 SSD settings, 241
  mSATA settings, 241
  NVMe SSD settings, 241
  on-board NIC, 603
  POST error messages, troubleshooting, 490-491
  RAID configuration settings, 255
  resource conflicts, 121
  SATA
    ports, 237
    settings, 241
  security, 910-911
  storage devices, configuring, 241
  system boots from the wrong device, troubleshooting, 116
  TPM considerations, 117
  troubleshooting, 131, 491
  viruses, 119
Unallocated status messages, 265
unattended installations, Windows, 765
unauthorized account access, 443
unauthorized camera activation, 444
unauthorized location tracking, 443-444
unauthorized microphone activation, 444
unauthorized root access/jailbreaking, 445
unavailable resources, troubleshooting, 612-613
unbuffered memory, 191
uncompressing files, 719
undervoltage, 986-987
undetected/nonfunctioning devices, troubleshooting with Device Manager, 789-790
unexpected app behavior, troubleshooting, 450
unexpected shutdowns, troubleshooting, 96
uninstalling apps/software, 794
unintentional network connections, troubleshooting, 459
Unknown status messages, 265
unlicensed ranges, wireless connectivity, 527
unlocking BitLocker encrypted hard drives, 940
unmanaged/managed switches, 554
unplugging computers, 161
unprotected systems, OS security, 935
Unreadable status messages, 265
untrusted sources, web browsers, 528
unused ports, disabling, 908
unwanted notifications, OS security, 935
updatedb command, Linux, 883, 891
updating
  apps
    failures, troubleshooting, 451
  Automatic Updates, 780
  boot orders, 777
  browsers, 531
  drivers, 123
  firmware, 118-120
  initiating updates, 736
  managing updates, 935
  OS, 777
    mobile OS, 441
    troubleshooting failures, 450
  PRI, 387
  PRL, 387
  software with Software Updater (Linux), 882
  system updates, macOS, 864
  Windows
    network settings, 833-834
    roll back Windows updates, 780
    Windows Update, 780-781
    Windows Update Assistant, 767
upgrading
  BIOS, 112
  CPU, 84
  memory, 193, 206, 425-426
  motherboards, 95
  power supplies, 170
  printers, 336
  processors, 84
  SSD, 241
  Windows, 765-767
UPnP (Universal Plug and Play), 608, 950
UPS (Uninterruptible Power Supplies), 989-991
upstream/downstream data, fiber networks, 523
urethane swabs, 157
USB (Universal Serial Buses)
  cabling, 38
  connectors, 38
  converters, 41, 46
  endpoints, 791
  expansion cards, 124-126
  flash drives, 207-208
  hubs, 40
  installing devices, 124
  locks, physical security, 904
  microUSB ports, 391
  miniUSB ports, 391
  "Not enough USB controller resources" error messages, 791

ports, 37
charging USB ports, 41
installing extra USB ports, 42
microUSB ports, 39
miniUSB ports, 39
power management, 127
sleep-and-charge USB ports, 41
troubleshooting shutdowns, 836
USB cabling, 38
USB connectors, 38
USB converters, 41, 46
USB-C ports, 43
USB hubs, 40
USB-PD, 38
versions, 37
printers, connectivity, 342-344, 359
removing USB devices, 41
scanners, 304
speakers, 295
troubleshooting devices, 126-128
USB-C ports, 391
USB-PD, 38
USB Permissions setting (BIOS/UEFI), 114
wireless NIC, 396, 584
user accounts
administrator accounts, 805
administrators, 921-922
guests, 921
managing
adding credentials, 802-803
certificate-based credentials, 801
Credential Manager, 801-804
editing credentials, 804
generic credentials, 801
Local Users and Groups tool, 804-805
recovering accounts, 805
removing credentials, 803
rights, 804
storing credentials, 801
UAC, 806
web credentials, 801
network configuration operators, 921
performance log users, 921
recovery options, 805
remote desktop users, 921
remote management users, 921
root users, 876
standard user accounts, 805
standard users, 921
UAC, 764, 806, 934
user interfaces
command-line interface, 653
GNOME, Linux, 879
GUI, 653
macOS, 859-862
shells, 859
Ubuntu, 880
users
authentication, printers/scanners, 355
BIOS/UEFI security, 910
concurrent users (share permissions), maximum number of, 929
educating, security, 912
end user acceptance of changes, 1001
environment variables, 738
EULA, 913
forums, Linux, 891
impersonation attacks, 918
managing, 921
new user/exiting user checklists, 996
passwords, 911
PHI, 914
PII, 914
power users, 921
privileges, commands, 734
profiles
security policies, 901
Windows, 686
using data
data caps, 399
limit notifications, 445
USMT (User State Migration Tool), 768
USS (Universal Security Slots), 440
utilities, macOS
Activity Monitor, 869
Boot Camp, 873
Console, 870-871
Disk Utility, 872-873
Keychain Access, 871-872
System Information, 871
Terminal, 874
UTM (Unified Threat Management) systems, 956
UTP (Unshielded Twisted Pair) cabling, 50, 560-564

V

VA (Vertical Alignment), LCD displays, 434
vacuum bags, 157
vacuums, 980
portable vacuums, 157
preventive maintenance, 158
toner vacuums, 157
valid licenses, 913
van Gogh, Vincent, 1012
vapor (phase-change) cooling, 80
variables, 741
data types, 743
declaring, 742-743
displaying, 729, 740
environment variables
accessing, 738-739
editing, 738
system environment variables, 738
user environment variables, 738
viewing, 740
initializing, 743
keywords, 742
naming, 742
PATH variables, 738
set command, 729, 740
use cases, 744-745
VBScript (.vbs), 735, 754
vCards, contact synchronization, 402
VDI (Virtual Desktop Infrastructures), 535
vendors (third-party), security, 907
ventilation, 167, 994
verifying
full system functionality, 497
hardware with Device Manager, 130-131
installations, 776-777
security certificates in browsers, 530

INDEX

versions of Windows, determining, 685
vertical lines (printing), troubleshooting, 363
VGA (Video Graphics Array) ports, 33, 36
vi command, 874
video
  adapters, 36, 485, 493
  AGP video adapters, power requirements, 171
  cabling, laptops, 436
  converters, 36
  editing workstations, system design, 476
  GPU, 280
  IGP, 280
  memory, 282
  overview, 280
  PCIe video cards, power requirements, 171
  ports
    adapters, 36
    analog signals, 33
    digital signals, 33
    DisplayPorts, 35-36
    DVI ports, 33, 36
    HDMI ports, 35-36
    Lightning ports, 43
    multipurpose ports, 37
    S-Video ports, 33, 36
    Thunderbolt ports, 43
    USB ports, 37-43, 46
    VGA ports, 33, 36
  projectors, 287-289
  subsystems, 280
  surveillance, physical security, 904
  troubleshooting, 284, 829-831
  video capture cards, 282
  video cards, 280
    AMD processors, 281
    installing, 283
    replacing, 433
  Video Options setting (BIOS/UEFI), 114
viewing
  amount of installed memory, 193
  environment variables, 740
  events
    logs, 798
    symbols, 799
  Linux processes, 886
  subnet masks, 1021
  taskbars in displays, 789
virtual apps, streaming, 539
virtual assistants, 389, 764
virtual desktops, 538
virtual memory, 256, 839
virtual networks, VNC, 956
virtual NIC, 603-605
virtual printing, 334
virtualization
  cross platform virtualization, 534
  desktops, 534-535
  emulators, 536
  host machines, 535
  Hyper-V, 77, 537, 769
  hypervisors, 535-536
  legacy software, 534
  NIC configuration, 603-605
  PC, 533
  requirements, 536
  resources, 536
  sandboxes, 534
  security, 537
  servers, 533
  snapshots/checkpoints, VM, 535
  support, 77
  test development, 534
  Virtualization Support setting (BIOS/UEFI), 115
  VM, 76-77, 205, 477, 535-537, 764
  workstations, system design, 477
viruses, 915-917
  antivirus software, 908
    Microsoft Defender Antivirus, 943
    mobile devices, 409
    reinitializing, 777
    rogue antivirus apps, 943
    Windows installations, 773
  BIOS/UEFI, 119
  boot sector viruses, 915
  incident response, 965
  mobile devices, 409
  Virus Protection setting (BIOS/UEFI), 114
  VM, 537
vishing, 918
VLAN (Virtual Local Area Networks), 580
VM (Virtual Machines), 76-77, 205, 477, 535
  external networks, 536
  Hyper-V, 764
  internal networks, 536
  security, 537
  viruses, 537
VNC (Virtual Network Computing), 956
voice recognition, physical security, 906
VoIP (Voice over IP), 520-522
voltage
  3.3V output voltage, 163
  5V output voltage, 163
  12V output voltage, 163
  110V vs. 220V input voltage, 163
  brownouts, 987
  current, 161-162
  DC power supplies, 166
  dual voltage memory, 192
  input voltage selectors, 166
  multimeters, 160, 572
  ohms, 161-162
  overvoltage, 986
  polarity, 160-162
  power supplies, checking, 174
  resistance, 161-162
  sags, 987
  spikes, 986
  surges, 986
  undervoltage, 986-987
  unplugging computers, 161
volume control, speakers, 295-296
volumes (drive partitions), 770
  adding to hard drives, 809
  boot volumes, 251, 814
  NTFS, 250
  RAW volumes, 251
  resizing partitions, 252
  simple volumes, 251
  spanned volumes, 251
  storage, volumes, 251

striped volumes, 251
system volumes, 251, 814
VPN (Virtual Private Networks), 446, 908, 954-955
VRAM (virtual RAM), 202
vulnerabilities/threats, security
access attacks, 919
backdoor attacks, 919
boot sector viruses, 915
botnets, 915, 919
brute force attacks, 919
cryptojacking/cryptomining, 915
DDOS attacks, 919
dictionary attacks, 911, 919
DoS attacks, 919
dumpster diving, 907
evil twin attacks, 919
impersonation attacks, 918
insider attacks, 919
keyloggers, 915
malware, 915, 917
MITM attacks, 920
password spraying attacks, 920
phishing, 918-919
piggybacking, 918
ransomware, 915
reconnaissance attacks, 920
replay attacks, 920
rootkits, 915
scareware, 919
shoulder surfing, 904, 918
Smurf attacks, 920
social engineering attacks, 912, 917
spear phishing, 918
spoofing attacks, 920
spyware, 915
SQL injection attacks, 920
tailgating, 904, 918
TCP/IP hijacking attacks, 920
Trojans, 915
viruses, 915-917
vishing, 918
vulnerability scanners, 920
whaling, 918
XSS attacks, 920
zero day attacks, 920
zombie attacks, 920
.VXD file extensions, 674

W

Wake on LAN, 169, 603
Wake on Ring, 169
wall jacks, RJ45, 565
WAN (Wide Area Networks), 552
wireless broadband (WiBro) connectivity, 526
WWAN, 608
WAP (Wireless Access Points), 576
warm bootups, 111, 494
warranties, asset management, 998
watts, 161-162, 170
wbadmin command, 733
WDS (Windows Deployment Services), 776
web browsers
ad blockers, 533
clearing caches/data, 530
configuration settings, 530
default browsers, 530
Edge, 532
Edge tile, Windows Start screen, 669
Internet Options Control Panel settings, 528-529
extensions, 530-531
Firefox, 532
Google Chrome, 532
password managers, 532
performance, 533
plug-ins, 530-531
pop-ups, 532
private browsing, 530
redirection, 531
rootkits, 531
security, 528-532
synchronizing, 530
troubleshooting, 455, 530-533
trusted sources, 528
untrusted sources, 528
updating, 531
verifying security certificates, 530
web credentials, 801
web servers, 622
webcams, 17, 306-307, 381, 436
facial recognition, physical security, 906
replacing, 439-440
WEP (Wired Equivalent Privacy), 602, 885, 959
WFX12V power supplies, 163
whaling, 918
while loops, 751-752
WiBro (Wireless Broadband), 526
Wi-Fi
analyzers, 409, 593
antennas, 436
calling, 389
connectivity, troubleshooting, 458-459
networks. *See* WLAN
Wi-Fi 5 (802.11ac) wireless standard, 395, 583
Wi-Fi 6 (802.11ax) wireless standard, 395, 583
WiGig (802.11ad) wireless standard, 583
wildcards, 706, 728
Windows (non-specific). *See also* Windows 10; Windows 11
32-bit OS, 655-656
64-bit OS, 655-656
activation clocks, 776
adding devices, 784
audio devices, 787
clock drift, 791
Device Manager, 785-790
Devices and Printers Control Panel utility, 785, 791
display settings, 788-789
"Not enough USB controller resources" error messages, 791
Sound Control Panel, 787
USB endpoints, 791
Advanced Boot Options menu, 819-820
Apply button, 671
apps
disabling, 822
repairing, 794-795
side-by-side apps, 764
uninstalling, 794
Apps & features (Settings > Apps), 794-795
Automatic Updates, 780
backups, 688, 781-782
balanced power, 836
baselines, 839

bootup
  Advanced Boot Options menu, 819-820
  process, overview, 814-815
  reboots, 835
  speeding up boot process, 826-827
  System Configuration utility, Windows, 820-824
  Task Manager, 824-826
  troubleshooting, 827-829, 832
CF cards, 379
checkboxes, 671
Close button, 671
command prompt, 698
compatibility mode, 768
Compatibility tab, 204-205
Component Services, 797
Computer Management console, 796
  disk maintenance, 810-811
  Disk Management tool, 807-809
  Local Users and Groups tool, 804-806
  ODBC Data Sources, 812-813
  Print Management console, 813-814
  Services and Applications section, 811
  Storage Spaces Control Panel, 810
  System Tools section, 797-800
  User Account Management section, 801-803
configuring, 783-784
context menus, 672
context-sensitive help, 672
Control Panel, 682-685
Cortana search feature, 678
Cortana virtual assistant, 764
Credential Manager, 801-804
data backups, 781-782
deploying, 775-776
device drivers
  installing, 786
  rolling back, 789
Devices and Printers Control Panel utility, 785, 791
dialog boxes, 670-672
digital signatures, 786
disabling apps, 822
Disk Cleanup tool, 810
disk maintenance, 810-811
Disk Management, 242, 245, 250-251, 771
display settings, 788-789
drop-down menus, 671
enhanced features, 764
Error Checking tool, 810
Event Viewer, 798-800
features, turning on/off, 795
File Explorer
  copying files, 681
  display options, 676-677
  file attributes, 679-680
  file compression, 681
  file encryption, 681
  indexing, 678
  moving files, 681
  paths, 674-676
  searches, 678
  starting, 719
File History backups, 782
files
  attributes, 679-680
  compression, 681
  copying, 681
  encryption, 681
  extensions, 672-674
  filenames, 672-673
  moving, 681
  paths, 674-676
  saving, 674
file systems, 771
folders
  attributes, 679-680
  compression, 681
  copying, 681
  encryption, 681
  moving, 681
  naming, 673
  subfolders, 672
formatting, 769
Group Policy, 720
hard drives
  maintenance, 810-811
  planning drive space, 770
high performance power plans, 837
Hyper-V, 764
indexing, 678
in-place upgrades, 765-767
installing
  antivirus software, 773
  backups before OS installations, 773
  clean installations, 765
  compatibility mode, 768
  corporate deployments, 775-776
  disabling interfering software, 774
  drivers, 772-773
  file systems, 771
  hardware, 772
  image deployments, 765
  in-place upgrades, 765-767
  licenses, 776
  multiboots, 765
  partitions, 769-770
  PCmover Express, 768
  phases of, 774
  preinstalling, 764
  recovery partitions, 765
  remote network installations, 765
  repair installations, 765, 779
  resets/restores, 765
  security scans, 773
  selecting networks, 774-775
  troubleshooting installations, 777-778
  types of installations, 765
  unattended installations, 765
  USMT, 768
  verifying installations, 776-777
  Windows Installation Assistant, 767
libraries, 672
licenses, 776
Local Users and Groups tool, 804-805
memory
  Memory Diagnostic tool, 206
  performance, 839
microphones, 293-294
Microsoft Store, 764
MMC, 796
multi-monitor taskbars, 764
network settings, 627-628, 631, 833-834
Notepad, 726

ODBC Data Sources, 812-813
OEM versions, 767
older apps, compatibility, 204-205
OneDrive, 764
OOBE, 774
Optimize and defragment tool, 811
partitions, 769-770
performance, monitoring, 838
  baselines, 839
  Performance Monitor, 841
  Reliability Monitor, 842
  Resource Monitor, 842
  Task Manager, 839-840
planning drive space, 770
power options, 836-837
PowerShell (.psl), 708-709, 735, 754
Print Management console, 813-814
printers
  connectivity, 359-362
  default printers, 345
  print drivers, 346-348
  printing in, 344
  print queues, 346
  sharing, 350
  testing, 346
profiles, troubleshooting, 832-833
Program Compatibility Wizard, 768
Programs and Features Control Panel utility, 794-795
quick formatting, 769
radio buttons, 671
ReadyBoost, 827
rebooting, 790
recovery, 688-689
ReFS, 810
registry
  backups, 781-782
  editing, 687
  regedit command, 728
  regedit.exe command prompt, 687
  regsvr32 command, 728
  regedt32.exe command prompt, 687
  subtrees, 686, 687
  troubleshooting, 830
  user profiles, 686
reimaging computers, 776
Reliability Monitor, 842
reloading, 779-780
reload OS, 688
remote desktops
  Remote Assistance, 843-845
  Remote Desktop Connection, 843-844
  starting, 723
repair installations, 779
Resource Monitor, 842
restore points, 783
roll back updates, 780
services, troubleshooting, 831
Services and Applications, 811
setup log files, 778
sfc, 779
shutdowns, troubleshooting, 835
snap-ins, 796-797
software
  installing, 792-793
  removing, 792
  uninstalling, 794
sound cards, 293
Sound Control Panel, 787
SRU, 780
Startup Settings menu, 819-820
Storage Space Control Panel, 810
subdirectories, 672
Sync Center Control Panel utility, 793
synchronization, 793
System Configuration utility, 820-824
system files, 814-815
System Image Recovery, 828
System Information window, 723
system instability, trouble-shooting, 835
System Restore, 783, 815-816
tabs, 671
Task Manager, 824-826
  measuring performance, 839-840
  Performance utility, 203-204
Task Scheduler, 797
textboxes, 670
threads, 839
troubleshooting
  black screens, 829-831
  bootups, 827-829, 832
  profiles, 832-833
  services, 831
  shutdowns, 835
  summary of steps, 836
  system instability, 835
  video issues, 829-831
UAC, 764
updating, 777
  Automatic Updates, 780
  roll back updates, 780
  Windows Update, 780-781
  Windows Update Assistant, 767
upgrading, 765-767
user account management
  adding credentials, 802-803
  administrator accounts, 805
  certificate-based credentials, 801
  Credential Manager, 801-804
  editing credentials, 804
  generic credentials, 801
  Local Users and Groups tool, 804-805
  recovering accounts, 805
  recovering user accounts, 805
  removing credentials, 803
  rights, 804
  standard user accounts, 805
  storing credentials, 801
  UAC, 806
  web credentials, 801
user profiles, 686
USMT, 768
versions, 685, 733
WDS, 776
WinRE, 688, 704, 764, 816-819
WRP, 779
Windows 8.1 Enterprise, 766
Windows 8.1 Home, 766
Windows 8.1 Pro, 766
Windows 10, 656
  Control Panel, 683
  desktop
    notification area, 667
    organizing, 668
    pinning apps to taskbar, 667

search function, 668
Show Desktop area, 667
shutdown options, 666
Start button, 664-665
Task View, 668-669
Enterprise edition, 657
File Explorer, 654
hardware requirements, 772
Home edition, 656
Hyper-V, 769
memory limitations, 193
memory recommendations, 193
Pro and Pro Education editions, 657
Pro for Workstations edition, 657
Recycle Bin, 669-670
shortcuts, 669
tiles, 669
Windows 10 Enterprise, 766
Windows 10 Home, 766
Windows 10 Pro, 766
Windows 10 Pro Education, 766
Windows 11, 656
Control Panel, 683
desktop
notification area, 667
organizing, 668
pinning apps to taskbar, 667
search function, 668
Show Desktop area, 667
shutdown options, 666-667
Start button, 664-665
Task View, 668-669
Enterprise edition, 657
File Explorer, 672
file paths, 676
Options button, 677
hardware requirements, 772
Home edition, 656
Hyper-V, 769
indexing options, 678
memory recommendations, 193
Pro and Pro Education editions, 657
Pro from Workstations edition, 657
Recycle Bin, 669-670
shortcuts, 669
tiles, 669
Windows 11 Enterprise, 766
Windows 11 Home, 766
Windows 11 Pro, 766
Windows 11 Pro Education, 766
Windows ADK, 775
Windows Compatibility Cookbook, 767
Windows Defender Firewall, 951-953
Windows Disk Cleanup, 258
Windows Hello, 442
Windows Installation Assistant, 767
Windows registry, 123, 830
Windows Storage Spaces, 255
Windows Update Assistant, 767
Windows Updates, 780-781
WinRE (Windows Recovery Environment), 264, 688, 704, 764, 816-819
winver command, 733
wiping
hard drives, 941
remote wipes, mobile devices, 441
wire (cable) strippers, 563, 572
wired connectivity, 594
Ethernet connectivity, projectors, 288
mobile devices
Lightning ports, 391
microUSB ports, 391
miniUSB ports, 391
mobile serial ports, 392
printers 342
proprietary vendor specific ports, 390
USB-C ports, 391
wireless antennas, 431, 576, 590-593
wireless AP
changing usernames/passwords, 607
configuring, 607
DMZ, 607-608
installing, 962-963
wireless bridges, 583
wireless cards
laptops, 413
replacing, 430-431
wireless connectivity
Bluetooth, 56
IR, 56
long-range fixed wireless, 526
mobile devices
802.11 wireless standard, 395
Airplane mode, 396
biometric security, 398
Bluetooth, 393-394
cellular data, 399
hotspots, 397
IR, 399
NFC, 398
RFID, 398
tethering, 397
two-factor authentication, 398
NFC, 56
power requirements, 527-528
projectors, 288
radio, 56
WiBro, 526
wireless extenders, 586
wireless networks
802.11ac (Wi-Fi 5) wireless standard, 583
802.11ad (WiGig) wireless standard, 583
802.11ax (Wi-Fi 6) wireless standard, 583
802.11b wireless standard, 582
802.11e wireless standard, 583
802.11g wireless standard, 583
802.11i wireless standard, 583
802.11n wireless standard, 583
AC addresses, 957
antennas, 590-593
AP, 583-584, 957, 960
as wireless repeaters, 587
default settings, 961
firmware, 962
installing, 962-963
passwords, 962
routers, 962-963
security, 959
SSID, 585-586, 962
Basic QoS, 608
bridges, 583
channel ID, 588-589, 608
content filtering, 608
data transfer speeds, 593
design, 585
desktop workstations, 582
device connectivity, 594
DHCP, 608

DMZ, 608
DNAT, 608
extenders, 586
external interference, 592-593
firewalls, 958
firmware, 608
frequencies, 581
intermittent wireless connectivity, 592
IoT, 609-611
IP filtering, 608
MDM, 958
multifunction devices, 583
NAT, 608
NIC, 583-584
overview, 581
port forwarding/mapping, 608
printer connectivity, 342, 351-352
repeaters, 587
routers, 583-584
security, 958
AP, 962-963
DMZ, 960
IP address filtering, 961
MAC address filtering, 960
TKIP, 959
WEP, 959
WPA2, 959
WPA3, 959
WPS, 961
signal strength, 459
site surveys, 592
SSID, 608
troubleshooting, 964
UPnP, 608
Wi-Fi analyzers, 593
WLAN, 552, 558, 957
WMN, 552
WWAN, 552, 608
Zigbee wireless standard, 610-611
Z-Wave wireless standard, 610-611
wireless NIC, 396, 431 601-602
Wireless option, AP configurations, 607
wireless printers, 351-353
wireless repeaters AP as, 587
wireless routers, 576
changing usernames/passwords, 607
DMZ, 607-608
installing, 962-963
IP filtering, 961
wireless security, 958, 963
DMZ, 960
IP address filtering, 961
MAC address filtering, 960
TKIP, 959
WEP, 959
WPS, 961
wireless standards 610-611
wiring standards 52 562
WISP (Wireless Internet Service Providers), 527
wizards troubleshooting with, 791
WLAN (Wireless LAN), 552, 558, 957
WMN (Wireless Mesh Networks), 552
work ethics (soft skills), 365
workgroups, 555-557, 775
workplace safety
environmental impacts, 981-982
equipment, 980
fire extinguishers, 979
fire safety, 979
government regulations, 978
lifting techniques, 981
MSDS, 979
OSHA, 979
personal safety, 981
trip hazards, 987
ventilation, 994
workstations
system design
audio/video workstations, 476
graphic/CAD/CAM workstations, 475
Pro for Workstations edition, Windows 10/11, 657
thick workstations, 479
thin workstations, 478
virtualization workstations, 477
wireless connectivity, 582
WPA (Wi-Fi Protected Access), 602
WPA2 (Wi-Fi Protected Access 2), 602, 959
WPA3 (Wi-Fi Protected Access 3), 602, 959
.WPS file extensions, 674
WPS (Wi-Fi Protected Setup), 961
.WRI file extensions, 674
wrist straps, antistatic, 144-145
writable media, optical drives, 298-299
Write permissions, 932
writing commands, 708
writing/exposing phase, laser printer imaging process, 325
written communication skills, 176-177
WRP (Windows Resource Protection), 779
wscript command, 733
WWAN (Wireless WAN), 552, 608

X

x64 processors, 68
x86 processors, 68
xcopy command, 706-707, 733
xDSL modems, 519
Xeon processors, 77
.XLS (.XLSX) file extensions, 674
XMP (Extreme Memory Profiles), 192
.XPS files, 334
XSS (Cross-Site Scripting) attacks, 920

Y

YB (yottabytes), 21

Z

ZB (zettabytes), 21
zero day attacks, 920
ZFS (Zettabyte File Systems), 881
ZIF (Zero Insertion Force) sockets, 80
Zigbee wireless standard, 610-611
.ZIP file extensions, 674
zombie attacks, 920
zooming in/out of objects, mobile devices, 384
Z-Wave wireless standard, 610-611

INDEX